10th Edition

Working with Young Children

Dr. Judy Herr

Early Childhood Consultant and Author
Professor Emerita, Early Childhood Education
School of Education
University of Wisconsin-Stout
Menomonie, Wisconsin

Publisher
The Goodheart-Willcox Company, Inc.
Tinley Park, Illinois
www.g-w.com

About the Author

The quality of this textbook reflects Judy Herr's intense dedication to early childhood education, with over 40 years of experience in the field: teaching, writing, consulting, and service. Judy supervised and administered seven children's programs in the Child and Family Study Center at the University of Wisconsin-Stout. She also served as the early childhood program director, graduate home economics program director, mentor to graduate students, and Associate Dean of the College of Human Development.

Judy has published numerous early childhood education books, curriculum guides, and journal articles. Her articles have been printed in journals such as *Young Children*, *Journal of Family and Consumer Sciences*, *Early Childhood News*, and *Texas Child Care Quarterly*. This text, *Working with Young Children*, has been published in English, Spanish, Chinese, and Arabic.

Judy has been a guest speaker at local, state, regional, national, and international conferences. She was invited to Pai Chi University in Korea as the Distinguished Invitational International Scholar. She has participated in the prestigious Management Development Program at Harvard University. She is active in professional associations, including the National Association for the Education of Young Children. Judy has received many awards, including the Shirley Dean Award for Distinguished Service to the Midwestern Association for the Education of Young Children. She was also named a Dahlgren Professor at the University of Wisconsin-Stout. Judy received an Outstanding Teaching Award at the University of Wisconsin-Stout.

The University of Wisconsin-Stout also awarded Judy the prestigious James Huff Stout Award for outstanding achievement. The award recognized her as a national and international educator, a prominent leader in early childhood education, a notable, prolific author, and an esteemed researcher.

Reviewers

The author and the publisher are grateful to the following reviewers who provided valuable input to this edition.

Donna Abbey
Teacher
Liberty High School
Renton, Washington

Amanda Abbott
Early Childhood Education Teacher and
    Center Director
Bristol-Plymouth Regional Technical
    School
Taunton, Massachusetts

Miskee Blatner
Career and Technical Education Teacher
Eldorado High School
Albuquerque, New Mexico

Irma Bode
Career Development Coordinator
Johnson County Public Schools
Wake Forest, North Carolina

Carlli Bryan
Teacher
New Smyrna Beach High School
New Smyrna Beach, Florida

Monica Carnahan
Teacher
Kingwood High School
Kingwood, Texas

Marnie Cunniff
Early Childhood Education Teacher
Bristol-Plymouth Regional Technical
    School
Taunton, Massachusetts

Megan Droste
Teacher
Cedar Falls High School
Cedar Falls, Iowa

Kayla Godbey
Office of Career and Technical
    Education
Kentucky Department of Education
Frankfort, Kentucky

Jill Harrison
Professor/Program Coordinator, Child
    Development
Delta College
Auburn, Michigan

Holly Hartman
Family and Consumer Sciences Teacher
Veterans Memorial High School
Corpus Christi, Texas

Beth Luhman
Family and Consumer Sciences Teacher
Blue Valley High School
Randolph, Kansas

Jamie Lynch
Early Childhood Education Faculty
WITC
Rice Lake, Wisconsin

Lisa McCauley
Child Guidance Teacher
Cypress Creek High School
Houston, TX

Rebecca McGrath-Hinkle
Career and Technical Education Early
    Childhood Education Teacher
Columbus City Schools
Columbus, Ohio

Alyson McIntyre-Reiger
Director
Advancing Connections
Indianapolis, Indiana

Diane Richards
Teacher
Trumbull High School
Trumbull, Connecticut

Ginger Voegel
Family and Consumer Sciences Teacher
Arthur Lovington Atwood High School
Arthur, Illinois

Karen Zellis
Family and Consumer Sciences Teacher
Brandywine High School
Wilmington, Delaware

Acknowledgments

The author and the publisher would like to thank the staff at the Child and Family Study Center, University of Wisconsin-Stout, for allowing photography of the children in their developmentally appropriate programs.

The tenth edition of *Working with Young Children* has been revised and updated to reflect the most effective practices for promoting children's growth and development and guidelines for developmentally appropriate practice. For instructor convenience, the chapters have been organized into lessons with corresponding review questions and auto-grading capabilities. The NAEYC Essentials for High-Quality Programs and Code of Ethical Standards have been updated. STEM activities and technology engagement have been added in all curriculum-related chapters. New social studies strategies are included to promote inclusion, acceptance, and enabling children of diverse cultures. The importance of the development of executive function and self-regulation is stressed. Recognizing the child's cultural background and home language is emphasized throughout the text. Recently published and classic children's books have been recommended for all classroom curriculum areas. New photographs appear throughout the textbook of children from birth through school-age. Under many of the pictures are questions to challenge students' thinking. In addition, content in individual chapters has been updated. Examples include:

- **Chapter 2: Types of Early Childhood Programs** includes a section on military child care.
- **Chapter 3: Child Development Principles and Theories** recognizes the historical influences on educating children of Beverly Prosser and Martha Bernal.
- **Chapter 9: Preparing the Environment** includes a section on infant and toddler environments.
- **Chapter 10: Selecting Toys, Equipment, and Educational Materials** now has a distinct section on infants and toddlers.
- **Chapter 11:** Reflects the most recent USDA guidelines.
- **Chapter 19: Guiding Art, Block building, and Sensory Experiences**, includes suggestions for promoting children's creativity and STEM.
- **Chapter 22:** includes the use of smart boards in teaching manuscript writing and the impact on emergence literacy.
- **Chapter 28: Guiding Field Trip Experiences** includes a section on virtual field trips.
- **Chapter 32: Engaging Parents and Families** includes strategies for family capacity building, engagement, and supporting military families.
- **Chapter 33: A Career for You in Early Childhood Education** includes expanded avenues for seeking employment.

Credentialing Partners and Support

Goodheart-Willcox appreciates the value of industry credentials, certifications, and accreditation. We are pleased to partner with leading organizations to support students and programs in achieving credentials. Integrating industry-recognized credentialing into a career and technical education (CTE) program provides many benefits for the student and for the institution. By achieving third-party certificates, students gain confidence, have proof of a measurable level of knowledge and skills, and earn a valuable achievement to include in their résumés. For educators and administrators, industry-recognized credentials and accreditation validate learning, enhance the credibility of programs, and provide valuable data to measure student performance and help guide continuous program improvement.

Working with Young Children is correlated to the Basic and Advanced Job Ready Early Childhood Education and Care credentials offered by NOCTI and to the Early Childhood Education certification offered by Precision Exams by YouScience.

NOCTI Certifications

Goodheart-Willcox is pleased to partner with NOCTI, a leading provider of industry certification solutions for CTE programs across the nation. With over 50 years of experience, NOCTI is a valuable partner in the CTE community's efforts to improve America's workforce. Goodheart-Willcox has created correlations between select products and the standards and competencies that make up the NOCTI credentials, to the benefit of states, instructors, and students working to achieve NOCTI credentials.

NOCTI certifications (knowledge-based and skill-based) are developed by national teams of subject matter experts as part of the process that meets personnel accrediting standards and requirements under ISO 17.024, resulting in credentials measuring skills and competencies critical for learner success outside the classroom. From online test delivery and psychometric services to digital badging and professional development, NOCTI uses the latest tools and methods to provide relevant solutions for those in CTE. For more information about NOCTI, visit www.nocti.org.

Precision Exams by YouScience Certification

Goodheart-Willcox is pleased to partner with Precision Exams by YouScience, correlating select Goodheart-Willcox titles to Precision Exams Certifications, to the benefit of states, instructors, and students working to achieve Precision Exams Certifications.

Precisions Exams Standards and Career Skill Exams™ are created in concert with industry and subject matter experts to match real-world skills and marketplace demands. Students who pass the exam and performance portion of the exam can earn a Career Skills Certification™. For more information about Precision Exams by YouScience, including a complete listing of their 150+ Career Skills Exams™ and certificates, please visit www.youscience.com/certifications/career-clusters/.

To see how *Working With Young Children* correlates to credentialing and certification standards, visit the Correlations tab at https://www.g-w.com/working-with-young-children-2024.

Student Tools

Student Text

Working with Young Children covers the knowledge and skills required to prepare students for a career in early care and education. The lesson-based structure includes extensive assessment opportunities and a selection of Workplace Connection features, which provide students with information about early childhood careers. The following supplemental materials to the text are available for students with access to digital resources. The workbook is also available in print.

Workbook

- Hands-on practice includes questions and activities.
- Organized to follow the textbook lessons to help students achieve essential learning outcomes.

Observation Guide

- Activities help guide students through the observation process that is fundamental to evaluating children's development.
- Chapters are coordinated for use with the text, providing forms and instructions to help students benefit from their time withchildren. Students will also have opportunities to plan, lead, and evaluate their own activities.

Companion Website

- For digital learners, e-flash cards and vocabulary exercises allow interaction with the content to create opportunities to increase achievement.

Instructor Tools

G-W Ignite

G-W Ignite provides a seamless user experience for both you and your students. The easy-to-navigate interface and class rostering capabilities make setting up a course easy and intuitive. Instructors can quickly and easily share assignments with students. Auto-graded activities and assignments make grading easier than ever, and rubrics are provided for ease of grading when required. Extensive reporting capabilities allow instructors to view students' progress and evaluate performance against learning outcomes and key standards. Students have their own My Progress dashboard where they can view grades and comments from their instructor.

G-W Ignite provides a complete learning package for you and your students. The included digital resources help your students remain engaged and learn effectively.

- The **Online Textbook** is a reflowable digital textbook that works well on all devices. It also works well with screen readers and accessibility tools.
- The **Workbook** content in digital format provides opportunities for students to reinforce their understanding of learning outcomes in the text. Instructors can easily assign activities and grade student work using the rubrics provided.
- The **Observation Guide** in digital format helps students log and evaluate their observations when working with young children.
- **Videos** dive deeper into key concepts with guided worksheets and quiz questions.
- **Drill and Practice Vocabulary Activities**, provided for all key terms in every lesson, provide an active, engaging, and effective way for students to learn the required terminology.
- Use the **Pretests**, **Posttests**, and **Exams** to assess students' knowledge of learning outcomes and key standards. These prebuilt assessments help you measure student knowledge and track progress in achieving learning outcomes.
- The **Instructor Resources** provide instructors with time-saving preparation tools such as answer keys, editable lesson plans, and other teaching aids.
- **Instructor's Presentations for PowerPoint®** are fully customizable, richly illustrated slides that help you teach and visually reinforce the key concepts from each chapter.

See https://www.g-w.com/working-with-young-children-2024 for a list of all available resources.

Professional Development

- Expert Content Specialists
- Research-Based Pedagogy and Instructional Practices
- Options for virtual and in-person PD

The instructional design includes student-focused learning tools to help students succeed. This visual guide highlights the features designed for the textbook.

Reading Advantage provides reading comprehension advice at the beginning of each chapter.

Case Study describes a real-world scenario with application questions to consider.

Essential Question provides a starting point for thinking about the material in the lesson.

Learning Outcomes identify the knowledge and skills to be obtained when the lesson is completed.

Key Terms lists the vocabulary words to be defined in each lesson.

Lesson Review Questions provides an opportunity to assess student learning.

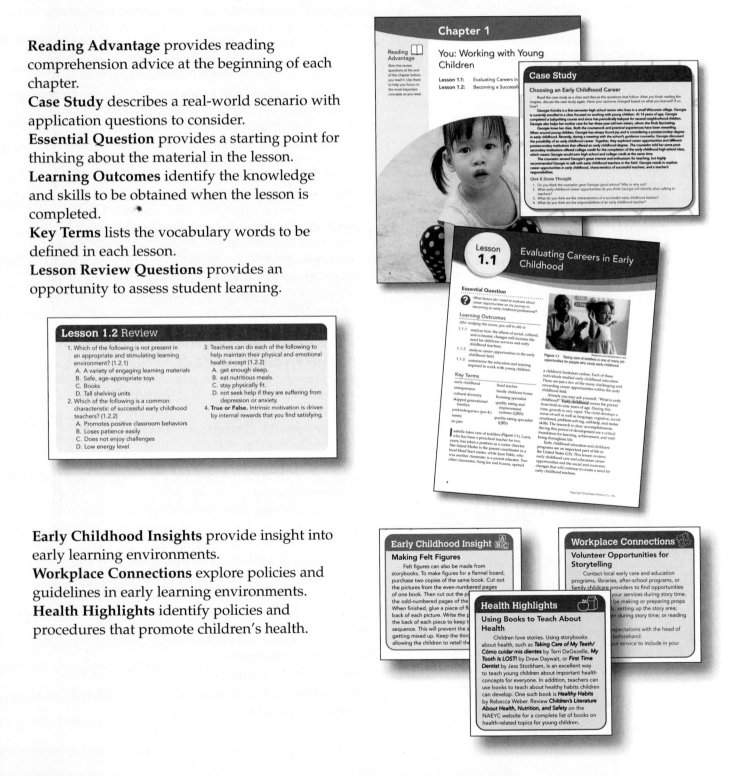

Early Childhood Insights provide insight into early learning environments.

Workplace Connections explore policies and guidelines in early learning environments.

Health Highlights identify policies and procedures that promote children's health.

Guided Tour

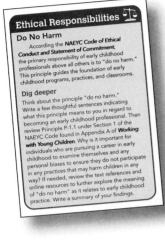

Ethical Responsibilities identifies ethical guidelines to be followed in early learning environments.

Safety First defines best practices to ensure a safe early learning environment.

Focus on Careers identifies specific career paths in early learning environments.

Summary provides an additional review tool and reinforces key learning outcomes.

Vocabulary Activity reinforces the vocabulary words learned in each chapter.

Critical Thinking questions develop higher-order thinking and problem-solving, personal, and workplace skills.

Core Skills questions develop higher-order thinking and problem-solving, personal, and workplace skills.

Portfolio Project develops higher-order thinking and problem-solving, as well as personal and workplace skills.

Chapter 20 Review and Assessment

Summary

Lesson 20.1

20.1-1 Early childhood programs must nurture a child's sense of joy and wonder. Books and storytelling promote children's cognitive and social-emotional development.

20.1-1 For optimum growth, it is important that they see and hear their home language in the early childhood setting.

20.1-2 Two major groups of books are picture books and storybooks.

20.1-2 Books in these groups are further divided into family life stories, animal stories, fables, and fairy tales.

20.1-3 Storytelling and language experiences support children's overall language and literacy development and should reflect the rich diversity of all children.

20.1-3 Teachers must select stories carefully so content matches the children's developmental levels, experiences, cultural backgrounds, interests, and needs. In addition, the content must be free of stereotypes and sexism.

Lesson 20.2

20.2-1 As part of preparing to read, teachers must think through how they will introduce and read the story, handle interruptions and maintain children's interest, and how they will end the story.

20.2-1 Teachers must collaborate with the parents or guardians of non-English-speaking children to learn key words and phrases to use when speaking with their children and labeling classroom areas and equipment.

20.2-2 Besides reading a book, there are several ways to share a story. Draw and tell, audio and video recordings, puppets, and flannel boards are a few options.

20.2-2 E-books and e-readers can provide children with new literature and language opportunities.

20.2-3 The library area is an important classroom area. Locate it away from traffic.

20.2-3 Choose books for the library area carefully. Consider children's development, experiences, and interests to stimulate enthusiasm for books and reading.

Vocabulary Activity

Choose one of the Key Terms in this chapter. Then use online resources to locate photos that visually show the meaning of the term you chose. Share the photo and meaning of the term in class. Ask for clarification as necessary.

Critical Thinking

1. **Compare and Contrast.** Prepare a bibliography of six children's books you might use in storytelling. Divide the books into groups based on the age of the intended audience. Then, compare the books' subject matters, illustrations, and writing styles. How do the similarities and differences between these books make them appropriate for their audiences?

2. **Identify.** Visit a local library or bookstore and survey the children's books or magazines available. Select one book or magazine and identify the key information about it, including its content (appropriate or inappropriate), recommended ages, quality of illustrations, writing style, cost, and durability features. Write a short book review, including all this information.

3. **Analyze.** Listen to an audio recording of a children's story and take notes about how the speaker reads the story. Analyze strategies the speaker uses to hold children's attention and assess whether these strategies were effective.

4. **Evaluate.** Video record yourself reading a book to a group of children. Evaluate your presentation. What parts were of most interest to the children? What storytelling strategies were most effective in holding the children's interest? If you told the story again, what would you change? Then, trade recordings with a classmate and evaluate each other's recordings. Compare your evaluations.

5. **Draw Conclusions.** Go to Storyline Online on YouTube. It provides read-aloud stories with famous storytellers. Listen to the book, *Skin You Live In* by Michael Tyler. What do you think appeals to young children about this book? What skills did the storyteller use to maintain the children's interest? What do you think a child will find appealing about this book? Describe why the inclusion of this children's book would make an important addition to the classroom. Could you use this site to download stories to a smart board? Why or why not?

Core Skills

1. **Writing.** Create a lesson plan for preschoolers that focuses on the development of their reading and language skills. How would you target the needs of this age group? If possible, implement your lesson plan in an early childhood program and assess its effectiveness.

2. **Reading.** Examine a book collection in an early childhood center. Browse all the books for dual-language (bilingual) teachings and those containing multicultural stories. Take notes about the cultures and languages that the collection covers. Then, identify two to three cultural or language gaps in the collection. Search online for books to fill these gaps. Choose three books and read them. Write a letter recommending that these three books be added to the center's collection.

3. **Writing.** Enlist the cooperation of a creative-writing teacher and an art teacher for a joint children's book writing project. Interview a preschooler to help you come up with a story idea. Then, using one of the storytelling strategies explained in the chapter, write a children's story, and create illustrations for it. Ask the creative-writing and art teachers to evaluate the illustrations and writing. After incorporating their feedback, share your story with the class.

4. **Research.** Conduct an online search for information about one popular children's book illustrator. Examples of popular illustrators include Tomi di Paola, Jack Kent, Patricia Polacco, Eric Carle, and Arnold Lobel. What influenced the artist to become an illustrator? How does the artist's work contribute to the enjoyment and understanding of a story? Get examples of the artist's illustrations. Discuss your findings and share your illustrations with the class.

5. **Speaking.** Choose a children's story that you find interesting and identify its target age range. Then, create an introduction for this story and practice reading the story as if to children within the intended age range. When reading, consider what strategies and props you could use when reading your introduction. Finally, implement these strategies and read your introduction and your story to the class.

6. **Technology.** Consider how a camera or digital device with video and auditory capabilities could be used to create a digital story. Then, choose one of these methods and create a digital story featuring an early childhood program. Your story should include the children as characters and should bring the center to life. Share your digital story at a parent-teacher conference or at preschool program functions and events. Include visual or audible captions for each picture, and be sure to get permission from people in the photos.

7. **Identify.** Go to YouTube and search for *The Hula-Hoopin' Queen* by Thelma Lynne Godin as read by Oprah Winfrey. Watch and listen to the video. Make a list of all of the effective strategies Oprah uses while reading the story. Discuss the strategies in class.

8. **CTE Career Readiness Practice.** Imagine that you are the director of a new preschool center. Recently, parents have been questioning the importance of storytelling for their children. They are complaining about how much time is scheduled for storytelling. You have planned a meeting to ensure that your staff is prepared to respond to the parents' questions. To prepare for this meeting, create fact sheets that outline what the staff must know and communicate about why storytelling is important in early childhood education. Also include sources that your staff can reference during this explanation.

Portfolio Project

How can early childhood teachers encourage parents to include storytelling activities at home? Write a brief letter to a preschool parent citing the benefits of reading to their child regularly. Include suggestions on the types of books appropriate for the age of the child. File a copy of the letter in your portfolio.

Brief Contents

Feature Contents

Health Highlights

Ethical Responsibilities

Safety First

Focus on Careers

Unit One
The Children and You

Chapters

Who you are and what you know affects your ability to work with young children. In this unit, you will explore current career opportunities in the early childhood field. You will also examine the professional dispositions and characteristics of successful early childhood teachers. Various types of early childhood programs will be described.

This unit will help you understand the characteristics of children of different ages. It will give you an overview of their physical, cognitive, social-emotional, and linguistic development. Each of these developmental domains supports each other.

You will also learn how to adapt your teaching skills to promote their strengths, developmental needs, and interests at different ages helping them achieve their full potential. This information will help you plan intentional, developmentally appropriate learning experiences.

You: Working with Young Children

Lesson 1.1:   Evaluating Careers in Early Childhood
Lesson 1.2:   Becoming a Successful Teacher

Case Study

Choosing an Early Childhood Career

Read the case study as a class and discuss the questions that follow. After you finish reading the chapter, discuss the case study again. Have your opinions changed based on what you learned? If so, how?

Georgie Kondra is a first-semester high school senior who lives in a small Wisconsin village. Georgie is currently enrolled in a class focused on working with young children. At 14 years of age, Georgie completed a babysitting course and since has periodically babysat for several neighborhood children. Georgie also helps her mother care for her three-year-old twin sisters, whom she finds fascinating.

Georgie loves her class. Both the coursework and practical experiences have been rewarding. When around young children, Georgie has always found joy and is considering a postsecondary degree in early childhood. Recently, during a meeting with the school's guidance counselor, Georgie discussed the possibility of an early childhood career. Together, they explored career opportunities and different postsecondary institutions that offered an early childhood degree. The counselor told her some postsecondary institutions offered college credit for the completion of the early childhood high school class, which means Georgie would earn high school and college credit at the same time.

The counselor sensed Georgie's great interest and enthusiasm for teaching, but highly recommended Georgie to talk with early childhood teachers in the field. Georgie needs to explore career opportunities in early childhood, characteristics of successful teachers, and a teacher's responsibilities.

Give It Some Thought

1. Do you think the counselor gave Georgie good advice? Why or why not?
2. What early childhood career opportunities do you think Georgie will identify when talking to teachers?
3. What do you think are the characteristics of a successful early childhood teacher?
4. What do you think are the responsibilities of an early childhood teacher?

Opening image credit: paulaphoto/iStock via Getty Images

Essential Question

? *What factors do I need to evaluate about career opportunities on my journey to becoming an early childhood professional?*

Learning Outcomes

After studying this lesson, you will be able to

1.1-1 analyze how the effects of social, cultural, and economic changes will increase the need for childcare services and early childhood teachers.

1.1-2 analyze career opportunities in the early childhood field.

1.1-3 summarize the education and training required to work with young children.

Key Terms

early childhood
entrepreneur
cultural diversity
skipped generational families
prekindergarten (pre-K)
nanny
au pair
head teacher
family childcare home
licensing specialist
quality rating and improvement systems (QRIS)
quality-rating specialist (QRS)

Isabella takes care of toddlers (**Figure 1.1**). Lucia, who has been a preschool teacher for two years, has taken a position as a center director. Her friend Marko is the parent coordinator in a local Head Start center, while Juan Pablo, who was another classmate, is a parent educator. Two other classmates, Sung Jee and Ivanna, opened

Rawpixel.com/Shutterstock.com

Figure 1.1 Taking care of toddlers is one of many job opportunities for people who study early childhood.

a children's bookstore online. Each of these individuals studied early childhood education. These are just a few of the many challenging and rewarding career opportunities within the early childhood field.

Already you may ask yourself, "What is early childhood?" **Early childhood** covers the period from birth to nine years of age. During this time, growth is very rapid. The child develops a sense-of-self as well as language, cognitive, social-emotional, problem-solving, self-help, and motor skills. The research is clear: accomplishments during this period of development are a critical foundation for learning, achievement, and well-being throughout life.

Early childhood education and childcare programs are an important part of life in the United States (US). This lesson reviews early childhood care and education career opportunities and the social and economic changes that will continue to create a need for early childhood teachers.

Copyright Goodheart-Willcox Co., Inc.

1.1-1 Social and Economic Changes

The social and economic changes in society occur in families, employers' attitudes, education attitudes, and studies. Career opportunities change along with these factors.

Growing Cultural Diversity

The 2020 US census shows that there has been dramatic growth in cultural diversity—the presence of different cultures or ethnicities. America is becoming more multiracial and nonwhite. For the first time in history, there is a decline in the white population with minority populations driving growth. The number of people who identify themselves as Hispanic or Asian has surged. The largest population increase was among Americans who identify as being more than one race or ethnicity.

Over the past decade, the Hispanic population has increased by about 23 percent. The Asian population increased by about 36 percent, which is about a fifth of the US total. Currently, one out of four Americans identifies themselves as Hispanic or Asian.

According to the census, the US population is now

- White—57.8 percent
- Hispanic—18.7 percent
- Black—12.4 percent
- Asian—6 percent

The number of young children from multicultural families is increasing. The latest census data shows Americans of two or more races or ethnicities are the fastest growing demographic. Over 10 percent of babies born in the United States have one white and one nonwhite parent. Populations of some groups are growing more quickly than others are.

Changes in Family Structures

A dramatic change has taken place in the early experiences of preschool children over the past several decades. Children are living in smaller, more complicated families and changing family structures. One of the most notable changes is in the increase in non-marital childbearing. Researchers estimate that 40 percent of births occur with single parents. There are also changes in family life, the economy, and public support that influenced the growth of early childhood education programs. Several trends support this prediction.

- In two-parent families, both parents work to meet the cost of living.
- Women are becoming more highly educated and now make up over 57 percent of the workforce.
- Both parents are employed full-time in almost half of households that include two parents.
- There is an increase of dual-income families because a second income is usually needed.
- Married couples are having fewer children.
- More young adults are getting married later in life. When they have children later, they are in a better position financially to afford early childhood programs.
- Smaller family size means some families have more money to divide. Therefore, they can spend more on childcare and early childhood education.
- Women are showing an increased commitment to their careers. They work during pregnancy and return to work after birth.
- Sixty-six percent of women with preschool children work outside the home.
- Many working women are widowed, divorced, or never married. They lack the option of a spouse caring for the child.
- Families are more mobile and may move away from relatives who would otherwise provide childcare support.
- More children being raised in skipped generational families in which they are raised by grandparents apart from their parents.

Families see the value of having children attend an early childhood program. The media have shared the importance of the early years and the success of publically funded programs such as Head Start. Eighty-four percent of children are in some type of nonparental care arrangement.

According to government statistics, the under-five population will rise modestly to 25.2 million in the next decade. So, there will be an increasing need for early childhood teachers (**Figure 1.2**).

Rising Cost of Childcare

The cost of childcare continues to rise. It is more expensive than college tuition in the majority of states, and only six percent of companies offer families a stipend or childcare benefits. As a result, many families are facing a dilemma. They are faced with three options, which include

- finding lower-quality childcare for less money;
- leaving the workforce to care for their children; and
- working from home if the employer allows this option.

Achieving quality, availability and affordability is often called the *trilemma of childcare*. The economics of childcare creates a trilemma for parents, teachers, and children. High-quality programs for children compensate teachers with a higher salary and better working conditions. These teachers are usually more

Rido/Shutterstock.com

Figure 1.2   Changes in family demographics, including multicultural families, is increasing demand for early childhood professionals. *What other changes do you think are increasing the demand for early childhood professionals?*

highly qualified and experience better working conditions. In these programs, affordability for parents becomes an issue.

Changes in Employers' Attitudes

Childcare is one of the most pressing issues faced by employers. Problems with childcare can negatively affect worker productivity and a stable workforce. Many childcare arrangements do not meet the needs of working parents. Single parents face even more challenges in emergency situations. They may not have backup in emergencies. As a result, some companies offer corporate or employer-sponsored childcare. Other childcare benefits may include

- partial subsidies to select childcare centers;
- flexible employee scheduling;
- predictable scheduling;
- parental leave; and
- working from home options.

By providing some type of childcare benefit, companies have reported tangible payoffs. Included are positive effects on recruitment, job satisfaction, loyalty, and productivity. Turnover and absenteeism are reduced. Other positive results are better public relations, tax benefits, ease of scheduling, and improved quality of the workforce.

On-site childcare provides parents the opportunity to

- observe and interact with their children during lunch breaks;
- feed or breastfeed their infants;
- save time in the drop-off and pickup process; and
- attend holiday and birthday celebrations.

In addition to on-site early childhood centers, employers may offer other means of childcare assistance. They may make arrangements with community childcare centers to provide slots for employees' children. The company may provide a resource and referral service, which helps match the employee's needs with services in the community. They may distribute lists of childcare providers, maps, and brochures to families. This type of service respects the employee's right to choose a suitable arrangement.

A few corporations hire early childhood specialists to provide sick childcare. They provide emergency backup arrangements that are provided for limited time periods. The average child is ill about eight times each year. As a result, sick children force parents to stay home from work. Emergency backup arrangements help reduce the parents' stress, guilt, and worry that occur when their children are ill.

Intergenerational care is another service a few corporations provide. This model is often called *dependent care*. It provides services for older adults as well as young children. These centers operate as both as a childcare center for children and an adult day program for older adults. These programs have positive benefits. The children learn from older adults, while the adults gain a renewed sense of self-worth while interacting with the children.

Changes in Education Attitudes

More than half of three-, four-, and five-year-olds are attending early childhood programs. In addition, many younger and older children are enrolled in programs while their parents work or attend classes. Using center-based care was the least popular form of nonparental care in the 1960s. Only 25 percent of three-, four-, and five-year-old children were enrolled in part- or full-day programs—some in Head Start. By the 1970s, Head Start had become so popular that many middle-class Americans began enrolling their children in early programs. Today, most three and four-year-olds attend an early childhood center-based program.

Most parents are becoming more aware of their children's developmental needs. As a result, they are seeking high-quality environments that will promote their children's growth and development. Most working parents search for early childhood programs that are licensed and accredited.

There is mounting evidence that early childhood professionals should be optimistic. The US Bureau of Labor Statistics projects employment to grow 2 percent annually through 2030. The US needs more trained teachers because of the importance of early childhood education and the growing population of three- to five-year-olds. A focus needs to be on providing quality programs. Quality can be enhanced with better-trained caregivers and teachers, lower child-to-staff ratios, and greater services.

Educational Studies

Early childhood programs are becoming more research based. The government is supporting research to ensure that spending of federal money is on effective evidence-based programs. Studies have confirmed the benefits of high-quality early education. These programs represent one of the best investments. The first five years of life are a critical period in development, and the benefits are long-term. Children who take part in early learning experiences are more successful in school. Quality early childhood programs benefit children from all socioeconomic levels by nurturing them and helping them reach their full potential. These programs also prepare the children to reach school ready to learn.

Children who get a good start in high-quality programs are less likely to have behavioral problems. They are also less likely to be referred to special education. One study surveyed the progress of children who attended a high-quality preschool program. Over the years, these students fared better than those who did not take part in early education. Fewer of these children committed crimes, required special education, or became teen parents. They also earned better grades. More graduated from high school, were employed, and enjoyed higher earnings. They made less use of financial-assistance programs and paid higher taxes.

This research is reinforced by other studies that showed the importance of brain development and early learning. According to research, early brain development depends on a stimulating and nurturing environment. As a result, most states have prekindergarten programs. **Prekindergarten (pre-K)**, sometimes referred to as *preschool*, are school-based programs for three- to five-year-old children.

Nationally, 70 percent of children are enrolled in a pre-k attend a school program. The remaining children attend Head Start, a for-profit or nonprofit early childhood center, or a faith-based program.

Benefits to the Economy

Quality early childhood programs do not only affect tomorrow's citizens, but they also influence tomorrow's economy. Studies show that preschool education is a sound economic investment. Over time, such programs pay for themselves. Every dollar invested in early education saves taxpayers future costs, and it also is an investment that pays great returns to children. Therefore, early care and education is cost-effective. Across the nation, states have caught on to the importance of offering early childhood programs for all young children.

High quality, publicly funded universal prekindergarten programs promote the well-being of the nation. By providing high-quality programs and closing the educational gap, they reduce inequality. The most positive effects of high-quality programs are with children who experience the most disadvantages. When they enter kindergarten, they score higher on tests. Investing in children has many important benefits that include

- lower crime rates;
- less dependency on temporary government financial assistance;
- reduced drop-rates;
- higher employment and earnings;
- less grade retention;
- less need for special education;
- higher graduation rates;
- less likely to be teenage parents; and
- lower rates of drug use.

1.1-2 Early Childhood Career Opportunities

Never have there been more career opportunities in early childhood. Early childhood programs occur in a variety of settings. Private schools, public schools, charter schools (independently run public schools with greater flexibility in their operations), homes, apartment buildings, centers, businesses, parks, and houses of worship are examples. As a result, early childhood specialists may choose from many alternatives. Professional nannies, au pairs, kindergarten teachers, Head Start teachers, preschool teachers, infant-toddler teachers, directors, licensing specialists, and tutors will be in need. You may find additional possibilities in business settings (**Figure 1.3**).

Due to demand and changes in licensing, the challenge of maintaining a qualified early childhood workforce will grow more difficult. Workers over 45 years of age will need to be replaced as they retire in the next 25 years. In addition, new teachers will be needed to keep pace with the continued growth of early childhood programs. For most early childhood education positions, a community college, technical college, college, or university degree is necessary.

Nannies and Au Pairs

There is currently a great demand for trained nannies and au pairs. The dual-career family has contributed to the increasing demand for nannies and au pairs. A **nanny** provides care in a child's home. Depending on the parents' needs, nannies live in the family's home or on their own. In addition to their wages, they may receive paid holidays and room and board.

An **au pair** (pronounced oh pare) is a person from another country who temporarily lives with a family and performs tasks like those of a nanny. In exchange for weekly pay, room, board, transportation, and an opportunity to learn the family's language, the au pair provides childcare and may do housework.

Prekindergarten and Kindergarten Teachers

More children than ever are being served in state-funded preschools, which require a post-secondary degree. Thus, there is a need for pre-K and kindergarten teachers in public and private schools. Even many early childhood centers hire kindergarten teachers. These centers provide all-day kindergarten programs for children of working parents. This allows the children to be in one setting for before- and after-school care rather than multiple settings.

Early Childhood Assistant and Associate Teachers

Besides the lead teacher, state licensing requirements may demand hiring an additional staff member. To achieve the required adult-child ratios for a group of young children, centers may hire an early childhood assistant or associate teacher. The role of the early childhood teacher or associate is to provide support for a lead teacher. The associate will also help provide a developmentally appropriate curriculum.

These positions may not require a degree in some states, although specialized course work or training in child development or early childhood education may be a requirement. For example, the associate teacher may have a *CDA® (Child Development Associate®) credential*. This credential shows the applicant has developed and demonstrated competence in areas supporting the healthy development of young children. The assistant teacher, sometimes referred to as a childcare aide, is typically an entry-level position. Assistants may have earned a high school degree and participated in a professional

development course or training program. This position may help the individual gain experience needed to advance to a lead teacher position. Many students work in these positions while working toward an early childhood education degree at a university.

Head Teachers and Directors

With the number of children attending childcare centers growing, the need for educated, qualified professionals is also growing. The US Bureau of Labor Statistics predicts an increased number of job openings for early childhood educators. Usually, the **head teacher** handles all aspects of class functioning. These include planning curriculum, maintaining a safe and stimulating environment, teaching children, and engaging parents. The director's responsibilities are broader. They must meet the required local, state, and federal requirements. They are also responsible for marketing the program, recruiting children, hiring and supervising staff, and managing the budget. Building maintenance is also the director's responsibility in some centers.

Family Childcare Home

Family childcare homes provide childcare for children ranging in age from six weeks to 12 years. Caregivers in these settings may work with one or several children at a time, including their own. This type of care allows the caregiver to work from home, and may attract parents because of the longer hours of operation and more homelike atmosphere. These providers are small business owners. They are caregivers, teachers, and administrators. They enroll children, collect fees, and ensure that their operation meets state licensing requirements.

Licensing Specialists

Because of the rapid increase in early childhood centers, the number of licensing positions are expanding. The state usually employs the **licensing specialist**. The role of

Early Childhood Career Opportunities

Careers in Childcare and Early Childhood Education Programs

- Au pairs
- Curriculum specialists
- Directors of early childhood and school-age child care programs
- Family childcare providers
- Nannies
- Teachers: childcare centers, early childhood programs, prekindergarten, kindergarten, elementary schools, and school-age childcare programs
- Assistant and associate teachers: childcare centers, early childhood programs, elementary schools, and school-age childcare programs

Related Careers in the Early Childhood Industry

- Childcare resource and referral specialists
- Early childhood consultants
- Early childhood educators (high school teachers, technical school instructors, community college instructors, and university professors)
- Early childhood researchers
- Licensing specialists
- Safety specialists
- Sick childcare specialist for corporate child care
- Special education teachers
- Staff trainers

Child-Related Careers in...

Business

- Designers of children's products: clothing, computer hardware and software, furniture, school supplies, sports equipment, and toys
- Salespeople of children's products
- Playground designers
- Safety testers for children's products

Community Service

- Children's librarians
- Children's art, dance, music, and sports instructors
- Health care: pediatricians, pediatric nurses, pediatric surgeons, pediatric dentists
- Social services: family or children's therapists, counselors, social workers, caseworkers
- Parent educators
- Recreation directors

- Religious education
- Directors or instructors

Publishing and Art

- Authors of books and magazine articles for children and parents
- Editors of books and magazines for children and parents
- Children's artists, illustrators, and photographers

Entertainment

- Writes and records children's music
- Coordinates birthday parties and special events for children
- Entertainers: actors, singers, clowns, magicians, puppeteers
- Writers, producers, and directors for children's TV shows, movies, and theater productions

Figure 1.3   Many career opportunities exist in early childhood. *Which careers appeal to you most?*

this person is to protect and promote the health, safety, and welfare of children attending centers.

Licensing specialists, sometimes referred to as *regulators*, make on-site visits to assigned centers. During each visit, the licensing specialist observes whether the center is following state licensing standards, which vary from state to state. These standards reflect the minimum requirements to operate legally. Licensing specialists monitor the number of children in the center, adult-child ratio, size of the facility, food service, and curriculum provided. They also monitor building safety, health practices, educational preparation of staff, and physical space.

Quality-Rating and Improvement Systems Specialists

Like the need for licensing specialists, most states and District of Columbia have introduced **quality rating and improvement systems (QRIS)**, or established standards or benchmarks that show programs exceed minimal state licensing requirements. Childcare centers, prekindergarten programs, Head Start programs, licensed family childcare homes, and school-age programs can all be evaluated. Each state's approach is unique. **Quality-rating specialists** evaluate and rate the achievement of benchmarks that exceed the minimal state licensing requirements. The most common areas include the following:

- licensing compliance
- accreditation
- ratio and group size
- teacher and director qualifications
- staff training
- assessment, environment
- family engagement
- health and safety
- provision for children's special needs
- program administration

After the in-depth study, a report providing detailed and descriptive information is shared. Programs achieving high-quality ratings may receive higher reimbursement rates, professional development, and technical assistance. Ratings help educate parents so they can make an informed decision when selecting their child's program. Programs communicate their rating levels on their websites and in program brochures.

Other Career Opportunities

Many other career opportunities exist for you in early childhood care and education. With this background, you will be qualified to hold a variety of positions. For example, a career as

Workplace Connections

Reviewing Licensing Standards

Obtain a copy of your state's licensing standards for childcare centers and family childcare homes. Review curriculum and equipment standards.

1. How would a childcare center or family childcare home prepare for an inspection by a licensing specialist in these areas?
2. How often do licensing specialists conduct on-site visits?
3. What could happen if a center or home cannot meet standards?

a parent educator might appeal to you. In this position, you would work with parents to help them learn competent and confident parenting skills (**Figure 1.4**). You might work days, evenings, or weekends. You could design educational materials or produce visuals to help parents better understand their roles and the nature of young children. You might even produce materials to share online on various platforms.

Knowledge of child development is also a requirement for community recreation leaders and children's art, dance, music, and sports instructors. This knowledge is helpful for those creating television shows, books, toys, music, and magazines for young children, too.

Social workers, counselors, and therapists must know about children's development to provide help. This is also true of health-care providers who treat children. Indeed, the demand for workers educated in early childhood far exceeds the current supply.

Finally, you might enjoy a career as an **entrepreneur**. This person creates and runs their own business. The most common early childhood entrepreneurship is a family childcare home. Family childcare providers run their businesses from their homes. They put in all the work, take all the risk, make all the decisions, and earn all the profit associated with their businesses. Consultants, store owners, designers of children's products, and entertainers are other examples of entrepreneurs.

The work available to you as an entrepreneur is limited only by your imagination. If you can shape your ideas into a career that meets a need of children and families, you will likely succeed. For example, you could start a business that specializes in providing substitute staff for childcare centers. When a center needs personnel to cover an absent staff member's job, the director could call you. Your responsibility would be to furnish a substitute teacher, cook, custodian, or office assistant.

1.1-3 Education and Training to Work with Young Children

As you can see, there are many opportunities for people who are interested in working with young children. What education and training are required for these jobs?

Major changes are facing education and training for working with young children. More entry-level positions require an associate degree from a technical or community college or a bachelor's degree from a college or university. A few entry-level positions, depending upon state licensing, may require little training or experience. For instance, some state licensing regulations may allow someone with a high

as-artmedia/Shutterstock.com

Figure 1.4 Parent educators present information that will help parents improve their nurturing skills. *In what other ways do you think parent educators might help parents?*

school education to work as a teacher's aide or playground supervisor. A teacher's aide would assist the teacher, help the children with their snacks, or supervise play activities.

Changes in education have been affected by preschools being offered and funded by the public schools. Preschool teachers typically need at least an associate degree. If teaching in the public school, you must have a license in early childhood education. An early childhood education license typically covers teaching pre-K through the third grade. While a CDA credential was once sufficient for teaching Head Start, times have changed. Today nationwide, 50 percent of Head Start programs require a teacher to have a bachelor's degree in early childhood.

Some people seek a **Child Development Associate (CDA) Credential**™. It is awarded for one of four settings: center-based infant-toddler; center-based preschool, family childcare homes, and home visitor programs. Candidates may apply for one credential at a time. This credential has limitations. Each separate credential requires another application, fee, and requires completion of the assessment process when applying for an additional credential. The CDA credential expires three years from the award date and requires renewal. Someone may only renew it for the original setting, age-level endorsement, and specialization.

The eight CDA Subject Areas identify the skills needed by early childhood professionals. These standards are divided into eight subject areas for caregiver behavior. The goals are divided into functional areas, which describe major tasks caregivers must accomplish to satisfy the competency goals. To be eligible for this credential, individuals must meet the following criteria:

- They have earned a high school diploma.
- They are juniors or seniors enrolled in a high school early childhood education or child development Career and Technical Education (CTE) program.
- Before application, candidates must complete 120 clock hours of professional education that covers the eight CDA Subject Areas.

- Within three years of application, candidates must obtain 480 hours of experience working directly with young children.
- Within six months of application, candidates must prepare a CDA Professional Portfolio that meets the requirements outlined in the CDA Competency Standards book.

The CDA credential is valid for three years from the award date. To renew, a teacher must apply within 90 days prior to expiration.

Most of the jobs described in this chapter require at least a two-year associate's degree in child development or a related area. While a CDA is limited since the credential expires, a diploma from a technical college, college, or university does not expire. For that reason, most students elect to attend a post-secondary institution. Another advantage is many high school programs are *dual credit*. With dual credit programs, academically qualified students simultaneously earn both high school and college credit upon successful completion of a course. This allows students to complete a postsecondary degree faster and saves money on college tuition. The courses may be taught by college faculty or qualified secondary instructors.

A bachelor's degree usually requires a minimum of four years of college. Directors of early childhood or childcare programs need a bachelor's degree (**Figure 1.5**). Some jobs require a graduate degree. These include consultants,

Prostock-studio/Shutterstock.com

Figure 1.5 If you hope to become a center director, you will need to pursue a college degree in early childhood.

researchers, and early childhood instructors or professors. Some large early childhood programs require director candidates to have earned a graduate degree.

Each state establishes its own qualifications for staff who work in early childhood settings. There is no uniform standard established by the federal government other than for Head Start. The qualifications will depend on the job you are seeking and the state in which you plan to work. It is important to know the minimum requirements for your state. You can ask the local agency that licenses childcare centers what those standards are.

Lesson 1.1 Review

1. Which of the following is not a social or economic change that has impacted careers in early childhood? (1.1.1)
   A. Growing cultural diversity
   B. Changes in family structures
   C. Dress codes in schools
   D. Rising cost of child care
2. Who handles all aspects of classroom functioning? (1.1.2)
   A. Head teacher
   B. Nanny
   C. Associate teacher
   D. Licensing specialist
3. A CDA credential may be obtained in each of the following settings except a (1.1.3)
   A. center-based infant-toddler program.
   B. second-grade classroom.
   C. family child care home.
   D. home visitor program.
4. **True or False.** Preschool teachers typically need at least a master's degree.

Becoming a Successful Teacher

Essential Question

What factors do I need to know about teacher roles, responsibilities, and characteristics in my aspiration to become an early childhood professional?

Learning Outcomes

After studying this lesson, you will be able to

1.2-1 summarize all aspects of teacher roles and responsibilities in early childhood care and education.

1.2-2 analyze personal characteristics that can help early childhood teachers care for and educate young children.

Key Terms

early childhood educator

advocate

developmentally appropriate practice (DAP)

ethical

ethics

professional development

intentional

intrinsic motivation

mentor

People who are considering careers in early childhood often have at least three major questions. First, they want to know whether there will be a need for people educated in early childhood. They want to know about the job responsibilities of early childhood educators. In addition, they ask about the personal characteristics needed to be successful in this field. This lesson summarizes teachers' responsibilities and characteristics of successful teachers.

1.2-1 The Teacher's Responsibilities

Most career opportunities in early childhood will be as teachers, assistant teachers, or teacher's aides. A more recent term is **early childhood educator**. This is someone who has achieved mastery of the knowledge, competencies, and early childhood skills. So, the individual meets the specialized educational qualifications of the profession and has acquired an associate's or bachelor's degree. These professionals are needed for childcare centers, preschools, prekindergarten programs, Head Start programs, and in early childhood programs in public and private schools. Because of this need, this book will emphasize the knowledge and skills needed to teach young children.

Your responsibilities as an early childhood teacher will be complex and demanding. You will have both direct and indirect influences on children. Directly, you will interact with children. Indirectly, you will influence children through the arrangement of space, so that every child, regardless of ability, thrives. You will need to provide developmentally appropriate learning experiences and embrace children with disabilities and their families by serving as an *advocate*. An **advocate** is a person who defends, supports, or promotes the interest of others. As an early childhood teacher, you will serve a dual role. Often you will play both the teacher and parent-educator role. Usually, the younger the child, the more support you need to provide to the parent in the transition from home to center. The parent may also seek advice on such aspects of child development as toilet learning, biting, thumb-sucking, and temper tantrums.

You will also need to be a friend, colleague, counselor, janitor, nurse, decorator, safety expert, and even a cook on some days. Not all your tasks will be pleasant. Sometimes your work may be unpleasant, such as changing messy diapers and cleaning up after a sick child. You will wipe noses and clean messes, such as spilled milk, dumped paint, or a leaky sensory table.

Challenging and *rewarding* are two words that can best describe the responsibilities of an early childhood teacher. You will face challenges with planning developmentally appropriate curriculum, designing culturally relevant teacher-made materials, and coping with challenging behavior in the classroom. You may become discouraged, particularly when behavioral changes are slow. Once the changes occur, however, the rewards are well worth the time and effort. Early childhood teachers usually feel useful, needed, and important (**Figure 1.6**). Working with young children is an act of hope for a better future. Most teachers also enjoy feeling loved by the children. For these reasons, most early childhood teachers thoroughly enjoy their profession.

MBI/Shutterstock.com

Figure 1.6   Affection from children helps make teaching in early childhood a rewarding career. *What other interactions with children would you find rewarding?*

Health Highlights

Health Policies and Practices

As an early childhood professional, you are responsible for all children's health and safety. Become familiar with your center's policies and practices regarding children's health and safety. This includes all forms and documents that should be in every child's file. Forms may include medical checkup and immunization records, accident or injury forms, and medication logs.

To Know How Children Grow and Develop

Teachers need to know what children are like. Regardless of your position, you will need a thorough understanding of child growth and development. You will need to understand the needs, skills, and interests of children at different ages. This understanding will help you prepare inviting and developmentally appropriate

environments for young children. Likewise, it will help you design educational experiences that promote children's growth in knowledge, skills, and self-confidence. Knowing the principles of child development will assist you in developing a curriculum that is challenging and interesting without being difficult or discouraging.

Understanding children's behavior will help you work effectively with individuals and groups of children. You learn that children behave the way they do because their behavior brings them pleasure. What happens to the child after acting determines whether they will continue this behavior. A child who throws a tantrum to get a second turn on a bike (and gets a second turn) will usually repeat this behavior. Thus, *you* teach children to behave the way they do. Most of what they learn they will learn from other people, including you.

As you work with young children, you will notice differences in behavior. Children can learn to be friendly, and they can learn to be aggressive. As a teacher, you need to teach children to interact positively. Your goal is to teach them to be cooperative and skillful in getting along with others. To do this, you will need to learn and use developmentally appropriate guidance and group management techniques.

To Plan a Developmentally Appropriate Curriculum

Teachers are responsible for planning a developmentally appropriate curriculum. **Developmentally appropriate practice (DAP)** is a framework or approach to working with young children. The knowledge of how children learn and develop at different ages and stages forms the foundation of DAP. To plan a developmentally appropriate curriculum, you need to know the typical characteristics of a particular age group. This will help you understand what the children can do. DAP involves making thoughtful decisions based on what is known about young children.

Using this approach, teachers can make decisions about the environment, activities, materials, tools, and interactions. Teachers base their planning on the child's:

- age
- skills
- strengths
- knowledge
- culture and ethnicity
- interests

Quality programs focus on the "whole child," matching practice with knowledge of child development and learning. Such programs emphasize the physical, cognitive, and social-emotional development, and can provide long-term, positive differences in the lives of young children. The knowledge in this book is critical for helping you make developmentally appropriate decisions.

Physical development is stressed in a quality early childhood curriculum. Young children develop a variety of skills through physical experiences that are a foundation for later learning. Coordination, stamina, flexibility, strength, and sensory awareness are all included (**Figure 1.7**).

Young children need to gain information to understand and function in the world. As a result, cognitive development is an important area of the child's development. Problem-solving through hands-on activities will be an important part of the children's learning.

Emotional development is also an important element of a developmentally appropriate curriculum. Young children need to understand themselves. Understanding their feelings helps children develop self-awareness and self-knowledge. To become emotionally literate, children need help in learning to recognize, label, and accept their feelings. They need to learn to assert their rights in culturally accepted ways without hurting others.

Children also need to develop social skills to interact effectively and get along with others. They must learn to regulate their own behavior according to society's rules and values. When in a group setting, they need to learn to carry out desirable actions. Taking turns when talking, respecting individual differences, and sharing toys and materials are all essential skills for developing social competence.

antoniodiaz/Shutterstock.com

Figure 1.7   Curriculum should include activities that help improve muscle strength and coordination. *What are two activities you might propose to help preschoolers improve their muscle strength and coordination?*

Your curriculum will need to be developmentally appropriate for the children. You will need to balance child-initiated activities with teacher-initiated activities. A broad knowledge of all the curriculum areas outlined in this book is important. You will find that an understanding of science, math, music, literacy, movement, social studies, art, dramatic play, and storytelling will influence what you do with children.

To Prepare the Learning Environment

A large part of the teaching process involves preparing an inviting, culturally relevant, and stimulating learning environment. Learning is an active process whereby children gain knowledge and develop new skills. The environment that you provide must encourage children to independently experiment, explore, and manipulate (**Figure 1.8**). Interaction with materials is a vital learning vehicle.

As a teacher, you will need to provide a variety of materials. These materials will encourage children to engage in positive social activities. They will also promote physical, cognitive, and social-emotional development. Lack of variety or quantity can lead to lags in development and behavior problems. For instance, if there are not enough interesting materials, children may fight over the few that

MBI/Shutterstock.com

Figure 1.8 It is up to you as a teacher to make learning an active process. ***In what ways do you think this teacher is engaging these children in active learning?***

they enjoy. Chapters have been included in this book to teach you how to arrange space and select toys, equipment, and supplies.

To Communicate Effectively

To be an effective teacher, you need to have good communication skills. These skills are important for ease in expressing ideas and gaining trust with children, their families, and your peers.

Positive communication skills will help you form and maintain a close relationship with the children in your care. Your words will inform, explain, and guide them. It is important to use proper grammar when speaking to children. This will help them learn the proper way to speak as well. Listening actively to what the children share is just as important as speaking.

Effective communication with families is also vital. Most early childhood teachers and caregivers have daily contact with the children's parents or guardians, either in person or electronically. Therefore, it is important to demonstrate effective electronic communication skills.

Early childhood teachers must also be able to form meaningful relationships with their colleagues. To provide a quality educational program for young children, all staff must work cooperatively. This requires open communication.

To Demonstrate Teamwork and Leadership

An important part of any employment is getting along with your coworkers. Staff in early childhood programs need to work as a team (**Figure 1.9**). To demonstrate characteristics of effective team members, help make your coworkers feel respected. Everyone enjoys feeling valued.

To demonstrate effective characteristics of leaders, you need to support your coworkers through your actions and your words. Empathize with them by recognizing and reflecting their feelings. Share ideas and information with them. Tell them when they have planned interesting activities. Praise them for meaningful interactions with the children. Furthermore, accept their style of caregiving.

MBI/Shutterstock.com

Figure 1.9 When staff members take and give suggestions on curriculum, they can give children the best care possible. *Why do you think teamwork is important in an early childhood setting?*

Even when team members work well together, conflicts will arise. Knowing how to resolve conflicts effectively is fundamental to teamwork. Being able to talk through a situation and work together to find a solution can be challenging. With practice, however, you can look at conflict resolution as just a regular part of working on a team.

To Manage Time Wisely

Rarely does an early childhood teacher have time to do everything he or she wants to do. Therefore, time management skills are essential. Time management skills help teachers work smarter, not harder. They help you organize your time, set priorities, and distinguish between important and urgent matters.

No matter what you accomplish, there is always more that you could do. You might want to make one more bulletin board, write a letter to a parent, or develop new teaching materials. Time-management skills will help you make choices and use your time wisely.

To Participate in Professional Organizations

The field of early childhood constantly changes. Joining a professional organization can help you keep up with current developments in the field. To enjoy the full benefit of membership, you must be an active participant.

Family, Career and Community Leaders of America (FCCLA) is an organization for middle and high school family and consumer sciences students. Members develop skills for life through character development, creative and critical thinking, interpersonal communication, practical knowledge, and career preparation. Participation can be at the local, regional, and national level.

The largest professional organization in early childhood is the *National Association for the Education of Young Children (NAEYC)*. This highly respected and credible organization was founded in 1926 to improve professional practice and preparation. With nearly 60,000 members and 52 affiliates. NAEYC is the primary organization for the early childhood field. This organization has local, state, and national affiliates. Membership services include annual state and national conferences. The organization also offers a journal, a magazine online resources, blogs, and discussion groups.

Becoming a member of a professional organization is important for your career. These organizations are sponsored locally, regionally, and nationally. Attending conferences, reading materials, and interacting with peers are part of being a professional. By participating, you will keep informed of teaching trends, issues, research, legislation, upcoming events, and new publications. **Figure 1.10** provides the names of major early childhood education professional organizations.

To Follow Ethical Standards

When you work with young children, you will face each day with decisions of an ethical nature. You will need to choose between conflicting options. To help you make these tough choices, you will rely on your **ethics**, or guiding set of moral principles. Your ethics will help you choose the option that is most **ethical**, or conforming to accepted standards of conduct.

People who work with young children should always model ethical behavior. They should also maintain the highest standards of professional conduct. For early childhood professionals, these standards are reflected in the Code of Ethical Conduct created by NAEYC. This code establishes

Professional Organizations

- American Montessori Association
- American Montessori Society®
- Association for Childhood Education International (ACEI)
- Council for Exceptional Children (CEC)
- Family, Career and Community Leaders of America (FCCLA)
- National Association of Child Care Professionals (NACCP)
- National Association for the Education of Young Children (NAEYC)
- National Association for Family Child Care (NAFCC)
- National Child Care Association (NCCA)
- National Head Start Association (NHSA)
- ZERO to THREE

Figure 1.10 Involvement in a professional organization can help you grow as an early childhood professional.

Ethical Responsibilities

Do No Harm

According the *NAEYC Code of Ethical Conduct and Statement of Commitment,* the primary responsibility of early childhood professionals above all others is to "do no harm." This principle guides the foundation of early childhood programs, practices, and classrooms.

Dig deeper

Think about the principle "do no harm." Write a few thoughtful sentences indicating what this principle means to you in regard to becoming an early childhood professional. Then review Principle P-1.1 under Section 1 of the NAEYC Code found in Appendix A of *Working with Young Children*. Why is it important for individuals who are pursuing a career in early childhood to examine themselves and any personal biases to ensure they do not participate in any practices that may harm children in any way? If needed, review the text references and online resources to further explore the meaning of "do no harm" as it relates to early childhood practice. Write a summary of your findings.

guidelines of responsible behavior to follow in relationship to children, families, colleagues, and communities. The foundation for the Code is a set of core values for the profession set forth by NAEYC. (See the Appendix A of this text to learn more about NAEYC's Code of Ethical Conduct.)

Professionals who follow the Code of Ethical Conduct ensure that programs for young children

are based on the most recent knowledge of child development and early childhood education. In their communities, these professionals serve as advocates for children, families, and teachers. They recognize that biases, opinions, and values can alter professional judgment. As a result, these professionals are always open to new ideas and suggestions.

Sometimes choosing ethical behavior is difficult. You might be called on to make a decision that is unpopular with families, children, or coworkers. A professional who behaves ethically follows the right decision, no matter what others do. Being ethically responsible might also mean taking action in some sticky situations. When this occurs, you are facing an ethical dilemma in which there is over one course of action. For instance, if you know a coworker is stealing supplies from the center, you may feel a powerful pull to report this unethical behavior to the director. You will have to weigh the importance of telling against the consequences of not telling. For many professionals, violating their ethics just to avoid conflict is too great a price to pay.

In a sense, much of this text deals with ethics. The chapters of this book will teach you the best practices for making day-to-day decisions while working with young children. Following these best practices will bring you into alignment with the Code of Ethical Conduct. As you study the chapters that follow, think about ethical dilemmas that might arise and ask yourself how you would handle these situations.

To Practice Lifelong Learning

Professional development is an ongoing process through which people update their knowledge and skills related to their professional lives (**Figure 1.11**). A teacher never finishes learning. To keep up with happenings in the field, you need to be a committed, lifelong learner. Conferences, workshops, in-service training, course work, journals, podcasts, videos, blogs, study groups, and books are all professional development activities that help teachers learn more about their field. In addition, taking part in one or more professional organizations is essential to learning recent developments in the field.

insta_photos/Shutterstock.com

Figure 1.11 Participating in online learning opportunities is an important part of continuing education for early childhood teachers. ***In what other ways might an early childhood professional participate in continuing education?***

Frequently introduce new materials in environment. Try using new activities and instructional strategies. Discuss the impact with your classroom colleagues and ask for constructive feedback. Some teachers find it helpful to keep a portfolio to assess their progress. The portfolio could contain photographs and videos of activities, room arrangements, and children's work.

1.2-2 Characteristics of Successful Teachers

Working with young children requires a special person. As an early childhood teacher, you will need to build on your own strengths and develop your own style. Each teacher is different. Some teachers are outgoing and lively. Other teachers may be reserved and naturally quiet. Both styles can be effective. Simply copying the style of another teacher will not make you a successful teacher. You must know yourself and develop a style that best suits your personality. When your style suits your personality, you will feel more comfortable working with children and adults. You will also find more enjoyment in your profession.

Although teachers may use unique styles, successful teachers have some common characteristics (**Figure 1.12**). These traits help teachers cope with the day-to-day situations that are naturally part of their work.

Passionate About Working with Children

The most important trait of an early childhood teacher is passion for children. The rapport established with each child determines the program's success. Every child requires understanding and acceptance. Each child's family cultural background, interests, needs, and desires requires respect.

As an early childhood teacher, you will need to show affection for each child with whom you work. You need to be kind, firm, and understanding. These actions affect how children feel about themselves and show children

Characteristics of a Successful Teacher

- Has a positive, caring attitude and a sense of humor
- Has a strong sense of ethical behavior
- Has passion for young children
- Relates easily and spontaneously to others
- Is kind, patient, and confident
- Is creative and resourceful
- Is dependable and reliable, and respects differences
- Is a keen observer, listener, and communicator
- Solves problems well and makes sound decisions
- Demonstrates inclusiveness, equity, and respects differences.
- Maintains open communication with parents, staff, and volunteers
- Promotes positive classroom behaviors
- Is compassionate and accepting of children's strong emotions, such as anger, love, and wonder
- Enjoys challenges and is willing and able to grow
- Takes initiative in the classroom
- Has knowledge of child growth and development, assessment, and child guidance
- Keeps abreast of changes in the field by reading, attending conferences, seminars, and courses
- Is a lifelong learner
- Becomes an active member of professional organizations
- Can juggle several activities at once
- Feels rewarded by even minimal progress
- Communicates and resolves conflicts well
- Has a lot of energy
- Understands the importance of self-care
- Uses reflection to improve practices

Judy Herr

Figure 1.12 Successful teachers have many positive characteristics. *What other characteristics can you add to the list?*

how to treat each other. As part of their social development, young children need to be taught that people and feelings are important.

Feeling loved, safe, valued, and emotionally secure helps children develop intellectually, socially, and emotionally. As you show children they are important, children will have confidence in themselves. They are more willing to try new activities and interact positively with others.

Patience

Effective teachers are also patient, allowing children time to explore, solve problems, and create. Young children often need extra time to complete tasks. Children also need the opportunity to repeat tasks. Much of a child's learning occurs as the result of repetition.

Children are naturally curious and may constantly repeat simple questions. Children do not always remember everything they have been told. Repeating information and reminding children of limits may seem tedious. When handling these situations patiently, however, teachers help children grow and learn while building their self-esteem.

Compassion

Compassionate teachers can accept others without prejudice. Being compassionate requires self-knowledge and self-acceptance. It involves accepting any emotion from others, such as anger, grief, joy, fear, love, or even hate.

A compassionate teacher does not simply observe a child's feelings. The compassionate teacher is sensitive to both positive and negative feelings the children express.

Teachers show compassion by affirming children for their successes. They also avoid actions that make children feel worthless, such as punishment and shaming. Compassionate teachers work to help children understand the feelings of others and motivate children to respect each other.

Confidence

Having confidence in your abilities helps you relax in the classroom. Teachers who are relaxed and natural are more successful with children. Children, especially the younger ones, can become easily excited. By remaining calm and self-assured, you will have a calming effect on the children.

Your ability to make sensible decisions affects your confidence. You need to feel sure the choices you make are in the best interest of the children. For instance, when it is raining, children should not be taken outside. Children may not always understand such decisions. If you stand by your choices with confidence, children will accept them.

Sense of Humor

People of all cultures and ages respond to humor. A sense of humor is helpful when working with children because they enjoy adults who can laugh. Laughter helps children relax and feel content. When children see a teacher with a positive, cheerful attitude, they are more likely to be positive and cheerful.

Keeping a sense of humor can also make your work more enjoyable. Seeing the funny side of children's actions and classroom incidents can be a rewarding experience. Seeing the humor and joy in situations can also help you cope with some of the daily stresses of teaching. Of course, you must be careful to laugh with, not at, children.

Commitment

The job of an early childhood teacher can be challenging. Demands on your energy will be high. You will find that meeting the demands of this field requires a serious commitment. To keep up with current developments in the field, you must constantly study. You will be expected to be an expert in child development, health, safety, child guidance, curriculum, and relationships. Parents will ask your advice on such issues as toy selection, toilet learning, and guidance.

Intentionality

Preparing for daily teaching is also time consuming. To be a successful teacher, you must be **intentional**. Intentional teachers act purposefully in helping children gain knowledge, interests, habits, and attitudes. To be an intentional teacher, you must carefully assess the children's knowledge, skills, and interests to plan a developmentally appropriate curriculum and environment. You must fully understand the goals of each activity. The activities planned for the day must address all areas of a child's development. Balance these activities so children are not constantly active or quiet. (**Figure 1.13**).

Creativity

Successful teachers constantly working at developing and growing their creativity. With patience and time, creativity can blossom. The result can be a more attracting, engaging, and educational environments for the children. Likewise, teacher feel self-satisfaction observing

Figure 1.13 Spending the time needed to plan a developmentally appropriate curriculum takes a firm commitment from a teacher.

the children's excitement as well as colleagues and parents' comments.

Creativity does not just happen. Creative teachers look for ideas everywhere. They are constantly searching by keeping their mind, eyes, and ears open. They observe their colleague's classrooms, attend conferences, and search curriculum guides. Carry a notebook and pen to ensure you do not forget new ideas. Take pictures with a smartphone or tablet to reference them for new ideas.

Intrinsic Motivation

Knowing that you really want to teach young children is important to your success. Your *intrinsic motivation* to learn all you can about young children and apply this knowledge in your early childhood practice is also key to your success. **Intrinsic motivation** is motivation that is driven by internal rewards that you find satisfying. Although you may have doubts, you need to feel that working with young children is rewarding. Hearing children make comments, such as "I love you" or "you're nice," should boost your self-esteem.

Questioning a career choice is not unusual. You will discover that even experienced teachers have days when they wonder why they chose this career. These questions are healthy. If they help you determine you belong in early childhood education, you will feel more confident and committed to your career choice.

Only you can decide whether teaching is really for you. You know yourself better than others do. To make this decision, carefully examine your own interests, feelings, and satisfactions (**Figure 1.14**). Studying the chapters in this book can help you in this process. Each chapter contains important concepts that you can explore and apply in settings working with young children.

Working with children will increase your insights. Provide yourself sufficient time, however. Until you understand how children grow and develop, how to guide them, and how to develop appropriate curriculum, you might not feel much self-satisfaction. Given time, though, you will discover the real joys and rewards of working with young children.

Mentors

Center directors often assign to a mentor to a new employee to promote their professional growth. A **mentor** is a more experienced teacher who encourages, guides, coaches, and influences the growth and development of a less-experienced person. They are a source of knowledge, offering support and encouragement.

Your mentor will have experiences from which you can learn. They can share any mistakes that they made when beginning teaching young children. Mentors can expand your networks by helping you make connections with professional organizations, other professional, and potential early childhood training opportunities.

Physical and Mental Health

Teaching young children is demanding, both physically and mentally. It requires you to be constantly alert to handle multiple tasks and model healthy social-emotional skills. Meeting these demands requires a self-care plan to reduce stress and improve the quality of your life. Eating

A Letter to a New Teacher

Dear Teacher:

As you begin working with young children, you will meet many new challenges and find new answers. This process will continue throughout your teaching career. You will find that being a good teacher is a matter of caring for yourself, the children you teach, their families, and your colleagues.

There will be many exciting and fulfilling days. The children will be experiencing many new discoveries. You will experience, their excitement, joy, and love of learning-and their energy will be contagious.

You will also have days that are discouraging and exhausting. Teaching is not an easy job. It can be physically, emotionally, and mentally exhausting. At times, you may feel like you are on a roller coaster. The costs may seem to exceed the rewards. Luckily, most of the time you will find teaching is rewarding and personally satisfying. Teachers of young children are stewards of the next generation. As a result, you will be influencing lifelong outcomes in children's behavior, health, and learning.

Changes in practice take time. When you end the classroom at the end of the day, have a conversation with yourself. Reflect on your actions. Also, respond on the ways the children responded to these actions. This process will affect your teaching effectiveness.

Remember you will only get out of a career what you invest in it. You must be aware of where you need development. Also, you must be willing to work overtime, if needed, and seek new answers. You must take advantage of professional development opportunities. Participation will improve your teaching skills—benefitting the children, their families, and your joy of teaching.

Try learning as much as you can about child development, child guidance, curriculum areas, the teaching process, families, and culture. Improving teaching effectiveness is a lifelong process. Becoming a self-mentor is important. Talking to your colleagues, reading professional journals, joining professional organizations, and attending conferences are several methods for self-improvement. Taking additional course work and obtaining advanced degrees will also strengthen your understanding of young children and improve your competence. Chances are, if you are actively involved, you will never lose your love and thrill of teaching.

Best wishes for the beginning of your teaching journey. Students who follow their hearts in selecting teaching as a career will most likely end up laboring at what they love. They will make the world a better place by making children and their families stronger and wiser.

Judy Herr

Figure 1.14   The author of this text offers some inspiring information to aspiring early childhood professionals. *What advice strikes you as most important?*

nutritious meals and getting enough sleep is important. You will also need to stay physically active and reduce stress. Seek counseling or other professional help if you notice problems with your mental health, such as stress, depression, or lasting anxiety. Keeping yourself physically and mentally healthy allows you to meet the challenges of your job.

Lesson 1.2 Review

1. Which of the following is not present in an appropriate and stimulating learning environment? (1.2.1)
   A. A variety of engaging learning materials
   B. Safe, age-appropriate toys
   C. Books
   D. Tall shelving units
2. Which of the following is a common characteristic of successful early childhood teachers? (1.2.2)
   A. Promotes positive classroom behaviors
   B. Loses patience easily
   C. Does not enjoy challenges
   D. Low energy level

3. Teachers can do each of the following to help maintain their physical and emotional health except (1.2.2)
   A. get enough sleep.
   B. eat nutritious meals.
   C. stay physically fit.
   D. not seek help if they are suffering from depression or anxiety.
4. **True or False.** Intrinsic motivation is driven by internal rewards that you find satisfying.

Summary

Lesson 1.1

1.1-1 Many social and economic changes are creating new opportunities in childcare and early childhood education.

1.1-1 The demand for quality early childhood education services is high.

1.1-2 Early childhood advocates work to expand the availability of early childhood programs.

1.1-3 Most jobs in early childhood require at least a certificate or a degree.

1.1-3 Qualifications vary from state to state. Requirements are increasing as prekindergarten programs are moving into the public schools.

Lesson 1.2

1.2-1 Most career opportunities in early childhood are as teachers or assistant teachers.

1.2-1 Teachers must understand principles of child growth and development.

1.2-1 Teachers develop curriculum and create classroom environments that meet children's developmental needs. They need communication, teamwork, and time management skills.

1.2-1 Joining professional organizations, continuing education, and following ethical principles are also important.

1.2-2 A successful teacher is on a continuous journey of self-discovery. They should develop a style that works well for them.

1.2-2 Most successful teachers have many traits in common.

Vocabulary Activity

Classify the list of terms into categories. Then pair up with a classmate and compare how you classified the terms. How were your lists similar or different? Discuss your lists with the class.

Critical Thinking

1. **Determine.** Early childhood teachers often assume a parent-educator role. Some school districts and youth service agencies provide parent education as part of their early childhood programs. Research types of parent-education activities available in the community. What role could early childhood educators play in providing parenting education to parents of young children? Write a brief summary.

2. **Identify.** Visit the website for the National Resource Center for Health and Safety in Childcare. To get information regarding licensing in your state, click on State Licensing and Regulation Information. Then click on your state on the map.

3. **Draw Conclusions.** Search the Internet to learn about the job duties of a licensing specialist. What are the educational requirements for this position? How is the job outlook for a licensing specialist over the next 10 years? Write a brief report to record your findings.

4. **Draw Conclusions.** Write an essay explaining your understanding of ethics. How will knowledge of ethical standards affect your work performance? Include thoughts on attitude, honesty, teamwork, professionalism, and personal responsibility. Refer to any previous ethical dilemma you have experienced.

5. **Identify.** Review a local childcare center's policies and practices regarding children's health and safety. What forms and documents does the center require for every child? What additional forms or policies might be added? Discuss your findings in class.
6. **Analyze.** What leadership characteristics do you demonstrate? How do you demonstrate characteristics of effective team members? Explain why collaboration among staff is necessary in the childcare classroom.
7. **Identify.** Review the qualities of a successful teacher given in Figure 1.13. Make a list of qualities from the chart that you possess.

Core Skills

1. **Reading.** Review the jobs listed on NAEYC's Early Childhood Education Career Center. The Career Center is free to all job seekers. It provides you with the best jobs and employers in the field. Make a list of jobs in which early childhood training would be helpful.
2. **Writing.** Write a one-page paper on why time-management is important in early childhood education.
3. **Research and Writing.** Investigate child advocacy initiatives currently being sponsored by your state or the nation. Prepare a written report on the aims of the initiatives, expected results of the initiatives, and what citizens can do to promote child advocacy initiatives.
4. **Research and Writing.** Research training programs for nannies. Note the location, course content, length, cost, and job placement opportunities for the programs. Compare these to certificate or degree programs in early childhood at a community or area college or university or other training program. Report your findings to the class.
5. **Research and Speaking.** Take a survey of early childhood teachers. Ask them to share the advantages and disadvantages of teaching. Share your findings with the class.

6. **Research and Speaking.** Search the Internet for information on any changes in the early childhood field. What reading materials, conferences, seminars, or courses are available to expand knowledge of the changes? Use presentation software to share your findings with the class.
7. **Research and Writing.** Staying committed to the job of early childhood educator can cause stress for even the most confident and easygoing individual. Research strategies on dealing with the daily stress encountered in this field. Create a database of "stress builders" and "stress busters." How can knowing how to handle stress affect your performance in high school and in future employment? Write a brief report of your findings.
8. **Writing.** Write a summary of how critical-thinking and problem-solving skills will help you in your early childhood education career.
9. **Research.** Research and evaluate entrepreneurial opportunities for early childhood development and early childhood services.
10. **CTE Career Readiness Practice.** Locate a person who works at a local childcare facility. Plan to job shadow or work with this individual as a mentor as you pursue your career. How can you benefit by having such a mentor in your life?

Portfolio Project

Create a portfolio. Get a folder or large manila envelope or create an electronic portfolio. Brainstorm unique items that can be added. Throughout the course, your teacher will designate items you will add, such as writing assignments, lesson plans, résumé, certificates, photographs, journal entries, and documentation of service hours.

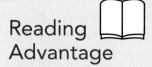

Chapter 2

Reading Advantage

Skim the chapter by reading the first sentence of each paragraph. Use this information to create an outline of the chapter before you read it. Take notes as you read the chapter using the outline.

Types of Early Childhood Programs

Lesson 2.1: Program Options and Sponsorship

Lesson 2.2: Program Quality, Licensing, and Accreditation

Case Study

Types of Childcare Programs

Read the case study as a class and discuss the questions that follow. After you finish reading the chapter, discuss the case study again. Have your opinions changed based on what you learned? If so, how?

The Barillas are both gainfully employed at two different companies. Six months ago, they had their first child. One parent had parental leave, which was expiring in three weeks, so they needed to find daily childcare from 8:30 a.m. to 4:30 p.m., Monday through Friday. One parent's company was a 45-minute drive in pleasant weather. The other parent rode a subway to and from work.

After talking with friends, families, and colleagues, they felt they had three options. One parent's company provided on-site childcare. The second option was a family childcare home that was located a block away in their neighborhood. The last option was an early childhood education center located a mile from their residence.

The Barillas decided the best approach to selecting a program was to visit each facility, observe the program, and talk to the teacher(s) and care providers. They found that there were distinct differences among the programs. All programs met state licensing requirements. The first program they visited was the corporate on-site childcare center located 45 minutes from their home at one parent's employer. All teachers in this program had four-year degrees. Next, they visited a preschool accredited by the National Association for the Education of Young Children. The teachers and care providers had either four- or two-year degrees. A childcare home was the last center they visited, at which the owner had a one-year certificate from a local technical college. Three other children were currently enrolled in the program: a two-, three-, and four-year-old.

Give It Some Thought

1. Were the Barillas using an effective approach for evaluating childcare options? Are there other factors they should have considered?
2. What factors do you think influence program quality?
3. How do licensing rules and regulations impact a program?
4. What are the advantages of each type of childcare—a corporate on-site center, family daycare home, and a preschool center?
5. Which of the three options would you select? Why?

Opening image credit: Weekend Images Inc./E+ via Getty Images

Program Options and Sponsorship

Essential Question

 What do I need to know about various types of early childhood programs, their benefits, and types of sponsorship when investigating career options in early childhood?

Learning Outcomes

After studying this lesson, you will be able to

2.1-1 **summarize** and assess the various early childhood programs available to parents and their children.

2.1-2 **differentiate** among the types of early childhood program sponsorship.

Key Terms

socioeconomic status (SES)

childcare centers

Head Start

Early Head Start

universal prekindergarten (UPK)

learning standards

school-age childcare programs

check-in services

parent cooperatives

laboratory schools

for-profit centers

nonprofit centers

Today, someone other than their parents care for most American children. Families rely on a variety of childcare services to meet family and work needs. According to the United States Census Bureau, most preschool-age children take part in some type of program. The number of continues to grow, which has driven up the demand for early childhood programs. Parents place their children in early childhood programs for two main reasons.

Many parents like the rich learning environment of a high-quality developmentally appropriate early childhood program. Brain research shows that children learn from the earliest moments of life. Their learning is most rapid in the first five years. High-quality programs stimulate learning in this period (**Figure 2.1**). Studies continue to show that children from high-quality programs did better in primary grades than other children in reading, math, and social skills. They also get along with their peers better and have fewer behavioral problems.

2.1-1 Early Childhood Program Options

Distinct differences exist among the many types of early childhood programs. Such

ucchie79/Shutterstock.com

Figure 2.1 A challenging environment can help children develop cognitively, emotionally, socially, and physically. ***What areas of development is this child's activity supporting?***

programs may differ in their philosophies, ownership, program offerings, and sources of support. They also vary in size, staff qualifications, hours of operation, facilities, and fees. They may vary in terms of quality, even when they are of the same type.

Some types of programs are more common than others. All of them, however, should be high-quality and designed to meet the needs of young children. Studies show that properly designed programs result in substantial long-term gains.

Access to early childhood programs varies and often depends on socioeconomic status. **Socioeconomic status (SES)** relates to a combination of social and financial factors that affect people's ability to meet basic needs, including access to early childhood care and education and other resources. Preschool children from families with higher socioeconomic status are more likely to attend early childhood programs. Preschool children from families with lower socioeconomic status have access to Head Start. Families with moderate socioeconomic status are challenged in finding affordable, high-quality programs. While they cannot afford private programs, their income level makes them ineligible for those that are federally funded.

Early Childhood Insight

NAFCC

The *National Association for Family Child Care (NAFCC)* is a professional organization for family childcare providers. It promotes high-quality early childcare and education. NAFCC is committed to improving the awareness and quality of childcare. The organization requires training and health assessments for accreditation. Other requirements include criminal background checks and an observation to verify that providers meet standards.

Family Childcare Homes

A popular form of childcare in the United States provided other than by a relative or parent is called *family childcare*. In this type of program, the caregiver provides care and education in the caregiver's home with a few children. Often the location of the home is in the child's own neighborhood. Most states require licensing or registration for family childcare homes. In those states, operating without a license or registration is against the law. The state could impose a misdemeanor offense and fine. Family childcare home programs are often popular for infants and toddlers, but children might range from infants to school-age. Children may attend up to 12 hours per day.

Home-based care is the most-used arrangement for infants and toddlers. Advantages usually include

- a home like environment;
- fewer illnesses since children are exposed to fewer children;
- continuity of care can be provided as child has the same caregiver throughout the day;
- more flexible hours;
- a caregiver who may speak the child's home (native) language; and
- siblings that may be cared for in the same environment.

Childcare and Early Childhood Centers

Childcare centers, or *early childhood centers*, are facilities that offer full-day children's programs. Most twenty-first century programs focus on loving care and education. The design of care meets the child's basic nutrition, health, and safety needs. The curriculum emphasizes the whole child, including social-emotional, cognitive and physical needs, and self-esteem.

Most centers provide for larger groups of children than family childcare homes. They operate on a schedule that is convenient for working parents. Many centers open early in the morning and remain open until six or seven o'clock in the evening. Some centers provide care for children 24 hours per day. For parents whose children need care during the evening or early morning hours, this service is most convenient.

Program

The program provided depends on the philosophy of the center and the educational background and skills of the staff. State licensing rules and accreditation guidelines also influence the program. For example, the National Association of for the Education of Young Children (NAEYC) defines early childhood groups as:

- Infants and toddlers: birth to 36 months
- Preschool: three- and four-year-olds
- Kindergarten: five- and six-year-olds
- Primary grades—first, second and third grades: six-, seven-, and eight-year-olds

Ideally, the program should meet the child's needs in all areas of development. The focus should be on the whole child and include a balance of engaging learning activities that promote their optimum development. See **Figure 2.2.**

Military Childcare Programs

The United States Department of Defense (DOD) childcare system offers the largest employer-sponsored childcare program in the United States. The need for military childcare has grown. A greater number of military spouses are working outside the home and the number of parents in the armed services has grown. In addition, the number of dual-military couples has increased. Childcare provides them with a quality-of-life benefit, which helps support recruitment and retention. Recent statistics show military childcare centers provide services to approximately 200,000 children of uniformed personnel and employs over 26,000 workers.

The Department of Defense has 850 child development centers around the world. There are programs across the United States and overseas. About 95 percent of these centers are accredited by the National Association for the Education of

Ignasi Soler/Shutterstock.com

Figure 2.2   Materials used in a Montessori school are designed to help children learn with little adult guidance. *What skills do you think children are learning from using these materials?*

Young Children (NAEYC). Children can attend child development centers, family childcare homes, or school-age care. The benefits of working in these programs are attractive. Military childcare employees receive paid leave, health and life insurance, retirement benefits, and tuition assistance. These benefits reduce turnover and enhance program quality.

Head Start and Early Head Start

In the 1965, the federal government designed an eight-week summer-school program to overcome the negative effects of low socioeconomic status for three-, four-, and five-year-old children. The original intention of the program was to prepare America's children from families with lower incomes in a few weeks to start elementary school ready to learn. The program was updated the following year when Congress authorized it as a year-round program. Today it also includes Early Head Start, Migrant and Seasonal Head Start, American Indian and Alaska Native Head Start, and Family and Community Partnerships. Programs are available to all children who have special needs, including those who have severe disabilities.

Head Start is complex. It provides a free, national comprehensive child-development program. The objective is to promote high-quality, comprehensive early childhood services. Head Start's focus is on providing children with social and cognitive school-readiness skills and requires parent involvement. It also provides a variety of medical, and social services to promote healthy development for children in families with lower socioeconomic status. For example, the program provides educational, nutritional, health, medical, dental, social, mental health, and other services. Parent participation is a requirement.

Head Start mainly provides services for three- to five-year-old children. It has specific performance standards that help define the quality of services for children and their families to strengthen its educational practices. The best evidence-based research on how young children learn and develop provides the foundation for these standards.

Head Start began serving children who experience homelessness in 2007. Children who experience homelessness lack a regular, fixed, or nighttime residence. It includes children living in cars, motels, or shelters due to economic hardship. Head Start also is required to provide services to the older and younger siblings of children who experience homelessness.

As of 2013, educational qualifications for Head Start teachers require a minimum of an associate's degree, which affected the need for a CDA credential. As a result, today over 62 percent of teachers in Head Start programs have earned a bachelor's degree.

Education

The curriculum design in a Head Start program meets the needs of each child, reflecting their values, language, and culture. One goal is to build self-esteem that will lead to future success in school. Staff encourage self-confidence, curiosity, and self-discipline in the children.

Staff members design a variety of learning experiences to meet the children's needs in all areas of development: cognitive, social-emotional, and physical. The staff and the child's entire family work as a team to plan curriculum and teach children. Parent involvement is the heart of the program.

Nutrition

Many children who take part in Head Start may not have nutritious meals available at home. Providing nutrition services is a vital part of the program (**Figure 2.3**). Federal rules require centers to provide at least one healthy snack and one hot meal every day. The nutrition program serves foods that reflect children's ethnicity and cultural preferences. The goal is to help children make healthful food choices and develop healthy eating habits.

Health

All children who attend a Head Start program receive a total health plan. This includes the provision of dental, medical, and mental health services. Prior to enrollment, many of these

University of Wisconsin-Stout; Child and Family Study Center

Figure 2.3   A well-organized, sanitary kitchen is an important link in providing good nutrition for children.

children have never visited a dentist. Children who have not already received childhood immunizations may receive them during their enrollment.

Parental Involvement

Head Start recognizes the parent as the child's first teacher. Supporting parental involvement is vital to the program's success. Parents are encouraged to help recruit new children, assist in the center, and take part in policy meetings. Thus, Head Start parents can influence administrative decisions.

Later in 1994, **Early Head Start** was introduced to promote positive outcomes and healthy families. Early Head Start includes year-around services for infants and toddlers. The focus of the program is on child development, family development, staff development, and community development. There have been many studies about the effectiveness of Head Start. In 2020, a study found that former students who attended Head Start benefitted from their participation. They had higher levels of education and income than those children who did not attend.

Universal Prekindergarten

Another type of early childhood education program is **universal prekindergarten (UPK)**. The state and federal governments fund these programs, which are usually housed in public

school systems. UPK is a voluntary program designed for three- and four-year-old children and available to interested families regardless of income level. Universal prekindergartens promote a high-quality literary-rich environment. Children benefit from being involved in this environment before they enter kindergarten. They then start kindergarten eager to learn and ready for success. When children lack quality early-learning experiences, they start school at a disadvantage as compared to others.

Studies show that pre-K benefits all children, but has greater benefits for children who experience disadvantages, although other children also receive substantive benefits. Large gains depend on high-quality pre-K programs.

Kindergarten

In 1837, Friedrich Fröbel opened the first kindergarten in Germany for children three through six years of age. The name he gave to his system of education was *kindergarten*, which means children's garden. Fröbel believed that self-development took place through creative activities, such as play. Children's education should be the based on their interests and active development. The children in Fröbel's kindergarten engaged in painting, drawing, stringing beads, block building, folding, cutting, and clay modeling. The children also cared for pets, sang songs, and gardened.

The first American kindergarten opened in Watertown, Wisconsin, in 1856 for German-speaking children in the home of Margarethe Schurz. This mother and teacher studied under Fröbel. Mrs. Schurz first opened the kindergarten for her own children and four of their cousins. In 1860, Elizabeth Peabody opened an English-speaking kindergarten in Boston, Massachusetts.

Today, kindergartens are different. In the past, they focused on the child's social and emotional development. Over the years, these programs have become more academic. Math, science, and early literacy are all included in the curriculum.

Kindergartens are part of most public and many private school systems. Attendance policies vary throughout the United States. Kindergartens are usually restricted to children who are at least four years old. The purpose of kindergartens is to prepare children for primary school.

Schedules

State and local governments determine the schedules for school programs. There are two basic scheduling patterns in kindergarten: half-day and full-day sessions. The half-day sessions usually run from two and one-half to three and one-half hours per day. Full-day sessions run from six to eight hours per day, which provides children with more time in a structured setting. Studies show that children attending full-day developmentally appropriate kindergarten programs have better preparation for primary-grade learning. They have stronger learning skills and understand appropriate behavior. Their learning in mathematics, literacy, and language skills was greater in comparison to those children attending half-day programs.

Goals

Goals for a kindergarten program vary from state to state. During the past decade, these programs have become more academic. Kindergarten programs focus more on areas such as math, literacy, and science than child-initiated activities. Goals may include developing:

- literacy skills that include oral language, phonological awareness, uppercase and lowercase letter knowledge, and print knowledge;
- math skills that include number sense, measurement, geometry, and calculating;
- life science that focuses on animals, the human body, and plants;
- earth science that focuses on weather, recycling, and the environment;
- social studies skills that focus on family life, lifestyles, and responsibilities to peers and society; and
- social learning skills that foster the development of self-esteem and self-worth; following directions, using time wisely, positive peer interaction, and developing independence.

Kindergarten curriculum may vary depending on a state's core learning standards and school district requirements. **Learning standards** are instructional tools that state boards of education agree on with the help of educators in the field. They represent the agenda that has been determined for teaching and learning. Learning standards help teachers set goals, plan curriculum, and evaluate the students and themselves.

School-Age Childcare

School-age childcare programs provide care for children before and/or after school **(Figure 2.4)**. Their purpose is to meet the needs of working families. Public schools, private schools, preschools, YMCAs, YWCAs, faith-based organizations, or childcare centers often sponsor these programs. Children from five to 10 years old most often attend. School age childcare programs help meet the child's social-emotional, cognitive, and physical needs. The programs provide a comfortable environment that supplements regular classes. They provide a snack and help with homework. They also play games and take part in other large motor activities.

Judy Herr

Figure 2.4 School-age early childhood programs provide activities and care before or after school.

As an alternative, some parents use **check-in services**. These services hire workers who call the home to check whether the child has arrived safely. This is a good option only for children who are mature enough to provide self-care until parents arrive.

Parent Cooperatives

Parent cooperatives are preschools, usually serving children from three to five years old. Parents typically form and run these schools. Parents bring a unique understanding of their child, which helps the teacher create a learning environment that meets the needs of each child. They assist in the classroom on a rotating basis as a requirement of enrolling their child in the program. Parents also attend meetings and assist with preparing budgets, hiring teachers, and setting program policies and goals.

Parent cooperatives provide developmental experiences for adults and children. Specifically, parents:

- obtain guidance in their jobs as parents;
- learn what children are like at different ages and stages;
- gain several free mornings or days each month;
- become familiar with creative activities, materials, and equipment; and
- gain a more objective picture of their child's development.

Due to these experiences, many parents have reported feeling a greater sense of self-satisfaction in their parenting roles. The number of parent cooperatives continues to diminish as participation of parents in the workforce increases.

Advantages and Disadvantages

There are many advantages to teaching in a parent cooperative. Since the parents help with making administrative decisions, collecting fees, and ordering and repairing equipment, the teacher can devote more time to the children and curriculum. Another advantage can be the special relationships that many times develop between parents and teachers.

A major disadvantage of a parent cooperative is the lack of control on the teacher's part. Although the teacher acts as an adviser, parents are usually responsible for making rules. There may be differences of opinion between teacher and parents. For instance, parents may feel that children do not have to help return toys to the storage place. The teacher may feel differently. This can cause problems for many teachers.

Sessions

Parent cooperatives usually operate full-day or half-day programs. Some programs only operate on selective days of the week, such as Tuesday and Thursdays or Monday, Wednesday, and Friday. Sometimes these groups are structured by the children's ages. For example, on Tuesday and Thursday mornings, a group of two-year-old children will be scheduled. On Monday, Wednesday, and Friday mornings, three-year-olds may attend. Other centers may prefer to use the *family-type* grouping. In this type of setting, children of mixed ages may all be included in one group.

Fees

Due to the parent's involvement, fees charged at a parent cooperative are usually less than at other programs. Hiring only a head teacher helps reduce operating costs. Parents serve as the classroom aides. Each parent typically assists in the classroom several times each month. In addition, parents volunteer to perform many of the service activities. They may clean and maintain the building, prepare snacks, prepare newsletters, and do some special jobs, such as painting the classroom.

Laboratory Schools

Laboratory schools, or university- and college-affiliated programs, are on a postsecondary or college campus (**Figure 2.5**). These schools are recognized for using evidence-based research to guide their educational programs. Most have a highly qualified staff, well-planned evidence-based curriculum, up-to-date facilities, and excellent equipment. A

SDI Productions/E+ via Getty Images

Figure 2.5 Laboratory schools have highly qualified staff, well-planned curriculum, and excellent equipment. ***What are the advantages and disadvantages of laboratory schools?***

primary purpose of a laboratory school is to provide a model program to support practicum experiences for future teachers. These programs also provide faculty and students with research opportunities. As a result, they are renowned for providing excellent educational programs.

One clear advantage of a laboratory school for students majoring in early childhood education are the participation experiences available. Some laboratory schools also have an observation booth for students majoring in early childhood, graduate students, and faculty doing research. Participation in the laboratory by observing professionals and working with young children helps them understand principles of child development and child guidance. For many students, participation promotes an interest in higher education.

By attending a laboratory school, children have many advantages. One advantage is the children get to experience peers, and sometimes teachers and practicum students from different cultural backgrounds. Along with the advantages, there are some disadvantages. The environment does not always provide consistency since there is a constant turnover of student teachers and practicum students. For the children, building a long-term relationship with consistent caregivers is challenging. Student teachers and practicum

students keep changing and their teaching strategies and guidance techniques can vary, which often causes confusion. Students enrolled in course work are assigned specific times and assignments. Sometimes there are too many adults in the classroom.

High School Early Childhood Programs

Some high schools provide career training for early childhood occupations. Like the laboratory schools, these programs train future early childhood professionals. Some have their own early childhood laboratory facilities where students can work with preschool children. The preschool program may operate two, three, or even five days a week with some operating for just a couple of hours. Preschool children of high school students, faculty, and community members usually attend the program.

An advantage of having a high school laboratory is students can plan, present, and evaluate the curriculum under the supervision of an experienced teacher who has a degree in early childhood education. Some high school students may observe the children while others work directly with the children. The following week, the students may shift responsibilities. Those who observed the preceding week work with the preschoolers while the other students observe. For children, this can be a disadvantage. Like attending a laboratory school, the children cannot build long-term relationships with consistent teachers.

2.1-2 Sponsorship of Early Childhood Centers

Operation and funding of early childhood programs vary. They can be either ***for-profit*** programs or ***nonprofit***. Most observers are unaware of the differences between for-profit and nonprofit operated centers. They all look alike from the outside. **For-profit centers** rely on parent fees to operate. They are businesses with private ownership in local communities. For-profit centers can also be part of regional or national chains, which experienced rapid growth during the last two decades of the twentieth century. After paying expenses, the remaining revenue is returned to the owners or stockholders.

An agency often sponsors **nonprofit centers**. Religious groups, universities, colleges, YMCAs, YWCAs, hospitals, and recreation departments sponsor the largest number of nonprofit centers. To qualify for nonprofit status, the center must operate for charitable purposes. Nonprofit boards are eligible for grants and government funding. Because of the additional funding, these programs can provide care that some families could not afford. If the center is profitable, dividends cannot go to private individuals. All profits must be returned to the organization.

Public Sponsorship

Publicly sponsored programs are nonprofit since they are eligible for local, state, and federal grants. Some of these funds may come through school districts. Other funds may come through social service agencies.

Head Start is an example of a publicly sponsored program. Most parents pay no fee for their child to attend Head Start. If parental income exceeds the federal guidelines for the program, however, a fee may be a requirement. Grants from the federal government cover most program expenses. Funding is usually provided annually.

State funds may help support programs designed for educational purposes. They may house these programs in a university, college, secondary school, or career and technical education school. Examples include childcare centers, preschool centers, laboratory schools, and high school early childhood programs.

Publicly funded early childhood centers, preschools, and laboratory programs may receive several forms of financial support besides parental fees. For instance, a publicly funded early childhood center may also receive funds from the United Way, community donations, and tuition. Likewise, a laboratory school on a college campus may receive tuition donations or scholarships through alumni groups.

Private Sponsorship

The largest group of privately sponsored programs are the privately owned centers. These centers rely on parent fees to cover most of the operating expenses.

The location of a privately sponsored program may be in a religious organization facility, hospital, or office building. Many of these programs are nonprofit and operate as a service to the community. A voluntary board of community members may govern them.

Independent owners operate many of these centers. Their motivation in operating a center is to provide a service that makes a profit.

For-Profit Care Corporations

Some early childhood centers are a part of chains run by large, publicly help for-profit corporations, although some of the smaller chains are privately held. There are 50 for-profit centers in North America, the largest is KinderCare Learning Centers with 1,480 centers and a capacity of 194,000 children. Other examples of for-profit chains include Bright Horizons Family Solutions, Primrose, and Learning Care Group. Midsize chains typically operate on a regional basis. Often, these centers are built and located in large cities and suburban areas. To make a profit in these centers, the enrollment must be high. A central administration sets policy. Some corporations hire curriculum specialists to develop curriculum guides, training manuals for directors, and provide in-service training to center staff.

Employer Sponsorship

Some employer-sponsored early childhood providers have extended their services. They may include special activities for school-age children and care for older adults and ill children. The employer may pay part or all the costs of the services. The center can be located on-site or at a nearby center.

Corporate-sponsored childcare is a coveted benefit. In the United States, employer sponsored childcare is limited. Only four percent of companies offer free onsite childcare. Another four percent of companies provide subsidized onsite care.

Employers sponsor childcare to reduce the conflict between family and work responsibilities. Studies show that there is lower employee turnover and absenteeism at companies that provide some form of childcare. At such companies, employees have better work attitudes, new employees are attracted, community relations improve, and the company receives good publicity. Moreover, there are tax incentives for companies who sponsor childcare for their employees.

Companies can provide childcare assistance in several ways (**Figure 2.6**). A company-owned, on-site childcare center is one option. Such a center may be at or near the workplace. With this type of program, the company may hire a director to run the program. Other companies may contract with childcare chains or firms specializing in childcare to operate the center.

There are advantages to an onsite childcare facility. These include:

- Parents can save time dropping off and picking up their children.
- Parents can observe their children interacting with others.
- Parents can attend special activities such as birthdays and holiday parties.
- Mothers can breastfeed their children.
- Parents can also spend breaks and lunch hours with their children.

In large cities, however, this model may not work. Employees who commute long distances to work may find it difficult to travel with children on public transportation or in car pools.

The off-site center is another option. When several companies form a group, they often choose this is the type of center. Each company may not have enough need for their own childcare center. By sharing a facility, they also share the costs and risks. The off-site location may be closer to the parents' homes. Therefore, transportation times are shorter. If space is available, this type of model may also serve other children from the community.

The vendor model allows companies to purchase space in a childcare center or several

Types of Employer-Sponsored Childcare Assistance

- Company-owned, on-site care center
- Off-site center sponsored by one or more companies
- Company-sponsored, vendor-provided centers
- Vouchers provided by company to subsidize care
- Sick childcare
- Referral services

Figure 2.6 Employer-sponsored childcare assistance helps families meet work-life balance. *Why do you think that employer-sponsored care is important to families?*

centers. This model is ideal for small companies. It is not as costly as opening a center. There are no costs for start-up, investment in a building, or center administration.

Companies respect parental choice when they use the voucher model. Parents receive a voucher or coupon worth a certain amount of money from the company. Some companies will pay for all childcare costs, while others pay only a portion. Parents who do not live close to the work site may prefer this model. Thus, it is a useful model for companies in large cities.

One disadvantage of the voucher model is that parents must declare the money they receive as income on their tax returns. The employee, however, can deduct the cost of childcare from federal taxes (and state taxes where allowed).

Some companies provide childcare for ill children. This benefit can take two forms. A center may provide services for children who are ill and cannot attend school. With this type of care, the health department as well as the state licensing agency must receive notification. This works best for children who are recovering from an illness, but are not well enough to return to school. The second form provides a nurse to provide care in a sick child's home. This allows the parent to go to work.

Finding a quality childcare program near home is a problem for many parents. To assist parents in this process, some companies provide a referral service that matches the parents' needs with centers. The company may hire its own resource specialist or contract a resource and referral agency.

Parents receive a list of community childcare centers along with information about each center from their employers. Included are the center's location, fees, and hours of operation, goals, enrollment capacity, policies, curriculum, staff qualifications, and special services. This information may also include maps showing the location of the centers to help parents in the selection process.

Lesson 2.1 Review

1. **True or False.** High school early childhood programs provide childcare in a private home with a small number of children. (2.1.1)
2. Head Start provides children with each of the following except (2.1.1)
   A. proper nutrition.
   B. curriculum-based education.
   C. dental and medical services.
   D. scholarships.
3. Publicly sponsored programs are funded by all of the following except (2.1.2)
   A. social service agencies.
   B. cooperating families.
   C. state funds.
   D. school districts.

Program Quality, Licensing, and Accreditation

Essential Question

What factors are important to developing and maintaining early childhood program quality to benefit children and their families?

Learning Outcomes

After studying this lesson, you will be able to

2.2-1 **identify** factors that influence the quality in early childhood programs.

2.2-2 **recognize** licensing rules and regulations that help keep centers safe.

2.2-3 **explain** the components of center accreditation and the steps centers must take to receive accreditation.

2.2-4 **summarize** the rating instruments used to measure the quality of childcare programs.

2.2-5 **identify** factors parents consider when selecting an early childhood program.

2.2-6 **explain** the steps families may take in choosing a quality early childhood program.

Key Terms

structural quality
process quality
teacher-child ratio
licensing rules and regulations

childcare license
accreditation
quality-rating and improvement systems (QRIS)

P arents who work outside the home must provide for their children's needs during working hours. For this reason, parents may enroll their children in early childhood programs. Parents pay to provide safe, nurturing, and stimulating care in a developmentally appropriate setting. High-quality programs help meet the child's developmental needs.

2.2-1 Factors Affecting Program Quality

Structural quality and process quality are the two dimensions used to measure quality in early childhood programs. **Structural quality** defines teacher qualifications, teacher-child ratios, and group size. **Process quality** defines the quality of relationships among the teachers and children, teaching strategies, curriculum, and learning environment. Early childhood programs vary in their practices and program quality. It is important to examine quality indicators to ensure that the needs and well-being of children are being met. The following factors influence the quality of programs:

- low teacher-child ratios;
- limited group size;
- educational background, experience, and knowledge of child development of the staff;
- adult-child relationships and interactions;
- assessment and curriculum that supports the child's home language;
- well-equipped and organized indoor and outdoor environments; and
- staff salary and benefits.

Teacher-child ratio refers to the number of children per teacher or caregiver. This number is important because teachers can be more responsive and interactive when there are fewer children in the group. They can also provide more individualized attention. See **Figure 2.7** for the adult-child ratios recommended for various

Recommended Adult-Child Ratios

Age of Children	Recommended Ratio	Maximum Group Size
6 weeks to 1 year	1 adult to 3 children	6
1 to 2 years	1 adult to 4 children	10
2 to 3 years	1 adult to 5 children	12
3 to 5 years	1 adult to 7children	14
5 to 6 years	1 adult to 10 children	20

Figure 2.7 Teachers and caregivers can provide more individualized attention to children when the early childhood program meets or exceeds the recommended adult-child ratios for quality care and education.

age groups by the National Association for the Education of Young Children (NAEYC). When there are many children per teacher or caregiver, the children's behavior and adult-child interaction are affected.

Group size also affects the quality of a child's experience. The age of the children should influence the size of the group, which can vary from state to state. Check the licensing guidelines for your state. These regulations mandate the minimum ratio and maximum group size. NAEYC has also suggested guidelines. When the group is under the recommended size, quality is usually better.

Staff qualifications are another factor affecting quality programs. Staff should have specific training in early childhood education and child development. A large national study showed that teachers with this background had better adult-child interaction skills, were more positive, and less authoritarian. Moreover, their environments were more stimulating, safer, and cleaner. As a result, the children enrolled in these programs showed greater cognitive and social skills. Recommendations suggest that full-time head teachers have a bachelor's degree in child development or early childhood education. Some teachers may have graduate degrees, although assistant teachers usually have less education than head teachers do.

Warm, caring, kind, encouraging, and intentional adult-child interactions are at the heart of a quality early childhood program. Through social interactions, young children learn to communicate, think, and reason. Their

confidence increases as well as their motivation, which will make them more engaged and successful learners.

Many state licensing rules and regulations have a minimum standard of 35 square feet of usable space per child, a requirement to which centers must legally adhere. People question where this number came from. Speculation is that it originated from codes applied to elementary schools and studies show this number is inadequate. Crowding tends to be associated with stress, which produces cortisol, and more upper respiratory infections. It is also associated with more behavioral problems and injuries. As a result, Federal childcare centers require a minimum of 48.5 square feet per child. A growing body of research over the last 10 years, however, recommends a range of 42 to 54 square feet per child.

2.2-2 Licensing Rules and Regulations

Licensing rules and regulations are standards set to ensure that centers follow uniform and safe practices. Depending upon the state, the department issuing the license may deviate. Licensing rules and regulations vary from state to state. Each state has minimal requirements that a program must follow to operate legally. They also specify conditions that affect the safety and health of the children. Licensing rules and regulations also protect parents, employers, and employees. Currently,

Ethical Responsibilities ⚖️

Maintaining Confidentiality

When talking with staff and family members, early childhood professionals have an ethical responsibility to maintain confidentiality regarding decisions and sensitive information about the children in their care.

Dig Deeper

Review the definition of *confidentiality* in *Webster's Collegiate Dictionary*. How does this definition compare to your understanding of confidentiality? Write a short essay about the meaning of confidentiality and your future as an early childhood professional. Why should confidentiality be a core value in your career as an early childhood professional?

every state in the United States has licensing rules and regulations to promote safe, healthful environments for children in out-of-home care. Many licensing systems exist because no two states are alike. Communities have different needs and vary considerably. These rules and regulations change in response to research, monetary considerations, and politics.

A **childcare license** is a state-provided certificate granting permission to operate a childcare center, early childhood center, or family childcare home. Many states require that centers post the license in their entryway. Most licenses include the center's name, period for which the license is effective, hours of operation, and number of children permitted to attend. States typically monitor programs with scheduled and unscheduled inspections. When a violation is noted, some states require that centers post a copy of the official violation in the entryway. Once the violation has been corrected, the posting can be removed. This is a way of communicating the status of the center to families, prospective employees, and the community.

Before opening a new center, the first step is to contact the state licensing agency to get an application. Not all programs require a license. Some licensing requirements depend on whether the children attend full-time or part-time. In some states, parent cooperatives, faith-based programs, and military programs are exempt from obtaining a license. Centers in public schools or university laboratory schools may be exempt in some states. It is important to study your state's standards carefully. Typically, centers must address the following topics in writing to get a license:

- admission procedures and enrollment records;
- written policies and record keeping;
- adult-child ratios;
- staff educational requirements;
- background checks;
- personnel policies;
- number of square feet per child for both indoor and outdoor spaces;
- daily schedule;
- transportation policies;
- emergency plans and drills for fire, tornado, hurricane, earthquake, and active shooter;
- exits, fire doors, construction materials, lighting, heating/air conditioning;
- health and safety requirements: hand washing and proper sanitizing of food preparation areas, toileting areas, toys, play equipment, diapering tables, sleeping and floor areas;
- foodservice and nutrition;
- parent involvement; and
- staff training and development.

If infants and toddlers are in the program, centers must address additional requirements, including feeding, diapering, and toileting. You can obtain your state's regulations or compare regulations from different states online.

Workplace Connections 🧩

School-Age Teacher Interview

Interview a school-age childcare teacher about the challenges of his or her job. Write your questions prior to the interview.
1. What does a typical daily schedule involve?
2. Write a report about the interview.

2.2-3 Center Accreditation

The best indicator of high-quality early care and education is *accreditation*. **Accreditation** is a voluntary program that improves the overall quality of the early childhood program. Accreditation systems require programs to exceed licensing requirements. The process involves conducting an extensive self-study. After the study is complete, outside professionals verify that the center meets quality standards and certifies that an early childhood program has met a set of professional standards. The National Association for the Education of Young Children (NAEYC) administers a voluntary professional accreditation system. This system, changed in 2018, is designed for early learning programs serving children from birth through kindergarten. They have also designed it for programs that serve school-age children in before-school and after-school care.

The purpose of this voluntary national system is to conduct a thorough evaluation based on recognized quality standards. The process helps strive for continuous quality improvement. Program accreditation assists families in their search for high-quality programs for their children. In addition, it helps assure parents that their children are receiving quality care.

NAEYC requires four steps to prepare programs for initial accreditation. These include *enrollment, application/self-assessment, candidacy,* and *site visit* to show how the program meets standards.

The first step involves submitting an enrollment form and fee. After receiving this information, NAEYC mails programs a self-study kit focusing on 10 categories of center operations. Administrators, teachers, and parents evaluate program quality and guide quality-improvement efforts using the tools in the kit. Their purpose for this process is to determine strengths and weaknesses. Programs need to develop improvement plans for the weak areas. See **Figure 2.8** for a list of standards for high-quality programs.

Step two, application/self-assessment, involves compiling evidence of how the program meets the 10 Early Childhood Program Standards. Applicants use the self-assessment tools to provide documentation on how their program meets the standards. Candidacy, the third step, is the time when materials and a fee are forwarded to the National Academy of Early Childhood Programs. In the final step, trained professionals conduct an on-site validation visit. A team of experts representing the Academy makes the decision about accreditation.

Quality early childhood education is a field that is changing continuously. Studies show NAEYC's accreditation process has improved

Early Childhood Insight 🄰🄱🄲

Training Requirements and Career Paths for Early Childhood Professionals

When working in the public schools, early childhood professionals will often need to meet licensing requirements in addition to having a degree.

- *Licensed and certified teachers* are required to have earned a bachelor's degree, fulfilled the student teaching requirement, and passed the state's required exam for teachers. Many states use the *Praxis*, which is a standard exam for students who want to become teachers.
- *Certified specialists* require an advanced

degree. Positions include elementary school counselor, school library media specialist, school reading specialist, and school psychologist. To become certified for these positions, a graduate degree (master's degree) is required in most states.

- *Curriculum specialists* develop new curriculum and revise existing curriculum. In nearly all states, these individuals are required to have a graduate degree in *curriculum and instruction*.

The 10 NAEYC Program Standards

Standard	Description
Standard 1: Relationships	The program promotes positive relationships for all children and adults. It encourages each child's sense of individual worth and belonging as part of a community and fosters each child's ability to contribute as a responsible member of society.
Standard 2: Curriculum	The program implements a curriculum that is consistent with its goals for children and promotes learning and development in each of the following areas: social, emotional, physical, language, and cognitive.
Standard 3: Teaching	The program uses developmentally, culturally, and linguistically appropriate and effective teaching approaches that enhance each child's learning and development in the context of the program's curriculum goals.
Standard 4: Assessment of Child Progress	The program is informed by ongoing systematic, formal, and informal assessment approaches to provide information on children's learning and development. These assessments occur within the context of reciprocal communications with families and with sensitivity to cultural contexts in which children develop.
Standard 5: Health	The program promotes the nutrition and health of children and protects children and staff from illness and injury. Children must be healthy and safe in order to learn and grow. Programs must be healthy and safe to support children's healthy development.
Standard 6: Staff Competencies, Preparation, and Support	The program employs and supports a teaching staff with the educational qualifications, knowledge, and professional commitment necessary to promote children's learning and development and to support families' diverse needs and interests.
Standard 7: Families	The program establishes and maintains collaborative relationships with each child's family to foster children's development in all settings. These relationships are sensitive to family composition, language, and culture. To support children's optimal learning and development, programs need to establish relationships with families based on mutual trust and respect, involve families in their children's educational growth, and encourage families to fully participate in the program.
Standard 8: Community Relationships	The program establishes relationships with and uses the resources of the children's communities to support the achievement of program goals. Relationships with agencies and institutions in the community can help a program achieve its goals and connect families with resources that support children's healthy development and learning.
Standard 9: Physical Environment	The program has a safe and healthful environment that provides appropriate and well-maintained indoor and outdoor physical environments. The environment includes facilities, equipment, and materials to facilitate child and staff learning and development.
Standard 10: Leadership and Management	The program effectively implements policies, procedures, and systems that support stable staff and strong personnel, and fiscal, and program management so all children, families, and staff have high-quality experiences.

National Association for the Education of Young Children (NAEYC)

Figure 2.8   The 10 NAEYC Program Standards provide a framework for centers in developing high-quality programs.

program quality. Program improvements are made in a smoother and easier process. **Figure 2.9** contains a list of organizations that have accepted standards for quality practice.

Standards for Quality Practice

Association	Types of Programs
National Association for the Education of Young Children (NAEYC)	Birth through kindergarten programs
National After-School Association (NAA)	School-age programs
National Association of Family Child Care (NAFCC)	Family childcare programs
National Association of Child Care Professionals (NACCP)	Childcare centers
National Early Childhood Program Accreditation (NECPA)	Birth to kindergarten programs
National Accreditation Commission (NAC)	Childcare centers, family childcare, and stand-alone school-age programs

Figure 2.9 These organizations have accepted standards for quality practice.

2.2-4 Quality-Rating and Improvement Systems (QRIS)

Research has demonstrated that early childhood programs improve outcomes for children. Concern over quality has resulted in accountability. States have implemented **quality-rating and improvement systems (QRIS)** that can help parents judge program quality. These systems—important tools for protecting children—assess, improve, and communicate the level of quality. The information collected by using these evaluation instruments tells teachers what the expectations are in quality environments. Many teachers will change their classroom practices to prepare for an evaluation.

Four *Early Childhood Education Rating Scales (ECERS)* were developed at the University of North Carolina. The purpose of the instruments is to determine how programs meet the three basic needs of children: protecting children's health and safety, building positive relationships, and providing stimulating learning experiences.

Each instrument focuses on a different setting, and is valid and reliable.

- The *Infant/Toddler Environment Rating Scale® (ITERS-R™)* assesses programs with children from birth to three years of age.
- The *Early Childhood Environment Rating Scale® (ECERS-R™)* assesses programs with children from three through five years of age.
- The *Family Child Care Environmental Rating Scale® (FCCERS-R™)* assesses children in homes that serve infants through school-aged children.
- The *School-Age Care Environment Rating Scale® (SACERS™)* assesses programs with children from five to 12 years of age. It assesses the before and after school group, and includes supplementary items for programs that enroll children who have disabilities.

Some states recognize early childhood programs that exceed minimal licensing requirements. They may have highly qualified teachers with better educational preparation. They may have better group sizes and better teacher-child ratios. These programs may be recognized online with more stars.

2.2-5 Selecting an Early Childhood Program

Selecting an early childhood program is one of the most important decisions that parents make. Comfort with their children's care and education can greatly affect the quality of family life (**Figure 2.10**). For this reason, parents need to make this decision carefully.

When searching for the right program, parents consider many factors. Each family makes this choice based on its own needs, priorities, goals, and budget. Many parents do consider some common factors, however. See **Figure 2.11** for a list of questions parents can use to compare programs.

Foremost, parents want their children to be safe and comfortable. They want a program that welcomes their child and promotes all

Rawpixel/iStock via Getty Images

Figure 2.10 Parents are greatly comforted when they see their children playing happily in the early childhood program they have chosen.

developmental areas. Cost and location are important, too. Working parents usually prefer the convenience of a program near their home or job.

Parents must choose a program they can afford. For example, parents with a lower socioeconomic status may need to use a public program or a private program with a lower fee structure. Program quality is a key factor. Parents are interested in the program's goals, activities, and schedule. Variety and balance among activities is desirable. Quality programs offer ample materials, equipment, and space. These programs also offer smaller group sizes and more adults within each group. This allows children to receive more attention and personal care.

Many parents ask about the training and experience of the staff. Studies that show staff members with early childhood education degrees and experience are often more sensitive to children's needs. They provide more stimulating, developmentally appropriate care and education. Well-trained staff members ensure that learning experiences are culturally meaningful and respectful for the children and their families.

Asking about staff turnover rates can help parents in choosing a program. Parents should avoid choosing programs with high staff turnover. First, frequent staff changes may be a sign of low staff wages or poor working conditions. These may indicate problems with the quality of the program. High staff turnover

also interferes with children's sense of security. To feel secure, young children need consistency and predictability. They also need to form close, caring relationships with the teachers or caregivers. Likewise, children need a predictable environment. Staff turnover disrupts the environment and prevents children from forming close relationships with caregivers.

Parents want a facility that is safe for their children. For example, many centers have a security system that helps them monitor who enters and leaves the building. For safety, the building should also have smoke detectors, carbon monoxide detectors, fire extinguishers, and evacuation plans. Parents also desire a facility that is clean and in excellent repair.

2.2-6 The Selection Process

Most parents follow the same process in selecting and early childhood program. As a teacher, you need to understand the important role you play in this process. Parents usually want to know about a program before they can choose it. Your role will be to help parents gain the needed information.

As parents begin a search, they want to identify options. Some parents start by contacting a childcare resource and referral agency for a list of licensed programs in their community. Other parents go online. Website ratings and number of children in a group is more important to parents with children under age one. Others search print or online telephone directories to identify programs in the community. Parents may also ask people they know about their experiences. Many parents seek the advice of other relatives, friends, coworkers, and neighbors who use early childhood programs. Parents often trust this more than information given by the program itself.

Next, parents may begin calling available programs. The first questions they often ask are about the age groups the program serves, whether openings exist in their child's age group, and what the hours of operation are. Then, parents might ask about fees and location.

Selecting Quality Childcare

Questions	Yes	No
1. Is the center accredited by the National Association for the Education of Young Children?		
2. Do the ratios and group size meet or exceed NAEYC's recommendations?		
3. Do the children appear to be happy, active, and secure?		
4. Does the center provide in-service training and continuing education for the staff?		
5. Are all staff members educationally qualified?		
6. Do staff members attend in-service training, professional meetings, and conferences on a regular basis?		
7. Are staff meetings conducted regularly to plan and evaluate program activities?		
8. Do staff members observe, assess, and document each child's developmental progress on a continuous basis?		
9. Does the curriculum support the children's individual rates of development?		
10. Does the staff value and include each child's family, culture, and language in the curriculum?		
11. Are the indoor and outdoor environments large enough to support a variety of activities?		
12. Is the environment inviting, warm, and stimulating?		
13. Is equipment provided to promote and challenge physical, cognitive, social, and emotional development?		
14. Are safe and sanitary conditions maintained within the building, classroom, and on the playground?		
15. Are teacher-child interactions warm, frequent, and positive?		
16. Are teachers using developmentally appropriate teaching strategies?		
17. Are multicultural perspectives incorporated in the curriculum and classroom environment?		
18. Are families welcome to observe and participate in the program?		
19. Is sufficient equipment available for the number of children attending?		
20. Do the teachers communicate in the child's home language?		
21. Does the climate in the center feel inviting and positive?		
22. Do teachers meet with families regularly to discuss the child's strengths, needs, interests, and progress?		

Figure 2.11   To help ease the parents' stress in choosing childcare for their children, you may wish to supply them with this questionnaire. *In what ways do you think these questions help ease parental stress when selecting an early childhood program?*

Parents who still have interest will ask about the program, staff, and activities. From there, they may arrange a visit to the program. A visit during program hours lets parents inspect the environment, observe the program, and meet the staff. Parents may want to see the entire facility, including the kitchen, restrooms, classrooms, and outdoor play areas. They will often ask to see the daily and weekly schedules as well as the menu for meals and snacks. Parents also want to observe the interactions of staff with children and other adults in the program.

After the visit, parents may have additional questions. Some parents may need to visit a program several times before making a final decision. They may also bring their child to see how the child responds to the environment. With this information, parents can decide which program will best meet the needs of their child and family.

Figure 2.12 lists factors that are important to parents when choosing childcare arrangements. Website ratings and number of children in a group were ranked more important by parents with children under age one. Likewise, the importance of time with other children increased with age.

Factors Affecting Childcare Choices

Factors Affecting Choices	Percentage of Importance
Reliability	87%
Available time for care	75%
Qualifications of staff	72%
Learning activities	68%
Location	60%
Time with other children	59%
Cost	55%
Recommendations	45%
Number of children in group	42%
Website ratings	27%

Source: Cui, J. and Natzke L., (2020), Early Childhood Program Participation 2019 (NCES 2020-075) US Department of Education, Washington DC, National Center for Education Statistics

Figure 2.12 Parents must consider many factors when selecting childcare arrangements for their children. *Talk to several parents you know who use early childhood education or care services. Which of these factors do they indicate are most important to them?*

Lesson 2.2 Review

1. ____defines the quality of relationships among the teachers and children, teaching strategies, curriculum, and learning environment. (2.2.1)
   A. Structural quality
   B. Teacher-child ratio
   C. Process quality
   D. Licensing rules
2. Licensing rules and regulations protect all of the following except (2.2.2)
   A. state officials.
   B. parents.
   C. employers.
   D. employees.
3. **True or False.** Accreditation systems require early childhood programs to exceed licensing requirements. (2.2.3)
4. Which is not one of the four rating instruments parents can use to measure the quality of early childhood programs? (2.2.4)
   A. The NAEYC Program Standards
   B. The Infant-Toddler Rating Scale®
   C. The Early Childhood Environment Rating Scale®
   D. The School-Age Care Environment Rating Scale®
5. Which of the following is not a common factor families consider when selecting a quality early childhood program? (2.2.5, 2.2.6)
   A. Safety and comfort
   B. Cost
   C. Program quality
   D. Proximity to elementary schools

Summary

Lesson 2.1

2.1-1 Many types of early childhood programs are available.

2.1-2 Each type of program takes a unique approach to meeting children's developmental needs and offers a variety of benefits.

2.1-2 Programs are sponsored in a variety of ways. The type of sponsorship may affect the goals and philosophies of centers.

2.1-2 Employers use a variety of ways to provide program benefits for their employees.

Lesson 2.2

2.2-1 The two dimensions for measuring quality in early childhood programs are structural quality and process quality.

2.2-1 Factors that influence program quality help ensure that the developmental needs of children are being met.

2.2-2 Families may look for programs that have been licensed by the state, ensuring that they follow state licensing rules and regulations.

2.2-3 Accreditation certifies that a program meets the NAEYC Early Learning Program Standards for measuring program quality.

2.2-3 NAEYC conducts a thorough evaluation based on recognized quality standards.

2.2-5 Families consider many factors in choosing the best program for their child, including safety and comfort, program goals, staff-to-child ratios, group sizes, equipment and materials, schedule, and fees.

2.2-4, Parents follow many steps and use many
2.2-6 criteria when selecting early childhood programs for their children, including quality-rating systems.

Vocabulary Activity

Write all the lesson terms on a separate sheet of paper. For each term, quickly write a word you think relates to the term. In small groups, exchange papers. Have each person in the group explain a term on the list. Take turns until all terms have been explained.

Critical Thinking

1. **Identify.** Visit a family childcare home. Ask the provider for the daily schedule. Identify instances of predictability that are provided for children.
2. **Draw Conclusions.** Arrange a visit to a school-age childcare program. Ask to review the curriculum. Write a report on what you learn.
3. **Determine.** Check the website of your state's department of education to find out your state's kindergarten requirements. The National Database of Childcare Licensing Requirements is a useful tool for obtaining information on each state.
4. **Analyze.** What are the benefits of Head Start for children who live in families with lower socioeconomic status?
5. **Analyze.** Analyze the two dimensions of program quality for early childhood programs. Use the text and online resources for your analysis. How does structure quality help support process quality? What evidence can you give to support your response?
6. **Compare and Contrast.** Search the National Database of Childcare Licensing Regulations to identify your state's requirements. How do licensing regulations in your state compare and contrast to the NAEYC Early Learning Program Standards?
7. **Identify.** Search for licensed and registered childcare programs by state, city, and region. Create a database of those in your area.
8. **Determine.** Write an essay outlining the value of center accreditation.

9. **Draw Conclusions.** Research the National Association for Family Childcare (NAFCC) organization. What are the goals of NAFCC? What eligibility criteria must providers meet? Describe the role of a NAFCC accreditation observer. Why do people like being a NAFCC accreditation observer? Write a summary of your findings.

10. **Compare and Contrast.** Identify, compare, and contrast criteria parents use to select the best childcare program for their children, including financial considerations.

11. **Identify.** Visit the NAEYC website to find information for parents on selecting early childhood care and education programs.

Core Skills

1. **Research and Speaking.** Research the political platform of Lyndon Johnson and the part the War on Poverty and Head Start may have played in his successful election. Has the United States government been completely supportive of Head Start since its inception? What changes have been made to the Head Start program through the decades, and what is in store for its future? Present your findings in a presentation to the class.

2. **Research and Writing.** Research kindergarten readiness. Some sources contain kindergarten checklists and other information for parents concerning their children's kindergarten experience. Write a brief article directed to prospective kindergarten parents about what to expect.

3. **Speaking.** Debate the advantages and disadvantages of teaching in a parent cooperative.

4. **Writing.** Privately sponsored childcare programs operated by a faith-based organization may include religious education as part of the curriculum. Describe your opinion about this subject. Should all students enrolled have to take part in the religious curriculum activities the program provides? Why or why not? Write a short essay detailing the advantages and disadvantages of this type of program.

5. **Research and Speaking.** Search online for large companies in the United States that provide some form of employee assistance for childcare. What type of assistance do these companies provide? What choices do employees have for childcare benefits, if any? What is the percentage of employees who take advantage of these benefits? Use presentation software to present your findings.

6. **Research and Writing.** Use the text and online resources to cite specific evidence about the various types of early childhood services. What are the various rules, regulations, and licensure requirements?

7. **Writing.** Visit the website for the National Association for the Education of Young Children. Review the 10 NAEYC Program Standards in Figure 2.10. Write an article on their importance and post it to the class website for peer and instructor review and discussion.

8. **CTE Career Readiness Practice.** Imagine it is five years in the future and you are starting your first full-time job. Your goal is to maintain health and wellness by developing a plan for handling workplace stress. Investigate and evaluate the resources on the link to the National Institute for Occupational Safety and Health on the Centers for Disease Control (CDC) website. Then write your plan for preventing job stress. How can dealing with teacher stress help improve relationships with parents and staff?

Portfolio Project

Write a short essay on your vision of a high-quality childcare center or preschool program. Include characteristics of the program you feel would best meet the needs of the children served by the program. These may include facility, curriculum, child-adult ratios, teacher qualifications and training, equipment, and accreditation. (Refer to Figure 2.10). What would encourage parents to enroll their children in this program?

Chapter 3

Reading Advantage

After you read the chapter, test your comprehension of new vocabulary. Write a sentence using each vocabulary word.

Child Development Principles and Theories

Lesson 3.1: Understanding Children's Development

Lesson 3.2: Historical Factors and Theories of Development

Case Study

Effects of Toxic Stress

Read the case study as a class and discuss the questions that follow. After you finish reading the chapter, discuss the case study again. Have your opinions changed based on what you learned? If so, how?

Tina Robinson, a single mother, arrived at the early childhood center carrying her nine-month-old daughter, Maya. Tina was visibly upset and crying. Immediately when she walked in the door, the teacher noted that Tina had a black eye, several bruises on her right arm, and her breath smelled of alcohol. Maya was also crying. Her mother was holding a bottle filled with an orange-colored liquid.

The teacher motioned for Tina to come into an office. There Tina confided that both she and her boyfriend had problems with alcohol. When her boyfriend had too much to drink, he became abusive. It particularly bothered him that Maya cried so much. It seemed to trigger his anger.

The teacher reached out to take Maya from her mother. Tina handed Maya and the bottle to the teacher, who commented about the orange juice. Tina responded by saying, "Oh, no, that is not orange juice. It is powdered drink mix. Orange juice costs too much."

Give It Some Thought

1. What are some aspects of Maya's home environment that are not conducive to healthy growth and development? If you were in this teacher's situation, how might you respond to Tina's comments about problems with alcohol and her boyfriend's abusive behavior?
2. How do you think Maya's environment will affect her development?
3. What do you think children need for healthy development?

Opening image credit: SDI Productions/E+ via Getty Images

Lesson 3.1 Understanding Children's Development

Essential Question

What do I need to understand about child development and brain development to be an effective care provider or teacher?

Learning Outcomes

After studying this lesson, you will be able to

3.1-1 **analyze** the areas and principles of child development.

3.1-2 **summarize** key factors about brain development, including nature and nurture, adverse childhood experiences (ACE), environment of relationships, self-regulation, and windows of opportunity.

Key Terms

development	maturation
milestones	adverse childhood experiences (ACEs)
infant	toxic stress
toddler	neurons
preschooler	axons
middle childhood	myelin
heredity	dendrites
environment	synapses
physical development	plasticity
gross-motor development	overstimulation
fine-motor development	cortisol
cognitive development	executive function
social-emotional development	windows of opportunity
cephalocaudal principle	
proximodistal principle	

Studying and understanding child growth and development are important parts of teaching young children. Knowledge of child development is a core consideration that informs decision-making. No two children are alike. Children differ in physical, cognitive, and social-emotional growth patterns. Even identical twins, who have the same genetic makeup, are not exactly alike. They may differ in the way they respond to play, affection, objects, and people in their environment.

Social and cultural contexts influence all human development and learning. Think of the children you know. Each is different from the others (**Figure 3.1**). Some always appear to be happy. Other children's personalities may not seem as pleasant. Some children are active. Still others are typically quiet.

To help all these children, you need to understand the sequence of their development and value their strengths. Knowledge of the areas of child development is basic to guiding and teaching young children. Linked to this is the understanding of healthy brain development.

Healthy brain development results from healthy human contact. Babies come into the world wired to form relationships. Early experiences with a warm, caring, responsive caregiver are critical. Positive stimuli are a major factor in brain development. These stimuli begin at birth. Therefore, it is vital for children to have responsive, loving caregivers. Young children need dependable, trusting relationships. They thrive in environments that are predictable and nurturing.

fizkes/Shutterstock.com

Figure 3.1 Knowledge of child development can help you understand how to work with children who have very different personalities. *How do you think social experiences and culture impact personality?*

3.1-1 Child Development

Child development is a scientific approach to studying children. **Development** refers to change or growth that occurs in children. It starts with infancy and continues to adulthood. Knowledge of child development is the foundation for working with young children. By studying child development, you will form a profile of children's developmental continuum. You will learn developmental milestones. **Milestones** are widely held expectations of what most children are able to do at a certain age. For instance, you will learn that two-year-old children like to run. They enjoy the sensation of moving their bodies. This means you should provide space for them to move freely. Likewise, you will learn that infants explore with their senses, often mouthing objects. Knowing this, you will need to make sure that all toys for infants are sanitized and safe.

Different names describe young children at approximate ages. **Infants** range in age from birth through the first year. **Toddlers** are children ranging in age from one up to the third birthday. (Because of an awkward style of walking, the name *toddler* describes this age group.) The term **preschooler** describes children ages three through five years. **Middle childhood** is the term that describes children between the ages of six and twelve.

The study of these basic patterns of child development has occurred for generations. Researchers are constantly discovering new information on how children grow, develop, and learn about themselves and their world.

Studying the basics of child development is just the beginning for you. Keep in mind that growing as a professional is a constant journey and lifelong process. Throughout your career, you will need to update your knowledge of the latest research and trends in this career field. You can do this by

- attending seminars, workshops, and conferences—in person and virtually;
- reading books and professional journals;
- taking part in on-line discussions;
- watching professional online videos;
- listening to podcasts;
- attending college classes; and
- having discussions with colleagues.

Workplace Connections

Teacher Interview

Interview an early childhood teacher. Ask the teacher how developmental and learning theories influence his or her teaching strategies. If the teacher mentions any theorists who are not discussed in this chapter, research them and their theories.

1. Does the teacher seem to focus equally on physical, cognitive, or social-emotional development?
2. Does the teacher adapt their teaching strategies to meet the needs of children who have developmental delays? If so, how?
3. Write a report on your findings to share with the class.

Areas of Development

Two major forces influence all areas of a child's development: *heredity* and *environment*. **Heredity** refers to the characteristics a child inherits genetically from parents. *Genes* are a blueprint for a child's potential development. Heredity determines when a child's brain and senses will be mature enough to learn certain skills. Environmental factors also affect learning. **Environment** includes the interactions, experiences, and events that influence a child's development. Children need opportunities to use their senses and try new things (**Figure 3.2**). As a caregiver or teacher, you need to provide an enriched environment that allows children to develop to their full potential intellectually.

The study of child development includes three major domains that overlap and interact with each other. These domains include *physical, cognitive,* and *social-emotional development*. Dividing development into these domains makes it easier to study.

Physical development refers to physical body changes. It occurs in a relatively stable, predictable sequence. It is orderly, not random. Changes in bone thickness, vision, hearing, and muscle are all included. Changes in size and weight are also part of physical development (**Figure 3.3**).

Physical skills, such as crawling, walking, and writing result from physical development. These skills fall into two main categories:

- **Gross-motor development** involves improvement of skills using the large muscles in the legs and arms. Running, skipping, and bike riding are examples of gross-motor skills.
- **Fine-motor development** involves improvement of skills using the small muscles of the hands and fingers. Grasping, holding, cutting, and drawing are some activities that require fine-motor development.

Environmental factors also affect what children can do physically. These factors include proper nutrition and developmentally appropriate toys, activities, and interactions.

Cognitive development, sometimes called *intellectual development*, refers to processes people use to gain knowledge. Language, thought, reasoning, and imagination are all included. Identifying colors and knowing the difference between one and many are examples of cognitive tasks.

Language and thought are a result of cognitive development. These two skills are closely related. Both are necessary for planning, remembering, and problem-solving. As children mature and gain experience with their world, these skills develop.

Social-emotional development is the third area of development. These two areas are grouped together because they are so interrelated. Learning to relate to others is *social development*. *Emotional development* involves feelings and expression of feelings. Trust, fear, confidence, pride, friendship, and humor are all part of

Nick Fedirko/Shutterstock.com

Figure 3.2 The activities that you provide infants and young toddlers help them develop cognitively. ***What skills is this toddler learning from this activity?***

bhowie/iStock via Getty Images

Figure 3.3 Changes in height and weight are two of the most obvious signs of physical development.

social-emotional development. Other emotional traits include timidity, interest, and pleasure (**Figure 3.4**). Learning to express emotions in appropriate ways begins early. Caregivers

and teachers promote this learning when they positively model these skills. A person's self-concept and self-esteem are also part of this area. As children experience success, their skills and confidence flourish. This leads to a healthy self-concept and sense of worth.

The physical, cognitive, and social-emotional areas of development are all interrelated. Each area affects and influences every other area. For instance, writing words requires fine-motor and hand-eye coordination skills. It also requires cognitive development. Language, a part of cognitive development, is necessary to communicate with others. It is also necessary for growing socially and emotionally.

Just as research has made known the areas of development, it also shows that development follows key patterns, or principles. Think about how these principles might influence how you promote children's development.

FatCamera/E+ via Getty Images

Figure 3.4   Learning to trust and show affection for others is a part of social-emotional development. ***What emotions are these children expressing?***

Principles of Development

Although each child is unique, the basic patterns, or principles, of growth and development follow a universal, predictable, and orderly trend. Through careful observation and interaction with children, researchers and those who work with children recognize major principles governing growth and development.

- ***Development tends to proceed from the head downward.*** According to the **cephalocaudal principle,** the child first gains control of the head, then the arms, then the legs. Infants gain control of head and face movements within the first two months after birth. In the next few months, they can lift themselves up using their arms. By six to 12 months of age, infants start to gain leg control and may be able to crawl, stand, or walk.

- ***Development also proceeds near to far.*** Growth begins from the center of the body

and extends outward according to the **proximodistal principle**. Accordingly, the spinal cord develops before other parts of the body. The child's arms develop before the hands, and the hands and feet develop before the fingers and toes. Fingers and toes are the last to develop.

- ***Development also depends on a combination of maturation and environment.*** **Maturation** refers to the sequence of biological changes in children, the foundation of which is their genetics. These orderly changes give children new abilities. Much of the maturation depends on changes in the brain and the nervous system. These changes assist children to improve their thinking abilities and motor skills. A rich learning environment helps children develop to their potential.

Children must mature to a certain point before they can gain some skills. For instance, the brain of a four-month-old has not matured enough to allow the child to use words. A four-month-old will babble and coo. By two years of age, however, with the help of others, the child will be able to say and understand many words. This is an example of how cognitive development occurs from simple tasks to tasks that are more complex. Likewise, physical skills develop from general to specific movements. For example, think about the way an infant waves its arms and legs. In a young infant, these movements are random. In several months, the infant will likely be able to grab a block with his or her whole hand. In a little more time, the same infant will grasp a block with the thumb and forefinger.

Understanding the areas and principles of development is important. Development occurs at varying rates from child to child. Individual variations occur. These may result from lack of experience or the cultural and linguistic context in which children live. As your knowledge of child development grows, so will your ability to plan a developmentally appropriate curriculum. Recognizing how the brain functions in development is equally as important. What should caregivers and teachers know about the brain, and how it influences development, behavior, learning, and health?

Early Childhood Insight ABC

Principles of Development

The principles of development will help you understand that the order or sequence of development in children is generally the same. Although there are many developmental norms, each child develops at their own *rate*. Development also occurs within the cultural context in which a child lives. In any classroom, you may find children the same age who have progressed to different levels in each developmental area. Knowing child development principles will help you observe the strengths each child has gained. It will also help you plan developmentally and culturally appropriate activities that promote the development of new skills.

3.1-2 Brain Development

Which is more important for the developing brain—*nature* or *nurture*? This is one of the oldest debates in the study of human development. Human development depends on the interaction between nature and nurture, often called *biology* and *experience*. Years ago, people thought that only genes contributed to brain development. Today, scientists who are unraveling how the mind works, say both factors are critical to healthy brain development. It is important to study these two factors together. Genes that children inherit from their parents set up the basic brain structures, while experiences determine how the connections work. The brain develops under the mutual influence of genetics and the environment.

The most effective living structure is the brain. Its purpose is to store, use, and create information. The development of the brain begins before birth and continues into adulthood. The young brain's architecture is experience-dependent and is both receptive to positive influences and vulnerable to damage. A distinguishing characteristic of the prenatal period is the brain's sensitivity to a range of harmful conditions. A woman's habits and health during pregnancy will influence the developing embryo. For example, prenatal alcohol or drug exposure has dramatic negative effects on the brain.

Pregnancy is the critical time for promoting healthy brain development. The basic architecture of the brain forms during pregnancy when the structures are forming. The spinal cord, neurons, and brain cells are forming just days after conception. The first twenty weeks of pregnancy lay the groundwork for a lifetime of well-being. The mother's nutrition, including appropriate amounts of iron and folic acid, also affect the brain before birth. The number of brain cells produced depends on the mother's nutrition. **Adverse childhood experiences (ACEs)** change the brain. After birth, **toxic stress** such as extremely low socioeconomic status, severe neglect, maternal depression, and exposure to violence can undermine the developing brain architecture and immune system. The lasting effects of toxic stress are built into a child's body, which can compromise their development, lifelong health, and opportunities. Toxic stress, if intense, frequent, or sustained, can interfere with the normal development of the immune system.

The purpose of the immune system is to protect the body. When children are in an environment that causes prolonged toxic stress, the result may be chronic inflammation. When this occurs, children live in a fright-or-flight mode. Over time, these inflammatory substances can damage organs and increase the risk of a host of health issues. This can lead to increased susceptibility to mental and physical illnesses. The long-term result may be asthma, obesity, hypertension, depression, diabetes, cancer, or cardiovascular diseases, and substance abuse. Long-term or chronic stress can cause lifelong behavioral and learning problems. Language deficits, attention disorders, cognitive impairments, and academic problems can occur.

There are differences in how children respond to stress. Some children seem to be more resilient than other children are. The reasons for such resiliency may be their genes, temperament, and early experiences. Sometimes, nurturing caregiver relationships buffer them from stress.

Figure 3.5 shows environmental influences affecting the developing brain. Some environmental influences are beneficial while others are harmful. The harmful influences affect the brain before and after birth. Prenatal exposure to alcohol, for instance, has potential lifelong effects on child's development.

For optimal brain development, children need excellent nutrition before and after birth. Timing effects are also evident with postnatal nutrition. The earlier malnutrition occurs, the greater the decrease in brain size. Studies show that adequate nutrition prenatally and during the first three years of life is critical to healthy growth and development.

Health Highlights

DHA and Brain Development

Overall, good nutrition is important to healthy development of infants. Some recent studies suggest that infants who are not fed breast milk—the ideal source of nutrients for infants—should receive DHA-fortified infant formula during feedings. DHA, or *docosahexaenoic acid*, is an omega-3 fatty acid that occurs naturally in breast milk and such other foods as fish and eggs. This fatty acid supports eyesight and brain development in infants and children. If parents have questions about DHA-fortified formula, care providers should encourage them to talk with their health-care provider.

Sophisticated technology allows scientists to look inside the brain and view its electrical activity. By taking and comparing pictures, scientists study rates of development. Brain chemistry studies show that young children's

Environmental Influences Affecting the Developing Brain

Harmful or Toxic Influences			Needed for Normal Brain Development
Airborne pollutants	Food insecurity	Prenatal infections	Oxygen
Alcohol	Housing instability	Radiation	Adequate nutrition
Malnutrition	Parent depression	Lead	Sensory stimulation
Drug exposure	Poor child care	Tobacco	Social interaction
Chronic stress	Poverty	Abuse and neglect	Physical and mental activity
Chemicals	Parental divorce	Family violence	
Diseases	Pesticides		

Goodheart-Willcox Publisher

Figure 3.5   Environmental influences such as pollutants and pesticides affect the developing brain.

brains are highly active. The most rapid development occurs during the first three years of life. Therefore, hours in infancy may have more impact on the brain's development than months in middle age. **Figure 3.6** illustrates how different parts of the brain control body functions.

In contrast to every other major body organ, the brain is not fully developed at birth. It is immature and underdeveloped, weighing about one pound, and builds over time. The brain reaches adult size before other body organs. It contains about 100–200 billion specialized nerve cells called **neurons**, which are the building blocks of the brain. Although these cells are present at birth, they are poorly connected. The key to building the brain structure is experience. Through experience, neurons connect to each other, strengthening the most used connections.

After birth, no new neurons form. They sprout narrow branching extensions called axons

and dendrites. **Axons** are long, thin fibers of the neuron or nerve cell. They usually conduct impulses away from the cell body. **Myelin**, which is a layer of white, fatty material, covers and protects axons. Myelin increases the transmission speed of impulses from cell to cell. **Dendrites** are short, hair-like fibers around the cell body that receive signals. With development, neurons move to specific regions of the brain. The neurons establish contact with one another, and the connections, or **synapses,** develop rapidly with stimulation. "Brain wiring" occurs as new links and connections form.

At first, there is an overproduction of neural connections. Over time, brain circuits become more efficient and more refined as cells that are not used require pruning. *Pruning* is often referred to as the "use it or lose it" principle. Through lack of use, the brain prunes some

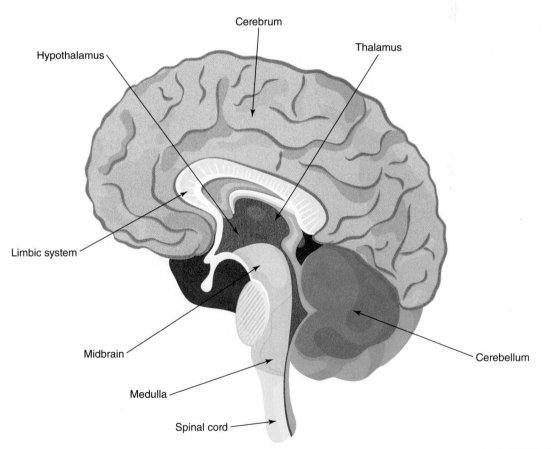

logika600/Shutterstock.com

Figure 3.6   This diagram illustrates how different functions are controlled by different regions of the brain. Connections between them are critical to healthy development. *What forms of stimulation can help form new connections in the child's brain?*

circuits while those that are repeatedly used become stronger.

These links result from the child's interaction with the world. They influence the ability of a child to learn, solve problems, get along with others, and control emotions. For example, the child's growing brain responds each time a caregiver provides sensory stimulation. This stimulation could be in the form of holding, cuddling, touching, rocking, talking, reading, or singing. When stimulation occurs, the child's growing brain responds by forming new connections. **Plasticity** is the ability of an infant's brain to change according to stimulation.

Quality programs can help reverse the damaging effects of stress. Early care has a long-lasting impact on how children develop. Science shows how an environment of supportive relationships shapes the architecture of a healthy brain. The number of brain connections children form and keep depends on the care they receive. Warm, nurturing, consistent, and responsive care will determine the brain's architecture. Children also need a stimulating environment to produce growth in brain cells. A wide variety of visual, auditory, and sensory experiences will help promote brain connections.

In contrast, adverse relationships that lack warm, responsive interactions can limit a child's potential. Some children are deprived of stimulation either intentionally or unintentionally. These children receive fewer touches, and caregivers speak to them to less often. They may also receive little visual stimulation. This neglect can impair brain development and the child's potential that can last a lifetime.

The problem for the caregiver is providing just the right amount of stimulation for each child. For example, the amount of stress created by negative experiences also affects brain development. **Overstimulation**, a flood of sounds and sights, is one factor that can cause harmful stress to infants. **Cortisol** is a steroid hormone that the body produces when it is under stress. Even daily stressors such as loud noises, being hungry, lack of attention, or too

much visual stimulation can increase a child's cortisol. High levels of this hormone wash over the brain like an acid. Over a long length of time, cortisol can threaten brain development. It can lead to problems with memory and regulating emotion. A child constantly exposed to stress can develop connections that trigger anxiety, fear, and mistrust. These children may grow up to be unhappy, sad, or even angry. They may also have problems with self-control. **Figure 3.7** contains a list of factors that can interfere with healthy brain development.

The science is clear. Healthy brain development depends on healthy human connections. Understanding brain development means understanding the importance of warm, supportive, safe, predictable, and dependable relationships with adults. High quality, early childhood programs can promote health and prevent disease. The caregiver's relationship will influence the wiring of the brain. Warm, responsive care appears to have a biological function. It helps children weather stress and develop resiliency the adverse effects of later stress.

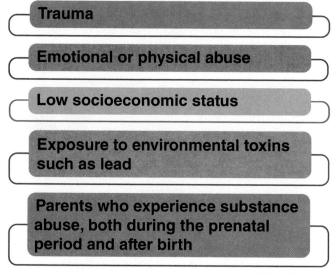

Risk Factors for Healthy Brain Development

- Trauma
- Emotional or physical abuse
- Low socioeconomic status
- Exposure to environmental toxins such as lead
- Parents who experience substance abuse, both during the prenatal period and after birth

Goodheart-Willcox Publisher

Figure 3.7   Exposure to stress-causing factors such as these can interfere with healthy brain development.

Environment of Relationships

Science reveals that a responsive environment of nurturing relationships shapes the architecture of a healthy brain. Caring and stable growth-producing relationships are the core of healthy brain development. The process begins prenatally and continues through adulthood. Beginning at birth, young children are helpless and are totally dependent on their caregivers inside and outside the family.

Through a serve-and-return interaction with caring and attentive people in their environment, children learn to think, feel, and act. Infants begin reaching out to others (*the serve*) by using facial expressions, babbling, and words. Much like a tennis game, the caregiver needs to *return* the serve by responding using gestures, sounds, and facial expressions. These give-and-take responses are biologically essential. If the caregiver repeatedly does not respond, the child's stress system can be activated and weaken the developing brain structure.

Relationships with caregivers help children define who they are and what they are capable of doing. Positive, responsive caregiving helps promote the development of cognitive skills, self-confidence, and persistence. Through these relationships, children are motivated to learn to self-regulate their behavior.

Self-Regulation

Self-regulation is the foundation of early childhood development. Often referred to as **executive function**, self-regulation is the ability to think before acting, which involves regulating self-behavior in socially and culturally appropriate ways. This critical task develops rapidly during the early years. Self-control involves developing the ability to monitor and control attention, emotions, and behaviors, which are crucial life skills for learning and development. Executive function involves the problem-solving skills needed to plan, start, and complete a task. Executive function also involves the ability to interact in positive ways with others. Children must learn to solve and control aggressive impulses without violence. Developing

cognitive flexibility, the ability to focus and ignore distraction, is an important task for the preschool years. Examples of self-regulation include

- focusing and controlling attention
- remembering directions
- controlling impulses
- self-monitoring and redirecting thoughts and behaviors
- delaying gratification
- thinking flexibility
- planning and organizing
- reasoning
- problem-solving
- employing memory strategies

Windows of Opportunity

The brain has a remarkable capacity to change, although timing is critical. The parts of the brain develop at different times and at different rates. Studies show that there are **windows of opportunity**, or a framework that identifies key neurological wiring opportunities. During these key times, children need appropriate stimulation for the brain synapses to link easily and efficiently. It is a time when appropriate learning experiences are most beneficial for the brain's rapidly developing organization.

After these key periods, chances for creating stable, long-lasting pathways in the brain diminish. Learning will continue to occur for the remainder of the person's life, although the skill mastery level may not be as high. **Figure 3.8** contains a list of brain functions and the approximate windows of opportunity for each.

Vision: Birth to Six Months

An infant's brain is not wired for sight at birth. The key period for developing vision is first six months of life. Covering newborns' eyes or keeping infants in a dark room during this time will affect their vision. Their sight may not develop normally. Once passed, this window of opportunity is impossible to recover. For this

Windows of Opportunity

Brain Function	Approximate Window of Opportunity
Vision	Birth to 6 months
Motor development	Prenatal to 8 years
Emotional control	Birth to 3 years
Vocabulary/speech	Birth to 3 years
Math/logic	1 to 4 years

Goodheart-Willcox Publisher

Figure 3.8 Windows of opportunity are key periods of time when appropriate learning experiences are most beneficial for rapidly developing brain organization. *At what ages do significant windows of opportunity develop for vision, speech and vocabulary, emotional control, motor development, and math and logic?*

reason, doctors examine a newborn's eyes after birth. If a cataract covering the lens of the eye is present at birth, removal of it is necessary.

Vision is one area that develops with little stimulation. Light and visual stimulation are a requirement during this period. Infants need interesting objects to look at, including toys and people. As you carry infants, point out and describe interesting objects, pictures, people, and places.

Vocabulary/Speech: Birth to Three Years

Infants must hear language to learn it. Children at this age have an incredible capacity for learning language. The speech children hear during their first three years of life will determine their adult vocabulary and ability to produce certain sounds. Infants who experience an environment rich in descriptive words are likely to develop an extensive vocabulary. Infants and toddlers who hear fewer words develop smaller vocabularies.

It is important for caregivers to speak in full sentences. Talk to children often. Tell them what you are doing, what they are doing, and what you will do next. Read them stories and play music. Engage them in social interactions that require language. Be sure to model good grammar.

The sensitive period for developing a second language is between birth and five years of age. After this time, learning becomes more difficult as the brain loses plasticity for these skills. Babies are equipped to speak any language at birth.

As early as six months of age, children filter out sounds that are necessary for their native language. To speak a second language without an accent, it is important to build these pathways at the same time they build their native language.

Emotional Control: Birth to Three Years

The critical period for emotional control occurs between birth and three years of age. Emotional development includes the abilities to identify feelings, manage strong emotions, and develop empathy. Severe stress or early abuse can damage a child's emotional development.

Infants and toddlers thrive in warm, nurturing, and stable relationships. In early childhood programs, infants and toddlers should have a consistent primary caregiver. Children need loving caregivers who can read their cues, respond promptly, and meet their needs in a nurturing manner. By using caring words, caregivers reassure children they are valued. Caregivers can also support emotional understanding by labeling children's feelings. Storybooks are effective in helping to promote this type of development.

Math/Logic Development: One to Four Years

The sensitive period for developing this skill does not begin at birth as it does for vision, vocabulary, native language, and emotional development. Rather, the critical timing for promoting brain connections related to math is from one to four years of age. Young children need chances for working with materials that offer an appropriate level of challenge. Blocks and rhythm instruments are examples of toys that encourage sensory exploration related to math. Caregivers can introduce experiences requiring matching and sorting by size, shape, and color. Learning how objects are alike and different is an important skill. When appropriate, caregivers need to introduce words to describe color, size, shape, and texture. They also need to introduce

math words, such as *bigger, smaller, more, less,* and *one more*.

Motor Development: Prenatal to Eight Years

Motor development requires complex brain networking. The window of opportunity begins before children are even born. The window lasts for the first eight years. This time allows for creation of stable, long-lasting structures. Young children need a variety of gross- and fine-motor activities to support motor development.

Lesson 3.1 Review

1. Which type of development includes changes in bone thickness, vision, and hearing? (3.1.1)
   A. Physical development
   B. Cognitive development
   C. Social-emotional development
   D. Heredity
2. **True or False.** Nature and nurture work together to contribute to healthy brain development. (3.1.2)

3. Each of the following is an example of executive function during the early years except (3.1.2)
   A. problem-solving.
   B. reasoning.
   C. object permanence.
   D. controlling impulses.

Lesson 3.2

Historical Factors and Theories of Development

Understanding historical influences and the theories about how people develop helps form your knowledge base in caring for and educating young children. Your beliefs about how children learn and develop will influence how you plan curriculum and how you teach young children. Erickson, Piaget, Vygotsky, Montessori, Dewey, and Gardner have influenced the content of this book.

3.2-1 Historical Influences on Early Childcare and Education

To understand early childhood education, the past is important. Many of the current practices have their roots in the past. Throughout history, differing viewpoints, committed educators, and changes in popular practice have all helped shape early care and education. Views and treatment of children have recycled. Today new and old traditions influence best practices in early care and education.

During the 1700s, children were raised in difficult and rigid environments. Children were treated as adults in early America. They received little attention and were expected to grow up quickly. Religious institutions controlled much of what people believed about children. Children were taught to read the Bible at an early age with their fathers serving as teachers. The focus was on religious and moral education.

In the 1800s, the movement toward an industrial society shaped life. In school, the basics of reading, writing, math, and citizenship were taught, but few children received formal schooling. Later in the century, improving the educational system became a priority. Free schools and libraries were built for children of all levels of society. Kindergartens were opened to help younger children, particularly those from families with fewer economic resources, succeed in school.

The 1900s included the scientific revolution. During this time, the work of several theorists contributed to the understanding of how young children develop and learn. This work helped guide the practice of parenting. Early childhood education became a public concern. Federal legislation was passed to meet children's needs. Childcare became an important profession. Printed books and newspapers became more affordable to the public. With these changes, knowledge began to spread quickly. The first printed information on childcare was imported from Europe and emphasized the mother's role.

In the twenty-first century, advances in education have been rampant. Use of technology occurs in every aspect of life. Curriculum, whether preschool, elementary, high school, or college emphasizes science, technology, engineering, and mathematics. Prekindergartens are being funded by local and state departments of education. Historically Black colleges, formerly housed in Home Economics departments, continue making contributions to the understanding of young children and cultural diversity. With the encouragement of Hispanic leaders, bilingual education programs are flourishing.

Many people contributed to the understanding of how children grow and develop. Some developed theories and published books. Some opened and worked in children's programs. Others showed leadership by introducing professional organizations. All their work and beliefs have shaped current practices about young children and early childhood education. **Figure 3.9** outlines historical influences on educating children.

Early Childhood Insight 🅐🅱🅒

Learning Standards

All states have developed a set of learning standards for children below kindergarten age. These standards are expectations for the children's learning. Learning standards affect curriculum planning, are research based, and linked to specific ages or developmental periods. The goal of learning standards is to provide guidelines that define the desired content and outcomes of young children's education. They define the foundational steps for learning. Effective standards should be developmentally appropriate in content and outcomes.

3.2-2 Theories of Development

Psychologists continue to study human development. They hold different theories about how people learn, grow, and develop. Some theories, once considered universal, people now recognize as varying by experience and culture. Over the past century, many researchers have provided theories that are practical guides. A **theory** is a principle or idea that is proposed, researched, and generally accepted as an explanation. Theories describe, explain, and predict behavior. They help you understand how, why, and when learning occurs.

Theories are useful decision-making tools. They are helpful for understanding and guiding developmental processes. Theories differ, and no single theory tells people everything. The theory of *nature* or genetics supports the idea that children mature as they grow older. Another theory, *nurture*, supports that their environment shapes children. Still, other theories support both environment and genetics as influences on children's learning and behavior.

Since a variety of theories exist, teachers and care providers need to understand these different approaches for working with children. Theories will help you form your personal values and beliefs about learning. They will also help you understand strategies for promoting children's development. Chances are you will choose parts from various theorists.

In this chapter, you will learn about five major theories on how children learn. These include theories of mid-twentieth-century psychologists Erik Erikson, Jean Piaget, Maria Montessori, Lev Vygotsky, and John Dewey. The final theorist, Howard Gardner, is a twenty-first-century developmental psychologist. They base these theories on observation and experiences with children. Think about the children you know as you read about theories that helped form today's ideas about working with young children.

Historical Influences on Educating Children

Date	Historical Influence
1632	John Locke, father of educational philosophy, claimed that children are born with a clean slate and molded by experience. Locke believed in the importance of nurture over nature. He also believed the main goal of education was self-control.
1801	Johann Heinrich Pestalozzi published *How Gertrude Teaches Her Children,* which emphasized home education. He believed all children are capable of learning and activities should focus on the manipulation of objects.
1826	Friedrich Froebel is known as the "father of the kindergarten." Froebel published *Education of Man,* which included the first system of kindergarten as a "children's garden." He advocated a play-based learning environment and introduced stories, finger plays, songs, sewing, and cutting.
1837	Froebel opened the first kindergarten in Germany.
1856	Margarethe Schurz opens a German-speaking kindergarten in her home in Watertown, Wisconsin. Schurz's program focused on Froebel's principles.
1860	Elizabeth Peabody opened the first English-speaking kindergarten in Boston, Massachusetts. Peabody adapted Froebel's approach and included individualized instruction by adapting activities to the children's abilities. She helped gain support for public kindergartens in the United States.
1896	John Dewey opened a laboratory school at the University of Chicago. Dewey supported a child-centered approach where children learn by doing. He believed children should be able to explore the world around them. He encouraged teachers to observe children use the children's interests for integrating subject matter into the curriculum. Through a purposeful curriculum, Dewey also encouraged the development of critical-thinking and problem-solving skills.
1900s	Arnold Gesell, the Director of Yale Clinic of Child Development, developed age-related norms that characterize children's tasks and behaviors. He found that children reach developmental milestones in a fairly predictable sequence and within a reasonable time frame. He believed a child's development was directed by the action of genes.
1907	Maria Montessori, an Italian doctor, opened her first school in the slums of Rome. She is well-known for her work with children with disabilities. Montessori stressed practical life tasks such as washing and dressing. Her schools emerged in America after her death in 1951. Today her theories influence how many early childhood programs are structured.
1911	Margaret McMillan, who had a background in social work, opened a nursery school in the slums of London. The child's overall welfare was the focus. Hygiene, active hands-on learning, and outdoor play were emphasized. McMillan was the first to write about the influence teachers could have on a child's brain development during this formative time.
1916	The first parent cooperative for children between 18 months and 7 years of age began at the University of Chicago.
1920s and 1930s	Many college home economics departments began nursery schools. The emphasis was on the whole child with children playing freely indoors and outdoors in carefully designed learning environments.
1923	Jean Jacques Piaget published *The Language and Thought of the Child.* He developed the cognitive theory of development, which focuses on how children's intelligence and thinking abilities emerge through distinct stages. According to Piaget, children play an active role in their own cognitive development.
1926	Patty Smith Hill founded the National Association of Nursery Education, which is now called the National Association for the Education of Young Children (NAEYC). Hill believed that kindergartens should be open to innovation as well as remain faithful to Frobel's ideas. She brought innovation to Froebel's kindergarten, establishing the foundation for modern kindergartens in the United States today. However, critics thought it was too rigid.
1940s	Benjamin Spock introduced a best-selling book on child care, *The Common Sense Book of Baby and Child Care.*
1942	The *Lanham Act* passed. Federally funded day care provided support to mothers working in defense plants.
1943– 1945	The Kaiser Company opened two child care centers in Portland, Oregon, to attract female workers during the war.
1944	*Young Children*, a journal for people working with young children, was first published.

Continued
Goodheart-Willcox Publisher

Figure 3.9 Many people and events have had great influence on the education of young children.

Historical Influences on Educating Children (continued)

Date	Historical Influence
1946	Mamie Phipps Clark was the first African American woman to earn a Ph.D. in experimental psychology, which she did from Columbia University. She is best known for her research on race, self-esteem, and child development. Clark and her husband founded the Northside Child Development Center in the basement of the Paul Lawrence Dunbar Apartments. The center was the first to provide therapy for Black children in Harlem. They also helped families in need of housing. Today, the center provides math tutoring, nutritional workshops, and parental training.
1950	Erik Erikson, who developed the psychosocial theory, published *Childhood and Society.* Erikson's work is the foundation of current beliefs about children's personality development. His theory covers the human life span.
1954	Inez Beverly Prosser was the first African American woman to earn a doctorate degree in psychology. Her historic academic work focused on the damaging effect of racism on African American children and how best to educate Black students. Prosser's work was referenced in the debates surrounding the *Brown v. the Board of Education of Topeka, Kansas* U.S. Supreme Court ruling of 1954, mandating integration in the nation's public schools.
1964	Martha Bernal was the first Latina woman in the United States to earn a doctorate degree in psychology. Bernal's work helped advance a multicultural psychology that promotes diversity in training, research, and practice. She provided clinical psychologists with training on mental health issues. While working at UCLA's Neuropsychiatric Institute, Bernal assisted with the development of behavioral interventions. Parents were given training and lesson plans to help with their children's behavioral challenges.
1965	The first *Head Start* pilot program was introduced as part of President Lyndon Johnson's War on Poverty initiatives. The focus was to alleviate the risks to children and families related to living in poverty through health, wellness, and education. Head Start has become the largest provider of medical services and education for children of low-income families.
1972	The Child Development Associate Consortium (CDA) was founded to develop professional training programs. The credential is competency based.
1978	Lev Vygotsky's book, *Mind in Society: The Developmental of Higher Psychological Processes,* was printed in English. Vygotsky believed historic and social forces shape intellectual ability and children use language to organize their thinking.
1983	Howard Gardner published *Frames of Mind,* which describes his theory of multiple intelligences. The teacher's role is to assess each child's abilities, interests, and goals as a foundation for curriculum development. Learning experiences should be comfortable for the children and stimulate their development in each of the intelligences.
1986	The National Association for the Education of Young Children (NAEYC) published a position paper, "Developmentally Appropriate Practice in Early Childhood Programs Serving Children from Birth to Age 8." The publication included standards for high-quality care and education for young children.
1993	Universal preschools began to emerge. The goal of public prekindergarten is to enable every child with the skills needed to succeed in school.
1996	The Family and Work Institute published *Rethinking the Brain*, which includes new research on brain development. The book shows the importance of early experiences.
1998	Head Start was reauthorized to provide additional resources for quality enhancement and technical assistance.
2000	The Reggio Emilia approach to education gained increasing attention. The child-centered curriculum is based on many of Piaget's and Vygotsky's theoretical principles. This approach emphasizes the importance of creating authentic learning environments. There is a focus on relationships among parents, teachers, and the community. Much of the curriculum focuses on projects that allow a child to explore a personally meaningful concept or theme. Children's work is carefully documented through transcripts of discussions and photographs of their activities.
2001	The *No Child Left Behind Act* became law. The law was designed to improve the quality of education and improve outcomes for all students. The law requires that teachers to be highly qualified and schools to be accountable for student achievement.
2003	Early Learning Standards defining what children should know and be able to know emerged.
2012	NAEYC published The Common Core State Standards: Caution and Opportunity for Early Childhood Education.
2014	Every state has Early Learning Standards, and most states have proposed changes to them. Most states have Kindergarten Entry Assessments (KEA).
2019	NAEYC adopted a position statement on *Advancing Equity in Early Childhood*.
2021	NAEYC adopted the Fourth Edition of *Developmentally Appropriate Practices*.

The Human Need for Safety

According to psychologist Abraham Maslow, the human need for safety must be met before growth and development occurs in other areas. This is especially true for young children. What does this mean for early childhood teachers and caregivers? Be alert to what causes children in your care to feel unsafe or have fear. Some children may cling to you for security. Others may act out by hitting or biting. Still others may react negatively to "strangers" in the room. On a continuing basis, look for ways to keep children feeling secure. For example, this may mean standing close to a child who fears strangers when a new person is in the room.

Erikson's Psychosocial Theory

Erik Erikson (1902–1994) proposed a theory of *psychosocial development*. He believed development occurs throughout the life span in a series of stages. Each stage represents a vital period in social development. His theory provided new insights into the formation of a healthy personality. It emphasizes the social and emotional aspects of growth. Children's personalities develop in response to their social environment. The same is true of their skills for social interaction.

Erikson's theory includes eight stages that reflect feelings people bring to tasks. At each stage, a social conflict or crisis occurs. These are not generally tragic situations; however, they require solutions that are satisfying both personally and socially. Erikson believed that each stage must be resolved before children can ascend to the next stage.

Maturity and social forces help in the resolution of the crisis or conflict. Therefore, teachers and parents play a powerful role in recognizing each stage. By providing social opportunity and support, teachers and parents can help children overcome each crisis. **Figure 3.10** contains the first four stages of Erikson's theory. These stages occur during the early childhood years. The paragraphs that follow summarize these early stages.

Stage 1: Trust Versus Mistrust

From birth through the first year of life, children learn to trust or mistrust their environment. To develop trust, they need to have warm, consistent, predictable, and attentive care (**Figure 3.11**). They need caregivers who will accurately read and respond to their signals. When infants are distressed, they need to be comforted. They also need loving physical contact, nourishment, cleanliness, and warmth. Then they will develop a sense of confidence and trust that the world is safe and dependable. Mistrust will occur if an infant experiences an unpredictable world and is handled harshly.

Erikson's Stages of Development During Early Childhood

Stage	Approximate Age	Psychosocial Crisis	Strength
I	Birth–18 months	Trust versus mistrust	Hope
II	18 months–3 years	Autonomy versus shame and doubt	Willpower
III	3–6 years	Initiative versus guilt	Purpose
IV	6–12 years	Industry versus inferiority	Competence

Goodheart-Willcox Publisher

Figure 3.10 According to Erikson, children's personalities develop in response to their social environment. During these stages, children experience a social conflict or crisis that they must resolve before moving to the next stage. *Give an example of a crisis a child may experience between the ages of six and eleven years of age. What factors may influence a child's success in handling the crisis?*

MBI/Shutterstock.com

Figure 3.11   These children build trust by forming a loving, caring relationship with their teacher.

Stage 2: Autonomy Versus Shame and Doubt

This second stage occurs between one and three years of age. During this stage, toddlers use their new motor and mental skills. They want to be independent from those with whom they bonded. They want to choose and do things for themselves. They are in the process of discovering their own bodies and practicing their developing locomotor (physical movement) and language skills.

During this stage, children need clear and consistent limits. They rebel against rules and are often negative when confronted by a caregiver. The objective of this stage is to gain self-control without a loss of self-esteem. Fostering independence in children is important. At this age, toddlers start to become self-sufficient. They need to learn to make simple choices and decide for themselves. To do this, toddlers need a loving, supportive environment. Positive opportunities for self-feeding, toileting, dressing, and exploration will result in **autonomy**, or independence. In contrast, overprotection or lack of adequate activities results in self-doubt, poor achievement, and shame.

Stage 3: Initiative Versus Guilt

Between three to six years of age, the third stage occurs. According to Erikson, it emerges because of the many skills children have developed. Now children have the capacity and are ready to learn constructive ways of dealing with people and things. They are learning how to take initiative without being hurtful to others. They are also busy discovering how the world works. Children begin to realize that they can influence the world, too. Challenged by the environment, children are constantly attempting and mastering new tasks. Aided by strong initiative, they can move ahead energetically and quickly forget failures. This gives them a sense of accomplishment.

Children at this stage need to create, take risks, and develop a sense of purpose. This happens when adults direct children's urges toward acceptable social practices. If children are discouraged by criticism, feelings of incompetence and guilt are likely to emerge. This can also occur if parents demand too much control.

Stage 4: Industry Versus Inferiority

The major crisis of this stage occurs between six and eleven years of age when children enjoy planning and carrying out projects. This helps them learn society's rules and expectations. During this stage, children gain approval by developing intellectual skills, such as reading, writing, and math. Successes in and out of school will make them feel competent.

The way family, neighbors, teachers, and friends respond to children affects their future development. Realistic goals and expectations enrich children's sense of self. Children can become frustrated by criticism or discouragement, or if parents demand too much control. Feelings of incompetence and insecurity will emerge.

Workplace Connections

Observing Erikson's Stages in Children

Observe infant, toddler, and preschool-age children at play in a childcare center. Try to identify activities or actions a child performs that show which of Erikson's stages of development the child is demonstrating.

1. Interview the center's staff to discover how they view Erikson's developmental theories.
2. What role do Erikson's theories play in the center's daily program?

Piaget's Cognitive Development Theory

Jean Piaget's (1896–1980) thinking has challenged teachers to focus on the ways children learn to know as opposed to what they know. His theory of cognitive development focuses on predictable cognitive (thinking) stages and

ages. Piaget believed that thinking was different during each stage of development. His theory explained mental operations, which includes how children perceive, think, understand, and learn about their world. He was interested in what knowledge is and how children acquire it.

Piaget's theory focuses on how thinking and language influence all aspects of life. He believed that children naturally attempt to understand what they do not know. They are little scientists and construct their own intelligence. Children gradually build knowledge through active involvement in first-hand experiences with people, places, and objects in their world. For example, by physically handling objects, young children discover that relationships exist between them (**Figure 3.12**). Terms Piaget used to describe these processes were *schemata*, *adaptation*, *assimilation*, and *accommodation*. These processes occur during each stage of development.

Schemata are mental representations of organized units of knowledge. As children receive new information, they are constantly creating, modifying, organizing, and reorganizing schemata. Piaget believed physical activity was important in the process of developing new schemes.

Adaptation is a term Piaget used for children mentally organizing what they perceive in their environment. When new information or experiences occur, children must adapt to include

Alina Demidenko/Shutterstock.com

Figure 3.12 According to Piaget, children construct their knowledge of the world through activities. *What activities might help a child develop the skill of conservation during the preoperational stage?*

this information in their thinking. If this new information does not fit with what children already know, a state of imbalance occurs. To return to balance, adaptation occurs through either assimilation or accommodation.

- **Assimilation** is the process of taking in new information and adding it to what the child already knows.

- **Accommodation** is adjusting what is already known to fit the new information. This process is how people organize their thoughts and develop intellectual structures.

Piaget's stages of cognitive development are the same for all children. Most children proceed through the stages in order. Each stage builds on a previous stage. The age at which a child progresses through these stages, however, is variable due to differences in maturation.

Although Piaget did not apply his theory directly to education, he did strongly influence children's early education. Many teaching strategies have developed from his work. Caregivers and teachers now know that learning is an active process. Providing children with stimulating, hands-on activities helps them build knowledge. Piaget's theory includes four age-related stages: *sensorimotor, preoperational, concrete,* and *formal operations*. The first three stages occur during early childhood and the early school-age years.

The **sensorimotor stage** takes place between birth and about two years of age. Infants use all their senses and motor activity to explore and learn. In this way, sensory experiences and motor development promote cognitive development. Babies' physical actions, such as sucking, grasping, and gross-motor activities help them learn about their surroundings. Movements are random at first. Gradually they become intentional as children repeat these behaviors. During this stage, children begin to learn **object permanence,** which is the knowledge that objects still exist even when they are out of sight. Through exploration and exposure to new experiences, children learn new concepts (**Figure 3.13**).

The **preoperational stage** takes place between ages two and seven. Children during

PixieMe/Shutterstock.com

Figure 3.13 This child is at the sensorimotor stage of Piaget's cognitive development and is using all senses to learn.

this stage are very *egocentric*. This means that they assume others see the world the same way they do. Children do not yet have the ability to see others' points of view. During this time, children learn representation skills, including language, symbolic play, and drawing. Children learn to use symbols and internal images, but their thinking is illogical. It differs greatly from that of adults. Children begin to understand that changing the physical appearance of something does not change the amount. They can recognize the difference between size and volume. They can stretch a ball of clay into a long rope. Even if the physical appearance changes, the amount of the object does not change. This skill is called *conservation*. At this stage, children can also classify groups of objects and put objects in a series in order.

During the ages of seven to about age twelve years of age **concrete operations,** the third stage of Piaget's theory of cognitive development, begins. Children develop the capacity to think systematically, but only when they can refer to actual objects and use hands-on activities. Then they begin to internalize some tasks. This means they no longer need to depend on what they see. Children become capable of reversing operations. For example, they understand that 3 + 1 is the same as 1 + 3. When presented with actual situations, children are beginning to understand others' points of view.

The fourth stage, **formal operations**, takes place from eleven years of age to adulthood. According to Piaget, young people develop the capacity to think in purely abstract ways. They no longer need concrete examples. Problem solving and reasoning are key skills developed during this stage.

Montessori Method

In the early 1900s, Maria Montessori developed her own method of education. She was the first woman in Italy to receive a degree in medicine. Early in her career, she was an assistant doctor at a clinic that served children with mental disabilities. Montessori's observations of these children indicated that they lacked stimulation.

Montessori brought her scientific skills to the classroom to determine the children's needs. She developed her theory of education while working with and observing these children. This theory stated children learn best by being active in well-planned spaces. Montessori soon learned these methods were usable with other children. This led to the development of the first Montessori School in Rome.

Knowledge of Montessori's theory and methods spread throughout the world. After a short period of popularity, however, interest in this method declined over the next 40 years. In the 1950s, there was a rebirth of the Montessori method. Magazines and television helped make this method known. Montessori received nominations for a Nobel Peace Prize three time. Today her philosophy, materials, and methods are in use in private and public schools throughout the world. By observing in Montessori programs, you will note a wide diversity. While some programs strictly adhere to Montessori's principles, others do not.

Montessori Approach

In her first schools in Rome, Montessori stressed proper nutrition, cleanliness, manners, and sensory training. Children also worked with special equipment she designed (**Figure 3.14**).

These materials were self-correcting and required little adult guidance. The teacher organized these materials from simple to complex to make learning possible. By handling and moving the materials, the children's senses were trained and they learned to think. They also learned number concepts as well as motor, language, writing, and self-help skills.

Montessori created interesting and beautiful environments to stimulate the children's senses. The tables, chairs, and tools were child-sized. Children's artwork was carefully matted and hung. This practice allowed the children to appreciate the work by observing the color and design. Children were also encouraged to take responsibility for the environment by being involved in real-life work. For instance, they washed and set the tables for lunch.

Montessori believed in self-education in multiage groups. The primary goal of the **Montessori approach** was for children to "learn how to learn" in a prescribed environment. After observing and analyzing the children, teachers would provide instructional materials in a prescribed sequence, which related to the children's physical and mental development. This self-directed learning approach allowed the child to interact with the environment by exploring materials. Montessori believed that this approach

Rawpixel.com/Shutterstock.com

Figure 3.14 According to Vygotsky, children learn the rules of social interaction through play. *What social skills do you think these two young peers are learning?*

would provide the child freedom within limits. It would also help the children to learn logically.

In Montessori schools, daily living exercises were designed to promote independence. Children must learn to care for themselves and learned self-reliance. Teachers provided little help. As a result, children learned to button, zip, tie, and put on coats and boots.

The purpose of sensory training was to help children refine their senses and help develop intelligence. They learned touch, taste, sight, and auditory discrimination. One piece of equipment for this training was a set of sandpaper blocks that vary in texture. The children were to rub their fingers across the blocks. Their goal was to correctly match blocks with like textures. Musical bells with varying tones were used similarly. Children matched bells that have like tones. Montessori schools still use teaching equipment like this today.

Montessori programs also stressed academics. Before introducing children to these experiences, however, they usually had to achieve mastery of sensory training. Then, to teach letter recognition, sandpaper letters were used. After the teacher introduced a letter, children were encouraged to trace the letter with their fingertips. Teachers taught numbers in the same manner. When children demonstrated knowledge of and interest in letters, they began reading instruction.

In addition to daily living exercises, sensory training, and academics, teachers planned artistic or cultural experiences, too. Exposure to artistic materials helped children learn about color and line. By playing with instruments and dancing, they learned music appreciation.

Observing in a current Montessori program, you typically will find

- well-planned spaces for children focused on beauty and order;
- child-sized tables and chairs;
- child-sized tools workbenches, hammers, saws, and scissors;
- materials and equipment carefully organized and within the child's reach;
- children assuming responsibility caring for the environment;

- scheduling that includes large blocks of time so children will not be interrupted; and
- teachers using observation to support children's needs and behavior.

Vygotsky's Sociocultural Theory

Both Jean Piaget and Lev Vygotsky (1896–1984) were *constructivists*. They believed that children build knowledge by being mentally and physically involved in learning activities. Piaget believed this happened through exploration with hands-on activities. Vygotsky believed that children learn through social and cultural experiences. He was interested in how the values, customs, beliefs, and skills of a social group were transmitted to the next generation. He believed that social interactions with peers and expert adults help children in this process. For this reason, families and teachers should provide plenty of social interaction for young children (**Figure 3.15**).

Vygotsky believed that language is an important tool for thought and plays a key role in cognitive development. He introduced the term **private speech**, or self-talk. This refers to when children "think out loud" as a means of guidance and direction. After learning language, children engage in self-talk to help guide their activity and develop their thinking. Generally, self-talk continues until children reach school age.

One of Vygotsky's most important contributions was the **zone of proximal development (ZPD)**. This concept presents learning as a scale. One end of the scale or "zone" includes the tasks that are within the child's current developmental level. The other end of the scale includes tasks too difficult for children to accomplish, even with help. In the middle are the tasks children cannot accomplish alone. Children achieve these tasks with guidance and encouragement from another knowledgeable peer or adult. The term used for this assistance is **scaffolding**. Just as a painter needs a structure on which to stand and paint a building, scaffolding provides the structure for learning to occur. For example, a teacher could scaffold a child's learning while constructing a puzzle. The

FatCamera/E+ via Getty Images

Figure 3.15 Vygotsky believed it is important to support language development. During storytelling, the teacher extends the experience by asking questions.

teacher might show how a piece fits or provide clues regarding color, shape, or size. The "zone" is constantly changing. In contrast to Piaget, Vygotsky believed that learning was not limited by stage or maturation. Children move forward in their cognitive development with the right social interaction and guided learning.

John Dewey: Progressive Teaching Theory

John Dewey (1859–1952), was an American philosopher, psychologist, and educational reformer, is credited with some of America's best educational practices. Until his death, at the age of 93, Dewey was a prolific writer committed to progressive education.

While at the University of Chicago, Dewey founded the *Laboratory School*. The school provided him a site to introduce and test his progressive teaching methods. He was opposed to the techniques used in the nineteenth and twentieth century. At the time, the American schools were authoritarian, rigid, and highly structured. Young children sat quietly in rows and spent hours, even days, memorizing information.

Dewey believed in progressivism. It was an educational theory that emphasized the child's nature and interests as opposed to those of the teacher. According to Dewey, children were social beings. They learned best while interacting and problem-solving with others. He also believed schools should be more democratic. Schools were to promote socially responsible citizens. This meant teachers needed to teach and model how to live in society.

Dewey's Approach

Like Montessori, Dewey supported a child-centered educational philosophy and the power of observation and play. One of his publications was entitled, *The Child and Curriculum*. To provide a quality curriculum, teachers carefully conducted a plan by using observation. Progress, achievement, behavior, and needs required regular documentation. A child's interests formed the basis for planning educational experiences. The intention of these real-life learning experiences was to prepare the child for the future.

Dewey thought teachers needed to ask themselves a series of questions during the curriculum-planning process. Included were:

- Is the experience based on the children's interests and/or needs?
- What is the purpose of the activity?
- What new knowledge and or skills will children gain?
- Will the children be physically engaged manipulating physical objects to learn concepts, knowledge and skills?

Many of Dewey's beliefs today are the basis for developmentally appropriate practices (DAP). Much like the focus on intentionality today, Dewey felt teachers needed to prepare learning experiences carefully. These experiences included *hands-on* and *minds-on* learning activities that involved the children's manipulation and exploration of objects.

Gardner's Multiple Intelligences Theory

Howard Gardner (1943-) has helped teachers rethink how they work with young children. He describes intelligence in terms of cognitive skills, talents, and abilities. Gardner's theory of **multiple intelligences** emphasizes that there are eight potential pathways to learning. Gardner believes intelligence results from the complex interactions between children's heredity and experiences. This theory focuses on how cultures shape human potential. Since publishing his theory in the 1980s, Gardner has continued to expand and revise parts of his theory.

Early Childhood Insight

Kohlberg's Theory of Moral Development

Lawrence Kohlberg, an American developmental psychologist, formed his theory on how children develop an understanding of moral concepts by interviewing children over a period of 20 years. Based on his research, Kohlberg determined that moral development occurred in six stages he grouped into three major levels.

- *Pre-Conventional Level:* At this level, children are very egocentric in their views on morality. They judge moral issues based on whether they will receive punishment. They do not understand that others have different viewpoints.
- *Conventional Level:* Children and adolescents at this level have a basic understanding of morality. They accept and obey society's moral rules even if there are no consequences.
- *Post-Conventional Level:* At this level, individuals may base moral decisions on their own views or principles over society's views. They hold mutual respect, however, for those values and opinions that differ.

Pre-Conventional Level	Conventional Level	Post-Conventional Level
Stage 1: Obedience and punishment orientation	Stage 3: Interpersonal accord and conformity	Stage 5: Social contract orientation
Stage 2: Self-interest orientation	Stage 4: Authority and social-order maintaining orientation	Stage 6: Universal ethical principles

Gardner claims that intelligence is pluralistic. Children learn and express themselves in many ways. In the process, they are using several types of intelligence. Each intelligence functions separately, but all are closely linked. According to Gardner, unless nurtured, a potential intelligence will not develop. Learning is best achieved by using a child's strongest intelligence. Gardner claims, however, that all children need opportunities to develop all areas of intelligence.

The multiple intelligence theory allows teachers to see the positive attributes of all children. Teachers also view Gardner's theory as a meaningful guide for making curriculum decisions. It gives them a chance to assess children's learning strengths. From this data, teachers can plan a wide variety of learning experiences to encourage various intelligences in all children. They can individualize their curriculum, environment, and approaches. **Figure 3.16** lists the intelligences currently endorsed by Gardner. The paragraphs that follow explain these intelligences. Other proposed intelligences, which are still under examination, may be added to Gardner's theory in the future.

Bodily-Kinesthetic Intelligence

Bodily-kinesthetic intelligence involves the ability to coordinate one's own body movements. This includes using parts of the body to solve problems, handle objects, and express emotions. People with this type of intelligence typically enjoy sports, dance, or creative drama. They can express themselves with their entire bodies. Children will benefit from creative-movement experiences and role-playing.

Gardner's Intelligences

Intelligence Type	Description
Bodily-kinesthetic	Ability to control one's own body movements and manipulate objects Use of fingers, hands, arms, and legs to solve problems, express ideas, construct, and repair
Musical-rhythmic	Ability to recognize, create, and appreciate pitch, rhythm, and tone quality Ability to use different forms of musical expression
Logical-mathematical	Ability to use logic, reason, and mathematics to solve problems Ability to apply principles of cause-and-effect and prediction Appreciation of patterns as well as relationships
Verbal-linguistic	Ability to use well-developed language skills to express thoughts, feelings, and ideas and understand others Sensitivity to sounds, rhythm, and meaning of words
Interpersonal	Ability to understand feelings, behaviors, and motives of others Ability to work effectively with others
Intrapersonal	Ability to understand personal strengths, weaknesses, talents, and interests Knowledge of skills, limitations, emotions, desires, and motivations
Visual-spatial	Ability to form mental images Ability to visualize the relationship of objects in space
Naturalistic	Ability to distinguish between living things such as plants and animals Ability to detect features of the natural world such as rock configurations and clouds

Figure 3.16 Gardener believes that a potential intelligence requires nurturing to develop. He also believes that children need opportunities to develop all areas of intelligence. ***Read Gardner's list of intelligences. Do you agree or disagree that children need opportunities to develop all areas of intelligence? Explain your response.***

Gardner suggests children with this type of intelligence process knowledge through a physical experience. They enjoy touch and creating with their hands. Therefore, teachers and caregivers should provide children with daily opportunities for hands-on manipulative activities. Clay, sand, dough, feely boxes, and other sensory activities help them develop fine-motor skills. Movement is also necessary for gross-motor skills and coordination. It is important for caregivers and teachers to provide activities involving physical challenges. These may include playing kickball, jumping rope, and moving to music.

Musical-Rhythmic Intelligence

Musical-rhythmic intelligence involves the ability to recognize musical patterns. It also includes the ability to produce and appreciate music. Since music evokes emotion, this is one of the earliest intelligences to emerge. Composers and musicians are examples of people with this type of intelligence.

Children with this type of intelligence love listening to and moving to music. They are drawn to the art of sound and appreciate all forms of musical expression. They have a well-developed auditory sense and can discriminate tone, pitch, and rhythmic patterns. As a result, they often cannot get songs out of their minds. You will hear them repeatedly singing or humming. This helps them understand concepts and remember information.

Activities to support musical intelligence can be included throughout the day. Offer opportunities for sound exploration through listening and singing. Use songs for directions and moving children from one activity to another. They love making the connection between their bodies and music. Play background music during self-selected play. Include songs during large- and small-group activities. Record the children creating their own music while singing or chanting. Explore rhythm by moving to recorded music. Use different instruments and instruments from other cultures to add variety.

Logical-Mathematical Intelligence

Logical-mathematical intelligence is more than just the ability to use math. It is the ability to use logic and reason to solve problems. Math experts have this form of intelligence. Scientists, composers, and computer programmers also use this type of intelligence in their work. This intelligence involves the ability to explore categories, patterns, and other relationships (**Figure 3.17**). It includes applying the principle of cause-and-effect.

Children with this type of intelligence take pleasure in problem-solving by finding patterns and relationships. They enjoy discovering similarities and differences. Teachers and caregivers should provide manipulatives for matching, measuring, and counting. Blocks can encourage the children's problem-solving and reasoning skills. Storybooks that show a sequence of events hold appeal for this type of intelligence. Water and sand activities with different-sized containers help teach the concept of volume.

Verbal-Linguistic Intelligence

Verbal-linguistic intelligence involves the ability to use language for expression. People with this type of intelligence have listening, speaking, reading, and writing skills. They demonstrate

Rawpixel via Getty Images
Figure 3.17 Children with logical-mathematical intelligence enjoy discovering similarities and differences.

sensitivity to the meaning, sound, and rhythm of words. Lawyers, poets, public speakers, and language translators have this type of intelligence.

Young children with this intelligence enjoy learning by talking, listening, reading, writing, learning languages, and playing word games. These children quickly learn the words to new stories, songs, and finger plays. They enjoy talking to other people and find the right words to express themselves. They can also speak in an interesting and engaging manner. They are also able to learn a second language with ease.

Environments rich with language opportunities can nurture verbal-linguistic intelligence. Children learn language in settings where it is used. Teachers need to follow the children's interests and then use these interests to engage children in meaningful conversations. Children's storybooks, songs, poetry, chants, riddles, and rhymes can serve as a means for learning new vocabulary words. Listening to and telling stories can also promote language development.

Interpersonal Intelligence

People with *interpersonal intelligence* display excellent communication and social skills. These people have a gift for understanding the feelings, behaviors, moods, and motives of others. They make friends easily and understand their intentions and desires. They use language to develop trust and bonds with others. They are also skilled in supporting others and empathizing with them. These skills are important for teachers, politicians, religious leaders, comedians, salespeople, and people working in the service industry.

These skills are nurtured in young children when caring behaviors are modeled for them. Teachers should keep this in mind. They can share experiences and provide the children with chances for verbal interaction. Children can act out stories from books focusing on emotions.

Intrapersonal Intelligence

Intrapersonal intelligence, or self-awareness, is the ability to understand the inner self. It involves knowing your strengths, limits, and feelings. It includes understanding your desires and motives.

The ability to organize groups of people is part of this strength. Communicating needs clearly is another aspect. Psychologists, social workers, religious leaders, and counselors are examples of people with this type of intelligence.

How can you foster this type of intelligence? In the classroom, share emotions that all children experience. These include joy, sadness, regret, and disappointment. Along with sharing classroom experiences, share storybooks as well as that contain emotional concepts.

Visual-Spatial Intelligence

Visual-spatial intelligence allows people to visualize the world in three dimensions. They use their vision to develop mental images. People who have this type of intelligence are observant and show a preference for pictures and images. Photographers, artists, scientists, and athletes are some examples. Architects, engineers, and surgeons also need this ability to see the relationship between objects in space.

Teachers can foster this intelligence by providing children with a stimulating environment. Building blocks, solving puzzles, and reading maps and charts strengthen this type of intelligence (**Figure 3.18**). Children like

snowcake/Shutterstock.com

Figure 3.18 Visual-spatial intelligence can be promoted through toys such as blocks and puzzles. *As a future teacher or caregiver, what other activities might you offer children to promote visual-spatial intelligence?*

to see, touch, and manipulate objects. Make and use visual aids wherever possible. For example, display all classroom schedules, recipes, and stories in charts. They can label shelving units with pictures cut from equipment catalogs.

Naturalistic Intelligence

Development of *naturalistic intelligence* occurs from the need to survive. This is the ability to classify living objects in nature, such as animals and plants. It depends on a type of pattern recognition. This strength also includes the ability to distinguish among types and brands of objects. Sailors, gardeners, zoologists, biologists, chefs, and farmers are people who have this intelligence.

To build on this intelligence, provide cooking activities, nature walks, and classroom animals. These activities help develop use of the senses to gather information. Planting and growing a garden help the children observe cycles. Children can collect rocks, seashells, flowers, leaves, seeds, and coins. In the classroom, they can sort and classify their findings. Post picture collections of plants, animals, bugs, fish, and seashells. Share books about natural events.

Making the Pieces Fit

You might think, "How will understanding the areas and principles of development, the brain, and theories help me when working with children?" The answer is both simple and complex. It is much like fitting together the pieces of a puzzle. To become a nurturing, responsive teacher, you must have insight into how children grow and develop.

The brain affects all aspects of growth and development. The areas and principles of development are similar for all children. Development generally progresses predictably for all children. Although each theory looks at development from a different angle, each offers a wealth of insight into how children develop and learn. On what do the theorists agree? Children learn best in a predictable, caring environment rich with opportunity for learning. In addition, caregivers help build the self-confidence and self-worth that children need to safely explore the world.

Lesson 3.2 Review

1. **True or False.** Children were treated as adults in early America. (3.2.1)
2. Which of the following is not a stage of Erikson's psychosocial theory that takes place during the early childhood years? (3.2.2)
   A. Trust versus mistrust
   B. Executive function versus inaction
   C. Autonomy versus shame and doubt
   D. Initiative versus guilt
3. The purpose of Montessori's daily living exercises was to (3.2.2)
   A. promote independence.
   B. teach pre-reading skills.
   C. promote trust between children and their caregivers.
   D. ease separation anxiety.
4. What term did Vygotsky use to describe assistance provided to a child by a knowledgeable peer or adult? (3.2.2)
   A. Zone of Proximal Development (ZPD)
   B. Private speech
   C. Scaffolding
   D. Multiple intelligences

Chapter 3 Review and Assessment

Summary

Lesson 3.1

3.1-1 Understanding and applying the principles of child development will help make you a successful caregiver or early childhood teacher.

3.1-1 The study of child development is divided into three main domains—physical, cognitive, and social-emotional development. This specialized body of knowledge informs teaching practices.

3.1-2 Brain development occurs rapidly during the first three years of life and is influenced by a number of factors.

3.1-2 The connections between nerve cells are created as a child interacts with the environment. The brain's structure is changed by learning new things.

3.1-2 Infant care and interaction with caregivers is crucial to brain development, and can affect lifelong outcomes in learning, behavior, health, and opportunity.

Lesson 3.2

3.2-1 High quality programs contribute to children's healthy development, behavior, learning, resilience, and opportunity.

3.2-1 New and old traditions influence best practices in early childhood education. So, understanding theories is important.

3.2-2 Theories help explain children's growth, development, and learning.

3.2-2 Understanding theories will help you plan an interesting classroom environment and learning experiences to best promote developmentally appropriate practices.

3.2-2 The theories of Erikson, Piaget, Montessori, Vygotsky, Dewey, and Gardner present differing views on how children grow, develop, and learn that can help inform how teachers and caregivers provide activities to support children's growth, development, and learning.

Vocabulary Activity

In small groups, create categories for the for the chapter Key Terms and classify as many of the terms as possible. Then, share your ideas with the other groups in the class.

Critical Thinking

1. **Create.** Create a digital photo file of children at various stages of maturation. Prepare a digital slide show of the photos and discuss the stage of development demonstrated in each picture.

2. **Make Inferences.** Visit an infant or toddler program. Observe and record strategies used by teachers to promote the development of trust.

3. **Execute.** Contact the public relations personnel of your school and research the legalities concerning taking pictures of children. Create a form to use when seeking permission to take and use photographs of children for educational purposes. Save the project in your portfolio.

4. **Draw Conclusions.** Observe a group of preschool children in a classroom setting. Record examples of how the teachers used scaffolding the children's learning.

5. **Analyze.** Review Gardner's theory of multiple intelligences. Analyze and describe the intelligence area that you believe is your strength. What evidence do you have that supports your belief? Investigate what other researchers say about the validity of Gardner's multiple intelligences. Do these comments change your opinion about the area of intelligence you regard as your strength? Why or why not?

Core Skills

1. **Research.** Use psychology references and websites to review theories of development discussed in this chapter.
2. **Math.** Search for information regarding the development of mathematical and logic abilities in infants and young children. What do researchers say about this subject? What role, if any, do worksheets and flash cards have in the development of these skills? What developmentally appropriate activities can be recommended for the development of these skills during the critical years between one and four years of age? Discuss your findings in class.
3. **Reading.** Read the information at the website *Zero to Three* about stimulating the infant's developing brain through touch, voice, movement, and vision.
4. **Research and Writing.** Search online for information concerning conditions in children that might cause development delays. Are these delays the result of genetics, accident, or disease? Are they always permanent? What treatments are available for children with developmental challenges? For genetic conditions, are any prenatal screenings available to detect the presence of the defect before birth? Write a brief report of your findings.
5. **Research and Writing.** Research the formation of Piaget's cognitive development theory. What early professional experiences led Piaget to propose his theory? What are the two major aspects of Piaget's theory? How did Piaget's early training as a biologist influence his beliefs concerning how individuals begin to learn? Write a short essay based on your research.
6. **Research and Speaking.** Search online for information regarding the appropriate age for introducing technology toys and games for young children. What can young children gain from playing with hi-tech toys? How might growth and development be affected when children engage more often in play with hi-tech toys than in creative and imaginative play with traditional play materials and equipment? Choose a side and debate the merits of each.
7. **Research and Writing.** Using online or print resources, research the biography of Maria Montessori. Write a one-page report detailing how Maria Montessori's early experiences in medicine led her to define a philosophy of early childhood education. Discuss her contribution to the way children are educated today.
8. **CTE Career Readiness Practice.** Examine and analyze Figure 3.9 in your text. How can this help you in working with young children? Then answer the following questions regarding information the author presented in this figure.
   A. Who opened the first English-speaking kindergarten?
   B. What act provided federally funded day care to mothers working in defense plants?
   C. When was the first Head Start pilot program introduced?
   D. Where did Maria Montessori open her first school?
   E. How did the No Child Left Behind Act affect education?

Portfolio Project

1. Using print or Internet sources, search for information on Piaget's conservation experiments. Attempt to duplicate the experiments with young children from a local preschool classroom, kindergarten, or early elementary school. What do the results of the experiments convey about a young child's development of conservation abilities? What about a young child's ability to think and reason logically? Write an essay of your findings and place a copy in your portfolio.

2. Research the work of Howard Gardner and how he came to develop his theory. For example, why is the work of Dr. Gardner relevant considering today's educational crisis? How can applying Dr. Gardner's theory to the classroom encourage greater success in today's students? Write a brief essay on how you would incorporate the use of the intelligences in education and activities for young children. Save a copy of the essay in your portfolio.

Chapter 4

Understanding Children from Birth to Age Two

Lesson 4.1: Physical Development During the First Two Years

Lesson 4.2: Cognitive Development During the First Two Years

Lesson 4.3: Social-Emotional Development During the First Two Years

Lesson 4.4: Culture and Teaching

Case Study

Environmental Effects on Toddler Development

Read the case study as a class and discuss the questions that follow. After you finish reading the chapter, discuss the case study again. Have your opinions changed based on what you have learned? If so, how?

The Contes are recent immigrants to the United States. Both are IT professionals. They enrolled their child in the Valders Early Childhood Center six months ago when arriving in the United States. Today, while entering their child's classroom, the Contes scanned the room for their child's primary caregiver, Robbie Nelson. While approaching her, the teacher glanced up and immediately detected a look of concern on their faces. With a warm smile, the teacher welcomed them and Carson, their sixteen-month-old child. After a pleasant exchange, one of the parents asked if they could schedule a meeting. Robbie indicated she would be happy to meet with them. Then she asked what day and time would best meet their needs. They asked if it could be soon, sometime that day or the next. Sensing they were concerned about something, Robbie volunteered to remain after her scheduled hours to meet.

When they arrived, Robbie suggested they meet in the teacher's lounge since it was empty. The three of them walked down the hall and into the lounge. Before closing the door, Robbie hung a sign on the door that said, "Private parent conference in session." Then she asked the parents to take a seat and offered them a cup of tea, coffee, or a bottle of water. Both parents wanted water. While Robbie walked to the refrigerator to get the water, she noted the nonverbal exchanges between the parents.

After sitting down, Robbie noticed that one parent appeared to be near tears. The other parent was trying to offer comfort by providing a light shoulder rub. Straight away one parent began expressing their concern. They had noticed all the other children in Carson's toddler program were walking. Likewise, the neighborhood children the same age and younger were already walking. Eventually the parents shared their concern about Carson's safety and the potential for getting hurt in their rental home. Because of their concern, neighbors gave them an old playpen that their children had used decades ago. To keep Carson occupied, the Contes provided an endless number of board books and toys, rotating them several times a week.

Give It Some Thought

1. Why do you think Carson is not walking?
2. Should the teacher have contacted the parents to discuss Carson's development? If so, when?
3. If you were Robbie Nelson, how would you encourage the parents to modify the child's environment?
4. How could you explain the progression of motor skills to the Contes?

Opening image credit: FatCamera/E+ via Getty Images

Physical Development During the First Two Years

Essential Question

What do you need to know about the physical development of children from birth to age two to promote their development as an early childhood professional?

Learning Outcomes

After studying this lesson, you will be able to

4.1-1 **analyze** the physical development of children in the first two years after birth.

4.1-2 **differentiate** among the various infant reflexes: rooting, sucking, Moro, Palmar grasp, Babinski, and stepping or walking.

4.1-3 **summarize** the motor sequence that occurs in the development of children from birth to two years.

Key Terms

reflex

motor sequence

pincer grip

Young infants are fascinating and, in many states, they can be enrolled in childcare at six weeks of age. During the first year of life, their development is rampant. Physically many infants learn to sit, crawl, scoot, stand, bend, and walk. Their brain also increases in size by over 100 percent. A toddler's growth and appearance continue to change. As they become more active, their baby fat will disappear and their body will look leaner and more muscular. Their hands become more skilled.

Growth is rapid during the first two years of life and tapers off somewhat by age three. The child's size, shape, senses, and organs change. Some changes are rapid; others are more gradual.

With each change, infants and toddlers gain new abilities. They spend much of the first year of life coordinating motor skills.

Through the repetition of motor actions, infants gain physical strength and coordination. For example, to be able to crawl, infants need to control their lower back and leg muscles.

As a caregiver, you need to be aware of physical changes in the first two years. Activities, nutrition, sleep schedules, and safety policies need to be adjusted as children grow. For instance, infants less than four months old have little muscle strength. Typically, these children enjoy being rocked or held for most of the day. They also enjoy sitting in infant seats and lying on mats. By 12 months, however, the infant's large muscles are more developed. Children need time and space for crawling, creeping, and walking.

4.1-1 Size and Shape

Newborn infants' body shapes are very different than they will be in 12 months. At birth they have bowed legs and a potbelly trunk with a large head. Infants grow at different rates. They grow faster during the first few months than ever again. An infant's weight may change almost daily. The average weight at birth is between 6 pounds 9 ounces and 7 pounds 9 ounces for a North American baby (**Figure 4.1**). Five months later, the infant will have doubled in weight. By one year, the typical child weighs about 22 pounds—or about three times their birth weight. By two years of age, most children weigh almost four times their birth weight. Nutrition is important for infants and toddlers. Well-fed children will grow taller than undernourished children.

Safety First

Preventing Sudden Infant Death Syndrome (SIDS)

Childcare providers who serve infants must be knowledgeable about reducing the risk of *Sudden Infant Death Syndrome*, or *SIDS* (sometimes also called *crib death*). SIDS can be defined as an unexplained death of a healthy baby, usually during sleep. Keeping up-to-date with state guidelines and recommendations by groups, such as the American Academy of Pediatrics, is essential for care providers. The incidence of SIDS in the United States has declined significantly since the American Academy of Pediatrics (AAP) began making their recommendations. Some states require caregivers to complete training for the prevention of sudden death syndrome. When caring for infants, always

- place infants on their backs for sleep, even for naps;
- provide a firm crib covered by a sheet;
- keep soft materials, such as comforters, pillows, and stuffed toys, out of the crib;
- make sure the sleeping area is a comfortable temperature to keep infants from becoming overheated; and
- offer the child a pacifier.

Judy Herr

Figure 4.1 While the average weight at birth for a single baby is 7 1/2 pounds, twins average about 5 1/2 pounds. *What factors do you think contribute to twins having a lower birthweight?*

The infant's length also changes rapidly. The normal range for full-term infants is between 18 and 22 inches. Twelve months later, the infant has usually grown 10 to 12 inches. During the second year of life, most children grow 2 to 6 inches more. By 24 months, most children measure 32 to 36 inches in height.

Body shape and proportions also change as a baby grows. The head and chest have a growth advantage after birth. Gradually, the trunk and legs will pick up speed. There are weight and height differences between males and females by two years of age. At this age, most males are slightly heavier and taller than females.

A newborn's head is disproportionately large at birth because the brain grows so rapidly before birth. The brain is 70 percent of its adult weight at birth, but the rest of the body is only 10 to 20 percent of adult weight. The child's head becomes more proportionate as the child grows in height.

4.1-2 Reflexes

At birth, the infant's physical abilities are limited to reflexes. **Reflexes** are involuntary, unplanned body response to certain stimuli. They are controlled by the lower-brain centers that govern involuntary processes such as heart rate and breathing. A person does not control these responses. Blinking when something is coming toward your face is an example of a reflex. Some reflexes, such as blinking, continue throughout life. Others appear in infants and disappear after a few months.

Doctors and others who work with children check reflexes to assess brain and nerve development. When normal reflexes are not present in infants, it may be a sign of brain or nerve damage. If these reflexes continue past the time they should disappear, brain or nerve damage may again be suspected. Professionals often test infants for the reflexes listed in **Figure 4.2**. Infants do not all acquire or lose these reflexes at the same time. The table shows the age range when each of these reflexes generally disappears.

There are two types of reflexes. *Survival reflexes* are necessary for life. These include breathing, rooting, sucking, and swallowing. Unlike survival reflexes, *primitive reflexes* will disappear during the first six months to one year. The *Babinski, Moro, palmar grasp,* and *stepping* reflexes are examples.

Rooting Reflex

Many of the infant's movements the first weeks are reflexes. These reflexes are needed for survival (**Figure 4.3**). The *rooting reflex* causes infants to turn their heads toward anything infant's that touches the cheek or corner of the mouth. When this occurs, it will trigger a rooting response. The infant's head and mouth will move toward the stimulus. This reflex helps the infant find the breast or bottle. It usually disappears around three weeks of age when it becomes voluntary head turning.

Sucking Reflex

The *sucking reflex* is present even in the uterus. It is a permanent reflex that helps the infant get food for survival. To test for the sucking reflex, place a finger or nipple in the mouth between the tongue and palate. When a nipple is placed in the mouth, the infant will move his or her tongue to the end and begin sucking. By moving the tongue toward the bottom of the nipple, milk will move

Some Newborn Reflexes

Reflex	Age of Disappearance
Rooting	3 to 4 months
Moro	6 months
Palmar Grasp	3 to 4 months
Babinski	8 to 12 months
Stepping	2 to 3 months

Figure 4.2 Doctors and others who work with children assess brain and nerve development by checking reflexes.

Hananeko_Studio/Shutterstock.com

Figure 4.3 The rooting and sucking reflexes help an infant get food. *What are the differences between rooting and sucking reflexes?*

into the mouth. With practice, this reflex becomes a skill.

The course of development for this reflex is from birth to six months. Rooting, sucking, and bringing the hands to the mouth are feeding cues exhibited the first weeks after birth.

Moro Reflex

The *Moro reflex* is sometimes referred to as the "startle reflex." It occurs when a newborn is startled by something loud, such as a noise or an abrupt movement. The infant will react by flinging the arms and legs outward and extending the head. Then the infant will quickly draw the arms together, crying loudly. This reflex peaks during the first month and usually disappears by two to four months.

Palmar Grasp Reflex

The *palmar grasp reflex* is easy to observe. When you place a finger in the infant's palm, the hand will immediately close tightly. The grip is tight enough that you can lift the infant into a sitting position. Do not try this, however. Since the infant has no control over this response, the infant may suddenly let go. This reflex can also be seen if you place a rattle or another object across the palm. The reflex weakens after the first three or four months after birth, although it prepares them for voluntary grasping. The grasp reflex disappears totally late in the first year.

Babinski Reflex

The *Babinski reflex* is present at birth in babies who were born at full term. To test for this reflex, stroke the sole of the foot on the outside from the toe to heel with a blunt instrument. The toes will fan out and then curl tightly and the foot twists in. This reflex prepares the child for voluntary walking. It usually lasts for eight to 12 months after birth.

Stepping or Walking Reflex

A *stepping or walking reflex* can be observed in full-term babies. When an infant is held upright with feet on a flat surface, the infant will lift one foot after another in a stepping motion. This reflex prepares children for voluntary walking. It usually disappears two to three months after birth and then shows up again at the end of the first year. Infants learn to step voluntarily late in the first year when they begin walking.

4.1-3 Motor Sequence

The motor development milestones are uniform, and physical development occurs in a predictable order. It begins at the head and chest and moves to the trunk and lower extremities. **Motor sequence** refers to the order in which a child can perform new movements. Each new movement builds on the previous abilities. Motor sequence depends on good health and nutrition, which supports the development of the brain and nerves. For this reason, movements develop in areas closest to the brain and spinal cord first.

In the first months after birth, head and trunk control develops. When this occurs, the infant can lift the head from a surface and watch a moving object by moving the head from side to side. At two months, the infant can cycle arms and legs.

By four or five months of age, an infant can roll over. Most infants are first able to turn from the stomach to the back. Soon after, the child will roll from back to stomach.

Most infants can sit upright alone at seven months of age, although some may sit by five months. Others may not accomplish this task until nine months of age. The infant needs to strengthen the neck and back muscles to accomplish this feat.

Gradually, infants can pull themselves into sitting positions. After this, *crawling* is the next skill in the motor sequence. This skill occurs shortly after the child learns to roll onto the stomach. To crawl, the child pulls with the arms and wiggles the stomach. Some infants may even push with their legs. Many people confuse the terms *crawling* and *creeping*. Crawling occurs when the infant's abdomen is on the floor.

Hitching is another movement used by infants. Before they can hitch, infants must be able to sit without support. From this position, they move their arms and legs, sliding their buttocks across the floor.

As the arms and legs strengthen, infants can creep. *Creeping* is a movement in which infants support their weight on their hands and knees. To creep, infants must develop control of their lower leg and back muscles (**Figure 4.4**). They then move their arms and legs to go forward. As arms and legs become stronger, infants can stand with help from an adult. Soon after, they can stand while supporting themselves with furniture.

George Rudy/Shutterstock.com

Figure 4.4   Creeping requires stronger leg muscles and better leg control than crawling.

With better leg strength and coordination, infants can walk when led by an adult. Soon after, they can pull themselves up into a standing position. Next, infants can stand with no support. Finally, they become true toddlers—able to walk without support or help. Walking requires the control of the back, neck, shoulders, legs, feet, and toe muscles. It is a skill that requires balance and coordination.

Walking requires intense practice and motivation for exploration. Gradually children's toes point forward and their steps become longer. Repetition of new movements promotes new connections in the brain.

There are stages of development for each skill that involves movement. To illustrate, when progressing toward mature motor skills, children show changes in movement. Picture the child's first attempts at walking. These actions are awkward. At first, it is difficult to maintain an upright posture. Next, there is an unpredictable loss of balance. Short steps are taken and the toes are pointed outward. The child keeps the legs spread to have a wide base of support.

Gradually the walking pattern appears smoother. The step length increases and the arm swinging decreases. The child also brings the legs closer together, decreasing the base of support (**Figure 4.5**).

The earliest hand movements are reflexive. By three to four months, infants enjoy swiping at objects. At this age, they still cannot grasp objects because they close their hands too early or too late. By eight months, hand-eye coordination improves. Now infants can purposefully pick up objects by using their finger and thumb in a **pincer grip**. By 12 months of age, they can transfer objects from one hand to the other.

Infants can begin scribbling with a crayon by about 16 months of age. They can make simple figures composed of vertical and horizontal lines by the end of the second year. By two years of age, the child is typically showing a preference for one hand or the other. Some children do not establish hand dominance until age four.

Children gain many other motor skills in the first two years. These skills are listed in *Appendix B*. The skills listed are milestones for each age group. They are considered milestones because about half of infants at that age achieve the skills. For this reason, you should not worry if a child cannot do every skill listed for his or her age. Wide variations exist. An infant may be slow to reach the skill of sitting. This does not imply the child will be late developing crawling or walking skills. You should, however, implement activities for the development of motor skills. Seek help for an infant who is way behind the milestones and may have special needs. For instance, if a 17-month-old cannot roll over, the parents need to make an appointment with a physician.

Walking Sequence

Immature Stage

- Upright position difficult to maintain
- Rigid appearance
- Loss of balance occurs frequently
- Short steps taken
- Toes turned outward
- Legs spread wide as base of support
- Arms held above waist

Mature Stage

- Upright position and balance maintained
- Step length increases
- Legs closer together, narrow base of support
- Relaxed appearance

Figure 4.5 As young children grow in maturity, their walking pattern becomes smoother. *What characteristics show a child's walk is becoming more mature?*

Health Highlights

Failure to Thrive (FTT)

Failure to thrive (FTT) is a term, not a disease, that describes either inadequate growth or insufficient weight gain. It happens more often with infants and toddlers when growth rates are the highest. Symptoms include lack of weight gain and height growth, as is typical of other infants and toddlers of the same age. Environment and health problems can cause it. Unplanned causes may be low birth weight. Environmental causes may result from poverty, parental withdrawal, improper feeding, and lack of social interaction. Health problems may be related to diseases such as gastric reflux, cystic fibrosis, and lead poisoning.

Diagnosing FTT is a team effort and begins with the child's doctor and parents. Team members may include nurses, dietitians, social workers, and early childhood providers. As an early childhood provider, you may be asked to talk about a child's eating patterns and social interactions with staff and family.

The goal in treating FTT is to restore a child's nutritional health. This may help avoid negative effects on brain development and other areas of growth and development. Early intervention may also provide children and families with continuing medical care, counseling, and education about feeding and social interaction.

If FTT is due to abuse or neglect, it must be reported to the proper authorities. Follow the reporting guidelines of your state and the facility in which you work.

Lesson 4.1 Review

1. During the first year, the infant brain increases in size over _____ percent. (4.1.1)
   A. 100
   B. 75
   C. 50
   D. 25
2. **True or False.** Doctors who work with children check reflexes to assess brain and nerve development. (4.1.2)
3. _____ requires stronger leg muscles and leg control than crawling. (4.1.3)
   A. Hitching
   A. Creeping
   B. Rolling
   C. Moving

Cognitive Development During the First Two Years

Essential Question

What do you need to know about cognitive development of children from birth to age two to become an effective early childhood caregiver or teacher?

Learning Outcomes

After studying this lesson, you will be able to

4.2-1 **identify** how children develop cognitively from birth to six months.

4.2-2 **summarize** the cognitive development that occurs from six to 12 months, including object permanence and infant sign language.

4.2-3 **analyze** aspects of cognitive development from 12 to 18 months, including the significance of reading to children for language development.

4.2-4 **discern** key changes in the cognitive development of children from 18 to 24 months, including the development of deferred imitation and telegraphic speech.

Key Terms

prelinguistic communication

preverbal gestures

infant sign language

holophrase

deferred imitation

telegraphic speech

At birth, most of an infant's movements are the result of reflexes. As infants grow, they learn how to make things happen for themselves. This sign of cognitive development shows that infants are becoming goal-oriented and adaptive. Soon they can coordinate the movements needed to grab a bottle and suck milk from it. They also begin to react differently depending on their needs. A baby may spit out a pacifier if he or she is not hungry. A hungry baby, however, may be content to suck on the pacifier.

Ability to see, hear, feel, taste, and smell are important to learning. Through these senses, children learn about many objects and concepts. All the senses develop during the first two years of life. An infant's sight and hearing develop especially quickly.

Playing is learning. Using all of their senses, they notice, take action, and explore materials and objects. While acting on them, they notice what happens. Often, the same interaction will be repeated over and over again.

As toddlers' attention span increases, and their oral language skills begin to expand. At the same time, their understanding of language develops faster than their speaking skills. Observe them.

4.2-1 Birth to Six Months

A newborn's vision is blurry at birth because the nerves, muscles, and the lens of the eye are just developing. The visual system will not develop unless exercised. Both eyes cannot focus on a single object. During the first few weeks after birth, infants appear to focus on objects in the center of their visual field. Their near vision is better developed than their far vision. They like to focus on objects held eight to 12 inches in front of them.

As their vision improves with age, infants show preferences for certain objects. Studies show that infants will gaze longer at patterned disks, such as checks and stripes, than at disks of one solid color. Infants seem to prefer bold colors rather than soft pastels. They also pay more attention to faces than to other objects. In fact, by two months of age, an infant will gaze longer at a smiling face than at a face with no expression.

As infants grow older, they tend to shift their attention to the face. At one month of age, infants appear to focus on the hairline. By two months, infants show more interest in the eyes. The adult's facial expression is most interesting to a three-month-old child. By four months, an infant can recognize a positive from a negative facial expression. These changes show children are giving thought to areas of the face that interest them.

Hearing also develops early in life. From birth, infants will turn their heads toward a source of sound. Loud noises startle a newborn. They enter the world communicating and often react to these noises by crying. These same newborns are lulled to sleep by rhythmic sounds such as a lullaby or a heartbeat. They also react to human voices while ignoring other sounds. By three weeks, a newborn can distinguish between the voice of a parent and that of a stranger. By eight weeks, infants also begin making vowel-like noises from the back of the throat called *cooing*.

During the first three months after birth, infants do not distinguish between themselves and surrounding objects. If infants see their hands moving, they do not think of themselves as making this movement. In their thinking, it could easily be someone else's hand.

Children this age experiment with reflex actions. Newborns suck everything that touches their lips. They even make sucking motions in their sleep. Gradually, children adapt such reflexes to objects in their environment. They learn to suck the breast, bottle, pacifier, and their own fingers in different ways (**Figure 4.6**).

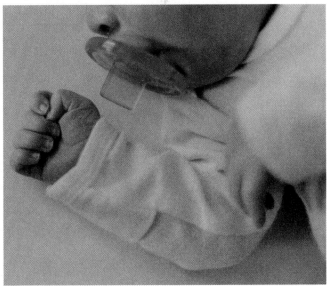

Rawpixel/iStock via Getty Images Plus

Figure 4.6 For very young babies, learning to suck a pacifier differently from the breast or bottle is a cognitive skill.

From three to six months, children start to focus on their surroundings. Before this age, a child would just gaze at objects. The infant now begins to examine objects more closely. By six months of age, the child can distinguish between familiar and unfamiliar faces.

Infants also start to learn that they can touch, shake, and hit the objects they see. They notice that toys make sounds. Memory, foresight, and self-awareness are all developing. The child learns that hitting the crib gym makes a noise. The infant also learns that their own movement caused the noise.

Infants from three to six months of age also begin to show judgment. For instance, they prefer the smell and voice of a parent to that of a stranger. As early as three days after birth, infants will respond to noise. Infants in this stage also try to locate noises by turning toward them. The infant will look around to explore the sources of sounds such as a doorbell, a dog barking, or an oven timer. Many times, though, they will turn in the wrong direction.

From birth, infants begin to use **prelinguistic communication**. They use facial expressions and sounds to express their states. During this stage, vocalizations increase. You will find that babies this age make many noises when you hold and play with them. They respond when their name is said, smile, and play peek-a-boo. Social interactions are becoming increasingly important.

Infants in this stage also respond in new ways to touch. If you blow on or kiss the baby's stomach, the child may smile or coo in response. Children this age also respond happily to light touches and tickling.

Infants think with their senses and movements. By four months, an infant will start using a predictable pattern to learn about objects. If you give a child an object, you will see this pattern. The child will first look at the object. Then the child will mouth it and try shaking it (**Figure 4.7**). The child may also try banging the object on the floor. This is the infant's way of learning what the object can do or how it can be used.

Toward the end of this period, body awareness develops. Infants may bite their toes while playing. If they have a tooth, the hurt this causes may surprise them. This does not stop

M-Image/iStock via Getty Images Plus

Figure 4.7   Mouthing is a major way that infants learn about objects. *What do you think infants learn from mouthing?*

infants from making the same mistake with other toes or fingers.

Early Childhood Insight

Object Permanence

You can test for object permanence by showing the infant an interesting toy. Then cover the toy with a towel or blanket while the child is looking.

If the child attempts to uncover the toy, the child shows an understanding of object permanence. This child also shows goal-oriented behavior.

4.2-2 Six to Twelve Months

Piaget's concept of *object permanence* is a gradual achievement that develops during this stage. This concept is the understanding that objects continue to exist even if the infant cannot see them. Before this time, anything out of sight was out of mind for the infant. For instance, if you place a rattle under a blanket, the young infant would not search for it. Now, the child understands that the rattle is still there even though it is covered.

Understanding object permanence shows that these infants are developing memory and goal-oriented thinking. The child will search under a blanket for a rattle that has been covered. This means that the child remembers that the rattle was there. It also means that the child takes actions with the goal of finding the rattle. If they cannot find the rattle in a few seconds, they give up.

Part of object permanence involves understanding that other people exist all the time. Before this stage, children would simply cry if uncomfortable and stop crying when needs were met. Now, children begin to understand that they can cry as a call to parents or other caregivers. They know that even if a person is not within sight, the person still exists. Their cry will call the person to them.

Crying to call a person is also a sign that infants are learning to communicate. Children learn that crying can get an adult's attention to soothe and comfort them. At this point, the child starts communicating in other ways. Regardless of native language, babies begin babbling by repeating consonant-vowel combinations, such as *dadada*. When infants *babble*, they will often listen for a response. If you make a noise in return, infants may answer back. Usually, infants will listen when spoken to and look up when their names are spoken.

Infants at about eight months of age are becoming better communicators and screen out sounds not used in their native language. They usually are using preverbal gestures. **Preverbal gestures** are intentional signals a baby uses to influence other people in their environment. For example, an infant may point to an object such as a cracker, bottle, or toy to signal you that they want it. When this occurs, you need to respond to them to show that language brings desired results. You may say, "Evan, you want your toy bear." This response will help promote the transition to the spoken language.

Some programs introduce infant sign language to help preverbal infants as young as six months of age to communicate their emotions and desires. **Infant sign language** includes modified gestures of American Sign Language. With ability to sign, infants can communicate before using vocal communication.

Signs often taught infants include *eat, more, bed, thank you, all done (finished), milk, diaper change, please,* and *help.* Signing reduces frustration, temper tantrums, and crying since the baby can communicate simple requests. Sign language will help the child make the transition to spoken language. There are developmental benefits of using sign language. These children often speak earlier and have larger vocabularies. Once they learn to sign, they are practicing and refining their motor skills.

Between 9 and 12 months, infants become more social and intentional about their goals. The child has definite ideas about what he or she wants (**Figure 4.8**). If confined, the child may cry to be taken out. Once out, the child may crawl across the room to get a forbidden object. At the same time, the child may ignore many interesting objects along the way.

These infants also begin to anticipate certain events. A child at this stage, they may express anxiety by crying when a parent puts on a coat. The infant has learned that when this happens, the parent will leave. When the child sees the parent enter the early childhood center, they may become excited and happy.

4.2-3 Twelve to Eighteen Months

Between 12 and 18 months, infants' hearing and speech continues to develop. They enjoy playing pat-a-cake and peekaboo games. Children at this stage like trial-and-error problem-solving. They experiment with objects to find new ways to use them. These might include rolling, hitting, tossing, or bouncing. These children express joy when they find toys can make noise. They begin to understand that the force they use affects the loudness or softness of noise in a toy.

Relationships between cause-and-effect fascinate young toddlers. For instance, the child loves to hit water and watch it splash. Children also learn ways to use cause-and-effect to reach goals at this age. For instance, children may learn that by pulling on a tablecloth, they can reach a plate of cookies.

DavidLongMedia/E+ via Getty Images

Figure 4.8   Using sign language, the child is communicating the word "eat." *How do preverbal children benefit from using sign language?*

Language is a change of behavior that occurs as a result of experience and maturation. It is also related to the child's environment. In Spain, for instance, children learn to speak Spanish, while children in Italy learn Italian. Language becomes a bigger part of communication at this stage. Before this time, some children may say a few words, such as *daddy* or *mommy*. Now, children learn to say many new words. Children's first words usually include objects that move and familiar actions. Included are words such as *mama, daddy, no, car, truck, dig, ball, up, down, bye-bye, wet, dirty,* and *hot*. Mostly, children use one or two words to communicate during this stage. They do not yet understand how to combine a series of words to form sentences.

Books become more important to children. Reading books to infants and toddlers helps them learn the meaning and cadence of words. During this stage, children will love to sit on your lap

and have you read a story. Young toddlers may be able to identify many pictures in simple books. As you point to the pictures, children may give the names of the objects. Most children at this age can understand even more words than they can say. They also enjoy hearing the same book over and over. Through repeated exposure, they learn new things.

Holophrases are commonly used in children's speech at this stage. A **holophrase** is a one-word utterance and gesture combined to express a complete thought. Before combining two words together, toddlers often used a gesture combined with a single word. To illustrate, the child may point to a purse and say the word "mama" to convey that it is their mother's purse. Likewise, children may point to a banana to say that they want to eat a banana. Holophrases reflect how much conceptual and neurological developed has occurred during the first year of life.

Workplace Connections

Age-Appropriate Books for Infants and Toddlers

Visit your public library, a bookstore, or go online to survey books suitable for infants and toddlers.

1. Compile a list of books you might use in an infant or toddler room.
2. Make a display of some of your favorite books for this age group for your class. Explain to the class why these books are age appropriate.

4.2-4 Eighteen to Twenty-Four Months

As children near their second birthday, there is a change in how they approach their environment. During this stage, children start to think before acting. They can apply what they know about objects to solve problems without as much trial-and-error. For instance, the child may know that standing on a stool in the bathroom helps the child reach the sink. This same child may apply this knowledge to get a cookie on the kitchen counter. Instead of a stool, the child may use a chair or even an open drawer. Children in this stage think in terms of actions.

Improved thinking skills and motor skills can make caring for toddlers in this stage exhausting. These children want to actively explore everything. They want to find out as much as they can about unknown places and objects; however, toddlers are not old enough to understand the dangers that may be involved in exploring. For instance, they may step in an open drawer to reach something without realizing that the drawer may fall. Therefore, you must continually watch toddlers and try to make sure their environment is as safe as possible.

Pretending is part of a child's world at this stage. A young toddler's pretending is often a form of deferred imitation. **Deferred imitation** is watching another person's behavior and then acting out that behavior later. For instance, a parent may tuck their child into bed each night and kiss the child on the forehead. At the center the next day, the child may tuck in a doll and give it a kiss on the forehead. Children may also pretend to be animals they have seen, such as dogs.

Children of this age now understand that symbols may represent other actual objects. For instance, a younger child might play with a doll by swinging it around and hitting things with it. Now, however, the child will hold the doll like a baby and cover it with a blanket (**Figure 4.9**).

Children are learning more and more words. At first, toddlers only add one to three words to their vocabularies each month. Between 18 to 24 months, however, their language begins

Mary.Toch/Shutterstock.com

Figure 4.9   This child is caring for a doll. *How do you think deferred imitation has influenced this child's actions?*

to explode. They may add as many as 10 to 20 unfamiliar each month. When their vocabularies reach about 200 words, they combine two words. The term used to describe these two-word phrases is **telegraphic speech**. For instance, the child might say "doggie bark" to let you know that they hear a dog barking. **Figure 4.10** shows typical two-word phrases used by toddlers during this stage.

Children are more confident and like to share what they know with you. As you read to them, they may point to objects to tell you what they are. They enjoy pointing to things that you name. For example, you may say to the child, "Touch your nose." Children at this age are quick to respond by pointing to parts of their bodies. Later, you may get them to point to other objects in the room.

Toddler's Typical Two-Word Phrases

Johnny hit.	My bear.	Big ball.
Hi daddy.	Give milk.	No milk.

Goodheart-Willcox Publisher

Figure 4.10   When toddlers use two-word phrases, they are using telegraphic speech.

Lesson 4.2 Review

1. **True or False.** A newborn baby can focus clearly on a single object. (4.2.1)
2. Piaget's concept of understanding that objects continue to exist even if the infant cannot see them is called _____ . (4.2.2)
   A. rooting reflex
   B. object permanence
   C. preverbal gestures
   D. infant sign language

3. Between nine and twelve months, infants become more social and _____ about their goals. (4.2.3)
   A. intentional
   B. tentative
   C. excited
   D. telegraphic
4. **True or False.** If a toddler sees their parent mowing the lawn one day and then pretends to mow the lawn at the early childhood center, the child is practicing deferred imitation. (4.2.4)

Essential Question

In what ways does social-emotional development from birth to age two influence or set the foundation for how children develop and learn in the future?

Learning Outcomes

After studying this lesson, you will be able to

4.3-1 **analyze** the role of temperament in the development of children from birth to age two.

4.3-2 **assess** the importance of attachment to social-emotional development of children during the first two years after birth

4.3-3 **summarize** the social-emotional changes that occur in children over time during the first two years after birth.

Key Terms

prosocial behavior
empathy
temperament
attachment
bonding

stranger anxiety
sensitive period
separation anxiety
joint attention

At birth, infants do not show a wide range of emotions. They seem to be basically comfortable or uncomfortable. To communicate this, they use movements, facial expressions, and sounds. By cooing, they show their comfort or delight. By crying, they show discomfort.

Security is an important developmental factor. It is critical for infants to develop trust in a responsive, familiar caregiver who can comfort them. They respond differently to a stranger than a familiar caregiver. With a familiar, consistent, and sensitive caregiver the infant expresses more emotions. They will smile, laugh, and babble more. Relationships are critical to their development. When something upsets them during play, toddler's return to and need emotional support from a familiar caregiver. They need to trust the adult will keep them safe and protect them.

Infants display a range of emotions in the first few months of life. The most reliable clues are infants' facial expressions. They show happiness when the corners of the mouth are pulled back and the cheeks are raised (**Figure 4.11**). Between six and nine months, infants will begin to show fear, anxiety, and anger. Signs of fear are the mouth opened with the corners pulled back, eyes widened, and eyebrows raised. By the end

SDI Productions/E+ via Getty Images

Figure 4.11 You can tell by her facial expression this young baby is content. *As a caregiver or teacher how might your actions influence the social-emotional development of infants and toddlers?*

of the second year, children are expressing their emotions in many more ways.

The beginnings of **prosocial behavior** (acts of kindness that benefit others) begin to emerge. **Empathy**, the ability to understand another's behavior, is observed in children with secure attachments. Children may react to another's crying by crying themselves. By 18 months, they may begin to provide comfort.

Socially, young children focus on a few adults who are close to them. This is especially true of infants. After their first birthday, children may take more interest in other toddlers. Adults, however, are still most important to children in this age group. As a caregiver or teacher, you need to realize that your actions will have a profound effect on children's social-emotional development. These children are ready for relationships. They need to be able to count on caregivers and teachers who will respond immediately to their distress signals. Healthy social-emotional development is a foundation for learning.

Modeling prosocial behavior in the classroom will influence children's behavior. If you are warm, helpful, and model kindness, children will notice and imitate this behavior.

4.3-1 Temperament

Even from birth, children differ in temperament or the ways in which they react to their environment. **Temperament** refers to the behavioral characteristics a child has at birth. It is the quality and intensity of the child's repeated pattern of emotions. Such factors as passivity, irritability, adaptability, and activity patterns are part of a child's temperament. These natural traits generally cannot be changed. It influences how comfortable children are with new people, experiences, and places. It also shapes how children learn and behave.

The research team of Alexander Thomas and Stella Chess who were both psychiatrists and university professors, studied temperament. They found that the quality of mood most children fall into is one of three types. These include

- *Easy or flexible*—children with predictable daily patterns are usually warm, pleasant, and friendly.
- *Difficult, active, or feisty*— children who are emotional, sensitive, and cry often, can be negative, and have irregular schedules.
- *Slow to warm up*— children who are shy, cautious, and often anxious when exposed to new people or experiences.

Temperament is a trait that influences how caregivers and teachers react and interact with children. If you care for infants, you need to adjust to the temperaments of different children. All infants need loving attention. If given patient, tender care, most children will grow to be happy and well-adjusted. This is even true of very irritable infants.

Teachers and caregivers need to use discretion when talking about temperament traits. Depending upon the culture, temperament traits may be viewed differently. The optimal traits for children differ. For example, a shy child may be viewed differently in the United States as opposed to in China, Korea, or Japan. When a child is shy in the United States, the teacher or caregiver may become concerned. In another part of the world, shyness may be considered a positive trait.

4.3-2 Attachment Patterns

Attachment and *bonding* are two terms that are often used interchangeably, but they are different. **Attachment** is a type of emotional bond between an infant and important caregiver that develops over the first years of life. It is a mutual pattern of responding and is one of the most important influences in a child's development. Strong attachment results from a caregiver's sensitivity to an infant's signals when needing attention. Its purpose is to make the child feel secure, safe, special, supported, and protected. While **bonding** is the closeness that people develop over time, it is unrelated to attachment. Often, the term bonding is associated with mothers and infants and is related to their everyday expressions of affection and love (**Figure 4.12**).

Prostock-studio/Shutterstock.com

Figure 4.12 Attachment between infants and their caregivers begins soon after birth. ***What are some characteristics of securely attached infants?***

Studies suggest attachment is a powerful predictor of a child's social and emotional development. Researchers have classified four types of attachment patterns:

- securely attached
- insecurely resistant attached
- insecurely avoidant attached
- insecurely disorganized attached disoriented

Most infants fall into the securely attached type of attachment. Secure attachment is an asset. *Securely attached* infants will use their caregiver as a base for exploration. They will venture out and look back to their caregivers for comfort. *Insecurely resistant attached* infants are easily upset and struggle to explore their environment. *Insecurely avoidant attached* infants are not upset

when left with a stranger. They do not have **stranger anxiety**, which is an expression of fear around unfamiliar people. They may resist their caregivers' efforts to comfort or hold them. *Insecurely disorganized attached disoriented* infants display conflicting behavior. These children may smile at their caregiver and then abruptly turn away.

Relationships are the key to promoting attachment and social-emotional development. Infancy is a **sensitive period** for when particular experiences can best contribute to development. The infant's brain development is dependent on environmental stimulation. Infants become attached to the people who care for them and are sensitive to their signals for attention. They know and recognize their loved ones. Included may be parents, caregivers, older siblings, and grandparents. Young infants learn that when they are hungry, wet, or frightened, they can depend on these people for care, comfort, and security. Basic trust is an important part of attachment. The quality of attachment depends on the adults who need to respond promptly, warmly, and consistently.

Infants show several early attachment behaviors. Beginning around two to three months of age, infants will respond to familiar people. They will single these people out for special attention. When approached, the infant may break into a broad, warm smile. Other examples of attachment behaviors are cooing, kicking, gurgling, and laughing. Crying and clinging are also attachment behaviors. These behaviors show the child is signaling to others.

Mobile infants need to feel secure to move and explore. As they adventure out, they turn back to look at the caregiver to check their safety. Exploring is important to the child's development as they learn about how the world works—a process that supports brain development. To feel comfortable, they must trust their caregiver.

Separation anxiety is another attachment behavior shown by infants and toddlers. This happens when a child protests because a familiar caregiver is leaving. The child often cries as a sign of distress. The first signs of separation anxiety appear at about six months of age. The reaction becomes clearer by nine months of age. By 15 months of age, separation anxiety is very strong. It will gradually weaken as the child ages.

As a caregiver or teacher, you need to be prepared for the attachment behaviors of children in this age group. Children between nine and 18 months of age will usually have the most difficulty beginning an early childhood program. To make the transition easier, you need to be responsive and emotionally available. Hold the child facing outward. In this position, the infant can focus on the environment as opposed to you, a stranger. You should also encourage parents to bring the child's favorite toy or blanket.

Some parents also experience separation anxiety, particularly when leaving their infant at the center. You will play an important role reassuring them. Keep the lines of communication open. You may want to send them a text message or even a photograph to show them their child is doing fine.

As children show separation anxiety, you need to remind yourself not to take the reaction personally. These children are simply fearful because their familiar caregivers are leaving them. They do not know what to expect next, and

Safety First

Shaken Baby Syndrome

Shaken Baby Syndrome (SBS) is a form of abusive head trauma that results in *traumatic brain injury (TBI)*. It is a preventable form of severe physical child abuse. Babies have weak neck muscles. Shaken Baby Syndrome happens when parents or caregivers violently shake an infant by the shoulders, arms, or legs, resulting in a whiplash effect. When shaken, the baby's fragile brain moves back and forth in the skull. The result is bruising, bleeding, and swelling. Inconsolable crying is often the trigger for parents or caregivers to shake a baby.

SBS occurs from the shaking alone or with impact on a surface. Infants ages newborn to four months are at the greatest risk for SBS. It is also the leading cause of child-abuse deaths. When parents or caregivers suspect SBS, it is important to report these suspicions to the proper authorities.

SBS can be fatal or cause a permanent disability. Some symptoms of SBS include:

- loss of consciousness and unresponsiveness
- breathing problems—irregular or no breathing
- no pulse
- vomiting, convulsions, or seizures
- uncontrollable crying

Providing positive parenting resources and offering parents various ways to calm their babies is the first line of defense against SBS. See the Centers for Disease Control (CDC) website for more information on how to prevent Shaken Baby Syndrome.

they are in unfamiliar surroundings with strange people. As children become more familiar with the center, its people, and its routine, they will show less distress.

Relationships are the heart of quality care and education. Caregivers and teachers need to be responsive, sensitive, consistent, predictable, and loving so children learn that their wants and needs are important. Secure attachment is important for an infant's emotional health and development. Studies show that having secure attachment to at least one person leads to better intellectual development and social relationships.

4.3-3 Changes Over Time

During the first two years after birth, you will see many changes in children socially and emotionally. As a caregiver, your actions will affect how these children change. Establishing trust is a key factor in social-emotional development. Trust develops when there is predictability. If you meet children's needs and encourage them to interact with others, children will learn to trust and care for others. They will feel safe and happy.

Birth to Three Months

At birth, newborns do not have very refined emotions. General excitement and distress are the only emotions they show. The child may show excitement by looking alert, smiling, or wiggling. Distress is shown by crying. When observing a child in this stage, you may notice that there are no tears when the child cries or that a social smile emerges when a caregiver speaks.

Three to Six Months

By three months, children respond to people with smiles and laughter. They may make joyful sounds as adults play with, hold, or feed them. During this stage, infants start to notice and smile at other babies. Crying is still used to show distress. Early in this stage, tears begin to appear. Later, children start to use distinct cries to signal different types of distress.

Six to Twelve Months

Infants in this stage become actively involved with their caregivers. At this stage, **joint attention** emerges when the infant attends to the same event or object as the caregiver. During this process, the adults need to provide verbal information. This interaction is important for early language development.

As adults play with and care for them, these children express happiness, joy, and surprise. They also make sounds in response to the speech of others. Infants in this stage also develop fear. You should not be surprised if a child this age cries at the sight of a stranger. By this age, children have also developed attachment to their caregivers. They may cry and even show anger when their caregivers leave them.

This stage may be the most difficult for the child's parents and for you. Separation anxiety starts to show. As a result, a child may start crying and clinging upon entering the center. When you try taking the child from the parent, the child may attempt to push you away. After the parent leaves, the child may continue to cry. Most children, however, will stop crying within a few minutes. This behavior may continue until 14 to 16 months of age.

Twelve to Twenty-Four Months

Early in this stage, children still show separation anxiety. Children in this stage also show anxiety and become upset because of something they think will happen in the future. For instance, this child may cling to a parent who will be leaving soon.

These children become more interested in exploring. Although they still fear the unfamiliar, they are curious about new places and objects (**Figure 4.13**). Children who feel secure are more likely to explore than those who feel unsure of their surroundings. By this age, children start to take more interest in other children. They like to play next to others, but they interact little with them.

Children become more aware of their own abilities at this point. This self-awareness is a source of joy and anger for children. Toddlers are proud and happy when they can do things for themselves.

Rawpixel.com/Shutterstock.com

Figure 4.13   Curiosity helps toddlers explore new objects. ***What factor influences whether children are willing to explore?***

Sometimes, however, they insist on doing things for themselves that they cannot do yet. This can cause frustration and anger for the child.

Children are rapidly developing new motor, cognitive, and social-emotional skills during this period. They are also likely to use strong-willed responses. Often, they use the word *no*. Toddlers like to know that they can make things happen, and they do not always want to do what adults want. Sometimes they may say *no* to you just to see what will happen. You will need to be kind but firm with these children. You must help them understand that there are rules that they must be follow. At the same time, you need to reassure the children that their wants and needs are important.

Lesson 4.3 Review

1. Temperament shapes how children _____ and behave. (4.3.1)
   A. think
   B. walk
   C. learn
   D. verbalize

2. At what age do children start to show the first signs of separation anxiety? (4.3.2)
   A. birth
   B. three months
   C. six months
   D. nine months

3. Joint attention emerges when _____. (4.3.3)
   A. an infant shows excitement
   B. there is predictability in an infant's life
   C. an infant attends to the same object as a caregiver
   D. an infant becomes more interested in exploring

Culture and Teaching

Essential Question

? *How can assessing your personal cultural identity and attitudes about human differences help you become a culturally competent early childhood caregiver or teacher?*

Learning Outcomes

After studying this lesson, you will be able to

4.4-1 **discern** how culture influences they ways in which children develop.

4.4-2 **illustrate** how interactions with teachers and caregivers influence infant and toddler development.

Key Terms

culture   cultural competence

For children and their families, culture plays an important role in learning and development. It is very crucial for teacher and caregivers to understand cultural elements that are different from their own. Such understanding will inform your teaching and caregiving practices and interactions with children.

4.4-1 Culturally Based Routines

Everyone has a culture. **Culture** is a shared system defining who people are and how they choose to live. It includes the values, beliefs, and practices of a particular group. It is the group's ideas and ways of doing things—such as traditions, language, customs, behaviors, and practices—that become a learned pattern of social behavior.

From birth, culture provides a framework that defines what a child should know and be able to do. A culture's unique socialization experiences influences how children grow and develop.

Cultural variations in childrearing practices can shape development. Movement patterns are examples. Parental beliefs and interactions influence these patterns. Both a stimulating environment and movement opportunities impact a child's development. Some cultures intentionally bounce their infants on their feet to gain muscular strength and promote walking. In other cultures, they do not encourage early crawling and walking.

Part of becoming an early childhood professional involves developing cultural competence. **Cultural competence** involves understanding your own cultural identity and attitudes about human differences, while acquiring knowledge and appreciation for other cultures. Teachers and caregivers need to develop strong and ongoing relationships with parents to learn about their cultural practices, hopes, and priorities for their child. For infants and toddlers, the following routines are culturally based and affect children's developmental outcomes:

- breast or bottle feeding, including frequency and feeding position;
- introduction of solid foods, including types and use of utensils;
- age toileting begins;
- being hand fed or spoon fed;
- sleeping practices;
- use of comfort objects, including timing and duration;
- discipline; and
- napping, including location, timing, and duration.

It is important that teachers and caregivers do not assume all families have the same child-rearing techniques. Prior to a child's enrollment in the program, you should schedule an interview with the parent(s). It should focus on welcoming the parent and discussing cultural beliefs and values. Home language, child-rearing practices, and goal setting are all important items to discuss. Also, an interesting question is to ask them is what they like best about their child. Chances are you will find some of the responses interesting.

4.4-2 Teaching Infants and Toddlers

Play is essential to the development of infants and toddlers. Watch them. They are little scientists and learn through all their senses. They will look, listen, touch, taste, and explore their environment. Infants and toddlers enjoy being play partners and are active learners from birth. Through their interactions with their environment and you, they are building brain architecture for lifelong learning and health.

Babies are wired for connection with others. From watching adults and others, they learn. They learn best in an interactional mode through nurturing, stable relationships with caring adults. Their brains need predictable and responsive caregiving, supportive relationships, and opportunities for learning. Each infant needs to be assigned one consistent caregiver for optimum development.

When an infant cries, babbles, or makes a facial expression or gesture, your presence is important. Infants have limited self-regulation capacities. So, they need your support to help manage their behavior and feelings. Show them you care by responding promptly, warmly, and consistently. Hold them tenderly. Talk to them, softly and sweetly. Help them identify their emotions. You can also rock them, sing to them,

or even distract them by shaking a rattle. Babies can develop multiple attachments to a variety of people—nannies, aunt, uncles, siblings, and caregivers. Secure attachments are important.

Interacting with infants and toddlers supports building the child's neural connections. Respond to the child's crying, babbling, or gesturing. When a child *serves*, you need to be supportive and *return*. If the infant babbles, then you need to return by babbling back. Likewise, if the toddler points to something, you need to name and describe the object. These give-and-take, serve-and-return interactions are important as they support healthy development. These actions help create neural connections that will build the baby's brain, which is rapidly developing.

Notice and follow a child's interests. Provide them with brightly colored toys with textures and interesting shapes. Talk to them, label objects, and help them build conceptual categories. If they need you to stop, they will let you know. They may turn their head or ignore you. Toddlers may even push your hands away.

Healthy toddlers are curious and always watch and study the behavior of others. They love to explore and problem-solve their environment. Their environment should provide powerful opportunities for learning with all five senses. Toddlers also are beginning to talk and verbally interact. When they talk, show them you value them. Model respectful interactions by looking at them and listening carefully. Tailor how you speak by modifying your words to fit the child's interests and strengths. This will make them feel important and stimulates their language development.

Provide toddlers with ample space to move, and materials to encourage pretend play as well as toys that challenge them. They love dolls, telephones, puzzles, stacking rings, jumbo crayons, and building blocks. Toddlers will want autonomy. Observe them. They want to explore and accomplish new things. They also want to do things by themselves, without others providing help.

Lesson 4.4 Review

1. _____ is a shared system defining who people are and how they choose to live. (4.4.1)
   A. Joint attention
   B. Culture
   C. Bonding
   D. Attachment

2. True or False. Cultural variations in childrearing practices can shape development. (4.4.1)

3. Which is *not* an example of a serve-and-return interaction that helps build neural connections for brain development? (4.4.2)
   A. Tossing a ball to a toddler after they point to the cat.
   B. Naming an object after a toddler points to it.
   C. Babbling back to an infant who is babbling at you.
   D. Taking a book off a shelf and reading it to a toddler after the toddler pointed to the book.

Chapter 4 Review and Assessment

Summary

Lesson 4.1

4.1-1 During the first year, infants typically triple their birth weight and grow 10 to 12 inches in height. Body shape and proportions also change.

4.1-2 Infants have many involuntary reflexes that are eventually replaced with voluntary movements.

4.1-2 *Survival reflexes* include rooting and sucking, while *primitive* reflexes include the Babinski, Moro, palmar grasp, and stepping reflexes.

4.1-3 Motor sequence is the order in which a child can perform new tasks.

Lesson 4.2

4.2-1 During the first three months, a newborn's vision gradually improves, they react to human voices, and begin cooing.

4.2-1 From three to six months, infants begin to show judgment and begin to use prelinguistic communications. Infants think with their senses and movements, and develop body awareness.

4.2-2 Object permanence develops from six to 12 months and infants begin babbling. They also use preverbal gestures communicate.

4.2-3 Infants at nine to twelve months are more social and may express anxiety when parents leave.

4.2-3 From 12 to 18 months, young toddlers continue to develop hearing and speech, are fascinated by cause-and-effect relationships, and use holophrases to communicate.

4.2-6 During 18 to 24 months, toddlers' thinking and motor skills improve and pretend play becomes part of their world. They begin to use two-word phrases.

Lesson 4.3

4.3-1 Each child is born with a unique temperament, or ways they react to their environment.

4.3-2 Strong attachment results from caregiver sensitivity to infant needs. Bonding develops over time, but is unrelated to attachment.

4.3-2 Attachment is a powerful predictor of a child's social-emotional development.

4.3-3 During the first two years, there are many changes in social-emotional development. Establishing trust is a key factor in this development.

Lesson 4.4

4.4-1 Teachers need to develop supportive relationships families to learn about their child-rearing techniques.

4.4-1 Teachers and caregivers must continually reflect on their own cultural identity and views about human difference to help develop cultural competence and inform their teaching and caregiving practices.

4.4-2 The understanding of child development is critical to informing teaching and caregiving practices.

Vocabulary Activity

Working in small teams, locate a small image online that visually describes or explains each of the Key Terms in the chapter. To create flashcards, write each term on a note card and paste the image that describes or explains the term on the opposite side.

Critical Thinking

1. **Distinguish.** Visit a childcare center serving infants. Observe and distinguish differences among them.
2. **Analyze.** Bring to class your baby books or albums in which your parents documented your milestones. Analyze photos and descriptions of infant reflexes and other important development such as lifting your head or rolling over were recorded. At what ages did these occur?

3. **Compare and Contrast.** Review infants' cognitive development in the first two years of life and then choose two age ranges to compare. Write a short story from the points of view of the infants in each range and try to describe the infants' environments according to their cognitive levels.

4. **Draw Conclusions.** Observe a parent playing with or caring for an infant. Record the child's age in months. Write an anecdotal description of the child's interactions with the parent. Share your observation with the class.

5. **Cause-and-Effect.** Analyze factors related to cultural diversity that might impact a child's development. Share any experiences you have had where your culture and another person's provided different reactions to a situation or problem. How did this affect the development of you and the other person?

Core Skills

1. **Research and Writing.** Research the reflexes of premature infants in comparison to those of full-term babies. Are there any differences that could influence the premature infant's development? Write a one-page report of your findings.

2. **Technology.** In small groups, search online for videos of infants creeping, crawling, hitching, standing, and beginning to walk. Choose one video for each stage in infants' motor sequence. Create a presentation incorporating these videos and showing how infants learn new motor skills. Narrate the video to your class and then lead a discussion about the videos you chose.

3. **Writing.** Write an article suitable for a parent newsletter or early childhood center bulletin that summarizes cognitive development during the first two years. Use your textbook and online resources as needed. Include what parents should expect regarding their child's intellectual development during this period. Additionally, offer suggestions for activities parents can try at home to interact with their child.

4. **Research and Speaking.** Research the "Mozart Effect" online. How much research is available linking listening to music with an increase in intelligence? How has music been shown to affect infants' moods and emotions? Research how the "Mozart Effect" has affected parents' perception of the importance of playing music for their infants. Share your findings in class.

5. **Research.** Research information about Jean Piaget's studies, particularly those involving object

permanence. Duplicate some of his experiments with infants, such as hiding a toy under a blanket. You might also drop an item off a high-chair tray to see if the infant will search for the toy. Create a classroom discussion forum to discuss your findings.

6. **Research and Speaking.** Research studies of infants who, for some reason, did not form attachments to others early in life. How did this affect their behavior as young children and as adults? How did it affect their social-emotional development throughout life? Give an oral report based on your findings.

7. **Writing.** Review this chapter's information about social-emotional development in infants and then think about the information from the perspective of a parent. For each of the age ranges listed in the text, make a list of facts you think parents would be interested in knowing about their children. Then, compile these facts into a pamphlet titled *The Social-Emotional World of Your Infant*. Include pictures of parent-child interactions to complement each fact.

8. **Research.** Research how cultures differ in their expectations and opportunities provided for young children. Identify one culturally based routine and describe how it can affect a child's developmental outcomes. Draw conclusions about how understanding cultural difference might influence your career as an early childhood professional.

9. **Research and Writing.** Use the text and online resources such as the NAEYC website to further research the role of cultural competence in early childhood classrooms. Write a short paper summarizing your findings.

10. **CTE Career Readiness Practice.** Suppose you are a journalist for a local newspaper, and your current assignment is to write a full-page public service announcement that captures student attention and warns about the effects of shaking on babies. In your research, be sure to identify documented cases where shaking resulted in physical harm to an infant.

Portfolio Project

Compile a list of resources that might be used to assist in parent communication. These may include websites, books, magazine articles, professional journal articles, newsletters, pamphlets, cooperative extension agency bulletins, and government information. Format your list as a bibliography and add to it throughout the year as you learn of additional resources. Keep a copy of the list in your portfolio.

Understanding Two- and Three-Year-Olds

Lesson 5.1: The Developing Two-Year-Old
Lesson 5.2: The Developing Three-Year-Old

Case Study

What Skills Should Two- and Three-Year-Olds Have?

Read the case study as a class and discuss the questions that follow. After you finish reading the chapter, discuss the case study again. Have your opinions changed based on what you learned? If so, how?

Geneva Corace just began working at Manitowoc's Early Learning Center. Although she earned an associate degree from a local community college, she lacked experience working with young children other than babysitting during the summer of her junior year of high school. The community college canceled all practicum experiences due a recent pandemic. As a result, Geneva felt she lacked valuable knowledge that could have been gained by participating in practicum experiences working with young children.

A three-year-old child named Glen was enrolled during Geneva's first week of employment. Glen came to group time and listened to a story, which he appeared to enjoy. On the play yard, he walked around, watched, and talked to other children who were playing. In the classroom, he sat still and observed while the other children were actively involved in the dramatic play, art, sensory, block building, and small manipulative areas. Glen appeared to enjoy snack and lunch and talking with the other children.

Geneva encouraged Glen to sit at the table in the art area with her. The table had crayons, colored markers, and paper. Unlike most children, he did not engage with the materials even when encouraged. From her course work, Geneva knew three-year-old children learn best when they attend to just one thing at a time. So, she gave him a crayon and piece of paper. He had a difficult time picking up and grasping the crayon, and he experienced difficulty drawing wobbly lines. Then Geneva gave him two baskets and a pile of red and yellow cubes to sort. She demonstrated by putting a red cube in one basket and yellow in another. Using a scooping motion with his palm, he attempted to pick up the cubes. He talked about the colors, other colors in the room, and his favorite colors. He seemed to enjoy one-to-one interaction with an adult.

The teacher met Glen's parent at the classroom door at the end of the day. Then she shared Glen's day, including his interest in storytelling and his enjoyment of lunch and snack with the other children. Geneva also told the mother that she sat with him at the art table, and he did not show interest in the classroom supplies and materials. She added, "This is not unusual since it is his first day." The mother responded by saying, "Glen does not have those things at home. I don't buy them for him as I want to keep the house clean. This morning when I dropped him off, I noticed children were playing with all types of things, even cutting with scissors. What should he be doing?"

Give It Some Thought

1. Do you think Glen's mother understands child development? Why or why not?
2. Why couldn't Glen pick up the cubes?
3. What are the widely held expectations for a three-year-old's fine-motor development?
4. What are the widely held expectations of receptive- and expressive-language development of a three-year old? Do you think Glen's language skills are stronger than his fine-motor skills? What makes you think this?

Opening image credit: FatCamera/E+ via Getty Images

Lesson 5.1

The Developing Two-Year-Old

Learning Outcomes

After studying this lesson, you will be able to

5.1-1 **describe** the physical development of two-year-olds.

5.1-2 **summarize** the cognitive development of two-year-olds.

5.1-3 **describe** the social-emotional development of two-year-olds.

5.1-4 **analyze** how the development of two-year-olds will affect your role as a teacher.

Key Terms

mock writing

language comprehension

expressive language

egocentric

empathy

To better understand two- and three-year-olds, you need to develop a mental picture. You need to understand how children in these age groups behave. Two-year-olds are active, demanding, and curious. They are gaining experience with exploring their environment. Three-year-old children tend to be calm. Generally, they try to please and conform. Within three years, they learn to move with confidence and speak with ease. Understanding these differences will help you plan programs that best meet the needs of each child.

5.1-1 Physical Development of Two-Year-Olds

Two-year-old children continue to grow physically, and are now about half their adult size. The rapid growth that occurred during infancy slows down. A typical two-year-old will grow two to three inches in height. Their birth weight has quadrupled, and they will add about five pounds in weight during the year. Their legs are growing longer and their smiles are showing more teeth. The brain now is about 80 percent of the adult size, and their head is proportionately larger than the rest of their body. Organs, such as the stomach, heart, and lungs, become stronger.

The digestive system matures slowly in children. The appetites of two-year-olds vary from day to day. Some days they may be excited about eating at snack time; other days they may reject their snacks. Likewise, what they eat at mealtimes may vary.

The coordination of two-year-olds' bodies is improving. They are less top-heavy and their center-of-gravity shifts downward. Teachers and caregivers much carefully plan the environment for two-year-olds to encourage sensorimotor exploration. Programs must provide equipment, space, and support so these children can achieve a variety of gross-motor skills (**Figure 5.1**). They can usually run and jump without falling. The fine-motor skills of these children are also improving.

Gross-Motor Development

Improved coordination and body control make playing with balls great fun for active two-year-olds. They can pick up a ball by bending at the waist and can kick a large ball. They can usually throw a ball without falling.

greenaperture/Shutterstock.com

Figure 5.1 Two-year-olds have improved muscle strength and coordination. They enjoy playing on playground equipment. *What types of activities help contribute to improved muscle strength and coordination of toddlers?*

Two-year-olds are full of energy and are in constant motion exploring. They have more control over leg and foot muscles and are continuously moving. Their walk is becoming more rhythmical and they are beginning to run. Stairs are not as challenging. They can walk up and down stairs, placing both feet on each stair. (Most children this age need to hold on to a rail as they step.) They can also stand with both feet on a balance beam. These children have the skill to walk on their toes. From a standing position, they can balance on one foot for a second or two. Jumping and walking backwards is also possible. They can jump several inches off the floor or bottom step with both feet. Most children this age can do a standing broad jump of about eight and one-half inches. In addition, most two-year-olds can sit on a riding toy and move it by pushing with their feet. Some are beginning to ride a bicycle.

Children at this age love to climb to the top of equipment, but they cannot always climb down. They also enjoy playing with large balls. Using both forearms to push, they will throw and catch a ball. They use little body rotation or footwork during this process. The arm and upper body skills develop gradually as the child grows.

Fine-Motor Development

Fine motor skills are movements in the fingers, hands, wrists and toes. Two-year-old children are rapidly developing hand and finger dexterity and control. They can insert keys into a lock and skillfully turn pages in a board book with thick pages one at a time. Most children this age can also string large beads or spools and lace cards. They can hold scissors properly. By two years of age, they can open and close scissors.

Hand preference is a complex skill, which requires practice. By this age, it is fairly well developed. Many children will use the same hand for most fine-motor activities, although children still switch hands for some activities. Alejandro, for example, draws with his right hand, but eats and throws a ball with his left hand.

You will see children using and enjoying writing tools at this age (**Figure 5.2**). At about 24 months of age, children can scribble by holding the writing tool in their fist. Later, they will hold it between their thumb and fingers. At first, their scribbles look like tangles of lines. By 30 months, children begin to use **mock writing** by making a series of wavy lines that imitate adult's writing. They also become more proficient at drawing horizontal lines, vertical lines, and circular strokes.

Two-year-olds become skilled at building with blocks. They can build towers of six to seven

yaoinlove/iStock via Getty Images Plus

Figure 5.2 Using chalk helps two-year-olds refine their fine-motor skills. *Name another activity that will help a two-year-old develop fine-motor skills.*

blocks. Often, they take delight in knocking them down. They can also use two or more blocks to make a train and push the blocks along.

Self-Help Skills

With a little help, two-year-olds can accomplish many self-help skills. At this age, they begin to cooperate in dressing. First, they can undress themselves, removing simple items of clothing, such as socks, shoes, and pants. They open snaps successfully. Next, they dress themselves. At first, this involves pulling on simple garments and opening and closing zippers. By 30 months, most children can unbutton large buttons, close snaps, and put on their socks, however, you will need to assist them as they try these skills.

By this age, children are capable of self-feeding and can drink from a cup or glass without help. They may spill, but their drinking skills improve with practice. Two-year-olds can drink using a straw. They can use short-handled spoons and forks to feed themselves, but may revert to eating with their fingers if hurried.

Children usually make strides in toilet learning during this time—a major task for toddlers. At two years of age, most children use the toilet or potty-chair with reminders. Accidents are common, however, since children need to learn the physical sensations that go with toileting. Between 24 and 35 months, children seldom have bowel accidents but may still have problems with wetting for several months. By 33 months, many children can use the toilet without help.

5.1-2 Cognitive Development of Two-Year-Olds

Conversation is important to promote a two-year old's cognitive development. The two-year-old's cognitive development focuses on three key areas. These include *language-comprehension skills, expressive-language skills,* and *math-readiness skills.* All these areas reflect the child's intelligence.

Language-Comprehension Skills

Language comprehension is a person's understanding of language. Some experts refer to this as *receptive* or *inner language.* This form of language is more advanced than expressive-language skills in children. For instance, a 20-month-old child may follow directions, however, this child may not say more than a few words.

Language comprehension grows rapidly in two-year-olds. Words referring to people and objects develop the fastest. The children also begin using *telegraphic speech* in which they use two or three words to make a sentence. For example, they may say, "bye bye" or mommy go." They may use words that are not real words. Children may often say the word "mulk" when wanting a glass of milk. They can understand and answer routine questions. While reading a story, you may point to a picture and ask, "What is that?" The child may respond by saying "Baby" (**Figure 5.3**).

Noun learning appears to precede verb learning. By 24 months of age, most children can identify at least six body parts. Children can point to these parts on themselves, others, or dolls. They enjoy playing games in which you state, "Find your toes" or ask, "Where are your eyes?" Children gradually associate objects with their uses. For instance, they know people use kettles and pans for cooking, keys open a door, and sponges can clean the table.

Many other new skills develop around 24 months. Children can comprehend the pronouns *I, my, mine,* and *me.* They can also provide answers to yes and no questions. They also use emotional identification. These children use emotional language to obtain attention, comfort, and support. Two-year-olds are more likely to pay greater attention to their own desires and feelings. By 36 months, young children are showing more interest in the feelings and desire of others.

By 30 months of age, they reach other milestones. When asked, children can give you one cracker. They also can understand sentences that are more complex and follow two-step commands. For instance, you can tell a child:

FatCamera/E+ via Getty Images

Figure 5.3 Two-year-olds will answer questions about pictures in the stories you read them.

- "Take off your coat and hang it in your locker."
- "Give Tunde a napkin and come back here."
- "Put the book on the shelf and sit down for storytime."
- "Go to the bathroom and wash your hands."

Children of this age can also give answers to "where" questions. For instance, you may ask a child "Where is your locker?" or "Where do you wash your hands?" They also enjoy completing the lines when listening to a familiar story.

Understanding the meanings of words continues through the second year. When picking up objects, two-year-olds can tell the difference between *soft* and *heavy*. Size concepts are also developing. Children understand such words as *big* and *little*. Children also start to understand words related to space. These include such words as *on, under, out of, together,* and *away from*. Speech has cultural influences, so expect variations.

Expressive-Language Skills

Expressive language is the ability to produce language forms. It is a tool that a person can use to express their thoughts to others. For most two-year-olds, expressive-language skills develop quickly. Like other aspects of development, it follows a sequence. The child's experiences affect the rate and content of expressive-language development. Therefore, it is important that you provide an environment that nourishes the child's language development. Teachers and care providers need to continuously provide and repeat vocabulary.

Speech usually involves simple sentences by two years of age. In the beginning, only two words may be used. This is *telegraphic* speech, which is the two-word stage of language acquisition. The characteristics of telegraphic speech include stating words in the correct order and using the most important ones. Examples are "Johnny hurt", "daddy go car", or "Tom dog." Later, the child will put three-word sentences together. Examples include "Tom go home," "I eat corn," or "See my truck." The child's sentences follow the word order of their native language.

Toddlers often overextend categories. For example, they may call everything with wheels a truck or car. Likewise, they may call all animals doggies. When this occurs, it is important that the caregiver provide the animal's correct name.

Two language strategies that are important for working with two-year-olds are called feeding-in and expansion. *Feeding-in* is a strategy where you provide the child's language. For example, if a child is building with blocks, the teacher might say, "You are building with blocks."

Expansion is a strategy used to expand the child's language. Typically, the teacher accomplishes this by reframing the child's utterance into a sentence. For example, if the child says "car" the teacher might say, "That is a blue car."

The vocabulary of the average two-year-old is 50 to 200 words. You will notice that children at this age often use words without fully understanding them. You might also observe that females often develop language skills faster than males.

Two-year-olds do not understand how to use grammar to form questions. Instead, they use the tone of their voice. They may ask in a questioning tone, "Grandma go?" or "Milk all gone?"

Two-year-olds often make negative sentences. They do this by adding the word no to positive sentences. For instance, a child may say "No milk" meaning that they do not want any milk. The child may say "Teacher no here" meaning that they cannot find the teacher.

Between 27 and 30 months, children may begin to use prepositions. For instance, children may say "Cookies in jar." Around this age, children also begin using plurals. They may request "cookies" or "crackers."

Two-year-olds also add modifiers to their vocabulary. *Some, a lot, all*, and *one* are used as quantifiers. *Mine, his*, and *hers* are used as possessives. *Pretty, new*, and *blue* are some adjectives that might be used as modifiers.

Between 31 and 34 months of age, children may begin adding *ed* to verbs to show past tense. At about the same time, present tense verb helpers appear. These include such terms as *can, are, will*, and *am*.

Early Childhood Insight 🄰🄱🄲

Body Language

Two-year-old children tend to use body language to let people know how they feel about their possessions. They can be very physical in their responses. They may push, hit, or shove another child who approaches their toys.

Math-Readiness Skills

Children develop math skills by interacting with others and with objects. When you ask, a child can give you "just one" of something. Children are beginning to learn to categorize and classify items. They understand size concepts such as *big* and *small*. Awareness of shapes, forms, and colors is also developing during this stage. Children sort objects by size, shape, and color.

5.1-3 Social-Emotional Development of Two-Year-Olds

Two-year-olds continue to grow socially and emotionally. At this age, children tend to show many negative attitudes. Children like instant gratification and find it difficult to wait. These qualities make patience an important quality as you work with two-year-olds.

Social Development

At the beginning of this developmental stage, children are interested in other children. They play next to each other; however, they do not play cooperatively (**Figure 5.4**). Children in this stage are more interested in adults. Therefore, they tend to act out adult experiences as they play. These

Aleksandar Pirgic/iStock via Getty Images Plus

Figure 5.4 Two-year-olds interact little as they play and are typically more interested in adults. *What types of adult experiences might two-year-olds act out?*

might include driving a car, sweeping, cooking, and talking on a cell phone.

The average two-year-old is possessive. Usually, these children do not want to share, and there is typically competition for toys. Although they have difficulty understanding the concept of sharing, two-year-olds may return a toy that belongs to someone else.

Despite their negativism and possessiveness, two-year-olds are usually affectionate. They may hug you and hold your hand. Two-year-olds thrive on love and caring from adults. They also enjoy helping you. Whether you are setting the table for lunch or picking up blocks, they are eager to participate.

Emotional Development

Children at this age are often referred to as in the "terrible twos." It is the beginning of temper tantrums, which is a normal way toddler's express frustration. Children at this stage like to control their surroundings. They lack the skills to say "I want that," "I am feeling angry," "I am frustrated," "I am hungry," or "It is mine." Because they cannot always do that, they tend to get frustrated and angry at times (**Figure 5.5**). Trying to do a task that is too hard for them may also cause anger. Not being allowed to do or have something may stir a full-blown meltdown.

Two-year-olds may have temper tantrums if they do not get their way. They may throw themselves to the ground and scream, cry, stamp, or kick. Their anger is not usually at any one person or object; they are simply frustrated. Children this age still have not learned appropriate ways of expressing anger. They also have other negative behaviors. They may hit, shove, kick, and bite. They also may grab other children's toys. For this reason, duplicate toys should be available in the classroom for children this age.

Fears become common at this age. Two-year-olds are often afraid of being hurt or harmed. Many of their fears have to do with their imagination. Two-year-olds cannot always separate pretend from reality, so they may be afraid of a monster from a story. A dream may frighten them because they think the characters are real. As a teacher, you need to comfort children when they are afraid. Even imagined fears are genuine to toddlers.

These children often show love and caring and need to receive love and caring in return. Two-year-olds need to know that people still care for them even if they get angry. They also need to know that they can depend on others. To build trust and security, children of this age need consistent routines. For instance, they may need to sit next to the same person or group of people at every meal or snack time.

Ann in the uk/Shutterstock.com

Figure 5.5 Ability to meet goals quickly is important to two-year-olds. If they do not get instant results, they often become angry and may begin to cry. *How should teachers and care providers handle the temper tantrums of two-year-olds?*

Two-year-olds show an abundance of laughter. Typically, these children find humor in something that is novel or surprising. Watch them. Not knowing what to expect, they will burst into laughter. They may laugh at books with exaggerated shapes and sizes of figures, such as Pinocchio with the huge nose or a cat wearing glasses. Children may come from different cultures, but laughter is universal.

5.1-4 Teaching Two-Year-Olds

The development of two-year-olds has a powerful effect on the way you teach and work with them. You need to be prepared to handle situations that are typical for them.

If you were to observe a group of two-year-olds, your first observation might be of their first word, "No!" They appear negative. Two-year-olds often use the word *no*. They may even mean "yes" when they say "no." For instance, you may ask "Do you want more milk?" The child may say "no" while extending his or her glass toward you for more milk.

Chances are you may become impatient with two-year-old children at times. They always seem to want their own way. Whether you want to read a story or take the children on a walk around the neighborhood, you are bound to find a two-year-old who refuses. The child may refuse to leave his or her present activity or to put on his or her coat. Working with two-year-olds requires gentle but firm guidance.

Two-year-olds are very **egocentric**. This means that they believe everyone else sees, thinks, and feels like they do. This does not mean they are selfish, but that they believe you think exactly as they do.

Prepare yourself for the dawdling behavior of the typical two-year-old. Be patient. These children insist on doing things at their own pace. Because of this, routines take longer. When planning a schedule, be aware of this type of behavior. Two-year-olds need plenty of time to move from one activity to the next. Therefore, you will need to be flexible and patient.

Upon entering a classroom of two-year-olds, you will first notice the noise. This is very common. When a child discovers a drum, the child will hit it repeatedly. Likewise, they may repeat a new vocal sound many times. If one child starts to clap and stamps their feet, the other children may join in. You will need to prepare for high noise levels and be able to control the noise from time to time.

Curiosity is another trait of two-year-olds. Children of this age need the opportunity to explore their environment. When you bring new materials into the classroom, the children will carefully examine them. If you ask them what toy they want, they may have difficulty choosing. Therefore, you should add only a few new items at a time.

Two-year-olds are developing **empathy**. Empathy is the ability to understand or feel what another person is experiencing. If a child is crying, they often will walk over and share concern by the look on their face. Otherwise, they may try to comfort them.

Gross-motor activity is a favorite of two-year-old children. They delight in movement and are not afraid to try out new equipment. They love to run and chase others. Adequate supervision is crucial when taking walks away from the center.

Two-year-olds like to act out life experiences. They especially like to imitate the activities of adults (**Figure 5.6**). They need a dramatic play

GordanD/Shutterstock.com

Figure 5.6   Teachers should provide many dramatic play materials so two-year-olds can act out such everyday experiences as preparing food. *What other themes might encourage toddlers to act out everyday experiences?*

corner. Housekeeping equipment, mirrors, dolls, dress-up clothes, toy telephones, trucks, and cars should all be included.

Two-year-olds need some routine in their day. They like to have things done the same way. These children look forward to certain parts of the day, such as story time. You need to be careful to follow a similar schedule from day to day. A few changes add interest, but children need to rely on a predictable schedule.

Because two-year-olds lack the language skills to express their intense emotions, they may also have temper tantrums. As you know, this is normal behavior. They need your help to build an emotional vocabulary. When an outburst occurs, it has nothing to do with your skill as a teacher; however, you may be embarrassed. What is important is how you handle the tantrum. It is vital that you remain composed and use a calm voice when speaking to the child. If the child is kicking, you may have to immobilize the child by holding their leg. If the child is a threat to the other children, move the child to another area of the room.

Lesson 5.1 Review

1. Which of the following is not a motor skill of two-year-olds? (5.1.1)
   A. Picking up a ball
   B. Kicking a ball
   C. Throwing a ball
   D. Catching a ball
2. **True or False.** Expressive language is more advanced in two-year-olds than language comprehension. (5.1.2)
3. Characteristics of a _____ include crying, yelling, and shouting. (5.1.3)
   A. temper tantrum
   B. reflex
   C. physical milestone
   D. language skill
4. **True or False.** It is important to allow plenty of time for transitions between activities when working with two-year-olds. (5.1.4)

The Developing Three-Year-Old

Essential Question

What do I need to know about the physical, cognitive, and social-emotional development of three-year-olds to become an effective teacher?

Learning Outcomes

After studying this lesson, you will be able to

5.2-1 **describe** how three-year-olds develop physically.

5.2-2 **summarize** how three-year-olds develop cognitively.

5.2-3 **describe** the social-emotional development of three-year-olds.

5.2-4 **analyze** how the development of three-year-olds will affect your role as a teacher.

Key Terms

fast mapping   self-concept
gender roles

5.2-1 Physical Development of Three-Year-Olds

For three-year-olds, playing is exploring. They are constantly moving, tasting, smelling, and touching. As a result, their body coordination shows great improvement (**Figure 5.7**). You will notice that the arms, hands, legs, and feet are all becoming more coordinated and stronger. Likewise, their bodies are becoming less top-heavy and they are taller and leaner. To stay upright, three-year-olds no longer need to keep their legs spread apart. Their walk appears more

natural as their toes point forward and their feet move closer together.

Gross-Motor Development

The motor skills of three-year-old children are improving based on the accomplishments of infancy and toddlerhood. Throwing, jumping, and hopping skills improve as a result of better coordination. The improvement of body coordination is also reflected in the climbing skills of three-year-olds. Their balance is improving. At this age, children are using alternate feet to climb and descend stairs. Going up stairs is easier than going down. These children can walk upstairs with alternating feet, but they cannot descend until about five years of age.

By 36 months of age, children can kick and throw a small ball. They can also catch large balls with their arms extended. Their catching skill gradually becomes more refined. Eventually, they can catch bouncing balls with their hands. This skill usually emerges toward the end of the third year.

Amorn Suriyan/Shutterstock.com

Figure 5.7 Three-year-olds often express silliness and a creative spirit.

Leg coordination and balancing skills also improve. Three-year-olds can start pedaling and steering tricycles. They can walk heel-to-toe for four steps and jump. They can balance on one foot for up to eight seconds. They can hop on one foot up to three times, and enjoy swinging on a swing.

Workplace Connections

Working with Mixed-Age Groups

Because of the differences in their abilities and behaviors, two-year-olds and three-year-olds are usually separated in a preschool or child care center. Some settings, such as child care homes, however, may have mixed-age groups in their programs. Interview teachers of mixed-age group programs in your area for their insights.

1. What are the challenges of working with mixed-age groups?
2. What are some advantages of combining the two age groups?
3. What considerations must be made for supervision, activities, and equipment?

Fine-Motor Development

The fine-motor skills of three-year-olds continue to develop. Cutting skills become more refined. The two-year-old could only hold and work scissors. However, a three-year-old can use the scissors to cut paper. They can cut five-inch squares of paper into two sections. Young three-year-olds can cut across the paper, but they cannot cut along a line. By 42 to 48 months, children can cut along a line straying only one-half of an inch away from it.

Three-year-olds have better drawing and art skills. Making use of their improved fine-motor skills, they often reproduce simple shapes as they draw. Their drawings represent six basic shapes—circles, squares, triangles, Xs, crosses, rectangles, and odd forms. If you show these children the shape of an X, they can copy the shape. They can also trace the shape of a diamond. They are starting to draw people with two to four body parts. They enjoy drawing faces, which usually include the mouth, eyes, nose, and/or ears. These features are not drawn in proportion, but they are usually placed in the correct position on the face. Three-year-olds lack the fine-motor coordination needed to create complex figures.

At this stage, children enjoy manipulating blocks and puzzle pieces. They can build towers with nine to ten cubes. They can also construct simple puzzles. If you observe them, you will note that three-year-olds usually prefer using one hand over the other. There are more right-handed than left-handed people, and some cultures discourage left-handedness.

Self-Help Skills

Three-year-olds become increasingly self-sufficient (**Figure 5.8**). Daily care routines now require little adult help. These children can turn the water faucet on and off if they can reach it. As a result, they can attend to routines such as washing and drying their hands and face, and can also brush their own teeth.

Three-year-olds become better at dressing themselves. They can help put on and remove clothing. They also now open buckles and put on shoes that do not tie. Three-year-olds need little adult help when their clothing has elastic waists or large button openings. They still cannot work large buttons and hooks. Three-year-olds have trouble telling the front from the back on clothing, too. They do well with clothing that has a design on the front or a label in the back.

At snack and mealtime, these children now feed themselves with little help. They also eat

christinarosepix/Shutterstock.com

Figure 5.8   Three-year-olds can turn the pages in a book to follow the story as they listen to audio books.

with silverware, although they sometimes revert to using their fingers. Using a knife, they can spread butter, jelly, and creamy peanut butter on bread. They can also pour liquid from a small pitcher. As a result, the children may enjoy assisting at snack time.

Another step toward independence is mastered at this age. Three-year-olds have almost full control over toilet routines, and are even able to get through a night without wetting. This accomplishment is made possible through improved motor control.

5.2-2 Cognitive Development of Three-Year-Olds

By the third birthday, the ability to think matures. Children move away from thinking only in terms of actions. They can solve simple problems. For instance, if you place an object under a cup and place nothing under another cup, the child knows which cup the object is under. If you switch the cups while the child is watching, the child still knows where the object is.

Children at this age still do not think logically. They are still egocentric as they have not yet learned to see things from more than one perspective. For instance, they do not realize that something that seems tall to them might seem short to an adult. They get confused about time concepts. These children may also become confused about cause and effect. For instance, if a bell rings before each snack is served, children may think the bell causes the snack to appear.

Even though thinking is still flawed, these children learn quickly. Their language-comprehension skills, expressive-language skills, and math-readiness skills continue to improve.

Language-Comprehension Skills

Understanding of language continues to grow in three-year-olds. The average three-year-old child uses 900–1000 different words. They can answer simple questions. On request, they can now give you two objects. These children can

also remember and follow three-part commands. For example, you might say "Go to the sink, wash your hands, and dry them with a towel" (**Figure 5.9**).

Three-year-olds expand their vocabularies rapidly by using **fast mapping**. They can absorb the meaning of an unfamiliar word after hearing it just once or twice in a conversation. They also are beginning, to understand the pronouns *you* and *they*. They understand such words as *who, whose, why, where, what, when* and *how*. They can provide answers to questions based on these words. For instance, you may ask the child, "Who lives at the North Pole?" Another question might be, "Whose teddy bear is this?" While reading a story you may ask, "Why is the girl crying?" These children will be able to answer such questions as "How will your mother bake the pie?"

Children at this stage are understanding more complex sentences. You may say, "After story time, we will go outside to play." During story time, they may recall an event from the day before. When story time is finished, the child may get up and move towards the door. They also are beginning to ask questions such as, "Can I have water?", "When is snack time?", "Where are the felt-tip markers", or "Where is Juan?"

Space concepts become clearer. While moving objects, children will understand your instructions that include such words as *toward, up, top,* and *apart*. Toward the end of the third year, children master more space concepts. They understand such ideas as *around, in front of, in back of,* and *next to*.

Expressive-Language Skills

Children's ability to produce language continues to increase. They become chatterboxes and may use over 900 words. Three-year-olds also have improved grammar. They may make sentences of four or five words and connections are appearing. They may even join sentences together with a conjunction. For instance, the child may say "The bunny died and we don't have it."

Three-year-olds are beginning to understand the difference between past and present tense.

Figure 5.9 Three-year-olds can follow your three-step commands. *Give an example of a command you might want a three-year-old to follow in a classroom setting.*

They like to make verbs past tense by adding *-ed* to them. These children make statements such as "I talked" or "Daddy walked," however, they do not yet understand that there are exceptions to this rule. They may use such past tense verbs as "runned" and "goed." They may even use the correct form, but still add *-ed*. For instance, they may say "ranned" or "wented."

Children start to understand possessive nouns. Three-year-olds may refer to mommy's car, daddy's hammer, and teacher's coat. Negatives are not fully understood by three-year-olds. They understand that such words as *no, not, can't, don't, nothing,* and *never* are negative. They use all negative terms, however, when they form negative statements. For instance, a three-year-old may say "Kelsie can't do nothing" or "Jackson can't never go nowhere."

During this stage, children start to use question words, especially *why, where,* and *when.*

These children may add on the question word to a regular sentence. For instance, they may ask "When Daddy is coming?" or "Why the cloud is moving?"

As these children play, they frequently talk out loud to themselves. For example, three-year-old Jenny is painting at the easel and saying, "Jenny is painting a picture. I need red. Where is the red? Now I need yellow. I need to paint with yellow."

Math-Readiness Skills

Three-year-olds continue to learn concepts basic to math. They start to understand the concepts *full, more, less, smaller, the same,* and *empty.* By 42 months of age, most children understand the concept of *largest.* These children like compare objects, saying one object is bigger or another is smaller.

Counting skills also begin at this stage. If you ask, a three-year-old can give you two objects.

These children can also count to three while pointing to corresponding objects. They may recite numbers in order higher than three, but they are not able to count that number of objects. They are also learning numerals differ from letters.

Children in this age group can distinguish between *one* and *many*. To check for this skill, place one chip on the table. Nearby, place a pile of chips. Ask the child to point to one chip. Repeat the question asking the child to point to many chips. Children who respond correctly have learned the difference between *one* and *many*.

Health Highlights

Delays in Speech and Language

Although children vary in speech and language development, there is a general time and age by which children master language skills. As with other development, language skills also develop from simple to complex. If teachers or care providers have concerns about the possible delay in a child's speech or language development, they should share these concerns with the parents or guardians. The parents should talk with their child's doctor. Sometimes a doctor will refer parents to a speech-language pathologist for further evaluation.

5.2-3 Social-Emotional Development of Three-Year-Olds

After the third birthday, children start to grow out of the temper tantrums and contrariness of the two-year-old stage. They become cooperative, happy, agreeable, and sociable. By this time, children are learning socially acceptable ways of expressing their feelings. They can use language more effectively to communicate with others. Also, they start to form friendships and begin taking turns with their peers.

Social Development

Three-year-olds are eager to help others, especially adults. They like to help with such tasks as passing out crayons and pouring water. They are learning new ways of showing concern for others. Three-year-olds are learning positive ways to get attention from others. They are more willing to accept attention from adults and children who are not well known. They adjust to new people more easily than two-year-olds do.

By the third birthday, children begin to play with, rather than next to, other children and often have preferred playmates (**Figure 5.10**). Although these children interact with each other, their play is not truly organized. For instance, they may play house and each child playing may be the daddy.

Children this age are not as possessive as two-year-olds. They will share with others, but dislike sharing too much. For this reason, three-year-olds usually play with only one or two friends. The children use language more to communicate with friends. For instance, they may say to a friend, "You play with the baby." To another child, they may say, "You can't play with us."

At three years of age, children are becoming aware that people look different. There are physical differences between males and females. They also begin to learn **gender roles**. To grow and learn, they need to explore different roles and materials that are usually defined as female or male. There should be no gender expectations. No longer does society think of particular skill behaviors and abilities with gender. Girls play with trucks, woodworking tools, pulleys, and wear blue. Boys cook, sew, play with dolls, and wear pink.

Emotional Development

Three-year-olds have strong, visible emotions. They get excited. They get angry. They get discouraged. They are beginning to understand, however, that there are appropriate ways to express these emotions. They realize that adults do not approve of such actions as temper tantrums. Also, they are eager to act in ways that please others. Therefore, children of this age are

gpointstudio/Shutterstock.com

Figure 5.10   Although their play is not organized, three-year-olds will play with each other. *How can using themes help organize the play of three-year-olds?*

developing control over their powerful feelings. Instead of striking another child, they may scream, "Stop it!"

Unlike two-year-olds, many situations no longer lead to angry outbursts among three-year-olds. Because they have improved coordination, three-year-olds are less likely to become frustrated when they cannot do something. They also have improved language skills. When children at this age can understand why something is happening, they are less likely to get angry. For example, a child may want a drink just prior to lunch. You can explain, "It's only a few minutes until lunch. You can have a drink then." When the child understands that he or she will have a drink soon, he or she is less likely to get angry.

Three-year-olds are likely to become angry when things do not go their way, however, they may direct their anger at objects. For instance, they may be angry at a pitcher if they spill their

milk. Children this age are more likely to express their anger in words. They do not push, hit, stump, grab, whine, or cry as much as two-year-olds do.

The three-year-old is beginning to develop a self-concept. Your **self-concept** is the way you see yourself. It embodies the question of *who am I*. A child's self-concept includes a set of beliefs about himself or herself. Ask three-year-olds to tell you about themselves. They will probably provide you with their names, possessions, and physical appearance. As a result, you might hear something like this: "I'm Kelly. I have a dog. I have a brother. I have black hair."

By this stage, children are not as likely to be frightened by objects that they know. For instance, the noise from a car will not frighten them; however, they are quite fearful of imagined dangers. They may be especially afraid of the dark. Children of this age also become more fearful of pain. They may be frightened a dog will bite them or they will be hurt during a doctor's visit.

Three-year-olds are affectionate, and they tend to seek affection in return. They may follow, cling to, or help an adult with tasks to gain attention, approval, or comfort. Three-year-olds still do not think in terms of the feelings of others.

Children learn to express their own feelings by watching surrounding adults. When you express surprise and happiness, they will also show these emotions. Likewise, if you give a hug to comfort someone who is sad, they will imitate your behavior.

5.2-4 Teaching Three-Year-Olds

Three-year-olds are typically happy, sociable, and agreeable (**Figure 5.11**). They are very eager to please. As a result, they are likely to accept your suggestions. They also adjust easily to new adults, classmates, and situations. For these reasons, you will find that most adults enjoy working with these children.

You can help three-year-olds develop grammar. There are two methods of providing grammatical prompts. You can recast the child's speech and correct the child's inaccuracy. For example, the child may say, "I gotted a new doggie." You can respond by saying, "You have a new dog." Likewise, you can use expansion. To illustrate, the child may say, "Blue ball." You can respond by saying, "You are throwing a big blue ball."

Three-year-olds enjoy playing. They still like playing alone, but they also enjoy playing in groups of two or three. You can introduce themes to their play. Some themes include treating and healing others. One child will help another who is injured or ill.

Happy Together/Shutterstock.com

Figure 5.11   Three-year-olds tend to be more content and agreeable than two-year-olds. *How might a three-year-old express signs of independence?*

The objects that you supply in the classroom will influence a three-year-old's dramatic play. Cooking supplies, tools, phones, and suitcases are popular. These children enjoy pretending to be cooking, making repairs, calling others, and taking trips.

Three-year-old children are becoming increasingly independent. They feel a need to do things for themselves. Signs of independence include such statements as "I can do it" or "Let me do it." These statements are healthy signs that the children are gaining confidence in their abilities.

Some three-year-olds need encouragement to become more independent. They may make such statements as "You do it" or "I can't." When these words are spoken, you need to provide encouragement. These children need to know that you value their independence. They need to feel that they can do things for themselves.

Lesson 5.2 Review

1. Which of the following is not a fine motor skill of three-year-olds? (5.2.1)
   A. Cut with scissors
   B. Manipulate a puzzle
   C. Draw simple shapes
   D. Jump with both feet off the ground
2. **True or False.** By using *fast mapping*, three-year-olds can absorb the meaning of an unfamiliar word after hearing it just once or twice in a conversation. (5.2.2)
3. **True or False.** Three-year-olds are eager to act in ways that please others. (5.2.3)
4. Which of the following objects do not encourage dramatic play? (5.2.4)
   A. Play clothes
   B. Toy food
   C. An electronic device
   D. A suitcase

Chapter 5 Review and Assessment

Summary

Lesson 5.1

5.1-1 Two-year-olds' motor skills improve as they explore the world. So, they may run for an object. They also may use words to show what they want.

5.1-2 Two-year-olds communicate in a variety of ways. They may use facial expressions, talking, walking, and running.

5.1-2 Two-year-olds can answer simple questions and follow simple directions.

5.1-2 They are beginning to learn basic math concepts related to size, number, shape, and color.

5.1-3 Socially and emotionally, two-year-old children are striving to be independent.

5.1-4 Planning a variety of activities to meet the physical, cognitive, and social-emotional needs of two-year-olds has a powerful effect on their development.

5.1-4 Two-year-olds need a predictable routine in their day.

5.1-4 Helping children learn vocabulary to express their emotions is an important job of early childhood teachers and care providers.

Lesson 5.2

5.2-1 Three-year-olds grow out of many of the problems of two-year-olds. They have better muscle control and coordination and successfully manage many self-help skills.

5.2-2 The thinking ability of three-year-olds is improving. These children have a growing understanding and use of language, and are also developing more refined concepts of number and size.

5.2-3 Socially and emotionally, three-year-olds are learning appropriate ways to express emotions. They are also beginning to play with others and forge friendships.

5.2-4 Plan a variety of activities to meet the physical, cognitive, and social-emotional needs of three-year-olds to encourage their independence.

5.2-4 Introducing themes into the children's play helps them interact more with others and encourages empathy.

5.2-4 Some three-year-olds require additional teacher encouragement to help build their confidence.

Vocabulary Activity

Work with a partner to write the definitions of the *Key Terms* from both lessons based on your current understanding. Then pair up with another team to discuss your definitions and any discrepancies. Finally, discuss the definitions with the class and ask your instructor for necessary correction or clarification.

Critical Thinking

1. **Draw Conclusions.** What routines could be introduced in the center to help two-year-olds feel secure? What strategies might you use to direct children and keep them together on walks and field trips? What safety measures are needed when considering a two-year-old's curiosity and tendency to explore his or her environment?

2. **Compare and Contrast.** How can dramatic play in the preschool help children understand the concept of gender roles? What toys, supplies, and equipment are needed? Compare the attitudes or beliefs of parents several generations ago with those of today.

3. **Evaluate.** Ask a three-year-old to describe themself to you. As the child explains, take notes about what elements of the child's life make up self-concept. What does the child think are his or her most important qualities? How does the three-year-old's self-concept differ from the self-concept of an adult?

Core Skills

1. **Writing.** Visit an early childhood care center and observe the motor skills of two- and three-year-olds. Write a report comparing the motor skills of the two age groups based on your observations.

2. **Listening.** Interview a teacher of two-year-olds and ask about the language strategies of *feeding-in* and *expansion*. Document how the teacher explains the difference between these two strategies. Ask about how these two strategies can be used together to encourage two-year-olds' language skills. Also ask about how, if at all, these strategies continue to be used for older children. After the interview, write a short summary of your findings and share with another classmate.

3. **Speaking.** Interview teachers of two-year-olds about tasks they allow children to perform in the classroom. How are the children encouraged to participate? What safety concerns should be considered when asking for a two-year-old's help?

4. **Math.** Refer to Appendix B. Observe the gross-motor skills of a group of three-year-olds in a preschool classroom. Then calculate the percentage of children who can perform each of the typical physical traits listed for children between two and three years of age. Do all the three-year-olds observed perform at the same level of gross-motor development? Explain how knowing these percentages can assist the teacher in planning physical activities for this age group.

5. **Speaking.** Interview an early childhood care provider or teacher about the differences in expression of emotions between two-year-olds and three-year-olds.

6. **Reading and Writing.** Visit a children's library and find books designed to help young children express their feelings in positive ways. Write a report on one of these books.

7. **Reading and Writing.** Search online for books about teaching self-help skills to three-year-olds. These books might talk about teaching three-year-olds to dress themselves, feed themselves, or brush their own teeth. Choose one book and read it, noting any places where the book seems to agree with or disagree with the information in this chapter. Finally, write a book review analyzing the information in the book and the writing style used to deliver that information.

8. **Research and Speaking.** Conduct an online search for information on math-readiness skills. What math concepts can children understand at the toddler stage? What type of activities can demonstrate and reinforce these concepts? Should two-year-olds be subjected to math worksheets? Share your findings with the class.

9. **Technology.** In small groups, review this chapter's information about teaching two-year-olds and teaching three-year-olds. Discuss how the teaching strategies are similar and how they are different and then create two scenarios that could be used to illustrate these similarities and differences. Act out these two scenarios and film them. Then, present your film to the class. Lead the class in a group discussion about how appropriate the teaching strategies are and about how they coincide with the children's development.

10. **CTE Career Readiness Practice.** In small groups or teams, debate the pros and cons of separating two-year-olds and three-year-olds in early childhood care and education settings. Identify text factors that support or interfere with each position.

Portfolio Project

1. Some three-year-olds, even those with above-average comprehensive and expressive language skills, may stutter when speaking. The website of The Stuttering Foundation is a useful resource for information about stuttering. Review this and other sources of information on stuttering and write a report of your findings. Include suggestions of ways to help children who stutter. Include these, along with a bibliography of your sources, in your portfolio.

2. Many parents who are not familiar with child development do not always understand why their children are acting the way they are or what they can expect of young children. Sometimes, it is the role of the teacher to communicate these expectations and facts. Review this chapter's information about two- and three-year-olds and then draft an easy-to-understand handout outlining the differences and similarities between two- and three-year-olds. Include a summary telling parents "what to expect" of their two- and three-year-olds. File a copy in your portfolio once you are done.

Chapter 6

Reading Advantage

As you read the chapter, write a letter to yourself. Imagine you will receive this letter in a few years when you are working at your future job. What would you like to remember from this chapter? In the letter, list key points from the chapter that will be useful in your future career.

Understanding Four- and Five-Year-Olds

Lesson 6.1: Physical and Cognitive Development of Four- and Five-Year-Olds

Lesson 6.2: Social-Emotional Development of Four- and Five-Year-Olds

Case Study

Deciding About Preschool

Henri is a four-year-old only child whose mother, Bobbi, recently began working in the community. She originally considered having her mother, who lives 15 miles away and has orthopedic problems, care for Henri. After talking with neighbors, friends, and relatives, Bobbi decided to enroll Henri in a neighborhood preschool program. They convinced her the preschool environment might be more socially stimulating and better promote the skills needed for kindergarten.

Henri's grandmother was upset over her daughter's decision. She wanted to care for Henri in her home. She told her daughter that if the roads were bad during the winter, he could stay overnight. Moreover, she felt that four-year-olds were too young to go to school. When they did, the grandmother claimed they frequently contracted contagious diseases and picked up negative behaviors.

The neighbor felt that Henri could become more independent participating in a high-quality program. She noticed that Henri still received unnecessary parental assistance while dressing, undressing, and at meal time. For eating, he only used a spoon. So, she suggested Bobbi contact the center director to make an appointment to tour the center. While there, she could also ask questions regarding the potential impact of Henri's participation on his health, behavior, and preparation for kindergarten.

Give It Some Thought

1. Do you agree with Henri's grandmother that she should care for him? Why or why not?
2. What questions should Bobbi ask the center director?
3. Do you think Henri would contract more contagious diseases and develop behavior problems by attending an early childhood program? Why or why not?
4. What dressing features should Henri's clothing have that would require minimal help if he attended an early childhood program? What self-help skills can most children accomplish at four years of age? What self-help skills should be expected of Henri by five years of age?

Opening image credit: FatCamera/E+ via Getty Images

Physical and Cognitive Development of Four- and Five-Year-Olds

Essential Question

What do I need to know about the physical and cognitive development of preschool children to foster children's development?

Learning Outcomes

After studying this lesson, you will be able to

6.1-1 **describe** the physical development of four- and five-year-olds, including gross- and fine-motor skills and self-help skills.

6.1-2 **summarize** cognitive development of preschoolers, including language comprehension, receptive- and expressive language, and math skills.

Key Terms

self-help skills	emotional language
passive voice	stuttering
receptive language	rote counting
expressive language	principle of cardinality
articulation	true counting

Your days with four- and five-year-olds will be filled with fun and challenges. *Preschoolers* (as four- and five-year-olds are referred to in this chapter) can handle many basic self-help skills; however, to keep growing and learning, they need new experiences and challenges. Preschoolers have many questions about the world around them. Helping them find answers to these questions can be rewarding.

6.1-1 Physical Development of Preschoolers

Increased body strength and coordination makes movement great fun for preschoolers. Physical skills become easier partly because body proportions are changing. Compared to their total height, toddlers have short legs, however, by five and one-half years, most children's legs are about half the length of the body. Their proportions are more like adult proportions (**Figure 6.1**). This makes running, jumping, and balancing easier for preschoolers.

Preschool children are growing in more than just size. Their bones are becoming harder and stronger. Their eyesight is getting better and their permanent teeth are forming beneath their gums. Some children in this age group may begin losing their baby teeth. These children need good nutrition to assure that their bones and permanent teeth form properly. For children this age, a healthy dietary pattern should include foods that are excellent sources of calcium and vitamin D, such as milk and other dairy products.

Gross-Motor Development

Four- and five-year-olds are using previously acquired skills to perform more complex movements. They improve their skills and engage in longer periods of play as their bodies become stronger and larger. At four years of age, children can hop on one foot for 20 or more feet without losing balance. By five years of age, they can also walk down stairs with alternating feet.

Judy Herr

Figure 6.1 Four-year-olds show individual differences in height. Both children are four years old. ***Observe a group of four-year-olds. What other differences and similarities do you see?***

Vadym Zaitsev/Shutterstock.com

Figure 6.2 Improved balance allows this five-year-old to walk forward and backward on a balance beam.

Four-year-olds can balance on one foot for about 10 seconds. They can walk backward, toe-to-heel, for four consecutive steps.

Large-muscle-coordination skills are better for preschoolers. Late in the fourth year, many children may begin learning how to skip. Most five-year-olds have developed this skill. Older four-year-olds may ride a bike with training wheels. If they have the opportunity, most children have developed this skill by five years of age. Five-year-olds can also walk forward and backward on a balance beam (**Figure 6.2**). They can climb fences and march to music. They can also jump from table height and land on both feet.

Throwing and catching skills also improve during these years. Preschoolers can bounce and throw a ball, with four- and five-year-olds having the ability to throw overhand. As they grow, they are becoming better at using their bodies to direct a ball as they throw. When throwing, preschoolers rotate their bodies and shift their weight from the back foot to the front foot, using both hands and visually tracking the ball. These children can catch a ball with two hands. A five-year-old can keep the hands close to the body until just before catching the ball. As the child's brain matures, there is better coordination of motor and visual systems.

Children this age enjoy working to improve their physical skills. They try to use their skills to the fullest. Now they do somersaults and jumping jacks and can carry objects while walking up and down the steps. Sometimes preschoolers may even become reckless. For example, they may try to ride scooters as fast as they can.

Fine-Motor Development

Children's fine-motor skills improve rapidly during the preschool years. They have developed a higher degree of control and precision. Their fingers, hands, and eyes are better at coordinating movement, so they find it easier to string beads and work with small game or puzzle pieces (**Figure 6.3**). When preschoolers build towers from blocks, the towers are straight and tall. By four years, most children can complete 12- to 18-piece puzzles. By five years, children can put together puzzles with 18 to 35 pieces. Five-year-olds are also becoming skilled at working clay, and may sculpt simple forms and figures.

Now children can usually grasp a writing tool with three fingers instead of a fist. This provides better control, so writing and drawing skills improve quickly. By four years of age, children's drawing forms are more refined. As a result, you will have an easier time recognizing what they are drawing. Preschoolers are recognizing the alphabet letters. They can tell writing from non-writing. They can also copy a square and print a few letters. Often though, they print the letters improperly. Letters that are mirror images are especially difficult for preschoolers. For instance, children may print *b* for *d* or even for *p*, and may place five or six horizontal lines on an *E*.

FatCamera/E+ via Getty Images

Figure 6.3 Four-year-olds have an easier time building a tower with blocks than younger children do. ***What skills are four-year-olds using when building with blocks?***

Five-year-olds show marked improvement in controlling a writing tool. They delight in copying triangles and tracing diamond shapes. They are also fairly skilled at staying within the lines when they color. Most five-year-olds enjoy printing their first names. They are capable of copying most letters and printing some simple words, but they may still have problems printing some letters properly. They are beginning to understand the link between letters and sounds.

Self-Help Skills

Preschoolers become more and more self-sufficient as they develop **self-help skills**—those skills and abilities that help them move toward independence. They are dressing and undressing themselves with very little help. Most of these children can tell the front from the back of clothing, however, you may need to give them reminders from time to time. By four years of age, most children can buckle belts and close zippers. By five years, many children can even button and unbutton fasteners on the backs of garments. They can also put shoes on the correct feet. Some five-year-olds can even tie their own shoelaces.

Self-feeding is easier for preschoolers, too. They enjoy helping with table-setting and serving food. They can use spoons and forks with ease. By four years of age, children are using their forks to cut some large pieces of food, and they may even try cutting foods with a dull knife. Most five-year-olds can cut soft foods with knives. After eating, children at this age can throw their napkins in a wastebasket and clear their plates from the table.

Preschoolers are also better are better at caring for their own hygiene. They have become more skilled at handling a toothbrush and brushing their teeth. They can also use a washcloth for wiping their hands and faces. Preschoolers become more skilled at brushing and combing their hair as well. They also can take care of their toileting needs, though they may still not be skillful at wiping.

Five-year-olds can choose appropriate clothing for the weather, if taught. They will also learn their own telephone number and those for the police and fire department. In their own home or the classroom, they know the places where familiar items are stored.

6.1-2 Cognitive Development of Preschoolers

Children in this age group make many gains in understanding the world around them. They become more skilled in thinking without having to act things out. As a result, they have a better understanding of symbols than younger children. Four- and five-year-olds also have increased language-comprehension and expressive-language skills. Language is a tool that can help children solve problems mentally.

Four- and five-year-olds now have the language skills to describe what they see and remember. You can test a child's recognition and recall skills. Show the child ten small, familiar toys. Then place the toys in a bag or box. Ask the children what items are in the bag. To recall the items requires the children to create a mental image. Although preschoolers can recognize all ten items, they probably will only recall four or five. This is because preschoolers have better recognition than recall skills.

Children start creating their own symbols at this age (**Figure 6.4**). They reflect this in their play. Instead of just imitating the actions of adults, preschoolers add their own ideas. For example, instead of using a bowl for mixing, they may pretend the bowl is a hat. New symbols also appear in art. Before the fourth year, children tend to scribble or just draw simple shapes. By five years, children make drawings that represent real objects. These drawings are simple and do not always represent what the child really sees. For instance, a hand may have six or even ten fingers. Four-year-olds often make drawings and then name them. By five years, children decide what they want to draw and then draw it.

Understanding symbols is important for developing more advanced cognitive skills.

fizkes/iStock via Getty Images Plus

Figure 6.4   Four- and five-year-olds enjoy adding their own ideas during cooperative play.

Symbols are a part of learning in language, math, science, social studies, and many other areas of education. Therefore, cognitive development during the preschool years helps prepare children for future learning during the school years.

Five-year-olds question constantly. They want to know the **how** and **why**. They are eager to learn about why things happen around them. They may ask, "Why do dogs bark?" or "Why do boats float?" With their endless string of questions, they are trying to make sense of their world. They still have flaws in their thinking like younger children and seldom do they see things from another's viewpoint. Through asking questions repeatedly, the thinking of five-year-olds becomes more and more logical. Their vocabulary keeps growing and they are beginning to use connecting words— words such as "but" and "when."

Your curriculum should support the children's cognitive growth. As you provide new experiences, the children's vocabularies will grow. They will learn new concepts. For instance, you may show the children a live bunny. These children will explore concepts about the bunny, such as size, body parts, color, and method of eating. Children may also learn new vocabulary words as you show the animal. For instance, you might explain that the bunny is timid. Each new experience helps the children grow intellectually (**Figure 6.5**)

SDI Productions/E+ via Getty Images

Figure 6.5   A visit from a librarian to read stories can promote children's cognitive development. *What cognitive skills can children develop by listening to stories?*

Language-Comprehension Skills

The language-comprehension skills of four- and five-year-olds are expanding with extraordinary speed. By kindergarten, they will understand an average of 3,000-5,000 words. When speaking, they use the appropriate level of volume, tone, and inflection. Their sentences are now grammatically complex and consist of three or more words.

New words related to space concepts increase their understanding. These include such words as **beside, bottom, backward,** and **forward**. They also understand such words as **down, low, different,** and **thin**. By the fifth year, the words **behind, ahead of, first,** and **last** are added to children's understanding. As you instruct children using these words, children will be able to understand and follow directions. For example, you may tell a child "Place the green block behind the blue block."

Children this age become even better at following three-step commands. These children will be able to follow the directions in the order that they are given. For instance, you may tell a child "Pick up the puzzle, put it on the table, and wash your hands." If you do not sequence the directions correctly, however, the child can become confused.

Children have a better understanding of the difference between plural and singular nouns at this age. For instance, you may tell the children to take a sandwich at lunchtime. The children understand that they are to take only one sandwich. If you tell them to take crackers, the children know that they can have more than one.

Children start understanding the passive voice at this age. In a **passive voice** sentence, the object of the sentence comes before the subject. An example of a passive voice sentence would be "The orange was eaten by Finley." Three-year-olds do not usually understand this word order. They think the sentence means that the orange ate Finley. Four- and five-year-olds understand that Finley ate the orange.

Because many words and phrases have more than one meaning, preschoolers may become confused about some statements. They tend to take literally such comments as "Anne just flew out the door" (**Figure 6.6**). You need to be careful about the phrases that you use around children of this age. For instance, a phrase such as "I'm dying of hunger" may frighten children.

You will note differences exist in children's language development. The children's heredity and environment influence these differences, although the sequence of development is similar across all cultural groups. Children who have heard more words will be better prepared to see them eventually in print.

Receptive-Language Skills

Receptive language refers to how a person understands language. It grows as the children are exposed to new words or known words used in new ways. Children at this stage of development listen for a variety of purposes. They listen for enjoyment, to learn what happens in a story, and how to perform a task. They also listen to interact with other children or adults.

Expressive-Language Skills

Expressive language is the ability to express thoughts to others verbally or in writing (**Figure 6.7**). Preschoolers become quite talkative.

Alessandro Biascioli/iStock via Getty Images Plus

Figure 6.7   Four-year-olds like to match alphabet letters using apps. ***What apps are available online to help children match letters and words? How can using such apps help children expand their expressive language?***

As their vocabularies and grammar skills improve, they enjoy talking to others. At this age, children are using more complex sentences. They tend to talk to you rather than converse with you. When you talk about one subject, a child may interrupt to tell you about something entirely unrelated. The child may even make two or three unrelated comments to you in the same conversation. The children can answer your questions. In later years, these children will become better at true two-way communication.

Early Childhood Insight 🄰🄱🄲

Imitation

You will notice that children in this age group will imitate your speech. You may hear one child tell another, "Christopher, we walk, we don't run, when we are in the hallway." For this reason, you need to be careful of your statements. You should never use words or statements that you would not want the children repeating.

Anne just flew out the door...

Vector Juice/Shutterstock.com; Goodheart-Willcox Publisher

Figure 6.6   Preschoolers may have trouble understanding figurative speech. ***Name several examples of figurative speech that you think might confuse children or cause misunderstandings.***

Articulation

Articulation is the ability to speak in clearly pronounced sounds. Articulation improves in

baona/iStock via Getty Images Plus

Figure 6.8   Children may imitate a phrase from television such as "My teeth feel minty fresh and tingly." These children do not always understand the meaning of the phrase.

many ways at ages four and five. Preschoolers can make most of the sounds needed to form words. Many children still have trouble making the *ch* sound and the *th* sound in words. Others may have trouble with the *s* sound, causing a lisp.

Some preschoolers also have stuttering problems. **Stuttering** includes repeating sounds or words and pausing for unusually long times while speaking. For most preschoolers, stuttering results from thinking faster than they can talk. As children's speech ability catches up to their thinking ability, the stuttering usually disappears.

Vocabulary

Vocabulary grows quickly over these two years. As a result, the children will speak in complete sentences. They do not always have clear ideas of the meanings of all the words they use and may make up their own meanings to some words.

Preschoolers have mainly concrete nouns and action verbs in their vocabularies. They are beginning to add some modifiers and adjectives. Words related to ideas or thoughts, however, are still not a big part of their vocabularies. For

example, children this age would be unlikely to use the words *freedom* or *unfair* unless they were simply imitating the words of adults.

Children of this age do imitate phrases they hear from adults or television (**Figure 6.8**). After a meal, a child may say "That was simply delectable!" This child is most likely imitating a statement heard at home or on television. If you ask, the child could not tell you what *delectable* means. Children might also use such words as *bionic* or *biodegradable*.

Children this age need to develop a vocabulary describing emotions, which is called **emotional language**. To help promote this type of language, teachers need to coach children to use words and verbally express their feelings in their home language or English. Feeding in emotional language is important. To illustrate, assume you are trying to open a jar of paint in the art area. The cover is tightly closed and difficult to open. Therefore, you may be feeling frustrated. Say, "I cannot open the jar and am feeling frustrated. Watch. I will try again."

Grammar

Children's grammar improves during these years. Children gradually learn there are exceptions to rules for past tense. They use such irregular verbs as *ate, ran,* and *went* properly. These children still put *ed* at the end of these words occasionally.

Children also learn how to properly form questions. The three-year-old would say "Why the sky is blue?" Four- and five-year-olds know to say "Why is the sky blue?"

Some grammar rules still give four- and five-year-olds problems. They especially have trouble using the proper forms of pronouns in sentences. For instance, a child may say "Him and me are going to the zoo." They also have trouble with noun and verb agreement. For example, a child may say "Tommy don't have a crayon."

Reading

Most four- and five-year-olds cannot read, but they are acquiring abilities that lead to the development of reading skills. These abilities are made possible as children begin to understand symbolism. Before children learn to read, they need to understand that a group of letters on paper can symbolize any object, from a ball to an airplane.

Four- and five-year-olds can recognize and name many letters of the alphabet. They can also recognize their own names. Children in this age group enjoy having stories read to them over and over again. As you reread stories, the children may pick out and say words they recognize. The children will also try to guess words they do not recognize. They tend to look at the first letter of a word and name any word that begins with that letter. For example, they may point to the word ball and say *baby*.

During this stage, a growing awareness of *environmental print* occurs. You seen this print around you in daily life in the form of signs and logos. Four- and five-year-olds can recognize common signs, such as fast-food restaurants, favorite cereals, and traffic signs.

Writing

Most four-year-olds are interested in writing their own names. They understand that letters make up words. Five-year-olds like to practice writing. They write their names on artwork, and will also copy words in the environment.

Math Skills

Number concepts become easier for children in this age group. Rote-counting skills increase quickly when adults provide the opportunity for counting and talking about number concepts. **Rote counting** is reciting numbers in their proper order. Most children gain this skill before they fully understand that each number represents a certain amount. Children at this age also understand the **principle of cardinality**. This principle is the last number in a counting sequence that designates the quality of items in the set. At four years of age, most children can rote count from one up to ten. By the end of the fifth year, most children can rote count to 20. Rote-counting skills develop at different rates for children in this age group. Therefore, you need to

observe children to make sure your curriculum fits their skill levels.

True counting, in which an object is counted for each number named, develops more slowly. For instance, a child may try to count ten objects. The child may touch one object and say "one," another and say "two," and another saying "three." However, the child may then point to another object three times in a row, saying "four, five, six." Children in this age group may count three or four objects; however, they have trouble counting more objects.

Children start to recognize numerals in this stage. A four-year-old usually recognizes the numerals *1, 2, 3, 4,* and *5*. Five-year-olds learn to recognize *6, 7, 8, 9,* and *10* as well. By five years of age, many children can enter their own telephone numbers on a phone. They are also beginning to write numerals.

Other math skills develop at this age. Children become better at recognizing shapes. About 80 percent of five-year-olds can recognize the square and rectangle shapes. Four- and five-year-olds also understand more terms related to size and number. These include *short, tallest, same size, first,* and *last*. They also learn positional and directional words, such as *front/back, on/off, over/under, up/down, inside/outside, above/below, in front of/behind, near/far, top/bottom,* or *before/after*.

Children start to understand money concepts during this stage. Most preschoolers can identify a penny, a nickel, and a dime. Children of this age do not yet understand the true value of money, though. If you ask a preschooler whether a nickel or a dime is worth more, the child is likely to choose the nickel. Since it is bigger, children think that it is worth more. They do not yet realize a nickel is worth five pennies, and a dime is worth ten.

Time concepts become clearer at this age. The children start to understand the difference between *today, tomorrow,* and *yesterday*. Many time concepts, however, are still confusing for children this age. They do not really understand how long an hour or a minute takes. They also get confused because time is described in so many ways. An adult may tell a child that puppet time is at 3:30, at half-past three, this afternoon, or in a few hours.

Lesson 6.1 Review

1. What is true about four- and five-year-olds throwing and catching a ball? (6.1.1)
   A. They can catch a ball with one hand.
   B. They do not visually track the ball.
   C. They have the ability to throw overhand.
   D. They do not use their body to direct their throw.
2. Which is a common task for four-year-olds? (6.1.1)
   A. Buttoning and unbuttoning fasteners
   B. Closing zippers
   C. Tying shoes
   D. Choosing appropriate clothing for the weather
3. **True or False.** Early childhood professionals need to be careful using phrases such as "I'm dying of hunger" around four- and five-year-old children. (6.1.2)
4. Each of the following is a reading ability of four- and five-year-olds except _____. (6.1.2)
   A. recognizing and naming letters of the alphabet
   B. picking out and saying words they recognize
   C. reciting numbers in their proper order
   D. trying to guess words they do not recognize

Essential Question

What do I need to know about the social-emotional development of preschool children to promote equity and respect for others?

Learning Outcomes

After studying this lesson, you will be able to

6.2-1 **analyze** social-emotional development of preschoolers, including gender stereotypes.

6.2-2 **explain** how you as a teacher can plan programs to meet the developmental needs of preschool children.

Key Terms

solitary play

empathy

gender stereotypes

Preschoolers continue to be helpful and cooperative. With improved language skills, children become more involved with one another. Friendships become more important. They know that a friend is a person who "likes you." Emotions are changing in children at this age. As they learn and grow, the causes of happiness, fear, anger, and sadness change. The ways children react to these emotions change, too.

6.2-1 Social Development

Companionship is important to preschoolers. Friendships, attention, and approval are important as well. Preschoolers, however, are also becoming more independent of adults. They like to play on their own or with other children. They may not always want you or other adults to participate in play. They may still need your help to get materials or settle disputes.

Children at this age start to value their friendships with others. They tend to have only a few friends. Young children tend to see things in terms of absolutes. For instance, you are either a friend or you are not. They also prefer friends of the same sex. Children in this age group become more willing to cooperate as they play with others. They are more likely than younger children to offer a favorite toy to a friend. Many children in this age group choose best friends, although they may change best friends often.

For four-year-olds, over one-third of a child's play is **solitary play**. By age five, however, play involves more and more interaction and cooperation. Play groups are still small—only two or three children—but children talk to each other more and do more as a group. Five-year-olds are sociable and enjoy competitive games. While playing, they insist on rules and like to define them for others (**Figure 6.9**).

Four- and five-year olds are developing social awareness. They are beginning to understand the emotions of others and see situations from another child's perspective. When Hiram is pushed off a tricycle, the other children understand how he feels.

Gender Stereotypes

Four- and five-year-old children have developed many gender-linked stereotypes of their culture. **Gender stereotypes** are the beliefs people have about male and female characteristics that are often based on their cultural beliefs about what is normal and appropriate behavior for males and females. During these early years, preschool children may quickly develop

Natalia Lebedinskaia/Shutterstock.com

Figure 6.9   Play becomes more cooperative for four- and five-year-olds. *Observe a group of four- and five-year-olds. Identify examples of cooperative play and social awareness.*

stereotypes as they attempt to navigate the world around them. First children identify themselves as a boy or girl. Then they begin thinking about qualities. For instance, girls are more likely to wear shirts with pictures of unicorns and mermaids, while boys are more likely to wear shirts with pictures of superheroes. Watch and listen. In the dramatic play area, children show knowledge of each sex. For instance, Melinda and Tunde were playing house with a doll. Melinda referred to herself as the doll's mother, and Tunde referred to himself as the doll's father.

With age, the children's stereotypes will become more flexible and may change. Boys may wear longer hair and girls like cars and trucks. Boys may decide to nurture a baby doll and girls may decide they like to play with cars and trucks.

Children now can accept supervision. They know their own abilities, and they realize that adults have reasons for rules. These children will accept your instructions, and they will ask your permission before doing certain activities.

Emotional Development

Four- and five-year-old children with good emotional regulation have better empathy for others. They are beginning to take another's perspective. When others are in distress, they can empathize. They begin to realize new ways of helping, comforting, and sharing. They still understand hugs and other physical signs of affection. They may hug another child who is sad to give comfort. They are realizing that helping others, however, is a way of showing love. These children may show love for others by sharing something or helping with a task. They may also seek this sign of love from others. For example, children may ask for help with a task even if they do not need it. The children are looking for assurance that you care.

Empathy is a motivator for prosocial behavior. Four- and five-year-olds can use words more as their language continues to develop. Lucas is a four-year-old with strong prosocial behaviors. He now can understand behavioral causes. He noticed that Pouneh was crying at the art table so sensed her unhappiness. To help relieve her feelings, he walked over to her. Then he said, "Pouneh, can I help you? Let me get you a brush so you can paint."

Four- and five-year-olds are beginning to develop a sense of humor. Laughter becomes a way of expressing their happiness. These children do not yet understand most verbal jokes, but they laugh at funny faces or actions. They also laugh at things they know are unusual. For instance, they may laugh at a dog that says "meow" in a story. The children also need excellent role models to learn that harm done to others is not funny.

Fear

Fears are still common, but most only last a few months. Causes of fears change during this stage. These children are still afraid of imagined creatures, such as monsters and ghosts. They may be especially fearful of dreams because they seem so real. Preschoolers also start to realize, however, that there is a difference between the real and the imagined. This helps children deal with some of these fears. For this reason, you may hear preschoolers firmly state "There's no such thing as dragons." They may ask you repeatedly "Was the story just pretend?"

The new knowledge preschoolers are gaining may create fears. They are becoming aware of more dangers; however, preschoolers do not know enough to understand what *is* and *is not* dangerous. Their imaginations are vivid. For instance, a child may learn that sharks live in the ocean. This may cause fear of being hurt in the ocean. The child may also become afraid of sharks in rivers, pools, and even bathtubs.

Five-year-olds are also more afraid of being hurt than are younger children. They know of more things that can hurt or injure them. They may be afraid of doctors and dentists because they are aware of pain or injuries associated with these professionals. They may also be afraid of high places and dogs because of prior experiences.

Children sometimes work through fears in their play at this age. For instance, a child who is afraid of dogs may pretend to be a fierce dog. A child who is afraid of heights may pretend to be a bird. For these children, play is therapeutic. It helps them act out some of their intense feelings and deal with their fears.

Often children have a fear of animals regardless of size. You should never force a fearful child to handle a pet or animal. Rather, demonstrate how to touch or pet the animal. For example, show a child how to gently pick up a baby bunny. Then you can ask if they would like to hold it. If the child refuses, you could say "that bunny is so little and you are so big." Then ask again. If the child still declines, discontinue the encouragement. Be patient as eventually the child may overcome the fear.

Anger

Like three-year-olds, children in this age group do not have as many causes for anger as toddlers do. They can become angry, however, if they cannot reach their goals. Four- and five-year-old children are more likely to use words and yelling rather than hitting or kicking to express anger. If they do express anger physically, they are more likely to take out their anger on objects or other children. They rarely respond to adults physically because they know this action is not acceptable.

Some preschoolers respond more physically to anger than others. Also, they may become angry more easily than others. They may use

pushing, hitting, or kicking to show anger. They may not have learned better ways of expressing anger from their adult role models or they could just want attention.

Jealousy

Jealousy can be a problem for some children in this age group. Four-and five-year-old children are most likely to become jealous of a new sibling. They may resent the fact that their parents are spending so much time with a new child. They may fear that their parents do not love them as much. Jealousy may surface in children in many ways (**Figure 6.10**). Children may regress to earlier behaviors, such as crying or having toileting accidents. They may also develop physical problems, such as stomachaches or nightmares. These children need to be reassured that they are still loved. Sometimes they may need a little extra attention away from home to make them feel special. Showing children that their sibling needs help from a "big sister" or "big brother" can make them feel better.

Sadness

Four- and five-year-olds learn that some situations are sad. They realize the concept of death. Their first experiences with death may be the loss of a pet. Preschool children do not understand that death cannot be reversed. As

Ann in the uk/Shutterstock.com

Figure 6.10 Children who are jealous of a new sibling may become withdrawn or show regressive behaviors at the child care center.

a result, it may take children a while to realize that the pet will not come back to life. Once they understand this, however, they often become sad.

Children are not always sure how to express sadness. Children may deal with sadness in play. They may pretend to be the lost pet or to talk to the lost pet. Frequently, they need help from adults to learn that it is okay to cry and talk about their feelings. They also need adults to model appropriate responses to sadness and to provide simple explanations.

Some children must also deal with the death of a close family member. These children need to have as much explained about the situation as they can understand. They also need help from adults in dealing with the loss and sadness.

6.2-2 Teaching Four- and Five-Year-Olds

Like three-year-olds, four- and five-year-olds are usually cooperative and helpful. These children are eager to please you (**Figure 6.11**). If you ask a child to help you, the child feels complimented. Children of this age enjoy feeling needed and important. They may even ask "Can I help you?"

Alexander_Safonov/Shutterstock.com

Figure 6.11 Preschoolers are eager to help you in such ways as caring for pets. *In what other ways can preschoolers be good helpers at an early childhood center and at home?*

Because these children like to help, you need to carefully select helpers. Choosing the same few helpers time after time can make others feel unimportant. Even children who do not volunteer need to be asked from time to time. These children may be too shy to ask, or they may not feel confident in their abilities to help. By choosing them, you can help build their self-esteem.

By this age, children become quite talkative. They still enjoy physical play, but they like to spend more time talking. You will enjoy carrying on extended conversations with them. These conversations may become a part of learning activities or story time. After you read a story, the children may enjoy retelling the story, and are capable of retelling the story in the proper sequence. Discuss word meanings with them and ask open-ended questions that require more than a yes, no, or one-word response. Model the use of new words.

Children are now more content playing with each other. You do not need to function as a playmate as much, however, strengthening their social skills will be some of your most important work. You will need to handle more disputes among children. At this age, children may have conflicts over group rules. They will look to you for advice on settling these problems. You may also want to add new ideas to play. Preschoolers enjoy playing some simple, organized games.

Some children may have imaginary playmates. For instance, child may come to school explaining that Ralph, his playmate, asked to come with him. He may provide space for Ralph on his cot at nap time. He may have conversations with Ralph throughout the day. This kind of play does not necessarily indicate problems. It is simply a way of using the imagination and having fun.

Children in this age group are often proud of their possessions and family members (**Figure 6.12**). They may like to bring favorite toys to the center. They may also call attention to new shoes or a new jacket. They may beam with pride when their parents visit the center. Children enjoy talking with you and others about their

fizkes/Shutterstock.com

Figure 6.12   Preschoolers are proud to have their siblings visit the center.

belongings. Asking children questions about something of theirs can help build their self-esteem.

Children of this age also enjoy working on projects. Their attention spans and goal-setting abilities are improving. Children's ideas for projects may come from playing with peers or from adult activities. Such projects as woodworking, cooking, and sculpting clay may be fun for these children. As they get older, they will engage for longer periods of time in these activities. The average time spent in most activities at this age is about seven minutes.

Lesson 6.2 Review

1. For four-year-olds, how much of their play is solitary? (6.2.1)
   A. None
   B. All
   C. About half
   D. Over one-third
2. **True or False.** Four- and five-year-old children are more likely to use hitting and kicking to express anger. (6.2.1)
3. **True or False.** A teacher should always choose the same few helpers. (6.2.2)
4. What is the average length of time that four- and five-year-olds are engaged in activities? (6.2.2)
   A. 2 minutes
   B. 5 minutes
   C. 7 minutes
   D. 10 minutes

Chapter 6 Review and Assessment

Summary

Lesson 6.1

6.1-1 The growth of four- and five-year-old children helps them become more independent and self-confident.

6.1-1 These preschoolers are becoming stronger and more coordinated as their gross-motor and fine-motor skills are refined.

6.1-2 Preschooler's thoughts become more adult-like, and their language comprehension skills improve quickly.

6.1-2 Much new knowledge helps prepare four- and five-year old children for later math learning.

Lesson 6.2

6.2-1 Children become more social with their peers at this age. They like to help and talk to adults, and seek adult favor and approval.

6.2-1 As children age, their gender stereotypes will become more flexible and may change.

6.2-1 Children are learning acceptable ways of expressing their feelings.

6.2-2 As a teacher, you will enjoy working with four- and five-year-old children. These children can be independent in terms of self-care.

6.2-2 Preschoolers are eager to help you and enjoy learning about new ideas.

Vocabulary Activity

With a partner, use online resources to locate photos or graphics that depict the chapter terms. Print the graphics or use presentation software to show your graphics to the class, describing how they depict the meaning of the term(s).

Critical Thinking

1. **Evaluate.** Play catch with a four- or five-year-old. Make sketches or written descriptions of the movements used by the child to catch and to throw. Report your findings to the class.

2. **Compare and Contrast.** Review the information about self-help skills for two- and three-year-olds. Then, in small groups, compare that information with the information in this chapter about self-help skills for four- and five-year-olds. How are the children's skills similar? How are they different? In what ways do children grow?

3. **Analyze.** Conduct an online search for preschool vocabulary lists, such as the *Dolch Basic Sight Vocabulary*. Analyze and compare several lists and print them out. How can knowing the expected basic vocabulary for preschoolers help you design appropriate language learning activities? What ideas have you learned from your research? Share your findings with the class.

4. **Draw Conclusions.** Write an opinion paper on using time-outs as a method of handling a preschool child's anger. What are the pros and cons of using this method in an educational setting? What role will consistency play in helping a child become self-disciplined? What should the ideal time-out area look like in a preschool classroom?

5. **Analyze.** Select one preschooler and write a profile describing the child's physical, cognitive, social, and emotional development. Is the student typical of others in his or her age group according to the characteristics discussed in this chapter? Does the child have any outstanding skills or abilities? Does the child demonstrate any delays in development?

6. **Produce.** Obtain a lesson plan for school-age children about a topic that interests you. Then, considering everything you have learned about four- and five-year-old children in this chapter, adapt and produce the lesson for the children. What would you have to change to make the lesson accessible? What parts of the lesson would be challenging?

Core Skills

1. **Research and Writing.** Using internet resources, research the physical benefits of gross-motor activities and active physical play for preschoolers. How much time do experts recommend preschoolers spend each day in active physical play? Use a publishing program to create a newsletter article encouraging families to promote healthful activities for their children. List suggestions for ways families can interact with their children to model healthful activity habits.

2. **Math.** Observe a four- or five-year-old while performing rote and true counting activities. How many numbers can the child recite in their proper order? How many objects can the child count for each number named? What difficulties, if any, was the child experiencing? Determine the child's skill level and create a math activity that will help the child practice rote or true counting. Share your math activities with the rest of the class.

3. **Speaking and Listening.** Interview an early childhood teacher about the artwork of four- and five-year-olds. Ask to see samples that show the types of symbolism these children use.

4. **Research and Writing.** Write a research report on recommended ways of helping four- and five-year-olds deal with death.

5. **Reading and Writing.** Go to the HealthyChildren.org website, which is sponsored by the American Academy of Pediatrics (AAP), and search for *Emotional Development in Preschoolers*. After reading the article, write a one-page summary of your findings. Exchange papers with classmates and check for correct grammar, spelling, and punctuation. Then, prepare a final draft of your report.

6. **Listening and Writing.** Observe and interview a four- or five-year-old you know. During the interview, take notes about the child's emotions and how he or she expresses them. Are there emotions the child expresses with actions, though not verbally? Are the child's stated emotions reflected in his or her behaviors? How do the emotions the child describes align with the information covered in this chapter? After the interview, write a short reflection about the experience.

7. **CTE Career Readiness Practice.** Use text or reliable internet or print resources to investigate the physical changes that occur from birth to age five. Compare the physical characteristics of a newborn with that of a five-year-old child.

Portfolio Project

Design a photo essay showing the self-help and gross- and fine-motor skills exhibited by four- and five-year-olds. Photos can be obtained from print sources or downloaded to the computer from a cell phone camera, digital camera, or scanner, and formatted into a slide show presentation. Write a brief narrative explaining each photo. Save the photo essay in your portfolio. (Be sure to follow proper copyright and permissions guidelines before taking or saving photos.)

Chapter 7

Reading Advantage

Before reading the chapter, scan the Key Terms in each lesson for words you can define. Based on your definitions, predict the content of this chapter. Review your predictions after reading the material.

Understanding Middle Childhood

Lesson 7.1: Physical and Cognitive Development in Middle Childhood

Lesson 7.2: Social-Emotional Development in Middle Childhood

Case Study

Can a long-term teacher of two-year-olds be successful teaching school-aged children in a third-grade classroom?

Pat Denk, who has a bachelor's degree in early childhood education, taught four-and five-year-old children for the past 25 years. Considering retirement, Pat recently moved to a new community in southwest Florida. One August morning, an ad appeared in the Naples paper seeking applicants for positions in the Lee County Schools. One part-time position appealed to Pat. It was working as an assistant teacher in a third-grade classroom with school-aged children for 20 hours a week. Pat called the number provided in the ad to get an application and provided the secretary with an email address.

Pat promptly received an application and immediately filled it out. Pat also prepared a cover letter showing interest in the position and returned it along with the application. Three days later Pat received a phone call to schedule an interview. On arrival for the interview, Pat was welcomed by the administrative assistant and asked to take a seat. The personnel director came into the reception area and, after an introduction, Pat was ushered into a conference room. There Pat was introduced to the principal of Three Oaks Elementary School. During the interview, both asked questions related to Pat's academic background, last teaching position, and teaching style. The final question was, "What did you learn in your last teaching position that you would bring into a third-grade classroom?"

Pat received a call two days later and was offered the position. When Pat thought about the position, it was frightening. Pat was hesitant to take the position due to a lack of clear understanding about the development of school-age children.

Give It Some Thought

1. Describe the development of school-age children: physical, cognitive, and social-emotional.
2. How would you describe school-age friendships to Pat? What are the differences in friendships between four-year-old children and school-age children?
3. How would the gross- and fine motor skills of school-age children differ from preschool children?
4. If you were Pat, would you take the position? Why or why not?

Opening image credit: kali9/E+ via Getty Images

Physical and Cognitive Development in Middle Childhood

Essential Question

How can understanding physical and cognitive development in middle childhood help me to better teach, guide, and care for children?

Learning Outcomes

After studying this lesson, you will be able to

7.1-1 **summarize** the characteristics of physical development in middle childhood, including gross- and fine-motor skills.

7.1-2 **analyze** potential health concerns of middle childhood.

7.1-3 **compare** aspects of cognitive development during middle childhood, including attention and memory, mental operations, and language and literacy.

Key Terms

visual perception	operation
farsighted	conservation
nearsighted	seriation
incisors	classification
rehearsal	

Middle childhood refers to the span of years between ages six and 12. Since this timeframe begins with the onset of formal schooling, it is often referred to as the *school-age years*. It is a time of important advances in every developmental area, including the child's identity. At this stage of development, children are making strides in becoming self-competent and self-aware.

During middle childhood, children become more self-sufficient and independent. They are interested and involved in many new activities. Peers and adults outside their families play an increasingly important role in their lives. Their circle of friends and acquaintances expands far beyond their own family members. These friendships and school-related activities are taking more and more of their time. As a result, they are learning to adopt new social rules and expectations.

Though developmental changes continue to occur throughout middle childhood, the changes are not as dramatic as they were during infancy and toddlerhood. During the school-age years, the brain undergoes changes that allow more highly developed thinking skills. As a result, the children are becoming better problem solvers. They are also growing in self-knowledge and understanding, and they are beginning to think about things from different points of view.

School-age children are beginning the process of entering the adult world and are attending more to their own needs. They are becoming better able to get themselves up in the morning, bathe, dress, and eat without adult help. Most families expect more of their school-age children because of their improved skills. Often children this age assist with cooking, dishwashing, and laundry chores. They are also capable of helping with younger siblings.

7.1-1 Physical Development

Physical development during middle childhood is not as rapid as during the first years of life. It slows considerably. Between the ages of six and 12, children experience steady physical growth (**Figure 7.1**). There are gradual and consistent increases in weight and height as bones broaden and lengthen. Heredity and environment account for most differences in physical growth. Heights will vary. A 3- to 6-inch difference is typical. Health care and nutrition are environmental factors that can affect both weight and height. In the United States, most children have adequate nutrients to grow to their full potential.

During this period, children are interested in their physical growth. They care more about what other people think of them. Therefore, their body size, shape, and physical abilities can influence how they feel about themselves.

pathdoc/Shutterstock.com

Figure 7.1   Children do not grow as rapidly during middle childhood as they do in the first years of life. *How do children in middle childhood change in height and weight?*

At the beginning of this stage, children have much better control of their large muscles than their small muscles. During the six-year span, children show continued improvement in skills learned earlier. They show gains in motor skills, agility, and physical strength. These skills are helpful for participation in games and sports.

Height

Variations in height among school-aged children are not unusual. Growth spurts are common, but there are also periods of slow growth. Males are usually slightly taller than females at the beginning of this stage. Until age nine, males keep this edge. Then the reverse occurs as females begin to grow slightly more rapidly than males. At 10 years of age, most females experience a growth spurt. This growth spurt occurs two years later in males. By ages 11 and 12, most females have surpassed males in height. During the lifespan, this is the only time females are typically taller than males. This difference can be a source of embarrassment for some children.

The typical six-year-old is almost four feet tall. During middle childhood, children usually grow about two to three inches per year. By the age of 12, the average child is about five feet tall. By the end of middle childhood, females may reach 90 percent of their adult height. At the same time, males may be about 80 percent of their adult height. Often children at this stage will feel awkward and they will compare their bodies to their friends. Some may be six or more inches apart in height.

Body proportions change during the school-age years. The upper part of the body grew fast during the first six years of life. Now the arms and legs grow more quickly. Children look less top-heavy and are longer-legged now than during the earlier years. Their bones have continued to lengthen and broaden. Muscle mass increases, making them stronger.

Weight

During middle childhood, children gain about 5–7 pounds per year. At age six, the average child weighs about 47 pounds. By age 12, this weight may double. Children gain about five to seven pounds per year during middle childhood.

There are weight differences between females and males. From birth through the preschool years, females usually weigh slightly less than males. Females catch up with males in weight by age 11. By 12 years of age, females usually weigh about three pounds more than males.

Gross-Motor Skills

By watching school-age children on the playground, you can see how their motor skills are becoming more refined (**Figure 7.2**). Physical growth and regular physical activity contribute to these changes. Gains in height and weight help with coordination. These children possess greater speed and accuracy of movement, with faster reaction times. Movements are more refined and fluid. Balance, strength and flexibility improve. This supports the children's refinement in running and ball skills.

Younger school-age children are constantly practicing and perfecting seven skills. These are jumping, hopping, balancing, throwing, catching, running, and sequencing foot movements. Their

running is faster. They can swim, ice skate, dribble a ball, and skip rope. With practice, they are more accurate in throwing, catching, and kicking. They can throw balls greater distances and swing at pitched balls. Batting increases in speed and accuracy.

Sex differences exist in gross-motor development. Moreover, these differences tend to increase with age. As they grow older, both males and females improve their gross-motor skills. Even though females usually surpass males in height and weight, males have more physical strength because they have greater muscle mass. Males are typically are stronger than females in skills emphasizing force and power. As a result, males may outperform females in jumping, hopping, catching, throwing, and batting. They can usually run faster and for greater distances.

Females typically outperform males in motor skills that require balance, coordination, agility, flexibility, and rhythmic movement. Some examples include playing hopscotch, dancing, and skipping. Females also have an edge in skills involving the use of the small muscles.

Fine-Motor Skills

Children show improvement of their fine-motor skills throughout middle childhood. They have better control of the small muscles in their fingers and hands. Their writing and drawings are more legible since they are using more wrist movement. They learn computer keyboard skills to express their thoughts digitally. Letters and words are more uniform and neater. Moreover, the spacing between letters and words improves. Handwriting and printing involve fine-motor and visual-perception skills. **Visual perception** involves the coordination of the eye and hand. To write, a child must see the differences in size, shape, and slant (**Figure 7.3**).

Improved finger dexterity allows school-age children to play musical instruments, such as a piano, guitar, or flute. Their hand-eye coordination skills are also improving. While grasping tools, they can control the motion and speed. This allows them to learn such skills as sewing and assembling models with small pieces.

patpitchaya/Shutterstock.com

Figure 7.2 Motor development continues to improve during the school-age years. ***Name two ways gross-motor skills improve for males and females.***

FD Trade/DigitalVision via Getty Images

Figure 7.3 With better control of the small muscles and hands, children's writing skills improve. *How does visual perception help improve fine-motor skills?*

7.1-2 Health Concerns

Middle childhood is often one of the healthiest periods for children. The lowest illness rates are for children between five and 12 years of age. Therefore, there are fewer sore throats, upper respiratory diseases, and middle ear infections than during the preschool years. One reason for this reduction is the body's developing immune system, which offers protection against disease. School-age children, however, are not illness-free. Many school-age children still have several upper respiratory illnesses each year.

Some chronic illnesses may surface during middle childhood. Ulcers, asthma, and diabetes are examples. *Asthma* is the most frequent cause of school absence. According to the American Lung Association, some of the common risk factors for developing asthma include family history, allergies, exposure to cigarette smoke, air pollutions, and obesity. Additionally, other risk factors include low socioeconomic status (SES) (often impacting people of various racial ancestries and ethnicities), and lack of health insurance. Asthma is a chronic inflammatory disease of the airways that causes labored breathing, gasping, coughing, and wheezing. Airborne irritants trigger it. Other irritants may include animal dander, stress, and exercise.

Many school-age children also experience headaches and acne as they approach adolescence.

Some children may develop hearing and vision problems. Lack of exercise is another problem. Others exercise too much, placing their bodies under stress. For these children, overuse can cause sprains, *tendinitis* (inflammation of a tendon), and even broken bones. A variety of other health problems occur even though most children are at their healthiest during middle childhood.

As in other stages of development, accidental injuries will occur. To reduce head injuries, children must wear helmets while biking, rollerblading, skateboarding, or using a scooter. Males are more likely to misjudge risky play activities, which can result in injury.

Hearing

Children's hearing is usually well developed by middle childhood. Awareness of mid-range sounds develops first, followed by high-range and low-range awareness. By 11 years of age, most children have the auditory awareness of adults.

Several factors can cause hearing loss. After birth, exposure to noise, trauma to the ear, and certain medications can cause severe ear infections. Ear infections can be a health problem. If left untreated, they can cause permanent hearing loss. For most young children, the number of ear infections decreases due to structural changes within the body. The eustachian tube, which connects the middle ear to the throat, has changed position. This change helps prevent bacteria and fluids from moving from the mouth to the ear.

Vision

Vision problems are common to school-age children. According to Prevent Blindness America, one out of four school-age children have vision problems. Left untreated, their learning ability and adjustment to school can be affected.

Many preschool children are somewhat **farsighted**. This means they can see objects in the distance more clearly than those that are close. During the middle years, though, their close-up vision improves and vision becomes more acute. By age six, most children are ready to read. They can see an object with both eyes at the same time. Their ability to focus improves.

Throughout middle childhood, nearsightedness is the most common vision problem. Being **nearsighted** means having ability to see close objects more clearly than those at a distance. The more time children are engaged in reading and close-up work, the greater their chances of becoming nearsighted. With corrective lenses, they can overcome nearsightedness (**Figure 7.4**). Estimates show that 25 percent of children will need to have their vision corrected by the end of the school years. It is important that children have regular vision checkups to detect any problems.

As a teacher, there are some signs you should observe in school-age children, including

- frequently rubbing eyes
- closing one eye to read
- consistently holding a book too close
- complaints of headaches
- avoiding printed materials
- avoiding computers
- using a finger to guide eyes while reading

If you observe any of these signs, make notes. Discuss them with the child's parents. Encourage them to see an ophthalmologist. Common refractive errors can be corrected with glasses.

Teeth

During middle childhood, children begin losing their primary or "baby" teeth. First and second graders often have toothless smiles! The first teeth to fall out are the central **incisors**, which are the lower and upper front teeth (**Figure 7.5**). The molars are the last to erupt. The first lower and upper molars usually erupt between six and seven years. By the age of 12, permanent teeth will replace all 20 primary teeth. At first, these permanent teeth appear to be out of proportion to the child's face. Gradually, the facial bones grow, causing the face to lengthen and the mouth to widen. These changes are to accommodate the larger permanent teeth.

Injuries to the mouth, face, and head are common to young children. They can lose a tooth or teeth during a mouth injury. Regardless of a tooth lost by accident or natural causes, the loss can have a psychological effect on some children. They become self-conscious. Calling attention to the change in their appearance may cause them to be uncomfortable.

A common health problem for school-age children is tooth decay. Children with poor dental hygiene habits are most susceptible to cavities. Also at risk are children who are in poor health and who eat many foods high in sugar.

As a teacher, you should promote good dental health. Begin by modeling proper care of your own teeth. Brush your teeth with the children after each meal. Eat a well-balanced diet and avoid foods high in sugar. Encourage parents to have their children receive regular dental checkups.

Flamingo Images/Shutterstock.com

Figure 7.4 Corrective lenses can overcome most vision problems. *What is the difference between being nearsighted and farsighted?*

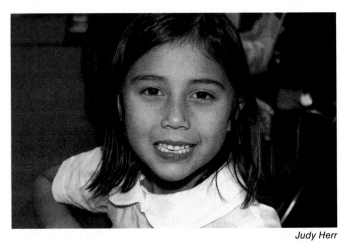

Judy Herr

Figure 7.5 You can tell by looking at the lower front teeth that Eva has entered middle childhood.

Physical Health and Fitness

Early childhood programs must set an example. Healthy meals include serving foods with healthy fats (like avocado and low-fat milk) in appropriate amounts. Nutrition education needs to be included in the curriculum. The daily schedule should include daily physical activity, including vigorous exercise. Children need unstructured time playing outdoors involving physical activity.

Health Highlights

Healthful Activities for School-Age Children

School-age children are rapidly growing and changing—and so are their activity and relationship needs. With ongoing concerns about childhood obesity and peer relationships, care providers must offer a wide range of healthful activities that promote all areas of development. Types of activities for school-age children should include

- vigorous gross-motor activities that increase physical fitness, such as outdoor games, running, biking, or team sports;
- healthful food choices to meet energy needs;
- time for quiet activities to be creative or to do homework;
- opportunities for community involvement that enhance social relationships; and
- time for developing independent relationships with the guidance and support of parents and care providers.

7.1-3 Cognitive Development

During middle childhood, children's cognitive skills ascend to new heights. They begin to think mentally using logic and symbols. They no longer rely only on what they can see or perceive. They begin to use logical thinking instead of only perception. In addition, their memory improves and they become sophisticated in handling new information. Their attention span has increased.

They can process and recall information more readily. These improved thinking skills allow them to engage in academic tasks. Reading, writing, science, and math skills develop continually throughout the school-age years (**Figure 7.6**).

Early Childhood Insight

Achievement and Motivation

The desire to achieve is an important influence on cognitive development during middle childhood. Achievement is often related to motivation. Some children have an internal desire to work hard and achieve. Others are motivated by the prospect of concrete rewards or social recognition. Whether the desire to succeed comes from within the child or externally, the motivation to do well influences performance. Studies show teachers need to exercise caution using extrinsic rewards. Even too much praise can be damaging. The teacher's goal should be to encourage internal motivation. They need to develop a desire within the child to learn, which will give them a sense of pride and achievement.

Attention and Memory

Critical to cognitive development is attention and memory. Memory becomes more controlled than during early childhood. The child's age, motivation, health, and attitude determine the effectiveness of memory. School-age children have learned to repeat information as a tool for improving memory. Attention also improves. Children now can ignore unnecessary information. They can focus their attention on the important aspects of a task, and can scan detailed tasks and decide what they must do first. These changes allow thinking skills to become more refined. School-age children are better at processing information. As a result, they are better problem solvers.

To remember information, school-age children often use a technique called *rehearsal*. **Rehearsal** involves the repetition of information after it is used. The following example illustrates rehearsal. Sidney is a typical six-year-old who can tell you his address and telephone number. In addition, he knows his grandmother's telephone number and those of several friends.

Judy Herr

Figure 7.6 Children learn to read and write during middle childhood. *How do children use the technique called rehearsal?*

To remember this information, Sidney usually writes the phone numbers down. You can see that while recording the numbers, Sidney's lips are moving. Then he repeats the numbers many times. This type of organization and process improves his memory.

Mental Operations

There are changes in reasoning and thinking during middle childhood. Gradually, school-age children change the way they process information. During the preschool years, children relied totally on what they saw or perceived. Sometimes their perceptions were flawed. Now their perceptions are more accurate because they begin to use logical thinking. An **operation** is the manipulation of ideas based on logic rather than perception. Between seven and eight years of age, children enter the stage of *concrete operations*. This means they use logic, but they base it on what they have experienced or seen.

Because they can now use logic in their mental operations, children learn several new concepts during the middle years. These include the concepts of *conservation, seriation,* and *classification.*

Conservation

Children gradually acquire the concept of conservation. **Conservation** means that the change in position or shape of substances does not change the quantity. If nothing is added or taken away, the amount stays the same. Such properties as weight, length, mass, and volume do not change. The appearance, however, may change. You can test a child's understanding of the principle of conservation with liquids, a series of objects, and pliable substances.

To illustrate the conservation of liquids, show a child two identical glasses. Fill each glass with the same amount of liquid. Ask the child if the two glasses have the same amount of liquid, and the child will say that they do. Next, pour the liquid from one glass into a taller, narrower glass. Again, ask the child if the two glasses have the same amount of liquid. Until about seven years of age, the child will probably say that the taller glass contains more liquid. Between seven and eight, when children enter the stage of concrete operations, they will say that the amount of liquid has not changed. Their logic has overruled their perception.

You can test a child's understanding of the conservation of length by using a series of identical objects, such as pennies. Place 10 pennies in two rows of five each. Place the rows side by side. Ask the child if the number of pennies in each row is the same. The child will agree that the two rows contain the same number of pennies. Next, spread the pennies apart in one of the rows. If the child is at the concrete level of operations, the child will say that the longer row still has the same number of pennies. If the child says that the one row has more pennies, the child is focusing only on the dimension of length. Rather than using logic, the child is relying only on perception.

A child's understanding of the concept of mass can also be tested. Show the child two balls of modeling dough that are the same size and shape. Ask the child if the two balls have the same amount of dough. The child will say *yes*. Then flatten one ball of modeling dough and repeat your question. The child who understands conservation will note that the amount of dough is still the same.

Figure 7.7 shows several conservation tasks. It lists the questions to ask children to test their understanding of conservation. Those children who have not reached the stage of concrete operations will respond by saying *no*. If the children respond by saying *yes*, they have reached the concrete operations stage.

Seriation

Seriation is the ability to arrange items in an increasing or decreasing order based on weight, volume, or size. Like conservation, seriation typically emerges between six and eight years of age. To illustrate, you may provide a child with a set of sticks of different lengths. Then ask the child to arrange the sticks from the shortest to the longest. Preschool children will lay the sticks haphazardly. Most school-age children will lay the sticks in an orderly fashion, from shortest to longest as requested.

Seriation can also involve sequencing the events in a story. After hearing a story, the child should be able to recall the sequence of events. As a result, the child will be able to retell the story. Likewise, following a recipe involves seriation. After preparing a simple recipe, the child should be able to recall the preparation steps.

Classification

Simple **classification** is the ability to group objects by common attributes, such as size, color, shape, pattern, or function. The typical preschooler can group objects by one attribute only. For instance, if given a group of different-colored shapes, the preschooler could sort by either color or shape. During the early school-age years, children can mentally handle two aspects of the problem, such as color and shape. For instance, they can sort blue squares into one pile and blue circles into another.

Conservation Task

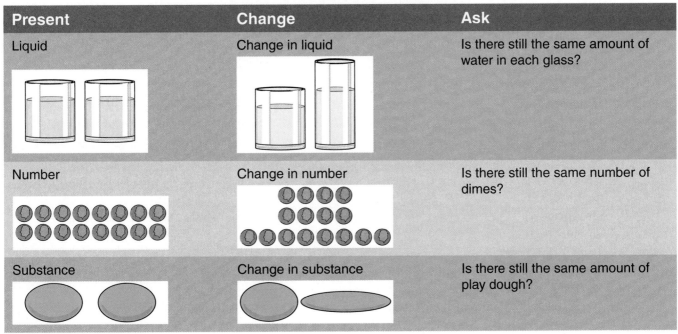

Present	Change	Ask
Liquid	Change in liquid	Is there still the same amount of water in each glass?
Number	Change in number	Is there still the same number of dimes?
Substance	Change in substance	Is there still the same amount of play dough?

Goodheart-Willcox Publisher

Figure 7.7 Children's understanding of the principle of conservation can be tested using liquids, objects, and pliable substances. *How might you assess a child's ability to use classification in the early school-age years?*

Language and Literacy

The ability to communicate improves gradually throughout middle childhood. Comparing language development to the preschool years, changes are more subtle. The child's vocabulary doubles between the ages of six and 12. As they learn to read, children learn many new words each day. Grammar skills improve. They learn sentence structure, using pronouns, plurals, and tense properly. Children during this stage are also moving from using only oral expression to using both oral and written expression.

Conversational skills and language play continue to develop during middle childhood. One form of language play for school-age children is telling riddles and jokes. Cognitive development links to humor. Using humor improves language skills. (**Figure 7.8**).

Children at this age are beginning to read and write. They have learned to recognize letters and sounds, and they can reproduce the letters of the alphabet. Reading is important for mental development because it provides the ability to access other people's ideas.

wavebreakmedia/Shutterstock.com

Figure 7.8   School-age children begin to develop a sense of humor.

Lesson 7.1 Review

1. **True or False.** By 12 years of age, males are more likely to be taller and weigh more than females. (7.1.1)
2. In which activity do females typically outperform males? (7.1.1)
   A. Jumping
   B. Skipping
   C. Hopping
   D. Throwing
3. Having the ability to see close objects more clearly than those at a distance is called being _____. (7.1.2)
   A. farsighted
   B. perceptive
   C. nearsighted
   D. visually disabled
4. By which age will permanent teeth replace all 20 primary teeth? (7.1.2)
   A. 10
   B. 11
   C. 12
   D. 13
5. Each of these factors determine the effectiveness of a child's memory except _____. (7.1.3)
   A. age
   B. motivation
   C. attitude
   D. height
6. What is *rehearsal*? (7.1.3)
   A. The ability to arrange items in an increasing or decreasing order based on weight, volume, or size
   B. The repetition of information after it is used
   C. The manipulation of ideas based on logic rather than perception
   D. The ability to group objects by common attributes

Social-Emotional Development in Middle Childhood

Essential Question

How do social-emotional connections with others change during middle childhood? What factors contribute to these changes?

Learning Outcomes

After studying this lesson, you will be able to

7.2-1 **summarize** the characteristics of social-emotional development in middle childhood, including self-concept, understanding others, friendships, aggression, and peer group activities.

7.2-2 **analyze** the roles of peer-group activities in social-emotional and cognitive development during middle childhood.

7.2-3 **summarize** moral development during childhood.

Key Terms

social comparison	microaggression
self-esteem	bullying
compassion	moral development
physical aggression	morality
verbal aggression	internalize
relational aggression	

School-age children are growing in self-understanding. Their self-concept is forming, which affects their self-esteem. They are experiencing many new emotions and becoming more aware of the feelings of others.

Social relationships become more complex during middle childhood. By choice, children in this stage are spending less time with their parents and more time with peers. Friendships

are becoming more important. The family, however, still plays a significant role in supporting the child's development.

7.2-1 Social-Emotional Development

As children enter school, they start to take a closer look at the world around them. They begin to make social comparisons. **Social comparison** is a process in which people define themselves in terms of the qualities, skills, and attributes they see in others. They identify personal strengths and weaknesses because of this comparison. A self-concept is formed. *Self-concept* is the view a person has of himself or herself. Though the child's self-concept has been forming since infancy, school-age children are more aware of who they are.

School-age children can describe their strengths and weaknesses in very concrete terms. To illustrate, Luis is seven years old. Recently, his teacher asked him to describe himself. He said, "My name is Luis. I am a boy, and I live in Breckenridge, Colorado. I am tall and have brown eyes and black hair. My hobbies are biking and skiing. I am good at them. I am not as good at using the computer. I swim at the recreation center with my friends. My friends like me. I try to be helpful to them. My teacher says that I am an excellent speller, so I help my friends with their spelling."

Luis's self-description refers to his sex, physical appearance, and some social comparisons. Luis, like other children his age, has extended the number of people he is looking to for information. During the preschool years, his references were primarily his family. Now his reference groups include classmates and teachers. The feedback he receives from these individuals influences his self-concept.

Self-Esteem

Self-esteem is the belief that you are worthwhile as a person. While preschool children usually have very high levels of self-esteem, this sometimes changes in middle childhood. To have healthy self-esteem, school-age children need to believe in themselves. By continually evaluating themselves, some children lose their confidence. Subtle messages echoed by adults and peers can promote or undermine self-esteem. Children's judgements of self-worth are based on:

- academic competence
- athletic competence
- physical appearance
- behavior
- social acceptance

As a teacher, you can play an important role in promoting children's self-esteem. A warm, nurturing attitude is important. Avoid making comparisons among children. By avoiding comparisons, you will be helping children develop confidence in their own abilities. Children will feel better about themselves (**Figure 7.9**).

Accomplishments need to be viewed in relation to a child's efforts and ability. In almost every classroom, at least one child has learned helplessness. These children think that, no matter how hard they try, they cannot be successful. You will spot them immediately. When faced with new experiences or challenges, they give up quickly. Before they attempt to try, they say "I don't know how" or "I can't do that."

Help children during middle childhood avoid feelings of helplessness. Encourage them to persist at hard tasks. Make them believe that with more effort, they can overcome failure. Say, "I know you can do this if you try harder." Likewise, celebrate when these children do succeed, even in small ways. Provide them with additional feedback on why they were successful.

Judy Herr

Figure 7.9   School-age children are becoming interested in taking music lessons and other creative activities. ***How might taking music lessons help improve a child's self-esteem?***

Understanding Others

With experience and maturity, school-age children make major advances in understanding others. They are developing *empathy*—the ability to understand the feelings of others. At the same time, they are feeling compassion toward others. **Compassion** is awareness of others' distress and wanting to help them.

School-age children focus more on others and less on themselves. They can describe another person's feelings and personality traits. Prior to this time, children used only physical descriptions of others. For example, when Ben was a preschooler, his grandmother asked him to describe his teacher. He said, "She has brown hair and brown eyes. She wears glasses, and she is pretty." When Ben's grandmother asked him to describe his teacher as an eight-year-old, the description went beyond physical traits. He said,

"He is really a happy person. He smiles a lot and says things like 'good job.' Sometimes he gets mad, like when Brian is being a jerk. Then he gets angry with him."

Ben has developed the ability to see another's viewpoint. His ability to imagine what his teacher was feeling or thinking is developing. This is an important developmental milestone. Getting along with others throughout life depends on being able to understand another person's point of view. Studies show that children with poor social skills have trouble identifying other people's thoughts and feelings.

Friendships

Friendships are valuable to a child's development. Friendships take on greater importance in the school-age years. During preschool, a friend was a convenient playmate who shared toys and activities. Preschool children may identify everyone in their class as a friend. With school-age children, choosing friends becomes a more selective process.

Friendships teach children how to communicate, cooperate, and commit emotionally. Friendships foster intellectual growth and provide emotional support and companionship. (Figure 7-10.) Without friendships, a child does not receive the important benefits of interacting with peers. This can be traumatic and lead to difficulties such as low self-esteem, the inability to develop social skills, and loneliness.

Aggression in Middle Childhood

Aggression can be observed when working with school-aged children. As early as kindergarten, patterns of aggression and bullying may emerge. *Aggression* is defined as hostile or violent attitudes toward another. It can be in the form of *physical, verbal, relational,* or *microaggression.* **Physical aggression** is physically harming another. Forms of physical aggression include kicking, slapping, pushing, and pulling hair. It can also include destroying another person's property. **Verbal aggression** is name calling, yelling, teasing, screaming, or swearing at another person.

Jose Luis Pelaez Inc/DigitalVision via Getty Images

Figure 7.10   School-age children are becoming more compassionate and aware of the feelings of others. *How have you observed compassion in school-age children?*

Relational or social aggression is defined as trying to harm the social relationships of another person. Examples include gossiping, spreading rumors, giving someone the silent treatment, or excluding them from social activities.

Microaggressions are disrespectful comments or actions that communicate a prejudice toward members of marginalized groups. Such groups include racial minorities, people with disabilities, or those of a different religion, gender, nationality, socioeconomic class, or citizenship. These comments, snubs, or insults take place in everyday conversations in the neighborhood, community, school, and in the play yard. Often, they are unconscious or unintentional and are communicated through comments, body language, or behaviors.

Disrespectful comments and actions are painful for children. No matter how subtle, there are consequences to discrimination. Microaggressions can cause a power imbalance by disregarding the child's identity. Cognitive and emotional reactions can result, impacting the child's ability to learn. Microaggressions can cause low self-esteem, mistrust of peers, feelings of exhaustion, inability to study, lack of participation, and a feeling of not belonging.

Bullying is another form of unwanted aggressive behavior. It involves using verbal and physical attacks that are directed to disturb another child. Making fun of someone's looks or speech is a common form. The children who bully lack skills in solving problems and managing their feelings. The target of the bullying typically appears weak and vulnerable.

7.2-2 Peer Group Activities

Peer group activities play an important role in the social and cognitive development of school-age children. Generally, they often consist of children who are of similar ages, attend the same school, and live close together. Socialization and productivity are important. They may join 4-H clubs, Big Brothers Big Sisters, Camp Fire, religious groups, or scouting organizations. Some are also involved in community service through such groups as K-Kids and Builders Clubs (part of Kiwanis) and the American Red Cross. Children

also may join team sports. Soccer, tag football, basketball, swimming, and hockey are some examples. In these groups, children learn how to cooperate with others to achieve goals, and they learn rules of group behavior.

Safety First

Preventing Sports Injuries

As children grow and develop their gross-motor skills, participation in team sports becomes more common. Along with such participation comes the potential for acute and chronic sports injuries. *Acute injuries* include fractures, strains, and sprains. *Chronic injuries* result from repetitive use and include tendinitis, stress fractures, and growth-plate injuries. The following includes some ways that parents, teachers, and care providers can help prevent pediatric sports injuries:

- learn about the types of injuries that can occur with specific sports;
- have children play a variety of sports to prevent overuse of certain body parts;
- learn the coach's philosophy about preventing sports injuries; and
- make sure children wear proper protective gear such as padding, helmets, and guards for shins, eyes, and mouth.

If children complain of pain during a sporting event, have them stop playing immediately. Have a medical professional check out the injury.

Games with Rules

Can you remember your middle childhood years? Chances are you were enjoying organized games with rules. Rules determine what roles children can play and their standards for conduct. If you were like most children, during recess you were playing hide-and-seek, four square, jacks, kick-the-can, and blind man's bluff. You probably played tag, jump rope, and hopscotch. You may have played basketball, football, soccer, and softball during physical education classes.

These games are important for children's social, emotional, physical, and cognitive development. They are a medium for developing negotiation skills and learning to cooperate.

Games also encourage children to take another person's perspective. From this, children learn why rules are important. Children often spend as much time working out the rules for a game as playing the game. These experiences help them develop their concepts of fairness and justice.

In recent decades, there has been a decrease in the amount of time children spend in child-organized games. More time is devoted to digital devices, video games, television, and adult-organized sports. As a result, some children may not as physically fit. In addition, they do not have as many opportunities to learn to follow rules.

Team Sports

With improvement in their physical skills, children enjoy taking part in team sports. Most experts agree the age to begin team sports is around six or seven. Soccer, swimming, gymnastics, football, softball, and basketball are common (**Figure 7.11**). Through participation in team sports, children often develop lifelong habits that contribute to a healthful lifestyle.

By participating in competitive sports, children benefit in many ways. These include

- building teamwork skills by working toward a common goal;
- learning to get along with their peers;
- engaging game strategies and other mental exercises;
- strengthening muscles and bones;
- engaging in activities that bring enjoyment; and
- forming a lifetime pattern for a healthful lifestyle.

There are also drawbacks to taking part in team sports. There is no safe sport. School-age children can acquire injuries. Bumps, bruises, and scrapes are common injuries. The most serious injuries are head and neck injuries, which usually result from playing football. To reduce injuries, children require instruction on the safe

MBI/Shutterstock.com

Figure 7.11   Friends tend to be of the same sex during middle childhood.

use of equipment. They also need to learn the importance of conditioning activities, such as stretching and warm-up exercises.

Critics of adult-organized team sports claim they resemble more work than play for children. Since the focus is often on winning, children may feel pressure from their peers, parents, and coaches to win at all costs. Because adults often control the game, children may not be developing decision-making and leadership skills.

7.2-3 Moral Development

Moral development is the process of acquiring the standards of behavior considered acceptable by a society. **Morality** involves understanding and using accepted rules of conduct when interacting with others. As children grow and develop, they **internalize** (or incorporate within themselves) standards of behavior. They learn the difference between right and wrong and understand how to make right choices.

Children learn moral awareness through playful learning and interacting with others (**Figure 7.12**). Social influence shapes their morality. Preschoolers begin to learn acceptable behavior through the use of rewards and negative consequences during social play. Some behaviors bring rewards, such as praise or attention. Children learn to repeat these behaviors. Variations in development may be due to experiences, individual differences, and cultural contexts.

Children in middle childhood are more aware of the world around them and more sensitive to the feelings of others. They become interested in equality, and they focus on the concept of equal shares as fairness. Cooperating and sharing with others is also important. As children develop more concern about others' needs, they want to help them. This desire influences their moral development as they internalize rules of conduct (**Figure 7.13**).

MBI/Shutterstock.com

Figure 7.12   School-age children enjoy participating in team sports. *What are from the pros and cons of children playing competitive sports?*

MBI/Shutterstock.com

Figure 7.13   Children during middle childhood internalize standards of behavior they learn from their parents and others. ***Give an example showing how children internalize standards.***

Lesson 7.2 Review

1. The belief that you are worthwhile as a person is called _____. (7.2.1)
   A. self-concept
   B. compassion
   C. social acceptance
   D. self-esteem
2. **True or False.** Bullying is unwanted aggressive behavior that involves using verbal and physical attacks to disturb another child. (7.2.1)

3. What is **not** a benefit of participating in team sports? (7.2.2)
   A. Develop leadership skills
   B. Strengthen muscles and bones
   C. Build teamwork skills
   D. Engage game strategies
4. What is one way children learn moral awareness? (7.2.3)
   A. Practicing fine motor skills
   B. Independent play
   C. Interacting with others
   D. Eating healthy snacks

Summary

Lesson 7.1

7.1-1 Physical development during middle childhood slows down. Gross-motor skills and fine-motor skills are improving.

7.1-2 Several chronic illnesses may surface during middle childhood.

7.1-2 Children's vision and hearing require regular checkups.

7.1-3 Cognitive development continues as children begin to think using logic and symbols. They can process and recall information more readily.

7.1-3 Memory improves and children's attention span increases.

7.1-3 Children gradually develop the mental operations of conservation, seriation, and classification.

Lesson 7.2

7.2-1 Self-esteem develops in important ways for school-age children.

7.2-1 Friendships and group activities take on greater importance.

7.2-1 School-age children are becoming more compassionate and understanding of people's feelings.

7.2-1 Bullying and other forms of aggression can be observed when working with school-age children.

7.2-2 Games with rules and team sports play an important role in the social-emotional development of school-age children.

7.2-3 Morality begins to develop during middle childhood as children internalize standards of behavior.

Vocabulary Activity

With a partner, choose two words from the *Key Terms* in each lesson to compare. Create a Venn diagram to compare your words and identify differences. Write one term under the left circle and the other term under the right. Where the circles overlap, write two to three characteristics the terms have in common. For each term, write a difference of the term for each characteristic in its respective outer circle.

Critical Thinking

1. **Analyze.** Arrange a visit to a local elementary school with a lunch program or a before- and after-school program for children. Analyze sample menus and calculate the number of proteins, carbohydrates, fats, vitamins, minerals, fiber, and calories in a typical meal. Does the meal contribute positively to the recommended daily allowances for children? What changes or modifications could you suggest to make the meal more healthful? Write a brief report of your findings.

2. **Make Inferences.** Consult a classroom teacher, physical education instructor, school nurse, dietitian, or social worker for suggestions on how to approach parents to discuss and find positive ways to promote physical health and fitness for their children. Write a sample of a tactful, professional, and informative dialog you might have with a parent to address a child's problem. Record possible parent reactions and your response to them.

3. **Draw Conclusions.** Conduct an online search for information about the effect of low socioeconomic status (SES) on a child's social and emotional development. For example, what research is available concerning aggression and depression in a child affected by SES? Draw conclusions about the challenges low SES in childhood presents to schools and communities. Create a database of information on available programs addressing this problem.

4. **Analyze.** School-age children learn moral behavior by interacting with others and through a system of rewards and negative consequences. In small groups, hold a discussion about what this means teachers should expect from school-age children. What does this mean for how teachers should educate children before the school-age years?

Core Skills

1. **Research and Writing.** Using print or online sources, research current statistics on the amount of time school-age children spend on sedentary activities such as playing video games, watching television, or using other digital devices. What is the recommended amount of time children should spend on active and passive activities to remain healthy and physically fit? Write a report of your findings. Read your report in class.
2. **Research.** Choose one of the chronic illnesses mentioned in this chapter and research it using reliable online or print resources. What are the common causes of this illness? What are the symptoms, and how severe can these symptoms be? What treatments are available for the illness and how do schools accommodate illness and treatment for students? After conducting your research, write a summary about what you have learned. Include a bibliography listing your sources.
3. **Math.** Visit an after-school program. Bring along 10 pennies and two balls of modeling clay or dough. Assess the ability of six- and seven-year-olds to conserve number and mass. Write a summary of your findings.
4. **Writing.** Visit an after-school program. Observe the children's social interactions and peer groups. Write a summary of what you observe.
5. **Speaking and Writing.** Interview a tutor or an educator with a tutoring center or service. Prepare a list of additional questions prior to the interview. Write your findings in a brief report.
6. **Research, Writing, and Speaking.** Conduct an online search for the following programs:

Action for Healthy Kids, Alliance for a Healthier Generation: Healthy Schools Program, CDC's Healthy Youth! Physical Activity, and Walking Works for Schools. Write a brief summary about each program. Include information about how the program encourages physical activity in schools. Present your findings to the class using presentation software.

7. **Technology.** As early as kindergarten some children experience bullying. In small groups, research programs that seek to combat or end bullying in schools. How do these programs seek to end bullying? What positive messages do they promote? What are the current statistics on bullying in schools? In your group, create an electronic presentation highlighting one anti-bullying program and describing its strategies and beliefs.
8. **CTE Career Readiness Practice.** One way to start solving a problem is to use *metaphors*—words or phrases that suggest a likeness or analogy to an object or idea. Presume you are a counselor or social worker whose primary responsibility is working with children who are struggling with aggression. You are not only teaching children how to interact and solve problems in acceptable ways, but also dealing with the emotional and social factors that accompany aggression or microaggression. For the terms *aggression* and/or *microaggression* think of as many metaphors as possible. In what ways do metaphors help you focus on the problem differently? How can this help lead to a solution?

Portfolio Project

Using print and online sources, search for resources on children's growth from ages six through twelve. Share your list in class. After viewing several resources from other students' lists, select those you feel are most useful. Compile a list of resources that could be distributed to families. Include a copy of your resource list in the school-age section of your portfolio.

Unit Two

Creating a Safe and Healthful Environment

Chapters

Your primary goal as an early childhood teacher is to keep children safe and healthy. Creating a safe, healthful, welcoming, valued, and inclusive environment requires careful planning and preparation.

As you read this unit, you will discover how to arrange the space in a center to promote safety, curiosity, the joy of learning, and fun. You will also learn criteria for choosing toys and equipment that will safely help meet your program goals.

This unit gives safety objectives to help you prevent accidents and illness. It also makes you aware of your responsibilities in detecting and reporting child abuse and neglect.

Guidelines for planning and serving nutritious meals and snacks are provided in this unit. Also, procedures are given for handling such medical emergencies as wounds, burns, and fevers.

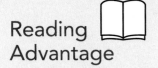
Preparing the Environment

Lesson 8.1: Space Planning for Early Childhood

Lesson 8.2: Organizing Early Childhood Spaces

Case Study

Preparing a Safe and Healthful Environment

Terry, who just graduated from college, was excited about sorting through the mail. The teaching contract from Menomonie's Early Learning Center had arrived for signature. Teaching at the newly constructed early learning center on the south side of town should be a wonderful experience. It pleased Terry to have an opportunity in Menomonie, as the local college had an excellent early childhood education program. This college would provide him an opportunity for advanced study.

The contract provided for 10 days of additional employment for arranging and setting up the classroom. Before opening day, Terry also needed to plan and provide an open house for the families and their children. The purpose was to have the children experience the environment prior to their first day of attendance.

Arriving on the first day, the center director told Terry all classroom furniture, equipment, and supplies had arrived. Everything had been inventoried, and it was already placed in the classroom. The director then introduced Terry to his colleagues, the other newly hired teachers and assistant teachers, the custodian, cook, and center administrative assistant. Overwhelmed, Terry returned to the classroom. What should be done first?

Give It Some Thought

1. What is the value of planned space?
2. How can Terry make the classroom environment attractive? What color choices are best for an early childhood classroom? Why?
3. What factors should influence space organization?
4. What are the basic activity areas of a classroom? How should they be arranged?

Opening image credit: miodrag ignjatovic/E+ via Getty Images

Essential Question

How can understanding the functions, furnishings, and color choices for early childhood classrooms help me determine effective arrangements that benefit children?

Learning Outcomes

After studying this lesson, you will be able to

8.1-1 **explain** the value of planned indoor and outdoor space.

8.1-2 **summarize** the areas of physical space in the center, along with the functions of each.

8.1-3 **analyze** criteria to consider when choosing playroom furniture.

8.1-4 **evaluate** factors to consider about color choices for early childhood centers.

Key Terms

isolation area	cubbies
staff room	cool colors
interactive whiteboard	warm colors
acoustic material	

Michiko is running. Sofia is hiding. No one saw Chang take the fish out of the bowl. There is no place for José to play with the blocks. The behavior of children in this classroom is affected by the classroom size, materials available, and the way the space is arranged.

In another classroom, the space is carefully organized. All the children are engaged in constructive play. The layout encourages active exploration, independent learning, and communication. It is an environment that reflects joy, curiosity, and learning that honors the children's cultural backgrounds. There are few, if any, behavior problems. Dakota is smiling. Noah is looking at books in a quiet corner of the classroom. At the same time, Wong and Marley are building a large block structure.

In a developmentally and culturally appropriate, well-planned environment, children grow and learn. The teacher is responsible for creating a pleasing environment where children and their families feel a sense of belonging. No one group should have privilege over another. The social identities, the strengths, needs, and interests of the children should shape the environment. The center design should promote self-help skills, independence, decision-making skills, joy of learning, and a sense of belonging. A nurturing, safe, and trusting environment is critical for children's social, emotional, physical, and cognitive development. (**Figure 8.1**).

8.1-1 Value of Planned Space

The early years are crucial for the cognitive development of children. It is essential to have sufficient floor space for children to move around furniture, equipment and their classmates. Check your state licensing standards. Most do not provide you with sufficient space for a high-quality program. A general rule of the thumb is that there should be a minimum of 50 square feet of usable play indoor space per preschool child. This figure does not include kitchens, closets, restrooms, built in cabinetry, staff areas, or entryways.

Before arranging a classroom, review the developmental objectives of the program. For example, toddlers do not have refined gross-

Jose Luis Stephens/Hemera/Thinkstock

Figure 8.1 Quality early childhood programs have ample space for children and teachers. ***Predict the consequences of too little space for children and teachers.***

motor skills. To promote safety and motor development, they need large, open spaces. They need to be able to find adults when they need them. It is important to plan classroom arrangements with these goals in mind.

An attractive, well-arranged classroom is welcoming and visually pleasing. The design conveys a sense of order and promotes children's learning individually, in small groups, and large groups. It encourages children to use materials and do things for themselves. It respects the children's

curiosity and nurtures a desire for exploring. It also molds their behavior. Predictable boundaries found in this type of classroom make the children more responsible. They know where to find classroom materials. They also know where to return them when they are finished.

Safety is an important concern in planning space. When children feel safe, they feel free to learn. Open spaces must be provided so adults can supervise the entire room. The ratio of caregivers to children also affects safety. If the number of caregivers is low, the room arrangement should be simple to make supervision easier.

The goals for a well-planned space include providing

- a physically safe environment for the children;

- children with areas that promote cognitive, emotional-social, and physical growth;

- an abundance of materials so children can make choices;

- adults with a space that is easy to supervise without blind spots;

- space that is pleasing to the eye for children, teachers, families, and volunteers;

Early Childhood Insight

The Influence of Space on Behavior

Studies show that the arrangement of space greatly affects teachers' behavior as well as children's behavior. In centers with well-planned space, teachers were more friendly, sensitive, and warm to children. These teachers taught their children to respect others' rights and feelings. In centers with poorly planned space, teachers were often less sensitive to their students.

- easy access to materials when needed so children can direct themselves (**Figure 8.2**); and
- a space with high activity and low stress where children can work, play, and interact comfortably.

8.1-2 Physical Space

The physical space of a center can be divided into seven main areas. These basic areas include the following:

- entrance
- director's office
- isolation area
- kitchen or kitchenette
- staff room
- restrooms
- preschool classroom
- infant-toddler room

Entrance

The exterior entrance to the center should convey a welcoming feeling and appeal to children

Olinchuk/Shutterstock.com

Figure 8.2 The infant-toddler classroom features low shelving units that allow children to choose and put away their own materials and equipment. *What areas of infant-toddler development are supported by having materials and equipment on low shelving?*

as well as adults (**Figure 8.3**). The entry area should ease the transition for the children to enter their playroom. It should also provide an area for families to interact. Plants, an aquarium, a display gallery of the children's artwork, and a bulletin board for families will enhance the appearance. The bulletin board may contain important parent information such as daily schedules, parent notices, and center events. The center's state licensing certificate should be framed and hung on the wall. If space permits, comfortable chairs and a sofa are welcome additions for families. These provide a place for parents to sit while waiting for a meeting with a staff person or the director. Often the entrance has a physical connection to the director's office, parents' resource area, and parents' storage area.

Parent storage can be located off the entrance. Addition of this feature is often occurs when planning a new facility or remodeling an existing center. The purpose of this area is for the storage of infant car seats and strollers. This area is particularly useful when one parent or caregiver drops the child off in the morning and someone else picks them up at the end of the day.

Director's Office

The director's office should be just inside the center's entrance in a visible location off the entrance. Storage for school records, children's records, and public relations material is typically in this location. Family interviews and conferences are another use for this office. Some directors also have a small table in their offices for teachers' meetings and planning sessions.

Isolation Area

Most states require centers to provide a special room or space for children who become ill or show signs of a communicable disease. Another name for this room is an **isolation area**, which contains a cot and a few toys. If the space is not available, a cot may be placed in the director's office when needed.

Kitchen

The size of a center's kitchen depends on the amount of daily food preparation. Even if meals

PhotoMavenStock/Shutterstock.com

Figure 8.3 This child care center has an entrance area that helps families feel welcome.

are not served, most centers have a small area with a sink, refrigerator, microwave, range with oven, and dishwasher for preparing snacks and cleaning dishes. Regardless of the kitchen's use, the local health department personnel should inspect it. They can tell you if the kitchen meets all legal requirements.

Floor coverings in the kitchen should be easy to clean. Vinyl coverings and ceramic tile are recommended floor coverings for the kitchen, restroom, and art area.

Workplace Connections

Security Measures for Early Childhood Centers

Security measures are essential for promoting the children's safety In early childhood centers. Every center should include the following:

- security cameras at the entrance;
- keyless entry pad for parents and staff;
- sign-in/sign-out to get an accurate accounting of the children in the building;
- a call station at the entrance allowing staff to communicate with delivery people, volunteers, or parents who may have forgotten the code; and

- a posted list of protocols to follow to prevent illness at the center.

1. Visit an early childhood center to observe their security measures.
2. Using the above information, create a checklist to use as you observe security measures at the center. Then, based on the information you observed, write a paragraph summarizing your opinion on the security of the center. Share your paragraph with the class.

Staff Room

Adults need an area to take a break from the children. This **staff room** should contain a locked storage space for personal belongings. A coatrack, sofa, and tables or desks should also be available. Most staff members prefer having secured storage for personal belongings. They also need access to a computer, professional journals, file space, and curriculum guides. Uses for this include planning or preparing materials or meeting with families or other staff members. Privacy is also important for the staff area.

Some centers and states have cell phone policies. Staff may *only* use personal cell phones in the staff room during break for telephone calls, text messages, or using the internet. This prevents a teacher from being distracted on the playground or in the classroom. Moreover, answering a telephone or responding to a text poses a safety threat. It also removes a teacher from the ratio needed for proper supervision.

Restrooms

Most states have laws requiring a certain number of toilets and sinks for a group of young children. Some states require at least one child-sized toilet for every 10 children; however, a higher ratio is more desirable. There are many times during the day when several children may have to use the restroom at the same time.

The size of the toilet fixture will vary with the size and age of the children. Check your state licensing requirement. Usually, group of two-year-old children would be comfortable with toilet fixtures 10 inches from the floor. Five-year-old children would find 13-inch toilet fixtures more comfortable.

If small toilets are unavailable, check early childhood catalogs. You can purchase sturdy toilet step stools for smaller children. There are also step stools available to use in front of the sinks that are too high for children to reach. Typically, sinks are not child specific, but sinks can be installed at child-appropriate heights.

For safety purposes, the water heater that supplies water to the children's restroom should be set on low heat. Restroom flooring should be easy to clean. Tile is recommended, but should not be slippery. For safety purposes, avoid having wax applied to the flooring in this area.

Indoor Environment

The classroom or playroom should be on the ground floor close to an exit. A rectangular room is the best shape because it allows for optimal supervision. This shape also allows for many more space arrangements than other shapes.

Studies show that aggression increases in programs that lack adequate space. Quality early childhood centers need to have enough space for children, furniture, and a variety of materials and equipment. The recommended amount of space varies from state to state. It can range from 35 to 100 square feet of indoor space per child. This amount should not include hallways or space taken up by equipment, built-in cabinets, diaper stations, closets, or toileting areas.

Walls

All walls should be painted with lead-free, washable paint. Many teachers like bulletin boards attached to the walls. This provides space to hang artwork and papers, as well as absorb sound (**Figure 8.4**).

An **interactive whiteboard**—a touch-sensitive board connected to a computer and projector—is common technology in preschool and kindergarten classrooms (**Figure 8.4**). Install whiteboards at either floor level or low on a wall to allow children to easily view the board. Integrating whiteboards in the classroom is a strategy for facilitating new skills and ideas. They are excellent for gathering children around a common activity and engaging them in meaningful learning. Whiteboards, which come with software, are useful in teaching in all content areas. Mathematical content such as shapes, measurements, and numbers are one example. This interactive process allows children to move objects on the board.

Floors

A recent trend for playroom floor coverings has been carpeting. Carpeting and carpet tiles are easy to maintain, add warmth, and provide a sound cushion for noise control. Carpeting can

Uses for an Interactive Whiteboard

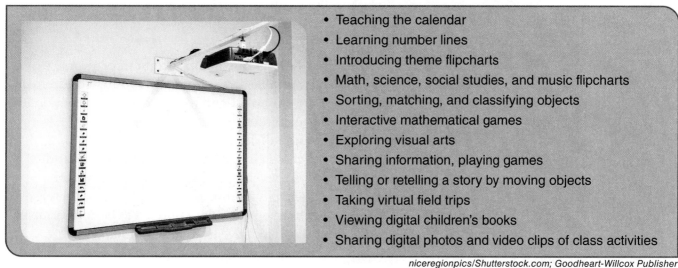

- Teaching the calendar
- Learning number lines
- Introducing theme flipcharts
- Math, science, social studies, and music flipcharts
- Sorting, matching, and classifying objects
- Interactive mathematical games
- Exploring visual arts
- Sharing information, playing games
- Telling or retelling a story by moving objects
- Taking virtual field trips
- Viewing digital children's books
- Sharing digital photos and video clips of class activities

niceregionpics/Shutterstock.com; Goodheart-Willcox Publisher

Figure 8.4 Interactive whiteboards allow science and social studies lessons to come alive for children and are a welcome addition to any classroom.

Ethical Responsibilities ⚖

Creating a Positive Environment

An ethical responsibility for early childhood professionals is to build a positive social and emotional environment that nurtures children. The foundation of this type of environment is a caring, trusting relationship with children that supports their needs. An essential need for children is to feel secure and to be able to trust those who teach and care for them.

Dig deeper

What does a caring social-emotional environment look like to you? What does an early childhood professional need to learn about the children with whom they work? What actions do they need to take to ensure an environment is supportive and nurturing? Write a reflective paper creating a word picture of what a positive social-emotional environment for children looks like for children and their teachers and caregivers.

also add visual appeal, comfort, and softness to a room. Use a tightly woven carpet that has a flat, firm surface. This will minimize balance problems for children while stacking blocks. Some centers have tile on the floor in the art,

water play, and eating areas, which is easy to clean and maintain. Restrooms typically have tile floors.

Windows

The location and placement of windows in the playroom should allow children to view the outdoors. Screens should be installed outside all windows, and all windows must open in case of fire.

Use drapes or blinds to help control light, and add interest, softness, and color to a room. Drapes or blinds also reduce glare, heating bills, and noise. One disadvantage of drapes is that they become easily soiled when children brush by them with dirty hands.

For a different effect, you might wish to hang a valance above each window. This can be a nice addition to a classroom if the colors complement the decor. Valances and drapes create softness and absorb sound. If you use valances instead of drapes, also use miniblinds or pleated shades to reduce glare.

Doors

Doors should be lightweight. Glass doors should utilize safety glass (**Figure 8.5**). To guard against injury, the doors should push out to open.

Courtesy of the UW-Stout Child and Family Study Center

Figure 8.5   Doors with glass panels provide a place for posting.

Doorknobs should be low enough so children can reach them. Install pinch guards on all doors to protect children's fingers and help avoid needless injuries.

Acoustics

Studies show that noise affects children's behavior. For this reason, use materials that reduce or eliminate noise.

Acoustic material deadens or absorbs sounds. Carpets, drapes, bulletin boards, pillows, stuffed toys, and sand are examples. The physical makeup of these materials helps them reduce or eliminate noise. For instance, carpeting will absorb the sound of footsteps.

If the classroom is still noisy after the addition of draperies, carpeting, and bulletin boards, consider installing acoustical tile on the classroom ceiling. If possible, the ceiling should

be a minimum of 10 to 12 feet high to reduce noise and provide a feeling of spaciousness.

Temperature

Temperature is important in planning a comfortable environment for young children. They cannot attend to or process information in an uncomfortable environment.

Usually, a temperature range of 68 to 70 degrees Fahrenheit will be comfortable and helps prevent the spread of disease. When planning vigorous physical activities, decrease the temperature. For children to be comfortable, adults may have to wear a sweater.

Humidity

Humidity, like temperature, influences the comfort of the environment. Usually, a 30 to 50 percent relative humidity range is comfortable for most people. As the temperature rises, decrease the relative humidity to maintain comfort.

Electrical Outlets

For safety purposes, electrical outlets should be above the children's reach. When outlets are not in use, insert safety caps to protect children. Many times, the location of electrical outlets influences room arrangements. For example, the music area might be located near an outlet to allow use of an audio system. For the safety of the children and staff, do not use long electrical cords. These can cause someone to trip or fall. Because of this danger, many states ban the use of long extension cords in the classroom.

8.1-3 Furniture

Furniture and cribs for classroom use should utilize strong, durable, and easy-to-clean materials. (**Figure 8.6**). Purchase tables that are the appropriate height for the children. Easels should be adjustable to fit each child who may use them. To check if an easel is the proper height, have the child stand next to it. Ask the child to touch the middle of the easel pad. If the child must bend or reach to touch the middle of the pad, adjust the easel.

soul_studion/Shutterstock.com

Figure 8.6   Furnishings should be durable and easy to clean. *What types of products can be safely used to clean furnishings in early childhood classroom? Use online resources to investigate.*

Workplace Connections

Storage in Early Childhood Centers

Survey the storage units in an early childhood center. Evaluate the types of units used.

1. Is the unit in good repair? Are there any safety hazards present?
2. Are there any classroom areas that need more storage? What type of additional storage units might be added? Check equipment and storage websites and catalogs for ideas.

Check chair and table heights in a different manner. Ask a child to sit on a chair and then push it under the table. If the table and chair are suited to the child, there will be room between the bottom of the table and the child's knees. The child should be able to place his or her feet flat on the floor.

Chairs

Children's chairs are often used in the art, dramatic play, and dining areas. Chairs should always be the proper height for the children. Most teachers prefer stackable chairs. The chairs should be light enough to move. They should have a tough finish and not require refinishing. Place an adult-sized rocking chair in the library or dramatic play area that children may use. Adults may also use this chair as a special place to hold or comfort a child.

Tables

Classroom tables should be hard, smooth, and washable. Tables should be light enough to move. Most preschool teachers prefer tables that are large enough to seat four to six children. Rectangular tables are often preferred over round tables. The rectangular shape allows children to have their own space, reducing the chance for aggression. To add interest to the classroom, consider using low, round tables in the library and dramatic play area.

Storage Units

Organize storage units for easy access of equipment and supplies to cultivate independence and self-regulation. Keep blocks, books, art supplies, games, and other classroom materials in storage units. Arrange these units to encourage children to independently remove and return materials. When children can reach it, they can use it. For flexibility, all storage units should have casters to move them easily. The casters should be equipped with locks so they do not move accidentally. For units without casters, hardware can be bought and easily installed. Keep in mind that you can attach pegboard or corkboard to exposed sides and backs of storage units to serve as bulletin boards.

Storage units should match the height of the children. The children must be able to reach the materials. Therefore, choose small, lightweight sections of cabinets.

If doors storage units need doors, sliding doors are best. When opened, swinging doors can cause safety hazards.

Lockers and Cubbies

Children can learn responsibility for their own belongings when they are provided personal storage space. Each child enrolled in the program should have a locker (**Figure 8.7**). Label lockers with a photograph, printed name tag, or other visual clue, depending on the age of the child.

Courtesy of the UW-Stout Child and Family Study Center

Figure 8.7   Use symbols or pictures on lockers and cubbies to help young children identify their space. *What do children learn from having personal storage space?*

Most lockers for preschool children are 10 to 12 inches wide and 10 to 15 inches deep. Each locker should contain a hook for hanging a coat.

The primary purpose of lockers is to store children's clothing. Finished artwork, library books, parent letters, and other valuable items also require storage. Many lockers have a top section for storage of these items. These are often called **cubbies**. If the lockers do not have cubbies, containers can be stacked to store the children's belongings (**Figure 8.8**).

Lockers and cubbies should have a protective coat of varnish or polyurethane. This coating will help prevent staining from muddy boots or wet paints. Locate lockers near the center entrance. This will save families time when dropping off and picking up children. It will save the class from disruptions when children must go to their lockers.

8.1-4 Color Choices for Early Childhood Centers

An attractive environment contributes to a child's well-being and appeals to the senses. The use of color can affect how children, teachers, and families feel about their classroom. Colors can help calm or stimulate young children. Because of the emotional effects of color, select colors carefully. The goal should be to create a room that looks pleasant and feels spacious. You can accomplish this by using **cool colors**, such as lighter shades of blue or green. Cool colors make a room appear larger. They create a feeling of openness. **Warm colors** make a room seem smaller. These colors include red, yellow, and orange. Studies show that children prefer warm

Courtesy of the UW-Stout Child and Family Study Center

Figure 8.8   Photographs help younger children identify their container.

colors until about age six. After the age of six, they start to prefer cool colors.

Other factors affect color selection. These include the amount of available light in the room and the amount of time spent in the room. For example, if the room does not have much light available, a warm color will help the room appear brighter.

Pay close attention to color. Many early childhood administrators and teachers feel color should be used with restraint (**Figure 8.9**). Early childhood centers are active places and contain many colorful materials, including toys, bulletin boards, posters, and clothing in the cubbies. To avoid overstimulation, off-white is often used for classroom walls. To avoid an institutionalized look, ceiling and flooring should not be white.

Children respond well to off-white. This color promotes positive feelings and is optimal for learning. The perception is that off-white rooms are clean and cool. White is also an excellent color for the eating, isolation, administration, and reading areas. It is also a good color for the restroom.

Light blue is sometimes used in child center classrooms. Children respond to this color by feeling comfortable, soothed, and secure. Therefore, the napping, reading, eating, and isolation areas often use light blue.

miodrag ignjatovic/E+ via Getty Images

Figure 8.9   This classroom has a neutral palette. *Why is it important to consider the effects of color on children when purchasing furnishings and equipment?*

Light green, like light blue and white, creates a positive response. It makes children feel calm, refreshed, peaceful, and restful. It is useful for isolation, napping, reading, and eating areas.

Yellow makes people feel happy, energetic, and cheerful. This uplifting color creates a sense of joy and optimism. It is a good color in art and music areas since it encourages creativity. Playground equipment sometimes is painted yellow or has yellow accents.

Lesson 8.1 Review

1. Why should open spaces be provided in a classroom? (8.1.1)
   A. The children need space to play.
   B. The adults need to be able to supervise the entire room.
   C. There needs to be more space for toys.
   D. The children need space to run.
2. **True or False.** The purpose of an isolation area is to store important children's records and public relations materials. (8.1.2)
3. Which table shape allows children to have their own space? (8.1.3)
   A. Round
   B. Triangular
   C. Rectangular
   D. Square
4. Which color promotes the feeling of being comfortable, soothed, and secure? (8.1.4)
   A. Light blue
   B. Off-white
   C. Light green
   D. Yellow

Essential Question

What factors do I need to know to arrange and organize indoor and outdoor play areas to foster creativity, safety, and diversity for children?

Learning Outcomes

After studying this lesson, you will be able to

8.2-1 **integrate** factors that affect the organization of indoor space in a center.

8.2-2 **summarize** the basic organization of activity areas and the arrangement of activity areas in the space.

8.2-3 **integrate** factors that affect the organization of outdoor space for a center.

Key Terms

traffic pattern
sensory table
guardrail
accessibility
aesthetic

unitary surfacing materials
loose-fill impact-absorbing materials
stationary equipment

Classroom arrangement reflects program quality. It also provides clues about expected behavior. A well-planned setting usually promotes knowledge across all content areas. The materials need to promote interesting play, provide children with choices, and reduce behavior problems. It should encourage social interaction with other children and adults, as well as active exploration. The children's developmental needs, strengths, interests, experiences, and program goals form the basis for a well-planned space. The classroom should also be attractive, inviting, and provide the children a sense of pride.

Children need space to build, move, sort, create, pretend, spread out, work, and interact with friends. They need diverse and interesting materials in sufficient quantities to keep them actively involved. They need a place to be quiet, be active, talk, and move. Space affects the activity level of children. The space also affects the choices children make and the way they carry out their choices. Space can even affect the children's concentration and the length of time they will remain with one activity. Therefore, space arrangements should appeal to the children's strengths, interests and emerging abilities; however, the space should be pleasing, comfortable and convenient for the staff, parents, and volunteers.

8.2-1 Factors That Affect Space Organization

An organized classroom can inspire children to take part in the activities of the day. Arrange the space to define the scope and limits of activities. Space will also affect the children's use and care of materials. Therefore, the space must provide for proper learning experiences.

When planning classroom space, you will need to consider many factors. These include licensing requirements, program goals, group size, ages of children, scale, and traffic patterns. These factors will greatly affect how the classroom is organized.

Licensing Requirements

All states, Native American Tribes and Tribal Organizations, and even some cities, have their own licensing requirements for early childhood centers. You will need to know your state's requirements before you begin planning classroom space. Requirements vary from state to state, although some common requirements exist. For example, they all require a minimum number of fire extinguishers, clear exits, and entrance doors that open to the outside. In addition, a minimum number of square feet of space must be available for each child.

Program Goals

The children's strengths, developmental ages, and interests are the basis of the program's goals. The goals a teacher selects should represent the major stages of development and growth. The environment, as well as planned classroom activities, should stimulate growth and development.

Early childhood caregivers and teachers concerned with all developmental areas might select the following program goals to promote:

- a positive self-concept
- independence
- problem-solving skills
- fine-motor coordination
- gross-motor coordination
- development of executive-function skills
- language and literacy skills
- prosocial behavior
- social justice
- an appreciation of cultural diversity and equity

After listing the goals for the children, review each goal. Decide how the classroom environment will support each goal. For instance, most teachers set a goal to develop independence in children. The arrangement of the room can help children achieve this goal. Materials, locker hooks, and shelving units should all be within easy reach for the children. This will encourage children to act without help from adults in many cases. **Figure 8.10** lists several ways to meet various program goals.

Program goals should also reflect state licensing requirements. Therefore, if the state requires that children receive one meal and two snacks each day, a program goal might state that children receive nutritious meals and snacks. Some states even specify how many toys are needed in the classroom.

Group Size

Group size is an important factor to consider when arranging space. It is an indicator of program quality. The viable space, ages of the children, and the number of caregivers all help determine the group size. Many children crowded into a small area will cause problems. Children are likely to feel stressed and engage in negative behavior when crowded. Likewise, a small number of children with too much space will also cause stress. Too much open space encourages children to run. You must strive to create an arrangement that will be the proper size for the group.

The more children there are in the group, the more space is needed. A good rule of thumb is to plan open space for one-third to one-half of the classroom. Additionally, the room arrangement needs to be simple. Children will feel safe and secure in this arrangement.

Arrange shelving units and other furniture with group size in mind. A good arrangement allows teachers and children to move easily through the room. It also allows for teachers to see children and children to see them easily. This will promote a relaxed setting.

Scale

The classroom environment must be in scale with the size of its occupants. Purchasing child-sized furniture is critical. Installing bulletin boards, toilets, water fountains, sinks, pictures, and other items at the children's level is important. One method to judge if the setting is in scale for children is for an adult to walk on his or her knees through the entire classroom.

How Goals Are Supported by the Environment

Goal	How Goals Are Supported by Environment
To promote independence	• Similar materials are stored together. • Drawers, shelves, and containers are labeled with outlines of contents. • Materials and equipment are easily accessible to children. • Coat hooks are low enough for children to hang their own clothing. • Individual storage is provided for each child. • Toilets and sinks are child-sized.
To promote a positive self-concept	• Equipment is developmentally appropriate. • Children's work is displayed. • Unstructured materials are available in each area. • A variety of materials are available for children to choose.
To promote problem-solving skills	• Equipment is developmentally appropriate. • Open-ended materials, such as blocks, are available. • A variety of materials are available for children to choose. • Materials are added and rotated to create interest.
To promote fine-motor coordination	• A classroom area is devoted to manipulative equipment. • Enough material to maintain children's interest is available. • Materials are easily accessible to children. • Materials are changed frequently to create interest.
To promote gross-motor development	• A classroom area is devoted to gross-motor activities. • An adequate amount of space is provided to encourage play. • The traffic flow does not interfere with the children's use of materials. • The area is located away from quiet activities.
To promote self-control	• Enough space is provided for children to use materials in each classroom area. • The classroom traffic flow permits children to work without interruption. • Noisy areas are located away from quiet areas. • Sufficient variety and quantity of materials are available in each area.
To promote language and literacy skills	• A book display space is placed at children's eye level. • Classroom materials are labeled. • A wide variety of multi-cultural materials, including books, puppets, and music are available.
To promote social skills	• Boundaries between areas are defined with low shelving units. • A sufficient number of materials are available to encourage cooperative play. • The area is set up to attract small groups of children.
To promote an appreciation of cultural diversity	• Dolls, puppets, puzzles, picture books, posters, and bulletin board figures represent various cultural groups. • Music and musical instruments reflect various cultural groups.

Figure 8.10   The program goals for an early childhood center guide the room arrangement and the materials in each area to support the development of children.

Anything positioned too high for the children should be noted and adjusted.

Traffic Patterns

The arrangement of a classroom centers around the **traffic patterns**, sometimes called *pathways*. This is the pattern children follow to move between areas in the classroom. It is important to arrange furniture to create a useful traffic pattern. For instance, children should be able to walk from the art area to the block-building area without going through the middle of the library area.

Program activities will affect traffic patterns. For example, most early childhood programs provide breakfast, snacks, and lunch. These meals may be prepared on-site or contracted. Some states do not allow food to be prepared off-site and delivered to the center. Whichever plan the program uses, the food will likely be made in or delivered to a kitchen. For this reason, the kitchen should be near a delivery door, which should be close to the eating area.

8.2-2 Organizing Basic Activity Areas

Classrooms arranged according to activity areas provide an ideal environment for active learning. Each activity area should clearly convey to the children what those choices are. For example, the art area should have an easel and art supplies. By displaying these materials in an inviting manner, the children will be aware of what is available to them. This gives them the chance to make their own choices.

Each activity area is a space of its own, and each area supports the program goals. Each area should be well defined, but the space should be flexible. Shelves placed in *U* or *L* shapes can create boundaries for classroom areas. When the shape of the space requires change, you can easily move the shelves.

Arrange activity areas by function. Think carefully of each area as wet or dry, active, or quiet (**Figure 8.11**). Place wet and dry activities far away from each other. Sensory and science

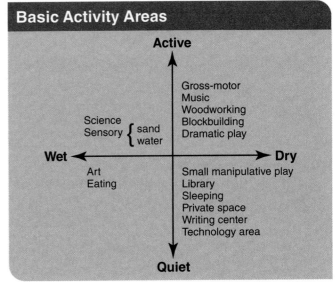

Goodheart-Willcox Publisher

Figure 8.11   The basic activity areas of an early childhood center are identified as active or quiet and wet or dry. *How can identifying activities as active or quiet or wet or dry help teachers plan the arrangement of a classroom in an early childhood center?*

activities are examples of wet/active activities. Art, eating, and cooking are types of wet/quiet activities.

Active activities should take place far from quiet activities. Woodworking, block building, music, and dramatic play are all active activities. Each of these could disrupt a quiet activity. Sleeping, reading, and small manipulative play are all examples of quiet/dry activities.

Most teachers prefer to map out two or three possible room arrangements. This helps them see what will work best and why. **Figure 8.12** shows some room arrangement principles.

Remember that rather than being static, room arrangements must be flexible. Rearranging the classroom areas is necessary when the children's strengths, interests, or developmental needs change. With changing interests, caregivers and teachers need to consider the addition and elimination of equipment and materials.

Some programs use the term *learning centers* instead of *activity areas*. This term, however, seems to imply that the children only learn in centers. On the contrary, learning takes place inside and outside of the center.

Principles of Room Arrangement

Whenever possible, arrange areas around the edges of the room. This allows the center of the room to be used for traffic flow.

Arrange shelving units so the teacher can clearly view the entire room.

Store objects together that are used for the same activities.

Place the art area near a water source and near windows for natural lighting.

Place quiet activities far away from active activities and traffic areas.

Place tables in art and manipulative areas.

Place dry activities far from wet activities.

Provide open space for blockbuilding and group activities.

Define areas by arranging storage units into *U* or *L* shapes.

Provide private spaces where children can be alone or with one or two children.

Figure 8.12   Following these principles of room arrangement can help you create flexible room arrangements.

Introducing Activity Areas

Children require an introduction to the activity areas in the classroom. They need to learn what

Workplace Connections

Diagraming Room Arrangements

Review the Principles of Room Arrangement in Figure 8.12. Visit a child care center classroom or survey a preschool classroom. Diagram or photograph the room's arrangement.
1. Determine if the principles are used in the room arrangement.
2. Discuss how effective the arrangement is in meeting the principles. Can a child who uses a wheelchair or walker easily navigate the space? Offer suggestions for any alterations that would provide for more efficiency in the classroom.

materials are in each area and what activities take place in that area. They also need to learn the safety and cleanup rules of the area. In programs that operate for nine-month sessions, introduce the children to the areas at the start of the session. In programs that operate throughout the year, introduce children to each area when they first enroll in the program. Older children who have been attending the program for a time may help the teacher introduce the areas to new students.

Children need to learn the routine for using and replacing materials. Carefully arranging materials will enable the children to help maintain the learning environment. To help children feel comfortable in using and moving about the areas, use labels, photos, and signs to direct children's attention (**Figure 8.13**). This then helps children become self-directed learners. Labels and signs also encourage children to return materials to storage areas. They can be taped to the storage areas to serve as reminders.

Block-Building Area

Blocks give children practice sorting, grouping, comparing, arranging, making decisions, hypothesizing, cooperating, and role-playing. Therefore, this area should be well-equipped and well-defined (**Figure 8.14**).

The best location for block building should be on a carpeted area. Carpeting helps by reducing

Goodheart-Willcox Publisher

Figure 8.13 With the help of labels and signs, children will learn to move around their environment easily.

PhotoMavenStock/Shutterstock.com

Figure 8.14 Block-building areas are very popular. Make sure this area is well equipped and spacious. *How do labels on shelving help children?*

the noise level. Define the area with low cabinets. Allow enough room for building. Children will need room to build structures that go around, up, and out.

To stimulate play, provide items other than blocks in the block-building area. Examples include plastic zoo and farm animals, people representing different cultures, traffic signs, wheeled toys, pulleys, and boxes.

Use low cabinets to define the area for storage of materials. Make sure there are enough shelves

to arrange the blocks according to shape. Place all block-building materials at the children's eye level and within their reach.

Place large, heavy blocks (and other heavy materials) on a bottom shelf or on the floor to avoid accidents. Save higher shelves for lightweight items. Label each shelf with the shape of the block that can be found there. Labels help children return the blocks to the correct shelf. Labels also provide matching practice and reduce cleanup time.

Art Area

Place the art area where there is access to a water source and good lighting. Arrange the space so groups or individuals can use the area. Use tables, chairs, easels, drying racks, and shelving units that are easy to clean and maintain. If possible, the floor covering should be tile to allow for easy clean-up. Label the shelves with the materials found there.

Dramatic Play Area

The dramatic play area may also be called the home living or housekeeping area. For younger children, arrange this area to look like a real home. A range, refrigerator, table, chairs, sink, and doll bed are basic furniture you may wish to provide. Some centers even include child-sized sofas.

You may wish to provide other props, such as dolls, kitchen utensils, cleaning tools, costumes, and dress-up clothes. For older children, other props may be added to help them investigate their world. For example, the area could be set up as a hair salon, bakery, fast-food restaurant, florist, or post office.

Sensory Area

The key piece of equipment in the sensory area is the **sensory table**, also known as a water or sand table. It can be purchased with a cover so it can be used for other purposes. The size of the table will depend on the amount of space available and depend on the age of the children. Two- and three-year-old children love the sensory appeal of water and sand. They usually enjoy pouring and scooping. A sensory table can give the children practice interacting with others.

Not all centers have sensory tables. Some centers use plastic wading pools or washtubs. Whatever container the center uses, locate it near a water source. Children and teachers enjoy adding water to the sand to change the feeling.

You can use other items in the sensory table, too. (Figure 8.15) Provide rustproof spoons, shovels, sand pails, measuring cups, funnels, tubes, strainers, and other kitchen items. Place shelving units near or under the table for storage. Items can also be stored in plastic buckets or laundry baskets.

Woodworking Area

After building wood sculptures, many children enjoy decorating them with paint. For that reason, locate the woodworking area near the art area (Figure 8.16). For the children's safety, place this area outside the line of traffic.

Items you may wish to provide at the woodworking bench include safety goggles, tools, wood scraps, and Styrofoam pieces. Hang a pegboard next to the woodworking bench, within children's reach. Use it to hang tools. To encourage the return of tools, paint outlines of the

Natalia Lebedinskaia/Shutterstock.com

Figure 8.15 This sensory table has extra built-in features to increase the children's enjoyment. *What materials and equipment might be used in a sensory table? Check the guidelines for your state.*

PIKSEL/iStock via Getty Images Plus

Figure 8.16 The woodworking table can hold the attention of children for extended time periods. *What safety materials should you provide for children in the woodworking area?*

tools on the pegboard. The children can replace tools by matching them with outlined shapes.

Sleeping Area

Most preschool children rest or nap after lunch. In fact, the licensing rules and regulations of most states require that children under age five rest or nap. Not all programs, however, have separate sleeping areas. For those that do not, a flexible room arrangement is key. Such an arrangement allows you to quickly and quietly alter the area during or immediately after lunchtime into a sleeping area. Allow sufficient space for sleeping. Some states require that two feet of open space exist between cots. Check your state's regulations.

Small Manipulatives and Mathematics Area

The small-manipulatives, or fine-motor, area should be in a dry, quiet area of the playroom. Table blocks, puzzles, plastic building pieces, parquetry blocks, stringing beads, lotto boards, sewing cards, and color cubes with pattern cards are some items you may wish to provide. These materials should represent various levels of difficulty. Many teachers also include math materials and equipment in this area. A table, chairs, and shelving unit are also useful in this area.

Literacy and Library Area

The literacy area should be in the quietest part of the classroom. Often this is next to the manipulative area. Choose colorful books, posters, and pictures that represent various cultural groups. In addition to providing books and magazines, you will want to promote language arts. For example, paper, pens, pencils, and washable felt-tip markers encourage writing skills. Shelving units, a table, and chairs are all useful in this area. Display books standing up with their covers showing (**Figure 8.17**). This allows easy access for the children. They will more likely choose a book to look at if they can see the cover. For comfort, pillows and beanbag chairs may also be part of the area. Many centers also carpet this area or add an area rug. Some children enjoy being on the floor to read.

Music Area

Culturally diverse rhythm instruments, puppets, and scarves, along with media players and audio systems are typical items in almost all music areas. The materials should encourage the children to experiment with sound, melodies, and rhythm. When space permits, some centers have a piano. For other centers, an autoharp or guitar is an option. The music area should also allow for movement, including creative dancing.

globalmoments/iStock via Getty Images Plus

Figure 8.17 Display books at the children's eye level in the library area. ***What is a benefit of displaying books at eye level for children?***

Private Area

Provide a private area in the classroom where children can go when they need time to themselves. This allows them the option of limiting contact with others when they choose. This reduces the pressure of being around others when they wish to be alone and promotes self-regulation. Set a classroom rule stating that children who go to the quiet space will not be disturbed by others.

Lofts are a unique way to provide private space and enhance the environment. Lofts designed with a platform higher above the floor can provide a play space or storage.

In programs where a wooden loft is not in the budget, large cardboard boxes and wooden crates can be used to create private spaces for children.

The private space should be small, allowing room for only one or two children at a time. The children in the private space should not be visible to other children in the room; however, the teacher must be able to see into the private space.

Science and Discovery Area

Place the science and discovery area in the wet, active area of the classroom. Most science areas contain at least one table where children can investigate materials using magnifiers and scales. Rocks, shells, leaves, plants, insects, and bones can all be part of this center along with a shelving unit. Small caged pets and project materials may also be located in the science area of the classroom. Check your state's rules and regulations to determine whether small pets are allowed in classrooms. Place science related books in this area. They can be story or informational books. If possible, place this area near a light and water source for growing plants.

Technology Area

The technology area should be in the quiet, dry part of the classroom to encourage digital play and interaction. A technology area might include a small area with tablets, computers, cameras, handheld devices, and a printer. Electrical outlets are a requirement for computers and printers.

Where you place the computer affects how often children will use it. Keep the monitors visible throughout the classroom. This placement increases children's curiosity about digital devices and encourages children to interact. It also helps the teacher supervise from anywhere in the classroom. Install software so it is easy for children to access on their own.

Finally, choose computer furniture designed for young children. Injuries or strains can occur if children must adjust their bodies to reach the mouse or keyboard from adult furniture. Position the top of the work surface two inches below the children's elbows. When seated, children should be able to see the center of the monitor by looking directly ahead. Having a few extra chairs in the area encourages the children to use the computers together. This allows children to explore and improve their social and language skills.

Eating Area

When space is available, provide a separate eating area. This area could also serve as a special interest area for cooking activities. It should be located near the kitchen and allow for easy service and cleanup.

If space is limited, have children sit at tables in other areas of the classroom. You will need to arrange the daily schedule to allow for this.

Figure 8.18 summarizes each classroom area and the furniture, materials, and equipment you may wish to supply in each. In each of the activity areas, include culturally diverse materials and artifacts whenever possible. Be sure to include such items such as artwork, fabric, jewelry, tools, utensils, toys, and children's books.

Materials and Equipment for Activity Areas

Classroom Area	Furniture	Materials and Equipment
Block building	labeled shelving units	large hollow blocks; solid unit blocks; wheeled toys: cars, buses, trucks, fire engines, tractors, planes; boats; traffic signs; small toy people of various ethnic backgrounds; community helpers; small, colored wooden blocks; zoo animals; farm animals; sea life, forest animals, dinosaurs
Art	adjustable easels shelving unit tables and chairs drying rack	clay, pencils, crayons, colored chalk, washable ink markers, paper, tempera paint, scrap paper and fabrics, tape, glue, paste, brushes, scissors, painting smocks, play dough rolling pins, cookie cutters, chalkboards, manilla paper, crepe paper, rubber cement, easel brushes
Dramatic Play	child-sized refrigerator, stove, sink, cupboard, and doll bed trunk or tree to hold clothes tables and chairs	child-sized cleaning equipment: broom, dustpan, and mops; doll clothes; telephones; mirror; dishes and cooking utensils; empty containers, tubs, buckets, and pans; dress-up clothes, costumes; purses, shopping bags, backpacks, suitcases; dolls of both genders and various cultures
Sensory	sensory table shelving unit (optional)	funnels, pitchers, hoses, spoons, sponges, measuring cups, containers, strainers, rotary beaters, water toys, scoops, shovels
Woodworking	woodworking bench	measuring tape, marking tool or pencil, saw, sanding blocks, screwdrivers, hammers, vise, nails, screws, scraps of soft wood and foam, glue, protective goggles
Sleeping	cots mats	blankets, pillows, soft music

Continued

Figure 8.18 The materials and equipment in an early childhood classroom may vary, but should include items supporting cultural diversity.

Classroom Area	Furniture	Materials and Equipment
Small Manipulative and Mathematics	shelving units table (optional depending on space) chairs (optional depending on space)	hand puppets, blocks, puzzles, plastic forms for joining, Lego® plastic building blocks, parquetry blocks, stringing beads, board games, sewing cards, colored cubes with pattern cards, bingo games, rods and blocks of different sizes, flannel board numerals, number puzzles, wooden numbers, magnetic numbers, measuring containers, scale, rulers, play money, cars, rulers, hour glass, Cuisenaire® rods, kitchen timers, giant dice, peg boards, colored chips, buttoning and zippering frames
Language and Literacy	table chairs rug soft pillows (optional) beanbag (optional) shelving shelving unit flannel board chalkboard whiteboard	picture books, children's magazines, child-authored books, charts, games, alphabet letters, pens, pencils, felt-tip markers, chalk, different-colored lined and unlined paper, photographs, word lists, picture dictionary
Music	piano (optional) shelving unit CD or media player	rhythm instruments; CDs; silk scarves or streamers for dancing; puppets for song activities
Private Space	loft TV box wooden crates	pillows
Science and Discovery	aquarium table shelving unit terrarium	magnets; microscopes; scissors; prism; measuring instruments; jars and other empty containers; collections of related objects such as leaves, nuts, rocks, and insects; magnifying glasses; small pets; scales; mirrors; thermometers
Eating	tables chairs	vases and centerpieces, place mats, plates, eating utensils, cups
Technology Center	child-sized computer workstations or tables and chairs extra chairs computer printer electronic tablet	software, printer paper, manuals for computer and software, typing stand, mouse, and wrist pads
Gross-Motor	balance beam steps walking boards jungle gym	balls, ropes, hula hoops, fabric tunnels, tumbling mat

Displaying Children's Work

Display the work of the children throughout the activity areas. Bulletin boards, wall hangings, clothesline, or appliance boxes can be used for display purposes. Place display areas at the children's height, allowing them to mount and view their own work.

You can make a wall hanging from a 36- or 52-inch-wide piece of felt, burlap, or sailcloth. The length of the hanging can vary. Hem each end of the hanging. Then insert a dowel through each hem.

You can use colored yarn or a piece of clothesline to display work. Use colored plastic clothespins to clasp work to the line.

A large appliance box can provide a freestanding-display area. The advantage of this type of display is that it is portable. You can use it in any area of the center. Even after assembly, you can move it.

Displays in the center lobby allow families and visitors to see the children's work. When organizing the displays, recognize all the children's work. To keep displays interesting, set a time limit for each display. Change the work often. Make sure the children's first names identify their work. Families enjoy seeing their child's work.

Controlling Clutter

The classroom sets the tone for learning. Controlling classroom clutter is essential for maximizing learning, preventing behavior problems, and promoting safety. Some classrooms feel visually uncomfortable. These rooms have too much clutter, which bombards the children with too much visual information. Excessively decorated classrooms cause sensory overload, particularly for children who are sensitive to external stimuli. Overstimulation triggers stress and anxiety in these children. When this happens, the brain decreases its ability to focus on what is important and stay on task. Stress from clutter also limits the ability of the brain to process information, which hampers the children's learning. Moreover, executive-function skills such as self-regulation, attention, and memory are impacted.

Intentional teachers understand the impact of a negative environment on children's learning and behavior. They also realize reducing environmental stress can enhance children's learning and affect their own satisfaction with teaching. These teachers constantly observe to see what is important. Unnecessary postings, toys, and materials are continuously edited from the classroom. Twenty to fifty percent of wall space should be free of any attachments.

Creating an Inclusive Environment

An inclusive environment reflects the uniqueness of children and their families. It supports each child by acknowledging the differences and similarities in people that make them special. An inclusive environment uses bilingual practices to support and help the children maintain their first language. Recognizing, promoting, and respecting the home language and culture of the children is important. It creates a sense of belonging, identity, and social harmony. Books, musical instruments, songs, games, alphabet charts, dolls, puppets, greeting cards, photographs of families, and posters all convey a trusting environment. The dramatic play area can also include dolls and eating utensils representing different cultures.

Effective environments for children who have disabilities and other diverse learning needs requires careful and intentional arrangement. To meet the needs of these children, teachers must carefully assess how the physical space, equipment, and class materials are organized both indoors and outdoors. The physical space needs to be organized to maximize the active participation of every child. Children using wheelchairs, canes, crutches, or walkers require ample space to easily navigate the classroom. They need to move independently in the space without assistance. Placing materials at their eye level and within easy reach on a shelf, allows children to independently access them.

Every child and disability are different. When enrolling a child who has a disability or other need, talk with the parents and professionals working with the child. You need to gain as much information as possible about the child and disability. Accommodations will vary depending on the disability. For example, a child with a hearing disability needs soft materials such as pillows, carpets, and drapes to absorb sounds. A child with a physical disability may need to have furniture arranged with wide aisles and a safe place to store their devices so other children do not trip on them.

8.2-3 Outdoor Play Environments

A well-designed outdoor play area can serve as a second classroom. Developmentally appropriate programs value outdoor as well as indoor play. Children need to take part in both indoor and outdoor activities. Many classrooms do not have the proper amount of space for gross-motor activities. Other activities such as science, art, and music can also take place outdoors during pleasant weather. The outdoor playground can fill these needs (**Figure 8.19**). Additionally, early childhood professionals must consider playground safety and playground design that is developmentally appropriate in meeting children's needs.

Planning Safe Playgrounds

The National Program for Playground Safety (NPPS) has identified four components that contribute to safe playgrounds. These components are *supervision, proper developmental design, protective surfacing and fall zones,* and *equipment maintenance*.

gpointstudio/iStock via Getty Images Plus

Figure 8.19   The playground is safe, developmentally appropriate and encourages risk taking. *Why is risk taking an important factor to consider for young children?*

Workplace Connections

State Requirements for Outdoor Space

Review your state's requirements for outdoor space. Visit a preschool or local early childhood center. Compare the amount of available outdoor space at the center to the state's requirement for available outdoor space. Draw a plan of the playground.
1. How is the playground space arranged?
2. Discuss the factors and challenges that may affect the amount of space available.

Supervision

Supervision is the first component. Proper supervision will minimize injuries and reduce unsafe behaviors. Playground design must ensure that all children are visible to the caregiver or teacher. Caregivers and teachers need ability to spread out and actively supervise children. According to *Safe Kids*, an organization aiming to prevent accidental childhood injury, 40 percent of playground injuries occur due to lack of supervision. Designing the playground into zones can promote safety. Each zone should reflect the type of activity occurring in the area. Zones may include gross-motor, quiet undisturbed play, sand and water, planting and digging, and wheeled-toy.

In outdoor areas, the required number of square feet per child varies from state to state. Usually, a minimum of 75 to 200 square feet per child is required to prevent unintentional injury. A rectangular space is most functional. Teachers and caregivers can see such a playground from end to end. *U-* or *L*-shaped playgrounds are discouraged since they are more difficult to supervise and arrange.

Proper Developmental Design

Proper developmental design is the second component. Playgrounds should be age-appropriate. Preschool children need equipment designed closer to the ground. Ramps on this equipment should have a **guardrail** for grasping. Platforms should be low, with only a few access points. When over three feet high, decks need a railing to prevent falls. The sand table or area should have a cover to protect the children from sun.

Make sure children of varying abilities have **accessibility**—or ability to access and use the playground and equipment. The playground should provide a range of play experiences. There should be an accessible path from the parking lot or early childhood center to the playground.

Protective Surfacing and Fall Zones

Protective or resilient surfacing or shock absorbers are the third component. Protective surfacing is essential for reducing life-threating head injuries. According to the NPPS, about 70 percent of head injuries result from children falling off equipment to the ground. All equipment, other than sandboxes and playhouses that have no elevated space, requires protective surfacing around and under it. This fall zone should extend at least six feet beyond the outer limits of stationary climbing equipment. To make sure your program is in compliance, check the licensing requirements in your state. Suitable shock-absorbing surfacing materials are energy absorbing and resilient. Never use concrete, asphalt, blacktop, grass, or packed dirt. They are unsuitable under or around equipment of any height. They have poor shock-absorbing properties.

There are two types of acceptable playground surfacing materials: unitary or loose fill.

- **Unitary surfacing materials** are rubber mats or tile systems, or a blend of rubberlike materials. A shock-absorbing surface forms when the loose-fill materials are poured in place at the playground site and cured. Synthetic grass with an under-padding is also a unitary surfacing material.

- **Loose-fill impact-absorbing materials** should be soft and resilient. Examples include gravel, wood chips or mulch, and sand. A minimum of nine inches of loose surfacing is required for sand, pea gravel, and wood mulch. Six inches of loose-fill material is required for shredded/recycled rubber. Manufacturers of these materials should be able to provide height-fall ratings for their playground products. This should reduce the chances of serious injury for falls up to 10 feet. See **Figure 8.20**.

The height of the equipment should determine the type of surfacing material to use. According to NPPS research, the probability of injuries double when equipment exceeds five feet in height. Over time, loose-fill materials will become displaced or erode. For optimal performance, these materials require frequent maintenance.

Equipment Maintenance

Equipment maintenance is the fourth component of safe playgrounds. Well-maintained playgrounds provide greater protection and help minimize risk. Conduct general inspections and look for loose screws or bolts, sharp edges, and broken and missing parts. Cap open pipes and remove tripping hazards. When using loose fill under equipment, rake and monitor the depth and distribution. If needed, add more fill. Inspections should also include checks for rotten lumber.

Designing the Playground

The playground design, like indoor space, requires in-depth study in terms of use and then broken into areas. A well-designed playground usually has empty space and a wheeled vehicle path. These two items aid movement through the playground.

gpointstudio/ iStock via Getty Images Plus

Figure 8.20 This loose fill will help protect a child who falls from the slide.

The wheeled vehicle path divides the activity areas of the playground. This path creates space between areas and makes moving about easier. Without a path, children may constantly be bumping into each other.

To determine where to lay the path, the teacher should kneel to be at the children's eye level. The path should be wide enough and clear enough so children can see all areas of the playground, even when outside school grounds.

Empty space should be in the center of the playground. Place the activity areas around the outside of the playground, surrounding the empty space. You may also need to leave empty space around some pieces of equipment.

When planning playground space, consider the following guidelines:

- Equipment should be far enough apart so a child using one piece of equipment cannot touch a child using another piece of equipment.
- All equipment should be visible to the teacher from any spot in the playground.
- Children should not have to walk through one area to get to another.
- One-third to one-half of the playground should be used for play equipment, and the remainder should be open space to encourage active movement.

In addition to paths and empty space, there are other factors to consider when planning an outdoor playground. Among items to consider are fences, the playground surface, landscaping, storage, wheeled toy paths, stationary equipment, space for a garden, a water source, and animal shelters.

Fencing

Most states require that playgrounds be fenced for safety of the children. Fences prevent children from wandering away or strangers from entering the playground area. Some programs are in areas that may be at risk for realistic fear. Fences surrounding these centers need to reduce visibility to the public. Fences should separate the play area from any hidden corners of the playground. This makes outdoor supervision easier for teachers. Covered sections or shade from trees should also be available for very warm and rainy days.

Selecting the proper fence requires careful thought. The goal is to purchase a fence that can keep children safe. The fence needs to be tall enough to prevent the children and intruders from climbing over it. The gate should securely fasten. There should be no sharp metal pieces or splintered wood to hurt children.

Five types of fences are commonly used for playgrounds: *chain link, wood, aluminum, vinyl,* and *iron*. Each type of fence has its good and bad points. For instance, because chain link is an open design, it is possible for the children to observe activities outside of the playground. This gives the playground an open feeling; however, some children can climb chain-link fences. This can be dangerous. In addition, many people feel that chain-link fences lack **aesthetic** (beautiful or pleasing in appearance) appeal.

Wood, aluminum, and vinyl fences that complement the center design are very pleasing to the eye. The fence design, however, should keep the children's safety in mind. Children should not be able to climb over or through a well-designed fence. Centers are now also using a manufactured wood product that will not warp, splinter, or require painting. Otherwise, the boards require sanding to prevent children from getting splinters.

Surfaces

A portion of the playground area should have grass. This is best for running and organized games. As you have learned, the best surface to use under equipment for safety is loose material such as bark nuggets, shredded bark, or sand. When children fall on such material, they receive fewer and less-severe injuries than when they fall on hard surfaces. A good cushion requires 9 to 12 inches of loose material.

The drawback to loose-fill materials is that they tend to pile up in one spot. They shift under the weight placed on them. In high traffic areas, they will thin out and pile up around the edges of the area. Therefore, the material must be raked or shoveled back into position often.

Infants and toddlers need opportunities for safe and age-appropriate outdoor play. The outdoor space for them should have two or more different types of surfacing. This surface could be grass, rubber cushioning, or even outdoor carpeting.

Landscaping

A well-landscaped playground makes for pleasant surroundings. In addition, landscaping can also be part of the science program by encouraging children to observe and make discoveries. Trees, shrubs, and flowers in a variety of sizes, colors, and growing cycles will interest children. Trees are also a good source of shade, beauty, and sound control. A well-landscaped playground gives children a place to be alone, as well as corners for play. Hilly areas on the playground are useful for developing gross-motor skills.

Before choosing flowers or shrubs, consult a landscape architect. Some plants are poisonous. A landscape architect can tell you which plants to avoid, and can recommend shrubs and flowers with several growing cycles. This ensures that children will always have a seasonal plant to study and view.

Storage Shed

Tricycles, wagons, scooters, shovels, rakes, balls, plastic wading pools, and gardening tools are just some of the items you may want to keep in a storage shed (**Figure 8.21**). The materials stored will vary with the climate of the area.

Arrange the storage space so that children can return materials themselves. Paint lines on the floor of the shed to outline parking spaces for wheeled toys. Use large barrels or baskets to store many types of materials. Hang rakes and shovels on wall hooks.

Wheeled Toy Paths

A path that children can use to push or ride wheeled toys is key for two reasons. The first reason is safety. A path with one-way traffic will prevent children from riding into each other. The second reason is protection of the outdoor play area. A path gives children a place to ride so they do not destroy grassy areas. Set limits regarding the use of wheeled toys and paths, and enforce these rules.

The paths should join at the storage shed. Children can then drive their toys directly into

Suggested Contents of a Storage Shed

Type of Contents	Examples
Water and Sand Play	rakes, shovels, scoops, trucks, cooking utensils, water hoses, empty cans with paint brushes, funnels, strainers, containers, wading pool, sponges
Wheeled Toys	wagons, doll buggy, wheeled cars and trucks, scooters, tricycles, road signs
Construction	cable spools, packing crates, large wooden blocks, sawhorses, wooden boxes, wooden planks
Carpentry	carpentry bench, hammer, saw, vise, clamps, nails, brushes, sandpaper, Styrofoam pieces
Science	gardening tools, seeds, worm jars, garden hose, animal feed, butterfly nets, bird feed, binoculars, magnifying glasses
Dramatic Play	dress-up clothes, fabric, tunnel puppet, stage puppets, folding table and chairs, cardboard appliance boxes, blankets
Art	easel(s), paintbrushes, paper, scissors, paste

Figure 8.21   The contents of storage sheds vary from center to center.

or out of the shed. Design the path with curves instead of sharp right angles to allow children to make easy turns on curves, keeping them from tipping over on sharp turns.

Stationary Equipment

Jungle gyms, slides, and tree houses are all **stationary equipment** set permanently in the ground for stability. For added appeal, place large pieces of stationary equipment in different corners of the playground. For safety reasons, spacing is also a requirement for pieces of stationary equipment that are designed for different age groups.

Sandbox

Children will play in sandboxes for long stretches of time. If the sandbox is in a sunny area, children are at risk for sunburn. Therefore, place sandboxes in shady areas. If there is little or no shade on the playground, build a roof over the sandbox for protection. Also, place the sandbox near a water source. By adding water to dry sand, children can build structures with more details.

Playground sandboxes require special care to protect the children's health. Prevent stray cats or other animals from using the sandbox as a litter box by purchasing or building a cover for the sandbox. When the sandbox is not in use, place the cover over it and fasten it securely

(**Figure 8.22**). Check the sand every day for spiders and other debris. Use the correct type of sand that is labeled as a safe play material, which is sterilized for children's use. Replace the sand every two years for safety.

Water

Water play is a pleasant activity for children during warm weather. Check your state licensing requirements. Sprinklers and portable pools are sometimes used. Regardless of the water source,

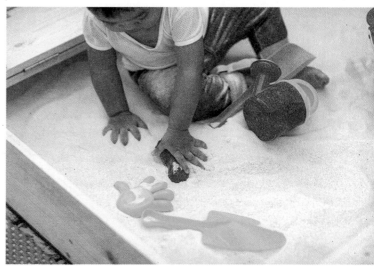

Teerat/iStock via Getty Images Plus

Figure 8.22   This sandbox must be covered with a tarp when not in use. *Why should the sandbox be covered when it is not in use?*

constant supervision is necessary. For safety purposes, empty portable pools and properly clean them with a sanitizer at the end of each day. Never leave children unattended around water tables or wading pools.

Animal Shelter

Playgrounds for young children often have animals. City zoning laws or state child care licensing rules determine the type of animals, if any, centers can have. Some states prohibit animals in early care and education programs. Turtles, fish, and some birds are carriers of *salmonella*, a bacterial disease that can infect children. It is important to check your licensing requirements before purchasing animals.

Before considering animals, check the children's health forms. Some children may have allergies to animals.

To shelter animals, use cages. These should be large enough for the animal, have a mesh floor to keep the cage tidy between thorough cleanings, and have a quality padlock to protect against vandals. Place the cages where animals will have protection from wind, sun, and rain. Provide adequate protection from extreme heat and cold, too.

Safety First

Helmet Safety for Riding Toys

According to the American Academy of Pediatrics, injuries from accidents with wheeled toys (tricycles, bicycles, and scooters) are the leading cause of visits to the emergency room for children and teens. Many of these injuries are head injuries, some of which lead to traumatic brain injury (TBI) or death. Along with close supervision, the best way parents, teachers, and care providers can help prevent such injuries is by requiring children to use approved safety helmets for riding wheeled toys. According to the United States Center for Disease Control and Prevention, using helmets reduces injuries by 80 percent. For helmets to prevent such injuries, they should fit properly. The Consumer Product Safety Commission (CPSC) recommends the following:

- Ensure all children have their own helmets (if shared, helmets must have nonporous linings and be easy to clean between users).
- Make sure the helmet meets CPSC standards.
- Wear the helmet low on the forehead (about two finger widths above the eyebrows) and parallel to the ground.
- Adjust the inner pads to fit the helmet snuggly on the head.
- Tighten the chin strap for a snug fit.
- Ensure the helmet does not move on the head.

Note that bicycle helmets are not suitable for all wheeled toys. Check the Consumer Product Safety Commission website for more information on helmet choices for other activities. In addition, children should also wear knee and elbow pads, especially on scooters.

Lesson 8.2 Review

1. How much space in a classroom should be open? (8.2.1)
   A. Zero
   B. One-fourth
   C. One-half
   D. One-half to one-third

2. Each of the following is a characteristic of the block-building area except: (8.2.2)
   A. Carpeting helps reduce the noise level.
   B. Plastic zoo animals and traffic signs can help stimulate play.
   C. Blocks are arranged on shelves for the best fit.
   D. Heavy blocks placed on lower storage shelves.

3. Each of these is an important characteristic of a private area except: (8.2.2)
   A. It is a place where children can go when they need time to themselves.
   B. It promotes self-regulation.
   C. It reduces the pressure of being around others.
   D. It is ideal for group play.

4. **True or False.** Playground equipment should be close together so children can easily play with each other. (8.2.3)

5. Which type of fence is the most dangerous for a child care center? (8.2.3)
   A. Wood
   B. Chain-link
   C. Vinyl
   D. Aluminum

Chapter 8 Review and Assessment

Summary

Lesson 8.1

8.1-1 Sufficient floor space is essential for children to move around furniture, equipment, and their classmates.

8.1-1 Program goals should guide space planning for safe, well-arranged, and visually pleasing classroom design.

8.1-2 The typical area divisions of the physical areas of the center include the entrance, director's office, isolation area, kitchen, staff room, restrooms, preschool classroom, and infant-toddler room.

8.1-3 Materials for classroom furnishings should be strong, durable, and easy to clean.

8.1-3 The use of color can affect how the children, teachers, and families feel about their classroom.

8.1-4 Color can be used to create a room that is pleasant, light, and spacious.

Lesson 8.2

8.2-1 Many factors affect space organization, including licensing requirements and the program goals.

8.2-1 Teacher created plans for space should reflect children's strengths, cultural backgrounds, interests, and experiences as well as program goals. In such a space, children are more relaxed and positive.

8.2-2 Properly organized space defines behavior expectations for children and frees them to play without interruption.

8.2-2 Each activity area is a space of its own. Carefully arrange activity areas by their functions.

8.2-2 Inclusive environments are supportive of children by acknowledging the differences and similarities that make them special.

8.2-2 Classrooms arranged according to activity areas provide an ideal environment for children's learning.

8.2-3 Factors that contribute to safe playgrounds include supervision, proper developmental design, protective surfacing and fall zones, and regular equipment maintenance.

8.2-3 When planning the outdoor playground, consider the distance between equipment, visibility of equipment to the teacher, children's ability to move safely from one area to another, and the amount of open space.

Vocabulary Activity

For each of the Key Terms, identify a word or group of words describing a quality of the term—an *attribute*. Pair up with a classmate and discuss your list of attributes. Then, discuss you list of attributes with the whole class.

Critical Thinking

1. **Create.** Draw a room arrangement that includes each of the basic activity areas. Include a center of interest for each area.

2. **Determine.** Plan a color scheme for a classroom. Be prepared to provide evidence to support your color choices for the space.

3. **Draw Conclusions.** Tour an area child care center. Prior to the visit, create a checklist to determine if common state licensing requirements are being met. Possible questions on the checklist may include: How many fire extinguishers are present? Are all the center pathways clear? Are space requirements being met? Record your responses during the tour. Draw conclusions about your findings and compare them to state licensing requirements. Discuss your findings with the class.

4. **Analyze.** Search for information regarding materials used for window coverings that would help reduce energy costs to heat or cool a room. Which of these materials or coverings are appropriate for a child care center classroom? What are the advantages and disadvantages of each? Which would you prefer if you were responsible for the selection? Write a brief analysis summarizing your findings.

5. **Analyze.** Brainstorm ways to create a space in the preschool room that is private and comfortable, yet

allows supervision and safety. Which of your skills in art, woodworking, or sewing could be used to help create the space? Why is a private space recommended for preschool rooms? Create a private space in the preschool room if one does not already exist.

Core Skills

1. **Research.** Research your state's licensing requirements as they apply to classroom space. For instance, how many square feet of space is required per child? How many toilets are required for a group of 40 children? Compare these requirements to NAEYC's.

2. **Speaking.** Interview early childhood teachers about space arrangement. Ask them what they like best about their classroom space. Ask them what they would like to change.

3. **Research.** Research the impact of color on learning performance. For example, what is the effect of color on eye fatigue, productivity, and accuracy? What is the difference between selecting colors for function rather than for aesthetic appeal? Is there any validity to the effect of color on blood pressure and on instances of aggressiveness by students? Discuss your findings in class.

4. **Research and Math.** Conduct an online search for classroom furniture, materials, and equipment for each of the classroom areas listed in Figure 8.20. Research at least two items for each classroom area. Investigate the price and how functional and safe each item would be for the classroom. Write a brief description for each item. Discuss your findings in class.

5. **Research.** What types of sandboxes are available from early childhood and preschool equipment sources? Research the cost to purchase and install an outdoor playground sandbox at your school. What factors affect the location of the sandbox in the playground? What school safety guidelines and policies must you consider when installing a sandbox?

6. **Writing and Math.** Make a scale drawing of a model preschool playground suitable for a toddler or preschool program. Include all pieces of stationary equipment, paths, empty space, storage facilities, and surfacing materials. Write a brief essay explaining what factors contributed to your choice of equipment and what safety features are included in the plan. Consult outdoor play equipment catalogs, building material suppliers, and other sources to estimate the cost of their project.

7. **Research.** Check your state's child-care licensing requirements by using the website for the National Resource Center for Health and Safety in Child Care and Early Education.

8. **CTE Career Readiness Practice.** The director of the early childhood center where you work overheard you explaining to parents the precautions they can take against SIDS. Your center has recently hired a new employee, and your director asks you to train this new employee on methods of preventing SIDS and on educating parents about these methods. In preparation for training, develop materials for the new employee, including
   - authoritative information about SIDS and what resources provide accurate information about it;
   - the precautions your child care center takes against SIDS; and a script in which you train the employee to talk with parents about SIDS.

9. **CTE Career Readiness Practice.** Imagine you are a new employee at a local early childhood center. Your employer asks you to research information on standards for playground safety and the relation of standards to the Consumer Products Safety Commission (CPSC). Write a report of your findings using sources such as the National Playground Contractor's Association (NPCA), the International Playground Equipment Manufacturer's Associations (IPEMA), the National Program for Playground Safety (NPPS), and the National Playground Safety Institute (NPSI). Once you have created your report, present it to the class and ask for feedback on how well you completed your employer's assignment.

Portfolio Project

It is important to include culturally diverse materials in the classroom to promote understanding of cultural diversity. Many schools ask parents to contribute items that help support this goal. Draft a sample letter asking parents to borrow and display items in the classroom. Include a request for parents to visit the classroom if they would like to share cultural information with the children. Have your teacher review your letter for appropriate grammar, clarity, and professionalism. File a copy of the letter in your portfolio under Parent Communications and/or Public Relations.

Chapter 9

Selecting Toys, Equipment, and Educational Materials

Reading Advantage

Read the chapter title and write a paragraph describing what you know about the topic. After reading the chapter, summarize what you have learned.

Case Study

Selecting Classroom Furniture, Materials, and Supplies

Charlie has a bachelor's and master's degree in early childhood education. After earning the bachelor's degree, Charlie accepted a position with a national childcare chain. The first position was working as a teacher for three years. Then Charlie was promoted to the position of center director and continued earning credits online to earn a master's degree. From working as director, the next promotion was to a regional director, with the responsibility for supervising eight centers. Recently, Charlie was promoted to the corporate office.

The new position involves the responsibility for ordering, updating, and coordinating the delivery of the toys, equipment, and materials for new and existing centers. The company has provided Charlie with a budget, depending on the number of classrooms and ages being served, for each new center. On file in the office, there was also detailed information on the classroom furniture, equipment, and materials for all existing centers with the dates purchased. There also was a list of vendors who were sources for toys, materials, and equipment and their typical bid prices.

Give It Some Thought

1. What selection criteria should Charlie consider for purchasing classroom equipment, toys, and materials?
2. How would Charlie determine the quantity of toys needed?
3. Why should Charlie select gender-neutral and multicultural toys and materials?
4. The corporate vice-president of operations told Charlie that the playground equipment had already been ordered and installed. But it needed to be carefully examined by the director and staff to ensure it was safe. What should Charlie inspect for?

Opening image credit: AsiaVision/E+ via Getty Images

Lesson 9.1

Selection Criteria and Technology in the Classroom

Essential Question

? *What do I need to know about developmentally appropriate, gender-neutral, and multicultural toys, equipment, technology, and educational materials to promote children's development?*

Learning Outcomes

After studying this lesson, you will be able to

9.1-1 **summarize** criteria for selecting developmentally appropriate toys, equipment, and educational materials.

9.1-2 **identify** toys and educational materials that are gender-neutral and teach children appreciation for people of all cultures.

9.1-3 **analyze** how to use technology in the classroom.

Key Terms

spectator toys

physical age

chronological age

developmental age

multicultural

Children construct their knowledge and learn about their world by playing with toys, exploring materials, and interacting with other people. They learn best when provided with a wide range of toys and educational materials that match their strengths, interests, cultures, and languages. A self-directed learning environment allows them to make choices. Toys that are responsive to their interests and culture play an important role in facilitating the learning process. For instance, children can learn speech and dressing skills while playing with toys. When playing with toys, children often interact with others, so they can learn about other people and explore their cultures. They make choices, solve problems, and apply some control over their environment (**Figure 9.1**).

Developmentally appropriate toys motivate and engage children as active learners. Simple toys, like building blocks, can promote cognitive growth. For example, if children do not build a strong foundation under their block building, the building will topple. This is a basic physics concept. If they join two semicircular pieces, they make a circle. Using blocks is a way for children to learn math concepts.

9.1-1 Selection Criteria

In early childhood programs, selecting toys and equipment for children is often the teacher's responsibility. The process needs to be intentional and individualized. In preparation, check your state's licensing requirements. You will need to assess the children's strengths, needs, interests, and cultural backgrounds. You will then need to

Art Stocker/Shutterstock.com

Figure 9.1 Toys help children build many skills. *How do developmentally appropriate toys help motivate and engage children as active learners?*

choose the materials that would best meet those needs. As you can see, this is an important job. Thoughtful planning and knowledge of age-appropriate toys representing cultural diversity are required. During the selection process, teachers often ask parents which toys have cultural meanings for them. Children will want some toys and materials to be like those in their homes. They need to feel celebrated with mirrors that reflect themselves. Classrooms need to reflect every child's, culture, identity, and their language to be developmentally appropriate.

Safety is a concern when selecting toys. Children throw, bite, pound, and hit toys without thinking of the consequences. So, all classroom equipment must withstand intense use. Choking and improper use cause most injuries in childhood. For this reason, many states' licensing requirements specify the use of a choke tube. Try inserting the toy in the tube. If you succeed, the toy is a choking hazard and would be considered developmentally inappropriate. Developmentally appropriate toys can help reduce the number of injuries. Age warnings on packaged products are not always reliable.

The program goals, budget, and curriculum will influence which materials you buy for the classroom. The number of children in the program and the available space and storage should also be considered. You will want to choose toys that are safe, appropriate, and interesting for the children. Guidelines for choosing educational toys are described in the sections that follow.

Program Goals

Classroom toys and equipment should reflect program goals. If a program goal is to have the children develop language skills, then language materials should be in the classroom. Books, pictures, alphabet cards, puppets, digital tablets, pencils, and paper can all be used to promote language skills.

Write your program goals on paper (**Figure 9.2**) or use a digital device. Make a list of items that promote each goal. Review the goals and lists. Take count of items you already have in

Program Goals

To develop a positive self-concept and view self as worthwhile

To develop a curiosity about the world

To develop sensory exploration skills

To develop prosocial behavior skills

To develop executive function skills

To value own rights as well as those of others

To develop language skills, both listening and speaking

To develop fine-motor skills

To develop gross-motor skills

To develop problem-solving skills

To develop creativity skills

To develop an appreciations for one's own culture and the cultures of others.

Figure 9.2 Understanding program goals helps early childhood professionals make wise choices about toys and equipment.

the classroom. Then decide in which areas more toys and equipment are required. You may find a planning sheet helpful for this task (**Figure 9.3**).

Toy Selection Planning Sheet

Program Goals	Available Toys	Toys Needed
To encourage sensory exploration	water table, shovel, cups, pitchers, scoops, clay, eggbeaters, feely box, harmonica, kazoo, guitar	bells, drum, texture matching games, pumps, funnels
To promote gross-motor skills	low climber, wagon cart, large rubber balls, planks, boxes, jungle gym	low slide, balance boards, bicycle
To promote technology skills	interactive whiteboard, digital tablet, audio recorder, printer, lap top computers	web cam, floor robot, digital, camera, digital microscope, books

Figure 9.3   This planning sheet helps teachers identify areas that are in need of toys and equipment.

Budget

When purchasing items for your class, you will need to stay within your budget. To do this, first purchase the basics, such as tables, chairs, and shelving units. You can continue adding items as your funds permit.

Teachers are often surprised at the cost of toys, equipment, and materials. The major portion of the budget for a new program is for furniture.

Balance

Examining program goals helps you decide what toys and equipment might be purchased. Before buying, however, review each item to decide if it will add balance to the items already available. Ask yourself the following questions: Can the item be used with other toys? Will it help children reach program goals that are not met sufficiently with current toys? Will it promote interaction with peers? Will it help balance toys for all areas of development—physical, cognitive, emotional, and social? Do the toys and equipment represent a variety of cultures? Books, dramatic play materials, musical instruments, recorded music, posters and displays need to reflect the cultures and languages of children attending the program.

Space

Keep in mind the space and storage requirements for any new items you are thinking about buying or building. This is especially true for large pieces of equipment. For instance, an indoor jungle gym is a useful item in many centers. If the space for storing it is not available,

Workplace Connections

Storage Space

Visit a preschool classroom and observe how the amount of storage space available affects the quantity and type of play materials and equipment in the classroom.

1. What strategies do the teachers employ to get the most use from their play space and storage space?
2. Write a brief report of your observation findings and discuss your findings in class.

it is a poor investment. It may end up being stored in another part of the building. If the location is inconvenient, the jungle gym will not be used very often.

Supervision

Quality supervision is vital to safety. Consider the number of staff available for supervision when selecting toys and equipment. Think about how each item will affect your ability to supervise children properly. You will have to consider each item individually, balancing safety and developmental needs. Safety is a primary concern. For example, you may want to buy swings for the playground. The state may require one adult supervisor for every 10 children. You can comply with state guidelines for ratios, but you might feel that more supervision is necessary for safety. You may decide, in this case, that the swings would be an unwise purchase.

The developmental stages of children also require consideration when choosing toys and equipment. This will affect the amount of supervision required. For instance, many five-year-old children can use blunt-nosed scissors with some guidance. Four-year-old children, however, require much more supervision for the same task.

Maintenance

All toys and equipment require maintenance. The care required varies with the type of toy or equipment and the amount of use. For example, a plastic jungle gym needs less upkeep than a wooden or metal one. Upkeep of equipment can become costly. Make sure schedule regular maintenance to keep the equipment safe for children.

Durability

Children's toys need to be durable. Children bang, drop, stand on, sit on, and lay on toys. When angry, they may even throw toys. Broken toys can pose a danger to children. For instance, a broken toy can have sharp edges that cut. It is usually best to buy toys and equipment that are well built. Toys can be expensive to replace. You want to buy quality toys that will last through much use.

Today, some manufacturers are focusing on manufacturing earth-friendly toys. The fast-fashion of the toy industry is plastic toys. It is important, however, to purchase brands that manufacture sustainable and earth-friendly choices. For instance, some turn plastic milk jugs into safe toys. Other toy manufacturers use rubberwood trees that no longer produce latex or nontoxic rubber. One manufacturer even saves walnut and coconut shells from incineration. Then they turn these shells into earth-friendly toys.

Wood and cloth are two materials that are durable, warm, and pleasurable to touch. Wood toys can withstand many years of use by many children. When buying wood toys, look for those made of hardwoods such as maple. The toys should also be split-resistant. To prevent injury, make sure the corners of the toys are have round edges.

Quantity

The quantity of toys can be as important when purchasing materials as the quality. In most classrooms, it is common to find two or more children playing with the same toys. To promote this type of cooperation, supply an ample number of toys and materials for children. If there is a shortage of play materials, undesirable behavior can result. Therefore, be certain you can purchase any toys you wish to add to the classroom in the amount necessary (**Figure 9.4**).

Variety should also be a consideration along with quantity. Is the item you wish to add to the classroom like existing items? Studies show that children who have exposure to a wide variety of toys are more imaginative and creative. To provide variety, rotate toys and equipment regularly.

When choosing toys, keep them simple. Children do not have freedom to express themselves if there is too much detail. Unstructured toys, such as blocks and paints, encourage the children to use their imagination.

The table in **Figure 9.5** suggests toys and equipment for a class of 15 children. These items represent a varied group of toys and equipment.

Child Involvement

Choose toys that will actively involve children. Toys should inspire children to explore,

LightFieldStudios/iStock via Getty Images Plus

Figure 9.4   Choosing duplicates of some toys helps discourage children from attempting to take toys from one another.

Suggested Equipment and Supplies for a Class Unit of 15 Preschoolers

Type of Materials and Equipment	Items to Select	
Indoor block building	• 400 hardwood unit blocks, including such shapes as units, half units, double units, quadruple units, pillars, large and small cylinders, curves, triangles, ramps, Y switches, X switches, floorboards, roof boards, hollow blocks, arches, tunnels, and beams	
Floor play materials	• 24 cars, airplanes, boats, fire engines, wagons, tractors, trains of assorted sizes, giant floor puzzles, farm animals, families • Hispanic, Caucasian, African, and Asian sets of wooden people	• 30 rubber, plastic, or wooden figures of farm and zoo animals; community workers: police officers, firefighters, and doctors; family members: mother, father, boy, girl, baby, grandparents • 1 rocking boat
Family living and dramatic play	• 8–10 rubber dolls representing all cultures and both genders; doll clothes and accessories; chest for doll clothes; baby bottles • 2 doll carriages • 1 doll bed, big and sturdy enough for a child to crawl into • 1 smaller doll bed or crib • Blankets, mattresses, pillows for doll beds • Furniture for household play: wooden stove, cupboard for dishes, sink, small table, and chairs • Dolls with different skin tones • Multi-cultural/international plastic foods	• Multi-cultural doll clothes • Kitchenware: plastic dishes, tea set, small cooking utensils, silverware • Housekeeping equipment: broom, mop, dustpan, brush, iron, ironing board, clothesline, clothespins • Full-length mirror • Dress-up clothes: men's and women's shoes, handbags, jewelry, hats, belts • Supplies for other dramatic play: office equipment, telephones, cash registers, firefighters' hats, badges, play money, stethoscope, doctors' bags and white coats, nurses' hats,
Table and perceptual activities	• Bingo and lotto games • 12 wooden inlay puzzles of varying degrees of difficulty • 1 puzzle rack • Pegs and pegboards • Matching games • Sets of small blocks (cubes, parquetry, interlocking, snap-in, number) • Cultural food puzzles • Multicultural puzzles	• Large table dominoes: picture sets, number sets • Nested blocks • Pounding peg board • Cuisenaire® rods, counting frames; abacus • Cards: geometric shapes • Lacing and stringing toys • Legos

Continued

Figure 9.5   Select a variety of toys and equipment in quantities that multiple children can use at one time.

Type of Materials and Equipment	Items to Select	
Art activities	• 2 easels • Drying rack for art materials • 24 easel paintbrushes with 1/2-in. and 3/4-in. handles • Splash mats for under easels • 75–100 quarts liquid tempera paint of various colors* • 8000 sheets white manila paper, 4000 sheets newsprint 24 in. by 36 in. • Paste and paste brushes • 20 packages finger paint paper or glazed shelf paper • 24 packages construction paper of various colors* • 4 clay boards, 2 plastic covered pails for storing clay, and clay • Aprons • Spill-proof cups	• Multicultural crayons, felt-tipped markers, and paper • 100 lb. flour and 40 lb. salt for dough • 18 blunt scissors, including some left-handed training scissors • 5 aprons or smocks • Miscellaneous supplies: orange juice cans, drying rack, florist wire, pipe cleaners, armature wire, colored toothpicks, transparent colored paper • 5 dozen crayons • Rolling pins • Transparent tape • Stapler and staples • Scissors and stamps • Colored pencils and washable markers representing all the skin tones
Music	• Media player, CD player, CDs • Autoharp® • Xylophone • Scarves, streamers • Rhythm instruments: kazoos, shakers, maracas, sticks	• Drums, triangles, tambourines, cymbals, tom-toms • Sleighbells for hands and feet • Balls, hoops • Multicultural rhythm instruments • Djembe drum
Woodworking	• 1 sturdy, low workbench with 2 vises • Tools: four 4-oz. claw hammers, two 12 in. crosscut saws, 1 hand drill, 1 rasp, 1 file, 2 screwdrivers, assorted nails with large heads, screws, 2 large C-clamps • Safety goggles	• Soft wood scraps, doweling • Sandpaper • Miscellaneous: buttons, washers, corks, wire, nuts, hooks and eyes, spools, bottle caps
Furniture	• 15 chairs, 8 in. to 12 in. in height • 3 adult-sized chairs • 3 tables, 18 in. to 22 in. in height, for snacks, meals, and tablework activities • 2 room dividers • 15 cots for resting	• 15 lockers and cubbies for hanging coats, hats, boots, extra change of clothes • Children's book shelf • Cabinets and shelves
Science and special projects	• Bar and horseshoe magnets • Children's cookbook • Magnifying glass • Large indoor and outdoor thermometers • Tubes • Seeds, rocks, shells, plants, leaves, bugs, insects • Animals: hamsters, mice, rabbits, fish, ducks, and gerbils (where permitted by law) • Picture collection: machines, animals, plants, and geography	• Books with science concepts • Tape measure, yardstick, rulers • Scales • Measuring cups and spoons • Dry cell batteries, flashlight bulbs, electric wire • Pulleys and gears • Hand mirrors • Hot plate and electric frying pan • Aquarium and terrarium • Cages for pets

Continued

Suggested Equipment and Supplies for a Class Unit of 15 Preschoolers continued

Type of Materials and Equipment	Items to Select	
Water and sand play (indoor and outdoor)	• Small pitchers, watering cans, measuring cups, bowls of various sizes, plastic bottles, medicine droppers, large spoons • Scoops and sifter sets	• Funnels, strainers, eggbeaters, ladles, straws, lengths of hose, brushes • Soap and soap flakes • Sponges
Outdoor equipment	• Covered sandbox, cans, buckets, spades, spoons, small dishes, colander • Jungle gym • Ladder box • Horizontal ladder • 5 tricycles • 3 scooters • 3 small wagons • 2 wheelbarrows • 6 10-in. and 12-in. rubber balls • 3 four-wheeled cars or "horses" manipulated by a child's feet • 2 sturdy doll carriages • 2 sturdy wooden packing cases (42 in. by 30 in. by 30 in.) • Spring bouncer • Walking boards	• 2 sturdy wooden packing cases (35 in. by 23 in. by 16 in.) • 24 hollow wooden blocks (5½ in. by 11 in. by 11 in.) • 12 hollow wooden blocks (5½ in. by 11 in. by 22 in.) • 12 low sawhorses • 8 small wooden kegs • Wooden ladders • Walking boards (balance beam) and flexible jumping boards • Lengths of sturdy rope and garden hose • Automobile and airplane tires and rubber inner tubes • Rubber balls of different sizes; beanbags • Plastic balls and bats
Language arts	• Picture books, fairy tales, storybooks, informational books, counting books and interactive books appropriate to the age, culture, and special interests of the children; books should include a range of poetry and prose, humor, fiction, and nonfiction	• Alphabet books and big books • Hand puppets • Flannel board • Felt board with felt figures • Lotto and picture games
Audiovisual technology	• Interactive whiteboard • Software • Audio recorder • Printer • Computer • Electronic tablet	• Video camera • Television • Media player • Digital microscope • Digital camera • Web cam
Posters	• Faces of the world	

manipulate, invent, and problem-solve. In this way, children learn for themselves. They learn to use their imaginations.

Spectator toys such as battery-powered cars and talking dolls require little action on the child's part. Avoid purchasing these types of toys. Besides being costly, their appeal with children is

quite often brief. Children will leave these toys for others that involve more imagination.

Choose simple toys (**Figure 9.6**). Too much detail limits imagination. Open-ended materials free children to use their minds and express their creativity.

Blocks, play dough, paint, sand, and construction sets are open-ended toys. Using

Tomsickova Tatyana/Shutterstock.com

Figure 9.6 Toys should encourage children to engage their senses. *What toys might you suggest to help children engage their senses?*

these items, children build structures, make designs, problem-solve, and play games. Children find endless ways to use such toys.

Use the checklist in **Figure 9.7** to define what skills children can learn from a specific toy. This task will help you see how a toy will affect children's development. This knowledge will be helpful when determining what to purchase.

9.1-2 Developmentally Appropriate Toys

Children's physical age and developmental age are often quite different. **Physical age** is an age determined by a birth date. It is also known as **chronological age**. **Developmental age** refers to a child's skill and growth level compared to

Checklist for Skills Learned from Toys

Skills	Yes	No
Will the children learn or improve *auditory discrimination*?		
Will the children learn or improve *balance*?		
Will the children learn or improve *color concepts*?		
Will the children learn or improve *counting*?		
Will the children learn or improve *fine-motor skills*?		
Will children learn or improve *gross-motor skills*?		
Will the children learn or improve *hand-eye coordination*?		
Will the children learn or improve *hearing-doing skills*?		
Will the children learn or improve *language concepts*?		
Will the children learn or improve *matching*?		
Will the children learn or improve *number concepts*?		
Will the children learn or improve *patterning and problem-solving skills*?		
Will the children learn or improve *seeing-doing skills*?		
Will the children learn or improve *self-esteem*?		
Will the children learn or improve *sensory discrimination*?		
Will the children learn or improve *sequencing*?		
Will the children learn or improve *social skills*?		
Will the children learn or improve *space perception*?		
Will the children learn or improve *strength*?		
Will the children learn or improve *throwing-catching skills*?		
Will the children learn or improve *visual discrimination*?		

Figure 9.7 Using a checklist such as this can help you ensure that you select toys and equipment that are developmentally appropriate in meeting children's needs.

typical skills for that physical age group. For example, Kathy may be four years old physically, but only functions as a two-year-old child. A child who functions as a four-year-old could string beads, however, Kathy can only do tasks two-year-old children can do. She lacks the hand-eye coordination needed to string beads. As you choose toys, remember the difference between physical and developmental age.

Toys are teaching tools. Those that suit children's developmental ages help them build self-esteem. For instance, Pedro will feel powerful as he learns to ride a scooter or as he pushes a wagon up a hill. When accomplishing this skill, Pedro gains a sense of control and builds an "I can do it" feeling.

Figure 9.8 lists several toys and equipment pieces that are appropriate for various age groups. The ages on the chart refer to developmental ages.

Gender-Neutral Toys and Materials

Gender-neutral toys and materials provide children with the opportunity to explore nontraditional roles. These toys do not lock children into play that is gender biased. For instance, males and females can be anything. Males can be nurses, preschool teachers, and stay-at-home fathers. Females can be airplane pilots, truck drivers, and plumbers. This type of play will also help children form potential ideas about careers.

As a teacher, it is important to set up an environment that is free of gender bias. Your attitude about toys will affect what children learn about sex roles. Attempt to introduce or suggest a variety of toys to all children, however, be matter-of-fact. For instance, you might suggest to Octavio that he should try playing in the kitchen. You might invite him to play with you in the kitchen to learn about preparing food for a family.

Multicultural Toys and Materials

Toys and materials that are **multicultural** represent a people from a variety of cultures. These items are an essential part of a cross-cultural curriculum that teaches and models respect for people of all cultures. Multicultural

Early Childhood Insight ABC

Toys and Self-Esteem

Toys that do not match the child's development can cause frustration. Lack of success with a toy can have a negative effect on the child's self-esteem. For instance, it is not likely that a two-year-old child could put together an 18-piece puzzle. The child may make several attempts at the puzzle, but soon will become frustrated and move on to a toy that is more rewarding.

toys and materials encourage children to explore the world's diversity. This helps them learn to appreciate and respect others by understanding similarities and differences.

In addition, the early childhood environment must help each child develop a sense of identity. The child needs help to understand and appreciate his or her cultural heritage. Each child needs to feel welcome and supported in the classroom. Thus, children need to see their heritage reflected among the program's toys and materials.

By choosing multicultural toys and materials, you communicate respect and appreciation for all cultures. **Figure 9.9** contains a checklist for evaluating a classroom for multicultural toys and materials.

Puppets, dolls, and people figures should reflect cultural diversity. Puzzles, books, and other toys should also be chosen with cultural diversity in mind. Pick items that show people of various cultures in positive and accurate ways. Art supplies should reflect a range of skin tones. Classroom decorations and bulletin boards should show people of all cultural groups and ethnicities. Recorded music and musical instruments should represent various cultures, too.

9.1-3 Using Technology in the Classroom

A critical issue that teachers face is the thoughtful and intentional use of technology in the early childhood classroom. Content may be delivered through music, movies, television, video

Developmentally Appropriate Toys and Equipment
(Ages 6 months to 36 months)

Type of Play	Six Months to One Year	One-Year-Old	Two-Year-Old
Block and Dramatic Play	Include: grasping toys foam blocks soft animals bucket and blocks	Add: large trucks interlocking blocks shape sorter	Add: unit blocks wooden figures people zoo animals farm animals
Gross-Motor Equipment	Include: push/pull toys beach balls activity gym sensory balls	Add: toddler stairs driving bench large foam blocks toddler barrel tire swing	Add: toddler stairs driving bench large foam blocks toddler barrel tire swing
Housekeeping	Include: soft dolls stuffed animals puppets acrylic plastic mirrors	Add: doll bed doll blankets doll mattress unbreakable doll wooden telephone	Add: simple doll clothes doll carriage child-sized sink, stove, pots, pans, aprons backpacks purses
Sensory and Science	Include: tub tub toys sensory mat musical mobiles	Add: sponges buckets funnels pitchers measuring cups scoops	Add: sand table water table
Creative Art and Books	Include: wall hangings mobiles board books	Add: large crayons hard books cloth books media player or CD player and CDs	Add: picture books blunt scissors paste finger paints play dough
Classroom Furnishings	Include: infant seat crib changing counter adult rocking chair cubbies high chair baby bouncer	Add: clothing lockers storage shelves book display cots discovery table	Add: bookcase block cart play table and chairs
Miscellaneous	Include: soft balls stroller standard crib and mattress music boxes mirrors rattles textured rattles	Add: stacking and nesting toys pull toys simple puzzles pop beads stacking cones pegboards	Add: more complex puzzles large wooden threading beads small cots rest mat and cover sheet

Figure 9.8 Toys and equipment that are appropriate for children's developmental ages help build self-esteem.

Multicultural Classroom Checklist
Does your classroom provide the following multicultural items?

Items	Yes	No
A variety of books containing accurate information about many cultures		
A culturally diverse collection of puppets, dolls, people figures, and posters that reflect the social identities of children in the classroom		
Puzzles and small manipulatives representing people from around the world		
Musical instruments from various cultures		
Musical recordings in various cultural styles and languages		
Art materials and supplies that reflect various skin tones		
Multicultural posters, pictures, and decorations		
Play money from other countries		
Culturally relevant foods, kitchen items, and furnishings for the dramatic play areas		

Figure 9.9   To ensure your classroom includes a variety of multicultural materials, use a checklist such as this.

games, and other applications, or *apps*. Media technologies include computers, smartphones, interactive whiteboards, digital tablets, and printers.

Computers and other digital devices use should foster the children's learning, imagination, and creativity. They should complement other activities and social interaction. Use of digital devices cannot replace physical activity or play with puzzles, blocks, books, and other materials.

The American Academy of Pediatrics (AAP) has amended their guidelines for media use for infants and toddlers. Media has benefits as well as risks for children. At a very young age, children are influenced by what they think and feel. It is acceptable for babies to video chat with families; however, a parent or caregiver must be interacting with them. The AAP discourages all other media use or screen time for children age two and under.

From the ages of two to five, parents or a teacher should participate with the child with any digital media use. Moreover, the AAP recommends limiting screen time for children ages of two to five to one hour or less per day. Only high-quality programs such as Sesame Workshop or PBS Kids should be viewed with a parent or teacher. While watching the media, caregivers and parents should help the children understand what they are seeing. Young children need one-to-one interaction to develop language and cognitive skills.

Computers and other digital devices are common in the early childhood classroom. Studies show benefits for children older than three years who use the computer. Digital devices can stimulate children's cognitive, language, and social development. These benefits are greatest when developmentally appropriate software is used with supporting activities. In studies, children who used a computer or other digital device had greater gains in nonverbal, verbal, problem-solving, and conceptual skills as compared to other children.

Place computers and other digital devices in a quiet area of the classroom. To encourage children to make digital activity time a social time, place two or three chairs at each digital device. This allows the children to seek help from each other to find solutions to problems.

Adults should use discretion in choosing digital technology. They can request free online trials, try out software at educational conferences, and consult with other early childhood professionals. Many programs exist, but not all are equal in terms of benefits for children. For instance, programs that model aggression are not appropriate for early childhood programs. Software that promotes learning is often preferred over programs that merely entertain. Two factors are vital—the program must be age-appropriate and easy to

Health Highlights

Preventing Computer Vision Syndrome

With increasing use of computers and other digital devices, some children are developing *computer vision syndrome (CVS)*. Symptoms of CVS can include eyestrain, dry eyes, blurred vision, headaches, neck ache or backache, and sensitivity to light. Extended periods of computer or device use, poor posture or ergonomics, and improper lighting can all lead to CVS. Although CVS does not cause permanent eye damage, there are ways to prevent its discomfort. The American Optometric Association makes the following recommendations for children's use of computers and digital devices:

- Make sure children have a comprehensive eye exam before starting school. This ensures that children have clear vision and can detect any conditions that affect eyestrain.
- Limit the amount of time children use a computer or other digital device. Encourage breaks every 20 minutes to minimize backache and eyestrain.
- Be sure to adjust the work area to fit a child's size. Children should sit no closer than 18 inches to the monitor or device to prevent eyestrain.
- Adjust the room lighting to eliminate glare on the screen.

operate so even nonreaders can understand what to do. Other qualities to look for include

- clear, user-friendly directions that children can follow without adult help;
- colorful, animated, realistic graphics to hold children's attention;
- logical sequences;
- frequent interactions with the child, including instant feedback;
- feedback that permits sufficient time for the children to respond;

- promotion of problem-solving skills by offering choices;
- investigation of concepts, such as numbers, colors, shapes, letters, or counting; and
- ability to save work so children can restart from where they left off.

By six years of age, most children can operate simple programs and follow instructions from a picture menu. They like showing others how to use digital devices.

Lesson 9.1 Review

1. **True or False.** Centers should purchase durable toys. (9.1.1)
2. Which toy should a center avoid purchasing? (9.1.1)
   A. Blocks
   B. Paints
   C. Talking dolls
   D. Play dough

3. Multicultural toys are important in a classroom for each of these reasons except: (9.1.2)
   A. They promote respect of all cultures.
   B. They encourage children to explore the world's diversity.
   C. They help children develop a sense of identity.
   D. They are affordable.
4. Two- to five-year-olds should be limited to _____ hour(s) or less of digital media use per day. (9.1.3)
   A. 1
   B. 2
   C. 3
   D. 4

Selecting Safe Toys and Playground Equipment

Essential Question

How do safety factors influence the selection and purchase of toys and equipment for early childhood centers?

Learning Outcomes

After studying this lesson, you will be able to

9.2-1 **analyze** safety factors to consider when purchasing toys.

9.2-2 **explain** how to select and maintain safe playground equipment.

9.2-3 **list** sources and methods for purchasing toys, consumable supplies, and equipment.

Key Terms

co-op (cooperative)	vendor
consumable supplies	bid

To promote safety, choose toys carefully. Serious injuries can result from poor toy selection. With normal use, many hazards are not immediately observable. For this reason, you must study each toy thoroughly before buying it. The safest toys are not always those that appeal most to children. Rather, the safest toys are those that meet the standards outlined in this chapter. **(Figure 9.10)**

9.2-1 Selecting Safe Toys

There are thousands of toys to choose from, and hundreds of new ones are available each year. Toys are supposed to be safe; however, over 217,000 children ages 14 and younger were treated

New Africa/Shutterstock.com

Figure 9.10 Choose toys carefully for safety. *How does the Consumer Product Safety Commission help reduce the risk of injuries and deaths from toys?*

in hospital emergency rooms in one recent year for playground-related injuries. Brain injury is one of the top diagnoses for playground-related injuries. According to the Consumer Product Safety Commission (CPSC), there are over 200,000 reported toy-related injuries each year.

The National SAFE-KIDS Campaign has reported the following:

- Falls and choking cause most toy-related deaths and injuries in children. Choking alone causes one-third of all toy-related deaths—most often from balloons.

- Forty-five percent of toy-related injuries are to the face or head.

- Children four years old and younger account for more than a third of all toy-related injuries and almost all deaths.

- Children under three years of age are at the greatest risk of choking because they tend to put objects—especially toys—in their mouths.

Focus on Careers

Preschool and Child Care Center Director

Preschool and child care center directors are responsible for all aspects of a center's program, including designing program plans, preparing and allocating budgets, and overseeing daily activities along with supervising and leading their staff members. Additionally, center directors hire and train staff (ensuring staff pass background checks), offer professional development opportunities for staff, maintain instructional excellence, establish center policies, communicate with parents and assist staff in such communication, and ensure their facilities meet all state regulations for maintenance and cleaning, program, and staff. They may work for independently owned centers, national chains or franchises, or public-school systems and Head Start programs.
Career cluster: Education and training.

Education: A bachelor's degree in early childhood education is a typical requirement for becoming a preschool or child care center director in most states. These positions may also require several years of experience in early childhood education.
Job outlook: The overall employment of preschool and child care directors is projected to grow 11 percent through 2030, which is faster than average for all occupations.

To learn more about a career as a preschool and child care director, visit US Department of Labor websites for the *Occupational Outlook Handbook (OOH)* and *O*NET OnLine*. You will be able to compare the job responsibilities, educational requirements, job outlook, and average pay for preschool and child care directors with similar occupations.

- Riding toys—including bicycles and scooters—cause many injuries in children.

Several federal laws regulate the manufacture and labeling of children's toys. Two of these laws are the *Child Protection and Toy Safety Act* and the *US Child Safety Protection Act*. The Child Protection and Toy Safety Act sets basic standards for toy manufacturers. The US Child Safety Protection Act mandates warning labels on toys that indicate whether the toys pose choking hazards to children younger than three years. Manufacturers must make sure toys and other children's products comply with all federal laws. Always check these labels carefully for warning recommendations.

The government agency that issues and enforces these laws is the US Consumer Product Safety Commission (CPSC). Its mission is to reduce the risk of injuries and deaths associated with consumer products. The CPSC is heavily involved in the safety of children's products. The CPSC also recalls or bans unsafe products, conducts product research, and informs and educates consumers about product safety. The letters "ASTM" are on some toys. This means the products meet national safety standards set by the American Society for Testing Materials (ASTM).

As a result of laws and standards, most new toys are developed with safety in mind. When used by children of an appropriate developmental age, these toys are generally safe. For example, small stringing beads are safe and useful for many four-year-old children. In the hands of a two-year-old, however, they present a risk of choking. Keeping inappropriate toys away from younger children is crucial.

Older toys are much more likely than newer toys to present safety hazards. This is because the toys were made prior to the most recent standards. They may contain the hazards addressed by these standards. Check older toys (or toys of an unknown age) very carefully for potential risks. Discard any items you find that contain any of the following safety hazards:

- *Breakable pieces.* For children under three years of age, toys must be unbreakable and able to withstand use and abuse.

- *Sharp edges or points.* Toys made with sharp edges or points are dangerous. Also hazardous are older toys that break and expose internal sharp edges or points. An example is a stuffed toy with sharp wires inside to stiffen its ears, legs, paws, and tail. Dolls that have hair or clothing held in place by straight pins are also dangerous.

- *Small parts.* For children under three years of age and under, all parts of toys smaller than 1 inch in diameter or 1½ inches long present a choking hazard (**Figure 9.11**). Check product labeling to verify whether a toy is appropriate for the children's use. For toys without a label attached, use a plastic choke tube to test the size. Any toy that fits inside the tube presents a choking risk for children under three years of age. Of particular risk are balls with a diameter of 1¾ inches or less and rattles that are small enough to be lodged in the throat or with pieces that can separate.

- *Toxic materials in or on toys.* For example, older toys or those produced in other countries may be painted with lead paint, which can be poisonous if ingested. Older art materials may contain toxic materials.

- *Electrically operated toys with heating elements.* Avoid these toys. They can cause burns, fires, or electrocution. Any electrical equipment should have a seal from a safety testing organization, such as Underwriters Laboratories, Inc. (UL).

- *Battery covers with no locking mechanism.* Children can remove these covers, which exposes the batteries. Batteries present a choking risk and are poisonous if placed in the mouth or swallowed. Also dangerous are battery covers with removable screws. If these tiny screws are lost during battery changes, a child might later find and swallow them. Instead, look for covers that incorporate the screws or other locking mechanisms as part of a single piece. Even safer is a single-piece cover that is attached to the toy. An attached battery cover eliminates the risk of choking on the cover itself.

- *Fabric products or toys that are not flame retardant or flame resistant.* The label will show whether a product resists or slows the rate of burning. If not, do not purchase the product.

- *Balloons.* Many children each year die from choking on uninflated balloons or balloon pieces. Inflated balloons that pop are hazardous if they are swallowed. Balloons should be avoided in the classroom.

- *Toys with small bead-like objects inside them.* If these toys are broken, the objects can fall out and pose a choking risk.

- *Pull toys with long cords or strings.* Cords and strings on toys should be too short to wrap around a child's neck, preventing the chance of strangulation. Strings should be 12 inches or less.

- *Plastic climbing equipment used indoors without proper surfacing.* Carpeting does not provide adequate protection from falls from indoor climbing equipment. The CPSC reports these falls are the leading cause for significant injuries in child care settings. For indoor climbing equipment, approved rubber flooring or tile is needed.

If you have a safety problem with a product, you have an ethical obligation to report it. Your report can help protect other children from the same danger. Call the CPSC or visit the CPSC website to report an unsafe product. The CPSC investigates the reports it receives from consumers. If the CPSC finds the product to be unsafe, it may issue a product recall or ban. The CPSC can also set new standards in response to reports of consumer safety problems.

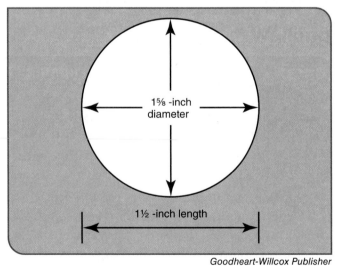

Goodheart-Willcox Publisher

Figure 9.11 The safest toys for children under age three years have small parts that meet these size standards.

Safety First

Shopping for Safe Toys

Although your daily routine at an early childhood center may involve checking toys for broken parts and other hazards, you also need to think about these factors when you buy toys. The Consumer Product Safety Commission (CPSC) offers tips on toy-shopping safety and information on toy recalls. Before you shop, check out the CPSC website.

9.2-2 Selecting Playground Equipment

Playground equipment may consist of stationary equipment, wheeled toys, wading pools or sprinklers, a shaded resting area, and animal shelters. Stationary equipment is the most costly and difficult to choose.

Selecting playground equipment may be the job of the director, however, the director often asks teachers for suggestions to help in this process. In other programs, a committee of parents, teachers, and directors choose the playground equipment. Everyone involved in the decision needs to know key points to consider.

Safety

For playground equipment, safety is always the primary concern. Many children are injured each year on outdoor playgrounds. Falls from swings, climbing devices, and monkey bars were cited most often in most equipment-related injuries. Choosing equipment with safety in mind can reduce the number of serious injuries. See **Figure 9.12** for a detailed list of playground surfacing materials. Visit the CPSC website for detailed information about specific kinds of equipment.

Avoid choosing new equipment that is unsafe and check existing equipment for dangers. Repair or remove any dangerous equipment at once. General hazards to avoid include the following:

- *Exposed pinch-crush parts on seesaws or gliders.* Children's skin or clothing can catch in these areas. In addition, a child might lose a finger or toe if pinched here. Remove equipment with exposed pinch-crust parts from the playground at once.

- *Head entrapment openings.* Measure the exercise rings or space between parts of equipment, such as rungs in a ladder. Openings should be smaller than 3½ inches or larger than 9 inches. Children can get their heads caught in openings between these sizes. Remove any rings or close the risers on ladders of unsafe sizes.

- *Open-end S-rings on swing sets.* These rings can pinch skin or catch clothing. You can close the S-ring by pinching the ring shut with a pair of pliers.

- *Hard swing seats.* Children can be injured if hit by a hard swing seat, such as those made of wood, metal, or hard plastic. Replace any hard swing seats with soft seats made of rubber or canvas (**Figure 9.13**).

- *Exposed screws, bolts, or sharp edges.* Cuts and scrapes can result from these hazards. Use your hands to feel all the equipment. Cover bolts, screws, or sharp edges with layers of duct tape. Recheck the area often and reapply tape as needed. In addition, exposed screws and bolts are a danger because a child's hair or clothes can catch on them.

- *Hot metal playground equipment.* The US Consumer Product Safety Commission (CPSC) advises adults to check for hot metal surfaces before allowing children to play on them. Solid steel slides, decks, steps, and railings in direct sunlight may reach temperatures high enough to cause serious burns. Unlike adults or older children, young children are at major risk since they do not react quickly. They may remain in place when in contact with a hot surface. The result could be second, or third, degree burns to the buttocks, hands, and legs.

Even if a piece of equipment is free from safety hazards, it may still not be safe for use by children in a particular program. Adults should consider each piece of equipment in terms of the following:

Surfacing Materials

Material	Advantages	Disadvantages
Pea gravel	• Readily available • Inexpensive • Drains easily • Easy to install	• Needs barriers to contain • Pea gravel not recommended for children under five years of age • Medium-sized gravel causes more superficial scrapes • Occasionally needs replacement • Becomes compact when wet
Wood chips	• Readily available • Inexpensive • Drains easily • Easy to install	• Needs barriers to contain • Compacts easily • Decomposes quickly so needs replacement periodically
Shredded rubber materials	• Inexpensive • More wheelchair accessible than loose fill	• Requires a good drainage system • May stain clothing if not treated
Safety-tested mat systems or rubber matting	• Easy to clean and maintain • Accessible for wheelchairs • Does not absorb water • Prohibits mold and fungus growth • Foreign objects are easy to see • Annual replacement requirements are lower	• The most expensive to install • Needs to be installed on a flat surface
Sand	• Inexpensive • Does not deteriorate • Easy to install	• Attractive to cats • Must be raked • Undesirable or harmful objects may become embedded
Synthetic turf	• Low maintenance • Constructed from antimicrobial materials • Provides a natural look • Available up to 12 feet fall heights	• Expensive

Figure 9.12   Protective surfacing materials such as these are essential for reducing life-threatening head injuries.

- Is the equipment safe for the children's ages and level of development? Some pieces of stationary equipment are designed for older children. Others are made for younger children. Programs with children of mixed ages need separate equipment for each age group.

- Is there enough room for the equipment on the existing playground? This includes room required around the equipment for safety. Pieces of play equipment should be spaced at least 6 feet apart. Equipment should not be placed too close to sandboxes, wheeled toy paths, fences, or sidewalks.

- Can the equipment be anchored properly? Equipment must be stable to avoid overturning, tipping, sliding, or moving in any way. The equipment needs to be anchored in concrete below ground level before it is used. The anchoring process needs to comply with manufacturer's specifications.

Appeal

If the equipment does not appeal to children, they will not use it. Before choosing equipment, teachers might ask children what they want to do on the playground (such as climb, swing, or

Olga Enger/Shutterstock.com

Figure 9.13   The safest swings have closed S-rings, rubber or canvas seats, steady anchoring, and adequate surfacing. *Explore the children's outdoor swings in local parks and playgrounds in your area. Can you identify any safety risks?*

run). Then they can choose equipment to allow children to meet their goals.

Equipment needs to accommodate several children at once (**Figure 9.14**). It should also be accessible for children with special needs. Colorful and interesting design attracts children's interest. Children prefer having a variety of equipment. They enjoy being able to push, pull, balance, swing, and slide. Children also like equipment on which they can climb or crawl in, out, under, and around. What they seem to like least is equipment with just one use.

Maintenance

When shopping for playground equipment, keep maintenance in mind. The program's staff will be responsible for repairing or replacing broken equipment. For safety reasons, children must not use or play near broken equipment.

Rawpixel/Shutterstock.com

Figure 9.14   Playing together enhances children's social skills and enjoyment of active play.

Safety First

Playgrounds for Children with Diverse Abilities

Children with diverse abilities may require a variety of playground modifications for accessibility and safety. For example, children with mobility problems may need wheelchair ramps or transfer systems. Consult the *Americans with Disabilities Act (ADA)* website for more information on accessibility for play areas.

Choose equipment that is durable. This equipment will withstand many years of heavy use. It will be less likely to break and need repair, which lowers maintenance costs.

For durability and safety, many of the newer playgrounds are constructed from plastic with metal and wood supports. This type of equipment combines the best features of each type of material. All-metal equipment is too hot in summer and too cold in winter. Over time, this equipment will also rust. All equipment made from natural wood will weaken, splinter, and rot. The plastic used for some equipment is a composite. It is made from sawdust and recycled plastic. It is weather resistant, so it will not splinter, warp, or rot.

Two other safety factors require consideration. Decks and platforms over 30 inches from the ground need to contain railings. Check opening sizes carefully on these railings and ladder rungs to prevent any child from entrapment. Safety experts recommend openings of less than 3½ inches or over 9 inches.

Cost

Of course, programs must follow their budget when making playground purchases. Some programs plan a fundraiser to help meet the cost of expensive items. Staff should search catalogs and websites of several companies to learn what is available. Programs should receive cost estimates from each company. They should ask about costs for delivery, assembly, and installation. Knowing the final cost helps the program set goals for obtaining the money needed.

9.2-3 Sources for Toys and Equipment

Before you begin selecting new toys and equipment, take an inventory of materials that are on hand. After you complete this task, compare the inventory with program goals. For example, you may note that there are too few manipulative toys. These, then should be at the top of the list for purchase. Evaluate all available sources to find the best selection and price (**Figure 9.15**).

Using your list, browse online and through catalogs to find items you need. Take time to look through various websites and all the catalogs at the center. Prices can vary a great deal, so consider all costs before ordering. For instance, does the shipping cost for an item make the purchase price too high? Some companies will not charge a shipping fee if the order is large.

Early childhood centers can also purchase equipment through a co-op. A **co-op (cooperative)** is a group of people or organizations who join for the mutual benefit of more buying power. Directors of several small centers sometimes form co-ops. One goal of the co-op is to purchase toys and equipment at the lowest cost. Companies will often give a discount on large orders. The directors share the savings with all those who are making purchases.

If time is available, you may wish to visit flea markets, garage sales, and discount stores. Materials can often be purchased at reduced prices. When buying used items, be extra cautious

Judy Herr

Figure 9.15 The exhibit area at an early childhood conference is a good source for toys and equipment.

regarding safety. Check for product recalls and know the safety standards for the objects you seek.

Toys can also be designed and built at the center. Older adults, scout troops, and others may volunteer to help. Many of these people are skilled in making puppets, doll clothes, dramatic play clothes, and wooden toys.

Buying Consumable Supplies

Clay, paper, paint, paste, glue, and other art materials are called **consumable supplies**. Once a consumable supply is used, it cannot be used again. To save money, some centers order these materials only once or twice a year. There are many ways to purchase these supplies.

If the order is large, the center may ask vendors to make bids on the sale. **Vendors** are the people who sell the supplies. Their **bid** is the price at which they will sell the items.

The center might also contact a vendor when placing a large order and ask for a 10-percent discount, plus free shipping. Many directors are surprised to learn that this can be done. This is very useful for stretching the center budget.

Lesson 9.2 Review

1. To what government agency should you report safety problems with toys? (9.2.1)
   A. CPSC
   B. ASTM
   C. U.S. Department of Education
   D. U.S. Department of Health and Human Services
2. Which of the following is *not* a safety hazard in toys? (9.2.1)
   A. Small parts
   B. Balloons
   C. Smooth edges
   D. Pull toys with long cords
3. **True or False.** Openings on all railings and ladder rungs of outdoor equipment prevent child entrapment. (9.2.2)
4. Which is an example of a consumable supply? (9.2.3)
   A. Truck
   B. Glue
   C. Play dough
   D. Doll

Chapter 9 Review and Assessment

Summary

Lesson 9.1

9.1-1 Following criteria for selecting toys, equipment, and educational materials is an important task.

9.1-1 Key factors to consider include program goals, budget, balance, cultural diversity, space, supervision, maintenance, durability, quantity, child involvement, and developmental age.

9.1-2 Toys should require active involvement of children and be developmentally appropriate They should also be nonviolent, non-sexist, multicultural, and safe.

9.1-3 Technology use requires thoughtful and intentional planning.

9.1-3 Media use has benefits and risks. Follow all guidelines for appropriate media use with young children.

Lesson 9.2

9.2-1 Safety is the primary concern when buying toys and playground equipment. Appeal to children, maintenance and durability, and cost are other important considerations.

9.2-1 Laws and guidelines help you to choose safe products for the children in your care. Make purchases only after reviewing the guidelines.

9.2-1 Understanding how to report unsafe toys and equipment to appropriate agencies is important for all early childhood professionals.

9.2-2 For playground equipment, safety is always the primary concern.

9.2-3 There are many sources for toys, equipment, and supplies. Knowing where and how to make these purchases can help teachers use the center budget wisely.

9.2-3 Purchasing large quantities of consumable supplies may require seeking bids from vendors.

Vocabulary Activity

Using a T-chart, write the *Key Terms* in the left column of the chart. Write the definition of each term in your own words in the right column of the chart. Compare your definitions with a classmate and with the text.

Critical Thinking

1. **Analyze.** Write a report on your favorite childhood toys. Analyze the characteristics of the toys and identify the value of each.

2. **Evaluate.** Choose a software item available for use in early childhood classrooms. Use online resources to research the features and benefits of the software. If possible, try using the software. Evaluate the software against the text guidelines. Write a summary of your evaluation to share with the class.

3. **Articulate.** How would you manage technology, media, and other resources to promote healthy development of the children in your care? Express your response in a short report to the class.

4. **Determine.** Search for five new toys and equipment that can be added to a preschool classroom. Choose items that will actively involve children. Do the items encourage children to explore, manipulate, invent, and problem solve? Are the items affordable when purchasing in quantity? Do the items represent a variety of toys and equipment? Discuss your findings in class.

5. **Create.** Based on the chapter criteria, create a design for an early childhood classroom and outdoor play area for 20 children. How much space would your classroom and outdoor play area require? What other factors do you need to consider about the space?

Core Skills

1. **Math.** Presume your center director has assigned you a specific amount of money to be budgeted for toy and equipment acquisition for the coming school year. Predetermine the percentages of the amount to be spent on each area. Select the materials to be purchased without going over budget. Create a spreadsheet to keep track of selections and amount of money spent. Figure out the percentages of your expenditures for each activity type after you have selected the materials for that area.

2. **Math.** Divide into teams. Your instructor will assign specific types of materials and equipment for classroom areas from Figure 9.5. Determine the cost of all the equipment for your assigned area if purchased new. Search websites and equipment catalogs for prices. Add the prices to total your section. Once all groups are finished, share your group's total with the class. Add all the group totals together.

3. **Research.** Use toy and equipment catalogs for early childhood education to investigate gender-neutral toys and equipment. Choose one item to review in detail. Write a summary about the item and indicate why you would choose this item to use in an early childhood classroom.

4. **Research.** Research the history of multicultural education in the United States. Ask a social studies teacher to share information about the struggle for equality in education during the last half of the twentieth century. What challenges still exist? How does this information affect a developmentally appropriate preschool program?

5. **Speaking.** Interview an early childhood program director about toy and equipment selection criteria. Write a report of your findings to post on the class website for peer and instructor review and comment.

6. **Writing and Speaking.** Write, perform, and video record short television public safety announcements regarding toy safety. Your school's technology or television department may help in shooting and editing the video. Videos should contain needed information in a concise and visual method. Show the videos to preschool parents at conferences.

7. **CTE Career Readiness Practice.** Presume you are a new employee at a local early childhood center. Your employer asks you to research information on toy safety standards for indoor and outdoor toy and equipment safety and the relation of standards to the Consumer Products Safety Commission (CPSC). Do the standards apply equally to all toys? What role does third-party testing and certification play in toy safety? Write a report of your findings using reliable online resources. Share your findings with your employer (your class and instructor) for review and comment.

Portfolio Project

Write a preschool parent newsletter article that shows your understanding of the skills children will develop from using toys. The article can explain developmental appropriateness and developmental age. It should also suggest toys that provide opportunities for learning and creativity. Refer to the Checklist for Skills Learned from Toys in 10.7 to explain how you would analyze a toy for its potential as a learning tool. Keep a copy of your article in your portfolio.

Promoting Children's Safety

Lesson 10.1: Early Childhood Safety Procedures
Lesson 10.2: Neglect, Abuse, and Liability

Case Study

What Dangers Can be Found in Early Childhood Centers?

Dangers can be found everywhere in early childhood centers. Dakota Kondra was just assigned a student teacher from a local community college. To prepare for the student's participation, Dakota printed a list of objectives and limits to promote the children's safety, including walking indoors and wiping up spills right away. When the student arrived for the orientation, Dakota stressed children need to have safety limits. They need to learn ways to play safely both indoors and outdoors to protect themselves and prevent injuries to others. Dakota also stated that children needed limits that were consistently enforced. For safety, they needed to wear helmets when riding tricycles and scooters outdoors. They also needed to learn to operate wheeled toys without accidentally hurting each other.

Give It Some Thought

1. What other safety objectives should Dakota share with the student teacher for providing a safe, healthy, and stimulating environment?
2. What safety precautions do early childhood programs need to follow?
3. What emergency phone numbers should be posted in the center? Why?
4. What sun safety precautions do early childhood centers need to follow to protect the children?
5. What does the term *liability* mean? How does liability apply to early childhood settings? Could the teacher be liable? Why or why not?

Opening image credit: recep-bg/E+ via Getty Images

Early Childhood Safety Procedures

Essential Question

What do I need to know about procedures for promoting and maintaining children's safety in an early childhood program?

Learning Outcomes

After studying this lesson, you will be able to

10.1-1 identify objectives for maintaining a safe environment for children.

10.1-2 outline ways to promote and practice safety in an early childhood program.

10.1-3 describe guidelines for promoting children's safety, including safe adult-child ratios, environment safety, fire safety and fire extinguishers, sun safety, weather and disaster emergencies, and procedures for treating poisonings.

Key Terms

limits

sun protection factor (SPF)

"**P**lease give me that broken toy," teacher Lucinda Goldstein said to the child. She immediately saw the danger of the unsafe toy. At the same time, the center director was checking the art supplies. In the kitchen, the cook was filling out the monthly safety and sanitation checklist. All these staff members were showing their concern for the children's safety by checking the safety of their surroundings.

Dangers can be found everywhere in an early childhood center (**Figure 10.1**). Electrical outlets, cleaning supplies, plants, woodworking tools, outdoor climbing equipment, and cooking tools can all cause injuries. Staff members must closely observe and remove these dangers. Failure to do so may cause accidents. Most accidents can be avoided.

Accidents are more likely to occur when a disruption occurs in the children's routine. Accidents also occur more frequently when staff are absent, busy, or tired.

10.1-1 Safety Objectives

The center staff is responsible for providing a safe, healthy, and stimulating environment for children. The basic objectives toward this goal include the following:

- Supervise the children at all times.
- Maintain at least the minimum adult-child ratio as required in your state.
- Develop and follow through with safety limits.
- Provide a safe environment.
- Practice fire safety.
- Protect children from extreme temperatures and the sun.
- Develop and practice plans for weather emergencies.
- Know emergency procedures for accidental poisoning.
- Recognize signs of child abuse and neglect and report any known or suspected cases.
- Teach children how to protect themselves from sexual assault.

The following sections will summarize procedures for meeting each of these objectives.

FatCamera/E+ via Getty Images

Figure 10.1 Young children can get into dangerous situations in seconds. Supervision is necessary at all times. *Give two examples of dangerous situations for young children.*

Supervise the Children at All Times

"It happened so fast—I just looked away for a moment," said the teacher. This teacher did not understand that children cannot be left alone for even a moment. A teacher who is responsible for a group of children should supervise constantly. He or she must be prepared to spot potential dangers. Young children do not always understand the concept of danger. As a result, teachers must protect the children.

Young children are fearless, unpredictable, and quick. They lack sound judgment because they lack experience and cannot see another's viewpoint. They may bite, throw, push, hit, kick, or shove. All these actions can endanger others as well as themselves. Young children may not recognize behaviors or actions that can cause injuries to themselves or others.

To properly supervise a group of children, keep your back to the classroom wall. Focus on the interior of the classroom. The entire room should be visible. Move closer to an area if you observe children who need help or redirection. Likewise, constantly observe children who are not involved in an activity. Be especially protective of younger children. Usually, younger children require more staff supervision than older children.

Bumps, bruises, and scratches can occur in overcrowded classrooms. Make sure there is enough space for furniture and equipment. Observe children as they play. Can they move from area to area without bumping into furniture or other children? If sufficient space does not exist, remove some furniture or rearrange the classroom.

Maintain Minimum Adult-Child Ratios

Adult-child ratio relates directly to safety. A classroom should never have fewer adults than required by state law for its age level and group size. Having more adults than the minimum is even safer and adds to program quality. These extra adults can step in quickly to protect children when unsafe situations arise.

The minimum number of staff members set by your state's licensing rules must be always present. Failure to comply may result in revocation of the center's license or a citation indicating the center was not in compliance. Remember, too, if there is an injury to a child and the staff/child ratios are lower than the requirement, center staff may be liable.

Develop Safety Limits

Limits are guides to actions and behaviors that reflect the goals of a program. Another name for limits is *rules*. The most important limits set by early childhood teachers involve safety issues. These limits protect the children. Make safety limits positive, simple, and clear for children to understand.

Some typical safety limits include the following:

- Walk indoors.
- Use blocks for building.
- Wipe up spills right away.
- Tell the teacher when equipment breaks.
- Always fasten your seat belt when riding in the center's van.
- Always use safety straps on equipment when available (Figure 10.2).
- Climb the ladder using both hands to go up the slide.
- Wear a bicycle helmet when riding bikes.
- Wash your hands before and after playing with dough or at the water table.

Children need reminders about the limits. Otherwise, they may forget or ignore them. For example, Eino may walk in front of moving swings. When this happens, say, "Eino, walk around the swings, not in front of them." Usually, this reminder will redirect a child. If Eino still cannot comply, you may have to say, "Eino, you need to stay away from moving swings." Do not allow anyone to continue swinging until Eino moves a safe distance away from the swings.

Teach children to wipe up spills promptly. Always keep paper towels within the children's reach. When children forget to wipe up a spill, remind them. Likewise, it is important to praise children who remember. Say, "Skyler, thank you for wiping up that spill. Now no one will slip and fall." Praise will encourage all the children to remember the limits. In time, you may hear the children remind each other of the limits.

Thien Woei Jiing/iStock via Getty Images Plus

Figure 10.2 Early childhood teachers should use safety straps when available on outside equipment.

10.1-2 Provide a Safe Environment

Closely observing children and setting safety rules for them to obey helps create a safe center. This is only part of the process. You must watch for hazardous situations. Toys, equipment, electrical appliances, hot water, and cleaning supplies can pose danger to children. Center vehicles and the building itself can also be hazardous to children.

Toys and Materials

A teacher's first job regarding toy safety is to choose items wisely. Picking safe toys and materials reduces the risk of serious injury.

Selection is just the first step. As a teacher, you must constantly supervise children using toys. Children often use toys in ways for which they were not designed. While most times this play is harmless, sometimes you must intervene for safety reasons. For instance, a wooden mallet for use with a pegboard might be dangerous if children use it to hit each other. A child can use a metal toy car safely for driving on the floor. This same car poses a safety risk, however, if the child throws it. You must teach children about safe toy use and repeat safety limits often. Be firm but pleasant when enforcing the limits.

Remember, a toy can be safe for one child, but dangerous for another. Accidents can occur when children use toys that are too advanced for them. For instance, five-year-old children love to play with large marbles. These same marbles are a choking hazard for younger children.

Check toys frequently for safety. To illustrate, check the seams of cloth infant toys for tearing and weak threads. If the toy lacks durability, remove it from the classroom. Depending on the condition and value, it can either be repaired or discarded.

Examine toys for sharp or splintered edges. Observe to see if any small pieces have broken off or splintered. If a toy requires repairs, immediately remove it from the classroom.

As a teacher, you must also stay informed about changes in safety standards. When new standards are issued, check current toys to be sure they conform. Discard items that do not meet the new standards.

Playground Equipment

Staff members have several duties related playground safety. First, they must be sure to plan the playground with safety in mind. For example, proper surfacing is a key safety concern (**Figure 10.3**).

Second, staff members must select safe playground equipment. Safer equipment eliminates many preventable accidents. Many products are available today to help children enjoy safe outdoor play.

onfilm/iStock via Getty Images Plus

Figure 10.3   An impact-absorbing surface was installed under this playground equipment to prevent serious injuries related to falls. ***What impact-absorbing materials are best to use on playgrounds?***

Third, staff must evaluate existing equipment for safety. Older equipment rarely meets current safety standards. This equipment often contains hazards not found on newer equipment. These hazards include head entrapments, sharp edges, hard swing seats, and all-metal slides. Staff should research laws on playground equipment safety. They must be sure their program complies with these requirements. Next, staff can seek tips from professional organizations regarding playground safety. These tips can offer extra protection by exceeding legal requirements.

Falls are the most common cause of playground injuries. Children fall off equipment because they lose their grip, balance, or slip. When falling, for protection they often extend their hand in an outward position. This can cause an elbow fracture. The National Program for Playground Safety (NPPS) estimates that 30 percent of all injuries occur because of poor maintenance. As equipment ages, it is likely to need upkeep and repair. For this reason, check all playground equipment often for dangers. Many programs devise a safety checklist to guide teachers in inspecting the playground. Teachers conduct weekly checks, fill out the checklist, and give it to the director. The director must then arrange for needed repairs or maintenance.

Finally, and perhaps most importantly, staff are responsible for supervising children on the playground. Even the safest equipment can cause accidents when not used properly. Limits must be set and enforced regarding equipment use.

Workplace Connections

Identifying Hazards

Survey the areas in the center that children access and then document all hazards. This may include slippery walkways, loose flooring materials, inappropriate equipment, poisonous landscape plants, and weed treatments.

1. What changes could staff make to create safe areas or reduce the hazards?
2. Should all early childhood centers be subject to the same types of hazards? Are some types of early childhood centers exempt by licensing? If so, which ones.

Children can be involved in setting these limits, if developmentally appropriate. Teachers must constantly observe children using the equipment and step in when needed. Staff should praise children who are practicing safety.

Transportation

Motor vehicle accidents pose the greatest threats to children's lives. They are the leading cause of death for children from two to 14 years of age. Due to safety concerns, the National Highway Traffic Safety Administration (NHTSA) recommends transporting preschool and school-aged children in 12- or 15-passenger vehicles. Vans, buses, and other vehicles owned by the center should have safety door locks and safety restraints installed according to manufacturers' specifications. Additional guidelines include the following:

- The same staff-child ratio must be maintained when children are being transported.
- The driver cannot be counted in the staff-child ratio when transporting three or more children under the age of two years.
- Staff must have a functioning cell phone for use in case of emergency.
- Transport all children in an approved Child Safety Restraint System (CSRS). Children must use the CSRS until they weigh over 50 pounds.
- Keep transit time under one hour whenever possible.
- Children up to age three should ride in a rear-facing car seat until they reach the manufacturer's height or weight limits.
- Children four to seven years of age should ride in a forward-facing car seat with a harness until they reach the seat's height or weight limits. Many seats can accommodate children up to 65 pounds.
- Children ages eight to 12 who have outgrown car seats need a booster seat, lap belt, and shoulder harness until the vehicle seat belt fits properly. Typically, this is when the child has reached the height of 4 feet and 9 inches.

Train all staff and parent volunteers on the proper use of child safety restraints. While riding in any center vehicles, children should be secured in a properly adjusted seat belt or child safety seat. Do not allow children to put their arms or heads out of the vehicle's windows. When several children are riding in a vehicle, extra adult supervision may be necessary.

Center vehicles should be adapted or designed for transportation of children with disabilities. Vehicles are also required to have equipment for emergency situations. A first aid kit for treating minor injuries should be in each vehicle. Moreover, a fire extinguisher and tools for changing tires should also be present in each vehicle. Vehicle drivers should be trained to correctly use these items. Check your state licensing requirements to ensure you are complying with their rules and regulations.

Building Security

Early childhood centers must take safety measures to control unauthorized access to the building. Some centers install keypads and assign ID codes to parents and staff (**Figure 10.4**). Computers may also be available for tracking when parents sign their children in and out of the center. A sign-in/sign-out system should also be available for anyone else who enters the center, and should include the name and telephone number of each person, and their purpose, such as guest, volunteer, or vendor. The time entering and exiting needs to be included.

Outside gates should have locks installed and be locked. Some centers also install observation cameras and observation windows. The cameras monitor the center's entrances and exits while the observation windows provide access for monitoring classrooms.

Many accidents that occur in centers involve the building and building fixtures. Windows, doors, floors, and stairs all may cause injuries. Doors should have rubber gaskets or pinch guards (plastic shields) to prevent finger pinching. They should open to the outside and have see-through panes. This will help prevent injuries by making the children inside the classroom visible to anyone opening the door.

Keep windows closed at all times unless gates or sturdy screens are in place. Keep floors dry. If wax is used, use a nonslip type. Cover stairways with carpet or rubber treads. Make sure stairways are well lighted and free of clutter. Install railings at the children's level on both sides of the stairs.

Sliding patio doors, doors with glass panels, and storm doors can all be dangerous. To protect the children, use only safety glass. Decals applied to sliding glass doors at their eye level warn children of glass they might not otherwise see.

Fans should be mounted and out of the children's reach. Cover all unused electrical outlets in the building with safety plugs. Avoid using extension cords.

UW-Stout Child and Family Study Center

Figure 10.4 A keypad entry system prevents unauthorized access to the building. *What other security precautions my early childhood centers take to prevent unauthorized building access? Use the text and online resources for ideas.*

10.1-3 Practice Safety

Fire Safety

To promote fire safety, check the center regularly for fire hazards. The best protection against fires is prevention. As a teacher, you need to become skilled in finding and correcting fire hazards. Study **Figure 10.5**. This safety checklist will help you identify potential hazards.

Check smoke alarms and carbon monoxide (CO) detectors at least once each month to make sure they are working. If smoke detectors are battery powered, change batteries when indicated. Most states require smoke alarms and CO detectors to be hardwired into the electrical system. Check your state licensing rules and regulations.

Carbon monoxide and smoke detectors should be installed and maintained in the center. Carbon monoxide is known as a silent killer. It is colorless, odorless, and tasteless. Symptoms include drowsiness, dizziness, confusion, and loss of consciousness. A sound, beep or chirp will sound when the detector is activated.

Fire Extinguishers

Each early childhood center needs several fire extinguishers. The director is often in charge of securing fire extinguishers for the center. Fire extinguishers are classified by fire type.

Fire Safety Checklist

Checklist	Yes	No
Exit passageways and exits are free from furniture, equipment, and toys.		
Locks on bathroom and toilet stall doors can be opened from the outside by center staff.		
Protective safety plugs are placed in on all electrical outlets.		
Permanent wiring is used instead of extension cords.		
Each wall outlet contains no more than two electrical appliances.		
A fire evacuation plan is posted.		
Fire drills are conducted at least monthly, some of which are unannounced.		
Flammable, combustible, and other dangerous materials (including hand sanitizers) are marked and stored in areas accessible only to staff.		
Children are restricted to floors with grade-level exits (no stairs).		
The basement door is kept closed.		
No items are stored under stairs.		
Smoke detectors are installed in each room and checked regularly.		
Smoke alarms, fire alarms, carbon monoxide detectors, and emergency lighting are checked at least once a month.		
Toys, chairs, tables, and other equipment are made of flame-retardant materials.		
Carpets and rugs are treated with a flame-retardant material.		
Emergency procedures and numbers are posted by each telephone.		
Evacuation cribs fit easily through the doors.		

Goodheart-Willcox Publisher

Figure 10.5   Regularly checking an early childhood center aganist a Fire Safety Checklist is an important task for staff and child care providers.

Prevent Carbon Monoxide Poisoning

Carbon monoxide (CO) is a deadly gas. It is odorless and invisible. Symptoms of poisoning include headache, fatigue, nausea, and dizziness. When such fuels as coal, kerosene, gasoline, natural gas, propane, oil, and wood burn incompletely, carbon monoxide forms. Heating systems and cooking appliances that burn fuel can also be a source of carbon monoxide when they do not function properly. Proper installation and venting along with regular professional inspection and maintenance of equipment can help prevent carbon monoxide formation.

Centers must meet state and local laws regarding carbon monoxide detectors. If centers use any source of fuels that can be a source of carbon monoxide, detectors must be installed to warn facility occupants when carbon monoxide is in the air. When the alarm goes off, immediately move to a fresh-air location and call emergency personnel.

- Class A fire extinguishers are effective against fires involving textiles, wood, plastic, and paper.
- Class B fire extinguishers are effective against flammable-liquid fires. Examples are gasoline, oil, oil-based paints (in cans), alcohols, and flammable gases.
- Class C fire extinguishers are suitable for fires in live electrical equipment.
- Class D fire extinguishers are suitable for combustible metals, such as magnesium, titanium, zirconium sodium, lithium, and potassium.
- Class K fire extinguishers are suitable for fires in cooking appliances that involve combustible fats and oils.

Rating system indicates the rating size of the fire that the unit can extinguish. A fire extinguisher with a 1-A rating must be capable of extinguishing a wood crib, shredded paper, and wood panels. The higher the number, the larger the surface that can be extinguished and the heavier the extinguisher. For example, a 10-A fire extinguisher is heavier and can extinguish a larger surface.

Before buying extinguishers, contact your local fire department. The fire chief can tell you which types and sizes of extinguishers is best suited for your center's unique needs. Schedule annual in-service training on fire extinguishers for staff members. Some directors prefer to have a local firefighter conduct this in-service. After this orientation, update all staff members yearly (and newly hired members) on fire extinguisher use.

Check the condition of each fire extinguisher monthly. Note any problems you find. Immediately replace any extinguisher with any of the following conditions:

- pressure gauge indicating a higher or lower pressure than recommended
- blocked nozzle or other parts
- missing pin or tamper seal
- dents, leaks, rust, or other signs of damage

Emergency Lighting

All early childhood facilities are required to have emergency lighting. This lighting is located in hallways, stairwells, and building exits. Some communities require fixed, mounted security lighting in these locations. For family child care homes, battery-powered emergency lights that plug into wall outlets to remain charged may be acceptable. Always check with the local fire marshal and state licensing rules to determine the type and location of emergency lighting. Because they are not safe, never use candles and fuel-operated lanterns in an early childhood center. Rather, use emergency lighting.

Fire Drills and Evacuation Procedures

Fires are a major concern in early childhood centers. The US Fire Administration estimates there are 325 fires annually in early childhood centers. State licensing rules and regulations require fire and disaster drills. States also require scheduling these drills at least once a month. Vary the time of day (including nap time) and day of week. These drills will prepare staff and children for an actual fire or other emergency. During drills, use the daily class roster to take roll. It is an important tool for checking on the evacuation of all children and their safe return indoors. In addition, most states require monthly inspection for fire hazards by trained staff and monthly checks of the emergency lighting system. Documentation must show that these inspections occurred.

Every center needs to have well-planned evacuation procedures. A fire inspector from the local fire department must approve changes. This approval usually occurs annually during the observation of a fire drill and building inspection for fire hazards. The procedures should include escape routes (and alternate escape routes), planned meeting places outside of the building, staff assignments, and location of alarms and emergency lighting.

The evacuation procedures should be posted in every room where they can be easily seen. In case of blocked routes, plan for alternative evacuation routes. See **Figure 10.6** for an example of procedures to use.

Post emergency phone numbers next to all center telephones. List the following emergency contacts, including names, telephone numbers, and emails or websites:

- Police 911
- Fire 911
- Fire/rescue
- Poison control
- Gas company
- Water company
- Local emergency manager

If you discover a fire in the center, sound the alarm immediately. Stay calm. If you panic, the children will panic as well. Evacuate children from the building at once, even if you do not see flames. Smoke, not fire, is responsible for more deaths. Leave the classroom lights on and close the doors. Do not lock the doors. Lights allow firefighters to see better in a smoke-filled structure.

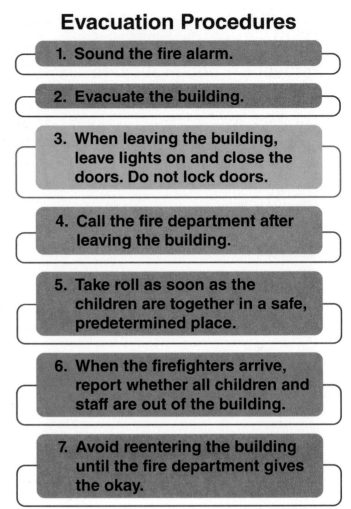

Evacuation Procedures

1. **Sound the fire alarm.**

2. **Evacuate the building.**

3. **When leaving the building, leave lights on and close the doors. Do not lock doors.**

4. **Call the fire department after leaving the building.**

5. **Take roll as soon as the children are together in a safe, predetermined place.**

6. **When the firefighters arrive, report whether all children and staff are out of the building.**

7. **Avoid reentering the building until the fire department gives the okay.**

Goodheart-Willcox Publisher

Figure 10.6 Following appropriate evacuation procedures in case of fire is essential to ensuring the safety of children and staff.

Take roll as soon as the children and staff have cleared the building and have reached the planned meeting areas. When firefighters arrive, inform the chief whether anyone is still in the building.

When making evacuation plans, remember that infants cannot walk and are therefore more difficult to move to a safe location than older children. Most adults cannot carry more than two infants at one time. Therefore, when ratios are higher than one caregiver to two infants, a careful plan needs to be made. Some centers practice by placing several babies in special evacuation cribs and rolling them out of the building. Wagons can be used for evacuating older children, if needed.

Plan and introduce fire and burn prevention into the curriculum, if developmentally appropriate. Remind the children to tell staff right away if they smell smoke. Explain that in a fire, clean air is near the floor. By crawling close to the ground, it will be easier to breathe. Teach the children what to do if their clothing catches fire.

Figure 10.7 shows the stop, drop, and roll technique. Also, share books about fire safety and firefighters. Since firefighters could be frightening to young children, invite one to come to the center. Encourage the firefighter to show the children his or her clothing and equipment.

Sun Safety

The sun's ultraviolet (UV) rays cause harm. The result can be skin damage, eye damage, and even cancer. The sun's rays are the strongest between 10:00 a.m. and 4:00 p.m. During these hours, limit the children's sun exposure as it is the most damaging. Before going outside, always check the UV index. You can retrieve this information easily on smart watches or digital phones.

Daily newspapers provide this information on the weather page. Otherwise, check the US Environmental Protection Agency's website.

Early childhood teachers need to teach children sun safety precautions. Always apply a broad-spectrum sunscreen 30 minutes before going outdoors. The American Academy of Dermatology recommends a broad-spectrum sunscreen with a *sun-protection factor (SPF)* of 30 or higher. **Sun protection factor (SPF)** is a number assigned to a sunscreen that is the factor by which the time required for unprotected skin to become sunburned is increased when the sunscreen is used. Apply generously wherever the skin is showing. For maximum protection, reapply every two hours if the children remain outdoors. Always reapply sunscreen after water play.

The American Academy of Dermatology recommends that babies under 6 months should be kept out of the sun's rays. Infants six months and older may have a broad-spectrum water-resistant sunscreen with an SPF of 30 or higher

1. STOP:
Do not move. Stop where you are.

2. DROP:
Drop to your knees.

3. ROLL:
Cover your face with your hands, and then roll over and over to smother the flames.

BNP Design Studio/Shutterstock.com

Figure 10.7   If clothing catches fire, the stop, drop, and roll technique should be used.

applied to their exposed skin, even on cloudy days. The sun's rays can penetrate through clouds. Follow the manufacturer's instructions on the product label. Some sunscreens are made just for infants and toddlers, and may cause less irritation to sensitive skin. Encourage parents to talk with their pediatrician for recommendations about the best sunscreen to use for their child.

While outdoors, seek shades for activities. Promote sun safety by teaching the shadow rule. If the children cannot see their shadows, they should seek shade or go indoors. They should wear hats and sunglasses designed to block UV radiation. Protecting the eyes with sunglasses having 99-percent UV protection is important. Wearing a hat with a three-inch brim will help protect the eyes, face, ears, and back of the neck.

Safety First

Sun Safety and Hydration for Infants

The American Academy of Pediatrics (AAP) recommends that babies be dressed in lightweight clothing when outdoors and in the sun. Clothing should have long sleeves and long pant legs to keep sensitive skin from direct sunlight.

It is important to note that babies are at greater risk for dehydration when outdoors in the summer heat. Because their internal "heating and cooling systems" are not yet well-developed, they do not sweat. Therefore, babies can easily become overheated. When taking babies and children outdoors, be sure to pack a cooler with bottles of formula or breast milk and water to keep them well hydrated.

Weather or Disaster Emergencies

Blizzards, hurricanes, floods, electrical storms, tornadoes, and earthquakes are examples of weather or disaster emergencies. All these conditions pose safety threats for the children and staff. Therefore, it is important to have an emergency plan for possible weather or disaster emergencies. The plans you formulate will depend on your geographical area.

In areas where natural disasters occur often, practicing evacuation drills with the children monthly is essential. Evacuation procedures need to become routine for the children so they remember them. Parent or guardian information should be stored in the director's cell phone and kept in case of an emergency. Children should be released only to contacts listed on the child's forms.

In some weather emergencies, you may decide to close the center. The center needs to have a plan in place for notifying parents of such an emergency. The center may need to make special arrangements for transporting the children in such instances.

Be prepared for weather emergencies. Always keep a battery-operated radio and flashlights in a convenient spot. For some weather emergencies, blankets, water, food, and a first aid kit should also be available. Some centers have a NOAA Weather Radio (NWR)—the fastest way to receive weather information from the National Weather Service, 24 hours a day, seven days a week.

Early Childhood Insight

Informing Staff About Toxic Substances

The Occupational Safety and Health Administration (OSHA) requires employers to keep early childhood teachers and care providers informed about the presence and use of any toxic materials in use in a facility. This includes ingredients in art materials and sanitizing products. Employers can get the latest information about such products from the Environmental Protection Agency (EPA) or the Consumer Product Safety Commission (CPSC).

10.1-4 Poisonings

Accidental poisonings are most common in children from one to three years of age. Studies show that children under five years of age account for almost half of poisonings that occur each year. Ingesting medications results in about 50 percent of these poisonings, which can affect many parts of a child's body. The National Safety Council claims that the average residence contains over 40 poisonous products. **Figure 10.8** lists many of these products. Under certain conditions, nearly any substance can be poisonous.

Children eat many things adults would not think of placing in their mouths. There may be times when you are not sure whether a child has eaten something. For instance, you see a child playing with an empty aspirin bottle. The child has powder around the mouth. When in doubt, always assume the worst. If the child has eaten the aspirin, failing to act may cause great harm.

If you suspect that a child in your classroom has eaten something poisonous, remain calm. Do not wait for a poisoning symptom(s) to occur. Rather, telephone the nearest poison control center immediately. If your area does not have a poison control center, call the nearest emergency room. Ask for instructions on treating the child.

Emergency Procedures for Poisonings

Poisoning emergencies often involve swallowing toxic substances. Other types of poisoning emergencies can occur. These include breathing toxic fumes and chemical injuries to the eyes or skin.

If any type of poisoning emergency occurs, follow these procedures. Do not rely on first-aid information, antidote charts, or product information. Often, this information is outdated or incorrect. The child may experience additional injury if you take the wrong action.

Always call 911 or your local emergency immediately if the child is drowsy, is unconscious, has difficulty breathing, or has seizures. Be prepared to provide specific information. You will be asked to

- provide your name, the center name, and your role;
- provide the name of the of the poisonous substance;
- report the amount of the substance consumed;
- report the child's health and weight;
- describe the child's symptoms; and
- identify any first-aid procedures you may have already administered.

Poisonous Substances

Home Cleaning	Personal Care	Plants and Medications	Other Poisons
Cleaners: ammonia, bleach, dishwasher detergent, dishwashing liquid, disinfectants, drain cleaner, dusting spray, laundry pods, lemon oil, spot remover, toilet bowl cleaner, window cleaner, drain cleaner	Cosmetics and personal care items: aftershave lotion, hair care products, makeup, mouthwash, nail polish and nail polish remover, perfume, sunscreen Soap Hand sanitizer	Flowers and plants: many varieties—consult a greenhouse for names or go online Medications: many prescriptions and over-the-counter drugs Vitamins	Mouse poison Paint and paint thinners Pesticides Insecticides Plant food Shoe polish Glue Lighter fluid Matches E-cigarettes Batteries/battery acid Candle wax

Figure 10.8   Many everyday substances are poisonous and need to be kept away from children. *How should poisonous substance be stored in a care center or early childhood classroom?*

If you suspect poisoning and there are no symptoms, contact the national toll-free Poison Help line at 800-222-1222 (in the United States), which will connect you to your local poison center. If the child removed the substance from a container, have the container with you when you call. Unless you know the exact amount, overestimating the amount consumed is better than underestimating it.

One of the leading causes of poisoning in young children is toxic plants. Many common household plants are poisonous. When eaten, many popular house and garden plants can produce toxicity ranging from minor to severe. They can cause skin rashes, upset stomachs, or even death. To prevent poisoning, check with your florist or go online and research before purchasing a plant for the classroom. Finally, teach children never to put any leaves, flowers, or berries into their mouths.

Health Highlights

Poison Proofing

The accidental poisoning of children can happen—anywhere, anytime—whether at home, at an early childhood center, or at a family child care home. Vigilant action is necessary to poison proof any area where children are present. Here are some tips to prevent accidental poisonings.

- Store poisonous substances in their original containers in locked storage. Make sure they are not used in any way that will contaminate play surfaces or food preparation areas. Always follow the manufacturer's directions when using any product.
- Store medications in a locked cabinet or room and out of sight and reach of children. Make sure medications are fitted with child-safety devices.
- Store medications away from food and toxic materials.
- Refer to medication labels to ensure giving children the proper dosage of necessary medicines as prescribed by the health-care professional.

Lesson 10.1 Review

1. Which of the following is *not* a typical safety limit? (10.1.1)
   A. Walk indoors
   B. Wipe up spills right away
   C. Use one hand to climb the ladder going up to the slide
   D. Wear a bicycle helmet when riding a bike

2. **True or False.** When selecting toys, you can assume a toy that is safe for a five-year-old is also safe for a three-year-old. (10.1.2)

3. Each of the following is a guideline to follow when transporting children *except*: (10.1.2)
   A. The same staff-child ratio must be maintained when transporting children.
   B. Transport all children in an approved Child Safety Restraint System (CSRS) until they weigh 30 pounds.
   C. Transport children up to age three in a rear-facing car seat until they reach the manufacturer's height or weight limits.
   D. Keep the transport time to under one hour whenever possible.

4. Which fire extinguisher is best for fires in cooking appliances that involve combustible fats and oils? (10.1.3)
   A. Class A
   B. Class B
   C. Class D
   D. Class K

5. What is the minimum sunscreen SPF that a child should apply? (10.1.3)
   A. 15
   B. 20
   C. 30
   D. 50

6. **True or False.** If a child ingests a poisonous substance, you should wait for symptoms to occur before calling the poison control center or 911. (10.1.4)

Neglect, Abuse, and Liability

Essential Question

? *What are the consequences for children and their families when early childhood teachers and care providers fail to understand the laws and regulations that guide the practice of early childhood care and education?*

Learning Outcomes

After studying this lesson, you will be able to

10.2-1 **recognize** the signs of nonaccidental physical injury, neglect, emotional abuse, and sexual abuse.

10.2-2 **analyze** strategies for mandated reporting, background checks, and protection education.

10.2-3 **teach** children how to resist child abuse.

10.2-4 **implement** strategies for helping families and promoting resilience.

10.2-5 **summarize** types of liability as an early childhood care provider, forms to use for documentation, and privacy law.

Key Terms

neglect

nonaccidental physical injury

emotional abuse

sexual abuse

incest

molestation

mandated reporter

statute

Children can also be in danger of neglect and abuse. Teachers and care providers must recognize the signs of neglect and physical, emotional, and sexual abuse. By law, teachers must report known or suspected child abuse and neglect.

As an early childhood teacher, you will need to be alert to any dangers that threaten the safety of the children. In addition, your program must have safety limits and procedures. The staff must also know their legal responsibilities for protecting the children in their care. Because safety standards vary from state to state, consult your licensing standards.

10.2-1 Neglect and Abuse

Child neglect and abuse is common and the rate of referrals continues to increase. Studies show domestic violence is more prevalent in homes with younger children. Many states reported that more than a quarter of children who experience abuse were younger than three years old. The highest rate of abuse is in babies younger than one year of age who often have head injuries. Twenty percent were between three to five years of age. Neglect was the largest category, representing about 75 percent of maltreatment. Physical abuse was the next largest category, followed by sexual abuse.

Neglect and abuse can happen in any family type or socioeconomic group. Certain situations increase the risk. The three leading factors are financial problems, substance abuse, and the stress of handling parental responsibilities. Single parenthood, isolation from others, and teen parenthood are other factors. Violence between parents can also lead to abuse of their children.

As an early childhood professional, you should be concerned about the health and safety of the children in your care. You do everything you can to see that the center is a safe place for them to be; however, the children are not in your care all the time. When they are away from the center, some children experience abuse. Because you are with the children for several hours a day, you may be the one to notice signs that a child is experiencing neglect or abuse. State law requires you to report known or suspected cases of child abuse. Follow your center's procedures for reporting.

Studies show that children who experience abuse often become troubled adults. These children may have developmental and learning delays. They are also more prone to physical illness and mental health problems. Children who experience abuse are more likely to have difficulties with attachment, regressive behavior, and anxiety. They may drop out of school, lack employment, and commit violent crimes. Exposure to violence also may impair their abilities for partnering and parenting. When these children become parents, they may also be at high risk for abusing their own children. There are four types of child abuse: neglect, nonaccidental physical injury, emotional abuse, and sexual abuse. Be aware of the signs.

Neglect

When children do not receive the basic needs of life, they experience **neglect**. Neglect takes many forms. A child who experiences neglect be deprived of proper food, medical and dental care, shelter, and/or clothing. Children who have been unsupervised may also be experiencing neglect. Neglect may or may not be intentional on the part of the person who abuses or neglects, but the potential for harm is possible.

Children who wear clothing that is too small or dirty may also be experiencing neglect. They may also wear clothes that are inappropriate for the weather, and may lack warm coats, gloves, or hats for the winter. Children with poor grooming may also be neglected.

Other signs of neglect may appear in a child's health. Neglect may cause children to be underweight or experience malnutrition. These children may ask to take food home. Constant fatigue, illness, or poor dental care may be other signs of neglect. These children may have bad body odor due to lack of bathing. Wearing dirty clothes could also contribute to bad odor.

Alert teachers should observe for signs of neglect. They must be sensitive to different child-rearing practices, cultural expectations, and priorities. Signs of possible neglect include the child

- often arrives early or is picked up late;
- displays passive or aggressive behavior;
- wears inappropriate or unclean clothing;
- always seems hungry;
- has a regression in toilet training;
- has unmet medical needs;
- experiences poor hygiene that results in odor;
- appears fatigued, falls asleep, or has a sudden change in self-confidence; or
- may have physical injuries or may not be treated for illness.

Tom is a child who is experiencing neglect. He often arrives early or is picked up late. His teacher observed that he seems small for his age. After observing him for several more months, she noted developmental lags. He appeared to be lagging behind many of his same-age peers. Often, he would ask when snack or lunch would be served. During cooking activities, he would try to eat or take food, and also complained about being hungry. Tom was lacking proper nutrition. As a result, he was constantly fatigued and sometimes fell asleep during class activities.

Observing these signs, Tom's teachers suspected neglect. They compared information and shared their concerns. As early childhood teachers, they knew they were required to report suspected child abuse. They knew Tom would never reach his full potential without proper nutrition and care.

Nonaccidental Physical Injury

The most visible type of child abuse is **nonaccidental physical injury** (Figure 10.9). This is physical abuse inflicted on purpose. It includes biting, scratching, throwing, burning, scalding, punching, and poisoning. Physical abuse can have lasting long-term effects on mental and physical health.

Signs of Possible Physical Abuse

Child has unexplained or repeated injuries (bruises, bites, cuts, welts, burns or scalds, bone fractures, or black eyes)

Child and parent provide illogical or conflicting explanations for injuries

Child complains frequently of pain

Child lacks ability to give or seek affection

Child seems afraid to go home

Child may have fading bruises after an absence from the center

Child displays fear of adults, including parents

Child wears clothing that can hide injuries, even when unsuitable for the weather

Child can be withdrawn or aggressive

Child appears anxious about routine activities, such as toileting, eating, and sleeping

Figure 10.9 Understanding the signs of possible child abuse is essential for all staff.

Children who experience physical abuse often come to school with bruises, bites, burns, or other injuries. They may frequently complain of pain. These children often refuse to discuss their injuries. The people who abuse them may threaten them with further harm if they tell someone. Other children may talk about harsh punishment they have received. Often these children come to the center wearing clothing to hide their injuries. Their clothing may be unsuitable for the weather.

Because of physical abuse, some children may show an unusual fear of adults. Amaya is one example. Her father abused her for two years. A teacher at Amaya's early childhood center contacted authorities with her suspicions. Amaya had an unusual fear of adults, especially her father. Whenever he came to pick her up, she backed away and avoided eye contact with him.

Child abuse was a suspicion for other reasons as well. Amaya often arrived at the center with visible bruises. She also wore long-sleeve turtleneck tops in warm weather. One hot summer day, her teacher was concerned that Amaya might be too warm. When she was changing Amaya's top, the teacher found many bruises. Amaya could not explain the injuries.

Emotional Abuse

Emotional abuse occurs when someone acts in a way to scare, control, or isolate another. Children can experience emotional abuse resulting from of insufficient love, guidance, and/or support from parents or guardians. The verbal and emotional assaults can affect a child's self-esteem. Parents or guardians may make excessive or inappropriate demands on the children, which can cause emotional harm to children.

Children who experience emotional abuse may repeat certain behaviors over several months. Look for the following signs:

- refusal to talk
- unusual or unpredictable behavior
- rare smiling or laughter
- excessive clinging or crying
- appearing withdrawn or showing destructive behavior
- lack of attachment to parent or caregiver
- poor motor coordination for age
- fear of adults

Sexual Abuse

Sexual abuse is forcing a child to observe or engage in sexual activities with an adult. Rape, fondling, oral-genital contact, attempted or completed intercourse, exposure to child pornography, exposure to "flashing," and indecent exposure are all forms of sexual abuse. Each of these acts involves adults using children for their own pleasure. **Incest** is sexual abuse by a relative. **Molestation** is sexual contact made by someone outside the family with a child.

There are many signs of sexual abuse. A child may have problems when walking or sitting. The child may complain of itching, pain, or swelling in the genital area. Some children who experience sexual abuse have bruises in the genital or anal areas. They may also have bruises in their mouths and throats. Some may complain of pain when urinating or may have blood in their underwear.

Children who experience sexual abuse commonly have poor peer behaviors. They may show extremely disruptive or aggressive behaviors. Often, they will regress to infantile behaviors, such as baby-talking, thumb-sucking, or bed-wetting. Some will show a lack of appetite. These children may express affection in improper ways (**Figure 10.10**).

10.2-2 Mandated Reporting

Health-care workers, social workers, school administrators, and teachers are **mandated reporters** of child abuse. This means the law requires them to report any known or suspected cases of child abuse or neglect to the appropriate county authorities or police. As a mandated reporter, you should read your state's **statute**, a formal document drawn up by elected officials. The statute will explain your legal responsibilities and the penalties for failing to make a report. To receive a copy of the statute, contact your local law enforcement office. Another source is the Childhelp National Child Abuse Hotline.

Follow your center's procedure for reporting child abuse and neglect to the proper authorities. Your program must comply with the law, but may also have other guidelines in making a report. For instance, you might need to complete certain paperwork and report the abuse to the director or health consultant. Some programs designate one employee to make all reports of child abuse for the program. In other programs, staff members report these cases themselves.

If you must make a child abuse report, do so immediately by telephone following your center's instructions. Include the name, age, and address of the child and the child's parents or guardian. Report the facts that led to your suspicion (**Figure 10.11**). After the telephone conversation, confirm the report in writing. Make a copy of the written report for the program and one for yourself. If you make the report in good faith, you will not be subject to legal action if they find your suspicions found not to be child abuse or neglect.

Should a child abuse case result in a trial, it may require you to testify in court. Your legal and ethical responsibility is to tell the court what you know about the case that will help the court protect the child.

Case Study—Reporting a Case of Abuse

In recent weeks, Bella's teachers began noticing some unusual behaviors that caused them to suspect she may be experiencing sexual abuse. Bella refused help with clothing and toileting needs. She would not allow teachers to help her remove her outdoor clothing. After observing an incident with another child, her teachers had even greater concern. Bella liked Jayden, one of the children in her group. The teachers saw her touching him inappropriately during group time.

After observing Bella's behavior, the teachers reported their suspicions of abuse. They realized if they waited for more proof, Bella could be at greater risk of abuse.

Figure 10.10 Bella's teachers carefully documented possible indicators of sexual abuse. *If you were Bella's teacher, what would you do? How would you handle reporting this case of suspected abuse?*

fizkes/iStock via Getty Images Plus

Figure 10.11 As mandated reporters, early childhood center staff are required by law to report suspected cases of abuse or neglect.

Background Checks

Early childhood programs need to protect themselves from potential child-abuse accusations. This is a licensing requirement of all states. A center needs to conduct a background check on every teacher, new employee, student teacher, janitor, kitchen staff, administrative staff, and volunteer working in the program. This check will determine if they have had any felony or child-abuse convictions. Some states require a onetime fingerprint check. Individuals convicted of crimes other than minor traffic violations may not be employed.

10.2-3 Protection Education

Planning for children's safety goes beyond the classroom. Children need to learn how to deal with dangers outside the classroom. They must learn about sexual abuse and learn how to protect themselves. The National Survey of Children's Exposure to Violence confirms that children experience exposure to violence in their daily lives. More than 60 percent of children experienced exposure to violence in the last year, either directly or indirectly.

Warning children about strangers has been a common practice for some time, however, only 10 percent of people who abuse children are strangers to the children they abuse. The other 90 percent are people whom the children know. These people may be neighbors, relatives, friends of the family, scout leaders, siblings, or parents. Most offenders are men, but may also be women. Additionally, according to the US Department of Justice, about 23 percent of perpetrators are children under the age of 18.

Before age eight, 3.0 to 4.6 percent of all children experience sexual assault. About 10 percent of these children experience assault by the time they are five years old. Assaults are reported for females far more often than males. Studies show that race, intelligence, family income, and social class do not appear to affect the occurrence of sexual assault.

Teach children to resist sexual attacks. They must first resist the offender by saying no. Then they must tell a trusted friend or relative about the attack. Role-play this process with the children. Give them phrases to use if they find themselves in trouble. The following are examples:

- If someone tries to give you a wet kiss, shake hands instead.
- If someone tries to get you to sit on their lap and you do not want to, say "No, not now."
- If someone wants to give you a hug and you do not want it, say "No thanks."
- If someone tries to touch your genitals, say "Stop. That is not okay."
- If someone rubs or pats your bottom, say "Do not do that."

Children may have trouble identifying sexual abuse. This is especially true with people they know. To combat this problem, explain to the children the difference between *good touch* and *bad touch*. A bad touch is any of the following: a touch the child does not want or like, a touch that hurts or makes the child uncomfortable, a secret touch, or any touch to a child's private parts (genitals). A good touch is wanted and appropriate. It does not make the child uncomfortable.

Suggest various scenarios and ask the children whether these are good or bad touches. In the classroom, encourage children to tell the other person when they do not want to be touched or if they dislike how a touch feels. Help them put these feelings in words. Intervene if a child persists with a touch after another child requests them to stop.

Children also need to learn how and who to tell if someone assaults them. Use puppets, charts, movies, or other materials to teach children this lesson.

10.2-4 Helping Families

Early childhood teachers are able to help families. Daily face-to-face contacts provide opportunities for recognizing families in crisis. Teachers can share parenting information on child development and management of behavior. They can also guide them in seeking community programs, resources, and services. These may include:

- parenting classes
- self-help or support groups
- financial planning
- family counseling
- help lines
- preventive health care programs for children
- nutrition for healthy living

Promoting Resiliency

Neglect and abuse cause children to feel vulnerable. Teachers can play an important role in helping children become resilient. The children benefit from developing a secure relationship with a trusting and supportive teacher. Knowing that someone cares can help children develop faith in themselves. They also learn that they are important. Over time, the teacher can foster resiliency by providing

- consistency and predictability;
- developmentally appropriate limits;
- responsive and stimulating care;
- encouragement for persisting and exploring new opportunities;
- positive expectations;
- problem-solving skills;
- praise for efforts and accomplishments;

- verbal expressions of caring; and
- labels for feelings.

Workplace Connections

Liability Insurance

Interview the director of an early childhood center to discover what type of liability insurance coverage is needed for programs for children.

1. What are the insurance limits for accidents, injuries, and other harm to children?
2. Do the individual teachers and aides need to have their own liability coverage? If so, how much does yearly insurance coverage cost?

10.2-5 Liability

By law, young children are not expected to care for themselves. This is the primary role of the staff at the center. The staff must ensure the children's safety and health. Education is a secondary function.

Center directors are liable for the acts of their employees. *Liable* means having a responsibility that is upheld by the law. Having liability means you can be punished for failing to uphold your legal responsibility. The extent of liability may vary, however. As a result, center directors should only hire individuals who are safety- and health-conscious (**Figure 10.12**). Once hired, the director needs to carefully observe new workers to ensure they use effective supervision techniques.

Types of Liability

Early childhood center staff can receive punishment by law for failing to follow state licensing rules and regulations. They can be liable for failing to

- obtain a signed health form from a licensed physician for each child;
- require all staff members and volunteers have a background check before working with children;
- keep medications in a securely locked location;

Figure 10.12   Safety-conscious staff members watch for danger in all situations.

- provide safe indoor and outdoor equipment;
- maintain the required adult-child ratios at all times;
- provide proper supervision;
- provide proper food storage;
- maintain fence and door locks in proper condition;
- provide staff with information about children's special needs;
- refrain from corporal (physical) punishment;
- provide a safe building;
- remove children who lack self-control and are a hazard to themselves as well as others; and
- cover electrical outlets.

Center directors and staff must constantly monitor the center environment. They must ensure that it is safe and healthy. New teachers will need constant support from the staff and director.

Forms

Every center needs forms related to the health and safety of the children. The licensing departments of some states provide and require standardized forms. Many of these forms direct the staff in the care of the children and protect staff members from possible liability. Two forms commonly used by centers are incident report forms and various types of release or permission forms.

Every center should have a standard *incident report form*. No matter how minor, any injury to a child requires a written report. Any information recorded on this form is useful if parents or guardians bring legal action against the center. Parents also need information about the details of a child's accident or injury. The parental signature on the form conveys that they received the report. **Figure 10.13** shows a sample form.

Centers use a variety of forms depending on state licensing and personal choice. Some states provide forms that can be downloaded and printed. Examples of forms that centers might use include

- Infant Feeding Chart
- Infant Sleep Chart
- Infant Sleep Position Waiver
- Medical Action Plans (asthma, diabetes, seizure, food allergy)

Accident and Incident Report Form
Child and Family Study Center

Child's Name: _Diana Smith_

Date of injury: _March 9, 20XX_ **Time of injury:** _10:30 a.m._ (a.m./p.m.)

Type of injury: (*bite, broken bone or tooth, bruise, burn, choking, cut, ear, eye, head, poisoning, scrape, sliver, sprain, other*):

Scraped elbow

Staff members present: _Antonia Mendoza (teacher), Jane McCarthy (teacher assistant) Elena Simpson (teacher)_

Witness(es): _Elena Simpson (teacher) and Jane McCarthy (teacher assistant)_

Description of the incident: (Include specific information, such as where the child was playing, with whom, and with what.)

While playing outdoors, Diana fell off a tricycle and scraped her elbow.

Description of injury: (Include specific information, such as type, location, size, severity of injury, and symptoms noted following injury.)

Diana's left elbow had a mild scrape with little bleeding after falling off a tricycle.

Action taken by staff: (Include all actions, such as treating injury, seeking medical advice or care, comforting child, and notifying director and parents.)

After ensuring Diana had no further injuries, Antonia Mendoza took Diana into the center building to the nurse's office. Antonia stayed and comforted Diana while the nurse gently washed the wound with soap and warm water. After air-drying, the nurse applied an over-the-counter antibiotic ointment and bandage. After this, Antonia took Diana to the restroom to wash her hands for lunch. Antonia notified the center director and Diana's parents about the injury and completed the Accident and Incident Report Form.

Antonia Mendoza

(Name and signature of staff member attending)

Adrian Smith

(Name and signature of parent or guardian to whom in injury reported)

Figure 10.13 After an accident or other incident, early childhood teachers or care providers must fill out an accident or incident report form following the center guidelines. *Why is this an important task for teachers and care providers?*

- Medical Administration Permission
- Emergency Medical Care
- Transportation Roster

Various *permission forms* should also be on file. Parents or guardians should fill out these forms at the time of the child's enrollment. Permission is usually required for such items as special screening tests, walks around the neighborhood, and field trips. To protect children from being picked up from the center by a stranger, unauthorized person, or even a noncustodial parent, a *transportation form* should be used. This form should contain the names, relationship, telephone numbers, and driver's license numbers of people who have permission to transport the child to and from the center. Staff should check the identification of anyone other than the parents who comes to pick up the child from the program. In the event a parent wants to add or remove an individual from the list, a new form needs to be completed.

Privacy Law and Early Childhood Programs

The *Family Educational Rights and Privacy Act (FERPA)* is designed to protect children. It is a federal law that states that the center cannot give a child's records to anyone other than parents without the parents' permission. The center should give a child's records only if the parents make the request in writing. After receiving the request, the center can release the materials within 45 days. **Figure 10.14** shows a form that can be included in each child's file.

Privacy Law

The information contained in this file is confidential and is not to be circulated outside the center without the prior written consent of the child's parents or legal guardian(s).

Under Public Law 93-380: Parents have access to all educational records. According to this law:

1. You are not allowed to provide the information contained in this file to anyone without the written consent of the child's parent or guardian.

2. You must advise parents or legal guardian(s) of their rights concerning their child's file.

3. Parents or legal guardians or legal guardian(s) have the right to read and review the file. Moreover, they may request a revision of information in their child's file.

4. Within forty-five (45) days, you are required to respond to a parent's request.

File reviewed by:

Name and Title	Address	Reason	Date
T. Smith, director	123 Gateway Ave.; Anytown, IL	Reviewed file materials after the parents provided them at the time of enrollment.	3/1/20XX
J. Rodriquez, head teacher	7890 Wake Dr.; Anytown, IL	Reviewed materials forwarded from the previous preschool to plan developmentally appropriate goals.	4/9/20XX
A. Chou, assistant teacher	890 Glenwood St.; Anytown, IL	Updated file to include information from the latest hearing screening test.	6/5/20XX
D. Williams, teacher	8690 Hwy 30; Anytown, IL	Introduced most recent assessment data and results of family conference.	7/8/20XX

Figure 10.14 Documenting who has had access to a child's confidential information is important for center staff to do to ensure the child's privacy is protected.

Parents have unlimited access to all their child's records kept by the center. Included may be screening information, developmental evaluations, parent meeting planning sheets, and summaries. Many teachers share all this information during parent meetings.

Lesson 10.2 Review

1. _____ is sexual abuse by a relative. (10.2.1)
   A. Neglect
   B. Incest
   C. Molestation
   D. Nonaccidental physical injury
2. **True or False.** Teachers need to prove that a child is being abused before reporting it. (10.2.2)
3. What is a good touch? (10.2.3)
   A. A touch the child does not want
   B. A touch that hurts the child
   C. A secret touch
   D. A touch the child does want
4. Teachers can foster resiliency by providing all of the following *except*: (10.2.4)
   A. Problem-solving skills
   B. Praise for efforts and achievements
   C. Inconsistency
   D. Responsive care
5. How can a parent access their child's record? (10.2.5)
   A. Calling the center
   B. Providing a written request
   C. Asking a teacher in person
   D. Asking the child to request the record

Summary

Lesson 10.1

10.1-1 Providing a safe environment for children requires time and attention to detail. You can find danger in every corner of the center.

10.1-1 Dangers can threaten both the physical and mental well-being of children.

10.1-2 Protecting children from dangers is the most important job of teachers and care providers.

10.1-3 Early childhood professionals need to be prepared for any emergency.

10.1-3 All center staff need to know how to use fire extinguishers and how to evacuate the children safely in case of a fire or other disaster.

10.1-4 Handling accidental poisonings is also a requirement. Be prepared to provide specific information when calling 911 or your local emergency number.

Lesson 10.2

10.2-1 Teachers and staff also need to recognize signs of child neglect and abuse including nonaccidental physical injury, emotional abuse, and sexual abuse.

10.2-2 Early childhood professionals are considered mandated reporters and must report suspected neglect and abuse to appropriate county authorities.

10.2-3 Teaching children how to resist child abuse is a responsibility of teachers and care providers.

10.2-4 Early childhood teachers have opportunities to assist families with information about community programs, resources, and services.

10.2-4 Teachers play an important role in helping children develop resilience.

10.2-5 Center staff can be held liable for failing to follow state licensing rules and regulations. It is important to know these rules and the extent of potential liability.

Vocabulary Activity

Create a T-chart on a sheet of paper and list the *Key Terms* in the left column. In the right column, list an *antonym* (a word of opposite meaning) for each term in the left column.

Critical Thinking

1. **Draw Conclusions.** In small groups, discuss the importance of supervision and draw conclusions about how to explain this concept to an overworked or overwhelmed parent or guardian.

2. **Compare and Contrast.** Research the required adult-child ratios for early childhood centers in your state or region. Then, research the required adult-child ratios in two other regions. Compare and contrast these ratios. What factors might contribute to the variation?

3. **Evaluate.** At the website for the National Program for Playground Safety, print checklists for *Playground Inspection* and *Playground Safety*. Arrange a visit to a local early childhood center and complete the checklists.

4. **Create.** Design an evacuation chart for the classroom.

5. **Analyze.** Use the text and reliable online resources to research sun safety precautions for an early childhood center. How do precautions differ for infants under six months of age to children who are older?

6. **Evaluate.** Using the poisonous substances chart in this chapter, conduct a safety check at home. List the poisonous substances you found.

Core Skills

1. **Writing.** Write a brief essay explaining how you will keep children safe under your supervision and care. Explain your understanding of the various factors that are part of this responsibility. These may include building, room, and equipment safety; proper supervision and management of children; reporting suspected abuse situations; and fire safety.

2. **Speaking.** Interview the local fire chief concerning the proper use of fire extinguishers.

3. **Research.** Conduct online research about *pica*, an eating disorder associated with eating nonfood items. How might preschool children be affected by pica? What is the possibility that children in your program will exhibit pica?

4. **Research.** Research information on the effects of emotional abuse on children. Find out about the following types of abuse: belittling, corrupting, isolating, rejecting, and terrorizing. Why is the loss of self-esteem from emotional abuse so devastating to young children?

5. **Research.** Many children who experience sexual abuse do not know how to describe their abuse due to lack of understanding or vocabulary. In small groups, research cases of child sexual abuse and take notes about keywords children used to describe their experiences. Also, research recommendations for how to handle suspected cases of child sexual abuse. Afterward, write a group report summarizing your findings and analyzing how they apply to early childhood care and education.

6. **Technology.** As mandated reporters, teachers should understand the steps for reporting a suspected case of child abuse. Search online or contact an anti-abuse organization to determine the steps for reporting child abuse in your state. Take notes about what you learn and then write a blog post or create a website outlining the information. View other classmates' posts or websites and offer feedback.

7. **Listening.** Interview a local early learning center director about the types of liability a center must consider. What are the most common liability issues the center faces? How does the center educate its teachers in handling this liability? What would happen if an accident occurred, and the center was held liable for the result? After the interview, summarize your findings in a short report.

8. **CTE Career Readiness Practice.** Suppose you work in an early childhood care center. One day, you notice one of your coworkers becoming frustrated with a fussy infant. Fearing that your coworker may shake the infant, you offer to hold the infant for a while. You finish the day saying nothing about the incident to anyone, but start to wonder if you should mention it to your supervisor. You ask yourself, "Did I act responsibly by not talking to my boss about my coworker's behavior? Could I be legally liable if abuse occurred and I didn't report it?" In small groups, discuss this scenario. What is the responsible thing to do in this situation? Role-play a conversation in which you respond to the dilemma appropriately.

Portfolio Project

Many states require a specific number of in-service continuing education credits be earned each year by early childhood professionals. A fire extinguisher demonstration would qualify for an in-service training activity. Ask a representative of an extinguisher company or your school's head custodian to give a demonstration. Following the demonstration, ask your teacher to sign a certificate documenting your attendance. File the certificate in your portfolio as verification of attending a professional educational activity.

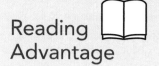
Planning Nutritious Meals and Snacks

Lesson 11.1: Nutrition Needs for Young Children

Lesson 11.2: Meals and Snacks for Children

Case Study

Encouraging Frankie to Eat Healthy Foods

Read the case study as a class and discuss the questions that follow. After you finish reading the chapter, discuss the case study again. Have your opinions changed based on what you learned? If so, how?

Mr. Kendra's class of four-year-old children just entered the lunch area. The children selected their usual places at the table. Then each child followed the pattern outlined on their place mat to place their silverware, napkin, glass, and plate. Within a few minutes, the center cook entered with a big smile, carrying a large tray with covered bowls of food. Carefully, the cook placed each bowl on the table so she would not spill and the children could serve themselves.

The teachers had taught the class about MyPlate to learn about the five main food groups and healthy food choices. The children began serving themselves, except for Frankie, who was attending the center for the first time. Frankie made no effort to take any food. Mr. Kendra, who was observing, tried encouraging Frankie to serve himself. After several attempts, Frankie responded by saying, "I only eat hamburgers, hotdogs, cheese, and peanut butter sandwiches. I am not eating any of that." When the milk pitcher was passed around the table, Frankie asked for a can of cola.

Frankie's teacher was puzzled. During the past nine years teaching four-year-olds, he never had a child who refused to eat anything. In the past, there had been children who had distinct preferences and may have served themselves only one food. Other children had not been exposed to a wide variety of healthy food and were picky eaters.

Give It Some Thought

1. What are the five major food groups that Frankie should choose foods from?
2. Why is using MyPlate an effective way to teach healthy eating habits? Why is the plate divided into four major sections?
3. Which types of foods do children prefer? Which do they reject?
4. What strategies can teachers use to encourage children to try a new food?
5. What curriculum strategies can teachers use to encourage healthy eating?
6. What can Mr. Kendra do to find out more about Frankie's eating habits?

Lesson 11.1

Nutrition Needs for Young Children

Essential Question

What do I need to know about nutrition and food guidance systems to help meet the nutritional goals of a healthy nutrition program?

Learning Outcomes

After studying this lesson, you will be able to

11.1-1 **integrate** goals for a healthy nutrition program.

11.1-2 **describe** nutritional challenges that influence children's nutritional needs.

11.1-3 **summarize** *The Dietary Guidelines for Americans* and *MyPlate* in helping children and their parents learn about healthy dietary patterns.

Key Terms

nutrition	allergy
nutrients	allergen
undernutrition	anaphylaxis
malnutrition	gluten
overeating	dietary pattern
diabetes	MyPlate
insulin	nutrient dense

It was lunchtime at the New Horizons Child Care Center. Nidda asked for a second serving of spinach, a food being served for the first time. Dominic said the potatoes were yummy. Isabella shared that her mother was sending oranges for her birthday treat. Throughout the meal, the teacher talked with the children and ate portions of the foods served.

The lunchroom was decorated with 12 large paper ice cream cones. Each cone represented one month of the year. The children's names and birthdays were written on paper scoops of ice cream. These scoops were placed in the cone that matched their birthday month.

On the other side of the lunchroom was a large carrot cut out of tagboard. Plastic measuring tape was pasted down the center. Each child's height was marked next to the tape.

In this classroom, children learn about nutrition both directly and indirectly. For instance, the variety of foods served and the teacher's comments about the food are *direct* learning experiences. Children learn about many types of food and that mealtime is a pleasant time. The positive attitudes and pleasing surroundings of the lunchroom are *indirect* learning experiences. By watching friends and teachers, children develop habits and attitudes about food. Many of their food attitudes and behaviors will carry into adulthood. Hopefully, they will establish a lifelong pattern of choosing healthy foods.

Teaching children about nutrition is an important responsibility. They need proper nutrition for their health, growth, and development. Behavior and learning ability also relate to nutrition. Studies suggest that young children who have learned to make healthy food choices may experience lifelong health benefits.

Teaching nutrition concepts requires a high-quality nutrition program. A quality program centers on the needs of the children, including their cultural backgrounds. Nutrition concepts should be integrated into all subject areas. Program goals should include:

- providing nutritious meals and snacks;
- introducing new healthy foods;

- encouraging healthy eating habits;
- involving children in meal activities;
- introducing culturally diverse foods; and
- providing nutrition information to parents.

To meet these goals, you will need to understand how the body uses food. In addition, you must know the various nutrients, functions, and their sources. Meal plans and food experiences also need to meet program goals for the children.

Health Highlights

Avoiding BPA

BPA, or *bisphenol A*, is an industrial chemical compound used in manufacturing hard plastic food containers since the 1960s. BPA is a type of synthetic estrogen, a hormone. It is used to make plastics hard, prevent bacterial contamination of food, and keep food cans from rusting. With surface scratches and exposure to heat or acid in foods, these plastics can leach small amounts of BPA into food.

Studies by the National Institutes of Health (NIH) and the Food and Drug Administration (FDA) indicate concern about the potential impact of BPA on health—especially for children. While uncertainty exists, studies continue to assess the long-term effects of BPA. Concern exists because BPA exposure can affect an infant's or toddler's brain, which will impact their behavior. There is also a possible link to type 2 diabetes, blood pressure, and cardiovascular disease.

BPA is found in household products such as plastic water bottles, food storage containers, plastic dishes, and food packaging. The health concern is that BPA migrates from the container to the food it contains. Freezers, microwave ovens, and dishwashers cause it to leech faster. The FDA advises parents and child-care providers to use porcelain or glass for heating foods and also check the recycle codes on the bottom of the container. Those with numerals 1, 2, 4, and 5 are less-toxic plastics.

11.1-1 Nutrition

Nutrition is the science of food and how the body uses food to support life. (Figure 11.1) **Nutrients** are the chemical substances in food that help the body grow, survive, and reproduce. Certain nutrients are required to build a strong body and mind. There are six groups of essential nutrients that people need for growth and maintenance of health. These are *proteins, carbohydrates, fats, vitamins, minerals,* and *water.* **Figure 11.2** lists some of the most important nutrients, their functions, and sources.

Food also provides the body with energy. Each food has its own energy value, which is measured in *calories*. Energy from food provides a heat source so that our bodies can function. It supports body processes, such as breathing and blood circulation. All body organs and systems need energy to function and stay healthy. Your body's physical and mental activities require energy, too.

The number of calories a person needs depends on age and activity level. Children need more energy than adults do in relationship to body weight. For instance, a moderately active four-year-old male needs about 1,400 calories per day. In contrast, a somewhat active 45-year-old

karelnoppe/Shutterstock.com

Figure 11.1   Knowledge of nutrition is needed for planning healthy meals and snacks. *What are the functions of nutrients?*

Nutrients, Functions, and Sources

Nutrient	Functions	Sources
Proteins	• Builds and repairs tissues, antibodies, enzymes, and hormones • Regulates fluid balance in the cells • Regulates many body processes • Supplies energy when needed	Meat, dairy, soy, poultry, fish, eggs, milk and other dairy products, peanut butter, lentils, whole-grains and cereals
Carbohydrates	• Supplies energy and regulates blood glucose • Helps the body efficiently digest fats • Provides dietary fiber	Sugar: Honey, jam, jelly, sugar, molasses Fiber: Fresh fruits and vegetables, whole-grain cereals and breads Starch: Breads, cereals, corn, peas, beans, potatoes, pasta, and rice
Fats	• Supplies and stores energy • Carries fat-soluble vitamins • Protects vital organs and body from shock and temperature changes • Contributes to satiety, feeling satisfied	Meat (marbling), fish, nuts, seeds, lunch meats, egg yolks, butter, margarine, cream, cheese, whole milk, olives, chocolate, salad oils and dressings
Vitamins	**Functions**	**Sources**
Vitamin A	• Helps promote growth and is an antioxidant • Helps keep skin, mucus membranes, and immune system healthy • Helps promote normal vision	Liver and other organ meats, salmon, egg yolk, butter, whole milk, cream, fortified margarine, cheddar cheese, dark green and yellow fruits and green leafy vegetables, fortified breakfast cereals
Thiamin (Vitamin B-1)	• Promotes normal appetite and digestion • Helps keep brain, nervous system healthy • Helps body release energy from food	Pork, other meats, poultry, fish, eggs, dried beans, green peas, yogurt, sunflower seeds, enriched or whole-grain breads and cereals
Riboflavin (Vitamin B-2)	• Helps red cell production • Helps keep skin, tongue, and lips healthy • Aids digestion; helps maintain healthy metabolism	Milk, cheese, yogurt, liver, meats, fish, poultry, eggs, dark leafy green vegetables, enriched breads and cereals
Niacin (Vitamin B-3)	• Helps keep nervous system, skin, mouth, tongue, and digestive tract healthy • Helps cells use other nutrients	Organ meats, fish, poultry, yeast, milk, peanut butter, dried beans, and peas, enriched or whole-grain breads and cereals
Vitamin C	• Helps keep gums and tissues healthy • Helps heal and repair wounds and broken bones • Builds the immune system • Helps body fight infection	Citrus fruits, strawberries, cantaloupe, broccoli, green peppers, raw cabbage, tomatoes, green leafy vegetables, brussels sprouts, cauliflower
Vitamin D	• Helps absorb calcium and phosphorus • Helps build strong bones, muscles, and teeth in children • Helps keep adult bones healthy	Fortified milk, butter, cheese, fish liver oils, liver, sardines, salmon, herring, perch, rainbow trout, egg yolk, sunshine
Vitamin E	• Helps body form red blood cells • Helps absorption of vitamin K	Liver and other variety meats, eggs, leafy green vegetables, whole-grain cereals, legumes, salad oils, other fats, and oils
Vitamin K	• Aids in blood clotting, and bone and heart health	Organ meats, pork, leafy green vegetables, cauliflower, broccoli, egg yolk

Continued

Figure 11.2   Understanding the functions and sources of nutrients can better prepare you to teach children about nutrition as well as plan healthy meals and snacks.

Minerals	Functions	Sources
Calcium	• Helps build and repair bones and teeth • Helps circulate and clot blood • Helps muscles and nerves function properly • Helps regulate the use of minerals in body	Milk, cheese, yogurt, kefir, buttermilk, other dairy products, dark green leafy vegetables, tofu, sardines, canned salmon.
Phosphorus	• Helps build strong bones and teeth • Helps regulate normal heartbeat, nerve signaling, and kidney function	Protein and calcium food sources such as meats and dairy products
Iron	• Combines with protein to make hemoglobin • Helps transport oxygen in blood • Maintains healthy cells, hair, and nails	Liver, meats, egg yolk, dried beans and peas, leafy green vegetables, dried fruits, enriched and whole-grain breads and cereals

Nutrient	Functions	Sources
Water	• Transports nutrients and oxygen to cells • Regulates body temperature • Moistens tissues of mouth, nose, and eyes • Flushes out waste products from kidney and liver • Lubricates joints	Water, beverages, soups, and most foods

male weighing 160 pounds needs about 2,600 calories per day. Thus, the child needs about 38 calories per pound while the adult male needs about 16 calories per pound. Children's physical growth is greater than adults' growth. Children are also very active. All their physical activities require a lot of energy.

11.1-2 Nutritional Challenges

Undernutrition, malnutrition, and overeating are medical problems that affect children's health and development. Children under the age of five are a vulnerable group. The effects of poor nutrition on their cognitive abilities have been proven in several studies. To plan nutritious meals and snacks, you need to know the effects of these problems.

Undernutrition means not eating enough food to maintain a healthy body weight and activity level. People get too few nutrients because they do not eat enough food. Undernutrition often results from fewer financial resources. **Malnutrition** is a lack of proper nutrients in the diet. It happens when nutrients are lacking from the diet. An unbalanced diet, poor food choices, or the body's inability to use the nutrients properly can be the cause.

Children who have these challenges are often shorter than their peers. Long-term nutrient deficiencies can slow, or even stop, growth. Other signs of poor nutrition include irritability, anxiety, digestion problems, bowed legs, sunken eyes, decaying teeth, low energy, and tiring easier than other children.

Overeating is the intake of more food than the body needs to function properly. Many factors contribute to overeating. There is a larger and more available supply of food, which often contains more highly processed and high-sugar foods. There also is a trend toward more snacking. Portion sizes are larger, which leads to overeating. Unfortunately, overeating can cause many health and emotional challenges. Overeating is one contributor to body weight. Other factors that impact weight include access to healthy foods, genetics, physical activity, poor sleep, and excess screen time.

Overeating and lack of physical activity affects every organ system in the body. It can lead to many other health conditions in adult life. These include hypertension (high blood pressure and related issues), diabetes, heart disease, asthma, sleep problems, and emotional health issues.

Poor body image can cause psychological issues such as poor self-esteem, depression, and anxiety. Children in larger bodies may experience bullying from classmates. It is important to discourage children and other staff members from making comments about a child's body weight or appetite.

Taking steps to encourage healthy habits may prevent excessive weight gain. Prevention is easier than treating obesity. Encourage all children to join in gross-motor play. According to *The Dietary Guidelines for Americans, 2020–2025,* preschool-aged children should engage in active play for at least three hours per day. School-aged children need at least one hour of moderate-to-vigorous activity daily. You can also discuss your concerns about a child's nutrition and physical activity with staff and their parents.

Meeting Special Nutritional Needs

As a teacher, one of your tasks is helping all child in your care to meet their nutritional needs. Most children of a certain age share similar nutritional needs, but some children have unique needs. These special needs are often created by a health condition, such as diabetes or food allergies or intolerances. When you understand the special nutritional needs of the children in your care, you can plan healthy meals and snacks for them.

Diabetes

Diabetes is a condition in which the body cannot properly control the level of glucose (sugar) in the blood. Along with obesity, type 2 diabetes is becoming increasingly common in young children. People with diabetes produce little or no **insulin**, the hormone that regulates blood sugar levels. Many children who have diabetes must take insulin to keep their blood sugar level within a healthy range. When blood sugar is too high or too low, it may be reflected in the child's behavior.

According to the American Diabetes Association, there is not a specific "diabetic diet." People with diabetes need to follow the same basic eating guidelines as other people. They need a varied healthy dietary plan with plenty of fruits, vegetables, and whole grains. The dietary plan should be low in saturated fat, added sugars, and salt.

Blood sugar fluctuates with food intake and physical activity. For this reason, the foods and portion sizes selected should reflect balance. Eating at regular intervals also helps the blood sugar remain steady.

Managing the planning and scheduling of snacks and meals for a child with diabetes can be challenging for a teacher. The parents of children with special dietary needs should provide written instructions. Chances are they have worked with a registered dietitian nutritionist (RDN) to develop a personalized meal plan for the child. Parents also need to tell you about the best spacing of meals and snacks for their children. With practice and communication, you can work together to meet the special food needs for children who have diabetes.

Food Allergies and Intolerances

Children with food allergies or intolerances may also have special nutritional needs. An **allergy** is the body's negative reaction to a particular substance which is harmless to most people. The body's immune system treats it as an invader and tries to fight it off. The offending substance is called an **allergen**. Sometimes the allergen is a substance in the environment, such as pollen, dust, or mold. Allergens can also be a pet's saliva and dander. Other times the allergen is a food or medicine. Food allergies are more common among children than adults. There is no cure for a food allergy. Avoiding the offending food is vital to prevent a reaction.

Food allergies most often begin during the first two years of life. For some children, allergens in food act like poison. Certain foods are more often triggers of a food allergy. The nine common culprit foods include wheat, soy, peanuts, tree nuts, fish, shellfish, eggs, sesame, and cow's milk. They cause 90 percent of food allergies (**Figure 11.3**). Corn, beans, and berries are other foods that can produce an allergic response. Exposure can occur from inhaling, touching, or

Mariya Rus/Shutterstock.com

Figure 11.3 Many children are allergic to peanuts and products that contain them. ***What other food allergies are common among younger children?***

ingesting. Cow's milk allergy is the most common allergy in infants and young children. Peanut and tree-nut allergies are also common. Exposure can cause a severe reaction. A lifelong avoidance of all tree-nuts or peanuts may be needed. Sometimes children may have multiple food allergies to different foods.

Because of the high incidence of peanut allergies, some centers and schools have created a "peanut-free environment." Families may be prohibited from bringing peanuts and peanut products into the facility. Most allergic reactions to foods occur within hours after contact with the allergen. Some occur within minutes.

An allergic reaction can range from mild to severe. Symptoms might include sniffles, skin rashes; abdominal pain; diarrhea, nausea, and vomiting; and swelling of the lips, face, tongue, throat, or eyes. Hives, trouble breathing, and nasal or respiratory congestion may also occur. Children may have trouble communicating a reaction.

The most severe allergic reaction, called **anaphylaxis**, is potentially fatal. Shock symptoms develop quickly, including weakness and collapse. Other signs include problems breathing, a drop in blood pressure, and severe itching and swelling. Abdominal cramping can also occur accompanied by diarrhea and vomiting. Seek immediate medical help for anyone with signs of anaphylaxis.

Health Highlights

Peanut Allergy and Infants

Food allergy experts have changed the recommendation for first-introduction of peanuts to children. According to *The Dietary Guidelines for Americans 2020–2025*, age-appropriate, peanut-containing foods can be introduced as early as four to six months. This includes infants with an egg allergy, persistent eczema, or both, as they are considered at a higher risk for peanut allergy. Parents need to discuss this with their medical provider. By introducing peanut-based products, the child's development of a peanut allergy could be warded off. The provider may take a blood test or skin prick to determine whether peanut should be introduced and the safest way to introduce them.

Gluten—a protein found in wheat, rye, barley, and oats *not* labeled gluten-free—can also cause health problems. Some children have gluten sensitivities or intolerances. Others may have a food allergy to some grains. Gastrointestinal problems, headaches, depression, fatigue, and skin issues can all relate to gluten sensitivities and intolerances. Any food using wheat flour as an ingredient contains gluten. Pastas, graham crackers, baked goods, breads and pastries, cereal and granola, and flour tortillas are common foods including gluten.

Food allergens can make meal and snack planning challenging for teachers. A child with food allergies requires a restricted dietary plan. The child must not eat even a trace amount of the food that is an allergen. You should offer a safe substitute that provides similar nutrients. Although allergic reactions to breathing in a small amount of peanut or tree-nut allergens is rare, sometimes breathing small particles of the offending food can cause a severe allergic reaction. This child cannot even be in the same room with the allergen, which means you must eliminate this food from the classroom.

Families are your best resource for meeting their child's special nutritional needs. Include a question on your enrollment forms regarding food allergies or intolerances. This will remind families to share the information with you. If a child has food allergies, get detailed notes from the family about what foods to exclude from the diet, which foods to offer as substitutes, and establish an emergency care plan that outlines what steps to take if an allergic reaction occurs. Always check enrollment records of a child who is new to the center before serving the child any food or drink. Read product labels to check the ingredients of foods and make sure to avoid **cross-contamination** (allergen-free foods coming into contact with other foods). Be mindful of children's food allergies as you plan menus for meals and snacks. If your center has a cook, share the information.

Workplace Connections

Handling Food Allergies and Intolerances

Interview an early childhood center or preschool director to discover how food allergies and food intolerances are handled.

1. Are special foods and meals supplied by the center or parents?
2. What precautions does the center take to ensure that someone does not accidentally expose a child to a food that could cause a severe reaction?

11.1-3 Dietary Guidelines for Americans

The *2020–2025 Dietary Guidelines for Americans* have been developed to help all Americans. Included are all ages and life stages, different racial and cultural backgrounds, and a range of socioeconomic statuses. The guidelines are based on scientific evidence that shows how diet promotes health and prevents diseases. These guidelines emphasize a *healthy dietary pattern*, rather than just focusing on food groups or nutrients in isolation. A **dietary pattern** is the combination of foods and beverage that

constitutes an individual's complete dietary intake over time.

The guidelines have been developed for people who are healthy, those living with diseases, and those at risk for diet-related diseases. The new guidelines are timely. Seventy-four percent of American adults have obesity or are overweight, and six in ten adults are living with one or more diet-related diseases.

This is the first time that *The Dietary Guidelines* have provided guidance by stage of life beginning at birth to older adulthood. The purpose is to promote health and prevent disease by following a healthy dietary pattern. This dietary pattern offers foods and beverages that provide minerals, vitamins, and other health-promoting components. A healthy dietary pattern has little added sugar, saturated fat, and sodium. A nutrient-rich dietary pattern with its health-promoting components lowers the risk of

- heart disease
- type 2 diabetes
- cancer
- obesity
- hip fracture

The latest guidelines have been developed with the growth of scientific knowledge. They emphasize it is never too early or late to follow a healthy dietary pattern. Studies show that the food and beverages that people consume have a profound impact on life-long health. The latest guidelines have four overarching guidelines. Included are:

1. Follow a healthy dietary pattern at every stage of life.
2. Customize and enjoy nutrient-dense food and beverage choices to reflect personal preferences, cultural traditions, and budgetary considerations.
3. Focus on meeting food group needs with nutrient-dense foods and beverages, and staying calorie limits.
4. Limit foods and beverages higher in added sugar, saturated fat, and sodium.

Key recommendations that support the four overarching guidelines include the following.

- *Added sugars.* Foods and beverages with added sugars should be avoided for infants and toddlers. For ages two and older, limit added sugars to less than 10 percent of the calories per day.
- *Saturated fat.* At age 2, limit saturated fat to less than 10 percent of calories per day.
- *Sodium.* Limit sodium to less than 2,300 mg per day or less for children younger than 14.

The core elements of a healthy dietary pattern include

- vegetables of all types—dark green; red and orange; peas, and lentils; starchy; and other vegetables;
- fruits, especially whole fruit;
- grains, at least half of which are whole grain;
- dairy, including fat-free or low-fat milk, yogurt, and cheese, and/or lactose-free versions, and fortified-soy beverages and yogurt as alternatives;
- protein foods, including lean meats, poultry, and eggs; seafood; beans, peas, and lentils; and nuts, seeds, and soy products; and
- oils, including oils and oils in foods, such as seafood and nuts.

Source: Dietary Guidelines for Americans 2020-2025

Using MyPlate to Teach Good Nutrition

To ensure good nutrition, children need to eat a variety of foods. Their specific nutritional needs differ from those of adults, however. The US Department of Agriculture (USDA) developed the **MyPlate** food guidance system with a set of online tools to help people plan nutritious meals to fit their individual needs. You can access it at the www.MyPlate.gov website. It contains recipes, videos, and a cookbook.

MyPlate can be used as a guide for teaching children and their families about planning healthful meals and snacks. MyPlate includes the five major food groups—fruits, vegetables, grains, protein foods, and dairy (**Figure 11.4**). Foods from each of these groups are essential for a healthy eating pattern. You will notice the plate is divided into four sections—fruits, grains, vegetables, and protein. The

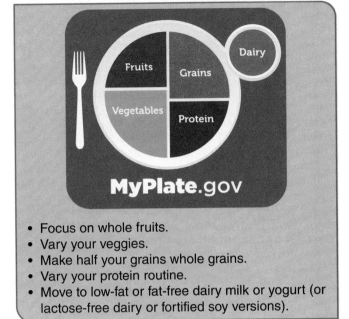

MyPlate Food Guidance System

- Focus on whole fruits.
- Vary your veggies.
- Make half your grains whole grains.
- Vary your protein routine.
- Move to low-fat or fat-free dairy milk or yogurt (or lactose-free dairy or fortified soy versions).

USDA

Figure 11.4 The MyPlate food guidance system is a set of online tools to help people plan nutritious meals and snacks.

size of each section represents the proportion of a meal each food should be. The circle next to the plate represents the dairy group. You can use the "MyPlate Plan" interactive tool on the MyPlate website to help determine calorie levels and food needs for all people, including children as young as age two. Choosing **nutrient-dense foods** (those options that are full of nutrients in relationship to calories and that have positive health effects) is important.

MyPlate's five major food groups send a simple message about how to divide a meal plate. It shows that half of a person's meal plate should be fruits and vegetables. **Figure 11.5** shows the food amounts from each food group necessary to plan daily meals for a four-year-old child.

Fruits

Like vegetables, fruit servings are measured in cups. They are major sources of vitamins C and A (**Figure 11.6**). Serve fruits fresh, canned, frozen, dried, slightly cooked, or in the form of 100 percent juice (limit juice to ½ cup daily). Juice should not be given to infants under 12 months. Use MyPlate's interactive tool, *MyPlate Plan,* to

Food and Nutrition Service
United States Department of Agriculture

MyPlate.gov

Start *simple* with **MyPlate** Plan

The benefits of healthy eating add up over time, bite by bite. Small changes matter. Start Simple with MyPlate.

A healthy eating routine is important at every stage of life and can have positive effects that add up over time. It's important to eat a variety of fruits, vegetables, grains, protein foods, and dairy or fortified soy alternatives. When deciding what to eat or drink, choose options that are full of nutrients. Make every bite count.

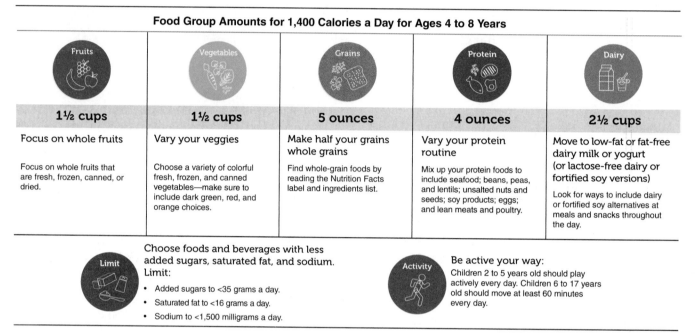

Food Group Amounts for 1,400 Calories a Day for Ages 4 to 8 Years

Fruits	Vegetables	Grains	Protein	Dairy
1½ cups	**1½ cups**	**5 ounces**	**4 ounces**	**2½ cups**
Focus on whole fruits	Vary your veggies	Make half your grains whole grains	Vary your protein routine	Move to low-fat or fat-free dairy milk or yogurt (or lactose-free dairy or fortified soy versions)
Focus on whole fruits that are fresh, frozen, canned, or dried.	Choose a variety of colorful fresh, frozen, and canned vegetables—make sure to include dark green, red, and orange choices.	Find whole-grain foods by reading the Nutrition Facts label and ingredients list.	Mix up your protein foods to include seafood; beans, peas, and lentils; unsalted nuts and seeds; soy products; eggs; and lean meats and poultry.	Look for ways to include dairy or fortified soy alternatives at meals and snacks throughout the day.

Limit
Choose foods and beverages with less added sugars, saturated fat, and sodium. Limit:
- Added sugars to <35 grams a day.
- Saturated fat to <16 grams a day.
- Sodium to <1,500 milligrams a day.

Activity
Be active your way:
Children 2 to 5 years old should play actively every day. Children 6 to 17 years old should move at least 60 minutes every day.

USDA

Figure 11.5   This MyPlate Plan for four- to eight-year-olds shows you how much food a child should eat to meet daily calorie needs. *How does the MyPlate Plan for a two-year-old differ? Use the MyPlate Plan tool to investigate your answer.*

Luiza Kamalova/Shutterstock.com

Figure 11.6   Serving a fruit or vegetable at snack time gives children one of their food requirements. *Name an example of a nutrient-packed fruit or vegetable.*

help choose food amounts for children. Rich sources of vitamin C include oranges, mango, strawberries, and kiwifruit. Deep yellow fruits, such as apricots, peaches, and cantaloupe, are rich sources of vitamin A. Serve several sources of vitamin C and vitamin A several times weekly. Serve whole or cut-up fruits more often than juice.

Vegetables

Foods from this group are measured in cups. As with other food groups, the age, gender, and activity level of a child are important factors in determining food amounts. Foods in this group are major sources of vitamins C, A, and potassium. (**Figure 11.7**).

Maples Images/Shutterstock.com

Figure 11.7   Vegetables provide good sources of vitamin A and vitamin C.

Vegetables are rich sources of nutrients and fiber. MyPlate divides this group into the following five subgroups:

- dark green vegetables, which include broccoli, spinach, asparagus, and kale;

- red and orange vegetables, including carrots, red peppers, tomatoes, and deep-orange winter squash;

- beans and peas, including kidney beans, soybeans, and lentils;

- starchy vegetables, such as green peas, corn, and potatoes; and

- other vegetables, including celery, onions, and zucchini.

When planning meals for children, vary your veggies. Make sure to include several sources of vitamin C and vitamin A weekly. Other vegetables are important, too. Vegetables should be served raw if children can chew and swallow them without choking. Otherwise, they should be cooked as little as possible to avoid losing nutrients in the cooking water.

Grains

The recommended number of ounce-equivalents from the grains group will vary depending on a child's age, gender, and activity level. An ounce-equivalent is the amount of some foods that are counted as an ounce. For example, a one-ounce slice of bread or one cup of dry cereal are each counted as one ounce-equivalent. A

three-year-old female only requires four ounce-equivalents from the grains group in a day.

Foods in the grains group include whole-grain and enriched breads. Also included are pancakes, pastas, crackers, oatmeal, grits, tortillas, rice, and cold cereals. Carbohydrates, iron, and B vitamins are the chief nutrients in these foods. Only whole-grain and enriched products should be served to children, but make sure at least half the grains are whole grains. Check labels on products to be sure. Also, if you make breads at the center, be sure to use whole-grain or enriched flour.

Choose breakfast cereals that are lower in added sugars. The USDA indicates cereals must contain no more than 6 grams of sugar per dry ounce. All cereals served must be whole-grain-rich, enriched, or fortified. Check the *Nutrition Facts* label on the cereal package. See the USDA website for an approved list of cereals.

Protein Foods

Like grain foods, the foods in this group are counted in ounce-equivalents and can vary by the age, gender, and activity level of a child. Protein is the most important nutrient supplied by foods in this group. Protein foods are also excellent sources of B vitamins, iron, and phosphorous.

Animal products provide the highest quality protein sources. These include lean beef, pork, and lamb. Eggs, seafood, and poultry are also included in this group. Dried beans, dried peas, lentils, soy products, and unsalted nuts and seeds are also included in the protein group. (Nuts and seeds should not be given to young children since they pose a choking hazard.) Plant sources can provide good sources of protein and are often a source of fiber. When served with milk, and dairy products, breads, or cereals, you can create a balanced meal.

Dairy

Children need at least two cups of fortified milk or dairy daily. The most important nutrients provided by this group are calcium and vitamin D. Riboflavin, vitamin A, protein, and phosphorous are also provided.

Milk is considered the best source of calcium in this group. Milk products such as cheese and yogurt are also good sources. Children ages one to two years need the fat that whole milk contains unless otherwise directed by the child's doctor. For children over two, low-fat (1%) or fat-free milk and other dairy products are better choices. They have all the nutrients found in milk, but much less fat and, therefore, fewer calories. Lactose-free cow's milk or calcium-fortified soymilk may be an option for children who have lactose intolerance. Other plant beverages are not considered equivalent in nutritional value.

Oils

Although some oils are necessary for good health, they are not a MyPlate food group. Oils are fats that are liquid at room temperature. Oils are found in nourishing foods such as fish, peanut butter, olives, and avocados. In fact, the fatty acids they contain are essential for good health. Margarine, salad dressings, and cooking oils are also in this category. All oils are rich in calories, and so are solid fats. Limit oil and fat intake to those oils that provide good health.

Foods that are high in fats or oils can be a source of excessive calories. High-calorie pastries, candies, bars, cookies, muffins, doughnuts, and other snack items provide the types of fats that may cause harm in later years. These foods are often also high in sugar. While children are growing, a diet high in fats and sweets can deprive them of the nutrients they need for forming healthy muscles, organs, and bones. These foods should be enjoyed as occasional treats rather than part of a daily eating pattern.

Hydration

Water is important for the body to function properly for people of all ages. It is healthy because it has no added sugar or calories. Water is good for the body as it helps the blood circulate and is good for the mind. It helps with focus, concentration, and is important for good oral health. It washes away bacteria that causes tooth decay. Water also moves nutrients throughout the body. It keeps the joints healthy, gives skin a glow, and rids the body of waste. When the body is not well hydrated, fatigue sets in. During the summer months, water is especially important for

Early Childhood Insight 🅐🅑🅒

Safe School Gardens

Planting a school garden is a great way to get young children interested in science, health, and eating nutritious vegetables and fruits. Research shows that when children take part in a school garden, they develop more positive attitudes about eating vegetables and fruits. Besides learning gardening skills, children also learn life skills such as leadership, teamwork, and cooperation.

Before getting started, it is important to locate a safe environment in which children and teachers can work. Care providers should make sure parents sign permission slips for their children to take part in the school garden. Here are a few more safety ideas to keep in mind.

- Choose a garden site on level ground with well-drained soil that gets sunlight for at least six hours per day.

- Have the garden soil tested for lead contamination.
- Use a safe water source for the garden. Public water systems are generally safe.
- Make sure children wear protective clothing and shoes. Sunscreen is essential when children work in the garden.
- Teach children to use gardening tools safely. Staff members need to monitor children closely when using such tools.
- Have children wear gloves while gardening. Make sure they thoroughly wash their hands after working in the garden.

For more information about school gardens, visit the website of the National Gardening Association.

the body's cooling system. It keeps the body from overheating.

Supplemental water is usually not needed during the first six months of an infant's life. After that, small amounts of fluoridated drinking water can be given. Slowly, water intake can be increased. It is recommended that children drink 8 ounces of plain, fluoridated drinking water for each year of their age. For example, a three-year-old should drink three 8-ounce cups.

Lesson 11.1 Review

1. **True or False.** A person only needs four out of the six essential nutrients to maintain health. (11.1.1)
2. Which medical problem involves the lack of proper nutrients in the diet? (11.1.2)
   A. Overnutrition
   B. Malnutrition
   C. Overeating
   D. Diabetes
3. What is an allergy? (11.1.2)
   A. A condition in which the body cannot properly control the level of glucose in the blood
   B. A protein found in wheat, rye, barley, and oats
   C. The body's negative reaction to a particular substance
   D. The hormone that regulates blood sugar levels
4. All of the following are overarching dietary guidelines *except*: (11.1.3)
   A. Follow a healthy dietary pattern at every stage of life.
   B. Customize and enjoy nutrient-dense food and beverage choices to reflect personal preferences, cultural traditions, and budgetary considerations.
   C. Focus on meeting food group needs with nutrient-dense foods and beverages, and staying within calorie limits.
   D. Encourage foods and beverages higher in added sugar, saturated fat, and sodium.
5. How many 8-ounce cups of water should a four-year-old drink every day? (11.1.3)
   A. Two
   B. Three
   C. Four
   D. Five

Meals and Snacks for Children

Essential Question

What do I need to know about planning and serving healthy meals and snacks that are appealing and provide multicultural experiences for children?

Learning Outcomes

After studying this lesson, you will be able to

11.2-1 plan healthy meals and snacks using such tools as the Child and Adult Care Food Program, food appeal, food preferences, and developmental readiness.

11.2-2 identify ways to include multicultural experiences when planning meals and snacks.

11.2-3 serve nutritious and appealing meals and snacks for children.

Key Terms

Child and Adult Care   neophobia
    Food Program
    (CACFP)

Nutrition is the most important part of a well-planned menu, but many other factors also contribute. For instance, scale food amounts to the children's appetites. Children manage best with small amounts of food. Their appetites often vary from day to day. One program for helping early childhood centers and family day care homes provide nutritious meals and snacks is the *Child and Adult Care Food Program (CACFP)*.

11.2-1 Child and Adult Care Food Program

The **Child and Adult Care Food Program (CACFP)** is administered by the USDA's Food and Nutrition Service. Through CACFP, participating centers and family child care homes receive reimbursement for the nutritious meals and snacks they serve to children. Each state has an agency (often the department of education) that administers the CACFP. To learn more about the benefits of CACFP and requirements for program participation, visit the USDA's CACFP website.

CACFP offers meal-pattern guidelines that recommend minimum food amounts from each food group. Participating centers and family child care homes must provide at least the minimum food amounts per meal or snack to be eligible for reimbursement. **Figure 11.8** lists food amounts for specific age groups for breakfast, snacks, and lunch or supper. Meal patterns for infants from birth to 11 months can be found on the USDA website.

Food Appeal

Children will eat more if the food appeals to them. Variety, texture, flavor, color, form, temperature, and food preferences all affect how much a child enjoys a meal.

Variety

Many children like variety in the foods served to them. A meal with all the same texture or color could be boring for children. When offering new foods, add the new food with a meal of familiar and well-liked foods. This is because children may be overwhelmed if given too many new foods at once.

Child and Adult Care Food Program (CACFP)
Child Meal Patterns

Breakfast

Food Components	Ages 1–2	Ages 3–5	Ages 6–12
Fluid milk	4 fluid ounces	6 fluid ounces	8 fluid ounces
Vegetables, fruits, or portions of both* (juice must be pasteurized, full strength)	1/4 cup	1/2 cup	1/2 cup
Grains (oz. equivalent)			
Whole-grain-rich bread	1/2 slice	1/2 slice	1 slice
Whole-grain-rich biscuit, roll, or muffin	1/2 serving	1/2 serving	1 serving
Whole-grain-rich, enriched, or fortified cooked breakfast cereal, cereal grain, and/or pasta	1/4 cup	1/4 cup	1/2 cup
Whole-grain-rich, enriched, or fortified ready-to-eat breakfast cereal (cold, dry)			
Flakes or round	1/2 cup	1/2 cup	1 cup
Puffed cereal	3/4 cup	3/4 cup	1-1/4 cup
Granola	1/8 cup	1/8 cup	1/4 cup

Snack

Food Components	Ages 1–2	Ages 3–5	Ages 6–12
Fluid milk	4 fluid ounces	4 fluid ounces	8 fluid ounces
Meat/meat alternates			
Lean meat, poultry, or fish	1/2 ounce	1/2 ounce	1 ounce
Tofu, soy product, or alternate protein products	1/2 ounce	1/2 ounce	1 ounce
Cheese	1/2 ounce	1/2 ounce	1 ounce
Large egg	1/2	1/2	1/2
Cooked dry beans or peas	1/8 cup	1/8 cup	1/4 cup
Peanut butter or soy nut butter or other nut/seed butters	1 tbsp.	1 tbsp.	2 tbsp.
Yogurt, plain or flavored, unsweetened, or sweetened	2 ounces or 1/4 cup	2 ounces or 1/4 cup	4 ounces or 1/2 cup
Peanuts, soy nuts, tree nuts, or seeds	1/2 ounce	1/2 ounce	1 ounce
Vegetables*	1/2 cup	1/2 cup	3/4 cup
Fruits*	1/2 cup	1/2 cup	3/4 cup
Grains (oz. equivalent)			
Whole-grain-rich bread	1/2 slice	1/2 slice	1 slice
Whole-grain-rich biscuit, roll, or muffin	1/2 serving	1/2 serving	1 serving
Whole-grain-rich, enriched, or fortified cooked breakfast cereal, cereal grain, and/or pasta	1/4 cup	1/4 cup	1/2 cup
Whole-grain-rich, enriched, or fortified ready-to-eat breakfast cereal (cold, dry)			
Flakes or round	1/2 cup	1/2 cup	1 cup
Puffed cereal	3/4 cup	3/4 cup	1-1/4 cup
Granola	1/8 cup	1/8 cup	1/4 cup

*May only be used to meet the vegetable or fruit requirement at one meal, including snack, per day.

Continued

USDA

Figure 11.8 The Child and Adult Care Food Program (CACFP) offers meal patterns that recommend minimum food amounts from each food group.

Child and Adult Care Food Program (CACFP)
Child Meal Patterns

Lunch or Supper

Food Components	Ages 1–2	Ages 3–5	Ages 6–12
Fluid milk	4 fluid ounces	6 fluid ounces	8 fluid ounces
Meat/meat alternates			
Lean meat, poultry, or fish	1 ounce	1-1/2 ounces	2 ounces
Tofu, soy product, or alternate protein products	1 ounce	1-1/2 ounces	2 ounces
Cheese	1 ounce	1-1/2 ounces	2 ounces
Large egg	1/2	3/4	1
Cooked dry beans or peas	1/4 cup	3/8 cup	1/2 cup
Peanut butter or soy nut butter or other nut/seed butters	2 tbsp.	3 tbsp.	4 tbsp.
Yogurt, plain or flavored, unsweetened, or sweetened	4 ounces or 1/2 cup	6 ounces or 3/4 cup	8 ounces or 1 cup
The following may be used to meet no more than 50% of the requirement:			
Peanuts, soy nuts, tree nuts, or seeds, as listed in program guidance, or any combination of the above meat/meat alternates (1 ounce of nuts/seeds = 1 ounce of cooked lean meat, poultry, or fish)	1/2 ounce = 50%	¾ ounce = 50%	1 ounce = 50%
Vegetables*	1/8 cup	1/4 cup	1/2 cup
Fruits*	1/8 cup	1/4 cup	1/4 cup
Grains (oz. equivalent)			
Whole-grain-rich bread	1/2 slice	1/2 slice	1 slice
Whole-grain-rich biscuit, roll, or muffin	1/2 serving	1/2 serving	1 serving
Whole-grain-rich, enriched, or fortified cooked breakfast cereal, cereal grain, and/or pasta	1/4 cup	1/4 cup	1/2 cup

*May only be used to meet the vegetable or fruit requirement at one meal, including snack, per day.

Source: Food and Nutrition Service, U.S. Department of Agriculture (USDA).

See the USDA website for further details about requirements for reimbursable meals.

Texture

The texture of a food affects the child's acceptance or rejection. *Soft, hard, chewy, mashed, chopped, crisp, creamy,* and *rough* are all textures. It is wise to combine textures when planning meals and snacks for young children. This makes the meal more interesting. For instance, at mealtime, serve one soft food, one crisp food, and one chewy food. Combine contrasting textures for a pleasing effect. This also provides you with an opportunity to include language concepts during meals and snacks.

Dry foods are hard for children to eat. Serve dry food only in combination with two or more moist foods.

Children often prefer foods that they can easily manipulate with their mouths. Soft, smooth foods are typically preferred to hard lumpy foods. Some meats are difficult for young children to chew. Their teeth cannot grind meat as easily as adults' teeth. Because of this, children usually prefer hamburgers. Chili, spaghetti, and casseroles are other ways of serving meat with varied textures.

Flavor

In accepting new foods, texture is more important than flavor. Children generally prefer sweet foods and may reject strongly seasoned foods. One rule of thumb is to use only half as much salt as noted in a recipe. Whenever possible, enhance the natural flavor of the food. This means that you should add only small amounts of sugar and seasonings.

Color

Children are attracted to color in their meals. Serve brightly colored fruits like mango or blueberries with less colorful options such as potatoes. Plan activities that encourage eating fruits and vegetables from all colors of the rainbow.

Food Forms

The shape, size, form, and visual appearance of food influences children. Serve most foods in bite-sized pieces. Children have poorly developed fine-motor coordination skills. They find it difficult to use spoons and forks well. Therefore, slice cooked carrots and other vegetables in large pieces rather than dicing them. Try adding diced vegetables to another food. For instance, add diced carrots to mashed potatoes.

Soup is also difficult for many young children to eat. They become tired from spooning. Children may get frustrated if they spill on clothing or the table.

Two methods make soup easier to consume. One method is to thicken the soup by adding solid ingredients or a thickener, such as flour. The second method is to let the children drink the soup from a cup.

Whenever possible, prepare foods so they can be eaten with the fingers. For example, serve chopped raw vegetables instead of a tossed salad.

Temperature

Variety in the temperature of foods served can be appealing, too. For a snack, offer a cold glass of milk with a room-temperature food, such as apple slices. At mealtime, serve a cold fruit or pudding with a warm casserole. For safety reasons, be sure to serve each food at its proper temperature (hot foods hot and cold foods cold). Keep in mind, however, that children are more sensitive to temperature extremes than adults.

Food Preferences

Children differ in their individual food preferences. For example, while some children enjoy spicy foods, others prefer milder flavors. Most children have at least a few foods they strongly like and some they strongly dislike. Although food preferences are personal, home life also influences them. One family may eat many vegetables, while another family might eat them less often.

As a teacher, you will quickly learn about the children's likes and dislikes. When possible, honor the child's preferences unless they are unhealthful. Suppose Courtney likes her sandwiches cut diagonally. Accommodating this food preference when possible will help mealtimes run more smoothly. Continue to offer disliked foods on a child's plate without pressuring them to consume the foods.

Health Highlights

Serving Milk in Early Childhood Programs

The USDA has changed the milk requirements to ensure that children receive the nutrients they need for growth and development. Requirements for children in early childhood programs include:

- Infants should not consume cow's milk or fortified soy beverages before 12 months of age to replace human milk or infant formula. Cow's milk does not have enough nutrients for infants. The higher protein and mineral content of cow's milk are hard on the infant's kidneys and digestive system to process.
- Toddlers 12 through 23 months no longer consume human milk or infant formula.
- Only plain whole cow's milk or fortified unsweetened soy beverage can be offered around twelve months of age to help meet calcium, potassium, Vitamin D, and protein needs.
- Toddlers can obtain needed nutrients from cow's milk or fortified soy beverage.

Developmental Readiness for Eating Solid Foods

According to the guidelines, infants between the ages of 4 and 6 months typically are ready to begin eating solid food. To prevent choking, the food must be developmentally appropriate. By this time, most infants have the necessary gross-motor, fine-motor, and oral skills to consume complementary foods. According to the USDA, signs an infant is ready include ability to

- control head and neck;
- sit up alone without support in a high chair or other safe, supervised space;
- bring objects to the mouth;
- grasp small objects such as foods or toys; and
- swallow food as opposed to pushing it back out onto the chin.

By six months, infants need an external source of iron in addition to breast milk or formula since their iron stores from birth will have been depleted. Serve them iron-rich foods such as meats, seafood rich in iron, and iron-fortified infant cereals. When children are being exposed to the flavors and textures of foods for the first time, repeated exposures are necessary.

11.2-2 Multicultural Experiences

Foods can bridge cultures. So, children need to be exposed to healthy foods from various cultures. This will help create community among a diverse group of children. Through repeated experiences, children will learn how food relates to social and cultural customs. Including foods from the children's cultures helps promote cultural identity and self-esteem. Foods from other cultures help children learn to taste new dishes and respect cultural differences.

Family members can also help you promote a multicultural approach to the food program. Encourage them to share recipes for snacks, meals, and holiday celebrations. Invite parents to prepare special foods from their culture for the class. Some parents may enjoy teaching children to help prepare the foods.

11.2-3 Serving Meals and Snacks

Licensing requirements outline how often and how much food must be provided for young children in child care centers. These requirements vary from state to state. As a rule, the number of hours a child spends at a center governs the number of snacks and meals served. In most states, children who attend fewer than four hours a day must be served a fruit juice or milk and a snack item. Children who attend five or more hours must be served both a meal and a snack. The amount of each food served to children is based on their age range as noted in the CACFP guidelines.

The decision to serve breakfast is often based on two factors. These are the length of the program day and the distance the child travels to reach the center. Centers with full-day programs or children who travel long distances often serve breakfast.

Breakfast

The purpose of breakfast is to break the 10- to 14-hour overnight fast. Breakfast provides energy for morning activities. Studies show that children who eat a nutritious breakfast perform better mentally and physically.

A nutritious breakfast should include a variety of foods in the amounts recommended for the child's age. The minimum recommendations of the CACFP are:

- 1 milk;
- 1 fruit, vegetable, or ½ cup of 100 percent juice; and
- 1 grain source, such as bread, hot or cold cereal, or pasta or noodles.

Fruit drinks or punches are not juice substitutes, even when fortified with vitamin C.

Self-Serve Breakfasts

Self-serve breakfasts are popular with center staffs. This is because children can eat their breakfasts as they arrive. They can choose what and how much to eat based on their own appetites. The self-serve breakfast gives children the chance to prepare their own breakfasts.

Safety First

Serving Food Safely

Along with serving nutritious, healthful foods, the foods you serve to children should be safe. Safe foods are cleaned properly and prepared or cooked to proper temperatures. They are also stored at proper temperatures. When serving prepared food to children, keep these additional safe food-handling procedures in mind:

- Use good personal hygiene. This includes following proper hand-washing procedures, wearing clean clothes, and restraining hair. In addition, follow local health department guidelines for personal hygiene.
- Avoid handling ready-to-eat foods with bare hands.
- Wear disposable foodservice gloves when preparing and serving food.
- Use serving utensils that are clean and sanitized. Hold utensils by their handles.
- Hold plates of food at their bottoms or edges and hold beverage cups by their handles or bottoms.

For more information on serving food safely in early childhood facilities, visit the USDA's website for the Child and Adult Care Food Program (CACFP).

Workplace Connections

Licensing Requirements for Serving Meals and Snacks

Investigate your state's licensing requirements or restrictions, if any, for serving snacks during the preschool or child care center day.

1. What foods, besides those listed in the text, are inappropriate to serve as snacks to young children?
2. Compare your findings to a preschool or child care center snack menu. Discuss your findings in class.

Many prepackaged breakfast foods come in child-sized servings. These include dry cereals, yogurt packs, and muffins. Juice and milk are also available in child-sized servings.

Snacks

Most children eat small amounts of food at one sitting. They may not be properly nourished by just eating three meals a day. Therefore, provide snacks between meals. Snacks satisfy hunger and help meet daily food requirements.

In most centers, snacks are served midmorning and again in midafternoon. Snacks should not interfere with a child's appetite for meals. Because of this, it is best to schedule snacks at least one and one-half hours before meals.

Plan a snack based on the menu for the day. Consider the nutrients, colors, and textures of the meals. Then choose snacks that complement the meals. Avoid fats, sweets, and highly salted foods such as potato chips, pretzels, and corn chips. Children usually enjoy simple snacks they can eat with their fingers. Suggestions for snack ideas are shown in **Figure 11.9**.

Lunch

To ensure that children receive the proper nutrients, be sure to include the minimum recommendations of the CACFP:

- 1 milk;
- 2 fruits, vegetables, 100% juice, or any combination;
- 1 grain source, such as bread, hot or cold cereal, or pasta or noodles; and
- 1 meat or alternate, such as poultry, fish, soy product, cheese, egg, cooked dry beans or peas, peanut butter (or similar nut or seed butter), or yogurt

Grains, protein-rich foods, and vegetables are often served together as one dish. They might be used in a casserole or stew, for instance. Combining food groups can make mealtimes more interesting than always serving each of these groups separately.

Snack Ideas by Food Group

Food Group	Snack Examples
Fruits	Fruits (use variety): pomegranates, cranberries, blueberries, apricots, sliced peaches, pineapples, tangerines, kiwifruit, sliced apples, sliced strawberries, papaya cubes, cantaloupe chunks, bananas, sliced red grapes, raisins (over age 1) Orange wedges Kebobs and salads Fruit juices (100% juice) Fruit in muffins, yogurts, and breads Stuffed dates or prunes
Vegetables	Vegetables (with or without dips): sweet and white potatoes, carrot sticks, broccoli, cucumber slices, cauliflower, radishes, peppers, mushrooms, zucchini, squashes, rutabagas, avocados, eggplant, okra, pea pods, turnips, pumpkin, sprouts, spinach, shredded carrot sticks Kebobs and salads Vegetable juices and juice blends (100% juice) Vegetable soups Stuffed celery, cucumbers, zucchini, spinach, lettuce, cabbage Vegetable spreads
Grains	Granola Rice cakes Dry cereal mixes (not presweetened) Roasted wheat berries, wheat germ, bran as roll-ins, toppers, or as finger-food mix Variety of breads (tortillas, pita breads, crepes, scones, pancakes, English muffins, biscuits, bagels, corn bread, popovers) and grains (whole wheat, cracked wheat, rye, oatmeal, buckwheat, rolled wheat, wheat germ, bran, grits) Toast (plain, buttered, with spreads, cinnamon) Homemade yeast and quick breads Waffle sandwiches Whole-grain and spinach pastas Pasta with butter and poppy seeds Cold pasta salad Rice (brown or white)
Protein foods	Meat strips, chunks, cubes Meatballs, small kebobs Meat roll-ups (cheese spread, mashed potatoes, spinach as stuffing) Meat salads (tuna, chicken, turkey, egg salad) Sardines Fish sticks and chicken nuggets Hard-boiled eggs Deviled eggs Beans and peas mashed as dips or spreads like hummus Bean, pea, or lentil soup 3-bean salad Chopped nut spreads Peanut butter or sunflower butter on, in, around, over, or with anything
Dairy	Milk Dips (yogurt, cottage cheese) Cheese (cubes, wedges, cutouts, faces, strips, slices) Milk punches made with fruits or juices Low-fat yogurt or pudding Cottage cheese with vegetables or pancakes Cheese fondue (preheated, no open flame in classroom) Low-fat cheese sticks

Figure 11.9   These snack ideas can help you plan for a variety of snacks to help meet the nutrition needs of the children you work with. *How might snack foods complement foods served during meals to meet the nutritional needs of children?*

Try including foods from various cultures. This will help the children develop an appreciation of other foods. The children will learn that people have different food preferences. For example, rice is an important staple in some cultures, while bread is in others.

When included, desserts should be part of the meal, like the vegetable or bread. They should not be treated as a special part of the meal. Never tell children they must eat everything on their plates in order to get dessert. This will only make desserts appear special.

Desserts that are high in fat and sugar and low in other nutrients should be avoided. For example, plain cookies and cakes have little nutritional value, but are high in calories. Instead, plan to use carrots or pumpkin in recipes to provide vitamin A. Custards and puddings are good desserts since they contain calcium and protein.

Figure 11.10 contains sample daily food plans for one meal and a snack. Note how each meal-snack pair complement one another.

Serving Safe Meals and Snacks

When planning nutritious meals and snacks, keep safety in mind. Remember that young children are learning how to chew and swallow. When they are in a hurry, they may gulp their food. This can create a risk of choking. To prevent choking, avoid serving foods that, if swallowed whole, could block children's windpipes. Foods to avoid include cherries with pits, hard or sticky candies, marshmallows, nuts, peanut butter by the spoonful, gum, popcorn, pretzels, raw celery, whole raw carrots, whole grapes, raisins (for children less than 12 months), and hot dogs (unless sliced lengthwise, then crosswise into bite-sized pieces).

Providing Water

Drinking water needs to be available to children throughout the day, both indoors and outdoors. Water should also be available at mealtimes, but it should never be a substitute for milk. Children need to learn to drink water as part of their daily routine. Water lubricates joints, makes muscles work, and cools down the body.

Promoting Healthy Eating Behaviors

Teachers are important role models for helping children develop healthful eating habits. Always sit at the table for mealtimes and snacks. You may notice that some children show **neophobia**, or the fear of something new, when encountering unfamiliar foods for the first time. Children need repeated exposure to accept new foods. Studies show that young children often must be introduced to a new food eight to 10 times to increase their acceptance. Therefore, teachers should provide many opportunities for children to try the same food.

Create a positive mealtime environment. Engage the children in interesting mealtime conversation. Talk about the tastes, colors, and textures of the foods being served. Encourage children to smell and feel the foods, if appropriate. Avoid pressuring children to eat a new food, as this may cause them to dislike the food. Instead, encourage them, beginning with acknowledgement. Notice and narrate. Make comments such as, "Shawn is enjoying the broccoli. She has just asked for another serving." Another example would be, "Roberto just finished his macaroni and cheese."

There are many ways you can encourage healthy eating behaviors. Introduce fun food preparation experiences featuring new foods. Plant a garden and include food-tasting parties in the curriculum. Involve parents by inviting them for breakfast, lunch, or a child's birthday. Parents can also be encouraged to prepare foods representing their culture in the classroom. These foods can be shared at snack time or mealtime.

Sample Menu for Lunch and Snack

Pattern	I	II	III	IV	V	VI
Snack	Orange juice Whole-wheat bread Butter	Apple wedge Cheese	Banana Milk	Hard-cooked egg Tomato juice	Apple juice Celery stuffed with peanut butter	Milk Peanut butter and cracker
Lunch	Ground beef patty Peas Carrot strips Enriched roll Milk	Roast turkey Broccoli Mashed potatoes Whole-wheat bread Milk	Fish sticks Scalloped potatoes Stewed tomato Whole-wheat bread Milk	Black-eyed peas with ham Mustard greens Purple plums Corn bread Milk	Scrambled eggs Spinach Cooked apples Biscuit Milk	Oven-fried drumsticks Corn on the cob Sliced tomato/green pepper rings Whole-wheat bread Milk

Pattern	VII	VIII	IX	X	XI	XII
Snack	Apple slices Cheese toast	Milk Pineapple Cottage cheese	Grapefruit juice Finger-size pieces of leftover meat	Milk Raw carrot strips, green pepper with dip	Tomato juice Flour tortilla with melted cheese	Fresh fruit in season (strawberries, melons, tangerines)
Lunch	Meatloaf Green beans Baked potato Carrot strips Enriched bread Pears Milk	Tuna sandwich on whole-wheat bread Tomato juice Raw cabbage (small pieces) Apricots Milk	Pinto beans with melted cheese Chili peppers, chopped Tomato, onion, lettuce Flour tortilla Milk	Meatballs in tomato sauce over spaghetti Zucchini Peaches French bread Milk	Lunch meat roll-ups Sweet potato Apple, banana, and orange salad Rye bread Milk	Swiss steak cubes Cauliflower Cooked carrots Whole-wheat roll Milk

Figure 11.10   These sample lunch and snack menus offer a variety of healthy foods.

Lesson 11.2 Review

1. **True or False.** The Child and Adult Care Food Program offers meal-pattern guidelines that recommend minimum food amounts from three of five food groups. (11.2.1)

2. What are signs that show an infant is ready to begin eating solid food? (11.2.1)
   A. Ability to control neck and head
   B. Sits up with support in a highchair
   C. Brings objects to the mouth
   D. Swallows food

3. **True or False.** Offering foods from the children's cultures helps promote cultural identity and self-esteem. (11.2.2)

4. Which food, if swallowed whole, has a high chance of blocking a child's windpipe? (11.2.3)
   A. Cherries with pits
   B. Cooked celery
   C. Hot dogs cut into bite-sized pieces
   D. Pudding

5. All of the following are ways to create a positive mealtime environment *except*: (11.2.3)
   A. Talk about the tastes, colors, and textures of the food
   B. Encourage children to smell the food
   C. Pressure children to eat a new food
   D. Throw a food-tasting party

Summary

Lesson 11.1

11.1-1 Teaching children about nutrition is an important responsibility. Children who learn healthy food choices can use the information their entire lives

11.1-1 Good nutrition promotes healthy growth, development, and learning.

11.1-2 Undernutrition, malnutrition, and overeating are food challenges children often experience.

11.1-2 Some children have special food needs due to health conditions such as diabetes or food allergies and intolerances.

11.1-3 To teach about nutrition, you must first understand how food is used by the body. You must also understand how nutrients fuel the body. You can then use this information to plan nutritious meals and snacks.

Lesson 11.2

11.2-1 MyPlate and the Child and Adult Care Food Program are a useful for planning menus.

11.2-2 Providing multicultural experiences helps children learn how food relates to social and cultural customs and helps promote cultural identify and self-esteem.

11.1-3 Food will appeal more to children if you consider the texture, flavor, color, form, temperature, and the serving size of the foods you plan to serve.

11.1-3 Teachers should provide many opportunities for children to try the same food. Children may need to be exposed to new foods eight to 10 times before they accept them.

Vocabulary Activity

Create flashcards to review the Key Terms for this chapter. On index cards, write the terms on one of the cards and the definitions on the other side.

Critical Thinking

1. **Determine.** Imagine that you are an early childhood teacher and that several of your children have and must manage their diabetes. In small groups, determine what safeguards you would put in place to supervise the children's management of their condition. Also, brainstorm ways you could explain diabetes to the other children.

2. **Analyze.** Review the text about factors that contribute to overeating. Analyze why overweight and other health and emotional challenges are easier to prevent than treat. How can early childhood professionals encourage healthy eating patterns? Write a summary of your findings.

3. **Compare and Contrast.** Search the websites for MyPlate and the American Diabetes Association. Compare and contrast food recommendations for children.

4. **Draw Conclusions.** Observe a group of children at lunchtime. Describe their food preferences. Draw conclusions about what is or is not lacking in their lunch menu based on the recommendations given in this chapter.

5. **Create.** Plan a breakfast, lunch, and snack menu for one week for a group of three-year-old children.

6. **Create.** Prepare a list of desserts that do not include added sugars or fats. List the nutritional information for each of these desserts.

Core Skills

1. **Speaking.** Interview a dietitian about the importance of a nutritious diet for children.

2. **Research and Speaking.** Conduct an online search for information on overeating in childhood and health challenges related to overeating. What has caused this growing problem in the United States? What are the physical and emotional effects on children? What is being done to help educate children and parents about preventing overeating in childhood and treating conditions that result from overeating? Use presentation software to discuss your findings in class. Include graphs and charts where possible.

3. **Listening.** Interview a teacher of young children about how he or she accommodates children with allergies in the classroom. What guidelines has the teacher put in place to protect these children? Are other children and parents accepting of these guidelines? What risks do children with allergies face daily, and to what extent can the child care center protect them?

4. **Research.** Conduct an online search to find out about protein in the vegan diet. Prepare a sample menu plan based on your findings. Share your menus in class.

5. **Research.** Search for information about the effects of food sources on the brain. Research one food from each of the nutrient sources listed in Figure 11.2. How does this food affect the brain? Prepare a chart of your findings. Share your findings with the class.

6. **Writing.** Write a summary of reasons why MyPlate suggests children should play actively every day.

7. **Research and Writing.** Download the MyPlate app. This easy-to-use app can help you make positive changes in choosing healthy foods.

Healthier eating will help you achieve a healthier lifestyle, which will contribute to your teaching practices and success.

8. **Research.** Use online resources to research various multicultural foods that contribute to healthy eating. Based on your knowledge of child development, what foods might be good to serve to preschool children? How would you introduce these multicultural foods to a group of young children?

9. **CTE Career Readiness Practice.** As a new employee at an early childhood center, you are taking initiative to serve healthy meals and snacks. Use the menu planner on the MyPlate website to plan healthful meals, compare food choices to recommendations for meeting nutrient needs, and identify ways to improve physical activities. Plan a one-week menu (meals and snacks) for the preschoolers at your center. Your menu should satisfy all the Daily Values a preschooler should consume. Print your menu and bring it to class.

Portfolio Project

Create a healthful choices snack recipe booklet for use in a preschool classroom. Collect at least 10 recipes that are low in sugar, fat, and sodium. Recipes should also contain nutritious ingredients such as fruit, vegetables, and dairy products. Assemble the recipes into a booklet with an appropriate cover and write an explanation about why each recipe is a nutritious choice. Be sure to include multicultural recipes. File the completed booklet in your portfolio, allowing room for additional recipes to be added later. Check out the Child Nutrition Recipe Box to assist you in this process.

Reading Advantage

Write all the chapter terms on a sheet of paper. Highlight the words that you do not know. Before you begin reading, look up the highlighted words in the glossary and write the definitions.

Guiding Children's Health

Lesson 12.1: Promoting Children's Health

Lesson 12.2: Caring for Illnesses and Injuries

Case Study

What Went Wrong?

When Carson entered the early childhood classroom, something immediately captivated his interest. So, he walked quickly by his teacher, Ms. Tinley, and went directly to the block-building area. There a group of children were engaged in building an elaborate castle, which intrigued him. Carson's grandmother stopped and talked to the teacher briefly before leaving for work. Meanwhile, Carson became engrossed in assisting with the block structure, and suggested adding a garage to park compact cars. The group of children continued building and discussing the structure until some guitar notes were played, indicating it was time to transition to a large group.

Ms. Tinley moved into the large, opened area of the classroom and the children sat in front of her. One of Carson's neighbors, Hussein, sat next to him. Ms. Tinley opened group time by reviewing a few reminders for the day. Then she held up a large, brightly colored book and said, "Today, I have a wonderful new book to share." After getting the children's attention and asking several motivating questions, Ms. Tinley began reading the book. About halfway through the book, she paused when she noticed Hussein's hand was held up. She smiled warmly and nodded at him to speak. He asked, "Why does Carson have all of those red dots on his face?" Ms. Tinley looked at Carson and immediately recognized the symptoms of chickenpox. She asked her assistant to take him to the director's office.

The director thanked the assistant and asked Carson to sit at the small table, which had books and child-sized puzzles. While Carson constructed a puzzle, the director opened his file and checked for contact information and began calling. There, she only found one contact. When there was no answer, she tried texting. Again, there was no response. For the next four hours, the director repeatedly tried making a telephone contact. Finally, there was an answer and a parent came to pick Carson up 30 minutes later.

Give It Some Thought

1. What should the teacher have done immediately when Carson entered the classroom?
2. What are the signs and symptoms of chickenpox? How long is the incubation period? How long should Carson be kept at home?
3. Since preschool children are prone to communicable diseases, do you think the other children were exposed? Why or why not?
4. Do you think something was missing on the emergency contact information form the director had for Carson? How could it be improved?

Opening image credit: lechatnoir/iStock via Getty Images Plus

Lesson 12.1

Promoting Children's Health

Essential Question

What do you need to know about health policies and sanitary control in early childhood programs to keep children healthy?

Learning Outcomes

After studying this lesson, you will be able to

12.1-1 describe the positive environmental factors that influence good health in children, including heredity and environment, and objectives for guiding children's health.

12.1-2 develop a workable health policy for an early childhood center.

12.1-3 explain the importance of sanitary control in early childhood programs.

Key Terms

policy

communicable diseases

sanitizing

disinfecting

standard precautions

Tu-Ling's health affects his performance, ability to learn, and behavior. Tu-Ling has a constant inner ear infection and is having trouble hearing. This hearing loss may affect the development of Tu-Ling's language skills, contact with peers, and general behavior.

Children attending early childhood programs experience more illnesses in the first two years of life than those cared for solely at home. A child's health is a key concern when planning, preparing, and maintaining a classroom environment (**Figure 12.1**). A healthy environment for young children starts with effective health policies.

fizkes/Shutterstock.com

Figure 12.1 Contact parents on health issues when appropriate.

To avoid disease transmission, stress personal hygiene and safe food-handling practices. Plan for emergencies such as control of head lice. Also, plan for sudden illnesses. In addition, obtain the knowledge and skills to provide first-aid treatment.

12.1-1 Healthy Children

There are many different definitions of *healthy*. Today, health extends beyond the absence of illness and disease to focus on physical, mental, and social-emotional well-being. Factors that affect one area of health also influence another. For example, a child living in an abusive home environment may experience frequent illnesses.

The Role of Heredity and Environment in Health

A child's heredity sets the limits for their health potential. Environment, however, plays an equally important role. The child's environment

284

Copyright Goodheart-Willcox Co., Inc.

comprises cultural, social, physical, and economic factors. These factors influence a child's dietary pattern, opportunities for exercise, and stress levels. These are all issues that affect health. Positive environmental factors that influence good health include

- good nutrition and dietary habits;
- daily physical activity;
- personal hygiene;
- regular medical and dental care (Figure 12.2);
- exposure to clean and safe environments at home and school; and
- respectful and stable relationships that provide predictability and consistency.

Poor nutrition and inactivity can lead to overweight and other health problems. This affects children's health negatively. Child abuse, violence, and low socioeconomic status also have a negative impact. Exposure to lead paint and chemicals can be harmful to a child's health. A lack of medical attention can interfere with optimal health and learning.

Objectives for Guiding Children's Health

Your responsibility is to protect, maintain, and improve children's health. Thus, you will need to create a healthful environment. Consider the following objectives:

- develop written center health policies and procedures that include the responsibilities of each staff member;
- review the children's health records to ensure that children receive immunizations;
- conduct daily health checks;
- recognize ill children when making daily health observations;
- isolate any children from the group who may have an illness;
- contact parents or guardians on health issues when appropriate;
- develop cleaning, disinfecting, and sanitation policies;

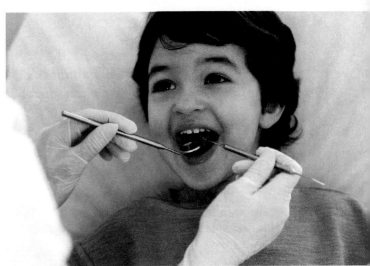

Iryna Rahalskaya/Shutterstock.com

Figure 12.2 Regular dental care is an essential factor impacting children's health. *How would you teach preschoolers to brush their teeth?*

- plan a safe environment to prevent accidents;
- provide first-aid treatment as necessary;
- develop a plan to care for sick children when waiting for their families or guardians to pick them up;
- take part in health-related in-service training; and
- include health in the curriculum.

12.1-2 Health Policies

A **policy** is a course of action that controls future decisions. It is important for your center to have health policies. These policies will help you make consistent decisions regarding the health of the children in your care.

In most states, licensing rules and regulations govern health policies for children in childcare and early childhood education settings. Their purpose is to protect young children and their caregivers or teachers. These rules and regulations address only the basic health requirements. Your center may have additional health policies that are more specific.

Medical Examination Policy

All children enrolled in your program should have a preadmission medical examination. This exam will help you learn whether the child

- is free from **communicable diseases**—illnesses that can be passed on to other people;
- has up-to-date immunizations;
- has any allergies; and
- has any health problems that require special attention.

Likewise, to provide the best environment for children, the staff must also be in excellent physical, mental, and social-emotional health. They should have health appraisal before their first day of work. A center must maintain a record of these examinations and up-to-date immunizations in the employees' files.

Immunization Policy

To protect all children, each child attending the center must have the proper immunizations. The only exception to this policy is when a child has an exemption by state laws for religious or medical reasons. Exclusion from the center is required for children who do not have proper immunizations or exemptions. Partial immunizations protect against many diseases. The American Academy of Pediatrics (AAP) suggests the following immunizations: Hepatitis B; diphtheria, tetanus, and pertussis (DTaP); measles, mumps, and rubella (MMR); inactivated polio vaccine (IPV); Haemophilus influenzae type b (Hib) vaccine; varicella (chickenpox) vaccine; and pneumococcal conjugate vaccine (**Figure 12.3**). Find out which immunizations are a requirement by law in the state where you live.

Immunizations for Young Children

Immunizations	Range of Recommended Ages
Hepatitis A (HepA)	1st dose,12 to 23 months; 2nd dose, 6 months later
Hepatitis B (HepB)	1st dose, birth; 2nd dose,1 to 2 months; 3rd dose, 6 to 18 months
Diphtheria, tetanus, and pertussis (DTaP)	1st dose, 2 months; 2nd dose, 4 months; 3rd dose, 6 months; 4th dose, 18 months; 5th dose, 4 to 6 years
Inactivated poliovirus (IPV) (polio vaccine)	1st dose, 2 months; 2nd dose, 4 months; 3rd dose, 6 to 18 months; 4th dose, 4 to 6 years
Haemophilus influenzae type b vaccine (Hib)	1st dose, 2 months; 2nd dose, 4 months; 6 months; 3rd dose, 12 to 15 months
Influenza	1st dose, 6 months; 2nd dose, separated by 4 weeks for children 6 months to 8 years; annual, after 9 years
Rotavirus	1st dose, 2 months; 2nd dose, 4 months; 3rd dose, 6 months
Measles, mumps, and rubella (MMR) vaccine	1st dose, 12 to 15 months; 2nd dose, 4 to 6 years
Varicella (chicken pox) vaccine	1st dose, 12 to 15 months; 2nd dose, 4 to 6 years
Pneumococcal vaccine (PCV13) (4-dose series)	1st dose, 2 months; 2nd dose, 3rd dose, 4 months; 4th dose, 12 to 18 months

Source: US Department of Health and Human Services, Centers for Disease Control and Prevention, 2022

Figure 12.3   All children, except for those with medical or religious exemptions, must have proper immunizations for protection from certain diseases.

Exclusion Policy for Illness

For the safety of all the children, centers need a policy concerning ill children. During the first year of attending group care, children may experience many infections. By the second year, respiratory illnesses decrease as the child's immune system becomes stronger. For example, your policy might state that parents or guardians should keep children at home if they have any of the following symptoms within the past 24 hours. The American Academy of Pediatrics (AAP) recommends that the following conditions require exclusion:

- an oral temperature over 101°F or rectal temperature of 102°F, unless the child's average temperature is above 101°F;
- diarrhea for children who wear diapers when stool is not confined in the diaper;
- diarrhea is causing accidents or stool frequency that exceeds two stools above normal in a twenty-four-hour period;
- vomiting two or more times in the previous 24 hours;
- severe, persistent cough or cold;
- drainage from open sores, eyes, nose, or ears;
- rashes, excluding diaper rash, with fever; or
- head lice, scabies, or ringworm until after the first treatment.

Per the center policy, inform parents or guardians to keep a child home for 24 hours after a fever subsides (**Figure 12.4**). Likewise, children should remain at home until free from diarrhea for 24 hours. Instruct parents or guardians to report all sickness to center personnel. When is it okay to stay in early childhood programs? With the onset of COVID, sick policies have become more stringent. Parents or guardians should check with their center's directors or teachers. They also need to check with their healthcare provider if the child has shortness of breath, cough, or lack of smell or taste.

Parents or guardians and teachers often disagree on criteria for when children should be excluded and can return to the center. Fueling this confusion, every state's licensing agency and

mytrykau/Shutterstock.com

Figure 12.4 Even after a fever subsides, it can take up to 24 hours for children to feel well enough to attend child care or preschool. *What other illnesses require children to stay home from child care or preschool?*

health department has created health policies and procedures. They may differ in what symptoms, diseases, and conditions that require children to be excluded from attending a childcare or early childhood program. Some policies are unique. So, it is essential to check your state's policies and provide the parents or guardians with this information.

Administering Medications

Children with mild illnesses may require medications. To protect staff and children in their care against lawsuits, centers should always require a signed release form for each medication. These policies must adhere to your state's licensing requirements, but they can exceed them. For instance, your state may require that you may only give a child a doctor-prescribed medication. You must follow this rule. Some states, however, prohibit administering medications.

A parent or guardian should transport medicines to the center or early learning setting and hand them to designated personnel. If the center does not have a nurse, the center director is usually responsible for storing and dispensing medicines at the proper time. A parent or guardian must bring medicine to school in the original labeled container and center staff should store it appropriately. Store refrigerated medications in a secure, labeled plastic bag. Then, store the bags in a locked container in the refrigerator at the appropriate temperature. Store nonrefrigerated medicines in a locked place out of the children's reach.

Medications must contain a label specifying the child's name, date, physician's name, drug name, dosage, and how often to administer the medication. Over-the-counter medications may include sunscreen, antihistamines, decongestants, cough medicines, and insect repellents, and require storage in the original containers and a label with the child's name. Check to ensure there are explicit instructions from the child's healthcare provider, the medication has not expired, and a release form is signed.

Always use caution when giving medications. Make sure to

- wash your hands and wear gloves if applying medication to open, oozing sores;
- read the label as you remove the medicine from storage to ensure you have the proper medication for the correct child;
- review the label to check for any special requirements, such as taken at mealtime;
- verify the child's name before giving the medicine;
- always read the label on the medication at least three times;
- use an accurate dosage spoon or medicine dropper to dispense liquid medications instead of using flatware;
- give the correct medication and exact amount prescribed at the prescribed time; and
- keep a record containing the child's name, date and time of day, the medication name, and the amount of medication.

Reading the label three times is important. First, read the label as you remove the medication from storage to be sure you have the right medication for the right child. Reread it as you dispense the medicine into the measuring device. Look at the label one last time before giving the medicine. Double-check it to see if it is the right amount, right medicine, at the right time, and for the right child. If you have questions about the

medication, call the parents or guardians or the prescribing doctor before giving the medicine.

Early Childhood Insight 🄰🄱🄲

Keeping a Medication Log

Early childhood teachers or center directors may need to administer medicine to children in their care. For each child, keep a special log that includes signed parental or guardian consent, a copy of the health-care provider's documentation for the child's need of medicine, the medication, name, dosage, time(s) it should be given, and other requirements, such as "with a glass of water." The log should also list signs of negative reactions and instructions for handling them. In addition, you may be asked to keep a checklist of medication brought to the facility by the parents or guardians.

Napping

One health policy that is a requirement to help prevent the spread of illness relates to napping. Children should not share cots or beds. Instead, provide each child with freshly laundered fitted sheets (**Figure 12.5**). Provide infants with clean sheets twice a week. Infants should sleep in a crib

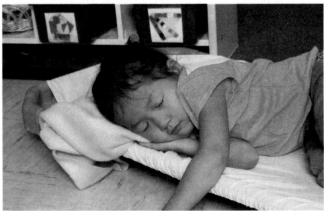

ktaylorg/iStock via Getty Images Plus

Figure 12.5   Clean and well-spaced cots can help prevent illness from spreading from child to child. *How often should bed linens be laundered for young children? What conditions might require more frequent laundering?*

free of stuffed animals and blankets. By the time they are 18 months, toddlers typically shift from two naps to one nap a day. They need fitted sheets and a blanket. Provide preschoolers with clean sheets once a week. It may be necessary to change sheets more frequently, such as when a child is ill, has perspired a lot, or has soiled the sheets.

Health Highlights

Doctor and Dental Visits

Parents or guardians may ask you to assist in preparing their children for doctor or dental visits. Note that it is not recommended that families and caregivers talk a lot about these visits in advance. Take your cue from the children.

- Provide age-appropriate information and be positive.
- Answer children's questions directly and honestly.
- Always provide comfort and assurance.
- Encourage family members to plan a fun activity (not a bribe) after doctor and dental visits are over.

Daily Health Inspection

To protect children's health, conduct an informal health inspection each day. Conduct this inspection as soon as each child and their parents or guardians arrive at school. Greet the child by name with a smile and welcoming comment at the classroom door. Check the child from head to foot. Take the child's temperature and observe for rashes, sores, swelling or bruising, changes in the appearance of the eyes, runny noses, flushing of the skin, coughing, sneezing, and a sweaty appearance.

Even after the health inspection at arrival time, observe the children throughout the day for symptoms of illness (**Figure 12.6**). If a child appears sick, contact the parents or guardians.

Preschool children are prone to **communicable diseases**. These include chickenpox, conjunctivitis (pink eye), influenza, and measles. Observe for symptoms of each of these diseases. Make sure all staff know this information. Post a communicable disease chart in the staff room (**Figure 12.7**).

Symptoms of Illness

Behavior Changes	Upper Respiratory, Fever, Ears, and Throat	Body Aches	Other
• Atypical behavior: more quiet, tired, fussy, or aggressive than usual • Frequent scratching of body or scalp • Lack of energy • Loss of appetite or refusal to eat • Frequent rubbing of eyes • Change in crying volume, pitch, or continuous and excessive crying • Severe drowsiness	• Breathing difficulties • Shortness of breath • Wheezing • Fever • Severe coughing or persistent cough • Congestion • Runny nose (a yellow or green discharge indicates infection; a clear discharge indicates allergies • Sore throat, spots on throat, difficulty swallowing	• Complaint of abdominal pain or cramping • Headache, stiff neck, or other neck pain • Achiness, general • Swollen lymph nodes • Earache	• Blood in stools • Diarrhea • Vomiting is green or contains blood • Change in color of urine or stools • Urine with a strong odor • Infected skin lesions • Sores • Skin rashes or spots • Redness or discharge from eyes • Seizure for the first time • Croup

Figure 12.6 Early childhood teachers and staff need to observe children for symptoms of illness throughout the day. *What symptoms are a cause for concern?*

Communicable Diseases

Disease	Incubation Period (Time from Exposure to First Signs)	Signs and Symptoms	Period of Communicability, Precautions, and Restrictions	General Information
Chicken pox (varicella)	10 to 21 days	Sudden onset, slight fever, raised pink or red bumps often appear first on scalp, then on face and body. Successive crop of lesions remains 3 to 4 days, leaving crusts and scabs.	Keep child home five to ten days until all lesions are crusted over, usually a week after onset of rash.	Mild disease in children. May be more severe in adults and in children with cancer, leukemia, and other high-risk conditions. Vaccine is available for prevention.
COVID-19	2-14 days	Symptoms typically appear 4-5 days after exposure. Runny nose, headache, sneezing, sore throat tiredness and persistent cough. May also include loss of smell and shortness of breath. Other symptoms include chest pain, nausea, vomiting, diarrhea, and rash. Symptoms range from mild to severe.	People are most contagious shortly before and after symptoms occur. Risk factors include being within six feet of someone with COVID-19 and being coughed or sneezed on by an infected person. The virus spreads easily among people.	Prevention involves physical distancing, by at least six feet, wearing a face mask, avoiding others when feeling sick, and handwashing. Avoid touching eyes, nose, or mouth with unwashed hands. Get vaccinated. COVID-19 can be spread even by people who do not have any symptoms.
Conjunctivitis (pink eye)	2 to 7 days	Redness in the white of the eye. May or may not have pus discharge. Eye irritation. Crusting of eyelids or lashes may occur. Often begins in one eye and the other eye becomes infected.	The contagious period depends on the cause, but is usually while inflammation or drainage is present. Keep child home during contagious period, and refer for medical diagnosis and treatment.	Most infections are viral by cause; some are bacterial. May spread person to person through hand to eye contact. Also, an early symptom for measles. Some symptoms may be an allergy and are noncommunicable.
Herpes simplex (cold sores)	2 to 12 weeks	Common viral infection. Blisters develop on face, lips, and other places.	Following recovery, the virus can remain in the saliva for up to seven weeks.	Child does not need to be excluded from the center.
Viral hepatitis type A (formerly infectious)	14 to 50 days (average 25 days)	Usually abrupt onset with fever, fatigue, loss of appetite, nausea, and abdominal pain. Jaundice is less common in children than in adults.	Most contagious during first week of illness and up to 1 week after jaundice. Keep child home. Avoid food handling or patient care while communicable.	Vaccine not available in all areas. May be confused with Hepatitis B. Differential diagnosis is important for prevention and control. Household contacts should be given immune serum globulin as soon as possible.
Influenza	1 to 2 days	Rapid onset with fever, chills, headache, lack of energy, muscle ache, sore throat, cough.	Communicable for 3 to 7 days after clinical onset. Keep child home until symptoms disappear. Noncommunicable 36–48 hours after treatment.	Vaccine is available and should be given to all children or persons with greatest risk of serious complications from the disease: the chronically ill and older adults.
Measles (rubeola)	8 to 12 days	High fever (101°F or more), with cough, runny nose and/or conjunctivitis. Blotchy rash appears 3 to 5 days after early signs, beginning on face and becoming generalized, lasting 4 or more days.	Communicable from onset or respiratory illness until 4 days after appearance of the rash. Keep child home until 5 days after the appearance of rash.	A very serious, highly contagious but vaccine-preventable disease.

Continued

Figure 12.7   Communicable diseases are easily transmitted from child to child.

Disease	Incubation Period (Time from Exposure to First Signs)	Signs and Symptoms	Period of Communicability, Precautions, and Restrictions	General Information
Mononucleosis, infectious	30 to 50 days	Characterized by fever, sore throat, fatigue, and inflamed posterior lymph nodes. May be accompanied by a headache.	Keep child home at the discretion of physician. Length of communicability is unknown.	The disease is usually mild and difficult to recognize in children. Use frequent hand washing.
Mumps	12 to 26 days, commonly 18 days	Fever, pain, and swelling about the jaws involving one or more salivary glands. Many infections occur without symptoms.	Keep child home until salivary gland swelling has subsided, or other symptoms have cleared.	Infectious early. May cause complications in adults. Vaccine available. Children should be excluded from the center until all symptoms have disappeared.
Pediculosis (lice)	Eggs hatch in a week; reach maturity in about 2 weeks	Excessive scratching on head or other parts of body. Light gray insects lay eggs in the hair, especially at the nape of the neck and around the ears. Lice are seldom visible to the naked eye.	Keep child home until treated and nits have been destroyed (should not need to miss more than 1 day of school).	Hair needs to be washed with a special medicated shampoo. Then it needs to be rinsed with a solution of vinegar and water. Avoid sharing personal belongings, such as clothing, head gear, combs, brushes, and bedding.
Ringworm (scalp, skin, feet)	Variable, 4 to 10 days	Scalp: Scaly patches of temporary baldness. Infected hairs are brittle and break easily. Skin: Flat, inflamed, ring-like sores that may itch or burn. Feet: Scaling or cracking of the skin, especially between the toes or blisters containing a thin watery fluid.	Communicable as long as active lesions are present. Keep child home until adequate treatment has begun.	Preventive measures are largely hygienic. All household contacts, pets, and farm animals should be examined and treated if infected. Ringworm is spread directly by contact with articles and surfaces contaminated by such infected persons or animals.
Rubella (German measles)	14 to 21 days	Mild symptoms, slight fever, rash lasting about 3 days, usually begins on face, enlarged head and neck glands common (particularly in back part of neck, behind ears).	Keep child home until 4 days after appearance of rash.	Highly communicable but vaccine-preventable disease. Complications are mild except in pregnancy, when fetal infection or damage may occur. If contacts include a pregnant woman, she should consult her physician immediately.
Pertussis (whooping cough)	7 to 10 days	Begins with upper respiratory symptoms. An increasingly irritating cough develops with a characteristic "whoop" and frequently occurs in spasms accompanied by vomiting.	Keep child home for 21 days from beginning of "whoop," or 5 to 7 days after onset of appropriate therapy.	Most dangerous to preschool children. Immunization is not recommended for children over 6 years of age. Susceptible contacts should be treated and observed for respiratory disease.
Scabies	30 to 45 days with first infections, several days with reinfection	Small, raised, reddened areas or lesions with connecting grayish-white lines. Marked itching. Most commonly found in the folds of the skin, finger webs, wrists, elbows, thighs, beltline, abdomen, nipples, buttocks.	Keep child home until under adequate treatment and no open lesions can be observed.	All cases, family members, and other physically close contacts should be treated for scabies simultaneously.
Streptococcal infections including scarlet fever (strep throat)	2 to 5 days	Sudden onset with high fever, sore throat; tender swollen glands with a fine, red rash present in scarlet fever. May also have headache, vomiting, and white patches on tonsils.	Keep child home for 7 days from onset if untreated; with adequate medical treatment, 24 hours.	Medication for symptomatic patients is recommended because of possibility of complications, including rheumatic fever. Culture survey rarely recommended.

Contacting Parents or Guardians

Children may arrive at the center in good health, but later show symptoms of illness or infection. When do you decide to contact a parent or guardian to pick up a sick child? The answer to this question depends on the disease and the center's policies. Most states require centers to have an isolation area for sick children. The care provider should remove the child from the classroom and wait with the child in the isolation area until a parent or guardian arrives.

Always contact parents or guardians when a child shows signs of illness. Describe the symptoms to the parent. If the child is very ill, the parent or guardian should pick the child up within a reasonable time. Programs need to have this clearly stated in their policies.

Each child's folder should contain emergency information. Record parents' or guardians' home, cell, and work telephone numbers. Also note the phone numbers of the family doctor and dentist. See **Figure 12.8** for an example of an emergency information sheet.

Emergency Contact Information
Child and Family Study Center

Child's Name _____   Birthdate _____

Home Address _____   Home Phone _____

Parent Name (guardian) _____

Home Address _____   Home Phone _____

_____   Cell Phone _____

Place of Employment _____   Business Phone _____

Email Address _____

Parent Name (guardian) _____

Home Address _____   Home Phone _____

_____   Cell Phone _____

Place of Employment _____   Business Phone _____

Email Address _____

In Case of Emergency
(Person to be called if the parent or guardian cannot be reached.)

Name _____   Phone _____

Relationship _____   Cell Phone _____

Name _____   Phone _____

Relationship _____   Cell Phone _____

Family Doctor _____   Phone _____

Address _____   Cell Phone _____

Family Doctor _____   Phone _____

Address _____   Cell Phone _____

Parent or Guardian Signature _____   Date _____

Goodheart-Willcox Publisher

Figure 12.8   Every child enrolled in an early childhood center must have a folder that contains emergency contact information. *How would you inform parents or guardians about an outbreak of head lice at the center?*

Parents or guardians should receive notification if their children have exposure to a communicable disease such as chickenpox, pertussis (whooping cough), measles, meningitis, or parasites, such as head lice, scabies, or ringworm. **Figure 12.9** shows an example of the communication. The communication should *not* include the name of the child who has the infectious condition, but *should* include a list of signs and symptoms of the illness or disease.

Personal Hygiene

Personal hygiene is the science that deals with promoting and preserving health. It is an essential component of a healthful environment.

Date: March 29, 20XX

Dear Parents or Guardians:

It is important that we work together to promote a healthful environment for young children by minimizing communicable diseases. Therefore, I want to inform you that today your child was exposed to conjunctivitis, sometimes referred to as "pink eye." Since conjunctivitis is highly contagious, please observe your child carefully. Signs and symptoms include the following:

- pink or red color in the white of the eye
- itching of the eye
- blurred vision and sensitivity to light
- thick yellow discharge in the eye that forms a crust, especially after sleep
- increase in tear production

If your child has any of the symptoms, please call your physician immediately. Moreover, if you have questions, please call the center.

Thank you for your cooperation,

Judy Gifford, Director

Goodheart-Willcox Publisher

Figure 12.9 One of the responsibilities of early childhood staff members is to keep parents or guardians informed when their children have been exposed to a communicable disease. *How would you approach informing parents or guardians about an outbreak of head lice at the center?*

When cleanliness is stressed, the body performs better. Fewer children and staff become ill with the prevention or control of many diseases.

It is important to stress the importance of good personal hygiene to all new employees and volunteers. In-service training, the employee handbook, or orientation meetings are ways to provide this information. All should follow essential habits of cleanliness. Good personal hygiene includes clean skin and care of the mouth, teeth, hair, hands, nails, feet, and ears.

Environmental Control

Early childhood centers need sanitary practices to keep the environment clean. Studies show that children in group settings have more upper respiratory infections. Germs are everywhere. Young children have not learned good hygiene practices. Infants drool everywhere and mouth toys. Older children forget to wash their hands after using the restroom, blowing their noses, or sneezing in their hands. They may share cups and food. These practices spread communicable diseases. Everyone is at risk—the children, teachers, support staff, and family members.

Environmental control is essential to prevent the transmission of diseases. Sanitary practices can remove bacteria and dirt. These are practical measures to help keep the center as germ-free and clean as possible.

Every center needs written health policies. These policies should include cleaning, sanitation, and disinfection procedures. To coordinate home and center practices, share these policies with families. Procedures should address handwashing, diapering, toileting, cleaning, disinfecting, and sanitizing. Handwashing is one of the most important sanitary practices.

Handwashing

Studies show that a child's success in school and life is directly related to their health and well-being. As an early childhood caregiver or teacher, your role is to protect the children's health and teach habits for healthy living. Medical experts agree that hand hygiene is the most effective practice for reducing illness in early childhood settings. Everyone—children, teachers, and staff—must practice good hygiene to prevent disease in early childhood settings. To promote handwashing, teachers need to display handwashing charts in the restrooms of children and adults. To encourage children to wash their hands methodically, teachers must carefully supervise and model hand hygiene.

When centers follow acceptable handwashing practices, studies also show there will be a reduction in many illnesses, such as diarrhea. Modeling handwashing teaches children the techniques and their importance. Teachers and children should wash their hands

- on arrival at the center;
- after handling classroom pets;
- after playing outdoors;
- after coughing sneezing, rubbing the nose, or handling a handkerchief or tissue;
- before handling food or eating;
- after checking for a dirty diaper, changing a diaper, or using the toilet;
- handling animals or cleaning up animal waste;
- when hands are dirty; before and after playing in the water table or sandbox; and
- after handling clay, play dough, paint, and other art materials.

Avoid using alcohol-based hand sanitizers if possible. They are not as effective as soap and water and are expensive, toxic, and flammable. There are risks with using these products because the ingredients include a high percentage of alcohol, which may be harmful if swallowed. This is a significant risk with young children, as they often put their hands in their mouths.

Children need to be taught to wash their hands properly. Use liquid soap for handwashing since bacteria from the previous user can grow on bar soap. Moreover, not all children have the dexterity to handle a soap bar. See **Figure 12.10** for the proper handwashing procedure.

Handwashing for Mobile Infants

Mobile infants' hands are in constant use handling toys, crawling, and eating.

How to Wash Hands

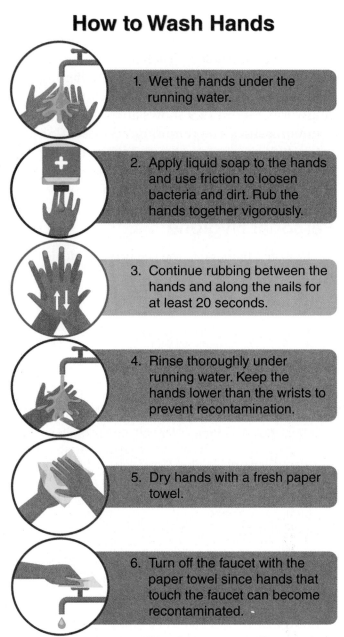

1. Wet the hands under the running water.

2. Apply liquid soap to the hands and use friction to loosen bacteria and dirt. Rub the hands together vigorously.

3. Continue rubbing between the hands and along the nails for at least 20 seconds.

4. Rinse thoroughly under running water. Keep the hands lower than the wrists to prevent recontamination.

5. Dry hands with a fresh paper towel.

6. Turn off the faucet with the paper towel since hands that touch the faucet can become recontaminated.

Goodheart-Willcox Publisher; elenabsi/Shutterstock.com

Figure 12.10   One of your responsibilities as an early childhood teacher will be to teach children how to wash their hands properly.

Handwashing is the most effective method of controlling the spread of communicable diseases. Water alone will not kill germs. To wash an infant's hands, moisten a damp paper towel and add a drop of a child-safe liquid soap solution. Lather the infant's hands for 20 seconds or as long as possible. Then moisten another disposable paper towel with water and rinse off each hand and dry. Using a clean paper towel, dry the infant's hands.

Handwashing for Toddlers

Chances are you are going to need to teach and assist toddlers with the handwashing process. Begin by squirting a drop or two of liquid soap on one of the child's hands. If needed, help them to wash and rinse their hands under warm, running water. The water should flow down from the wrists to the fingertips. After rinsing, give them a paper towel to dry their hands. If needed, help.

Handwashing for Preschool Children

Preschool children may need a reminder to wash their hands following the procedure in Figure 12.10. They may also need supervision. After applying liquid soap, encourage them to rub their hands together to create a soapy lather. Then they need to scrub both the fronts and backs of each hand. After this, they should wash the area between their fingers before rinsing under warm running water. This process should take twenty seconds. To help the children estimate the time, teach them to sing "Twinkle, Twinkle, Little Star" twice while washing their hands.

Safety First

Be Safe with Hand Sanitizers

The Centers for Disease Control and Prevention (CDC) recommends washing hands that are visibly soiled or contaminated using soap and water. Soap and water are more effective for removing all kinds of germs, including COVID-19, from the hands. Hand sanitizers with at least 60 percent alcohol can be used for children over two years of age *only* when soap and water are unavailable. Alcohol is the ingredient in hand sanitizers used to clean and may be toxic if ingested by young children.

Ventilation

Ventilation is a factor in maintaining a healthy indoor environment for young children and their teachers and caregivers. It is an important strategy the Center for Disease Control and Prevention (CDC) recommends to help prevent the spread of the COVID-19 virus and other infectious diseases. An effective ventilation system can reduce the number of virus particles in the air either in a childcare home or early childhood center. Opening or even cracking a screened window reduces the virus particles by increasing the airflow. If the climate allows, you could also consider having classroom activities outdoors.

Cough Etiquette

A cough responds to something irritating tissues in the airway between the nose and lungs. Cough etiquette is essential for adults and children in early childhood settings to prevent the spread of serious respiratory illnesses such as influenza, whooping cough, and COVID-19. The CDC recommends that you cover your mouth. Use a disposable tissue to cover your mouth and nose when coughing or sneezing. Discard the used tissue in a wastebasket and wash your hands with soap and water for at least 20 seconds. If you do not have a tissue, cough, or sneeze into your upper sleeve, not your hands. Always wash your hands immediately after coughing, sneezing, or blowing the nose. If the child is over two years of age and soap and water are not available, use an alcohol-based sanitizer that contains at least 60 percent alcohol.

12.1-3 Cleaning, Sanitizing, and Disinfecting

Preventing the transmission of diseases in an early childhood center is a challenge. It occurs from the contamination of hands, toys, diapering tables, highchair trays, kitchen counters, and food preparation equipment. Just as you must take care in handwashing, you must also take care in wiping up spills, and cleaning surfaces, toys, and outdoor equipment. After each use, you much clean and disinfect toys in an infant and toddler room (**Figure 12.11**). Wash stuffed toys at least once a week or when soiled. Toys for toddlers who do not wear diapers require weekly cleaning

DeymosHR/IShutterstock.com

Figure 12.11 All toys must be cleaned, sanitized, and disinfected after every use. *What is the difference between sanitizing and disinfecting?*

Health Highlights

Sanitizing Surfaces

Keeping surfaces free of harmful bacteria and viruses can be a challenge in an early childhood setting. Soap and water are the best way of cleaning followed by sanitizing. A simple sanitizing solution of 1/4-cup bleach with hypochlorite to one gallon of water can be used to sanitize indoor surfaces. Prepare a fresh bleach mixture daily and place it in an opaque spray bottle. Adjust the setting to produce a heavy spray and apply when children are not in the area. After spraying the solution on a surface, wait two minutes before wiping to kill an infectious agent. Another option would be to allow the surfaces to air-dry since chlorine evaporates. Commercial sanitizers are also available; however, check with state and local guidelines to make sure the products are safe to use around children, adults, and food.

or when soiled. Check your state's licensing requirements for their recommendations.

According to the CDC, playground equipment requires routine cleaning and sanitizing, but does not require disinfecting. You can use common household cleaning products but check the product label to make sure the product is registered the Environmental Protection Agency (EPA). Wearing rubber gloves and eye protection, prepare a solution of 1/3 cup of chlorine bleach per gallon of cool water or four teaspoons per quart of water. To reduce fumes, add bleach to the water. Begin the cleaning process by washing the items using a liquid detergent in warm water. Then using a low-pressure garden hose, remove the dirt and germs from the surface. Rinse thoroughly.

Regularly clean high-touch surfaces constructed of metal or plastic such as slide railings, monkey bars, swings, and climbing handles. Disinfecting or cleaning wooden play structures, benches, or tables is not recommended. You should contact manufacturers to find out what they recommend for these items. Otherwise, if the wrong product was used, it may void the warranty. Since these recommendations are constantly changing, check with the CDC.

Cleaning removes dirt, but it does not kill germs. **Sanitizing** reduces germs. The process removes dirt or soil *and* bacteria. As previously mentioned, an inexpensive and effective way to sanitize surfaces is to make a solution of household bleach and water. Check the instructions on the bottle. Manufacturers use two types of instructions, one for sanitizing and the other for disinfecting. Sanitizing solutions use *less* bleach. The manufacturer's instructions will list the amount of bleach to use for sanitizing and disinfecting. Follow the manufacturer's instructions. Mix a fresh solution daily and pour the bleach solution into labeled spray bottles. Since a poisonous gas can result, never mix bleach with other household chemicals such as toilet cleaners or ammonia products.

All surfaces that food touches require sanitizing, including flatware, high-chair trays, tables, counters, and computer keyboards. Toys and pacifiers that children put in their mouths also require sanitizing. After cleaning and rinsing, the toys will require disinfection.

Disinfecting is the process of destroying or inactivating germs. Disinfect toys after every use. Surfaces that children and staff often, such as tables and chairs, require daily disinfection. Disinfect cots and cribs weekly or when changing soiled linen. Disinfect restroom surfaces, kitchen surfaces, doorknobs, and kitchen sinks one or more times daily. Vacuum play areas daily. Remove any spilled food immediately. Hard surfaces require washing, rinsing, and then disinfection. Different states have different rules about disinfecting solutions. Check your state childcare licensing regulations to make sure you comply.

Prevention from Exposure to Blood

The US Department of Labor's Occupational Safety and Health Administration (OSHA) protects workers' safety. Federal laws require staff protection from accidental exposure to blood-borne pathogens. These include any microorganism that can cause infection, such as HIV or Hepatitis B. The law requires programs to develop and practice **standard precautions** (also known as *universal precautions*). Otherwise, children could be unknowingly infected with HIV, Hepatitis B, or some other infection. Hepatitis B can survive for at least a week or longer in a dried state.

Consider all bodily fluids to be potentially infectious and contaminated. Wear either disposable latex, vinyl, or utility gloves and use them only once. Remove them without touching the outside with your hand and discard them. Then follow appropriate handwashing procedures.

Blood-contaminated materials, such as furniture and toys, require immediate cleaning and disinfecting. Separately wash blankets, sheets, pillows, stuffed toys, towels, and other center materials containing any child's bodily fluids. If the fluids are on a child's clothing, remove the clothing and seal it in a plastic bag marked with the child's name. Send the soiled clothing items home for laundering.

Lesson 12.1 Review

1. **True or False.** To protect, maintain, and improve children's health, it is necessary to identify objectives for creating a healthful environment. (12.1.1)
2. What will a preadmission medical exam not help you learn about a child who is being enrolled? (12.1.2)
   A. If they have up-to-date immunizations
   B. If they have any allergies
   C. If they have any health problems that require special attention
   D. If they will contract chickenpox
3. How long should a child remain home after a fever or diarrhea subsides? (12.1.2)
   A. 12 hours
   B. 24 hours
   C. 36 hours
   D. 48 hours
4. How often should you disinfect toys? (12.1.3)
   A. Once a week
   B. Once a day
   C. After each use
   D. Once a month

Caring for Illnesses and Injuries

Essential Question

What do I need to know and be able to do to prevent and care for illnesses and injuries of children in my care?

Learning Outcomes

After studying this lesson, you will be able to

12.2-1 **analyze** guidelines for controlling the spread of foodborne illnesses.

12.2-2 **summarize** how to prepare a kit of basic first-aid supplies and treat various types of medical emergencies.

12.2-3 **implement** ways to promote proper oral hygiene and handle dental emergencies.

12.2-4 **describe** the caregiver's or teacher's responsibility when caring for children with certain illnesses, including allergies, asthma, diabetes, epilepsy, human immunodeficiency virus (HIV), and disease due to air pollution.

12.2-5 **explain** why it is essential to monitor air quality before taking children outside.

Key Terms

foodborne illness	first-degree burn
first aid	second-degree burn
wound	third-degree burn
abrasion	head lice
epinephrine auto-injection	asthma
capillaries	epilepsy
rabies	human immunodeficiency virus (HIV)
burn	

acquired immunodeficiency syndrome (AIDS)

Air Quality Index (AQI)

First-aid training is essential for every early childhood caregiver or teacher. All teachers are responsible for keeping children safe and responding to medical emergencies. Young children are vulnerable to unintentional injuries and accidents—cuts, bruises, bites, fractures, puncture wounds, splinters, and choking. Some children have unique health concerns and may have a medical emergency related to allergies, asthma, diabetes, or epilepsy. Others may have sunburn or head lice. First-aid training helps teachers and caregivers feel secure and stay calm, allowing them to provide a quick initial response to medical emergencies. First-aid training will provide an awareness of illnesses and provide caregivers with the tools for assessing casualties and providing the best initial treatment for an injured or ill child. It can prevent death or further injuries.

12.2-1 Controlling Foodborne Illness

Foodborne illness is caused by eating food containing harmful bacteria, toxins, parasites, or viruses. People who eat these foods can become very ill. They can have painful symptoms, including stomach pain and cramps, diarrhea, bloody stools, nausea, vomiting, severe headaches, or fever.

Young children and pregnant women are at high risk of getting these diseases. As a teacher or center director, you should take precautions to prevent these illnesses among your staff and the children. Foodborne illness often results from improper food preparation, handling, or storage. Using safe food-handling techniques will prevent many of these illnesses.

When preparing food, keep your work area clean. Avoid transferring harmful bacteria from one food to another. This can occur when your utensils touch a contaminated food and then touch another food. When foods touch a contaminated counter, appliance, or towel, this can also happen. Keeping these items clean will prevent the spreading of contaminants (**Figure 12.12**).

Cook all meat, poultry, seafood, and egg dishes thoroughly. This will kill any harmful bacteria in these foods. Learn federal recommendations and your state's requirements for institutional food preparation. Your center and the agencies that found it may set additional policies.

Andrey_Popov/Shutterstock.com

Figure 12.12 A refrigerator that is clean and kept at 40°F helps control the transmission of foodborne illness.

growth. Never leave perishable foods out at room temperature for more than two hours. Discard foods left out longer than this. This applies to plates of food, baby food, formula, and breast milk as well.

If foodborne illness should occur at your center, seek medical help for those affected. Alert any parents whose children may have eaten the contaminated food.

12.2-2 First Aid

In every preschool or childcare center, injuries, and illnesses occur. Sometimes, it may just be a scratch or bumped knee. At other times, it may be a sudden high temperature.

First aid is the immediate treatment given for injuries and illnesses, including those that are life-threatening. First-aid training provides the knowledge and skill needed to handle emergency medical care. With the proper training, you will know how and when to treat illnesses and injuries. You will also know when it is necessary to seek professional medical help.

All employees in early childhood care and education should have certification from the American Red Cross. This certification may have been gained through prior course work or previous employment. If an employee does not have certification, acquiring certification must be a condition of employment.

Health Highlights

Safe Food Temperatures

Caring for Our Children, fourth edition, indicates taking the following precautions for keeping foods safe to eat:

- Serve foods promptly after preparation or cooking and maintain temperatures of not less than 135°F for hot foods and not more than 41°F for cold foods.
- Hold fully cooked and ready-to-serve hot foods no longer than 30 minutes before serving. Promptly cover and refrigerate.
- Fully cook to heat all raw animal foods to 145°F or above for 15 seconds for fish and meat; 160°F for 15 seconds for chopped or ground fish, chopped or ground meat, or raw eggs; and 165°F or above for 15 seconds for poultry or stuffed fish, stuffed meat, stuffed pasta, stuffed poultry, or stuffing containing fish, meat, or poultry.

Store foods at safe temperatures, too. Foods that are cold (below 40°F) or hot (above 140°F) are safest. According to the USDA, temperatures between 40°F and 140°F promote bacteria

Schedule the first aid in-service training session for all center personnel each year. Include administrative assistants, custodians, cooks, and bus drivers in the training session. Training should focus on updating personnel on first-aid procedures of the American Red Cross.

Early Childhood Insight 🄰🄱🄲

Sprains, Strains, and Fractures

What is the difference between a sprain and a strain? A sprain is a stretch or tear of a ligament, while a strain is a stretch or tear of a muscle or tendon. The usual treatment for a minor sprain or strain is RICE: *rest, ice, compression* (such as an elastic bandage), and *elevation*. If the injury seems more severe, or when a bone fracture is obvious, do not move the child. Call for medical help immediately. Early childhood staff learn more about treatment for sprains, strains, and fractures by becoming certified in first-aid procedures.

First-Aid Supplies

To administer first aid, you will need some basic supplies. Most pharmacies and school supply catalogs sell first-aid kits that include these basic supplies. You may also purchase your supplies separately from a pharmacy and put them together in a kit.

Store all first-aid items in one area. Keep them out of children's reach. Do *not* keep first-aid supplies in a locked cabinet. You may not have time to search for a key during an emergency.

Each month, check the contents of the first-aid kit. Make sure all first-aid kits have the necessary supplies (**Figure 12.13**). To do this, check the contents against a list. Many programs have one person responsible for this duty. Replace any supplies that have run out.

If some children have special health needs, you will need additional supplies. An antihistamine or bee sting kit may be a requirement for children with allergies. Children with diabetes may need sugar or honey. For emergency preparedness, always take a first-aid kit on field trips.

Wounds and Their Treatment

A **wound** is damage to the surface of the skin or body tissue. Basically, there are two types of wounds. A *closed wound* is an injury to the tissue directly under the skin surface. It does not involve a break in the skin. An *open wound* is a break in the skin.

Closed Wounds

Children usually get closed wounds from falling, being struck, or running into objects. Most closed wounds involve the soft tissues under the skin. The most common type of closed wound is a bruise.

Common signs of a closed wound are discoloration, tenderness, and pain in the damaged area. To help control the pain, apply a cold cloth or pack to the injured area (**Figure 12.14**).

Open Wounds

Cuts and scrapes that injure the skin are open wounds. Open wounds cause two first-aid problems. First, there may be rapid blood loss. If this is the case, the injured child may go into shock. Second, exposed body tissue may become contaminated and infected.

Some open wounds bleed freely. This reduces the danger of infection. Other wounds bleed very little. These are more likely to become infected.

Open wounds on the top skin layer require simple treatment. To clean the wound, wash your hands and put on disposable gloves. Then clean the wound with gentle soap and water. Gently pat the wound dry. Apply an antibiotic cream or petroleum jelly and a clean bandage. If the wound is deep or does not stop bleeding in a short amount of time, seek medical attention.

Abrasions

An **abrasion** is a scrape that damages a portion of the skin. Children usually get abrasions from falling and handling rough objects. It is common to have several children in a classroom with skinned knees, scratched arms, or rope burns.

Bleeding from an abrasion is often limited to blood flow from broken **capillaries** (small

Basic First-Aid Supplies

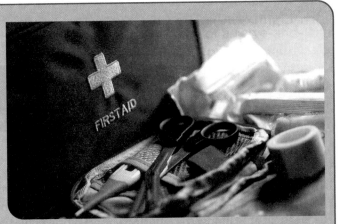

- List of emergency phone numbers
- Current American Academy of Pediatrics first-aid chart
- Individual adhesive bandages in 1/2-inch, 3/4-inch, and round sizes
- 2-by-2 inch sterile first-aid dressings, individually packaged for burns and open wounds
- 4-by-4 inch sterile first-aid dressings
- Gauze bandage, 2 inches by 5 yards
- Adhesive tape or surgical tape, 1 inch wide
- Disposable paper tissues
- Disposable instant cold packs
- Antibacterial cleaning pads
- Tweezers for removing splinters
- Blanket
- Blunt-tipped scissors for cutting tape and bandages
- Safety pins
- Hydrocortisone cream for insect bites
- Flashlight
- Sterile eye wash
- Box of temperature strip thermometers for use on the child's forehead
- Non-contact digital (never touches the child) thermometer

- Alcohol wipes
- Cotton swabs
- Absorbent cotton balls
- Disposable powder-free latex or vinyl gloves
- Eye patch
- Sterilized water
- Cold pack
- Up-to-date first-aid manual
- Scissors
- Flashlight
- Plastic bags
- Liquid soap to wash injury
- Note pad and pen or pencil

bernie_photo/iStock via Getty Images Plus; Goodheart-Willcox Publisher

Figure 12.13 All early childhood centers must keep first-aid supplies on hand to care for minor injuries and illnesses. ***How often should you check the supplies in a first-aid kit?***

veins). Bacteria or dirt may still enter the wound, however, and infection can still occur. Dirt particles may slow down the healing process. Sometimes abrasions heal around the particles, forming a permanent scar.

Cuts

Cuts, or incised wounds, on body tissues are often caused by broken glass, metal, or sharp edges. Bleeding can be heavy if a blood vessel has been cut. Nerves, muscles, or tendons can also be damaged if the cut is deep. When this occurs, emergency medical care will be necessary.

UW-Stout Child and Family Study Center

Figure 12.14 Cold packs help reduce swelling in closed wounds.

Puncture Wounds

Puncture wounds are made by sharp objects, such as nails, splinters, thumbtacks, and even sticks. The force at which the object meets the skin must be strong to puncture the skin. Bleeding is often light. As a result, the wound is not flushed out and could be dangerous. Infection may set in. Harmful bacteria such as tetanus may grow in the presence of moisture and warmth and be carried within the body. Care for the wound by first washing your hands, and then putting on disposable gloves. Use a clean bandage or clothe and apply pressure to stop the bleeding After the bleeding stops, clean the wound with clear water. If dirt remains, use a fresh piece of gauze or a clean washcloth to remove it. Apply a thin layer of antibiotic cream. Cover with a bandage to keep the wound clean. Watch for signs of infection when you reapply the ointment and change the bandage daily. If the bandage becomes wet, dry, or comes off, the dressing needs to be changed. Communicate with the parents or guardians. They will need to contact their pediatrician to determine if the child needs a tetanus booster.

Splinters

Children often get splinters, and it will be your job to remove them. A pair of sterilized tweezers is the best tool for this process. To sterilize tweezers, store them in a jar of rubbing alcohol. You can also soak them in alcohol or boil them for 10 minutes. A third option is to hold the tip of the tweezers in a flame and wipe the carbon away with a clean cloth before using.

First wash your hands and then the splintered area with soap and water or alcohol. Then remove splinters at the same angle they entered the skin. Do not put any ointment or antiseptic on the wound. Cover with a sterile bandage. If you cannot remove a splinter, contact the child's parent(s) or guardian, and seek prompt medical help.

Bites

According to the American Academy of Pediatrics (AAP), human and animal bites are a frequent cause of emergency room visits for children. Bites are a type of puncture wound and are common. If a child in the program receives a bite, thoroughly wash the injured areas. If there is a break in the skin, however, consult a doctor at once. This is especially important if the bite was from an animal. There is a danger of an infection, such as **rabies**, a disease caused by a viral infection of the nervous system and brain.

Open Wound Care

Care must be taken so an open wound does not become infected. Some open wounds require medical attention (**Figure 12.15**). As the teacher,

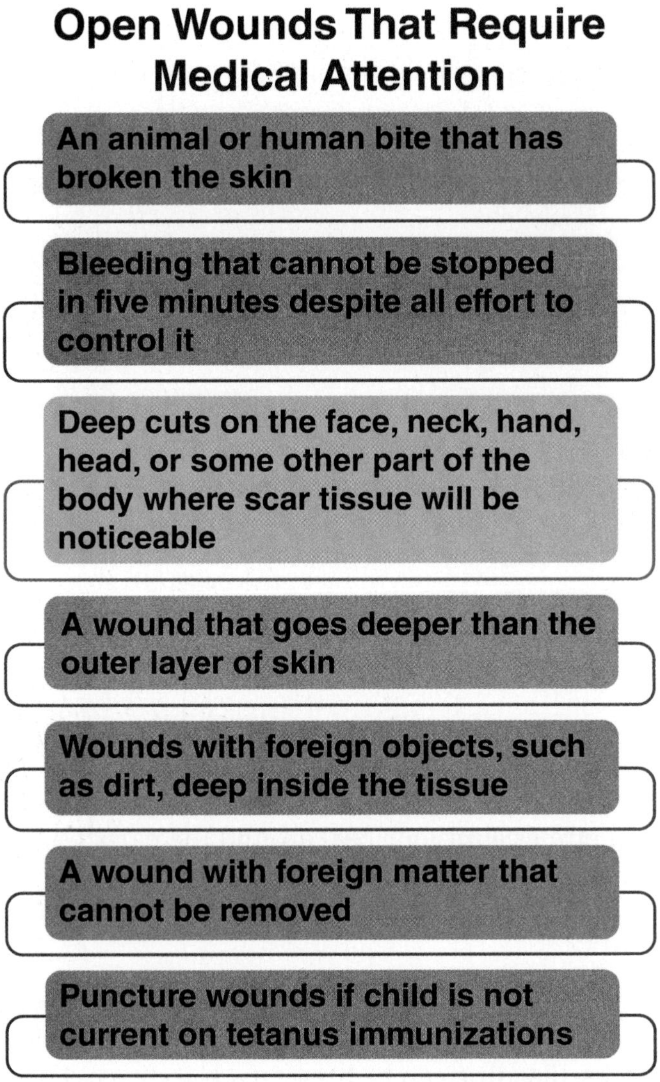

Open Wounds That Require Medical Attention

An animal or human bite that has broken the skin

Bleeding that cannot be stopped in five minutes despite all effort to control it

Deep cuts on the face, neck, hand, head, or some other part of the body where scar tissue will be noticeable

A wound that goes deeper than the outer layer of skin

Wounds with foreign objects, such as dirt, deep inside the tissue

A wound with foreign matter that cannot be removed

Puncture wounds if child is not current on tetanus immunizations

Goodheart-Willcox Publisher

Figure 12.15 Some open wounds require immediate medical attention. *For what types of injuries would you seek medical attention?*

you can usually treat minor wounds such as abrasions and slight cuts. First, wash the area with antibacterial soap and warm water. Then, as you apply a sterile bandage, bring the wound edges together. This will help prevent scarring.

Assume that any loss of blood is harmful. To control severe bleeding, place a sterile gauze over the wound. Press on the wound with the palm of your hand. The object is to control the bleeding by pressing the blood vessels against something solid, such as a bone or muscle.

If there is no sign of a fracture, elevate open wounds of the leg, arm, neck, or head. To elevate, raise the injured area above the level of the child's heart. The force of gravity will help reduce blood pressure in the injured area, slowing blood loss.

Insect Bites and Stings

Mosquito bites appear on the skin after it has been punctured. The mosquito uses its mouthparts to puncture the skin and feed on the victim's blood. White, puffy, and reddish bumps result from the invasion within a few minutes. The skin usually clears up in a couple of days.

Wasps, bees, hornets, yellow jackets, and fire ants are all stinging insects. The stings are painful to all children. For children who are allergic to insect stings, a sting can be fatal. React quickly when a child has been stung. Most deaths from insect stings occur within two hours of the incident.

If a child is stung, scrape the stinger away with your fingernail. Avoid using tweezers to pull the stinger out. This might squeeze the stinger and release more toxins into the skin. After removing the stinger, watch for signs of an allergic reaction.

A rash or swelling usually shows a mild allergic reaction. Anaphylactic shock can result from an extreme allergic reaction. Watch the child closely for signs of anaphylactic shock. If you notice any of the signs, get prompt medical help. Symptoms of anaphylactic shock include

- difficulty breathing
- swelling of the tongue and throat
- a rapid or weak pulse
- dizziness or fainting
- loss of consciousness
- skin reactions, including pale skin, itching, hives

Children who are allergic to stings and have been stung before may have their own medication and *epinephrine auto-injector* equipment. An **epinephrine auto-injector** is a medical device that includes a spring-loaded needle and prefilled syringe of epinephrine—a drug used to treat potentially life-threatening allergic reactions. A pharmacist or doctor can show you how to use this auto-injection device. It is also important to read the patient information that comes with the device prior to the need to use it. This information will include the directions for using this equipment.

Make sure you have the epinephrine auto-injector available for emergencies. When you leave the classroom to go to the lunchroom, outdoor play area, or on a field trip **ALWAYS** take the medication and injection equipment with you.

Head Lice

To maintain a healthy environment, you will need to recognize head lice. They most often affect children. **Head lice** are small, six-legged tan-colored, tiny insects about the size of a sesame seed. These insects feed on the blood supply on the human scalp. They have no wings, do not fly, but crawl. They have a hook-like claw at the end of their six legs. With these hooks, they attach themselves to the hair shaft. Short legs and large claws help them keep their grip on the hair. They produce small round gray-white eggs, called *nits*. Nits look like grains of sand and are deposited near the scalp since the eggs require warmth for hatching.

It is difficult to see head lice with the naked eye, however, there are several signs you can recognize. Look for the following:

- Head lice cause a constant itch on the scalp, especially behind the ears and at the base of the scalp. Often the child will have infected scratches or a rash on the scalp.

- Small, gray-white eggs are attached to individual hairs. Usually, a magnifying glass will help reveal these.

- In severe cases, lymph glands may swell in the neck or under the arm.

Head lice can spread through close, head-to-head contact. It is less common for them to be transported via combs, brushes, hats, headgear, bedding, or other objects close to the scalp.

If one child in your classroom has head lice, other children and staff members may get it, too. Send notices home to all parents if even one child has been infected with head lice. A county or city nurse will conduct daily inspections at a center with an outbreak in some areas Children and staff members infected with head lice should remain out of the program until they receive treatment.

The best way to get rid of head lice is to seek medical help. Most healthcare providers prescribe a medication that kills lice and nits. Over-the-counter treatments are available, too. All family members should receive treatment for head lice. Apply the treatment following the package instructions.

In addition to treatments for head lice, wash hats, scarves, clothing, bedding, towels, and furry toys in hot water and dry them in a dryer using a hot-air cycle. Items that cannot be washed can be dry-cleaned or sealed in a plastic bag for two weeks, which is the life cycle of a louse. Vacuum upholstered furniture and mattresses. You can treat grooming aids, such as combs and brushes, by soaking them in a bleach solution for one hour.

Burns and Their Treatment

A **burn** is an injury caused by hot boiling liquids, excessive sun exposure, radiation, electrical current, or chemical agents. Burns can also be caused by fires, including flames from candles and matches. They vary in size, depth, and severity. Burns are generally classified by degree or depth. There are three classes: *first-degree burns, second-degree burns,* and *third-degree burns.* A person can have more than one type of burn from a single accident. Scalding is an example as it can cause all three burn levels.

Children are commonly burned by hot liquids, cooking and electrical equipment, open fires, matches, chemicals—strong detergents and acids, and overexposure to the sun. When developmentally appropriate, you should teach children to stop, drop, and roll if their clothes catch fire (**Figure 12.16**).

First-Degree Burns

First-degree burns are injuries that affect the first layer of skin. They are the least severe of all burns. They may result from brief contact with hot objects, overexposure to the sun, or scalding by hot water or steam. Common signs include red, non-blistered skin or mild discoloration, pain, and swelling. Healing is usually rapid and occurs within seven to 10 days. Because the burn does not go deep, there is no scarring.

Special medical treatment is generally not needed for first-degree burns. Cool the wound under cool running water or use a cool, wet compress to help relieve some pain.

Goodheart-Willcox Publisher; Passakorn sakulphan/Shutterstock.com; 3DMI/Shutterstock.com; Alexander Kondratenko/Shutterstock.com; Gts/Shutterstock.com; Kolonko/Shutterstock.com; Aleks vF/Shutterstock.com

Figure 12.16 Take care to keep children safe around items that cause burns.

Second-Degree Burns

Second-degree burns are marked by pain and are more serious. They go beyond the top layer and cause damage to underlying layers of skin. They are caused by extreme overexposure to the sun, contact with hot liquids, and contact with flash fires from gasoline, kerosene, and other products.

Second-degree burns are painful, and cause blistering, swelling, and discoloration. Over several days, the burn is likely to swell a great deal. Due to the severity of these burns, they require medical treatment. Do not treat the burn by breaking blisters or placing an ointment on the burn. This may cause infection. If infection arises in the wound, a second-degree burn can quickly become a third-degree burn.

Third-Degree Burns

Third-degree burns are the most severe. They destroy the skin layer and nerve endings. Open flames, burning clothing, immersion in hot water, contact with hot objects, and live electrical wires can all cause third-degree burns.

Third-degree burns are severe. Call 911 immediately. These wounds require prompt medical attention. An ambulance should be called at once.

Sunburn

A sunburn is a red, painful reaction after exposure to the sun's ultraviolet rays. Children can get first- or second-degree burns. There is usually a three- to 12-hour lapse in time between exposure and the development of sunburn. Sunburns rarely require a hospital stay, but they can cause a child to be out for several days due to swelling, pain, nausea, chills, headache, and fever. Sunburn also raises the risk of skin cancer and premature aging later in life.

Protect the children in your care from sunburn by using the A, B, C's of sun safety—*away*, *block*, and *cover-up*. Keep babies younger than six months away from direct sunlight and in the shade. Their skin burns quickly since it is thinner. According to the Food and Drug Administration (FDA) and the American

Academy of Pediatrics (AAP), you should not apply sunscreen on babies younger than six months because they are at greater risk for side effects, such as a rash. For children older than six months, block the sun's rays with broad-spectrum sunscreens that provide a *sun protection factor (SPF)* of 30 or higher. Apply sunscreen to all exposed areas of skin 30 minutes before going outside. Use a lotion-type sunscreen on children. Avoid spraying sunscreens since children are at risk of breathing in the ingredients. If outdoors, often apply throughout the day. Reapply sunscreen after swimming, heavy sweating, or two hours of sun exposure. Hats and sunglasses also protect children from damaging sun rays (**Figure 12.17**). Schedule outdoor play periods to avoid sun exposure from 10 a.m. to 2 p.m. when the sun's rays are most intense and particularly harmful.

Choking

While choking can occur among people of all ages, children are at the highest risk. Young

Judy Herr

Figure 12.17 Sunscreen, hats, and sunglasses help protect children from sunburn. *Why is sunscreen not recommended for infants younger than six months?*

children are more likely than adults to put small objects, such as toys, buttons, and coins, in their mouths. Children younger than four years are more likely to choke on high-risk foods such as hard or round foods. They are less likely to chew food well or sit still while eating. Children are also more likely to stuff their mouths with too much food. All these actions increase the risk of choking. **Figure 12.18** contains a list of choking hazards.

The best way to prevent choking is to protect children from choking hazards. Infants should have their heads elevated during bottle-feeding. Keep small toys and other objects that pose a choking hazard out of the reach of children younger than four years. Avoid offering foods that are choking hazards. Prepare and cook foods to the right texture, size, and shape for the children's development. Supervise mealtimes carefully. Have children sit while eating and eat only a small amount at a time.

Choking Hazards

Foods	Toys and Objects
Caramels	Batteries
Carrots	Dice
Celery	Game pieces
Cherries	Jacks
Cough drops	Jewelry
Grapes	Marbles
Gum	Nails
Hard candy	Paper clips
Hot dogs	Pen or marker caps
Olives	Safety pins
Peanuts	Vending machine toys
Popcorn	
Pretzels	
Ice cubes	
Cheese cubes	

Goodheart-Willcox Publisher

Figure 12.18 Although choking can occur at any age, young children are at the highest risk. *What is the difference between the American Red Cross and the American Heart Association emergency procedure for choking?*

When the brain goes without oxygen for over four minutes, a result can be brain damage or even death. Therefore, when choking occurs, program staff must respond quickly. All staff members need to know what techniques to use to treat choking and how to perform them. If the child can speak, cough, and breathe, encourage the child to cough. The child should be able to cough up the object. If, however, you see the child cannot breathe or speak, take immediate lifesaving emergency steps.

The American Red Cross and the American Heart Association teach emergency procedures to relieve choking. Their recommended techniques differ slightly. The American Red Cross recommends a "five-and-five" response. This means delivering five back blows between the shoulder blades with the heel of one hand, and five abdominal thrusts should follow this. Place a fist thumb-side against the middle of the abdomen, just above the navel. Cover the fist with the other hand. Then give up quick, upward abdominal thrusts. Continue the back blows and abdominal thrusts until the object is forced out, or the child can breathe or cough; otherwise, the child will become unconscious.

For simplicity in training, the American Heart Association recommends only the abdominal thrust procedures. According to both organizations, these procedures should be followed for children one year or older. The procedures differ slightly for infants under a year of age.

Back blows and abdominal thrusts relieve most choking incidents, but cardiopulmonary resuscitation (CPR) is sometimes needed (**Figure 12.19**). Newly hired staff should be required to attend pediatric first-aid training, which focuses on techniques for choking relief and CPR for infants and children. The American Red Cross or the American Heart Association will certify members who successfully complete the course. All staff must complete refresher courses for these techniques yearly to keep their certifications current. The director can offer these trainings as an annual in-service.

AlpakaVideo/Shutterstock.com

Figure 12.19 Staff training on CPR is essential.

Workplace Connections

Health-Related Early Childhood Careers

Research various careers in the health field that relate to the care and education of children. Information on jobs can be located in the school's guidance or career center. Another source is the online *Occupational Outlook Handbook (OOH)* published by the United States Bureau of Labor Statistics.

1. What are the educational requirements for each career? How much background in child development and education is needed for each career?
2. What is the job outlook over the next 10 years for each career?

12.2-3 Oral Hygiene

Good oral hygiene is an important part of overall health and begins with regular toothbrushing. The American Dental Association recommends brushing a baby's teeth using fluoride toothpaste the size of a grain of rice. Otherwise, bacteria from the mouth mix with milk sugars and can break down the tooth enamel. Healthy baby teeth are essential for chewing, clear speech, and providing a space underneath for permanent teeth.

The National Center on Early Childhood Health and Wellness claims children usually have all primary teeth by the time they are two or three years old. They stress five ways primary teeth are essential for young children's health and development. These include:

- maintaining good health
- maintaining good nutrition
- helping with speech development
- holding space for permanent teeth
- promoting self-confidence

Brushing Teeth

Babies should have their teeth brushed twice a day with fluoridated toothpaste the size of a grain of rice. Until age two, young children tend to swallow toothpaste instead of spitting it out. After each snack or meal, have children over the age of two brush their teeth. They should use a soft-bristled brush to avoid damaging the gums. Children at the age of two can use a pea-sized amount of fluoride toothpaste on their brush. All toothbrushes should be labeled, age-appropriate size, and replaced every three months. For younger children, use symbols they can quickly identify. The child's name can be placed on older children's brushes. After use, store the brushes to allow air to circulate them. To prevent contamination, the brushes should not touch one another or contact any surface.

Dental Emergencies

Dental emergencies include cut or bitten tongues, lips, and cheeks; knocked-out permanent teeth; and broken teeth. With any of these problems, take quick action and remain calm.

If a child complains of a toothache, help the child rinse the affected area with water. Apply cold compresses if the face is swollen. Urge the parents to take the child to a dentist.

If a child has a cut or bitten lip, tongue, or cheek, apply ice to the injured area (**Figure 12.20**). Hold a clean gauze or cloth over the area if you see blood. Gently apply pressure. Contact the child's parents or guardian if the bleeding does not stop in 15 minutes. If the cut is severe, take the child to an emergency room.

To provide emergency care for a knocked-out permanent tooth, use the following procedure:

1. First, find the tooth. If it is a baby tooth, apply clean gauze to the tooth socket to control bleeding. Since reimplantation may cause problems, a baby tooth is not reimplanted.

2. Pick the tooth up by the crown, not the roots. If the tooth is dirty, rinse it gently with milk. Do not use water. Avoid unnecessary handling. Keep the tooth moist by placing the tooth in a container of cool, clean milk. Do not put the tooth in mouthwash, alcohol, or saltwater.

3. Avoid trying to place the tooth back in the tooth socket, which could cause accidental choking.

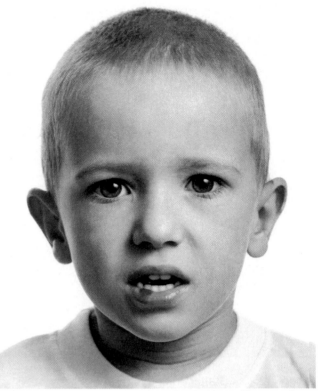

Ilya Andriyanov/Shutterstock.com

Figure 12.20   Ice can help relieve pain and swelling on an injured lip.

4. Call the child's parents or guardian. The child must see a dentist immediately to have the tooth successfully reimplanted If the dentist is unavailable, directly go to the hospital emergency room.

If a child breaks or chips a tooth, report it to the parents or guardian. They can decide whether to consult a dentist. Gently clean the injured area with warm water. Use a cold compress to reduce swelling.

12.2-4 Caring for Children Who Become Ill

Whenever children become ill, move them into a separate area at once (**Figure 12.21**). Every early childhood center needs an *isolation area* or room. Some states require that centers have isolation rooms. Because of a lack of space, some centers do not have a special room for this purpose. Instead, these centers use a cot in the director's office for emergencies.

Chubykin Arka/Shutterstock.com

Figure 12.21 Children who show signs of illness should promptly be isolated from other children. ***What signs of illness require immediate isolation?***

When children become ill, they may vomit, develop diarrhea, or develop a fever. Early childhood workers need to know how to handle these signs of illness.

After a child has vomited, they need to rest and keep warm. Remove the child from the group and contact the parents or guardian. The child may request food or drink; however, only provide sips of water. Any other foods may prompt more vomiting. Record the number of times the child vomits and the amount thrown up. Report this information to parents or guardians when they arrive.

Diarrhea may be caused by a virus, foodborne illness, or allergies. Many diseases cause diarrhea that lasts for two or three days. Chronic diarrhea may be a symptom of infection, inflammation of the intestines, or allergies. Chronic diarrhea may last for up to 10 days.

With diarrhea, a child will have an increased number of stools compared to the child's normal pattern. The stool may be loose, watery, and unformed.

Children who have diarrhea require isolation. Remove them from the classroom and contact their parents or guardian. They should be diarrhea free for 24 hours before returning to the center.

Temperature Emergency

Temperature measures body heat. The human body typically maintains an average internal temperature of 98.6°F. Typical temperatures range from 97°F to just under 100°F. For this reason, it is essential to have each child's average temperature recorded on a health form.

A slight change in a child's temperature signals that the body is preparing against illness. A temperature of at least two degrees above average is significant. Most, but not all, young children will run a higher fever than adults. A fever is a sign of infection, illness, or other conditions.

A child may have a slight rise in temperature for several reasons. For example, the presence of infection raises a child's temperature. Too much physical activity will raise the temperature. Sometimes, children will have a low-grade fever after an immunization. The temperature may also vary depending on the time of the day. Temperatures are somewhat lower in the morning than in the evening.

To take a child's temperature, you need a thermometer that is quick, easy to use, and provides accurate readings. Although they are more expensive than other thermometers, digital thermometers are preferred (**Figure 12.22**). There

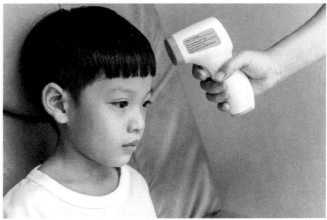

Illonajalll/Shutterstock.com

Figure 12.22 At many centers, temporal artery (forehead) thermometers are used to get a temperature reading quickly and easily.

are three types of digital thermometer options, including:

- **Digital thermometers.** The most common type uses electronic heat sensors to record body temperatures and has a digital display that shows the temperature reading. In less than one minute, most digital thermometers can record temperatures from the mouth, rectum, armpit, or forehead. A rectal thermometer is the most accurate thermometer for infants three months or younger.

- **Temporal artery thermometer.** The temporal artery (forehead) thermometer is the preferred thermometer, since it is the most accurate. It uses an infrared scanner to measure the temperature of the temporal artery in the forehead. It is also the safest and the most convenient thermometer. It takes a gentle swipe across the child's temporal artery on the forehead to accurately measure a child's temperature. On the negative side, accuracy may be affected if the scanner is held too far away from the forehead.

- **Digital ear thermometers.** These thermometers use an infrared scanner to measure a child's temperature in the ear canal. Note that earwax or a small ear canal can cause inaccuracy in temperature readings.

Contact the parents or guardian immediately if a child has a fever. Report any other unusual behavior.

Special Health Concerns

Children may have other special health concerns. Require all parents or guardians to complete a health questionnaire on admitting their children to the center. If a child with a special physical condition is enrolled in the program, you will need to make plans for this child's health and well-being. Begin by discussing the child's condition with the parents or guardians. Be sure you understand the condition and what type of emergencies may arise. Find out what approach the center needs

to take. Does the child require a special diet, medications, or specific exercises? Also, ask the parents or guardians for suggestions on how to help the child feel comfortable. Follow parental or guardian instructions and keep careful records about dietary needs, medications, physical activity, and rest. These records give the child's parents or guardians and doctor a complete picture of how the child is doing or what changes they may want to make.

You will probably encounter several common health concerns among the children in your class. Some of the most common of these include *allergies, asthma, diabetes, epilepsy, human immunodeficiency virus (HIV)*, and *air-pollution-related illnesses*.

Allergies

An *allergy* is the body's reaction to a substance in the environment, which is called an *allergen*. Smoke, dust, mold, mildew, pet dander, pollen, and certain foods are common allergens. Reactions to an allergen include sneezing, runny nose, coughing, itchy or watery eyes, headache, skin rashes, hives, diarrhea, and vomiting. Some allergies are seasonal, while others are continuous. Ask parents what the allergens are and try to avoid exposing the child to these. Medications may be needed to treat the symptoms of allergies.

Asthma

Asthma is a chronic inflammatory disorder of the airways. Symptoms include coughing, wheezing, rapid or labored breathing, shortness of breath, and chest tightness. Ask parents or guardians what conditions trigger their child's attacks and try to prevent these conditions. Examples include smoke, cold air, exposure to an allergen, and overexertion. Find out what medications should be given and when. For older children, ask the child to tell you right away when an asthma attack is starting so you can administer medications. For younger children, you will need to observe carefully for signs of an attack.

Diabetes

For a child who has diabetes, the body cannot properly control the level of sugar in the blood. Having too much or too little sugar in the blood can cause serious health problems. Children who have diabetes cannot regulate blood sugar because they do not produce insulin. They must balance their food choices, intake, and activity levels. Many children with diabetes must also monitor their blood sugar throughout the day and take insulin injections as needed. You will probably need to help with these procedures.

Ask the child's parents or guardians about your role in managing the disease. Learn the signs of an insulin reaction such as low blood sugar; the body's response to an insulin imbalance. If a reaction occurs, offer juice, sugar, glucose tablets or glucose gel, or candy to help raise the blood sugar level quickly. Always keep these items handy. In severe cases, a child may pass out. Take the child to an emergency room or call an ambulance at once.

Epilepsy

Epilepsy is a condition in which a person has periodic seizures. There are two types of seizures. *Grand mal seizures* consist of repeated convulsions or jerking over the entire body. *Petit mal seizures* are milder than grand mal seizures. They consist of a few brief muscle twitches and a sense of confusion. Ask the child's parents or guardians what medical treatment should be given to prevent seizures. Have them describe the seizures and how to avoid them. With a grand mal seizure, protect the child from self-injury. Help the child lie down and monitor the child's breathing. Contact the child's parents or guardians and doctor after every seizure. Describe what occurred before, during, and after the seizure.

Human Immunodeficiency Virus (HIV)

Human Immunodeficiency Virus (HIV) is a virus that breaks down the body's immune system. This virus eventually leads to the disease **acquired immunodeficiency syndrome (AIDS)**. AIDS further destroys the immune system and, over time, can be fatal. Most children with HIV got the virus from their mothers during pregnancy, birth, or breastfeeding. It can also be acquired through contact with an infected person's blood.

Hugging, touching, or being near someone with HIV does not spread the disease. Children with HIV can attend early childhood programs unless they have open sores, uncontrollable nosebleeds, bloody diarrhea, or are highly likely to expose others to blood-contaminated bodily fluids. Ask parents or guardians about the treatment, diet, and activity level recommended for children with HIV. These children have weakened immune systems and have trouble fighting even common illnesses. Alert the parents or guardians about communicable diseases of other children in your class right away.

12.2-5 Air Pollution and Illness

Air pollution, linked to climate change, is a public health threat. Diseases of the heart, lungs, and cancer have been associated with pollution. Young children who breathe polluted air have their development and health put at risk. Polluted air is poisoning. Children's lungs are in the process of developing. After birth, eighty percent of their tiny air sacs will grow. These tiny air sacs, called *alveoli*, transfer oxygen to the blood. Healthy lungs are essential as they contribute to overall health.

Children's health is more at risk than adults since they breathe more rapidly. As a result, they inhale more pollutants. When children are exposed to polluted air, they can develop respiratory problems. Polluted air emissions result from forest fires, traffic, coal-fired power plants, pollen, dust, mold spores, industrial plants, inefficient wood-burning stoves, etc. Studies also show that pediatric asthma is associated with forest-fire events.

Pollution can irritate the throat and cause coughing, congestion, and phlegm. Other health problems for children may include:

- itchy eyes
- sore throat
- sneezing
- runny nose
- fatigue
- emphysema
- bronchitis
- reduced resistance to infections

The American Academy of Pediatrics (AAP) recommends using the **Air Quality Index (AQI)**—a system for reporting how clean or polluted the air is—to minimize exposure and restrict outdoor time for children. Before taking the children outside, constantly monitor the air quality. The lowest pollution levels are typically between noon and six in the evening. The higher the level of air quality, the greater the level of pollution. When the AQI is within 0–50, air-quality conditions are good. With numbers ranging from 51 to 100, air quality conditions are moderate. It is unhealthy for sensitive groups, such as children, to go outside when air quality conditions range from 101 to 150. The AQI should be included in the center policies. It can help educate parents, staff, and volunteers on protective education.

Indoor and outdoor sources both cause air pollution. Windows should remain closed if near forest fires. The children's health can be improved by reducing air pollutants. Centers may decrease the children's symptoms indoors by using a portable air cleaner with a HEPA filter.

Health Highlights

Food Allergies

Food allergies are increasing, especially among children, and peanut allergy is the leading cause. Peanut allergies also cause the most severe reactions, including potentially life-threatening conditions. For children who are allergic, peanuts act like poison. Exposure can happen through inhaling, touching, or ingesting.

To keep children safe, you must be able to recognize allergic reactions and react quickly. The best way to handle children with food allergies is to partner with parents. Learn as much as you can from them and create an individualized care plan. Together, develop a plan of action to ensure the health and safety of their child.

A child with a severe allergy to peanuts may keep an EpiPen® at the center. An EpiPen is an *auto-injecting device* that a doctor prescribes. It provides a single dose of *epinephrine*, which is used in the case of a severe allergic reaction. Children with severe peanut allergies often wear small packs around their waists that contains an EpiPen. These pens travel with the child whenever possible because they always need to be accessible. So, they should move with the child from the classroom, to the lunchroom, on field trips and to the playground.

EpiPens must always be accessible and storage should remain unlocked. These pens need to be readily available. Proximity is essential since just a few seconds can save a life. In an emergency, lay the child down and remove the gray activation cap. Then, use enough force to jab the black end into the child's thigh. If the child is wearing pants, go through the clothing. Hold the pen in for 15 seconds and keep the child lying down. Call 911 immediately. Tell them that you have a child experiencing anaphylaxis and administered an EpiPen. Tell them to bring more epinephrine.

Some centers that have a child with a peanut allergy have created a "peanut-free environment." Their goal is to reduce exposure and create a safe environment. Peanuts are not allowed in any form. Additionally, children in these centers are not served ice cream, items prepared at home, or commercially baked items. Even though these items may not contain peanuts, they could have been cross-contaminated during preparation.

Lesson 12.2 Review

1. **True or False.** Foodborne illness only affects young children and pregnant women. (12.2.1)
2. Within how long after an incident do most deaths from insect stings occur? (12.2.2)
   A. 1 hour
   B. 2 hours
   C. 8 hours
   D. 24 hours
3. **True or False.** All burns are severe and require immediate professional medical attention. (12.2.2)
4. What is the "five-and-five" response to choking? (12.2.2)
   A. Deliver five back blows
   B. Deliver five abdominal thrusts
   C. Deliver abdominal thrusts for five seconds
   D. Deliver five back blows and five abdominal thrusts
5. How many times a day should babies have their teeth brushed? (12.2.3)
   A. Once a day
   B. Twice a day
   C. After every meal
   D. Three times a day

6. What should you do when caring for a knocked-out permanent tooth? (12.2.3)
   A. Place the tooth back in the socket.
   B. Rinse the tooth with water.
   C. Apply clean gauze to the tooth socket.
   D. Pick the tooth up by the roots.
7. Which is the safest and most convenient thermometer? (12.2.4)
   A. Temporal artery thermometer
   B. Digital thermometer
   C. Digital ear thermometer
   D. Infrared thermometer
8. If an insulin reaction occurs, what should you give a child? (12.2.4)
   A. Sugar
   B. Protein
   C. Water
   D. Insulin
9. When is the ideal time to take children outside? (12.2.5)
   A. When the AQI is within 0-50
   B. When the AQI is within 51-75
   C. When the AQI is within 76-100
   D. When the AQI is within 101-150

Chapter 12 Review and Assessment

Summary

Lesson 12.1

12.1-1 Understanding the role of heredity and environment for children's health and setting objectives for guiding children's health are essential for early childhood centers.

12.1-1 Knowledge about immunizations, symptoms of illness, and communicable diseases is essential for early childhood professionals.

12.1-1 Protecting, maintaining, and even improving health is a major responsibility of a teacher. The teacher and early childhood staff are trusted with the well-being of the children.

12.1-2 Setting workable health policies is the first step in guiding children's health. Policies should include requiring all children enrolled to have medical exams and immunizations.

12.1-2 The health policies should also address the process for contacting parents or guardians regarding health-related issues.

12.1-3 Maintaining proper personal hygiene and using the proper handwashing procedure are essential for the children and the early childhood staff.

12.1-3 Keeping the center clean and sanitary and properly ventilated is important aspect of controlling the spread of disease.

Lesson 12.2

12.2-1 Following guidelines for controlling foodborne illness is essential for all early childhood staff.

12.2-2 All newly hired early childhood staff must attend pediatric first-aid training and acquire certification from the American Red Cross or the American Heart Association.

12.2-2 Early childhood staff must know how to care for injuries, including open and closed wounds, burns, insect bites and stings, and head lice.

12.2-2 Early childhood staff must be able to identify different types of burns, how to treat them, and which require medical treatment.

12.2-2 Knowing how to prevent choking is essential. Helping children who are choking requires the ability to use back blows, abdominal thrusts, and CPR.

12.2-3 Assisting children with proper oral hygiene and knowing how to handle dental emergencies, such as knocked-out teeth, are the responsibility of teachers and care providers.

12.2-4 Caring for a child who is ill requires isolating them from others and knowing how to accurately take a child's temperature.

12.2-4 Teachers and care providers are often responsible for caring for children who have special health concerns, including allergies, asthma, diabetes, epilepsy, HIV, and illness due to air pollution.

12.2-5 Using the Air Quality Index (AQI) helps teachers monitor pollution levels in the outdoor air prior to taking children outside to help minimize children's exposure to pollutants.

Vocabulary Activity

Work in pairs to write a *simile* for each of the terms. Remember that a simile is a direct comparison of two items or factors that are *not* alike. When creating a simile, the comparisons are introduced by the words *like*, *as*, *seem*, or *appear*.

Critical Thinking

1. **Identify.** Check the website for the National Resource Center for Health and Safety in Childcare and Early Education for health tips suggested for childcare centers.

2. **Cause and Effect.** Design a handwashing lesson plan and present it to the children. Study the children closely following the lesson to determine the effectiveness. Share your findings in class.

3. **Identify.** Visit the school cafeteria to observe the strategies practiced to reduce the incidence of foodborne illness. What training is provided to foodservice workers to teach them these critical strategies? What clothing or hair requirements do you see? How are food preparation surfaces treated or cleaned and what precautions do foodservice workers take when serving the food to students?

4. **Draw Conclusions.** Visit the KidsHealth website to learn more about allergies and asthma. Prepare a presentation on your findings.

Core Skills

1. **Research and Speaking.** Investigate the possibility of becoming certified in First Aid and CPR through your school's Physical Education or Health departments. The instructors may be certified through Red Cross or the American Heart Association to train and certify you. Interview area childcare directors to find out if they provide training and/or recertification each year for their employees. How much does a certification class cost? Who pays for the classes? Share your finding in class.

2. **Math.** Research the cost of commercially prepared first-aid kits available in local stores, at medical supply companies, and online. Compare the cost of the commercial kits with the cost of obtaining all the supplies and creating your own first-aid kit. Which is more cost-effective? Do any of the items have expiration dates?

3. **Writing.** Write a paper identifying signs of good health in children. Contrast these with symptoms of illness in children.

4. **Research and Writing.** Research epidemics and pandemics, such as influenza, typhus, tuberculosis, and COVID-19, have affected the United States over the last century. What was the nation's response to these incidents? What medical and public health policies or agencies were developed to avoid similar health crises in the future? How has education been affected by public policies designed to avoid the spread of disease? Write a report of your findings.

5. **Speaking.** Interview the school nurse or other health professionals about the immunizations listed in Figure 12.3. What are the symptoms of each disease that the immunizations prevent? What may result if children contract these diseases? Prepare additional questions to ask during the interview.

6. **Speaking.** Interview an early childhood center director about food safety requirements and policies followed by the center. Ask whether the center has ever had an outbreak of foodborne illness and, if so, how it was handled.

7. **Research and Writing.** Research information on a child's reactions when stung by an insect. How does epinephrine treat the symptoms of anaphylactic shock? Write a brief report of your findings.

8. **CTE Career Readiness Practice.** The ability to read and interpret information is a critical workplace skill. Presume you work for an early childhood center. Check your state's licensing standards about required naps or rest periods. Are they based on the number of hours a child is in attendance? Depending on the child's age, what types of cribs, cots, or sleeping mats are used at the center? How far apart should cots be placed? How often are these items to be cleaned and disinfected? How often is the bedding changed for infants, toddlers, and preschoolers? After reading and interpreting the information, write a report summarizing your findings.

Portfolio Project

Attend an in-service session on children's health presented by the school nurse or a public health nurse. Find out about symptoms of illness, treatment, responsibilities, policies, illness prevention, abuse, sanitation, reporting, and forms. Ask your teacher to sign a certificate to document your attendance following the in-service session. The certificate can be filed in your portfolio to verify attending an in-service activity.

Unit Three
Guiding Children

Chapters

As you work in an early learning center, guidance will be a routine part of your experiences with children. Children need positive role models to learn how to get along with others, stay safe, and develop executive function skills.

In this unit, you will learn how the quality of a teacher-child relationship will influence behavior. You will study and practice successful techniques for guiding children throughout the day. You will gain insight into methods for handling guidance problems such as anger, aggression, negativism, and fear. You will also help children develop responsibility.

You will learn the risk factors for challenging behaviors and guidelines for establishing and enforcing limits throughout the classroom. This unit will also teach you ways to guide children through daily routines such as dressing, eating, and napping.

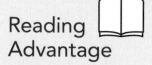
Developing Guidance Skills

Lesson 13.1: Foundations of Child Guidance

Lesson 13.2: Effectively Guiding Children

Case Study

Preparing for Guidance

Ricardo was enrolled in the local technical college. As part of his course work, Ricardo was assigned to assist one day a week in a local early childhood center. On the first day, he arrived at the center ten minutes early and went immediately to the director's office. Mrs. Rodriguez, the center director, welcomed him and asked for a copy of his background check to place on file. Then she walked him to his assigned classroom and introduced him to the head teacher.

The teacher, Ms. Garcia, stepped aside and greeted him. Briefly, she told him about the class, including the number of children, ages, other staff working in the classroom, and the focus of the current curriculum theme. After this, Ms. Garcia provided him with a copy of the center's written guidance policies. Today, she wanted him to read the policies and observe as this would give him an opportunity to learn the children's names, classroom routines, and guidance techniques. Then she walked over and motioned for him to sit on a chair. When Ricardo sat down and Ms. Garcia returned to observe a group of children, he began reading. When he finished, he began observing the classroom interactions.

Ricardo noted that one of the teaching assistants gave a child a warning. She told Hinata, if the blocks were used as guns again, Hinata would need to leave the block area. The teaching assistant walked away and went to a table in the art area. There she sat on a chair where her back faced the block-building area. Hinata continues using a block as a gun.

Give It Some Thought

1. Why do you think Ms. Garcia gave Ricardo a copy of the guidance polices?
2. Do you think the children's parents or guardians should be provided a copy of the guidance policies? Why or why not?
3. Do you think the teaching assistant should have continued observing Hinata after giving her a warning? Why or why not?
4. Should a teacher sit with her back to a group of children? What could be the consequences?

Opening image credit: Liderina/iStock via Getty Images Plus

Essential Question

What do I need to know about child guidance to be an effective early childhood teacher or caregiver?

Learning Outcomes

After studying this lesson, you will be able to

13.1-1 **understand** the differences between guidance versus punishment.

13.1-2 **list** personality traits of effective early childhood teachers.

13.1-3 **explain** why is important for a teacher to be culturally competent.

13.1-4 **describe** the principles of both direct and indirect guidance.

Key Terms

discipline	bicultural
guidance	cultural competence
prosocial behavior	implicit bias
open-ended questions	indirect guidance
child observation	direct guidance
nonverbal behavior	

Alicia sat in the corner looking at a library book. Slowly, she ripped a page from the book. On the other side of the room, Wyatt knocked Matteo's block tower over. Then he sped to the art table and grabbed Ryder's play dough. At the same time, Bella entered the room, greeted another child, and threw her coat on the floor.

A child's misbehavior is a form of communication. It often results from stress or home behavior as opposed to being intentional. When children's needs are not being met or they lack the skills to solve problems, behavioral problems may emerge. The behavior is serving a purpose and is the child's resolution to a problem.

Understanding and guiding children's behavior is a complex process. It requires knowledge of child growth and development. It also requires understanding each child's temperament, family, and cultural background.

Today, classrooms are more culturally diverse and the children bring their own culture into the classroom. So, learning is a constant process that never ends. As a teacher, you need to create a learning environment that represents every single child in the context of their lives. The classroom needs to be a mirror in which they see themselves. Families have different beliefs and values. By partnering with them, you will grow skills and confidence in your ability to guide young children. During this process, you will learn that changes in behavior often take time.

13.1-1 Discipline: Guidance Versus Punishment

The terms *discipline, guidance,* and *punishment* in an early childhood setting may be confusing. One definition of the word **discipline** is training that develops self-control. This definition is what early childhood teachers refer to as *guidance,* a positive form of discipline. However, the term discipline has changed somewhat over time to include more negative tones. A second definition is *strict control used to enforce obedience.* This meaning suggests punishment. Punishment may include abusive behaviors instead of guidance techniques. It should *never* be used in an early childhood setting.

Safety First

Written Guidance Policies

Well-defined written guidance policies that support positive social behavior and help reduce challenging behavior are a requirement for early childhood programs. All staff, families, and volunteers need to receive these policies. The policies should outline strategies for positive, appropriate, and consistent expectations for guiding children's behavior. Staff members should sign an agreement saying they will follow and implement the policies. A written policy should include

- a physical environment designed to minimize stress and conflict;
- age and culturally appropriate expectations for children's behavior;
- positive guidance techniques such as redirection, specific limits, consistent rules, planning to prevent problems, and encouraging positive behavior;
- examples of ways for dealing with repeated negative behavior or denying privileges for school-age children; and
- the guarantee that information about children and their families is kept confidential.

For additional information about written discipline policies, contact your state licensing agency. Chances are these policies vary somewhat from state to state. You might also check out resources on staff-child interactions published by NAEYC.

sturti/E+ via Getty Images

Figure 13.1 Younger children often require more guidance than older children. *Give a situation where a younger child may need more guidance than an older child.*

Punishment does not help young children to learn positive ways of controlling their behavior. Studies show that physical punishment promotes children's aggression. **Figure 13.2** shows the difference between guidance and punishment.

Goals of Guidance

Effective guidance is nonpunitive. It works to build a positive relationship with children.

Guidance comprises a system of direct and indirect actions an adult uses to help children develop internal controls and socially acceptable behavior (**Figure 13.1**). This is a form of discipline that can be used in any situation. It involves helping children learn self-discipline by taking personal responsibility for their actions. Guidance teaches children the difference between acceptable and unacceptable behavior. The intent is to teach children social-emotional skills to function in positive ways.

In contrast, *punishment* is a form of discipline that does little to respect children, which is a hurtful penalty for unacceptable behavior.

Guidance Versus Punishment

Guidance	Punishment
• builds self-esteem	• lowers self-esteem
• respects	• degrades
• gives hope	• angers
• encourages	• discourages and embarrasses
• is loving and caring	• denies affection
• teaches	• controls behavior thorough fear
• helps develops self-control	• may reinforce poor behavior by getting attention

Figure 13.2 Learning the difference between guidance and punishment can help you effectively guide children to learn positive ways to control their behavior.

Guidance should always maintain the children's self-esteem and produce a desired change in behavior. *Self-regulation* and *self-control*, which promote executive function, are the long-term goals of guidance. The children learn self-discipline by directing their behavior without external control. These are helpful lifetime skills. Studies show that positive social behavior links to later academic success.

Another goal of guidance is to promote *prosocial behaviors* among the children. **Prosocial behavior** is a term psychologists use to refer to behaviors that promote the well-being of other people. They are voluntary acts of kindness. Children with prosocial-behavior skills show cooperation, sharing, and helping. Their prosocial behaviors usually center on concern for friends and approval. These behaviors usually emerge by the third year of life.

The following are examples of prosocial behaviors:

- accepting, acknowledging, and respecting others' feelings;
- expressing powerful emotions in acceptable ways;
- responding to others' emotions verbally and/or comforting them;
- helping others;
- cooperating with others in play and cleanup time;
- sharing toys, materials, and ideas;
- sharing warmth and affection;
- comforting others;
- caring how actions affect others; and
- inviting others to take part in activities.

13.1-2 Guidance and You

The heart of guidance lies in relationships. Children develop in a model of relationships. They need caring, warm, and nurturing teachers who consistently guide and support them. Human love is powerful! Children need teachers whom they can trust to provide a reliable presence. The healthier the relationships children have, the more likely they are to thrive.

As a teacher, your personality will affect the behavior of the children in your care. Researchers have conducted studies to determine the effect that specific personality traits have on children's behavior. These studies show that effective early childhood teachers are warm, affectionate, and nurturing. They create a caring classroom community. They encourage, support, and show interest in children. These teachers use more suggestions than commands. Children respond faster to suggestions than they do to commands.

According to research, teachers should often interact with the children and ask **open-ended questions.** These questions require more than one-word answers. Children in this type of environment will show certain positive characteristics. These include independence, verbalization, cooperation, task persistence, and high self-esteem (**Figure 13.3**).

Model prosocial behaviors. Use words and actions that show children you value them. Children rely on their environment for behavioral clues. They need affirmation. Young children will imitate your example, so model attentive, warm, friendly, and respectful behaviors. Studies also note that uncooperative teachers have more hyperactive, disruptive, and bored children. Children in the classes with talkative teachers tend to be shyer. Nurturing teachers have children in their classes who interact easily with others.

Teachers can also influence aggressive and attention-seeking behavior by the children. This behavior occurs most often with permissive teachers. Such teachers often cannot get involved with or stop aggressive and attention-seeking behavior. The children who behave this way may see the teacher's lack of involvement as permission to engage in such behavior.

Preparing for Guidance

There are some general guidelines for developing effective guidance skills. Study these guidelines. They will help you become an effective teacher.

One of the first steps toward effective guidance is observing the children. You need to see what they are unable to say. So, watch carefully and note how individual children behave and act out

fizkes/Shutterstock.com

Figure 13.3   This child will learn a great deal through interaction with the teacher. *How can using open-ended questions promote positive characteristics in children?*

in certain situations. Use the process of **child observation** to gather information. Look for clues when observing their behavior. Sometimes, you will know immediately what they are unable to say. Other times, you will have to guess.

Ask yourself how you respond to each of the children in your class. Do you have any biases? Are you expecting certain behaviors from children based on culture, temperament, parent's educational level, gender, personality, or appearance? The stereotypes you hold may affect your perception of a child. For example, do you always expect Clarice to model positive behavior because her parents are doctors? Being honest about your attitudes and how they may influence your interactions will allow you to be more objective.

13.1-3 Culturally Appropriate Variations

The experience that children know best is their family. Their participation in an early childhood program may be their first experience learning about routines, behaviors, and practices that differ from home. Some family traditions, religious beliefs, or social class may pose guidance challenges. Therefore, it is important to learn about and understand the children's families and their *culturally appropriate variations*.

Cultural influence on child development is considerable. Culture is a powerful driver for development. It affects how quickly children reach developmental milestones. Cultural norms affect how children are raised, including what values and behaviors are appropriate. Culture is the people's way of life and a defining feature of a community. It may be reflected in the language, vocabulary, human behavior, and human emotions. Culture affects children's behavior, beliefs, and how they relate to others. Culture even influences how they think about themselves.

Children learn from studying others' behavior. Beginning at birth, they will watch their parent's or guardian's conversation style. This style will vary. In America, children tend to be self-focused, take turns talking, and talk about themselves. Not all cultures rear their children with Western beliefs. For example, children take a more passive role in other cultures, such as Korea and Japan. Their conversations will be brief. Children in Native American communities tend to hold back before responding to questions in a classroom setting. Children from India are careful about drawing attention to themselves.

The definition of a productive member of society differs from culture to culture. There are basic child-rearing patterns. Cultural norms reflect what values and behaviors are appropriate. Cultural elements include:

- home language, speech, and writing symbols
- religious beliefs and traditions
- marriage customs—arranged, free, or same-sex
- gender roles
- foods—types, preparation, and eating tools
- games and leisure pursuits
- clothing
- greetings

The expression of family and cultural variations can occur in several ways. One example is children's nonverbal behavior. **Nonverbal behavior** comprises actions rather than words. These can include facial expressions, eye contact, touch, gestures, and physical closeness. For example, it is common for people in some cultures to look down to show respect. In these cultures, a child who speaks in a soft voice and maintains less eye contact reflects respect and courtesy. A teacher who was unaware of this behavior could interpret it as disrespectful.

Biases are acquired early in life by observing parents, teachers, siblings, grandparents, and others. There is an intergenerational transmission. You will need to examine your own lens of bias and learn more about cultural differences to help all children grow—socially, emotionally, and cognitively. The curriculum in teacher education programs emphasizes the importance of thinking and acting in a culturally competent way. Teachers are prepared to include all children, discovering and building on their strengths.

When differences exist between the center and home rules, it is more difficult for children. They need to become **bicultural** by learning the rules of the center's culture while maintaining those of their home culture. Five-year-old Tunde, for example, is from Nigeria. During his first day attending the center, he used his hands to eat rather than flatware. Some children told him he had to use flatware. Mrs. Wong, his teacher, immediately explained the eating ritual used in Tunde's home country. She believed in integrating his cultural norms and values into the classroom to make him feel more comfortable. So, Tunde continued using his hands to eat. Over time, he began to integrate the eating practices the other children used in the classroom.

Cultural competence is needed to be a successful teacher. It involves the ability to understand and respect the values, attitudes, and beliefs of cultures beyond your own. Cultural competence requires great care and thoughtfulness when working with children of a different culture. A person's cultural values influence their perceptions of acceptable child guidance practices. Not all parents hold the same views, and agreement is not always possible. To create a supportive environment, teachers need to understand and respect cultural differences. Begin by forming meaningful relationships with parents or guardians. Relationships are at the heart of learning and teaching. Educate yourself about the children's cultures in your classroom. Listen and observe. Read, talk with people of different cultural backgrounds, and eat in culturally diverse restaurants. This process will help you understand and respect other's traditions and cultures.

You will also need to carefully examine your own inherent biases to become a culturally competent teacher. **Implicit bias**—a bias or prejudice that is present but not consciously held or recognized—is hard to measure. It is the thoughts and feelings that are outside of an individual's conscious awareness. These biases influence an individual's perception, judgment, and actions. It impacts their reaction toward others. People often discriminate unintentionally or hold prejudices. They may favor one group of people over another.

Remember the children always watch and learn from you, and you are impacting their social learnings. Your biases are shown through your observations of children's behavior and how you respond. This can cause changes in their own beliefs and sense of belonging to the classroom community.

Sharing Observations

Another essential guideline is to plan with other teachers. Sharing observations, feelings, and suggestions will help you better understand the children. One teacher may add to your observations (**Figure 13.4**). As a result, you will better understand why a child refuses to take part in art activities, is always angry, or shoves other children on the playground.

stock_photo_world/Shutterstock.com

Figure 13.4   With the help of other teachers, you can learn more about the children in your center. ***How do you think collaborating with other teachers might help you guide children's behavior?***

Avoid talking to other staff when you are teaching unless it is necessary. The children's needs should always come first. Alertness to these needs requires your full attention. Save other comments for after program hours.

Finally, sit with the children. You will be closer to their level. As a result, the children will find it easier to interact with you. Do not interrupt an activity unless you can add to knowledge or safety. Let the children begin interacting with you. Remember that to develop independence and self-confidence, never do for the children what they can do for themselves.

13.1-4 Principles of Direct and Indirect Guidance

Child guidance consists of direct or indirect actions to help children develop appropriate behavior. **Indirect guidance** involves outside factors that influence behavior. A classroom layout is a form of indirect guidance. Indirect guidance will be discussed later in the chapter.

Direct guidance involves nonverbal (physical) and verbal actions to guide children's actions. Nonverbal actions, or body language, include *facial expressions*—such as eye contact, a smile, or even a surprised look—and *gestures*, such as gently touching a child's arm or nodding. Your words are also a form of direct guidance. Another example is sitting or squatting to get down to the child's level. This conveys the message that you are interested, you care.

Body language is a useful tool for direct guidance. When guiding children, get down on their level for greater impact and look them in the eye. This will allow them to see your facial expressions and gestures, which can convey a variety of messages ranging from approval and reassurance to disapproval and sadness. Placing a hand on a child's arm or shoulder may help redirect their attention and behavior.

Your nonverbal actions need to reinforce what you communicate verbally. Watch that your words match your nonverbal signals. For example, if you are asking a child to stop a behavior, your facial expression should also convey disapproval. Children become confused when adults' words give one message and their actions another. Following the principles in **Figure 13.5** will help you develop direct-guidance skills.

Use Simple Language

Young children have a limited vocabulary so you need to carefully choose your words. To communicate clearly, use language they can understand. Consider the ages of the children and adjust your vocabulary to fit their developmental level. For instance, two-year-olds usually learn the word *big* before they learn *large*. Therefore, use the term *big* with these children. When working with three-year-olds, you might use the word

large. This depends, however, on their level of development. With four- and five-year-olds, again adjust the level of your vocabulary. With these children, you might say *huge*.

Early Childhood Insight

Tone of Voice

According to Merriam-Webster, *tone of voice* is how a person speaks to another person. It is how you sound when you say words aloud to another person. When guiding children, it is important to use a calm, firm tone of voice when you speak with them. A calm tone of voice can help you focus on helping children learn appropriate behaviors and encourage self-regulation.

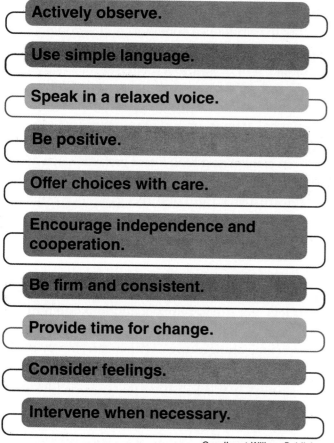

Direct Guidance Principles

- Actively observe.
- Use simple language.
- Speak in a relaxed voice.
- Be positive.
- Offer choices with care.
- Encourage independence and cooperation.
- Be firm and consistent.
- Provide time for change.
- Consider feelings.
- Intervene when necessary.

Goodheart-Willcox Publisher

Figure 13.5 Using these principles will help you develop your direct-guidance skills. *Choose one of the principles of direct guidance and describe how you might effectively use this principle with young children.*

Speak in a Relaxed Tone of Voice

Speak in a calm and relaxed, clear *tone of voice*. Children will listen to this type of voice. Save loud, high-pitched voices for emergencies. Since loud, high-pitched voices are associated with powerful emotion, you will gain the children's attention. If you raise your voice during the normal course of the day, children will become used to this level. When an emergency occurs, you may fail to gain their attention. In addition, when you raise your voice, the children will also raise their voices. The classroom will become a very noisy place.

Be Positive and Provide Cues

Guide the children by telling them what to do instead of what not to do. Children will feel more comfortable with a positive comment. For example, instead of saying "Don't put that puzzle on the floor," say "Put the puzzle on the table" (**Figure 13.6**). This will remind the children of the rule that puzzles in the classroom are used on a table.

Teacher cues are also important in helping children develop appropriate social behavior. These cues may be verbal or nonverbal. During playtime, you may notice that Annabelle is observing Mayra playing with blocks. Her teacher might suggest, "Mayra, Annabelle looks like she would like to help you build with the blocks." At

Using Positive Guidance

Negative	Positive
"Don't put the puzzle on the floor."	"Put the puzzle on the table."
"Don't touch anything!"	"Place your hands in your pockets."
"Do not run."	"Please walk."
"Quit screaming."	"Use your indoor voice."
"Don't drip paint."	"Wipe your brush on the container."
"Don't get paint on your clothes."	"Put on a painting smock."
"Do not rip the pages."	"Turn the pages carefully."
"Do not walk in front of the swing."	"Walk around the swing, please."

Goodheart-Willcox Publisher

Figure 13.6 Using positive comments to guide children's behavior results in positive responses from children.

lunchtime, Daniela says, "I want more rice." As a reminder, the teacher says, "Daniela, what magic words should you use to have the rice passed?"

Offer Choices with Care

New, unskilled teachers sometimes confuse offering a choice with giving a direction. For example, when it is lunchtime, the teacher may say, "Do you want to go in for lunch?" By asking this question, they give the child a choice. If the child is not interested in eating lunch, they may answer by saying, "No."

You should offer children a manageable choice only when you want them to have one. Here, it would be better to say, "It is time for lunch now," or "We need to go inside for lunch now." Make sure that once you offer a choice, the child may carry through with their choice. For example, you might ask a child if they prefer watering the plants or feeding the fish. If the child chooses to feed the fish, accept the choice. Avoid trying to get children to change their minds. When you do this, you are telling them that there really was no choice.

Encourage Independence and Cooperation

Give children the least amount of help they need. In this way, they will have opportunities to learn independence. For instance, encourage children to dress and feed themselves. Encourage them to share responsibility for keeping the classroom orderly and tidy.

Some children begin school dependent on others. At home, these children have an adult or sibling to attend to their needs. As a result, they come to school expecting the teacher to dress them, pick up after them, and intercede. Encourage independence from the start in order to change this behavior. For instance, when Kaito reports Lorenzo is teasing him, ask Kaito how he feels when this happens. If he says he does not like it, tell him to share his feelings with Lorenzo. Likewise, if Talia does not want to share her clay, Kaito must tell Talia he is mad because she will not share.

Children only become independent if allowed the opportunity. Many people are surprised at the competence of three-, four-, and five-year-old children who have the opportunity to do for themselves (**Figure 13.7**).

These children must also learn to help each other. Encourage children to work with each other. When Toby tells you he cannot zip his coat,

Seahorse Photo in BKK/Shutterstock.com

Figure 13.7 Young children are good at doing tasks for themselves when you give them a chance. *Why do you think it is important for children to begin learning independence skills at a young age?*

say, "Ask Joanne if she can help you." If Lucinda cannot tie her shoe, say, "Ask Luis to help you tie it." These experiences help the children to learn prosocial behaviors.

Be Firm

Be firm and speak in a quiet voice when disciplining children. Some children are very demanding. When you tell them they cannot do something, they may cry. Some may throw temper tantrums. If it is behavior that you cannot allow to continue, you must stand firm.

When a child throws a tantrum, you may feel like giving in. If you do, the child will probably use the same method again when they want their way. Effective guidance requires firmness. For example, Sam may be angry and hit Lucinda. You will need to be firm. Say, "You look angry, but I cannot let you hit Lucinda."

Be Consistent

Consistency is a key element in effective guidance practices. Children are good at testing adults. If they feel an adult is not firm in disciplining, they will repeat their unacceptable behavior. They may want to find out what will happen if they continue to repeat their unacceptable behavior. For this reason, give discipline and approval consistently. For instance, do not discipline children one day and praise them the next for running to the door at playtime.

Make sure that you are also consistent from child to child. Children quickly develop a sense of fairness. If you tell one child to pick up the toys at cleanup time, all children should have to clean up. When you are not consistent, children will challenge your requests.

Provide Time for Change

Young children need time to change activities. It is essential to provide them with ample time for a change. Without this time, children can become confused. By allowing time, you will provide children with an adjustment period. For instance, when children are preparing to go outside during cold weather, allow them time to put on their coats, hats, and mittens. This time will allow them to prepare themselves for new activities and surroundings.

Consider Feelings

Although it is not always included in daily lesson plans, learning about feelings and emotions is an essential part of any early childhood program. Children need to recognize, understand, and learn to express their feelings.

Young children can have powerful feelings, which often center on control of their environment. The feelings may relate to their bodies, siblings, eating, friendship, and toileting.

It is best to discuss feelings in small group settings or alone with a child. For some children, talking about feelings and emotions is difficult. Your responsibility is to help them understand and express their feelings (**Figure 13.8**).

Facing someone else's pain is also difficult for young children. You will observe that children do not know how to deal with the pain of others. When a new child begins school and cries over separation from parents or guardians, the other children rarely get involved. Some may pretend not to see or hear the child. Others may have a pained look on their faces. This shows sensitivity. Although they may feel sympathy, they tend not to get involved. Usually, if a child is bleeding, they will only get involved. They will bring the child to you for a bandage; however, they will not usually console the child.

globalmoments/iStock via Getty Images Plus

Figure 13.8 Many children do not know how to handle their feelings. They may require your help to feel good about themselves.

Teachers are behavior models for children. You can model kindness, respect, and compassion to teach peaceful living. Show the children how to help and empathize with others. For instance, if Avery is crying, put your arm around his shoulders. By modeling warm and responsive actions, you will teach the children a way to comfort each other. They will learn that a hug can help mend crying.

Young children also need to learn how to handle mistakes. When a child spills milk or breaks a toy, do not overreact. Instead, show the child how to handle the mistake. The child will then know not to fear mistakes. Remind the child who spilled the milk that it needs to be cleaned up. If needed, show the child how to do this. Depending on the situation, you may wish to help clean up.

Intervene When Necessary

To be an effective teacher, you will need to know when to intervene to teach expectations (**Figure 13.9**). Observe children carefully before saying anything. Allow them to explore on their own. Interrupt only when you can add to their knowledge or promote their safety. For example, if a four-year-old says, "Cows give eggnog at Christmas," clarify this statement. Unless you intervene, children who are listening may believe this comment.

Safety intervention will often require words and action. If Jamie is not careful climbing up the slide, you will need to walk over and review the limits with her. Make clear the dangers of falling. Intervention would also be required if you were observing a group of children and noticed that a child was in danger of being hurt. It is important to intervene before this happens by redirecting the play or providing help.

You may also need to intervene for health purposes. Remind children to dress appropriately for outdoor play in the winter. Encourage children to cover their mouths with their arms when they cough. When cooking, remind children not to use the cooking utensils to taste the food.

Children need to learn to be friends with all the children. Thus, do not allow children to be excluded from play because of age, culture,

veryulissa/Shutterstock.com

Figure 13.9 The teacher may have to intervene if one child tries to take another's toy. *What are other behaviors that may require the teacher's intervention?*

or gender. When Emerson says, "Only girls can come into the playhouse," it is essential for you to intervene. One way to handle, say "This school is for everyone." By doing so, you will give the children the words they need to defend their right to take part.

You must also intervene when children are impolite. Sometimes you will hear a child say, "I do not like you," or "You are ugly." When this happens, you need to intervene. Point out to the child that such words can hurt another's feelings. With young children, that may end the behavior.

Property arguments may also require intervention. Classroom property does not belong to the children, but to the center. Therefore, the children must share it. During a property argument, you may have to be the mediator since children need to practice resolving conflicts. Remind the children to share. If this does not work, give the equipment to one child for a set time period. Then give it to the other child for another time period. For instance, tell Justice that she may play with the truck in the morning and Mark may play with it in the afternoon. Then make sure each child has a turn.

It is important for children to learn that they cannot grab materials from others. No matter how strong the child's feelings, others have rights.

Children need to take turns painting at the easel, taking part in cooking activities, and watering plants (**Figure 13.10**). While children learn and develop, you will need to intervene. That is why in many early childhood classrooms, you will hear a teacher saying many times a day, "You can have a turn next," or "After she is finished, you can paint." From your modeling, children will learn social, emotional, and cognitive skills.

Indirect Guidance

You will recall that indirect guidance involves outside factors that influence behavior. The physical setup of a center and daily schedule are forms of indirect guidance. They can indirectly influence both the children's and teachers' behavior.

For example, a well-planned facility makes supervision easier and supports positive behavior. If you can supervise properly, it will help you feel relaxed and in control. The children will feel safer knowing that you are protecting them.

To carefully supervise young children, an open classroom is best. Stand with your back toward the classroom wall. You should be able to view the entire room. Such an arrangement will allow you to actively observe and give help when needed. It will also reduce your fatigue, since you will not have to continually run back and forth between areas.

The physical setup of the facility promotes a healthy, safe environment. In one large room, you see everything that happens (**Figure 13.11**). Therefore, you can step in when dangerous situations arise. For instance, the behavior of two-year-old children needs close monitoring. Many two-year-olds use body language. They will hit another child instead of saying "I do not like that." With the proper physical arrangement, you can see such situations occurring and step in immediately.

Young children, and especially two-year-olds, rarely have well-developed gross-motor skills. They often stumble, trip, or fall. To reduce the number of these accidents, large, open areas are best. For instance, place shelving units around the outside walls of the room instead of in high-traffic areas.

The physical setup of the facility can also promote children's independence. Independence

Zabavna/iStock via Getty Images Plus

Figure 13.10   These children will need to take turns using the shovel.

Krakenimages.com/Shutterstock.com

Figure 13.11   This teacher has positioned herself so she can see all the children. *Why is it essential for the teacher to have all children in sight?*

should be a learning objective of every early childhood program, no matter the ages or abilities of children in the program. For example, you should encourage toddlers to use the restroom if they have developed control of their bowels and bladders. For this reason, the bathrooms should be next to the classroom. The installation of sinks, toilets, paper toweling, or hand dryers should be at the children's level.

To encourage children to hang up their coats, provide low hooks for hanging coats and hats. Low shelf units and sinks will encourage children to help with cleanup. All toys and materials should have a designated place in the classroom. Placing a picture of the item on a shelf or container is one way of assisting the children. Mark the containers. This visual clue helps children replace toys and equipment to the proper storage place.

Through these arrangements, you will save the time and energy needed for assisting the children. You will also have more time to observe, plan meaningful activities, and interact with the children.

Workplace Connections

Classroom Observation

Visit a local early learning center or Head Start classroom and observe how manners are modeled and taught. Write a brief report of your findings and discuss your observations in class.

1. Were children learning good manners by imitating the teacher's behavior? What instances of verbal and nonverbal modeling did you observe?
2. Were active listening techniques and other guidance techniques used in the classroom? If so, describe your observations.

Lesson 13.1 Review

1. Guidance _____. (13.1.1)
   A. uses strict control to enforce obedience
   B. helps children develop internal controls and socially acceptable behavior
   C. includes abusive, punitive behaviors to enforce obedience
   D. should never be used in an early childhood setting

2. Each of the following is an example of a prosocial behavior except _____. (13.1.1)
   A. helping others and sharing kindness, warmth, and affection
   B. responding to others' emotions by comforting them
   C. expressing powerful emotions in an unacceptable way
   D. inviting others to take part in classroom activities

3. Each of the following is an example of children's behavior with permissive teachers except _____. (13.1.2)
   A. aggressive behavior
   B. attention-seeking behavior
   C. unfriendly behavior
   D. respectful behavior

4. Each of the following is an example of how culture influences child development except culture _____. (13.1.3)
   A. affects how quickly children reach developmental milestones
   B. influences how children are raised, including appropriate values and behaviors
   C. impacts classrooms that have more hyperactive, disruptive, and bored children
   D. influences children's behavior, beliefs, and how they relate to others

5. All describe cultural competence except cultural competence _____. (13.1.3)
   A. involves forming meaningful relationships with parents or guardians
   B. involves the ability to understand and respect the values, attitudes, and beliefs of cultures beyond your own
   C. has little to do with becoming a successful early childhood teacher
   D. requires educating yourself about the children's cultures in your classroom

6. Each of the following is an action useful for direct guidance except _____. (13.1.4)
   A. body language, such as facial expressions and eye contact
   B. standing next to children to get their attention
   C. touching a child's arm or nodding
   D. using actions and words that give the same message

7. Which of the following is not an example of a positive guidance statement? (13.1.4)
   A. "Put the puzzle on the table when you use it."
   B. "Do not get paint on your shirt."
   C. "Please pass the rice."
   D. "Adrian, Darra looks like she would like to help you build with blocks."

8. Which of the following is not an example of how physical setup can indirectly promote appropriate behavior? (13.1.4)
   A. A well-planned facility helps you supervise properly and support positive behavior.
   B. An open classroom helps you view the entire room and give help to children when needed.
   C. An open classroom provides too much space for toys and equipment, often causing young children to stumble, trip, or fall.
   D. Installation of sinks, toilets, paper toweling, or hand dryers at children's level promotes independence.

Effectively Guiding Children

Essential Question

 What do I need to know and implement about effective guidance techniques to successfully guide children and promote positive self-concept?

Learning Outcomes

After studying this lesson, you will be able to

13.2-1 **differentiate** among various techniques for effective guidance.

13.2-2 **summarize** ways to promote a positive self-concept in children.

Key Terms

verbal environment	I-message
positive reinforcement	prompting
consequence	redirecting
natural consequence	modeling
logical consequence	

Children need to develop responsibility for their behavior to live successfully in a democratic society. Teachers in early childhood programs must promote a social environment that supports positive behavior to help them build self-esteem and confidence. A teachers' first step is planning and arranging an environment that will guide appropriate behavior. Then the teacher must introduce, model, and consistently reinforce appropriate expectations, such as reasonable classroom limits or rules. Through guidance, the teachers' responsibility is to help children build new behaviors such as kindness, the ability to delay self-gratification, and develop self-control. To be successful, teachers must establish effective guidance techniques.

13.2-1 Techniques for Effective Guidance

As an early childhood teacher, you will teach children by intentionally modeling acceptable behaviors. Likewise, the children in your classroom will also teach each other. Whatever effect you have on the children's behavior, the children will affect others.

There are specific guidance techniques that can be useful in guiding children's behavior. These techniques include creating a positive verbal environment, using positive reinforcement, and using consequences. In addition, you will want to include *warning, time-out, I-messages, praising, affirming, suggesting, prompting, persuading, redirecting, modeling, listening, ignoring,* and *encouraging.*

Positive Verbal Environment

The **verbal environment** includes all the communication that occurs within the setting. An adult or child may make these exchanges. In addition, the verbal environment includes the nonverbal communication of actions rather than words. Eye contact, facial expressions, gestures, and touch are examples. What people say and how they say it determines whether the environment is positive or negative.

Teachers need to create an encouraging classroom by using positive words. They can help create a positive verbal environment by using active-listening skills and modeling appropriate behaviors. They can start by preparing the environment before the children arrive at the center. This would allow them to give the children their full attention when they enter the classroom. When engaging in a conversation, caregivers should use the children's names and words to share their interests. They need to know you love and respect them. Modeling words such as *thank you, please,* and *excuse me* throughout the day show children how teachers want them to behave. Likewise, these teachers should be sincere and constructive when praising children.

Positive Reinforcement

Rewarding appropriate behavior can help shape the children's behavior. This technique is called **positive reinforcement**. For instance, if you thank a child for holding the door, the child will most likely hold the door again. You have provided a positive reinforcement of the child's behavior. Positive messages will encourage the child to repeat the behavior. Repeated positive reinforcement will cause repeated behavior.

You must be careful when using positive reinforcement that you are rewarding behaviors you want the child to repeat. Teachers sometimes do not realize they are rewarding children for unacceptable behavior. For instance, laughing at a child who is acting silly during group time reinforces the child's behavior. The child sees this reaction as a reward. It encourages the child to repeat the behavior (**Figure 13.12**).

fotostorm/iStock via Getty Images Plus

Figure 13.12 The teacher needs to provide children with positive reinforcement for putting their toys away. *How would you affirm a child for putting away their toys?*

Using Consequences

Consequences are important in molding children's behavior. A **consequence** is a result that follows an action or behavior. Consequences can be very influential in shaping behavior. There are two types of consequences: *natural consequences* and *logical consequences.*

Natural consequences are those experiences that follow naturally because of a behavior. They do not require anyone's intervention. For example, the natural consequence of forgetting to put away an art project is that someone might throw it away during cleanup time. The natural consequence of forgetting to put on your gloves is that your hands will get cold. Natural consequences can be very effective in guiding children's behavior, but avoid using them if a child's safety is at risk. For instance, if a child runs into the street without stopping to look for cars, a car could hit the child. Here, an adult must intervene to ensure the child stops and looks before crossing a street.

Use *logical consequences* when you cannot use natural consequences to guide behavior. **Logical consequences** are those that an adult deliberately sets up to show what will happen if a child does not follow a limit. The consequences should relate to the unacceptable behavior as much as possible.

When using logical consequences, first make the children aware of the limits. Then they need to know the consequences of choosing not to follow the limits. For example, if Jules drives his scooter into Lucas, tell him to stop. Remind him of the consequence if he does not stop. The consequence might be that he will have to give up his turn on the scooter. If Jules runs into Lucas again, enforce the consequence. Thus, Jules will learn that driving into others is not acceptable behavior.

Warning

When children cannot follow a limit, you must remind them they are misbehaving and their behavior will have consequences (**Figure 13.13**). You are *warning* the children. Warn only once. If the behavior continues, proceed with the consequences. Effective warnings contain only two parts. First, state the misbehavior. Then state the consequences. Examples include:

- "Joel, keep the sand in the sandbox. If you throw it again, you will lose your turn."

- "Tunde, either choose a place in the circle, or I will choose one for you."

- "Hinata, do not use blocks as guns. If you use the block as a gun again, you will need to leave the block area."

These warnings provide children an opportunity to change their behavior. After giving the warning, provide time for the child to comply. If the child does not comply, follow through with the consequences.

Take-A-Break

Take-a-break is a guidance technique that involves moving a child away from others for a short period. Use take-a-break when you cannot ignore a child's disruptive behavior. The child needs time to calm down. In some classrooms, teachers use this technique when a child is out of control with anger or frustration and is harmful to others. To protect the other children, the teacher moves the angry child to a quiet place away from the group. This is one way of allowing the child to gain self-control. Only use take-a-break for as long as it takes the child to become calm. You should never use take-a-break as a form of punishment because it does not teach acceptable behavior skills.

UW-Stout Child and Family Study Center

Figure 13.13 The teacher will have to warn the child that he cannot take sand from his friend. *How are warnings helpful in guiding children toward positive behaviors?*

Take-a-break can be an effective guidance tool for some children. Four- and five-year-olds usually understand the purpose better than younger children. By this age, most children can understand that their behavior can have negative consequences. Take-a-break is an example of a logical consequence.

To be effective, tell children in advance what behaviors cause take-a-break. If you decide to use take-a-break, carry it out in an unemotional, direct way. Simply state the limit that someone has broken a rule and say "take-a-break." Promptly remove the child to an area away from the group, but within your vision. Say nothing further. You do not want to reward the child with added attention. Limit the time to a few minutes. If the child returns to the group and the behavior continues, add another minute to the time.

Not all teachers agree with the use of take-a-break. Some feel the technique should seldom be used, if at all. Others feel that take-a-break provides time for children to think about the skills they need to function more appropriately in the classroom. If used, take-a-break should never be punitive. Rather, it should be a time for children to reflect on their actions.

I-Messages

When a child misbehaves, use an I-message to communicate your perceptions and feelings. An **I-message** tells children how you feel about their challenging behavior in a respectful manner. It does not place blame on the children, which would cause them to feel they are a bad people. Instead, it helps the children learn how others view their actions.

Your I-message statement should include three parts:

1. naming the child's specific behavior;

2. identifying your feelings about the behavior; and

3. naming the effects of the behavior.

After you state the I-message, you should then say what you want the child to do. For instance, you may say, "When I see you hitting Yasser, I am unhappy because you are hurting him. I want you to stop hitting Yasser." Note that in this example, the behavior is hitting. It makes you feel unhappy, and the effects cause another child to be hurt. I-messages show the child how others perceive their actions.

Effective Praise

Studies show that not all praise is equally successful. *Effective praise* is sincere and constructive. It is specific and individualized to fit the situation and child. Praise acknowledges the child's actions or progress. It is thoughtful and does not interrupt the child's activities. Effective praise recognizes the child's positive behaviors and encourages the child to persist at a task. This type of praise may compare a child's progress to past performance.

Effective praise aims to make the child feel competent and valued. Young children thrive on effective recognition. When you say "I like the way you helped, Cedric," you tell the child he is important. This is verbal praise (**Figure 13.14**). Nonverbal praise can also be successful. A smile, wink, or pat on the back are types of nonverbal praise. Displaying a child's work on a bulletin board is also a form of praise. Some teachers paste

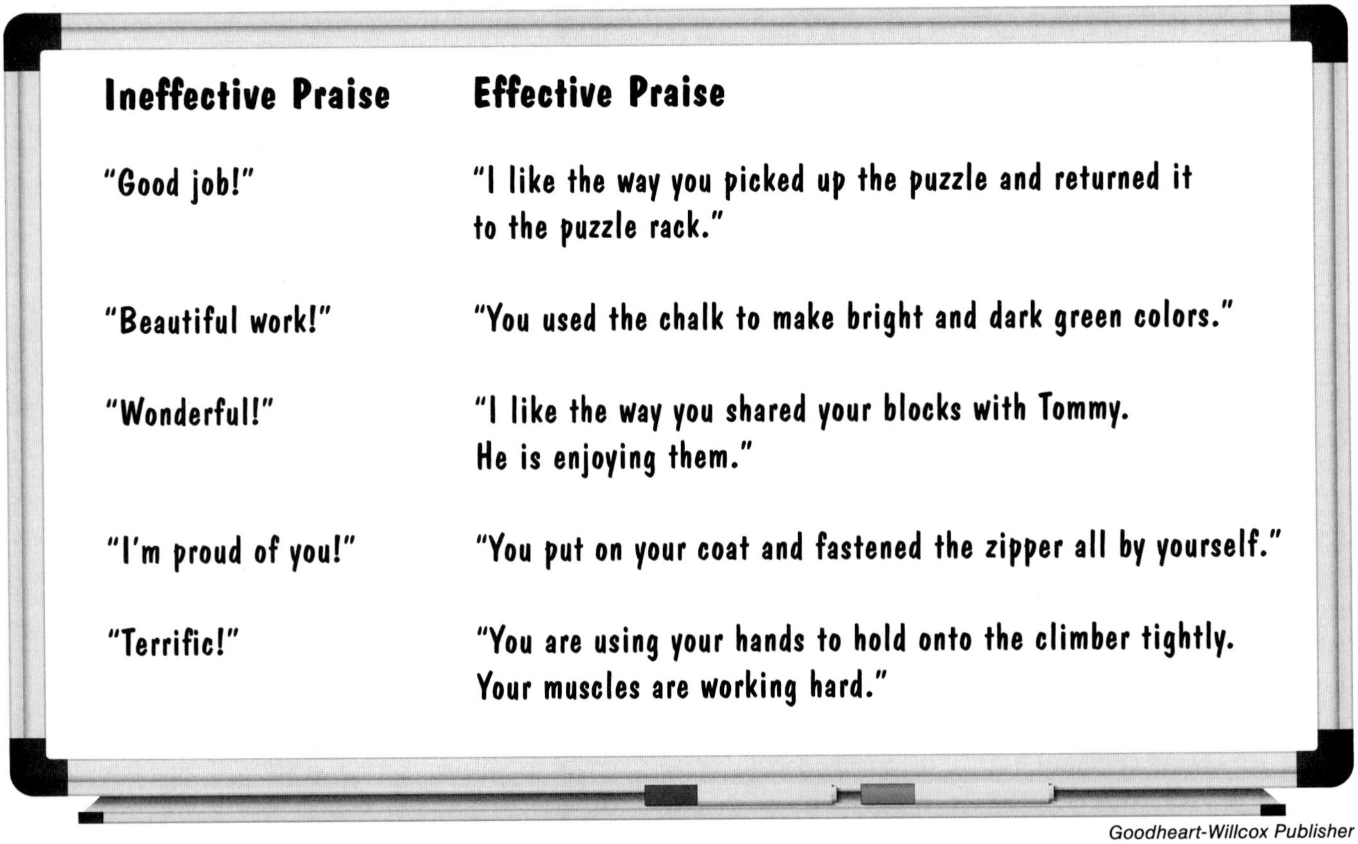

Ineffective Praise	Effective Praise
"Good job!"	"I like the way you picked up the puzzle and returned it to the puzzle rack."
"Beautiful work!"	"You used the chalk to make bright and dark green colors."
"Wonderful!"	"I like the way you shared your blocks with Tommy. He is enjoying them."
"I'm proud of you!"	"You put on your coat and fastened the zipper all by yourself."
"Terrific!"	"You are using your hands to hold onto the climber tightly. Your muscles are working hard."

Goodheart-Willcox Publisher

Figure 13.14 Effective praise is specific and acknowledges the child's actions or progress.

a star or sticker on children's artwork. This is also a form of nonverbal praise.

When praising young children, remember:

- Make praise age appropriate.
- Give praise immediately. It is most effective to praise children while still in the act.
- When praising, always establish eye contact.
- Do not overuse praise. If you do, it will be ineffective.

Affirmation helps the children by identifying and labeling positive behavior. Like adults, children love acknowledgment, and they repeat behaviors that receive it. A teacher might use such affirmations as "You enjoy helping others" or "Raul enjoys having you share the toys with him." When you affirm behaviors, children are likely to repeat them.

Ineffective praise—or *empty praise*—may be more damaging than helpful because it is repetitive and not genuine. Frequent use of ineffective praise can lead children to base their feelings of self-worth on adults' opinions of them. Examples of empty praise include sayings such as *good job, super, terrific,* and *fantastic.* What does a good job mean? It would be better to say, "I liked the way your picked up all the blocks and returned them to the shelves."

Questioning

Teachers may use a multi-turn conversation to help young children understand their behavior. As they learn acceptable and unacceptable behaviors, young children develop self-regulation skills. When teachers observe inappropriate behavior, they need to ensure the child understands the classroom rules. Using open-ended questions, teachers can help them elicit different types of thinking. The purpose of questioning is to help the children engage in higher-level thinking skills while reflecting on their behavior. For example:

Teacher: Looks at Charlie and asks, "Why did you knock down Kris's block structure?"

Charlie: "Because I wanted to."

Teacher: "In our classroom, we are responsible for what we do."

Charlie: "I know."

Teacher: "How do you think it made Kris feel?"

Charlie: "Mad or bad. But he had all the blocks."

Teacher: "What should you say to Kris if you want to use some blocks?"

Charlie: "Ask to please use some blocks."

Teacher: "Now, what do you need to do?"

Charlie: "Say I am sorry. Won't do it again."

Children like Charlie often have not had opportunities to practice social skills. Children like him need to learn to use verbal skills rather than physical actions. His teacher needs to help him to learn to understand and guide his behavior.

Suggesting

Suggesting means placing thoughts for consideration in children's minds. This often leads to action. For instance, after Cassidy spills her milk on the table, you may need to suggest she clean it up. To do this, say "Cassidy, here is a sponge." This will probably be enough to encourage Cassidy to wipe the spill. If not, you may have to add, "You need to wipe up the milk." During snack time, you may suggest to the children that they try a new fruit. You can do this directly or indirectly. Simply stating "This fruit is delicious," is enough to encourage some children to try the food. A more direct approach may work for other children. For example, you may say, "Taylor, try this fruit today. It is delicious."

Always make suggestions positive. Lead children's thoughts and feelings in a desirable direction. If you tell the children to listen carefully to the story, they will probably follow your advice. In contrast, if you tell the children that they are noisy and behaving poorly, they will likely continue to act this way. Negative suggestions usually produce negative behavior.

Effective teachers use suggestions many times each day. You will have many daily opportunities to mold behavior through suggestion. For example, Darlene may forget to put the blocks back on the shelf. A suggestion may work here. Corinna may drop her coat on the floor as she enters the room. A suggestion may work here as well.

Prompting

Children often need **prompting** to stop an unacceptable action or start an acceptable one (**Figure 13.15**). Prompting prepares children for transitions. Prompting differs from suggesting because it requires a response. Examples of verbal prompting include the following:

- "Moses, do you remember where we keep the play dough?"
- "Glenda, what must we remember when riding bikes?"
- "Michelle, do you remember where you put your painting?"

Prompting can also be nonverbal. You may place a finger over your lip at group time to signal "Quiet, please!" Limits printed on a poster board (if age appropriate) are nonverbal prompts. Frowning can show your disapproval. Even turning a child around to attend to group activities is prompting.

Make prompting simple and noncritical. Prompt in a calm, impersonal manner. You may ask a child, "What are you supposed to be doing?" or "What should we be doing before we have a snack?"

Prompts may often require repetition before the children develop acceptable behavior. For instance, children new to the center may need prompts for several days to hang their coats on the hook before this behavior develops. Once the child complies, praise this behavior.

Persuading

By *persuading*, you encourage children to act or behave in a certain way by appealing to their basic wants and needs. Seeing things from their point of view will give you an idea of the best way to approach a situation.

Link children's behavior with their feelings. For instance, you might persuade children who hang back from activity to join by appealing to their need to belong. You might say, "We are having such fun, Elizabeth and Miguel. Will you join us?"

A child who interferes with another child's activities also needs some persuasion. You can persuade the interfering child by helping them understand the other child's feelings. For instance, you may say, "Kenny, Joanie is afraid that you will knock her building down if you keep jumping."

Redirecting

Children often need redirecting to a substitute activity. When **redirecting**, you divert, or turn, their attention in a different direction. One way to redirect is through distraction. A child who cries when a parent leaves the center may need a distraction. Choose an interesting toy or book to distract the child's interest away from the parent.

Redirection encourages children to express themselves in more socially acceptable ways. For example, an active child may constantly push other children. To help this child release energy, provide activities that are physically demanding. Playing with a punching bag, carpentry tools, or play dough will provide an outlet for extra energy. The key to redirecting is providing an appealing substitute.

Modeling

Children learn by imitating others. When they see others helping, sharing, and cooperating,

Ridofranz/iStock via Getty Images Plus

Figure 13.15 The teacher had to prompt and assist this child to wear a helmet. ***Why do children often need prompts?***

they are likely to act in these ways. Whenever you speak or move, you are **modeling** behavior. Modeling involves both verbal and nonverbal actions. It is a powerful tool when working with young children. At an early age, children realize the actions of the surrounding adults. Thus, it is important to set a good example. Social-emotional development is an important part of the early childhood curriculum. Much of what children learn results from watching others and imitating their behavior. Set an example by modeling prosocial behavior (**Figure 13.16**).

Listening

By listening to important people, such as teachers, children form beliefs about themselves. Listening involves giving children your full attention. Let them know you are there to listen and their ideas are important. As a result, your actions should make the child feel good. They may feel you like them and they are important. With time, your relationship will deepen. You will get to know the children better; likewise, they will get to know you better.

Listening is more effective when you are at eye level with the child. Nodding and letting the children talk without interruption conveys your attention. Educators call one type of listening **active listening**. Through active listening, you first listen to what the child is saying to you. Then you respond to the child by repeating what the child said. This lets the child know you have heard what they said and you accept it. It does not mean, however, that you solve the problem (**Figure 13.17**).

For instance, Salvatore was playing in the housekeeping area. He wanted to use the broom that Anna Maria was using. He asked Anna Maria, "May I have the broom?" Anna Maria responded, "No, I am using it. Besides, I had it first." Salvatore got angry. He ran over and shared the incident with the teacher's aide. The aide listened carefully to what Salvatore was saying. Then the aide repeated what Salvatore had just said to make sure she heard correctly. The aide said, "You are angry because Anna Maria will not let you use the broom." Salvatore was learning that people will listen to him and accept his

feelings; however, he needs to solve the problem himself.

Health Highlights

Signs of Unhealthy Self-Esteem

Self-esteem involves the feelings people have about their self-value. Patterns of healthy and unhealthy self-esteem can start when children are young. These healthy patterns will also impact how children perceive their accomplishments. Interactions with parents and teachers strongly influence children's self-esteem. Although self-esteem can vary as children grow, there are some signs that show unhealthy self-esteem even in young children. These often include

- resistance to trying new things;
- negative self-talk;
- hard to develop friendships;
- fear of failure;
- low tolerance for frustration;
- giving up easily; and
- lack of persistence.

Teachers and care providers can help promote healthy self-esteem in several ways. Providing a safe environment is top on the list. Being a positive role model and using positive self-talk is important. Giving positive affirmations honestly gives children a boost to their self-esteem.

Ignoring

Do not encourage inappropriate behavior. When a child can gain your attention by whining, crying, or throwing a tantrum, you have reinforced the child's behavior. The child will probably continue this behavior rather than control it.

If a child's inappropriate behavior is not dangerous, avoid giving the child attention. Do not look directly at the child. Avoid acknowledging the undesirable behavior. Educators call this *ignoring*. In contrast, praise children when they model acceptable behavior.

Ignoring is inappropriate when the child's behavior is harmful, either verbally or physically, to

Figure 13.16 Modeling is used in many situations at the center.

(characters) Colorfuel Studio/Shutterstock.com; (bicycle) NotionPic/Shutterstock.com;Goodheart-Willcox Publisher

Liderina/Shutterstock.com

Figure 13.17 Active listening is a nonverbal skill that helps children develop healthy self-esteem.

the child or others. Likewise, it is wrong to ignore a child who is damaging property. If you choose to ignore the behavior, tell the child what the behavior is that you are ignoring. Also, tell the child the behavior you desire. Then, do not look at the child. Be sure you do not acknowledge the behavior through your actions or words. When the child models acceptable behavior, praise him or her.

For example, Mrs. Garcia has noticed that whenever Miranda wants something, she whines and uses baby talk. Mrs. Garcia tells Miranda that she will not pay attention to her until she uses her "big girl" voice. Mrs. Garcia also shows Miranda what she means. Miranda continues to whine and use baby talk, so Mrs. Garcia ignores Miranda's requests. Eventually, Miranda sees there is nothing to gain and uses the appropriate words, and Mrs. Garcia responds to Miranda's request.

Changing a young child's behavior is usually not a quick process. The behavior may become worse before it improves! It is important to be patient. Unless you ignore unpleasant behavior 100 percent of the time, it is likely to reoccur.

Encouraging

Encouraging is a guidance technique that helps children believe in themselves. By *encouraging* children, you recognize their efforts and improvements. You may observe that successful teachers often use this technique. They want children to focus on their own work and feel good about themselves. The following are encouraging phrases you may use include

- You can do it all by yourself!
- You know how it works.
- I know you can fix it.
- You were able to do it last week.
- You must be pleased.
- I like the way you are listening.
- You remembered how to set the table.

13.2-2 Promoting a Positive Self-Concept

When guiding children's behavior, your actions should always promote a positive self-concept in each child. A child's self-concept includes the qualities the child believes they possess. It results from the beliefs, feelings, and perceptions a child has of themself (**Figure 13.18**). Children's self-concepts reflect the feelings others have for them and their confidence in themselves. A child's self-concept develops gradually and continues into adulthood.

During early childhood, another part of the self-concept emerges. This is *self-esteem*. Self-esteem involves making judgments about your worth and feelings. It answers the question "How worthy am I?" It is the belief that you are a worthwhile person.

Children's behavior mirrors their self-esteem. A child who lacks confidence may reveal feelings of inadequacy. For instance, the child may not be willing to try new activities. They may withdraw from an experience, show little curiosity, or appear overly anxious or overly dependent. This child may also be hostile, seek attention, or perform poorly.

Children with positive self-esteem perceive themselves as able and important. They accept and respect themselves as well as others. These children can often judge their own skills and cope with problems they confront. Typically, they are more objective and understand other people's behaviors.

You can promote or undermine a child's self-esteem through your words and actions. In many subtle ways, a teacher affects how children feel about themselves. Your reactions may give children the feeling that they are bad or annoying. For instance, you may need to ask children to be quiet. Consider the message the children will receive. If you ask them to be quiet because they are too noisy, they may feel they are bad people because they make too much noise. If you ask them to make less noise because it is disturbing you, the children see they can help you by being quiet. They do not feel they are bad, noisy people.

If a child spills juice, do you call the child clumsy or react negatively by scowling? Instead, do you accept this as typical behavior for a young child and help wipe up the spill? Caring adults can separate children's needs from their own. They can see the difference between their needs and the children's.

Every day you provide subtle messages in verbal and nonverbal feedback. These signals can either promote or decrease children's sense of self-esteem. You can make children feel appreciated, worthy, loved, and secure by being accepting, concerned, and respectful. Helping young children grow to respect themselves, as well as others, is difficult. Listen carefully to what you say and how you say it. Consider the impact your words have on the children. Watch the subtle ways you interact with them. Your message should always convey to children that they are important. Ask yourself the questions shown in **Figure 13.19**.

Children's behavior reflects their self-concept. Their self-concept is a reflection of their stress-coping abilities. Children who spend time with nurturing and supportive adults develop more effective coping skills. Gradually, the children learn their choices influence their lives. They also learn that all choices have consequences.

There are many ways you, as a teacher, can promote the development of positive self-esteem. You can plan activities that focus on making children feel good about themselves and their abilities. **Figure 13.20** describes several activities you can use to help children feel good about themselves. You can also provide children with experiences with which they will have success.

Waridsara_HappyChildren/Shutterstock.com

Figure 13.18 A child with healthy self-esteem is not afraid to explore different types of play. *How might you encourage a young child who appears to lack confidence?*

Teacher Checklist for Promoting Positive Self-Esteem

Questions	Yes	No
Do I observe children carefully before speaking?		
Do I consistently maintain limits to create a safe, predictable environment?		
Do I develop special ways of connecting with the children – smiling, winking, waving or thumbs up?		
Do I visit with families in their neighborhoods to learn more about their culture?		
Am I an open-minded person?		
Do I recognize and value differences in children?		
Do I constantly strive to gain more knowledge about the world and share it with the children?		
Do I provide the children with choices so they may become independent decision makers?		
Am I constantly trying to increase my human-relations skills?		
Do I state directions in a positive manner?		
Do I encourage parents to share their feelings, knowledge, and culture with me?		
Do I encourage children and families to share pictures of their cultural celebrations?		
Do I avoid showing favoritism?		
Do I listen to the children?		
Do I help children sort out their mixed emotions?		
Do I plan developmentally appropriate activities?		
Do I respect cultural differences in young children?		
Do I permit enough time to complete activities?		
Do I call attention to positive interactions between and among children?		
Do I make expectations clear?		
Do I acknowledge the child's attempts at tasks as well as accomplishments?		
Do I encourage children to use self-statements of confidence?		
Do I encourage children to share their emotions in positive ways?		
Do I use praise effectively?		
Do I constantly work on my implicit biases that impact children's behavior?		
Do I engage children in problem-solving to avoid and resolve conflict?		

Goodheart-Willcox Publisher

Figure 13.19 The teacher's behavior can promote or hinder the development of positive self-esteem. *Why do you think it is essential for teachers to continually analyze their actions and behaviors as they learn to guide children effectively?*

Building Positive Self-Esteem

After an outing, make an experience chart. Include children's names and their exact words.

Provide a special chair and crown for each child on his or her birthday. Take a digital photo of the child to share with families.

Record children's stories from circle time on a large piece of poster board titled Our News.

Make charts of children's likes. For example, you might chart children's favorite colors, animals, toys, foods, or activities.

Make charts of hair and eye color to reinforce concepts of similarities and differences among people.

Record children telling their own stories.

Make height and weight charts.

Add a full-length mirror to the room.

Label children's lockers and artwork with their names.

Make a mobile or bulletin board with the children's pictures or names.

Provide children with family face puppets of various cultures. Encourage children to act out imaginary family situations using the puppets.

Outline children's bodies on large sheets of paper for them to decorate and display.

Provide dramatic play kits to encourage children to try new roles and roles they find interesting. For example, a carpenter kit could include a hat, an apron, a hammer, nails, and boxes of wood scraps.

Display children's art work at their eye level.

Use children's names frequently in songs and games.

Introduce learning experiencs that are challenging but not too difficult, allowing the children to succeed.

Offer just enough assistance for success.

Use words and actions that show children you value them.

Goodheart-Willcox Publisher

Figure 13.20   These activities are quite useful for helping children build positive self-esteem. *Observe an early childhood classroom. How many of these activities (or similar activities) do you observe in this classroom? How do they appear to influence the children's behavior?*

Lesson 13.2 Review

1. Each of the following is an example of positive reinforcement *except* _____. (13.2.1)
   A. thanking a child for holding the door
   B. laughing at a child who is acting silly during group time
   C. praising a child for putting block away in the proper location
   D. praising children when they use such words as *please*, *thank you*, and *excuse me*

2. Consequences that an adult deliberately sets up to show what will happen if a child does not follow a limit are known as _____ consequences. (13.2.1)
   A. natural
   B. important
   C. logical
   D. acceptable

3. Each of the following is important to remember when praising children except _____. (13.2.2)
   A. give praise when parents or guardians are present to be most effective
   B. make praise age-appropriate
   C. always establish eye contact when praising children
   D. do not overuse praise because it will be ineffective if you do

4. Placing thoughts for consideration in children's minds is *called* _____. (13.2.2)
   A. prompting
   B. questioning
   C. suggesting
   D. persuading

5. Encouraging children to act or behave in a certain way by appealing to their basic wants and needs is *called* _____. (13.2.2)
   A. prompting
   B. questioning
   C. suggesting
   D. persuading

Chapter 13 Review and Assessment

Summary

Lesson 13.1

13.1-1 Guidance is a positive form of discipline, or training that helps children develop self-control.

13.1-1 Punishment is a form of discipline that does little to respect children and is a hurtful penalty for unacceptable behavior.

13.1-1 Effective guidance should maintain children's self-esteem and produce a desired change in behavior.

13.1-1 Self-regulation and self-control, which promote executive function, are the long-term goals of guidance. The children should learn to direct their own behavior without outside control.

13.1-2 Teachers need to address their implicit biases. Every teacher needs to examine their own biases and develop an understanding of other cultures. The children are watching, and you are teaching them social learning.

13.1-4 Child guidance may be direct or indirect.

13.1-4 Direct guidance involves physical and verbal actions. The direct guidance principles described in this chapter will help you guide children's behavior more effectively.

13.1-4 Indirect guidance involves outside factors that influence behavior.

13.1-4 Important factors that indirectly affect guidance are the physical layout of the classroom, an engaging curriculum, and a predictable daily schedule.

Lesson 13.2

13.2-1 Guidance techniques to promote a positive environment include positive reinforcement, natural consequences, warning, take-a-break, I-messages, praising, affirming, suggesting, prompting, persuading, redirecting, modeling, listening, ignoring, and encouraging.

13.2-1 Using positive reinforcement and other effective guidance techniques help shape children's behavior.

13.2-2 When teachers model appropriate behavior, love and respect children, and sincerely give constructive praise, children are more likely to repeat positive behaviors.

13.2-2 When guiding children's behavior, your actions should always promote positive self-esteem in each child.

13.2-2 A child's self-esteem includes the qualities the child believes they possess.

Vocabulary Activity

For each of the terms, draw a cartoon bubble to express the meaning of each term as it relates to the chapter.

Critical Thinking

1. **Evaluate.** Conduct a self-observation. Video record your interactions with children. First, listen to your interactions. Were they positive? Did you help the children in identifying and labeling positive behavior? Then review the video to evaluate how you demonstrated effective nonverbal communication skills.

2. **Create.** Write your own guidance policy. Contact local childcare centers to view their guidance policies before beginning the assignment. Ensure the policies include the qualities and behaviors that you are trying to establish that will model prosocial behaviors and strategies to handle inappropriate behaviors. Include a description of the difference between guidance techniques and abusive behaviors.

3. **Assess.** Observe a teacher interacting with children for one hour. Record all incidences of verbal guidance. Assess the verbal guidance. Was it positive or negative? How did the children respond to the guidance? Share your findings with the class.

4. **Create.** Search the online catalog for the National Association for the Education of Young Children for resources on guidance and discipline of young children. Create a bibliography listing these resources. Post your bibliography to the class website for peer and instructor review.

Core Skills

1. **Speech.** Practice verbal guidance techniques by showing a friend how to use a puzzle. Then discuss the effectiveness of your verbal guidance with your friend. What improvements might you make?

2. **Research and Writing.** Research the educational trend favoring open classrooms in the 1960s and 1970s. Write a report about the events or situations that led to encouraging this trend. Explain what an open classroom is and what it is not. Describe how this trend fell out of favor, but explain how some philosophies followed at the time remain in education today.

3. **Writing.** Write a short, reflective essay on your understanding of the role of guidance principles and techniques in managing children's behavior. Explain the concept of positive guidance. Describe your beliefs about the role it plays in helping children develop self-control, self-regulation, and manage emotions. Summarize your feelings about how learning these techniques will help you in your future career.

4. **Writing.** What makes an outstanding teacher? Think about the teacher who affected your life the most. Describe the teacher's skills in using guidance techniques?

5. **Reading.** Locate books written for children to help them deal with behavioral problems. Suggested books and authors may include: *We Don't Eat Our Classmates* by Ryan T. Higgins; *That's Mine!* by Michel Van Zeveren; *Theo's Mood* by Maryann Cocca-Leffler. A series of behavior books have been written by Elizabeth Verdick and Marieka Heinlen which include: *Feet Are Not for Kicking, Germs Are Not for Sharing, Hands Are not for Hitting, Teeth Are Not for Biting,* and *Words Are Not for Hurting* and *Goldilocks for Dinner* by Susan McElroy Montanari and Jake Parker. Discuss how reading a story about another child with problems may be an effective tool for helping children recognize their own difficulties.

6. **Writing and Speaking.** Using a digital tablet with recording capabilities or video recording equipment, create a short educational movie promoting the use of effective guidance techniques. Write a script that explains the techniques listed in the text and their effects on children. Record children and student teachers in the early childhood center interacting and demonstrating the various techniques. Use editing, writing, interviewing, organizational skills, and other skills in creating the video.

7. **CTE Career Readiness Practice.** Presume you are a teacher at a local preschool. Write an article for a parent newsletter explaining the strategies you will use in the classroom to help children become independent. Explain in your article why developing independence skills is essential for preschoolers. Offer suggestions on how parents can encourage children to practice these skills at home. Include examples of the tasks that preschoolers can perform by themselves.

Portfolio Project

Select one child in a childcare center, preschool, early learning program, or Head Start program. After gaining permission from the center director, write a brief profile of the child, focusing on the child's typical behavior and use of social skills in relationships with other children. Identify any guidance issues you have seen displayed by the child and describe any intervention used to handle these guidance issues.

If possible, interview the child's family to get additional insights into the child's behavior. File the writing example in your portfolio.

Chapter 14

Guidance Challenges

Lesson 14.1: Understanding Behavior Challenges

Lesson 14.2: Strategies for Handling Specific Behavior Challenges

Case Study

What Happened?

Valentine's Day was three weeks away, and it was always Ms. Wang's favorite holiday. So, she began introducing the holiday early. Today she had three different related activities for the children to choose from. They could prepare cards for a favorite person, decorate Valentine cookies, or decorate empty shoe boxes to be used as mailboxes.

Because the children were so engaged, Ms. Wang changed the schedule by eliminating outdoor play. The children continued working, and some went to a second Valentine related activity. But those children wanting to make Valentine mailboxes had to wait since that table only had two chairs. Then suddenly the noise level elevated and some children began running in the classroom.

Johnny, using a closed clinched fist, hit Hiram in the face. He was angry, as he wanted Hiram to finish his mailbox so he could take his chair. Hiram was crying, which immediately got Ms. Wang's attention. She rushed across the room with a stern look on her face. Then Ms. Wang picked up Johnny's hand and walked him to a chair in the back of the classroom. The chair had the words "Time-Out" stenciled on it. After this, she picked up a timer and set it for 15 minutes. Ms. Wang told Johnny that when the timer went off, he could get up, but he could not make a Valentine mailbox.

Give It Some Thought

1. Why do you think the children became overstimulated? If you were the teacher, what would you have done differently?
2. What is the purpose of classroom routines?
3. When does anger occur in children like Johnny? Did the teacher handle the incident appropriately? If not, what should she have done?
4. Do you think it is appropriate to punish the child by making him sit in a time-out chair for 15 minutes? Why or why not?
5. How far in advance is it appropriate to begin preparing for holidays with preschoolers?

Opening image credit: AleksandarGeorgiev/E+ via Getty Images

Essential Question

What do you need to understand about children's behavior challenges to best help them cope?

Learning Outcomes

After studying this lesson, you will be able to

14.1-1 identify situations and feelings that cause tension and challenging behaviors in children.

14.1-2 analyze the impact of stress on children's behavior, including teacher and family stressors, effects of stress, and signs of stress.

14.1-3 summarize ways to communicate with families about stress.

14.1-4 identify ways to help children cope with stress.

Key Terms

overstimulated	resilient
frustration	regression
onlookers	context
stress	

All behavior is goal-directed and purposeful. Four-year-old Emma is an example. She is tattling on the other children. After arriving at the center, she told the teacher that Toby had pushed her the day before. During snack time, she announced loudly that Luis did not take the muffin he touched. Later, during cleanup time, she told the teacher that Jafar did not put away his puzzle.

Hoa does not like to take a nap during naptime. He begins crying every day after lunch as naptime approaches. Yolanda, who is usually very cooperative, has been less so in the weeks following the birth of her new brother. Rather than taking turns, she has become bossy on the playground. The teacher has also seen her hitting other children.

During your teaching career, you will likely have several children in your classes who will model behavior like that of Emma, Hoa, and Yolanda. Many times, behavior problems will be disruptive to the class. The behavior may be harmful or it might infringe on the rights of others. Mishandling of classroom pets, equipment, and materials may also occur.

14.1-1 Tension and Challenging Behaviors

Children engage in challenging behaviors for a variety of reasons. *Tension* is often the cause of disruptive behavior. Overstimulation, changes in routine, long transitions, too many children in a group, insufficient space, and loud noise are just a few causes of tension in children. Because children do not know how to handle tension, they often react with disruptive behavior such as pushing and disturbing other children, running, and using loud voices (**Figure 14.1**). This behavior may be appropriate at home. They lack the skills in masking their feelings and expressing them in words.

Helping children deal positively with tension-causing events is a key role of the teacher. You will need to understand situations and feelings that cause tension in children. Recognizing behavior patterns that result from tension is also

Figure 14.1   Some children cry and withdraw from the group when they feel tension. *What is your role as a teacher in such situations?*

nimito/Shutterstock.com

Workplace Connections

Activity Survey

Conduct a survey of the early learning programs in your area to discover how they handle the period between Thanksgiving and New Year's Day. Ask if special activities, guests, or entertainments are planned that differ from the regular schedule.

1. Do children display more energetic or atypical behavior during these time periods, even if holiday events are not part of the program?
2. Do parochial and secular programs differ in their programs' focus during this holiday period?

important. Then you will need to help children deal with this tension. With this information, you will be able to effectively guide and help children grow and develop executive function skills.

Causes of Behavior Challenges

There are many causes of inappropriate behavior in children. These include certain stressors and frustrations that children do not know how to handle. In addition, there are physical problems that can cause tension in children. Children who have delayed executive-function skills can display challenging classroom behaviors. Awareness of situations and emotions that produce tension is important. This knowledge will allow you to avoid these causes, or reduce their effects.

Carefully observe the children. This is the best approach for preventing behavior problems. You will see the very earliest signs, which vary from child to child. Children fidget, cry, bite fingernails, clench their teeth, or even whine. When this happens, respond so their behavior does not escalate.

Overstimulation

Children can become overexcited, or **overstimulated**, by many things. For instance, simply playing with other children can

overstimulate some children (**Figure 14.2**). Usually, the larger the group of children, the greater the likelihood that overstimulation will occur. You may want to limit the number of children that are in a certain classroom area at any time. This will help prevent the chaos that occurs when a large group of children play together. For example, post a sign in the block-building area limiting the space to four children at any given time. Print the word and numeral. If you have dual-language learners in your classroom, print both in all languages. For younger children who do not read, make a simple

Gala Kovalchuk/Shutterstock.com

Figure 14.2   As the other children look on, the center director is carefully supervising the overstimulated child. *How can you help reduce the likelihood of children becoming overstimulated?*

sign showing four stick people. It will serve the same purpose. Post similar signs in other classroom areas.

Some children become overstimulated when there are program changes. Holidays, such as Halloween and Valentine's Day, can be overstimulating times for children. Avoid introducing holiday decorations and activities too early. When this happens, the children may get keyed up long before the event occurs. Likewise, some children become overstimulated if transitions between activities take too long.

Overstimulation can also result from having too many planned activities. When this happens, some children have a hard time making choices. Instead of staying with one activity, they run back and forth between several. Their activity and excitement, in turn, can affect others.

If a child is overstimulated, they need to calm down. Help them find a space where they can be alone and become calm. Then spend time with them until you feel they are no longer overstimulated.

Breaks in Routines

Routines are important to children. They create order and stability. Routines let children know what to expect and when. If a center or teacher does not follow routines, children become confused and behavior problems can arise. For instance, Jimmy takes a nap at 12:30 p.m. every day. If there are interruptions to the schedule, he may become overtired. This may result in disruptive behavior. If a child's family follows a different routine at home from that of the center, this can affect the child's behavior. Family members may experience behavior problems at home, because the child does not know what to expect next. In addition, you may see more behavior problems after weekends and holidays when the child readjusts after being away from the center for a few days. Talking with the family members about these problems may help them adjust their schedule to match the child's routine more closely at the center.

All children need consistent daily schedules. Active activities need to follow quiet activities (**Figure 14.3**). If children sit still too long, they

kali9/E+ via Getty Images

Figure 14.3 After a quiet activity, such as story time, children need periods of active free play.

may lose interest in the activity and become disruptive. Likewise, if children remain active too long, they may become overstimulated and disruptive. When changes in routine are necessary, such as a planned field trip, prepare the children ahead of time. Talk to them about what will happen. Also, explain to the children what your expectations are before, during, and after the trip.

Noise

Noise affects children differently than adults. Children are less likely to ignore irrelevant sounds. Noise-induced hearing loss in young children can harm their language acquisition, speech, and social interactions. It also affects their cognitive and social-emotional development. In particular, children with very sensitive ears are upset by noise. For example, these children will cover their ears or cry when a smoke alarm goes off. Likewise, if an ambulance drives by with its siren wailing, some children will cringe. While some children may try only to escape the noise, others may react to the stress by pushing or hitting others.

To avoid the problems caused by noise, control the volume of video, audio, and computer sounds. Be selective in choosing rattles, squeaky, and musical toys whose sounds are too loud. Noise can cause hearing loss. Also, pay attention to the volume of your own voice. In frustration, you may raise your voice or yell. Unfortunately, this causes a chain reaction. As the volume of your voice increases, the children's voices also become louder. This, in turn, will affect children who are sensitive to noise. The result will be chaos.

Waiting Time

Waiting time is difficult for young children. They are developing the ability to self-regulate, but often lack the ability to manage their impulses. Often, they begin leaving the group or behave poorly when they must wait for long stretches of time. By nature, they are usually in motion. Therefore, if children are waiting too long for a story, they may start pushing or hitting. This behavior is not the children's fault; however, it may gain the teacher's disapproval.

Be creative when lining up to go outside or to the lunchroom. Ask the children who are wearing a certain color to go first. You could also ask children who are wearing a certain type of shoes or those who have a particular color of hair or eyes to go first. This requires the children to listen and is a distraction from disruptive behavior.

Manage your time wisely. Cut down on waiting time by being prepared. If you are going to read a book for a large group, choose it in advance. Place it where it will be convenient. Likewise, prepare materials for all group activities in advance. If the children are actively involved in self-selected activities, it will reduce waiting time and resulting behavior problems.

Frustration

Children sometimes feel they are not in control. They feel defeat or discouragement by a problem that is too big for them. These feelings are called **frustration**. Most children go through peaks of frustration between the ages of one and three. Frustration causes tension in children (**Figure 14.4**). To control frustration, carefully plan each day's activities. The activities you choose should be developmentally appropriate. They

Workplace Connections

Activity Timing to Avoid Behavior Challenges

Conduct an experiment in an early childhood, childcare, or Head Start program to determine the optimum time that four-year-old children should spend on specific activities to avoid behavior challenges. An example may be to spend 20, 15, and 10 minutes respectively on different days on gross-motor, fine-motor, and circle-time activities.

1. How long should free play or discovery time activities be conducted?
2. What suggestions could you make for future scheduling?

should reflect the strengths, interests, abilities, and experiences of the children in the center.

Some children arrive at the center full of energy. These children need to be active. Provide wheeled toys, block-building materials, and woodworking activities for them. Other children prefer quiet activities, such as books, puzzles, stringing beads, or play dough. By observing the children in your program, you can provide the proper activities, materials, supplies, and equipment.

Juanmonino/iStock via Getty Images Plus

Figure 14.4 Being in control is important for young children. When they are not in control, they may become frustrated. *As a teacher, what actions can you take to help reduce frustration in children?*

Forcing children into activities they are not prepared to join or interested in can result in frustration. A better approach is to allow the children to choose.

Conflicts often arise over toys, which creates frustration. Therefore, make sure that several kinds of interesting toys are always available to children. Whenever possible, you should purchase several toys of the same kind. To prevent conflict, always buy more than one telephone, wagon, scooter, or car.

Select materials and equipment to match children's developmental level. This allows the children to feel successful and develop an "I can do it" attitude. Working with mixed-aged groups presents unique problems. Include open-ended materials such as blocks, Legos, play dough, and sand. Children of all ages will play with these, but in different ways (**Figure 14.5**). Provide puzzles, small manipulatives, and books for a range of abilities.

Acknowledge the child's feelings and try to help them find a solution. When necessary, redirect children to materials that match their abilities. Repeated failures will cause frustration, which may lead to angry tantrums. An angry child may pinch, hit, push, kick, bite, or destroy property.

As an adult, you may become frustrated. When this happens, try to relax. Carefully watch your words and actions. If the children sense you are upset, they, in turn, may become more upset. They need to feel that you are calm and in control.

Physical Problems

Poor health or other physical problems can cause tension and behavioral problems in children. One teacher, Mr. Lee, had such a problem in his center. During Liam's first day at the center, Mr. Lee and several other teachers

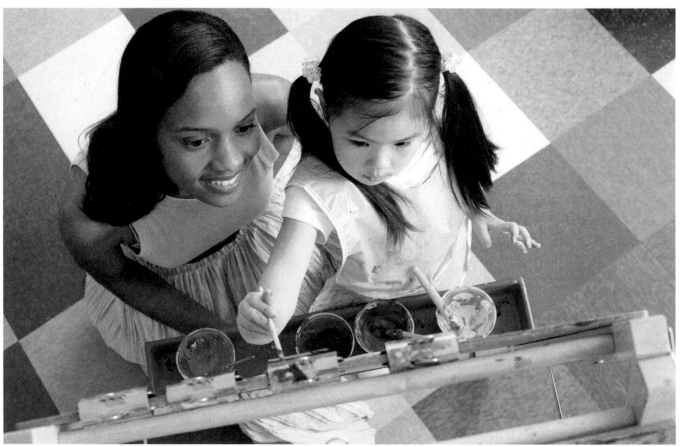

Juice Dash/Shutterstock.com

Figure 14.5   Paints are sensory materials that appeal to children of many ages. *Why do you think that painting and other activities help children deal with frustration?*

observed Liam. He ignored all directions and suggestions from Mr. Lee. Liam also appeared to have a high anxiety level.

Liam's behavior became a source of frustration for Mr. Lee. More than once, he wondered whether Liam should even be in the center. He feared that other children would copy Liam's behavior. Mr. Lee was also concerned about his ability to handle Liam's behavior. This concern continued for several weeks.

Mr. Lee finally decided to ask the center director to observe Liam's behavior. After observing Liam, the director determined a possible cause for Liam's problem. First, the director noted that Liam did not respond to many of the verbal requests made by Mr. Lee or other children. The director also noted that while interacting with others, Liam closely watched their faces when they spoke. The director suspected that Liam had hearing loss. For added information, the director then picked up two wooden blocks, stood behind Liam, and clapped them together as hard as she could. While several other children either jumped or turned to see what was happening, Liam did not respond.

Before sharing these observations with Liam's father, Mr. Lee repeated the clapping incident. Liam failed to respond. In addition, other staff members tried speaking to him when they were out of his field of vision. Again, each time he did not respond. At this point, the center director shared these observations with Liam's father. She encouraged Liam's father to have his hearing tested.

Luckily, for Liam, his father, the staff, and other children in the center, a hearing specialist was able to identify the cause of Liam's behavioral challenges. After having a hearing test, Liam received a hearing aid. His behavior improved dramatically. At the same time, his speech also improved.

Children may be overly active or tense due to other health problems (**Figure 14.6**). A child who is in constant pain due to a lack of dental or medical care may act inappropriately.

Medications can affect some children's behavior. Observe for symptoms such as dilated pupils, drowsiness, slurred speech, poor

MAOIKO/Shutterstock.com

Figure 14.6 Pain from this child's head injury may cause him to be tense and uncooperative. *What are other physical problems that may cause tension in children?*

coordination, and general irritability. In many states, parents are required to report to the staff when their children are on medication.

Prolonged or recurring illness or hospitalization can cause frequent absences from the center. When this occurs, some children are not able to maintain their friendships. Coming back to the center is difficult for them. This may cause some children to become **onlookers**. This means they watch others, but tend not to get involved. Other children may become aggressive. By acting out, they hope to gain the other children's attention. Onlookers and aggressive children need your help. Observe them carefully. Focus on their needs.

An onlooker needs to get involved. Encourage this child by suggesting activities to try. If the child does not respond, gently take the child by the hand, and walk them to an appealing activity. You may have to sit down and play with the child for a while; otherwise, involve other children in the activity.

Aggressive children need a calming influence. Direct these children to activities in which they can release energy. For instance, direct the aggressive child to woodworking, sculpting, or water play activities.

Poor or inadequate nutrition can also affect behavior. Millions of children rely on early childhood centers for regular meals. The lunch the center provides may be their healthiest meal of the day. Studies show that between one-fourth and one-third of preschool children do not receive the caloric intake recommended for them. Children who do not have the proper caloric intake or nutrients may be inattentive and sluggish. This may also affect their motor skills.

14.1-2 Stress and Behavior Challenges

Stress is the body's reaction to physical or emotional danger signals. It is a part of life. A stress reaction often takes the form of tension. Mild or occasional stress is not a problem. Constant stress, prolonged stress, or the piling up of many stressors, however, can threaten a child's ability to cope. Chronic stress has biological consequences. It creates the dysregulation of the immune system. This undermines healthy development by increasing the child's vulnerability to infections and chronic illnesses. It can affect the way a child thinks, feels, and acts, and it can be present in any setting where a child needs to adapt and change.

The early childhood years lay the foundations for life. Early in life, children watch how their parents, peers, siblings, grandparents, and teachers cope with stress. Children learn their responses to stress from these adults. As a result, children vary widely in how they handle stress. Children who learn negative-coping skills may become more prone to stress. They may become illness-prone, withdrawn, anxious, aggressive, or angry. In contrast, some children learn positive-coping strategies, which become lifelong resources. These children are **resilient**—they bounce back quickly from stress.

Both negative and positive events can cause stress. One negative event that can cause stress in children is a change in family structure due to divorce. Even the most amicable divorce is a major stressor for young children because it disrupts family stability. Other negative stressors include abuse, neglect, rejection, separation, fights, and food insecurity. Death or illness of a family member and living in an unsafe home or neighborhood are also negative stressors. Positive events that can cause stress may include a new activity, parties, vacations, overnight visits with friends or relatives, the birth of a sibling, or a new pet.

Starting preschool, childcare, or Head Start, or changing to a new early childhood program

Safety First

Policy on Aggressive Behavior

Aggressive, disturbing behavior in children happens in early childhood settings. Even with the most careful planning, children sometimes act out. As an extension of the written discipline policy, a facility should include procedures to follow when an act of aggression occurs. The policy procedures may include training staff in the following strategies:

- redirecting children to more acceptable behavior;
- caring for children who experience the aggressive acts from other children;
- avoiding guidance techniques that reward children who act aggressively;
- ensuring the safety of other children;
- redirecting children to a "safe place" if they are unable to control actions;

- communicating regularly with parents to discuss guidance at home and center;
- providing children who act out a quiet place;
- notifying parents of all children involved, especially if another child or staff member was hurt or bitten;
- completing a behavior incident report if the act caused an injury requiring first aid or other medical attention;
- reviewing staff-to-child ratios to determine if enough staff was present to prevent the act; and
- examining the room arrangement and activity plans to avoid potential sources of conflict.

can be stressful for some children. In many early learning centers, children also move among different classrooms as they get older. Adjusting to new teachers, playmates, and surroundings can take time. Learning a new routine can also cause tension. This stress should subside as the child adjusts to the new center or classroom. Helping children feel safe and welcome is the most helpful way to ease this discomfort.

In poor-quality programs, however, the stress continues. Programs with low adult-child ratios and large group sizes cannot adequately meet children's needs. Adults in these programs often lack the necessary time to nurture each child's development. These programs often lack enough toys, materials, and equipment for the number of children enrolled. The facilities may be inadequate in other ways, too.

Teacher Stressors

Like children and their families, teachers also experience stress. This is particularly true when the ratio of children to adults is high. Teachers may experience burnout, emotional exhaustion, depression, and physical illnesses. Studies show these factors can affect teacher-child interactions, which can increase behavioral challenges. Most teachers claim behavioral issues in the classroom affect their job satisfaction.

Family Stressors

As the primary social unit, the family can serve as a buffer from stress. It can also be a source of many stressors in a child's life. The influences of family can be positive or negative, depending on the family dynamics. Family harmony is important for the health of all the members. Stress within the family disrupts this harmony and affects all family members, including young children. Stress can also strain family relationships, which children can sense.

Family crises cause major stress within a family. See **Figure 14.7** for a list of family stressors. What other factors can you identify? In any of these situations, disruptions in daily family life will occur, at least for a time. Resulting changes in routine can upset infants as well as older children. These children lose a sense

Possible Family Stressors

- Birth or adoption of a sibling; blended families
- Marriage, separation, divorce, or remarriage of parents or guardians
- Custody, visitation, or child support issues
- Stay-at-home parent or guardian entering the workforce
- Family member moving into or out of the home
- Chronic illness or injury of family member
- Serious illness of self or family member
- Death of a friend, family member, or pet
- Moving to a new home and/or city
- Military deployment of a parent
- Friend or extended family member(s) moving away
- Parent or guardian loss of employment
- Financial or legal problems in the family
- Substance abuse or addiction of a family member
- Exposure to violence (unsafe neighborhood)
- Relationship problems
- Incarceration of a family member
- Becoming homeless
- Arguing, fighting, or violence among family members
- Abuse or neglect of self or family member
- Emotional problems—depression, low self-esteem, anxiety, anger, or guilt

Goodheart-Willcox Publisher

Figure 14.7 Family stressors will cause disruptions in daily family life. *Why do you think handling family stressors is difficult for young children?*

of predictability and security when they do not know what to expect next. This can cause children to become irritable, have problems eating and sleeping, and become clingy or demanding. These are normal responses to stress.

In some families, the stressor is a temporary condition. For example, the loss of a parent's job may be short-lived as the parent seeks a new job. With other stressors, family life may change permanently, such as with a death or divorce. Extra support from teachers, friends, extended family, and the community may be necessary to cope with a permanent stressor.

Constant activity from morning to night causes another, less intense type of stress. In a family with this schedule, as parents and older siblings rush to meet their obligations they may overlook a young child's needs. Both children and adults need time to unwind and be together as a family. Family time and relaxation help people ward off the harmful effects of stress.

Handling family stressors of any type is difficult for young children. The intensity of a child's reaction will depend on how threatening the stressor is to them. Children feel worse if they believe they are the cause of a divorce, separation, death, or other family crisis. Feeling their behavior caused the problem leads children to feel guilty. Explaining that is the problem is not a child's fault can be helpful.

Effects of Stress

Prolonged stress in early childhood can undermine healthy brain development. Children depend on their environment for experiences that will promote optimal brain development and resiliency. Stimulation from caregivers and teachers also influences the wiring of the brain. That is why consistent, predictable, warm, loving, and responsive care is necessary.

Good beginnings can last a lifetime. Healthy relationships promote brain growth and healthy social attachment. A strong, secure attachment to a nurturing caregiver or teacher appears to provide a protective biological structure. It buffers children from the effects of stress. Studies show that children with strong, secure attachments have fewer behavioral problems when confronted with stress throughout life.

Signs of Stress

Stressful situations vary in duration and severity. These situations raise the body's anxiety levels. Stress can lead to biological, emotional, behavioral, and mental consequences. Severe stress negatively affects children's ability to control and focus their own thinking. Early childhood teachers have the responsibility of making stress manageable for children.

The disruption of family stability is often visible in the children's behavior. A frequent sign of stress is regression. **Regression** is showing behaviors that were typical at earlier stages of development. Toileting accidents and thumb-sucking are examples. A child who has used the toilet successfully for some time may begin to have accidents. They also may begin wetting during naptime. Additionally, a child who had given up thumb-sucking might revert to self-soothing with this habit.

In addition to regression, many other behavior changes can indicate stress in children. Awareness of the common signs of stress listed in **Figure 14.8** is also helpful. Sometimes, however, these behaviors can be unrelated to stress. Knowing the typical behavior of each child in your class will help you note these behavior changes.

14.1-3 Communicating with Families About Stress

A partnership with families is important to support children's development. Two-way communication between teachers and families is vital. Teachers should realize the important role families play in children's lives and vice versa. Before addressing challenging behaviors, the teacher must establish a trusting relationship with parents or guardians.

Create a positive environment for engagement. Build on the family's strengths. Let the parents or guardians know they are "welcome" and take time to get to know them. Greet them at the door with a smile and warm

Possible Signs of Stress in Young Children

Physical Signs		Emotional Signs	
• Accident proneness	• Hair twirling	• Anger	• Irritability
• Bed-wetting	• Headaches	• Anxiety	• Poor judgement
• Biting	• Hitting	• Baby talk	• Nightmares
• Clinging to parent/ guardian or teacher	• Kicking	• Crying spells	• Pounding heart
• Eating too much or too little	• Indigestion	• Detachment	• Screaming
	• Nose picking	• Excessive aggressiveness or laziness	• Stuttering
• Fingernail biting	• Prone to illness		• Tattling
• Frequent colds and infections	• Respiratory tract illness	• Inability to focus	• Temper tantrum
		• Inconsolable	• Whining
• Grinding teeth	• Stomachache	• Insomnia	
	• Thumb-sucking		

Goodheart-Willcox Publisher

Figure 14.8 Knowing typical behaviors of each child in your care can help you identify when behaviors are a sign of stress.

welcome. Likewise, at the end of the day, do the same and share something special their child did that day. If you listen to what they have to say, family members will respond more positively to a conversation and provide you with more information. Parents or guardians feel validated when you communicate effectively. To communicate with parents:

- choose words the parents or guardians will understand;
- speak softly and slowly;
- be attentive by looking the parents or guardians in the eye and giving them your full attention;
- invite the parents or guardians to share their perception of the child's behavior;
- listen carefully; and
- thank the parents or guardians for the information and encourage them to keep you informed of any behavioral changes.

You will need to learn the **context** in which each child develops. This includes the family's culture, language, structure, customs, beliefs, environment, and preferences for their child. Before enrolling the child, meet with the parents or guardians. Discuss your expectations and ask them to share theirs. After this initial meeting, continue working on building a relationship. Be available. Take advantage of daily arrival and departure time. Welcome them by smiling and addressing them by name. Send notes home to the family. Share advances in the child's development and interests.

Families have a responsibility to support children through times of stress and crisis. Children depend on and turn to family members (especially parents or guardians) to protect them from the effects of stress. Parents or guardians can often provide the comfort children need to overcome stress. By their example, they teach children how to cope with stress and handle problems.

As a teacher, you can help children handle stress when you are aware of family situations that could affect the child's behavior. Ask parents or guardians to keep you informed of any major family events, such as births and deaths. Events that change the structure of the family are also important, such as marriage, separation, divorce, or a death in the family. Children need the loving support of family and teachers through these times of adjustment.

If a child's behavior changes suddenly, share with the family any signs of stress you observe. Ask what they think might be causing the stress. Work with family members to plan ways to help the child and address the troubling behavior. As with other guidance issues, children benefit the most when there is a consistency of guidance between parents or guardians and teachers.

Recognize, however, that crises in the family will affect parents, too. During a divorce, for example, children are not the only ones hurting. Parents or guardians suffer the loss as well. While your focus is on helping the children, you want to approach this task in the most sensitive and relevant way. Listen to the parents or guardians and offer kind words to let them know you understand that they must be hurting. If family members seem open to suggestions, you may be able to refer them to community resources that can help.

14.1-4 Helping Children Cope

Stress affects children as much or more than it affects adults. Unlike adults, however, children lack the skills to understand and handle the pressures. As a teacher, you can help children develop positive responses to stress.

When you note changes in children's behavior, observe them more carefully. Calmly accept the children's behavior, if possible. (Of course, hurtful, or unsafe behavior is an exception to this. You must be gentle but firm to stop these behaviors.) Criticizing children for their response to stress only leads them to feel more stress. For example, scolding children for thumb-sucking in response to stress may make them feel badly about themselves. Talk to the children about their feelings. Reassure the children that you care about them. Offer comfort, warmth, and encouragement.

Human love is the best therapy. Your relationship with children is powerful. Provide a supportive, affectionate, and consistent environment. Be a role model. Smile, hug, and

Health Highlights

Helping Children Cope with Trauma

When traumatic events threaten their safety, young children may feel the effects strongly. Physical, psychological, and sexual abuse may be intentional. Natural disasters, wars, or accidents can also cause stress.

Along with parents or guardians, teachers and care providers are among the most important adults in helping children recover from natural disasters and other traumatic events. Empathetic teachers and care providers are crucial in providing a safe, stable environment. A sense of safety and belonging contributes to the ability of children to cope with trauma.

According to the US Department of Education, teachers and care providers can help children cope with trauma in the following ways:

- make the child feel welcomed and supported;
- show you care by reassuring children that they will be okay;
- show empathy for what children are going through and take time to listen to them;
- help children feel welcome if they have been displaced from their homes; and
- provide a variety of ways for children to express their reactions to disasters and tell their stories of survival. Using the creative arts often helps students express emotions.

For more information about ways to help children cope with trauma, visit the website for *The National Child Traumatic Stress Network (NCTSN)*. Other organizations that include helpful resources are the *National Association for the Education of Young Children (NAEYC)* and the *National Association of School Psychologists*.

touch. Children exhibit less stress when teachers are attentive (**Figure 14.9**). Observe carefully and really listen to the children. Talk with them

Krakenimages.com/Shutterstock.com

Figure 14.9 Children are better able to handle stress when their teachers care about them enough to listen attentively. *What actions can you take to show children that you care?*

about their feelings. Help them recognize, label, and clarify their feelings. Teach children coping behaviors. Use effective praise and acknowledge the children's actions, feelings, and progress. Correct any misconceptions children have about themselves or their feelings to help children see themselves as positive, worthwhile people.

It is important to praise children for their efforts rather than their outcomes. If you do, they are more likely to stick with a task. This will help them understand that everyone makes mistakes. Furthermore, they will maintain a steady sense of self-esteem.

Lesson 14.1 Review

1. Which of the following is *not* a reason why children react disruptively then they experience tension? (14.1.1)
   A. Children do not know how to handle tension.
   B. There are too few children in a group.
   C. They lack skills in masking their feelings.
   D. They lack skills in expressing their feelings with words.

2. Each of the following is an event that causes tension in children *except* _____. (14.1.1)
   A. overstimulation
   B. changes in routines
   C. using quiet voices
   D. long transitions

3. What is stress? (14.1.2)
   A. Dysregulation of the immune system
   B. The body's reaction to physical or emotional danger signals
   C. Vulnerability to infections and chronic illnesses
   D. Negative coping skills

4. Prolonged effects of stress _____. (14.1.2)
   A. promote brain growth
   B. promote healthy social attachment
   C. undermine healthy brain development
   D. buffer children from the effects of stress

5. Which of the following is *not* an effective way to discuss stress with families? (14.1.3)
   A. Choose words the parents or guardians will understand.
   B. Speak softly and slowly.
   C. Listen carefully.
   D. Confront them about their lack of proper guidance skills.

6. Each of the following is a step you can take to help a child deal with stress *except* _____. (14.1.4)
   A. praise children for the outcomes of a task rather than their efforts
   B. provide a supportive, affectionate, and consistent environment
   C. use effective praise and acknowledge children's actions, feelings, and progress
   D. praise children for their efforts with a task rather than their outcomes

Essential Question

What actions can you take to effectively guide children who have challenging behaviors?

Learning Outcomes

After studying this lesson, you will be able to

14.2-1 describe specific behavior challenges and strategies for handling challenges in the early childhood classroom, including negativism, stealing, temper tantrums and anger, biting, tattling, body exploration, thumb-sucking, and fear and anxiety.

Key Terms

negativism   mirror language

Teachers of young children will face specific behavior challenges. They must provide a warm supportive environment and be intentional role models. Teachers should provide children with developmentally appropriate feedback on their behavior and with reminders that relate to classroom rules for safety and respect. In a caring way, teachers must help children to identify their strong emotions and an awareness of other's perspectives. This takes time and practice. During the process, children need to develop self-reflection skills. Often the teacher will use questions related to their behavior beginning with the words *how, what* or *why* as successful teaching strategies. The ultimate goal is for the children to learn to control and regulate their own behavior.

14.1-1 Specific Behavior Challenges

Young children often behave in a socially unacceptable way when they are tense. Negativism, defiance, theft, anger, biting, lying, name-calling, exploration of the body, thumb-sucking, and fear are all possible reactions to tension. These reactions remind us that children are people, too. You must deal with and guide their behavior, just as you would an adult.

Negativism

Negativism among preschool children is typical, particularly between two and three years of age (**Figure 14.10**). Children of this age may oppose every request you make—a typical characteristic of negativism. At this age, they

Seahorse Photo in BKK/Shutterstock.com

Figure 14.10 Young children may resist your requests to end their free play. *Why is it not uncommon for children to oppose teacher requests?*

want to become more independent. A "no" in many cases is a child's attempt at independence. For instance, you may say, "Pick up the block." The child might look at you and say "No."

Accept a young child's negative behavior; however, keep in mind all health and safety regulations. For example, children must wash their hands before eating. If a child refuses to do this, take the child by the hand and walk the child to the sink. Tell the child "You need to wash your hands." Let the child know, through your voice and body language, that you expect cooperation.

A negative child cannot be hurried. If hurried, opposition will be stronger. Given time, most children outgrow this stage of development.

Workplace Connections

Handling Negative Behavior

Imagine that a child in your care refuses to pick up blocks or put away toys. Consider whether you would allow the blocks or toys to remain out on the floor or table, or encourage other children to clean up for this child.

1. What are some possible solutions for handling this negative behavior?
2. Would there be any consequences for the child's negative behavior?

Stealing

Preschool children do not understand the difference between *mine* and *yours*. When children under three years of age take something, they are not stealing. At this age, children do not understand the concept of stealing. Before considering the needs of others, preschoolers attempt to meet their own needs. The desire for something appealing may combine with a young child's natural impulsiveness. As a result, they may take items that do not belong to them.

Small objects, such as toy cars and puzzle pieces, may vanish from the classroom. When you notice these items missing, warn the other teachers. Ask them to observe the children closely.

Strategies for Handling Stealing

Help children learn to respect the possessions of others. If you see a child take something, do not ask why they stole it. Likewise, do not lecture about stealing. Instead, make the child return it. Otherwise, the child may keep taking things from others. Remember that preschoolers do not understand ownership.

A helpful way to teach children about ownership is to respect their property rights. For example, before trying Jodi's new puzzle, encourage children to ask her permission to use it. If you see another child looking at Jodi's toy, say, "Why don't you ask Jodi if you can use it?"

Strategies for Minimizing Stealing

You should also try to minimize opportunities for stealing. When children bring toys or other items from home, problems can occur. If the center policy allows children to bring toys to the center, there need to be clear rules. It is best for children to leave their toys in their cubbies and only take them out for naptime or show-and-tell. To avoid potential problems, many centers have a policy stating that children should not bring toys from home.

Temper Tantrums and Anger

A child's temper tantrums can have a variety of triggers. Tantrums may occur when the child is tired, hungry, overstimulated, ill, or when the child wants something. The greatest number of tantrums typically occurs at about 18 months of age. After this age, there is a sharp decline. Age also affects how a child will project anger. Young children often use their whole bodies to express anger. By age two, children may hold their breath for as long as they can. Screaming, kicking, hitting, pounding, and hitting their head against a wall are other ways children may express anger. By the age of three, verbal conflict is more common among children, while four-year-olds often engage in name-calling.

Identify the Source of Anger

Anger usually draws attention to something that annoys the young child. For instance, children may become angry when other children push or hit, someone takes something that belongs to them, they feel rejected, or they experience teasing and other verbal conflict. When anger occurs, you need to help the child learn to deal with it. Identifying the cause can help you use strategies to guide children effectively.

Strategies for Dealing with Anger

When children display anger, begin by discouraging behavior that hurts. Teachers and care providers should not allow children to hit each other, although children may still try. When they do, safety should always be the first concern. Stop them immediately. Say, "I am sorry, but Antonio does not like that." At the same time, you might have to hold the child's hand or arm. The child may try to hit you. Stop that action also. For older preschoolers, you may also use comments. For example, you may say, "You are usually kind. We cannot treat our friends this way." When young children are upset, they need help calming down.

Ignoring outbursts is also a successful technique when dealing with an angry child. Of course, ignore these behaviors only if there is no threat to the health and safety of other children. If children can get attention or gain control through outbursts, they will keep using this behavior. For example, if Marina cries and yells for another cookie and then receives one, she will cry and yell again. In contrast, if she does not receive the cookie, she will learn that her outburst is unacceptable.

The children need to express their feelings and assert their rights in socially acceptable ways. You can redirect anger. Tell the child it is okay to feel this way and encourage the use of words. Use **mirror language,** which helps children feel accepted and understood. Whenever possible, use the child's own words. If the child has not spoken, reflect on their emotions. For example, you could say, "Frankie, you are feeling really angry right now."

Children can release anger through activities such as finger painting, modeling with clay, punching a punching bag, hammering, and playing at the sensory table (**Figure 14.11**). All these activities involve use of children's hands,

Julie Senkevich/Shutterstock.com

Figure 14.11 Children can release energy through physical activity. *What physical activities might you provide for children to help them positively cope with anger?*

arms, and legs. They will redirect their anger and energy into physical movements. Remember to have enough supplies and equipment for these activities. Use a minimum of rules.

Surprisingly, noise can also help relieve aggression. Yelling, beating drums, dancing to loud music, crying, and making animal noises can all help children relieve stress and anger. Remember, however, that noise can be catching. If several children make too much noise, the rest of the group may also become noisy.

Whenever possible, catch children before they react angrily. For instance, if you see that Camilla is going to kick over Mateo's blocks, stop her. Then say, "Camilla would you like it if Mateo knocked over your blocks?" A question like this will force Camilla to think about what she was going to do.

Biting

Biting is quite common in young children. Babies and toddlers may bite when they are teething. Young children often bite when they are feeling frustrated or angry. This behavior is not unusual with two-year-olds. For many children, biting is only a temporary problem. Biting usually peaks just before children can use words. Children may bite because they cannot express themselves using words. For them, biting is a form of body language. Typically, property is the main source of conflicts that result in biting.

Early Childhood Insight

Helping Children Manage Anger

Helping children learn to manage anger is a challenge in the early childhood setting. Children are learning about their world and have limited language skills. Once you identify why children are angry, you can take steps to help them manage their anger. Early childhood teachers and care providers should:

- provide a stable, secure environment;
- tell them it is okay to feel angry;
- help children label and understand their angry feelings;
- explain emotions and encourage children to talk about anger-inducing situations;
- use stories to help children learn to understand and self-manage their anger; and
- avoid labeling or blaming a child.

Biting can be a reason for a class meeting. For instance, Molly Crown called a class meeting in her classroom at group time. She said, "We have a problem in our classroom. We cannot bite our friends. Biting hurts. When you think someone is going to bite, hold up your hands and say *stop*."

Molly's meeting was successful. Whenever a child held up their hands and said "stop," the impulse of the child to bite was broken. It also signaled to the teacher that there was a potential problem.

Strategies for Handling Biting

Early childhood teachers and caregivers are responsible for the safety of all children. Because biting is a typical behavior often seen in children under three years of age, you need to help the children who bite and protect other children from getting bitten. Start by keeping playtime simple for children who are likely to bite. Limit the number of playmates they may have at any time. Large groups often create stressful situations; biters become anxious and then bite. If there is a second adult, separate the larger group into two smaller ones.

You need to respond quickly to prevent children from hurting each other. Remove the biter to make the child who is the target of the biting feel safe. Place the biter in a quiet place for a couple of minutes. Isolation of a biter sometimes helps to curb this habit. When the child bites another, say, "No biting. Biting hurts. Paula does not like that." Then say, "I can't let you bite Paula or anyone else so you must sit over here." Make the child sit for a few minutes, but no longer. Then, remind the child that biting is not allowed and allow the child to return to the play area.

Do not forget the child who was the target of the biting. This child also needs to feel secure. To provide security, observe constantly. Never allow a child to bite back. Always reinforce the biting rule. Biting back does not prevent biting—it only creates behavior that is more aggressive by modeling the behavior you want to extinguish.

Continued observation of a child who does the biting is important. Observe them to find out what triggers the behavior. It might be when the room is noisy. Sometimes it occurs when another child takes a toy from them.

Tattling Versus Telling

Tattling seems to occur in many classrooms and is a typical behavior for many young children. Frequently, the child who tattles is insecure and tattles to get your attention. As a teacher, you may find tattling irritating, but you need to listen to the children. You want the children to be aware that classroom limits are important. Tell the children that they do not need to let you know each time another child misbehaves.

In contrast, *telling* is informing the teacher of dangerous situations. For example, a child may tell the teacher that another child has fallen off the bicycle, has a nosebleed, or is crying. Likewise, a child could tell the teacher that another child is struggling with zipping their coat and needs help.

Strategies for Handling Tattling

To prevent tattling, try to build children's self-esteem. This, in turn, will make them feel more secure. For a child who is insecure, stay close while supervising. Knowing that a caring adult is nearby is helpful.

Try to have a daily one-to-one time for listening and talking with each child. This may be during free play or small-group time. During this time, provide the child feedback by recognizing their positive qualities. To illustrate, you may say, "Sharice, I like the way you help Marco" or "Eileen, Journey enjoys having you help with the puzzle." Positive reinforcement will help prevent the children's need to tattle.

Ignore tattling behavior, if possible. If Jared tattles to you that Abbas has taken his scissors, comment by saying, "You need to tell Abbas to return your scissors." This encourages Jared to speak to the child who has misbehaved. Likewise, if Christopher tattles that Haven has taken his bicycle, encourage problem-solving. Say, "Haven has taken your bike. What should you do?" (**Figure 14.12**). If Blair always talks about other children, set a limit by saying, "I enjoy talking with you, but we shouldn't talk about others."

Exploring the Body

Children begin to explore their bodies early in life. It is common for one-year-olds to explore their genitals during diaper changing. As children begin to gain control of their body functions, interest in the genital area grows. By age three, children are aware of sex differences. By age four, children who must use the restroom may hold the genital area. When this occurs, remind the children to use the restroom. By five years of age, children may begin to manipulate their genitals. Some children may rub their genitals to reduce irritation caused by tight clothing.

Strategies for Handling Body Exploration

Exploration of the body is normal behavior in development; however, it is not socially acceptable to engage in such behavior in public. Therefore, it is important to guide children away from public display of body exploration.

ampak/iStock via Getty Images Plus

Figure 14.12   To help prevent tattling, encourage children to problem solve with each other.

During naptime, you might see children touching themselves. When this occurs, never shame or threaten the child. Whenever possible, remember to use a positive approach when guiding young children. You can do this by firmly telling a child privately that this behavior is impolite in public.

Thumb-Sucking

Like adults, children feel certain tensions. To relieve the tension, some children may suck their thumbs. There usually are patterns. Children may suck their thumbs when they are tired, bored, anxious, angry, or sad. Babies are born with a need to suck for self-soothing. Studies show that almost half of all infants suck their fingers or thumbs. By 18 months, thumb-sucking usually reaches its peak. Then the behavior becomes less frequent, especially during the day. By four or five years of age, peer pressure at school may stop the habit. Children of this age will sometimes engage in thumb-sucking if they are tired, so they may continue sucking their thumbs before going to bed. Moreover, children may revert to thumb-sucking if they feel anxious or stressed.

Many parents or guardians are concerned about thumb-sucking. Encourage them to accept this behavior as a normal stage of growth for preschool children. Most children outgrow thumb-sucking. The American Dental Association (ADA) claims most children will stop thumb-sucking between the ages of two and four. They recommend avoiding putting pressure on the child since it can have the opposite effect. Long-term thumb-sucking is problematic, especially beyond the age of six. It can change the size and shape of a child's palate. This disrupts the growth of their mouth and alignment of permanent teeth.

Strategies for Handling Thumb-Sucking

Supplying a pacifier is a way to satisfy an infant's urge to suck. One advantage of a pacifier is that it does not place pressure on the roof of the mouth or the jaw. When they are ready, most children give up their pacifiers. In fact, some children may have an intense sucking need for only the first few months of life. When children stop using their pacifiers, parents or guardians and caregivers can take them away permanently. If a child reverts to sucking fingers or thumbs, however, return the pacifier.

If you notice thumb-sucking, do not pull the thumb out of the child's mouth. This guidance may not be successful. In some cases, it might cause anxiety that increases the child's thumb-sucking. During the first three years, the harder you try to stop thumb-sucking, the stronger it becomes. Instead, accept and ignore the behavior. In this way, children will usually stop thumb-sucking between four and five years of age.

Attending an early learning program may help curb thumb-sucking for some children. At the center, the child will find many new interests and friends. As a result, you may not notice thumb-sucking. Many times, children will only suck their thumbs when they lie down for naps or are tired.

Fear and Anxiety

All children experience fear and anxiety. It is a normal part of growing up. Infants have stranger anxiety. They will recognize a familiar face, but are fearful of a new face. Toddlers have separation anxiety. When a parent or guardian leaves them at the center, they will cling and cry. By three years of age, most children have many kinds of fear. Some fears will be real while others will be imaginary. As children grow, they keep their real fears but outgrow their imaginary fears.

Common childhood fears include falling from high places, putting faces in water, loud thunder, heights, the dark, people in uniforms, fire engines, ambulances, dogs and big animals, and getting shots. Fear of the unknown is also common in young children. You may see this fear on the first day of school. Children may cry, cling, and refuse to leave their parents or guardians. As the teacher, be prepared for this fear. Inform family members in advance that this is a common fear.

Strategies for Handling Fear

Understanding children's fear is important in guiding young children (**Figure 14.13**). Fear of the dark is quite common among young children.

andresr/E+ via Getty Images

Figure 14.13 Teachers need to be prepared for fears on field trips that may be caused by unfamiliar sights or sounds. *What preparations could you make?*

You may notice this fear at naptime or when showing a video. Understand that this behavior is due to unfamiliar surroundings. These children cannot sleep or concentrate on videos. Instead, they may focus on scary images formed by the shadows in the darkened room. Help these children by keeping a small night-light turned on during these times. Then the room will not be very dark. Also, allow children to keep a familiar stuffed toy or blanket near them for comfort.

Accept children's fears. For young children, even the silliest fear is real. When a fire engine passes the playground and a child cries, give the child immediate attention. The child needs to feel safe. You may wish to hold the child's hand, kneel and put your arm around the child's shoulders, or hold the child on your lap. When you do this, you are meeting the child's immediate need of protection. After the crisis passes, talk to the child about the fear.

Children may need to act out situations to conquer their fears (**Figure 14.14**). For instance, Devan's grandmother died in the hospital. When Devan came back to the center, he asked two other children to play hospital with him. Devan played the role of a doctor while one

friend played the nurse. This was Devan's way of handling the fear he felt when his grandmother died at the hospital.

Talking with children can also help them control fear. For example, Mark visited his cousin Dakota. After returning to school, Mark told his teachers that the house had ghosts. As a result, Mark said that he was never returning. Mark's teacher was observant, and talked to Mark about

fizkes/Shutterstock.com

Figure 14.14 Playing hospital helps many children deal with their fears of hospitals and doctors.

his visit with Dakota. The teacher explained that sleeping in strange places is often frightening because it is new.

Sidney was afraid of the new bunny. Fortunately, the teacher was understanding. He helped Sidney face her fear by introducing the bunny in gradual steps. First, the teacher asked Sidney to place a carrot in the cage. Then he encouraged Sidney to watch the bunny eat. The next day the teacher encouraged Sidney to touch the bunny's fur. Sidney continued this for about one week. Her teacher did not rush Sidney. Finally, the teacher asked Sidney if she wanted to hold the bunny. Sidney said *yes*. Sidney's teacher carefully and slowly took the rabbit from the cage and placed it on Sidney's lap.

When children feel unsafe or strange, they may reject a person or situation. For example, a child may greet a new aide with "Go away, I hate you." If this happens, do not scold the child. Telling the child that they like the aide will not help either. Instead, accept the child's feelings. You may say, "Miss Brown is our new teacher. When you get to know her, you will learn to like her."

Children will sometimes hit others when they are afraid. For instance, a resource person visited a group of four-year-olds. This person brought a large snake to show the children. When Ariel saw the snake, she began to act aggressively. She hit Charlie and Morgan. The teacher then stepped in and explained to Ariel that her friends might be frightened, too. She then explained to Ariel that this type of snake was not dangerous. There was no need to fear it and hitting is never an acceptable behavior.

Lesson 14.2 Review

1. What will happen if you hurry a negative child? (14.2.1)
   A. The child will comply with your request.
   B. The child's opposition will be stronger.
   C. The child will become more independent.
   D. The child will cooperate with all directions.
2. Each of the following is a strategy for handling stealing and helping children to respect the possessions of others *except* _____. (14.2.1)
   A. make children return stolen objects instead of lecturing
   B. minimize opportunities for stealing
   C. teach children about ownership by respecting their property rights
   D. if you see a child take something, ask them why they stole it
3. Which of the following is *not* an effective strategy for dealing with children's tantrums and anger? (14.2.1)
   A. Tell children it is not okay to feel angry.
   B. Discourage a behavior that hurts others.
   C. Ignore outbursts when there is no threat to health and safety of others.
   D. Help children label and understand their angry feelings.
4. Steps teachers can take to help children manage their behavior include each of the following *except* _____. (14.2.1)
   A. providing a stable, secure environment
   B. explaining emotions and encouraging children to talk about anger-inducing situations
   C. using stories to help children learn to understand and self-manage their anger
   D. telling children that it is not okay to feel angry
5. Each of the following is an effective strategy for handling biting *except* _____. (14.2.1)
   A. keeping playtime simple
   B. expanding the number of playmates
   C. dividing children into smaller play groups
   D. isolating children who bite from others for a few minutes

Summary

Lesson 14.1

14.1-1 As a teacher of young children, at times you will be challenged while guiding the children. Your goal is to guide children so they learn appropriate social-emotional skills.

14.1-1 Common causes of tension challenges include overstimulation, changes in routine, too many children in a group, crowded surroundings, and loud noise.

14.1-1 Frustration and physical problems can also cause guidance challenges.

14.1-2 Knowing how stress affects young children is essential.

14.1-2 Stress can have many causes, including changes or problems within the family.

14.1-2 Young children do not know how to handle stress well. As a result, they most often express stress through their behavior, which is a form of communication.

14.1-3 If adults see a child shows signs of stress or anxiety, they can offer the help the child needs. Although family events can be a source of stress, families can also serve as a buffer for children during times of stress.

14.1-3 Teachers can also experience stress, which can impact the quality of your interactions with young children.

14.1-3 Your role as a teacher will be to help children and families deal positively with tension-causing events. Knowing more about common family stressors and signs of stress will help.

14.1-4 You can help by modeling coping skills and providing an extra measure of comfort and reassurance for the child.

Lesson 14.2

14.2.1 You will face other challenging behaviors in the classroom, including negativism, stealing, anger, biting, exploring the body, tattling, thumb-sucking, and fear.

14.2.1 Handling each of these challenging behaviors requires guidance skills and techniques that are unique to each situation.

14.2.1 As a teacher, you will need to create ways to guide children as they learn skills for appropriate behavior.

Vocabulary Activity

Individually or with a partner, create a T-chart on a sheet of paper and list each of the terms in the left column. In the right column, list an *antonym* (a word of opposite meaning) for each term in the left column.

Critical Thinking

1. **Create.** Prepare a checklist of ways to avoid overstimulation of children.
2. **Cause-and-Effect.** Create teacher strategies for reducing waiting time during transitions.
3. **Analyze.** Search online for guidance tips and resources related to the guidance challenges described in this chapter. Analyze the tips and resources for their potential effectiveness. Choose two tips and explain how you might implement them in an early childhood classroom
4. **Draw Conclusions.** Visit an early childhood center. Observe the children behavior for any signs of stress. Describe the signs you see. Draw conclusions about the teacher's response to the children's stress. Discuss your findings when you return to class.

5. **Evaluate.** Locate children's books that deal with typical situations that may cause a child stress. After reading a story to the children, ask the children how they would feel in a similar situation. Did the children respond as you thought? Why or why not? How was the story helpful for the children? Some suggested books are: *Theo's Mood; Finding Kindness; A Boy and a Bear; When I Feel Angry; The Very Angry Day That Amy Didn't Have; The Berenstain Bears and Mama's New Job; Good Night Gorilla;* and *I Like Myself* among others.

Core Skills

1. **Speaking.** Interview four parents or guardians to learn what problems they have guiding their children. How do they cope with their guidance challenges?

2. **Writing.** Research common fears among children and compose a report that summarizes your findings. Post your findings to the class website for peer and teacher review.

3. **Writing.** Pair up with another student to write a possible dialogue between a teacher and a parent or guardian to show how you would handle communicating with parents about a child's stressful behavior. Your instructor will assign specific scenarios, such as aggressive behavior related to a divorce; regressive behavior related to a new baby; or anxiety and fearfulness related to a family member's serious illness and hospitalization. Role-play the dialogue for the rest of the class.

4. **Speaking.** Interview the health instructor to discover how the subject of students' health challenges is treated. What strategies or precautions are taught to students to help them avoid health risks? How is the subject of blood-borne pathogens approached?

5. **Research and Writing.** Conduct online research for information on the effects of family stress on preschoolers. Research answers to the following questions: What stressful life events in a family most affect children? How do children typically manage these events? What are the effects of family stress on a child's behavior and on academic performance? How can a preschool teacher use this information to help a child deal with stress? Write a summary of your findings.

6. **Listening.** Interview an early learning teacher about their experience dealing with one of the specific problem behaviors covered in this chapter. Ask the teacher to describe the behavior and to explain how they recognized it. How did the teacher handle the problem? What strategies did they use? Looking back, would the teacher have handled anything about the situation differently? After the interview, compare notes with a classmate. Discuss the two experiences you heard about.

7. **CTE Career Readiness Practice.** Imagine that you work in an early childhood center. Emery, one of the children, arrives at class sullen and withdrawn. Emery refuses to hang up his coat and join other children in a parachute activity, and will not come to the circle for story time. Emery responds with "no" to any suggestions made by the teachers and will not even participate in snack time. List the steps you would take in analyzing Emery's behavior and determining a solution to the problem.

Portfolio Project

Write a brief article for a guidance advice column in the parent newsletter. Choose a topic such as handling fears, biting, or tattling. Use your digital device and a language-translation app to convert the file to another language. File a copy of your printed articles in your portfolio.

Establishing Classroom Limits

Lesson 15.1: Understanding Limits

Lesson 15.2: Putting Limits into Action

Case Study

Establishing Limits: The Power of Prevention?

Kai Wang and Zara Yang, college friends and recent graduates, were hired as co-teachers for a new preschool classroom opening in a San Francisco suburb. On their first day of preparation, they brainstormed a to-do list. It included everything they needed to complete prior to the opening of the school year the following Monday. After their brainstorming session, Kai and Zara agreed to prioritize the tasks on their list. After reviewing each item, Kai and Zara agreed establishing classroom limits is the top priority.

Kai and Zara discussed what they had learned in their Child Guidance class at the university. Both agreed that limits were powerful influences on the social climate of the classroom. Children feel safer when they know what their teachers and care providers expect of them. To be effective, limits need to be short, clear, and positively stated as well as culturally and developmentally appropriate. Their professor also emphasized the necessity of stating limits positively, and that they should tell the child what to do, rather than what not to do. Limits impact the social climate and learning environment of the classroom. Knowing expectations helps children feel safer.

Give It Some Thought

1. Do you think establishing limits is as important as Kai and Zara? Explain.
2. Do you agree with Kai and Zara's professor that limits should be short and positively stated? Why or why not?
3. What limits would you have for the cooking area? Block-building area? Art area?
4. How could limits help prevent challenging behavior? Explain.

Opening image credit: Africa Studio/Shutterstock.com

Lesson 15.1 — Understanding Limits

Essential Question

What do you need to know about establishing and enforcing classroom limits to protect children's health and safety?

Learning Outcomes

After studying this lesson, you will be able to

15.1-1 **summarize** the reasons for establishing classroom limits.

15.1-2 **list** guidelines for establishing classroom limits.

15.1-3 **describe** methods for enforcing limits.

Key Terms

limits   flexible limits

consistency

Limits are guides to actions and behaviors that are necessary for children in early childhood settings. Sometimes they are called rules. Limits promote safety, respect, responsibility, and self-discipline. In early childhood programs, clear and reasonable limits serve as a shorthand to state the center's goals. Limits should focus on actions and behaviors that reflect goals. As a teacher, you will have input in suggesting limits for the center.

Every area of the classroom will need to have limits. As the classroom teacher, it is your responsibility to explain and enforce limits. You will need to explain these limits at the children's level of understanding. The staff and children should know the reasons for the limits, and each adult working in the classroom should understand and enforce them. The limits should also be posted in the teachers' lounge and the classrooms.

15.1-1 Establishing Limits

There are three reasons for establishing classroom limits. First, according to the law, the center must protect the children's health and safety. Limits are boundaries that a teacher establishes to help the children learn respect for others and develop self-regulation. Limits help make the classroom a safe place for the children. Second, children feel free to explore when they know their teacher will stop them if they go too far (**Figure 15.1**). Thus, they feel protected from mistakes. Finally, limits help children develop self-control. As children learn to accept and obey limits, they gradually come to learn that limits are part of life. One of the center's goals should be to develop socially responsible behavior in young children. Establishing limits will help the center reach this goal.

Workplace Connections

Communicating Limits to Families

Brainstorm ways to communicate to families the limits their child will have to follow while attending an early childhood education program. Plan a parent meeting or orientation session that focuses on limits.

1. How can family members become part of the process of communicating and enforcing limits with their preschool children?
2. Should children be exposed to the limits all at once or gradually? Are there any exceptions?

lisegagne/E+ via Getty Images

Figure 15.1 Enforcing limits about the use of safety equipment allows this child to explore a woodworking project more freely. ***Why do you think it is important for children to have the freedom to explore within protective boundaries?***

15.1-2 Guidelines for Setting Limits

When setting limits for children, make the limits short and positive. Focus on positive behaviors and avoid attention to negatives ones. Use familiar language and short, simple sentences the children can understand. You and the children need to have the same understanding of what the limit means. Be sure the words you use describe the exact behavior you desire. Children are often confused by such general words as *be nice, stop it,* or *behave*. These words can have many meanings and do not say precisely what you want. State the limits in terms of the positive behavior you expect.

Set limits that are reasonable and developmentally appropriate. This means that children can act. Limits should serve a useful purpose. Give children specific reasons for each limit. If you cannot think of a reason for having a limit, rethink it. Try to determine whether your expectations are really that important. Unreasonable limits can cause young children to feel angry.

Avoid making too many limits. Having a few well-established limits is better for the children and you. If you have too many limits, the children will forget them. You, too, may have trouble remembering and enforcing them.

Define both acceptable and unacceptable behavior. Decide how to deal with unacceptable behavior. Usually, the best approach is to stop such action firmly and quickly; however, you may find that the child will become angry (**Figure 15.2**). This anger may show in several ways. The child may resist the set limit, cry, yell, or stare at you.

The entire staff regularly will need to reexamine the classroom limits. Children's behavior will change as they grow and develop. Therefore, limits should change as the children

globalmoments/iStock via Getty Images Plus

Figure 15.2 Undesirable behavior should be stopped, even if the child becomes upset. *How might you handle this situation when the child becomes upset?*

change. The entire staff must discuss any limit changes. Discuss what changes are necessary and why. If you determine that a limit no longer fits the group's needs, discard it.

Limit changes also require discussion with the children who are preschool age or older. When an issue arises, invite the children to discuss the problem. They need to be accountable to their peers. Begin by stating the issue. Then ask the children to think of ways of solving it. During the discussion, encourage the children to state the limits positively. Write out each new limit, calling attention to the printed words. If there are dual-language learners, also write the limit in their language.

15.1-3 Enforcing Limits

Children follow limits best when teachers enforce the limits with **consistency**. This means that the consequence of the limit is the same every time. Consistency helps children know what you expect of them; however, children will often test these well-established limits. You should feel comfortable with this testing process. At the same time, you should also maintain your position. Do not be afraid or back down. For

example, if you said each child may do only one painting, make sure no child paints two. Friendly reminders may also be helpful, such as "When you are finished, Shandrel wants a turn to paint a picture."

Enforcing limits also requires that limits be flexible. **Flexible limits** allow you to adapt to the needs of an individual or situation. For instance, your limit states that children must wear smocks in the art area. If an art activity is not messy, you might be flexible about this limit and allow the children to work without a smock. Your limits must be flexible enough to handle such situations, although you might want to share the reason for relaxing the limit (**Figure 15.3**).

The way you react to children who break limits affects children's feelings of security. Children feel secure knowing the limits protect them; however, when one child violates a limit, this may threaten another child's security. For instance, a child may express their anger violently, such as by hitting or kicking. That child is violating a limit. You must tell the child that hitting is wrong. The child who was hit is also affected and has lost some security. You need to reassure and pay attention to this child. Giving attention to the injured child shows that hitting is not a good way to gain attention.

UW-Stout Child and Family Study Center

Figure 15.3 Limits may need to be adapted to an individual child's needs or situation. In this center, the teacher has tied the scissors to the table so children cannot walk away with them. *Give an example of when a limit might need to be adapted.*

Lesson 15.1 Review

1. Each of the following is an important reason for having limits in an early learning center *except* _____. (15.1.1)
   A. Limits promote safety, respect, responsibility, and self-discipline.
   B. Limits are only essential in certain areas of the early learning center.
   C. Limits that are clear and reasonable support the goals of the center.
   D. Limits should focus on actions and behaviors that reflect goals.

2. Which of the following is *not* a reason for establishing classroom limits? (15.1.2)
   A. Centers must protect children's health and safety according to law.
   B. Limits help children to feel free to explore, knowing teachers protect them from mistakes.
   C. Limits are boundaries that teachers develop for their own peace of mind.
   D. Limits help children learn respect for others and develop self-regulation.

3. Each of the following is a guideline for setting limits for children *except* _____. (15.1.2)
   A. Define only acceptable limits, so children do not forget them.
   B. Set limits that are reasonable and developmentally appropriate.
   C. Make limits short and positive.
   D. Avoid making too many limits.

4. Consistency with reinforcing limits is important for each of the following *except* _____. (15.1.3)
   A. consistency helps children know what you expect of them
   B. consistency keeps children from testing the limits
   C. consistency means the consequence of a limit is the same every time
   D. children follow limits best when teachers enforce them with consistency

5. Each of the following describes flexible limits *except* _____. (15.1.3)
   A. flexible limits allow you to adapt to the needs of an individual
   B. flexible limits allow you to adapt to the needs of a situation
   C. enforcing limits requires that limits be flexible
   D. flexible limits allow for inconsistency

Essential Question

How can you differentiate among important limits, communicate them to children, and evaluate whether established limits require changes?

Learning Outcomes

After studying this lesson, you will be able to

15.2-1 **differentiate** among useful limits for various classroom areas and activities.

15.2-2 **summarize** ways to communicate limits.

15.2-3 **analyze** ways that teachers and care providers should evaluate limits.

Key Terms

sensory table   pre-reading skills

Just telling the children something is not teaching them. Early childhood teachers must be role models and display consistent behavior. Their goal is to guide and teach young children to identify and develop positive behaviors. Young children need to learn to control their emotional impulses, direct their behavior, and respect others. During this process, they need to know what to expect and develop confidence in their ability to meet these expectations. Opportunities need to be available in the program to practice these skills continuously.

Limits are essential in providing children with a sense of security. They communicate expectations of desirable behavior and define unacceptable behaviors by establishing boundaries. Limits must be equitable and fair, promoting the children's safety and respect for each other and the classroom environment. They must be for specific classroom areas and activities. Limits must also be developmentally appropriate and stated in words that are understandable to the children.

15.2-1 Limits for Specific Areas and Activities

The limits you set may differ greatly from those set at another center. This is because no two centers are alike. Equipment, facilities, and staff vary among centers. Similar activities take place at many centers, however, regardless of location. For instance, science, math, dramatic play, cooking, block-building, and reading occur at most centers. You can use general guidelines for some of these areas and activities.

Sensory Play

In some classrooms, sensory play is a daily activity. Many centers use a **sensory table** to hold a variety of items for this activity. During a typical week, the center may use ice cubes, snow, colored water, or soapy water in the sensory table. Pebbles, shells, small stones, dirt, and sand are other options for use in the sensory table.

Depending on the material in use, the limits may change somewhat. For instance, a child would not need to wear a smock for protection when playing with dry sand; however, the smock may be necessary with ice cubes, snow, or water. Be sure to wipe up all spills immediately to prevent slips and falls.

Limits for sensory play might include

- Wear smocks for all wet or messy activities **(Figure 15.4)**.

MartinPrescott/E+ via Getty Images

Figure 15.4 Wearing smocks during messy activities will keep children clean and dry.

- Wipe up splashes and spills immediately.
- Keep sensory materials inside the table.

Early childhood centers do not allow eating or throwing sensory materials, but you must positively state this limit positively. If a child does not follow the limit, they must face the consequences. For example, you might say, "Jacques, I cannot let you throw sand. It could get in someone's eyes and hurt them. If you choose to throw sand, you have to stop playing here." If Jacques keeps throwing sand, stop his play immediately and offer him a choice between more acceptable activities.

Safety First

Safety Sense for Sensory Tables

Sensory tables can provide much enjoyment to toddlers and preschoolers. They can present some safety concerns, however. The two biggest concerns are choking hazards and bacterial contamination. Ensure that all items you put in the sensory table are large enough not to cause choking. When children are through playing, make sure they wash their hands. Then clean all washable items in water with mild soap. Be sure to clean and sanitize all parts of the sensory table as well.

Dramatic Play

Dramatic play is sometimes referred to as imaginative or pretend play. Provide materials in this center that promote curiosity and expand the children's vocabulary and language development. The setting should be nonsexist and multicultural. It should also reflect all children and be arranged to accommodate children with diverse needs. Participation in dramatic play helps children better understand themselves and others around them. It also allows children to express and work out their feelings. To provide the children with the least restrictive environment, limits can include

- Respect the participation of others.
- Wipe up all spilled water.
- Put materials away correctly after use.
- Be a good friend to everyone.

Small Manipulative Activities

This area of the classroom contains games and small objects. Children learn to build, compare, sort, arrange, and match with these materials. Such materials can also help children achieve mastery with color, number, size, and shape concepts. As children use small manipulatives, they also develop fine-motor, hand-eye coordination, and math skills.

Usually, there are few limits in this area. Suggested limits include the following:

- Return toys to their assigned place on the shelf after use.
- Keep games and puzzle pieces in the classroom area (**Figure 15.5**).
- Take turns or share materials.

Cooking

Children learn about food by participating in cooking activities. Cooking allows children to feel a sense of accomplishment. Tasting, smelling, touching, listening, and seeing help build language, number, sequence, and physics concepts.

FatCamera/E+ via Getty Images

Figure 15.5 The limit that small manipulatives cannot leave the designated classroom area makes cleanup much simpler. *What might you say to two children who are arguing about small manipulatives they both want to play with at the same time? Discuss your thoughts with the class.*

You must address the limits concerning health and safety precautions. Therefore, the following limits are a requirement:

- Wash hands before cooking.
- Wear an apron or smock.
- Wipe up spills immediately.
- Only teachers pick up hot cooking utensils, pots, pans, or foods.
- Everyone assists with cleanup.
- Eat prepared foods only during lunch or snack time.

Early Childhood Insight 🅰🅱🅲

Cooking-Area Limits

Supervision is a requirement during all cooking activities. Whenever electrical appliances are in use, *never* leave the activity area! If you need more supplies, signal for another teacher or care provider to get them for you. Always use pot holders and hot pads with cooking appliances. Only teachers should pick up hot foods or cooking utensils, pots, and pans.

Block Building

Block building encourages children to be productive and creative. It also provides children

with a way to release energy. The children's safety is essential in this area, and close supervision is always a requirement. Limits must stress safety. Because of this need, building activities should occur only during a set time period.

Limits for block-building activities might include

- Use blocks for building only.
- Keep blocks in the block-building area.
- Touch only your own building projects unless you ask permission.
- Return blocks to the storage shelves after use.

Music

All children enjoy music. It is a universal language. By participating in music activities, children can develop self-expression, listening, language, and coordination skills. Music, like other activities, needs specific limits that promote safety, respect, and responsibility. Limits for the music area include

- Select the rhythm instruments you want to use.
- Use musical instruments only for creating sounds.
- Return rhythm instruments to their assigned places on the shelves after use.

Art

For children, art is usually a pleasurable activity. Therefore, they generally spend much time playing in this area. During the self-selected activity period, art occurs almost daily in most centers.

Encourage children in the art area to explore materials. Avoid telling them what to make, and do not compare their artwork with others. Most centers use only the following limits:

- Wear smocks for messy activities.
- Wipe up spills immediately to prevent slips and falls.
- Return art materials to the shelf after use.
- Work only with your own materials (**Figure 15.6**).

MBI/Shutterstock.com

Figure 15.6 Children can only paint on their own paper during art.

Book Corner

In the book corner, children can develop *pre-reading skills* and motivation to become readers. **Pre-reading skills** include letter knowledge, concepts of print, phonological awareness, and language skills. Encourage children to explore the books in this area. They will learn about themselves, their family, culture, and community. They will also learn about other cultures. Limits for the book corner might include

- Handle books gently.
- Turn one page at a time.
- Give torn books to the teacher for repair.
- Return books to the shelf after use. (**Figure 15.7**).

To encourage the children to explore, rotate books regularly. Some teachers rotate books on a weekly basis, leaving several favorites to carry over. Control the number of books available at any given time. When too many books are in the area, it can become cluttered. Likewise, a child may have difficulty locating a favorite book.

MBI/Shutterstock.com

Figure 15.7 Children need to learn to wait their turn during a group story time. ***How can you encourage children to take turns during group story time?***

Science

All children need science activities. These activities encourage them to discover their environment. As they observe and question, they will see relationships and make conclusions.

Science activities require careful planning. Include a variety of classroom and outdoor activities. Emphasize hands-on activities that allow children time to explore their surroundings (**Figure 15.8**). Encourage the children to participate by observing, touching, and questioning during these activities.

As a teacher, you will need to demonstrate some of the limits in this area. For example, you will need to show the children how to hold a bunny, water a plant, or feed classroom pets. You will also need to demonstrate the equipment used for the children. You may even have children assist with cleaning the animal's housing.

Limits for the science area might include the following:

- Feed pets and water plants only with a teacher's supervision.
- Handle pets with care.
- Wash hands after touching pets, feeding, or cleaning cages.
- Keep science equipment in the area.

Nadya Chetah/Shutterstock.com

Figure 15.8   Hands-on activities encourage children to become involved in the world around them. *What are some examples of hands-on activities you might offer children to explore music, science, art, and books?*

Playground Activity

On the playground, children can express themselves in creative ways. They can build ships, houses, forts, and other objects with wooden crates, cardboard boxes, and other materials. Through play, children develop motor-coordination skills, social skills, a sense of cooperation, and self-regulation skills.

The primary concern of the teacher is the children's safety. Limits must be set and enforced if children are to play happily and safely on the playground. These limits will vary, depending on the equipment and the children's abilities.

Wheeled Toys

Tricycles, bicycles, scooters, wagons, and other wheeled toys can pose dangers with improper use. For this reason, safety limits are a requirement regarding the use of these toys. These limits include

- Always wear proper safety gear when riding (**Figure 15.9**).
- Each wheeled toy can only have one rider at a time.
- Sit on the seat to ride.
- Ride only on the wheeled toy path.
- Watch for other riders or walkers.

Swings

Swings are not available on all playgrounds because they require constant teacher supervision. If swings are available, specific limits must include

- Only one child is on a swing at a time.
- Sit in the center of the swing.
- Use both hands to hold on.
- Stay on the swing until it has stopped.
- Only teachers push children on swings.
- Keep clear of moving swings.

Slides

Slides are a source of hazard for young children. Accidents happen when children bump into each other. Injuries happen when children teach children how to correctly and safely use the jungle gym. Include the following limits for jungle gym use:

- Use both hands to hold on.
- Make sure you do not step on another child when climbing.
- Only four or five children may use the jungle gym at a time.

Sandboxes

Sand play appeals to young children. When not in use, keep the sandbox covered to repel cats, pigeons, spiders, ants, and other insects. Rake the sandbox to remove any debris such as fallen leaves. After being wet, the sand must be thoroughly dry before covering it to prevent the growth of bacteria. If the children play in a sandbox with contaminated sand and then place their hands in their mouths, they could develop pinworms. As a result, set these limits:

- Sand and sand toys stay in the sandbox.
- Touch only your own sand structure unless you ask permission.
- Report seeing insects and animal feces in the sandbox to the teachers.
- Wash hands after playing in the sand.

15.2-2 Communicating Limits

What method can you use to communicate limits to young children? As you have already read, limits need to be short, simple, and reasonable. Some teachers make this task easier by first dividing their limits into three categories. These categories include

1. Be safe.
2. Be kind and respectful.
3. Be neat and responsible.

When reminding children about certain limits, the teachers begin by using one of the three categories. **Figure 15.10** shows examples of this method.

US-Stout Child and Family Study Center

Figure 15.9 When riding wheeled toys, helmets are a must. *What other safety issues should you enforce with children regarding riding wheeled toys?*

stand up as they go down the slide, or when they slide headfirst. For these reasons, many center playgrounds do not have slides. Programs that have slides need to set these limits:

- Only use the steps to climb to the top of a slide.
- Use both hands when climbing up the steps.
- Wait until the person in front of you is off the slide before you slide down.
- Slide down sitting up and feet first.
- Get off the slide as soon as you get to the bottom.

Jungle Gyms

Jungle gyms are very appealing to young children. Since children are adventurous, any activity on this equipment requires careful supervision. Teachers and care providers must

Communicating Limits to Children

Category	Examples
Be safe!	• Use both hands to hang on to the swing. • Sit at the table while using scissors.
Be kind and respectful!	• Say please when you want something. • Say thank you when someone helps you. • Hold the door for others.
Be neat and responsible!	• Hang your jacket in the locker. • Wear your smock while painting.

Figure 15.10 Some teachers make the task of writing limits easier by dividing them into three categories.

15.2-3 Evaluating Limits

Classroom limits *are* essential. They help centers comply with state licensing rules and regulations. Limits help show respect for the rights of others. Boundaries are necessary to keep children safe and to promote the children's health. Staff need to evaluate individual classroom limits by asking themselves the following questions:

• Is the limit necessary?
• Does the limit respect the rights of individual children?
• Does the limit support the children's safety or health?
• Does the limit support the children's development?
• Does the limit support the children's learning?
• Do the children and staff know and follow the limit?

If the answer is *no* to any of these questions, the staff and center director need to evaluate the limit. Sometimes, stating limits in simpler terms is necessary, so the children understand them. At other times, the limits are no longer necessary. Additionally, you may need to introduce new limits to promote respect and support the children's learning and development.

Ethical Responsibilities

Building Trust and Respect

In one of its *Core Values*, NAEYC states that members "Recognize that children and adults achieve their full potential in the context of relationships that are based on trust and respect." In this chapter, you have learned how early childhood professions are responsible for setting limits that are essential in helping children build trust and respect. Additionally, early childhood professionals must work to build trust and respect with family members and their coworkers.

Dig Deeper

What does trust and respect mean to you? Explore actions you can take to build relationships on a foundation of trust and respect. What strategies might you use to build trust and respect with parents or guardians and coworkers? Write a reflective paper on strategies you might use to personally build trust and respect with others.

Lesson 15.2 Review

1. When may limits change for sensory play? (15.1.1)
   A. Limits may vary depending on state law.
   B. Limits may change when children are too noisy.
   C. Limits may change depending on the materials in use.
   D. Limits may change when children break the rules.

2. What types of materials should be provided in the small manipulative activity area? (15.1.1)
   A. Materials that help children learn to build, compare, sort, arrange, and match.
   B. Materials that promote curiosity and conversation.
   C. Materials that require children to use math skills.
   D. Materials that require children to use pre-reading skills.

3. Each of the following is a suggested limit for children's small manipulative activities except _____. (15.2.2)
   A. return toys to their assigned place on the shelf after use
   B. take turns or share materials
   C. keep games any puzzle pieces in the small manipulative area
   D. wear a smock for all messy or wet activities

4. Which of the following is *not* a health and safety precaution that is important for children's cooking activities? (15.2.2)
   A. Only teachers clean up.
   B. Wash your hands before cooking.
   C. Wear an apron or smock.
   D. Wipe up spills immediately.

5. Which of the following is *not* a category of limits to use when communicating with children? (15.2.2)
   A. Be safe.
   B. Be good.
   C. Be kind and respectful.
   D. Be neat and responsible.

6. Each of the following is a reason for evaluating classroom limits *except* _____. (15.2.3)
   A. limits help centers comply with state licensing rules and regulations
   B. limits are necessary to keep children safe and to promote the children's health
   C. limits show respect for the rights of teachers
   D. limits show respect for the rights of others

Chapter 15 Review and Assessment

Summary

Lesson 15.1

15.1-1 Limits focus on actions and behaviors that reflect the goals of the center.

15.1-1 Limits promote safety, respect, responsibility, and self-discipline.

15.1-1 Both the staff and children should also know the reasons for the limits.

15.1-2 Limits must be made for all classroom areas and activities.

15.1-2 Limits may need to be flexible to adapt to the needs of an individual or situation.

15.1-2 It is important that all staff members have input into setting limits.

15.1-3 Limits that are consistently enforced and fair help create a relaxed center atmosphere at the center.

15.1-3 As a classroom teacher, it is your responsibility to explain and enforce limits.

Lesson 15.2

15.2-1 Limits are essential in all areas of the classroom.

15.2-2 Limits may vary and change depending on children's developmental level.

15.2-2 Teachers and care providers need to explain limits at the children's level of understanding.

15.2-2 Dividing limits into three categories—be safe, be kind and respectful, and be neat and responsible—can make it easier for children and teachers to remember the limits.

15.2-3 Teachers and care providers should review limits regularly and revise as necessary.

Vocabulary Activity

On a separate sheet of paper, list words that relate to each of the Key Terms. Then, work with a partner to explain how these words are related.

Critical Thinking

1. **Make Inferences.** Children need rules to be enforced consistently. At the same time, they also need flexible limits. Working with a partner, discuss the difference between a flexible limit and a limit that is enforced inconsistently. Give two examples of each. Afterward, share your examples with the class.

2. **Analyze.** Discuss and analyze ways in which limits may change as children grow. Give some specific examples.

3. **Determine.** Role-play the following scenes that might occur in early childhood programs. Determine how you would respond as an early childhood teacher.
   A. Toby is in the book corner. While looking at a book, she accidentally tears a page.
   B. Damarion goes down the slide. When he reaches the bottom, he continues to sit there.
   C. Erik knocks down Alicia's castle in the block-building area.
   D. During a cooking activity, Hoang accidentally spills his milk.

4. **Compare and Contrast.** Collect classroom limits from two centers. Discuss the similarities and differences between the two sets of limits. Why do you think these differences exist?

5. **Draw Conclusions.** Imagine that you are an early learning teacher and have set the limit that all children must help clean up after cooking activities. One day, a parent comes to you complaining that this limit is unfair and too harsh. The parent says his son doesn't like cleaning and complains about it at home. Draw conclusions about how you could respond to this parent. How could you explain your limits while acknowledging the parent's concern?

6. **Analyze.** Visit a local library and talk to a librarian in the children's section. What limits does the library set on children's use of books? How do they enforce these limits? In small groups, share your findings and analyze how the library's limits could be incorporated into an early learning center.

7. **Identify.** Check the website of the National Network for Child Care for information on guidance, discipline, and appropriate limits for children of various ages.

Core Skills

1. **Writing.** Give an example of a limit that is stated negatively. Rewrite the limit, so it is stated positively.

2. **Writing.** Create a classroom discussion forum to share ideas on handling guidance issues and to provide feedback on one another's ideas.

3. **Research.** Survey area preschool and child care teachers to discover how often music activities are conducted in the classroom. Do children have daily access to musical and rhythm band instruments, or are they used only on special occasions? What limits have been established for music activities? Observe a preschool class during music time. Are children following the established limits? Discuss your findings in class.

4. **Writing.** Locate pictures of two pieces of outdoor play equipment. Write limits for each piece.

5. **Technology.** In small groups, choose one activity area and write a set of limits for that area. Then, imagine that you are early childhood teachers and are trying to communicate these limits to parents so that they enforce similar limits at home. Use presentation software or another digital software to create a visually appealing product displaying these limits. Make your product interactive. Present your product to the class and then ask for feedback.

6. **Writing and Speaking.** Review the three categories for communicating limits and then write a short drama in which an early learning teacher uses these categories during communication. Write the most realistic scenario and then share your drama with the class. Lead the class in a discussion about how to use categories for communicating limits.

7. **Listening and Writing.** Interview an early childhood educator about limits. Ask what is easy and difficult about setting and enforcing classroom limits. How do this educator and other staff members evaluate whether the limits are on target or require change? Write a summary of your interview.

8. **CTE Career Readiness Practice.** Presume you are an early childhood educator. Your interpersonal skills—your ability to listen, speak, and empathize—are a great asset in working with coworkers and children. One of the other teachers is having trouble with one child always taking another's blocks and destroying others' building projects. The teacher asks for your advice. What would you tell her? How would you incorporate limits into this conversation?

Portfolio Project

Create a list of the ten limits you feel are most important in an early childhood setting. Explain why you included each item on the list and give an example of the type of behavior you are trying to control with each limit. Write a brief reflection on your understanding of the need for limits and how they contribute to the goal of helping a child become self-disciplined. File the list in your portfolio.

Chapter 16

Handling Daily Routines

Lesson 16.1: Understanding the Daily Schedule

Lesson 16.2: Implementing Daily Routines and Transitions

Case Study

Ensuring Smooth Transitions

This was a rewarding week for Denzel Brown. He was assigned to student teach in a kindergarten classroom with 20 five-year-olds. Although he had spent time on Thursday with his cooperating teacher, Ms. Smith, reviewing the children's individual folders containing family background information and planning the curriculum for the first week of school, he had not met the children.

On Friday, Ms. Smith and Denzel physically rearranged the classroom areas, placed name tags on the children's lockers, and posted the daily schedule for the parents to view. After this, they introduced an array of interesting materials to stimulate the children's curiosity and thinking in each activity area.

Denzel woke up early on Monday, which was the opening day of school. He showered, ate breakfast, and dressed. Leaving home, he felt excited and anxious since this was his first day. When he arrived at the school, the principal met him in the lobby. She said, "I am sorry, but Ms. Smith is ill today. She called me early this morning, and I hired a substitute teacher to assist you." Although Denzel was nervous, he felt his studies and academic accomplishments in early childhood education had prepared him for this day.

The children arrived. Some seemed confident, many excited, but a few appeared shy. Once they began exploring the different classroom areas, they became deeply engaged with the materials and other children. Denzel looked up at the clock and recognized that it's time for transitioning into another activity. He wasn't sure what to do. Using his loudest voice, he yelled, "Children it is time for large group, but first you need to use the bathroom." A few children heard him and walked to the open area of the classroom, but not the bathroom." The others kept playing.

Give It Some Thought

1. Was transition time effective? If not, why?
2. What are four methods could teachers use for making transitions? What transition strategy would you have used if you were Denzel? Why?
3. Do you think the children should receive a five-minute warning before transitioning to the next activity? If so, why?
4. Why do you think the children first walked to the open area of the classroom, but not the bathroom?

Opening image credit: MBI/Shutterstock.com

Essential Question

How do daily routines affect the functioning of early childhood centers and promote children's social-emotional, self-help, and learning skills?

Learning Outcomes

After studying this lesson, you will be able to

16.1-1 **explain** the importance of a daily schedule including arrival time, large group activities, small group activities, self-selected activities, meals and snacks, and nap time.

Key Terms

routine   hyperactivity
schedule

The young child's brain needs predictability to reduce stress. Chaotic environments cause stress in young children. So, it is important for them to have regularly scheduled routines. **Routines** are everyday experiences, such as dressing, undressing, eating, napping, brushing teeth, and toileting. They promote the children's social-emotional, self-help, and learning skills. Routines at early education centers reassure children by providing a predictable pattern. By following a *schedule*, children know the order of daily events. They also know what to expect with each event. This offers them emotional security. When children feel emotionally secure, they are more likely to explore their environment.

Daily routines provide opportunities for children to develop independence. Young children feel great satisfaction in doing things for themselves (**Figure 16.1**).

VastiChaya/Shutterstock.com

Figure 16.1 Teaching children how to put on their clothing allows them to be more independent. *How does independence benefit children?*

Daily routines will need your guidance. The children will need to learn the classroom schedule and daily routines. Before understanding time, children learn to understand a sequence of events. For instance, Jules and Merena, twin three-year-olds, began attending a local preschool. When their older sister asked what they do at preschool, Jules responded in this way: "First we play; then we hear a story; then we have a snack; then we go outside; and then mama comes to get us."

16.1-1 The Daily Schedule

A well-planned **schedule** provides the framework for the day's activities. State and local standards affect the daily schedule. Your teaching philosophy and the parent's beliefs will also affect the schedule. Schedules for early childhood programs vary by type of program. For instance, the sequence of events in an all-day program will not be the same as in a half-day program. Factors such as the length of the program's day and the time children arrive will also require consideration.

Schedules also vary with the amount of time given to different curriculum areas. Viewing a program's schedule, you can tell what is important.

A well-planned schedule should help prevent conflicts and meet the children's needs. Health and safety are important factors. To feel comfortable and secure, children need consistency and predictable routines.

The design of the daily schedule should include basic routines. **Figure 16.2** shows the segments of a typical schedule. Include time for both indoor and outdoor play. Consider the weather when deciding how much time to allow for outdoor play. Remember to plan time for eating and resting or napping, too.

When planning the daily schedule, include large blocks of open time. At least half of the day should be set aside for self-selected activities. Young children enjoy selecting activities and deciding how long to remain with each activity. Many preschool children have short attention spans. Differences also exist in the speed at which they complete projects. By providing larger blocks of time, you will be meeting these children's individual needs.

All centers need to post a visual daily schedule. Most centers post schedules on a bulletin board outside the classroom door and inside the classroom. Additionally, some centers or classroom teachers post their schedules on their websites. This information is helpful for parents or guardians, volunteers, and staff. Teachers often orally review the schedule with the children at the beginning of each day.

Arrival Routines

The children's arrival should follow a consistent routine so they know what to expect. Their arrival requires the teacher's full attention.

A typical arrival routine begins with the greeting of each child. Bend down to the child's level, make eye contact, and give a warm smile to make each child feel welcome. Tailor your welcome to the needs of individual children. In the process, check the children's emotional and health status. Then direct the children to store their outer garments and other belongings in their cubbies. They can then move to a self-selected activity until all the children have arrived.

When enrolling in an early childhood program, children react differently to separation from their parent or guardian. Some will remain silent while others cry. Some will refuse to enter the room, and others will bring favorite toys from home. Children vary in the duration of their separation anxieties. Some children will feel comfortable in a day or two. For other children, this may take a week or even several weeks. As a teacher, recognizing and responding to these anxieties is vital. Your caring, understanding, and

Scheduling Segments for a Full-Day Program

I. Arrival, greetings, and self-selected activities
II. Cleanup, toileting, and handwashing
III. Snack, cleanup, and handwashing
IV. Self-selected activities and cleanup
V. Teacher-structured large group activity
VI. Outdoor self-selcted activities
VII. Cleanup, toileting, and handwashing
VIII. Lunch, cleanup, handwashing, and toothbrushing
IX. Transitioning for nap time: quiet music or story time
X. Toileting, handwashing, and nap
XI. Self-selected activities, indoor or outdoor
XII. Cleanup, toileting, and handwashing
XIII. Snack, cleanup, and handwashing
XIV. Outdoor free time
XV. Departure

Figure 16.2 Schedules for full-day programs may vary from center to center, but most include these basic routines.

support will be critical in helping the children make this transition.

Large Group Activities

Most programs include time in the schedule for large group activities. Teachers may refer to this segment as *group time, story time,* or *circle time.* Often, teachers use this time for stories, music, fingerplays, and discussions. If developmentally appropriate, teachers also use it for discussions about the weather and calendar.

Schedule large group activities when the children are well rested and nourished, such as mid-morning. Since not all children arrive at one time, avoid scheduling group time at the beginning of the day. Problems can also occur when the schedule includes large group time just before lunch. Usually, the children are under the most stress at this time of day. They are becoming tired and hungry, which could impact their behavior.

Group time should take place in an area where there are few distractions. The children should sit away from books, puzzles, and other materials that could be a distraction. Many programs have a carpeted area for group time. Some teachers prefer using individual carpet squares. A teacher or aide may prearrange the squares prior to a large group activity to ensure the children are not sitting too close together. It will also ensure that the children are sitting near the teacher and not blocking the view of others.

A key to the success of group time is teacher organization and readiness. Immediately engage the children with a fingerplay, puppet, or song. This will help captivate the children's attention. Always end group time before the children lose interest.

Small Group Activities

Schedule small group activity periods for 15 to 20 minutes. Typically, the four to six children in the group have similar interests or abilities. During this time, the children work with a teacher or aide. The purpose may be to teach specific concepts such as colors, alphabet letters, numbers, shapes, or sizes.

Self-Selected Activities

The largest block of time in the schedule is for self-selected activities. Other names for this activity time may be *self-directed activities, free choice,* or *free play.* Depending on the climate, you may schedule the activities indoors or outdoors. A variety of developmentally appropriate activities should be available.

When longer play periods are available, children engage in more involved activities. Larger blocks of time help promote the development of the children's attention spans. These longer time periods are also valuable to you. As a teacher, you can engage in conversations with the children, asking questions, and assessing learning.

Meals and Snacks

A half-day or two-hour preschool program usually provides a 15-minute snack period. Centers that operate full-day programs usually provide lunch. Typically, they allow a half hour for lunch. The time needed for snacks or lunch will vary depending on the age and the number of children in the group.

Early Childhood Insight 🄰🄱🄲

Responses to the Schedule

There will be differences in each child's response to the schedule. For some children, the pace may be too fast, and they may feel stressed. Other children may become bored if the pace is too slow. Children's reactions often depend on the number of hours they spend at the center. Children attending full-time may feel differently from children attending part-time.

Nap Time

Check your state's regulations on rest or nap time. States usually require children under the age of five in a full-day program to have a rest or nap time. Usually, the schedule includes this time after lunch. Since sleep needs are individual, this time needs to be flexible, as some children will sleep longer than others.

Departure

The center is legally responsible for the safety of all children enrolled. Only individuals authorized in writing by the family may pick up a child. Otherwise, the child could be put at risk. It is the teacher's responsibility to always err on the side of a child's safety. Check to see if an individual picking up a check has authorization. Always ask to see the individual's driver's license or photo identification unless you are acquainted with the individual.

For the children's protection, they need to be in the custody of an adult, not a minor. Siblings should not drop them off or pick them up. Clear policies are essential for protecting the children's safety and the center against negligence. These policies should include that the authorized individual picking up a child at departure must:

- Sign the child out using the designated computer or notebook. Record the child's name, date, departure time, and their name. Early childhood centers are required to track drop-offs and pick-ups.
- Inform the teacher that the child is leaving.
- Encourage the child to put away the toys or materials they are playing with.
- Check the child's cubby for artwork, written communication, and personal items.

The adult should arrive before closing time to pick the child up. Often children need a few minutes to finish what they are doing. If the child is not picked up on time, some centers impose a late fee.

Focus on Careers

Occupational Therapy Assistant

Occupational therapy assistants work under the direction of occupational therapists. The goal is to help clients develop, recover, improve, and maintain skills necessary for daily living and working. They collaborate with occupational therapists in developing and carrying out the treatment plan to meet the needs of individual clients. Occupational therapy assistants

- help clients do therapeutic activities, such as stretching and other appropriate exercises;
- encourage clients to complete their activities and tasks;
- guide children who have developmental disabilities in play that promotes coordination and socialization; and
- record client progress and report to occupational therapists.

Occupational therapy assistants may work in educational services in the state, local, and private facilities. They also work out of physical offices, hospitals, and nursing facilities. Others provide their services through home health care.

Career cluster: Health science.

Education: Associate's degree from an accredited occupational therapy assistant program.

Job outlook. Employment for occupational therapy assistants is expected to grow 34 percent from 2020 to 2030, which is much faster than average for all occupations.

To learn more about a career as an occupational therapy assistant, visit the US Department of Labor websites for the *Occupational Outlook Handbook (OOH)* and *O*NET OnLine*. You will be able to compare the job responsibilities, educational requirements, job outlook, and average pay for people with similar occupations.

Lesson 16.1 Review

1. Each of the following is true about daily routines for children *except* routines _____. (16.1.1)
   A. promote social-emotional, self-help, and learning skills
   B. reassure children by providing a predictable pattern
   C. require very little teacher guidance
   D. offer predictability to reduce stress

2. A typical arrival time does *not* include which of the following? (16.1.1)
   A. Large group story time.
   B. The teacher's full attention.
   C. Eye contact at the child's level and a warm greeting.
   D. Self-selected play until the arrival of all the children.

3. Each of the following is true about departure time *except* _____. (16.1.1)
   A. only individuals authorized in writing by the family may pick up a child
   B. teachers are responsible for keeping children safe
   C. children may be picked up by an unauthorized adult as long as it is clear that the child recognizes the adult
   D. teachers must ensure individuals picking up children are authorized

4. Which of the following is *not* required of authorized individuals who are picking up a child at departure? (16.1.1)
   A. Authorized individuals must sign the child out using the designated notebook or computer.
   B. Authorized individuals must encourage the child to stop what they are doing and gather their belongings to leave.
   C. Authorized individuals must check the child's locker or cubby for artwork, written communication, and personal items.
   D. Authorized individuals must always inform the teacher that the child is leaving.

Essential Question

How can you successfully implement daily routines and transitions in an early childhood program?

Learning Outcomes

After studying this lesson, you will be able to

16.2-1 **guide** children successfully through the daily routines of dressing and undressing, eating, napping, toileting, and cleanup.

16.2-2 **utilize** transition techniques to move smoothly from one activity to another.

Key Terms

pica	visual signal
dawdling	novelty transition
induce	auditory signal
transition	

Predictable routines create a daily framework that provide security for young children. Routines are the repeated parts of the day that remain a constant in the daily schedule, such as large group and outdoor play. Self-care tasks such as washing hands, eating, dressing for the outdoors, brushing teeth, toileting, and napping are also examples of everyday routines. During these daily routines, many valuable learning opportunities occur. Children practice new skills and learn problem-solving skills. They can also learn new health, nutrition, math, social studies, science, and language concepts.

Orderly, consistent, and flexible transitions from one routine to the next are essential to promote positive behaviors. Successful changes require thoughtful planning and need to be developmentally appropriate. Teachers may use visual, auditory, visual and auditory, or environmental signs to get the children's attention. They must also prepare children for approaching transitions by providing enough time. Teachers may say, "Children, in five minutes we will clean up to go outdoors."

16.2-1 Daily Routines

Throughout the day, many routines take place in the center. As a teacher, you will need to know how to handle basic routines. These include dressing and undressing, eating, napping, toileting, and cleanup. Encourage the children to become as independent as possible in carrying out basic routines.

Some classrooms have routines within routines. At circle time, for example, you may begin with a song, read, and discuss a book, and then the children will go outside.

Dressing and Undressing

As a teacher, you will want to encourage preschool children to independently dress and undress themselves as much as possible. Begin by telling the children what you expect of them. This is important. When four-year-old Mohamed hands you his coat, refuse to help him put it on. Instead, tell Mohamed he can dress himself. If needed, prompt him by providing verbal instruction. Once his coat is on, do not forget to praise him for his accomplishment. This will help him to enjoy becoming independent (**Figure 16.3**).

Children should hang up their coats. You may notice that many of the children simply lay their coats in their lockers. Do not allow this. For

myboys.me/Shutterstock.com

Figure 16.3 Letting children know they can dress and undress themselves helps children build independence.

instance, if you see Alexandra lay her coat in the locker say, "Alexandra, you need to hang your coat on the hook." If she does not understand, show her how to hang it on the hook. Then take the coat off the hook and let Alexandra hang it herself.

Label lockers so children can find their own spaces. The labeling method you use will vary with the ages of the children. Staff members usually write names on the lockers for infants. This helps both teachers and families. For two-year-olds, use a picture of the child. Names and symbols are helpful to three-year-olds. If children cannot recognize their names, they can find their symbols. Give each child a unique symbol. Most four- and five-year-olds can recognize their names.

Suggestions for Families

Dressing can be time-consuming and frustrating for teachers and children. For this reason, some centers provide families with a list of clothing suggestions for the children. The list usually includes the following:

- Send an extra set of clothing for your child to keep at school to use in an emergency. For instance, a child might trip and fall in mud, rip a pair of pants, or have a toileting accident.
- Attach labels to the inside of your child's clothing. It is common for several children to have the same style and size of clothes. Labeling helps prevent confusion.

- Select clothing for your child with oversized zippers, buttons, or snaps. This makes dressing easier for children who do not have well-developed fine-motor skills.
- Boots and shoes should fit properly and slide on and off easily.
- Shoelaces should not be too long because they can be a tripping hazard and are hard for children to tie. You may want to choose shoes with hook Velcro® closings, which are easier for younger children to manage independently.
- Consider buying elastic-waist pants and shorts instead of snap or button types. They are easier for children to handle during toileting.

Demonstrating Dressing Techniques

Buttoning, zipping, pulling on boots, tying shoes, and putting fingers in gloves are all actions that teachers or care providers can demonstrate for children. Demonstrating at the child's eye level is the most effective. Sometimes verbal guidance is all a child requires. At other times, you may need to start an action and allow the child to finish the process. The child will feel a sense of accomplishment. For example, Amari can put on his coat but cannot get the zipper started. Start the zipper and have Amari finish zipping it by himself.

Tying Shoes. Tying is a skill that requires advanced coordination. As a result, most children do not learn this task until five years of age (**Figure 16.4**).

There are several methods for teaching children how to tie shoes. One method is to place the child on your lap. From this angle, the child can observe the process. For most children, the easiest technique to learn is to loop each string like a bunny ear. Tie these loops into a double knot. Encourage the child to repeat this process.

Many parents purchase shoes that fasten with Velcro instead of tie with laces. Bring shoes with thick ties to the center to teach these children how to tie them. Let them use these shoes to practice. This will help them learn tying skills, or you can let them practice on a shoelace box.

Robie Online/Shutterstock.com

Figure 16.4 Most kindergarten children have the coordination necessary to tie shoes. *How would you explain to a young child how to tie shoes?*

Boots. Boots that are too small can be hard to put on. When this happens, place a plastic bag over the child's shoes or feet. This will help the boot slip on and off more easily.

Some centers keep a box of surplus boots. When a child is wearing boots that are too small, the teacher can make an exchange. Boots from this box are also handy if a child forgets to bring boots from home.

Children can practice putting on and taking off their own boots, or they may practice using the extras in the box.

Coats. To demonstrate putting on a coat, lay the child's coat, button or zipper side up, on the floor. Have the child kneel at the collar end. Tell the child to place their hands and arms into the sleeves. Then tell the child to put it over their head. Use your own sweater or jacket to demonstrate this for the children (**Figure 16.5**).

Eating

Nutritional services that centers provide may vary. Some centers serve only lunch, while others may also serve breakfast. Centers serving breakfast may use an open-ended concept. In the morning, children arrive at different times. The open-ended concept allows each child to have a nutritious breakfast when they arrive. Snacks may be the only food served in centers that only operate for two or three hours. Some centers require that children bring their own bag lunches. While most centers provide older children with meals, they require parents to provide infant formulas, breast milk, or baby foods.

As a teacher, you will have many concerns during mealtime. A major concern is serving nutritious meals that children will like.

You will also want children to enjoy eating and practice their table manners. Making mealtime pleasant and orderly is another concern of teachers. This means making meals appropriate for the ages, abilities, and interests of children. It also means teaching rules of etiquette during meals. The best way to teach etiquette is to

1. The child kneels at the collar end of the coat.

2. The child puts their hands in the coat sleeves.

3. The child flips the coat over their head.

4. The child puts their arms all the way into the sleeves.

ONYXprj/Shutterstock.com; Goodheart-Willcox Publisher

Figure16.5 Children can use this technique to learn how to put on a coat.

model it. When you want more potatoes say, "Will you please pass me the potatoes." Make sure to say, "Thank you," after a child passes the dish.

You will notice that children's appetites change. Their appetites may be influenced by illness, stage of development, physical activity, and a body's individual nutrient needs. Emotions can also affect appetite. For example, if Lila has cried since her parents dropped her off this morning, she may not be hungry at lunchtime. Appetite changes will require you to be flexible regarding the children during meals.

Infants and Toddlers

Infants and toddlers have definite food likes and dislikes (**Figure 16.6**). It is not unusual for them to spit out or refuse foods they dislike; however, they will eagerly eat foods they enjoy.

The Centers for Disease Control and Prevention (CDC) recommends that teachers and care providers teach children age one and older to drink water from a cup rather than a sippy cup. Inform parents and recommend them to use the same practice at home. At first, children may take only a few swallows. Spilling will occur for several months. Later, children will enjoy using cups by themselves. To help these children, provide spill-proof cups.

Once children become mobile, their interest in food may decrease. During this stage, some

Oksana Kuzmina/Shutterstock.com

Figure 16.6 Infants can use facial expressions and body language to communicate their food preferences. *What do you think this infant is expressing about food?*

children are too interested in moving to sit still for very long. Even if placed in a high chair or feeding table, they may try to get out and continue with their play.

Provide finger foods to infants and toddlers whenever possible. By picking up small bits of food, the child will develop fine-motor skills and hand-eye coordination skills. It also gives them a sense of accomplishment and helps them in developing independence.

Interest in self-feeding using spoons may occur between 15 and 18 months of age. You will need to be patient with children who are learning to feed themselves. You may have to help them fill their spoons. Since spilling occurs often, the children should wear bibs. Also, expect children to spill food on the feeding tray, high chair, and floor. Wipe up the spills immediately so others do not slip on them.

Two-Year-Olds

Two-year-old children are developing fine-motor skills and are becoming skilled at handling cups and spoons. Provide these children with child-sized spoons and small, unbreakable cups. Fill the cups only halfway. If they spill a drink, there is less to clean up.

Use child-sized pitchers (16 ounces) filled with water for two-year-olds. Encourage the children to fill their own cups. This is a good hand-eye coordination exercise. Watch carefully and provide support (**Figure 16.7**).

Three-Year-Olds

By the age of three, children have developed distinct food preferences. They may refuse to eat certain foods because of their color, shape, or texture. Your attitude will help children accept these foods. In addition, family food attitudes and preferences can influence what children may eat. Other children can also influence food preferences. Some children who flatly refuse to eat vegetables at home may enjoy eating them with their peers.

Three-year-olds are capable of assisting with mealtime. Ask them to first wash their hands and then set the table. Make place mats.

Alter_photo/iStock via Getty Images Plus

Figure 16.7 Supervise three-year-olds as they pour their own drinks. They may need help handling the pitcher.

Using a permanent marker, make outlines of the plate, glass, fork, and spoon on rubber washable placements. These patterns will help children set the table properly with minimal adult assistance. Provide forks and spoons to help the children develop handling skills. Use unbreakable glasses with weighted bottoms to help prevent spills. Use pitchers with lids and pour spouts. Serve the food in shallow bowls, which will allow the children to see what is in them.

Have children serve themselves. As a rule, tell children to fill their water glasses only halfway. Keep portions small. If children want more food, they may ask for second portions.

Keep a wet sponge on the table for spills. When children spill, accept this as a normal occurrence. Avoid scolding the child. Instead, guide the child in wiping up the spill.

Four- and Five-Year-Olds

Four- and five-year-olds like to help at mealtime. They may ask to set the table, serve, and assist with after-meal cleanup. They may also enjoy helping to prepare the meal. If appropriate, encourage them to do so. For a classroom activity, have them prepare pudding, rolls, or other simple foods (**Figure 16.8**). Later, serve these foods for snack time or lunch.

Older children enjoy talking at the table. You may wish to help them begin conversations. Mention activities they have seen, heard, or done. They will begin talking with each other and naturally move on to other subjects.

Limits

Limits for eating depend on the ages of the children. However, general limits might include
- Tasting all foods before asking for seconds of food or milk.
- Remaining at the table until everyone has finished.
- Wiping up your own spills.
- Eating food only from your own plate.
- Saying "please" when asking to have food passed or served to you.
- Saying "thank you" after someone has served or passed you food.

Eating Problems

Eating problems are common during the preschool years. These problems usually peak at three years of age. Eating will remain a problem for 25 percent of four- and five-year-olds. In most cases, problems will end somewhere around the sixth birthday. *Food refusal, dawdling, pica,* and

kohei_hara/E+ via Getty Images

Figure 16.8 Children enjoy helping to clean and prepare foods they will eat later. *What other food preparation tasks might preschool children do?*

vomiting are all eating problems that can become serious.

Food Refusal. Young children tend to be *neophobic*. They initially often do not like new foods. With time and repeated exposure, they may learn to accept and enjoy them. Food refusal problems are related to a lack of interest in food. Food refusal often begins between one and two years of age. At this time, children's need for food decreases. Some children may need only one meal a day. Refusing food because they lack an appetite is not a problem. Children who do not eat even when they need food, however, have food-refusal problems.

Lack of exercise or energy, excess energy (**hyperactivity**), and illness can all cause a lack of interest in food. These fairly common problems sometimes cure themselves. There are actions you can take, however, to help children with food refusal problems (**Figure 16.9**).

To encourage children to eat, serve small portions. Avoid pushing the children to eat. Instead, talk with the families of children who have food problems. Find out what these children eat at home. Despite mealtime refusal at the center, these children may be getting proper nourishment at home.

tylim/iStock via Getty Images Plus

Figure 16.9 If a child often refuses food, try serving smaller portions. *Why is it important for teachers and care providers to talk with parents or guardians when a child shows a pattern of refusing food?*

Do not provide extra snacks to children who refuse to eat breakfast and lunch. If you do, they will not be hungry at mealtime.

Pica. Pica is a craving for nonfood items. Young children may be curious and put nonfood items into their mouths. Cravings include paper, soap, rags, grass, and even toys. This condition is uncommon in most preschool children, although there is a *pica-autism* connection.

If you think a child may have this problem, ask other staff members to observe the child. Compare your observations. In some cultures, there are some nonfood items people view as having healing properties. Discuss the problem with the center director. You may want to schedule a conference with the family to discuss the problem. A combined effort between parents, teachers and, and medical professionals may solve the problem if necessary.

Dawdling. While one child eats only one or two bites, the other children may have finished an entire meal. It is common to have several children who eat slowly in a group of preschoolers. This is called **dawdling**. Some may hold food in their mouth for a long time, failing to chew or swallow it. Others are so busy talking at the table that they forget to eat. Still others may push the food around on their plates or play with it. These children lack interest in food.

Many times, dawdling is an attempt to gain attention. Therefore, do not urge or threaten dawdling children. Instead, provide these children with small portions of food. After being given a reasonable amount of time to eat, clear the table without comment. Children will learn that if they want to eat, they must do so in a timely fashion.

Vomiting. Young children can **induce** (to produce on purpose) vomiting. If a child in your class vomits often without other signs of illness, the child is possibly inducing it.

If you are sure a child is not sick, ignore repeated vomiting. Clean up the mess quickly, without emotion. If the child notices any concern, the vomiting may begin again to get your attention.

You should, however, share the child's behavior with the family. Find out if this behavior also occurs at home during or right after a meal. If it does, you will need to work with the center director and parents or guardians to solve the problem.

Rest or Nap Time

"Will you require my child to take a nap or rest?" Parents or guardians who are thinking of enrolling their child in a center often ask this question. Some children may have outgrown napping at home. Your response will depend on your state's childcare licensing regulations and center policies.

Most states require that preschool children nap or rest for at least one hour (**Figure 16.10**). A center can expand that requirement if they wish. For instance, if a state requires all children under the age of five to have naps or rest, a center may expand that rule to require all enrolled children to have a nap or rest. In any case, you should check your state's guidelines for requirements.

Most early childhood centers have a set nap or rest time. At the end of this time, most children are awake. If not, wake them gently. You may note that a particular child needs to be awakened every day. If this happens, the child may not be getting enough rest at home. This requires a discussion with the family. Check with your center director to find out who is responsible for talking to the family. If you are asked to contact

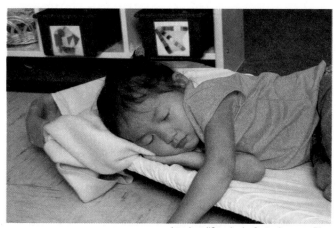

ktaylorg/iStock via Getty Images Plus

Figure 16.10 Many states require naps. *What are the state regulations in your state regarding rest or nap time for young children?*

the family, use a positive approach. Share your observations with the family. Try to arrive at a solution together.

Rest Time or Nap Time Rituals

Schedule quiet activities before rest or nap time. Children often enjoy hearing a story. Select stories that will soothe the children. Four-year-olds may like to look at books until they fall asleep. They may also enjoy listening to soft music.

Lack of rest can cause irritability in young children. Most preschool children, tired or not, can postpone sleep at nap time. Younger children may simply cry. Older children, however, may make repeated demands for your attention. They may request to go to the restroom or have a drink of water. In most cases, these are only pleas for attention.

Rest Time or Nap Time Guidance

Plan ahead to prevent children from making too many demands at rest or nap time. First, have the children use the toilet, brush their teeth, wash their hands, and have a drink of water before they lie down. Ask if anyone needs a tissue or wants to look quietly at a book. Make sure they have their blankets and stuffed toys. After this, cover them. Do not be surprised, however, if a child still asks for another drink of water or trip to the bathroom. These rituals seem natural to most two- and three-year-old children. They sincerely believe their needs are real. However, if you allow children to meet these needs before rest or nap time, they will have an easier time getting and staying settled (**Figure 16.11**).

Not all children will fall asleep. Their need for sleep varies. It is common for some five-year-olds to remain awake if required to take a rest or nap. Five-year-olds will cooperate, however, if nap time limits are stated clearly and enforced.

Children who do fall asleep may tell you they had bad dreams while sleeping. Others may cry out in their sleep. When this happens, calmly approach the child. Let the child know you are near. One way to do this is to hold the child's hand or straighten the covers.

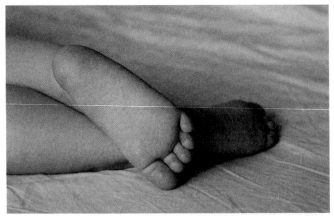

Mila Usmanova/iStock via Getty Images Plus

Figure 16.11   Allow children to remove shoes and socks at nap time. They will be more comfortable and relaxed.

As a teacher, it is important to respect the children's need for sleep. Because it is difficult for some children to fall asleep, try to remain as quiet as possible. Avoid talking to other teachers during nap time.

Workplace Connections

Stories at Nap Time

Locate storybooks that will promote a calming atmosphere for nap time. Practice reading the stories aloud using voice inflections that will soothe and comfort children as they begin to fall asleep.

1. Contact local preschool classrooms or early childhood centers to read a story before nap time.
2. Was the story calming to the children? Share the results of your experience.

Toileting

Across cultures, families use an array of options in handling toileting, and use a variety of toilet-learning techniques. Parents typically meet the toileting needs of infants using diapers. In the United States, some children wear them until they are three years old. Diapers are not an option, however, in developing countries.

Infants cannot control *elimination*, bowel, and bladder release. For them, elimination is a reflex action. The first few weeks after birth, infants eliminate many times each day. They may cry when it happens. The number of eliminations will decrease as the infant gets older; however, the volume increases. By 28 weeks, a child may remain dry for one to two hours. When they eliminate, however, the diaper is usually soaking wet. The diaper may leak unless it is changed immediately. Check diapers often and change them when wet to prevent diaper rash.

When should a child learn to use the toilet? This is a good question, but there are no specific answers. Talk with the parents or guardians. Children differ in their toilet-learning needs and schedule. Some children use the toilet as early as two years. Others may not have full bladder and bowel control until three years or later. For some children, toilet learning will take just a few days. Other children may require several months. Females tend to achieve control slightly earlier than males. Both nap time and nighttime control will typically take months longer to achieve.

Different cultures have varying opinions on when children should learn to use the toilet. One belief system is not right and another wrong. Cultures in Africa, China, and India support practices that begin within the first 12 months of life. Western cultures begin later, focusing on a more child-centered approach, following the child's own timetable. Benefits of early training include reduced incidence of diaper rash and urinary tract infections. The American Academy of Pediatrics recommends that the process begins when a child demonstrates an interest, usually between 18 and 24 months of age. Because of the diverse views, it is important to engage each child's parents or guardians in conversation about toilet learning.

Toilet-Learning Timetable

Children cannot learn to perform toileting functions until their central nervous systems are ready. This rarely occurs until after two years of age. At this age, most children can stay dry for up to two hours. They should be able to express their need to use the toilet. Some may pull down their pants and sit on the toilet. Others will tell you they have to use the bathroom.

Each child in the center will have their own toilet-learning timetable. Never force children

Health Highlights

Using Potty Chairs

Because non-flushing toilets, or potty chairs, can pose a significant sanitation risk, take special care when you use them. If used, potty chairs should be made of nonporous plastic material that is easy to clean and disinfect. Do not use wooden potty chairs because they are not durable and may be difficult to clean and disinfect. Keep the following guidelines in mind when using potty chairs:

- Empty, clean, and disinfect the potty chairs after each use.
- Clean and disinfect potty chairs in a sink that is used *only* for this purpose.
- Use potty chairs *only* in the bathroom area.
- Keep potty chairs out of children's reach when not in use.
- Wash your hands thoroughly according to accepted standards when assisting children with toileting, or cleaning and disinfecting potty chairs. Wear disposable vinyl gloves (or utility gloves that must be washed with soapy water and dried after each use) when cleaning and disinfecting potty chairs. Remove the gloves when finished and follow up with the proper hand-washing technique.

to develop self-regulation. When they are ready, they will achieve control of their bodily functions. Instead, praise them as they become better at keeping themselves dry. Controlling elimination is one step toward independence and is a real accomplishment.

Certain factors may affect a child's toilet-learning timetable. Illness, a new baby in the home, or weather changes are common factors. Remember, too, that toileting accidents are common during a child's first few weeks at the center. Accidents may indicate the emotional stress the child is feeling in a new environment. Another factor is the toilet-learning attitudes and practices at home. In some homes, adults may overreact to children's toileting accidents

by showing their disapproval. These children may feel ashamed by their failure to control elimination. In the center, you need to be sensitive to children's feelings following an accident. Quietly help them change clothes.

Toileting Guidance

As a teacher, keep a matter-of-fact attitude in toilet teaching. Shaming and scolding have no place in helping a child develop control. Instead, provide children with the facilities and encouragement to stay dry.

Have toilet seats or potty chairs available. If you provide a seat for the toilet, also provide a step stool to help the children reach the toilet comfortably. Not all children like to sit on the toilet. Some fear they will fall into the toilet and be flushed away. These children will prefer the potty chair.

During toilet learning, the child's clothing should be easy to manage. Pants that pull down easily work better than those that are hard to unfasten. In case of accidents, it is a good idea to keep several extra pairs of underwear and clothing for each child at the center.

Children often provide clues when they need to use the toilet. Some start wiggling. Others cross their legs. When you notice these signs, provide reminders to the child. You can remind the child by saying, "It is toilet time again," or "Louis, do you need to use the toilet?" After children use the toilet, remind them to flush the toilet and wash their hands. At the same time, make sure to wash your own hands (**Figure 16.12**).

Remember to use praise whenever a child expresses an interest in using the potty. Patience is the secret to success. Even after the child seems to be successful with toilet learning, accidents and near-misses will happen. Be prepared with cleaning materials including sanitizers.

Cleanup

Cleanup is an important routine in early childhood classrooms. Children learn to be responsible for themselves, their belongings, and classroom materials and equipment. Cleanup time can be stressful for a new teacher. Consider Carlos, who recently began teaching

Tips for Guiding Toilet Learning

Each child has their own toilet-learning timetable. Never force children to learn before they are ready.

Maintain a matter-of-fact attitude.

Stay with the child.

Praise children as they become better at keeping dry.

Always be positive and never shame or scold.

Make toilet seats or potty chairs available.

Watch for clues that children provide when they need to use the toilet.

Use lots of positive encouragement.

Handle accidents casually.

Coordinate consistent routines between home and the center.

Figure 16.12 Following these tips for guiding toilet learning can help the process go smoothly for children and their teachers or care providers. *Why do you think "patience" is the key to success with toilet learning?*

in a preschool. He frequently raises his voice, scolding or nagging the children to help with cleanup. Carlos's frustration is not uncommon. The following suggestions may be helpful.

Cleanup Guidance

Try to maintain a positive attitude toward cleanup. Scolding or nagging the children usually is ineffective. You will discover that some children are unresponsive and do not want to take part.

Begin by setting firm ground rules and then follow through. All children should take part in cleanup. You must deal individually with a child who refuses to participate. You may say, "Tanya, you need to put the puzzle away." Watch Tanya closely. If she walks away from the table, take her hand. Then say, "Tanya, come. You need to return the puzzle to the tray." If Tanya still refuses to put the puzzle away, she needs help in understanding the consequences. Explain that if she fails to put the puzzle away, she will not be able to play with the puzzles.

You will find that some children need encouragement or reminders. You might try saying:

- Help me put the blocks away.
- Show me where the puzzles are stored.
- Do you remember where we hang these dress-up clothes?
- Timmy, you worked hard making your block structure. Now show Malcolm how to put the blocks away.
- Move your milk away from the side of the table so it is not spilled.

Foster independence by visually assisting the children in seeing where materials and equipment belong. For instance, in the woodworking area, paint a silhouette of each tool on a piece of poster board. Hooks in the dramatic play area should be available for hanging dress-up clothes. To assist the children, attach an eight-inch loop of string to each item of clothing. On the block shelves, provide separate sections for each shape and size of blocks. The manipulative area needs to have separate, transparent containers for different types of pieces.

Young children enjoy pleasing others. They will work hard to win your approval. Thus, it is important that you praise the children's efforts at cleanup. Praise their efforts by saying, "Jia Li, I like the way you are helping Frankie put the blocks away," or "Ampario, I like the way you are picking up the puzzle pieces."

16.2-2 Transitions

Transitions are changes from one activity to another or movements from one place to another. They occur many times during the day. Children may go from self-selected activities to using the bathroom to snack time to outdoor play in just a few hours. Plan transitions carefully to help children get through the daily routine without a fuss.

Tell the children in advance that a transition will occur (**Figure 16.13**). Many teachers provide a warning before transitioning to the next activity. The amount of time the children require to make a transition depends on their ages. While two-year-olds may only need two minutes, four- and five-year-olds may need four or five minutes to finish a project or complete a puzzle. The warning signal may be sounding a bell, playing the piano, or rapidly turning the light off and on. This will allow children time to finish what they are doing.

There are four basic methods for making successful transitions. You may use concrete objects, visual signals, novelty, or auditory signals. You may use several types of transitions in one day. Remember to be consistent. Young children respond better if they know what to expect. Therefore, it is best to use the same transition for individual activities. For instance, play the same cleanup song every day to let the children know it is cleanup time.

AaronAmat/iStock via Getty Images Plus

Figure 16.13 The teacher is preparing the child in advance that a transition will occur. *Why do you think it is important for teachers or care providers to give children advance warning about transitions?*

Concrete Objects

Using concrete objects as a form of transition involves children moving items from one place to another. This technique directs a child's attention from one activity to another. Examples include

- "Leon, please put your picture in your cubby." This will direct Leon from an art activity to a new activity.
- "Darra, hang up your coat." Darra will move from an outdoor activity to an indoor activity.
- "Shilpa, put these washcloths on the restroom hook." This signals the end of cleanup.

Visual Signals

Using **visual signals** is another transition method. This method involves informing children of a change through signals they can see. For instance, when you show the children a picture of lunchtime, the children move to the lunch table. After story time, you might hold up a picture of outdoor play. This will serve as a signal to the children that it is time to put on outdoor clothing and wait at the door for you. See **Figure 16.14** for other examples of visual transitions.

The first few times you use visual signals, you will need to explain them to the children. After you use them several times, the children will know what to expect.

Novelty Transitions

Novelty transitions involve the use of unusual, new actions or devices to move the children from one activity to another. *Locomotion* is one type of transition. The children use motion to make their transition. For instance, ask the children to pretend they are elephants. Have them walk like heavy elephants to the snack table, or ask them to tiptoe lightly like tiny monkeys. Likewise, they may hop like kangaroos.

Using locomotion is limited only by imagination. Children can march, skip, crawl, jump, or walk backward. Before introducing a novelty transition, however, consider the abilities of the children. For instance, do not ask a group of two- or three-year-olds to skip. They will not

Using Visual Transitions

Visual Transition Method	Application of Method
Construction paper	Use to break children into small groups. Place a piece of blue, red, green, or yellow construction paper at each table. Divide children into four groups and assign each group one of these colors. Have groups find their tables.
Hand motions	Use on playground to motion children indoors or to a specific area.
Blinking lights	Use to gain children's attention or to warn children to complete an activity.
Clock	Use with older children by telling them "When the big hand is on the 12, it will be lunchtime."
Words	Use to dismiss children from a group. Make a name card for each child. Hold cards up one at a time. Children are dismissed when they see their names.
Whistle	Use outdoors to alert children it is time to go inside.

Figure 16.14 There are many visual transition methods that help children move from one activity to the next. **Which method might you use to let children know it is time to line up to go outside?**

have developed this skill yet. Instead, you could ask them to crawl or take big steps.

Transportation is another type of novelty transition. The children can move like freight trains, jets, buses, or cars. Each time you introduce a locomotion or transportation transition, get involved with the children. Model the movement you want them to make.

You can also use identification games for novelty transitions. For instance, you may direct the children from one activity to another by asking, "Who is wearing red today? You may go into the bathroom and wash your hands before we have our snacks." Continue using other colors that the children are wearing until every child has departed from the group.

Novelty transitions can also be made using single alphabet letters. Direct the children to another activity by asking, "Whose name starts with the letter *T*? You may go outside." Continue calling out letters until all the children are outdoors.

Auditory Signals

Auditory signals inform the children of a change through the use of sound. A bell, timer, autoharp, tambourine, guitar, or piano can all inform children of a transition. Some teachers use a simple song or chord of music as a transition signal. For example, when Mr. Andrews plays "Mary Had a Little Lamb" on the piano, the children know it is time to clean up.

Auditory signals also need to be developed for individuals. There will be times when you may wish to signal only one child. For instance, you may quietly tell a child to clean up or go to the snack table. This is called an *individual transition*.

Auditory signals are quite useful for providing warnings. For instance, a ringing bell tells the children that playtime will end in five minutes. At the end of the five minutes, they know it is time to clean up.

Safety First

Safety Policy for Departure

Every early childhood facility must keep records about which people the parents or guardians have authorized to pick up children from the facility. Such records include the names, addresses, telephone numbers, email addresses, and photo identification of individuals with authorization. Photos can be from driver's licenses or photos the parent supplies. This information is kept in the child's file at the early childhood facility. Teachers and care providers should not accept telephone authorization to pick up a child. This helps prevent noncustodial parents and other unauthorized individuals from gaining access to a child. Note that parents or guardians should make contact with the child's teacher or care provider on arrival or pick up.

Lesson 16.2 Review

1. With dressing and undressing, encourage preschool children to do each of the following *except* _____. (16.2.1)
   A. independently dress and undress themselves as much as possible
   B. tell them what you expect of them for dressing and undressing
   C. hang up their coats in their locker when they hand them to you
   D. praise children for their accomplishments with dressing and undressing

2. Which of the following is *not* an example of a limit for eating to use with young children? (16.2.1)
   A. Sampling food from the plates of other children.
   B. Remaining at the table until everyone is finished.
   C. Wiping up your own spills.
   D. Saying "please" to have food passed or served to you.

3. Pica is when _____. (16.2.1)
   A. children do not like new foods
   B. children crave nonfood items
   C. children are not hungry at mealtime
   D. children eat too slowly in a group

4. Each of the following is an example of supplies or clothing that can help children during toilet learning *except* _____. (16.2.1)
   A. pants that pull down easily
   B. extra underwear and clothing
   C. books to read while on the toilet
   D. special toilet seats or potty chairs

5. A _____ is a transition that involves the use of unusual, new actions or devices to move children from one activity to another. (16.2.2)
   A. novelty transition
   B. visual signal
   C. auditory signal
   D. concrete object

6. Which of the following is *not* an example of a policy that keeps children safe during departure from the center? (16.2.2)
   A. Records about which people have authorization to pick up children.
   B. Photo identification of individuals who have authorization to pick up children.
   C. Acceptance of telephone authorization to pick up children.
   D. Requirement for parents/guardians to make contact with the teacher at pick up.

Chapter 16 Review

Summary

Lesson 16.1

16.1-1 A daily schedule and routines provide structure for each day. Within this structure, children can develop independence and learn responsibility.

16.1-1 A well-planned schedule provides the framework for the day's activities.

16.1-1 Schedules for early childhood programs vary by type of program.

16.1-1 The daily schedule must be planned to meet the children's physical and psychological needs.

16.1-1 The daily schedule includes such routines as arrival time, large group activities, small group activities, self-selected activities, meals and snacks, and nap time.

Lesson 16.2

16.2-1 Health and safety are important considerations. For comfort and security, children need to have consistency and predictable routines.

16.2-1 Teachers and care providers guide children to achieve success through such routines as dressing and undressing, eating, napping, toileting, and cleanup.

16.2-1 Each of the daily routines presents its own challenges and problems.

16.2-1 Using positive guidance strategies will help you teach children about responsibility and help them achieve independence.

16.2-2 Teachers and care providers use transition techniques to help children move smoothly from one activity to another.

16.2-2 Transition types that teachers may use include concrete objects, visual signals, novelty transition, and auditory signals.

Vocabulary Activity

For each of the Key Terms, identify a word or group of words describing a quality of the term—an *attribute*. Pair up with a classmate and discuss your list of attributes. Then, discuss your list of attributes with the entire class to increase understanding.

Critical Thinking

1. **Make Inferences.** What routines did you engage in as a young child? How did these routines provide you with a sense of security?

2. **Evaluate.** Both children and parents benefit when parents know about the routines that go on in the early learning center. In small groups, discuss ways that early childhood workers can keep parents or guardians updated about the center's routines. Evaluate two to three effective methods.

3. **Draw Conclusions.** Practice putting on your sweater or jacket using the technique outlined in the chapter. Would you make any adjustments to the directions? Why or why not?

4. **Evaluate.** Observe children during cleanup time. Record the techniques the teacher uses with the children to encourage them to take part. Discuss your findings with your classmates. How effective or ineffective were the teacher's strategies to encourage the children to clean up?

5. **Analyze.** Contrast the costs of dolls, diaper alternatives, potty seats and chairs, storybooks, pictures, and posters designed to promote toilet learning. Which of these products, would be useful for teachers to use in an early childhood program? Share your findings in class.

6. **Defend.** Do early childhood centers have the right to decide if nap or rest time should be included in the daily schedule? Explain your answer. Give evidence to support your reasoning.

7. **Compare.** Ask parents what clues their children use when they need to use the toilet. Compare these to the clues you observe.

8. **Evaluate.** Select music that would provide a soothing environment for nap time. You may access musical sources on the internet or check out CDs from the public library. If you have a personal media player, create a playlist of songs to be used during nap time. (Be aware of copyright infringement laws and use only music that is free from restrictions.)

Core Skills

1. **Listening and Speaking.** Interview experienced teachers about their successful nap time techniques. Present this information as an oral report.

2. **Research.** Research the value of free play activities in an early childhood program. What types of activities are encouraged during free play or self-selected activities? What routines are incorporated into free play? What is the philosophy behind encouraging children to engage in activities that interest them during the daily preschool or child care center schedule? Write a brief report of your findings.

3. **Research and Writing.** Conduct research about how to handle feeding problems for children under five years of age. Summarize your findings in a written report.

4. **Speaking.** Obtain permission from parents or guardians to photograph children as they master self-dressing skills such as zipping, tying, and buttoning. Create an electronic photo album for each child to document their growing skills. Present your photos as a slide show in class.

5. **Listening.** Interview a teacher of young children about what methods they use to signal transition time for the children. What type of transition does the teacher use? How well does this transition work? Has the teacher tried other methods that did not work as well? After the interview, write a short summary about which transition the teacher prefers and why.

6. **Research and Speaking.** Conduct an online search for information that ties eating problems in young children to the development of other problems, such as eating disorders and stress. What triggers may exist that result in a young child's food refusal behavior? Does anorexia exist in young children? What effect can stress have on the eating habits of the young? What is the significance of this information for teachers and parents of the young child? Share your findings in class using presentation software.

7. **CTE Career Readiness Practice.** Imagine you are a new employee at a local early childhood center. Your employer values your creativity and fresh take on planning activities for children, so she asks you to think about incorporating etiquette in the daily routines of toddlers and preschoolers. She asks you to brainstorm possible etiquette rules and determine those that are appropriate for the early childhood setting. She also asks you to create a program that incorporates these rules into the routine. Create a weekly program that includes the existing activities for toddlers and preschoolers and opportunities for introducing etiquette. Once you have created your program, present it to the class and ask for feedback on how well you completed your employer's assignment.

Portfolio Project

Using print or online sources, search for information on teaching good manners to young children. How early should manners and etiquette training begin in a child's life? After a review of the information, create lists of the most important basic manners and basic table manners for preschoolers. Use a desktop publishing software to create a handout or pamphlet for families. File a copy of the handout or pamphlet in your portfolio.

Unit Four

Learning Experiences for Children

Chapters

In this unit, you will learn how to plan an emergent curriculum that promotes the optimal development of the whole child. Providing a variety of learning experiences helps children learn and grow. As you read this unit, you will learn techniques for guiding the following types of experiences: art, storytelling, puppetry, writing, math, science, technology, social studies, food and nutrition, music and movement, and field trips. Each chapter will give you guidelines for planning and supervising activities. You will also discover what types of supplies and resources you will need to conduct these activities.

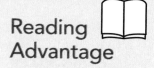
Observing Children: A Tool for Assessment

Lesson 17.1: Understanding Assessment

Lesson 17.2: Technology and Observing Children

Case Study

How Vital Is Assessment?

Beatrice earned an early childhood degree from a four-year college twenty years ago. After graduation, she worked as a head teacher in a child development center. Before the birth of her first child, she left teaching to be a stay-at-home mom. Now that Beatrice's children are older, she has decided to return to teaching and was surprised to see how differently the process of observing, recording, and assessing a child's growth and development was conducted.

On Beatrice's first day of teaching, she noticed that the other teacher, Hunter, was engaged in taking notes about the children working in the writing center. Then Hunter picked up a digital tablet to take pictures of their writing samples. Later Beatrice observed him writing an anecdotal record about another child. When she walked by Hunter, he held up the digital tablet, and she read, "Toby built a block structure that keeps falling. He tried to rebuild it six times by rearranging the blocks. On the seventh attempt, he stabilized the structure." Then Hunter added a comment, "Tony's persistence demonstrates he is making progress developing emotional regulation and executive-function skills."

After all of the children had departed at the end of the day, Beatrice asked Hunter the question troubling her: "Why do you spend so much time recording information on each child instead of direct teaching?" He explained and then said he needed to write a learning story before leaving for the day. Beatrice was surprised how the assessment process had changed since she graduated from college.

Give It Some Thought

1. How would you define assessment? What is its purpose? How is the data used?
2. What is the difference between summative and formative assessment?
3. Predict types of assessment tools teachers might use in an early childhood setting.
4. What digital devices can be used for collecting data on children's learning?
5. What do you think the purpose is of learning stories?
6. What do you think should be included in a child's portfolio?

Opening image credit: Trendsetter Images/Shutterstock.com

Understanding Assessment

Essential Question

What do I need to know about assessment to accurately identify children's strengths and needs and plan authentic curriculum?

Learning Outcomes

After studying this lesson, you will be able to

17.1-1 describe what assessment is and list its purposes.

17.1-2 analyze the factors to consider in choosing a method of assessment.

17.1-3 analyze the advantages and disadvantages of various assessment tools, including anecdotal records, checklists, participation charts, and rating scales.

Key Terms

assessment	anecdotal record
authentic assessment	interpretation
evaluation	checklist
developmental milestones	participation chart
	rating scale
formative assessment	artifact
summative assessment	learning story
standardized test	chronological

Young children are fascinating to watch. Just ask any new parent or proud grandparent! A young child's awkward attempts to try new skills or early efforts at conversation can be captivating. Observing children is something everyone enjoys doing. Children are charming, creative, active, and emotional.

Observation also serves another purpose. It provides vital information about each child's strengths, needs, interests, abilities, behaviors, and learning styles. Observation is one of the oldest and best methods for learning about children. Most of what educators know about child growth and development results from some form of observation. It is impossible to measure many behaviors of children in any other way. A one-year-old, for instance, cannot answer questions orally or in writing, but someone can observe the child's behavior (**Figure 17.1**).

As a student of child development and early education, much of what you will learn about children will come from observing them during daily activities. As part of your educational requirements, you may observe the children in your program or a specific aspect of a child's behavior or development. Informally observing children outside of school may also be a requirement.

FatCamera/E+ via Getty Images

Figure 17.1 Teachers observe largely through their eyes and ears. *How can you use assessment data from an observation?*

Jafar, a student majoring in child development, was assigned his first observation. He was amazed at the developmental differences he observed within the group of three- and four-year-olds. Jafar noticed Mateo was doing an 18-piece puzzle, but Hunter was asking for help with a puzzle with only four pieces. Standing at the easel, Sebastian was printing his name across the top of his art project. Next to him was Isabella. She drew a circle in an upper corner of her work and exclaimed, "That's my name!"

Each of these children is unique. If you were the teacher in this classroom, how would you plan a curriculum that would be developmentally, culturally, and linguistically responsive? How would you support the needs of each child in the class? To begin the process, you would need to gather information. Knowledge of individual children's strengths, needs, interests, and abilities is the basis for *best practice*. This involves observation. You would need to determine each child's developmental stage and uniqueness. With this information, you gain insight into their abilities, interests, behavior, and how you can best promote their learning. Assessments also inform program quality and the need for improvement. Assessments tell you what is or is not working. The data gathered would help you support teaching and learning. It will help you plan curriculum, environment, and interactions sensitive to the children's needs.

Assessment data is used to

- identify a child's strengths;
- chart a child's development over time;
- select equipment;
- reorganize the classroom;
- align the curriculum with the children's strengths, knowledge, and skills;
- screen children for disabilities or special learning needs;
- plan interactions that will scaffold learning;
- assess kindergarten readiness;
- evaluate the effectiveness of a program;
- provide feedback to families on their child's continuous progress and learning;

- identify program strengths and weaknesses to improve the learning process;
- communicate the children's learning and development; and
- help children reflect on their own learning.

17.1-1 Assessment

Assessment comes from a Latin word meaning *to sit beside and get to know*. It is a systematic process that evaluates someone's abilities, interests, strengths, and temperament. It involves continuously observing, recording, gathering information, and documenting children's strengths, growth, behavior, and academic progress. Assessment is challenging as it needs to be appropriate for each child's age, culture, language, and developmental level. It should also address all developmental areas, and it can occur indoors and outdoors. During the process, the teacher will note the children's favorite activities and materials. For example, when assessing children in the writing area the teacher will observe letter awareness, letter formation, stages of child's writing, first letters, and alphabet knowledge.

Authentic assessment is more informal and embraces observations that occur during daily play-based activities and routines. This type of assessment is best because it most accurately shows how children apply what they know in daily situations. Authentic assessment obtains information on children's developmental status, strengths, health, interests, behavior, and learning styles that teachers can use to make sound decisions.

Sometimes the terms *assessment* and *evaluation* are used interchangeably, but they are two different processes. While assessment is the process of collecting information or data, **evaluation** is the process of reviewing the information and finding value in it.

Purposes of Assessment

Information and data from assessment informs teachers about children's development and learning. They find out what the child knows, believes, and understands. They intentionally use the collected data for planning a developmentally appropriate curriculum. Assessment results keep the teachers and the curriculum responsive to the needs and interests of the children. An authentic assessment responds to the children's language, experiences, and developmental status. The assessment process involves gathering information when children are performing tasks in natural settings. Assessment should include all developmental areas—physical, social-emotional, linguistic, cognitive, and artistic. Assessment should provide data on each child's unique needs, strengths, and interests. It also charts progress over a period of time.

During the assessment process, teachers gain insights into children's learning styles and needs (**Figure 17.2**). What are their strengths and weaknesses? What materials and equipment do they use? How do they interact with others? What does the group know? What are they able to do? What are their interests and dispositions? What are their needs, and how should teachers group them for instruction? Teachers who have excellent assessment skills will make better decisions and plan an intentional curriculum.

kali9/E+ via Getty Images

Figure 17.2 Each child has unique strengths, needs, and interests. *Name three purposes of assessment.*

You can identify individual behavioral problems through ongoing purposeful assessment. When you observe and record specific examples of a child's behavior, their behavior patterns become clearer. When this happens, you can make plans to remedy a problem when it arises. For example, suppose there have been many instances of pushing and shoving in the dramatic play area. By observing and evaluating, you may realize that more classroom space is necessary for this activity (**Figure 17.3**). If this is impossible, you may decide to limit the number of children in this area at one time to prevent the undesirable behavior.

Assessment also allows you to identify children who might have special needs and monitor their progress. Perhaps a child has a hearing or disability. Maybe a child has an emotional or behavioral problem that requires counseling. You can help identify these needs and assist the family with appropriate follow up and, if needed, evaluation.

Through assessment, you can identify where the children are in their development continuum. Record data on each child regularly. In this way, you can see how each child is progressing. This information will help you make better curriculum planning decisions. It will also help you decide how to select equipment and create an environment that stimulates each child's development.

Regularly share the information gained through ongoing assessments with families. It can be a focus for parent conferences. Parents want to know how their children are progressing. The factual assessment data will assure them that you know, understand, and care about their child. Parents can also share the information on their child's strengths, interests, and habits with you.

A primary purpose for assessment is to evaluate your program. Information obtained through assessment can help your staff determine if your program is effective in meeting its goals.

When to Do Assessments

As a teacher beginning a new year, you will need to do an initial assessment. This will provide entry data and a baseline to use for each child. You cannot assume all children of a

SDI Productions/E+ via Getty Images

Figure 17.3 Teachers can quickly record what they see during classroom activities. *How can assessment be used to identify classroom problems?*

given age are alike. Developmental differences will exist. Culture, economic status, ethnicity, and home background will affect each child's development. Therefore, the purpose of an initial assessment is to create and document a "snapshot" of each child in the group. **Documentation** refers to recorded evidence. The most common way to gather this information is by observing children during play and gaining information from their families. You will want to learn as much about the children as possible during your initial assessment. Study the existing folders on each child. Review home background information forms. Read the notes from past parent conferences. If possible, visit each child's home. An alliance with families is important. Families can give you useful information on a child's learning needs and interests.

Besides this initial assessment, you will need to do ongoing assessments on individual children and the group. A single assessment is not an exact assessment of ability or performance. It is just an indicator.

Ongoing assessment may take more time, but it will also provide more in-depth information. The information gained will be useful in tracking each child's progress and documenting change. It

should provide evidence of a child's learning and maturation. This information will also be helpful in making decisions for enriching or changing the curriculum and classroom environment when necessary.

Enter data on nearly a daily basis. You can gather it during classroom activities. Watch children as they work on art projects and listen to them as they tell stories. Observe children as they construct puzzles, write, play in the dramatic play area, or build with blocks. Listen in on children's conversations. Discreetly, take notes on individual children, especially during free-choice activities. This is when children are most likely to reveal their personalities and personal interests. These notes will provide meaningful assessment information.

Formal and Informal Observation

Observation is the intentional act of carefully observing a child's behavior in a particular setting. It must be done carefully since it is the basis for making professional decisions. You can use two different methods of observation for assessing young children—*formal* and *informal*. They differ in the conditions for using them. Formal methods include standardized tests and research instruments. Because of research, developmental milestones for children have been identified. **Developmental milestones** are characteristics and behaviors considered normal for children in specific age groups. Some educators refer to these as *emerging competencies*.

Developmental milestones will assist you in comparing and noting changes in the growth and development of children (**Figure 17.4**). They will also help you as you observe young children in preparation for your career working with young children. The developmental continuum from birth to age 12 is included in the *Appendix B* of this book. These traits are valuable tools for assessing children's developmental status. They also form the basis for planning a developmentally appropriate curriculum.

While formal observation methods provide important information, they require specialized training for recording data on carefully designed forms. Training is also needed for analyzing and interpreting the data.

Phovoir/Shutterstock.com

Figure 17.4 Reviewing developmental milestones will help you assess the children's progress in your care. ***Why do preschool teachers usually use informal observation methods to collect data?***

Preschool teachers usually use informal observation methods to collect data. These methods are easier to use and more appropriate for program planning. They include observing children in the classroom, collecting samples of their work, interviewing parents, and talking with children.

Health Highlights

Observing Developmental Milestones

Parents, teachers, and care providers all play critical roles in promoting the healthy development of children. Through observation, they can see how children are growing and developing according to developmental milestones (see Appendix B). Educators, teachers, and childcare providers should know how to identify children who are not developing according to normal patterns. In such cases, they should talk with parents or guardians about seeking further developmental screening by a pediatrician or other trained professional.

17.1-2 Choosing a Method of Assessment

There are four considerations for choosing a method of assessment. First, the method chosen depends on the type of behavior you want to assess and the amount of detail you need. Another consideration is whether the information needs to be collected for one child or the entire group. A third consideration is the amount of focused attention required by the observer. Finally, they must consider the children's cultural, linguistic, and ethnically diverse backgrounds.

Two terms that relate to assessment are *summative* and *formative*. Each assessment has its own intention. **Formative assessment** occurs over time. It is an ongoing gathering of information during daily play activities to find out what the children know and can do. This data is essential for improving instruction and supporting children's learning. It informs the teacher on teaching practices to support the children's learning. The goal is to build a joyful, engaging, and responsive classroom that meets every child's needs.

Summative assessments are formal, standardized methods educators use to measure a child's learning against a benchmark. A **standardized test** is a form of summative assessment designed to determine the child's achievement. A teacher administers a standardized test with specific instructions to the child and compares the score against state or national norms. These results typically are shared with schools' administrators and parents. Most standardized assessment instruments have limitations. They do not provide a total picture of the child's learning and development. If used, they need to be culturally and linguistically appropriate.

There are commercial developmental screening instruments that early childhood programs can purchase. These instruments are usually for children one month to six years of age. The purpose of these instruments is to identify infants, toddlers, or preschool children with developmental delays. A focus may be on the developmental areas—gross-motor, fine-motor, language comprehension, and social-emotional growth. A teacher, doctor, social worker, or parent may administer the test.

Some methods of assessment will require more of your attention. For example, it is difficult interacting with children when you are writing an anecdotal record. Narratives need to be rich in information with detailed behavioral accounts. Checklists, video recordings, and participation charts are easier to use while working with the children.

Usually teachers use a variety of methods for gathering information about the children's learning. Since no one method is the most effective or reveals everything, teachers may use several methods. They obtain more complete information by using several types of assessment collecting information on all developmental domains. This strategy provides a holistic view of the child. Multiple sources of information also reduce the possibility of error when making evaluations.

Workplace Connections

Determining Use of Formal Assessment

Interview area preschool teachers and other early childhood education professionals. Ask them how often they use formal assessment methods, including standardized tests.
1. Write a brief report of your findings.
2. Share your report with the class.

17.1-3 Assessment Tools

Early childhood teachers use several types of assessment tools. These include anecdotal records, checklists, participation charts, rating scales, samples of products, photographs, and audio-video recordings. Teachers can also interview families to get powerful information.

Anecdotal Records

The simplest form of direct observation is a brief, factual narrative account of a specific incident called an **anecdotal record**. Often, an anecdotal record is used to develop an understanding of a child's behavior. Anecdotal records do not require charts or special settings. They can be used in any setting and require no special training. All you need is paper, a writing tool, a camera, or a digital tablet to record what you see and hear in a factual, objective manner. The observation is open-ended, continuing until everything is witnessed. It is like a short story because it has a beginning, middle, and end. These narrative assessments convey more in-depth meaning in ways a checklist cannot.

Recording the incident requires a careful eye to capture all the details. You will need to be a neutral observer and note facts only. Include who was involved, what happened, when it happened, and where it occurred. It needs to be done promptly and accurately. Otherwise, important details may be forgotten. **Figure 17.5** shows the contents of an anecdotal record.

Contents of Anecdotal Records

Identifies the child and gives the child's age

Includes the date, time of day, and setting

Identifies the observer

Provides an unbiased, accurate account of the child's actions and direct quotes from the child's conversations

Includes responses of other children and/or adults, if any are involved in the situation

May include pictures of a child creating a block building, art, writing sample, etc.

Goodheart-Willcox Publisher

Figure 17.5 Anecdotal records can be recorded in any setting, but you must record what you see and hear in a factual, objective manner.

When you use the narrative form of observation, your eyes and ears act like a video camera. You will record pictures of the children playing, learning, and interacting. During your observations, you will record how children communicate, both verbally and nonverbally. You will record how they look, what they do, and what they say. Physical gestures and movements will be noted. You will also detail children's interactions with people and materials. Record as many details as possible.

Young children move quickly, so you will need to be efficient. This means it may be necessary to use abbreviated language. Consider writing just the letter **R** for Ricardo's name. Because hard evidence is important, you may also consider capturing evidence using a digital tablet, camera, or cell phone. For example, observing Alexander in the writing center you note the letters **b** and **s** are being written backwards. Alexander is also interchanging uppercase and lowercase alphabet letters. The most efficient way to record this is to take a photograph.

Anecdotal Records Must Be Objective

During the observation process, it is important to record only objective statements. To be objective, a statement must pass two tests. First, it must describe only observable actions or facts. Do not include generalizations about the motives, attitudes, and feelings of the children. The recorded information must be non-evaluative. An anecdotal record should *not* include an interpretation of why something happened, nor imply that what happened was wrong, right, good, or bad. Also, avoid labeling. Judgments or conclusions should not be inferred at this point. The following example is a narrative observation:

Sophia arrived at school, holding her mother's hand. She strolled over to her locker, removed her coat, and hung it on a hook. She turned to her mother and said, "You go to work." Sophia's mother hugged her and said, "After work I'll take you to the dentist." Sophia looked at her mother and started to cry. She said, "I'm not going to the dentist. I'm staying here." Sophia's mother reached out and hugged Sophia. Sophia continued crying and hung onto her mother.

The teacher walked over to Sophia and whispered in her ear. Then the teacher put out her hand and said, "Come and look, Sophia. We have a new friend at school today. Chloe brought her new hamster." Sophia stopped crying and took the teacher's hand. Together, they walked over to see the hamster. Sophia's mother watched her for a moment and then left the room.

Notice that only an objective description of the observed behavior is recorded. The statements do not include causes, emotions, explanations, feelings, goals, motives, desires, purposes, needs, or wishes.

Interpretation of the Data

A second process begins once the narrative data is recorded. This process involves combing through and interpreting the data. An **interpretation** is an attempt to explain the observed behavior and to give it meaning. Why did the child behave as he or she did? What might have been the child's motives? Did someone or something cause the child to act in this way? This interpretation takes knowledge and skill. It should not be attempted without a thorough understanding of how children grow and develop. The observation itself serves no purpose without interpreting the behavior to give meaning to the data.

Though an observation may be factual and unbiased, various interpretations are sometimes made. Since no two people are exactly alike, no two people will interpret facts in the exact same way. Each person who interprets a child's behavior may determine different motives for the behavior based on their own personal experiences. Their personal feelings, values, and attitudes may also influence the interpretation of behavior.

To illustrate, an observer wrote the following about Demarco:

Demarco picked up the pitcher of milk. He moved the pitcher toward his glass. He hit the glass and tipped it over. The milk spilled.

In reviewing the observation of Demarco, you might interpret his behavior in several ways. These may include

- Demarco was careless.

- Demarco was inexperienced in handling a pitcher.
- Demarco was not paying attention to what he was doing.
- Demarco lacked the strength needed to lift the pitcher.
- Demarco lacked the hand-eye coordination necessary to pour from the pitcher.

To decide which interpretation is most accurate, you will need to observe Demarco frequently. You would also need a thorough understanding of how children grow and develop.

Figure 17.6 shows a form for an anecdotal record, although many teachers just use a note card or plain piece of paper. Teachers who record incidents throughout the year have a means of assessing progress. A series of records over time can provide rich details. The records can be extremely valuable in noting progress, strengths, needs, and interests.

Advantages and Disadvantages of Anecdotal Records

An important advantage of using an anecdotal record is that it is the easiest method of use. It requires no special setting or time frame. Anecdotal records can provide a running record over time, showing evidence of a child's growth and development. Therefore, teachers who record incidents throughout the year have a means of assessing progress.

There are also disadvantages to using anecdotal records. Because the incident observed is based on the observer's interest, they may not provide a complete picture. This means the records may not always be accurate. If the observer writes the incident at the end of the day and is poor at recalling details, important information may be missed.

Checklists

Another form of assessment is the *checklist*, which can cover a wide range of children's

Sunshine Early Childhood Center
Anecdotal Record

Child's Name: Carrie Date: 10/9/XX

Child's Age: 3 Years 9 Months

Setting: Dramatic Play Time: 8:30 to 8:45

Observer: Geneva Peterson

Incident:

Carrie went directly to the dramatic play area when she arrived at the center. She placed the cash register on a table. After this, she displayed empty food containers on a table. Tony entered the area. He stepped behind the cash register and said, "I want to play with this." Carrie said, "No, it's mine. I had it first." Then, using her arm, she hit Tony and began pushing him. Tony looked at Carrie, shrugged his shoulders, and walked away. As Tony walked away, Carrie smiled.

Interpretation:

Goodheart-Willcox Publisher

Figure 17.6 Although anecdotal records are recorded in an objective manner, they require interpretation to give meaning to the data. *What interpretations would you make about the data in this anecdotal record?*

abilities. **Checklists** record the presence or absence of specific behaviors. They are easy to use and are especially helpful when many different items require observation. They often include lists of specific behaviors to identify children's skills and knowledge. Depending on their function, they can vary in length and complexity. Checklists may cover any developmental domain—physical, cognitive, or social-emotional. A carefully designed checklist can tell a lot about one child or the entire class.

Early childhood staff may develop checklists to survey one child or a group of children. They list the targeted behaviors in a logical order, grouping similar items together. Therefore, you can quickly record the presence or absence of a behavior. Usually, a check indicates the presence of a behavior.

Checklists require structuring. You may purchase commercially prepared checklists. Some teachers working in childcare or early childhood centers structure their own. **Figure 17.7** shows a typical checklist for observing individual children. The developmental continuum found in the Appendix of this book may be adapted as checklists for assessing individual children or groups of children. **Figure 17.8** shows a checklist for assessing the gross-motor skills of a group of children.

You can even design checklists for the children to do a self-appraisal. This appraisal can be completed every month or two. Title the checklist, "I Can." Include items such as:

- hang my clothing in my locker
- assist with clean up
- be kind to others

Checklist Sample

Name: Wyatt Anderson
Program: Sunshine Childcare Center
Child's Age: 3 Years 6 Months
Date of Observation: 2/9/XX
Observer: Sally Olm

✔ Equals "Yes"; **X** Equals "No"

Fine-Motor Skills	Yes	No
Cuts paper	✔	X
Pastes with a finger	✔	X
Pours from a pitcher	✔	X
Copies a circle from a drawing	✔	X
Draws a straight line	✔	X
Uses finger to pick up smaller objects	✔	X
Draws a person with three parts	X	✔

Goodheart-Willcox Publisher

Figure 17.7   Checklists can be used to observe a child for developmental milestones.

Gross-Motor Skills Group Assessment—Three-Year-Olds
✔ Equals "Yes"; x Equals "No"

Gross-Motor Skills	Henry	Ed	Jo	Vicki	Cari	Deb
Catches ball with arms extended	✔	✔	✔	X	✔	X
Throws ball underhanded	X	✔	X	X	✔	X
Completes forward somersault	✔	✔	X	X	✔	✔
Rides tricycle skillfully	✔	✔	X	✔	✔	✔
Throws ball without losing balance	X	✔	✔	✔	✔	X
Hops on one foot	X	✔	X	X	X	✔

Goodheart-Willcox Publisher

Figure 17.8   A checklist can also be used to assess the overall skill level of a group of children.

- play well with others
- share toys with other children
- clear my place after breakfast, snack, and lunch

Advantages and Disadvantages of Checklists

One advantage of a checklist is that there are no time constraints in collecting the data. You can quickly record information anytime during program hours. You can use checklists in most situations. They are easy to use and efficient. It is easy to analyze data from checklists and use this information to plan instruction.

A disadvantage of using a checklist, however, is the lack of detailed information. Checklists lack the richness of the more descriptive narrative. Because of the format, you can only note particular behaviors. The observer may miss important aspects of behaviors, such as how a child performs a behavior and for how long. A checklist only notes the presence or absence of a behavior.

Participation Charts

You can develop a **participation chart** to gain information on specific aspects of children's behavior. Participation charts have a variety of uses in the classroom. For instance, they can help determine children's activity preferences during self-selected play (**Figure 17.9**).

Richard, a teacher with much experience, uses participation charts to record the time each child falls asleep at nap time. He also charts the amount of time each child sleeps. He records this information several times a year. After collecting the data, he decides if the staff should make a change in the nap-time schedule. With Richard's data, the center staff can adjust the length of the nap time to reflect the children's needs.

Sometimes teachers find that children's preferences do not match their needs. To illustrate, Randy has weak hand-eye coordination skills. A participation chart shows he spends most of his time listening to stories and music and watching other children play. To meet Randy's needs, the teacher could introduce him to interesting art activities, puzzles, and other small manipulative learning aids. These materials will help advance Randy's skills in hand-eye coordination, which will be necessary for reading and writing.

Rating Scales

Rating scales, like checklists, record something specific, and early childhood professionals can use them to gather data quickly. With rating scales, teachers and care providers can record the degree to which a quality or trait is present on a numerical scale. Rating scales require you to make a judgment about the quality of an observed behavior. Where a checklist only

Activity Preferences During Self-Selected Play

Time	Bryce	Tina	Saul	Ting	Bergetta	Tanya	Hunter	Shawn	Janus	Vida
9:00 - 9:10	b	dp	a	st	m	dp	a	b	st	s
9:10 - 9:20	b	dp	a	st	m	dp	a	b	st	s
9:20 - 9:30	b	dp	m	m	dp	dp	s	b	st	s
9:30 - 9:40	b	st	m	m	dp	dp	b	b	m	a
9:40 - 9:50	b	m	m	m	dp	dp	b	b	m	a
9:50 - 10:00	b	m	s	m	dp	dp	b	b	m	a

a=art; b=block-building; dp=dramatic play; m=manipulatives; s=sensory; sc=science; st=storytelling

Figure 17.9 By using a participation chart, you can assess children's activity preferences during self-selected play. *How can teachers use participation charts to better meet children's needs?*

shows the presence or absence of a trait, a rating scale tells how much or how little is present. As a result, the observer's implicit biases could hamper objectivity.

A major role of a teacher is to support the development of executive-function skills. You can develop a rating to assess these skills. You could list these traits could in three categories, such as *never, sometimes,* and *often*. Every two or three months you can revisit the scale to monitor children's progress. You could use the following descriptors:

- controls impulses
- recalls prior knowledge
- focuses attention
- follows directions
- follows classroom rules
- thinks critically
- recalls prior knowledge
- poses questions based on prior knowledge

- problem solves
- collects evidence
- stays organized

The data you collect on this assessment will provide important information for intentionally individualizing interactions and program planning.

Advantages and Disadvantages of Rating Scales

Rating scales are easy to use, require little time to complete, and gather data quickly. You can easily develop them for all classroom activities. Some scales contain key descriptors with only a numerical range. Others define the behaviors. Rating scales only include fragments of actions, which is a disadvantage. To choose a rating, observers should have a good understanding of the behavior they are rating. **Figure 17.10** shows a typical rating scale.

Social/Emotional Rating Scale

✔ Equals "Yes"; x Equals "No"

Child's Name: _____   Date:_____

Child's Age:_____ Years _____ Months _____

Observer: _____

Behavior	Never	Sometimes	Usually	Always
Shows increased willingness to cooperate	X	X	✔	X
Is patient and conscientious	X	✔	X	X
Expresses anger verbally rather than physically	X	X	X	✔
Has strong desire to please	X	✔	X	X
Is eager to make friends and develop strong friendships	X	X	✔	X
Respects property rights of others	X	X	✔	X

Goodheart-Willcox Publisher

Figure 17.10 In contrast to checklists, rating scales require the observer to make a judgment about the quality of what they are observing. *How do you think an observer's opinion could hamper the objectivity of a rating scale?*

Documenting Children's Work

Collecting *artifacts* and analyzing the children's work systematically over time is another assessment tool. An **artifact** is a tangible object a child creates that provides evidence of learning; it requires a date. Artifacts provide a rich picture by telling a story. They reveal what a child knows, areas of growth, strengths, and interests. Artifacts also can disclose a child's feelings, thoughts, and skills. For example, a piece of artwork shows how the child thinks about the world. You might analyze the painting of a tree for the color, size, placement of paper, and drawing.

Documentation is the process of collecting artifacts. It is a powerful source of knowledge for teachers. It should show tangible evidence of progress. Products collected may include artwork, stories dictated or written, audio and video recordings, photographs, and records of conversations.

Early childhood educators, teachers, and care providers can collect and compare documentation samples over time. To illustrate, Shouta could make only random scribbles on paper at the beginning of the year. When Shouta's teacher asked him to describe his work, he explained it. The teacher discovered the sample showed more than Shouta's scribbles. He said, "There is my name. That is how to write it. I wrote my mother's name and my sister's." Now he can draw a circle. A comparison of the two samples shows the progress Shouta has made in fine-motor and hand-eye coordination skills.

Store a child's products in a folder or portfolio in chronological order, if possible. (**Chronological** refers to the order in which events happened.) This will save you time when evaluating progress or sharing the materials with families or the child.

You can keep assessment artifacts and data in different forms. You may preserve samples by photographing, sketching, video-recording, audio-recording, or diagramming children's products. These methods are especially useful for large structures such as block displays and three-dimensional artwork that you cannot store conveniently. Teachers often explore different forms of documentation to see what is the most effective for them.

Learning Stories

A **learning story** is a form of strength-based observation and documentation that a teacher records in a story format. Teachers become story tellers. They observe the actions and behaviors of a child during play and take notes. The focus is on the child's dispositions for learning and thinking. Then they capture the child's words and actions in a narrative form, creating a child-centered story to celebrate. During the process, the teacher usually takes pictures or video-records the child engaged in an activity. After, the teacher views the notes and photograph or photographs. Then the teacher will write to the child a positive, encouraging, strength-based learning story recognizing the child as a competent explorer.

After writing the story and attaching the photograph(s), the teacher reads it to the child. They discuss and talk about possible ways to extend the play. Questions such as, "What would you do differently?", "Could you add more materials?", "What did you learn?" or "What if…? During your discussion, the child will see that you value their work.

The teacher will also ask whether the child wants to share the story with classmates. If the child agrees, the teacher might it at group time or post it on a documentation board. The teacher should provide copy of the story to the child's family asking for comments. The teacher might write or say, "This is a wonderful story I wrote about Carson playing in the block-building area today. Read it and make any comments or ask questions. You might even want to write Carson a note sharing your feelings." Make sure to write the story in the child's home language. Some teachers have volunteer interpreters that assist with the process. Other teachers go online for a translation.

Great stories have a title, and no two look alike. This is an example of a simple learning story:

To Carson:

I loved watching you working in the block-building area today with Amos. You were learning information about math, such as size, shape, and weight. You were so patient as you carefully and slowly studied each block before adding it to your building. Then the top block on the building kept falling off. You were very patient and asked Amos for his advice. You were curious why it kept falling. So, carefully you studied its size and shape. Then you put the block down knowing it was too heavy and long. This did not stop you from completing the building. You were very calm, kept going, and trying other blocks. I admired that you kept searching and found a lighter-weight block that did not cause the structure to topple. Then you had a beautiful look of satisfaction and joyfulness on your face.

I think you learned how important it is to keep trying. Instead of giving up, you were persistent and kept trying other-sized blocks. Like you, good learners are persistent and stick with a task.

What's next tomorrow? I will add some books on buildings and shapes to the block area. I also will add some additional blocks so you can use engineering skills and expand your play.

Documentation Boards

Some classrooms have documentation boards hung in the entry or entrance to the classroom. The purpose of the board is to share the children's accomplishments, field trips, and classroom celebrations. Photographs of each child engaged in a self-selected activity might be one week. Another week, the board might feature the children's individual artwork. Group photographs could also be featured. Pictures of the children planting a garden are an example. Under the photograph, you might add a title, "We Planted a Flower Garden." Then you could print, "We learned:"

- A flower is a plant.
- Most flowers have a smell.
- Flowers need sun, soil, water.

Lesson 17.1 Review

1. What process is informal and embraces observations that occur during daily play-based activities and routines? (17.1.1)
   A. Assessment
   B. Authentic assessment
   C. Evaluation
   D. Documentation

2. What is an ongoing gathering of information during daily play activities to find out what the children know and can do? (17.1.2)
   A. Assessment
   B. Summative assessment
   C. Evaluation
   D. Formative assessment

3. Which assessment tool would you use to determine the degree to which a quality or trait was present? (17.1.3)
   A. Anecdotal record
   B. Checklist
   C. Rating scale
   D. Participation chart

4. **True or False.** The purpose of a documentation board is to share the children's accomplishments, field trips, and classroom celebrations. (17.1.3)

Lesson 17.2
Technology and Observing Children

Essential Question

 Why is confidentiality an ethical obligation when using observation for assessment purposes, especially when using technology and portfolios?

Learning Outcomes

After studying this lesson, you will be able to

17.2-1 **evaluate** how technology can be used in the assessment process.

17.2-2 **summarize** the use of portfolios in documenting children's development.

17.2-3 **summarize** guidelines for observing children.

Key Terms

visual documentation   ePortfolio
portfolio

Collecting all the data necessary to assess learning and creating individual portfolios for each child can be overwhelming and time-consuming. With tablets, laptops, smartphones, and digital cameras, teachers are increasingly adopting technology as an efficient and reliable method of documenting learning. Digital technology and documentation are more accurate, cost and time-effective, flexible, and provide improved and immediate feedback. Using technology to create digital records of the child's growth and development also has ease of mobility. The use of technology allows information to quickly pass from one program to another program. Some teachers send this information home at the end of the year to provide the families with tangible evidence of their child's growth and development.

A child's portfolio is a record-keeping system designed to provide documentation of their skills, such as what they know, can do, and how. Portfolios allow teachers to date, save, track, and refer to what the children have learned. Early childhood educators use this information to construct a picture of the child and plan the curriculum. The portfolio is also a valuable tool to use at parent conferences. It provides families with visible documentation of their child's strengths, interests, and needs.

17.2-1 Using Technology for Assessment

Digital tablets and smartphones are changing documentation in early childhood. Technology is a very convenient tool for recording children's development by capturing live action. Making video and audio recordings using a digital tablet is an excellent way to make learning visible and preserve information. Recordings may focus on an individual child, a small group of children, or an entire class. Videos can preserve both action and speech. Audio and video recordings may show children telling stories, acting out stories, or explaining their projects. Teachers can also record dramatic play interactions and music experiences. By viewing or listening to the recordings, it is possible to note progress in language, speech, and self-confidence. The children might also enjoy viewing or listening to the recordings.

Since most people can type faster than they can write, digital tablets are helpful for recording assessment while observing. You can preload a developmental checklist on a digital tablet. Open the document and check the milestones the child has reached. Later, you can download this information into the child's portfolio.

Digital cameras or phone cameras are valuable tools for assessment. Photographs can make learning visible to everyone, including the children, colleagues, volunteers, and classroom visitors. At first, you may find using the camera is challenging. The subjects or artifacts may be too distant. With practice, you can refine your skills.

Some teachers who have become comfortable with technology take digital photographs daily. They may send a photograph to a parent. When all the children are taking part in an activity such as planting a garden or participating in a field trip, they may send it to the parents with information on what the children are learning.

Early Childhood Insight 🅰🅱🅲

Using Digital Videos for Anecdotal Records

Be careful that the video camera or digital tablet does not become intrusive. If necessary, you may want to ask other adults, such as teacher aides, teachers, or parent volunteers, to assist with the recording. This will allow you to be included in the recording. By reviewing the recording, you can self-evaluate your own interactions with the children.

Visual Documentation Using Technology

You have probably heard the phrase "seeing is believing." **Visual documentation** refers to collecting, photographing, or recording samples of a child's work that portray learning and development. Visual documentation provides a record that you and others can study. Other assessment methods, such as rating scales, checklists, and anecdotal records, involve on-the-spot interpretation. This can make it difficult to be completely objective when recording the children's behavior.

Digital devices are convenient for visually documenting children's development. Such

technology can photograph children's engagement in creating artwork, participating in dramatic play, or taking part in field trip activities. You can use digital devices to take pictures of a child's accomplishments, such as artwork or building-block structures. In an infant program, use the digital camera to record self-feeding, playing peek-a-boo, sitting up, creeping, or walking. With toddlers and preschool children, digital devices are helpful in recording self-help skills such as dressing or brushing teeth. It is important to date all pictures you take with a digital device for visual documentation. You should also record a brief description to show its significance.

Once you download the digital image files, teachers can print or save them for later use. For instance, teachers can use digital devices to take pictures of classroom activities. They can download and print these photos for use in a portfolio. Teachers might want to feature classroom photos on the bulletin board to share with families before filing them. Some teachers, particularly those teaching infants and toddlers, create weekly posters.

Safety First ✥

Video Recording and Photographing Safety

Be sure to consult parents, families, or teachers before video recording or photographing children. Many centers require written consent to be on file before staff can video record or photograph children for educational purposes. Some families do not want images taken of their children for privacy reasons.

17.2-2 Portfolios

Place materials you collect for documentation as a part of ongoing assessment in each child's portfolio. A **portfolio** is a collection of materials that documents a child's strengths, abilities, and progress over time. Portfolio items may include

- teacher observations and other records gathered through assessment;
- samples of the children's paintings, drawings, and writing samples;
- photographs of developmental milestones, block-building constructions, science projects, and children engaged in activities;
- developmental checklists, rating scales, interest scales, and anecdotal observations;
- conference notes;
- parents' comments and completed questionnaires;
- audio or video recordings of children speaking, singing, telling a story, and responding to questions; and
- a list of the child's favorite books, songs, and fingerplays.

Depending on the collection of materials, the contents of a portfolio may be difficult to store. You can store it in a variety of forms. Some teachers prefer three-ring binders. Others prefer to use boxes or large folders or an **ePortfolio** (a digital portfolio collection) to show their collection of assessment evidence. Teachers who prefer using an ePortfolio maintain a computer file on each child.

Portfolio Contents

Carefully plan and organize the content in a child's portfolio. It should be more than a file of anecdotal records, photographs, checklists, and questionnaires. Most teachers include work samples as artifacts. Examples include art projects, audio recordings of conversations, and child-dictated stories. Work samples can provide evidence in all developmental areas. In addition, the portfolios include summaries of parent conferences and parent questionnaires. **Figure 17.11** shows the contents of a typical portfolio.

For each child, teachers include work products that reflect unique skills and interests. For instance, if Thomas built a complex and interesting block structure, you might photograph it to include in his portfolio. Likewise, you may record stories that children dictate to you.

SDI Productions/E+ via Getty Images

Figure 17.11   Teachers collect samples of work in a portfolio that reflect a child's skills and interests, documenting evidence of a child's progress in learning and development. *How can using a portfolio enhance family involvement?*

A portfolio should be continually growing, documenting evidence of a child's continuous progress. Over time, this method provides a vivid picture of each child's growth and development. Visual documentation included in a child's portfolio is a helpful tool when conferring with families. It should be a summary of a child's development. The information gained from evaluating the portfolio can guide teachers in making curriculum decisions, structuring interactions, setting up the classroom, and purchasing classroom supplies and equipment.

Family Involvement in Assessment

Families, too, will gain from reviewing the child's strength-based portfolio with the teacher. They are their child's first and most important teachers and partners. During the portfolio review with families, ask them to tell their stories. You need to know more about the family unit to provide authentic caring. What is the child's life like outside the classroom? What is the family composition? You need to know about their language, cultural practices, literacies, and values. What traditions are important? They need to share their observations. A family scrapbook is one way to do this. This knowledge will help you intentionally plan an authentic curriculum.

Other questions teachers might ask include

- Who is the primary caregiver?
- What expectations do you have for your child?
- What does your child enjoy doing?
- How do you guide and discipline your child?
- How do you handle toilet learning?
- When and where does your child sleep?
- How does your child interact with his siblings and the neighborhood children?
- What are your expectations of the early childhood program?
- What are your hopes and goals for your child?

Often, families do not speak up. Some are uncomfortable, while others may not want to upset their child's teacher. Teachers, however, need them to describe what their child needs and share their child-rearing practices. Many child-rearing variations can impact the child's development and classroom life.

By reviewing the portfolios of children in a program, you should be able to identify the unique characteristics of each child. For instance, according to Mark's portfolio, he remains in the cooking area until the snack is prepared every day. Often, he provides the teachers with other methods of preparing the foods. J'Miah develops elaborate and imaginative buildings in the block-building area. During self-selected play, Maria always chooses the same theme. She dresses like a superhero in the dramatic play area. The hamster and rabbit fascinate Blake. He wants to learn more about different animals, their eating habits, habitats, and behaviors.

17.2-3 Guidelines for Observing Children

During your study of young children, you will observe them in many situations. Whether on the playground, in a classroom, or on a field trip, your behavior as an observer is important. You should observe at different times of the day, both individually and in groups. It is important to follow specific guidelines, whether inside or outside an early childhood facility, preschool center, prekindergarten program, or in your school's laboratory.

Whenever you gather data about children, you must use special care. You must keep the information collected *confidential*. This is perhaps the most important guideline for you to follow. Though you can discuss a child's behavior in your classroom, you must refrain from doing so outside that setting. Whenever you are talking, other people are listening. The information you share could be embarrassing or even damaging to a child, parent, teacher, or the creditability of the program. Never use such public forums as Facebook or Instagram to post classroom activities.

To protect confidentiality, avoid using a child's full name during classroom discussions. Only permit first names. This practice will help protect the real identity of a child. It also prevents information about a particular child from leaving the classroom.

While you are observing, do not take your coats, books, and other belongings into the classroom. Young children are especially curious about purses and bags. Such items may cause an unnecessary distraction. Cosmetics and medications could endanger their safety.

During your observation time, observe without interfering. Avoid talking to the children, other observers, or the staff. It is likely, however, that your presence will spark the curiosity of some children. A child may ask you what you are doing. If this happens, answer in a matter-of-fact manner. You might say that you are watching the children play or that you are writing notes on how children play.

One of the best ways to learn about young children is to observe them and to make a note of their behavior (**Figure 17.12**). By sharing your observations with other class members, you will see children as they really are. These records will help you understand children and become a better early childhood professional.

SDI Productions/E+ via Getty Images

Figure 17.12   By observing children and recording their behavior, you will become a better early childhood professional. *What guidelines should you follow when observing children?*

Lesson 17.2 Review

1. **True or False.** Visual documentation provides a record that involves on-the-spot interpretation. (17.2.1)
2. What items should not be included in a child's portfolio? (17.2.2)
   A. Art projects
   B. Audio recordings of conversations
   C. Child-dictated stories
   D. Standardized test scores
3. When observing children, what guideline should you follow? (17.2.3)
   A. Take your coat and bag into the classroom
   B. Post classroom activities on Facebook
   C. Avoid talking to the children
   D. Refer to children by their full name

Chapter 17 Review and Assessment

Summary

Lesson 17.1

17.1-1 Teachers primarily use assessment data for planning a developmentally appropriate curriculum and interactions to advance each child's development and learning.

17.1-1 Assessment keeps the teacher and curriculum responsive to the needs and interests of every child.

17.1-1 Initial assessments provide a baseline of development.

17.1-2 Teachers consider many factors when choosing assessment methods, including children's cultural, linguistic, and ethnically diverse backgrounds.

17.1-2 Teachers use formative and summative assessments to analyze and evaluate children's progress in learning and development.

17.1-3 Anecdotal records, checklists, participation charts, rating scales, learning stories, and documentation boards are assessment tools that early childhood programs commonly use.

17.1-3 Every assessment method has advantages and disadvantages.

17.1-3 Documenting children's work reveals much about their growth and development and learning progress.

Lesson 17.2

17.2-1 Technology is a convenient tool for recording children's development, making learning visible, and preserving information.

17.2-1 Digital tablets are helpful for recording an assessment while observing.

17.2-1 Visual documentation provides a record of children's learning and development that can be studied.

17.2-2 Materials that have been collected during the assessment process should be placed in a portfolio, which is a growing document of a child's continuous progress.

17.2-2 A variety of items can be collected and placed in a child's portfolio, including samples of work, documentation of developmental milestones, assessments, and conference notes.

17.2-2 Involving families in the assessment process helps teachers intentionally plan an authentic curriculum.

17.2-3 As an early childhood teacher-in-progress, it is essential to monitor your behavior and follow guidelines for observing children.

17.2-3 Once data is recorded, it can be interpreted. Information you collect on children must be kept confidential.

Vocabulary Activity

Read the text passages that contain each *Key Term*. Then write the definitions of each term in your own words. Double-check your definitions by re-reading the text and using the text glossary.

Critical Thinking

1. **Create.** Prepare a checklist for a group of children to assess color recognition skills.

2. **Evaluate.** Develop a Math Readiness Skills Group Assessment checklist for two-year-olds. Refer to the chart of math readiness developmental milestones in the Appendix B or search online for reliable information. Use your checklist to evaluate the math readiness skills of a group of children. How effective was the checklist assessment? Share your results with the class.

3. **Create.** In small groups, choose one developmental domain to create a checklist for. Determine what milestones or activities signify growth in this developmental domain. Afterward, compare checklists with groups who studied other domains. How do the checklists differ? Would the checklists complement each other in a classroom? Why or why not?

4. **Compare and Contrast.** Video record a group of children interacting. Show the recording to classmates. Have each class member write a narrative of what they see. Compare and contrast the contents of the narratives.

5. **Analyze.** Check NAEYC's position statement in early childhood programs on the organization's website. How does this statement relate to observation in early childhood programs?

6. **Create.** Develop a participation checklist for the use of outdoor play equipment.

7. **Draw Conclusions.** Get permission to make a video or audio recording of a small group of children. Recordings can be children telling stories, acting out stories, or explaining their projects; dramatic play interactions; or music experiences. Be sure permission slips are on file. Share your recordings with the class and discuss what you can learn about the children from these recordings.

Core Skills

1. **Research.** Research journals and online for information about the observation of young children. Which materials do you find most useful and why?

2. **Technology.** Video record a group of children playing and then, using the appendix of developmental milestones in this text, identify what milestones the children have achieved or are achieving. What milestones are the children approaching? Also, play your video for a partner and compare analyses.

3. **Writing.** Observe a child for 15 minutes and write an anecdotal record of the observation. Compare and discuss the results. Which records contained the most detail? Which records contained only objective statements? Did any of the records contain interpretive statements? If so, what were they?

4. **Math.** Using Appendix B, develop a rating scale to assess the motor skills of four-year-olds. Then use your checklist to observe and assess the motor skills of one or more four-year-olds? How helpful was your checklist in documenting children's motor skills? Write a summary of your findings.

5. **Writing.** Writing skills are essential in careers related to child development. Write anecdotal observations on the same child for a specified time period from different vantage points. Then trade papers to compare the observations for accuracy. Be sure to check grammar, spelling, sentence structure, etc. Type the final copies and add them to your portfolio.

6. **Writing.** Observe a child in a classroom setting and use the learning story format to record the child's words, actions, and behaviors in a narrative format during the observation.

7. **Speaking.** Interview an early childhood teacher about how they develop and use portfolios.

8. **Research and Speaking.** Conduct an online research project on the trend toward using student portfolios as an assessment tool. Use the search terms *educational portfolios* or *student portfolios* to find information on using portfolios in the classroom. Why is portfolio use increasing? How can portfolios be fully integrated into the curriculum? What research supports the use of portfolios in education? Use presentation software to present your findings.

9. **Speaking.** In small groups, review the guidelines for observing children in this chapter. Then, create a short drama to illustrate each guideline. Assign each group member a part in the dramas and practice the dramas ahead of time. Perform your short dramas for the class. Then lead a class discussion on which guidelines you illustrated and why these guidelines are important.

10. **CTE Career Readiness Practice.** Interview a person who has done many assessments of children. How does the information you learned from the interview compare to information presented by the author of your text? Write a detailed summary of your interview.

Portfolio Project

1. Collect samples of the different assessment tools used in early childhood education for your portfolio. Design your own forms using those in the book as examples. If your school has a graphic arts department, get permission to use those facilities for printing the forms. Write a brief explanation for each type of assessment tool.

2. Attend a demonstration of technology tools and equipment with your school's technology coordinator. These may include video recording, digital photography, sound recording, and digital programs and apps that you can use to create electronic portfolios.

Chapter 18

Reading Advantage

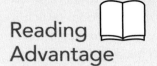

Read through the list of *Key Terms* at the beginning of each lesson. Write what you think each term means. Then look up the term in the glossary and write the textbook definition.

The Curriculum

Lesson 18.1: Foundations for Curriculum Planning

Lesson 18.2: Developing the Curriculum

Case Study

What Is an Effective Curriculum?

The Mounds Early Childhood Center has scheduled a faculty in-service, which will focus on evaluating their curriculum approach. For the past year, the teachers' discussions before and after program hours focused on the amount of time needed for planning a curriculum that provides positive outcomes for children. The debate often questioned how they could work smarter, not harder. Two very vocal teachers with opposing viewpoints, Geneva Peterson and Jamal Wilson, convinced the director to bring in a consultant.

The director agreed, scheduled an in-service training, and hired a local college professor to facilitate the session. The consultant's assignment was to share the pros and cons of each curriculum approach. During the in-service training, the teachers were respectful and accepting of views that differed from their own.

Geneva and a group of teachers were opposed to a commercial approach. They indicated that by continuing to provide a thematic approach, the children's interests and curiosity would be stimulated. The curriculum would continue to focus on all developmental domains. Based on the assessment data, it could be intentionally tailored to every child's strengths, interests, cultural backgrounds, and linguistic needs. Moreover, themes could provide all children, especially dual-language learners, with an enriched language environment and deeper conceptual understandings.

While Geneva agreed that a pre-planned curriculum might save time, Jamal argued that it definitely would. Jamal added that some commercial curriculum models focus on learning theorists, emphasizing how children learn and develop. A few teachers joined him in expressing that a preplanned curriculum would save time and, with training, might lower their stress levels. They also thought there would be fewer classroom behavioral problems with lower stress levels. They felt, however, that in-service training would be needed if a commercial curriculum becomes the focus. Others, like Geneva, were convinced that a teacher-planned curriculum would be much more effective in meeting the children's diverse individual needs.

Give It Some Thought

1. Do you agree with Geneva or Jamal's suggested approach to the curriculum? Why or why not?
2. What are the advantages of a preplanned curriculum? Disadvantages?
3. What are the advantages of a commercial curriculum? Disadvantages?
4. Would one approach be better at helping children develop executive function skills? Why or why not?

Foundations for Curriculum Planning

Essential Question

What do I need to know about foundational factors that influence the development of effective curriculum in order to meet the learning and developmental needs of all children?

Learning Outcomes

After studying this lesson, you will be able to

18.1-1 **develop** program goals.

18.1-2 **apply** ways to meet program goals.

18.1-3 **identify** who is involved in curriculum development.

18.1-4 **summarize** how assessment is used in curriculum planning.

18.1-5 **explain** the content- and process-centered approach to curriculum development.

18.1-6 **analyze** factors to consider when planning the curriculum.

18.1-7 **explain** the role of early learning standards.

Key Terms

home language
program goals
content- and process-centered approach
direct learning experience
indirect learning experience
teachable moment
engaging activities
field-sensitive learner

field-independent learner
visual learner
auditory learner
impulsive
cautious
infusion
early learning standards

Reading a story, feeding a bunny, singing songs, and playing outdoors are all parts of the curriculum. Cooking, scribbling on paper, building with blocks, and playing in the dramatic play center are also part of the curriculum. Curriculum emerges from the play of children. It is what happens in the classroom or center, including all the activities, materials, and equipment used (**Figure 18.1**). Curriculum may result from planning or be accidental. It may emerge from the teacher's interactions with the children and the children's interactions with each other. Even room arrangements, classroom equipment, and materials reflect the curriculum.

A developmentally appropriate early childhood curriculum is play-based, joyful, and based on the children's strengths. It is also evidence-based and is consistent with research on how children develop and learn. It comprises a wide range of concepts, experiences, and materials designed to meet the developmental needs of a group of children. These include their social, emotional, physical, and cognitive needs.

Maples Images/Shutterstock.com

Figure 18.1 Age-appropriate play materials should be part of the curriculum.

The curriculum also considers and respects families' culture, ethnicity, and linguistic backgrounds. Curriculum should develop, support, and encourage strong collaborations with the child's family and community. It involves determining what children need to do and what they need to know. A good curriculum also focuses on children's learning styles and characteristics. It is based on the premise that play is an important part of the curriculum.

Health Highlights

Teaching About Health Through Daily Routines

As you plan lessons on various themes, look for ways to include developmentally appropriate health topics and healthy behaviors. For example, you might teach preschool children about hand washing after a lesson on handling small animals or before a lesson that involves food. What are some other ways that you can incorporate health education into the daily program?

Children with disabilities and children with a **home language** other than English have not had equitable learning opportunities. Home language is the first language a child learns to speak. Every child needs equitable learning opportunities to help them reach their potential. A developmentally appropriate curriculum tailors learning experiences to children's ages, stages of development, interests, needs, abilities, experiences, and linguistic and cultural backgrounds. It looks at children and focuses on their strengths to provide positive outcomes and equitable learning. If the curriculum is not equitable, it is not developmentally appropriate. The curriculum should provide the children with an opportunity to make meaningful choices. It also requires thoughtful, intentional planning. Teaching and learning are most effective when built on children's existing understanding. This chapter will describe the factors to consider when planning an appropriate curriculum.

18.1-1 Developing Program Goals

Before curriculum planning can begin, it is necessary to determine the goals of the program. In an early childhood program, the program goals outline the philosophy of the center. **Program goals** are broad statements of purpose that state the desired end results—what the children are to achieve. Some people describe goals as the "why" of the curriculum.

Program goals are based on child development and focus on the whole child. Goals to promote optimal development for children in an early childhood setting might include the following:

- to develop a positive identity;
- to develop executive-function skills;
- to develop a positive attitude toward learning and the joy of learning;
- to develop critical thinking and problem-solving skills (**Figure 18.2**);
- to respect and understand cultural, ethnic, and linguistic diversity;
- to develop an understanding of one's own emotions;
- to develop effective language skills, both receptive and expressive;
- to develop fine-motor and gross-motor coordination skills;
- to develop a curiosity about the world and see oneself as a learner;
- to develop positive social skills, including cooperation and interdependence;
- to develop respect for one's own rights as well as the rights of others; and
- to develop an understanding of the relationship between people, events, and objects.

Each of these goals is broad. The goals relate to all four areas of development since a developmentally appropriate curriculum focuses on the whole child.

UW-Stout Child and Family Study Center

Figure 18.2 Teacher-made materials are a good way to promote problem-solving skills. *What might be some other ways that teacher-made materials benefit children?*

18.1-2 Meeting Program Goals

Teachers, available resources, activities, and the environment all influence whether the center meets its program goals for children. A strong curriculum supports the child's development through play and structured activities. For example, if one of the goals is to create independence, teachers need to provide children with a minimum of help. This environment will give the children many opportunities to grow in independence. Classroom activities should be play-based and interactive. The teacher's role is to introduce experiences just above the child's current level ability to scaffold their learning. Children should make choices and participate in most activities without an adult's assistance.

The classroom environment, including room arrangement, can also foster the development of independence. Placing coat hooks, paper towels, shelving, and equipment within children's reach is helpful. Teachers should mark the shelving units to show children where to return toys. This allows the children to act on their own and learn by doing or discovery. They do not have to always depend on teachers for help.

18.1-3 Who Plans the Curriculum?

Curriculum development can involve one person or several staff members. In small centers, the head teacher is often the person in charge of planning the curriculum (**Figure 18.3**). Teachers have firsthand knowledge of their children's interests, needs, abilities, learning styles, and prior experiences. They also have information on the children's culture, ethnicity, and linguistic backgrounds. In some centers, a wide range of additional people are involved in the process. The process may also include directors, teachers, aides, parents, and sometimes even the center nutrition coordinator or cook. Each of these people can contribute helpful information in planning the curriculum. In large organizations, the center

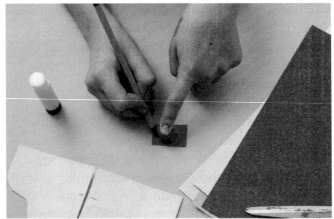

Katrinaqq/Shutterstock.com

Figure 18.3 Using a self-planned curriculum allows teachers to create their own games for the children. *Do you think a self-planned curriculum has advantages over a preplanned commercial curriculum? Why or why not?*

may hire a curriculum specialist to help plan the curriculum.

The center director usually plays a key role in curriculum development. In most centers, the director supervises all center activities. Therefore, the director's position usually includes curriculum supervision.

There is no single curriculum that is better than others; however, children who attend intentionally planned programs learn the most. Some early learning corporations provide the directors of their centers with preplanned curriculum units. Each director is responsible for introducing the curriculum to the teaching staff. After modifying it to fit the children's needs, the teachers are required to use the curriculum.

A preplanned or scripted curriculum has both advantages and disadvantages. For a staff with little training or experience, a preplanned curriculum can be helpful. Activities, procedures, and suggestions are often outlined in detail. Having these curriculum ideas at their fingertips saves teachers time and energy.

A preplanned curriculum may have more disadvantages than advantages. It may not factor in assessment data for every child in your classroom. The curriculum needs to be based on the learners' strengths so it can build on what the children already know and can do. It needs to be culturally relevant, interesting, and challenging. Experienced teachers may feel stifled or limited by a preplanned curriculum. Because of their experience, they are more likely to observe a mismatch between children's needs, interests, abilities, ethnicity, and the curriculum. If this happens, experienced teachers are likely to feel frustrated.

18.1-4 Assessment: An Important Step in Curriculum Planning

Every child is unique, even though there are many similarities within age groups. Although researchers study and provide the domains of development, learning does not occur in one area

Workplace Connections

Investigating Curriculum Planning

Interview a curriculum coordinator or center director who oversees curriculum to discover what this position entails.
1. What are the challenges of designing and selecting a curriculum? How difficult is it to meet the needs of the administration, teachers, parents, and state learning requirements?
2. What advice or suggestions does the curriculum director have for designing and choosing an effective curriculum that addresses diversity and equity?

or domain. They are all linked. Development is characterized by continuity and change. For this reason, continuous assessment is necessary to plan a curriculum that is both individualized, equitable, and developmentally appropriate for all children. Children of different races, cultural backgrounds, and dual-language backgrounds need to see themselves in the curriculum.

The assessment process should provide you with useful information on all developmental levels for planning a curriculum. The first assessment supplies data on what the children already know and what skills they have achieved. It should identify their strengths, needs, and interests. This data can help you tailor the curriculum to individual children and groups of children with like needs, providing them an opportunity to learn. It can also be helpful for informing parents of their children's progress.

Assessment should
- be based on the children's activities at the center;
- occur during daily play-based activities;
- rely on multiple sources;
- highlight the children's strengths, interests, and capabilities;
- highlight what the children know and what they can do;

- include collections of the children's work, such as artwork, writing samples, and projects; and
- include teachers' observations and summaries.

18.1-5 The Content- and Process-Centered Curriculum

Though there are several approaches to curriculum planning, the most popular method is the **content- and process-centered approach**. In this approach, learning is a constant process of exploring and questioning the environment. It stresses a hands-on, playful, and interactive curriculum. This approach includes all areas of child development—social-emotional, physical, and cognitive. The teacher uses a wide range of age-appropriate materials, supplies, and experiences to enrich the environment (**Figure 18.4**). Materials and equipment match the children's cultural and linguistic backgrounds, and their development.

Basic learning materials are a key part of the content- and process-centered curriculum. The teacher chooses and structures the materials. They may include puzzles, games, sand, water play, block-building, books, music, and materials to promote dramatic play, math, and science study.

The physical environment requires careful planning and preparation with the content for learning. It should be based on an assessment of children's developmental strengths, needs, interests, abilities, and experiences. Once the physical environment is prepared, the children assume responsibility by choosing most of their own activities. They largely determine the use of time, space, and equipment.

A good curriculum is intentional and includes *direct* and *indirect learning experiences*. Teachers plan and customize **direct learning experiences** with a specific goal in mind. For instance, they may plan a carpentry learning activity to promote the development of fine-motor skills,

UW-Stout Child and Family Study Center

Figure 18.4   In this process-centered environment, a child learns more about firefighters by trying on a firefighter's outfit and playing in a mock fire truck.

hand-eye coordination, and to teach the use of safety goggles. Likewise, they may plan the room arrangement to foster the independence needed for this task and call attention to the activity.

Indirect learning experiences occur on the spur of the moment. For example, while watching Reina, Carlos may learn how to button his coat. Amal may learn how to paint by watching Kelsie. While mixing paint, Aabida may learn that adding red paint to blue paint makes purple paint.

In teaching, timing is important. A **teachable moment** is an unexpected event the teacher can use as a learning opportunity. It occurs when the children are curious and responsive to being taught. These occasions are not planned; however, skilled teachers can take advantage of them by observing and listening. They can make the most of the moment by capturing the children's attention. They can then share important skills, concepts, and ideas. These opportunities happen throughout the day.

Many teachable moments start with a new discovery. Others start with mistakes. A teachable moment is an opportunity for children to learn why something happens or how to do something. Examples of teachable moments may include the following:

- Without advance notice, Huda's mother brought in a basket of baby bunnies.
- Mai tripped on some blocks.
- Amparo had a bike accident and was not wearing her helmet.
- Sonia said that play dough feels "sticky."
- The class gerbil gave birth to babies.
- The tulips bloomed in the flower garden.

18.1-6 Factors to Consider in Curriculum Planning

As you plan a curriculum, there are several important factors to keep in mind. You must engage in intentional decision-making. First decide what skills and content you need to cover. There are three important questions to ask as you determine the content of the curriculum. The learning activities you select need to be balanced. In addition, you need to consider various learning styles and learning characteristics.

Choose the Skills and Content to Cover

As you begin planning the curriculum, you must decide what skills and content to cover. Three basic questions can help you with this process. First, consider the question: *Is the information worth knowing?* To answer this question, think about the cultural context. In some societies, a certain learning outcome may be important. Ask yourself if the outcome will help the children better cope with their surroundings.

Children in the United States must at some point learn to read. In this culture, there is great emphasis on reading. As a result, teachers in early learning centers read many stories to young children. Through listening, children learn to enjoy literature and build knowledge There is a

relationship between a child's success in school and their vocabulary. In some societies, these skills may not be as important at this stage of development. They stress other skills important to their culture.

Secondly, consider the question: *Is the information testable?* In other words, can the child see firsthand that the information is true (Figure 18.5)? Many times, teachers choose activities based on personal appeal. They like the activity. For instance, activities that relate to dinosaurs have long been included in the curriculum for very young children. Think about the activity based on this question: Will two-year-old children ever see a live dinosaur? This activity is not testable. Depending on the age and cognitive development of the children, another activity might be more appropriate. Instead of reading a book about dinosaurs, choose one about an animal children have knowledge of or may have a chance to see at the zoo.

Here is another example. If you were going to do a unit on foods, making butter would be a testable activity. To begin this activity, tell the children they can make cream into butter. Then show the children the consistency of cream. After this, give each child an unbreakable container filled with whipping cream. Show them how to shake the container. Tell the children to keep shaking until the mixture becomes thick. After

Tatevosian Yana/Shiutterstock.com

Figure 18.5 Information on bubbles is testable if children can blow and catch bubbles.

the cream has turned to butter, let each child taste the butter. This will help them test their knowledge.

The third basic question remains: *Is the information developmentally appropriate?* A learning activity that requires giving scissors and paper to three- and four-year-olds is appropriate. Children this age can use scissors properly. This activity would be inappropriate for children 18 to 24 months old. Children need to experience success to be motivated.

Workplace Connections

Identifying Activities for Preschoolers

Work in a group to brainstorm a list of typical preschool activities. Write the results on a large sheet of paper.

1. What activities on your list are developmentally appropriate for most two- to three-year-olds and four- to five-year-olds? Why?
2. What vocabulary, concepts, and skills may emerge from engaging each activity?

Balance Learning Activities

An appropriate curriculum does not happen by chance. It is thoughtful and focused. An appropriate curriculum needs to contain a balance of learning activities supporting all *developmental domains,* or areas of development. You must choose these activities with care and specific goals in mind. Activities designed to keep children busy are not productive. Likewise, just because children prefer a certain activity does not mean it should always be repeated in the curriculum. Evaluate each activity to be sure it is engaging. Active learning is essential for joyful learning. **Engaging activities** connect the children's strengths, interests, experience, and developmental level.

A good curriculum includes a balance of structured as well as unstructured learning activities. Examples of child-guided unstructured activities include block-building, collages, water play, and sand play. Children should spend most of their time in self-initiated play with unstructured activities. This type of play allows them opportunities to practice newly developed skills.

Similarly, it is also important to include *structured,* or close-ended, learning activities. These activities indirectly prescribe children's actions. Stringing beads, working puzzles, and cooking are all examples.

Whenever possible, also plan a balance of indoor and outdoor learning activities **(Figure 18.6)**. The climate where you live will determine whether this is possible. During extremely hot and cold weather or in poor air quality, the children should remain indoors. When this happens, provide children with gross-motor activities appropriate for indoors.

In warmer climates, weather permitting, you can move many indoor learning activities outdoors. Painting, water play, science, and story and music time are all possible to do outdoors.

Balance active and quiet learning activities. Planning too many active sequential learning activities may overstimulate some children. The result can be chaotic and result in behavior problems. To prevent this, follow active learning activities with quiet ones. For example, active outdoor play followed by a story and small group would be a good balance.

A3pfamily/Shutterstock.com

Figure 18.6 Outdoor activities allow children to get fresh air and work off excess energy. *Why do you think it is important to balance indoor and outdoor activities?*

Too many quiet learning activities in a row also have a drawback. Children will get restless. The results can be just as chaotic as too many active learning activities. Children may lose interest in the activities and wiggle, talk out of turn, and distract others.

Consider Learning Styles

Basically, children learn through observation, play, interacting with others, and direct instruction. When planning activities for young children, consider the diversity of individual learning styles. Basic learning styles include *field-sensitive, field-independent, visual learner,* and *auditory learner.*

Field-Sensitive Learners

Field-sensitive learners like to work with others (**Figure 18.7**). In a group setting, they are helpful. They will volunteer and assist others in picking up blocks, setting the table, and finding a place for a puzzle piece. Field-sensitive children will also try to gain your attention.

When introduced to a new activity, field-sensitive children want a model to follow. They may ask you to show them how to do the activity. If there is not a model or demonstration, they may wait. When someone else begins, they will observe. After this observation, they will begin their work.

Field-Independent Learners

Field-independent learners like to try new activities. These children are curious and enjoy discovery. You do not need to urge them to try new activities. In most cases, field-independent children will be the first to try new activities and will rarely contact the teacher for help. They

Pressmaster/Shutterstock.com

Figure 18.7 Field-sensitive children enjoy playing with others.

enjoy engaging in new tasks without directions or assistance from the teacher.

Field-independent children prefer to work on their own (**Figure 18.8**). They enjoy competition, however, and individual recognition. Field-independent children are also task orientated. When engaged in an activity, they generally do not notice what is going on around them.

Visual Learners

Visual learners depend a great deal on the sense of sight. These children notice small changes in the environment. When a new plant appears on the science table, they are the first to notice. Visual learners enjoy looking at environmental print, books, and other objects.

Auditory Learners

Auditory learners are those who learn best through hearing. These children are the first to hear a fly in the classroom or a snowplow outdoors. Auditory learners enjoy listening. To meet their needs, include music, stories, and poems in the curriculum.

engagestock/Shutterstock.com

Figure 18.8 Field-independent children enjoy working alone.

Variations in Learning Styles

You may find that learning styles vary from program to program. Last year more children might have been field-independent, while this year more children are field-sensitive. The number of children who are primarily visual learners may also vary from year to year. This information is important for planning a program that relates to the children's learning styles.

Most children use a combination of senses, using both visual and auditory input to learn. Plan activities that involve several senses to provide for the children's needs (**Figure 18.9**). For example, while reading a book, also show the pictures. Using this method, children should retain more knowledge. They will also find activities more satisfying.

Consider Learning Characteristics

The children in each classroom have a wide range of learning characteristics. Some work slowly and others quickly. Some children are attentive, and others bore easily. Some are quick decision-makers, while others take more time.

Evaluate children's learning characteristics in relation to your own. If you work quickly, keep this in mind as you plan the curriculum. When demonstrating for children, slow down so they can understand concepts. Avoid reading or talking too fast.

Use caution when planning group learning activities. If Joey works extremely slowly and Koresh works quickly, being in the same group may frustrate both. It is better to place children with others who work at a similar pace.

Some children have long attention spans. They can pay attention and sit still for long periods of time. Other children, however, are easy to distract. To hold their interests, plan novel and interesting group activities. For instance, during story time, use a variety of teaching methods. During one week, use a variety of media. You can use flannel-board figures, puppets, smart boards, draw-and-tell charts, books, and visual storytelling to tell a story.

Children also make decisions in different ways. Some children are extremely quick to make

MBI/Shutterstock.com

Figure 18.9   Showing and talking about a new activity appeals to a child's visual and auditory senses. *Why is it important to be sensitive to children's diverse learning styles?*

decisions. This type of decision-making is called **impulsive**. When given the chance, impulsive decision-makers act immediately.

Other children are very slow to make decisions. This type of decision-making is called **cautious**. These children approach a new activity carefully. They study the environment before they begin.

Remember that not all children complete activities in the same amount of time. Children move and learn at different rates. As a teacher, you will need to be aware of individual learning styles and characteristics when planning the curriculum.

Respect Cultural Diversity

Families are becoming more diverse. It is important to infuse cultural diversity into teaching strategies, the learning environment, and children's experiences. It is important to embrace differences. **Infusion** is the process of integrating multiculturalism into all curricular areas. Your curriculum choices of books, board games, poetry, musical instruments, holiday celebrations, cooking experiences, and classroom resource people should reflect multiculturalism. The pictures, posters, books, music, and bulletin boards in the classroom should also represent a variety of cultures. Classrooms need to be culturally, linguistically, and ethnically appropriate for every child.

Respecting Home Language

The world is shrinking for all children. So, there is value in learning more than one language. Teachers need to provide support for multilanguage learners. There is a strong correlation between a child's school success and their vocabulary. The curriculum must respect the child's home language and affirm and value all children. By respecting their home language, you are also showing an appreciation for the child's family.

18.1-7 Consider Early Learning Standards

Early learning standards are guidelines (or a framework) for educators and caregivers to use that inform their decisions about their approach to curriculum development. The purpose of early learning standards is to improve professional practice by promoting high-quality learning environments for young children. Early learning standards provide the overarching framework from which educators and caregivers build their curriculums to meet the needs of children at the state or program level.

Effective early learning standards reflect all *domains* and *sub-domains* of early development and learning. They outline required learning by showing what children should know and be able to do. Standards help educators and caregivers in prioritizing reasonable learning expectations for children's growth and development. They must be developmentally and culturally appropriate. Standards also need to be adaptable to meet the needs of children with diverse abilities and disabilities. Standards also include sample behaviors and developmental milestones that help inform curriculum decisions.

Studies show that early childhood settings are influential on a child's future success in school and life. As a result, all states and territories in the United States have developed early learning standards for infants, toddlers, and preschool children to create a common method of communication for teachers. There are also some national standards, including Head Start's *Child Development and Early Learning Framework*. Some states provide the standards in several languages. An example is Wisconsin, which has English, Spanish, and Hmong versions of early learning standards.

Approaches to the use of standards vary from state to state. In most states, standards are not intended to be used as a checklist, assessment tool, or curriculum. They represent common, agreed-on outcomes for teaching and learning. Teachers should use standards as a framework for planning quality learning experiences for young children. Most high-quality early childhood programs already meet state standards.

States have designed their state standards to guide families. Families can use the indicators provided as a guide to help them promote their children's development. Understanding these indicators can also be helpful for family members when partnering with their child's teacher. Go online to learn more about the early learning standards in your state.

Lesson 18.1 Review

1. What are broad statements of purpose that state the desired end results—what the children are to achieve? (18.1.1)
   A. Program goals
   B. Early learning standards
   C. Direct learning experiences
   D. Teachable moments

2. Which factor does not influence whether a center meets its program goals for children? (18.1.2)
   A. Available resources
   B. Parents
   C. Environment
   D. Activities

3. Who is usually involved in curriculum development? (18.1.3)
   A. Aide
   B. Nutrition coordinator
   C. Parent
   D. Director

4. Assessment should _____. (18.1.4)
   A. occur during daily play-based activities
   B. rely on one source
   C. highlight the children's weaknesses
   D. highlight what the children don't know

5. **True or False.** Content- and process-centered approach is a constant process of exploring and questioning the environment. (18.1.5)

6. Which type of learner likes to work with others and volunteer often? (18.1.6)
   A. Field-independent
   B. Visual
   C. Field-sensitive
   D. Auditory

7. What are early learning standards? (18.1.7)
   A. An unexpected event the teacher can use as a learning opportunity
   B. Broad statements of purpose that state the desired end results
   C. An activity that connects the children's strengths, interests, experience, and developmental level
   D. Guidelines for educators and caregivers to use that inform their decisions about their approach to curriculum development

Developing the Curriculum

Essential Question

What questions might you ask yourself when creating a developmentally appropriate curriculum to meet the needs of young children?

Learning Outcomes

After studying this lesson, you will be able to

18.2-1 **summarize** the role of emergent curriculum in planning the curriculum.

18.2-2 **illustrate** the use of themes as a basis for planning curriculum.

18.2-3 **write** a block plan and create a lesson plan for one week of a program.

18.2-4 **analyze** ways the curriculum is evident in the learning environment.

18.2-5 **summarize** the role of documentation in planning curriculum and practices to support all children.

Key Terms

emergent curriculum	block plan
theme	lesson plan
spiral curriculum	learning expectation
web	motivation
concept	closure

A teacher's role in building a meaningful curriculum for each child is complex, and it involves a constant process of addressing the children's strengths, interests, and needs. It is challenging since there is a wide range of individual differences in any early childhood classroom. For each child, development occurs at uneven rates. Their skills will vary from day to day and week to week. Often there may be a regression in skills before reaching a new milestone.

Building a developmentally appropriate curriculum to meet the children's needs is a reflective, thoughtful process. Early childhood teachers need to constantly reflect on their practices to promote a healthy, supportive, and challenging environment. Before teaching, they need to ask themselves, "What does the assessment data tell me? What are the children interested in learning? How can I set up the environment to stimulate their curiosity?" While teaching, teachers observe and provide the support each child needs to *scaffold* their learning. After teaching, effective teachers reflect on how they can improve their teaching strategies. Detailed written plans are helpful in guiding their teaching.

18.2-1 Emergent Curriculum

The **emergent curriculum** is child-centered. It is a curriculum that "emerges" from the children's interests and experiences. It involves both the participation of teachers and children in decision-making. Initially, the teacher carefully listens and observes to take clues from the children. These observations help identify the themes of children's interest. It also helps the teacher plan curriculum that is personally meaningful to children. The intent is to provide an appealing, play-rich environment. This environment will stimulate the children to become involved with the materials and interact with each other. From this experience, children will construct their own knowledge.

The curriculum might emerge from events, things, and people in the environment. The teachers follow the direction of the children's interests in planning the curriculum. For example, a classroom of three-year-old children may notice a fire truck across the street from the center. They may become curious about fire trucks and the role of firefighters. As a result, the teacher might select a theme of firefighters, and may even sit down with the children and find out exactly what they already know and what they want to learn.

The emergent curriculum responds to the children's changing interests. Teachers observe the children carefully and continuously so they can see what the children are playing with, as well as what they are avoiding. For example, children may avoid the small manipulative area of the classroom. The teacher will think about how to make the environment more appealing. New or more stimulating small manipulative materials may be set out on the tables to capture the children's attention.

Themes should emerge that have a meaningful connection to the children's lives. There is no time frame for the length of a theme. A theme may be a day, a week, or a month or more. The length depends on the children's interests, available resources, and teacher's planning. Children learn through repetition, and repetition reinforces understanding and retention.

18.2-2 Themes

As teachers plan their curriculum, they often use a *thematic approach*. Themes provide child an opportunity to learn about their interests. A **theme** is one major topic or concept around which the teacher plans the classroom experiences and projects. Themes are concept organizers. They help integrate learning across the curriculum—science, math, language, social studies, technology, and creative arts. Connecting activities using a theme allows children to

- actively investigate their world;
- stretch their imaginations;
- build on previous learning;
- construct knowledge; and
- form more in-depth concepts.

A thematic approach also helps make the curriculum more interesting and varied. A well-planned theme links children's interests to subject matter in all content area and accelerates learning. Themes are also beneficial in helping dual-language learners to learn a second language.

Themes help teachers organize their planning and integrate state standards. Successful themes must be worthy of study with ample content. They need to focus on the process of learning and skills development. Successful themes consider the children's age, strengths, abilities, interests, needs, and experiences. Themes should also be culturally sensitive and supported by factual information. They depend on the availability of support materials. Also consider the time of the year. After choosing a theme, the teacher must research the theme. Then, meaningful goals, vocabulary, and activities require thoughtful development (**Figure 18.10**).

The number and types of activities supporting skills and content will vary with the theme. For example, a theme on apples may include a trip to an orchard. A bulletin board might show the three colors of apples. The teacher might read books, such as *Johnny Appleseed*, at group time.

An apple theme also lends itself to scientific investigation. What happens to apples when they go through processing? Applesauce, baked apples, apple muffins, and apple butter could be prepared. An art activity might include making apple prints from sponges cut in the shape of apples. Lotto games could be made using the three colors of apples. Apples of various sizes and colors could be placed on the science table. The apples can be cut apart and studied under a microscope. Math can be embedded by counting the number of seeds in the apple. Books related to the apple orchard and apples can be placed in the reading corner, dramatic play, and science area of the classroom. **Figure 18.11** lists other examples of themes.

Seldom do all planned activities relate to the theme. Some themes will have more related resources than others. Stories and bulletin board displays are the only two activities that nearly always relate to the theme. Themes should be

Activities for a Puppet Theme

Fine-Motor Development	Language, Storytelling, and Dramatic Play
Handling puppets	Creating a puppet story
Making puppets	Telling a story using a puppet
Paper bag puppets	Putting on a puppet show
Sock puppets	Telling a shadow puppet story
Paper plate puppets	Learning new vocabulary related to puppets
Stick puppets	Looking at pictures of puppets at group time
Milk carton puppets	Setting up a puppet stage with a variety of puppets
Spoon puppets	

Art	Social Studies/Sensory Table
Designing and making puppets	Attending a marionette show
Constructing a puppet stage	Providing a variety of puppets made from different materials

Goodheart-Willcox Publisher

Figure 18.10   Using themes to connect activities helps children thoroughly explore their world and build on their learning.

flexible and open in terms of length and time. They may be one day, a week, or even several weeks. Themes should never be preplanned for months ahead due to children's developing interests and needs.

STEM and STEAM

Enrich the curriculum and prepare the children for the future by integrating STEM learning concepts in the curriculum. STEM represents the areas of math, science, technology, and engineering concepts and establishes life-long thinking skills. A more recent term is *STEAM*, which also includes the arts. Why STEM or STEAM? Educators need to prepare children for the future since occupations in these fields will increase the fastest. STEM helps children learn new ways of thinking and to become critical thinkers and problem solvers. These skills will prepare them for technology-focused professions.

Theme Ideas

Themes should have a meaningful connection to the children's lives. They should build off the

Workplace Connections

Observing Preschoolers

Observe a group of preschoolers at a local early learning or Head Start center to identify themes that might interest the children.
1. In what events, objects, books, equipment, or people in the environment are the children interested?
2. Has the teacher followed the direction of the children's interests in planning the current curriculum?

children's interests and actual life experiences. Certain themes appeal to certain age groups (**Figure 18.12**). Very young children's interests center on their immediate surroundings. As children grow, their circle of interests becomes larger, like a spiral. A curriculum based on this concept is called a **spiral curriculum**. It begins with the child, followed by their interest in family, friends, community, and community helpers. After this progression, themes become more diverse and complex.

Examples of Themes

Alphabet Letters	Directions	Friends	Seasons
Animals	Exercise	The Garden	Fall
Farm Animals	Explorers	Flowers	Spring
Flying Animals	Fairy Tales	Plants	Summer
Pets	The Family	Trees	Winter
Water Animals	Mother	Gestures	Shadows
Zoo Animals	Father	Hats	Shapes and Sizes
Books	Parents	Health	Signs and Pictures
Brushes and Brooms	Sisters	Holidays/Celebrations	Telephones
Bugs	Brothers	Homes	Toys
Camping	Grandparents	Hospitals	Transportation/Travel
Clothes	Aunts	How I Care for Myself	Land
Colors	Uncles	The Library	Water
Community Helpers	Cousins	The Supermarket	Air
Doctors	Fantasy and Reality	Restaurants	Watches and Clocks
Firefighters	The Five Senses	Machines	Water
Nurses	Feelings	Measuring	Weather/Temperature
Police Officers	Foods	Money	We Create
Postal Workers	Fruits	Music	We Dance
Computers	Grains	Numbers and Counting	We Sing
Cooking and Baking	Proteins	Our Town	Wheels
	Dairy	Puppets	
	Vegetables	Safety	

Goodheart-Willcox Publisher

Figure 18.11 Successful themes must provide essential content for learning experiences. ***Choose one theme and name three activities you might do to help support the theme.***

Observe the children to identify their interest in a theme. You will find that two-year-old children are interested in their immediate world. Themes, such as sight, sound, touch, taste, and smell are appealing to them. Families, colors, shapes, pets, farm animals, and foods are also good themes for two-year-olds. When a theme changes, so does the environment that stimulates the children's curiosity. For each classroom area, plan a variety of activities that relate to the theme you choose. This will keep the young children interested and engaged.

Three-year-old children are interested in their families; however, they are also becoming interested in their neighbors and their community. Themes based on the supermarket, bakery, library, post office, fire station, and police station are of special interest to children of this age. Their interests are growing in the spiral outside of their immediate surroundings. If you watch and listen to them play, you will learn what appeals to them.

Three-and four-year old children also enjoy themes related to animals. Opposed to individual animals, these themes can focus on groups of animals. Groups might include farm, forest, water, and zoo animals. Bugs, birds, dogs, and cats can also have appeal for young children.

Sample Ideas—A Spiral Curriculum

Themes for Two- and Three-Year-Olds

All About Me
- I'm Me, I'm Special
- My Family
- My Friends
- My Home
- My Senses
- My Toys
- Foods I Eat
- Colors in My World

Concepts I'm Learning
- Big/Little
- Up/Down
- Soft/Hard
- Wet/Dry

Things That Go
- Cars
- Trucks
- Trains
- Airplanes

Shapes I See
- Circles

Themes for Three- and Four-Year-Olds

All About Me
- My Senses
- My Feelings
- My Home
- My School

People in My World
- My Family
- My Friends

Community Helpers
- Police Officers
- Firefighters
- Medical Doctors
- Nurses
- Pharmacists
- Ambulance Attendants
- Garbage Collectors
- Carpenters
- Plumbers
- Painters
- Auto Mechanics
- Farmers

Community Service Workers
- Bankers
- Grocery Store Clerks
- Meat Cutters
- Bakers
- Librarians
- Restaurant Chefs
- Restaurant Wait Staff
- Hair Stylists and Barbers
- Gas Station Attendants
- Photographers

Themes for Four- and Five-Year-Olds

My Body
- Good Health
- Exercise
- Nutrition

Communications
- Speaking
- Listening
- Reading
- Puppets
- Acting
- Writing
- Radio
- Television
- Digital Tablets
- Fairy Tales

My World
- Pets
- Plants
- Flowers
- Insects and Spiders
- Seeds

Safety and Transportation
- Air
- Land
- Water

Tools at Work
- Gardening
- Carpentry
- Mechanics
- Cosmetology
- Dentistry
- Art

Goodheart-Willcox Publisher

Figure 18.12   A spiral curriculum is based on children's growing interests.

Four- and five-year-old children enjoy themes related to a wider variety of topics. Themes can be grouped into a few broad categories. For instance, broad themes might include *My World*, *Things I Like to Do*, *Things That Move*, and *Transportation*. These categories could be broken down to contain a few subthemes. *My School*, *My Home*, *My Feelings*, and *My Family* are just a few examples of subthemes in *My World*.

Brainstorming is an effective strategy to use with older preschool children. During group time or during a class meeting, ask them to generate ideas for themes. Print each suggested theme on a large chart. After the children have finished generating the list, let them vote. Create a list showing the things the children already know and want to know.

Workplace Connections

Surveying Early Childhood Educators

Using the lists of themes from Figure 18.11, survey early childhood educators in your area to determine which of the themes they have used in their classrooms.
1. Which themes were most engaging for the children? Which themes, if any, were challenging?
2. Which themes provided the most opportunities for expanding on the children's vocabulary, concepts, and skills?

Holiday Themes

Use caution when planning holiday themes for children. Think about the children in your group. Is the theme appropriate to every family in the group? The celebration of some holidays can offend some families. Introduce holiday themes celebrated by all the children's families.

The activities planned around holiday themes are also often quite stimulating for children. If this excitement goes on for weeks, behavior problems could arise. More guidance will be needed. Some teachers prefer to integrate holidays into broader themes. They may include Thanksgiving in a

celebration theme, Valentine's Day in a friend's theme, or Halloween in a fall season theme.

A theme can last any amount of time. Some themes may last a couple of days or a week. You can plan other themes that can be carried out for a month or longer. A theme about community helpers could go on for months by featuring many different community helpers. Children's attention spans, needs, interests, experiences, and available resources are major factors affecting theme length.

Sometimes themes are repeated. A child may have a theme, such as tools in a prekindergarten program. The kindergarten teacher may repeat this same theme. When this happens, parents often express concern that the children are not learning anything new. If this occurs, emphasize that young children learn through repetition. Chances are that their learning is being expanded by the development of more in-depth concepts.

Older preschool children can provide input into theme building. They can identify a theme they want to study. After, they may even provide suggested activities and field trips that will help them develop agency. Likewise, the activities they suggest will motivate them to persist.

Early Childhood Insight

Celebrating Holidays—Use Caution

Because preschool children lack a clear concept of time, you must exercise caution when celebrating holidays at the center. If a holiday theme is introduced too early, children may become too excited. For instance, if Halloween is introduced the first week of October, but does not actually happen until four weeks later, children will become confused. They will not know when to expect Halloween.

Developing Themes Using Webbing

An effective method for developing themes is to brainstorm with colleagues and use resource books. To make this possible, many centers have curriculum guides or resources to use as references for background information. If you do not have these references, visit a local library, or conduct an online search. While referring to resources, you might draw a web. A **web** is a planning tool or map that outlines major concepts and ideas related to a theme.

Drawing a web is a simple method for listing concepts related to a theme. For example, when developing a theme on puppets, consult a resource. List all concepts you might include (**Figure 18.13**). The major headings in a puppet web could be *vocabulary, movement, types, stages, materials,* and *characterization.*

After drawing up a web, writing objectives is the next step. Study the web for objectives that you can develop. For instance, when using the web in Figure 18.13 as a basis, children might be expected to

- identify the types of puppets;
- develop skill in moving puppets with rods, wires, strings, and hands;
- enjoy a puppet show;
- learn new vocabulary words: *marionette, shadow,* and *dummy;*

- construct puppets from a variety of materials;
- express their own thoughts and feelings using puppets; and
- practice using a puppet behind a puppet stage.

Workplace Connections

Use of Holiday Themes

Interview area preschool teachers and other early childhood education professionals to discover how often holiday themes are used in the classroom.

1. What holidays are celebrated? Are the themes appropriate to everyone in the group?
2. How far in advance is the holiday theme introduced?

Concepts Based on the Theme

Curriculum themes are an important medium for helping children form concepts. A **concept** is a generalized idea or notion. Learning basic

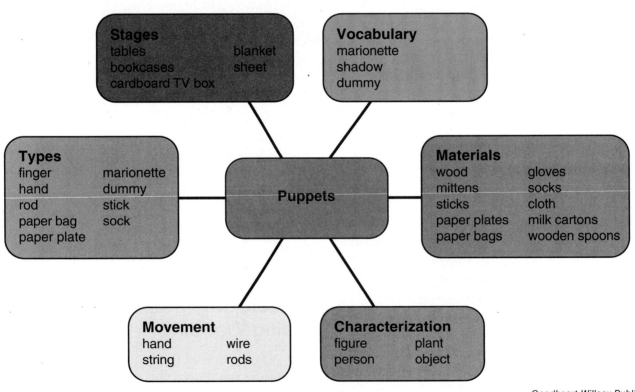

Goodheart-Willcox Publisher

Figure 18.13   Creating a web can help you organize major concepts and ideas related to a theme.

concepts helps the children understand their world. By forming concepts, they learn to group experiences in a meaningful and efficient way.

Concepts can be developed around a theme. To do this, review your web and then write the concepts. For instance, if your theme is birds, concepts might include the following:

- There are many kinds of birds.
- Some birds are pets.
- Birds hatch from eggs.
- Most birds fly.
- Birds live in nests, trees, houses, and cages.
- Birds have a head, body, wings, a beak, and feathers.

18.2-3 Written Plans

After considering your curriculum approach, theme, concepts, vocabulary, skills, and activities, written plans need to be developed. Many centers require two types of written plans. A **block plan** is an overall view of the curriculum. It outlines the general plans. A **lesson plan** is more detailed than a block plan and may list one or more early learning standards. It outlines specific actions and activities that will be used to meet the goals and objectives. Lesson plans are more likely to be developed for scripted lessons when adults provide directed instruction.

Block Plan

A block plan is key to planning a balanced curriculum. Without this written block plan, you may overlook some curriculum areas. You may think these areas were covered, but without a written record, you cannot be sure.

A block plan usually includes days of the week, time periods, and scheduled activities. **Figure 18.14** shows a sample block plan.

Keep block plans on file. You can use them as a reference to review what has happened during the year. The plans also contain a variety of learning experiences that you may use in future years, if appropriate.

To write a block plan, follow these steps:
1. Review your program goals.
2. Review your observations and assessment of the children.
3. Note the children's strengths, needs, and interests.
4. Consider the availability of resources.
5. Select a theme.
6. Develop concepts.
7. Select activities and record them on the block plan.

Lesson Plans

Lesson plans are more detailed than block plans. While a block plan gives just the title of a book, a lesson plan provides step-by-step directions for sharing the book. The writing process helps you think through the experience. **Figure 18.15** contains a sample lesson plan for cooking applesauce. Through cooking, children gain knowledge and skills. A cooking activity integrates literacy, language, math, science, and social studies. Lesson plans contain

- developmental goals
- learning expectations
- materials needed
- motivation
- procedures
- closure/transition
- self-evaluation

Lesson plans help teachers intentionally think about and organize their teaching. Writing effective lesson plans is a skill that you learn much like other skills. With practice, you will gradually increase your skill. Some programs only require weekly block plans. Teacher education programs usually require written plans for course work and student teaching. Writing a lesson helps to ensure success, particularly for large-group activities and students in enrolled in education programs.

Block Plan—Morning Session: Two-Year-Olds

Week: August 27–31   **Theme:** My School

Day	9:00–10:10 Self-Selected Play/Centers	10:10–10:25 Large Group	10:25–10:40 Snack	10:40–11:00 Small Groups			11:00–11:30 Outdoors
				Group 1	**Group 2**	**Group 3**	
Monday	• watercolors • water and toys in sensory table • tunnel • tennis shoes color match game	My School story cards *If You're Happy and You Know It* (song)	crackers tomato juice	stringing beads	table blocks	stringing beads	sand toys
Tuesday	• crayons and markers • goop in sensory table • driving wheel • tuff blocks	Short walk around the neighborhood	banana milk	table blocks	stringing beads	table blocks	balls
Wednesday	• play dough • Styrofoam® pieces in sensory table • balance beam • color clowns	*Little Red Wagon* (song) My School	apple and cheese milk	book: *Where Is It?* by Tana Hoban	puzzles	feely box	painting with water
Thursday	• soap-flake finger-painting • water in sensory table • rocking boat	Tour of school *Little Red Wagon* (song)	veggies and dip milk	feely box	book: *Where Is It?* by Tana Hoban	puzzles	bubbles
Friday	• roller painting • sand in sensory table • crawling cubes	*If You're Happy and You Know It* (song) Tour of school	SunButter® and crackers milk	puzzles	feely box	book: *Where Is It?* by Tana Hoban	rocking boat

Figure 18.14   A block plan includes the days of the week, time periods, and scheduled activities. *Why is it a good idea to keep the block plans you create on file?*

A Sample Lesson Plan

Date: 9/21 **Time: 10:00 A.M.** **Group: Four-year-olds** **Activity: Cooking Experience—Applesauce** STEM Areas: Math, Science, and Technology	*Based on the Wisconsin Model Early Learning Standards. Permission granted by: Wisconsin Department of Public Instruction. (2017). Wisconsin early learning standards (5th ed.). Madison, WI: WI Department of Public Instruction.*

Developmental Domain: Cognition and General Knowledge

  Sub-Domain A: Exploration, discovery, problem-solving

Developmental Expectation: Children in Wisconsin will develop their capacity to use cognitive skills as a tool to acquire knowledge and skills. These Skills include reasoning, reflection, and interpretation.

Performance Standard A.EL.1: Uses multi-sensory abilities to process information.

  Sub-Domain B: Mathematical thinking

Developmental Expectation: Children in Wisconsin will understand and use early mathematical concepts and logical thinking processes to extend their learning.

Performance Standard B.EL.4: Uses the attributes of objects for comparison and patterning.

Performance Standard B.EL.5: Understands the concept of measurement.

Developmental Goals: The goals of this activity are intended to help children to

- practice following directions
- practice personal hygiene by washing hands before and after cooking experience
- observe the beauty of an apple
- learn the parts of an apple: seed, core, flesh, peel, and stem
- count the seeds in an apple

- practice using a peeler as a tool
- develop safe cooking habits
- taste the ingredients in applesauce
- taste cooked apples
- observe the changes in texture and color when heat is applied to the apples

Learning expectations:

With use of the given materials and by completing the cooking experience, children will be able to (a) peel apples safely, (b) measure ingredients, and (c) describe the differences between fresh apples and cooked apples (attributes).

Materials needed:

- recipe chart
- measuring cup and spoon
- kettle

- bowl
- mixing spoon
- microwave oven

- 6 peelers
- 12 apples
- 1 cups of sugar

- 3 tablespoons of cinnamon
- water (as needed)

Motivation/introduction:

Set up the housekeeping area with recipe chart, cooking utensils, and tray with food. Ask "What can we make from apples?" Listen to responses. Tell the children, "Today we are going to make applesauce."

Procedure:

1. Tell the children to wash their hands.
2. Review the recipe chart step-by-step.
3. Cut an apple in half. Show the children the parts of an apple: seed, core, flesh, skin, and stem.
4. Demonstrate how to use a peeler as a tool, stressing safety.
5. Pass out apples and peelers, again explaining safety.
6. Encourage children to observe and feel the apples.
7. Peel apples.
8. When apples are peeled, focus children's attention back to recipe chart. Proceed by following directions step-by-step until the mixture is ready for a heat source.
9. Discuss each of the ingredients, allowing children to taste them if they wish.
10. Ask individuals to measure the sugar, cinnamon, and water.
11. Direct children's attention to the applesauce as it cooks. Clarify the process by asking questions, such as, *"How are apples different?"*
12. Serve the applesauce as a snack.

Closure/transition:

Assign cleanup tasks to the children. Have the children wash their hands. Tell the children the applesauce will be eaten at snack time. Then prepare the children for outdoor play.

Self-evaluation/Assessment:

This portion of the plan is completed after the activity. Two questions should be answered: *"What did the children learn? What would you do differently if you repeated this activity?"*

Goodheart-Willcox Publisher

Figure 18.15 Lesson plans provide the details for carrying out activities. They support early learning standards and developmental goals.

Early Standards

Most states' early learning standards recognize that child development occurs across multiple domains, including

- general cognition
- language and literacy
- social and emotional development
- physical and motor development
- approaches to learning

The example used in Figure 18.15 is from the *Wisconsin Model Early Learning Standards (WMELS).*

Developmental Goals

Developmental goals are statements that tell the "why" of the activity. They are more specific than program goals. See Figure 18.15 for examples of goals for cooking applesauce with a group of four-year-olds. To write developmental goals for a lesson plan, consider each activity. Ask yourself, "What can the children learn from this experience?" Then write the lesson plan, as outlined above, including all the learning involved.

Safety First

Teaching Children About Safety Through Daily Routines

In planning lessons on several themes, look for developmentally appropriate ways to teach about safety and safe behaviors. For example, during block play, you could teach children how high to build block structures for safety, and why it is unsafe to throw blocks because they could hurt someone. What are some other ways you can incorporate safety education into daily lessons?

Learning Expectations

Learning expectations describe the expected outcome of an activity. They are used for planning teaching strategies. There are three parts to learning expectations. These parts are the conditions of performance, the behavior, and the level of performance. **Figure 18.16** includes examples of each part of the learning expectation.

Learning Expectations

Conditions of Performance	Behavior	Level of Performance
States the conditions under which the child will perform. Examples include	States what the child will be able to do. Examples include	States the minimum level of achievement. Examples include
• Given a three-piece puzzle…	• …the child will cut…	• …four inches…
• Given crayons and a pencil…	• …the child will draw…	• …at least three feet…
• Given a set of blocks…	• …the child will construct…	• …two out of three times…
• Without the aid of a teacher…	• …the child will sing…	• …within a five-minute period…
• Given farm animals…	• …the child will match…	
• After listening to the story…	• …the child will climb…	
	• …the child will jump…	
	• …the child will skip…	
	• …the child will stack…	
	• …the child will predict…	

Goodheart-Willcox Publisher

Figure 18.16   Learning expectations describe the outcomes of activities or what you expect children to be able to learn and do. *Choose an activity you might want to do with children. Write one or more learning expectations for this activity.*

The *conditions of performance* list what materials, equipment, or tools the child will use. Items may include puzzles, paper, scissors, beads, or any other materials and equipment found in early childhood settings. The conditions of performance can also include what the child will be denied. For example, they may need to construct a puzzle without the aid of a teacher.

Behaviors are any visible activities by the child. It tells what the child will be doing. When choosing behaviors, avoid words that are open to many interpretations. To *know, understand, enjoy, believe,* and *appreciate* are all words that can mean many things. For instance, how will you judge if a child understands? **Figure 18.17** lists useful verbs for writing learning expectations.

The *level of performance* states the minimum standard of achievement. It should note how well you want the child to do. The level of performance many times is understood. Therefore, it is not always included as part of the learning expectation.

Materials

Under the materials section of the lesson plan, list everything you will need for the activity. For example, if you are going to make instant pudding, include *milk, pudding mix, bowl, wire whisk, spoon, scraper,* and *measuring cup*. If you are going to do a finger-painting activity, list *paint, paper, aprons,* and *wet sponge.*

Motivation

Motivation describes how you will gain the children's attention. The best devices are items that interest the children. You may use a picture of a cat as motivation before reading a story about cats. Motivation devices include pictures, puppets, alphabet letters, tapes, resource people, cards, artwork, photographs, animals, stuffed toys, clothing, and masks.

Procedures

The procedures section resembles a cookbook. It provides simple step-by-step directions. The directions should be in order. If necessary, number each step to remember the order. Include each of the developmental goals in the procedures. For example, if a goal is to have each child taste the ingredients, this should be a step in the procedures. **Figure 18.18** shows an example of procedures for an activity. The sample lesson plan also contains procedures.

Sample Behaviors for Learning Expectations

answer	feed	measure	replace	take
ask	find	mix	return	taste
brush	finish	move	run	tell
button	follow	name	say	throw
catch	follow directions	open	select	tie
choose	group	paint	separate	touch
climb	hold	paste	sequence	turn
close	jump	peel	show	use
collect	label	pick	sing	use two hands
color	list	place	skip	wait
count	locate	pour	solve	weigh
cut	make motions	print	sort	wipe
describe	mark	put in order	stack	write
draw	match	recall	stand	zip

Goodheart-Willcox Publisher

Figure 18.17 Choose specific verbs that show the behaviors children should be able to do. *Why should you avoid using words that can be open to interpretation when writing learning expectations?*

Procedure Chart

Activity: Visual perception
(This type of activity encourages children to see fine differences between and among objects.)

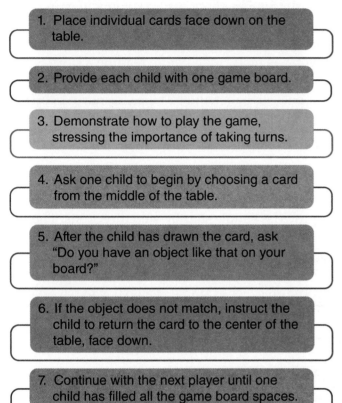

1. Place individual cards face down on the table.

2. Provide each child with one game board.

3. Demonstrate how to play the game, stressing the importance of taking turns.

4. Ask one child to begin by choosing a card from the middle of the table.

5. After the child has drawn the card, ask "Do you have an object like that on your board?"

6. If the object does not match, instruct the child to return the card to the center of the table, face down.

7. Continue with the next player until one child has filled all the game board spaces.

Goodheart-Willcox Publisher

Figure 18.18 A procedure chart outlines step-by-step directions for activities and include developmental goals.

Closure/Transition

Closure refers to how an activity will end. It might include cleanup tasks or sampling of food items at snack time. *Transition* refers to the movement from one activity to another. Sometimes closure and transition are the same task. For example, at the end of a creative drama activity, you may ask the children to walk like heavy elephants to the snack table.

Evaluation

A staff who provides a quality early childhood program is continually evaluating curriculum outcomes. In some centers, staff set aside time daily for this purpose. Many early childhood programs, however, do not have the resources to do this with the entire staff. Instead, staff members will evaluate the activities they conducted on their own. This process involves three steps:

1. evaluating the learning experience;
2. evaluating the children and their responses; and
3. evaluating your own teaching strategies.

It is important for children to feel success as it promotes their interest and persistence.

When evaluating the learning experiences, ask yourself whether the activity was appropriate for the age group. If, for example, children had trouble cutting paper, there could be several reasons for it. Were the scissors in good repair? Scissors with dried glue on the cutting edge will not cut properly. Left-handed children need left-handed scissors. Paper thickness could also be a problem. Children who are learning to cut need lightweight paper and proper tools.

Successful learning activities give children the chance to test their knowledge. For example, children will learn more about making applesauce by taking part in the activity than if they only watched an adult make it.

Your teaching skills are only effective if the children learn. Therefore, it is important to study the children and their responses to activities. First, see that the children reach the objective. If they did not, think through the activity. Ask yourself, "What could I have done differently?" Likewise, if there were behavior problems, try to reflect on the cause and how you could prevent such behaviors in the future.

Lack of organization can affect the outcome of an activity. If you forget some ingredients for a cooking activity, leaving the group to gather them could affect outcomes. During your absence, a child may mix the ingredients. Without properly measuring the ingredients, the product may not turn out.

Figure 18.19 includes a sample evaluation form for an activity. Your center may have a similar evaluation form, or you can create one using these questions. Completing this form can

A Sample Activity Evaluation

Activity: Story: "Never Talk to Strangers"

Group: Five-year-olds

I. **The Activity: Selection and Development**

    A. **Was the content (concept) worth knowing?** The content is valuable for five-year-old children since it deals with personal safety. With the increased incidence of child abuse, this is an important topic.

    B. **Was it developmentally appropriate?** Although fantasy was involved in the story, almost all the children were able to understand the content.

    C. **Was it interesting to the children?** All the children but Don listened and responded. During the repetitive sentences, the children repeated, "Never talk to strangers."

    D. **Did the activity include opportunities for the children to use or "test" their knowledge?** After the story, the children were asked questions. These included

- Is your grandmother a stranger?
- Is your neighbor a stranger?
- Is a man you never saw before a stranger?
- Who is a stranger?

    E. **What would you suggest as a follow-up experience?** Children's books related to child abuse will be read tomorrow. The game "Good Touch and Bad Touch" will also be introduced.

II. **The Children: Responses**

    A. **Did all the children become involved? If not, why?** Except for Don, all the children actively participated in the activity.

    B. **Were there behavior problems? If so, do you have any insight as to what caused them?** If Georgie and Carson had been separated during the story, Georgie may have paid better attention. Likewise, Carson found Georgie's behavior disturbing. He tried to move away from him, but another teacher made him sit down.

III. **The Teacher: Strategies**

    A. **Were you well organized?** Yes, the book was placed so I could easily find it. During the outdoor play period, an individual carpet square was laid out for each child. Approximately 10 inches were left between each square. This spacing probably helped maintain group control.

    B. **Were you satisfied with the effectiveness of your teaching strategies in reaching the learning objective? If not, why?** I should have practiced the story beforehand. In addition, I should have held the book so all the children could view the pictures.

    C. **Did you effectively guide or manage the group?** Yes, except for Georgie, I managed the group effectively.

    D. **Did you introduce the concepts in a stimulating manner?** The cover of the book appealed to the children. After the story, two children asked to have it read again.

    E. **Did you involve the children in the closure of the activity?** Yes, I did. The children were involved through a series of questions. Concepts of strangers and safety were both discussed.

    F. **What strategies would you change if you were to repeat this activity?** First, I would separate Georgie and Carson. I would also practice reading the book to myself several times before sharing it. This would make me less dependent on the words in the book. As a result, I would feel confident enough to share the pictures with the children.

Goodheart-Willcox Publisher

Figure 18.19 Completing an activity evaluation helps you analyze the success of an activity and identify areas you may want to change or improve.

help you reflect on an activity and evaluate it. After using the form a few times, you may find that you can remember the three parts of the form, including the specific questions. At this point, you might write your evaluations on index cards. In time, you will go through this process mentally.

At first, you may find the evaluation process time-consuming. You will learn, however, that it is useful. With evaluation, you will improve your teaching skills as well as the curriculum.

Workplace Connections

Designing an Evaluation Form

Design your own evaluation form using Figure 18.19, *A Sample Evaluation of an Activity*, in the book as an example. Use your form to evaluate an activity in a local early learning center.

1. Was the activity interesting to the children? Was the teacher well organized?
2. How effective was the evaluation form?

18.2-4 The Classroom Learning Environment

The curriculum theme should be apparent to anyone who walks into the classroom. For example, if the theme is flowers, the bulletin boards, posters, and books should reflect the theme. The posters could be pictures of flowers with names printed under them. The science tables should contain a wealth of materials for experimentation and investigation. For example, children can study a variety of different flowers, leaves, bulbs, and seeds under the microscope. They can learn the parts of a plant—petals, stems, leaves, buds, shoots, seeds, bulbs, and roots. They can compare the color, shape, size, and smell of each flower. Seeds, pots, and soil should also be available for planting. A scale should be available for the children to weigh the bulbs. Books about different types and care of flowers should be available. The children can learn the names of some flowers and conditions for growing.

Themes are more valuable if they involve concrete, firsthand experiences. A wealth of materials and activity choices is necessary to support a theme. Place books and computer software, if available, in the storytelling and language area. In the manipulative area, flower puzzles can be available. Children might sequence the different stages of growth of a flower. In the art area, you might place flower shapes for children to cut out and flower stickers for collage work. Flower shapes can also be cut out and hung on the painting easel. Place pots, vases, artificial flowers, and containers in the dramatic play area where the children can create arrangements. A garden prop box could contain gloves, seed packets, a sun hat, and watering cans.

During group time, share fingerplays and books on flowers. If the climate and space permit, plant an outdoor flower garden. Take a field trip to local flower gardens or a greenhouse. Another option is to invite a florist or gardener to the classroom. Learning experiences should promote whole child's development. They should be meaningful and facilitate active play, exploration, and inquiry.

18.2-5 Documenting Children's Learning

Teachers should continuously document the children's learning since development is uneven. Documentation should show verbal or visual evidence of the children's experiences. It shows what children are learning from the curriculum and how. Examples of documentation may include photographs, children's artwork, videos, teacher observations, learning stories, and samples of children's work. Documentation is important both to the children and their parents or guardians. Children can note that their teacher and families value their work and take pride in their accomplishments, which helps build their confidence. Parents or guardians gain a better understanding of what the children are learning and how their development is progressing. Documentation also encourages teacher dialogue with family members.

Lesson 18.2 Review

1. Which of these is not a characteristic of *emergent curriculum*? (18.2.1)
   A. Child-centered
   B. It "emerges" from the children's interests and experiences
   C. It involves both the participation of teachers and children in decision-making
   D. It involves rote learning techniques

2. **True or False.** A web is a planning tool or map that outlines concepts related to a theme. (18.2.2)

3. What is a block plan? (12.2.3)
   A. A detailed plan that includes early learning standards
   B. A plan that outlines specific actions and activities that will be used to meet the goals and objectives
   C. A plan more likely to be developed for scripted lessons when adults provide directed instruction
   D. An overall view of the curriculum

4. Which is not a part of a learning expectation? (18.2.3)
   A. Condition of Performance
   B. Motivation
   C. Level of performance
   D. Behavior

5. **True or False.** The classroom environment should reflect the curriculum theme. (18.2.4)

6. How often should a teacher document a child's learning? (18.2.5)
   A. Weekly
   B. Monthly
   C. Continuously
   D. Yearly

Chapter 18 Review and Assessment

Summary

- -

Lesson 18.1

18.1-1 Programs goals are essential for planning developmentally appropriate curriculum that provides children with joyful, engaged learning.

18.1-1 Goals should allow every child to flourish and reach their potential.

18.1-2 Teachers use a variety of methods and activities to meet program goals.

18.1-3 Directors, teachers, aides, families, and nutritional coordinators are often involved in curriculum planning.

18.1-4 Assessment provides useful information on children's developmental levels that early childhood professionals use for curriculum planning.

18.1-5 A content- and process-centered approach to curriculum involves hands-on, interactive activities that support all developmental domains.

18.1-6 Teachers consider many factors in curriculum planning, including skills and content.

18.1-6 As you plan the curriculum, your goal is to stimulate the children's curiosity, stretch their imaginations, and thirst for knowledge.

18.1-6 While developing the curriculum, balance the learning activities and consider individual learning styles and characteristics.

18.1-7 Before planning the curriculum, the center staff need to review the state's early learning standards. After that, review the center's goals. Finally, review the children's assessment information, which identifies their strengths, needs, interests.

Lesson 18.2

18.2-1 An emergent curriculum is child-centered and emerges from children's interests and experiences. Both teachers and children help make decisions about curriculum that is meaningful to children.

18.2-2 Themes help teachers organize curriculum content around children's interests. Activities, concepts, and vocabulary words are often selected based on a theme.

18.2-2 Teachers often use a web to help outline major concepts that relate to a theme.

18.2-2 Integrating STEM and STEAM concepts through activities helps children learn critical-thinking and problem-solving skills.

18.2-3 Written plans are developed that include a variety of activities for all the classroom areas.

18.2-3 Block plans are essential in developing and executing a curriculum that meets children's needs.

18.2-3 Lesson plans provide the details for implementing the activities identified on the block plan.

18.2-3 After the curriculum has been introduced, the last step is evaluation to improve teaching plans, skills, and the environment.

18.2-4 The learning environment should support the curriculum theme and be apparent to anyone who walks into the environment.

18.2-5 Documentation helps teachers intentionally plan a developmentally appropriate curriculum. The data helps them to identify and individualize practices to support every child.

Vocabulary Activity

Classify the *Key Terms* into categories. Then pair up with a classmate and compare how you classified the terms. How were your lists similar or different? Discuss your lists with the class.

Critical Thinking

1. **Compare and Contrast.** Research the early learning standards for your state and for one other state. Read both sets of standards carefully and then compare the early learning standards. How are they alike? How do they differ? Then, compare your finding to the Head Start Early Learning Outcomes. Do you think one set of standards is more effective than another?

2. **Cause and Effect.** Early learning standards can greatly impact curriculums. Interview an early childhood teacher and ask how standards are incorporated into the curriculum. Present the information you learn to the class.

3. **Determine.** Determine ways to teach self-help skills to preschoolers through direct and indirect learning experiences. First, plan a direct learning experience to teach preschoolers self-help skills, such as how to button their coats, wash their hands, or brush their teeth. Then, plan several indirect learning experiences and teachable moments that could be used as a learning opportunity for reinforcing the self-help skill.

4. **Draw Conclusions.** Review the web for a puppet theme in Figure 18.13 in the text. After reviewing the web, find a partner and draw conclusions about how the web could be adapted for activities with a group of two-year-olds. Plan developmentally appropriate activities that will address all the concepts in the web.

5. **Evaluate.** Using the criteria in the text, write five learning objectives for preschoolers. Then, exchange papers with at least two classmates. Evaluate your classmates' learning objectives and provide feedback about what they can do to strengthen these objectives. Implement the feedback you receive.

6. **Analyze.** Visit an early learning center and observe the materials, decorations, and objects in the space. Ask the teacher what themes the children are studying and then analyze how the classroom environment reinforces these themes. Write a short essay about the role of classroom environment in curriculum and theme.

Core Skills

1. **Speaking.** Interview an early childhood center director or teacher about curriculum planning. Who plans the curriculum in the early childhood center? What are the program goals, and how were those program goals developed? How did they conduct the assessment process during planning and what factors contributed to the curriculum currently in place? Deliver a presentation covering the information you learned during the interview.

2. **Research.** In small groups, research information about children's learning styles and characteristics. Take notes about learning styles that were not covered in this text. Choose three unfamiliar learning styles and research them in-depth, including their descriptions, prevalence, and ideal learning environments. Create a digital presentation detailing these learning styles. At the end of your presentation, lead a class discussion about the benefits for parents and teachers knowing a child's

learning style. What could result if a child could learn only using or never using his or her preferred style?

3. **Social Studies and Writing.** Research three countries and cultures other than your own to discover how culture affects the educational system. What countries or cultures have little or no emphasis on education because of cultural expectations for their children? Which have developed requirements based on high expectations for education and learning? Write a four- to five-page essay comparing these cultures and explaining how their values and beliefs affect their education system.

4. **Technology.** Select a theme from the list in the text for three-year-olds. Then, use a digital program to create a block plan for a morning session. Make sure you add a variety of large group activities that directly relate to the theme. Always check your block plan for accuracy, grammar, and spelling.

5. **Writing.** Select an activity from the block plan you created for item 4 and create a detailed lesson plan for this activity following the lesson plan format in this chapter. Be sure to think through all aspects of the activity and its benefits for children. Always check your block plan for accuracy, grammar, and spelling.

6. **CTE Career Readiness Practice.** At a recent parent-teacher conference, one of the families in your center suggested you incorporate a lesson on preparing pancakes. Intrigued by the idea, you wrote a lesson plan for it and planned a follow-up meeting with the parents and families to learn more about their idea. What questions would you ask the family members? What answers would you need in order to write your lesson plan and present it to the center director? Role-play the interview with a classmate and then write a comprehensive lesson plan based on your classmate's answers to the questions.

Portfolio Project

Select several of your own lesson plans to add to your portfolio. Selected plans should contain all eight steps of lesson design. Plans should be developmentally appropriate for the age of the children for which the lessons were designed. You may wish to document the presentation of a lesson by including photographs of your teaching and the children participating. A self-evaluation of the lesson should also be included along with a teacher evaluation, if available.

Guiding Art, Block Building, and Sensory Experiences

Lesson 19.1: Foundations of Art

Lesson 19.2: Painting Activities and Art Techniques

Lesson 19.3: Block Building, Sensory Experiences, and Woodworking

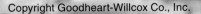

Copyright Goodheart-Willcox Co., Inc.

Case Study

What are appropriate comments to make about children's artwork?

Pedro, a new early childhood major, was assigned to do a practicum experience at the Meadows Early Childhood Center in Miami Beach. When he arrived at the center, the director welcomed him and walked him to a classroom with three-and four-year-old children. The head teacher showed him where to store his backpack and then gave him a brief background on the group of children. Then she told him that his assignment today was to be an observer and facilitator in the art area.

Being assigned to the art area was going to be interesting. His college course in children's art taught him that art was a medium for children to express their feelings, ideas, and knowledge in a visual form. He walked to the art area, pulled out a chair, and sat down. Then immediately, he began a conversation with a child named Edmund. He asked, "What are you making?" Edmund responded by saying, "I just drew an apple." Pedro responded by saying, "Apples are not purple." Then Edmund looked up at him with a puzzled look and said, "But my apple is purple."

Give It Some Thought

1. Is there a difference between being an observer and a facilitator? If so, describe.
2. Do you think Pedro's comment to Edmund is appropriate? Why or why not?
3. Are there any open-ended questions Pedro could ask Edmund about his art? If so, provide some examples.
4. Do you think that Pedro's comments fostered divergent thinking or cultural appreciation? Why or why not?
5. Which one of the three stages of art skill development do you think Edmund is at? What makes you believe this?
6. Beginning with dots, what is the progression of children's drawing movements?

Opening image credit: rogkoy/iStock via Getty Images Plus

Foundations of Art

Essential Question

? *What do you need to know about strategies for guiding art and the stages of art development to provide experiences for children that promote their physical, social-emotional, and cognitive growth?*

Learning Outcomes

After studying this lesson, you will be able to

19.1-1 explain how art experiences promote physical, social-emotional, and cognitive growth.

19.1-2 describe strategies for guiding art experiences.

19.1-3 identify the stages of art skill development.

19.1-4 compile a list of art supplies needed for a well-stocked classroom.

Key Terms

tactile	process-centered art
product-centered art	water-soluble

Preschool children are curious about their world. They thrive on hands-on experiences that encourage creative exploration. For them, art activities are a language. Using their imaginations, young children can think, plan, and turn their ideas into creations. Their need for movement, self-expression, and achievement is fulfilled by working with art materials. Like physical development, there is a sequence to developing drawing skills. While developing basic skills using art media, young children are expressing feelings and ideas.

19.1-1 The Importance of Art Experiences

Art promotes social-emotional, and cognitive growth in children. Art promotes physical growth through the movements involved in painting, coloring, drawing, scribbling, and playing with clay (**Figure 19.1**). All these motions improve fine-motor and visual-perception skills. Art activities promote motor development, hand-eye coordination, and problem-solving skills. In turn, these skills promote growth in other areas. In addition, art experiences help children:

- Develop positive self-esteem.
- Express feelings and ideas.
- Develop language skills.
- Experience the creative process.
- Learn to identify shapes.
- Learn the names of colors.
- Observe color, shape, texture, and line composition.

MBI/Shutterstock.com

Figure 19.1 Children improve hand-eye coordination during art activities that use small muscles. *How can art activities promote social skills?*

Art promotes cognitive growth. Experiences with art also help children learn responsibility. For example, children learn that they must put on their smocks before painting to protect their clothing. They also learn that they must put their work in a safe storage space when they finish it. Learning to work and share with others is stressed. In many programs, several children will share one container of paint, a box of crayons, or felt-tipped colored markers. They learn to respect the property of others. They also learn to value the work and ideas of others. While painting in group painting experiences, they develop skills in planning and turn taking.

Art experiences also promote emotional growth. Through a creative activity, children learn a means of communication other than verbalization. They can transform their feelings and ideas into a visual form. For example, pounding at the woodworking bench, hitting play dough, or scribbling with crayons allows angry children to express their frustrations in an acceptable way. Children also have the chance to choose their own activity. For instance, during a painting session children decide what they will paint. Their choices—a pet, a friend, or a flower—often express their feelings. Through art, they learn to communicate feelings nonverbally.

Finally, exploring, experimenting, and problem-solving with many materials and tools promotes children's cognitive growth. Through this process, they use the skills of an investigative scientist. They learn important concepts, such as color, size, texture, and shape. By manipulating and controlling tools, children learn such skills as drawing and cutting. They learn that cutting takes things apart while taping and stringing helps put materials together. Visual and **tactile** skills (those that relate to sight and touch) also develop. For example, rolling, rubbing, pounding, and tearing can change how an object looks and feels. Children also learn visual discrimination skills, cause-and-effect relationships, and experimentation.

There are two types of art experiences. One type is **product-centered art**, which focuses on a model and step-by-step instructions by the teacher. The children all copy the model, resulting in a finished product planned by the teacher. This type of art is **not** developmentally appropriate. **Process-centered art** focuses on creating and is developmentally appropriate. The child's interests and development are directing them. It results in the children's unique and creative work. This type of experience is developmentally much more valuable and requires no adult input. It promotes the child's problem-solving abilities, creative thinking, imagination, and curiosity.

Health Highlights

Art Therapy for Young Children

Young children—like older children and adults—can experience events and trauma that make it difficult to cope. Life challenges, such as experiencing natural disasters, can cause emotional stress. Art therapy is a creative process that combines art and psychotherapy. In this process, children can use various art mediums to express their thoughts and feelings. If parents or guardians and care providers note a child is experiencing emotional challenges after a traumatic event, they should seek advice from the child's doctor and a professional art therapist. These professionals can help determine if the child will benefit from art therapy.

19.1-2 Strategies for Guiding Art Experiences

As a caregiver, you must be creative in your approach to art. You must observe in order to find new ways to expand children's learning experiences. Creative growth is promoted through careful choice and experimentation with *open-ended art materials* (those that can be used in many ways). A good art program encourages children to think, discover, and express their ideas. It also provides them with time to experiment and explore new materials and techniques. These experiences should involve all five senses: sight, smell, taste, touch, and hearing.

Helping children during unhurried and unstructured art activities is an important task.

Model respect for the children's work using focused attention and language. Value their efforts. Support them with gentle questions and positive comments. If done properly, children will accept your help. If done improperly, however, children will come to think of you as an intruder. Tasks done for or forced on children often cause tension and displeasure.

To foster independence, start each session by telling the children what supplies and tools are available that day. Encourage them to use the supplies (**Figure 19.2**). For instance, if they have never worked with cotton balls, tell them "I think you will enjoy painting with cotton balls. They are very soft."

As you walk through the class, observe what the children are doing. However, it is best not to ask young children what they are making. They might just be experimenting with different tools and supplies. In this case, they do not know what they are making. Keep in mind that some children lack the language skills needed to explain their artwork. Always focus on the process when commenting on the children's art experiences. Your goal is to make the children feel successful and confident. Make comments, such as those listed in **Figure 19.3**.

Let children decide when their work is finished. Take them at their word. Do not urge them to fill up space or add to their work. This decreases their pride and confidence.

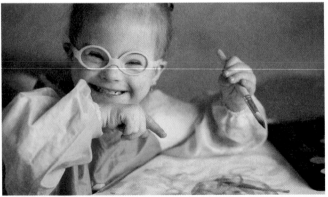

Eleonora_os/iStock via Getty Images Plus

Figure 19.2 Provide new supplies and tools to use during art activities and show the children how to use them. *What supplies and tools might foster independence?*

Commenting on Children's Art

"You're using a purple crayon."

"Your work has interesting lines."

"I see you are putting a lot of thought into creating your collage."

"What happened when you mixed red and yellow?"

"What a beautiful star you're making."

"I noticed you have used a lot of red, is that your favorite color?"

"You must really like green."

"Tell me about your art."

"That type of brushstroke feels smooth, doesn't it?"

"These colors look happy."

"Tell me about your painting. It looks so interesting."

"Look! You mixed blue and yellow together and now you have green."

Figure 19.3 When commenting on children's art experiences, always focus on the process.

Model art appreciation by offering feedback to the children about their work. However, avoid singling out one child's work as being the best. Instead, use praise that invites everyone to respect everyone else's work. For instance, you might say "Mary loves red and blue," or "Mark's colors are cheerful colors." Hanging the children's work tells them that their work is valued.

In preschool children's artwork, color does not play an important part. Often, there is no relationship between the colors chosen and the objects in the artwork. Children choose colors they like as opposed to colors that mirror real life. They may paint an apple bright pink or an elephant red. Studies show that children have color preferences. Preschool children are most fond of bold colors, as opposed to pastel colors and muted blends. Study their art work. Red, blue, and yellow are favorites. They also like orange, purple, and green. (**Figure 19.4**). Brown, white, and black are often labeled ugly. You may wish to maintain a large supply of primary colors, red, blue, and yellow, which all colors stem from. These three colors cannot be made with pigments of other colors.

Talking About Art

Conversations about art are important learning experiences for young children. They activate the children's interest, engagement, and are a great strategy for promoting literacy and language development. Young children love to share and talk about their art. When talking with them, use

kali9/E+ via Getty Images

Figure 19.4   Often there is no relationship between the colors children choose and the objects in the artwork. *Why do you think color does not play an important part in children's artwork?*

descriptive terms that include the language of art—color, line, size, and shape. Instead of making comments such as "Beautiful!" or "Nice!" regarding their work, share what you like or find interesting. You might comment about how the colors make

Focus on Careers

Art Therapist

Art therapists work in many different settings. Many art therapists work with children and students in schools, while others work in a variety of medical settings. Art therapists combine their knowledge of art, psychology, therapy, and counseling to help their clients understand themselves and work toward specific goals to deal with their challenges. For instance, if a child has experienced a trauma such as a natural disaster, home fire, or medical trauma, the art therapist will use their skills to develop strategies to help the child cope with the thoughts and feelings about the traumatic event. Art therapists must have excellent communication skills and the ability to recognize problems.

In addition to working directly with their clients, art therapists conduct assessments, create treatment plans, and write reports about their clients' progress. Sometimes, they may consult with colleagues to discuss client concerns.

Career cluster: Health science.

Education: Individuals interested in a career in art therapy must first earn a bachelor's degree in studio art or psychology. After this, the individuals must earn a master's degree in art therapy. The majority of accredited art therapy programs require students to submit a portfolio of their artwork. Graduate programs also require that students complete an internship to gain experience working with patients.

Job outlook. Employment for art therapists is projected to grow 10 to 15 percent between 2020 and 2030, or faster than average for all occupations.

To learn more about a career as an art therapist, visit US Department of Labor websites for the *Occupational Outlook Handbook (OOH)* and *O*NET OnLine.* You will be able to compare the job responsibilities, educational requirements, job outlook, and average pay for people with similar occupations.

you feel, or introduce comparison words like *lighter* or *darker*. Questions you ask include:

- How did you make your collage?
- How did you use the brush to make that stroke?
- What would happen if _____?
- What makes this piece of art so beautiful?

19.1-3 Stages of Art Skill Development

Children move through three distinct stages as they build their drawing skills. These stages are scribble, basic form, and pictorial drawing (or *first drawings*). Knowing these stages helps child care workers plan activities that reflect children's skill level. See **Figure 19.5** to learn how a child's drawing movements progress from simple to more complex.

Scribble Stage

The first stage is called the *scribble stage*. This usually occurs between 18 months and three years of age. Children's motor control and hand-eye coordination are not well developed yet. However, they can make dots, lines, multiple lines, and zigzags. Often, they hold the drawing tool with their fist. They may also appear to be drawing with every moving part of their body. In the scribble stage, children do not connect the marks on the paper with their movements. Their scribbles are by-products of the experience and are meaningful. They enjoy the physical sensation of moving a marking tool across the page.

To help children in this stage, make them aware of their movements. Comment on how hard they press their pencils, how fast they move their arms back and forth, or how large they make their movements. Such remarks help children make the connection between their actions and the art they create.

Comments about the look of children's artwork are also helpful. For example, you may say, "This is a long red line" or "This line has a curve." As you speak, trace some lines with your finger. The children's attention will focus on the form they have created.

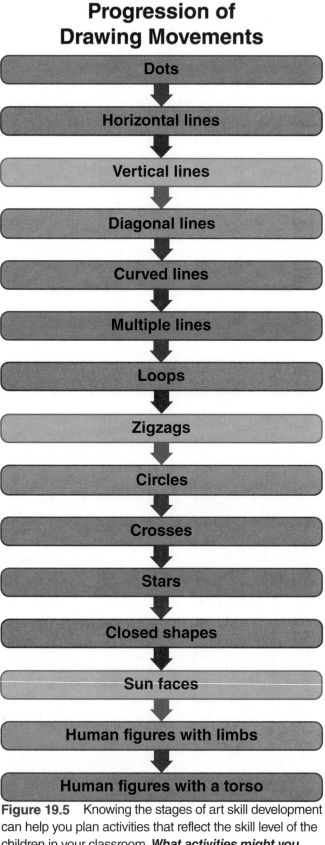

Progression of Drawing Movements

Dots

Horizontal lines

Vertical lines

Diagonal lines

Curved lines

Multiple lines

Loops

Zigzags

Circles

Crosses

Stars

Closed shapes

Sun faces

Human figures with limbs

Human figures with a torso

Figure 19.5   Knowing the stages of art skill development can help you plan activities that reflect the skill level of the children in your classroom. *What activities might you use for children who are in the scribble stage? Basic forms stage? Pictorial drawing stage?*

Basic Forms Stage

The second stage in art skill development of children is *basic forms*. This often occurs around age three. In this stage of development, children learn and recognize basic shapes such as circles, rectangles, and squares. They now have more control over their movements and better hand-eye coordination. As a result, they can control the size and shape of a line. During this stage, they use lines to create circles. They are enjoying their ability to create forms by combining scribbles.

At this stage, you can tell what the children's pictures represent. They see the connection between their movements and the marks they make. Before this time, children's scribbles resulted from the sheer pleasure of moving their arms and hands. Now children connect those motions to their artwork. Children may even name their drawings at this stage. They also start to feel pride in their work.

As in the scribble stage, you can help the children understand and talk about their work by commenting on their movements. For example, say, "You are moving your arm in big circles." You might describe the product. Say, "You have drawn a big picture."

Pictorial Drawing Stage

The third stage of art development occurs during the third and fourth year (**Figure 19.6**). During the pictorial drawing stage, children can draw marks that are representational of pictures. Drawing becomes another vehicle for communication. They attempt to mimic their view of the world. Using their increasing skill with basic forms, they combine shapes to represent objects or people. Study the art and you will notice their physical limits. The drawings are often large. The placement of their objects is random. Color is unrealistic. First, they draw humans with tadpole-shaped circles for a head and lines for limbs. After that, crudely drawn human figures emerge, which include a torso with straight lines for arms and limbs. This artwork will begin with heads, followed by limbs. Gradually, their drawings become more realistic. They add full torsos, eyes, eyebrows, noses, ears, and fingers as their perception and memory improve. Often, the children will place these

Judy Herr

Figure 19.6 First drawings represent a child's view of the world. Colors are often unrealistic. Notice that the sun is blue.

figures in context by adding the sky and ground. Animals, trees, houses, cars, boats, and airplanes now emerge in their artwork.

Overtime, children's drawings become more intentional and accurate. Their thoughts, thinking, and capacity to express themselves is rapidly changing. They add more details. To the human figure, they now may add eyelashes, ears, teeth, and hair. They may even label their pictures. After drawing a picture of a dog, they may label it. Often, they may reverse the letter "d".

There are cultural variations in art. In some cultures that highly value artistic skills, adults encourage the children to express themselves through drawing. They provide models for their children to imitate, and positive reinforcement and feedback.

19.1-4 Art Supplies and Tools

You have the option of buying or making many of your own art supplies and equipment. Most teachers need to purchase the basic tools: scissors, paintbrushes, cookie cutters, easels, and paper punches. You can purchase many of these items at school supply stores, catalogs, websites, or large discount stores.

Safety First

Buying Nonhazardous Art Supplies

The *Labeling of Hazardous Art Materials Act* requires the labeling of all art materials that pose a chronic hazard to children and others. The law applies to such children's art supplies as paint, crayons, chalk, modeling clay, colored pencils, glue sticks, and other art products.

When buying art materials for children, look for the statement "Conforms to ASTM D-4236" on the product label. This ensures that the products meet the *American Society for Testing Materials Standards* (ASTM). For more information about art supplies, consult the Consumer Product Safety Commission website.

Tempera Paint

Many early childhood centers use washable tempera paint. It has a slight odor and tastes chalky. When dry, painted surfaces may crack and peel. You can purchase tempera paint in both liquid and powdered form. Many teachers prefer liquid over powdered tempera because it does not require mixing. Since liquid tempera is much more expensive, however, many teachers still use powdered tempera. Powdered tempera paint is **water-soluble** (dissolves in water). The thickness of the mixed paint varies from a sticky paste to a runny fluid. To avoid drips and runs, mix the paint to the consistency of thick cream. Consistency will also affect the color. The colors should be bright and rich.

Some teachers mix enough paint to last for a week or two. Usually, teachers only mix a small amount of paint daily to eliminate waste because of drying. Whichever you prefer, remember to put the powdered paint in the container *before* you add the liquid. To avoid paint that is too thin, add only a small amount of liquid to the tempera while stirring constantly. This will make a very thick paste. Then slowly add more liquid until you get the desired thickness. You can also add powdered detergent to thicken the paint.

Brushes

Provide children with several paintbrushes. They should range in size from ½ to 1 inch wide. The youngest children should use the widest brushes. As their fine-motor coordination improves, give them smaller brushes. Older children with improved fine-motor coordination skills, may enjoy using other tools to apply paint. Provide them pieces of string, cotton swabs, sponges, and feathers.

Easels

Provide sturdy, adjustable easels as a place to paint, and place brushes and paint in an attached tray. Clamps or hooks at the top of the easels hold the paper in place. Adjust the height of the easel, so children do not need to stretch or stoop to paint. Also, adjust the easel so the painting surface angles or slants outward. This reduces the dripping and running of paint, and also reduces cleanup time.

Crayons, Chalk, and Felt-Tip Markers

Children enjoy using crayons, chalk, and felt-tip markers; however, these items are harder to use than paint. These tools require pushing hard with small muscles that are not well-developed in young children. Paint, however, flows easily.

Crayons come in regular and kindergarten sizes. Kindergarten-size crayons are round and large. These crayons do not break easily, nor do they roll easily off tables or other surfaces. Crayons should be nontoxic. Store them in bowls, trays, baskets, or boxes.

Chalk is available in both an art and chalkboard form. Art chalk comes in a variety of sizes. As with crayons, you can purchase chalk in large, fat sticks. Choose basic colors that are clear and brilliant. Store chalk in baskets, boxes, trays, or bowls.

Felt-tip markers come with washable or waterproof inks. Always buy washable felt-tip markers for early learning centers. Be sure that any markers you buy have tight caps to prevent them from drying out. Remind children to replace the caps after use.

Paper and Painting Surfaces

Children can use many types of paper and painting surfaces successfully for art activities. Newsprint, manila paper, construction paper, wallpaper, cardboard, and old newspapers are options. See **Figure 19.7** for other alternatives.

The least costly paper is newsprint. It is durable and easy to use. To determine the size of the paper, remember younger children have poorer muscle control. As a result, they need large surfaces on which to paint or draw. A good size for easel painting is 18- by 24-inch sheets.

Coloring Books

Coloring books contain images created by adults. Studies show that coloring books have a negative effect on children's creativity by blocking their creative self-expression. For this reason, avoid relying heavily on coloring books for children under six years old. With the limitations of designs in a coloring book, children lose the value of art as a form of expression. They become self-conscious and doubtful about their artistic talents.

For example, Sara colors in the outline of a kitten in a coloring book. The next time her teacher asks Sara to draw something, she recalls the perfect kitten from the coloring book page. She knows she could not draw that perfect kitten. She becomes frustrated and says, "I cannot draw very well." The frustration occurred because she knew her work looks like a child's as opposed to an adult's work. As a result, Sara may lose interest in the creative process of drawing.

For more enriching art experiences, however, rely on activities that allow children to explore interesting materials and experience cause and effect. Such experiences encourage children to be creative and better engage their interest in art.

Paper Alternatives for Art Activities

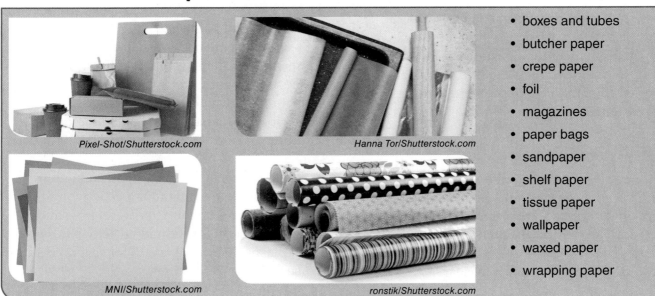

Pixel-Shot/Shutterstock.com

Hanna Tor/Shutterstock.com

MNI/Shutterstock.com

ronstik/Shutterstock.com

- boxes and tubes
- butcher paper
- crepe paper
- foil
- magazines
- paper bags
- sandpaper
- shelf paper
- tissue paper
- wallpaper
- waxed paper
- wrapping paper

Figure 19.7   Paper for use in art activities comes in many forms. Some of these types of paper can be obtained for little or no cost.

Paste and Glue Sticks

Paste and glue sticks work well for adhering to lightweight paper. Paste can be prepared or purchased. Teachers often prefer to prepare their own paste (**Figure 19.8**). To improve bonding strength, add small quantities of glue to your paste. When using glue sticks, consider the children's safety. To prevent a choking hazard, make sure to check the cap size. For young children, water-soluble adhesives are the best.

Early Childhood Insight

Preventing Glue Messes

Take precautions when using white glue. Glue is difficult to remove from clothes, carpeting, art tools, and art tables. Cover the surfaces with newspapers or washable plastic table cloths. Wipe up spills immediately. Children should wear smocks. If children use glue, provide small squeeze bottles or pour small quantities into shallow pans or jar lids. Wipe the bottles immediately after the children finish using them. Glue cleans up easily while it is still moist. Once dry, glue is difficult to cleanup. It is better to use glue with older preschoolers who are less likely to spill the glue.

Glue

The best all-purpose adhesive is a white liquid glue. The children can use it on heavyweight paper, cardboard, fabric, plastic, and wood. Glue is more permanent than paste and is often more costly. If purchased by the gallon, it is a better value. Many building supply stores carry glue in gallon containers.

Cleanup Tools

Keep cleanup tools in the art area so they are available when spills occur. Small buckets, sponge mops, and various sizes of sponges are useful. Keep supplies within children's reach. Cut mop handles down so they are child sized. This will encourage children to assist in cleaning.

Paste Recipe

1 cup cold water
1 cup flour*
2 1/4 cups boiling water
1 teaspoon powdered alum
3/4 teaspoon oil of wintergreen (optional)

Mix the cold water with the flour, stirring until smooth. Continue stirring while adding boiling water. Cook mixture on low heat in a double boiler until smooth. Add the alum and stir. At this time, the mixture should look slightly bluish-gray and shiny. Remove from heat and add oil of wintergreen for an interesting smell. Store in a cool place.

To reduce the risk of Salmonella or E. coli bacteria, bake the flour prior to the activity. Preheat the oven to 350 degrees. Spread the flour on a cookie sheet. Bake for a minimum of 5 minutes.

Figure 19.8 Preparing your own paste can be more economical than purchasing paste ready-made. *What factors may impact whether you purchase or make your own paste?*

Space and Storage

Well-planned space is a requirement to encourage children to use the art area. Storage and display areas for artwork are part of a well-planned space. Bookshelves can store staple supplies. These supplies include paper, scissors, paste, glue, collage materials, crayons, markers, chalk, tape, and paint.

Containers are necessary to store paint, paste, scissors, and collage materials (**Figure 19.9**). Many centers use plastic cups and plastic bowls to store tempera paint. Shallow dishes, including empty frozen food containers, can hold paint during painting activities. After use, cover the paint for storage.

Paste containers may be small enough for one child or large enough for a group to use. The size will depend on the activity. Empty squeeze bottles are useful for individual activities. Foil or small plastic dishes are useful for several children to use together at one time.

Store scissors within easy reach. You may purchase special scissor holders through supply catalogs. Otherwise, store scissors in baskets.

Collage materials require the organization to appeal to children. Sort and place them in clear plastic boxes, shoe boxes, plastic dishpans, or baskets. Then, place these containers on a shelf within eye level of the children.

Jamie Lynch

Figure 19.9 Store materials in individual containers. *Why does storage of art materials require good planning?*

Lesson 19.1 Review

1. Each of the following are ways art experiences promote social growth *except* _____. (19.1.1)
   A. develop positive self-esteem
   B. express feelings and ideas
   C. learn to identify color names
   D. transform feelings into a visual form

2. _____ promote(s) creative growth through careful choice and experimentation. (19.1.2)
   A. Art therapy
   B. Imagination
   C. Structured art materials
   D. Open-ended art materials

3. Each of the following is important to do when conversing with children about their art *except* _____. (19.1.2)
   A. use descriptive terms that include the language of art
   B. make comments such as "beautiful," "nice," or "great"
   C. introduce comparison words like *lighter* or *darker*
   D. share what you like or find interesting about their work

4. During the _____ stage, children's motor control and hand-eye coordination are not yet well developed. (19.1.3)
   A. basic forms
   B. pictorial drawings
   C. scribble
   D. first drawings

5. During the _____ stage, drawing becomes another vehicle for children's communication. (19.1.3)
   A. scribble
   B. basic forms
   C. intentional drawings
   D. pictorial drawings

6. Which of the following is *not* true about mixing tempera paint to the desired consistency? (19.1.4)
   A. Add the liquid to the container before you add the powdered paint.
   B. Add only a small amount of liquid to the tempera while stirring constantly.
   C. Continue adding more liquid while stirring until you get the desired thickness.
   D. Add powdered detergent to thicken the tempera paint.

7. Which of the following summarizes the controversy concerning the use of coloring books? (19.1-4)
   A. With coloring books, children become more self-aware and secure about their artistic talents.
   B. Coloring books have a negative impact on children's creativity and block self-expression.
   C. Coloring books encourage interest in the creative process of drawing and painting.
   D. Coloring books provide more enriching experiences for children.

Essential Question

 What do you need to know to create a variety of painting, molding, and collage activities for young children?

Learning Outcomes

After studying this lesson, you will be able to

19.2-1 plan a variety of painting activities using a number of painting mediums.

19.2-2 develop a variety of molding activities using clay, doughs, and other molding materials.

19.2-3 create cutting and collage activities using a variety of materials.

19.2-4 analyze ways to display children's work.

Key Terms

convergent thinking	texture painting
divergent thinking	salt painting
string painting	spice painting
mono-print painting	Plasticene®
chalk painting	collage

Painting is magic to young children and provides them with a safe outlet to their express feelings and ideas. The process gives them critical sensory input that promotes the development of neural connections. Touch, sight, sound, and smell are all stimulated depending on the activity. Math, visual perception, science, language, and fine motor skills are promoted. Painting also provides a hands-on activity that promotes the development of problem-solving abilities. When working with art, young children develop *convergent* and *divergent* problem-solving

skills. With **convergent thinking,** there is only one correct way or approach. When faced with a task or problem, employing **divergent thinking** allows the child to think creatively and use their imagination to discover new possibilities and evaluate results. This process enhances their problem-solving skills, creativity, confidence, and enjoyment of the artistic process.

19.2-1 Painting Activities

To learn what painting means to young children, listen and watch. You will note that most children find their work pleasing. The artwork of a two-year-old is different from that of a four-year-old. Children's paintings change from simple dots and strokes to crude figures as they move through art development. Some children enjoy moving the tools. Other children enjoy the feelings and visual aspects.

Consider some children you might meet. Noah, a two-year-old, seems to be fascinated by the painting process. He dips his brush and paints, making large circles over his entire paper. Noah's friend Chantou delights in moving the brush back and forth. When dipping the brush into different colors, Chantou ignores the cleaning process.

Georgie is curious and loves the classroom art area. The teacher observes Georgie' sustained interest in experimenting with mixing paint colors. These are teachable moments for promoting the scientific method. The teacher asks Georgie intentional questions, such as: "What will happen if we mix red and yellow together?" How can you make the color pink? What happens when you add white to blue?"

Thiago, an active three-year-old, makes large dots and zigzags all over the paper. Thiago pays little attention to the paint color but carefully observes his strokes. Harper, another three-year-old, paints different colors on top of each other. As a result, Harper's paper becomes soaked. She uses her hand to feel the paint. Then Harper removes the painting from the easel. During this process, it tears. This does not bother her. Like most three-year-olds, Harper is interested in the process, not the product. She paints one color on top of another and enjoys observing the changes in the layers of colors.

Dakota, a highly verbal five-year-old, is comfortable handling the brush. Dakota paints a man by making a circle face, and then paints straight lines to represent legs. Dakota uses a smaller circle for a mouth, two large round dots for eyes, and a V-shaped figure for a nose. While painting, Dakota keeps renaming the figure and inventing related stories. First, Dakota tells a child standing close by that the figure is a police officer, but claims the same figure is a firefighter.

Children like Dakota are not unusual. Some comment to themselves as they paint. They appear to be carrying on a conversation with their painting. These comments are useful. They tell you what the child feels and thinks. Sometimes children are eager to discuss their artwork; other times they are not.

There are many types of painting activities that children will be eager to do. Included are easel, finger, string, texture, salt, mono, spice, and chalk painting. From these experiences, children learn to apply the correct amounts of paint and to recognize color and shapes. They also learn about colors, sizes, shapes, and textures.

Easel Painting

Easel painting should be a daily activity in all early childhood programs. Provide an easel, paper, brushes, and washable tempera paint. Children can use easels indoors and outdoors. Position the easels to invite social interaction among children, and adjust them to the correct height for the children. Provide brushes with long handles (about twelve inches) in a variety of sizes and materials on the easel tray. The size of

Workplace Connections

Observing Children as They Paint

Observe two- through five-year-olds during painting activities. Record characteristics of the children's processes for creating art. Photograph the finished artwork and label the photos by the child's age and name spelled according to family preferences.
1. What activities were the children engaged in?
2. Compare your photo with those of other students in your class.

the paper you give the children will depend on the activity and age of the children. For young children, provide large sheets of newsprint. Sheets of this size will encourage the use of large muscles. On special occasions, you may wish to provide colored paper and white tempera.

To ensure success in easel painting, plan the session ahead of time. Provide only a small amount of paint since children often spill. Pour only enough washable tempera paint to cover the bottom of the container. This will save cleanup time. Make only one color of paint available for early experiences and toddlers. When adding a second color, provide a brush for each container.

Permit only one child to use each side of the easel at a time. Encourage children to wear smocks. Push long sleeves above their elbows to prevent paint from getting on their clothing. Encourage the children to paint in different positions, such as standing up or sitting down. You might also position the paper at different angles.

Teach young children how to use the paintbrush. Gently dip the brush into the paint container (**Figure 19.10**). Then wipe the brush on the side of the container. This will rid the brush of extra paint. As children gain skill, give them smaller brushes and pieces of paper with which to work. Wash brushes after use. Until you plan to use them again, place the brushes with handles down in a storage container. This allows the bristles to dry.

Figure 19.10   Provide children with a variety of tools for applying paint. ***Why is it important to teach children how to use painting tools?***

Finger Painting

Finger painting is a hands-on, open-ended sensory experience that provides a cool, squishy sensation. It promotes self-expression and the release of feelings. It is one of the most satisfying experiences for young children. Some may resist their first experience because they fear getting dirty. After having the chance to observe, these same children may begin painting with one finger. Later, when they become comfortable, they will use their hands and arms as brushes.

Since finger painting can require a lot of cleanup, cover the tables if they are not washable. Otherwise, provide a plastic cover. The children should always wear aprons or smocks during this activity. Provide wet sponges and rags to facilitate the cleanup process.

Finger painting requires more supervision than most other painting activities. For this reason, work only with four children at a time. Children need to stay at the table until they finish painting. They must wash their hands immediately after painting.

See **Figure 19.11** finger-paint recipes. You can also make finger paint from soap flakes whipped with water or shaving cream. Children enjoy using a variety of paints.

Provide children with paper that has a shiny surface. This can be finger-painting paper, butcher paper, shelf paper, or freezer wrap.

Early Childhood Insight

Rainbow Stew

Prepare individual bags of "Rainbow Stew" for each child using the following recipe: Mix 1/3 cup granulated sugar, 1 cup cornstarch, and 4 cups cold water. Cook this mixture until thick, then divide into individual bowls and add food coloring. After cooling, carefully spoon some of each color side by side into a zip-type plastic bag and seal. The children can squeeze the bags to mix colors and enjoy the sensory experience while creating their own rainbow.

Finger Paint Recipes

Speedy Finger Paint	Blender Finger Paint	Cornstarch Finger Paint

1 cup laundry starch
 	
3 cups soap flakes
 	
1 cup cold water
 	
    Mix all ingredients together. If colored finger paint is desired, add food coloring or colored tempera paint.
	1-pound powdered tempera paint
	
	1/4 cup liquid starch cup water
	
	1 tablespoon powdered laundry detergent
	
	    Place ingredients in blender. Mix until finger paint is blended well.
		1 cup dry starch
		
		1/2 cup water
		
		1-1/2 cups boiling water
		
		3/4 cup powdered laundry detergent
		
		    Mix starch and 1/2 cup water in heat-resistant bowl. Add 1-1/2 cups boiling water while stirring rapidly. Blend in 3/4 cup powdered laundry detergent until smooth. Add food coloring if color is desired.

Figure 19.11   Making finger paints from everyday materials is cost effective. *What might be a benefit of making finger paint from soap flakes?*

String Painting

To prepare for **string painting**, cut several pieces of heavy yarn or string. Place a tray, or trays, of colored tempera paint and paper on the table. Show the children how to slide the yarn through the paint and across the piece of paper. Another technique is to place the string in a folded piece of paper and pull it out.

Mono-Print Painting

A **mono-print painting** starts with finger painting over an 8- by 12-inch or larger piece of paper. After this, place a similar-sized piece of paper over the finger painting. Pat the papers together and then pull them apart.

Chalk Painting

To make a **chalk painting**, dip chalk into water and draw on construction paper. Use chalk at least one inch thick. Choose a paper color based on the color of chalk you are using. Add vinegar to the water to deepen the color of the chalk.

Texture Painting

Make paint for **texture painting** using liquid tempera or mixing powdered tempera with liquid starch. To this mixture, add sand, sawdust, or coffee grounds. For best results, the paint should be thick.

Salt Painting

Materials for **salt painting** include construction paper or cardboard, paste or glue, cotton swabs or tongue depressors, and salt mixed with dry colored tempera in shakers. Have the children spread paste or glue on the paper. Then have them shake the salt mixture onto the glue or paste. Shake off excess mixture and set aside to dry.

Spice Painting

Spice painting results in a scented painting. Prepare the mixture by adding a small amount of water to liquid glue. Give children enough glue to spread over their pieces of paper. They can use their fingers to do this. Then have them shake spices onto the paper. When dry, their artwork will look as interesting as it smells.

Cinnamon, onion powder, garlic powder, and oregano make aromatic paintings. For texture, use bay leaves, cloves, or coffee grounds. The center's budget may dictate which and how many spices you can use.

Utensil Painting

Utensil painting materials include cookie cutters, potato mashers, whisks, toothbrushes, pastry brushes, and spatulas. Create a thick paint using tempera paint with added detergent and pour it into a tray. Provide the children with a variety of paper sizes.

Object Painting

Collect objects that children can paint, such as pine cones, rocks, shells, and pieces of unfinished wood scraps. Provide the children with tempera paint and brushes.

19.2-2 Molding

Young children love molding materials. Play dough, Plasticene®, and clay are open-ended materials that children can mold or form. Children enjoy the tactile appeal of these responsive materials. Because children can reshape them, molding materials stimulate the imagination and allow children the freedom to change their minds. You will observe them poking, rolling, stretching, pounding, squeezing, coiling, flattening, tearing, and attaching pieces to the clay or play dough. Children may turn it into a ball, snowman, cat, pancake, or snake. Often the children will use accessories such as pans, cookie cutters, and rolling pins to make pies, cookies, and other "baked goods" from these materials.

Molding materials are shared materials; therefore, it is important that children wash before and after use. Children's play with molding materials reflects their level of development. Two-year-old children pull, beat, push, and squeeze. When children are about three years of age, they make balls and snake-like shapes. By age four, children can make complex forms, some of which they name. By age five, children will often announce what they are going to make before they begin.

Regardless of age, children have fun developing their fine- and gross-motor coordination skills. Play dough and clay provide an emotional outlet for the children to express and explore their feelings. Working with these materials also helps them make important mathematical, artistic, and scientific discoveries. This play also encourages their language and literacy skills.

Clay is available at local art-supply stores, online, or through school catalogs. It is available in two colors, white or red. When wet, the white clay appears grayish. Since red clay can stain clothing and carpeting, most teachers prefer white. After properly mixing clay, store it in a plastic bag, diaper pail, or garbage pail to prevent drying. Use clay on a vinyl tablecloth or tile to save on cleanup time.

Play dough is soft and pliable, and it has a softer texture than clay. It offers little resistance to pressure and responds easily when touched. Each type of play dough has distinct features. Provide the children with several types by using the recipes in **Figure 19.12**. When preparing play dough, you need to be careful to reduce the risk of Salmonella or E. coli. Spread the flour on a cookie sheet or cake plan. Preheat the oven to 350 degrees. Bake the flour for a minimum of five minutes before mixing it with the other ingredients.

You can vary these play doughs even further by adding pebbles or sand. Scented oils, such as peppermint and wintergreen, add a fragrant smell. Certain smells may boost attention and learning. Others may increase the ability to think creatively.

Many teachers use Plasticene® for modeling. **Plasticene**® is a putty-like modling material available in one-pound packs. It is an oil-based, commercially manufactured modeling compound. It is available in many bright colors including blue, green, orange, red, and yellow.

Unlike play dough and clay, Plasticene® does not dry out. It can be rolled up and used repeatedly. It requires little care, even when children use it daily. If Plasticene® is cold, it may be hard for young children to manipulate. So, you will need to give them a smaller piece. Teachers claim it has one disadvantage. It can leave an oily residue on the children's hands and table surfaces. For this reason, some teachers do not make it available to the children.

Play Dough Recipes

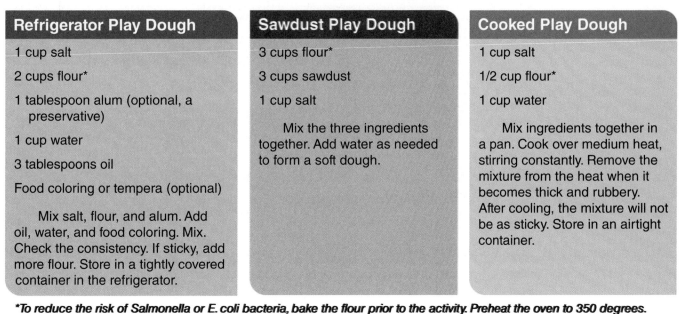

Refrigerator Play Dough

1 cup salt

2 cups flour*

1 tablespoon alum (optional, a preservative)

1 cup water

3 tablespoons oil

Food coloring or tempera (optional)

   Mix salt, flour, and alum. Add oil, water, and food coloring. Mix. Check the consistency. If sticky, add more flour. Store in a tightly covered container in the refrigerator.

Sawdust Play Dough

3 cups flour*

3 cups sawdust

1 cup salt

   Mix the three ingredients together. Add water as needed to form a soft dough.

Cooked Play Dough

1 cup salt

1/2 cup flour*

1 cup water

   Mix ingredients together in a pan. Cook over medium heat, stirring constantly. Remove the mixture from the heat when it becomes thick and rubbery. After cooling, the mixture will not be as sticky. Store in an airtight container.

*To reduce the risk of Salmonella or E. coli bacteria, bake the flour prior to the activity. Preheat the oven to 350 degrees. Spread the flour on a cookie sheet. Bake for a minimum of 5 minutes.

Figure 19.12   Each type of play dough has different features. *Why is it important to bake the flour before making play dough?*

19.2-3 Cutting

Children need time, supplies, and space each day for cutting. Young children learn to cut because they enjoy using scissors. At first, children just snip in a straight line. Provide strips of construction paper or wrapping paper. The paper should be long enough so the children may hold fast to one end of it. Avoid heavy wrapping paper, corrugated paper, or vinyl paper. These materials are developmentally inappropriate for young children. Children do not have enough fine-motor strength to cut through these materials. As children progress, they may wish to cut in curves. This requires more refined hand-eye coordination skills.

Have children work with one type of paper. This allows them to achieve mastery with handling one type of material and a cutting tool. Children between two-and-a-half and three years begin using a scissors. They need blunt scissors that open and close easily. This type of scissors prevents puncture wounds. Three and four-year-old children need quality blunt scissors with special nonstick blades. These scissors can cut through sticky materials such as stickers, cellophane tape, and glue. Older four- and five-year-old children are becoming proficient at cutting. Provide children who are left-handed with proper scissors. Mark these scissors with colored tape so the children can identify them. Periodically check scissors to ensure they are working properly.

19.2-4 Collages

The term **collage** refers to a selection of interesting materials mounted on a flat surface. Collages are creative two-dimensional arrangements of many materials. Making collages gives children the chance to make choices and create visual meaning. They decide what materials, colors, and textures to use and where they will place them. Two-year-olds may paste layers of materials on top of each other. Collages also introduce many materials of contrasting colors and textures to children. **Figure 19.13** lists materials that children can use in collages. Consider the children's ages when choosing collage materials. For instance, buttons, beads, or

Objects for Art Activities

Object Categories	Objects
Metal	foil, tinsel, trays
Cardboard	colorful cardboard, corrugated, packing boxes, shoe boxes, tagboard
Fabric	burlap, carpet pieces, cloth scraps, felt, netting, pom-poms, shoe laces, string, yarn
Paper	bows, bags, can labels, cartons, confetti, cups, baking cups, colored construction paper, gift wrapping, gift boxes, greeting cards, magazine pictures, napkins, newspaper, plates, ribbons, shoe boxes, stickers, tissue paper, wallpaper, waxed paper
Nature	acorns, bark, flower petals, leaves, pinecones, sea shells, seeds, twigs, walnut shells, wood shavings
Plastic	beads, buttons, clear plastic trays, foam packing, large jewelry beads, picks, straws, tape, tiles
Miscellaneous	craft spoons, features, glitter, ice cream sticks, sponges

Figure 19.13   Making collages gives children an opportunity to practice decision-making and create visual meaning.

other small objects are inappropriate for children younger than three. These tiny items can present a choking hazard. Whatever materials you decide to use, you must carefully supervise the children.

The base for a collage should be a heavyweight material. Construction paper or cardboard is ideal.

Arrange collage materials in attractive shallow containers. These may be baskets, paper, cookie sheets, or clear plastic trays. This will allow the children to view the materials. The children can browse through the containers, choosing items for their collages. Some children will use the pieces as they are. Others will prefer cutting, tearing, or breaking them into different size pieces.

Remember to provide adhesives. Paste is good medium for younger children to use. As children gain skills in making collages, they can use liquid starch, rubber cement, and white glue. Liquid starch works well on tissue paper. Rubber cement or white glue is a better choice for heavier materials, such as buttons. To add interest, tint white glue with tempera paint.

Young children enjoy exploring paste. They often apply an excessive amount of paste to paper. Then they will pick the paste up and spread it over their fingers. They enjoy the feeling of rubbing this medium over their fingers. When children apply paste to paper, their approach is much like finger painting. They will use sweeping motions. Gradually they will develop wrist action.

Teachers often keep a portfolio for each child that includes the child's art, and the date it was created. This is one way to document a child's growth, development, and learning. Displaying the completed art projects in the classroom or entry art gallery invites a celebration of the children's creations by parents and center visitors.

Each area of the classroom should include related children's books. See **Figure 19.14** for art exploration books and multicultural art books.

19.2-5 Displaying Children's Work

Children need to know their teachers, care providers, and family members value their artwork. Displaying children's work shows respect for them and their development. Children should always have a choice, however, in whether they want to save their work.

Print the children's name and the date on their work for identification purposes. Provide drying racks in the classroom away from traffic areas. Then, if the children want to take their work home, they will not soil their clothing or the family vehicle.

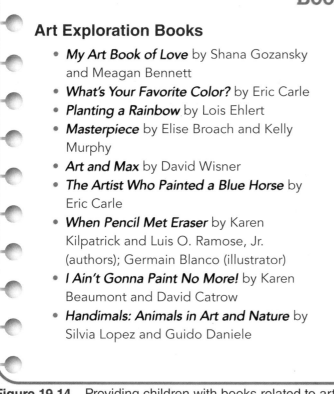

Books for Art

Art Exploration Books

- *My Art Book of Love* by Shana Gozansky and Meagan Bennett
- *What's Your Favorite Color?* by Eric Carle
- *Planting a Rainbow* by Lois Ehlert
- *Masterpiece* by Elise Broach and Kelly Murphy
- *Art and Max* by David Wisner
- *The Artist Who Painted a Blue Horse* by Eric Carle
- *When Pencil Met Eraser* by Karen Kilpatrick and Luis O. Ramose, Jr. (authors); Germain Blanco (illustrator)
- *I Ain't Gonna Paint No More!* by Karen Beaumont and David Catrow
- *Handimals: Animals in Art and Nature* by Silvia Lopez and Guido Daniele

Multicultural Art Books

- *Black is Brown is Tan* by Arnold Adoff (author) and Emily Arnold McCully (illustrator)
- *Crayola® Diwali Colors* by Mari Schuh
- *Crayola® Ramadan and Eid al-Fitr Colors* by Mari Schuh
- *The Magic Paintbrush* by Julia Donaldson and Joel Stewart
- *Shades of People* by Shelly Rotner and Shelia M. Kelly
- *To Be an Artist* by Maya Ajmera, John D. Ivanko, and the Global Fund for Children
- *From Wax to Crayons* by Robin Nelson
- *The Big Orange Splot* by Daniel Manus Pinkwater
- *Golden Domes and Silver Lanterns: A Muslim Book of Colors* by Hena Khan and Mehrdokht Amini

Figure 19.14   Providing children with books related to art helps captivate their interest in all aspects of art.

Bulletin boards are a way that centers can share and display the children's work. To be effective, position bulletin boards low enough for the children to benefit from seeing their work. Often teachers will print a title that represents the collective work. For example, titles could be *Easel Paintings*, *Finger Paintings*, and any other type of painting. Teachers might also take pictures of children working with an art medium. They can post these pictures on the bulletin board so family members can see and take pride in them.

Bulletin boards are also an important way of conveying information to classmates, families, friends, and the community. The children's work helps teach them about the curriculum. For example, you could title a bulletin board *Developmental Stages of Children's Art*. Then post an example of each of the stages. Likewise, you could make a bulletin board titled *The Value of Children's Art*. Then you could list all the skills children can learn or develop by participating in the artistic process.

Lesson 19.2 Review

1. What type of painting is an open-ended sensory experience that promotes the release of feelings and is very satisfying for children? (19.2.1)
   A. String painting
   B. Mono-print painting
   C. Finger painting
   D. Texture painting

2. Liquid tempera paint mixed with liquid starch, with added sand, sawdust, or coffee grounds is called _____. (19.2.1)
   A. salt painting
   B. texture painting
   C. spice painting
   D. finger painting

3. Each of the following is a benefit of using molding materials **except** _____. (19.2.2)
   A. language and literacy skills
   B. independence and self-help skills
   C. fine- and gross-motor coordination skills
   D. an emotional outlet to express feelings

4. Which of the following is the **best** material to provide children when they are learning to use a scissors? (19.2.3)
   A. Heavy wrapping paper or vinyl paper
   B. Construction paper or wrapping paper
   C. Corrugated paper
   D. Lightweight fabric

5. The term _____ refers to a selection of interesting materials mounted on a flat surface. (19.2.4)
   A. portrait
   B. tempura
   C. molding
   D. collage

6. **True or False.** Children should **not** have a choice as to whether or not their work is displayed. (19.2.5)

Block Building, Sensory Experiences, and Woodworking

Essential Question

What essential knowledge and skills do you need to plan effective block-building, sensory, and woodworking experiences for young children?

Learning Outcomes

After studying this lesson, you will be able to

19.3-1 analyze the benefits of block building.

19.3-2 identify the benefits of sand and water play for children.

19.3-3 develop woodworking activities suitable for young children, including safety and types of equipment and materials.

Key Terms

bridging   emergent writing

Block-building, sensory, and woodworking experiences are essential for children's development. Block-building is a vital classroom activity that encourages children to use their imaginations and problem-solving skills. In the block-building area, they are young architects at work. They develop essential math concepts as they work with number, comparisons, lengths, and balance. Executive-function skills are also promoted by practicing taking turns, sharing, and cooperating with others. While sensory play encourages learning through exploration, it also promotes social interaction, problem-solving skills, cognitive growth, and motor skills. It influences how children learn about the world and helps build the nerve connections in the brain's pathways.

Woodworking is a hands-on, three-dimensional activity returning to early childhood classrooms. It was almost removed from early childhood programs due to fears of lawsuits. Now children are required to wear safety glasses and receive instruction on the proper use of all tools The woodworking area of the classroom should provide children with a sturdy wood bench and carpentry tools for building and repairing. Working in this area, children show remarkable levels of engagement. They develop mathematical thinking, knowledge of technology, and the strength and coordination to handle the tools during the process.

19.3-1 The Benefits of Block Building

Blocks promote twenty-first century skills. They are important open-ended, two and three-dimensional, learning tools for young children from infancy through the primary grades. Children have been using blocks in classrooms since the mid-1800s. Today they are probably the most popular materials in early learning centers. The number of blocks, props, and shapes increase as the children get older. Playing with blocks captivates children's interests and challenges their thinking skills. During the process, they are developing engineering concepts by planning and constructing. While building with blocks, children are in constant motion, reaching, stretching, and changing body positions. Likewise, they can see the effects of their actions.

As children work with the blocks, they are improving their eye-hand coordination skills, strengthening their muscles, and developing problem-solving skills. Through block play, children also learn many new STEM vocabulary words, math concepts, and science concepts. Playing with blocks also promotes their spatial sense and geometric thinking. Their block constructions show what they are thinking, feeling, and understanding about the world. **Figure 19.15** lists the many ways that block play promotes learning in the four developmental domains.

Workplace Connections

Observing Block-Building Activities

Contact area centers to arrange a visit to observe children during block-building activities. Identify the ages of the children, the blocks the children are using, and any accessories children use with block play. Compare the block-building activities and stages you observed with those observed by other students in your class.

1. Does the teacher schedule sufficient time, 50–60 minutes, for block building?
2. Does the teacher offer targeted feedback? If so, provide examples.
3. Did any children name their structures or create stories about them?

Stages of Block Building

Children's block play becomes more complex as they grow older. The stages of block building include the following:

- *Stage One: Carrying.* At one to two years of age, children carry the blocks around and do not engage in construction. They enjoy filling containers with blocks and dumping them out.
- *Stage Two: Building.* From two to three years of age, building begins. The children will either stack the blocks vertically or lay them in horizontal rows (**Figure 19.16**). They strive to build towers higher until they fall, and their "roads" become longer and longer.

  They usually keep building until they run out of blocks or space. They may also combine horizontal rows of blocks.
- *Stage Three: Bridging.* Simple bridging occurs. **Bridging** is the process of placing

two blocks vertically a space apart. Then a third block is added. Children build these bridges repeatedly.

- *Stage Four: Enclosing.* Children begin to construct square enclosures. They enjoy building houses, apartments, barns, stores, caves for animals, and other types of buildings. Naming begins at this stage.
- *Stage Five: Making Decorative Patterns.* By four years of age, children build more intricate buildings. These buildings are now higher, wider, and more elaborate. Children begin to choose blocks carefully to carry out their designs.
- *Stage Six: Naming.* The children name their structures and include dramatic play by about 4 1/2 years of age. For example, they may build structures such as an airport for toy airplanes. Barns, grocery stores, garages, zoos, and spaceships are other popular structures.
- *Stage Seven: Symbolizing.* By age five, children engage in representational play. They decide what they want to build before construction. Their structures become more symbolic and they use them in dramatic play. The children will build stores, garages, houses, and barns. Structures will now be complex. They may have two or three levels and include walls and ceilings. Once built, their play becomes more creative by adding props and accessories. Often, the children like to play with the same structure for several days.

Adding writing materials such as paper, tagboard, pencils, washable felt-tip markers and measurement devices to the block-building area during stage seven will promote **emergent writing**. The children can make signs to communicate messages, identify functions, or show ownership. Older children may even draw maps or building designs before construction. Some children may want to label or write about their structures. Other children may want to take a picture of the structure with a digital camera. They also find joy in replicating models that you have built.

Learning Through Block Play

Domain	Learnings
Physical Development	• Developing fine- and gross-motor skills • Building hand-eye coordination skills • Increasing motor coordination and strength by lifting, pulling, carrying, stretching, pushing, and stacking
Cognitive Development	• Understanding object-space relationships • Understanding balance, weight, and measurement concepts • Understanding the function of objects and structures • Exploring shapes, sizes, heights, weights, and proportions • Practicing planning and problem-solving skills • Developing organizational skills • Understanding mathematical concepts, such as *larger than* or *smaller than* • Understanding language concepts related to direction and relationship in space, such as *over, under, same, different, beside, on top of, next to, in front of, in back of* • Experimenting with gravity, balance, action/reaction, and cause and effect • Developing skills in predicting, comparing, sorting, and classifying • Developing creative expression • Negotiating and resolving conflict • Thinking about another's point of view
Emotional Development	• Gaining self-confidence • Finding a sense of accomplishment and success • Developing patience and tolerance • Expressing feelings through role-playing • Building self-regulation skills
Social Development	• Improving cooperation skills by learning to compromise and negotiate • Practicing turn-taking and sharing skills • Learning to respect the work of others • Developing friendships

Figure 19.15 Blocks are generally the most popular materials in early learning centers. *Why do you think blocks are so popular with young children?*

The following books can be showcased be in the block-building area:

- *When I Build with Blocks* by Niki Alling
- *If I Built a House* by Chris Van Dusen
- *Houses and Homes* by Pam Holden
- *Look at that Building! A First Book of Structures (Exploring Our Community)* by Scot Ritchie
- *Architecture for Kids* by Mark Moreno and Siena Moreno
- *Let's Build* by Sue Fliess and Miki Sakamoto
- *Mighty, Mighty Construction Site* by Sherri Duskey Rinker and Tom Lichenheld
- *Construction Site Mission: Demolition!* by Sherri Duskey Rinker and AG Ford
- *The Construction Alphabet Book* by Jerry Pallotta and Rob Bolster
- *Little Excavator* by Anna Dewdney

FatCamera/iStock via Getty Images Plus

Figure 19.16 These children are at stage two of block-building. They will either stack or lay the blocks vertically. *Why do you think it is important to add writing materials in the block-building area during stage seven?*

Types of Blocks and Accessories

Blocks come in a variety of materials, including wood, cardboard, plastic, rubber, and foam. Square and rectangular blocks made from lightweight materials are best for younger children. Select blocks of different shapes, colors, sizes, weights, and materials. The basic geometric shapes include circle, square, rectangle, and triangle to teach geometry concepts. Combining lines and/or curves creates each block. For example, you explain a square to the children as a figure created by connecting four lines of equal length.

Children from three to six years of age prefer unit blocks made from wood in a variety of shapes and sizes. You cannot have too many blocks. Block sets need to include a variety of shapes and sizes. Use blocks for math-related concepts, such as counting, patterning, arithmetic, and building geometric shapes (**Figure 19.17**).

Kindergarten-age children enjoy tabletop blocks. Large dominoes, Lego® blocks, Duplo® blocks, alphabet, and parquet and bristle blocks. Building plans are also available from early childhood catalogs. Children this age also enjoy reference books, such as building construction and architecture.

Place props in the block area to encourage play and stimulate the children's imaginations.

They enjoy having accessories to use with block play. Usually, they prefer simple figures such as small farm and zoo animals, multicultural people, cars, and trucks. Often, they will want to recreate a setting they have experienced. After a field trip to a farm, children may build a barn. Other settings may include airports, firehouses, parking garages, a zoo, racetracks, train stations, and bus stations. With ramps, cars, and trucks, children also enjoy exploring motion. To maintain their interests, occasionally rotate the accessories. To facilitate sharing and cooperative efforts, always buy two of each item.

Stimulate block-building play by being present in the classroom area. Sit back and observe the connections the children are making. When appropriate, call attention to the children's work to extend their learning. Capture the moment to add scientific vocabulary. Interpret and expand on what they do. With repeated exposure, they will learn to use scientific thinking and understand new vocabulary words. Avoid asking the children what they are making. They may just be exploring the aspects of blocks and do not have a plan in mind. Instead, you might ask, "Does your block building have a story?" When necessary, teach structural techniques. For example, ask "Could you add a second floor to your structure?" If the structure falls, you might add, "The block you put on top was too heavy so your structure fell down." Follow up by asking, "What will you do to keep the structure from falling again."

If space permits, encourage the children to carry over their block-building activities for others to see and enjoy. Leave the structure standing, but encourage the children to make a sign. If they cannot write, you can make the sign for them. The sign may say something like "Do not touch" or "Unfinished." When the children return to school, the sign will serve as a visual memory aid.

Begin by labeling the children's constructions using their words. For example, Morgan was building a boat and said, "This is Grandpa Anselmo's new boat." Four- and five-year-old children often enjoy creating and dictating a story for you. If your classroom does not have the space

Common Blocks

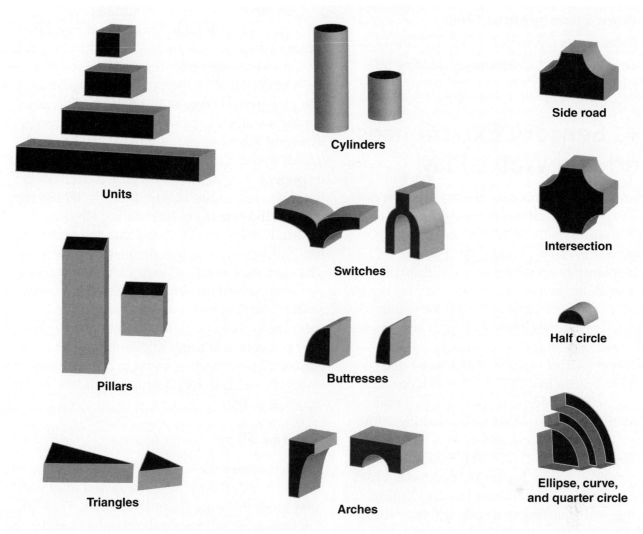

Figure 19.17 When choosing blocks for your classroom, be sure to select blocks in different shapes, colors, sizes, weights, and materials.

to save constructions for several days, take photos or make movies of the structures. Then you can place the photos on a bulletin board with the dictations.

Children need to share and showcase their block structures. Create an exhibit to document the children's block-building experiences. Using a digital camera, take pictures showing the steps the children used. Invite parents, friends, and extended families to review. Otherwise, you might want to create a digital narrative using iMovie or VideoShow.

When children are exposed to informational and architectural books, they develop an interest in architecture. With children four years of age and older, you could even sketch blueprints for buildings. Place fiction and nonfiction books on construction in the block-building area. They will help clarify and extend science and mathematical concepts and promote the thinking of engineering principles. Examples include:

- *Builders and Breakers* by Steve Light
- *Building a House* by Byron Barton
- *When I Build with Blocks* by Niki Alling
- *Billions of Bricks* by Kurt Cyrus
- *What to Do with a Box* Jane Yolen and Chris Sheban

- *Look at that Building! A First Book of Structures* by Scot Ritchie
- *Perfect Square* by Michael Hall
- *Cubes, Cones, Cylinders & Spheres* by Tana Hoban
- *Dreaming Up: A Celebration of Building* by Christy Hale

19.3-2 Sensory Experiences: Sand and Water Play

Sand and water play are *sensory experiences*. These experiences can build a foundation for understanding mathematics, chemistry, and physics concepts. Sand and water play are developmentally appropriate for children of all ages and ability levels. Like paint and play dough, water and sand are basic materials for young children. Fortunately, these materials are almost always available at little expense.

Most preschool programs offer water and sand play. Both activities can occur indoors and outdoors. Children find pleasure in these unstructured and fluid materials. Working with sand or water is relaxing and relieves tension. This type of play fosters a child's imagination, creativity, and experimentation. **Figure 19.18** includes a list of sensory table accessories for fantasy, floating, pouring, and squirting or dribbling. Water and sand play also encourage social interaction as children play side-by-side or with others.

Sand Play

An outdoor sandbox should have an 8- to 12-inch ledge around it. This gives the children a place to display their molded sand forms. It will also provide seating for the children.

Outdoors, place the sandbox in a quiet area of the playground (**Figure 19.19**). If possible, place it near a water source so children can moisten the sand. Children can use moist sand to pack molds and cans and to create castles. Moist sand is preferable to dry sand because it does not get into the eyes, shoes, or hair as easily. By placing the sandbox far from the building entrance, children will bring less sand into the center. As the children walk across the playground, some of the sand should fall off their clothes and shoes.

Place an indoor sensory table near a water source, too. Locate the indoor sensory table in or near the art area on flooring that you can clean easily. Ceramic tile and linoleum are excellent choices. Sensory tables come in different sizes to meet the needs of each group of children and the space available.

Water Play

To prevent the spread of illness, children need to wash their hands before and after water play since these are shared materials. They take joy in playing with water both indoors and outdoors. Watch them. They will splash, pour

Sensory Table Accessories

Category	Accessory Items
Floating	Boats, corks, foam, jar lids, meat trays, paintbrushes, rubber balls, sponges, wood pieces, pans of ice
Pouring	Bottles, buckets, cardboard tubes, plastic tubing, funnel cups, ice cube trays, ladles, measuring cups, measuring spoons, pitchers, pots, pans, scoops, sifters
Squirting and Dribbling	Hoses, margarine tubs, meat basters, medicine or eyedroppers, plastic tubing, spray bottles, sifters, spoons, water pumps, whisks, rotary egg beaters
Fantasy	Airplanes, trucks, cars, motorcycles, toy boats, plastic people, plastic animals, dolls, muffin tins, bread tins, cookie cutters, rubber, or plastic people

Figure 19.18 Working with sand or water in the sensory table can be very relaxing for children. *How does sand and water play help encourage social interaction?*

DGLimages/Shutterstock.com

Figure 19.19   Provide children with a variety of materials for water play to encourage mathematical concepts, social skills, and problem-solving skills.

back and forth, and make waves. In the process, they are learning physics concepts related to flow and motion. With careful supervision, water play is another activity that is developmentally appropriate for all children. Water play is about physical science. It can take place indoors or outdoors using a water table, plastic bins, laundry tubs, or wading pools. For variety, fill the tub with snow, ice, or bubbles. For interest, add food coloring or liquid detergent.

A sensory or water table should have a splash control. For safety, the frame of the water table should have rounded edges and the table should have casters. It is wise to purchase a table with a drain and valve. This will assist you in filling and draining the table if you need to move to a water source. For safety, the tables and accessories require daily disinfection when used with water.

Children should wear plastic aprons during water play to protect their clothing. Cover the floor with a plastic mat or covering to protect any carpeting. Only use unbreakable accessories in a sensory table.

Safety First

Water-Table Safety

Water tables give children much enjoyment. As an early childhood teacher, make sure you use the following safety guidelines:

- Fill the water table with fresh water before the children begin to play.
- Permit only children without cuts, scratches, or sores to play at the water table with others. In addition, if children are sick, they should not play at the water table to avoid spreading illness.
- Require children to wash their hands before and after using the water table.
- Constantly supervise children at all times when they are at the water table.
- Make sure that children do not drink water from the table.
- Clean and sanitize the water table and all toys that are used in it before the next water-play activity.

A sensory table promotes the understanding of scientific concepts such as buoyancy, density, flow, and motion. As children pour water, they promote their physical and hand-eye coordination skills. They also learn mathematical concepts, social skills, and problem-solving skills. **Figure 19.20** shows the concepts that children can learn from sand and water play. You need to promote the children's active involvement. Motivate them to observe, predict, and describe what is happening.

Children can learn many vocabulary words by playing with water. You need to be intentional and engage the children in meaningful conversation. For instance, you could place a chunk of ice into the water table. From this experience, children could learn that ice is frozen water; ice can melt; melted ice is water, ice can be picked up; ice is cold; and ice melts in warm places. When children hold ice in their hands, it melts. Other concepts children can learn about water include opposites such as *fast* and *slow*; the difference between *drip* and *drop*; and objects can *float* and *sink*. In addition, the children can learn the following words:

- leak
- measure
- mopping
- pour
- scoop
- shower
- splash
- spray
- swish
- sprinkle
- squeeze
- squish
- stir
- trickle

Each classroom area should include related children's books. The water and sensory area could include

- *Hey, Water* by Antionette Portis
- *Water Is Water* by Miranda Paul and Jason Chin
- *Tap Tap Bang Bang* by Emma Garcia

19.3-3 Woodworking

Children enjoy woodworking activities and, for safety, they should always wear googles and have close supervision. Hammering is usually their first interest. When provided with the proper tools, children may pound nails for 20 minutes. Developmentally, woodworking can be a valuable experience. It promotes hand-eye coordination, fine- and gross-motor development, and creative expression. Woodworking provides the children with an emotional release. It also encourages children to experiment and develop problem-solving skills.

If properly used, carpentry tools are safe for children (**Figure 19.21**). Teachers need to show them how to safely use the tools. In some classrooms, teachers demonstrate hammering golf tees into large foam board pieces. Some teachers have a large tree stump cut from softwood for their classroom. They place a can of large roofing nails and a hammer near the stump to encourage participation. Children who are using a hammer for the first time may want you to start the nail.

Teachers need to carefully choose tools for the woodworking bench. They should be lightweight and have handles that are easy for the children

Concepts Developed Through Sand and Water Play

Sand Play	Water Play
• Sand can be dry or wet.	• Water flows when poured.
• Sand absorbs water.	• Water takes many forms.
• Wet sand is heavier.	• Water dissolves some foods.
• Sand can be used in many ways.	• Water can be held in a container.
• Objects can be buried in the sand.	• Some items float on water.
	• Some materials absorb water.

Figure 19.20   Children learn many concepts through sand and water play.

bbettina/iStock via Getty Images Plus

Figure 19.21 Proper safety equipment should be provided for woodworking activities. **Why is it important for teachers to show children how to use woodworking tools?**

to grip. Examples of woodworking tools include claw hammers, screwdrivers, hand drills, pliers,

sandpaper blocks, a vise, and saws. Mount tools the children use frequently on the wall next to the woodworking bench. Thin nails with large heads are easiest for children to use. Wood glue should also be available.

Each area of the classroom should include related children's books. The woodworking area could introduce:

- *Whose Tools Are These? A Look at Tools Workers Use* by Sharon Katz Cooper and Amy Bailey Muehlenhardt
- *What Can You Do with a Toolbox?* by Anthony Carrino, John Colaneri, et al
- *Let's Build* by Sue Fliess and Miki Sakamoto
- *Tool Book* by Gail Gibbons
- *Building a House* by Byron Barton
- *If I Built a House* by Chris Van Dusen

Lesson 19.3 Review

1. Each of the following is a benefit of block building *except* _____. (19.3.1)
   A. blocks promote twenty-first-century skills
   B. blocks are learning tools for young children from infancy through primary grades
   C. block play promotes learning in two of the four developmental domains
   D. blocks captivate children's interests and challenges thinking skills
2. By what age do children begin to build intricate buildings? (19.3.1)
   A. Five
   B. Four
   C. Three
   D. Two
3. Each of the following is a concept children can build a foundation of understanding through sand and water play *except* _____. (19.3.2)
   A. reading
   B. physics
   C. mathematics
   D. chemistry
4. Each of the following is a concept children can learn by playing in sand *except* _____. (19.3.2)
   A. sand can be wet or dry
   B. sand absorbs water
   C. wet sand is lighter than dry
   D. sand can be used in many ways
5. Developmentally, woodworking promotes each of the following *except* _____. (19.3.3)
   A. hand-eye coordination
   B. reading and writing
   C. creative expression
   D. fine- and gross-motor development

Chapter 19 Review and Assessment

Summary

Lesson 19.1

19.1-1 Art promotes physical, social-emotional, and cognitive growth in children.

19.1-1 Through their own creativity, children express their ideas, their emotions, and learn to think critically. An effective art program fosters the children's independence, responsibility, honors experimentation, and a joy of creating.

19.1-2 Teachers need to model an appreciation of the children's creative work by taking an interest, asking thought-provoking questions, and providing positive feedback to them about their work.

19.1-3 Children move through distinct stages as they build their drawing skills: the scribble stage, the basic forms stage, and the pictorial drawing state.

19.1-3 Knowing these stages helps early childhood teachers plan activities that reflect children's skills level. Assessment data is needed to determine what types of activities, materials, and techniques will be introduced and used.

19.1-4 Art supplies Include tempera paint, brushes, easels, crayons, chalk, felt-tip markers, paper, paste, glue, and glue sticks.

19.1-4 Child-sized cleaning tools that are stored within children's reach, encourage children to assist with cleanup.

Lesson 19.2

19.2-1 Teachers can plan a variety of painting activities for children, including easel, finger, string, texture, salt, mono-print, spice, and chalk painting.

19.2-1 Children's paintings change from simple dots and strokes to crude figures as they move through art development.

19.2-2 Molding materials stimulate imagination and allow children to change their minds.

19.2-2 Along with molding materials, teachers need to provide a variety of accessories to encourage children's creativity.

19.2-3 Children need time, supplies, and materials for cutting each day to promote hand-eye coordination.

19.2-3 Teachers supply developmentally appropriate scissors.

19.2-4 Collages give children an opportunity to make choices and create visual meaning.

19.2-5 Displaying children's art helps them know their artwork is valued and respected.

Lesson 19.3

19.3-1 Block building supports twenty-first century skills such as engineering concepts, spatial sense, and problem-solving skills.

19.3-1 Children improve hand-eye coordination skills and strengthen their muscles through block play.

19.3-1 Blocks come in a variety of materials, such as wood, cardboard, plastic, rubber, or foam.

19.3-2 Sensory experiences such as sand and water play build a foundation for understanding mathematics, chemistry, and physics concepts.

19.3-2 Sand and water play is relaxing for children and fosters imagination, creativity, experimentation, and social interaction.

19.3-3 Safety is essential for woodworking activities. Children must wear goggles for eye protection.

19.3-3.1.1 Woodworking promotes hand-eye coordination, fine- and gross-motor development, and creative expression.

Vocabulary Activity

In teams, create categories for the Key Terms in this chapter and then classify as many of the terms as possible. Share your ideas with the rest of the class. Are your classifications similar or different? Why?

Critical Thinking

1. **Analyze.** Analyze the following statement about art: "Possibilities and discoveries are deeply involved in the concept of 'art.' Art is not 'crafts.' Creative art must be open-ended, no matter how messy it might be. Art is more than drawing, painting, cutting, and gluing. It's an attitude expressed from your emotions and your surroundings." Write a one-page paper about the advantages or disadvantages of creative art in preschool programs. File the completed paper in your portfolio.

2. **Evaluate.** Identify types of constructive play discussed in this chapter. Then, evaluate ways to implement strategies to encourage constructive play. What are some ways discussed to stimulate block-building play and teach structural or engineering-related techniques? What methods can you use to save children's structures?

3. **Draw Conclusions.** Review the different art materials covered in this chapter, including the various finger-paint recipes and the different blocks listed. In small groups, discuss why so many different types of art materials exist. Draw conclusions about what situations might call for each type of art material.

4. **Compare.** Visit the Consumer Product Safety Commission website and locate information about art product safety standards and voluntary standards for art materials, paints, and paper. Also, review information concerning the American Society for Testing Materials Standards (ASTM). After researching art product safety, compare the standards published by the Consumer Product Safety Commission with the standards presented in this text and at your preschool center. Prepare a presentation of your findings.

5. **Determine.** Determine the pros and cons of using coloring books or coloring pages in a developmentally appropriate curriculum. What is the position of NAEYC on using coloring books? What other fine-motor skill tasks might children be exposed to that would help them develop skills without affecting creativity and self-esteem?

6. **Create.** Choose at least two children's books from each of the lists in the chapter to begin your reference file for your early childhood career. For each book, create a digital file that includes the following information: book title, author(s), illustrator(s), year of publication, and a brief evaluative summary about the book. (As an alternative, you might consider keeping an index-card file.) Continue to build your reference file of books throughout this course.

Core Skills

1. **Speaking.** Create a library of art supply resources for early childhood classrooms. You can begin by conducting an internet search for suppliers and viewing their current catalogs. Once you have compiled 10 to 20 items for your library, present your list of items to the class and explain your rationale for choosing each one.

2. **Financial Literacy.** Prepare each of the tempera paint recipes given in the chapter. Compute the cost to make each recipe. Compare these costs to the cost of purchasing pre-made tempera paint products. Finally, organize your data into a PowerPoint presentation to deliver to the class.

3. **Writing.** Collect recipes for making homemade play doughs. Contact area early learning centers for their favorite recipes. You may also find recipes in resource books or online. Write a paper comparing the qualities of cooked versus uncooked recipes of play doughs and determining which type you most prefer for preschool use.

4. **Math.** Obtain geometric models of shapes and multidimensional figures such as cubes and cylinders from a math instructor. Arrange a display for kindergarten children and allow them to handle the shapes and models. Have children engage in drawing and painting activities and observe them to see if they incorporate the models into their artwork.

5. **Writing.** Practice composing letters that both request and thank businesses for free and donated items. Write a sample letter asking for the donation of items that are overstocked or damaged but still useful for an arts program. Include examples of items and projects for which they would be used. Businesses may have materials they do not realize could be used for creative art. Write a sample business letter thanking the business for its donations.

6. **Research.** Conduct an online search for information about the role of sensory education in Maria Montessori's method. Why did Montessori believe that educating the senses was an important part of a child's education? What types of activities did Montessori design for sensory exploration? What equipment or materials are used for sensory experiences in the Montessori method? Write a brief report to share with the class.

7. **CTE Career Readiness Practice.** Imagine that you are the codirector of a brand-new preschool center in your community. You have been put in charge of acquiring and accumulating art supplies for the preschool center, and you have been given an allowance of $50 per week for all art supplies (including writing tools, crayons, paper, and so on). Visit a local store or search online for what art supplies you would buy within the first three weeks of the center opening. Calculate your costs carefully and prepare a plan to present to the other director.

Portfolio Project

Write a description of your favorite art activity to teach. Explain why it is your favorite and why you think children would enjoy taking part in the activity. Then write a complete lesson plan for teaching the activity. Include a sample of the project and photos of the steps involved in the art activity.

Chapter 20

Reading Advantage

As you read the chapter, take notes on a presentation software program. Make one slide for each of the main headings. List three to four main points on each slide. Use the finished presentation to study for tests.

Guiding Storytelling and Language Experiences

Lesson 20.1: Storytelling and Children's Books

Lesson 20.2: Reading and Telling Stories to Children

Case Study

Storytelling and Becoming an Effective Early Childhood Teacher

Jamie Thompson was looking forward to her children's literature course. On the first day of class, the instructor said, "Children who were listened to, talked to, and read to regularly will be academically more successful." He said it is essential that storytelling opportunities be integrated into all curriculum areas. Young children need to hear language to become competent speakers, readers, and writers.

As part of the course requirements, each student was required to give a class presentation. Jamie chooses the topic of storytelling. She understands it is a critical part of the early childhood education curriculum from her readings. But she questions what her classmates need to know about the subject and what format should be used for the presentation. After much thought, she decided to create a digital slide presentation since her classmates would retain more information by seeing and hearing. After carefully researching the topic, she developed her presentation and focused on selection, illustrations, steps in reading stories, and various storytelling techniques.

Give It Some Thought

1. Why do you think storytelling is important?
2. What are the four types of children's books? What is the process for selecting them?
3. Why do you think illustrations and pictures are necessary in children's books?
4. What are the steps to follow when reading aloud to young children?
5. How can teachers achieve variety in storytelling?
6. How can dual-language learners be supported in storytelling?

Lesson 20.1 Storytelling and Children's Books

Essential Question

What do you need to know about children's books and how to select them to capture children's interests and promote language and literacy?

Learning Outcomes

After studying this lesson, you will be able to

20.1-1 **summarize** the importance and advantages of storytelling.

20.1-2 **describe** the four types of children's books.

20.1-3 **discuss** the process for selecting children's books.

Key Terms

storytelling	folktale
verbal fluency	nursery rhyme
picture book	informational text
storybook	fictional book
family life stories	review
animal stories	monolingual
fable	dual-language learner
fairy tale	bilingual
concept picture book	visual literacy
picture storybook	funds of knowledge

The words *once upon a time* convey imaginary creatures and magic for young children. The art of oral storytelling has delighted millions of children throughout the ages. By inviting children to share in a make-believe world of adventure, the storyteller stimulates wonder and fosters curiosity. Storytelling provides a wonderful educational tool for fostering a positive view of self and others.

Storytelling is the oldest form of teaching and every culture tells stories. It is an essential skill for early childhood teachers. It involves reciting a story or reading from a book. In most centers, storytelling is routine. Teachers need to read frequently to individual children, small groups of children, and the entire class, as it creates a rich sense of community (**Figure 20.1**). Storytelling is a valuable experience for children since words have a powerful impact on their development. They can develop a love for both stories and books because of daily storytelling sessions. This enhances their language development, which prepares them for thoughtful conversations. It also encourages them to talk about their own feelings.

Story books can take children on a journey to places they will never forget. Stories promote listening skills and enhance children's imagination. They help young children understand the emotions expressed by other people. Children develop an understanding of customs and culture through traditional stories. Studies show listening to stories is important for developing eventual success in reading. Language is a critical competency.

Teacher-created stories can be told without books. A well-told story captivates the children's attention and creates a sense of wonder. Stories without books can be told at any time, inside and outside the classroom.

FatCamera/iStock via Getty Images Plus

Figure 20.1 Storytelling is an enjoyable time for teachers and children. *Why should storytelling be part of the daily schedule at an early childhood center?*

20.1-1 The Importance of Storytelling

Regular storytelling promotes children's cognitive, social, and emotional development. It promotes vocabulary development and **verbal fluency** (the ability to speak easily and well). Storytelling helps young children to:

- understand the diverse people and places in the world
- gain positive perspectives, get along, and respect other people and cultures
- develop competent emotional expression
- develop a positive attitude toward books
- improve listening skills
- develop sound discrimination skills
- build correct concepts of objects and form new ideas

- build vocabulary and oral-language skills
- associate written and spoken words
- understand that print carries meaning
- understand that letters make words
- learn that people read English from left to right across the page
- develop an appreciation of printed words
- learn the difference between everyday conversation and written language
- understand that letters can be capital or small
- develop a sense of community in the classroom
- develop a desire to read (**Figure 20.2**)

Carefully chosen stories are a key part of the storytelling experience. Stories that reflect a child's home, culture, and community values help them understand themselves and others.

Hakase/iStock via Getty Images Plus

Figure 20.2 Children's desire to read is often rooted in early storytelling experiences. *From your experiences, why do you think this is true?*

Children learn the words that describe feelings and experiences they have. They learn to think about familiar situations in new ways. Stories invite children to explore and find joy and wonder about their world.

Stories also provide models of acceptable behavior and positive relationships. Using children's books to introduce problematic situations is a developmentally appropriate method of guiding children's behavior. When exposed to a variety of characters, children learn that other people often feel the same way they do. They learn how people express their feelings. They become more understanding of others' needs and challenges. They may also learn how to make good choices.

Storytelling is a critical part of the curriculum. It helps children learn reading skills. Listening comprehension precedes reading comprehension. Young children need to hear language first before learning to become readers and writers.

As a teacher reads aloud from a book, children learn how reading a book in English works. They follow the pages from left to right and from top to bottom. By watching the storyteller read, children learn the relationship between spoken and printed words. They also learn to listen. Books help children learn alphabet letters, numerals, and language.

Storytelling is also a pleasant form of relaxation. Listening to a story is a quiet activity. Children are not moving about or interacting with other children.

Workplace Connections

Early Learning Storytelling Sessions

Survey local early learning, preschool, or Head Start centers to find out the average length of a story session and how often they schedule daily storytelling activities. Write a brief report of your findings. Share your report with the class.

1. What does the teacher do to prepare for storytelling?
2. What classroom setup (location of children and teacher) provides the most effective story time experience?

20.1-2 Books as a Source of Stories

Children's books are an important source of stories for young children. There are two major groups of books: *picture books* and *storybooks*. Most books fit in these groups. **Picture books** have single words or simple sentences and simple plots. They convey meaning in both art and text. They are usually the first books family members and teachers share with young children. Some picture books are wordless, which allows the teacher or children to tell the story. Picture books promote the child's speech and imagination. These books also help children define who they are, and connects them to societal values.

After picture books, teachers introduce storybooks to young children. **Storybooks** often fit in the following categories: family life stories, animal stories, and fairy tales. These books also contain pictures, but they have more words and more complex plots than picture books. They help children understand how others feel, act, and think. Most storybooks center around the themes of achievement, love, and reassurance. A book that uses all three themes is *Peter Rabbit*. In the story, Peter has an adventure but safely returns home (achievement). His mother tucks him into bed and gives him tea (love and reassurance). Examples of other such stories include *Little Bear*, *Mike Mulligan and His Steam Shovel*, and *Little Tim*.

Selecting the right book is important. Books are like mirrors reflecting life experiences. Children see themselves in literature and love experiences that relate to their own lives. Books can help them develop a positive racial identity in a diverse society. Their race and cultural heritage are an important part of who they are, and they need to build relationships across races. Likewise, books are important for promoting the understanding and acceptance of children with diverse disabilities.

Family life stories contain the theme of social understanding. The children in these stories usually have challenges. Some challenges may be funny; some are serious; however, all problems reach resolution with love and concern. These stories help children develop social understanding by sharing the problems, troubles, and feelings of others. Examples include *Johnny Crow's Garden*, *My Dog Is Lost*, *My Grandpa*, *Timid Timothy*, and *Will I Have a Friend?*

Young children also enjoy **animal stories**. In these stories, animals often have some human qualities. Usually, the animal hero has some unusual success or ability. Examples include *Little Brown Bear*; *All About Dogs, Dogs, Dogs*; *Nothing but Cats, Cats, Cats*; and *Angus and the Cat*. **Fables** are simple stories where an animal is the main character and often points out a moral lesson.

Fairy tales are another type of book enjoyed by older children. **Fairy tales** have a theme of adventure, excitement, and achievement. The characters or heroes perform hard tasks in order to succeed. They must confront giants, witches, or other obstacles. Kindness and goodness win out over evil. *Three Billy Goats Gruff*, *Three Little Pigs*, and *Cinderella* are popular examples of fairy tales. These books are predictable. To help children make sense of the stories, the author provides obvious clues, pictures, and repeated phrases.

Health Highlights

Using Books to Teach About Health

Children love stories. Using storybooks about health, such as *Taking Care of My Teeth/Cómo cuidar mis dientes* by Terri DeGezelle, *My Tooth Is LOST!* by Drew Daywait, or *First Time Dentist* by Jess Stockham, is an excellent way to teach young children about important health concepts for everyone. In addition, teachers can use books to teach about healthy habits children can develop. One such book is *Healthy Habits* by Rebecca Weber. Review *Children's Literature About Health, Nutrition, and Safety* on the NAEYC website for a complete list of books on health-related topics for young children.

20.1-3 Selecting Children's Books

Storytelling is an art that requires study and practice. The key to success is choosing the right book. Choose books that reflect the rich diversity of all children. They should help children see themselves, including their race and cultural heritage. You need to know what the children's lives are like inside and outside the classroom to select the appropriate books. Books should also help them develop an understanding of themselves and others. School-aged children need exposure to America's rich and diverse history.

Concept picture books, picture storybooks, folktales, nursery rhymes, and informational and fictional books should all be included. **Concept picture books** consist chiefly of pictures used with prereaders. The images play an essential role in telling the story. These books teach young children early concepts such as shapes, numbers, colors, and alphabet letters. **Picture storybooks** are books that combine words and pictures to tell a story, or they may contain poetry. **Folktales** are stories typically passed on by word of mouth to stimulate the children's imaginations and share cultural traditions. The *Three Little Pigs*, *The Gingerbread Boy*, *The Three Billy Goats Gruff*, and *The Little Red Hen* are examples.

Nursery rhymes are short rhymes for children that often tell a story and are used by cultures worldwide. Their rhythmic structure helps children remember and retain words. Many examples are included in a *Mother Goose* book, such as *Itsy-Bitsy Spider*. **Informational texts** are helpful since they inform children about the natural or social environment and do not include characters. Topics include trains, airplanes, insects, plants, water, museums, and farm animals. These books stimulate knowledge, vocabulary, and comprehension skills. **Fictional books** contain illustrations and text that work together to tell a story. They are essential since they stimulate the children's imaginations and can take them to magical worlds.

Children also enjoy books that have dramatic elements. They enjoy "seeing" and "feeling" the events. Stories that mirror the children's emotional experiences will engage their hearts and minds. A story is only good if children enjoy it. If the story is to be an effective classroom activity, the teacher should also enjoy and value it. Otherwise, sharing it in an interesting way and with enthusiasm will be difficult.

Selecting storybooks is often hard for new early childhood teachers. Be intentional, equitable, and fair. You cannot leave finding good books to chance. One successful method is to look for award-winning books.

- The *Caldecott Medal* is an annual award for the most distinguished American picture book.
- For exceptional African American children's literature, check the winners of the *Coretta Scott King Book Awards*.
- The *Newberry Medal* is an annual award to the author who has made the most distinguished contribution to American literature for children.

Public libraries have many useful lists and descriptions of books, called *reviews*. **Reviews** will help you find titles, authors, and publishers of fiction and nonfiction children's books. You can order reviews from the American Library Association Children's Service. Likewise, you can also obtain a list of award-winning books through an online search.

Most children are **monolingual** and speak only one language. The number of children who are **dual-language learners**—or children who are learning two or more languages at the same time—is increasing. You may even experience children where there are several languages in their home, especially if there is an extended family. Every language is special, and you will need to support all dual-language learners in your classroom. Unless you make a continuous effort to support both the home language and English, **bilingual** (children who fluently use two languages) children will struggle. They could lose the ability to understand and speak their home language. See **Figure 20.3** for a list of popular bilingual children's books. These children need environmental supports. They need to see, hear, and speak English and their home language.

It is important to provide the children with access to high-quality multicultural literature. Sociological literature emphasizes the importance of representing all races. Studies show that children identify race as early as six months of age. Children internalize bias between two and five years of age. Children need to identify with characters in a book. Otherwise, they may assume that their lives are not very important.

There is a serious problem in children's literature that lacks diversity in showing children's backgrounds. Changes need to occur in the publishing world. It is essential that children's literature reflect, celebrate, and honor all lives. In relationship to the population, cultural diversity is exceptionally low in children's books. Approximately 50 percent of illustrations or pictures show people from a white background. The second largest category of illustrations was animals. Multicultural books reflecting the demographics of the world are also necessary. More people representing diverse ethnicities and cultures need to write books for young children that show their heritage.

Race, diversity, equity, and inclusion are all important when selecting classroom books. Children need to hear their voices in the narration of a book. They need to see people who look like themselves. Characters should represent their cultural background. Bonding with multicultural

Bilingual Children's Books

- *Bravo!* by Ginger Foglesong Guy and Rene King Moreno
- *Colores Everywhere!: Colors in English and Spanish* by Madeline Budnik
- *The Cazuela that the Farm Maiden Stirred* by Samantha R. Vamos (author) and Rafael López (illustrator)
- *Floating on Mama's Songs/Flotando En La Cancion De Mama* by Laura Lacamara (author) and Yuyi Morales (illustrator)
- *Counting with Frida/Contando Con Frida* by Patty Rodriguez and Ariana Stein
- *My Grandma/Mi Abuelita* by Ginger Foglesong Guy and Vivi Escriva
- *Manners at School/Modales en la Escuela* by Carrie Lynn Finn (author) and Chris Lensch (illustrator)
- *No More, Por Favor* by Susan Middleton Elya and David Walker (illustrator)
- *Ten Little Puppies/Diez perritos* by Alma Flor Ada and F. Isabel Campoy; English translation by Rosalma Zubizarreta
- *The Very Hungry Caterpillar/La Oruga Muy Hambrienta* by Eric Carle
- *I Need a Hug/Necesito un abrazo* by Aaron Blabey
- *The Three Little Pigs/Los tres cerditos* by Patricia Seibert
- *Big Brown Bear/El gran oso pardo* by David McPhail
- *Words Are Not for Hurting/Las palabras no son para lastimar* by Elizabeth Verdick and Marieka Heinlen
- *Jobs Around My Neighborhood/Oficios en mi vecindario* by Gladys Rosa-Mendoza
- *My House/Mi Casa* by Gladys Rosa-Mendoza
- *My Senses/Mis Sentidos* by Gladys Rosa-Mendoza
- *We Are All Alike…We Are All Different/Todos Somos Iguales…Todos Somos Diferentes* by Written and illustrated by the Cheltenham Elementary School Kindergartners and Laura Dwight
- *My Colors, My World/Mis Colores, Mi Mundo* by Maya Christina Gonzalez
- *ABC Spanish* by Aless Baylis

Figure 20.3   Books that support the home language and English are essential to helping bilingual children maintain the ability to understand and speak both languages. *What are the possible outcomes for children when there is lack of support for dual-language learners?*

books is important for children. These books carry children into different worlds, where they learn that all people have similarities and differences. People have different customs, languages, habits, working, and living behaviors.

Racial Understanding

Storytelling is a vehicle for tackling sensitive issues and developing pride in identity. Children need to value and celebrate diversity. They need to understand there are differences among people. Home languages, skin color, dress, gender, ability, food preferences, and family type are examples. Books such as *My People; Home is Window; All Are Welcome; Families; Amazing Grace; Happy in Our Skin; Hair, It Is a Family Affair; The Big Umbrella*, and; *The New Neighbors* are excellent classroom additions.

Fictional Content

Stories should reflect the children's developmental levels, backgrounds, and experiences. When choosing books for children, consider the content, illustrations, vocabulary, durability, and length of the book. Familiar objects, people, and situations make stories more interesting to children. Stories about children with backgrounds and activities like their own are special favorites.

Most preschool children cannot separate fact from fiction. Therefore, it is important to look for realistic stories. Some children are not ready for fantasy stories until they are four or five years old. Avoid books where animals or inanimate objects, such as trees and flowers, behave like humans. They should not be read to very young children who need concrete, factual, information.

Illustrations and Pictures

Illustrations are as important as the narrative in children's books, since they have an equal opportunity for telling and embellishing the story. They should be engaging and promote **visual literacy**—the ability to interpret information presented through images, such as pictures, photographs, symbols, and videos. A

Safety First

Choosing Stories Wisely

As an early childhood teacher, you will select books and stories for a variety of children. Books and stories can have a strong emotional impact on young children. Always consider the age, developmental level, interests, and cultural background of the children to whom you will tell a story. Although a classic tale such as *Little Red Riding Hood* may be fun for four- and five-year-olds, it may be truly frightening for two- or three-year-olds.

children's book should integrate the illustrations and text. The illustrations should inspire and represent the narrative. Illustrations should create interest, arouse children's imaginations, and develop an appreciation for art. Children will establish feelings and emotions by looking at the illustrations of the characters. Too much detail and shading or lack of color will confuse the children. Make sure the characters reflect the racial and cultural heritage makeup of the children in your classroom. The illustrations in a book for young children should be easy to recognize and help them make sense of the story so they can almost tell it by themselves. Children will be more interested if they can "read" the story by looking at the illustrations.

Inspiring pictures also help the children anticipate what happens next in the story. Children respond best to pictures with bright colors and large, clearly defined objects. Pictures should:

- be large, colorful, and plentiful
- represent the written word
- reflect actions
- avoid unneeded detail
- have realistic and attractive colors

Vocabulary

Writing a children's book is difficult. In an entire book, the author introduces only a few words. A good book creates a sense of wonder. It uses words most children of a certain age can understand. Although a story should introduce only a few unfamiliar words, building children's vocabularies is a goal. People think with words. The more words and richer the child's vocabulary, the more accurately the child will think and speak.

Books for young children should include repetition, rhythm, and rhyme. Repetition of some words will increase the children's enjoyment. This rhythm of word sounds is one major reason children enjoy stories, such as *Mother Goose* tales. Rhyming words, which have sounds in common, are also important.

Durability

Allow children to carry, hold, and turn the pages of a book. This requires the book covers and pages to be sturdy. Covers made of strong, washable material are best. Pages should be easy to manipulate without damaging the book. The page surface should be dull to prevent glare. The book's binding should lay flat when the book is open.

Length

Book length varies with children's ages and their interest in books. Infants and toddlers may stay with a book for just a few minutes. Their books are often only a few pages long. Two-year-olds will maintain interest in a book for 5 to 8 minutes; three-year-olds from 6 to 10 minutes; four-year-olds from 8 to 12 minutes; five-year-olds from 10 to 15 minutes. This interest relates to the number of pages in the book.

Selecting Books Based on Age

Age plays an important part in choosing books for children. **Figure 20.4** outlines some factors to consider for different ages.

Infants need durable picture books. The book should be constructed of firm cardboard, washable cloth, or vinyl. It should have a large, colorful, simple picture on each page with a contrasting background. Under the simple picture, there may be no words, a single word, a few words, or short sentences. Older infants enjoy handling books and often will look at the pictures upside-down.

Considerations for Children's Books

Age Group	Book Considerations
Toddlers	• Thick pages • Large, clearly defined pictures • Brightly colored pictures of simple, familiar objects and routines
Two-Year-Olds	• Imitate familiar sounds • Repeat children's own experiences • Contain large pages with big pictures • Include the familiar • Simple plots
Three-Year-Olds	• Include things and people outside of the home • Explain the who and why • Interpret the child's own experiences • Contain repetitive sound words
Four-Year-Olds	• Include humor in reality • Contain new words • Explain the how and why • Include exaggeration
Five-Year-Olds	• Add something to their knowledge • Take them beyond the here and now • Contain new information and relate it to familiar facts

Figure 20.4 Age plays an important role in how you select books for children.

Toddlers need durable picture books, too. Firm cardboard books with thick pages allow for easier handling and carrying them around. Pictures should be large and clearly defined. These pictures should represent simple items in children's surroundings. Toddlers may enjoy pointing at and touching objects in the pictures. They also enjoy books that have rhyme and repetition.

Two-year-olds prefer books about things they know, do, and enjoy. They respond enthusiastically when books mention favorite activities, such as running, eating, and dressing. Their favorite subjects also include animals and small children. Books for two-year-olds should still be durable with many large, clearly defined drawings. The pictures should represent familiar actions and sounds. The colors should be realistic.

Three-year-old children may request stories by title. They show a preference for stories about familiar subjects and happy endings. They also enjoy learning about people outside the home. Stories about community helpers such as police officers, mail carriers, and garbage collectors also bring enjoyment to children. Three-year-olds want to know what these people do and why (**Figure 20.5**). Pictures should be realistic, simple, clear, and show action. The number of sentences on each page should be few.

Four-year-old children are less self-centered than younger children. These children are becoming more curious about the world around them. They want to know how and why things work. At this age, children enjoy short, simple stories that use exaggeration and lots of action. Four-year-olds often enjoy pranks in books. Looking at the pictures can help them experience the story. Pictures should be colorful and show action.

Five-year-old children like stories that give them added knowledge. They will frequently memorize favorite stories word for word. They prefer stories that take them beyond the here and now. These children want new information and relationships along with familiar facts. They now appreciate fantasy trips beyond the confines of their world. Examples of these books include *Little Red Riding Hood*, *Peter Rabbit*, and *Goldilocks and the Three Bears*. Children of this age will tell you their likes and dislikes.

Avoiding Stories That Reinforce Stereotypes

It is important to choose age-appropriate stories that build on the children's **funds of knowledge**—the background experiences a child comes to school with. It includes the cultural

UW-Stout Child and Family Study Center

Figure 20.5   Children enjoy looking at books that contain familiar subjects. *Why do you think it is important for pictures and illustrations to be realistic, simple, and clear?*

practices and bodies of knowledge embedded in their family's daily routines. Selecting antibias stories that are free from stereotypes is essential, too. *Stereotypes* are generalizations about people based on one characteristic, such as sex, gender, race, culture, nationality, religion, profession, or age. Some picture books misrepresent gender. Avoid stereotypes because they are unfair and they affect how children perceive themselves. Read stories and study illustrations carefully before using them. Stereotyping is often easiest to spot in pictures. Inspect these illustrations closely since they have more impact on children than words. Refer to the child as "friends" or "children" as opposed to "girls and boys" to avoid common stereotypes.

Children's stories need to be free of sexism. *Sexism* is any action, attitude, or outlook used to judge a person based only on the sex of that person. In the past, many books did not show females who possess a full range of interests

and skills. Conversely, few males were shown in the roles of teachers or nurses. Most traditional children's books showed adult females wearing aprons and doing housework, while adult males went off to work outside the home. Young females were often passive and helped around the home. At the same time, young males were often portrayed as active and adventurous.

Study the ratio of males to females in the illustrations. There should be as many females as males. Notice the descriptions of characters and what kinds of activities the pictures show them doing (**Figure 20.6**). Books that avoid sexism

A   artisticco/iStock via Getty Images Plus

B

Dynamic Graphics/Dynamic Graphics Group via Getty Images Plus

Figure 20.6   Books that show men involved with their families and women in interesting jobs do not promote sexism.

will describe females as lively people who do interesting things. Likewise, these books will show males as caring people who are interested in homes, families, and friends.

Through books, children can also gain an understanding of people who have different skin colors, food preferences, family compositions, and languages. Knowledge of the differences among people can promote acceptance. The illustrations or pictures and narrative should positively depict people of all ethnicities and cultural groups.

Finally, search stories for stereotyping of older people. You must give children a realistic and positive picture of older adults. Stories should describe warm, pleasing, and active relationships between older people and children. In this way, children can learn to know and admire older members of their community.

Lesson 20.1 Review

1. Each of the following is true about storytelling *except* storytelling_____. (20.1.1)
   A. is the oldest form of teaching
   B. promotes listening skills
   C. limits thoughtful conversations
   D. enhances children's imaginations

2. Which of the following does *not* show how books reflect life experiences? (20.1.2)
   A. Books are like mirrors that reflect life experiences.
   B. Children learn to express their thoughts but not their feelings.
   C. Books help develop a positive racial identity in a diverse society.
   D. Children can see themselves in books.

3. What theme is used in family life stories? (20.1.2)
   A. social understanding
   B. cognitive understanding
   C. physical understanding
   D. emotional understanding

4. Why should teachers choose books that they enjoy and value? (20.1.3)
   A. To introduce dramatic elements for children.
   B. To mirror children's emotional experiences.
   C. To be able to tell a story in an interesting way with enthusiasm.
   D. To provide information and fun stories for the children.

5. Which of the following is *not* an important reason for teachers to have multicultural and bilingual books in the classroom? (20.1.3)
   A. Multicultural and bilingual books are only important for dual-language learners.
   B. Bonding with multicultural and bilingual books is important for children.
   C. Children learn that all people have similarities and differences.
   D. Children learn that people have different customs, habits, and working and living behaviors.

6. Which of the following is *not* a function of illustrations and pictures? (20.1.3)
   A. Illustrations and pictures should be engaging and promote visual literacy.
   B. Illustrations and pictures should create interest and arouse children's imaginations.
   C. Illustrations and pictures are more important than the narrative of a story.
   D. Illustrations and pictures confuse children then they have too much detail and shading.

Reading and Telling Stories to Children

Essential Question

What do you need to know about reading stories to children and storytelling methods to enhance children's language and literacy?

Learning Outcomes

After studying this lesson, you will be able to

20.2-1 **outline** the steps to follow when reading aloud to children.

20.2-2 **explain** a variety of storytelling methods.

20.2-3 **describe** how to display and integrate books into all classroom areas.

Key Terms

props	draw and tell
intonation	e-book
print referencing	flannel boards

Reading and telling stories to children requires preparation. Teachers need to prepare carefully to gain and hold the children's attention. First, teachers must select a book or story that appeals to the children's interests and adds to their knowledge. After choosing a book, teachers need to decide whether to read or tell a story. Once upon a time, there were not as many options for sharing. But today, teachers have access to more titles, types of children's literature, storytelling strategies, and technology. They can effectively use books, puppets, whiteboards, videos, draw-and-tell, and flannel boards. By using an app with a digital tablet, teachers can create self-made stories. For instance, they can take pictures on a field trip, during classroom activities, and celebrations and introduce them during story time.

After selecting a story, teachers need to plan strategies to create interest and hold the children's attention. They need to plan an introduction that will capture the children's interest. If unfamiliar with the book, teachers need to practice reading or telling and ending the story. During the process, they often create voices for the characters in the story. Handling interruptions, maintaining interest, and ending the story are other skills that compelling storytellers need to develop.

20.2-1 Reading Stories to Children

Good oral reading needs to be intentional, which takes time and effort. You need to take several steps before reading stories to young children. First, choose a story that you love and the children will enjoy. Then become familiar with the story. After reading the story several times, prepare the second step by planning an introduction. For instance, when reading the story of *The Little Engine that Could*, introduce the story by saying, "In this story, the little engine does something very, very special for the children. Look and listen carefully to find out what the little engine did for them." The story's success lies in your ability to be interesting and enthusiastic.

Preparing to Read

Excellence in storytelling is about practice. Read the story several times so you know it well. Then a quick glance at the page should remind you of the text. This leaves your eyes free for contact with the children. There is no best way to learn stories. Each person will develop their own method.

Oral reading skills are essential when storytelling. One way to build these skills is to practice reading in front of a mirror. Another method is to set up a digital tablet to video-record your presentation.

Using these methods, you can correct any problems you notice. For example, record yourself and then ask the following questions:

- Did I convey enthusiasm about the story?
- Did I use gestures?
- Did I keep the tempo lively?
- Did I smile and maintain eye contact appropriately?
- Did I suggest different voices and volumes for unique characters?
- Did I speak more slowly in serious parts and faster in exciting parts?
- Did I ask follow-up questions in a pleasant voice?

After you are familiar with the book, decide whether you want to *read* or *tell* the story. *Reading* the story has its advantages when working with young children. They can look at the drawings or photographs as they listen to the story. Reading stories may also get some children interested in reading. As they watch you, the children will learn the link between printed and spoken words. The advantage of *telling* a story is that you can better dramatize action and characters.

A comfortable setting for the children and teacher is necessary for a successful reading time. Children must be free from distractions, and feel safe and secure. They should sit in a group to listen. Some teachers like to have the children sit on carpet squares or pillows. Others may use a colorful quilt. Such seating arrangements prevent children from moving around and help them focus more on listening. You need to relax your body by finding a position that is comfortable. Make sure all the children can see the book and you.

Story groups should be small (**Figure 20.7**). You may wish to divide children into two or more groups, based on age and interest. This also allows the children more interaction.

FatCamera/E+ via Getty Images

Figure 20.7   In small groups, children are free to interact with the teacher. ***Why do you think smaller groups are important for storytelling experiences?***

Most children need a settling-down time. To help children get ready to listen, some teachers recite a fingerplay. Another technique is to talk to the children using a puppet. Other teachers simply discuss the events of the day.

Introducing the Story

Begin stories by setting the mood. Ask questions, make personal comments, or show the book cover to get children involved in the story. Ask children to predict what the story is about. Setting the mood should be brief. A few sentences are often enough.

A personal comment is one way to introduce a story. You may share where you learned about the story. For example, "This is a story that my grandmother told me as a child." You can set a humorous mood by asking, "How many of you like to laugh?" You might hold the book up and show the cover. The picture on the cover should suggest the story content.

Props are also good for introducing stories. **Props** are any items that relate to the story and attract children's attention. To introduce *Peter Rabbit*, for example, you may bring in a live rabbit, a stuffed rabbit, or a picture of a rabbit (**Figure 20.8**).

Store props in a storytelling apron. As you introduce a story, pull props out of the apron pocket one at a time. You can use a storytelling bag the same way. The bag is also useful for storing books in the reading area.

Props for Introducing Stories

Type of Prop	Book Title
A red balloon	"The Red Balloon"
A red apple	"The Apple Is Red"
A doll	"William's Doll"
A black cat	"The Tale of the Black Cat"
A purple crayon	"Harold and the Purple Crayon"

Figure 20.8   Using props to introduce stories helps engage children's interest. ***Identify one of your favorite storybooks. What props might you use to engage children with this story?***

Explain any words the children do not know before you begin the story. For example, before reading *The Gigantic Elephant*, define the new word *gigantic*. You might say that "gigantic" means *very big*. With older children you could introduce the words "enormous" or "huge."

Before you start, create a feeling that you are about to share something special. Use your voice to create enthusiasm when introducing the book. A smile on your face can also create excitement.

If you have dual-language learners in the group, support them. Introduce unfamiliar words in the story and connect them to the children's home language. Verbal clues and predictable gestures will help children become involved while you read the story.

Reading the Story

Read stories with pleasure and feeling to show the children you value and enjoy reading. Maintain eye contact with the children. Pause before introducing a new character or idea. Use facial and body movements, **intonation** (the rise and fall of the pitch of the voice), and gestures to aid the children in understanding the story.

Read the story in a normal speaking voice. Speaking too softly or at a high pitch may cause the children to lose interest. Think of your voice as a tool. To add interest, you can whisper or shout when appropriate. By lengthening your dramatic pause, you can let the children savor the words. You may mimic a sound or adjust your pace to reflect the story or change the pitch of your voice. For example, in the story of *Goldilocks and the Three Bears*, project yourself into the characters. Use a high pitch for the baby bear and a low pitch for the papa bear.

Occasionally point out the illustrations. Encourage child participation by predicting outcomes, such as "What will happen next?" Another technique is to ask opinions, such as "What would you do if you were Red Riding Hood and saw the wolf in grandmother's clothes?" Ask about previous parts of the story. For example, you might say "What did Tim Mouse say to his mother?" Children will remember the story if they are involved. Use repeated gestures and phrases.

When the children are listening to a story, they usually focus on the illustrations as opposed to the print. You will need to use **print referencing** to call attention to the print. Nonverbally, run your finger directly under the print. Otherwise, you could say, "Look, there is a letter C. Carson's name begins with that alphabet letter."

Handling Interruptions

Interruptions happen often when telling stories to young children (**Figure 20.9**). The children will ask such questions as, "Why is baby bear brown?" Accept these interruptions and answer questions patiently. There may be children who continue to ask many questions. If this happens, say, "Vjay, please save your questions until after the story."

Wiggling children can distract other children. Do not make an issue of this. It is best to ignore the wiggling and keep reading. A positive response is to praise children who sit still. For example, you may say, "Jace, I like how quietly you are sitting." This will strengthen Jace's actions. It will also encourage wigglers to sit still.

Maintaining Interest

You can see children's interest in a story in their laughter, stillness, and expressions. If children do not appear to like a story, talk faster. You might use more emphasis or skip some details. You can also restore interest by asking the children simple questions about the story. To quiet a bored or disruptive child, ask, "Remy, what color is baby bear?" Sometimes, no matter what you do or say, a book does not have holding power. If this should happen, end the story. You may say, "Children, this is not the right story for today."

Ending Stories

Ending a story is as important as introducing it. The children need to know when the story has ended. Therefore, the ending should be clear. You may ask a question about the story, such as "What did you like best about the story?" You may also ask a question about the characters, the plot, or the setting. For older children, create an environment that encourages *possibility thinking* by asking "what if" questions that are open-ended, requiring more than a one-word answer.

A simple "Thank you for listening" may be enough at times. You may also wish to give the children something to take home after some stories. Teachers do this most often for special occasions. For example, after reading *Winnie the Pooh*, you may wish to give the children a printed copy of the book cover. Encourage them to go home, share the cover, and retell the story to their family members.

Be prepared to read the same story repeatedly. A story will only have informational impact if you read it again. You will be pleased to hear, "Please read us that story again." This request tells you the children enjoyed the book.

Evaluating Your Performance

After reading a story, you will need to evaluate your methods. Children's reactions are

kali9/iStock via Getty Images Plus

Figure 20.9 Do not be annoyed by interruptions. Young children like to ask questions and make comments on stories they are hearing. *Why do you think it is important for teachers to accept interruptions and patiently answer children's questions?*

good feedback. The more children respond to a story, chances are the better your storytelling strategies. If the children lose interest, you may have talked too fast or too slow. In other cases, you may have spoken so carefully that you forgot to add expression and vary the tone.

Note your strengths and your weaknesses. When the children laugh, smile, and watch you closely, you have used strategies that hold their interest. Build on your strengths as you plan literature experiences in the future. In addition, review the tips for effective storytelling in Figure 20.10.

Supporting Dual-Language Learners

Early childhood classrooms are becoming increasingly more diverse. Today, nearly twelve million children live in a home where family members speak a language other than English. In three decades, according to the United States Department of Education, this number has more than doubled. At home, one in five young children speaks a language other than English. Their presence varies state by state. The number of bilingual speakers is expected to increase in the coming years. The United States Census Bureau's population projections have identified 2044 as the crossover year. At this time, no single racial or cultural group will be a majority.

After English, Spanish is the most dominant language in the United States followed by Chinese. Federal data show that three quarters of the nation's English language learners (ELL) are Spanish-speaking. There is not another language that accounts for more than three percent of dual-language learners.

The best time to promote bilingualism is during the formative years, infancy through early childhood (ages zero through eight). Bilingualism begins early in life. Infants begin their linguistic journey in the womb. After birth, they are capable of recognizing words across all languages. After 12 months, this ability gradually diminishes.

Children learn through the lens of their own cultures. Collaborate with the parents or guardians of non-English-speaking children to

Tips for Effective Storytelling

- Choose a book that is developmentally and culturally appropriate for the children.
- Use a good introduction to establish the mood of the story.
- Explain unfamiliar words.
- Encourage child participation.
- Tell the story with a conversational tone.
- Use eye contact.
- Convey enthusiasm.
- Demonstrate good posture.
- Use different voices for characters to create interest.
- Pronounce words clearly.
- Use a lively tempo.
- Allow comments to be added to story.

Figure 20.10   Using these tips to evaluate your storytelling skills can help you build your skills.

understand their culture. Ask them to provide you with keywords and phrases to use when speaking to their child. Seek their assistance in labeling classroom areas and equipment. For consistency, some teachers use one color for English and another color for a second language. Choose and read books that represent the home languages of all children in your program. Use pictures to convey meaning. Emphasize and repeat important words. Multicultural books for the classroom may include

- *The All-Together Quilt* by Lizzy Rockwell
- *Alma and How She Got Her Name* by Juana Martinez-Neal
- *Last Stop on Market Street* by Matt de la Pena
- *Feast of Peas* by Kashmira Sheth (author) and Jeffrey Ebbeler (illustrator)
- *In the City* by Chris Raschka
- *My Bed: Enchanting Ways to Fall Asleep Around the World* by Rebecca Bond (author) and Sally Mavor (illustrator)
- *Out the Door* by Christy Hale
- *The Paper Kingdom* by Helena Ku Rhee and Pascal Campion
- *Ready to Fly: How Sylvia Townsend Became the Bookmobile Ballerina* by Lea Lyon and Alexandria LaFaye (author), Jessica Gibson (illustrator)
- *Saturday* by Oge Mora
- *When the Babies Come to Stay* by Christine McDonell (author) and Jeanette Bradley (illustrator)
- *Llama Llama and the Billy Goat* by Anna Dewdney

Use your community as a resource. You may want to partner with a librarian at the local library. They can lend you multicultural children's library books. Likewise, they likely have access to interlibrary loans from which they could obtain books for the classroom. You may also want to build family engagement by introducing families to the library and librarians.

Teaching About Books

Books enthrall young children. As you read, you are teaching children about books. They learn a book has front and back covers. On the front cover, there is a title. An author is the person who writes a book, and the author's name is also on the cover. The illustrator prepares the drawings. Books have a beginning and an ending. Inside the book, there are pages. Each page has a top and bottom. People read books written in English from left to right and from top to bottom.

Children watch how you handle a book. From this, they learn how to handle a book. During the story, be sure to carefully turn the pages one at a time.

20.2-2 Achieving Variety in Storytelling

Besides reading stories aloud, there are other creative methods that help storytelling come alive. Guidelines for these methods are like those for reading aloud. First, decide whether you will read from a book or make up your own story. Next, record yourself practicing the story in front of a mirror until you know it well. This will help you prepare to perform as a storyteller.

Younger children will stay interested longer when you use several strategies during story time. As an early childhood teacher, you will need to learn several storytelling strategies.

Studies show that infants and young children seem to process only one stimulus at a time. Sounds appeal to them more than visuals. The younger the child, the more dominant their auditory preference will be. In fact, infants prefer sounds almost totally to visuals. Four-year-olds prefer sounds to visuals except for familiar objects. When familiar objects are associated with unfamiliar sounds, they pay more attention to the objects.

Adults can process both sounds and visual images together; however, they prefer visual information. Why do children pay more attention to sounds? The research claims that visual stimulation is somewhat stable, but sounds disappear. Perhaps for this reason, infants will look at pictures longer when teachers or family members pair them with unfamiliar sounds.

Draw and Tell

Draw and tell or *chalk talk*, is one storytelling method. As the storyteller tells the story, they make drawings on a chalkboard, dry-erase board, poster board, or an 18- by 24-inch newsprint pad. You can purchase textbooks containing draw and tell stories from school supply stores, catalogs, or online. Some early childhood educators prefer to find a storybook and adapt it. They may delete, combine, or add illustrations. As a rule, use no more than five sheets of paper.

Prepare draw and tell stories so you can use them more than once. Cover original light tracings with clear laminate. Use grease pencils to draw in the outline and fill in the color. After telling the story, clean the clear laminate by wiping it with a piece of felt or window cleaner.

Audio and Digital Storytelling

Audio books and stories appeal to young children. They contain sound effects and music. Audio stories often include an illustrated booklet that children can use to read along with the story. Many audio books of popular stories are available through streaming services, too.

Digital storytelling describes the practice of using digital tools to tell a story. It combines tradition with technology. Classroom teachers can create videos for storytelling using a digital tablet. With practice, you will be more skilled, and it will be easier to create stories. You can use a digital tablet to record special events, field trips, and classroom guests. It can also capture the children retelling, recreating, and acting out stories. Some teachers even provide props, such as picture cards, to facilitate the process.

Older children can be the producers of digital storytelling. They often enjoy using props. During this process, children will learn more about technology, expand their vocabularies, and increase oral fluency skills (**Figure 20.11**). You can load a digital recording to a computer and transfer it to a personal media player.

Puppets

Puppets are always magical to young children. Having puppets tell a story is a useful change of pace, and puppets help children in constructing and expressing their understanding of stories. Use a puppet as a listener who remarks and asks questions about the story. You can make puppets from tin cans, tongue depressors, socks, and other inexpensive materials. A mitten also makes a good puppet. Cut eyes, a nose, and a mouth from construction paper or felt and paste

Figure 20.11   Even young children who do not yet read can follow along in a book while listening to an audio recording. ***Do you think children benefit more from digital storytelling or printed books? What are the benefits of using both?***

them onto the mitten. Use the mitten puppet with the story **The Lost Mitten**. You can use stuffed animals in the same manner. For example, you could use a brown teddy bear to tell the story of **Little Brown Bear**.

Coordinating the puppet's actions and words takes practice. After you tell the story, place the puppet in the language and library area. You might also place a puppet theater in this area. The more children listen to puppet stories, the more they will want to use them. Providing an attractive puppet theater with a wide variety of interesting puppets will encourage puppetry.

Individual or Group Stories

Given the chance, children can be clever storytellers. After a field trip, guest visit, or other special event, ask children to record a story about that special time. You might have the children work together in small groups. Video the children's ideas as they tell their stories. Seeing their own words helps children understand the link between spoken and written words. You could write the ideas on the board, a piece of poster board, or paper. You can also record these stories with a video recorder or digital tablet with audio and video capabilities. Later, you can play the recordings for the children to reflect on and enjoy. If developmentally appropriate, the children may want to draw pictures to accompany their story.

Big Books

Big books are oversized books, 24 by 36 inches in size, and come in either hardcover or softcover. They come in many classic titles and new titles. Early childhood teachers may prefer reading these books to the entire group of children at circle time. Big books contain enlarged text that allows the children to see the print and the illustrations to draw them into the story. Using shared reading with predictable text helps children build sight word knowledge and reading. Teachers will often use their fingers to underline and call attention to the printed word and directionality. **Figure 20.12** contains a list of big books.

E-Books and E-Readers

You can successfully use technology in the classroom. Media provides children with new opportunities to experience literature and language. Some classrooms have e-readers with e-books to complement classroom books. Most e-readers include a dictionary. When children encounter an unfamiliar word, they can press on the word to call up its definition. They can also adjust the font size. Unlike a laptop or digital tablet, e-readers do not require daily charging. Most e-readers have a long battery life and can go days to weeks without recharging.

E-books should not replace the hands-on experience of using books in print. Classrooms should have both printed copies and digital copies of books available. Children need the tactile experience of handling print copies. They like to look and listen to the same book repeatedly.

You can purchase children's e-books online from bookstores. Sometimes you will also find free e-books available online. Usually, teachers will download several books on each device.

Teacher-Created Digital Stories

Teachers can use a video recorder or digital tablet with video and audio capabilities

Big Books

- *Big Fat Hen* by Keith Baker
- *Big Red Barn* by Margaret Wise Brown (author) and Felicia Bond (illustrator)
- *Mouse Paint* by Ellen Stoll Walsh
- *Caps for Sale* by Esphyr Slobodkina
- Eating the Alphabet by Lois Ehlert
- *If you Give a Pig a Pancake* by Laura Numeroff (author) and Felicia Bond (illustrator)
- *The Wheels on the Bus* by Raffi
- *Zoo-Ology* by Emmanuelle Grundmann and Joelle Jolivet
- *Brown Bear, Brown Bear, What Do You See?* by Bill Martin Jr. and Eric Carle
- *Freight Train* by Donald Crews
- *Sheep in a Jeep* by Nancy E. Shaw and Margot Apple
- *It Looked Like Spilt Milk* by Charles G. Shaw
- *The Napping House* by Audrey Wood (author) and Don Wood (illustrator)
- *My Friend Rabbit* by Eric Rohmann
- *When It Starts to Snow* by Phillis Gershator (author) and Martin Matje (illustrator)
- *My House/Mi Casa* by Rebecca Emberley

Figure 20.12 Using big books at story time allows the children to see the print and the pictures.

to create digital stories. They create stories by downloading photographs into a digital presentation. Digital stories can focus on pictures taken on field trips, classroom activities, or events such as holiday parties. You might start a story at the beginning of the year and wait until the end of the year to tell a story. Families enjoy digital stories involving their children at special events.

Using an app with a digital tablet, self-made stories can create a new type of literary experience. The stories can be tailor-made to meet the needs of the children. One advantage of a digital tablet is that you can make the text larger so it is easier for the them to read. You can add sounds, even music, and digital photographs. You can also record the children interacting.

Afterwards, share the recording and ask the children to watch and reflect. Promote their thinking by asking what they were feeling.

You can also use a tablet to have children reflect about a topic or event. Record the children interacting. Afterward, share their record. Have them watch the video. Then ask them to tell you what they saw and felt.

Flannel Boards

A flannel-board story is one of the most popular listening activities for young children. **Flannel board**, or *felt board*, storytelling uses characters and props cut out of felt and placed on a felt background (**Figure 20.13**). Teachers may purchase flannel boards from school supply stores, catalogs, online, or may make them. To make a board, you will need a piece of foam insulation board, 27 by 17½ inches. You can buy this material at a lumber supply company. To prepare the board, cover it with two contrasting pieces of felt or heavy flannel, 29 by 19½ inches. The two pieces provide different-colored backgrounds for felt figures.

Pieces of heavy paper, cardboard, felt, or textured fabrics can show major characters or objects. These may be hand-drawn, bought, or cut out of storybooks. Flannel-board books contain many stories. They also often contain patterns for characters and props. You can purchase these from school supply stores and exhibit areas at early childhood conferences.

A quick way to make figures is to purchase pattern-transfer books at sewing and craft stores. School copy machines can make the figures larger or smaller. When preparing figures, consider the size of your flannel board and always try to make the figures an appropriate size. For example, a dog should be larger than a cat; likewise, a cow is larger than a dog. Include ethnicity and cultural diversity when preparing human figures.

Use a nonwoven interfacing fabric to prepare figures for the flannel board. Hold the fabric in place and trace over the patterns with a black felt pen. Fill in the areas you wish to brighten with fluorescent paint or crayons. You can embellish the pieces with wiggly eyes, yarn for hair, liquid glitter, sequins, and other interesting items.

Early Childhood Insight

Making Felt Figures

Felt figures can also be made from storybooks. To make figures for a flannel board, purchase two copies of the same book. Cut out the pictures from the even-numbered pages of one book. Then cut out the pictures from the odd-numbered pages of the second book. When finished, glue a piece of flannel on the back of each picture. Write the page number on the back of each piece to keep track of the story sequence. This will prevent the story order from getting mixed up. Keep the third book intact, allowing the children to retell the story.

Choosing and Presenting a Flannel-Board Story

Use the same criteria for selecting flannel-board stories as you do for storytelling. Consider the children's age, experience, and interests. Popular books that lend themselves to flannel-board presentations include *The Very Hungry Caterpillar* by Eric Carle, *Brown Bear, Brown Bear, What Do You See?* by Bill Martin Jr. and Eric Carle, and *Polar Bear, Polar Bear, What Do You Hear?* by Bill Martin Jr. and Eric Carle.

Judy Herr

Figure 20.13 These felt figures are placed on the flannel board as the story is told. *How do you think children benefit from flannel board stories?*

Before you present a flannel-board story, you will need to do some advance preparation. Begin by practicing reading the story script aloud several times. Check your flannel-board figures and place them in order of use. Keep the figures on your lap in a flat box or basket when you tell the story. Avoid placing the figures on the floor because a curious child may pick them up. This could interfere with the success of the story.

Place the figures on the flannel board one at a time. Like writing, the figures should follow a left-to-right sequence. Practice telling the story and placing the flannel figures on the board. For emphasis, look directly at the figures as you place them on the board. Create drama and suspense with pauses.

After you finish telling a flannel-board story, leave the assembled board in the book area. The children will enjoy using the flannel-board figures to retell the story or create new tales. By observing and listening, you can assess their understanding of the story. You may even want to encourage the children to create their own stories by providing them with figures from a variety of stories.

Retelling Stories

Retelling stories to young children is important for their language development. It relates to their ability to both receive and express information. Children need to hear and speak to develop language. If they can say it, later they can write and read it.

Through listening, children develop vocabulary and a sense of the story structure. While listening to a story again, children often reflect on and share their own life experiences. You might have to prompt them by intentionally asking age-appropriate, open-ended questions that require critical-thinking. These questions never require a yes, no, or one word answer, and they invite meaningful conversations. Open-ended questions probe children's ideas. They require children to pay attention, think, and reason. Children have motivation to respond since there are no right or wrong answers. For example, you might ask:

- "How did the story begin?"
- "What was your favorite part of the story? Why?"
- "What was the story about?"
- "How did the main character solve the problem?"
- "What happened in the story?"
- "What did you like about the story?"
- "What character would you like to be? Why?"
- "What will happen next? How do you know?"
- "I wonder what would happen if . . .?"
- "What happened at the end of the story?

Provide children with wait time after asking the question. After the child responds, you may have to expand on the child's comments by adding clarification or information. Likewise, you may have to rephrase the child's response into a complete sentence. There also will be times that you will need to rephrase the child's response using standard academic English. You can use children's responses to assess their comprehension skills. Consider what the children say about the story details, sequences, and characters. Include these comments in your evaluation.

A child's funds of knowledge will influence their response to questions. Funds of knowledge are embedded in their family and friends, family values and traditions, home language, household chores, favorite TV shows, community, family occupations, and educational activities. Young children bring their funds of knowledge with them to the center.

20.2-3 Displaying Books

An important area of a classroom is the library area. Books, flannel boards, recorded music, and other storytelling equipment are in this area. Arrange the books so they appeal to children. The book covers should be visible to attract the children's interest (**Figure 20.14**). Arrange the books so they do not fall after removing one book.

globalmoments/iStock via Getty Images Plus

Figure 20.14 Displays that show book covers encourage children to look at books on their own. *What are the benefits of displaying books throughout the activity centers in the classroom in addition to the library area?*

Locate the library area away from traffic. Dividers should separate it from the rest of the classroom. This provides a quiet atmosphere. Scissors, crayons, and painting should not be allowed here. These limits should prevent misuse of the books.

Choose books for the library area carefully, and consider each child's developmental needs.

You may wish to include books on topics children in the group are facing, such as going to the doctor or dentist, the birth of a new sibling, making friends, and dealing with the death of a pet. Some books, such as the children's favorites, can remain in the area continually. Rotate other books frequently. Fun books should always be available. Add new books often to stimulate children's interest and enthusiasm. You might consider borrowing books from friends, parents, and public libraries.

Focus on Careers

Librarians and Library Media Specialists

Librarians and library media specialists who work with children generally work in school or public libraries. Their responsibilities may vary depending on the library. Librarians and library media specialists may create and use databases of library materials; organize library materials; research new books, materials, and equipment for purchase; teach children about using library resources; and plan programs for various audiences, such as story time for children. Additionally, they may also train and supervise library technicians and other library staff.
Career cluster: Education and Training.
Education: The education and training requirements for librarians and library media specialists require a master's degree in library science.
Job outlook. Employment for librarians or library media specialists is expected to grow 9 percent through 2030, which is about as fast as average for all occupations.

To learn more about a librarian or library media specialist, visit US Department of Labor websites for the *Occupational Outlook Handbook (OOH)* and *O*NET OnLine.* You will be able to compare the job responsibilities, educational requirements, job outlook, and average pay for librarians with similar occupations.

Integrate literature throughout all areas of the room. Put books about housing and transportation in a basket in the block-building area. Place shape, color, texture, and design books in the art area. Math books can be placed in the small manipulative and math area. Place books related to water and sand in the sensory area and songbooks in the music area. Put books about animals, birds, insects, dinosaurs, plants, trees, seeds, gardens, seasons, earth, and sky in the science area. Books about healthy food, healthy bodies, and families can go in the dramatic-play corner, and put books about fitness and sports in the large-motor classroom area. The language and literacy area needs to include an extensive selection of quality books.

Lesson 20.2 Review

1. Which of the following is **not** a step to take before reading stories to young children? (20.2.1)
   A. Choose a story you love and the children will enjoy.
   B. Become familiar with the story.
   C. Plan your introduction to engage children.
   D. Take little time and effort for oral reading.

2. Each of the following is a way for building oral reading skills **except** _____. (20.2.1)
   A. reading the story several times until you know it well
   B. practicing reading the story in front of a mirror
   C. choosing the storybook just before you read it to children
   D. using a digital tablet to record yourself reading the story

3. Which of the following is **not** a way to support dual-language learners during storytelling? (20.2.1)
   A. The best time to promote bilingualism is during infancy and early childhood.
   B. The best time to promote bilingualism is during the school-age years.
   C. Collaborate with parents and guardians to understand children's culture and home language.
   D. Choose and read books that represent the home languages of all children in your program.

4. _____ is a storytelling method in which the teacher makes drawings on a chalkboard, dry-erase board, poster board, or newsprint while telling a story. (20.2.2)
   A. Puppetry
   B. Digital storytelling
   C. Flannel board
   D. Draw and tell

5. Each of the following is a reason for developing teacher-created digital stories **except** _____. (20.2.2)
   A. digital stories can help meet the needs of children
   B. digital stories can help children reflect on their physical skills
   C. digital stories allow for making the text larger and easier for children to read
   D. digital stories can focus on class field trips, activities, and special events

6. Each of the following is key to arranging books in the classroom **except** _____. (20.2.3)
   A. arrange books only in the library area to prevent books from being misused
   B. choose books carefully considering developmental needs and children's interests
   C. rotate books frequently and add new books to stimulate children's interest and enthusiasm
   D. integrate literature throughout all areas of the room

Summary

Lesson 20.1

20.1-1 Early childhood programs must nurture a child's sense of joy and wonder. Books and storytelling promote children's cognitive and social-emotional development.

20.1-1 For optimum growth, it is important that they see and hear their home language in the early childhood setting.

20.1-2 Two major groups of books are picture books and storybooks.

20.1-2 Books in these groups are further divided into family life stories, animal stories, fables, and fairy tales.

20.1-3 Storytelling and language experiences support children's overall language and literacy development and should reflect the rich diversity of all children.

20.1-3 Teachers must select stories carefully so content matches the children's developmental levels, experiences, cultural backgrounds, interests, and needs. In addition, the content must be free of stereotypes and sexism.

Lesson 20.2

20.2-1 As part of preparing to read, teachers must think through how they will introduce and read the story, handle interruptions and maintain children's interest, and how they will end the story.

20.2-1 Teachers must collaborate with the parents or guardians of non-English-speaking children to learn key words and phrases to use when speaking with their children and labeling classroom areas and equipment.

20.2-2 Besides reading a book, there are several ways to share a story. Draw and tell, audio and video recordings, puppets, and flannel boards are a few options.

20.2-2 E-books and e-readers can provide children with new literature and language opportunities.

20.2-3 The library area is an important classroom area. Locate it away from traffic.

20.2-3 Choose books for the library area carefully. Consider children's development, experiences, and interests to stimulate enthusiasm for books and reading.

Vocabulary Activity

Choose one of the Key Terms in this chapter. Then use online resources to locate photos that visually show the meaning of the term you chose. Share the photo and meaning of the term in class. Ask for clarification as necessary.

Critical Thinking

1. **Compare and Contrast.** Prepare a bibliography of six children's books you might use in storytelling. Divide the books into groups based on the age of the intended audience. Then, compare the books' subject matters, illustrations, and writing styles. How do the similarities and differences between these books make them appropriate for their audiences?

2. **Identify.** Visit a local library or bookstore and survey the children's books or magazines available. Select one book or magazine and identify the key information about it, including its content (appropriate or inappropriate), recommended ages, quality of illustrations, writing style, cost, and durability features. Write a short book review, including all this information.

3. **Analyze.** Listen to an audio recording of a children's story and take notes about how the speaker reads the story. Analyze strategies the speaker uses to hold children's attention and assess whether these strategies were effective.

4. **Evaluate.** Video record yourself reading a book to a group of children. Evaluate your presentation. What parts were of most interest to the children? What storytelling strategies were most effective in holding the children's interest? If you told the story again, what would you change? Then, trade recordings with

a classmate and evaluate each other's recordings. Compare your evaluations.

5. **Draw Conclusions.** Go to Storyline Online on YouTube. It provides read-aloud stories with famous storytellers. Listen to the book, *Skin You Live In* by Michael Tyler. What do you think appeals to young children about this book? What skills did the storyteller use to maintain the children's interest? What do you think a child will find appealing about this book? Describe why the inclusion of this children's book would make an important addition to the classroom. Could you use this site to download stories to a smart board? Why or why not?

Core Skills

1. **Writing.** Create a lesson plan for preschoolers that focuses on the development of their reading and language skills. How would you target the needs of this age group? If possible, implement your lesson plan in an early childhood program and assess its effectiveness.

2. **Reading.** Examine a book collection in an early childhood center. Browse all the books for dual-language (bilingual) teachings and those containing multicultural stories. Take notes about the cultures and languages that the collection covers. Then, identify two to three cultural or language gaps in the collection. Search online for books to fill these gaps. Choose three books and read them. Write a letter recommending that these three books be added to the center's collection.

3. **Writing.** Enlist the cooperation of a creative-writing teacher and an art teacher for a joint children's book writing project. Interview a preschooler to help you come up with a story idea. Then, using one of the storytelling strategies explained in the chapter, write a children's story, and create illustrations for it. Ask the creative-writing and art teachers to evaluate the illustrations and writing. After incorporating their feedback, share your story with the class.

4. **Research.** Conduct an online search for information about one popular children's book illustrator. Examples of popular illustrators include Tomi di Paola, Jack Kent, Patricia Polacco, Eric Carle, and Arnold Lobel. What influenced the artist to become an illustrator? How does the artist's work contribute to the enjoyment and understanding of a story? Get examples of the artist's illustrations. Discuss your findings and share your illustrations with the class.

5. **Speaking.** Choose a children's story that you find interesting and identify its target age range. Then, create an introduction for this story and practice reading the story as if to children within the intended age range. When reading, consider what strategies and props you could use when reading your introduction. Finally, implement these strategies and read your introduction and your story to the class.

6. **Technology.** Consider how a camera or digital device with video and auditory capabilities could be used to create a digital story. Then, choose one of these methods and create a digital story featuring an early childhood program. Your story should include the children as characters and should bring the center to life. Share your digital story at a parent-teacher conference or at preschool program functions and events. Include visual or audible captions for each picture, and be sure to get permission from people in the photos.

7. **Identify.** Go to YouTube and search for *The Hula-Hoopin' Queen* by Thelma Lynne Godin as read by Oprah Winfrey. Watch and listen to the video. Make a list of all of the effective strategies Oprah uses while reading the story. Discuss the strategies in class.

8. **CTE Career Readiness Practice.** Imagine that you are the director of a new preschool center. Recently, parents have been questioning the importance of storytelling for their children. They are complaining about how much time is scheduled for storytelling. You have planned a meeting to ensure that your staff is prepared to respond to the parents' questions. To prepare for this meeting, create fact sheets that outline what the staff must know and communicate about why storytelling is important in early childhood education. Also include sources that your staff can reference during this explanation.

Portfolio Project

How can early childhood teachers encourage parents to include storytelling activities at home? Write a brief letter to a preschool parent citing the benefits of reading to their child regularly. Include suggestions on the types of books appropriate for the age of the child. File a copy of the letter in your portfolio.

Reading Advantage

Before reading, skim the chapter and examine how it is organized. Look at the bold or italic words, headings of different colors and sizes, bulleted lists or numbered lists, tables, charts, captions, and boxed features.

Guiding Play and Puppetry Experiences

Lesson 21.1: Understanding Play

Lesson 21.2: Socio-Dramatic Play and Puppetry

Case Study

How Should Play Be Supported?

Jayden and Alsea were hired as co-teachers in a new corporate early learning center. They had assistance from the corporate staff and enjoyed unpacking the equipment and materials and arranging the new classroom. Both teachers were pleased that everything was free of stereotypes. They discussed how powerful play was when children were actively engaged in exploring during the process. The program opened the following Monday, and after the children left Friday afternoon, the teachers evaluated the program. Although both teachers were pleased with the overall program, they had philosophical differences in the teachers' role supporting play.

Jayden believed a teacher should be a stage manager. First, they should carefully set up the environment and, after that, be minimally involved. He felt it was an opportune time for teachers to use their time wisely by engaging in housekeeping tasks, texting assessment data for their children to the parents, and preparing new activities. Being straightforward, Alsea said, "Jayden, you are the key to promoting meaningful play. It would help if you were more involved; otherwise, classroom behavioral problems or safety issues could emerge." Alsea believed the teacher should take on the role of a leader, observing, assessing, and adding new materials to enrich the children's interest and involvement. She also felt teachers needed to gently steer some children by making deliberate attempts to help them learn to play and interact with their peers. And, whenever possible, the teacher should scaffold the children's learning.

Give It Some Thought

1. Which teacher's philosophy do you think best represents your own regarding the role of the teacher in supporting children's play? Why?
2. Do you think, like Alsea, that children can be coached to improve their play behaviors? If so, provide some examples.
3. How would you describe an intentional teacher's roles and strategies in supporting children's play?
4. What is the difference between dramatic play and socio-dramatic play?
5. What is the difference between associative and cooperative play?

Lesson 21.1

Understanding Play

Essential Question

? *What do you need to know about the stages of play and material use in play to provide effective play experiences for children?*

Learning Outcomes

After studying this lesson, you will be able to

21.1-1 describe the stages of play.

21.1-2 explain the stages of material use in play.

Key Terms

agency

dramatic play

socio-dramatic play

unoccupied play

solitary play

parallel play

associative play

cooperative play

personification

manipulative stage of play

functional stage of play

imaginative stage of play

Play provides a valuable vital link to learning that promotes the necessary skills to help children thrive in the twenty-first century. Collaboration, communication, creative innovation, and confidence are all promoted. Play is an activity that helps children explore and make sense of their world and is essential for optimum child development. During this process, they exercise and develop their body and brain. For young children, play is magical and the best way to learn. It is an important part of their day and is essential for optimal child development. The social and emotional competencies children develop by playing are important for self-regulation and success in school and life.

Young children love the joy of pretending and playing make-believe. Such fantasy play keeps them engaged and focused. It provides opportunities for growth and development. Play also encourages **agency,** which allows them to make choices that influence events in the context of their learning. They assume role taking, experimentation, social interaction, and discovery. Young children are actors without stage fright. They say what they feel and feel what they say. By observing children at play, you will gain insight into their cognitive, physical, and social-emotional development. Play is a window into their minds and development.

Dramatic play is a form of play in which a single child imitates another person or acts out a situation (**Figure 21.1**). **Socio-dramatic play** involves several children imitating others and acting out situations together. It is the most complex form of play seen in early childhood settings and is seldom observed before age three.

MartinPrescott/E+ via Getty Images

Figure 21.1 This child is practicing using a saw while pretending to build something. *Why is playing in the woodworking center beneficial for children?*

21.1-1 Stages of Play

Children go through several stages of play before they can take part in socio-dramatic play. The first stage of play, which begins at birth, is **unoccupied play**. There is no purpose to this type of play, but infants make random movements. The second stage of play, or *solitary play*, is followed by *parallel play*. Finally, children learn to engage in *associative* and *cooperative play*. Thus, as children grow older, solitary forms of play decrease while social types increase.

With **solitary play** or *independent play*, infants most often play by themselves. This type of play is also often common in toddlers. Children's play is basically exploratory and there are improvements in their concentration and persistence. Solitary explorations involve the child gathering information. Until about nine months of age, infants explore single objects. After this, they can examine multiple objects at once.

Parallel play is typical of two-year-olds, although it occurs at any age. With parallel play, children play beside each other, but not with each other. It may involve all the children in similar activities, but there is little or no interaction among the children. Children in this age group focus more on using play materials on their own, even though they are not interacting with each other.

Associative play is the first type of social play in which children pay attention and interact with one another while engaging in a similar activity. It occurs around three or four years of age. The play is loosely organized, so there is not a definite goal, division of labor, or product. Any communication that occurs is related to the common activity and may involve exchanging play materials.

Cooperative play, or *social play*, occurs between two or more children. At this stage, children are beginning to understand how to get along. As children grow socially and emotionally, they begin playing with their peers for short time periods. Gradually, they learn to respect the property rights of others. This is a clue that they are gaining social skills (**Figure 21.2**). Children learn that they need permission to use other's materials. They are also more willing to

SDI Productions/E+ via Getty Images

Figure 21.2   Children learn social skills such as cooperation in socio-dramatic play. *How do you see these two children building their social skills?*

share with others. During this process, they are improving their reasoning and problem-solving skills.

It is at the cooperative play stage that socio-dramatic play begins. As children participate in cooperative play, they become more interested in social relationships. As this occurs, they learn how to develop and maintain peer relationships and work together. From this grows socio-dramatic play, which becomes increasingly complicated with social scenarios.

Children who are aggressive and uncooperative may have problems with cooperative play. To be successful in cooperative play, they need to give affection, be friendly, be kind, and consider other children's motivations. They also need to understand the viewpoint of others.

As you observe children in these four stages of play, you will notice that many engage in *personification*. **Personification** means giving human traits to nonliving objects. For instance, children may talk to dolls or puppets. They act as if the toys can hear what they say. They act out many everyday situations. A child may say, "Mommy is going to feed you now." While speaking to a puppet, a child may say, "You're going to go for a walk now." They will use exaggerated movements and voices. This is typical behavior for most young children.

21.1-2 Stages of Material Use in Play

Children move through three stages of material use in their play. Each stage of material use during play reflects the child's knowledge.

The **manipulative stage** is the first stage of material use. A child at this stage handles props. For instance, when given a baby bottle, children in the manipulative stage will unscrew the cap and then screw it back on.

During the second stage, or the **functional stage,** the child will use a prop as intended while playing with other children. Using a doll bottle, the child will pretend to feed a doll.

The **imaginative stage** is the third stage of material use in play. Children in this stage do not need real props (**Figure 21.3**). They can separate purpose from use. The child's imagination leads the way. Instead of feeding the doll with a bottle, they may use their index finger, a stick, a clothespin, or a pencil. Likewise, if a child needs a broom to sweep the floor, they may use a yardstick.

Many times, children at the imaginative level come up with unique ideas for their socio-dramatic play. They may use a toy to represent a dinosaur, a doll carriage for a grocery cart, or a paper bag as a chef's hat. When dramatizing a

Luis Louro/Shutterstock.com

Figure 21.3   A large box might be used as a playhouse, a race car, or recreational vehicle. *How do you think this child is using the box for dramatic play?*

Ethical Responsibilities ⚖️

Building Relationships with Children

Over 40 years ago, NAEYC developed *The Code of Ethical Conduct and Statement of Commitment* for early childhood teachers serving young children. Principle P-1.7 of the *Code* states, "We shall strive to build individual relationships with each child; make individualized adaptations in teaching strategies, learning environments, and curricula; and consult with the family so that each child benefits from the program…"

NAEYC's goal is to promote high-quality learning environments by focusing on a teacher's responsibility to children. One challenge that teachers continually face is balancing the needs of one child with the group of children.

Dig Deeper

Why do you think teachers have an obligation to protect, care, and build positive relationships with the young children in their classrooms? How can consulting with the family better enable teachers and care providers to build relationships with and meet the needs of individual children through teaching strategies, the environment, and the curricula? Explore online resources to locate more information on the NAEYC *Code*. How can this help you in your role as an early childhood educator to build healthy relationships with children? Reflect on this information and write a summary regarding how this information is helpful to you.

restaurant theme, they may make paper money to buy food.

Some children find it difficult to get involved in a role if there are no real props. In a restaurant scene, for instance, some children will play the role of servers. Children at the manipulative or functional stage cannot play the role without the use of paper and pencil. Children who have reached the imaginative stage of play might use their hand for the paper and use a finger as a pencil. Not all young children can reach the imaginative level.

Lesson 21.1 Review

1. A form of play that involves several children imitating others and acting out situations together is _____. (21.1.1)
   A. agency
   B. dramatic play
   C. socio-dramatic play
   D. projection
2. Play encourages _____, which allows children to make choices that influence events in context of their learning. (21.1.1)
   A. agency
   B. dramatic play
   C. socio-dramatic play
   D. projection
3. A type of play in which children play beside each other, but not with each other is known as _____. (21.1.1)
   A. associative play
   B. cooperative play
   C. parallel play
   D. solitary play
4. During the _____ stage of material use, a child will use a prop as intended while playing with other children. (21.1.2)
   A. functional
   B. imaginative
   C. manipulative
   D. cooperative
5. Each of the following is a way children will use materials during the imaginative stage of play *except* _____. (21.1.2)
   A. children can come up with unique ideas for socio-dramatic play, such as using a doll carriage as a shopping cart
   B. children can separate purpose from use with play materials
   C. children will pretend to feed a doll using a doll bottle
   D. children's imaginations lead the way in how they use play materials

Essential Question

What do you need to know about socio-dramatic play and puppetry to effectively guide children's play?

Learning Outcomes

After studying this lesson, you will be able to

21.2-1 **summarize** the benefits of socio-dramatic play.

21.2-2 **demonstrate** how to use three types of puppets.

Key Terms

projection
role-playing
coaching

prop box
puppetry
conflict

Play is essential for optimal development, learning, and resiliency. Social-dramatic play and puppetry experiences are two types of make-believe play that the children will find joyful. Each offers its own benefits. Socio-dramatic play is the most advanced form of play and constantly changes depending upon children's interests. It allows children to recreate many roles or events they have seen or experienced from a storybook. Props, costumes, and scenery can be involved. Children learn to take different perspectives with a teacher' guidance and age-appropriate materials. By expressing their ideas and thoughts, children learn to use their imaginations and develop problem-solving, social-emotional, and language skills.

Puppetry is a type of play that allows a child to imitate others. Storytelling comes alive with puppets. They allow children the opportunity to explore emotions, thoughts, and situations. A child's puppet may become a police officer, a mad dog, a friend, or even a troll. They enjoy having conversations with puppets. Through play, a child often shares their inner world. The child uses the puppet to express their emotions—happy, sad, humor, anger, and jealousy. This technique is known as **projection**. Puppets also help children improve their language and social skills and boost self-confidence.

21.2-1 Socio-Dramatic Play

As children engage in socio-dramatic play, they mimic adult roles. They may play at being a spouse, parent, doctor, or police officer through the process of *role-playing*. **Role-playing** allows children to try out a variety of roles. As one child plays the role of a hairstylist, another plays the role of the customer. Each role follows social rules determined by the group of children. Children engaged in role-playing often give specific instructions for roles. A child might say, "You be the doctor, and I'll be the baby." Conditions are also common. For example, a child may say, "I'll play, but I have to be the bus driver."

Benefits of Socio-Dramatic Play

Children benefit from participating in socio-dramatic play. From this type of play, children grow cognitively, physically, socially, and emotionally, and develop self-regulation skills. Play also supports the building of resilience.

Play is the cornerstone of learning **(Figure 21.4)**. Studies reveal a strong connection between play and cognitive development. Children's roles range from babies to parents to bears to astronauts. Their imaginations allow

Value of Play

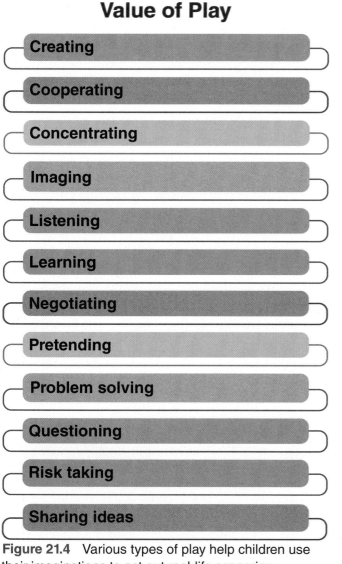

- Creating
- Cooperating
- Concentrating
- Imaging
- Listening
- Learning
- Negotiating
- Pretending
- Problem solving
- Questioning
- Risk taking
- Sharing ideas

Figure 21.4   Various types of play help children use their imaginations to act out real-life scenarios.

them to act out what they cannot yet be in real life. During this type of play, children make choices. By doing so, they learn decision-making and problem-solving skills **(Figure 21.5)**. Children also develop language and literacy concepts as they engage in play. They learn unfamiliar names for equipment and gain new ideas from other children. As children generate plots and new storylines, their language skills, creativity, and imaginations develop.

The play actions of children—through such tasks as sweeping floors, dressing dolls, cooking, and pretending to paint furniture—promote physical development. Building structures that enhance socio-dramatic scenes also helps develop physical skills.

Judy Herr

Figure 21.5   Cognitive development occurs as this child uses a mixer in the dramatic play area. *What cognitive skills do you feel this child is learning?*

Socio-dramatic play promotes social-emotional development. Children try out different social roles. Sometimes children act out negative feelings and situations that disturb them. Through these experiences, children learn about human relationships. They learn what kind of behavior upsets another child. They also learn how to get along with others and discover essential social skills, gradually learning how to balance their play to satisfy and please others.

Play Themes

Themes for socio-dramatic play vary. The play themes often focus on everyday situations that children experience **(Figure 21.6)**. Play is a dialogue with the materials provided in their environment. Children may imitate auto mechanics fixing cars, cooks making dinner, or painters working on a house. Teachers will often provide props that complement a unit of study and the children's interests.

Themes change with age. The emphasis in three-year-old children's play is on process. There is no preplanned plot or theme. Because there is no firm separation between real and pretend play,

Workplace Connections

Socio-Dramatic Play—Observing Four-Year-Olds

Observe four-year-old children at an early care and education, early learning, or Head Start center during socio-dramatic play. Answer the following questions and share your observations in class.

1. What was the theme of the play?
2. What is the role of rules in this type of play?
3. What props could be added to extend the play?
4. How did the teacher "coach" the children?

children become what they imitate. Routines are important. Many three-year-old children always begin their day with the same activity.

Four-year-old children are more likely to take part in socio-dramatic play. Their play no longer centers primarily around the home. Play now involves more aggressive behaviors. Four-year-olds like to imitate ghosts, monsters, or TV action heroes. As you watch their socio-dramatic play, you will often notice that children exaggerate the traits of the characters they are playing. For example, to role-play a firefighter, children need all the props: helmets, boots, water-proof jackets, water hose, a play fire extinguisher, play hammers, and walkie-talkies.

Children's roles change frequently. One moment a child may be a career worker, and the next moment a helpless baby. Children may be included in or excluded from play based on their interests and willingness to accept roles.

The socio-dramatic play of five-year-olds is becoming increasing complex. It reflects games with rules, as well as fears and hostile feelings. At this age, the child usually can tell the difference between reality and fantasy. As a result, you may hear the child say, "This is just pretend."

Themes for Dramatic Play

Occupational Roles		
Architect	Farmer	Photographer
Archaeologist	Fisher	Police officer
Artist	Firefighter	Post office clerk
Baker	Florist	Restaurant server
Barber	Garbage collector	Sailor
Builder	Grocer	Scientist
Bus driver	Hairstylist	Shoe salesperson
Carpenter	Housekeeper	Teacher
Computer operator	Librarian	Truck driver
Cook	Mail carrier	Window washer
Doctor	Mechanic	Veterinarian
Dentist	Nurse	
Disc jockey	Office worker	
Doctor	Pharmacist	
Explorer	Pilot	

Other Themes	
Airport	Nursery
Animal hospital	Pet show
Bakery	Pizza parlor
Beach	Post office
Birthday party	Radio station
Camping	Restaurant
Coffee shop	Sandwich shop
Costume shop	Supermarket
Explorers	Spa
Fairy tales	Store
Farm/ranch	Taco stand
Gardening	Television station
Hat shop	Theater
Hospital	Vet Clinic
Ice cream parlor	Zoo

Figure 21.6   Play themes often focus on everyday situations children experience.

Real-life roles and folk heroes are part of five-year-olds' socio-dramatic play. Queens, kings, nurses, doctors, firefighters, store associates, farm workers, teachers, and characters such as Big Bird, Chewbacca, and Batman are all frequent themes. Children are also quite interested in romance. So, they like to act out fairy tales such as *Cinderella*.

Workplace Connections

Observing Gender-Based Differences in Socio-Dramatic Play

Observe a group of three-year-olds during socio-dramatic play. Share your observations in class.

1. Did you note any gender-based differences in the themes chosen for role-playing?
2. Did you observe some situations in which girls and boys are playing together and portraying nontypical roles?

The Teacher's Role

The primary role of the teacher is to be a planner. The teacher needs to act as a resource person who provides materials and space. Studies show that in classrooms where the teacher provides props that relate to the theme, children spent more time in socio-dramatic play (**Figure 21.7**).

The quality of toys and activities in the classroom will also affect the time spent in socio-dramatic play. Provide interesting props. Real props will also enhance play. For example, instead of supplying small plastic firefighter helmets, provide real helmets from a local fire station. Change props often to maintain interest.

The teacher's role also includes listening, coaching, observing, modeling, and reinforcing. Listening helps you find out what is meaningful to the children. This information will help you create an inviting environment. *Observing* requires the teacher to observe the children, their

PhotoMavenStock/Shutterstock.com

Figure 21.7 The teacher's role is to provide an environment that stimulates the child's curiosity. *In what ways might children use the items in this image for dramatic play?*

interactions, and their use of materials. They also observe to see if the children are having trouble joining a group. **Coaching** requires that you provide children with ideas for difficult situations. For instance, a child may not want to be a baker because there is no baker's hat. You may then suggest that the child use a paper bag as a hat.

In *modeling*, you show the children the appropriate behavior to use during their socio-dramatic play. In a shoe store scene, a child may not know how to sell shoes. You may say, "Would you like to buy some shoes today?" Watching you, the child has a chance to model this behavior for the other children.

Verbal guidance is helpful. Remaining outside of the play, you may offer comments and suggestions. For example, you may see a child unable to get involved in play. You may say to the child, "Your child looks hungry. Shouldn't you go to the store and buy some food?" This statement may encourage the child to take the role of the parent. It should also get the child involved in dramatization with the children who have set up the grocery store.

Ask the children open-ended questions to stimulate their thinking and play. Questions may include

- What other materials could you use?
- What would happen if…?
- What will you do next?
- What other materials can be added?
- What can you do tomorrow?

Reinforcing is necessary to reward the children's positive behaviors during socio-dramatic play. The teacher may make positive comments directly to the children who are modeling the desired behavior. If Skylar just gave Kohinoor a turn to use the cash register in their restaurant, say, "Skylar, I like the way you are giving Kohinoor a turn."

Scheduling

Scheduling dramatic play during self-selected play periods is best. These periods must be long enough for the children to carry out their ideas. Many programs allow the first hour in the morning for this type of play. For children arriving, the dramatic play center is usually a welcoming area of the classroom.

Avoid scheduling too many activities. This affects the number of children who take part and remain in socio-dramatic play. If few children are playing, the schedule may include too many activities. Reduce the number of activities. Schedule only activities that complement each other. Blocks, woodworking, puppets, and art activities all encourage dramatic play.

Equipment and Setup for Socio-Dramatic Play

The first decision in arranging for socio-dramatic play is to decide on the location of the play area. Children spend more time in socio-dramatic play when the area is in the center of the classroom. Small areas promote quiet, solitary play. Large, open areas promote more socio-dramatic play.

Age-appropriate materials promote the quality of socio-dramatic play. To promote harmonious play, provide plenty of these materials and store them in accessible play areas.

Prop Boxes

Extend children's play by providing prop boxes. A **prop box** contains materials and equipment that encourage children to explore various roles. Boxes that are the same size, clearly marked, and made of lightweight cardboard can be stored and carried with ease.

Prop-box themes might include an office worker, shoe shop owner, painter, hairstylist, post office clerk, baker, grocer, firefighter, florist, librarian, chef, fast-food worker, doctor, painter, or carpenter. Each prop box should contain materials for one role (**Figure 21.8**) Integrate books to reinforce the theme. The materials should be nonsexist and multicultural. To illustrate, a prop box for a hairstylist should include styling tools and products for all people. It should also include hair-care items for people of various cultural groups. In addition, integrate books that could reinforce the theme. **Figure 21.9** lists examples of books to include in the dramatic play area.

Hair Stylist Props

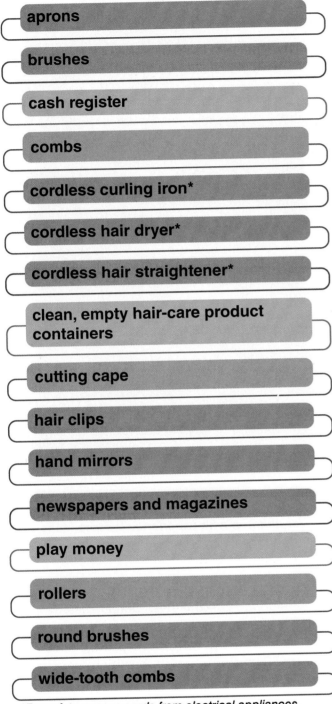

- aprons
- brushes
- cash register
- combs
- cordless curling iron*
- cordless hair dryer*
- cordless hair straightener*
- clean, empty hair-care product containers
- cutting cape
- hair clips
- hand mirrors
- newspapers and magazines
- play money
- rollers
- round brushes
- wide-tooth combs

*For safety, remove cords from electrical appliances.

Figure 21.8 Props for a hair stylist help children explore a career and an everyday experience. *What prop boxes might you want to include in a dramatic play center? Describe what would you include in one of the boxes.*

Costume Corner

Every dramatic play area should have a costume corner. Rotate costumes to complement current studies. For instance, if the theme of the week is community service, provide clothing to reflect this. For example, include clothing for firefighters, nurses, doctors, and post office clerks. If Halloween is the theme, provide a variety of Halloween costumes. Make sure the costume corner contains clothing and accessories that authentically represent a variety of cultures. Before including clothing items for dramatic play, consult with parents and family members that represent the cultures in your classroom to ensure you understand the cultural significance of the clothing. Some parents may be able to make contributions.

Store these costumes after use. Lightweight cardboard boxes are great for storage. Mark each box clearly so it is easy to locate.

Workplace Connections

Resource Survey

Survey early childhood equipment catalogs or online resources for furniture and props to use in a preschool housekeeping area. List the minimum equipment and props needed for a functional housekeeping area and calculate the total cost.

1. What types of props are available? What is the price range for each type?
2. What would be the total cost for equipping a dramatic play center?

Housekeeping Area

Every early childhood classroom should have a housekeeping area. Dramatic and socio-dramatic play often occurs in this area. Supply child-sized furniture and equipment. Include kitchen utensils, furniture, and other household items that complement current themes. To keep interest, rotate equipment often.

Outdoor Play Area

The outdoor play area needs equipment that promotes socio-dramatic play, too. Include a jungle gym, sandbox, housekeeping items, toy cars and trucks, sawhorses, wooden boxes, planks, and boards. Accessories such as tents, large blankets, and hats are also useful. With these materials, older preschool and kindergarten children can build forts, houses, and ships.

21.2-2 Puppetry

Puppetry involves the use of puppets in play. A *puppet* is a figure designed in likeness to an animal, human, or mythical figure. The magic of puppets captivates young children. Think how children have found joy watching puppets used in television programs such as *Mr. Rogers' Neighborhood* and *Sesame Street*. Puppets come in several sizes and shapes. People make puppets move by using their fingers, hands, and wrists. Puppets can appear to express emotions if they have movable mouths, legs, arms, and in some cases the eyes and mouth move.

Puppets can say things, do things, and hold things. They are powerful learning tools for young children. With a puppet, a self-conscious child can act out feelings such as anger and love. While using the puppet, the child often becomes the character and loses himself or herself. All children can learn how to communicate feelings and thoughts using puppets (**Figure 21.9**). They may say things to a puppet that they will not say to a person. By listening, teachers may learn what makes children angry, sad, or happy.

For teachers, a puppet can be a teaching aid. They can use puppets effectively in almost every area of the curriculum. **Figure 21.10** points out some of the values of puppets. Often, teachers use puppets to motivate children, to encourage them to share their thoughts, and to spark ideas. Group time can begin with a puppet. Teachers can change the appearance of a puppet for special occasions. For instance, a puppet might wear green for St. Patrick's Day.

Puppets can help children solve problems. When children cannot cooperate in cleanup, the

UW-Stout Child and Family Study Center

Figure 21.9   Children can use puppets to express their feelings. *Why can puppets play an important role for children who experience loss, sadness, or catastrophe?*

puppet can say, "I feel bad when all the children do not help pick up the toys." Sometimes, a teacher may use a puppet at group time to ask the question, "How can we get everyone involved at clean-up? The children will then give suggestions. The teacher might also use puppets to give suggestions, such as, "Tell Ricardo you want a turn."

Puppets are effective for teaching emotional and social skills, which are key lifetime competencies. Often a teacher will use two puppets, one on each hand at group time. One puppet can express an observed classroom problem, and the other will respond by providing positive suggestions.

Puppets and Curriculum

Curriculum Area	Value of Puppets
Art	• Offers emotional release • Provides sensory stimulation • Promotes fine- and gross-motor development • Encourages problem solving and decision making • Provides for exploration of materials
Math	• Encourages thinking through problems • Introduces concepts • Promotes the development of classification skills • Encourages measuring, ordering, and counting skills
Social studies	• Promotes communication skills • Models sharing and cooperation with others • Models critical-thinking skills • Demonstrates concepts, such as friendship and self-esteem
Language arts	• Encourages development of language skills • Encourages listening and speaking skills • Promotes the development of concepts such as *above, below, under, over, in front of,* and *behind*
Dramatic play	• Offers emotional release • Promotes listening skills • Promotes agency • Encourages problem-solving skills • Promotes decision-making skills • Promotes self-expression and creativity • Provides opportunities to gain self-confidence as group members • Provides opportunities to express feelings
Science	• Introduces concepts • Promotes classification of food, animals, and objects • Explores the value of the five senses • Demonstrates differences and changes in texture, shape, and size • Provides for exploration of animal and nature themes

Figure 21.10   Puppets can be used throughout the early childhood curriculum.

Types of Puppets

Puppet types include *hand, mascot,* and *"me" puppets.* The value of each type depends on the needs and interests of the children.

Hand Puppets

Hand puppets are the easiest to use since there are no strings or rods to work. You can work a hand puppet by placing your second and third fingers in the puppet's head. This position allows you to relax your hand to be able to spread the puppet's entire body open. Place your thumb in one of the puppet's arms and the fourth and fifth finger in the other arm.

You can hold hand puppets in front of your face or over your head. This allows you to work the puppet from a sitting, standing, or kneeling position.

Mascot Puppets

Some teachers choose to have a mascot puppet in their classroom. A mascot puppet is typically large. It usually remains in the classroom all year. Therefore, the construction should be sturdy to withstand handling from the teachers and children.

Mascot puppets are useful for many classroom routines. They can help introduce new activities and class members. You might also use puppets as teaching tools. A puppet can model proper classroom manners. For this reason, the puppet should have an expressive face and a forceful personality. The mascot puppet can also teach classroom rules. If a child neglects a rule, the teacher may have the mascot puppet provide a reminder.

Mary Arntson, a teacher of three- and four-year-old children, created a mascot for her classroom. She called him Mr. Dosendorf. Each day she used him for opening the morning meeting, during larger group times, and again for transitions. She kept him on a shelving unit where he could "observe" the entire room. Throughout the day, he provided the children with reminders. For example, when Eilian started running across the room, Mary used Mr. Dosendorf to provide a friendly reminder. She picked up Mr. Dosendorf and walked over to Eilian. Then Mr. Dosendorf said, "We walk in the classroom."

Teachers often use puppets to make storytelling come alive. They may use a puppet to introduce a story. Likewise, they may use puppets to teach children manners during breakfast, lunch, or snack.

"Me" Puppets

Older preschool and kindergarten children can also learn how to make "me" puppets using their own hands. To make "me" puppets, you will need nontoxic, washable markers; felt pieces; fake fur; construction paper; and double-stick tape. Show how to make a "me" puppet using your own hand. Line the inside opening between your index finger and thumb with a red marker. This line will be the puppet's lips. Using another colored marker, add the puppet's eyes. Use a piece of construction paper, fleece fabric, or a hair scrunchie for the hair. With double-stick tape, attach the hair to the top of your knuckle.

Show the children how the puppet can open and close its mouth and talk when you move your thumb. Urge the children to make a variety of puppets, including people and animals. School-age children may enjoy making "me" puppets on the first day of school. After making their puppets, each child can share something about himself or herself. This might include age, hobby, grade in school, or favorite books or toys.

Making Puppets

Many teachers make their own hand and mascot puppets using store-bought or self-designed patterns. **Figure 21.11** contains a list of materials for making puppets. You can even make a puppet from an old man's sock. After cutting the fabric, sew on the mouth, eyes, ears, nose, and other parts. It is quicker to attach these parts with glue, however, this method is not durable. In fact, many times the parts will fall off once the glue has dried. Sew all seams with a 1/4-inch seam allowance. The seams on a hand puppet should be on the outside of the puppet.

Constructing puppets fosters creativity. The children can use paper bags, socks, or gloves to make puppets. They can decorate paper bags with washable felt-tip markers or stickers.

Puppet Stage

A puppet stage is not always a requirement; however, most classrooms have a lightweight, portable stage. The puppet stage should be easy to fold and store.

Materials for Making Puppets

Fabrics and Notions	
buttons	suede
fake fur	terry cloth
felt	velour
gloves	velvet
hats	
material	
mittens	
ribbons	
socks	

Household Items	
aluminum foil	foam balls
bags	packing paper
brooms	paper plates and cups
boxes	pictures
coat hangers	plastic bottles
construction paper	plastic packing materials
drinking straws	pliers
envelopes	tongue depressors
flyswatters	wooden spoons

Figure 21.11   Teachers can use everyday materials for making puppets.

Teachers can order puppet stages through most equipment catalogs. Generally, they are wooden, and as a result, they are often quite heavy. Teacher-made puppet stages have the advantage of being more portable and less expensive.

Puppet Tree

Many teachers opt to have a puppet tree or rack in their classroom to make puppets visible and continuously available. Often children enjoy having a puppet on each hand. This allows them to have a one-to-one and back-and-forth conversation. For a shy child, a puppet can be their voice. With a puppet, children can be happy, excited, frightened, jealous, joyful, sad, angry, or happy.

Early Childhood Insight

Making a Puppet Stage

A cardboard cutting board is an excellent puppet stage. You can purchase these at fabric shops. If the board is too tall for children, you can cut it to the correct height. To make the stage more interesting, paint or apply wallpaper to the cutting board. You can also cover it with contact paper or fabric. Make sure that the covering is not overstimulating since the focus should be on the puppet, not the stage.

You might also use a tension curtain rod in creating a puppet stage. Simply gather the curtain onto the rod and place the rod in a door as a temporary stage. Use a simple curtain in a solid color that will not be distracting.

Safety First

Safety with Puppet Materials

When choosing materials to make puppets for or with children, make sure the materials and construction methods are safe. Choose washable materials and construction methods that are not choking hazards for children. In addition, keep all toy safety practices in mind as you create puppets.

Writing Puppet Stories

Not all puppet stories are found in books. In fact, teachers write many puppet stories. These stories are often contemporary and designed to meet the children's interests, stimulate their curiosity, and promote language development.

To begin writing a puppet story, select a theme. Using a theme will help you decide the order of the events in the story. You can base themes on friends, relatives, other people, or animals. Personal experiences are another useful theme, as are manners, safety, friendships, vacations, holidays, and center experiences. **Figure 21.12** lists some other theme ideas for puppet stories.

Developing a plot is the most challenging aspect of writing a puppet story. The children must be able to follow the action of the story. The events should occur logically. Begin with the theme and include the story's events and problems. Remember, it is the problems that add interest and tension to the story.

End the story by resolving the *conflict*. In a story, a **conflict** includes two or more forces that oppose each other. Conflict adds interest. When developing scenes of conflict, think in terms of synonyms and antonyms. Make a list of opposites. For example, opposite pairs might include: ugly-beautiful; poor-rich; weak-strong; soft-hard; kind-mean.

The ending of a puppet story finishes the picture for the children. The ending should make clear that the story is over. It should leave children with the story's most important point. The following books can be purchased in sets with puppets:

- *Birds* by Carme Lemniscates
- *Bug City* by Dahlov Ipcar
- *Bug Zoo* by Disney Books (author) and Andy Harkness (illustrator)
- *Beware of the Crocodile* by Martin Jenkins, and Satoshi Kitamura
- *Pete the Cat and His Four Groovy Buttons* by Eric Litwin (author) and James Dean (illustrator)
- *Pete the Cat: I Love My White Shoes* by Eric Litwin
- *Baby Penguin's First Waddles* by Ben Richmond
- *Owl* by Madeline Tyler
- *Turtle* by Madeline Tyler

Theme Ideas for Puppet Stories

Odin's Broken Tooth

My Dog Heidi

Kelsi's Hamster

My Cousin Pilar

Bobby's Friend Eric

Christmas at Aunt Shareece's

My Favorite Gift

A Trip to the Zoo

Jeffrey and Eva's Grandmother

Figure 21.12   Using a theme can help you order the events in a puppet story.

Working Puppets

When using a puppet in the classroom, the puppet should always model proper grammar skills for the children. When the puppet speaks, use a strong, elevated voice and face the children. When the children or you speak, hold the puppet still, facing the speaker. Use eye contact with the puppet and children. Your face should mimic the story and emotions.

You can model three basic types of movements with hand puppets, including movement of the fingers, wrists, and arms. The fingers can create slight movements in the puppet's arms and head. Make waist movements using the wrist. Use arm movements to show locomotion movements. **Figure 21.13** explains the various finger, wrist, and arm movements that you can use in puppetry.

Telling a Puppet Story

Practice the story and be comfortable working with the puppets. You will then be ready to tell the children a puppet story. Begin by creating the story setting and preparing the children.

Movements for Puppetry

Finger Movements

- The puppet's head can nod *yes* by moving the fingers up and down inside the puppet's head. This movement can also mean *I understand* or *I can do it*.

- The idea of *me* or *mine* can be expressed by pointing the fingers inside the puppet's hands toward the puppet.

- The puppet can gesture for someone to *come here* by waving one hand toward the body.

- Clapping and jumping up and down can express joy or enthusiasm.

- Pointing can convey such ideas as *you* or *over there*.

- Waving can be used to say *good-bye* or *hello*.

- Rubbing the puppet's hands together can mean the puppet is cold or thinking of doing something sneaky.

- Thinking can be expressed in a number of ways. The puppet can cross its hands or tap its head lightly.

Wrist Movements

- To show a *no* movement, rotate the puppet back and forth.

- To show a seated puppet, pivot the wrist, changing from a front to a side view. After this, the wrist needs to be bent, allowing the puppet to rest on a seat.

- To show a bow from the waist, bend the wrist down. At the same time, use the finger to make the puppet point toward itself.

- To show a puppet reading a book, model left to right progression skills by pivoting the wrist to mimic this action. At the same time, slowly move the fingers in the puppet's head to show reading action.

- To make a puppet appear to be looking for something, move the wrist back and forth. Using some arm movement, the puppeteer can make the puppet look to the sides of the stage and above and below it.

- To show a lifting movement, bend the wrist down as in bowing and grasp objects with the hands using hand and finger movements.

- The fingers can be used to mimic sneezing, crying, and snoring (move the puppet's head up and down slightly).

Arm Movements

- To mimic running, move the wrist up and down in a rapid, choppy motion. At the same time, move the puppet quickly across the stage.

- To mimic walking, hold the puppet upright and straight. As the puppet is moved across the stage, move its arms up and down.

- To mimic hopping, each hop needs to be deliberate. For variety, have the puppet hop in circles, returning to the ground as the last motion for each hop.

- To mimic flying, use broad arm movements. The puppet should always face the direction that it is flying.

- To mimic fainting or falling, use a broad arm movement and have the puppet land on its back. The speed at which the puppet lands is dependent on the desired effect. The best effect is acquired by freezing the puppet's movements for a few seconds before falling.

Figure 21.13   The various finger, wrist, and arm movements used in puppetry is essential for telling an effective puppet story. *Why do you think practice is important when telling puppet stories?*

The room should set the mood for a story. For a birthday theme, you might place colorful balloons next to the storyteller. A Valentine's Day event might include a valentine's box set next to the storyteller. Likewise, you could enhance a Halloween story with dimmed lights. This preparation establishes the mood of the story for the children to enjoy the presentation.

The first few minutes of a puppet story set the tone of the story. Attempt to gain the children's attention. You might do this using recorded music, clapping, or having the children sing a song; however, keep some surprises for later in the story.

Puppet Voices

To develop your puppet's character, use a special voice. Since puppets are not people, their voices should not be like human voices. Pitch is important. If you are using two puppets, one should have a low-pitched voice and the other a high-pitched voice.

The children should be able to hear the voices of the puppets clearly (**Figure 21.14**). Voices should also be constant. Each puppet should have the same voice throughout the story. If a puppet begins with a high-pitched voice, it should finish with one.

The voice should match the puppet's size and character. For instance, a huge tiger should have a booming voice. Likewise, a spider should have a tiny voice. A puppet of an older person may have a slower voice than that of a child.

SDI Productions/E+ via Getty Images

Figure 21.14   Puppet voices should be clear and consistent.

Lesson 21.2 Review

1. Each of the following is a benefit of socio-dramatic play *except* _____. (21.2.1)
   A. self-regulation skills
   B. cognitive development
   C. resilience
   D. projection

2. Which of the following is *not* an example of how social and emotional development are promoted through socio-dramatic play? (21.2.1)
   A. Children learn how to get along with others.
   B. Children generate plots and new storylines.
   C. Children are able to try out different social roles.
   D. Children are able to learn about human relationships.

3. _____ requires the teacher to provide children with ideas for difficult situations. (21.2.1)
   A. Observing
   B. Reinforcing
   C. Modeling
   D. Coaching

4. Which of the following is *not* an example of how can puppets help teachers to better understand children? (21.2.2)
   A. By listening, teachers may learn what makes children angry, sad, or happy.
   B. Puppets can be used to encourage children to share their thoughts and to spark ideas.
   C. Children may say things to a puppet that they would not say to a person.
   D. For the teacher, using a puppet is ineffective as a teaching aid for most curriculum areas.

5. Each of the following shows conflict as an effective element in a puppet story *except* _____. (21.2.2)
   A. conflict adds interest to the puppet story
   B. conflict is unrelated to the theme of the story
   C. conflict is two or more opposing forces
   D. conflict should be resolved at the end of the story

6. Each of the following is true about puppet voices *except* _____. (21.2.2)
   A. a puppet should have a different voice throughout the story for interest
   B. puppet voices should not be like human voices because they are not people
   C. a puppet's voice should match its size and its character
   D. if a puppet begins with a high-pitched voice, it should finish with one

Chapter 21 Review and Assessment

Summary

Lesson 21.1

21.1-1 Play is vital and essential for optimal development, learning, and resiliency.

21.1-1 Through play, children learn collaboration, communication, creative innovation, and confidence.

21.1-1 Children go through several stages of play before they begin to take part in socio-dramatic play, including parallel, associative, and cooperative play.

21.1-2 Children move through three stages of material use in their play, including manipulative, functional, and imaginative stages.

21.1-2 During the manipulative and functional stages, children use props.

21.1-3 Children do not need real props during the imaginative stage. They often come up with unique ideas.

Lesson 21.2

21.2-1 Socio-dramatic play and puppetry experiences are two types of make-believe children find joyful. Each offers its own benefits to children's learning and development.

21.2-1 Socio-dramatic play helps children develop cognitively, physically, socially, emotionally, and develop self-regulation skills.

21.2-1 Teachers serve several roles during socio-dramatic play, including observer and coach.

21.2-2 Puppets are powerful learning tools for young children and can help them solve problems.

21.2-2 Puppetry experiences provide children the chance to explore emotions, thoughts, and situations.
Types of puppets include hand, mascot, and "me" puppets. The value of each type depends on the needs and interests of the children.

21.2-2 Teachers can make puppets from store-bought or self-designed patterns using common materials.

21.2-2 Children can use their creativity to make puppets with paper bags, socks, or gloves.

21.2-2 Teachers often write their own puppet stories.

21.2-2 Teachers must prepare the children for the story, using a variety of actions to set the tone.

Vocabulary Activity

Divide into two teams. Play charades to act out the meaning of each Key Term in this chapter. Each team member will draw a slip of paper with one term. As team members identify the terms, the team gets a point. The team that acts out and identifies the most terms within wins the game.

Critical Thinking

1. **Draw Conclusions.** In a world of television, computers, and apps, why do children still need to play? In your own words, explain why dramatic play is critical to a child's development.

2. **Compare and Contrast.** Observe groups of two-year-old and four-year-old children, taking notes about how they play. Then compare the methods and types of play for each age.

3. **Evaluate.** Four-year-old Harper was just enrolled in a preschool program and has spent a lot of time watching other children in the dramatic play area. Harper seems to lack the skills to join in and interact, and the other children in the area seem to ignore Harper. Presuming that you are a worker at this center, evaluate the situation. What might be some reasons Harper is not playing with the other children? What are some strategies that you could use to get Harper involved?

4. **Make Inferences.** As children grow older, they need less guidance in their play than at earlier ages. Young children do not, however, grow out of the need for adult supervision and provision. What do preschool children need from their teachers and caregivers to maximize their play? Think of answers in both material and nonmaterial terms.

5. **Create.** In teams, imagine that the center director has asked you to create prop boxes for children's roles as zookeepers, painters, bakers, and carpenters. Identify props that can be used for these roles (ideally, for several roles in each box) and then create a virtual prop box using a store website.

Core Skills

1. **Technology.** Visit a local early childhood center and observe the socio-dramatic play area. What types of play do you notice? What stages of play do you observe? After your visit, create a presentation that outlines the stages of play and their observable characteristics among children. Your presentation should be informative and easy to follow.

2. **Social Studies.** Using reliable print or online resources, research what experts say about the importance of the educator's role in socio-dramatic play. Why is it important to intentionally plan play environments for learning? How can the dramatic play area be designed to reflect all children's abilities and cultural backgrounds? What strategies should educators use facilitate children's play and social interactions? How can guided play extend children's learning? How can teachers use guided playful experiences to help support self-regulation and executive function skills? Summarize your findings and share your report with the class using a digital presentation.

3. **Research.** Play, including the use of puppets and puppetry, is often used to help traumatized children handle their emotions. Through print or online resources, research how puppetry is used for these children. Why do therapists find puppets useful in situations where children have experienced abuse or catastrophes? Why might children respond better to a puppet than to a human voice? What programs currently use puppets and puppetry routinely when working with children? Discuss your findings in class.

4. **Writing.** Review the information in this chapter about writing a puppet story and then select a theme for a puppet story you would have found interesting as a child. Following the steps outlined in the text (select a theme, develop a plot, resolve the conflict), write a puppet story. After writing, share your story with a peer and give each other feedback. Revise your puppet story and then share it with the class.

5. **Speaking.** Ask a speech instructor at your school to teach you a variety of voice techniques suitable for puppets. Practice these voice techniques and make recordings so you can hear how you sound. After listening to the recordings, critique your own style and alter or add modifications for a more effective puppet voice.

6. **CTE Career Readiness Practice.** Imagine that you are the main puppeteer for an early childhood center and that several workers at the center have asked you for tips on using puppets to teach their children. You schedule a brief training session for the end of the week. What topics would you cover in this session? How would you help the workers understand puppetry and build competency with the basics they need to know? In your mind, what skills are vital to puppetry and what skills might be reserved for a more advanced follow-up session?

Portfolio Project

Using a camera or another digital device with recording capabilities, create photographic essays of children engaged in socio-dramatic play. Identify the age and stage of development of the children and any theme they are using. Write a short anecdotal observation to explain what is happening during the play period, how long the session lasted, and what props or equipment were used. (Be sure to get parents' permission to take the photos.) Creatively mount your photo essay with captions. File a copy of the essay in your portfolio.

Chapter 22

Guiding Manuscript Writing Experiences

Lesson 22.1: Understanding Writing Skills and Systems

Lesson 22.2: Promoting Writing Skills and Experiences

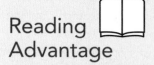

Reading Advantage

Take two-column notes as you read the chapter. Fold a piece of notebook paper in half lengthwise. On the left side of the column, write the main ideas. On the right side, write subtopics and detailed information. After reading the chapter, use the notes as a study guide. Fold the paper in half so you only see the main ideas. Quiz yourself on the details and subtopics.

Case Study

Promoting Print Knowledge

Abba Goldstein observed the children at the writing table and noted the individual differences in print awareness. He smiled as he watched Felix, who had recently learned that he could make print happen and found joy by flexing his muscles. Abba knew learning occurs in a developmental continuum, and the span between birth and eight years of age is the most important for literacy development. Abba also recognized that the children in his classroom were much more diverse than when he began teaching 10 years ago. The neighborhood changed, and now some children speak English or Spanish with different proficiency levels, which is a change from the past when the majority spoke English. Some children spoke both languages.

Over the weekend, Abba read an article in a professional journal on promoting print knowledge. The article's first two lines read, "Children need interaction with print, which should be highly visible throughout the classroom to encourage writing. This will help them develop a working knowledge of the alphabet system." The remaining content stressed strategies for promoting a print-rich environment. After completing the article, Abba reflected on his practices. He realized that his classroom environment was in need of an update to reflect the strategies in the article. Then, too, many of his teacher-made or commercially purchased examples of environmental print were only in English, so they required an update, too.

Give It Some Thought

1. Why is it essential for Abba to create a print-rich environment?
2. What emergent literacy sequence do children follow in learning to write alphabet letters?
3. Why do children need to learn the concept of print?
4. What teaching strategies can Abba use to promote print awareness?
5. What materials should be available in a writing center to encourage alphabet awareness and writing?
6. Why should Abba create documentation boards to display the children's writing samples?

Understanding Writing Skills and Systems

Essential Question

What do you need to know about emergent literacy, manuscript writing, and writing systems to understand and promote children's writing?

Learning Outcomes

After studying this lesson, you will be able to

22.1-1 summarize emergent writing, including stages children go through as they develop writing skills.

22.1-2 analyze prewriting skills and what children need to learn about the concept of print.

22.1-3 evaluate writing systems and tools necessary for children to develop writing skills.

Key Terms

emergent writing	manuscript writing
early scribbling	concept of print
controlled scribbling	hand-eye coordination
mock writing	conventions of print
letter string	

"Writing before kindergarten?" asked a concerned visitor, who was observing two children sitting at the writing table. "Preschool children can't even read yet." This person was unaware that children can informally learn to write at this age. Only minor attention is given to correct spelling, form, and style during the preschool years. Instead, the emphasis is on a readiness to develop needed skills and attitudes for writing. As children explore, they learn how symbols and meaning combine. Art and play activities are critical in children's growth as symbol makers. Handwriting emerges from drawing, print awareness, and alphabet knowledge. Learning to write results from maturation, exploration, and practice at scribbling and drawing forms. It also results from observing and interacting with other children, parents, and teachers.

Children will come to your program with different experiences. At home, some children will have many books, paper, and writing tools. They also observe their parents reading and writing. Other children will have limited exposure. They may lack resources and writing and seldom see their parents reading and writing.

22.1-1 Emergent Writing

Emergent writing is a term that explains a child's knowledge before learning to write words. Writing is a complex and lengthy process. Children move through several stages as they develop their writing skills. The **early scribbling** is the beginning of the journey. These marks may occur around the child's first birthday. The child grips the writing tool with their entire hand. During this stage, children have more interest in the physical experience of drawing on paper than in the markings. A two-year-old will make markings using a crayon, chalk, or felt-tip marker. During this process, the child is observing how the tool works. After finishing, the child may label the drawing and say things such as, "That is my dog" or "That is a car." Early scribbling is a faster process than controlled scribbling.

The second stage is **controlled scribbling**. Children now use symbols or drawings to represent ideas or words. These markings are becoming intentional and some scribblings look like drawings. When observing children at this stage, you will note that they use a combination of *sticks*, *dots*, *circles*, and *wavy lines* in their scribbling. In this **mock writing,** the children are experimenting with form. There are wavy lines with a left-to-right progression. There is no message, and the writing contains elements of actual letters. Encourage the children to tell you about their writings or drawings.

Gradually, scribbling becomes more controlled as the child begins to use a precision grip, holding the writing tool using their thumb and fingers. Eventually, this scribbling leads to the **letter strings.** The children now can use tools to write strings of alphabet letters and letter-like forms that do not make words. Children often capitalize these letters, may write them upside down, and copy them from the environment. Some letters may reflect reversals, which are common in preschool and kindergarten children. For example, the letters *R* and *S* may be backwards. The letters *M* and *W* are alike, but one letter faces up and the other down. When writing, the child often reverses them. They also may print words upside down.

After letter strings, children will produce letters found in their own names. Then they will focus on environmental print to write words with beginning and end letters. Examples include *hat*, *bat*, *Tom*, and *car*. As you observe, you will find the letters "*b*" and "*d*" are frequently reversed at this stage. When this occurs, teachers offer clues. They may say the letter *b* has a *bat* followed by a *ball*. The letter *d* has a ball, or circle, followed by a bat, or straight line. Words also often run together. After this, children write simple words with beginning and end letters.

For preschool children, learning to write is like learning to speak. Literacy will emerge gradually. Children must first observe others in the process and then imitate what they see. You should immerse them in a print-rich environment. You must introduce children who are not ready for writing to activities that will help them prepare. They need activities that promote fine-motor development and hand-eye coordination

skills. Eventually, as their coordination improves, these children will become interested in writing.

Manuscript writing, or print script, is a simple form of calligraphy. These simple strokes look like the printed words children see every day in books, in newspapers, on street signs, on billboards, and on digital devices. Print script does not require the sustained muscle control needed for cursive writing. It involves unconnected letters that are made of simple, separate strokes. Vertical lines (|), horizontal lines (—), diagonal lines (/), and circles (O) are used to compose the strokes. Children who lack well-developed fine-motor skills can make these basic stokes. Because of the separate strokes, this process takes more time than cursive writing; however, manuscript writing is more legible. Children can create their letters at a faster rate.

Teachers do not formally teach manuscript writing in the preschool setting. Most young children are not developmentally ready for this task. This text includes manuscript writing to introduce readiness activities and the sequence by which children should learn manuscript, and teach educators and caregivers of young children correct letter formations and the importance of promoting writing. All teacher-made materials should be prepared using the proper manuscript format, whether they are hand printed or computer generated (**Figure 22.1**). Your work will then serve as a model for children. It may also stimulate older children to identify individual letters of the alphabet and to write.

22.1-2 Concept of Print and Prewriting Skills

There are many reasons to encourage writing in preschool, especially with children who are ready for the task. Children need to learn the **concept of print,** which is the awareness of how print works. The objectives of learning the concept of print include

- the differences in the formation of letters
- letters have names and shapes
- words are made of groups of letters
- letters represent sounds

UW-Stout Child and Family Study Center

Figure 22.1   Teacher-made materials must be carefully prepared to serve as models for the children to copy. All letters must be accurately produced.

- letters in the English language go from left to right and top to bottom
- letter/sound associations
- the spelling of words relates to their sound
- there are spaces between words
- print carries a message

Four elements are necessary if children are to meet these objectives. These include interest, enthusiasm, a print-rich environment, and the support you give to each child.

Prewriting Skills

Manuscript writing is mainly a perceptual and motor skill. To accurately interpret what they see, children need visual-perceptual skills. They also require fine-motor and hand-eye coordination skills. Children need enough fine-motor coordination to hold a writing tool and make basic strokes. Their hands and eyes need to work together. Early childhood teachers must include activities that promote these skills in the daily routine. This will ensure that children learn the basic skills needed to learn manuscript writing.

Fine-Motor Activities

Fine-motor activities are those that encourage children to use the small muscles in their hands and fingers. **Figure 22.2** lists the materials

used in these activities. Observe the children's interest and success with these materials. Provide interesting developmental materials. Practice should provide the children with the fine-motor coordination skills necessary for manuscript writing.

Hand-Eye Coordination Activities

Hand-eye coordination is muscle control that allows the hand to do a task in the way the eye sees it done. **Figure 22.3** lists activities that promote this type of coordination. These activities will promote the development of writing skills. Therefore, they should be always available for use.

> ### Health Highlights
>
> #### Impact on Hand-Eye Coordination
>
> Developing hand-eye coordination is an important task for children in early childhood. Excellent vision and physical movement are the keys to achieving mastery of this skill. If children show poor hand-eye coordination when drawing, writing, and manipulating objects, problems with vision or physical movement may be the cause.
>
> Teachers and care providers should encourage parents and guardians to take their children for routine eye exams to identify any vision problems that can affect learning. Talking with their children's pediatrician can help identify problems with physical movement.

22.1-3 Manuscript Writing Systems

There are several manuscript writing systems available for teachers to use. The differences in these systems are minor. These systems include the shapes of the letters, the slant of the letters, and the directions in which you make the strokes for forming the letters. Research does not support one system over another. Whatever system you use, be a skillful and consistent model.

Materials Used in Fine-Motor Activities

- easel paints
- finger paints
- lacing boards
- play dough
- plastic or wooden alphabet letters
- putty
- puzzles
- rubber stamps and ink pads
- sand
- table blocks
- threading beads
- small, wheeled toys
- snap beads
- water play with sponges
- white and colored paper

- building blocks
- buttons and buttonholes
- chalk boards
- clay
- crayons, pencils, chalk, felt-tip markers

Sasiistock/iStock via Getty Images Plus

Figure 22.2   Fine-motor activities encourage children to use the small muscles in their hands and fingers. *What other activities can you think of that will help children develop fine-motor skills?*

Zaner-Bloser is perhaps the most widely used system in preschools and kindergartens. **Figure 22.4** introduces this system. It was selected for this text because of its common use and the ease with which children can learn to print using it.

Graphic Writing Tools

Provide a variety of graphic writing tools for young children. Chalk, crayons, washable felt-tip markers, and colored and lead pencils are examples. Until three years of age, children are interested in making something happen with a writing tool. They enjoy scribbling and may hold a writing tool in each hand. They often use colored felt-tip markers and soft lead pencils. These very young children hold the writing tool in a *fisted grasp* and use their shoulder and arm muscles to produce a marking. With time and practice, they will gain better control of the writing tool using a *pincer* grasp, which involves the coordination of the index finger and thumb.

Besides moving the shoulder and arm muscles, three- and four-year-old children start to use their wrists to move the writing tools. These children enjoy using a variety of writing tools, including chalk, crayons, felt-tipped markers, and colored lead pencils. Children's controlled scribbling emerges into letter-like forms. They produce circles, crosses, horizontal lines, and vertical lines. Gradually, children will use the tools to write the letters of their names. At this stage, children do not use correct spacing or position. They may also invent their own spellings for words.

By five years of age, children are beginning to use a mature *tripod pencil grip* on the writing tool using their thumb, middle, and index fingers. Some enjoy writing their names and drawing simple stick figures, suns, and snow figures.

Activities That Improve Hand-Eye Coordination

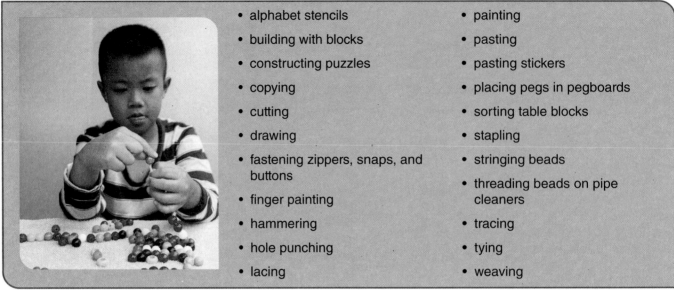

- alphabet stencils
- building with blocks
- constructing puzzles
- copying
- cutting
- drawing
- fastening zippers, snaps, and buttons
- finger painting
- hammering
- hole punching
- lacing

- painting
- pasting
- pasting stickers
- placing pegs in pegboards
- sorting table blocks
- stapling
- stringing beads
- threading beads on pipe cleaners
- tracing
- tying
- weaving

UW-Stout Child and Family Study Center

Figure 22.3   Hand-eye coordination is muscle control that allows the hand to do a task in the way the eye sees it done.

A B C D E F G H I
J K L M N O P Q R
S T U V W X Y Z
a b c d e f g h i
j k l m n o p q r s
t u v w x y z
1 2 3 4 5 6 7 8 9 10
? ! " " ' ,

© Zaner-Bloser, Inc.

Courtesy of Zaner-Bloser

Figure 22.4   The Zaner-Bloser writing system is easy for children to use and for teachers to teach. ***How do you think this chart helps children learn to form letters?***

Five- and six-year-olds exhibit superb control of writing tools and can form both upper- and lowercase letters. They like to draw more complex objects, such as flowers and houses. At this age, children are learning the **conventions of print**. This includes standardized spelling, word spacing, and upper- and lowercase letters.

Workplace Connections

Observing Children with Writing Tools

Collect crayons, pencils, chalk, and colored felt-tip markers of various thicknesses and set them out for children to use during group art time. Put out only the thick or thin utensils at a time. Observe how children handle these tools. Compare the line quality produced by the children using each type of tool. Write a brief report of your findings.

1. Which tools are preferred and are easiest for children to use?
2. Does the thickness of the writing tool relate to a child's ability to use the tool effectively?

Paper

Provide a variety of papers to encourage children to write. Young children enjoy making choices, so offer colored paper and white paper. Most preschool children lack the muscle control and hand-eye coordination to use lined paper. Use large, unlined pieces of paper such as newsprint instead.

Safety First

Safe Writing Tools

When selecting writing tools for an early childhood writing center, choose *nontoxic* chalk, markers, paints, crayons, pens, and pencils. For ergonomic safety, young children also benefit from using thicker writing tools to support better grip for developing muscles. Special weighted pencils or pencil grips are also helpful for children who have difficulty grasping. Because some writing tools have sharp points, careful supervision by teachers and care providers is a must.

Manuscript Sequence

There is a sequence in how children usually learn alphabet letters. First, children recognize whether a line is curved or straight. Next, they learn to distinguish round letters (O, C) and curved letters (S, D). Then they learn to recognize curved letters that have intersections, such as B and R. Finally, letters with diagonal lines (K, X) and horizontal lines (L, H) are recognized.

Certain letters are easier for children to form. The sequence recommended in the Zaner-Bloser method follows the similarities in lowercase letters. This is because children use lowercase letters more. Zaner-Bloser recommends the following sequence:

litoadcefgjqusbhprnmvywkxz

1, 2, 3, 4, 5, 6, 7, 8, 9, 10

LITOADCEFGJQUSBHPRNMVYWKXZ

The easiest letters are those made of straight lines or circles. You can follow this sequence as you design written materials.

Lesson 22.1 Review

1. _____ is a term used to explain a child's knowledge before learning to write words. (21.1.1)
   A. Early scribbling
   B. Controlled scribbling
   C. Mock writing
   D. Emergent writing

2. A stage when children use a combination of sticks, dots, circles, and wavy lines is called _____. (21.1.1)
   A. controlled scribbling
   B. mock writing
   C. letter strings
   D. emergent writing

3. Simple strokes that look like the printed words children see every day in books, in newspapers, on street signs, on billboards, and on digital devices is _____. (21.1.1)
   A. controlled scribbling
   B. mock writing
   C. manuscript writing
   D. controlled scribbling

4. Each of the following is an example of what children need to learn about the concept of print *except* _____. (21.1.2)
   A. the differences in the formation of letters
   B. there are no spaces between words
   C. the spelling of words is related to their sound
   D. print carries a message

5. To meet the objectives of the concept of print, the teacher must provide each of the following elements *except* _____. (21.1.2)
   A. interest
   B. enthusiasm
   C. a print-rich environment
   D. maturation

6. What two activities should teachers provide to encourage children to build skills in manuscript writing? (22.1.3)
   A. Gross-motor and fine-motor activities.
   B. Gross-motor and hand-eye coordination activities.
   C. Fine-motor and hand-eye coordination activities.
   D. Hand-coordination activities.

7. Which of the following is *not* an example of a major difference among writing systems? (22.1.3)
   A. The directions in which the strokes are made.
   B. The shapes of the letters.
   C. The slant of the letters.
   D. A skilled and consistent model.

8. In the sequence in which children learn alphabet letters, they learn letters with _____ last. (21.1.3)
   A. curved letters with intersections
   B. diagonal and horizontal lines
   C. straight and curved lines
   D. round and curved letters

Essential Question

How can you use teaching strategies to provide a print-rich environment that encourages children's success with writing?

Learning Outcomes

After studying this lesson, you will be able to

22.2-1 summarize basic guidelines that help children develop writing skills.

22.2-2 apply strategies that promote print awareness for children.

22.2-3 summarize how a teacher uses environmental print to promote print awareness.

22.2-4 describe how a teacher creates a print-rich environment to encourage children to develop writing skills, including techniques for writing, group experiences, space for writing, and documentation boards.

Key Terms

writing center	alphabet letters
print awareness	environmental print

Learning to write is a complex developmental process for young children in which teachers play an essential role. Teachers need to communicate to children that writing is valued and necessary by planning and introducing a print-rich environment. Signs and labels show the children the power of written words. The classroom needs to contain a defined space called a writing center for children to build writing skills. A **writing center** must have writing tools, papers, non-toxic markers, magnetic alphabet letters, alphabet blocks,

and books, such as a picture dictionary. This center needs to be organized to encourage children to intentionally focus on print, develop fine motor skills, and practice their developing writing skills. They need to discover different non-toxic writing tools and mediums in the process. Pencils and tools can be placed in containers where they will be easy to access. Materials should also be rotated to maintain and support the children's interests, developmental levels, and classroom curriculum or themes.

Learning the alphabet needs to be meaningful. Through practice and support from their teachers, young children will learn about letter size, proportion, spacing, line quality, and reversals. Teachers can promote print awareness during story time while reading to the children and sharing their love of print. Print awareness is an important skill that will contribute to a child's later reading success. Reading and writing require mastering the alphabet.

22.2.1 Developing Writing Skills

Proper writing skills are based on a few basic guidelines. With practice and maturity, children learn the importance of letter size, proportion, spacing, and line quality. You must be able to guide them through common problems, such as letter reversals. Likewise, it is important to develop the ability to work through unique situations faced by left-handed children.

Size and Proportion

To provide useful models for children to imitate, perfect your own writing skills. You must use the correct letter size and proportion.

Lowercase letters are always half the size of uppercase, or capital, letters. This rule holds true no matter how small or how large the writing is, and no matter where the writing appears (name tags, charts, boards, or games).

The size of the children's writing reflects the development of their fine-motor and hand-eye coordination. First writings are typically large. The letters vary in size and proportion. As the children's coordination skills mature, their writing decreases in size. Within any classroom, there will usually be a wide range of skills. Look at the writings in **Figure 22.5**. Kathryn's writing is mature for a four-year-old child, with letters that are similar in size and proportion. Amy's writing shows some variation in both size and proportion. Given time, Amy will develop the skill to make letters of proper proportion and size. Jena's writing almost looks like a scribble. Even though Jena is the same age as Kathryn and Amy, she lacks the skills to write her name legibly. Jena needs many more hand-eye and fine-motor activities.

Goodheart-Willcox Publisher

Figure 22.5 These writings show three levels of writing skill. Jena requires extra practice to bring her skills up to a higher level. *Observe a child practicing their writing skills at an early childhood center. What characteristics about the child's writing do you see regarding letter size and proportion, spacing, line quality, and reversals?*

Early Childhood Insight

Left-Handed Children

About 10 percent of the world's population is left-handed. A series of activities can assist you in learning a child's preferred writing hand. Ask children to pick up a piece of paper, throw a ball, pick up a fork or spoon, or place pegs on a pegboard. To avoid stressing the use of one hand over the other, center objects in front of children. If a child repeatedly uses their left hand, they show a preference for that hand. Place left-handed children at the end of the table. Such placement prevents the problem of bumping arms with a right-handed child when eating and working.

Spacing

Achieving proper spacing between letters and words is difficult for many beginning writers. Proper spacing requires more fine-motor control than most preschool children have. To help children gain control, have them write the letter *O* between words. However, this may still be too difficult for some preschool children. If so, direct them to place their index finger on the paper after the word. Then have them write the first letter of the next word to the right of their finger. Unless a child's fingers are unusually large, this should produce proper spacing.

Line Quality

Observe the line quality of children's writings. If a line wavers, this usually means immature coordination. Wavering lines can also result from writing too slowly or moving fingers, but not the pencil. When this happens, the writer is trying to draw rather than write. Most often, wavering lines are a sign the child lacks enough muscular control to apply constant pressure to the writing tool. To remedy this, have children use more arm action and relax their grips. Illegible writing is another common problem. Pencil lead that is too fine or too hard may cause of illegible work.

Reversals

Young children have difficulty learning the direction in which letters face. Preschool and kindergarten children often reverse letters in the early stages of writing. For instance, one letter becomes another letter. Children will print *b* when they intend to write *d*. Some letters are written backward. The letter *J* may have its tail reversed. The letter *S* is difficult for them to orient correctly. Children may also write the letters of a word in reversed order. For instance, Mark may write his name *kraM*.

You can guide children with reversal problems by pointing out differences in direction. If the child confuses the letters *b* and d, say "*b*, line, then circle." This tells the child that *b* contains a straight line first and then a circle. If the child is having a problem writing *d* correctly, say "*d*, circle, then line." After receiving these directions, some children will repeat them aloud when writing *d* or *b*. Gradually, reversals will disappear.

Practice

Children need many opportunities to practice their writing. Be selective in what activities you provide to promote this skill. Be careful that these practices do not become meaningless drills. During practice, show children how to hold the writing tool properly. First, ask children to watch the way you pick up a pencil. Place the pencil between your middle finger and thumb. Lightly rest your index finger on the top of the pencil. Show the children how the index finger controls the heaviness of the letter (**Figure 22.6**).

22.2-2 Print Awareness

Print awareness is the understanding that print carries a message. Reading to children is important for promoting the development of print awareness. It is essential to share your interest and joy of books. Use these strategies:

- Point out alphabet letters when working with individuals and groups of children.
- Label classroom lockers using the children's home language(s).
- Choose large story books, big books, with easy-to-read print for story time.
- Call attention to the special features of the book cover, such as the title and author's name.

US-Stout Child and Family Study Center

Figure 22.6   Teachers often assist children in their early writing experiences. *Why is it important for teachers to model proper letter formation for early writers?*

- Point out the organization of books, including the direction of the print.
- Show how books written in English are read from top to bottom and left to right.
- Point out the relationship between the written and spoken word.
- Show words are strings of letters without spaces.

Alphabet Letters

A system of letters of a language spoken or written in order is called **alphabet letters**. In a print-rich environment, children will see alphabet letters everywhere in the classroom; however, they also need your encouragement to write. You will need to display letters and charts at their eye level. Add pencils, markers, note pads, and magazines to the dramatic play area. Create different themes for the dramatic play area. Examples include the supermarket, library, pizza parlor, restaurants, and library.

Children attempt to write their own names first. You can make laminated sheets with their first name. Provide them with a grease pencil and a piece of felt. Once they have practiced tracing the letters, you can clean the sheets and use them again.

22.2-3 Environmental Print Show-and-Tell

Teachers need to surround preschoolers and kindergarteners with print for them to associate meaning with it. **Environmental print** is in the child's natural environment. It includes the print, symbols, numbers, and colors on commercial signs, labels, calendars, coins and bills, containers, books, billboards, road signs, grocery ads, fast food signs, cereal boxes, restaurant menus, and license plates. It is also on television, books, magazines, books, and fabric. You might send a letter home to children's families, encouraging them to have their child look around their home and identify items that they can read. Examples will typically include small boxes of such items as cereal, crackers, and toothpaste. The children can then bring these items to school for show-and-tell. Each child can read and talk about the print on their object. At the end of the session, attach these items to a "We Can Read" board in the writing area of the classroom.

You can use classroom curriculum themes to introduce environmental print. For example, a restaurant theme could have note pads, menus, and even a cash register with play money. A cooking theme could have recipe charts, measuring spoons, and cups with numbers. A grocery store, like a restaurant, could have a cash register, play money, grocery coupons, and clean, empty food boxes. Another theme could be the alphabet. Teachers can make alphabet charts or purchase them from a school supply catalog, or even online.

Take a picture of every child in your class. Mount the pictures using either glue or rubber cement on the tagboard. Post the chart in the writing center. Children will print their names and, possibly, their friends' names. Using a felt-tip marker, you can also make individual cards with the children's names printed on them.

During large group when telling a story, point out the features of a book, such as the title and author's name. If the print is large and you are working with four- and five-year-olds, review the letters. If there is an illustrator, include their name and contribution to the book.

22.2-4 Early Experiences in Writing

Early experiences often determine whether children like or dislike an activity. For this reason, start slowly and provide activities that children will not find frustrating. Since most children have an interest in the letters of their own names, begin by encouraging children to copy their first names. Most children have had experience writing or watching adults write their names. Early childhood teachers should stress that children learn the proper letter forms. Do not capitalize all the letters. Children can become confused if they see their names written in different ways at school and at home. For instance, write the name *Tait* using an uppercase *T* followed by lowercase *a*, *i*, and *t*.

Techniques for Encouraging Writing

The environment is the third teacher in the classroom that encourages writing. So, your major role is to intentionally prepare a print-rich environment that will encourage children to scribble and write. Children experience more success in developing print awareness in a print-rich environment. Some children will learn to recognize names and other words in their environment. To encourage the development of alphabet knowledge, you will need to use many teaching tools.

Provide children with copies of their names (**Figure 22.7**). Then make a bulletin board containing the children's pictures. Under each picture, place the correct name. Children will learn to write their own names first, followed by family members and pets.

Other practices to provide a print-rich environment and encourage writing include using place mats at mealtime. Print the child's first name, using their home language, on the place mat. In addition, print their names in the upper-left corner of all papers. You can also encourage writing by printing labels for classroom materials and furniture. Label cots, toothbrushes, cubbies, tables, windows, doors,

Wutikda/Shutterstock.com

Figure 22.7 Four- and five-year-olds enjoy printing their names.

clocks, sinks, shelves, and curtains, as well as other items. Label these items in English and the home languages of children in your program.

Make children aware of printed names other than their own. Do this by printing all the children's names on poster board cards. At transition times, place all the cards in a small basket. Then draw one name at a time, allowing the children to identify the name.

Encourage children who are ready to print their names on their artwork (**Figure 22.8**). To prepare them for the left-to-right progression required in reading, tell children to print their names in the upper-left corner of their artwork. Gradually, the children will learn they must place letters in a certain order. They will follow the left-to-right, top-to-bottom patterns of written English.

Always use the correct terminology. For example, when writing capital letters, call them *capital* or *uppercase* letters. Do the same

Judy Herr

Figure 22.8 The printing on this artwork is typical of five-year-olds. Children tell us how important their work is when they print their names on it. *How would you help guide and encourage a child who struggles with letter reversals?*

for lowercase letters. You might hear the children refer to them as big letters or small letters. Comment back by providing the proper terminology. For example, say, "Big letters are called capital or uppercase letters." Likewise, provide the correct small letters, which are called lowercase letters.

Provide children with sandpaper letters—a technique originally introduced by Montessori. You can purchase these letters from early childhood catalogs or online. By feeling a letter, the children learn its form and shape. Another technique is to print the manuscript letters on paper and laminate the paper or cover the paper with clear sheet protectors. Give children grease or china-marking pencils to trace the letters. Remove their markings with a piece of felt or window cleaner. The covered sheets are reusable. You might also purchase wooden puzzles that require children to match corresponding uppercase and lowercase letters.

Your classroom should reflect a love and joy of writing. Think of every way possible to create a print-rich environment so children learn that print carries meaning. Create and place signs around the room, such as post travel posters in the block or reading areas. Place books about writing in the writing area and library. Encourage the children to dictate stories as well as thank-you notes. Post these in the classroom. Make dramatic play into a literacy event. To illustrate, you could set up an office or grocery store for four- and five-year-olds. Print labels and signs for children who are dual-language learners, and make the signs in their home language and English. Introduce a cash register with play money. You could also add message pads and pencils in this area to encourage writing.

Make the print more meaningful by reading classroom labels, charts, lists, and signs to the children. Use print to inform children of anything new in the classroom. This could include new pets, new pieces of equipment, new staff, volunteers, or a new child. Develop cooking charts to show the children the ingredients and cooking sequence. Use a calendar to mark important upcoming events such as children's birthdays, field trips, and holidays. Prepare menus for the dramatic play area. Encourage print awareness by surrounding the children with print (**Figure 22.9**).

Group Experiences

There are many group situations in which you can encourage writing. Write in the children's presence. Encourage the children to dictate invitations, letters, birthday cards, holiday cards, or thank-you notes to you. As they dictate, record their message in print. It is important for the children to watch as you model writing. Point out the letters and read the message back to them. Follow the correct manuscript format. Call attention to the use of an uppercase letter at the beginning of a sentence, a question mark or a period at the end, and an uppercase letter at the beginning of proper names.

When reading books to the children, comment about the text. Point out alphabet letters in the title and author's name. Encourage the children to talk about or retell the stories.

Take digital photographs on a field trip. Print and share the photos with the children. Encourage the children to provide the script for each picture. When finished, staple the dictated sheets together to create a book. Print a title sheet with the name of the field trip. Place the book in the writing center so the children can review their experiences.

Make a set of name cards if you are teaching three- and four-year-olds. On one side, paste and picture and write the child's name. On the other side, just print the child's name. Use the cards at the end of group time. You could make a transition by showing a card. If the child does not recognize their name, show the side of the card with the picture and name. Show only the name if the child already knows their name.

Children need supportive adults to encourage them to explore and feel good about their writing. When children scribble or write, always praise their efforts. If they cannot print their own name, print it in the upper left corner. Then, display their work in a prominent place.

Space for Writing

A space for writing has appeal, especially for four- and five-year-olds. This space should be attractive, inviting, and located in the literacy area. Use bookshelves, screens, or mobile bulletin

UW-Stout Child and Family Study Center

Figure 22.9 Place paper and pencils in different classroom areas to encourage writing. ***What items might you place in the dramatic play area to encourage writing?***

boards to separate the literacy area from other classroom areas. This allows the privacy and quiet required for writing. Provide a variety of writing tools, such as crayons, pens, large and small pencils, colored pencils, chalk, markers, scented felt-tip markers, and pencil erasers. Provide plain paper of many sizes, postcards, stationery, writing folders, envelopes, picture dictionaries, and models of the alphabet. Avoid using lined paper since most preschool and kindergarten children lack the control to write between the lines. Use magnetic letters and letters from alphabet puzzles for tracing. Also, place rubber stamps with washable ink pads in this area. For school-aged children, provide draw and write journals.

Add teacher-made materials to the writing center. You can hang charts containing alphabet letters or words related to the current theme in this area (**Figure 22.10**). Also, display books on writing

Studio.G photography/Shutterstock.com

Figure 22.10 Classroom puzzles and activities promote an interest in alphabet knowledge.

(**Figure 22.11.**) Exhibit individual photographs of the children with their names written under them and place them in the writing area. Children enjoy looking at photographs of themselves and their

Children's Alphabet Books

Book Title	Authors and Illustrators	Appropriate Ages
Chicka Chicka Boom Boom *Chica Chica bum bum* (Spanish edition)	Bill Martin Jr. and John Archambault (authors) Lois Ehlert (illustrator)	Ages 1–4
Animalphabet	Julia Donaldson (author) Sharon King-Chai (illustrator)	Ages 3–5
Classic Munsch ABC	Robert Munsch (author) Michael Martchenko (illustrator)	Ages 1–3
Bears Awake! An Alphabet Story	Hannah E. Harrison (author)	Ages 3–5
Eek! A Noisy Journey from A to Z	Julie Larios (author) Julie Paschkis (illustrator)	Ages 2–6
Z Is for Moose	Kelly Bingham (author) Paul O. Zelinsky (illustrator)	Ages 4–8
Alpha Oops!: The Day Z Went First	Althea Kontis (author) Bob Kolar (illustrator)	Ages 4–8

Figure 22.11   Children's alphabet books promote early writing skills and print awareness.

classmates. Their interest will help them develop letter- and name-recognition skills.

Today Montessori Apps are available for tracing letters at the Apple App Store and on Google Play. They can be used either on cell phones or other digital devices. Although some children will enjoy the novelty of interacting with technology, there are some cons. By using their hands with materials, children engage in active learning. They experience the kinesthetic feel of sandpaper letters. Besides Montessori, there are other computer alphabet programs available, such as *Dr. Seuss's ABC* and *Curious George Pre-K ABCs.*

Teachers also need to display materials that encourage printing. These materials include alphabet models, sandpaper letters, and sandboxes. Using a sandbox, children can practice tracing various alphabet letters with their index fingers. Large chalk or white boards can also be useful. Children can make large, free movements that give writing a smooth quality.

Charts and other labels throughout the classroom can be useful displays for the children to copy. Prepare recipe charts for cooking activities. Record attendance, classroom helpers, the daily schedule, and small group membership on charts.

When there are dual-language learners in the class, teachers need to make labels, charts, recipes, and teaching aids in both languages. They should also encourage children to write in both languages. Providing multiple opportunities for the children to practice writing is essential. Teachers should encourage the children to write in both English and their home language.

Watching children's writing progress will be exciting as well as rewarding. Observe the appearance of simple letter shapes in a child's writing. Let the children know that you are interested. Celebrate these accomplishments by hanging the child's work in a prominent place.

Documentation Boards

Many teachers use *documentation boards* to display the children's writing artifacts. You can make them using bulletin boards, poster board, or other types of boards. Each documentation board provides a place to display samples of a particular child's work. By examining samples created over time, progress will be clear. Documentation boards can convey to family members the importance of children's scribbling and the process used to learn to write.

Lesson 22.2 Review

1. Wavering lines in children's writing can result from each of the following *except* _____. (22.2.1)
   A. immature coordination
   B. writing too slowing or moving the fingers
   C. lack of muscle control to apply constant pressure
   D. using less arm action and a tight grip on the writing tool

2. Each of the following is an example of a reversal *except* _____. (22.2.1)
   A. letters that are reversed
   B. letters are written backward
   C. letters result in wavering lines
   D. letters of a word in reversed order

3. Which of the following is *not* a strategy to teach print awareness to children? (22.2.2)
   A. Pointing out alphabet letters when working with individuals or groups of children.
   B. Pointing out the organization of books, excluding the direction of the print.
   C. Labeling classroom lockers using children's home languages.
   D. Choosing large storybooks with easy-to-read print for story time.

4. Print found in a child's natural environment is called _____. (22.2.3)
   A. environmental print
   B. conventions of print
   C. print awareness
   D. manuscript writing

5. During large group storytelling, each of the following is a way to introduce children to environmental print about books *except* _____. (22.2.3)
   A. point out the title and the author's name
   B. review the print letters and show how books written in English are read from top to bottom and left to right
   C. have children trace their names on laminated cards
   D. introduce the illustrator and describe their contribution to the book

6. Each of the following is an item in a writing center to encourage children to print *except* _____. (22.2.4)
   A. books about writing and draw-and-print journals
   B. pictures of the children with their names printed in their home language
   C. sandpaper letters for tracing, including upper- and lowercase letters
   D. lined paper

7. A place to display children's writing artifacts is called a _____. (22.2.4)
   A. print-rich area
   B. documentation board
   C. draw-and-print journal
   D. environmental print area

Chapter 22 Review and Assessment

Summary

Lesson 22.1

22.1-1 Learning to write is a complex, individual, developmental process.

22.1-1 Teachers need to be intentional in planning a print-rich environment so children can see the importance of letters and words, which are the basic building blocks of print.

22.1-2 Children move through several stages as they develop writing skills, including early scribbling, controlled scribbling, and mock writing.

22.1-3 Manuscript writing, or print script, does not require sustained muscle control. Children who lack well-developed fine-motor skills can make the strokes necessary for print script.

22.1-3 The concept of print involves the awareness of how print works.

Lesson 22.2

22.2-1 A few basic guidelines help children learn proper writing skills, including letter size, proportion, spacing, and line quality.

22.2-2 Print awareness is understanding that print carries a message.

22.2-2 Reading to children is important for promoting the development of print awareness.

22.2-3 Curriculum themes, photos of children on poster board with their names, and talking about books and letters are ways teachers can help children focus on environmental print.

22.2-4 Space for writing is located in the literacy area and should include a variety of writing tools and materials.

Vocabulary Activity

Working in pairs, locate a small image online that visually describes or explains each of the content and academic terms in this chapter. Create flashcards by writing each term on a note card. Then paste the image describing or explaining the term on the opposite side.

Critical Thinking

1. **Compare and Contrast.** Obtain writing samples from a group of five-year-olds and then review the samples in small groups. Compare the letters' sizes, formations, and thicknesses as you look at the samples. If you were supervising these children, what would you have each of them practice?

2. **Evaluate.** Create two sets of tracing alphabet cards for the children to use. Make one set using uppercase letters. Use lowercase letters for the second set. Once you have compiled your cards, trade with a partner and evaluate each other's cards. Make a note of any feedback you receive.

3. **Analyze.** Using the information about early writing experiences for children, create a "writing suitcase." Your writing suitcase should include a variety of graphic writing tools and paper. As you compile your suitcase, analyze why each object will be helpful. Finally, present your suitcase to the class and explain why you chose the materials you did.

4. **Identify.** Besides learning through manuscript writing experiences, children learn about letters from the signs and everyday letters they see. Identify all equipment and fixtures in your classroom that could have labels attached. Prepare the labels and consider what labels will be most helpful to the children.

Core Skills

1. **Writing.** Write an article for a preschool newsletter about the development of handwriting skills in preschoolers. Explain the progression of development. Offer suggestions for activities parents can do at home with their child to promote and encourage writing abilities. Include information on the role of letter recognition and the awareness of symbols and print in the learning process.

2. **Technology.** Practice making letters following the Zaner-Bloser writing system. Once you feel comfortable writing a few letters, create a video tutorial about writing letters in this system. In your tutorial, illustrate the correct line strokes and directions. Present your digital tutorial to the class.

3. **Writing.** Practice manuscript writing by making separate letters and paying careful attention to size and proportion, spacing, and line quality. When you finish, check your letters for these qualities and assess yourself based on the criteria given in this chapter. How exact were your proportions? How consistent was your spacing? Write a brief paragraph reflecting on what you have learned.

4. **Listening.** Listen to a presentation (digitally or in person) by an occupational therapist about the development of handwriting skills. What psychological and physical reasons may affect children who have difficulty in handwriting? What techniques are used with children who have visual, learning, or sensory challenges to help them learn to compensate for their disabilities? How can therapists, teachers, and parents collaborate to support and encourage children with writing difficulties? Try to answer these questions based on the presentation. If you cannot find the answers to your questions, ask a question at the end of the presentation, or look at other sources.

5. **Reading.** Many books suggest materials that teachers can create to foster learning and manuscript writing in a preschool classroom. Locate one of these books online or at a local library and read some materials and crafts suggested. List at least ten of these items and choose two to create. After creating these materials, bring them to class and explain their use and benefits.

6. **CTE Career Readiness Practice.** As a new staff member at a local preschool center, you are excited when the director of the center charges you with creating a print-rich environment and expanding the writing center. Set a date to meet and discuss your plan. To create a plan, use the following steps:

   - Identify the goals of creating a print-rich environment. What is the purpose of encouraging writing experiences in the preschool?
   - Write a summary of the goal for your coworkers.
   - Delegate the parts of the plan. Assume there are seven workers on the team. Who will handle each aspect of the plan?

Portfolio Project

Work with other students to create letter cards from a variety of textural materials. Suggestions include sandpaper' foam craft sheets; textural fabric such as corduroy, burlap, or fleece; small bubble wrap; plastic perforated shelf liner; and corrugated cardboard. Create the entire alphabet and numbers 1 through 10. Allow the child care lab children to handle and use the cards throughout the year for tracing and sensory experiences. Divide the cards up at the end of the year so each child care student will have a variety of examples to file in his or her portfolio.

Chapter 23

Guiding Mathematical Experiences

Lesson 23.1: Understanding Math Goals and Assessment

Lesson 23.2: Equipment and Activities for Math

Case Study

How Can Teachers Guide Math Experience?

It is 8:30 a.m. on a Monday in early September. Ms. Jones, the headteacher, looked around the classroom and saw mathematic opportunities everywhere. She understood that learning mathematics could be a playful journey that empowers young children. They need tactile, auditory, and visual learning experiences to understand math concepts. She saw Santiago sitting in the math area, playing with a stack of wooden table blocks. She walked closer to watch and listen to him before interacting.

Ms. Jones is interested in assessing Santiago's understanding of one-to-one correspondence. Sitting next to Santiago, she asked, "Santiago, how many blocks do you have?" Santiago looked up, smiled, and proceeded to place eight blocks in a row, and then began one-to-one tagging. Santiago put his finger on the first block and said, "one," and continued counting the second and third blocks. When Santiago got to the fourth block, he counted it twice, tagging it with his finger twice and saying, "four, five." Then he continued to the next block and said, "six, seven, and eight," while tagging the block with his finger three times. Santiago looked up at his teacher and said, "I have eight blocks." Ms. Jones noticed that Santiago could orally communicate the sequence of numbers but could not count the actual number of blocks. Santiago was either saying the numerals too quickly or moving his finger too slowly.

Now Ms. Jones moved closer, looked at Santiago, and said, "I think you counted some cubes more than once. Count them again. This time count each block only once as you say the number." The second time Santiago successfully counted the blocks.

Give It Some Thought

1. What are the goals of early math experiences?
2. How can teachers assess children's mathematical skills?
3. What is the one-to-one correspondence principle? What is cardinality?
4. What is the one-to-one counting principle? How can teachers promote it?
5. Do you think Ms. Jones would find using children's literature to teach math concepts an effective strategy? Why or why not?

Opening image credit: Shelly.Au/iStock via Getty Images Plus

Essential Question

What do you need to know about the goals for early math experiences and assessing children's math readiness skills prior to planning learning activities?

Learning Outcomes

After studying this lesson, you will be able to

23.1-1 **identify** goals and objectives of early math experiences.

23.1-2 **apply** the use of two basic assessments to determine the math skills of children.

Key Terms

mathematics
playful learning
specific task assessment

"One, three, five, two" and similar phrases can often be heard from young children. They are searching for meaning as they echo these words. Reciting numbers is a key step in learning math concepts. **Mathematics** is the study of numbers, arithmetic, measurement, and geometry. For young children, math is everywhere. Learning math is an active process of thinking about and organizing experiences to make sense of their world. This process involves reasoning processes, problem-solving, and communication. It takes time to develop mathematical conceptual understandings.

Children construct math concepts by relating new experiences and information to what they already know. Meaningful learning requires the ability to see patterns. Classroom equipment, materials, activities, and teacher support must provide opportunities for the children to understand patterns through play.

Early math experiences for children should focus on exploration, discovery, and understanding. Children develop concepts by exploring hands-on materials, three-dimensional objects, and the discovery of their relationships. Math concepts are usually taught and developed informally in the day-to-day playful activities in early childhood classrooms or playgrounds. These include art, block-building, cooking, games, dramatic play, music, sensory play, and storytelling (**Figure 23.1**). Almost every activity area in the classroom promotes math exploration. In addition, teachers can plan special activities such as a shape hunt. Math can also be taught at the snack table or by lining up to go outside. The teacher may ask the first person in line to raise their hand. After that, the teacher could ask for the last in line to raise their hand.

The teacher's role is to create a rich environment and interact with the children to develop mathematical thinking through *playful learning* (**Figure 23.2**). **Playful learning** describes a learning setting that may include free play, teacher-directed play, or play in a group setting.

Children may learn shapes, color, and order (logic) concepts through art activities or by playing with blocks. Cooking activities teach how quantities are related and ordered. For instance, you might tell a child, "Beat the eggs first, add the sugar second, and add the vanilla last." Classroom games provide an engaging opportunity to learn the concepts of *first* and *last*, as well as high and low numbers. If dice are used in games, addition concepts can be taught to the older children. While playing board games, children learn the more dots on the dice the

Nadezhda1906/iStock via Getty Images Plus

Figure 23.1 Games help children learn many math concepts. ***What games can you suggest to help encourage the development of math concepts?***

Studio.G photography/Shutterstock.com

Figure 23.2 Teacher-made materials can promote math concepts.

farther they go. Five is more than two and seven is more than five. Dramatic play offers many teaching opportunities. For example, as children play "store," they can learn about money. Songs,

stories, and fingerplays can also contain numbers and math language.

Other ways to include math concepts in the daily routine include asking "Are there enough chairs?" "Is everybody here today?" or "Is there a cookie for each child?" You can introduce math concepts in any appropriate situation. For example, you may introduce counting concepts by remarking "Kelsie brought three kittens to school."

Transitions (time between scheduled activities) are an excellent opportunity to present new math concepts. For example, while pointing at the clock, you might say, "It's two o'clock and time to go to the library." At cleanup time, one-to-one relationships can be taught if there is one puzzle for Xavier and one for Riley to put back on the shelf. After group time, you may have the group of children wearing red use the bathroom first.

23.1-1 Goals of Early Math Experiences

Well-planned environments provide developmentally appropriate play experiences that also help promote math skills. These experiences should help form concepts such as color and shape recognition, classification, measurement, counting, time, temperature, space, and volume concepts (**Figure 23.3**). Math gives children the tools to explain and understand their world. Math experiences should stress:

- observing and describing concrete objects
- making connections between new information and prior knowledge
- recognizing colors, patterns, and attributes
- developing a mathematical vocabulary
- developing spatial awareness
- classifying sets of objects
- labeling set sizes
- comparing objects and using terms that describe quantity, such as *more than* and *less than*
- copying patterns
- recognizing shape concepts
- recognizing and writing numerals
- using logical words such as *all*, *none*, and *some*
- using one-to-one correspondence
- estimating quantity and measurement
- developing problem-solving skills

23.1-2 Assessing Math Ability

Before planning math activities for children, remember almost any activity can be mathematical. To plan the environment or activities, first, determine the children's skill levels to find out where they are in mathematical comprehension. To do this properly, teachers need to assess children individually. Two common forms of assessment are *observation* and *specific task assessment*. The information gathered from these

Ethical Responsibilities ⚖

Using Appropriate Assessments

NAEYC Principle P-1.5 states, "We shall use appropriate assessment systems ... to provide information on children's learning and development." In the early childhood classroom, educators may use various types of **formative assessment** to help evaluate and monitor children's progress with various skills and to identify needs to use in planning additional activities. The results of such formative assessments also help educators communicate with parents or caregivers about their children's progress in learning and development.

Dig Deeper

When assessing children's progress with math skills, educators often use checklists, observations, and samples of children's work to assess children's progress and their needs. Choose one form of assessment for evaluating children's math skills. Describe how you would conduct this assessment. How might you use this assessment in planning further math activities and experiences for children? What ethical factors contribute to the successful use of this assessment and how will the results be communicated to families?

processes will determine the children's current level of mathematical knowledge. This information is useful in to determining each child's developmental progress in math. It will assist you in planning developmentally appropriate math activities, selecting appropriate equipment, and establishing a math rich environment.

Assessment by Observation

Observation involves informal viewing of a child during self-selected activities. Specific behaviors to watch for include:

- identifying colors and shapes
- sorting and classifying objects (**Figure 23.4**)
- counting objects
- setting a table correctly
- pouring liquids and carefully watching the amount poured

Strategies for Teaching Mathematical Concepts

Refer to times when the children will eat lunch, take a nap, and play outdoors.

Use teaspoons and cups to measure ingredients for cooking and feeding pets.

Divide portions using language such as "This half of the sandwich is for Raul; the other half is for Ali."

Count the children at group and snack time.

Give children an order of events for the day, such as "First we have group time and then playtime. Then we have snacks and go outdoors."

Keep score when children are playing games such as beanbag toss. Begin by using small blocks, tees, or other small objects to represent points. Later, use numbers.

Place a cash register with play money in the dramatic play area.

Place books with math content on the library bookshelves and in the small manipulative area.

Read counting picture books. Encourage participation by allowing the children to practice aloud counting and identifying numerals.

Provide board games containing linear patterns, such as Candyland®

Introduce finger plays and poems that encourage counting, such as "Five Little Monkeys."

Provide children with three-dimensional objects to group according to their likenesses and differences.

Review the calendar daily during large group time.

Hang a large thermometer outside your classroom door where the children can view it. Call attention to it during group time.

Discuss the temperature of foods at snack and lunch times.

Prepare and introduce lotto games with different colors, shapes, and sized figures.

Make obstacle courses outdoors that require under, over, around, and across.

Cut sponges into circles, squares, triangles, and rectangles. Let children use them as tools to apply paint.

Measure the children and record heights on a chart.

Provide puzzles that help children identify shapes and match colors as they complete the picture.

Figure 23.3 Activities that support math concepts can be used throughout the daily routines. *Give an example of a math activity to use with a daily routine.*

- constructing patterns
- writing numerals

Through observation, you can determine a child's strengths and needs. If you notice that a child cannot sort objects, you will need to provide sorting activities.

Mcimage/Shutterstock.com

Figure 23.4   A teacher can observe this toddler playing with a shape sorter to assess his math readiness skills. ***How can you use observation to assess a child's math readiness skills?***

Specific Task Assessment

Specific task assessment involves giving children set activities to determine their skills and/or needs. Examples include

- Present a child with crayons and say, "Tell me the colors." After the child has replied, say, "Now count these for me."

- Show a child one group of four pennies and one group of seven pennies. Then ask the child, "What group has more pennies?"

- Present a child with circle, diamond, square, and rectangle shapes. Say, "Find the square." Then have the child identify each of the remaining shapes.

As with observation, specific task assessment provides information for use in planning math activities.

Lesson 23.1 Review

1. Which of the following is *not* a goal of math experiences? (23.1.1)
   A. Recognizing colors, patterns, and attributes.
   B. The spelling of words is related to their sounds.
   C. Using logical words such as *all*, *none*, and *some*.
   D. Developing spatial awareness.
2. Each of the following is a behavior teachers observe to help determine a child's strengths in math readiness *except* _____. (23.1.2)
   A. identifying colors and shapes
   B. sorting and classifying objects
   C. improving hand-eye coordination
   D. pouring liquids and carefully watching the amount poured

3. _____ involves giving children set activities to determine skills and/or needs. (23.1.2)
   A. Playful learning
   B. Mathematics
   C. Problem-solving
   D. Specific task assessment

Equipment and Activities for Math

Essential Question

What do you need to know about math equipment and activities to create effective math experiences for young children?

Learning Outcomes

After studying this lesson, you will be able to

23.2-1 **analyze** a variety of three-dimensional objects that promote math experiences.

23.2-2 **contrast** math experiences that promote the development of key math concepts.

Key Terms

collection	number
attribute	stable order
parquetry blocks	cardinality
classification	rational counting
matching	sequencing error
sorting	coordination error
sequencing	tracking error
recognizing	subitize
set	number sense
empty set	numerals
rote counting	spatial relationships
one-to-one correspondence	

Math is a lifelong skill that helps children make sense of their world. The importance of early experiences in math has been demonstrated in research on children's learning. The curriculum for math is extensive. It encompasses color, shape, size, temperature, space, classification, counting, volume, numeral, and time concepts. Almost any activity for young children can be mathematical and should stress exploration, discovery, and understanding. Young children require an engaging and encouraging classroom climate as well as repetitive experiences to help them develop mathematical understandings and concepts.

Teachers need to thoughtfully plan and create an interesting environment and classroom climate. It should fuel the children's curiosity and cognitively challenge their thinking. A teacher's first step should be to carefully design and introduce a developmentally appropriate small-manipulative area to promote the development of math concepts and skills. This area should include wooden puzzles, counting sticks, wooden pattern blocks and boards, peg boards, threading laces, board and card games, and play money. Additionally, early childhood education teachers need to continuously integrate math teachings throughout the day into playful learning and across the curriculum. By asking questions such as, "How," "Why," and "What if?", educators encourage children to explain their thinking.

23.2-1 Math Equipment

Encourage children by providing an active, stimulating environment to foster mathematical thinking. Use concrete experiences. Provide the children with a collection of three-dimensional objects that promote physical and mental activity. A **collection** is a group of items, including those for counting, observing, creating, sorting, discussing, construction, and comparing. From these experiences, children can construct math concepts. **Figure 23.5** lists many materials for learning math concepts. If these materials are available in the classroom, children can

Supplies for Math Activities

Measurement

- measuring spoons and cups
- rulers, yardsticks, and tape measures
- egg timers
- weight and balancing scales
- thermometers, indoor and outdoor
- line measures 0 through 10
- measuring worms
- measuring containers of various sizes and types
- alarm clock; stopwatch
- egg timer
- calendars
- light and heavy objects; rocks, pennies, corks

Geometry

- shape sorting toys
- geo boards
- primary shape puzzles
- shape sorter toys
- centimeter cubes
- counting shape stacker
- plastic chains with removable links
- felt cutouts of various shapes and sizes
- magnetic shapes
- geometric puzzles

Manipulatives

- pegs and pegboards
- felt shapes of different colors and sizes
- magnetic numerals and shapes
- centimeter cubes
- buttons for counting
- empty spools
- colored wooden dominoes
- giant counting rods
- plastic chains with removeable links
- dice
- sequencing puzzles
- counting frame
- measuring worms
- primary shape template set
- jigsaw and geometric puzzles
- puzzles with numerals or numeral inserts
- patterning games

Counting

- abacus
- buttons for counting and sorting
- counting frame
- counting sticks
- dice
- giant counting rods
- tactile numbers
- play money
- felt-covered numerals
- light and heavy objects; rocks, pennies, corks
- magnetic numbers

Board and Card Games

- Cards: go fish, war, crazy eights
- Hi Ho! Cherry-O®
- Bingo
- Candy Land®
- Alphabet Bingo®
- Count Your Chickens!®
- Matching

Accessories

- play money
- cash register
- flannel boards

Figure 23.5   The use of three-dimensional objects available throughout the classroom help promote math concepts.

continually explore and develop mathematical understandings. Early math achievement is a predictor of later school success.

23.2-2 Mathematical Activities

A quality curriculum provides a rich environment. It also provides developmentally appropriate materials and activities to help children explore key concepts. Math activities for preschool children should promote the development of many skills. For example, children should learn to identify, classify, and understand the concept of a *set*. Children should also learn to count and recognize numbers and understand the concepts of *space, size, volume,* and *time.* The art of curriculum design is matching children's needs to their interests. This requires keen observation skills, listening skills, and a thorough understanding of child development.

Color Concepts

Color is a math concept since it helps children learn to discriminate among objects. Using color, children can classify, pattern, and sequence (**Figure 23.6**). Identifying colors also seems to promote language development. It requires the skill to recall a name and associate it with a visual image. Then, as the children's language skills grow, their skill at naming colors improves.

Studies show children learn to identify colors before shapes; however, it is not uncommon for a preschool child to confuse color and shape. For

Maryna Auramchuk/iStock via Getty Images Plus

Figure 23.6   Color helps children learn to discriminate among objects. *What are some informal ways to encourage color recognition at the early childhood center?*

example, you may ask a child to name a shape, and the child will answer with the color name.

By age two, many children can match a color to a sample. Some three-, four-, or five-year-old children, however, cannot match colors. Color blindness may cause this problem. You can identify color blindness through careful observation of children as they try to learn colors. Children who are color-blind see shades of green and red as grayish brown. They may even see all colors as gray. A child with color blindness may dislike sorting activities with colored beads or blocks. If you notice a child has a problem, report it to the center director. Often, the director can discuss the problem with the child's parents or guardians. The parents or guardians should decide if their child needs testing for color blindness.

The National Eye Institute (NEI) reports that more males than females are color blind. There are three types of color blindness. The most common is red-green, followed by blue-yellow color blindness. Total color blindness is the complete absence of color vision.

Color concepts can be taught formally or informally. You can teach children to name colors using different-colored blocks. Hold up a blue block and ask for the name of the color. Continue by asking the children to point out other blue objects around the room. Repeat these steps using the rest of the blocks.

Color recognition can also be taught at transition times. For instance, at the end of story time you may say, "All the children who are wearing red may go to the bathroom." Repeat this using different colors until you have excused all the children.

Sorting objects by color can teach color concepts. Provide each child with a small bag containing several colors and shapes cut from poster board. The children can sort by color and then by shape.

Charts are another way to teach color concepts. Charts also teach children the usefulness of graphing and the importance of the printed word. For example, you can make a chart labeled *Eye Colors*. Divide a piece of poster board into four even, vertical sections. Then divide the poster board into enough horizontal sections for every child in the class. Have each child in the class look at the chart and determine their eye color. If the children are able, encourage them to write their name under the color that matches their own eyes (**Figure 23.7**). If the children cannot write, give them pictures of themselves or round faces cut out of poster board. After all the children have finished, ask, "Which eye color is the least common?" Then ask, "What eye color is the most common?" You can also prepare charts for clothing and colors. Types of shoes such as ties, buckles, or Velcro® could also be a chart.

You can also graph color shapes on charts. For example, cut basic shapes from colored poster board. Using a felt-tip marker or pencil, divide the poster board into four equal horizontal sections. Next, divide the poster board vertically into five or six sections. Glue a different shape in each box in the first vertical column (**Figure 23.8**). Then give the children shapes to match. Other topics for graphs include hair color, favorite color, favorite food, clothing colors, and kinds of pets.

A feely box or bag is useful for teaching color. Place colored buttons, paper, felt strips, or blocks into the box or bag. Have children draw an object from the box or bag and identify its color.

Color sightings in the classroom are a fun way to teach color concepts. To conduct a color hunt, ask a child to choose a color. Then have other children point out objects of the same color found in the classroom.

Discussion helps children learn to recognize colors. Have a child choose a color. Then ask the child what thoughts the color suggests. One child may choose red and say, "Red makes me think of fire trucks and valentines." Another child may choose blue and say, "Blue makes me think of the sky." Yet, another child may say, "I like yellow because it is my parent's favorite color."

Other activities you can conduct to teach color concepts include the following:

- Hold up a piece of green construction paper. Ask children wearing green to stand up. Repeat using different colors each time. To add interest for four- and five-year-old children, give more complex directions. For instance, say, "If you are wearing blue, stand on one foot."

Eye Colors

Brown	Blue	Green	Hazel
Pablo	Josefina	Harper	Jamal
Parker	Luis	Reina	Jayden
Aaliyah	Pouneh	Sofia	Layla
Marco	Adila	Darius	Vjay

Figure 23.7   This chart can help children understand the concept of eye color.

Match the Shape

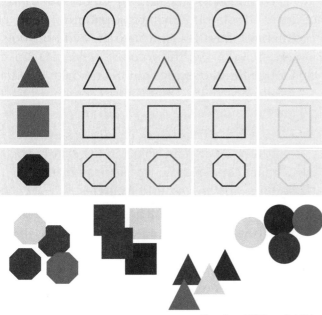

Goodheart-Willcox Publisher

Figure 23.8 This chart helps children learn to identify shapes and colors through matching. ***What other ways can you think of to teach shapes and colors to children?***

- Pour all your crayons into a basket or box. Then set out several empty baskets or boxes—one for each color of crayon. Encourage the children to sort the crayons by color.
- Display several identically colored shapes on a flannel board. Then add one that is the same shape, but a different color. Ask the children, "Which one does not belong?" You could also do this activity using different shapes.
- Play "I Spy" with a group of children. First, note a brightly colored classroom object. Then say, "I spy something yellow." Encourage the children to take turns guessing what object you are thinking about. If they cannot guess it, give them more clues. The child who guesses correctly starts the next game.

Shape Concepts

Geometry is the math content area for developing shape concepts. It is part of the child's environment in the form of traffic signs and buildings. These concepts often confuse young

Health Highlights

Color Vision Deficiency

Color vision deficiency describes a range of vision problems people have with seeing color. For example, some people have trouble telling colors apart, while others see only gray, black, and white. Problems with color vision are more common in males than in females. Most color vision problems in children are inherited and are present at birth.

Color vision deficiency provides a challenge for children's reading and general learning. These vision challenges can cause children to do poorly in school and develop low self-esteem. When a family history of color vision problems exists, parents should have their child checked for color vision problems during a routine eye exam.

Teachers and care providers can help children by:

- Labeling clothing and possessions with recognizable symbols.
- Teaching children the color names of common objects. For example, grass is "green" and pumpkins can be "orange or white."
- Labeling crayons, markers, and pencils with the color names or symbols.
- Using the buddy system. Pair a child who has color vision deficiency with a child who has normal color vision to do color-related activities.

children. At first, they will say circles and squares are the same figures because both have closed boundaries. Over time, they will notice features of the boundaries themselves. Typically, roundness is the first shape-related concept that children learn.

The skills needed to name and draw shapes do not develop at the same time. Children can most often name shapes before they can draw them. Circles are the easiest shapes for children to copy, followed by squares, then rectangles and triangles. Most children cannot copy shapes other than circles until they are about four years of age. Before this, their copies have round corners and distances of uneven length.

To teach basic shape concepts, use geometric language and vocabulary to describe their attributes. An **attribute** is the quality, characteristic, or feature used to describe something such as color, size, shape, or number. Use words such as corners, same, different, length, angles, and sides. Introduce a variety of activities that stress touching, holding, and matching shapes. You can define *shape* as what "goes around the outside," or the outline of the object (**Figure 23.9**). To help children grasp the critical attributes of a shape, have them trace around the outside of the shape. Ask questions while working with shapes, such as:

- How would you describe a circle?
- What shape has three corners?
- What shapes have four corners?
- What is the difference between a circle and a square?
- How do you know a shape is a triangle? How did you figure that out?
- What do you know about shapes?
- Where do we see circles in our classroom?

Some teachers prefer to use **parquetry blocks** to teach shape concepts. These blocks are geometric pieces that vary in color and shape. When the children are familiar with the blocks, hold up a block and ask the children to find a block with a similar shape. Next, build a simple design with three or four blocks. Show the children how to combine shapes to form new shapes. For example, show children how to form a rectangle by using two identical squares. A square

can be cut diagonally to form two triangles. Ask the children to copy it. You can also follow this activity with parquetry-patterned cards. The child can match the correct block to the pattern.

Other activities to encourage the identification of shape include

- Cut geometric shapes out of one color of poster board. Ask the children to name and sort the shapes.
- Place a circle on a flannel board. Ask the children to name an object in the classroom of that shape. Repeat this activity using squares, rectangles, and triangles.
- Provide each child with an example of a string with colored beads in a pattern. It may be three red beads followed by two yellow representing a pattern. Then provide a string with a knot tied at one end. Encourage the child to recreate the pattern. For the children that have trouble, use only one yellow bead and a green bead. Repeat the pattern. For children who correctly repeat the pattern, vary the number of beads. You can also change the bead size and shape.
- Use jump ropes, masking tape, or chalk to make shapes on the floor. Ask children to name the shapes as they walk, march, or walk backwards over the figure.
- Give each child a shape cut out of poster board. Then have the children move around the classroom to find another child with an identical shape. This activity is most useful with four- and five-year-old children.
- Introduce a game called "It's in the Bag." The aim of this game is to help children name shapes by touch. Begin by placing a variety of poster board shapes or blocks in a paper bag. Hold up one shape and ask a child to find its match by feeling in the bag.
- Plan a treasure hunt. Instruct children to find shapes around the room. For example, you can point out a round classroom clock as a circle.

Shape concepts are harder to teach than color concepts. Since color descriptions are used more often in everyday conversation, they may be easier for children to understand. For example, children often hear phrases such as a *black puppy*, *yellow socks*, *red shirt*, and *green room*.

Floortje/iStock via Getty Images Plus

Figure 23.9   Children need to focus on the outlines of these shapes before they can identify them.

Workplace Connections

Recognizing Shapes with Food

Design a snack or food preparation activity that incorporates shape recognition and identification. Investigate food items and recipes that are best suited to teaching children about shapes. The best food items may be recognizable shapes or odd shapes. Present your lesson plan to the class.

1. Which food shapes did children identify most easily? Which were more difficult?
2. After choosing a recipe, create a lesson plan for preparing the recipe and list ways you will craft the cooking experience into an opportunity to learn math.

Mariya Chichina/iStock via Getty Images Plus

Figure 23.10 The simplest matching activities involve putting objects that are exactly alike together.

Classification

Classification is the process of mentally sorting and grouping objects or ideas by a common attribute. Attribute examples include size, color, shape, pattern, or function. This is one of the first skills displayed by young children. If the object belongs to a class, it has one or more features in common with another object. Classification allows people to cope with large numbers of objects.

Matching is a form of classification. It involves putting like objects together (**Figure 23.10**). **Sorting** also involves classification. It is the process of physically separating objects based on unique features. **Sequencing** is ordering real-life objects from shortest to tallest or tallest to shortest.

Children begin to learn classification skills in their first few weeks of life. By two months, children begin to classify experiences as pleasant or unpleasant. Being held is a pleasant experience, while hearing loud noises may startle the child and be unpleasant.

Infants gather information to make classifications by using their senses through repeated experiences. This gives them the ability to relate past and present experiences. This process is known as **recognizing**. Recognizing is a simple form of classification.

First classroom experiences with classification should involve only one feature. Often, this feature is color, size, or shape. Provide items with obvious differences. For young children, this might include size, length, height, shape, color, or thickness.

Some useful classification tasks for young children include

- Provide children with a set of blue and red buttons. Have them sort the buttons into piles by color.
- Give children a set of checkers. Have them sort them into two piles by color.
- Give children pictures of known and unknown objects cut from old magazines. Ask them to sort the pictures into "I don't know the name of" and "I know the name of" piles.

As children build classification skills, increase the number of common features in the activities (**Figure 23.11**). You can do this in two ways. Either increase the number of items for children to classify, or increase the number of groups into which they can sort items.

Advanced activities include classifying classroom items according to function. For example, some items are used for listening, some for talking, and some for writing. As another activity, give children a set of fabric squares. Ask the children to sort the materials into piles of striped, plaid, polka-dotted, and solid fabrics.

poplasen/iStock via Getty Images Plus

Figure 23.11 This child followed his teacher's pattern when stacking the shape blocks. ***How do children benefit from following patterns?***

UW-Stout Child and Family Study Center

Figure 23.12 Many everyday items can be used to teach the *set* concept. ***Look around your classroom or home. What everyday objects can you find that you could use to teach the set concept?***

Notice that after children learn classification skills, they watch and describe features of objects. First a child may say an apple is round and red, yellow, or green. Later, the child may classify it as good food. Finally, the child may say the apple belongs to a group of foods known as "fruit."

Sets

Before children learn to add and subtract in elementary school, they need to understand sets. A **set** is two or more objects that are alike in some way and, therefore, belong together. Common features of a set may be color, shape, size, material, pattern, texture, name, or use.

A key objective of early math activities is to have children learn to organize objects. Objects belonging to a set are its members. A set can have a few or many members. A set of glasses is often a certain number, such as four or twelve. A set with no members is called an **empty set**.

To understand the concept of a set, children first need to learn about sets that have like members. It is best to teach this concept in small groups. You will need sets of objects that have like members, such as puzzle pieces, blocks, crayons, and squares of colored paper (**Figure 23.12**). Introduce one set of objects at a time. Say, "What are these? These are all blocks. We call them a set of blocks." Then introduce the remaining sets. Repeat the process. Stress the concept of set. To conclude the activity, ask, "What are some other sets in the room?"

Teachers can strengthen the concept of a *set* by asking a small group of children to divide themselves into a set. First divide the children into sets of light- and dark-haired children. Encourage them to regroup themselves into different sets. They might divide by age, the color of eyes, or the color of clothing.

Teach the concept of an *empty set* during snack time. Provide each child with a plate holding a banana sliced into five pieces. Tell the children to eat one piece of banana. Explain that they now have a set of four banana pieces. Tell the children to eat another piece. Ask the children how many pieces remain. Tell them that is the number of members still in the set. Keep going until all the pieces are eaten. Then explain that a set without any members is called an empty set.

Counting

Counting or recognizing number words is a basic math skill. Math is necessary to include in the curriculum because it is a key problem-solving tool. In the beginning, the child may only be engaged in **rote counting**. This is reciting numbers without understanding the quantity correspondence between an object and a number. Remember to include the children's home languages. Use fingerplays and songs as tools to learn new math concepts and words. This will encourage English-speaking children to count in their classmate's native languages, too.

The foundation for understanding counting is called one-to-one correspondence. **One-to-one correspondence** is the understanding that one group has the same number as another. It is the most basic part of the concept of numbers.

Opportunities for counting are everywhere inside and outside the classroom. A **number** is a system for recognizing quantity. It is essential to say number words in a **stable order**. Numbers must be said in the same sequence, as each number has a fixed meaning. For example, the number three is one less than four. Likewise, the number two is one less than three. Studies show that finger counting is an easy tool for young children to use to develop mathematical understanding.

Children love to count. They may start developing oral-counting skills as early as two years of age. Two- and three-year-olds learn to count at least up to their ages. They count objects by pointing to them as they say the numbers one by one. Most four- and five-year-olds can count higher. These children touch an item each time they say a number. Sometimes they forget which items they have counted. They might skip several items or touch (count) an item more than once. Gradually they will learn the concept of **cardinality**. This means that the last number of the counting sequence tells how many objects exist in a set. This number will not change regardless of the order in which the children count the objects.

Children's first exposure to counting is by listening to adults count objects. In time, children repeat these counting words. After they know the names of the numbers, they can later learn to identify written number words (two) and numerals (2).

The ability to count occurs in two stages: rote and rational counting. Children learn *rote counting* before rational counting. Rote counting is the recitation of numbers in order. This skill involves memory, not understanding. **Rational counting** involves attaching a number to a series of grouped objects (**Figure 23.13**). For example, a child has a box of crayons sitting on the table. If you ask the child for some crayons, they may place them on the table one at a time. As the child

Tatyana Abramovich/iStock via Betty Images Plus

Figure 23.13 Rational counting involves attaching a number to a series of objects. In this puzzle, they showed the number of objects for each matching numeral on the puzzle map. *What type of activity or game might you create to help children learn rational counting?*

places each crayon, they assign it a number in a sequence.

The *one-to-one correspondence principle* states that objects should only be counted once. When a child counts an item more than once, this error shows a lack of one-to-one correspondence skills. Young children experience three types of counting errors.

- A **sequencing error** occurs when the child may say the same number more than once, skip it, or say it out of order.

- A **coordination error** occurs when the child is counting a series of objects. The same object may be labeled with more than one number word or it may not have been counted. Often the child needs to learn to count carefully and slow down or does not understand that each object should be counted only once.

- **Tracking errors** occur when the child recounts an item that was counted earlier. One technique for helping these children is to place the uncounted items together. The counted items can be moved to another surface area.

Many children you teach will recite numbers in their correct order; however, often they will not understand the meaning the numbers represent. Children usually become skilled at rote and rational counting during kindergarten. Now they can **subitize**, which means they can provide immediate and accurate numbers without the need to count them. If you show them a plate with three crackers and asked them how many were on the plate, immediately, they would say three without counting.

Three-year-old Taylor has developed typical number skills for age three. The following activities illustrate Taylor's understanding:

- The teacher places seven pennies on the floor and asks Taylor to count them. Taylor counts from one to nine before touching the last penny.

- The teacher then arranges the pennies in a circle. Again, the teacher asks Taylor to count them. Taylor becomes confused several times and must begin again.

- Next, the teacher places seven pennies in a pile and spreads out seven pennies more. When asked which pile has more pennies, Taylor points to the pennies that are spread out.

Guided play is a powerful teaching tool for a teacher to scaffold a child's learning of one-to-one correspondence skills. *Scaffolding* is the process of helping a child move from being unable to achieve a task to being able to do work with guidance, interaction, and/or questions. For example, Iman was trying to line up a row of alphabet blocks. Then began quickly counting them. By the time Iman reached the third block, he said five. Mrs. Briones, Iman's teacher, stood by, watching quietly. To support and guide Iman's learning, she said, "Iman, you counted too quickly. Let's try a new way."

Mrs. Briones pulled up a chair next to Iman and made a suggestion. She said, "Count them again trying a new way." She pushed all the alphabet blocks to the left side of the table. One by one, she had Iman pull a block to the right side of the table and count it.

Always expose children to rational counting using concrete objects. The simplest way to do this is through physical guidance. Use buttons, books, disks, table blocks, counting sticks, or crayons. Lay the objects in a straight line. Then model counting the objects for the child. After this, guide the child by taking their hand and touching each object as they count it. At first, you may have to help the child count aloud.

Another teaching strategy is to make a number list of a series of numbers in order. You will need to make the number list developmentally appropriate. For example, with a group of four-year-olds, you might record the numerals one through five. The children may understand that four is one more than three. But they may not understand that five is precisely one more than four. You may need to increase or decrease the quantity of numerals used depending upon the child's level of understanding.

After children have had many counting experiences, test their understanding. Send a child to get four crayons, two pieces of paper, or three blocks. Remember two things. First, children learn math through repetition. Secondly, provide children with experiences that are challenging. This means that experiences should be just beyond their current level of understanding.

Identifying Numerals

In order to read and write, children must develop **number sense**, the understanding of how numbers work. They must be able to recognize written numbers and their symbols. **Numerals** are the symbols that represent numbers. Each numeral represents a quantity. Each numeral serves as shorthand for "how many."

Children learn numerals through informal and naturalistic experiences. They gain these recognition skills with continual exposure to numerals. Children see numerals at home, at school, and in the community. They can also find numerals in the grocery store, on signs, and on TV programs and commercials. Children can also see them with calculators, digital tablets, computers, clocks, and watches.

A pleasurable activity for teaching number symbols is to have the children take part in a number walk. To do this, collect 10 sheets of 9 by 12-inch paper. Number the sheets from 1 to 10. Laminate these sheets to increase durability. Then place the papers in a circle on the floor at random. Play some familiar music and ask the children to walk through the path of numbered pieces. When you stop the music, ask the children to tell the name of the number on which they are standing.

Another way to teach symbols is to set up a grocery store in a dramatic play area. Collect empty food boxes and containers. Wash and sanitize the containers. Check empty cans to ensure there are no rough edges. Then attach stickers with price tags ranging from one to five cents. This activity can also include a toy store or ice cream shop. Look for numbers on measuring tools, calendars, books, and puzzles.

A number line is yet another way to teach numbers. This teaching aid is based on units of length instead of objects. Make a calendar using a number line and refer to it daily during group time. After children learn to count, they will represent numbers in different ways. Eventually they can print the numerals.

Workplace Connections

Recognizing Numerals in the Classroom

Look for examples of numerals that already exist in an early learning classroom, such as room numbers, clocks, thermometers, number charts, puzzles, and birthday or height charts.

1. Are the numerals consistent in style on both commercial and student- or teacher-prepared items?
2. Do you notice any differences, particularly in the numbers one, two, and four? What effect will the different styles or types have on children who are attempting to learn to recognize numerals?

Space Concepts

Spatial relationships refer to the position of people and objects in space relative to each other. These concepts begin developing early

Early Childhood Insight

Writing Numerals

Prekindergarten and kindergarten-aged children should write numerals in their symbol form. Since children often find numerals hard to write, you may see many reversals. These problems are common and children usually self-correct them in time. It may surprise you to learn that children often prefer to write numbers more than alphabet letters. Have children practice by writing in numerals on calendars or charts.

in life. From birth, children begin developing relationships between people and objects.

Describing the position, direction, location, and shape of objects in space is an important part of early math experiences. **Figure 23.14** lists space concepts to introduce. Prepositions are abstract—they represent a location in space. To help the children learn the meanings of prepositions, use concrete examples. Since children's awareness of location and space grows out of their own bodies, have them move physically.

You can teach space concepts during cleanup time, art time, block-building, and other activities. Some experiences for teaching space concepts include

- Play the game "Simon Says" using the words listed in Figure 23.14. Give directions to the children, such as, "Place your finger on top of your nose" and "Raise your right hand above your head." Using simple concepts often works well, even with two-and-a-half and three-year-old children. When using a new concept, you may have to model it for the children. You can also use an animal puppet, stuffed toy, or doll to lead the game. To get the children more involved, allow them to take turns using the puppet and giving directions.

- Place several pictures of fruit on a flannel board. Then ask, "Which piece of fruit is below the orange?" "Which piece of fruit is above the apple?" "Which piece of fruit is beside the grapes?"

Space Concepts

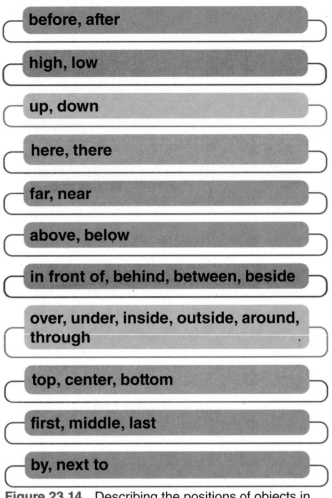

before, after

high, low

up, down

here, there

far, near

above, below

in front of, behind, between, beside

over, under, inside, outside, around, through

top, center, bottom

first, middle, last

by, next to

Figure 23.14 Describing the positions of objects in space is an important part of early math experiences.

- Give each child three different items, such as a block, a penny, and a button. Then give the children verbal directions using space words: "Place the penny on top of the block." "Place the button under the block."
- Use familiar circle games such as "Hokey Pokey" to teach space concepts.
- Stack five familiar items, such as a penny, stick, rock, clothespin, and puzzle piece, on a table. Then ask the children questions about the items: "What item is at the top?" "What item is at the bottom?" "What item is in the middle?" A stack of colored blocks or puzzle pieces can teach the concepts of top, bottom, and center.

- Conduct a shape scavenger hunt. Before the children arrive, hide different shapes either in the classroom or outdoors. Conduct the hunt with a small group, large group, or the entire class. Make a graph using a large poster board. Across the top, draw an example of each shape you hid. Down the left side, write the children's names. If developmentally appropriate, have the children use a washable marker to show the shapes they found. When every child has recorded this information, analyze the data with them. *Data* refers to the information collected. It is a tool for the children to summarize what they have learned and to collect and organize information. Ask open-ended questions that prompt children to think through their thoughts and learn from one another. Include questions such as: *How many children found every shape? How are the shapes the same or different? How can we find out how the shapes differ? How many children found three shapes? How many children found all the shapes?*

Remember that children need repetition to maintain any skill. Unlike adults, children do not tire easily from repetitive experiences. Your enthusiasm and support are important.

Size Concepts

Children develop size concepts only through experience. Introduce and stress the words in **Figure 23.15** to teach children about size. You can use these words throughout the day. To show children how big something is you can measure it with a scale, ruler, or tape measure. A tape measure, ruler, or yardstick can measure how tall, low, wide, or narrow something is.

Volume Concepts

An early childhood program should offer many opportunities to explore volume. Sand tables and water tables are useful for this task. Provide many containers of varying volumes and shapes for measuring. During the children's play with these materials, introduce volume concepts such as *empty, full, little, much, a lot,* and *some.* When children use these concepts, they think about their world in terms of quantity.

Materials that Teach Size Concepts

- big, little
- large, small
- long/tall, short
- wide, narrow
- big, bigger, biggest
- small, smaller, smallest
- inches, feet, pounds
- smaller than, bigger than
- thick, thin
- high, low
- large, larger
- longer, taller, shorter

FatCamera/E+ via Getty Images

Figure 23.15 Use of proper terms and visual aids will help children grasp the size concepts. *What potential visual aids can you find in your classroom to help children grasp size concepts?*

Time Concepts

"Is yesterday Valentine's?" Makoto, a four-year-old, asked one of the other children. Makoto's question is common of a young child. Since young children cannot see or feel time, it is a hard concept for them to understand. *Time* can stand for so many situations. Past, present, future, and soon are all examples of time concepts. Others include hours, days, tomorrow, yesterday, and today.

Studies suggest that young children have only a vague concept of time. In fact, the average five-year-old child knows only the difference between afternoon and morning, and night and day. Children usually cannot read the time on a watch or clock until about age seven.

You can use routines to teach time concepts to young children. For example, you might say: "After lunch, we take naps." "Your parents will come to pick you up after outdoor playtime." "Before large group time, we need to put our toys away." You can offer time experiences to children by using the correct time words. Include words such as those in **Figure 23.16**.

Time Concepts

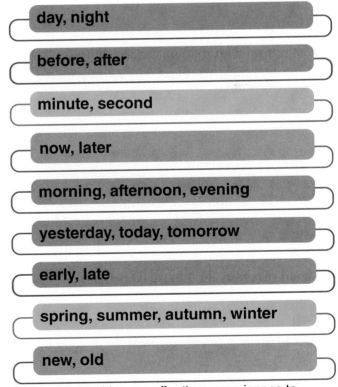

- day, night
- before, after
- minute, second
- now, later
- morning, afternoon, evening
- yesterday, today, tomorrow
- early, late
- spring, summer, autumn, winter
- new, old

Figure 23.16 You can offer time experiences to children by using the correct time words.

Children should also learn about the passing of time. For example, you may ask, "Do you remember the clown that came to school?" or "How did we make the play dough last time?"

Many activities can be used for teaching children time concepts. They include

- Provide children with a large, month-long calendar. Use the calendar each day during a large group activity. Review the days of the week and use such words as *yesterday*, *tomorrow*, *last week*, and *next week*.

- Encourage children to play with a toy alarm clock.

- Hang a large classroom clock at the children's eye level.

- Use a cooking timer during cooking experiences. Some teachers also use a timer to give children a warning before they change activities. For example, the teacher may set the timer and say, "In five minutes, it will be time to clean up."

- Provide time-recording equipment, such as a stopwatch, an alarm clock, a wristwatch, an egg timer, and an hourglass. Place these items on a table where children will explore them.

- Make a chart showing the birthdates of each child in the class. Depending on the developmental appropriateness, post a picture of the child or their printed name.

Temperature Concepts

Cooking and outdoor activities help introduce temperature concepts. To teach these concepts, words include such as *thermometer*, *hot*, *cold*, *warm*, and *cool*.

Small-Manipulative Center

Well-planned early childhood classrooms usually have a small-manipulative area to promote mathematical concepts. In this area, there are shelving units, tables, and child-sized chairs. Typically, the teacher places developmentally appropriate materials on the table daily prior to the children's arrival. Often, children will place their belongings in their lockers and go directly to the small-manipulative area. The materials displayed look appealing to them.

Puzzles are an example of a learning tool to on the tables prior to the children's arrival. By interacting, children will learn to identify shapes, search for patterns, and think about spatial relationships. Observe each child and ask yourself, "Is the child being challenged?" If not, introduce puzzles that are more difficult. Rotating the puzzles is important to maintain the children's interests.

Board games should always be available in the small-manipulative area for preschool children. Studies show there is a positive relationship between board games and numerical ability. Hi Ho! Cherry-O®, Candy Land®, Chutes and Ladders® are some examples of games children enjoy.

Card games should also be available. There are a wide variety of games available in early childhood catalogs, online, or in areas designated for children's playthings in large stores. Popular examples include go fish, Memory®, crazy eights, and Uno®. Card games help children focus on colors, numbers, and shapes.

Using Children's Literature

Using children's literature is a very important strategy for teaching math concepts to young children. Books enhance children's natural interest and curiosity about math. Books also help children see numbers in many contexts. They are a meaningful tool for exploring, thinking, and developing math concepts. **Figure 23.17** lists books you can use in the classroom to teach math concepts.

If you have dual-language learners in your classroom, consider their funds of knowledge. Read and make available children's literature in their home language. Engage with their families. You may even have to research online or work with a translator to say and write the numbers in the child's home language.

Books for Teaching Math

- *How Much Does a Ladybug Weigh?* by Alison Limentani
- *Inch by Inch* by Leo Lionni
- *One Fox* by Kate Read
- *My First Book of Patterns* by Bobby George and June George
- *Ten Dogs in the Window: A Countdown Book* by Claire Masurel (author) and Pamela Paparone (illustrator)
- *Just How Long Can a Long String Be?!* by Keith Baker
- *One Foot Two Feet* by Peter Maloney and Felicia Zekauskas
- *Round Is a Tortilla* by Roseanne Greenfield Thong (author) and John Parra (illustrator)
- *Which Is Round? Which Is Bigger?* by Mineko Mamada
- *Shapes* by Anne Woodhull (author) and Shelley Rotner (photographer)
- *Cubes, Cones, Cylinders and Spheres* by Tana Hoban
- *One Shoe Two Shoes* by Caryl Hart (author) and Edward Underwood (illustrator)
- *Five Minutes* by Liz Garteb Scanion and Audrey Vernick (authors); Olivier Tallec (illustrator)
- *Exactly the Opposite* by Tana Hoban
- *Up, Down & Other Opposites* by Ellsworth Kelly
- *Squares and Other Shapes* by Josef Albers (author) and Meagan Bennett (designer)
- *Perfect Square* by Michael Hall
- *Square and Other Shapes* by Josef Albers (author) and Meagan Bennett (designer)
- *Two Mice* by Sergi Ruzzier

Figure 23.17 Using children's literature helps enhance children's natural interest and curiosity about math. *Review one of the books from this list. How might you use this book to enhance the children's curiosity about math concepts?*

Lesson 23.2 Review

1. A _____ is a group of items, including those for counting, observing, creating, sorting, discussing, construction, and comparing. (23.2.1)
   A. math concept
   B. collection
   C. manipulative
   D. thermometer

2. Studies show children learn to identify _____ before shapes. (23.2.2)
   A. numbers
   B. letters
   C. colors
   D. textures

3. _____ refer to the position of people and objects in space relative to each other. (23.2.2)
   A. Time concepts
   B. Classifications
   C. Measurements
   D. Spatial relationships

Summary

Lesson 23.1

23.1-1 Goals for math experiences in the early childhood setting should focus on exploration, discovery, and understanding.

23.1-1 Young children require repetitive basic experiences to help them develop critical-thinking and problem-solving skills.

23.1-2 Two common forms for assessing math readiness skills are observation and specific task assessment.

23.1-2 Through observation and specific task assessment, teachers can assess children's abilities and identify their needs for developing math skills.

Lesson 23.2

23.2-1 A stimulating environment, books, games, and routines will promote their understanding. With such a foundation, they can build more advanced mathematical thinking skills as they get older.

23.2-2 Teachers need to plan an interesting environment that fuels the children's curiosity and cognitively challenges them. They can integrate math teachings into playful learning, directed play, and group activities.

23.2-2 For younger children, math experiences can be informal. Many daily events, such as play experiences and routines, lend themselves to informal math experiences. Older children enjoy playing board games with their peers.

23.2-2 Teachers can use a variety of objects, materials, and experiences to create math activities to meet children's needs.

Vocabulary Activity

With a partner, choose two of the Key Terms from each lesson. Search online to locate photos or graphics that show the meaning of these terms. Print the photos or graphics and show them to the class. Explain how they show the meaning of the terms.

Critical Thinking

1. **Identify.** Review a school equipment catalog or go online. List at least five pieces of equipment that can be used to teach space concepts. For each piece of equipment you identify, explain why it helps teach space concepts and describe how effective you think the piece of equipment would be.

2. **Create.** Create a file folder activity or game that incorporates color concepts suitable for a preschooler. Examples might be the color matching of items; sorting of colored items; sequencing of colored shapes in varying sizes; and games in which the child advances to a certain color. After creating your game, play the game with a preschooler. Analyze how well the preschooler understands the game. Was the game too easy for the child? too difficult?

3. **Determine.** Research activities that can teach children the concept of a *set*. Activities can be found online or in books of activities for teachers. For each activity, determine why the creator thinks it is effective. Describe the rationale.

4. **Evaluate.** In small groups, create a weeklong plan for teaching children counting concepts. Your plan should contain activities for each day of the week and should have specific instructions for each activity. After creating your plan, trade plans with another small group. Evaluate the other group's plan, noting any feedback you would suggest they implement.

5. **Compare and Contrast.** Brainstorm methods used to help young children understand size concepts. In small teams, make a list of 10 to 12 methods and then trade methods with another team. Compare and contrast the methods you chose and the methods another team chose. Are there any of the other team's methods that you would add to your list?

Core Skills

1. **Research.** Conduct an online search for information about kindergarten readiness regarding math knowledge. What should a child know and be able to do mathematically before entering kindergarten? What are the major benefits of entering kindergarten with the knowledge of basic math concepts? If children entering kindergarten are not prepared for math activities, what resources are available to help them?

2. **Writing.** Write an article for the preschool newsletter to describe the math curriculum of the early childhood lab. Even if math is not formally taught in the program, what activities contain elements that promote an understanding of math concepts? How do these activities relate to overall program goals? What suggestions do you have for activities parents can do at home to promote their child's math knowledge?

3. **Technology.** Search online to locate sources for math equipment and manipulatives for early childhood programs. Select several items that would meet the early childhood program goals for math. Then write a brief description of the concepts that children would learn from using the items and explain how the goals will be accomplished. Create a digital "wish list" of items you propose for a math area in an early learning center and present your wish list to the class.

4. **Research and Speaking.** Search for reputable information on the teaching of math concepts to preschoolers. Some sources for information include Constance Kamii, a renowned professor of early childhood education; Jean Piaget, learning theorist; The High Scope Educational Research Foundation; and the National Council of Teachers of Mathematics, among other sources. Read at least three reliable sources and use them to create a lesson plan for developing preschoolers' math and problem-solving skills. If possible, implement the lesson plan in an early childhood classroom.

5. **Reading.** Visit a local library or look online to research and compile a bibliography of children's literature that includes mathematics. Read at least two of these books and write brief book reviews that stress their mathematical value.

6. **CTE Career Readiness Practice.** For several months, your center has received complaints that children are not prepared for identifying and writing numerals in kindergarten. As a result, they have asked you to research kindergarten recommendations for numeral writing and draft a plan to help the center meet these recommendations. Determine kindergarten recommendations, including what children should be able to do and know. Then, draft a month-long schedule of activities that will help the children in your center meet these recommendations. Organize your plan into a presentation and deliver it to the class.

Portfolio Project

Work with other students to construct a set of number cards. What items, especially textural items, might represent the numbers besides stickers? Allow the children to handle and use the cards throughout the year for math experiences. Divide the cards up at the end of the year so each of you will have a variety of examples to file in his or her portfolio.

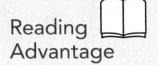
Guiding Science and Technology Experiences

Lesson 24.1: Science and Technology in the Classroom

Lesson 24.2: Teaching Science Basics

Lesson 24.3: Teaching Science with Food, Gardening, and Animals

Case Study

Strengthening Science and Technology Curriculum

Rena has just returned from the state early childhood conference in Denver, Colorado. Studying the conference program, she realized her classroom curriculum in science and technology needed to be strengthened. This was the curriculum area that she lacked the most confidence in teaching. So, she attended five engaging sessions. She recorded detailed notes to later share with her colleagues during each session. Rena's goal is to integrate science and technology throughout the curriculum. On Monday morning, upon returning to the classroom, Rena was enthusiastic about the ideas she had gleaned. Her primary focus was to deepen the children's understanding of science concepts while promoting a lifelong interest.

After the children left, a colleague approached Rena in the workroom and asked what she had learned at the conference. Rena responded, "Listening to experienced classroom teachers who loved science was rewarding. In a nutshell, teachers must provide abundant science materials, equipment, and thoughtful questioning. They need to guide the children's thinking and engage all their senses, so they learn to think like scientists. The teacher's questions should capture the children's attention and support the child's problem-solving process."

Give It Some Thought

1. Why should young children study science and technology?
2. What type of science and supplies do you think Rena should have in her classroom to help promote the children's understanding of their world?
3. What technology could be used to promote science and technology concepts?
4. What questions could Rena use to help focus the children's attention?
5. What field trips would help the children learn science concepts?
6. How could Rena use books on science and technology in the classroom?

Opening image credit: Saiistock/iStock via Getty Images Plus

Lesson 24.1 Science and Technology in the Classroom

Essential Question

What do you need to know about science and technology to encourage children's curiosity and interest in science and technology concepts?

Learning Outcomes

After studying this lesson, you will be able to

24.1-1 **summarize** the meanings of the terms *science* and *technology.*

24.1-2 **outline** the procedure for planning science activities, including the role of the teacher.

24.1-3 **summarize** the procedure for planning the technology area and activities, equipment and materials, and the role of the teacher.

24.1-4 **describe** how to integrate science and technology throughout the classroom environment, curriculum, and daily routines.

Key Terms

science	science table
technology	app
STEM	

Two-year-old Ricardo's first contact with a butterfly was accidental. His study of the bug was brief but intense. It involved mainly the senses of sight and touch. Quickly, Ricardo picked the butterfly up and said, "What's dat?" His mother replied, "It's a butterfly." This experience opened the world of natural science to Ricardo. Later, whenever he saw a butterfly or a moth, he repeated his new word, "butterfly." At school, Ricardo's teacher placed a butterfly under

a digital microscope for him. She encouraged Ricardo to look at it and tell her what he saw.

Science and technology are part of everything people do. Much of what children learn relates to science concepts. Their first learnings are often simple but meaningful. You can help form children's science concepts through science experiences and thoughtful conversations. Capturing the children's curiosity about science during daily classroom routines will help them develop respect for their environment, too, and they will be discovering the wonders of the natural world.

Technology is changing the way people communicate and learn, and children are a part of this interconnected world. Digital life is here to stay, and new technology continues to bring new opportunities. Technology is crucial to literacy development. It can be an effective tool for promoting learning and development in the infant, toddler, preschool, kindergarten, and after-school classrooms. Children use technological tools to figure out their uses. This skill is important to function in a digital environment. When they use technology, they are actively engaged in making decisions.

24.1-1 What Are Science and Technology?

Science is the study of natural processes and their products. It is a body of information containing a collection of facts. Science is a way of thinking and trying to understand the world. For children to understand their world, they must explore new materials and question, which leads to active learning. For this reason, early childhood experiences should use a hands-on approach. A hands-on approach allows children to be involved in and think about the sights, sounds, touches, and smells of their environment. Your role as a teacher is to nurture their curiosity and sense of wonder. Provide a rich, inviting, and supportive environment filled with hands-on activities. Children need these experiences with materials, ideas, and events to open their imaginations.

Science is a creative field of study. It requires the development of curiosity and imagination. As children watch, study, wonder, or question, they learn about science. Science is a way to gain an understanding of why events happen the way they do. Studying science inspires children to be aware of and involved with their surroundings. They can investigate answers to such questions as, *"How will it change?"* and *"What will happen if…?"* As children try to make sense of what is happening, they are building theories.

Science involves observing, questioning, investigating, hypothesizing, exploring, measuring, comparing, classifying, predicting, and making thrilling discoveries. The focus for young children should be on observing and exploring (**Figure 24.1**). Young children enjoy these tasks because they see the world from a fresh point of view. They have no preset ideas of how the world and nature work. Much of their learning in science and technology occurs informally. They may be

SDI Productions/E+ via Getty Images

Figure 24.1 Children learn to observe and explore as they view living things such as fish in a tank. ***What are some ways you might encourage children to explore the world around them?***

playing with blocks, water, cooking, observing the bunny, or in the outdoor garden.

All attempts to gain information begin with observation. By using their senses, children observe relationships between events. They start to group information and make generalizations. Studies show that science activities enhance the curiosity of children. Children also build skills in picking out similarities and differences. Vocabulary growth is supported. Children improve their language skills and general knowledge as concepts such as *round, triangular, big,* and *small* are discussed. This promotes reading-readiness skills. Fine-motor skills and hand-eye coordination improve as children measure items, collect samples, and handle objects. Weighing and counting items also enhance math skills.

Technology and science are interrelated. Science is a way of thinking that focuses on understanding how and why things happen, while **technology** focuses on using tools to make things happen, identify problems, and make things work. Technology is a way of *doing*.

Young children are growing up in a world with technological tools. As a result, emphasis is being placed on STEM. What is STEM? It is an acronym originated by the National Science Foundation. **STEM** stands for the disciplines of *science, technology, engineering,* and *math*. STEM is a curriculum focusing on integrating the four disciplines that will help prepare children to live and work in the twenty-first century. STEM education is important if the United States is to remain a world leader and compete in a global economy. Most jobs in the future will require an understanding of science, technology, engineering, and math. In some early childhood settings, STEAM is used. This includes the addition and integration of *art*.

Through STEM-related activities, children develop problem-solving skills and discover how things work. During this hands-on and minds-on process, children explore and apply engineering solutions. These experiences should spark their interest in science, technology, engineering, and math that could lead to a STEM career.

Technologies are constantly changing. Daily, children observe the adults in their lives using smartphones, digital tablets with multi-touch screens, ATM machines, digital cameras, wireless internet connections, personal media players, computers, and e-book readers. Many of them, too, are using powerful digital tools every day of their lives, whether watching television, playing with apps on a computer, or talking on the telephone. Young children must be competent in using developmentally appropriate technology to enhance their learning. When used wisely, technology can support relationships and learning. Its use promotes social, cognitive, literacy, language, and math skills.

24.1-2 Planning Science Activities

Some of the most successful science experiences are unplanned. For instance, you might bring in a flower you found on the way to the center. This can be the starting point for a discussion about flowers. As an ant moves across the floor, you can watch, study, and discuss it. If the wind rises suddenly, blowing debris around the playground, you can discuss the wind.

Science can be found in every area of the curriculum; however, most science experiences require planning. Focusing on a theme helps children learn about their world by structuring and organizing information. You will need to schedule events, prepare, and provide materials, and continuously add to the science area to spark children's interests. You will find that science activities mesh well with an integrated curriculum. You may plan a food or sensory activity that teaches a science concept. Fingerplays, stories, field trips, math activities, physical activities, and art projects can all teach science concepts.

Giving children time to play with, examine, and try the science materials and equipment will also teach science concepts (**Figure 24.2**). Science activities offer children the opportunity for:

- observing and exploring
- asking questions
- using tools to improve observations
- noting differences and likenesses

FatCamera/E+ via Getty Images

Figure 24.2   Having the chance to play with, examine, and use science equipment will promote children's growth in scientific knowledge.

- developing new questions
- making predictions and solving problems
- drawing conclusions
- building theories to explain what they see
- providing explanations, communicating, and sharing
- collecting samples, recording data
- developing new interests and skills
- listening to sounds
- viewing videos
- looking at books
- collecting and analyzing pictures

When planning science activities, it is important to consider what space, equipment, and materials you will need.

Science Area

Teachers need to create an environment that promotes science. In planning space for science activities, many teachers choose to create a science area. A *science area* is a space for science. Often placed near a window, the science is generally set apart from other classroom areas, tables, shelves, storage cabinets, and other creative spaces. A science area is best near a kitchen to allow access to both heat and water sources, which are quite important for many science projects. Provide a gathering area for discussions and STEM-related stories.

An outdoor science area may also be useful. This area may contain a garden space with plants and an area for conducting weather tests. Some centers raise small animals, such as rabbits and baby chicks. Store garden tools, insect nets, and water tubes in an outdoor shed for children to use in the outdoor area.

Equipment and Materials

Equipment and materials for a science area need not be costly. You can acquire most items obtained at little or no cost. Two factors play heavily in the selection process. First, consider the safety of the item. Then, decide whether the children have the skills necessary to use the item. See **Figure 24.3** for a list of common science supplies.

Most early childhood centers have a **science table**. The purpose of this table is to display science-related items and create a learning environment rich in materials. The teacher often acquires items to place on the table. The science table should have a focus that provides direction for advancing the children's learning. For example, place a group of plastic reptiles on the science table next to resource books showing pictures of the reptiles. This will allow the children to compare the model reptiles with those in the books. Finally, place concept-related literature books on the table. You can also encourage the children to bring their own items to display on the science table. Children often enjoy adding to collections of leaves, nuts, rocks, shells, insects, nests, cocoons, or seeds.

Science Supplies

Supply Types	Supply Items
School Supplies	• globes, paints, clay, chalk, markers, straws
	• colored paper, colored pencils, construction paper, chart paper
	• scissors, paste or glue, string, yarn, twine, craft sticks, blocks
	• bubble solution, magnetic marbles, string slime, magic sand, table tripod, magnifier
Scrap Items	• pocket mirrors, cameras, large spoons, clocks and watches, locks and keys
	• sawdust, fabric scraps, metal scraps, wood scraps
	• flashlights, watering cans, funnels, airplane and automobile parts
Classroom Pets	• hamsters, harmless snakes, frogs, birds, rabbits, fish, spiders, mice, guinea pigs, gerbils
	• animal homes, cages, aquariums
Nature Items	• stones, rocks, river rocks, seashells, pinecones, leaves, plant bulbs, seeds, flowers, cattails, butterflies
	• soil, sand, logs, birdfeeders, wind socks, bug boxes, root-viewer growing kits
Tools	• hammers, nails, rulers, tape measures, saws, screwdrivers, screws, bolts, wrenches, air pumps, safety glasses
	• trowels, vice, pliers, levers, ramps, pulleys, wheels, magnets
	• magnifying glass, binoculars, thermometer, eye dropper, balance scale, tweezers, prisms, microscope
Household Items	• salt, sugar, food coloring, jars, spoons, corks, tongs, funnels, strainers, cloth pieces
	• scales, measuring cups and spoons, pots and pans, empty containers and trays, egg time, flashlights, cardboard tubes, mirrors

Figure 24.3 Common science supplies are generally available for little to no cost. *How could you obtain science supplies for no cost?*

The science table should capitalize on the child's fascination with the world. It should motivate children to explore on their own. So, arrange the materials in a visually appealing way and change them often. If collections remain on the table too long, children become bored and lose interest. Be creative and display items in a tent, store setting, cave setting, booth, trailer, pushcart, or wagon.

The science table should sit away from the wall, allowing children to move about the table freely. They should experience the sensation of touching, smelling, hearing, and observing as they explore.

Centerpieces at the snack or lunch table also promote children's interest in nature. A bowl of pinecones or gourds or a flower bouquet brings the world of science indoors. These items will encourage science discussions during snack and mealtime.

Playground equipment can teach science concepts. For example, pedaling a bike creates the energy needed to move it. Using a teeter-totter shows the law of balance.

Explore concepts with high-quality fiction and non-fiction children's storybooks. Examples of high-quality children's science books include

- *Flashlight* by Lizi Boyd
- *What Will Grow?* by Jennifer Ward (author) and Susie Ghahremani (illustrator)
- *Seeds Move* by Robin Page
- *Sprout, Seed, Sprout* by Annika Dunkee (author) and Carey Sockocheff (illustrator)
- *How Apples Grow* by Jill McDonald
- *The Very Hungry Caterpillar* by Eric Carle
- *A Rock Is Lively* by Dianna Hutts Aston (author) and Sylvia Long (illustrator)
- *A Bird Is a Bird* by Lizzy Rockwell
- *Tadpole to Frog* by American Museum of Natural History
- *The Big Book of Bugs* by Yuval Zommer
- *The Happiest Tree: A Story of Growing Up* by Hyeon-Ju Lee
- *Caterpillar to Butterfly* by American Museum of Natural History

- *Do You Know Which Ones Will Grow?* by Susan Shea (author) and Tom Slaughter (illustrator)
- *The Velveteen Rabbit* by Margery Williams (author) and Charles Santore (illustrator)
- *The Snowy Day* by Ezra Jack Keats
- *Water Is Water* by Miranda Paul (author) and Jason Chin (illustrator)
- *Something Smells* Blake Lilane Hellman (author) and Steve Henry (illustrator)
- *If You Find a Rock* by Peggy Christian (author) and Barbara Hirsch Lember (photographer)
- *Looking Closely in the Rain Forest* by Frank Serafini
- *Hey Water* by Antionette Portis
- *Good Night, Veggies* by Diana Murray (author) and Zachariah Oltora (illustrator)
- *Our Solar System* Peter Roop (author), Connie Roop (author), and the American Museum of Natural History

The Teacher's Role with Teaching Science

As a teacher, see if your state has learning guidelines or standards for science. Your role is to promote an understanding and lifelong interest in science. You need to offer space, materials, and activities that encourage discovery. For safety reasons, you must provide constant supervision. You also want to learn when to let children work independently and when to step in and guide their explorations. A simple suggestion often helps a child who is frustrated. Unneeded input can sometimes stifle curiosity, however, and destroy a child's desire to continue experimenting.

The activities you plan should include materials for all children. Children should have ample hands-on activities in which they play, explore, and tinker with new materials. This process allows children to discuss relationships and concepts among themselves. They want to understand and build theories on how the world works.

Activities should promote the development of the following five basic process skills:

- observing and exploring objects using all five senses
- drawing conclusions from observations based on experience
- classifying objects into sets based on one or more observable properties
- comparing sets of objects by measuring and counting
- communicating by describing objects, relationships, and occurrences

Provide many opportunities for children to practice observing. Children enjoy watching and wondering. Going on field trips, viewing videos, looking at pictures, and viewing objects on the science table are good ways to help children build on powers of observation.

To encourage children to explore, use mirror talk. Tell them what you see them doing. Ask open-ended questions that model the inquiry process. Help them see themselves as learners. Asking too many questions is not always a useful technique. Instead, ask fewer questions that require more thought. Open-ended questions promote discussion and require decision-making skills. Closed-ended questions (sometimes called *single-answer questions*) demand few decision-making skills and are most often answered with a yes or no. **Figure 24.4** outlines how open-ended and closed-ended questions are used. Poor questioning techniques encourage children to guess rather than use thinking skills.

Children may need time to answer open-ended questions, and a teacher should give positive responses to all answers. When someone offers a better answer, explain how it adds to other answers. Children also need to be heard. Being listened to strengthens a child's desire to take part.

The teacher sets the tone for learning science in the classroom. A simple rule is to base activities on children's questioning. Do not give answers to questions children have not asked. Let the children use process skills as well as listen, watch, or read about science. Teachers who control the activity do little to promote questions. To create the right climate, provide hands-on materials for all children, study their interactions with the materials, and listen to them talk to each other. Finally, ask questions to focus on their thinking and scaffold their learning. As you listen, try to identify patterns in their observations. See **Figure 24.5**.

24.1-3 Planning Technology Activities

As technology becomes more and more a part of people's worlds, young children need to become knowledgeable about the use of technological tools. Technology is important for literacy development. It can help promote learning and social interaction in the early childhood classroom. Using technology, children can discover, create, and display their learnings in meaningful ways. For this reason, most early childhood teachers include a technology area or computer center in their classrooms.

Technology items early childhood teachers most frequently purchase include smart toys, computers, digital tablets, printers, and digital cameras. While smart toys and smart boards may be integrated into various curriculum and classroom areas, teachers often set apart a technology area.

The Technology Area

The technology area, also known as a *computer area*, is a space for children to learn about using technology. Safety should be the first consideration when setting up a technology area. A technology

Open-Ended and Closed-Ended Questions

Open-Ended	Closed-Ended
What are you observing?	What color is it?
How could you classify these?	Can you classify these by shape?
What happens to a hamburger when it is fried?	Has the hamburger changed color?

Figure 24.4 Using open-ended questions helps promote discussion and decision-making skills. *How can you use open-ended questions to encourage children to observe, draw conclusions, classify, compare, and describe items in their environment?*

Questions to Encourage Thought

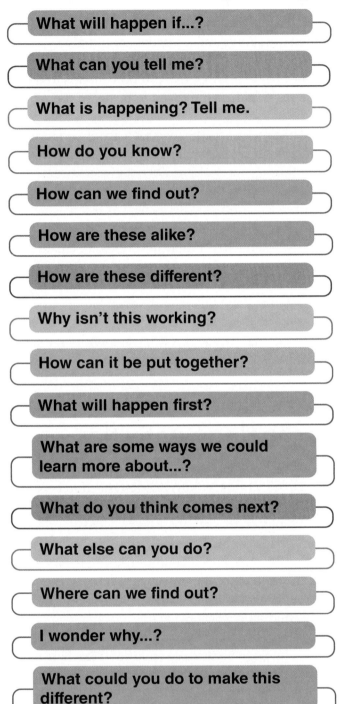

- What will happen if...?
- What can you tell me?
- What is happening? Tell me.
- How do you know?
- How can we find out?
- How are these alike?
- How are these different?
- Why isn't this working?
- How can it be put together?
- What will happen first?
- What are some ways we could learn more about...?
- What do you think comes next?
- What else can you do?
- Where can we find out?
- I wonder why...?
- What could you do to make this different?

Figure 24.5 Developing effective questioning techniques helps teachers guide children's thinking. *What other questions can you think of that would encourage the children's thoughts?*

Natee K Jindakum/Shutterstock.com

Figure 24.6 A dry, quiet corner is the best place for a technology area. *What other activity areas could be adjacent to the technology area?*

area should be in a *quiet, dry* area of the classroom with a low-traffic to avoid interruptions (**Figure 24.6**). Place computer tables against walls next to grounded electrical outlets. This will avoid electrical cords becoming tripping hazards.

Technology areas may include one or more laptops or digital tablets on child-sized computer tables with a color printer, paper, headphones (to reduce distractions), and an internet connection. To avoid glare from sunlight hurting children's eyes, place computers away from direct sunlight.

A computer table should be safe, accessible, and large enough to accommodate two or three chairs. Extra chairs encourage verbal interaction and cooperation among children. When two or more children work together, peer mentoring and collaboration occurs. These children provide verbal and physical help to each other, which contributes to their technological literacy and cognitive and social development.

Equipment and Materials

As a teacher, you should be intentional about selecting, integrating, and using technology. Many early childhood teachers feel challenged in selecting technology and software. New hardware and software choices with new products emerge daily, and technology areas can be a challenge to plan and arrange.

When selecting technology equipment, consider the children's development. Mouses should be child-sized to fit in the children's hands. Otherwise, children cannot perform basic tasks. Keyboards should contain large key labels and limited keys.

Depending on the ages of the children, you may have to change mouse settings on the computer to cater to a lower speed. You may also have to adjust the computer volume and brightness.

Many children use cameras in the technology area. Safety should be the major consideration in choosing children's cameras. Low-cost, waterproof digital cameras with rubberized grips are ideal. Rubberized grips absorb the shock if a child accidentally drops the camera. The camera's shutter button should be on the front face of the camera, making it easier for the children to operate. For safety, screw the tab to hide the batteries and memory cards.

Technology goes beyond computers and other digital devices. If you have access to an old radio, computer, record player, or telephone, take these devices apart to let the children see the parts. **Figure 24.7** lists equipment for children's technology areas.

Teachers must also choose software, which can be a difficult and time-consuming task. There are few standards surrounding the labeling and marketing of educational software, and thousands of different apps and programs are available and forthcoming for children. An **app** is an *application* or a piece of software that runs on the internet from a phone, computer, digital tablet, or another type of handheld device. These apps include activities involving math, music, art, language and literacy, creativity, memory, and problem-solving. Apps vary in quality, so it is important to try them yourself before sharing them with children.

Do your homework when selecting apps. Tens of thousands of apps have educational labels, but research is lacking in showing their effectiveness. Software should be age appropriate in interest, appeal, skill level, and content. It should engage, motivate, and inspire children to achieve. When software is developmentally appropriate, children's social and cognitive abilities improve. Opportunities for success should be embedded in software programs, and programs should be child friendly to encourage unlimited discovery and exploration. Software should be clear, friendly, and understandable, and contain voice and visual cues telling the children what to do. **Figure 24.8** lists other software selection criteria for teachers.

Technology for the Classroom

- audio recorders
- color printer
- computers
- digital cameras
- digital telescope
- digital keyboard
- digital tables
- e-readers
- headphones
- interactive whiteboard
- internet connection
- keyboard
- mouse
- personal media players
- scales
- smart boards
- smart toys
- video recorders

Figure 24.7 Technology goes beyond computers and other digital devices.

Software Selection Criteria

- Is age-appropriate in interest, skill level, and subject matter
- Relfects the children's experiences in the real world
- Content is built around an educational goal
- Vocabulary is age-appropriate
- Provides simple, clear, spoken instructions
- Is easy to navigate for independent use
- Teaches a process, skill, or concept
- Encourages curiosity, exploration, discovery, and investigative processes
- Increases complexity by building on learning
- Allows for trial and error
- Looks colorful, simple, and uncluttered
- Features realistic scenes and color animation
- Includes figures in appropriate size and proportion
- Avoids sterotypes, and cultural and gender biases
- Includes diverse family forms, ages, and abilities
- Promotes peer and/or teacher-child interaction

Figure 24.8   Software programs should be child-friendly and encourage unlimited discovery and exploration. *Why do you think selecting software can be a challenging experience for teachers?*

The Teacher's Role with Technology

Beyond creating a technology area and selecting hardware and software, teachers foster technology learning by guiding children's experiences. Technology activities are not bound to subject areas. You can integrate them to support and enrich learning objectives in every curriculum area. Software with media-rich content can help children learn language, science, social studies, and math concepts. As teachers guide technology experiences, they should ensure that children use technology in moderation. As with other self-selected activities, teachers should set time frames and limits for technology use.

The American Academy of Pediatrics (AAP) published new recommendations for children's media use in 2020. Other than video chatting with family members, avoid screen time for children less than 18 months of age. Beginning around 18 to 24 months of age, some high-quality programing can have educational value for children. The AAP recommends that parents watch programs with their children to help them understand what they are viewing. *Sesame Workshop*® and *PBS* are examples of high-quality programming.

Limit screen time for children two to five years of age to one hour of high-quality daily programing. Again, parents should watch with their children to help them understand what they are viewing and make applications to the world around them. Place consistent limits on children ages six and older in terms of usage and types of media.

As a teacher, set the stage by introducing the children to digital devices. Begin by familiarizing children three years of age and older with the technology area of the classroom. Small, informal groups of two or three children work best. Start by naming the hardware—the computer, the printer, the keyboard, and the mouse. Show the keys and buttons and how they are controlling the digital device. Show children how to hold and use a mouse and place their hands over a child-sized keyboard or screen. Review etiquette for using a digital device, including that the child must be gentle when using a device. Otherwise, it could break.

After this basic introduction, let the children explore, experiment, and create with a simple, easy-to-run, developmentally appropriate program. After demonstrating the program, most children should use the software without frustration. Young children are intellectual explorers. Their attention spans, creativity, and problem-solving skills increase when they are in control.

If a child experiences difficulty using a digital device, focus the child's attention and learning. Ask "what" questions instead of "why" questions. By asking a "what" question, you begin a conversation. For example, if you ask, "Why did the device shut down?" the child might say because they pushed a button. But, if you ask, "What happened?", you invite the child to explain.

When introducing technology, teach new vocabulary words for hardware and software. Describe *hardware* as a category of machines made with metal and plastic. *Software* can be described as programs that run on hardware. Additional terms that children need to learn include *computer, printer, mouse, cursor, screen, keyboard, touch screen, digital camera, interactive whiteboard, e-reader, scanner, flash drive,* and *smart pens.*

24.1-4 Integrating Technology into the Classroom

Children grow up with digital technology, which can have a positive or negative impact on development. The best way to teach children about technology use and skills is to integrate technology into every classroom and curriculum area. You can do this in endless ways. A digital telescope with built-in lighting might magnify three-dimensional objects as children learn shapes, and a digital scale in the science area might teach children about weight. Recorders, headphones, e-readers, and microphones for special occasions might complement storytelling experiences; and an electronic keyboard can promote music learning. Smart boards can encourage social interactions, and digital cameras can record children's successes at art and block-building. A digital tablet with video and audio capabilities might accent dramatic play.

In choosing how to integrate technology into the curriculum, teachers need to be mindful. The tools must support the developmental level and ages of children in the classroom. With appropriate use, technology is an effective tool that promotes development in all areas of the early childhood curriculum. It also promotes critical-thinking skills. Teachers should consider the technology available when planning integration.

Video Recorders

Video recorders and cell phones capture moments on film. All video recorders have video capabilities and most have audio capabilities. Video recordings can commemorate field trips, birthday celebrations, dramatic play, music, movement, block-building, art, cooking, and storytelling. Besides making children feel accomplished and special, these recordings can please parents. You could send deployed military parents a copy of their child's birthday celebration. Recordings of other activities can be revisited by children either in a group or individually.

Digital Cameras

People of all ages find photography interesting. Photographs are valuable because they help children revisit their science experiences. Pictures help children reflect on their learning. After building a tower, they can take a picture to solve design problems or to savor the satisfaction of the project. First experiences in photography should allow children to take pictures of anything they want to remember. Before the children take pictures, teach them how to point the camera and press the shutter button. Display photographs of block-building constructions or art pieces in the classroom, make them into a book, or send them home. Sharing and exchanging information between home and school strengthens relationships.

Computers

Computer programs can support learning in several subject areas, including art, language, social studies, math, and science. For example, some computer programs contain digital stories that are printed in a large-size font to promote early literacy development. Teachers need to select quality software programs for computers to be effectively integrated into the curriculum.

Interactive Whiteboards

An *interactive whiteboard* is a touch-sensitive flat screen that is mounted on a wall. The whiteboard enlarges content displayed on a computer and can be used in many ways. Interactive whiteboards can be used for circle and small group time to personalize learning. They can track daily routines, such as helper and attendance charts, classroom limits and responsibilities, and daily weather charts. Interactive whiteboards can display stories during storytelling and prepare for and conclude field trips. For example, before taking a field trip to the zoo, children could watch a video of panda bears eating and interacting with other bears in their cages.

Digital Tablets

Digital tablets and phones are part of the context of young children's lives. They enable children to play programs or record moments in a variety of settings (**Figure 24.9**). Some digital tablets can connect to the internet and run software. Others have audio and video capabilities that allow children to record each other telling stories, building with blocks, dancing, singing, or taking part in classroom celebrations. There are some highly recommended apps that adults can use to teach and interact with infants, toddlers, and young preschoolers. These apps include Elmo Calls by Sesame Street, Dr. Seuss's ABCs, and Elmo Monster Maker. The latter is interactive and open-ended and allows differences in creating the monster's bodies.

Internet

Use the internet as a teaching tool. The internet is home to a wealth of educational information about a variety of topics. Children can access online educational programs or they can view pictures or video clips related to learning. As a teacher, you can use the internet to gather information on almost any topic or classroom theme.

Media Players

Media players are digital devices that contain audio or video files, including music, audio books, and sometimes videos. Media players can support the language and library area of the

UW-Stout Child and Family Study Center

Figure 24.9   The timer shows when these children's turns using the digital tablet ends. ***Why should teachers set time limits for children's use of digital devices?***

classroom by housing digital stories. Children may want to listen to the same story repeatedly. Encourage repetition since it will build language and conceptual skills.

E-Readers

E-readers are digital devices that hold *e-books*, or books that are available in a digital format. You can download e-books onto e-readers, digital tablets, and sometimes computers. For school-aged children, using e-readers is helpful, since many e-readers link to a digital dictionary. When children need help with a word, they can simply highlight it. Many organizations, such as the International Library Association, contain collections of e-books specifically designed for children from three to 13 years of age. As much as possible, teachers should provide e-books that are multicultural and printed in many languages.

Focus on Careers

Teacher Assistant

Teacher assistants work under the guidance of a licensed teacher to provide students with additional attention and instruction. They may help reinforce lessons and gather materials and equipment teachers need to prepare and execute lessons. They may also observe and provide feedback to teachers about children's learning progress. Along with discussing and helping to develop lessons, teacher assistants may help children use digital devices and software programs. They may also supervise children during outdoor play and during snack and mealtimes.

Career cluster: Education and Training.

Education: The education and training requirements for teacher assistants may vary by state and employer. Entry-level workers typically need a high school diploma. To work in a public school, however, teacher assistants need at least two years of college coursework or an associate's degree. Some employers may require candidates pass a state or local assessment.

Job outlook. Employment for teacher assistants, is expected to grow 9 percent through 2030, which is about as fast as average for all occupations.

To learn more about a career as a teacher assistant, visit US Department of Labor websites for the *Occupational Outlook Handbook (OOH)* and *O*NET OnLine.* You will be able to compare the job responsibilities, educational requirements, job outlook, and average pay for people with similar occupations.

Lesson 24.1 Review

1. Each of the following is a focus of technology *except* _____. (24.1.1)
   A. using tools to make things happen
   B. making things work
   C. understanding how things happen
   D. identifying problems

2. **True or False.** Children develop problem-solving skills when performing STEM-related activities. (24.1.1)

3. _____ questions promote discussion and require decision-making skills. (24.1.3)
   A. Single-answer
   B. Open-ended
   C. Review
   D. Reflection

4. The acronym STEM stands for _____. (24.1.3)
   A. science, trigonometry, English, and music
   B. synchronous, tacit, experiential, and memorization
   C. science, technology, engineering, and math
   D. scaffolding, teaching, environment, and multicultural

5. A technology area may include all of the following except _____. (24.1.4)
   A. digital tablets
   B. a water table
   C. computers
   D. an old camera

6. What is the most important consideration when integrating technology in your classroom? (24.1.4)
   A. Proper placement
   B. Most up to date
   C. Developmentally appropriate
   D. Durability

Lesson 24.2 Teaching Science Basics

Essential Question

How can you use various strategies to incorporate basic science concepts into the classroom, curriculum, and daily experiences for children?

Learning Outcomes

After studying this lesson, you will be able to

24.2-1 **summarize** methods for using children's senses to teach science concepts.

24.2-2 **explain** ways that teachers can incorporate the science of color into everyday experiences.

24.2-3 **articulate** ways to teach science through the use of elements and objects, including water, air, the environment, weather, magnets, wheels, and children's growth.

24.2-4 **summarize** various ways to teach science concepts through field trips and guided walks.

Key Terms

feely box	secondary colors
primary colors	palpable

Teaching basic science concepts to young children is through the senses—feeling, smelling, hearing, and tasting. Children can also learn science concepts through color, water, weather, the environment, magnets, wheels, and even growth charts. One of the best vehicles for teaching science basics is through a well-organized science center. It should be in a low-traffic classroom area, capturing the children's attention and inspiring engagement. The children will learn as they compare, classify, measure,

and test. Books should be added to the center to extend their experiences.

Teachers need to observe the children's interactions. If required, activities may require accommodations and modifications for children who have disabilities. Teachers need to carefully monitor the children's behavior for signs of frustration and boredom. When necessary, the environment or teaching strategies require adjustment to maintain the children's interests. Equipment and materials may need changes or additions to existing ones. To add variety to teaching science basics, you can take children on guided walks around the neighborhood and field trips.

24.2-1 Teaching Science Through the Senses

Science is based on what people feel, smell, see, hear, and taste. As children learn more about their senses, they also learn how to explain their surroundings. For example, while peeling an orange, a child can see and smell the orange. After it is peeled, the child can feel it and taste it. By peeling an orange, a child can learn the following concepts: we see with our eyes; we smell with our noses; we feel with our skin; and we taste with our tongues.

Feeling

Feeling is a fun and important sense to explore through science activities. Whenever time permits, provide opportunities for children to feel several objects in the classroom. Construct a **feely box** by cutting a circle in a box large enough for the children to put their hands in. A feely bag can also be used. It should be opaque and easy

604

Copyright Goodheart-Willcox Co., Inc.

to reach into without exposing the contents. A feely box or bag contains different objects and materials. Let each child reach into the box and try to identify an object. If they cannot identify it, provide clues. For example, if the item is a spoon, you may say, "It is used to eat cereal in the morning."

Children can also build a sense of touch by feeling fabric samples of varying textures (**Figure 24.10**). These may include velvet, leather, flannel, knit, burlap, felt, and cotton. Encourage the children to explain what each piece feels like. You might add other materials, such as pinecones, bark, leaves, fake fur, sandpaper, glazed paper, sponge, pebbles, and cork. To add variety, place the materials on the science table where the children can sort them based on like textures.

Smelling

Preschool children need to learn that objects can be identified by their smells. One method for teaching this is to collect items in the classroom that have distinct odors, such as tempera paint, markers, crayons, play dough, bar soap, sawdust, and gerbil food. Place a small amount of each item in a container, such as a small paper cup. Explain to the children that the game you will play involves naming items by smell.

Food can also be used in a smelling activity. For example, you could place ketchup, mustard, applesauce, orange juice, and other common foods in containers and repeat the same steps.

Figure 24.10 Children can also build their sense of touch by feeling varying textures.

Seeing

The sense of sight is just as important as the sense of smell. A teacher can promote seeing experiences by playing games such as "I Spy." After saying "I spy something green. It is small and round. It is in the art area," pause to allow the children to identify the object. If the children cannot guess, give more clues.

Children can also build visual memory skills by naming what is missing from a group. Use this activity for one child or small groups of children. Collect common classroom objects such as crayons, blocks, puzzle pieces, paintbrushes, and toy cans. Gather the children, show them the objects, and explain that you will remove one object. Instruct the children to close or cover their eyes. Remove one object, then have them open their eyes and tell you what object is missing.

There are many variations to this game. You may increase the number of objects. You might place three or four objects in a sequence and ask which objects are out of sequence. You may remove two or three objects from the group and have a child name what is missing.

Hearing

Hearing is another sense that helps children understand and explain their environment. To help children become more aware of this sense, use an audio recorder.

Teach the concept that each person's voice sounds different from any other. Record the voice of each child. To encourage the children to talk, ask each child to tell you about a family member, a favorite person, a pet, or have them tell a story. After you have recorded all the children in the classroom, play the recording to the group. Ask the children to identify each child's voice by name.

Tasting

Children can build tasting skills by exposure to a variety of food. Plan a tasting party using several common foods. Blindfold a child and give them a small sample of some food. Ask the child to name the food. Repeat the activity with all the children in the group. Some teachers prefer to do this as a group activity, providing a sample of each food for all the children at the same time.

24.2-2 Using Color to Teach Science Concepts

Color is a part of science that children observe daily. A way children describe their world is by naming colors. Color also serves as a basis for grouping. Children can learn the **primary colors** (red, blue, and yellow) in the science area. They can match red, blue, and yellow toys, such as beads or blocks, with similarly colored boxes. Introduce **secondary colors** (purple, green, and orange) next; and again, using toys, the children can match the color of the toy to the container.

Some teachers have special color days. For example, Monday may be orange day. To prepare for this day, send a note or letter to parents or guardians. Ask the children to wear the color of the day. This may be a hair ribbon, pin, barrette, or any article of clothing. You may also use a nature walk to observe colors. The kitchen staff may coordinate snacks with the color of the day. For example, serve orange slices, carrots, or cantaloupe on an orange day.

Mixing colors is another way to teach color concepts (**Figure 24.11**). Children learn how colors are made by mixing primary colors to make secondary colors. Thus, as children learn color concepts, they notice their surroundings. One way to show the mixing of colors is to overlap colored cellophane. Another way is to set up jars or clear plastic glasses in the science area. Have the children fill the jars with water, and then place drops of food coloring in each container. Stress color comparisons by using terms such as *lighter than, darker than,* or the *same color as.*

24.2-3 Using Elements and Objects to Teach Science

Elements, objects, and field trips can be used to teach science concepts. Air, weather, water, magnets, field trips, and guided walks can all

UW-Stout Child and Family Study Center

Figure 24.11   Mixing colors is part of the science curriculum. *How might you promote the concept of color in the science curriculum?*

be effective for teaching basic scientific concepts and literacy skills. Regardless of the topic in the science curriculum, children must be engaged and develop a positive attitude. When engaging their hands and minds, they are learning to explore science and construct knowledge. During this process, they need encouragement to think like scientists—questioning, experimenting, predicting, and drawing conclusions.

Using Water to Teach Science Concepts

Water delights almost all children. As young children play with water and accessories, they learn about science concepts by trying to make sense of what happens. Some concepts taught with water include

- Water is a clear, colorless liquid with no taste or smell.
- Water can be found in ponds, lakes, rivers, and oceans.

- All living things need water to survive.
- People, animals, and plants need water.
- Water flows when poured.
- Water takes three forms: liquid, vapor, and solid.
- Frozen water is called *ice* and *steam* is a vapor form of water.
- Water makes objects wet.
- Water can be held in a container.
- Some items float when placed on water.
- Some materials mix with water, and others absorb water.

Water Equipment and Accessories

In programs without water tables, consider using large washtubs, sinks, foodservice bussing tubs, or plastic swimming pools. You can also create water tables using supplies around the center (**Figure 24.12**). When putting together a water table, supply water table accessories. Include funnels, spoons, sprinkling cans, nesting

UW-Stout Child and Family Study Center

Figure 24.12 This water table is transparent, allowing children to observe the contents.

cups, plastic containers, eggbeaters, measuring cups, strainers, corks, sponges, plastic tubing, soap, and food coloring.

To avoid excessive cleanup, put a shower curtain or plastic tablecloth on the floor to protect it. Plastic aprons can protect the children's clothes.

Fill the container with water based on the children's experience and age. (Younger children only need two or three inches of water.) Provide the children with accessories and allow them to experiment freely.

Water Activities

Besides letting children experiment with water tables, teachers can plan activities to teach children about water and water properties. A teacher can freeze water for children, teaching the concepts that ice is frozen water, ice can melt, melted ice is water, ice can be picked up, and ice melts in warm places.

Children can also learn that some materials absorb water. Use sponges, terry cloth, tissues, paper towels, cardboard, plastic wrap, wax paper, newsprint, finger paint, and plastic to teach this. You may wish to make a chart listing the materials and noting whether they absorb water. From using these materials, children should learn that some materials soak up water while others repel water.

Water can teach children about floating. Fill the water table half full. Provide items, such as wooden blocks, pencils, paper, plastic alphabet letters, metal spoons, and aluminum foil. Record each item that floats on a chart. Children will learn that some items float on water and others do not.

Through observation and participation, children can also learn what materials dissolve in water. Fill several small pitchers with water. Then have each child fill several plastic glasses. Give each child a material that dissolves in water, such as salt, sugar cubes, or baking soda. Also supply items that will not dissolve, such as cooking oil, or rice. Then let each child stir the mixture. Ask the children, "What happens when you add _____ to water?" Encourage the children to discuss the results as they add each item to the water.

Children may also paint with water, an activity best suited to the outdoors. Provide the children with cans of water and wide paintbrushes. Have the children paint surfaces such as a cement sidewalk. Then ask them what happens to the water. Try this in different weather. Children will see that on hot days the water evaporates and on wintry days it freezes.

Workplace Connections

Experimenting with Ice

Conduct the following experiment while working with a group of children in a preschool or early learning center. Provide children with Styrofoam, plastic, metal, and paper cups; ice cubes; and a variety of wraps and paper, such as wax paper, aluminum foil, bubble wrap, freezer paper, or plastic wrap. Let each child wrap an ice cube in selected material(s) and place it in the cup of their choice. Have children describe the results of their choices 30 minutes later as they examine the condition of their ice cube.

1. What observations did the children make?
2. What science concepts did this experiment teach?

Using Air to Teach Science Concepts

Every day, children have experiences with air. They watch airplanes and birds, fly kites, and blow bubbles. They feel the wind blow against their bodies and clothing. Experiences with air help children learn about their world and about the science concepts that control air and wind. Teachers can foster the learning of science concepts by teaching about air and teaching about wind.

Teaching About Air

Children can learn many science concepts about air. Bubble solutions can also teach children that air takes up space. You can buy a prepared solution or use the recipe in **Figure 24.13**. Give each child a straw and a paper cup. Using a

Bubble Solution Recipe

- 1/2 cup glycerin (purchase from drugstore)
- 2 cups water
- 3 tablespoons liquid detergent

LightField Studies/Shutterstock.com

Figure 24.13 Making bubbles helps children understand the concept that air takes up space.

pencil point, make a hole about one inch from the bottom of the cup. Have the children place a straw in the hole, and then have them dip the open end of the cup in the bubble solution. Finally, ask them to remove the cup from the solution and, with the cup in an upside-down position, blow into the straw. Encourage the children to blow bubbles. Ask them, "What is inside the bubbles? How did you get air inside the bubble? How can you make the bubble larger? How can you make the bubble smaller?"

Use clear containers, such as aquariums or glass mixing bowls, to conduct another experiment. Fill the containers with water. Assign containers and pass straws to each child. Tell the children to place their straws in the containers and blow. Ask, "What happens when you blow air through the straw into the water?" (Be sure to caution the children against drinking soapy water.)

Safety First

Balloon Ban

Because balloons are an aspiration and choking hazard, children should not have access to them in the early childhood facility. Young children might chew on uninflated or under-inflated balloons of all types (as well as latex or vinyl gloves) and suck pieces into their airways. Teachers and caregivers must be sure to keep latex or vinyl gloves used for diaper changing out of the reach of children.

Teaching About Wind

Most children can identify wind. To teach the concept that wind makes objects move, use thin strips of newsprint or crepe paper streamers. Take the children outside on a windy day and hand out the streamers. Show them how to hold the streamers. Ask, "What happens to the streamer when the wind blows? What direction is the wind moving? What happens when you run fast while holding the streamers?"

Teaching About the Environment and Weather

Children learn science concepts by learning how to take care of the earth. They need to learn to preserve the earth by keeping it clean (**Figure 24.14**). Set the stage by recycling in your classroom. To do this, place four bins labeled *paper*, *glass*, *metal*, and *plastic* in a classroom area. Encourage the children to sort items.

Children also learn science concepts by observing the weather. Teaching about weather helps develop environmental awareness, and snow, wind, rain, thunderstorms, and rainbows all appeal to young children. Develop a weather felt board to use at group time. Include figures of children; clothing for all seasons; and weather elements, such as clouds, sun, snow, and raindrops. Each day a child can select clothing and symbols to represent the weather.

Using Magnets to Teach Science Concepts

Magnets are an important classroom tool and have many applications to engineering. They will intrigue the children. Through a combination of teacher guidance and play, children best learn concepts about magnets (**Figure 24.15**). Teachers need to buy quality magnets, such as those at science equipment or school supply stores. Buy a variety of magnets, including horseshoe, ceramic, bar, rod-shaped, and disk magnets.

Children find magnets magical. As they explore and play with them, they will observe:

- Magnets attract some objects, but not others.
- Some magnets are big; others are small.
- Some magnets are stronger than others.
- Magnets pick up objects made of iron.

TAGSTOCK1/iStock via Getty Images Plus

Figure 24.14   Children should be encouraged to recycle. *What ways might you encourage recycling and taking care of our environment in the early childhood classroom?*

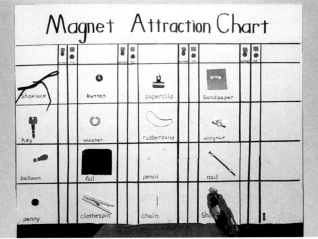

Judy Herr

Figure 24.15   Charts are also useful for learning magnet concepts.

To aid in building these concepts, place several magnets on a table. Collect objects that magnets will pick up and others they will not. Types of objects magnets attract include metal screws, staples, nails, paper clips, and other small metal objects. A magnet will not pick up objects that do not have iron content. Such objects include paper, cloth, buttons, small plastic toys, wooden pencils, crayons, shoelaces, and aluminum dishes.

Place a variety of horseshoe and bar magnets in a small box. In a second box, place chalk, toothpicks, paper, nails, paper clips, plastic spoons, and other objects. Have the children name each object and predict whether the magnets can lift it.

Children require careful supervision while working with magnets. Small magnets can be choke hazards. If two or more magnets are swallowed, they can stick together, form a blockage in the intestines, and require surgery for removal. Also, be cautious when allowing children to play with toys that contain magnets because the magnets can detach. Finally, carefully monitor any of the small metal objects when working with magnets. Screws, paper clips, and nails can all be choking hazards.

Using Wheels to Teach Science Concepts

Children see wheels every day. They may travel by car, truck, bus, or train to the early childhood center. There they see wagons, tricycles, scooters, and other toys with wheels. At home, they might see machines with wheels, such as vacuum cleaners and lawn mowers. Perhaps on a trip to the airport, they have seen people pulling suitcases with wheels. All these experiences should help them learn about the uses of wheels.

Children can learn the following concepts about wheels:
- Wheels are round and come in different sizes.
- Wheels roll.
- Wheels usually turn on an axis.
- Wheels can be made of metal, wood, rubber, or plastic.
- Wheels can help make work easier for people.

- Wheels help move people and things.
- A pulley is a wheel that is connected to a rope to move things.
- Tricycles, wagons, cars, trucks, buses, planes, and motorcycles have wheels for movement.

To learn these concepts, children require exposure to many types of wheels. To help children learn to identify a wheel, use a feely box or bag. Place cubes, balls, wooden blocks, and rubber wheels in the box. Ask one child at a time to feel in the box and find the wheel.

Another way to teach children about wheels is to cut out and hang pictures of wheels from magazines. Include fire engines, cars, trucks, tractors, wagons, airplanes, golf carts, scooters, and roller skates. Then cut out and hang pictures of other types of transportation. These might include motorboats, sailboats, skis, rafts, sleds, ice skates, donkeys, elephants, and horses. When you have finished, ask the children to point out the pictures with wheels.

Using Science to Teach About Children's Growth

Children undergo rapid physical changes during the preschool years. Often, these changes are more **palpable** (recognizable) to parents and teachers than to the children themselves. One way to teach science is to help children understand their own bodies—how they grow and their different traits. To do this, teachers can use photographs and drawings of the children.

One scientific concept to introduce is *recognition*, people can be differentiated by their unique physical traits. To teach this, take pictures of each child using a digital or instant camera. Then show each child their picture. Encourage the child to tell you about the picture. If he or she does not respond, ask specific questions about the photo, such as, "What are you wearing in the picture? What color eyes do you have? What color hair do you have?" Some children may find it hard to link a photo with themselves. For instance, twins might see themselves in a mirror or a picture and identify their siblings. Experiences like these are helpful for showing children they have unique physical traits.

A growth chart can teach measurement concepts (**Figure 24.16**). Make a chart by outlining and cutting out a shape, such as a carrot from a piece of poster board. Use orange for the carrot and green for the stem. Glue a tape measure vertically down the center of the carrot. Hang the carrot to a door, wall, or bulletin board. Then, have each child stand next to the tape and record the children's heights on the poster board.

24.2-4 Teaching Science Through Field Trips and Guided Walks

Field trips promote curiosity, supply opportunities for discovery, and encourage interaction with the environment. During field trips, children can observe how machines make work more precise, easy, and orderly. For example, on a trip to the fire station, children could point out the fire alarm system, ladder, ax, hose, and fire extinguisher.

Guided walks with a focus can also help the children learn about science. Topics for these walks could include colors, seeds, rocks, footprints, animals, insects, plants, or leaves. On rainy days, children can take a walk to study earthworms, puddles, or rainbows. **Figure 24.17** lists field trip locations and objects to observe there.

MIA Studio/Shutterstock.com

Figure 24.16   Colorful growth charts are a fun way to teach children about measurement. *How can learning about their growth and physical traits benefit children?*

Science Field Trips

Location	Science Concepts Studies
Lumber company	Nature of wood and sawdust
Automobile and bike shops	Workings of motors, gears, chains, wheels; use of tools
Grocery stores	Forms of foods
Vacant land	Insects, plant life, animal shelters
Commercial laundry	Effects of cleaners, heat, starch
Produce market	Nature of fresh fruits and vegetables
Interior decorating shop	Nature of fabrics, use of colors
Television and radio studios	Production and transmission of images and sounds
Fire department	Mechanics of trucks, engines, ladders
Animal hospital	Care of pets
Toy shop	Nature of toy materials, such as plastic, wood
Excavation site	Nature of soil, rocks, building materials
Zoo	Birds, insects, animals
Botanical gardens	Plant life
Museum	Rocks, geological formations, other science concepts

Figure 24.17   Science field trips and guided walks promote curiosity and offer children opportunities for discovery and engagement with the environment. What science-related questions could you ask on a walk around the neighborhood?

Lesson 24.2 Review

1. Which of the following is *not* a method for teaching science through the senses? (24.2.1)
   A. A bag with several objects of different textures
   B. An art display with photos of flowers
   C. A recording of animal calls
   D. A writing worksheet on the letter *A*
2. **True or False.** Placing four bins labeled paper, glass, metal, and plastic in a classroom area is an example of using color to teach science concepts. (24.2.2)
3. Which of the following activities would be appropriate for teaching science through the elements? (24.2.3)
   A. Playing a game of tag
   B. Observing icicles melting
   C. Reading a book about ducklings
   D. Matching same-colored objects
4. Field trips offer all of the following benefits for learning science *except* _____. (24.2.4)
   A. taking a nap
   B. promoting curiosity
   C. supplying opportunities for discovery
   D. encouraging interaction with the environment

Teaching Science with Food, Gardening, and Animals

Essential Question

How can you incorporate science concepts through the use of food, gardening, and animals in the early childhood classroom?

Learning Outcomes

After studying this lesson, you will be able to

24.3-1 **summarize** multisensory methods for teaching science concepts about food.

24.3-2 **analyze** ways to teach science concepts about gardening, including observing and planting seeds and gardens.

24.3-3 **contrast** ways to incorporate science concepts about animals and classroom pets.

Key Terms

subterranean	germinate
loam	nocturnal

Young children are natural scientists who can be introduced to science concepts through simple, hands-on experiences. Food, gardening, and animals can all be used to teach scientific concepts. Teachers must be intentional and purposeful in planning the teaching environment, activities, and strategies. To be successful, they must connect with the children's interests and build on their strengths to purposefully provide stimulating activities. Multiple options for engagement also need to be available to include children with diverse needs.

Formats for teaching science concepts vary with the children's ages. One-to-one interactions are typically used with infants. The infant may be sitting on the floor, on the caregiver's lap, or in a high chair. With toddlers' teachers may interact with more than one child at a time. Older children are usually in small groups with more focused experiences. Regardless of the format, moment-to-moment interactions are essential for scaffolding the children's scientific learnings, whether observing or petting an animal, preparing food, or gardening. Teachers need to use cues, hints and prompts to gain the children's attention and scaffold their learning, mastering new concepts and skills. Successful teachers provide encouragement and the least amount of help for a child to master a new skill.

24.3-1 Using Foods to Teach Science Concepts

Science experiments children can eat are both fun and educational (**Figure 24.18**). By preparing and cooking foods, children learn through a multisensory approach. They learn how solid materials can change. When heated, some foods become softer and some firmer. Heat may also change the color of food and blend its flavors. One example of a science project that involves foods is baking bread. You must follow a process when baking. This process involves:

- reading the recipe
- collecting all the ingredients, pans, and utensils
- measuring and mixing the correct amounts of ingredients
- setting the correct oven temperature
- observing the change in matter
- checking when the bread should be removed

Teachers may also use several other cooking projects. Some teachers prefer to tie

Prostock-studio/Shutterstock.com

Figure 24.18   Making pancakes is a science experience that involves a process and a product.

these experiences to weekly themes or units. For example, teachers may plan a unit on fall, Halloween, or Thanksgiving. Cooking experiences in these themes can focus on pumpkins, squash, apples, or cranberries. Activities could include

- preparing food in different ways (boiling, baking, broiling)
- using many kitchen tools (mixers, food processors, blenders)
- examining the insides of foods (peeling a potato, slicing an apple)
- observing the way foods change during preparation

Figure 24.19 lists foods that can be prepared easily in the center. During cooking experiences, children can learn that food varies in size, shape, feel, smell, and color. Some foods are heavier than others. One way to teach these concepts is to supply children with carrots, celery, apples, bananas, oranges, and pears for snacks. Have them discuss the differences among these foods.

24.3-2 Using Gardening to Teach Science Concepts

The study of gardening helps children understand where food comes from. Seeds can help them build an interest in growing and tending to living things. (**Figure 24.20**). There are four types of seeds including nuts, legumes, cereals, and spices. By five or six years of age, most children can identify common seeds such as watermelon, apple, and peach seeds. Many children do not know they are eating seeds when they eat bananas.

Nuts are seeds inside of a hard shell that come from fruit trees. Few children know that walnuts, pecans, hazelnuts, pistachios, almonds, and cashews are all nuts. Grains are small dried seeds people also eat. Examples of grains include rye, corn, rice, wheat, and oats. Many cereals are made from these grains. Cereal grains are also ground into flour and used for baking bread and other products. Some spices that flavor foods

Foods Children Can Prepare

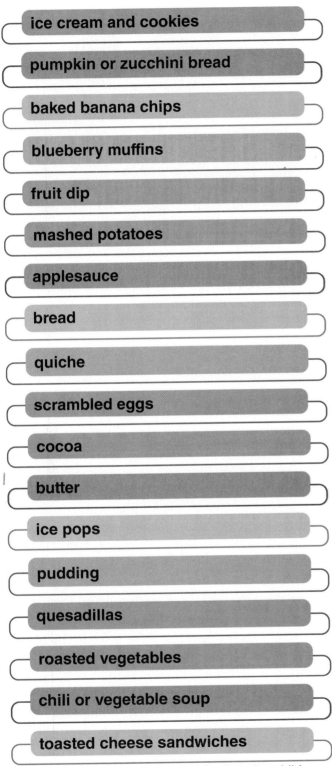

- ice cream and cookies
- pumpkin or zucchini bread
- baked banana chips
- blueberry muffins
- fruit dip
- mashed potatoes
- applesauce
- bread
- quiche
- scrambled eggs
- cocoa
- butter
- ice pops
- pudding
- quesadillas
- roasted vegetables
- chili or vegetable soup
- toasted cheese sandwiches

Figure 24.19 Preparing simple foods helps children learn that foods have a variety of characteristics.

Rawpixel.com/Shutterstock.com

Figure 24.20 Gardening can teach children science concepts. *Identify three science concepts children can learn through gardening experiences.*

also originate from seeds. An example is vanilla, which comes from the vanilla bean.

Teaching About Seeds

To teach children about seeds, teachers can introduce science experiments using seeds during snack or lunchtime. Talk about only one type of seed at a time. For example, ask the children, "What color is the orange? What is inside the orange?" Then give each child an orange that you have peeled. Show the children how to pull the orange apart. Encourage the children to look for seeds. Ask questions about orange seeds, such as "How many seeds are there in your orange? Are the seeds the same size? How do the seeds look? How do the seeds feel?" Tell the children to place their seeds on the science table when they are finished eating. Introduce a new type of seed during the next snack time or lunchtime and use the same steps. You can encourage children to compare the seeds from the fresh fruit in terms of size, color, and texture. Place all seeds collected from fresh fruit on the science table.

Children can also learn about seeds by having a seed party. Collect nuts that can be eaten: peanuts, walnuts, pecans, and a coconut. Ask the children to help you crack the seeds and remove the meat. As they sample the meat from each seed, discuss the flavors and talk about which seeds are **subterranean** (underground).

Pumpkin seeds, sunflower seeds, soybean seeds, and mixed nuts may also be used. Roast or sauté some seeds. Ask questions during the roasting process such as, "Which seeds are labeled **nuts**? How does cooking change the taste? How does cooking change the texture?"

Health Highlights

Nut and Seed Allergies

Some children have severe allergies to peanuts, tree nuts, and some seeds. Be sure that you know about all children's health records before you introduce nuts. Some children cannot even sit at a table where nuts are being served without having an allergic reaction. If any children have nut allergies, avoid introducing activities that involve nuts.

Observing Seeds

Children also learn by observing seeds. A nature or seed walk can teach children that seeds come from the fruits of plants. Before leaving on the walk, give each child a paper bag with their name printed on it. You may prefer to wrap a piece of packing tape with the sticky side out on each child's wrist. The children can stick the seeds they discover to the sticky tape. Walk to a park or other area where seeds are plentiful and encourage the children to collect seeds. When the group returns to the classroom, ask each child to choose three seeds to add to the science table. Save the rest of the seeds for an art display.

Place magnifying glasses on the science table next to the seeds. Encourage the children to use the glasses to view the shapes, sizes, colors, and textures of the seeds. This activity should help the children notice the seeds' differences and similarities.

Planting Seeds

Planting seeds indoors and outdoors teaches children concepts about plants and their growth (**Figure 24.21**). Container gardens, dish gardens, vase gardens, bulletin-board gardens, and outdoor gardens are ideal for young children.

Kirin_photo/E+ via Getty Images

Figure 24.21   These children are using a magnifying glass to study the shape, size, color, and texture of plants and seeds. *How might the similarities and differences among the seeds lead to similarities and differences among plants?*

Container Garden

To create a container garden, have children plant bean, corn, carrot, and radish seeds in individual containers. Use paper cups, tuna cans, milk cartons, or clay pots. If possible, use transparent recycled containers so the children can observe root growth below the surface. Write the children's names on the containers and provide soil for the children to use for planting. The best mixture for growth is garden soil or **loam** (a type of soil with ideal amounts of clay, silt, and sand). Both soils supply nutrients for the plant and provide good moisture and drainage control. Have children fill the containers with soil and then let the children choose seeds to plant. Show them how to use their fingers to make holes in the soil. Add the seeds and cover with soil and label each container with the seed name. Using a watering can, show the children how to dampen the soil.

Most seeds will grow when given proper moisture and temperature. When the seedlings emerge from the surface of the soil, place the containers where they will receive sunlight. Encourage the children to check the containers daily. Ask questions such as "What seeds sprouted first? Do all plants have similar leaves? How many leaves does each plant have?" From this experience, the children should learn:

- Seeds planted in soil and given water, warmth, and sunshine will grow.
- Some seeds **germinate** (sprout) earlier than others.
- As plants grow, their sizes and shapes change.
- Many plants droop or die if they do not have water.

Dish Garden

Children can also create dish gardens. Make a dish garden using pineapple, turnip, carrot, or beet tops. First, cut the tops off about one and one-quarter inch below the leaves. Then place the tops in clear, shallow dishes with water and sand. Put the dish on the science table where the children can observe the growth.

Vase Garden

For a vase garden, collect an onion, potato, sweet potato, or avocado pit and a jar large enough to hold the vegetable. Suspend the vegetable on toothpicks (**Figure 24.22**). You may have to add small amounts of water from time to time. As the vegetable sprouts and evaporation takes place, the water level will decrease. Students can observe the roots and stems as they grow.

Bulletin-Board Garden

Plants can also grow in resealable plastic bags. Hang one bag for each child on a bulletin board

Saslistock/iStock via Getty Images Plus
Figure 24.22 Many vegetables grow with little care if suspended this way. *What are some other vegetables you could suspend and grow this way?*

that is decorated like a garden. With help, each child can plant a seed in a bag. Start by folding a paper towel and soaking it. Put the wet towel inside the bag and place a bean seed between the side of the bag and the paper towel. In time, the seed will sprout and its roots will fill the bag.

You can also grow flowers in these bags. Fill the bags with potting soil instead of a paper towel. Add flower seeds. After the seeds sprout, move the plants to indoor pots or an outdoor garden if the weather permits.

Outdoor Garden

When space allows, grow an outdoor garden. The space and the children's ages and interests may influence what you grow. You might grow a flower garden, a simple vegetable garden, or both. Let the children take part in caring for the garden and enjoying its end results.

Figure 24.23 is an example of what children may learn by observing the seeds they plant in a flower garden. You may wish to print the children's comments on a large sheet of paper to document their learning.

24.3-3 Using Animals to Teach Science Concepts

Animals also teach children about science concepts. For example, children can learn how different animals look and feel, what they eat, how they should handle animals, and how animals respond to their environment. Pets can help teach children responsibility, empathy, and respect for all kinds of life.

Maintaining a healthy environment is important. Take care prior to introducing a pet into the classroom. Check your state licensing rules and regulations to see if and what classroom pets they permit. Before bringing an animal into the classroom, a veterinarian needs to check the animal. Written evidence should show the animal is free from disease and proof of any required vaccinations. Keep a copy of the pet's health certificate on file in the director's office.

Teachers must supervise all interactions between children and pets. While animals can

Our Flower Garden: What We Learned from Observing

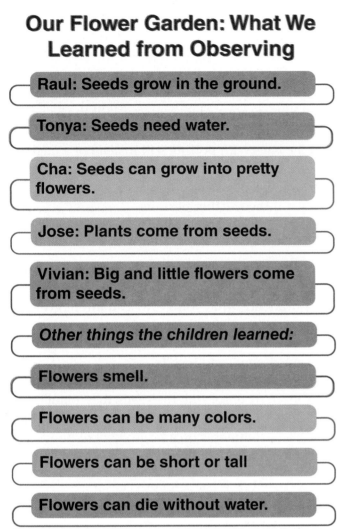

Raul: Seeds grow in the ground.

Tonya: Seeds need water.

Cha: Seeds can grow into pretty flowers.

Jose: Plants come from seeds.

Vivian: Big and little flowers come from seeds.

Other things the children learned:

Flowers smell.

Flowers can be many colors.

Flowers can be short or tall

Flowers can die without water.

Figure 24.23 Children learn many science concepts by observing the seeds they plant in a flower garden.

be educational and entertaining, children can get sick from handling them. Their immune systems are still developing and animals may carry germs such as E. coli and salmonella in their droppings and on their skin. Cats, dogs, and ferrets may carry rabies. Teachers must also prevent exposure to a particular animal for a child who is allergic. Each child's medical record needs to be checked prior to enrollment. If a child has a severe allergy to a pet already in the classroom, the animal will need to be removed.

The Center for Disease Control and Prevention (CDC) recommends the following animals *not* be introduced in a school or early childhood setting:

- amphibians
- apes
- bats
- chickens
- coyotes
- ducks
- foxes
- frogs
- lizards
- monkeys
- raccoons
- reptiles
- skunks
- snakes

Confine animals to a particular classroom area as opposed to roaming freely. The CDC also recommends that you carefully supervise children when handling or interacting with animals to reduce their chance of illness. After handling animals, their habitat, or food, children need to wash their hands with soap and water. To reduce the chance of illness, teachers should always supervise this process.

The staff needs to show the appropriate way for feeding and interacting with classroom pets. The children's behavior needs to be respectful and caring. After observing and comparing animals, children can draw conclusions from their experiences (**Figure 24.24**). Experiences with animals should teach children the following concepts:

Side Show Stock/iStock via Getty Images Plus

Figure 24.24 Having classroom pets gives children a chance to observe, care for, and learn about pets as a part of their daily routine. *What can children learn about pets by nurturing and caring for them?*

- There are many kinds of animals.
- Animals are fun to watch.
- Animals, especially pets, require care.
- Pets depend on humans for proper care.
- There are many kinds of animals; some are small and some are large.
- Animals need water, proper food, water, shelter, exercise, and loving care.
- Animals can be identified by the sounds they make.
- Animals have different body coverings, such as feathers, scales, fur, smooth skin or a shell.
- Animals move in different ways. They may fly, swim, walk, run, crawl, creep, or hop.
- Animals have different numbers and kinds of legs. Some have two legs, some four, some six, some eight, and some have none.
- Animals can be identified by the different sounds they make.

Many animals can be used as classroom pets. Classrooms pets make it easier for children to observe and learn science concepts about animals. Early childhood programs have housed hamsters, snakes, toads, frogs, fish, rabbits, and guinea pigs. Other classroom pets might be a gerbil, mouse, or bird. **Figure 24.25** lists the average life span of some common classroom pets.

Average Life Span of Classroom Pets

Type of Pet	Life Span
Mouse	5 years
Hamster	2½ years
Gerbil	6 years
Guinea pig	6 years
Rabbit	10 years

Figure 24.25 The life span for classroom pets can vary. *Is there a benefit to having classroom pets with shorter life spans versus longer life spans? What are the benefits of each?*

Hamsters

A healthy hamster is chubby and has a shiny coat and bright eyes. The average life expectancy of a hamster is one to two-and-one-half years. Buy hamsters only from pet stores that handle healthy animals. (*Note:* One strain of hamster spreads a form of meningitis.)

Each hamster needs a wire, rustproof cage. Since hamsters can chew through many materials and escape through small holes, a wire cage prevents escape. Make sure the cage has an exercise wheel, and wood shavings spread on the floor for cage litter. Replace the litter daily, and remove uneaten food and soiled bedding, too. You should also place newspaper in the cage for the hamster to shred for nesting. Provide hamsters with nutritious food. You can buy a hamster mix containing cracked corn, seeds, grain, and pellets at a pet store. Because hamsters have two pairs of gnawing teeth, they enjoy chewing pieces of softwoods or dog biscuits. Gnawing helps keep the hamsters' teeth at a healthy length. Hamsters also require fresh water in a special bottle that you can purchase at a pet store. The bottle prevents spilling and ensures that the animal has a constant supply of water (**Figure 24.26**).

Hamsters are **nocturnal** by nature. This means they usually sleep during the day and are awake at night. When awakened and picked up, they may nip. As a result, only allow children under the age of six to observe hamsters. They

Early Childhood Insight

Classroom Animals

All animals brought into the classroom should receive humane care and treatment. Children should always see teachers and care providers handling and caring for animals properly. Try to provide for the basic needs of classroom animals. These needs include food, water, light, air, proper space for movement, and exercise. Before purchasing pets for your classroom, check your state's licensing rules and regulations. Some states do not allow pets in the classroom. Health is the primary reason, since some children are allergic to pet dander.

Shawn_ang/iStock via Getty Images Plus

Figure 24.26 Note the water bottle in this gerbil's cage. It can be used for hamsters and rabbits, too.

should not handle them. Even children over six years of age need teacher supervision when handling a hamster.

Fish

Fish are ideal pets for some teachers because they require less attention than most other pets. If you would like fish as classroom pets, you will need to decide whether to buy tropical or freshwater fish. Freshwater fish are less costly and have easier care requirements. You can keep the fish in a fishbowl rather than in an aquarium.

An aquarium is a requirement for tropical fish. Most teachers prefer 20-gallon aquariums since they are easier to maintain than smaller tanks and children can see the fish more easily. Maintain a water temperature between 70°F and 80°F at all times. To ensure this range, purchase a thermometer and a self-regulating aquarium heater.

The water will need to be changed to remove organic wastes. A water change will remove odors, improve water clarity, and increase the amount of oxygen. Speak with salespeople at your local pet store to get details on properly setting up and maintaining the aquarium.

Set the tank on a sturdy table away from sunlight. Then fill the tank with water and allow it to settle. There should be a half gallon of water for every inch of fish in the aquarium. Wait one week for the water to reach the correct temperature and pH balance. Then add the fish.

Talk to the salespeople at your pet store to find out exactly what, how much, and how often you should feed your freshwater or tropical fish. They probably will recommend fish food and/or brine shrimp.

Rabbits

Rabbits are sociable, intelligent, and affectionate. When called, they come. They can be trained to use a litter box. Not all teachers enjoy having a rabbit indoors, however, because rabbits are messy and their cages require cleaning more often.

Keep rabbits in large wire cages that allow plenty of room for movement. For shelter, place a wooden box at one end of the cage. Wood shavings or straw should cover the bottom of the cage for bedding.

Always place rabbit cages indoors. Traditionally, some early childhood programs have introduced an outdoor hutch for their pet rabbit. This forces the animal into social isolation. A predator or vandal can harm the rabbit or cause it to have a heart attack.

Because rabbits are hearty eaters, they require large amounts of food and water. You can buy rabbit feed at a pet store. Rabbits also eat leafy vegetables, including lettuce, cabbage, and celery tops. You may wish to omit cabbage and other strong-smelling vegetables from their diet to control the unpleasant odor of strong-smelling urine.

Exercise caution when handling a rabbit. Rabbits have sharp toenails and may scratch to protect themselves if they are afraid. Dropping a rabbit accidentally may cause a broken back and legs. Therefore, it is important to teach the children how to safely handle a rabbit.

Guinea Pigs

Most early childhood teachers agree guinea pigs make good pets for young children (**Figure 24.27**). They are easy to handle and rarely bite. Also, guinea pigs are very gentle and enjoy having children hold and cuddle them. Even very young children can easily observe, care for, and handle guinea pigs. These pets have heavy bodies

Pavel L Photo and Video/Shutterstock.com

Figure 24.27 Guinea pigs have always been a favorite pet of young children and their teachers.

and tight skins; they can be easy to pick up by placing a hand under the pig's body.

Wire cages provide good housing for these animals, although the floor of the cage must be flat. Unlike other animals, guinea pigs cannot walk on wire flooring. recommendations for cage sizes are about two and one-half to three feet in length, one and one-half feet deep, and one and one-half feet wide. Doors on cages need to fit tightly to prevent the animals from escaping. Include spaces to hide, exercise, and sleep. Place a small cardboard box inside the cage for sleeping.

Food for a guinea pig is like that for rabbits. Guinea pigs enjoy pellets or grains, including corn, wheat, and oats. Add grass, alfalfa, clover, and carrots for variety. Most teachers who have guinea pigs for classroom pets recommend pellets as the most convenient type of food. Pellets should include vitamin C, which is very important to the guinea pig's diet.

Lesson 24.3 Review

1. Which of the following is *not* part of the baking process when teaching science concepts? (24.3.1)
   A. Setting the correct oven temperature
   B. Reading the recipe
   C. Observing the change in matter
   D. Cleaning the oven
2. Each of the following is a seed *except* _____. (24.3.2)
   A. bananas
   B. tomatoes
   C. nuts
   D. wheat
3. _____ is the term for when seeds sprout. (24.3.2)
   A. Germinate
   B. Pollinate
   C. Grow
   D. Photosynthesis
4. Which animal does the CDC *not* recommend be introduced in the classroom? (24.3.3)
   A. Fish
   B. Guinea pig
   C. Frog
   D. Mouse

Summary

Lesson 24.1

24.1-1 Science is a way of thinking that focuses on understanding how and why things happen, while technology is a way of *doing* and focuses on using tools to make things happen, identifying problems, and making things work.

24.1-1 Studying science inspires children to be aware of and involved with their surroundings.

24.1-3 Young children are natural scientists who can be introduced to science and technology through simple, hands-on experiences.

24.1-3 To teach science and technology, teachers must know the equipment and material that promote the development of science concepts.

24.1-4 Technology can be successfully integrated into all classroom and curriculum areas. A technology area can be placed in a low-traffic area of the classroom.

24.1-4 Young children's social, cognitive, literacy, language, and math skills are promoted using technology in the classroom.

Lesson 24.2

24.2-1 Teaching basic science concepts to young children is best done using the senses—feeling, smelling, hearing, and tasting. A classroom's science center can incorporate senses with activities and supplies that stimulate each of the senses.

24.2-2 Teachers can bring the science of color into daily curriculum through the science center, art projects, and meal times by emphasizing a specific primary or secondary color and mixing colors using different media.

24.2-3 Water tables, bubbles, kites, and outdoor activities can all be effective hands-on ways for teaching about the elements. Engineering concepts can be incorporated into the classroom using magnets and wheels, while using growth

charts teaches young children about their own and others' growth and development.

24.2-4 Field trips and guided walks provide opportunities for young children to explore and observe the science concepts taught in the classroom.

Lesson 24.3

24.3-1 Teachers can use foods in many ways to teach science concepts, including cooking projects, edible experiments, heating and freezing, and comparing food items.

24.3-2 Studying gardening establishes an awareness of how food is grown. Teachers can do many science experiments using seeds such as comparing and identifying different types of seeds. Planting and cultivating a garden allow young children to observe how plants grow.

24.3-3 When animals are incorporated into the classroom teaching, children can learn how different animals look and feel, what they eat, how they should handle animals, and how animals respond to their environment.

24.3-4 Classroom pets can help teach children responsibility, empathy, and respect for all kinds of life. Teachers must take care in choosing classroom pets and be mindful of children's allergies or any state licensing requirements. A classroom pet requires the proper care and supplies and a designated area within the classroom.

Vocabulary Activity

Read the text passages that contain each Key Terms. Then write the definitions of each term in your own words. Double-check your definitions by rereading the text and using the text glossary.

Critical Thinking

1. **Analyze.** Research manufacturers or stores for children's science and technology equipment. All

equipment and supplies should be appropriate for a preschool, early learning, or Head Start classroom. Choose five pieces of equipment and write a brief description about the concepts children would learn from using the items. How could a teacher reinforce this learning? How could learning be assessed?

2. **Evaluate.** Research and list at least 10 software games intended for children between three and five years of age. For each game, note how educational it claims to be. Play the games with several children and then evaluate each game's effectiveness. What were the children's reactions to the game? Could the game be improved?

3. **Draw Conclusions.** Imagine that a parent at your preschool center recently donated five digital cameras and two video and audio recorders. In small groups, create a plan for how these new devices will be integrated into the curriculum and used effectively. Draw conclusions about how you would incorporate them, teach children to use them, and explain to the parent how they are being used.

4. **Create.** Create a lesson plan that promotes the development of preschoolers' science and technology skills. If possible, implement the lesson plan in an early childhood education classroom and assess its effectiveness.

5. **Analyze.** Contact a science teacher in your school or community and ask about science lessons he or she thinks would be suitable for preschoolers. After obtaining this list, analyze ways to adapt each lesson to the correct developmental level. What steps would you have to include or expand? What equipment and materials would you need to take out of the lesson? Explain your reasoning.

Core Skills

1. **Technology and Speaking.** Based on the guidelines in this chapter, use graphics-editing software to draw a digital sketch of a science and a technology area as you would design them. In your drawing, include equipment and where it would be placed. Present your drawing to the class and ask for feedback.

2. **Science.** Ask a physics instructor to help you adapt a lesson about the physics of wheels for your preschool program. Many physics classes test movement theories with wheeled projects, such as a mousetrap car. Preschoolers may be interested in seeing these wheeled projects work. Choose one idea the physics instructor provides and adapt it into a lesson plan for preschoolers.

3. **Social Studies.** Survey local school science labs about whether they would welcome a visit from the preschoolers in your program. Of the labs that respond, choose one for a field trip. Make a list of the objects and equipment children might observe in the labs. What concepts could be taught? Enlist the support of instructors in chaperoning the children. After the field trip, be sure to discuss with the children what they learned.

4. **Research.** Research your state's rules and licensing restrictions relating to having animals in the classroom. What types of animals are allowed? Contact area preschools, child care centers, Head Start programs, prekindergarten, and early learning programs to discover if they have classroom pets. If they have pets, who cares for the pets during weekends and vacation periods? Discuss your findings in class.

5. **Research and Writing.** Research the difference between a therapy animal and a service animal. How are therapy animals trained and certified? What is the science behind therapy animals' positive effects on children? What science concepts could children learn after exposure to a therapy animal? Write a report of your findings.

6. **Research.** Review the CDC's Kidtastic podcast, "Wash Your Hands if You Pet a Bunny." Was the content meaningful for preschool children? Explain.

7. **CTE Career Readiness Practice.** Imagine you were hired as a consultant to design a technology curriculum for a preschool classroom. On further inquiry, you discover that the preschool wants technology to be integrated into every curriculum area. Draft a plan outlining how you would suggest they incorporate technology. Justify your plan with information about how the technology will reinforce important concepts. Prepare a four-minute pitch for the director and classroom teachers to gain their support for your plan.

Portfolio Project

Write a brief essay to explain your understanding of the value of teaching science concepts through the use of food. How can food activities help children meet the overall goals of a program? How can food activities be used to teach children good nutrition principles? What general and specific science concepts can children experience through their hands-on participation in food activities? Share your essay with the class and save a copy in your portfolio.

Chapter 25

Reading Advantage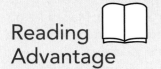

Predict what you think will be covered in this chapter. Make a list of your predictions. After reading the chapter, decide if your predictions were correct.

Guiding Social Studies Experiences

Lesson 25.1: Developing the Social Studies Curriculum

Lesson 25.2: Implementing the Social Studies Curriculum

Case Study

Helping Children Develop Social Competence

Today is Amelia's "All About You Day" celebration. When she arrived at her classroom, she saw a beautiful celebration poster that her teacher had created and positioned so everyone entering the classroom could see. It read, "Amelia's All About You Day." Posted on the chart were photographs of Amelia happily engaged in everything she loved to do in the classroom: looking at books, playing with her friends, engaging in science experiments, building with table blocks, assisting in preparing snacks, singing with her classmates, creating art, and writing. With a smile and look of satisfaction on her face, Amelia looked up and, one by one, admired each photograph. Then she looked up at her mom and said, "That is all about me. Ms. Smith always lets us take this home. We can show our family."

Celebrating each child's day was an essential part of the social studies curriculum for Ms. Williams. She had purchased a wooden children's chair from a secondhand store, colorfully painted it, and stenciled the words "Celebration Chair" on the back. On a child's special day, they get to use the beautiful chair. Ms. Smith also creates and decorates a crown for each child with their name on it, which they joyfully take home at the end of the day.

Ms. Williams believes in a language-rich environment focused on likenesses instead of differences for promoting social studies concepts. Her strategy is to create a community where everyone learns from others. So today was Amelia's day to share the items she brought from home at morning meeting time. As she shared photographs from home, she talked about how her family celebrated different events. After sharing the photos, she said, "I have something special." Removing a piñata from a huge bag, she said, "This is a piñata. We hang one on a tree for celebrations. My mom places a scarf over our eyes so we cannot see. We take turns. If it is your special day, you go first. They give you a big stick. You try to hit the piñata hard. If it breaks, candy comes out. We share. Everyone gets some." Then Ms. Williams said, "Children, Amelia's mother said we should hang this piñata outside and break it open. Let's go outside and see if we can open it."

Give It Some Thought

1. Do you like the way Ms. Williams handles celebrations? Why or why not?
2. Why are social studies experiences essential for young children's development?
3. What should be the teacher's role in designing and guiding social studies?
4. Why do teachers like to include morning meetings? What topics should they include?
5. What is the role of the teacher in promoting the development of friendships?
6. How can multicultural books and activities promote children's social development?

Developing the Social Studies Curriculum

Essential Question

What do you need to know about social studies to develop a successful social studies curriculum?

Learning Outcomes

After studying this lesson, you will be able to

25.1-1 **summarize** the importance of social studies experiences.

25.1-2 **outline** the role of the teacher in designing and guiding social studies experiences.

Key Terms

social studies	voluntarily
social development	antibias curriculum
emotional intelligence	incidental learnings

Young children approach classroom life eagerly and positively. They are interested in everything that goes on and are always full of questions. Many young children's questions are about their world, including the people they know, the words they hear, and the places they have been. For instance, they might ask:

- Where is Wyoming?
- How does the police officer help me?
- Why doesn't that child have a daddy?
- What is Passover?

Many of these questions arise naturally during daily classroom activities. Children's questions might relate to social skills, cultures, families, careers, holidays, current events, history, or geography. These questions all revolve around *social studies* as a curriculum area.

The field of **social studies** includes subject matter that helps children learn about themselves as well as other people. Social studies share life's lessons. It does not focus on one topic or subject. Children learn about families, peers, and people in the community. In addition, they learn positive group-living skills, such as cooperation and responsibility (**Figure 25.1**). They also learn kindness, morality, forgiveness, friendship, and how to live in a democratic society and tolerate differences. These skills are necessary for a child's success in school and life.

Young children build social studies concepts as they explore the world around them. Children may learn key social studies concepts when they walk around the neighborhood; look at many types of housing; or role-play doctors, mail carriers, grocers, or parents. The processes of making and eating cultural foods, hearing a story about community helpers, or taking part in tasks for maintaining the classroom may also

FatCamera/E+ via Getty Images

Figure 25.1 Through social studies experiences, children learn to accept themselves and get along with others. *How do children build social studies concepts through the world around them?*

promote understanding of social studies concepts. Watering flowers, feeding classroom pets, and putting blocks away teaches children about the core of social studies concepts, which focuses on getting along in one's world.

25.1-1 Importance of Social Studies

Children need to understand and appreciate how other people live, including other people's lifestyles, languages, and viewpoints. Social studies helps children gain skills for living. They learn social and emotional literacy skills. **Social development** is the ability to make friends with others, cooperate, and resolve conflict. **Emotional intelligence** is the ability to understand your own emotions and recognize their causes, listen to others, and express emotions positively. Social-emotional intelligence is the ability to control impulses, identify and label feelings, manage stress, ability to wait, relate to the feelings of others, and resolve conflicts. By learning social studies concepts, children will:

- develop self-respect, positive identity, and family pride
- develop respect for and listen to others
- develop an understanding of their own emotions and express emotions positively
- develop self-control and independence
- learn to share ideas and materials, negotiate, and compromise with others (**Figure 25.2**)
- learn skills for developing friendships
- develop healthy ways of relating to and working with others
- develop a positive racial identity and build relationships across races
- develop skills for self-management in a group
- gain the attitudes, knowledge, and skills needed for living in a democracy
- develop respect for other people's feelings, ideas, cultures, and property
- learn about the roles people have in life
- learn to appreciate the past and its relationship to the present

Pressmaster/Shutterstock.com

Figure 25.2 Children can learn about developing friendships through social studies concepts in the curriculum. *How can social studies help children develop respect for others?*

- learn the purposes of rules and learn to follow them **voluntarily** (by one's own will)

The primary value of the social studies curriculum is that it enables children to better understand their world, their place in it, and ways to respect the rights of others. Studies show that strong social-emotional development is a foundation for all later growth and development.

25.1-2 The Teacher's Role in Social Studies

The key to a good social studies program is your skill as a teacher. Exposure to positive teachers impacts a child's development. For all children to feel respected and safe, early childhood teachers need to be socially and emotionally competent. Your image of each child should be someone you see as capable. Show them you see and value them. Model patience, love, kindness, friendship, compassion, respect, fairness, and tolerance of others.

Your goal is to have the children develop resiliency and become socially and emotionally strong. To accomplish this, you will need to teach them to think highly of their heritage and culture. Develop a nurturing relationship with each child and among children. It is important to be observant and available to step in and guide the children.

Your interests will determine the degree to which you will include social studies in the curriculum. Through your education, you will understand the need to use community resources, the teachable moments, themes, group participation, observations, and evaluations to enrich social studies concepts.

To provide quality learning experiences, you will need to make daily observations. These routine checks should provide data showing the children's strengths, interests, abilities, attitudes, and knowledge. From this data, you can determine what children need to know and what behaviors need to change, which will help you develop the curriculum.

Determine the Children's Needs, Interests, Abilities, and Experiences

Every group of children brings a wide variety of interests to the classroom. Some children may be interested in airplanes, trains, or geography. Other children may prefer to study community helpers. To determine children's interests, you can:

- observe the children during play, noting their use of material, equipment, and types of play that stimulates their interests and relates to their strengths, and abilities (**Figure 25.3**)
- interact with the children casually, asking them what they enjoy
- ask the children's parents or guardians to share their children's interests with you
- observe the children's choices of books

As with interests, the skills of every group of children should influence the social studies program. In any classroom, there will be many levels of cognitive, physical, social, and emotional development. As a teacher of young children, you will need to match materials and equipment with each child's ability level. You can determine children's ability levels by:

- observing children's social skills as they play with other children

Nikos Vlasiadis/Shutterstock.com

Figure 25.3   Children learn about the roles people have in life.

- reviewing the children's developmental and health records
- structuring a variety of tasks for children to complete, noting their success
- discussing the children's interests with parents or guardians

There is no shortcut for gathering data to determine children's skill levels. Gathering data is an intentional process that takes time. This information, however, is essential for planning a developmentally appropriate social studies curriculum.

Develop the Curriculum

Once you identify the children's strengths, needs, interests, abilities, and experiences, you are ready to plan the curriculum. The traits and developmental experiences of the children will influence how you design and implement your curriculum. These traits can be observed and used as a starting point for planning social studies activities. **Figure 25.4** lists these characteristics and their implementations. As you develop a social studies curriculum, you should consider involving children in planning, using themes, exploring community resources, inviting resource people, and promoting incidental teachings.

The curriculum needs to have an **antibias** focus. The curriculum emphasis needs to have

Activities Related to Children's Characteristics

Characteristics	Implementations
Interest centered on immediate environment	Provide opportunities to explore the center or school play yard and neighborhood.
Enjoys opportunities for self-expression	Provide small group opportunities whenever possible.
Shows interest in people with whom he or she is acquainted	Include resource people with whom the children have indicated an interest.
Learns best through direct experiences	Provide concrete materials and hands-on activities.
Enjoys pretending	Provide opportunities and props for dramatic play.
Tends to be egocentric (self-centered: *I* or *me*)	Provide consistent modeling and verbal guidance in respecting others' rights and following rules.

Figure 25.4 Developing activities based on children's needs, interests, abilities, and experiences is essential for an effective social studies curriculum. *How can children benefit from involvement in planning the curriculum?*

a many-culture approach, honoring diversity by teaching children about respect. An antibias curriculum embraces differences and acts on unfairness and bias. Provide gender-neutral play spaces. These spaces will allow children to engage in roles or materials without gender expectations. The goal is to have every child develop self-respect and a group identity, which will help them achieve their fullest potential.

Involve Children in Planning

Encourage children to take part in curriculum planning. This process will help them organize their thoughts, express their ideas, and experience the results. During the planning process, allow children to make important choices and involve all children in the group. You may find that some children are shy and may feel better if given a chance to plan individually or in a small group.

Young children can plan the following aspects of their activities:

- whom to play with
- materials needed for an activity or project
- places to visit
- people to invite to the classroom
- how to celebrate birthdays, holidays, celebrations, and other classroom events

Workplace Connections

Investigating Social Studies Curriculums

Contact local preschools and early childhood learning centers to learn about the role that social studies play in their curriculums. Find out if social studies is formally taught as a separate curriculum area, or if teachers integrate it with other curricular areas and daily routines.

1. What materials or equipment are used to promote the understanding of social studies concepts?
2. What are the most popular and most successful social studies themes used at the different programs?

Use Themes

Many teachers use themes when planning a social studies program (**Figure 25.5**). Social studies can help integrate learning opportunities from many unfamiliar concepts and subjects. While social studies typically does not occur at a particular time each day, a variety of daily experiences will help children learn these concepts.

Explore Community Resources

Community resources can play a large part in teaching children social studies concepts. Look closely at your community resources for a variety of learning opportunities. Record the

MintImages/Shutterstock.com

Figure 25.5 A pet theme can be the basis for teaching many social studies concepts.

names of stores, museums, art galleries, theaters, community services, community workers, and housing groups that may be of interest. The people providing these services might also have suggestions for curriculum objectives and goals.

Promote Incidental Learnings

When developing a social studies curriculum, structure the classroom to promote **incidental learnings**. The word *incidental* suggests these experiences are unplanned. Incidental learnings are learning experiences that happen during a normal day. Watch for everyday happenings that can teach children a concept. For example, you could point out paint that has dried out when the can's lid was left off or plants whose leaves were yellow for lack of watering. These situations cause children to question and learn on their own.

Every classroom has unique incidental learning experiences. These learning experiences can result from:

- classroom and playground repairs
- classroom rules
- school workers such as custodians, bus drivers, or office workers
- handling an argument
- happenings in the local community

Evaluate the Curriculum

Evaluation is a key part of a social studies curriculum. The evaluation process will help you identify what goals have been met, what new goals should be introduced, and whether any current goals require modification. The children can take part in this process. For example, you may ask them the following open-ended questions:

- What did you like best?
- Why did you like it?
- What did you learn?
- What do you want to learn more about?
- What would you like to do again?
- Why would you like to do that activity again?

Lesson 25.1 Review

1. The field of _____ includes subject matter that helps children learn about themselves as well as other people. (25.1.1)
   - A. mathematics
   - B. multiculturalism
   - C. social studies
   - D. community

2. **True or False.** Studies show that strong social-emotional development is a foundation for all later growth and development. (25.1.1)

3. A(n) _____ curriculum embraces differences and acts on unfairness and bias. (25.1.2)
   - A. antibias
   - B. democratic
   - C. intergenerational
   - D. ecological

4. _____ are learning experiences that happen during a normal day. (25.1.2)
   - A. Social studies
   - B. Curriculum
   - C. Community resources
   - D. Incidental learnings

Implementing the Social Studies Curriculum

Essential Question

What do you need to know about social studies concepts to create and implement an effective social studies curriculum?

Learning Outcomes

After studying this lesson, you will be able to

25.2-1 analyze ways to include multicultural and intergenerational studies, democracy, ecology, change, gender-neutrality, community living, current events, celebration concepts, and friendships in the curriculum.

25.2-2 explain the importance of morning meetings.

Key Terms

perception	morning meeting
cultural identity	ecology
self-identity	gender-neutral
omission	self-regulation
gerontology	

Implementing a social studies curriculum is more complex than ever before in history. The United States is becoming more diverse—culturally, linguistically, ethnically, and racially. Some children speak multiple languages, while others speak one. Some children have identified disabilities, while others are highly gifted. As a result, helping young children to build social studies concepts is extremely complex. To be effective, teachers must commit to becoming lifelong learners and develop the habit of reflecting on their practices.

A classroom learning environment and community of learners that operate fairly and equally allows every child to experience success and a sense of belonging. Children need teachers who can implement a strength-based approach to curriculum. Their teachers also need to affirm their racial, cultural, and linguistic backgrounds while building social studies concepts.

25.2-1 Building Social Studies Concepts

Young children want to find out about their world. They touch, taste, smell, see, and hear to learn. They form perceptions from such activities. **Perceptions** are ideas formed about a relationship or object resulting from what a child learns through their senses. Repeated experiences form a set of perceptions, which give rise to concept formation. For instance, if a young child sees a black-and-white cow, the child may later call a black-and-white dog a cow. Given proper feedback, the child will learn the difference between a dog and a cow.

Concepts are building blocks. They help children to organize, group, and order experiences and to make sense of the world. Once learned, concepts help children communicate with each other. Children with well-formed language skills form useful concepts.

Personality, experiences, language skills, health, emotions, and social relationships all affect the formation of accurate concepts. A variety of experiences help form more in-depth concepts, and the feelings and emotions surrounding them affect all these experiences. Therefore, by having contact with others, children learn to view other people's ways of thinking.

Social studies activities help form many concepts. These include multicultural concepts, intergenerational concepts, democracy, ecology, change concepts, geography, community living, current events, holiday concepts, and friendship concepts.

Multicultural Concepts

Social scientists use the word *culture* to describe all the aspects of people's lives. This includes a group's ideas and ways of doing things: traditions, language, beliefs, and customs. It is what people do every day. Culture is a learned pattern of social behavior. Studies show that children typically are aware of their own **cultural identity**—or feeling of belonging to a group—around four years of age.

A child's culture is a lens through which the child judges the world. Culture influences feelings, thoughts, behavior, and affects the way children grow and learn. Culture imposes order and meaning on all experiences. A child's culture impacts their **self-identity,** which is whom they believe themselves to be. Culture affects children's lifestyles and eating habits. Culture often becomes inseparable from a person's way of living and thinking. As a result, children may not realize that their behaviors differ from those learned in other cultures.

A multicultural perspective is extremely important in planning a social studies curriculum. Studies show that children's attitudes toward their own identities and other cultural groups begin to form. They are aware of skin color early in life.

When planning a *multicultural curriculum,* a teacher's goal is to help each child develop:

- respect for oneself as a worthwhile and competent human being
- acceptance and respect for others' similarities and differences
- an appreciation of the child's own culture and ethnicity
- the skill to interact positively with all people
- an understanding that there are many ways to do things

You can meet these goals by involving parents or guardians. They can help by providing family background information, planning appropriate activities, and selecting related learning materials, including books like those listed in **Figure 25.6**. Your behaviors will also influence the success of your social studies curriculum. You can strengthen the multicultural concepts

Multicultural Books for Promoting Social Studies Concepts

- *When Lola Visits* by Michelle Sterling (author) and Aaron Asis (art)
- *Happiness* by Mariahadessa Ekere Tallie (author) and Ashleigh Corrin (illustrator)
- *The Joyful Nook* by Todd Parr
- *Mama Panya's Pancakes: A Village Tale from Kenya* by Mary and Richard Chamberlin (authors) and Julia Cairns (illustrator)
- *Jamal's Journey* (Middle East) by Michael Forman
- *Fiesta!* by Ginger Foglesong Guy
- *Families* by Shelly Rotner and Sheila M. Kelly (authors)
- *Home* by Carson Ellis
- *The Wooden Camel* (Kenya) by Wanuri Kahiu (author) and Manuela Adreani (illustrator)

- *The Smile Shop* by Satoshi Kitamura
- *Pino and the Signora's Pasta* by Janet Pedersen
- *Little Red Ruthie: A Hanukkah Tale* by Gloria Koster (author) and Sue Eastland (illustrator)
- *Sunny* by Celia Krampien
- *The Five Forms* (China) by Barbara McClintock
- *The Story of Little Babaji* (India) by Helen Bannerman (author) Fred Marcellino (illustrator)
- *My First Ramadan* by Karen Katz
- *In a Village by the Sea* by Muon Van (author) and April Chu (illustrator)
- *The Wheels on Tuk Tuk* by Kabir Sehgal and Surishtha Sehgal (authors) and Jess Golden (illustrator)

Figure 25.6   Choose books carefully to meet the multicultural needs of the children in your classroom. *How can involving families in choosing books, equipment, and other classroom materials benefit children?*

taught in the classroom by involving children's families, selecting and preparing appropriate materials, and planning activities to encourage a multicultural perspective.

When selecting children's literature for the classroom, exercise caution. Always base your selection on quality and complement the existing books in the classroom library. To capture the children's curiosity, there needs to be a good storyline. Then ask yourself, "Can the children see themselves in the story?" Books for supporting the social studies curriculum should help the children see themselves. The books should mirror different facets of their identity such as context, race, culture, and experiences. In addition, books should introduce children to new things, places, people, and experiences.

Involving the Family

Family can play a key role in meeting multicultural goals for children. As a teacher, study the cultural background of each child. Parents, guardians, or other family members are the best resources for this task. They can provide you with information on their culture's parenting beliefs and practices. Meeting and talking with parents can provide knowledge of the family and their needs, customs, concerns, and hopes. Parents can also share their heritage by taking part in classroom activities. They can share stories, games, songs, dances, foods, and holiday observances related to their culture (**Figure 25.7**).

Selecting and Preparing Materials

Select materials that reflect the cultural heritage and backgrounds of all children. The following are items useful for reaching this goal: cooking utensils; flags; weavings; traditional games; and ethnically diverse children's books, musical recordings, pictures, and videos.

Teachers should examine materials for their appropriateness in teaching social studies concepts. Note biases if they exist in any materials. Then, develop teaching strategies to overcome the bias.

Be sure to watch for stereotyping when selecting materials for classroom use.

Figure 25.7 The children's cultural backgrounds can be shared in the classroom. *How can parents share their cultural heritage by participating in classroom experiences?*

Stereotyping ignores individual differences. Take care when choosing games, books, puzzles, videos, classroom decorations, and visual aids.

An omission is another bias found in some teaching materials. **Omission** implies that some groups have less value than other groups in society. Excluding a group's cultural presence in teaching materials is an example of omission. All groups must be included and respected. To build self-esteem in children, share with them positive role models from all cultural backgrounds.

Health Highlights

Communicating in Native Language

Oftentimes, children or their parents speak a language other than English. An early childhood facility should have at least one staff member who can communicate with children and their parents in their native language. This helps parents and their children feel included and can help avoid miscommunication about issues such as children's health needs. If no staff members speak a family's native language, work with the parents to find a translator to help express their needs.

Planning Activities to Encourage a Multicultural Perspective

Studies show that children are more likely to focus on differences than on similarities among people. As a result, focus on people's similarities. In the curriculum, include activities that show how all people have similar ways of living within a family or other social group. Emphasize that all people have similar needs, including food, clothing, and shelter. Language, art, and music are ways of expressing various attitudes, feelings, ideas, and knowledge.

Plan special activities that focus on similarities. For example, schedule a "special day" for a particular child. During group time, the child may share his or her favorite toy, food, or color. Ask each child to bring in family photographs and use these photos to observe similarities. Cooking and eating a variety of cultural foods is another way of stressing multicultural concepts. Consider celebrating a "Cultural Day." Encourage the children to wear clothing, showing their family's culture. Serve traditional foods for lunch and snack.

Intergenerational Concepts

Young children's concepts of older adults are not always positive. A teacher asked a group of preschool children about older adults and growing older. Their comments included:

- "Well, they sure have a lot of extra skin."
- "My grandpa fixes my bike."
- "They walk slow and have to sit a lot."
- "They're sick."
- "You get bald if you are old."
- "They help you make cookies."
- "They can't hear well."
- "They talk loud."

Such responses show the need to include intergenerational concepts in the early childhood curriculum.

The number of older adults in American society is steadily growing. With this growth, there is a need to inform all people about the benefits of aging, as well as the problems older adults may face. Negative stereotyping is one of the greatest

problems facing older adults. These views about growing older have also been noted by children.

Studies show children form attitudes early in life. These feelings and thoughts remain a potent force in a person's life. Children's attitudes toward older adults are based on their families' views. Lack of knowledge may cause negative stereotyping of older adults. Another reason may be the lack of contact with older people. For many children, their only contact with older adults is with their grandparents. Young children need to learn from and about a variety of older adults for these attitudes to expand.

Including intergenerational concepts in the program can encourage children to view older adults more positively. The goals for such a program are listed in **Figure 25.8**. Interactions with older people should be included. Books, videos, and pictures used in the classroom should all portray older people without bias. These materials should show the varied interests, abilities, mobility, and health of older adults.

Involving Older Adults in the Classroom

Early childhood teachers can invite older adults to take part in the classroom. For example, older adults may help with projects, work with children who need special attention, read stories, or direct small groups of children. The roles taken by older adults depend on the needs of the teacher, children, and the older person. Intergenerational contacts can benefit both the young and old. Contact with older adults will affect the formation of positive concepts about them.

Intergenerational programs that focus on developing positive concepts of older adults must consider the needs of older people. Like other programs using volunteers, successful programs require careful planning. Consider the following guidelines:

- Ensure that each older adult has a definite role to play in the classroom.
- View each older person as an individual, using his or her special talents, interests, and training.
- Maintain close communications between the administration, teachers, and the older volunteer.

Goals for an Intergenerational Curriculum

- Encourage social integration of the young and old.
- Increase awareness that older adults vary in health, abilities, mobility, and interests.
- Challenge the stereotypes of older adults as being inactive, unhappy, incapable, or immobile.
- View the actions and traits of older adults in a wide variety of roles.
- Develop an appreciation of others' points of view.
- Promote growth of healthy, positive attitudes toward aging.
- Promote healthy development of self-concept to reduce the fear of growing older.
- Provide opportunities to learn how all people, including themselves, change as they move through the life cycle.

Rus Limon/Shutterstock.com; Goodheart-Willcox Publisher

Figure 25.8 Building relationships with older adults benefits children and older adults. *How can intergenerational concepts and activities help children view older adults positively?*

- Design and provide training and sharing opportunities for the older person.

Intergenerational programs benefit adults and children. Both often enjoy the growth of caring relationships. Adults have the chance to observe children's interests as they share their special talents with them. The children gain an understanding of and appreciation for older adults. In some cases, children are living with or being raised by their grandparents. Recommended books to the classroom library include

- *The Truth about Grandparents* by Elina Ellis
- *Thank You Omu!* by Oge Mora
- *Stand Tall, Molly Lou Melton* by Patty Lovell and David Catrow
- *Our Favorite Day* by Joowon Oh
- *Julian Is a Mermaid* by Jessica Love

Selecting and Preparing Materials

There are increasing numbers of resources for teaching **gerontology** (the study of older adults) to young children. Use care when choosing them. Books and other materials

Safety First

Safety Requirements for Intergenerational Care

As with separate child and adult care facilities, licensing and regulations for intergenerational programs sharing the same site must follow local, state, and federal regulations. It is important to note that sometimes the regulations for fire and building safety, immunizations, staff-to-client ratios, and nutritional requirements are not the same for children's programs and adult programs. Most states will require separate licensing for programs sharing the same site.

should depict older adults positively. They should also show pleasing relationships between children and older adults.

If materials are limited, use your imagination to design your own. Cut pictures from magazines or take photographs of active older adults. Then combine several pictures and use them to tell stories. After you tell the story with the pictures, let a child volunteer to retell the story.

Planning Activities for Developing Intergenerational Concepts

The curriculum needs to contain concepts about older adults that will foster positive ideas about them. There are many themes where these concepts can be shared (**Figure 25.9**). For instance, using the theme "Me, Myself, and I" children could focus on their own aging. They could bring pictures of themselves as babies to school. These pictures can serve as a basis for a talk about growth and development. You might also discuss other eventual body changes. Height and weight records could be compared from the beginning of the year to the end. Children could then guess what other changes will occur as they continue to grow. If developmentally appropriate, the children could also make booklets about things they liked to do when they were younger, things they enjoy doing now, and the things they think they might like to do when they are older.

If daily contact is not possible, arrange opportunities for interaction with older adults. Arrange field trips to visit older neighbors or an assisted living facility. You can do seasonal activities, such as singing holiday carols or making May Day baskets. Other classroom activities include having the children use drawings or pictures cut from magazines to form a large collage or mural depicting older adults in positive, active roles (swimming, jogging, skiing, nurturing). Add a caption such as, "It can be fun to be a grandparent" to the collage.

Democracy Concepts

Before age five, children's concepts of living in a democratic society are usually based on the information they receive from the media, home, and center. By this age, children can usually point out the flag and pictures of the president. They may also recognize the national anthem and the Pledge of Allegiance.

To help children learn governmental concepts, design group activities based on the function of a democracy. Engage them in group decision-making. Such activities will help children understand the purposes of rules and laws and the majority rule. (**Figure 25.10**). Some sample activities that help build governmental concepts include:

- When your class gets a new pet, let the children vote on its name.
- During cooking, let the children vote on what type of food to make.

Themes That Can Contain Concepts of Older Adults

People	Places and Activities
• Community Workers	• Celebrations and Holidays
• Families	• Clothes
• Friends	• Crafts
• Grandparents	• Games
• Grandparents' Jobs	• Hobbies
• Helpers	• Homes
• Me, Myself	• Music
• My Favorite Older Person	• Nursery Rhymes
• Neighbors	• Our Town

Figure 25.9   Including themes about older adults helps children view older adults.

UW-Stout Child and Family Study Center

Figure 25.10   This child is learning democracy concepts by voting for a dramatic play area theme. ***What activities help build governmental concepts for children?***

- When a new toy arrives, let the children outline rules for its use.
- Encourage the children to suggest field trips they would like to take.
- Let children plan the sandwiches they will have on a picnic.
- Let the children vote on plans for choosing and naming a new classroom pet.

Ecology Concepts

Ecology is the study of the chain of life. It is the study of organisms, the environment, and how organisms interact with the environment and one another. Ecology focuses on water, land, air, grass, trees, birds, animals, and insects. To develop ecology concepts, children need excellent observation skills. Using these skills, they can build an appreciation of their environment. They can also learn about the interdependency of all life on the planet. Because of these activities, children will develop a social concern for the environment.

Sample activities that focus on ecology include:

- Taking children on a trip around the block and help them appreciate nature. As you walk, point out plants, trees, flowers, gardens, shrubs, and birds.
- Keeping plants and animals in the classroom or the playground (**Figure 25.11**).
- Providing magazines that children may use to cut out pictures they feel are beautiful. Let each child explain the beauty of a picture.
- Making bird feeders and hang them outside a classroom window where the children can observe.
- Building a terrarium in a closed container to represent a model of a forest.
- Setting up a recycling center in the dramatic play area.

Change Concepts

Children need to learn that change is constant and affects their lives. To help children learn this

SUKJAI PHOTO/Shutterstock.com

Figure 25.11   Giving children their own plants helps them learn the importance of caring for the environment.

concept, use nature and the family. Taking part in these experiences will help children learn to accept change.

People are always changing. To help children understand how they have changed, include concepts about changes they have experienced. You might try:

- Showing a video about babies.
- Recording the children's height and weight at the beginning of the year, at midyear, and at the end of the year. Discuss with the children how they have changed.
- Collecting a variety of baby clothes and toys. Place these items on a table where the children can explore them.

Early Childhood Insight

Teaching Change Concepts

By observing nature, children learn to understand the concept of change. Plan a nature walk. During the walk, point out cherry trees budding, leaves turning colors, flowers blossoming, acorns dropping, or fruit ripening. Each of these experiences should help children understand all things change.

Gender Concepts

A teacher's goal should be to create a safe, gender-neutral classroom. **Gender-neutral** means roles not referring to either sex but only to people in general. Young children have constant exposure to gender stereotypes, which they recognize and internalize by two years of age.

Stereotypes can have a strong negative impact on children. To avoid stereotypes, teachers need to reflect on their words and actions. It takes effort and time to change how you think, feel, and talk about gender. A curriculum requires planning and implementation in which children can act outside of traditional gender roles.

Teachers need to train themselves to use gender-neutral language. Instead of using "girls and boys" when talking to the entire class, teachers now use neutral terms, such as *friends, children, everyone, kindergartners,* or *preschoolers.* For example, they can help promote a gender-neutral classroom by selecting storybooks and classroom photographs that counter stereotypes, where females are engineers and doctors and males are chefs and care for infants. Sharing and valuing these books will provide children with a more complex understanding of gender. The following children's books promote gender-neutral concepts:

- *Ada Twist, Scientist* by Andrea Beaty (author) and David Roberts (illustrator)
- *A Fire Engine for Ruthie* by Lesléa Newman (author) and Cyd Moore (illustrator)
- *Annie's Plaid Shirt* by Stacy B. Davids (author) and Rachael Balsaitis (illustrator)
- *Jacob's New Dress* by Sarah and Ian Hoffman (authors) and Chris Case (illustrator)
- *William's Doll* by Charlotte Zolotow (author) and William Pene du Bois (illustrator)

Geography Concepts

Young children are geographers as soon as they become mobile. They explore space, play in water and snow, and dig in the dirt. They note differences in wet and dry sand and begin to form some concepts about the earth.

The earth is home to many people. The relationship of humans to the earth is important for children to understand. They need to learn the earth provides humanity's food, shelter, and raw materials. Since these concepts are quite complex, formal lessons are most often first introduced in elementary school. There are, however, some informal activities to use with younger children (**Figure 25.12**). For instance, you could allow children to dig in a sandbox or a garden area and play in a sandbox with cars, trucks, bulldozers, pails, and shovels. You might also play readiness games that use symbols to prepare children to read maps. Finally, you could design a bulletin board that maps out the neighborhood surrounding the center. Children can study this board and then help "navigate" a field trip through the neighborhood.

Community Living Concepts

During the preschool years, children are becoming more and more aware of the world outside their homes and families. They are ready to explore their communities and to learn about

US-Stout Child and Family Study Center

Figure 25.12   An igloo was constructed by the children using sanitized plastic milk containers.

the people they will meet there. To foster these concepts, explore with children the neighborhood around the center. What buildings and businesses will they find? Who are the people they will meet? What do these people do? How can they help you? Answering these questions with the children will help them develop community living concepts.

Plan field trips to places in your community that provide services for people. These might include the library, museum, police station, fire station, post office, train station, radio or television station, or assisted living facility. Introduce the children to the people who work in these places. Introduce these people as *community helpers* because they help people live together in the community. Police officers, firefighters, postal workers, and librarians are some of the community helpers that might speak with the children.

Also, plan visits to various workplaces in the community so the children can see how people work. There are probably many businesses in a local neighborhood that would interest the children. You might plan to have them visit a grocery store, restaurant, farm, pet store, hair salon, or doctor's office.

You can also invite people in various careers to visit your class and talk about the work they do. They can bring samples of the materials or tools they use in their work. You might invite a dentist, doctor, nurse, teacher, musician, artist, veterinarian, chef, or other workers to visit. These activities will also develop career awareness concepts.

Current Events Concepts

Preschool children are usually unaware of events outside their own environment. Therefore, they need encouragement to share events affecting their own lives. Show-and-tell, sometimes called *Sharing Time*, is one activity that helps children understand current events. Some events children may share include personal achievements, family events, and special celebrations.

Some classrooms develop a current events bulletin board titled *News*. Children can display cards, pictures, invitations, newspaper pictures, drawings, and paintings. Add items such as pictures of the children's classroom activities or field trips.

Celebration Concepts

Almost every culture has celebrations throughout the year, such as holidays. During holiday celebrations, families and friends share excitement and fun as they join to eat, sing, and interact in other meaningful ways. These celebrations teach children about their own culture and other cultures. They provide opportunities for meaningful learning about similarities and differences. These learnings will help children form a sense of cultural identity. For these reasons, celebrations are a key part of your social studies curriculum.

Carefully choose and prepare for celebrations. Classroom celebrations need to connect to and support a child's home experiences. Holidays are personal and highly valued events. Talk with parents or guardians. Let them know you welcome their involvement. Prepare a questionnaire to learn what events parents or guardians would like to have celebrated (or not celebrated) at the center. Ask parents what involvement they would like to have. Family members may have time to share a family recipe, song, dance, tradition, or story from their culture. Be aware that some families may be hesitant to share personal information. **Figure 25.13** shows an example of a family celebration survey.

For each celebration, provide age-appropriate experiences and activities. They should be culturally sensitive and non-stereotyped. Provide hands-on activities to make the experience more meaningful. Teach children the social importance of the holiday. Children will also begin to learn concepts about the continuity of life. They will also learn families have different ways of celebrating.

Remember that children differ in their abilities to understand holiday and celebration concepts. It is difficult to make holidays meaningful and developmentally appropriate for young children because they are based on complex concepts. Two-year-olds do not grasp

Family Celebration Survey

Dear Families:

When planning holiday celebrations, it is important that we support the child's home environment. We want to honor the holidays of all children and encourage your participation. Therefore, it would be helpful if you could respond to the following questions.

A. What does your family celebrate and who is involved?

B. How would you feel if the center introduced celebrations that are not part of your family's traditions?

C. What celebrations do you feel the center should include?

D. What celebrations you prefer the center should exclude?

E. Would you be willing to contribute to the classroom holiday celebrations? If so, how?

(Check those that apply.)
_____ share artifacts
_____ play an instrument
_____ dance
_____ sing
_____ share records
_____ share photographs
_____ share folk art
_____ cook and share recipes with the children
_____ play games
_____ Other:

_____
_____
_____

Parent Name: _____ Date: _____
Telephone number: _____ Email Address: _____

Thank you for your participation.

Figure 25.13   Having families complete a survey about their celebration preferences and customs can help you plan an effective curriculum. *What questions do you think are important to ask parents?*

the concept of a *holiday* but catch the excitement from their caregivers and families. Three-year-olds view holidays in terms of their families' own experiences. They need holiday activities that are accurate, concrete, and related to their home experiences. Four-year-olds begin to understand simple information related to holidays. They can recall celebrations from the previous year. Four-year-olds can also note similarities and differences in celebrations. By five years of age, children understand people celebrate holidays in different ways. They enjoy decorating, preparing food, and celebrating holidays with family and friends.

When introducing celebration concepts, observe some precautions. Avoid introducing a holiday celebration over one week before it occurs; otherwise, the children may get confused. They do not have a well-developed concept of time. Choose celebrations that represent many cultural groups. For instance, you may celebrate more than one Jewish holiday. Consider celebrating

Passover in the spring and Yom Kippur or Rosh Hashanah in the fall. May Day, Three Kings' Day, Juneteenth, Ramadan, Chinese New Year, Diwali, and Kwanzaa are other cultural holidays you might want to celebrate. If you have children in your classroom who have come from other countries, ask what holidays and celebrations they enjoy. Learn to include these in your curriculum, too. Also, consider including a "Special People's Day." Invite parents, guardians, grandparents, uncles, aunts, neighbors, and volunteers to join the celebration.

Consider family diversity when planning Mother's Day and Father's Day. Not all children have a father and mother. As a result, many programs prefer to celebrate *family day* instead. Invite parents or guardians, grandparents, stepparents, siblings, or even aunts or uncles to take part in classroom activities. Likewise, the child could make a picture, card, or gift for any of these people.

Involve the children in your planning for holidays and special events (**Figure 25.14**). Their input may surprise you. Chances are they will suggest special foods, songs, books, or games. They may even suggest inviting special people. You may expand upon their ideas by introducing new foods, customs, fingerplays, songs, and stories.

Holidays are sometimes difficult to plan and implement for young children. Therefore, some teachers plan *classroom celebrations*. These celebrate any milestone a child has achieved. For instance, you can place a bulletin board with the title *Classroom Celebrations* in the classroom. Take a digital photo of the first time a child is successful in tying shoes. Post the photo on the bulletin board with a caption such as "Dallas lost a tooth today." Other examples for photographs include sitting up alone, walking, printing, riding a tricycle, cutting paper, walking a balance beam, zipping a coat, or even helping a friend. Other occasions to celebrate might include birthdays, the birth of a new sibling, or a new child in the program. After you take the picture, you may want to digitally forward it to the parent(s).

Sverre Haugland/Image Source via Getty Images

Figure 25.14 This child is carving pumpkins since they celebrate this holiday tradition in their home. *How can children be involved in planning activities for special events?*

Workplace Connections

Center Policies and Practices for Holiday Celebrations

Review a local early learning or Head Start center's policies and practices regarding children's holiday celebrations. Find out how holidays are selected, celebrated (or not celebrated), and what cultural groups are represented. Write a brief report of your findings.

1. How early should a holiday be introduced to the children?
2. Are children and parents involved in the planning for holidays and special events?

Friendship Concepts

Friendships are formed by people who talk, spend time together, and usually have similar interests. They are a vital part of growing up. Friendships provide children enjoyment and satisfaction. Friendships also provide opportunities for children to develop socially, emotionally, and cognitively. Most friendships develop from children's peer relationships.

Relationship success depends on the child's abilities to share, communicate, empathize, take turns, and cooperate. Young children view other children as being desirable or undesirable, friends or non-friends. Friendships are valuable as they provide children with:

- affection and companionship
- identity
- a diversity of perspectives
- stimulation
- security and a sense of belonging
- social comparison
- opportunities to lead and follow

Friends choose to be with each other when they have a mutual liking for one another. They share common activities and interests. In friendship concepts, children practice social problem-solving. Children's abilities to make and keep friends gauges their competence. During early childhood and until school age, friends are ever-changing. Over time, the expectations of friendship change and similar interests are of prime importance.

Acceptance by others depends on a child's own behavior, language, and play experiences. Preschool children will reject those children who are disruptive or aggressive. Peers who are withdrawn or shy can be ignored. Children typically have more friends if they have developed self-regulation. **Self-regulation** is the ability of a person to regulate their behavior in socially and culturally appropriate ways. Self-regulated children are better at exercising control over their actions and are less impulsive. They are also better at controlling their frustrations, managing their emotions, sharing, taking turns, and staying focused. The thoughts and feelings of others are important to these children.

Children learn to get along with others through peer interactions, on-the-spot coaching and modeling from their teachers, and time with friends. Children need to consider the well-being of others while interacting. This is difficult since they are generally *egocentric*. This means they think about what they want from other people, not about what they can do for them.

Friendship issues are challenging to some preschool and kindergarten children. As a teacher, you will play an important role in helping children develop friendships. You will need to coach them in appropriate prosocial behavior. You can do this by coaching and helping children see what they are doing and how their actions affect others. You will need to be specific so the child understands. Below are some examples of clear coaching for friendship concepts:

- If a child grabs another child's clay, say, "Ask Juan if you can play with some of the clay."
- If a child has a ball and another child is trying to grab it, say, "Tell Marena you don't like it when the ball is taken from you."
- If a child offers another child blocks in the construction area, say, "Say thank you to Daya. Tell her you like it when she offers you blocks to play with."
- If a child working in the dramatic play area asks another child if he wants to play, say, "You made Hong happy when you asked him to play."
- If a child is trying to paint on the easel where another child is working, say, "Ping, you will need to wait your turn. Mateo is still using the easel. He gets mad when someone paints on his picture. Ask him to tell you when he is finished."
- If a child who is shy and standing off to the side is watching children work at the art table, say, "Cameron would like to make a collage. Here is a chair for him. Please pass some collage materials to Cameron."
- If a child walks into the center for the first day, say, "Say hello to Tunde. Today is Tunde's first day at school."

Friendships are one of life's pleasures, and the early years are key for developing skills in growing and maintaining friendships. These skills are important since there are long-term risks for being friendless. Friendless adults are more likely to suffer depression, heart disease, and other medical problems.

25.2-2 Morning Meetings

Morning meetings can encourage democracy concepts. **Morning meetings**, sometimes referred to as *class meetings* or *gathering times*, promote a caring community at preschool, kindergarten, and school-age levels. These meetings help create and model a democratic environment. Morning meetings can be unscheduled or scheduled.

The purpose of morning meetings is to address the concerns of the learning community. This includes children and staff. During these meetings, teachers hold children accountable for their behavior and work. The children take part in discussion and problem solving. This helps them develop an understanding of the democratic process. They also develop important life skills in citizenship.

Some teachers use the morning meeting to provide a structure for the day. Riley, a teacher of four-year-old children, holds a daily morning meeting. To make each child gain a sense of belonging, Riley begins with a greeting that sets the tone for the entire day. Riley reviews the schedule, additions to the classroom environment, and special events. Riley also reviews expectations and promotes rules. After this, Riley presents problems to the group and encourages the children to discuss them and make recommendations. By being engaged in rule making and simple group decisions, children learn to solve social problems. They also develop communication skills and experience feelings of belonging, trust, and security. This all leads to a sense of community and helps build democratic concepts.

Lesson 25.2 Review

1. _____ are ideas formed about a relationship or object resulting from what a child learns through their senses. (25.2.1)
   A. Perceptions
   B. Gender concepts
   C. Multiculturalism
   D. Community
2. **True or False.** Self-regulation is the ability of a person to regulate their behavior in socially and culturally appropriate ways. (25.2.1)
3. Which of the following is **not** a community helper? (25.2.1)
   A. Postal carrier
   B. Police officer
   C. Insurance salesperson
   D. Firefighter
4. Morning meetings can encourage _____ concepts. (25.2.2)
   A. gender
   B. democracy
   C. geography
   D. celebration

Chapter 25 Review and Assessment

Summary

Lesson 25.1

25.1-1 Social studies concepts help young children understand the world in which they live.

25.1-1 Children's social development and emotional intelligence benefit from learning social studies concepts.

25.1-1 As children learn about people and customs that differ from and are like those in their own families, they begin to accept and appreciate differences. They learn there are differences in race, language, color, gender, and age.

25.1-2 Young children need their teachers to see, hear, know, and acknowledge them.

25.1-2 A teacher must identify the children's strengths, needs, interests, abilities, and experiences before they plan the curriculum.

Lesson 25.2

25.2-1 Information from families helps develop the curriculum using various themes and taking advantage of community resources. Incidental learnings also provide an opportunity to teach social studies concepts.

25.2-1 Effective social studies programs introduce children to different cultures, and generations of people.

25.2-1 Children can learn about basic democracy principles, friendship skills, ecology, and geography by studying social studies concepts.

25.2-1 Exposure and daily experiences with anti-bias literature will help children better understand themselves and others better.

25.2-2 Morning meetings encourage democratic concepts. These meetings help create and model a democratic environment. Morning meetings can be unscheduled or scheduled.

Vocabulary Activity

Draw a cartoon depicting one of the content or academic terms in this chapter. Use the cartoon to express the meaning of the term. Share your cartoon with the class. Explain how the cartoon shows the meaning of the term.

Critical Thinking

1. **Identify.** As a class, choose one theme and brainstorm related activities that could be used in various social studies areas. After compiling a list, identify the activities that could most smoothly be integrated into the theme. Think in terms of what concepts and themes will be easiest for children to grasp.

2. **Make Inferences.** Brainstorm a list of community resources. Include museums, art galleries, stores, and services that are available in your community. Then, make inferences about what children could learn by visiting these places. How realistic is a visit to one of these locations? How educational would a visit be? Write two to three paragraphs recommending or not recommending visits to these places.

3. **Evaluate.** When multicultural books are chosen, they need to be evaluated for authenticity. Using reliable online or print resources, and research guides for evaluating books with multicultural content. Then, locate two children's books with a multicultural perspective and evaluate them according to the criteria in one guide you found.

4. **Compare and Contrast.** Ask a group of preschoolers what they think about older people. Then, compare and contrast their comments to those listed in this chapter. How similar are the statements? How different are they? Do they reveal any stereotypes?

5. **Draw Conclusions.** While young children cannot fully understand scientific and ecological principles, they can learn ecology concepts that can help them take care of the environment.

Find posters or lesson plans for ways to teach preschoolers about caring for the environment. Choose at least three resources and draw conclusions about what they teach children and whether the level of detail they include is appropriate.

Core Skills

1. **Research and Speaking.** Research three cultures and gather the information that will help you understand, appreciate, and teach children about these cultures. Learn about the aspects of these cultures, including traditions, languages, beliefs, customs, clothing, foods, family structures, and roles of family members. Organize your notes into a presentation and deliver your information to the class. In your presentation, suggest ways to adapt the information for young children.

2. **Listening.** Interview an older adult about what school was like they were young. What instructional methods did teachers use to present social studies concepts to students? How much homework was required? What discipline methods were used? Write a short essay to compare and contrast educational methods and social studies lessons of the past with those used today.

3. **Social Studies.** Interview a social studies teacher about the possibility of creating mini-democracy lessons or activities suitable for preschoolers. Enlist the advice of an early childhood teacher to adapt the lessons and make them developmentally appropriate. Include hands-on opportunities when presenting the lessons to the preschoolers. Compare your experiences with those of other students.

4. **Science.** Explore the possibility of creating a worm farm. Conduct an online search for websites that give directions for making farms in quart-size, plastic, transparent jars by layering soil, sand, and food or compost. Collect the food or compost to feed the worms. What ecological principles can be taught through this project? Share your findings in class.

5. **Research and Writing.** Discussions of current events may prompt questions about war, terrorism, or natural disasters. This can cause stress in young children. Conduct an online search for information on handling these questions and other traumatic events to help children feel safe. What materials or programs exist to help children who are victims of stressful situations? How can these topics be addressed in an early childhood program at a level a child can understand without causing further anxiety? Write a brief report of your findings.

6. **Writing.** Interview individual children in an early learning, childcare, or Head Start center and ask for information about their interests and abilities. Observe the children during play and interact with them casually to learn more about them. After observing, use your notes to write a children's story about a new child at the center being introduced to all the children you observed. In the children's story, highlight the interests and abilities of each child and model prosocial ways for children to interact.

7. **CTE Career Readiness Practice.** As a new employee at an early childhood center, you are glad when your director assigns you a research project for the betterment of the center. Your task is to find reliable, current research about teaching geographical concepts to children. In your research, identify what kindergartens expect preschoolers to know about geography. Also, locate three reliable sources detailing how children learn these concepts and what resources are available. Prepare a summary of your research for your director, and include a bibliography.

Portfolio Project

Many young children learn social studies concepts through listening to and reading books. Books about geography, ecology, current events, and making friends are just a few of the types of literature that can aid children in developing these concepts. Visit a local library or search online for literature that exposes children to social studies concepts. Try to find at least three books that address each of the social studies concepts covered in this chapter. For each book, record the title, the authors and illustrators, and the topics covered. Also, write a brief summary of how the book could be incorporated into a lesson. File your list and summaries in your portfolio.

Chapter 26

Reading Advantage

Describe how this chapter relates to a chapter you read earlier in the semester.

Guiding Food and Nutrition Experiences

Lesson 26.1: Understanding Nutrition Experiences

Lesson 26.2: Implementing Food and Cooking Experiences

Case Study

Planning Food and Nutrition Experiences

Isabella, a student teacher from the local community college, was assigned to a group of three- and four-year-olds for the next eight weeks. Unfortunately, Mr. Garcia, her cooperating teacher, was ill last week, so he could not meet to review Isabella's responsibilities. Today was her first day participating in his classroom. When she arrived, she noticed Mr. Garcia was hurrying to get everything ready before the children came. Isabella immediately asked how she could help. Mr. Garcia told her to check the block plan posted in the entry to the classroom. It would provide her with an overview of the daily activities and assigned responsibilities. She carefully studied the block plan and saw her name penciled behind snacks—vanilla pudding with bananas. The activity was scheduled immediately following rest time.

Just before the children got up, Isabella went into the kitchen. She saw that the center cook had left two boxes of pudding and the bananas on the counter. Then she found a large serving tray. On it, she placed a large pitcher of milk, a huge mixing bowl, a large mixing spoon, and a spatula. She carefully carried the tray into the classroom, noticed an empty table, and placed the tray on it. Four children came and sat at the table. Isabella explained that they were going to prepare pudding for a snack. She opened the pudding boxes and let a child pour them into the mixing bowl. Then she looked down at the tray, and there was not a measuring cup. So, she excused herself and said she needed to get something from the kitchen and would be right back. When she returned to the classroom, she saw that a child had tried to pour the milk. The plastic pitcher was heavy and slipped, and the entire amount of milk was in the bowl.

Give It Some Thought

1. How could a detailed lesson plan have helped Isabella? Should the table have been cleaned before beginning the activity? Should the teacher and children have washed their hands? If so, why?
2. What math, science, language, and social studies concepts could have been intentionally included in the activity?
3. What is the value of including food and nutrition experiences as part of the early childhood curriculum?
4. Why is it essential to include multicultural cooking experiences for children in early childhood programs?
5. How would you teach Mr. Garcia's class to set the table, serve food, and clean up?

Opening image credit: Asia-Pacific Images Studio/E+ via Getty Images

Essential Question

What do you need to know about food and nutrition experiences, state and local regulations, and ways to work with parents to create successful nutrition and food experiences for children?

Learning Outcomes

After studying this lesson, you will be able to

26.1-1 **summarize** the value of food and nutrition experiences for children.

26.1-2 **explain** the impact of local and state regulations on the food environment.

26.1-3 **identify** ways to work with parents to best serve children's nutritional needs.

Key Terms

food and nutrition experiences

nutrition concepts

Food and nutrition experiences involve many activities: preparing foods, setting the table, eating snacks and meals, and cleaning up. These activities help provide learning experiences that prepare children for an independent and healthful life. Taking part in food and nutrition experiences also builds feelings of independence, responsibility, and worthiness. These activities provide opportunities for teaching nutrition concepts. **Nutrition concepts** are basic concepts that will help children develop lifelong healthy eating habits. These habits should promote a healthful diet, including appropriate portions of vegetables, fruits, whole grains, dairy products, poultry, fish, beans, eggs, meats, and nuts.

26.1-1 The Importance of Food and Nutrition Experiences

The preschool years are an important time to develop lifelong healthy eating habits. Experiences with food and nutrition promote the development of the whole child. Cognitive, physical, social, and emotional development are all affected. Studies show that feeding practices can be a stronger factor in the growth of young children than genetics or ethnic background.

Cognitively, children learn observation and critical-thinking skills by participating in food and nutrition experiences. By measuring, comparing, analyzing, and observing the change in ingredients and by predicting outcomes, children learn science and math concepts. By learning cooking vocabulary and the names of food preparation tools, children also develop language skills. By following a sequence of visual illustrations and directions provided on recipe charts, children develop left-to-right progression skills that are necessary for reading and writing.

Physically, cooking experiences promote the development of large and small muscles. Young children develop muscular control by rolling, kneading, peeling, chopping, whipping, sifting, and stirring. They also develop hand-eye coordination skills by measuring, spooning, dicing, cutting, and peeling.

Socially and emotionally, food and nutrition experiences promote self-esteem. Children take pride by participating in an "adult" activity (**Figure 26.1**). By taking turns and sharing utensils and ingredients, young children learn cooperation skills. By participating in food and nutrition experiences with their peers, they also

Alvarez/E+ via Getty Images

Figure 26.1 Preparing their own nutritious snacks is fun and promotes feelings of competence for children. ***What nutritious snacks might you consider preparing with children?***

learn about foods from their own and other cultures. Finally, by taking part in cooking activities, children learn independent living skills they can use throughout their lives.

Food and nutrition experiences also teach nutrition concepts, which are useful throughout life. Teaching nutrition is an important part of guiding food experiences. For instance, children learn that a wide variety of foods are available to meet the needs of their bodies. This concept can be taught by introducing children to many foods during snack and mealtime. These experiences can also teach children that they can eat foods in several ways. For example, they can eat apples raw or cooked. They can be made into applesauce, apple butter, apple bread, apple pancakes, apple pie, apple juice, apple cider, baked apple, and apple dumplings. **Figure 26.2** highlights other nutrition concepts young children learn through food and nutrition experiences.

26.1-2 Impact of Regulations on the Food Environment

In the United States, approximately one-third of preschool children consume most of their food in childcare or early childhood settings. Local,

state, and federal regulations will influence the food environment in these settings. In most cases, the federal ***Child and Adult Food Program (CACFP)*** requirements are more stringent than local or state regulations. Some state regulations follow only broad guidelines. There may be no specific guidelines on the types or serving sizes of foods. In some centers, parents provide the food and it is not uncommon to find potato chips, cookies, candy, a can of soda, or even marshmallows in lunch bags.

Another cause for concern may exist in centers without commercial kitchens. In some states, local health department regulations may mandate prepackaged foods. To conform to local health regulations, prepacked foods may be served rather than fresh produce. This may affect the nutritional value of the food served. It will also affect a child's acceptance and consumption of a wide variety of fruits and vegetables.

Check your state licensing requirements regarding food brought into the center. Some states allow commercially prepared foods to be brought into the center occasionally as part of a birthday or holiday celebration. For these purposes, food must arrive unopened as packaged by the bakery or manufacturer; otherwise, the center staff cannot accept it.

Nutrition Concepts for Young Children

Nutrition is how our bodies use the foods we eat to produce energy, growth, and health.

There is a wide variety of food available. Foods come from both plants and animals.

The same food can be used to make many different dishes.

Foods vary in color, flavor, texture, odor, size, and shape.

Foods are classified into basic food groups:
- ✓ grains
- ✓ vegetables
- ✓ fruit
- ✓ protein foods
- ✓ dairy

A good diet includes foods from each of the food groups.

There are many factors that enhance the eating experience:
- ✓ aesthetics of food
- ✓ method of preparation
- ✓ cleanliness, manners
- ✓ celebrations
- ✓ environment/atmosphere

We choose foods we eat for many reasons:
- ✓ availability
- ✓ taste
- ✓ family and personal habit
- ✓ aesthetics of food
- ✓ advertising and mass media
- ✓ social and cultural customs
- ✓ convenience
- ✓ health

Figure 26.2 By teaching important nutrition concepts, children learn that a variety of foods are available to help meet the needs of their bodies.

26.1-3 Working with Families

Families must know how they can influence their children's eating habits. These influences can be direct or indirect. For instance, the snacks that families provide for their children are a *direct* influence. The atmosphere of the home at mealtime is an *indirect* influence. Several methods are useful for working with families in this key area of child development.

Many centers have lending libraries. These libraries are a good way to share nutrition information with adults. Families may check out pamphlets, magazines, and books to learn or update their nutrition knowledge. They may also share recipes (**Figure 26.3**).

Family meetings, workshops, and discussion groups are useful methods for interacting. Here, family members and teachers can discuss reliable information on nutritional needs of children, suggestions for dealing with common mealtime problems, and resources in the community for food.

Some centers find that a weekly or monthly newsletter is an excellent way to keep families informed and involved. Such a newsletter can contain helpful information: home food activities that reinforce concepts children learn at the center and suggestions for menu planning, serving, and stressing good nutrition. It is important to always share the weekly center lunch and snack menus with families. Most states require that centers post this information for families to access. Family members can use this information to coordinate home meals with those served in the center. Send home a family letter such as Figure 26.3. The letter will inform them about what older preschool and school-age children can learn from cooking experiences. It can also encourage family members to see the value of cooking and have the children cook at home.

Family Letter

Dear Families:

Today the children made scrambled eggs with spinach as part of a cooking activity. They learned how to include vegetables in an egg dish and practiced many basic cooking skills. Try making the recipe at home for breakfast or as a part of a quick dinner—your child would love the chance to show off their new skills. Some skills we covered today include how to:

- chop
- crack eggs
- whisk
- measure wet and dry ingredients
- use a cooktop safely
- scramble
- toast
- cool food safely
- season food
- set a table

Ask your child about our activity today. Here are some questions to encourage the conversation:
- What did you make today?
- What steps did you follow to make scrambled eggs with spinach?
- Do we have the kitchen tools we need to make scrambled eggs with spinach at home?
- What could we serve with these scrambled eggs to include another food group?

Make meals and memories together! Cooking is a skill your child will use for life.

USDA United States Department of Agriculture

Figure 26.3 Cooking with children encourages family bonding and teaches life skills.

Sanest_Photo/Shutterstock.com

Figure 26.4 This child is preparing pizza for a snack. *What other snack options might you prepare with children?*

Early Childhood Insight

Foods from Home

As an early childhood educator, you must talk with families about safe foods to bring from home. At times, families may want to contribute food and baked goods for a special class project. Many states' licensing rules and regulations do not allow home-prepared food to be brought into the center. Check your state licensing regulations. If this is the case in your state, you must inform families. Tell them to bring only whole or packaged foods, such as commercially made foods and baked goods. Also, talk with families about proper storage temperatures and safe transportation of foods that require refrigeration.

Health Highlights

Nutrition Policies and Resources

According to federal guidelines, early childhood facilities must have a written nutrition plan. This plan should be shared with *all* staff members, including the foodservice staff and students' families. The plan should link food and feeding experiences with those that children experience at home. Early childhood teachers work with foodservice staff and families to ensure that meal plans and food-related activities fulfill the nutritional requirements of children. Resources for planning meals and food-related activities may include

- nutritionists at local and state health departments or hospitals
- cooperative extension nutritionists and WIC
- USDA Child and Adult Care Food Program
- USDA Child Care Nutrition Resource System (part of the Food and Nutrition Information System)
- organizations such as the Dairy Council, American Heart Association, American Dietetic Association, American Academy of Pediatrics, and many more

Lesson 26.1 Review

1. Which of the following is *not* part of food and nutrition experiences? (26.1.1)
   A. Cleaning up
   B. Preparing foods
   C. Eating a snack
   D. Naptime after lunch

2. Basic ideas that will help children develop lifelong, heathy eating habits are _____. (26.1.1)
   A. healthful practices
   B. the food pyramid levels
   C. nutrition concepts
   D. the five food groups

3. **True or False.** Positive food and nutrition experiences promote positive self-esteem. (26.1.1)

4. Which of the following might be an example of a local or state regulation regarding food and nutrition in an early childhood center? (26.1.2)
   A. Parents send in cookies, soda, and potato chips in their child's lunch.
   B. The center provides vegetables and hummus for a snack.
   C. Children help prepare for snack by setting the table.
   D. Only commercially prepackaged food can be brought into the center for birthday celebrations.

5. Which of the following is a direct influence on a child's eating habits? (26.1.2)
   A. A parent serving apples and cheese for a snack
   B. A child watching television during breakfast
   C. A family having lunch at a picnic table
   D. Siblings preparing dinner together

Implementing Food and Cooking Experiences

Essential Question

What do you need to know about foods and cooking to prepare effective cooking and eating experiences for children?

Learning Outcomes

After studying this lesson, you will be able to

26.2-1 **summarize** nutrition activities to use with young children.

26.2-2 **outline** the procedure for conducting cooking experiences.

26.2-3 **explain** why it is important to include multicultural foods in menus.

26.2-4 **teach** children to set a table, serve food, and clean up.

26.2-5 **examine** various eating problems encountered in young children, including food insecurity, challenging appetites, and food refusals.

Key Terms

portable kitchen	mitigate
mesh	quench
food insecurity	

Nutrition and cooking experiences are an important part of the early childhood curriculum. Children learn to develop healthy eating habits by participating in nutrition activities, while cooking teaches them food-preparation skills and safety practices. Cooking is a multisensory experience that emphasizes sights and sounds, and smells. By participating in cooking experiences, children develop and practice cognitive skills such as basic math,

science, and language. Children develop teamwork skills as they take turns during preparation. Cooking experiences also help them develop observational and critical-thinking skills, motor skills, problem-solving, creativity, and self-confidence. Children also learn proper hygiene as they wash some foods and clean up after food preparation.

Often, children are picky eaters. Engaging them in nutrition and cooking experiences helps them try new foods and learn to make healthy food choices. Providing early and frequent exposure to a variety of foods should encourage them to develop healthy eating habits. Exposing children to foods from many different cultures is also important. This familiarizes them with foods people from other cultures eat. Moreover, learning cooking skills will also help them in the future.

26.2-1 Nutrition Activities

Introduce classroom activities that reinforce nutrition concepts. Using grocery flyers or magazines, cut out pictures of nutritious foods. Laminate or cover the pieces with clear contact paper and place them in a basket. The children can sort the images into food groups or create collages. Another activity would be to provide paper plates with cut-out foods. The children can follow the MyPlate diagram to select a plate of healthy food. If you desire, they could glue the foods on the plate and take them home to share with their family.

Consider creating a food chart on a poster board with three columns. The headings should include three categories: *Anytime, Sometimes,* and *Once in a While*. Let the children sort through the food pieces. Anytime foods include healthy foods such as almost all vegetables, fresh, frozen, or canned without added sauce or butter; skim milk, low-fat, and fat-free cottage cheese; lean meats and other protein sources. Examples of sometimes foods include vegetables with fats and sauces, white bread, biscuits, peanut butter, nuts, and baked chips. The once-in-a-while group of foods would include French fries, hash browns, whole milk, fried chicken, hamburgers, bacon, cookies, ice cream, chips, and soda.

26.2-2 Cooking Experiences

Children enjoy cooking experiences, which also help them learn about healthful eating. Cooking is a STEM activity that promotes science, technology, and math. Children learn the vocabulary of cooking. Words such as *stirring, measuring, mixing, spreading, cutting,* and *pouring* extend their vocabularies. Children also learn basic math concepts such as *shape, size, number,* and *temperature change.* By exploring similarities and differences in food, they develop critical-thinking skills. By finding new ways to combine ingredients, they also learn creative-thinking skills.

By taking part in food and nutrition experiences, children learn how to use cooking utensils and work as a team. They learn to use can openers, vegetable peelers, and egg beaters. Children learn left-to-right progression skills as the teacher helps them read recipes. Cooking is also a natural way to learn how to organize ingredients and follow directions (**Figure 26.5**).

The key to an effective food and nutrition program is presenting cooking activities positively. It is quite easy for food experiences to become tense and unproductive. There may be children who refuse to eat. Other children refuse to help with cooking tasks. Still other children may overeat or help to a point where others cannot participate. Set several simple limits to promote happy, relaxed cooking experiences:

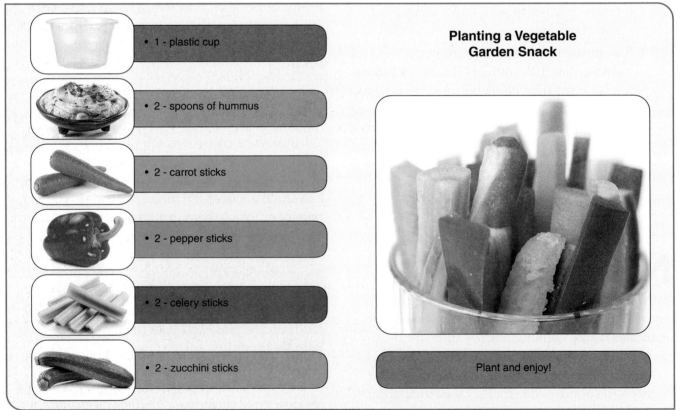

* 1 - plastic cup
* 2 - spoons of hummus
* 2 - carrot sticks
* 2 - pepper sticks
* 2 - celery sticks
* 2 - zucchini sticks

Planting a Vegetable Garden Snack

Plant and enjoy!

(Left to right and top to bottom) koosen/Shutterstock.com, MaraZe/Shutterstock.com, Khumthong/Shutterstock.com, Tauleo/Shutterstock.com, MarcoFood/Shutterstock.com, SOMMAJ/Shutterstock.com, Yummy Pic/Shutterstock.com

Figure 26.5   Even young children can follow recipe charts that are written using picture symbols.

Safety First

Avoiding Choking Hazards

When creating developmentally appropriate food plans for children, avoid foods that can cause children (especially those under four years of age) to choke. Examples of high-risk foods include hot dogs; raw carrots, sliced or in strips; nuts and seeds; hard pretzels, potato chips, large amounts of peanut butter; chunks of meat and other foods that cannot be swallowed whole; whole grapes; cherry tomatoes; melon balls; or hard candy. These foods are risky because they can partially or totally block a child's airway. To serve, slice them into pieces less than one-half inch.

- Schedule quiet, relaxing activities just before mealtimes.
- Provide child-sized tables, chairs, and serving tools.
- Eat with the children.
- Make positive comments about the food.

- Encourage children to serve themselves.
- Expect some accidents. Children will spill drinks and drop food. Involve the children in clean up. Be prepared by keeping damp sponges handy in all food preparation and eating areas. Encourage children to clean up their messes.
- Read children's books about food to prepare and relax them. **Figure 26.6** contains a list of good food books for preschool children.

Safety for Cooking Experiences

Most teachers understand the value of cooking experiences. Cooking experiences are also an opportunity for children to learn about safety. Teachers should do all they can to keep children safe during cooking. To increase learning and decrease safety and health hazards, follow these guidelines:

- Have all cooks wash their hands in warm, soapy water and wear aprons.
- Clean and disinfect all work surfaces.

Good Books About Food

- *Little Taco Truck* by Tanya Valentine (author), Jorge Martin (illustrator)
- *Dozens of Donuts* by Carrie Finison (author), Brianne Farley (illustrator)
- *Goldilocks for Dinner* by Susan McElroy Montanari (author), Jake Parker (illustrator)
- *Round as a Tortilla* by Roseanne Thong (author), John Parra (illustrator)
- *Pete's a Pizza* by William Steig (author, illustrator)
- *Fry Bread: A Native American Family Story* by Kevin Noble Maillard (author), Juana Martinez-Neal (illustrator)
- *Before We Eat, From Farm to Table* by Pat Brisson (author), Mary Azarian (illustrator)
- *Grow! Raise! Catch! How We Get Our Food* by Shelly Rotner (author)

- *A Gluten-Free Birthday for Me!* by Sue Fliess (author), Jennifer Morris (illustrator)
- *Bread Bread Bread* by Ann Morris (author), Ken Heyman (illustrator)
- *Mr. Crum's Potato Predicament* by Anne Renaud (author), Felicita Sala (illustrator)
- *I Eat Fruit!* by Hannah Tofts (author)
- *I Eat Vegetables!* by Hannah Tofts (author)
- *Rah, Rah, Radishes!* by April Pulley Sayre (author)
- *Soup Day* by Melissa Iwai (author)
- *The Vegetables We Eat* by Gail Gibbons (author)
- *Let's Go Nuts! Seeds We Eat* by April Pulley Sayre (author)
- *We Eat Food That's Fresh!* by Angela Russ Ayon and Cathy June
- *Yummy! Good Food Makes Me Strong!* by Shelley Rotner and Sheila M. Kelly

Figure 26.6 A variety of books are useful for teaching about food experiences with young children. *Which books might you prefer?*

- When using recipe cards, print short, clear, sequential instructions. Food labels, picture symbols, numerals, short phrases, and single words make recipes easy for young children to "read."

- Place the recipe, ingredients, cleanup supplies, and utensils on a tray before the activity begins (**Figure 26.7**).

- Use large, stable, unbreakable bowls for mixing ingredients.

- Have the children sit when using sharp utensils such as strong plastic knives and peelers.

First Experiences

First food experiences should be developmentally appropriate. They should revolve around simple recipes you can serve at snack time and require no cooking (**Figure 26.8**). For these recipes, children can shake cream to make butter or prepare instant pudding. Measuring the ingredients before the experience will help ensure success. Success is important to children wanting to take part in future activities. As children progress to more complex food experiences, the teacher should make careful plans and introduce children to cooking.

Planning

Teachers should plan a series of developmentally appropriate cooking experiences that gradually become more complex. This might

Onjira Leibe/Shutterstock.com

Figure 26.7 Preparing food on a tray before snacks helps the experience go more smoothly.

Anna Kraynova/Shutterstock.com

Figure 26.8 This young child is tasting watermelon for the first time during snack time. *What other foods might be good to introduce to children in the area in which you live?*

be preparing the same food in several different forms or each time adding something new. For example, children can add berries to instant vanilla pudding and later can add other types of fruit.

As you select recipes, be aware children's food allergies. Common culprits include cow's milk, milk products, wheat (and gluten), soy, peanuts and tree nuts, fish, shellfish, sesame, and orange juice. You should also observe children's families' beliefs about food. Some families avoid certain foods in their diets.

Limit the number of children participating in any activity, usually no more than four to six children. Children may have to take turns. Some teachers schedule cooking during small-group activity times to naturally limit the number of children. Smaller groups also encourage children to take turns.

Collect enough tools and unbreakable equipment to involve all children. Plastic bowls and blunt tools are best. Each child should have a tool when you schedule activities such as peeling apples. For cutting, provide strong plastic serrated knives. Always supervise children carefully when using cutting tools.

Cooking

Once it is developmentally appropriate, teachers should begin teaching children to cook. Some teachers create a portable kitchen in their classrooms. A **portable kitchen** is a kitchen that you can move from one location to another. When creating a portable kitchen, place ingredients, tools, and other equipment on a low table so all children can watch. Place your portable kitchen near an electrical outlet so you can use portable appliances such as an electric skillet or a hot plate rather than a cooktop on a range. To prevent accidents, turn pan handles away from children. Remind children of safety rules.

Start the activity by telling the children what you are going to make. Then have all cooks (including you) wash their hands with soapy water. After this, explain the sequence of steps you will use. Discuss the different sizes of measuring cups and spoons. Ask simple questions, such as "Which cup holds the most?" If you have not prepared a recipe chart, write the steps on a board or large piece of paper. The children will enjoy following the directions.

As the children move through the preparation steps, encourage them to observe and talk about what is happening. Point out the changes in food because of blending, cooking, or freezing. Ask children to predict what will happen. Include science, math, language arts, and social studies concepts if they **mesh** (fit well) with the experience. Introduce new foods, processes, and equipment.

Cleanup is an important part of the cooking experience. Involve children in returning equipment and ingredients to the kitchen and washing tables and dishes.

Tasting

After cooking, tasting helps children learn about new foods. Compare new foods with familiar foods. For example, compare a lime with a lemon, or compare a sweet potato with a white potato. Discuss food temperatures and textures. Many teachers use these activities as part of an interest center. This limits the number of children who can be involved. For safety reasons, an adult should be part of any tasting activities (**Figure 26.9**).

Onjira Leibe/Shutterstock.com

Figure 26.9 Adults often overestimate how much food a child can eat. *What food amounts are appropriate for children?*

26.2-3 Multicultural Cooking Experiences

Many young children have had limited exposure to cultural foods. Introducing them to foods enjoyed in other cultures can promote an acceptance of human differences. Multicultural snacks and meals should be healthy, varied, and, if possible, new. Many children may have eaten pizza, tacos, or French bread. They may not have tasted fried rice, sweet chicken, naan bread, and many other cultural foods. Two ideas for promoting multicultural cooking experiences include compiling a classroom cookbook and holding a bread-tasting party.

Make sure the children experience foods from many cultures. Russian, English, Caribbean, Mexican, Italian, Chinese, German, and French should be included. Try to have the recipes reflect the children in your class. Choose easy, quick recipes. Guacamole dip from Mexico, Crepes from France, or banana bread from South America are some examples.

Classroom Cookbook

Menus can emphasize the likenesses and differences among families. To vary menus, you can create a classroom cookbook. Ask families to provide a simple recipe for a main dish, salad, bread, or dessert. As children eat the food, talk about the food and about how it is similar or different from other foods. Use the recipes you collect for a classroom cookbook. Consider typing up the cookbook to use as a gift for parents or guardians. Other than a title, leave the cover blank. Then each child can decorate the cover.

You can also invite parents or guardians, aunts, uncles, or grandparents to come to the classroom and prepare a favorite recipe from their family. They can either demonstrate or encourage the children to take part in the preparation. After the food is prepared, the children can taste and discuss its appearance, flavor, and texture.

Bread-Tasting Party

Bread is a food that people eat worldwide. It is a staple in almost every diet. People may eat bread plain or with other foods. Breads have different textures and flavors. To teach children about multicultural foods, you can plan a bread-tasting party with a few different types of breads. Encourage the children to use all of their senses. They can look at, smell, touch, and taste the different types of bread. Examine the breads and discuss how they are alike and different. Observe their color, shape, texture, and size. Then taste the breads and discuss the textures and tastes. **Figure 26.10** contains breads representing different cultures.

26.2-4 Serving and Eating Foods

Part of the early childhood curriculum is serving and eating foods. Mealtimes should be a pleasurable experience for young children. They are learning to appreciate and accept a wide variety of foods and developing healthful habits. Consistent mealtime routines are important so children know what others expect of them. Encourage them to set the table. Use place mats with their names to promote name recognition.

Outline where the plate, glass, unbreakable utensils, and napkin should be placed.

A teacher or staff member should sit at each table as a role model for serving and eating food and encouraging language development The children should take responsibility for serving themselves and wiping their spills. Teach them to use the magic mealtime words, "please" and "thank you." When mealtime is over, the children need to assist with cleanup by clearing their dishes, utensils, and napkin. After that, they need to wash their hands and brush their teeth.

Setting the Table

When taking part in cooking experiences, educators should expect children to take turns setting the table. This routine provides experiences in counting and in spatial relationships. Teachers often list this task on a chart, along with other tasks that children can do around the classroom.

Begin teaching children to set the table by explaining rules. Before they set the table, the children must wash their hands. Then they must wash the table with a sponge or cloth and soapy water. After this, they may take part in setting the table.

Place mats that show the positions of eating utensils, napkins, plates, and glasses are quite helpful for beginners (**Figure 26.11**). These mats also help children learn the space relationships of eating utensils. You can also use printable placemats using the same technique to teach the children table-setting skills.

Teach children to place the plate on the middle of the place mat. Then have them place the fork to the left of the plate. Place the napkin next to the fork. After this, have them place the knife to the right of the plate (if you are using knives) and place the spoon next to the knife. Finally, have the children place the glass at the tip of the knife.

Small centerpieces are a pleasant addition to the dining table. Those made of unusual materials can become the focal point of conversations. Centerpieces may be something the class has made.

Bread Types

Barbarajo/Shutterstock.com

- Injera
- Lavash
- Lefse
- Marble rye
- Multigrain
- Naan
- Pancake
- Panettone
- Pia boa
- Pita
- Popover
- Potato
- Pretzel
- Pumpernickel
- Rice
- Rye
- Scones
- Soda
- Sourdough
- Tortillas
- Vienna
- Waffles
- Wheat-bran muffins
- Whole wheat

- Amish Friendship
- Anadama
- Bagels
- Baguettes
- Banana
- Belgian waffles
- Biscuits
- Boston Brown Bread
- Bread rolls
- Breadsticks
- Brioche
- Ciabatta

- Challah
- Chapati
- Cornmeal
- Crepes
- Cuban
- Dosa
- Egg
- English muffins
- Flatbread
- Focaccia
- French
- Fry bread

Figure 26.10   Because bread is a common food among cultures, introducing a variety of breads offers an opportunity to discuss how breads are alike and different.

Seating

The children should sit at a comfortable-sized table. They should always sit upright while eating and have sufficient room to manage food and eating utensils. Teachers should always sit face-to-face with the children at their eye level during snack and mealtime. This position provides opportunities for teachable moments, such as modeling positive social interactions and manners. Reinforce the use of such words as *please* and *thank you*. To illustrate, the teacher can use effective praise after hearing one child thanking another. The teacher's response might be: "It pleases me to hear you say thank you."

Encourage children to respect and care for others while sitting at the table. For example, the teacher may say, "Eva, will you please ask Jeffrey if he wants more pizza?" If Eva asks Jeffrey and passes the pizza plate to him, the teacher can

UW-Stout Child and Family Study Center

Figure 26.11 To teach children proper table setting, templates can be made on plastic place mats. ***How do children benefit from learning to set the table?***

comment, "It was kind of you to pass the pizza to Jeffrey." Likewise, the teacher can encourage children to use expressive-language skills at mealtimes with comments such as, "Nicole, if you would like another taco, ask Luis to pass it to you."

Workplace Connections

Promoting Positive Table Behavior

Role-play appropriate and positive table behavior for preschoolers. Arrange time after the presentation for preschoolers to practice appropriate and positive table behavior. Discuss your observations.

1. How closely did preschoolers imitate the table behavior modeled?
2. Did the preschoolers improve with practice?

Serving, Eating, and Language Development

The teachers need to be role models at the table. They should always take small bites and chew foods thoroughly before swallowing. This will help prevent potential choking incidents. To foster independence, children should serve

themselves and others. Place serving dishes on each table. Serving dishes should be the proper weight, size, and temperature for young children to handle. To encourage independence, provide small pitchers, allowing the children to pour their own juice, water, or milk.

Serve milk with each meal. Some children prefer liquids to solid food. They will often drink their milk right away and then ask for more. Always allow plenty of time for eating.

Eating should be a social time. During the meal notice and narrate. When Antonio passes the carrots to Silvia say, "Antonio, thank you for passing the carrots to Silvia." When Tunde carefully pours his milk say, "Tunde, I liked the care you took while pouring your milk."

Ask open-ended questions during meal and snack times. Examples might include

- What does _____ smell like?
- Tell me what it tastes like?
- What else could you make with _____?
- What would happen if?
- Where is _____ grown?
- How was this food prepared?

Cleaning Up

Cleaning up is also part of the eating routine. Children one year and older can begin to learn how to clean up after themselves.

Place a utility cart and garbage can next to the eating area. After the main meal is over, have the children take their plates to the cart. Ask them to throw napkins and other disposable items in the trash. You may wish to have the older children scrape the food scraps from their plates directly into the trash, too. If you are serving dessert, they may keep their eating utensils and glasses. When children finish eating dessert, they should then take all their dinnerware and eating utensils to the cart.

26.2-5 Eating Challenges

No doubt you find that some children have poor eating habits that make food and nutrition experiences challenging. Often, children learn these habits from others. If parents, relatives, and peers have poor eating habits, chances are that young children will have them, too.

You can use food and nutrition experiences to model and encourage good eating habits. By tasting all foods in front of children, you will encourage them to do the same. You can also model positive attitudes toward eating. Offering constructive comments is another way to improve eating habits. For instance, you might say, "Seth, I'm glad you tried the peas today. You probably found out how good they taste."

The United States Department of Agriculture (USDA) has described behavioral milestones for children two to five years of age, which may vary with individual children (**Figure 26.12**).

Changing Appetites

Children do not eat the same amount of food every day. If a child is very active or has a light breakfast, the child will probably have a big appetite. If the weather is hot or a child has just eaten before coming to the center, they probably will not be very hungry. Fatigue and illness can also cause a change in children's appetites. Sometimes huge appetites in children may be because of a lack of food at home. About fifteen percent of children live in a household with **food insecurity** (absent or inconsistent access to nutritious food). Their families have insufficient resources to gain sufficient food for healthy living.

If a child's lack of appetite at mealtime continues for a length of time, observe the child. Ask these questions:

- Is the child getting enough nutrients?
- Is the child eating too much at snack time?
- Is the child paying attention at mealtime?
- Is the child being properly reinforced at mealtime?
- Is the child always tired at mealtime?

After observing the child, you may notice one of these problem areas. For instance, if the child is always tired at mealtime, provide them with a quiet period before eating. If the problem continues, contact the child's parents or guardians.

Behavioral Milestones for Eating

Two-Year-Olds	Three-Year-Olds	Four-Year-Olds	Five-Year-Olds
• Can use a spoon and drink from a cup	• Makes simple either/or food choices	• Influenced by TV, media, and peers	• Has fewer demands
• Can be easily distracted	• Pours liquids with some spills	• May dislike many mixed dishes	• Will usually accept the available food
• Growth slows and appetites drops	• Comfortable using fork and spoon	• Rarely spills with spoon or cup	• Eats with minor supervision
• Develops likes and dislikes	• Can follow simple requests, such as "Please use your napkin."	• Knows what table manners are expected	
• Can be very messy	• Starts to request favorite foods	• Can easily be sidetracked	
• May suddenly refuse certain foods	• Likes to imitate cooking	• May suddenly refuse certain foods	
	• May suddenly refuse certain foods		

Figure 26.12   Understanding behavioral milestones for eating can help you use effective strategies for children with eating challenges.

Refusing Foods

Young children may refuse to eat foods for several reasons. Consuming too many liquids is a leading cause. Too much liquid can make a child feel full and displace other foods in the diet. To **mitigate** (lessen) this problem, limit milk and juices to snack and mealtimes. Offer water between meals to **quench** (satisfy) thirst.

Children may dislike foods that they have tried. They may also reject foods that are prepared in an unfamiliar manner. More often, however, children are copying the actions of others they have seen refusing to eat a certain food. Children need you to be a positive model for healthful eating.

Improper portion size can be another problem. Adults often overestimate how much food children can eat. This is one reason preschool children should serve their own food. Young children have internal signals that tell them when they are full. Pushing children to eat may cause them to ignore their internal cues, which may lead to overeating.

Pushing children to eat has another consequence—children may refuse the food just to see your reaction. In this way, eating can quickly become a power struggle. To avoid this situation, take a matter-of-fact approach to mealtimes. Provide nutritious foods and let the children choose which foods and how much of each food they will eat. Avoid becoming emotionally involved in their food choices.

Workplace Connections

Handling Food Refusals and Picky Eaters

Survey area programs that serve meals and snacks to young children. Investigate the ways staff handle food refusals and picky eaters.

1. What strategies are successful in getting children to eat a suitable portion of nutritious foods? Which methods do not work?
2. What effect does a picky eater's behavior have on the other children at the table?

Lesson 26.2 Review

1. Which of the following would *not* be a good category on a food chart? (26.2.1)
   A. Anytime
   B. Once in a while
   C. Never
   D. Sometimes

2. Each of the following is a simple limit that promotes a happy, relaxed cooking experience *except* _____. (26.2.2)
   A. encouraging children to clean up their messes
   B. scheduling mealtimes after outside playtime or active games
   C. making positive comments about the food
   D. eating with the children

3. How many children should participate in a cooking activity at one time? (26.2.2)
   A. No more than four to six
   B. The whole class
   C. No more than eight to ten
   D. It depends on the number of adults supervising

4. Which is an example of a simple recipe that would be appropriate for a first food-preparation experience? (26.2.3)
   A. Beef stew
   B. Steamed bao buns
   C. Tamales
   D. Turkey and cheese roll-ups

5. **True or False.** Serving multicultural foods in the classroom causes children to develop food intolerances. (26.2.4)

6. Children can begin to learn how to clean up after themselves after mealtimes _____. (26.2.5)
   A. at three years old
   B. at two years old
   C. when they begin to walk
   D. at one years old

7. Which of the following is a leading cause for young children refusing to eat? (26.2.6)
   A. Consuming too many liquids
   B. Overeating
   C. Too much exercise
   D. Boredom

Summary

Lesson 26.1

26.1-1 Food and nutrition experiences help young children to develop lifelong healthy-eating habits. These experiences promote children's cognitive, physical, social, and development and teach vital nutrition concepts.

26.1-2 Approximately one-third of preschool-age children consume most of their meals in early childhood settings. Local and state regulations vary widely and can influence the safety and nutritional value of the food programs provide, such as requirements about the use of prepackaged food. The foods consumed at the child care center can influence the child's preferences and choices.

26.1-3 Families directly and indirectly influences their child's eating habits. Centers can educate families on nutritional needs and offer guidance regarding mealtime difficulties and even resources in the community for food through a center-established lending library, newsletters, pamphlets, meetings, and discussion groups.

Lesson 26.2

26.2-1 Guiding food and nutrition experiences includes teaching basic nutrition concepts, planning for cooking experiences, setting tables, eating, and cleaning up. The skills children learn through these experiences are useful throughout their lives.

26.2-1 Introduce nutrition concepts in the classroom using activities that challenge children to identify and group food options.

26.2-2 Cooking is a STEM experience that promotes science, technology, engineering, and math. Setting limits is important for cooking experiences with young children to promote learning as well as ensure safety.

26.2-2 Food and nutrition experiences also involve interactions, movement, and activity. Children may become excited and require extra supervision. For this reason, the experiences must be well planned and limited to small groups of children. Having small groups allows you to provide enough space and tools for the children to use and share and the proper supervision.

26.2-3 When planning for first food-preparation experiences, teachers should select simple recipes, such as ones with a few ingredients and no cooking, and introduce more complex food experiences as developmentally appropriate.

26.2-4 Incorporating multicultural foods can promote acceptance of cultural differences and expand children's food experiences. Creating a classroom cookbook that incorporates dishes from the children's cultures and planning a bread-tasting party are two ways to introduce multicultural foods to young children.

24.2-5 Children develop responsibility, self-reliance, and social skills when they fully participate in mealtimes by setting the table, serving themselves, using appropriate manners, and cleaning up.

24.2-6 Sometimes teachers face eating challenges with the children. To solve these challenges, be a positive model. Reinforce positive eating habits and never turn eating into a power struggle. Let children choose what and how much they want to eat.

Vocabulary Activity

Write all the Key Terms for this chapter on a separate sheet of paper. For each term, quickly write a word you think relates to the term. In small groups, exchange papers. Have each person in the group explain a term on the list. Take turns until all terms have been explained.

Critical Thinking

1. **Draw Conclusions.** Choose one of the nutrition concepts covered in this chapter and draw conclusions about how you would teach that

concept to a young child. What activities would you use? How would you reinforce the concept after it was learned? Design a brief lesson plan for teaching this concept.

2. **Analyze.** Interview a registered dietitian about the nutritional needs of young children and how they are met through proper meal and snack planning. Prepare a list of questions ahead of time and take notes about the answers. After the interview, analyze the dietitian's answers. How can having accurate information about nutrient needs for specific age and growth stages help you plan food activities for children? How can you dispel nutrition myths among parents of these children?

3. **Cause and Effect.** Watch a Saturday morning television program designed for young children and compile a list of the food advertisements shown during the program. Do these ads convey positive messages about good nutrition? Negative messages? In a written report, summarize your findings and describe what effect you think the food advertisements might have on children.

4. **Create.** Choose an early childhood or childcare center and identify all of the cultures and ethnicities represented by the children. If your center contains less than three cultures, choose additional cultural backgrounds that you know are prevalent in your community. From this list of cultures and ethnicities, create a list of at least two foods from each culture that you could have children prepare in a classroom setting. List other multicultural foods you could have parents bring in for the children to taste.

Core Skills

1. **Writing.** In planning food and nutrition experiences, it is important to involve parents. In small groups, design a nutrition newsletter to be sent out to parents. What topics are most important for parents to understand? What questions do parents often have? Determine the columns and special features you want to include and then divide up the parts of the newsletter in your group. Write your part of the newsletter and then organize all your articles into one. Print copies of the newsletter for your class.

2. **Technology.** Search online for cooking activities for young children. As you search, evaluate each website by looking through the suggested activities and then rating them based on age-appropriateness; availability of ingredients and equipment; nutritional content; amount of adult help needed; relationship to program goals; and length of time. Compile the sites you recommend and any ideas you find interesting or useful into a class spreadsheet.

3. **Reading and Writing.** Choose a simple recipe to use with young children. Read the recipe carefully, making note of any complicated instructions or words that might be unfamiliar to young children. After reading, rewrite the recipe in chart form, making it understandable to young children by simplifying vocabulary and instructions.

4. **Math.** Contact a school cafeteria manager for several nutrition-conscious recipes that might appeal to young children. Determine the serving sizes appropriate for children and calculate the ingredient measurements needed for that size of a yield. What modifications will need to be considered? Will baking or cooking times need to be reduced for smaller pan sizes?

5. **Research.** Conduct an online search to find out more about food insecurity in your area. What factors influence food insecurity? What actions could you take as an educator to help reduce problems caused by food insecurity? Use presentation software to share your findings in a report to the class.

6. **CTE Career Readiness Practice.** Parents' Day is coming up at the early childhood center where you work, and you want the children to show their skills at preparing food, setting the table, and cleaning up. To prepare for the day, you need to create a plan for teaching and reinforcing these concepts over the next two weeks. In small groups, create a two-week series of activities to cement children's understandings of food preparation, setting the table, and cleaning up. Delegate which of you will direct each activity and present your plan to the class.

Portfolio Project

Create a recipe booklet for use in a preschool classroom. Collect at least 10 recipes that represent food products children can prepare by themselves or with very little help. Determine suggested age groups for each recipe added. Assemble the recipes into a booklet with an appropriate cover. File the completed booklet in your portfolio, allowing room for additional recipes to be added later.

Chapter 27

Reading Advantage

After reading each section, answer this question: If you explained the information to a friend who is not taking this class, what would you tell them?

Guiding Music and Movement Experiences

Lesson 27.1: The Role of Music and Movement Experiences

Lesson 27.2: Integrating Music and Movement Experiences

Case Study

Music and Movement Experiences in the Early Childhood Classroom

"Good morning to you, good morning to you, good morning Emanual, good morning to you." *Every day Eva Mizumo, who has been teaching preschoolers for over 25 years, uses songs and chants to welcome the children into her classroom. She has found music an excellent tool for introducing new children's names, building a sense of community, and teaching language, color, music, and math concepts.*

One morning when Eva was singing with the children, Luis Garcia brought his four-year-old son, Marcus, into the classroom. Eva nodded, smiled at Luis, and continued singing. But Luis remained and appeared to have a concerned look on his face. When group time was over and the children went to individual learning centers, Eva approached Luis wondering if he wanted to talk about something. Luis looked up and, with a serious look, said, "I am concerned about the lack of recognition of racial and cultural diversity. I can't understand why you do not sing songs in Spanish and English. Many children in this class are bilingual, and others could learn Spanish." Eva responded by saying, "I cannot speak Spanish." Then Mr. Garcia said, "We could help you by translating and taping Spanish songs. Some parents may even enjoy coming into the classroom and teaching the children Spanish songs."

Give It Some Thought

1. How would you have responded to Mr. Garcia? Why is it important for Eva to recognize racial and cultural diversity?
2. If you were Eva, how would you involve the parents? How could Eva learn Spanish?
3. What should be the contents of a music center? What multicultural instruments should be included?
4. What concepts can Eva teach the children using music and movement experiences?
5. What finger, hand, arm, and whole body movements can Eva teach?

Opening image credit: Liderina/Shutterstock.com

The Role of Music and Movement Experiences

Essential Question

How can music and movement experiences be supported in the early childhood classroom?

Learning Outcomes

After studying this lesson, you will be able to

27.1-1 **summarize** the importance of music experiences for children.

27.1-2 **design** a music center.

27.1-3 **outline** the teacher's role in music experiences.

27.1-4 **demonstrate** the use and purpose of rhythm instruments in an early childhood program.

Key Terms

music	whole song method
boisterous	phrase/whole
tempo	combination method
vitality	autoharp
phrase method	

On a rainy afternoon, Mrs. Oh notices that the children in her classroom are restless. They need some activity. She decides to guide them in a movement activity using a piece of music designed to promote movement.

Mrs. Oh tells the children to listen closely. Then she encourages them to move the way the music makes them feel. While observing the children, she sees that fast music makes them quickly hop up and down while slow music makes them tiptoe, taking tiny steps.

After the activity, Mrs. Oh feels she has achieved her goal. The children gained practice in listening. They also released pent-up energy and played cooperatively with each other. The activity included both music and movement. This type of activity promotes a sense of community.

27.1-1 Importance of Music and Movement Experiences

Music is a way of expressing ideas and feelings through sound. It is a powerful form of communication through which every culture speaks (**Figure 27.1**). Music is an important form of communication between adults and children. Adults often rock babies to sleep with soothing lullabies or play musical games with young children, such as *Ring-Around-the-Rosy, London Bridge,* and *Pat-a-Cake.* When adults incorporate

Liderina/Shutterstock.com

Figure 27.1 Children of all ages love to make music. *Why do you think music is such a powerful form of communication?*

music into their play with children, they help convey messages and communicate feelings. They pass on aspects of their culture and an appreciation for music. Through music, adults also teach children language skills, creativity, coordination, social interaction, and music basics.

To nurture the whole child, teachers use music of all cultures and styles with young children. Music is important because it:

- invites children to listen and express their emotions
- engages the brain by stimulating neural pathways in the brain
- exercises the brain and helps develop working-memory skills, which promote executive-function skills.
- builds a sense of community
- provides an opportunity to learn and use language concepts and vocabulary
- helps children connect with their feelings
- provides an opportunity to practice math skills, such as counting, size, and shape.
- provides relaxing background for playing, eating, and sleeping
- calms angry feelings and releases tension and energy
- can be used to express feelings through movement and dance
- can be used to manage behavior
- makes learning fun
- promotes attention control and development of listening skills
- helps build an understanding of musical concepts, including *loud/soft, high/low, fast/slow, up/down*
- helps build an appreciation of different cultural backgrounds (such as by encouraging children and their families to share their songs)
- helps build a sense of community as a social activity
- helps children learn about their own cultures and those of others

Music is a universal language. It is everywhere, and its power goes beyond words. Music experiences can increase creativity when teachers urge children to experiment, explore, and express themselves. Music—which can sound happy, soothing, sad, **boisterous** (loud or active), or relaxing—enhances the expression of feelings and thoughts. Music also helps children develop an awareness of the feelings of others. For young children, music is often a natural form of expression.

Language skills improve as children take part in music activities. As children listen and sing, they learn unfamiliar words and sounds and explore new concepts. Children also experiment with **tempo**, which is the speed of the music and the sound quality of the music. They enjoy singing their favorite songs and creating new ones. They also enjoy making sounds using their body and moving to music—stamping, clapping, whistling, marching, snapping, and singing.

Music activities help children grow cognitively through memorizing words to songs and learning to sing musical notes. Children also learn to compare musical concepts, such as loud/soft and fast/slow. They also learn songs to tell stories. Other concepts children learn through music include

- Music is a language made up of sounds.
- Music is a way of expressing ideas and feelings.
- Musical instruments each have their own sounds.
- Music can be used to express different moods
- Music can be played with a radio, digital tablet, CD player, record player
- Mobile phone and Bluetooth® speakers.

Music also appears to strengthen pathways in the brain. Researchers have found a link between music and the development of spatial intelligence. This type of mental ability helps children process math and science concepts.

In addition, children develop physically as they move during rhythmic activities and play instruments. Music experiences can also help children build positive self-concepts. As children learn about their culture and develop new skills, they gain self-confidence. Children also learn to respond to moods expressed by music, becoming more at ease with their emotions.

Children respond to and enjoy many forms of music experiences. They delight in listening to music and stories about music. They enjoy singing and vocal exploration to experience the different ways the voice can sound. They also like moving to music, playing rhythm instruments, and even making them. With their instruments, children enjoy making sounds (**Figure 27.2**). Four- and five-year-old children might even create their own songs, dances, and movements. When they do, video-record them and play back the recordings for their enjoyment.

27.1-2 The Music Center

To encourage music and movement activities in children, design and decorate a *music center* where children can learn and practice these

skills. Place a music center in an open section of the classroom to allow room for freedom of movement and children with diverse abilities. The active section of the room is best. Having dramatic play and block-building areas nearby encourages creative play. Provide beanbag chairs and pillows so children can sit and listen to music.

Display instruments on a table or open shelf so the children can easily access them (**Figure 27.3**). Include drums, kazoos, melody bells, clackers, maracas, rhythm sticks, guitars, tambourines, cymbals, and recorders on the shelf or table.

When buying instruments, look for quality. Quality instruments produce the best sounds. You can buy instruments and other supplies can through local music stores, school supply stores, catalogs, and online. Purchase music of

Smailik12/iStock via Getty Images Plus

Figure 27.3   This inviting display of instruments encourages the involvement of children. *Why do you think drums and other rhythm instruments are so appealing to children?*

FatCamera/E+ via Getty Images

Figure 27.2   Children enjoy listening to drums, such as the bongos shown here.

all cultures and styles. Consult online resources, your cellphone, or the Yellow Pages (or the Yellow Pages website) to get the names, addresses, and telephone numbers of music supply businesses. You will find a list of these businesses under such headings as *school supplies, music instruments, music, piano,* or *music dealers.*

Parents are also an excellent source for instruments. Many parents are happy to lend or give instruments to the program. Using instruments from many cultures helps to promote multicultural awareness.

The music center should also contain pictures of dancers, instruments, and singers. Choose pictures that represent the cultures of children in your classroom. Local music stores may be happy to supply you with these (**Figure 27.4**). Celebrate diversity by adding a multicultural library to teach respect and tolerance for others. Include recordings such as:

- *Multicultural Movement Fun* by Kimbo
- *Multicultural Children's Songs* by Ella Jenkins

Contents of a Music Center

- Autoharp, piano, or guitar
- Music for children, such as *Kids in Motion*; *Kids in Action*; *Shake Rattle Rock*; *We All Lie Together Volume 1 and 2* by Gregg & Steve
- Personal media player
- Pictures of dancers, instruments, and singers
- Rhythm sticks, tambourines, maracas, triangles, castanets, bongo drums
- Finger symbols, wrist and ankle bells
- Musical scarves, shake and ribbon bells, and wrist ribbons
- Brass symbols and hand bell
- Sound-producing objects (clocks, containers filled with pebbles)
- Songbooks
- Scarves, ribbon

Figure 27.4   The music center should include a variety of Instruments, equipment, songbooks, ribbons, scarves, and pictures of people dancing and using instruments.

- *Children of the World: Multicultural Rhythmic Activities* by Kimbo
- *Multicultural Rhythm Stick Fun* by Kimbo

Some centers even have mobile listening and storage centers. This unit has shelves, cubbies, and room to store headphones. Song books that could be stored in the cubby include:

- *All You Need is Love* by John Lennon and Paul McCartney
- *I Got Two Dogs* by John Litgrow
- *The Snowman's Song* by Marilee Joy Mayfield
- *Wheels on the Bus* by Raffi
- *When I Grow Up, I Want to be a Song* by Danielle LaRosa
- *Hush Little Bunny* by David Ezra Stein

Usually, the mobile storage units come with wheels, so they are portable. Some teachers whose centers are in warmer climates will roll them outdoors where there is much more space for movement activities.

27.1-3 The Teacher's Role in Music Experiences

The teacher's role in music experiences is to encourage musical expression. Children need surroundings in which they can explore, sing, and move to the music. Children may be nonparticipants, distant observers, close observers, limited participants, or eager participants. The extent of their participation and the time they will spend in musical activities will vary. It will depend on their age, interest, ability, and experiences.

Music does not require an introduction at a set time and place. Interweave it throughout the day. For instance, children respond better to musical directions than spoken directions. For this reason, many teachers use music to make announcements, provide transitions, and direct cleanup activities. Teachers may use music to welcome and say goodbye to the children. It is also important that surroundings promote and support music. Recorded music, personal media players, rhythm instruments, and singing all invite children to share music. Teachers' roles in music and movement experiences include encouraging discovery, encouraging nonparticipants, selecting songs, creating songs, teaching songs, singing with children, and accompanying singing.

Dual-language learners require support in music experiences. Introduce unfamiliar words. Then connect these words to the child's home language, which should prepare them to follow along with the music.

Encouraging Discovery

Musical instruments fascinate young children, so another role of the teacher is to promote children's interest in instruments and their sounds. This helps children grow in awareness. To promote the children's interest, you must also show interest. For example, during a group play activity, you may ask one of these questions:

- How can you make a different sound?
- How was this sound different?

- Can you make a faster sound?
- Can you make a slower sound?
- Can you make a louder sound?
- Can you make a softer sound?

You may also increase music awareness by asking children to listen to each other play instruments. Place four or five instruments on a table during free choice play periods. Otherwise, introduce the instruments at group time. A comment like "Here are some instruments that you may wish to play" may be all you need to arouse children's curiosity.

To encourage the children, comment on their efforts. Such statements as "You are making some interesting sounds," "Your sounds are beautiful," or "You found a new way" build positive self-concepts. You may also encourage children by prompting. For example, you may say, "Show me how you made that sound."

Early Childhood Insight 🅰🅱🅒

Using Music Responsibly

Using music responsibly in the classroom means maintaining high standards of ethical conduct regarding the music you use and record. In the United States, it also means following copyright laws.

Most music written since 1922 in the United States is copyright protected. This means the composer or publisher of the music has exclusive legal rights to reproduce, publish, sell, or distribute the creative works (also called *intellectual property*). Using music responsibly means legally purchasing and using music according to copyright owner's' guidelines. Here are some terms related to copyright that you should know.

- *Public domain*—a term that indicates a created work is not protected by copyright and is free for all to use. For example, because *Mary Had a Little Lamb* was written before 1922, it has no copyright and is free to use. The best way to identify public-domain music is to look for the copyright date and publisher on an original printed piece of music.

- *Royalty-free*—this term refers to music that is sold by the copyright holder for a one-time fee. Note that fees and terms of use can vary.
- *Out-of-print*—this term means the publisher is no longer printing a created work. It does not mean the work is in the public domain or that you are free to use it. In such instances, contact the publisher for permission to use or reprint such a work.

If you purchase and download music to use in the classroom, be sure to use reliable sites. There are many potentially deceptive download services that charge a subscription fee for music to which they have no legal right. This puts you at risk of downloading music illegally and facing the consequences of such actions.

For more information about the use of copyrighted music, see the *Music Education Copyright Center* hosted on The National Association for Music Educators website.

Encouraging Nonparticipants

In every group of young children, there are some children who choose to observe. These children prefer to listen to and watch the group. Nonparticipating children usually need more time to take part in music activities. Handle these children with patience. Try to stand next to such children during movement activities. With a smile on your face, slowly take their hands and swing to the rhythm. Then continue to encourage participation by nodding and smiling at them, showing your approval and enthusiasm. A skilled aide can also help encourage children who do not want to take part.

Selecting Songs

When choosing songs for young children, respect the children's ages, abilities, experiences, and interests (**Figure 27.5**). Simplicity is the key. The best songs for young children:

- tell a story
- have repetitive, easy-to-learn phrases

- have a developmentally appropriate vocabulary
- have a strongly defined and attractive mood or rhythm
- have a range of only one octave (most children are comfortable with the range from C to A or D to B)
- encourage active involvement
- relate to children's level of development

Selecting success-oriented songs is the key to involving the children. Begin by choosing songs you enjoy. To arouse children's interest, you must convey enthusiasm for a song. Have an expressive face and know the song well. Encourage the children to clap the words of their favorite songs. Children will not tire of a well-loved song. They will repeat it over and over once they know it.

Most children enjoy many types of songs, such as songs about familiar objects, families, lullabies, holiday songs, and songs with actions. Songs are rich stories about the world. Some songs are best for older children. Others, because of their content, are best for younger children, such as *Twinkle, Twinkle, Little Star*.

UW-Stout Child and Family Study Center

Figure 27.5 Children love outdoor games that involve singing and moving. *Why do you think success-oriented songs are key to involving children in singing and movement?*

Children's songbooks are available at bookstores, at professional conference exhibits, from early childhood catalogs, and online. These books can be sources for new songs. You can also use the songbooks along with the piano, guitar, or autoharp. If possible, keep several of these books to use as resources.

Workplace Connections

Creating Song Lists

Create lists of songs suitable for teaching toddlers, preschoolers, and young school-age children. Review children's songbooks and recordings for song ideas and interview early childhood educators about their favorite songs for young children.

1. What were early childhood educators' favorite songs? Why?
2. Why is it important to choose quality songs for children's music experiences?

Creating Songs

The best way to create a song is to use a melody you know with unfamiliar words. For example, *Baa, Baa, Black Sheep*; *Twinkle, Twinkle, Little Star*; and *The Alphabet Song* all share a tune that you can use for other songs. Changing words to this tune is a good way to teach language skills. You can translate some of the children's favorite songs from English into other languages.

Teaching Songs

The teacher's attitude about music influences children's responses. If you, as a teacher, are thrilled by and enjoy music, the children will likely also enjoy music. When teaching a song, know the song well and try to sing clearly, using expression, proper pitch, and rhythm. Use a CD or an audio file to learn the song. Sing with **vitality** (liveliness) and zest. When you do, the children will learn by imitating your voice. There are three methods for teaching songs: the phrase method, the whole song method, and the phrase/whole combination method.

The **phrase method** of teaching is used with longer songs and younger children. First, prepare the children by telling them what to listen for. For example, say, "I'm going to sing you a song about a dog named Wags. I want you to listen carefully and tell me what Wags does."

After this introduction, sing the entire song. Then stop and talk about the song. Next, sing short sections and have the children repeat these sections after you. Keep singing, increasing the length of the sections until the children know the song. After the children appear comfortable, drop out. This will prevent them from depending on you to lead songs.

The **whole song method** is used to teach songs that are short and simple, with a repetitive theme. Tell the children to listen to you. After they have listened to you sing the song once, ask them to sing with you. Repeat the song a few times to be sure the children know the words.

The **phrase/whole combination method** is done by teaching key phrases. Sing a key phrase and have the children repeat it. Continue until you have introduced a few key phrases in the song. Then sing the whole song and have children join in when they can. Repeat the song until children have learned all the words. Stress key phrases with rhythmic movement or visual props to make them more meaningful (**Figure 27.6**). An example would be *Johnny Pounds with One Hammer*. As the song is sung, both you and the children can mimic a pounding action.

UW-Stout Child and Family Study Center

Figure 27.6 This prop for *Five Green Speckled Frogs* helps children learn and remember the song. *Think of a song for children you enjoy. What prop could you create to accompany the song?*

Singing with Children

Teachers often find singing with young children fun. However, it is not uncommon for novice teachers to be shy about singing before a group of children. This fear is needless. Young children are not critics. They enjoy hearing their teachers sing.

Enthusiasm is the key factor in creating a positive experience. Your delight in music will be catching. Share an expressive face. Remember to smile and enjoy yourself. If you do, you will see children smiling and enjoying themselves, too.

Avoid forcing children to take part. Singing is a learned behavior, and whether singing alone or in a group, it takes some courage. Preschool children will usually join in group singing. By age five, most children will be comfortable singing alone. When children feel ready to take part, they will. Meanwhile, try to make music an enjoyable experience for them. As a result, the children's natural creativity will blossom.

When singing with or to children, use a light, pleasant singing voice. Children find it easier to match the tones of human voices than to match pianos or instruments. Therefore, for children up to age three, use instruments as little as possible.

Accompanying Singing

Many early childhood teachers like to play the piano, autoharp, ukulele, or guitar while children sing. Instrument availability and your playing skills will affect the choice. Remember, though, that your enjoyment of the music is much more important than flawless playing.

Some teachers do not use instruments even if they are skilled. They believe playing instruments detract from the total experience. Children's attention wanders. To avoid this pitfall, use the autoharp, ukulele, or guitar. With these instruments, children will see your facial expressions and lip movements. They will feel your involvement in the activity.

Piano

Early childhood centers often use electric pianos for accompaniment in some classrooms since they take up less space and never need tuning. A piano has a clear sound and can play melodies and accompany singing. You do not need advanced playing skills for successful music experiences. Children seldom notice missed chords or unpleasant notes. Instead, they notice enthusiasm and delight.

Autoharp

An **autoharp** is a simple chording instrument used to accompany singing. The autoharp is more useful than a piano for several reasons. It is not as costly as a piano, and it is portable. Teachers can take it to class picnics, on field trips, and out on the playground.

Learning to play an autoharp is quite simple. Begin by positioning the instrument so you can read the identification bars. Use your left hand to press the chord bars. Strum the strings with your right hand. For each beat, strum one chord. Many teachers have learned to play within a few hours by using a self-instruction book.

Guitar and Ukulele

The guitar and ukulele are string instruments. They are more difficult to learn to play than the autoharp. Like the autoharp, they are portable. Teachers can move the guitar or ukulele to the playground or take on a field trip. For this reason, it is often a favorite of many early childhood teachers.

27.1-4 Rhythm Instruments

Many children taking part in music activities use rhythm instruments. By playing rhythm instruments, children can express their feelings. Children who have expressed little interest or skill in singing may respond better to musical instruments (**Figure 27.7**).

Rhythm instruments can be used to:
- build listening skills
- create music
- accompany the beat of a sound or recording
- classify sounds
- discriminate between sounds
- project music or mood
- experiment with sounds
- organize sounds to communicate feelings and ideas

Liderina/Shutterstock.com

Figure 27.7   Children can have fun with rhythm instruments without worrying about their musical talents. *How can children benefit from playing rhythm instruments?*

- develop classification skills by learning the difference between *quiet* and *loud*, *hard* and *soft*, and other sounds

Your role as a teacher is to purchase instruments and create objects used for music. Rhythm instruments can be store-bought or made by teachers, parents, volunteers, and sometimes even children. Handmade instruments often will not have the same quality as store-bought instruments. Handmade instruments, however, serve a purpose by exposing children to many sounds.

Introducing Rhythm Instruments

Teachers can use rhythm instruments during individual or group experiences. Before giving children instruments to play, set rules. The following guidelines are suggested for using rhythm instruments in a group:

- Quietly hand out the instruments. This prevents children from getting too excited and becoming disruptive. One method that works well is to choose one child to hand out the instruments. This prevents children from struggling with one another to get their favorite instruments. Some teachers prefer setting the instruments in a circle to prevent crowding.

- If you have a variety of instruments, introduce only one at a time. The number of different instrument types should be limited to two, three, or four to keep the volume lower.

- Explain to the children that the instruments must be handled with respect and care. The instruments will be taken away from children who abuse them.

- After the children have instruments in their hands, allow them a few minutes to experiment. Most children will want to play their instrument right away. Use a signal, such as beating a drum, raising your hand, or playing the autoharp to have the children stop.

- Rotate instruments after children have had time to experiment. This gives each child a chance to play all the instruments.

- After the activity, have the children return their instruments to the box, table, or shelf where they belong.

Building Rhythm Instruments

Some teachers have the time and resources to make rhythm instruments. Instruments that teachers can make include sandpaper blocks and sticks, bongo and tom-tom drums, rattlers and shakers, rhythm sticks and bells, and coconut cymbals.

Sandpaper Blocks

Children of all ages can use sandpaper blocks. For this reason, they are often the first rhythm instruments used in the classroom. Some classrooms contain one pair of sandpaper blocks for each child.

Safety First

Instrument Safety

Musical instruments with small parts should be inaccessible to children three years of age and under. Shakers and rattlers and other instruments with parts smaller than 1-1/4 inches by 2-1/4 inches are potential choking hazards. Because choking still occurs during the preschool years, teachers and care providers must be vigilant in their supervision when making or using musical instruments with children.

Sandpaper blocks can be used for sound effects. They make a soft swishing sound and are played by rubbing the two sandpaper blocks together. See **Figure 27.8** for instructions on making sandpaper blocks.

Sandpaper Blocks

Materials
- 2 blocks of soft pine, 4 by 3 by 1 inch in size
- Several sheets of coarse sandpaper
- Colored enamel paint
- Thumbtacks or staples
- Strong glue (epoxy based)
- 2 straps of leather or flexible plastic, 4 to 4-1/2 inches long
- Scissors
- Hammer

Procedure
1. Sand the wood to remove all rough edges.
2. Paint the blocks a bright color to make them attractive and to prevent the wood from becoming soiled.
3. Glue the straps to each block to form handles:
4. Cut the sandpaper to fit the bottom and sides of each block:
5. Attach the sandpaper to the blocks with thumbtacks or staples. (As sand is rubbed off the paper, replace with new sandpaper.)

Figure 27.8 It takes just a little effort to make these inexpensive sandpaper blocks.

Sandpaper Sticks

Purchase rough sandpaper and wooden doweling 1 inch wide and 12 inches long for each stick. To construct the sticks, wrap and glue sandpaper around each of the dowels. Leave a small section for use as a handle. Then sand the end of the sticks smooth. Direct the children to scrape the dowels back and forth across each other to make a sound. These sticks, like the sandpaper blocks, will need to have the sandpaper replaced from time to time.

Bongo Drums

Bongo drums are a favorite of many preschool children. With a drum, children can create many tones by hitting the drumhead near the rim, in the center, and elsewhere.

To construct bongo drums, collect a pair of scissors, string, a piece of rubber, an empty coffee can with both ends removed, a hammer, and a large nail.

Use the plastic lid from the coffee can to trace two circles on the rubber. Allow an extra inch to pull over the edges. Cut out the circles. Take the hammer and large nail and punch holes around the outside edge of each circle. After the holes have been punched, place a rubber circle over each end of the can. Then lace the rubber circles to each other using string.

Tom-Tom Drums

Making tom-toms can be a group project for the children. You will need round oatmeal boxes (with lids) and tempera paint, watercolor markers, or construction paper. One way to get all the empty oatmeal boxes needed is to ask parents to send them from home. To make the tom-toms, tell the children to tape the lid on the box. After this, give them tempera paint, watercolor markers, or colored construction paper and paste to decorate their tom-toms. If needed, the children can use a rhythm stick for a drumstick.

Tin can tom-toms can be made with large empty coffee cans. Use the plastic top to cut three sheets of wrapping paper two inches larger than the top of the tin for each tom-tom. Glue the three sheets together. Stretch the glued paper over one end of the coffee can. Secure the paper with a large rubber band or string.

Focus on Careers

Music Therapist

Music therapists plan, direct, and coordinate evidence-based music therapy interventions that positively influence an individual's physical, cognitive, psychological, or behavioral status. They may engage clients in therapeutic music activities to improve communication, cognitive function, or controlling impulses. They may sing and play musical instruments such as the guitar or keyboard, and may also include dance and movement activities. They also help clients reflect on their musical experiences. Music therapists may work in medical or school settings. Many work with customized treatment programs for specific areas, including intellectual or developmental disabilities, physical disabilities, and wellness. Music therapists document objectives and strategies to help clients meet their goals.

Career cluster: Health sciences.

Education: Music therapists are typically required to have a bachelor's degree and successfully complete an internship. Some employers may require board certification in music therapy.

Job outlook. Employment for music therapists is expected to grow 10 percent through 2030, which is about as fast as average for all occupations.

To learn more about a music therapist, visit the US Department of Labor websites for the ***Occupational Outlook Handbook (OOH)*** and ***O*NET OnLine***. You can compare the job responsibilities, educational requirements, job outlook, and average pay for music therapists with similar occupations.

Rattles and Shakers

Making rattles and shakers is a simple activity in which the children can take part. To collect supplies for making instruments, ask parents to send a round saltbox to school with their children.

To make the instrument, give each child a handful of dry beans, corn kernels, or rice. Show the children how to pour them into the box. Then give each child a strip of tape to seal off the pour spout on the box.

After the box has been filled and the spout taped closed, the children can decorate their rattlers. Give the children tempera paint, washable markers, crayons, colored construction paper, and paste. After the rattlers have been decorated, put them on display. Encourage the children to explore the variety of sounds made by the different materials.

Rhythm Sticks

Rhythm sticks are always made in matching pairs. Wooden doweling from ¾ to 1 inch in diameter is needed. Cut the doweling into 12-inch lengths. Sand each end of the doweling. Add a protective coat of shellac or enamel paint.

Rhythm sticks can also be made from bamboo. This type of wood will produce a hollow sound. An excellent source for bamboo is a local carpet dealer. To make the rhythm sticks, cut the bamboo into 10- to 12-inch pieces. Tape each end of the stick with tape to prevent splinters.

Teach the children to play with rhythm sticks, holding one stick in each hand. They should hold one stick steady while striking near the top with a second stick. (**Figure 27.9**).

Jingle sticks are rhythm sticks with bells attached to each end. The bells can be attached with a small cup hook. After placing the bell on the hook, use pliers to force the cup hook closed. You may wish to paint the sticks bright colors. This may make them appealing to children.

Daria Kolpakova/iStock via Getty Images Plus

Figure 27.9   Children quickly learn to play rhythm instruments properly.

Rhythm Bells

Materials needed to make rhythm bells include strips of elastic 1/2 to 3/4 inch wide and 5 inches long. Also gather five to six bells for each strip of elastic and a needle and thread.

Sew the ends of the elastic together by overlapping the ends. This can be done by hand or on a sewing machine. On one side of the loop, sew on five or six small bells. Vary the size of the bells on the loops for a variety of sounds. The children will then learn that the sounds made by bells of different sizes vary.

Coconut Cymbals

Cymbals made of coconut halves offer many sounds. They can sound like horses galloping when clapped together. They can also be hit with a rhythm stick to make fast, light music.

To make coconut cymbals, buy several large coconuts at the supermarket. Each coconut will make a pair of cymbals. First, drain the milk from the coconuts. Then cut each coconut in half with a sharp saw and remove all the meat. Sand the outside and inside edges of the shell until smooth. After this, shellac or paint both sides of the shell.

Buying Rhythm Instruments

Many teachers do not have time to make all the instruments needed for their programs. As a result, some instruments will have to be bought.

Buy instruments that are sturdy (Figure 27.10). For instance, buy maracas that are constructed in one piece. Otherwise, the handles may come loose. Triangles should hang from sturdy holders. If the holder is not strong, the instrument may twirl around when a child is trying to strike it. Jingle bells should always be attached to elastic. This makes them flexible enough to use as either wrist or ankle bracelets. Check drum and tambourine heads to make sure they are durable and fastened firmly. The skins should be free from cuts or holes.

Try to buy instruments in several sizes. This allows for a good mix of tones. Usually smaller instruments have higher tones. Larger instruments have deeper tones.

FatCamera/E+ via Getty Images

Figure 27.10 Center instruments get much use, so they must be durable. *What other rhythm instruments might be easy to make?*

Lesson 27.1 Review

1. Researchers have found a link between music and the development of _____ intelligence, which helps children process math and science concepts. (27.1.1)
   A. interpersonal
   B. musical
   C. spatial
   D. community

2. **True or False.** Using instruments from many cultures does not promote multicultural awareness. (27.1.2)

3. The teacher's role in music experiences is to encourage _____. (27.1.3)
   A. musical expression
   B. group time
   C. mathematical concepts
   D. ecological concepts

4. Rhythm instruments can be used for each of the following **except** _____. (27.1.4)
   A. building listening skills
   B. creating music
   C. improving reading skills
   D. experimenting with sounds

Lesson 27.2 Integrating Music and Movement Activities

Essential Question

What do you need to know about integrating music and movement activities to help children develop their skills and feel successful?

Learning Outcomes

After studying this lesson, you will be able to

27.2-1 **analyze** considerations for scheduling music activities.

27.2-2 **plan** a variety of music activities, including listening, singing, mouthing, and chanting.

27.2-3 **summarize** how to teach various movement activities.

27.2-4 **describe** movement activities that promote children's development.

Key Terms

speech skills

chant

body percussion

auditory discrimination skills

pantomiming

Successfully integrating music and movement activities in the classroom is an important skill. Music is a universal language and a form of communication that every culture speaks and it often plays a key role at social activities. It is an activity that ignites all areas of child development, and teachers can schedule it throughout the day. Listening, singing, mouthing, and chants are all types of musical experiences. Movement, another type of music activity, helps children develop concepts of time, space, and weight awareness. Children can use the expression of body movements, rather than words, to tell stories. Through these experiences, children learn basic skills such as concentration, listening, and the recall of information.

27.2-1 Scheduling Music

Music should be scheduled throughout the day. It fits in well after a story, at the start of the day, after a snack, and during free playtime. It can be used during waiting times, such as the end of the day, a bus ride on a field trip, or before and after lunch. Music can be used to remind children of rules they may have forgotten. For instance, if Sam and Gail did not hang up their coats, you may sing "At school we hang up our coats, hang up our coats."

Besides these impromptu uses, music should also be scheduled as a group activity for four- and five-year-old children. This should occur at the same time every day, since children thrive on consistent schedules.

Scheduling Group Music

Group music activities help build group feelings and pride. A group setting is an excellent way to introduce new songs and instruments. These activities should focus on the group, not the individual.

Group time should be fairly brief. Schedule 7 to 10 minutes for two- and three-year-olds. You may later extend the period up to 15 minutes for four- and five-year-old children. Some centers schedule two short music periods. Early childhood programs may have to adjust their music time to meet the children's attention spans and developmental levels.

You will need to be well-organized for a successful group music experience. The following suggestions may help:

- Always be prepared. Ensure you have collected all the instruments, music, and other accessories needed.

- Use the same signal to call the children together for group music time. This signal may be a song, an autoharp chord, a beat on a drum, or a piano tune.

- Have the children sit in a circle or semicircle so they can see you and you can see them. To help children sit in the proper places, mark the floor with chalk, tape, or carpet squares.

- Require all adults in the classroom to take part. Their support encourages children to join in, too. These adults can also sit on the floor with the children and help them learn words and responses to the music.

- Switch between active and quiet music activities. If you always require children to listen to music, they may become bored. Likewise, they may tire quickly from, or become too excited by, activities that involve a great deal of movement.

- Reward children for positive behavior. Tell them what type of behavior you expect: sitting quietly, waiting for their turns, holding instruments correctly, and singing clearly at the proper volume. Ignore disruptive behavior if it only involves one child. If the child continues to be disruptive, ask another adult in the group to remove the child. Separate children who act up when they sit together during group time.

- Use familiar songs that include fingerplays every day. Such songs are favorites because children find it easy to take part.

- Remember, you are the leader of voice volume which is contagious. To gain the children's attention, sometimes use a soft voice; even a whisper can have a dramatic effect.

Scheduling Individual Music

Group music activities may stress conformity. Children are not as free during these times to

express their creativity. For this reason, individual music activities are also an important part of the music experience.

During self-selected play, encourage children to interact with the music. Play music during this period. Make rhythm instruments, the piano, an audio recorder, and a CD or personal media player available throughout the day (**Figure 27.11**). It is also a good idea to station a teacher or other adult in the music area. An adult's presence will encourage children to enter the area and engage in musical experiences.

27.2-2 Music Activities

Listening, singing, playing rhythm instruments, and moving to rhythm are all music activities. An excellent program contains all these

Surachetkhamsuk/iStock via Getty Images Plus

Figure 27.11 Many children love listening to music.

activities and includes repetition. Young children enjoy listening to and singing the same song over and over.

Listening

All music activities involve listening. The ability to listen is important for learning. Good listening skills help children build proper speech habits, an extended attention span, and reading readiness skills.

Listening to music can enrich the imaginations of young children. It can also help them relax and release pent-up feelings. Listening can take place when singing or when playing rhythm instruments, the piano, or a personal media player.

Children need to be taught how to listen. As a teacher, you need to give them reasons for listening. For example, you may say, "Listen to this music and tell me how it makes you feel." After playing the music, let the children express their feelings. The games in **Figure 27.12** can help young children develop listening skills.

Fingerplays are another useful method for teaching listening skills. Choose fingerplays based on developmental levels. For example, a fingerplay for two-year-olds should be short and contain simple words.

Teachers who enjoy fingerplays may wish to purchase their own fingerplay books for their professional libraries. They can purchase these books at a professional conference, a bookstore, or online. You can also download fingerplays from the internet.

The words of a fingerplay reinforce movements. Likewise, the movements reinforce words. Using body movements, the children learn how to express emotion.

Listening Games

What's the Sound?

Record sounds from different parts of the home. These may include running water, flushing toilets, ringing telephones, closing doors, or sounds made by scissors, doorbells, washing machines, radios, and electric garage door openers. Play each sound back to the children and ask them to name the object making the noise.

Body Sounds

Tell the children that you are going to play a body sound game. Tell them to close their eyes or cover them with their hands and listen carefully. Then stomp your feet, snap your fingers, slap your thigh, smack your lips, and clap your hands. Have the children guess how you are making the sounds.

Instrument Sounds

Provide the children with a box or basket of rhythm instruments to explore. Then ask the following questions:

- What instrument sounds like jingle bells?
- What instrument sounds like a church bell?
- What instrument sounds like the tick of a clock?
- What instrument sounds like thunder?
- What instrument has a loud sound?
- What instrument has a quiet sound?

Guess the Instruments

Let the children become familiar with the classroom instruments. Then, based on developmental level or age of the child, choose a few instruments to use in a game called "Guess the Instrument." With two-year-old children, choose only two instruments. These should have very different sounds. As the children progress, add more instruments. To play the game, tell the children to cover their eyes and listen to the sound made by the instrument you are playing. Then they can guess what instrument you are playing. After children are familiar with the game, older children may want to play the teacher's role. In this event, you, too, should cover your eyes and take part.

Figure 27.12   You can teach children how to listen; however, you need to give them reasons for listening. ***Why do children need reasons for listening to music?***

Some teachers prefer to file fingerplays under specific themes. For example, you could file "Two Little Apples" with units on apples, fall, or nutrition. You might file "Roll Them" under *transitions*, *movements*, or *body concepts*. Size concepts or numbers would be good themes for using "Here's a Ball." Consider filing "Lickety-Lick," a childhood favorite, under *science concepts*. You could use it for teaching these concepts during cooking experiences (**Figure 27.13**).

Singing

Children's best musical instruments are their voices. Their voices are always with them. Even very young children make musical cooing and crying sounds. These tones vary in strength and pitch. Singing is a behavior that children learn. As children take part in singing experiences, they learn voice control.

Workplace Connections

The Role of Music in Early Childhood Programs

Survey area preschool and childcare teachers to discover the role music education plays in their curriculums.
1. How often are music activities conducted in the classroom?
2. Do children have daily access to musical and rhythm band instruments, or are they used only on special occasions?

After children babble, tonal patterns emerge. Most children can sing by age two. They often sing as they dress, eat, and play. By this time, singing is a meaningful activity.

Fingerplays

Two Little Apples

Two little apples hanging high in the tree. (Place arms above head.)

Two little apples smiling at me. (Look up at hands and smile.)

I shook that tree as hard as I could. (Make a shaking motion.)

Down came the apples. Mmmmmmm, so good. (Make a falling motion with arms. Hold hands to mouth, pretending to eat.)

Roll Them

Roll them and roll them. (Roll hands.)

And give your hands a clap. (Clap hands.)

Roll them and roll them. (Roll hands.)

And place them in your lap. (Place hands in lap.)

Here's a Ball

Here's a ball. (Make a small circle with thumb and index finger.)

And here's a ball. (Make a large circle by using both thumbs and index fingers.)

A great big ball I see. (Make a huge circle with arms.)

Shall we count them? Are you ready? One, two, three.

Lickety-Lick

Lickety-lick, lickety-lick. (Make a big circle with the left arm by placing hand on hip. Place the right hand inside the circle.)

The batter is getting all thickety-thick. (Stir with the right hand.)

What should we bake? What shall we bake? (Gesture by opening hands.)

A great big beautiful cake. (Extend arms to show a big cake.)

Figure 27.13 Using fingerplays with specific themes allows you to teach specific concepts. *How do movements support fingerplays?*

Children's singing skills vary a great deal. In a group of two-year-olds, there may be children able to sing in tune and make up tunes. Other children cannot master these skills until they are three or four years old.

You may notice that children who stutter often sing clearly. These children can improve their **speech skills** through singing (**Figure 27.14**). Children also learn to sing through mouthing and chants.

Mouthing

Children's mouths can make coughing, gurgling, sipping, kissing, and hissing sounds. With their mouths, they can make an animal, train, plane, machinery, and traffic sound. As children compare these sounds, they will learn that some are fast, others are slow, some are loud, and some are quiet. Thus, exploring mouth sounds can add to knowledge. As children explore these sounds, they learn about others. Joining a variety of sounds can produce unique music.

To encourage children to make sounds, bring pictures to a group activity. For instance, collect pictures of large, medium, and small dogs in several poses. The dogs might bark, show their teeth, or play with their owners. Show the children each picture. Ask them to mimic the sounds a dog would make in each instance. You can use pictures of other animals, people, machines, cars, trucks, and other objects. These activities will help children become sensitive to sounds.

Chants

A **chant** is a group of words spoken with a lively beat. It is a song with word patterns, rhymes, and nonsense syllables in one to three tones repeated in a sequence. "Teddy Bear, Teddy Bear, Turn Around" is a chant. Mother Goose rhymes are also chants. Chants are an important form of early childhood singing. Children learn to speak together in unison by chanting.

Chanting is a beneficial activity for all children. They learn to share the joy of language. They also learn to cooperate. Chants provide opportunities to practice auditory discrimination skills. The rhythmic response to chants is helpful for children who are learning English as a second language. Chanting is also good for children who speak nonstandard English. Shy children can develop self-confidence and self-expression by chanting.

Kali9/E+ via Getty Images

Figure 27.14   Singing along to music helps many children correct speech problems. ***Investigate how singing can help children improve their speech.***

Like singing, you will need to model chanting for the children. Begin by repeating it aloud several times. When the children feel comfortable, encourage them to join you.

27.2-3 The Teacher's Role in Movement Experiences

For learning, movement is an important nonverbal tool that often includes math and language concepts. Movements provide opportunities for children to stretch their imaginations. They can walk like elephants, crawl like worms, or pilot an airplane. Children almost always enjoy these experiences.

Movement activities should provide children with the chance to:

- explore the many ways their bodies can move
- practice combining movement with rhythm
- discover they can express many ideas through movement
- learn how movement is related to space (**Figure 27.15**)
- develop respect for others' ideas

Some children will take naturally to movement activities. Other children may feel more self-conscious or embarrassed. To help these children, begin with some short, simple movement activities. Knowing what type of responses to expect can help you prepare.

Understanding Children's Responses

Studies show that two- and three-year-old children's responses to movement vary. Most two-year-old children actively respond to the rhythm, but at their own tempo. Their response may be to repeat the same basic movement throughout the entire activity. For example, a two-year-old may simply jump up and down during an entire song.

By age three, children have gained greater motor coordination. As a result, they have more control over rhythmic dance-like responses. Three-year-old children will probably use many

SolStock/E+ via Getty Images

Figure 27.15   Children like to discover what their bodies can do through movement activities.

responses. They may circle with their arms, run, and jump during the same recording. The mood of the music will encourage children to express their emotions through movement.

Between ages four and six, muscular coordination keeps improving, and their interest in movement and space increases. Watching children at this stage, you notice they skip, run, climb, clap, and dance to music. Now they do these movements to the beat of the music. If the beat is fast, their movements are quick. They move more slowly to slow beats.

Preparing for Movement Experiences

To prepare for movement activities, first select your activity. **Figure 27.16** lists many movements. Then stand in front of a full-length mirror and practice the movements. Do each movement in the activity. Repeat the movements several times.

In the classroom, your role will be that of a facilitator and supporter. Children learn best when they can see and hear. Rather than simply explain, you may have to act out certain movements. For instance, in the fingerplay "Two Little Apples," during the line "Way up high in the apple tree," place your hands high above your head. Reinforcing the words with actions also adds interest.

Body Movements

Finger Movements		Hand and Arm Movements		Whole Body Movements	
Cutting	Rolling	Bouncing	Rolling	Bending	Running
Folding	Rubbing	Carrying	Shaking	Bouncing	Scooting
Holding	Smoothing	Catching	Slapping	Climbing	Shaking
Patting	Snapping	Circling	Squiggling	Crawling	Spinning around
Petting	Tickling	Clapping	Stretching	Creeping	
Pinching	Touching	Dropping	Sweeping	Dancing	Shuffling
Pointing	Typing	Grabbing	Swinging	Galloping	Skipping
Poking	Wiggling	Lifting	Throwing	Hopping	Sliding
Pulling		Punching	Twisting	Jumping	Swaying
		Pulling	Waving	Leaping	Twirling
		Reaching		Rocking	Walking
				Rolling over	

Figure 27.16 When using movement activities, be prepared to act out certain movements.

Teaching Movements

Most movement activities encourage children to explore, create, and express their own way of moving. A tambourine can capture children's interest before and during the activities. Tambourines are very useful. You can play them loud or soft, slow or fast. They can represent a galloping horse or a frightened kitten.

For successful movement activities, you will need to follow specific guidelines:

- Choose a time when the children are calm and well rested.

- Define space limits. There needs to be enough open, clear space. If you have limited space, move chairs and furniture to the side.

- Tell children they need to stop when the music stops.

- For variety in movement experiences, provide props such as paper streamers, balls, and scarves (**Figure 27.17**).

- Use movement activities involving personal media players, rhythm instruments, and verbal instructions.

- Allow children to get to know activities by repeating many of the experiences.

- Stop before signs of fatigue appear.

JenJPayless2/Shutterstock.com

Figure 27.17 Using props adds an additional dimension to movement activities. *What guidelines are important to follow for successful movement activities?*

You can use almost any music for movement experiences. You may want children to be involved in planning some movement activities. Ask the children to suggest movement activities and to bring in their favorite music. After the group experience, place these pieces of music in the music center. This will give children the chance to listen to the music again.

Early movement activities should be simple—stomping feet, clapping hands, patting thighs, and snapping fingers are all simple movements. These are called **body percussion**. These movements involve using the body to make rhythm. Children can use body percussion to learn to do more than one movement at a time. Body percussion also helps children build **auditory discrimination skills**—the ability to detect unique sounds by listening.

Stomping feet to music has always been a favorite activity of young children. To stomp correctly, children should bring their legs back and stomp down and forward.

Children should be taught to clap with one palm held up steadily. You should refer to this palm as the *instrument*. The other hand serves as the *mallet*. Children should clap with arms and wrists relaxed and elbows out.

The thigh slap is easy to teach. Relax your wrist for modeling the thigh slap. With arms relaxed, move your hands to slap your thigh.

When teaching children to snap their fingers, hold your hands high. Tell the children to follow you. Snap once. Have the children repeat this action. After they have mimicked your action, have them do two snaps and then three snaps. Keep this up as long as they can repeat your action.

After children have learned to stomp, clap, slap, and snap, you can have them combine two actions. They might "snap, snap, snap," and then "clap, clap, clap." Depending on the skills of the children, you may gradually introduce all four levels of body percussion during one experience.

27.2-4 Movement Activities

Children learn to explore and express their imaginations through movement activities. One of the first movement activities should focus on listening to a drumbeat. A drum is the only instrument needed for the activity. First, tell the children to listen to the drum and see how it makes them feel. For two-year-old children, provide one steady beat. With older children, you may vary the rhythm: fast, slow, heavy, soft, big, small. Then ask them to respond. Encourage them

to run, crawl, roll, walk, hop, skip, and gallop. After experience using the drum, you can use many more movement activities with or without music. The key is to encourage the children to use their bodies to express themselves.

Partner Activities

Partner activities are best for four- or five-year-olds. Instruct the children to choose partners. You will also need a partner to demonstrate. With your partner, move under, over, and around each other. Then have the other children mimic your movements.

Time Awareness Activities

Use a drum to provide a beat that tells the children to run very fast or quickly. After they have done this well, tell them to run very slowly. Then tell them to jump on the floor quickly. Again, follow this request by having them jump slowly.

Space Awareness Activities

Tell the children to stand facing you. Make sure there is enough space between each child so they can make movements freely. Stress your instructions with actions as you tell them to repeat the following actions:

- Lift your leg in front of you.
- Lift your leg backward.
- Lift your leg sideways.
- Lift your leg and step forward.
- Lift your leg and step backward.
- Lift your leg and step sideways.
- Reach up to the ceiling.
- Reach down to the floor.
- Stretch to touch the walls (**Figure 27.18**).
- Move your arm in front of you.
- Move your arm behind you.

Weight Awareness Activities

Children can learn the differences between *light* and *heavy* using their own body force. To begin this activity, give verbal directions and show the actions. Tell the children to focus on

FatCamera/iStock via Getty Image Plus

Figure 27.18 Reaching helps make children more aware of the space around them.

the weight of their bodies as they make the movements. Give the following instructions:

- Push down hard on the floor with your hands.
- Push down softly on the floor with your hands.
- Lift your arms slowly into the air.
- Lift your arms quickly into the air.
- Walk on your tiptoes.
- Stomp on the floor with your feet.
- Kick your leg as slowly as you can.
- Kick your leg as hard as you can.

Dance Activities

Combining time, space, and weight movements, children can learn to form movements into dance. To teach this concept, have the children:

- Walk around quickly in a circle on the floor.
- Walk around slowly in a circle on the floor.
- Tiptoe slowly around the circle.
- Tiptoe quickly around the circle.
- Jump hard around the circle.
- Move your arms in a circle above your head.
- Move your arms in circles everywhere.

Word Games

Word games can help children move in ways that express feelings. To play word games, tell the children to move how the words you say might feel. Use such words as *happy*, *sad*, *angry*, *sleepy*, and *lazy*. After they have moved to these words, remind them to use their bodies and faces. Keep repeating the words (**Figure 27.19**).

Moving Shapes Activities

Four- and five-year-old children enjoy the moving shapes game. As with other movement activities, children will need ample space. Give children the following instructions:

- Try to move like something big and heavy: an elephant, tugboat, bulldozer, airplane.
- Try to move like something small and heavy: a fat frog, a giant turtle, a bowling ball, a brick.
- Try to move like something big and light: a cloud, beach ball, parachute.
- Try to move like something small and light: a snowflake, hummingbird, feather, butterfly, bumblebee, a tiny snake.

Pantomiming

Pantomiming involves telling a story with body movements rather than words. It is best

Liderina/iStock via Getty Images Plus

Figure 27.19 Children often express joy when engaged in music activities.

for use with four-, five-, and six-year-olds. Begin by telling the children they are going to get imaginary presents. Tell them to show you the size of their box. The children should show you a shape made by outlining with their hands and arms. Continue with the following statements:

- Feel the box.
- Hold the box.
- Unwrap the present.
- Take it out of the box.
- Put it back into the box.
- Rewrap the present.

Another pantomime children enjoy is acting out an occupation. Tell the children to think about a job. Then have them show how the worker acts. Sometimes this is fun to do one by one. Have one child act out his or her occupation while the rest of the class tries to guess it. Other variations could relate to how animals behave. One example could be to show how a dog acts. Include movements such as begging for a treat, chewing a bone, shaking hands, chasing a cat, and wagging its tail. Use your imagination to include other animals.

Pretending Activities

Pretending is an activity best used with older children. Tell the children to pretend they are crying, singing, boxing, driving, cooking,

---

Workplace Connections

Charting Music Activities

Design a classroom chart with the four categories of music activities—listening, singing, rhythm instruments, and moving to rhythm—listed at the top of each of the four columns. Keep track of the lessons and activities presented to the preschoolers during the class by listing each activity under a specific area.

1. Which areas may need more emphasis based on your review of the chart?
2. What activities could be planned to emphasize these less-developed areas?

---

laughing, typing, scrubbing, painting, playing an instrument, flying, playing cards, or building a house. There are many songs that children can act out as they sing. Classics include *Here We Go Round the Mulberry Bush* or *This Is What I Can Do*. The music to *Peter and the Wolf* provides the same opportunity for drama and movement.

Another pretending activity involves telling the children to imagine there is a box in front of them. Then tell them they are outside the box and should crawl into it. After crawling into the box, tell the children to crawl out of it. Continue by telling them to crawl under and beside the box.

Lesson 27.2 Review

1. Early childhood programs may have to adjust their music time to meet the children's attention spans and _____ levels. (27.2.1)
   A. interpersonal
   B. musical
   C. developmental
   D. reading
2. **True or False.** Good listening skills help children build proper speech habits, an extended attention span, and reading readiness skills. (27.2.2)
3. The teacher's role in movement experiences is that of a facilitator and _____. (27.2.3)
   A. enforcer
   B. supporter
   C. friend
   D. dance expert
4. One of the first movement activities should focus on listening to a(n) _____. (27.2.4)
   A. electric guitar
   B. saxophone
   C. drumbeat
   D. flute

Summary

Lesson 27.1

27.1-1 Music is a universal language and a form of communication that every culture speaks.

27.1-1 In the early childhood classroom, music can teach many skills, including math, science, social studies, and language. It promotes all areas of development–social-emotional, cognitive, and physical.

27.1-2 To encourage music and movement activities in children, design and decorate a *music center* where children can learn and practice these skills.

27.1-2 Place a music center in an open section of the classroom to allow room for freedom of movement and children with diverse abilities.

27.1-3 The teacher's role in music experiences is to encourage musical expression.

27.1-4 By playing rhythm instruments, children can express their feelings.

27.1-4 Children who have expressed little interest or skill in singing may respond better to musical instruments.

27.1-4 Rhythm instruments include sandpaper blocks, sandpaper sticks, bongo drums, tom-tom drums, rattles and shakers, rhythm sticks, rhythm bells, and coconut cymbals.

Lesson 27.2

27.2-1 Music should be scheduled throughout the day. It fits in well after a story, at the start of the day, after a snack, and during free playtime.

27.2-2 Listening, singing, playing rhythm instruments, and moving to rhythm are all music activities. An excellent program contains all these activities and includes repetition.

27.2-3 In the classroom, the teacher's role in movement activities is that of a facilitator and supporter.

27.2-3 Rather than simply explain a movement activity, you may have to act out certain movements. Children respond to what they see and hear.

27.2-4 Movement provides children with opportunities to pretend and exercise.

27.2-4 Movement activities can be easily combined with music activities for meaningful experiences.

Vocabulary Activity

Draw a cartoon for one of the Key Terms in this chapter. Use the cartoon to express the meaning of the term. Share your cartoon with the class. Explain how the cartoon shows the meaning of the term.

Critical Thinking

1. **Identify.** Review equipment catalogs for musical instruments and other props and items that would encourage music activities. Identify affordable objects and, in particular, multicultural instruments and equipment. Make a list of items for your music center and the projected costs.

2. **Analyze.** Select a simple song and translate it into Spanish or another language. Teach the translated song to children or your classmates and then analyze in small groups what the translated song taught or could teach children. What advantage or disadvantage does a translated song have as compared to a non-translated song? Explain.

3. **Create.** Create a music lesson plan based on rhythm instruments. Your plans should include goals and objectives for the activity and a description of how you would introduce and explain the activity. Present your lesson to a small group of your classmates and then evaluate each other's lesson plans based on effectiveness, safety, and fun.

4. **Determine.** In teams, construct two teacher-made rhythm instruments. Examine the instruments in your team and determine what types of activities you could introduce using these instruments. Outline objects for at least three activities using your two instruments.
5. **Make Inferences.** Select one movement activity and make inferences about how it would benefit young children. What concepts could children learn from this activity? How could the activity best be conducted? Write a brief reflection on how the activity would be best used.

Core Skills

1. **Science.** Research information about music and its effects on brain development. What research can you find to support the view that educators who use more movement, singing, and music will improve their students' learning efficiency and retention? Write a brief report of your findings.
2. **Speaking and Writing.** Select a song using the criteria in this text, and then teach the song to your class. Use methods covered in this chapter for teaching and write a short rationale explaining your teaching method before the lesson. Evaluate your teaching and the class's response.
3. **Technology.** Create two songs that could be used for daily transitions in the classroom. Record the songs using a computer or other equipment to create a digital media file. Then, use the transition song for a day to signal breaks between activities.
4. **Research.** Conduct an online search for information about popular children's music composers and performers. Composers and performers might include Raffi, Ella Jenkins, and Greg & Steve, among others. What philosophies did these music educators follow in their work? What topics do they address in their songs for children? Share examples you find of the composers' work. Why is their work appealing to young children?
5. **Social Studies.** Research the historical and the current role of drums in world cultures. What kinds of drums are unique to specific cultures? How were drums used in historical cultures? Locate and display pictures or samples of the drums you encounter in your research. Which drums would be most beneficial to use in an early childhood program?

6. **Listening and Speaking.** Contact a music teacher and cooperate in designing an activity that will introduce children to various musical instruments. While planning the activity, listen carefully to how the music teacher explains the music learning process and take notes about what considerations the teacher takes into account while outlining an activity. Conduct the activity with a group of children, and then deliver a brief speech about what you learned from cooperating with the music teacher.
7. **CTE Career Readiness Practice.** Presume that you are the director of an early childhood center and have just hired three new employees from different cultural and educational backgrounds. Your three new hires are skeptical about the prominent place that movement has in your curriculum and you schedule a meeting to explain to them why you have incorporated so much movement into each day. To prepare for the meeting, research articles and reliable information about the benefits of movement for preschool children. Rehearse a speech you would give to these employees and prepare a bibliography the employees could reference.

Portfolio Project

Write an observation of a preschool lesson using music and movement. What were the goals and objectives of the lesson? What did the children do during the activity? Were teacher directions clearly stated? Were the children able to follow directions and take part in the activity? Document the activity. Take a photograph or record the experience on an electronic tablet while children are participating. File the observation in your portfolio.

Chapter 28

Guiding Field Trip Experiences

Lesson 28.1: Field Trip Foundations

Lesson 28.2: Implementing Field Trips

Case Study

Planning Field Trips to Support Safety and Learning

Mr. Davis is excited about the curriculum theme on farm animals for next week. He ordered new puzzles and informational bilingual books, which he knew the children would enjoy. He believes there is a commonality among three-year-olds with their interest in animals. While developing the theme, Mr. Davis recorded his goals, and then he began creating a web. Carefully, he attempted to connect all domains of child development and curriculum areas for purposeful learning. He plans to support the theme goals by taking his group of twelve three-year-old children on their first field trip to a local farm. Instead of scheduling the trip in the morning, he planned it for after the children's nap on Tuesday afternoon.

Planning for a field trip must always be intentional. Once Mr. Davis had completed his flow chart, he began writing a detailed lesson plan for the field trip. There were so many things to think about. He thought about taking a pre-trip but then decided against it because of the amount of time it would involve. Instead, he called the farm owner and confirmed the time of the trip and the number of children in the group. Then he continued working on the plan and added attention focusing questions to capture and hold the children's attention during the trip. When the lesson plan was finished, he reviewed it and added the words "digital tablet." Mr. Davis wanted to take photographs of the children at the farm. He would print the pictures and laminate them for protection. Then he would place them in the classroom for the children to sequence the trip events or use to tell a story.

Give It Some Thought

1. Why are field trips important to young children?
2. Would Mr. Davis's field trip to a local farm be an appropriate choice for a first trip? Why or why not?
3. What is the purpose of taking a pre-trip? What might be some disadvantages of planning a field trip late in the afternoon?
4. What safety precautions would be needed for a bus trip to the farm?
5. Could there be any advantages for the children to take a field trip to the farm compared to a virtual trip? Explain.
6. How else could Mr. Davis use the digital photographs taken on the field trip?

Opening image credit: Rawpixel/iStock via Getty Images Plus

Lesson 28.1

Field Trip Foundations

Essential Question

? *What do you need to know about the importance of field trips for children's learning and ways to provide for success with first fieldtrips and children's safety?*

Learning Outcomes

After studying this lesson, you will be able to

28.1-1 describe the importance of field trips.

28.1-2 summarize points of consideration for first field trip experiences, including safety and reducing children's fears.

28.1-3 outline the process for selecting a field trip.

Key Terms

apprehensive   chartering

mini-trip   resource people

theme walks

"**A**pples grow on trees," announced Karla after a recent field trip. Alberto replied, "I know that, and I know something else. Apples are grown in special places called orchards." Hearing the conversation, Robbie added, "Orchards can have red, green, or yellow apples." By going on a field trip, these children expanded their concept of an apple.

Mr. Garcia, after hearing the children's comments, promoted further learning by saying, "It sounds like you know a lot about apples." All the children agreed. Mr. Garcia then suggested they write a story about the trip.

From the field trip, the children learned many concepts related to apples. They learned about color, size, shape, and plant growth. When planning the field trip for the children, Mr. Garcia had two major goals. The first was to expand the children's concepts of apples. The second was to introduce *orchard* as a new vocabulary word.

28.1-1 The Importance of Field Trips

Young children have limited experience in understanding their world. Much of what they understand comes from books, pictures, television, the internet, and movies. Although these media help children learn about their world, they do not replace actual experiences. To fully understand their world, young children need concrete experiences to connect them with their community. Nothing is as valuable as real-life learning. Young children need to see, hear, feel, taste, and smell the world around them (**Figure 28.1**). The more senses children use, the more they are likely to learn.

MarsBars/iStock via Getty Images Plus

Figure 28.1 First trips are often theme walks, such as this child exploring a rock using a magnifying glass. *How can field trips extend children's learning?*

Children gain firsthand experiences during field trips. They look at, listen to, smell, touch, and feel their world. As children connect words and concepts with actual objects, people, and places, vague concepts become clearer to them. Field trips also help children:

- develop keener observation and perception skills
- learn new vocabulary words
- clarify concepts as new information is learned
- learn about the people and locations in their community
- take part in multisensory experiences
- gain new insights for dramatic play
- learn about and stimulate interest in their environment
- practice following directions in a group
- add elements of realism to their play

28.1-2 First Field Trips

For young children, field trips can be novel experiences. Children may be unfamiliar with the idea of a field trip and thus may be **apprehensive** (anxious) about what will occur. For this reason, children's first field trips should be short, nonthreatening neighborhood events.

Reducing Fear During First Field Trips

The first excursion for an infant or toddler may be exploring the other classrooms in the center. Even if the first trip for three and four-year-olds is a simple walk around the block, some children may be hesitant to leave the building. They may fear their parents will come for them while they are gone. Teachers should relieve children of their fears by reassuring them that this will not happen.

To provide security, remind children of their daily routine. Say, "First, we are going to walk around the block. When we return, we will have a story. Then it will be snack time. After that, we will play outside, and then it will be time to go home." Knowing a familiar routine will help prevent some fears.

After taking a few trips around the neighborhood, you may take a **mini-trip**. Usually, a mini-trip is short and involves only a few children. You can take these trips only if the center has enough staff and volunteers to meet staff ratios. An example of a mini-trip would be taking a walk to a neighborhood library to return or check-out books. Otherwise, you might take a trip to a local grocery store to purchase ingredients for fruit smoothies. While at the grocery store, the children can see and talk about objects they know well.

First field trips can build or hinder children's confidence. Therefore, first trips need to intentionally planned to match the children's developmental needs and interests. Two-year-olds do best with short trips. Three-year-olds can take longer trips that may extend to an hour or two in duration. For longer field trips, allow time for slow walking and resting. Lengthen the trip time, sometimes up to several hours, for four- and five-year-olds. When planning trips, teachers should carefully handpick trips they think children will be interested in and add to their knowledge.

Theme Walks

One good "first" field trip is a theme walk. **Theme walks** are simple field trips involving walks near the center based on a theme. A center's neighborhood will contain many interesting and meaningful opportunities for children to learn about the world. Most children enjoy walking, and exercise is good for their bodies. Theme walks also provide an opportunity for children to sharpen their observation skills.

Theme walks may center on many topics: numbers, colors, people, occupations, buildings, flowers, trees, or cars. For best results, focus on only one theme during each walk.

Before starting a theme walk, talk about what children might observe. If the theme is *buildings*, tell the children to observe the types of buildings they see. They may see houses, apartments, offices, stores, and service stations.

Color is also a wonderful concept for a theme walk. Depending upon the children's developmental level, choose one or more colors. The children should watch for throughout the walk. Ask two- and three-year-old children to look for only one color. Older children, especially five-year-olds, may enjoy looking for many colors. A fun walk for these children would be to record as many colors as they observe.

A shape walk is a way to teach children about shapes. Before leaving the classroom, review with the children what shapes they are to observe. As with colors, the number of shapes children are to observe depends on their ages.

Theme walks based on numbers and letters may also be useful learning experiences. The children will see numbers and/or letters everywhere as they walk. They will see numbers on license plates, street signs, store windows, billboards, passing trucks, and houses. The children's ages, skills, and abilities should determine the quantity of numbers or letters to observe.

People walks can teach many social concepts. The children will see that people may be tall or short and have different-colored hair and eyes. Children will also notice that some people wear glasses or have beards or long hair. Two-year-olds can usually identify a baby, cars, trucks, and buses. Three-year-olds can usually distinguish differences among people based on dress, hair color, and height. Four- and five-year-olds may describe the actions of people they have observed. During occupational walks, children observe what people are doing. They may see a bus driver, truck driver, bank teller, street sweeper, construction worker, or house painter.

A building or architectural walk may be especially interesting for older children. As you approach buildings, note their purposes. When children see a gas station-garage combination, discuss why large windows and large doors are part of the architecture. (Large windows are required to see customers; large doors are necessary for cars and trucks.) You may also encourage children to imagine what is inside the building.

To gain the most on these theme walks, carry a smartphone to take notes, a camera, a video recorder, or even a digital tablet with audio and

video capabilities. Record observations that you can discuss when the children return to the classroom. These observations make good discussion topics for lunch, snack, or group time. By listening to the children's discussions, you will discover their interests and what they learned.

Workplace Connections

Teacher Interview for Field Trips

Contact local early childhood teachers to get suggestions for their most successful field trips. Interview the teachers to find out what trips they suggest for each of the age groups between two and six years old.

1. How much preparation and cost were involved in planning the field trips?
2. Which trips were most successful and why? What expectations were communicated to the children and volunteers?
3. Could the sites meet the needs for children with diverse abilities? Why or why not?

28.1-3 Selecting Trips

Thoughtful planning is essential for a successful field trip. The trip you select will depend on the ages of the children, the children's interests, the location of the site, and the budget available. Centers within walking distance of many potential sites will take more trips than those centers in more isolated areas. If located in large cities, centers may have the option of using public transportation. Some large for-profit and Head Start centers may have their own vans or minibuses to provide transportation.

Teachers sometimes select field trips based on the season or weather. A trip to a pumpkin patch or an apple orchard is a fun fall event. Take trips that require walking, such as a trip to a zoo, during warm weather. Be sure to schedule alternate dates in case of bad weather.

At other times, teachers choose field trips based on the curriculum themes the children are studying. For instance, while children are studying about farms, food, or machinery, a trip to a farm may be a good choice. While learning about health, a trip to a dentist's office, doctor's office, or hospital may be engaging for children. **Figure 28.2** lists many field trip suggestions based on themes.

Suitability

Put the child first in all of your planning. Before choosing a trip, ask yourself, "How appropriate is this trip for the children?" Consider the developmental level of the children. For five-year-olds, a trip to a television studio may be both fun and educational. This same trip would be inappropriate for two-year-olds. Two-

year-olds are more interested in objects closer to their immediate surroundings. For example, pets, animals, babies, parents or guardians, and grandparents are topics that capture their interest.

Field trips for children under 24 months are often simple walks around the neighborhood. For safety, use strollers for these children. Many centers purchase special strollers that transport up to six children. These strollers are available with adjustable seats and water-resistant canopies for sun protection. This allows one teacher to handle several children at a time (**Figure 28.3**).

When selecting field trips for young children, safety is a major consideration. Avoid crowded

Field Trip Suggestions

Field Trip	Related Themes
Airport	Air transportation or airplanes
Animal shelter	Pets, dogs, cats
Apple orchard	Apples, fruits
Aquarium	Fish, water, water animals
Artist's studio	Careers, art
Bakery	Foods, community helpers
Bird sanctuary	Birds
Bookstore	Reading, books
Botanical gardens	Flowers, plants
Butcher shop	Foods, careers, tools
Cafeteria	Nutrition
Car dealer	Transportation, car, truck, wheels
Car wash	Cars, trucks, water
Carpenter's shop	Careers, construction
Circus	Animals, careers
Construction site	Buildings, construction, tools
Dairy farm	Food, farm animals, machinery
Dance studio	Movement, communication, careers
Dentist's office	Health, careers, teeth
Doctor's office	Health, careers, "My Body"
Family garden	Plants, vegetables, food
Fire station	Community helper, fire safety
Garage	Tools, careers, machines
Greenhouse	Plants, spring, flowers, food
Grocery store	Food, community helpers
Hair salon	Health, "I'm Me—I'm Special"
Hatchery	Animals or fish
Hospital	Health, careers, people and places
Laundry	Health, careers, clothing
Library	Community helper, books
Nature preserve	Flowers, trees
Orchard	Food, nature
Park	Nature, "My Community"
Pet shop	Pets, animals, careers
Photography studio	Communication, careers, art
Planetarium	The universe, planets
Police station	Community helper, safety
Post office	Community helpers, communication
Potter's studio	Art, careers
Poultry farm	Food, farm animals, eggs
Radio or TV station	Communication, careers, listening
Retail store	Clothing, careers
Train station	Transportation, careers
Veterinarian's clinic	Pets, animals, health, careers
Zoo	Animals, homes

Figure 28.2 Teachers choose some field trips based on classroom themes.

Think Stock Images/Stockbyte/Getty Images

Figure 28.3   Children enjoy exploring museum exhibits. *What other types of exhibits might children enjoy?*

locations. Crowds may be overwhelming for some children. It is also difficult to supervise children in a crowded setting. Trips to the zoo and a children's museum usually involve large groups of people. In these cases, select days that will not be as busy. Ask family members and other available volunteers for help when you cannot avoid crowds cannot.

Choose trips that provide learning through participation. Children enjoy touching and experiencing things. When planning a trip to a strawberry farm, let the children pick and taste the berries. Likewise, a trip to an apple orchard could provide children with opportunities to pick and taste apples.

Cost

When selecting a field trip, always figure out the costs. This helps you decide if the trip is the best use of your resources. You may feel the cost of **chartering** (hiring) a bus to the zoo is more than your budget allows. You may decide that you could spend the money necessary for chartering a bus more wisely on classroom materials. If most of the children have already

Early Childhood Insight

Accessible Field Trips

When planning field trips, consider the special needs of children in your care. Visit the field-trip site before you schedule the trip to ensure it is accessible and safe for all children. Is it accessible for students who use mobility devices such as wheelchairs, crutches, two-wheeled seated walkers, or who have vision impairments? Evaluate these issues before confirming field-trip plans.

had this experience, use the money for some less costly trips. This would give the children new experiences.

Costs for transportation vary depending on the type used, duration, and distance. For centers that own their own vans, the costs of most field trips are minimal. Never ask staff or parents to drive their private cars. This type of arrangement has too many risks and is illegal. In case of an accident, legal problems can arise, such as a lawsuit against the driver and/or center for damages.

Public transportation, such as the city bus or subway, is often less costly than a chartered bus. However, there are disadvantages to public transportation. Crowded trains can be noisy, which can be stressful for children. There is also the danger of injuries to children or losing them during the trip. Accidents often happen as children enter or exit buses or trains. Therefore, some teachers elect not to use public transportation for their children. If they do, extra staff and volunteers will be necessary.

If you decide to charter a bus, call several reputable companies. Check to see that the company meets any state safety inspection guidelines. Explain where you intend to go, the length of your stay, the number of passengers, and request prices. Ask them to send you the price quote in writing. After you receive all the quotes, compare them to find the company that will provide the best service for the least amount of money. By thoroughly examining costs for a field trip, you can get the most for your resources.

Most field trips involve little or no expense, particularly if the site is within walking distance. Sometimes the only costs are admission and/or transportation. If there is an admission fee, call in advance and ask if group rates are available for early childhood centers. You may get a generous discount or free admission.

Health Highlights

Training Staff for Transporting Children

A driver or other staff member must have training to transport children. According to state and federal guidelines, at least one staff member on the vehicle should have a valid pediatric first-aid certificate and training in rescue breathing and managing airway blockages. In addition, follow mandated staff-to-child ratios to properly supervise children during transportation.

Resource People

Teachers may select field trips based on the resource people available. **Resource people** are visitors to a classroom or a field trip hosts (**Figure 28.4**). Promote STEAM in your curriculum by inviting a diverse group of community workers as resource people. Construction workers, architects, masons, and engineers are examples. Workers should represent different cultural backgrounds and ethnicities. Encourage them to bring the tools they use to perform their jobs. If the workers cannot come to the classroom, explore methods for connecting with them.

Resource people might also be people you talk to at a field-trip site, such as adults at work, a local florist, a farmer at a farmer's market, a firefighter, or a worker at a supermarket. While at these places, children can bring back materials for the dramatic play corner. Examples may include receipt pads, store coupons, and silk flowers. At

ChameleonsEye/Shutterstock.com

Figure 28.4   Firefighters are nearly always at the top of the list of interesting resource people. *What other community-resource people might be of interest to children?*

the farmer's market, you may purchase fresh vegetables and fruits that the children can have later for a snack or lunch.

Family members, including parents or guardians, grandparents, great-grandparents, aunts, uncles, neighbors, siblings, and friends are some of the most valuable resource people. Ask them what interests and hobbies, photos, crafts, clothing, and foods they would share. You can do this personally or through a questionnaire. Select only people who enjoy children. They should represent many cultural groups, both sexes, and a variety of ages. Compile a list of these people along with their interests and hobbies. During the year, select people from the list who complement your curriculum.

Your resource person is an expert in their field and may feel uncomfortable interacting with young children. They will appreciate having information about the group of children. It is your responsibility to provide an orientation before meeting the children. This step is necessary for making the experience a success for both the children and the resource person. To prepare, share with them:

- the number of the children in the group, ages, and interests
- the length of the children's attention spans
- what you think the children already know about the topic
- suggest questions they may ask the children
- the importance of keeping words simple

Warn the resource people that children often become very excited when they have class visitors. They are proud of their guests, their classroom, and their classroom friends. Because of the stimulation, they may exhibit overly active behavior.

If possible, suggest to resource people that they provide "hands-on activities" for the children. For example, if a grandmother is willing to demonstrate how she paints, encourage her to let the children try painting, too. If a person plans to share playing the drums, ask that each child have the chance to hit the drum.

If the resource person is coming to the center, confirm the date and time of the visit a few days before. Explain where visitor's parking is

> Dear Firefighter:
>
> Thank you for showing us your fire truck. We enjoyed sitting in the truck. Thank you for showing us the truck's parts. Thank you for sounding the siren. Thank you for showing us a firefighter's clothing. We enjoyed trying it on, too.
>
> Love,
> Juan Rubio's Class

Figure 28.5 Build a positive image of the center in your community with a thank-you note to resource people.

available and how to enter the building. Let them know if you require them to have identification for entry.

With the children, build anticipation before the resource person visits. Explain who is coming and what they will be sharing. With older preschool children, help them generate a list of questions to ask. Follow up with a discussion of respectful behavior when guests are in the classroom.

After a resource person has visited the classroom or hosted a field trip, always send a thank-you note or some other form of appreciation (**Figure 28.5**). You may write a personal note, or children who can write may wish to express their own thanks. The thank-you note could be an e-mail that included a picture of the children at the site. Younger children may choose to dictate thank-you notes to you. Other forms of thanking people include sending children's artwork or freshly baked cookies.

Appreciation may also take other forms. For instance, in February, make and mail handmade valentines to all resource people who took part in the program during the year. Recorded thank-you notes, songs on a CD or digital file, and videos or photos of the children at the site are other thoughtful ways to thank resource people.

Lesson 28.1 Review

1. Which of the following is a benefit of field trips for young children? (28.1.1)
   A. Napping on the bus
   B. Silently listening to lectures
   C. Taking part in multisensory experiences
   D. Feeling apprehensive about new places

2. Which of the following is *not* an example of a theme walk? (28.1.2)
   A. Observing forms of transportation and how many wheels each has
   B. Walking quietly to the library to check out books
   C. Finding the objects that are the color red
   D. Identifying the types of buildings along the sidewalk

3. Young children may feel _____ about going on their first field trip. (28.1.2)
   A. sad
   B. lonely
   C. sleepy
   D. anxious

4. **True or False.** Transportation costs are not a factor in planning for field trips. (28.1.3)

5. _____ are subject experts who either visit a classroom or host field trip groups. (28.1.3)
   A. Volunteers
   B. Grandparents
   C. Resource people
   D. Teachers

Implementing Field Trips

Essential Question

What do you need to know and what actions do you need to take to prepare for a safe, successful field trip?

Learning Outcomes

After studying this lesson, you will be able to

28.2-1 **plan** a field trip from pre-trip planning to follow-up activities.

28.2-2 **describe** the process of making and taking virtual field trips.

28.2-3 **analyze** the importance of creating field trip albums and displays.

Key Terms

chaperones	behavioral expectations
"trip" bag	virtual field trips
insulated	

Thoughtfully chosen and carefully planned field trips can enrich the early childhood curriculum. Review your center's policies and procedures before planning a field trip. When possible, take a pre-trip. Visit the site to identify walking paths, parking, and how you can the needs of children with diverse abilities. Find out what day of the week and time is best for the host at the site. Arrange for transportation, if needed, and get parental permission forms signed. After this, plan your educational goals and make a list of your behavioral expectations. Prepare the children for the field trip by discussing what to look for, rules to follow, and questions they might want to ask.

On the trip, you can use a digital tablet or cell phone to record the highlights. After the trip, the children can revisit it by replaying the video and looking at the photographs in an album. Teachers can plan and offer virtual field trips when there is a lack of funding, supervision, or logistics.

28.2-1 Planning a Field Trip

A successful field trip for young children requires careful planning. Give consideration to safety, types, scheduling, adult-child ratio, behavioral expectations, educational goals, and the children's preparation. As a teacher, you need to think about all these factors. Visit the site ahead of time to prepare for the field trip. This will help you plan educational goals for the field trip.

Pre-Trip

The success of any trip depends on preparation (**Figure 28.6**). After setting goals, always make a pre-trip if you have never been to the site. This visit will give you a chance to:

Pintau Studio/Shutterstock.com

Figure 28.6 The best field trips will be those the teacher has planned well. *What factors must a teacher plan for to have field trip success?*

- describe the purpose of the trip to the tour guide
- explain the children's interests and their need to engage their senses
- prepare the tour guide for the questions the children may ask
- locate bathrooms
- check for any potential dangers
- ask if pictures or video clips can be taken and used to introduce the trip
- observe and identify objects to look for and use as teaching opportunities
- revise the trip goals if necessary
- identify specific vocabulary words to be introduced
- determine how many adults or **chaperones** (people who accompany others to ensure correct behavior) you will need to provide maximum security

Keep a field trip file. In some centers, teachers maintain their own files. In other centers, the director maintains a file for use by all personnel.

This file may be a notebook, a folder, or a digital file. Information to collect for each trip includes

- name of site
- telephone number
- address
- website
- contact person (tour guide), telephone number, and email address
- costs
- distance from the center in blocks or miles
- dangers
- special learning opportunities
- locations of bathrooms and water sources

After the trip, write an evaluation. Ask yourself, did the trip meet your educational goals? Was it worth the time and expense? If not, explain why. Make notes about how to improve the trip for another time.

Permission slips signed by parents or guardians must be on file for each child before a trip (**Figure 28.7**). For convenience, some center directors use one form for all trips and walks if state licensing permits. Parents fill in and sign

Estero's Early Learning Center Field Trip Permission Form

Child's Name_____   Date _____

Parent/Guardian Name_____   Business Phone _____

Cell Phone _____

Parent/Guardian Name_____   Business Phone _____

Cell Phone _____

Home Address _____   Home Phone _____

Home email _____

In consideration of (child's name)_____

acceptance as an enrollee in Estero's Early Learning Center, I hereby give permission for my child to participate in any walks or field trips planned and supervised by the staff. I understand that various modes of transportation may be used for these trips, and I will be informed of each trip before it occurs.

Signature: _____   Date: _____

Signature: _____   Date: _____

Figure 28.7   Permission slips from parents, such as this one, are necessary when planning a field trip.

this at enrollment time. This saves the staff's time in obtaining permission slips for each trip. Busy parents will also benefit from this timesaving method.

Before the trip, plan your "trip bag." A **trip bag** should include the essential supplies that you will need to take along. Paper tissues; a basic first-aid kit; pre-moistened towelettes; a garbage bag; emergency telephone numbers; and a cell phone. Many centers also require that you take a folder with a class list, copies of emergency forms, and signed permission slips. Depending on the length of the trip and the weather, take snacks and refreshments for the children. In hot weather, children often become thirsty. Make sure water or some other nutritious drink is on hand. **Insulated** (protected from extreme temperatures) jugs are a good way to transport liquids. Many centers use individually labeled water bottles.

Field trips often involve added safety risks and responsibilities for early childhood centers. Before taking field trips, teach the children pedestrian safety. Practice taking short walks near the center. Before leaving the center, explain the rules the children must follow when crossing the streets. When approaching a crosswalk, review these rules with the children. Carefully observe traffic signals when crossing intersections. Make sure you consistently enforce and follow the rules. This is important since children learn by experience and imitation.

Workplace Connections

Designing Pre-Trip Activities

Design a pre-trip activity to help children understand what to expect on a field trip. For example, you could seat the children in a circle and start the game by saying, "I'm going on a trip to _____; and I'm taking _____." Insert examples such as *bakery* and *coat*. Let the children add their items.

1. What activities would help children know what to expect during a field trip?
2. What safety measures and expectations should be communicated during these pre-trip activities?

Scheduling

When planning a field trip, you must decide when the trip will take place. Midmornings are the best time to schedule field trips. This time of day works best for several reasons. First, children are usually well-rested. They often find it easier to listen, observe, and follow instructions. Second, children arrive at different times during the morning. Some parents may bring their children to the center at 7:00 a.m. Others may not bring their children until 8:00 or 9:00 a.m. If you schedule the trip too early, you will deprive some children of the experience. Also, in colder climates, early morning temperatures can be too cool for children. This is a key consideration for trips that require walking (**Figure 28.8**).

Afternoon field trips are also difficult to plan. Most preschool children require a nap. Also, children may not be able to attend the trip if their parents pick them up in the early afternoon.

Field trips should begin after a quiet activity. This helps children avoid excess excitement or overstimulation during the trip. Overstimulated children are very active and difficult to manage.

One question that teachers often ask is, "What is the best day for a field trip?" The answer to this question depends on the group and attendance. First, study the behavior and routine of the

Olga Listopad/Shutterstock.com

Figure 28.8   A trip to an apple orchard is most enjoyable in the warmth of late morning sunshine. *What discussion might you have with the children to help prepare them for a trip to the apple orchard?*

group. Some groups are always tired and restless by Friday. Choose a day early in the week for such a group. Monday may not be a good day, depending on the program. The children may be tired because of weekend activities. Second, consider the days children attend. If trips are always scheduled on the days they do not attend the center, you may deprive some children of going on the trip.

The right day for a field trip may also depend on the site. If you must make formal arrangements, ask the contact person to suggest a day. Many resource people prefer midweek. This allows time to prepare for the visit.

Intentionally plan around the children's needs, children's schedules, and resource people's schedules. This takes time. However, a well-planned field trip produces the greatest amount of learning and pleasure for the children.

Adult-Child Ratio

To ensure safety and the success of the trip, provide enough chaperones. The most desirable adult-child ratio is based on the number of children in the group, the age of the children, the nature of the field trip, and the dangers involved (**Figure 28.9**). Center staff can often handle walks around the block. You may need more adults for trips using public transportation or for visits to places with potential dangers.

Provide as many adults as possible to promote safety. For two-year-olds, there should be one adult for every two children. Assign an adult to every four three-year-olds, five four-year-olds, and six five-year-olds for optimal safety. If some children require close watching, adjust this ratio. Many times, teachers group children based on their temperaments. For instance, if Charlie and Renee misbehave when together, place them in different groups. If a child has difficulty following rules, you may assign the child to one adult. Often, teachers recruit an "extra" adult who is not assigned to any specific children. This adult can relieve a teacher to handle emergencies or give children one-to-one contact as necessary.

When you need more adults for field trips, invite family members. Many programs maintain lists of parents or guardians and other volunteers

UW-Stout Child and Family Study Center

Figure 28.9 Field trips can have many hidden dangers. For this reason, extra adult supervision is required.

who have an interest in helping on field trips. Be sure to follow your state's licensing requirements for volunteer participation. When the need arises, give these people several weeks' notice. Family volunteers may have to make special arrangements at work. Prior to the trip, provide the volunteers with information regarding the trip. Be sure to include the time of departure, arrival at the site, length of stay at the site, events occurring at the site, and arrival time back at the center. In addition, tell volunteers about the behavioral expectations.

Behavioral Expectations

Behavioral expectations require planning and discussion with children before the trip. Expectations for the children to follow will vary with the children and the nature of the trip. Some expectations may apply to all trips. Regardless of the type of trip, expectations are most often the same in most early childhood programs.

For best results, state all expectations positively. Tell the children exactly what they must do. For example, tell the children to place their hands at their sides when they are in a store.

The first expectation for field trips is that all children must always wear an identification tag. These tags should be durable and reusable. Children should wear them on all field trips. The tag should include the center or school name, address, telephone number and the child's first name. This information is helpful in case a child wanders from the group and it provides the child's name for the resource person at the field site.

The second expectation for field trips is that children should speak softly. To ensure this, teachers need to set a good example. Speak in a low-key voice to avoid overstimulation.

The third expectation is that children must remain with their assigned group and adult supervisor on field trips. Then each adult will know the names of the children they supervise.

Many teachers prefer children to follow the "hold-your-partner's-hand" rule. However, this is not always useful. It is unfair to interested children to have partners whose attention is not on the learning experience. Also, constant physical contact can cause stress for some children.

Instead of holding hands, children can hold on to a walking rope to keep them together as a group. To make this rope, purchase several 20-foot pieces of rope. With each piece of rope, loop and tie handles at 2-foot intervals. Show the children how to hold on to the handles and explain expectations during the trip. This technique keeps children from wandering.

Educational Goals

For the most benefit on a field trip, carefully plan educational goals with a clear focus. For example, a trip to a local auto repair shop may have several goals, including to:

- observe mechanics at work
- learn about the care of cars
- see how machinery works
- learn vocabulary words: *technicians, wrenches, ramps,* and *hoist*

During the pre-trip visit, discuss these goals with the resource person.

Children's Preparation

Preparation for children may begin a few days before the trip. Introduce the trip by putting up displays, reading a book, sharing a video, looking at the pictures, or simply talking about the trip.

On the day of the trip, tell children what to observe (educational goals) and how to behave (behavioral expectations). Give each child their identification tag and assign them to their adult guides. After this, encourage children to use the bathroom. Explain that a bathroom is not always available on walks or some field trips.

Family Preparation

Staff should always inform families at least one week before field trips. A newsletter, calendar, or posting a notice on a bulletin board or classroom door are all useful methods (Figure 28.10). Email can be useful, too. Inform the parents or guardians of the date, location, address, and exact times you will leave and return. In case of emergency, you should also provide them with the name and telephone number of the person at the site. This will help family members plan their schedules for dropping off and picking up the children.

Field trip
to
Perkin's Pumpkin Farm
23 Half-Day Road
Streamwood

Tuesday, September 23
We will leave the center at 10:00 a.m.
We will return to the center at noon.

Figure 28.10 Placing this notice on a center bulletin board helps remind families of an upcoming field trip. *How else might teachers notify parents to give reminders about a field trip?*

You should also notify parents or guardians in advance if they must pay any costs for the trip. Most centers do not ask families to pay an additional fee for field trips. They usually include the cost in the tuition. Let family members know if you will need them to provide any special items, such as special clothing.

Post a sign on the classroom door on the morning of the field trip before children, and their family members arrive. Note from where and what time you will depart and return. This will also serve as a trip reminder for parents, guardians, and center staff.

Share trip goals with children's families. This information may help them plan related home experience, such as discussions and books that complement the trip.

Follow-Up Activities

To help children clarify their learning, plan follow-up activities. Once you return to the center, talk with the children about what they saw, heard, and experienced. Plan an activity that reinforces the learning that occurred on the trip. Read books related to the trip. A class thank-you note could be a follow-up activity.

Review the classroom scene after the trip to the apple orchard described at the beginning of the chapter. Apples were served and discussed at lunch. Then the experience was used as a basis for writing a story. After a trip to a bakery, children could bake bread or cookies. The children could make ice cream or butter after a trip to a local dairy.

28.2-2 Virtual Field Trips

Virtual field trips do not replace a field trip, but they are inspiring to use to prepare for or review a trip. Due to a lack of funding, supervision, or logistics, some centers cannot offer actual field trips. Teachers in these programs have the option of offering virtual field trips (VFTs) to support the children's interests and expand their social worlds beyond the classroom. **Virtual field trips** are technology-based experiences that allow children an educational excursion without leaving the classroom. Virtual field trips can focus on people, places, animals, or objects. They range in complexity. Simple trips could consist of photographs, videos, video conferences, digital presentations, and internet resources. For more complex trips, teachers can utilize the integration of photos, videos, and audio.

Two types of VFTs exist. One type is a ***predeveloped VFT***. A predeveloped VFT has been prepared by an outside source. There are many examples of free predeveloped VFTs on various children's sources. A drawback to a predeveloped virtual field trip is that a teacher cannot easily change the content to make it developmentally appropriate. Some museums offer VFTs and their services are accessible to anyone using the internet.

The second type of virtual field trip is a ***teacher-created VFT***. Some sites, such as shoe factories, clothing factories, or canning factories, are too dangerous for children to visit. In these cases, after obtaining permission, a teacher may go to such sites and record a virtual field trip using a digital audio/video device. They may also take photographs for a VFT.

Hospitals, dental offices, farms, hatcheries, florists, and auto repair shops can all be featured in teacher-created VFTs. The number of potential trips is endless. After recording them, teachers can use these clips in the classroom and share them with the children. The teacher may also invite the site coordinator to describe the video and answer questions.

Some teachers use teacher-created virtual field trips as an introduction to an on-site field trip. When making the pre-visit, they capture photographs or create a video. These VFTs can motivate and direct children's attention to relevant people and objects before going on the trip. After viewing the virtual field trip, the children can identify objects to look for and questions they can ask on the trip.

Interviewing someone digitally would be another type of virtual field trip. A digital interview or call could be used to:
- interview a children's author who can also read a story to the children

- interview a children's musician who can sing with the children
- talk with community helpers
- talk with a classmate who is ill and cannot attend school
- see a classmate's new sibling

28.2-3 Classroom Field Trip Albums and Displays

Photography is a powerful communication tool, which teachers can use as a curriculum. Using photography, capture the moment during field trips to communicate the children's learning. A picture is worth a thousand words. After the trip, children enjoy looking at photographs and reliving the experience. Prepare them for your role as a photographer by taking pictures in the classroom, so they get familiar with the camera. Otherwise, they may act unnatural when you are taking pictures on the trip. Children are often easily distracted and unpredictable. As a result, you may have to take many pictures so that you can delete less-desirable images. When selecting

photos for the album, make sure to include every child. Tips for photographing the children include
- Be ready.
- Vertical images are often more appealing since the background is reduced.
- Get close to and at the level of the subjects.
- Focus on the height of the tallest child when photographing more than one child.
- Focus on the child's eyes when photographing one child.
- Use natural lighting or flash.
- Take many pictures, since pictures can be deleted.

View the photographs with the children. Agency can be supported through the photographs taken. Ask the children what photographs they would like to display. While viewing the photographs selections together, ask questions such as:
- What do you like about these photographs?
- What did you learn on the field trip?
- What else do you want to learn about (_____)?
- Was there something else we should have taken a picture of?

Follow-Up Activities

Trip	Activities
Apple Orchard	• Taste a variety of apples. • Make applesauce or apple muffins. • Read stories about apple orchards. • Serve apple butter, baked apples, or some other form of apple.
Fire Station	• Place puzzles and stories related to the role of firefighters in the classroom. • Read stories about firefighters. • Place firefighters' clothing in the dramatic play area. • Act out fire safety procedures.
Hair Salon	• Provide a prop box containing hair rollers, combs, brushes, towels, and a hair dryer with the cord removed. • Place dolls with hair and combs in the dramatic play area. • Hang up a mirror and have children compare the ways they wear their hair.

Figure 28.11   After returning to the classroom from the field trip, it is essential to plan activities that reinforce what children learn.

After a field trip, create a display table that documents the children's learning. Place the table where it is convenient for family members to see when entering the classroom. On the table, create a display by placing photographs and any artifacts the children collected during the field trip. You can also use the display table for photographs and artifacts the children collect on theme walks or when resource people visit the classroom.

Lesson 28.2 Review

1. Which of the following is **not** a good way to prepare young children for a field trip? (28.2.1)
   A. Reading books about the topic of the field trip
   B. Surprising them on the day of the trip
   C. Explaining safety and behavior expectations
   D. Introducing them to adults who will be attending the field trip

2. The appropriate adult-child ratio on a field trip with a class of four-year-olds is _____. (28.2.1)
   A. one adult for every six children
   B. one adult for every three children
   C. one adult for every five children
   D. one adult for every two children

3. Which of the following is **not** an example of a virtual field trip (VFT)? (28.2.2)
   A. A cartoon about a rabbit that talks
   B. A presentation about the lifecycle of rabbits from a forest preserve district
   C. A recording of the teacher visiting to a plant that produces pet rabbit food
   D. A videoconference call with a veterinarian about caring for rabbits

4. Which is an example of an object that a teacher may include in a display about their trip to a nature center? (28.2.3)
   A. A blurry photograph of some of the children running in a field
   B. The kickball the children use during outside playtime
   C. A child's sock that was left on the minibus after their trip
   D. An acorn the children found along the trail

5. **True or False.** When taking group pictures of children, horizontal images are often more appealing since the background is reduced. (28.2.3)

Summary

Lesson 28.1

28.1-1 Field trips provide concrete experiences for young children to fully understand their world through their senses and to learn new concepts in immersive environments.

28.1-2 Young children may feel apprehensive about their first field trip. Teachers can relieve children's fear by explaining the routine and answering any questions. They may start with theme walks around the neighborhood or short mini-trips to familiar local places, such as a library or a grocery store. Field trips can build in complexity and duration as children develop.

28.1-3 Teachers have many components to consider when planning field trips, such as the ages of the children, the children's interests, the location of the site, and the available budget for the trip. Transportation availability and cost are also factors. Resource people at a field trip site can help personalize the trip or presentation to the interests and developmental level of the children.

Lesson 28.2

28.2-1 Teachers must prepare in advance for successful field trips. When choosing a field trip location, they may take a pre-trip to visit the site and plan filed trip activities and details. In addition, their preparations will include handling logistical details, setting educational goals, introducing the trip's topic and establishing behavior expectations with students, and getting parental permission.

28.2-1 Teachers should reinforce what the children experienced and learned on the field through follow-up classroom activities.

28.2-2 Virtual field trips (VFTs) may help children prepare for or review a field trip's topics or may replace an actual field trip if one is not possible due to lack of funding, minimal supervision, safety concerns, or logistical challenges. Some organizations create VFTs for schools, while teachers may create their own VFT about a certain person, topic, or location if one is unavailable.

28.2-3 Taking pictures during field trips allows teachers to create albums and displays for the children to revisit their trip and recall their learnings through photographs and other trip artifacts.

Vocabulary Activity

In teams, play *picture charades* to identify each of the Key Terms in this chapter. Write the terms on separate slips of paper and put the slips into a basket. Choose a team member to be the *sketcher*. The sketcher pulls a term from the basket and creates quick drawings or graphics to represent the term until the team guesses the term. Rotate turns as sketcher until the team identifies all terms.

Critical Thinking

1. **Compare and Contrast.** Brainstorm 10 possible local field trip sites. For each site listed, find out the address, phone number, website, contact person's name, teaching opportunities, and price information. Make a database of the information and then compare your options.

2. **Analyze.** Interview an early learning center director for information about liability and accidents that may occur when a child is on a field trip. Does the center's permission slip absolve the center or individual teachers from a lawsuit for damages? What situations may cause special concern on field trips? Write a brief report of your findings.

3. **Evaluate.** Review the Americans with Disabilities Act of 1990 to learn what accessibility requirements for businesses you may visit for field trips. As part of pre-trip preparations for a field trip, visit a site and check to see if the business or location complies with ADA guidelines. Make sure parking, building access, hallways, aisles, viewing areas, and restrooms are all in compliance.

4. **Draw Conclusions.** Plan a field trip for your class. Consider the children's ages, curriculum learning, and schedules. Draw conclusions about what field trips would be best suited to the children and the center's resources. Outline the plan for your field trip, including all the factors covered in this chapter.

5. **Create.** Imagine that you have just taken your class on a field trip to the grocery store, where they learned about different produce and breads. In small groups, create two or more follow-up activities that could reinforce these lessons after the field trip. Share your activities with the class.

Core Skills

1. **Social Studies.** Start a file of ideas for field trips that young children could take in your community. What locations would be open to children visiting? What are the teaching opportunities involved in each?

2. **Financial Literacy and Math.** Calculate the total cost of a field trip for 20 four-year-olds and their adult chaperones to a museum 35 miles from the school. The admission charges are $10.00 for children and $15.00 for adults. Determine the number of chaperones necessary and include their admission in the calculations. Include transportation costs.

3. **Writing.** Write an article describing an upcoming field-trip experience for the family newsletter. Include the goals of the trip, the names of resource people and chaperones, and what the children will learn from the trip.

4. **Listening.** Interview a teacher or early learning center director about safety guidelines that teachers and staff should follow on all field trips. How do teachers enforce these guidelines, especially in a public place? Make a list of guidelines and tips for enforcing them. Share your findings with the class.

5. **Speaking.** With a field trip resource person's permission, video record a field trip and its informational presentations to create a mini-movie of the experience. Edit the video and insert an introduction, voiceovers for explanations and additional information, interviews with the speakers and the children, and conduct a follow-up activity.

6. **Technology.** Take photographs during a preschool field trip and then upload the pictures to a classroom computer. Make sure each child appears in at least one picture. Select pictures that best represent the trip and prepare a slide show using presentation software for the parents to enjoy. Include children's quotes about the trip and highlight what the children learned during the experience.

7. **CTE Career Readiness Practice.** Imagine that you have been asked to train new members of your center staff on planning appropriately for field trips. Using the information covered in this chapter, create an outline of what you need to teach the new staff. Create staff handouts they can keep for ready reference. Also, create a digital presentation to briefly train the staff. What information must the staff know? What content will you specifically mention, as opposed to allowing them to learn on their own?

Portfolio Project

1. Design a questionnaire to be filled out by potential resource people. Include spaces for information about the person's interests, career, or work they would share with the children. It should also include the person's experience with children and contact information. Finally, include any notes about the field-trip location or special needs when visiting the classroom, such as a table for displaying items. File a copy of the questionnaire in your portfolio.

2. Search for websites that offer pre-developed virtual field trips. Choose three of these field trips, and then brainstorm a list of ten other virtual field trips that could be created based on these examples. File your list of ideas in your portfolio.

Unit Five

Programs, People, and Your Career

Chapters

Some early childhood programs are geared toward preschoolers. However, you may also choose to work with younger children (infants and toddlers), school-age children, or children with diverse abilities. In this unit, you will discover what special qualities teachers in infant-toddler programs and school-age programs need to promote strong, healthy development. You will learn special strategies for providing nurturing care and learning experiences for these children. This unit will also introduce you to children with diverse abilities. You will understand how such needs as speech and hearing disorders, health disorders, and giftedness may affect your role as a teacher.

Parents and family members are very much involved with the care, education, and guidance of their young children. You will want to keep them informed of everything that is happening at the center. Family involvement can be the key factor in the success of a program.

A world of career possibilities is open to early childhood teachers. It's up to you to choose a career path that fits your goals and to find a teaching position that will start you on your path. This unit will help prepare you for seeking an early childhood position. You will read about how to prepare a résumé and find available positions. You will also discover ways to make a positive impression in an interview and be offered the job you desire.

Programs for Infants and Toddlers

Lesson 29.1: Understanding Infant and Toddler Caregiving

Lesson 29.2: Curriculum and Parent Involvement

Case Study

How Should a Teacher Respond?

Malena's mother is the president of a large company. She married for the first time at 38 years of age. Two years later, she had Malena, which was stressful since her husband was in the military. When she enrolled Malena in the infant program, she confided that she had role overload. Today was the third day in a row that she was late for picking up her four-month-old infant. As usual, she apologized and wrote a check for the late fee. When she handed the check to the teacher, she said, "my assistant thinks maybe I should get another type of child care since I am always late for pick up. She also thinks I need to interact with Malena more to promote her development. This is confusing to me. When I was young, my mother only picked up her children and responded to them when they cried, were fed, changed, and bathed. Otherwise, they were put in a playpen."

Malena's mother continued, "My assistant also tells me touch is essential for an infant. She said I should be holding and providing more cuddling and lap time so Malena can develop a sense of well-being, trust, and intimacy. She suggested that I play a serve-and-return game and provide Malena with tummy-time. Help me; I have never heard of these games." Ms. Smith explained to her how touch helps build the architecture of the child's brain. She then escorted her into the library and provided her with some articles on parent-child interaction.

Give It Some Thought

1. Why do you think Malena's mother shares this information with the teacher?
2. If you were Ms. Smith, how would you describe the importance of touch to Malena's mother?
3. Should Malena's mother learn the "serve and return" game? If so, how would you describe the game and its benefits to Malena?
4. How you would explain tummy-time and its importance for Malena's development? Why do you think the American Academy of Pediatrics recommends tummy-time?
5. Do you think center care is the best option for Malena's optimal development? Why or why not? What other child care options might Malena's mother consider?
6. How do you think Ms. Smith feels about Malena's mother being late for pick up three nights in a row? Explain.

Opening image credit: fizkes/iStock via Getty Images Plus

Lesson 29.1 Understanding Infant and Toddler Caregiving

Essential Question

What do you need to know about infant and toddler caregiving to provide developmentally appropriate, safe care for young children?

Learning Outcomes

After studying this lesson, you will be able to

29.1-1 **list** the characteristics of a nurturing infant-toddler caregiver.

29.1-2 **state** guidelines for proper infant-toddler care.

29.1-3 **design** a functional and developmentally appropriate infant environment.

29.1-4 **design** a functional and developmentally appropriate toddler environment.

29.1-5 **describe** developmentally appropriate care for infants, including feeding, oral health, diapering and toileting, napping, and handling the challenges of caring for infants and toddlers.

29.1-6 **handle** the routines of infants and toddlers.

29.1-7 **select** toys that are safe and developmentally appropriate for infants and toddlers.

Key Terms

continuity of care (COC)

serve and return

mirror neurons

adjoining

stunted

demand feeding

sportscasting

sudden infant death syndrome (SIDS)

stranger anxiety

wariness

separation anxiety

overfamiliarity

locomotive

At a local early learning center for infants and toddlers, Ian is learning to walk. Hayden just stood for the first time and Pouneh has just begun exploring books. Working with infants and toddlers can be exciting and rewarding (**Figure 29.1**). Infancy and toddlerhood are unique and challenging stages in the life cycle. Studies have shown the best time to influence lifelong health, learning, and behavior is during the early years. During this time, children build a foundation for more advanced skills.

A child's genes and environment influence brain development. At birth, the infant's brain is hardwired to learn. Studies show the brain's growth is more rapid from birth to age three than at any other period in life. The brain is the only organ in a child's body that will change after birth in response to the child's experiences, negative and positive. Early experiences shape the architecture of a young child's brain and have a lifelong impact on their learning, behavior, and health.

Learning how to work with infants and toddlers takes as much training and expertise as preschool and school-aged children. As an infant-toddler teacher, your nurturing and support play an important role during this most critical time. Providing a warm, safe, stimulating, and nurturing environment promotes optimal development. Offering developmentally appropriate activities can form and strengthen the connections in the brain, which increase lifelong learning potential. As you watch a child learn and develop, you will feel satisfaction knowing your efforts have made a difference. You should acknowledge and share the joy of each new skill the child demonstrates.

anek.soowannaphoom/Shutterstock.com

Figure 29.1   Infants and toddlers grow and change rapidly. They are constantly learning new skills and making new discoveries. *What are some ways that caregivers can build their relationships with infants and toddlers?*

29.1-1 Characteristics of Infant and Toddler Caregivers

As an infant-toddler caregiver, your behavior will influence the children's lifelong learning potential. Infants develop in an environment of responsive relationships and positive experiences. Nurturing, stable, and positive relationships with caring caregivers are essential to healthy development in young children. Relationships will affect all areas of a child's development— behavioral, cognitive, social, and emotional.

Caring, daily relationships are the heart of early brain development. During this formative period, children will rely on their day-to-day interactions with you to feel secure, learn, develop, and thrive. From these interactions, babies will build expectations on how they will be treated.

Infants and toddlers will react based on the ways you treat them. Growth-producing relationships depend on positive, engaging, and sensitive social interactions. Your modeling will teach them how to think, feel, and act. If you are consistently warm, trusting, and loving, the children will be warm, trusting, and loving. Touch, smile, make eye contact, and speak affectionately to the children.

Talk. Talk. Talk. Describe actions, things, feelings, accomplishments, and people with a tone of voice that shows enthusiasm, warmth, and interest. Conversing indicates that you are interested. The infant will absorb more language and language skills, the more you talk.

Develop a loving and trusting relationship. Engage the child by speaking with a loving voice, smile, and by using their names. Cuddle them, rock them, hug them, nuzzle them, talk and sing to them, and play with them. Likewise, be patient, flexible, and accepting while working with them. Infants and toddlers need warm, caring, responsive caregivers. Caregiver presence and responsiveness promotes trust, confidence, and the ability to buffer stress (**Figure 29.2**).

Ryan Kowadla

Figure 29.2   All areas of this young child's development are nurtured by the affectionate, responsive caregiver.

To be an effective infant-toddler caregiver, you must have a high energy level, be healthy, loving, and enjoy children. You must always be readily available to comfort and protect the children and must be able to handle many situations and understand feelings. Part of your responsibility includes nurturing social connections and emotional development. Young children need help in learning to express feelings, such as joy, love, anger, pleasure, satisfaction, and sadness.

Infants enrolled in early learning centers need predictability, security, and a stable relationship with a caring teacher. When infants and toddlers are attached to a teacher, they approach learning opportunities more confidently. High staff turnover can undermine a child's potential to establish clear expectations. One consistent caregiver must be available to maximize their development. Infants and toddlers need **continuity of care (COC),** a practice where at least one teacher follows a group of children for several years. With time, it allows the child to become securely attached to the teacher. Although this practice is beneficial, it is not widely used. The practice is not only beneficial to children, but also to their families to develop closer bonds.

Infant-toddler teachers need to recognize an infant's signals and provide consistent guidance and pleasurable interactions. To provide a consistent and trusting environment, all center staff must agree on what is acceptable behavior. In most cases, having only a few limits for children increases the chances they will consistently be followed.

Finally, an infant-toddler caregiver needs to be aware of the most recent research in the infant-toddler field. Read professional journals, books, and articles. Attend professional workshops and conferences in person or online. Watch videos produced by professional organizations. Another important way to stay informed is to discuss your observations and needs with other infant-toddler caregivers and your colleagues. Never forget that positive relationships are grounded in the knowledge of race and diversity.

29.1-2 Guidelines for Infant-Toddler Care

In order to provide a quality infant-toddler program, consider the following general guidelines:

- Provide the children with a safe, interesting, and nurturing environment.
- Nurture love and affection.
- Develop warm, pleasurable, engaging, and trusting relationships with them and their families.
- Respect the cultures and diversity represented by the children and their families.
- Provide sensitive and responsive caregiving so the children feel valued and respected.
- Individualize experiences for each child's personality, interests, and cultural background.
- Care for each child promptly and affectionately.
- Respond to children's distress or discomfort signals immediately.
- Follow a consistent and predictable daily routine in providing for children's needs.
- Encourage curiosity and problem-solving skills by providing opportunities for the children to explore.
- Engage in language-rich play by narrating events and asking questions.
- Use the children's developmental stages to plan activities and scaffold their learning.
- Help children develop trust, respect, and a positive regard for their world.
- Avoid overstimulation. Too many new experiences at one time can overwhelm young children, particularly infants.
- Plan experiences for infants and toddlers to master new skills.

In addition to these guidelines, an infant-toddler caregiver should take care to meet infants' and toddlers' needs in ways they understand. For infants, this means playing the developmental game of **serve and return** which shapes the brain's architecture. Like a lively game of tennis, volleyball, or ping-pong, an infant will *serve*, or reach out for interactions with you beginning early in life with cooing. Later the infants will use babbling, gestures, cries, or facial expressions for serving. These *serves* will tell you a lot about the child's interests, needs and ability. Watch for them and then acknowledge, support, and encourage, the infant's lead. *Return* the serve by responding appropriately with eye contact, facial expressions, verbal comments, the same type of gestures, words, or a hug (**Figure 29.3**). If an infant points to something, give it a name.

Infants will learn best through these responsive, playful interactions with you. These back-and-forth interactions teach turn taking and are the key to a strong brain. They promote the development of social and language skills, which strengthen proper neural wiring in infants' brains. Having a responsive teacher makes the infant feel more secure. Some educators call these interactions the *three T's*—*tuning* in, *talking* more, and *taking* turns.

Like adults, infants have **mirror neurons**. These are nerve cells that allow us to mimic the feelings and body movements of other people that surround us. Mirror neurons can be positive or negative. Think about looking someone in the face who is wearing a broad smile. Chances are you are going to return the smile. If someone is crying with a frown on their face, mirror neurons will duplicate this look. To promote positive feelings, teachers need to focus on the positive.

Early Childhood Insight 🄰🄱🄲

Infant Feeding Areas

The most convenient infant feeding area is near the entrance to the center. Parents arriving with baby food and bottles must have the teacher label and refrigerate them at once. Equip this area with high chairs, feeding tables, a heat source, and comfortable, adult-sized chairs.

29.1-3 Infant Environments

Providing a quality, nurturing environment for infants cannot be left to chance. Environment planning needs to be *intentional*, as often the environment is referred to as the third teacher. An environment for infants should be attractive and comfortable for infants as well as for their caregivers. These environments should address daily routines by including areas for feeding, diapering, cuddling with a caregiver, sleeping, and playing.

The diapering area should be positioned next to a sink, and the floor surface should be washable to allow for easy cleaning and disinfecting. To prevent back strain for adults, changing surfaces and storage areas should be waist high, which is usually between 28 and 32 inches. The American Academy of Pediatrics recommends that changing tables be free of restraining straps, since cleaning and sanitizing these straps presents caregivers with a challenge. Place a mirror on the wall or ceiling next to the changing surface so children can look at themselves. Laminated pictures on the wall or ceiling provide visual stimulation.

Sleeping areas usually use the most space because cribs take a large amount of floor space. Be sure to check your state's licensing regulations.

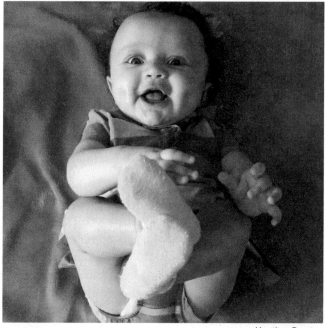

Heather Preston

Figure 29.3 This infant is engaged in playing the developmental game of serve and return with a teacher. These interactions are essential for the child's healthy development. ***What are the benefits of serve and return activities?***

While some states require separate napping rooms, others require napping areas in the same room. Some states also set the distance needed between cribs. The sleeping area should be **adjoining** (next to) the diapering area. Do not worry about light. Infants do not need a dark room in which to sleep. A dimmer switch should be installed in this area to control lights used in the diapering area.

Infants also need their own play area (**Figure 29.4**). They need to be safely out of the way of older children. Floor space to practice tummy time is necessary, while mobile infants and toddlers need clearly defined learning areas to explore. To ensure safety, use low dividers to make a crawling area. For comfort and warmth, cover the floor with densely woven, washable carpeting.

Health Highlights

Wearing Shoes in Infant Play Areas

Infants may spend much of their playtime on the floor. Teachers, care providers, and other children need to remove or cover their shoes when in the infant room. Wearing "street" shoes in the infant play areas may introduce disease-causing agents. When infants touch these surfaces and then put their hands in their mouths, they become ill. As an alternative to removing or covering shoes, teachers and care providers might keep a special pair of shoes or slippers just for use in the infant play area.

Oksana Kuzmina/Shutterstock.com

Figure 29.4 Infants need a safe place to play and explore their toys. *Why do infants need their own play area in an early childhood center?*

29.1-4 Toddler Environments

Balancing safety and health concerns is important in designing spaces for toddlers. Toddlers need more open areas than infants. When they are not sleeping, they are usually moving. Toddlers' environments should include receiving, playing, napping, diapering, and eating areas. Infants and toddlers may share napping, diapering, and eating areas (**Figure 29.5**).

A receiving area should be located near the main entrance where parents and children enter. This area should contain a bulletin board for family information and lockers or hooks to hold children's outdoor clothing. When standing in the receiving area, you should have a clear view of all other areas, especially the play area. Provide interesting equipment in the room to encourage children to play and help ease separation anxiety. Toddlers need a play area that allows them to move freely. To provide this, leave one-third to one-half of the total space open. In crowded areas, some children may find it hard to play. As a result, they may cry and grab. If children do not have adequate space, they will bump into each other.

Although a tile floor is easier to maintain, some teachers prefer a carpeted floor in the play area. Carpeting has two advantages. First, it provides a cushion for falls. Second, it is warmer for crawling children. If carpeting is on the floor, it should have a tight weave and be washable.

The layout of a classroom should encourage play. Since motor development is critical to toddlers' overall development, the middle of the room should be open. This area can contain portable equipment such as tunnels, bolsters, and gyms. In one section of the play area, there should be equipment that encourages toddlers' rapidly developing physical skills. Open areas and equipment for crawling, walking, and climbing should be available. Scaled slides, tunnels, carpeted platforms, cardboard boxes, and low shelves all invite exploration and climbing. Arrange equipment so that the caregivers can see all areas of the classroom. Toddlers also need some private space where they can rest and observe. This space may include a small loft, a tunnel, a cabinet with a door removed, or even an enclosed corner of the room.

UW-Stout Child and Family Study Center

Figure 29.5 The diapering area should be organized with each child's supplies. In this area, diaper-changing policies should also be posted.

The outdoor play area should connect to the indoor play area. This outdoor area should have a large grassy space for running and crawling. Grass, like carpeting, helps cushion falls.

A well-planned center for toddlers will include activity areas that are around the outer walls of the room. You can group similar activities into centers. Each center should contain equipment and materials that offer the child a choice of activities. An interesting, well-equipped room drives learning. It stimulates the toddlers' curiosity, encouraging them to explore and investigate. Art, sensory, fine-motor, gross-motor, music, and language areas can be included in a toddler program. When planning the activity centers, ask yourself the following questions:

- Does the room arrangement encourage active exploration?
- Are the toys and books developmentally appropriate and represent diversity?
- Is there enough space for the children to play comfortably?
- Are the materials at the children's eye level and within their reach?
- Are heavy toys stored on bottom shelves?
- Are the children provided choices so they can pursue their own interests?
- Are a variety of toys presented, including those for solitary play and those supporting cooperative play?

- Are toys gender-neutral?
- Are the toys safe and checked frequently for sharp edges, loose pieces, and small parts that could be swallowed?
- Are toys rotated so the children are exposed to new toys?

29.1-5 Caring for Infants and Toddlers

In an infant-toddler center, as in a preschool center, each child has their own rhythm. Some children will go about routines quickly; others will move slowly. As a caregiver, you must be sensitive to the children's needs and messages. You should also adjust your own rhythm to each child's rhythm.

All infants and toddlers, regardless of their rhythms, require caregivers to meet their needs promptly if they are to learn trust. Meeting these children's needs includes providing consistent care to help children learn they are special. Without consistent care, children may have difficulty trusting adults and other people. In providing consistent care, caregivers should meet needs appropriately. **Figure 29.6** lists appropriate and inappropriate caregiver practices.

When meeting the needs of infants and toddlers, routines are more important than they are with preschoolers. Daily routines and schedules should be predictable, yet flexible, to give children a sense of security and help them

---

Workplace Connections

Comparing Licensing Standards

Locate a copy of the licensing standards for childcare or early learning centers in your state. Compare the amounts and types of equipment and supplies required for infant-toddler programs with those for preschool programs.

1. What are the major differences in requirements between the two types of programs?
2. What items do the two types of programs have in common?

Appropriate and Inappropriate Caregiver Practices

Appropriate	Inappropriate
Caregivers interact face-to-face with individual infants frequently.	Infants are left unattended for long periods of time without adult attention.
Toys are picked up immediately after discarded to be sanitized. After being sanitized, they are reintroduced into the environment.	Toys that were mouthed by one child are left on the floor.
Caregivers are constantly talking, singing, and using nonverbal language with the children.	Infants are left to entertain themselves.
Caregivers recognize and provide for individual differences in children's sleeping and eating needs.	All children must conform to a rigid schedule for sleeping and eating.
Caregivers interact verbally and nonverbally while diapering.	Diapering is a hurried, nonverbal routine.
Each child is assigned a primary caregiver to receive predictable care.	Children are passed from one caregiver to another and provided with little consistency or predictability.
Adults consistently model warm, loving, sensitive, nurturing behavior.	Adults often display unfeeling and chilly behavior.

Figure 29.6   Meeting children's needs requires caregivers to provide consistent care. *Why is it important to coordinate center routines and home routines for infants and toddlers?*

know what to expect each day. Much of infant and toddler care will revolve around routines such as feeding, diapering, toileting, and preparing for nap time (**Figure 29.7**). For infants especially, coordinating center and home routines is important. Teachers should record infants' eating, elimination, activity, and nap patterns during the day. Infant-toddler caregivers should be knowledgeable about age-appropriate routines

aldomurillo/E+ via Getty Images

Figure 29.7   Routines such as feeding are an important part of a curriculum for infants. *Why do you think it is important for caregivers to hold infants during feeding?*

regarding feeding, diapering and toileting, and napping. Parents should provide the center with information daily, such as by giving caregivers an infant's daily record (**Figure 29.8**).

Feeding Infants

At no time do children grow faster than during their first year of life. Nutrition is very important for infants. If infants do not get the nutrients their bodies require, their growth and development can be **stunted** (hindered or delayed). Infants should be fed every two to four hours. By either fussing, crying, or moving their lips, the infant will tell you when they are hungry. Feeding an infant in response to these signals is called **demand feeding**. As caregivers learn the children's schedules and signals, they can feed infants before they begin crying.

Throughout infancy, babies rely on either breast milk or iron-fortified infant formula. Most feedings in childcare or early childhood centers will be by bottle. Caregivers should always hold infants while feeding them with a bottle. When feeding an infant, make eye contact, smile, and make small talk about the present. Feeding is a time for nurturing social, emotional, and

Infant Daily Record

Infant's name: _____ Parent's name: _____

Day/Date: _____ Time of arrival: _____

Parent's signature: _____ Time of departure: _____
  (filled in by parent) (filled in by staff member)

Baby seems: ❏ Normal, typical
❏ Bit fussy
❏ Not acting as usual

Baby slept: ❏ Soundly
❏ Woke up several times
❏ Did not sleep well

Baby ate:

Food/Drink	Amount	Time
_____	_____	_____
_____	_____	_____
_____	_____	_____

❏ Nothing this morning

Bowel movement number: _____

❏ Regular ❏ Irregular

Number of wet diapers: _____

Diet change for today: _____

_____

Special instructions: _____

Medicine taken today: _____

Time _____ Amount _____

Time _____ Amount _____

Medicine to be given today: _____

Time _____ Amount _____

Time _____ Amount _____

(See medication form for details)

Bottles:

Time	Food/Drink	Amount
_____	_____	_____
_____	_____	_____
_____	_____	_____
_____	_____	_____
_____	_____	_____
_____	_____	_____

Foods:
_____
_____
_____
_____
_____

Diaper checks and changes:

Time	Description
_____	_____
_____	_____
_____	_____
_____	_____

Medication given: _____ _____
  (Time) (Caregiver)

_____ _____
  (Time) (Caregiver)

Activities, accomplishments, skills shown today:
_____
_____
_____

Caregivers' initials: _____

Figure 29.8 An infant's daily record can help to coordinate home and center schedules.

language skills. When corporations have on-site care, some mothers may come to the center to breast-feed their infants and take advantage of this time. If this is the case, provide mothers a quiet, comfortable place to breast-feed.

Caregivers should immediately label and refrigerate all bottles containing breast milk or formula. The center for Disease Control and Prevention (CDC) and the American Academy of Pediatrics (APP) recommend that breast milk should not stay at room temperature for longer than four hours. In addition to these guidelines, consider the room temperature, which should not be over 77° Fahrenheit. If the temperature is over 77°, do not let milk sit out at all.

Bacteria are all around. Once a child has put his or her mouth on the bottle, bacteria from the mouth and saliva can enter the milk or formula. This causes the milk or formula to spoil even more quickly. After one hour, discard any milk or formula remaining in a used bottle.

Many infants prefer their bottles at room temperature. When taking a bottle from the refrigerator, place it under a stream of warm running water or use a bottle warmer to bring the bottle to room temperature. Never place a bottle in the microwave. Microwaves heat unevenly and may warm one part of the milk or formula enough to scald the baby's mouth. Excessive heat can also destroy living substances and nutritional content in breast milk.

A milestone in infant development is introducing solid food. According to the American Academy of Pediatrics, introduction of age-appropriate solid foods generally occurs when infants are about six months of age, or when their birth weight doubles (about 13 pounds). Introducing solids before four months of age is not recommended. When introducing solid foods, the infant should try one food at a time to ensure they do not have food allergies. Then wait three to five days between introducing each new food.

To eat solid foods, infants must be able to sit in a high chair and have good head control. The infant must also be able to transfer food from the front to the back of the tongue to swallow Showing an interest in foods and eagerness for feeling are other signs infants may be ready

for solids. The risk of becoming overweight is higher for infants who begin eating solid foods before *four* months of age. Expose infants to a wide variety of healthy soft foods, flavors, and textures, including pureed fruits, vegetables, and meats. Most parents use store-bought jars of baby food; others make their infants' foods at home. As a caregiver, serve children the breast milk or formula and the solid baby foods the parents provide. When serving baby foods, use a clean spoon to remove the desired portion from the jar or container. Put this into a small serving dish. Replace the lid and refrigerate the jar. Use the jar within two to three days and discard any uneaten food in the serving dish at the end of the feeding. This will prevent the food from growing bacteria from the baby's saliva.

Talk with parents about feeding practices, preferences, and habits. Ask parents which foods to offer as well as when to offer them. Unless safety is a concern, try to follow the parents' wishes regarding feeding. Discuss with your center director how to proceed. The director can inform you of center policies and advise you how to handle the situation. It is often best to inform parents of the risks involved and suggest a more appropriate option. For instance, propping an infant's bottle is an inappropriate practice. It creates a choking risk and deprives the infant of the personal attention and social contact needed when eating. It also promotes ear infections. If parents ask you to prop their child's bottle, tell them the center's policy is to hold infants during feedings.

Meeting infants' nutritional needs will be an important part of your job as a caregiver. Very young infants have an innate ability to self-regulate their food. They express their hunger by moving their mouths, rooting, or crying. It is important to feed infants on demand rather than on a set schedule. Feed each child when they are hungry, not when it is convenient. Responsive feeding will help foster self-regulation.

Older infants may cry for food, grunt and point at the food they want, or respond positively to a caregiver's offer of food. After nine months of age, offer infants two to three snacks a day. Encourage them to use fingers and spoons to feed themselves.

By the same token, do not force an infant to eat. Watch for cues that the infant is full or does not want more. These cues include crying in response to the bottle or spoon, turning the head away, closing the mouth tightly, and stopping sucking from the bottle. If you see these or other signs of refusal, respect the infant's cues and end the feeding.

Feeding Toddlers

Feeding practices for toddlers can differ from feeding practices for infants. Toddlers learn to wash their hands before and after eating. Many toddlers crawl on the floor and later use their hands to feed themselves. Before eating, always wash toddlers' hands. If child-sized sinks are not available, use a small pan of water at the table. At first, you may have to assist the children in swishing their hands as well as wiping them on a paper towel or cloth. Apply a small amount of liquid soap to a dampened towel and wipe the child's hands. Rinse the hands with a clean towel moistened with water. Finally, wipe the child's hands with a dry paper towel.

At about one year of age, toddlers begin to develop self-feeding skills. They begin exercising control over their food choices. Serve toddlers finger foods whenever possible. They are easy

for children to handle. Always provide many sizes and shapes of foods so children can practice picking them up. Be sure to cut food into small pieces to prevent choking. Examples include cubes of pear, cooked green peas, chopped cooked eggs, banana pieces, and cheese.

For feeding, seat toddlers in high chairs, at eating tables, or on low chairs placed in front of low tables. Toddlers will need some table space on which to move their food. Children of this age love to explore their food. Before eating, toddlers may smell, touch, and push around their food. Encourage this behavior; talk with the children about the food. Exploring food can give children important sensory experiences that foster cognitive growth (**Figure 29.9**).

Oral Health

Oral health is vital to overall health. Good oral health habits are vital for infants and toddlers. Healthy oral habits, beginning in infancy, build a foundation for a lifetime of good health. It is critical in preventing tooth decay. During childhood, caring for teeth is important. Cavities can be one of the most common chronic diseases for children. Untreated, they can cause pain and infections.

staticcnak1983/E+ via Getty Images

Figure 29.9   Toddlers can feed themselves with a spoon, but expect a mess. Use bibs to protect their clothing. *How do toddlers benefit from self-feeding?*

Caregivers should never place infants and toddlers in a crib to sleep with a bottle in their mouth. When given a bottle in bed, infants may fall asleep with the bottle in their mouth. The milk from the bottle will build up around the teeth and causes a plaque buildup. This can lead to "baby bottle decay" which most often affects the front teeth, but can also affect the infant's gums.

Teething Basics

Teething often is a painful experience for young children. Drooling, irritability, crying, and swollen gums are classic signs of teething. Most infants will begin teething at approximately six months of age, but it can begin anytime between three and twelve months. First the two bottom teeth, lower incisors, usually emerge in the infant's mouth. After this, the top two teeth, upper central incisors, will emerge a few weeks later.

According to the American Academy of Pediatrics, there are two safe options for treating teething pain if the baby is uncomfortable during teething. One is to rub the infant's gums with a clean finger, applying a slight amount of pressure. The other is to provide the infant with a teething ring constructed of firm rubber to chew on. Sometimes teething rings can be slightly chilled, but avoid giving the child a frozen teething ring as it can hurt.

Caring for Teeth

The American Dental Association recommends that children learn dental routines early in life. Brushing should begin as soon as an infant's first tooth appears. This usually occurs around six months of age, although some children do not receive their first tooth until 12 or 14 months of age. Teeth are at risk for decay as soon as they emerge. For infants, begin by placing a small amount of fluoride toothpaste (no larger than a grain of rice) on a child-sized, soft-bristled brush. Brush lightly and remember to replace a toothbrush every three to four months. Infants should have their teeth brushed twice a day, in the morning and at night.

Brush toddlers' teeth after meals. If the center's sinks are not low enough, you may use step stools for the children. Before brushing teeth, both the caregiver and toddler should wash their hands. After this, provide each child with their own toothbrush. On the brush, place a pea-sized amount of toothpaste. Then encourage the toddler to brush all teeth.

Pacifier Use

The majority of infants have a need to suck, which they usually find calming. Providing a pacifier can satisfy this need. Introduction of pacifiers should not occur during the few weeks of life; otherwise, nipple confusion may occur that could interfere with breastfeeding. For babies who use a pacifier, the best time to offer it is at nap times and bedtime. Check pacifiers for wear and tear by looking at the rubber. Look to see if it is frayed, torn, or discolored. If it is, tell the parents it needs replacement.

Workplace Connections

Investigating Diapering Policies and Practices

Investigate a local early childhood center's policies and practices regarding diapering.
1. Does the center have a specific diaper check routine?
2. Does the staff follow proper handwashing procedures?

Diapering and Toileting

Caregivers will change diapers many times each day. For this reason, diapering should be a pleasant experience. During diapering, give a child all your attention. Look into the child's eyes with gentle kindness and respect. Smile, sing, and talk softly to the child. Diapering can be a wonderful time for personal interaction. Diapering is also a time to use **sportscasting**, which is a way of communicating with the infant reflecting on your observation. It is a here and now moment. You may say such things as, "You look so happy today" or "Once I took the dirty diaper off, you stopped crying."

Many centers follow a diaper-checking routine. Infants need frequent diaper changes because they eliminate often. For infants' health and comfort, caregivers need to change soiled diapers promptly. Unchanged diapers may cause chafing, diaper rashes, infections, or discomfort. In baby girls especially, bacteria may cause a bladder infection. Your center needs specific policies regarding diapering. These policies might be checking each child's diaper once every hour or half-hour, unless the child is sleeping. In addition, you should check diapers before feeding and after naps. After introduction of solid food, there will be fewer wet diapers. When diapering, you may encounter many disease-causing germs that live in body fluids. Thorough handwashing will reduce the spread of these germs. Therefore, all staff should follow proper handwashing procedures before and after each diaper change (**Figure 29.10**). When washing hands, use warm water and liquid soap.

Safe and Healthy Diapering to Reduce the Spread of Germs
Keep a hand on the child for safety at all times!

1. **PREPARE**
   - Wash your hands thoroughly. If your center uses disposable gloves, put them on.
   - Cover the diaper changing surface with disposable liner.
   - If you use diaper cream, dispense it onto a tissue now.
   - Bring your supplies (e.g., clean diaper, wipes, diaper cream, gloves, plastic or waterproof for soiled clothing, extra clothing) to the diapering area.

2. **CLEAN CHILD**
   - Place the child on diapering surface and unfasten the diaper.
   - Clean the child's diaper area with disposables wipes. Always wipe from front to back.
   - Keep soiled diaper/clothing away from any surfaces that cannot be easily cleaned.
   - Securely bag soiled clothing.

3. **REMOVE TRASH**
   - Place wipes in the soiled diaper.
   - Discard soiled diaper and wipes in the trash can.
   - Remove and discard gloves, if used.

4. **REPLACE DIAPER**
   - Slide a fresh diaper under the child.
   - Apply diaper cream, if needed, with a tissue or freshly gloved finger.
   - Fasten the diaper and dress the child.

5. **WASH CHILD'S HANDS**
   - Use soap and water to wash the child's hands thoroughly.
   - Return the child to the supervised area.

6. **CLEAN UP**
   - Remove liner from changing surface and discard in the trash can.
   - Wipe up any visible soil with a damp paper towels or baby wipe.
   - Wet the entire surface with disinfectant; make sure you follow the directions on the disinfecting spray, fluid, or wipe. Choose disinfectant appropriate for the surface material.

7. **WASH YOUR HANDS**
   - Wash your hands thoroughly with soap and water.

Source CDC
Centers for Disease Control and Prevention
National Center for Emerging and Zoonotic Infectious Diseases

Figure 29.10 It is essential for center staff to follow proper handwashing procedures before and after each diaper change.

Use liquid soap because bar soaps, when wet and jelly-like, harbor microorganisms. A soap dispenser may be most convenient. Remember, microorganisms may also grow in liquid soap. Clean a soap dispenser each time it is refilled.

In many centers and some states, policy recommendations indicate to use lightweight, disposable gloves for all diaper changes. Put on these gloves before touching soiled clothing or diapers. Gloves help reduce infectious agents under the fingernails and on the hands. Safe and healthy diapering is important to reduce the spread of germs (Figure 29.10). The diapering procedure should be posted in the changing area, and followed for all diaper changes. If teachers speak multiple languages, the centers should post the procedure in multiple languages, too.

While changing the diaper, check for signs of *diaper rash*. Diaper rash is a skin rash that occurs in the baby's diaper area. It may result from infrequent diaper changing. The wet, damp diaper promotes the growth of bacteria that can irritate and infect the skin in the diaper area. Itching, redness, and discomfort are common. If you notice any signs of diaper rash, notify the parents that same day.

Keeping an infant clean and dry will prevent many cases of diaper rash. Check infants' diapers often and change them promptly. If diaper rash does occur, use a tissue to apply any diaper rash creams. The parents or caregivers can supply this ointment. To prevent diaper rash, some families prefer to apply creams with every change when no rash is present. Follow the family's instructions on this matter. If a rash worsens or will not clear up, advise the parents or caregivers to seek their doctor's advice.

During the diapering process, children's hands often stray into the area covered by the diaper. After each change, use soap and water to wash the child's hands. This will prevent the transfer of fecal organisms into the play area. Then record the diapering information on the child's daily record. You will need to note time of the check or change and whether the child urinated or had a bowel movement. If a child had diarrhea, note this along with the amount, color or odor, and consistency. Record any skin irritation.

Do not be shocked if, as a child grows older, they object to having a diaper changed. Many times, this objection occurs because the child is having fun playing and wants to avoid this interruption. When this occurs, there is no harm in waiting a few minutes. Wait until the child finishes with an activity, and then gently guide them to the changing area.

Some toddlers may show an interest in toilet learning. For these children, coordinate efforts between the center and home. Discuss the toilet-learning process with parents or guardians and explain that it will be easier for the child if the home and center routines are consistent.

As with diapering policies, toileting policies can help ensure children's health. The National Association for the Education of Young Children (NAEYC) does not recommend the use of potty chairs. If a center decides to use potty chairs, they should be construction of either plastic or a nonporous synthetic product. Do not use wooden

Health Highlights

Sanitary Diaper-Disposal Containers

Containers for sanitary diaper disposal follow specific guidelines for the early childhood classroom. Note these guidelines:

- Use disposal containers with tight-fitting covers that release easily without touching them with your hands. Step cans are one type. Simply step on the release to open the can.
- Stainless steel diaper disposals are less porous and may contain odors better.
- Use washable containers. Line them with plastic liners or garbage bags. Some teachers prefer using special scented bags that can mask smell.
- Store soiled diapers in disposal containers away from other waste receptacles.
- Keep disposal containers out of children's reach.
- Empty containers into the outdoor trash daily or as often as necessary throughout the day.

potty chairs since they are difficult to sanitize. When using a potty chair, clean it after each use. Children should wash their hands after using a potty chair (**Figure 29.11**). Finally, wash your hands with warm water and soap.

Napping

All children need sufficient sleep, though amounts vary among children. Newborns sleep 16 to 20 hours a day, waking only for feedings every few hours. (**Figure 29.12**). Most infants need at least two naps a day ranging from one to three hours. Without adequate sleep, a child can become cranky and difficult to handle. This can negatively influence other children and staff in the center. An infant may show you signs of being ready for sleep. They may rub their eyes, yawn, look away, or fuss.

When planning a nap-time schedule, check preferences of parents or guardians. Some keep their infants up late and wake them early in the morning. They want their children to sleep at the center so they are awake and alert at the end of the day. Others who may have to travel some

UW-Stout Child and Family Study Center

Figure 29.12 Caregivers should be able to see sleeping infants from the play area. ***Why is it important for caregivers to continually monitor infants during nap time?***

distance to get home, prefer a sleepy baby at the end of the day. Their goal is to have the baby sleep on the way home to avoid any distraction while driving.

Stagger nap times to meet the individual needs of the children. This type of scheduling also allows time to feed and rock each child to

Studio Romantic/Shutterstock.com

Figure 29.11 Young toddlers may need help washing their hands correctly.

sleep. Individual needs will often mesh with group needs. After developing a schedule that fits the individual needs of all children, it is necessary to be consistent.

When putting infants down for naps, certain precautions will help reduce the risk of **sudden infant death syndrome (SIDS)**. SIDS is the death of a healthy infant due to unexplained causes. It is the leading cause of death for infants between one and twelve months of age. SIDS is most likely to occur in infants that are one to four months old, but it can occur until a child is one year of age. To help prevent SIDS, always place infants on their backs on a firm mattress to sleep. Never place soft items, such as quilts, pillows, and stuffed toys in a crib with an infant. Avoid letting the baby get too hot. Cover them with a light blanket only up to their chests, or use a sleep sack or other sleep clothing that does not require additional covers. A caregiver needs to visually check sleeping babies continuously.

29.1-6 Challenges in Caring for Infants and Toddlers

Caregivers are likely to encounter several challenges when caring for infants and toddlers. Some of these challenges include crying as a means of communication, stranger anxiety, and separation anxiety.

Crying as a Means of Communication

Crying is an early means of communication that demands action. Infants may cry to express needs, cope with frustration, or get attention. They may also cry when they feel lonely, uncomfortable, neglected, or overstimulated. Regardless of the reason, you should never ignore crying. Always remember that the crying has some meaning for the child (**Figure 29.13**).

Studies support the theory that an infant's crying should always receive prompt attention. Crying is the strategy infants use most for self-soothing. According to these studies, when a caregiver promptly answers these cries, the crying frequency decreases.

You will observe that babies have different crying behaviors. Some babies cry more often and with greater strength. Other babies may seldom cry. All babies have various reasons for crying.

As a caregiver, you need to learn the meaning of each child's cries. By listening to how a baby cries, you will soon learn about their needs. A short and low-pitched cry usually means the baby is hungry. A loud and sudden high-pitched shriek followed by a flat wail is a cry of distress. Typically, the pitch and duration of cries reflect the intensity of disturbance. Sometimes the types of cries overlap. For instance, a baby may wake up hungry, making lip movement, and will cry for food. If you do not quickly respond to this need, the baby

Reasons for Infant Crying

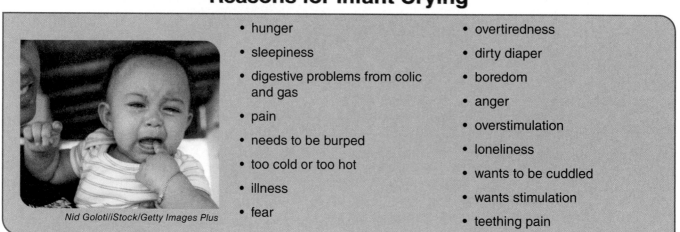

- hunger
- sleepiness
- digestive problems from colic and gas
- pain
- needs to be burped
- too cold or too hot
- illness
- fear

- overtiredness
- dirty diaper
- boredom
- anger
- overstimulation
- loneliness
- wants to be cuddled
- wants stimulation
- teething pain

Nid Goloti/iStock/Getty Images Plus

Figure 29.13 Infants cry to express their needs. Caregivers should never ignore crying.

may then cry with rage. You will also learn which cries show fussiness, soiled diapers, boredom, or discomfort related to being too cool or warm.

Always respond to a child's crying by first trying to solve the problem. If the infant is wet, change their diaper. Likewise, if the child is hungry, feed them. If you cannot find an obvious reason for the child's crying, check the infant's daily care record. Perhaps the baby is sleepy, teething, reacting to medication, or catching a cold. A baby may also cry out of a feeling of loneliness, wanting to play, or wanting to cuddle.

You can comfort tired, crying babies in several ways. Some enjoy being held; others love to be rocked or caressed. Often, you can comfort a child simply by speaking or singing softly. Talk to the infant's parents or guardians to coordinate home and center child-rearing practices. Each culture may have different customs, beliefs, and attitudes toward child rearing. For example, cultures respond in different ways to crying. Some parents will nurse, some will provide a pacifier, and others will talk with and snuggle the baby.

Stranger Anxiety

Usually between seven and nine months of age, infants begin to show fear of strangers, or **stranger anxiety**. Ricardo is an example. He was a friendly and happy child no matter whom he encountered. Then at about seven months of age, he began to discriminate between familiar and unfamiliar adults. When approached by an unfamiliar adult, he often would frown, cry, turn his head away, and display **wariness**, or cautious fear.

Emilio's behavior is typical of a child experiencing stranger anxiety, which show evidence of increasing cognitive functioning. These behaviors indicate that Emilio is trying to make sense of the world by distinguishing between strangers and familiar people. When seeing an unfamiliar person, Emilio experiences fear.

Working with young children, you will observe that not all children react like Emilio. Significant differences exist in how children show stranger anxiety. Some infants who have had experience with strangers will react less intensely. Other infants will show more anxiety with males or with females.

Besides strangers, you will notice that some children react strongly to sudden movements, noises, or strange objects. To help support children, let them explore at their own pace. Allow them to stay near you until their upset feelings have subsided. Meanwhile, gradually expose them to new objects in the center.

Separation Anxiety

Between nine and 18 months of age, after gaining an understanding of object permanence, many children will start experiencing *separation anxiety*. This is a feeling of fear of the unknown and distress at separation from a parent or other significant person. It can include crying, protesting, clinging to a family member, trying to follow a parent or guardian, withdrawing, or begging a parent or guardian not to leave. Separation anxiety is a sign that children are learning and developing close relationships with their family. It does not only happen at the beginning of the day; it may also occur at pickup time.

Separation anxiety is often strongest among children of this age who enter an early childhood care setting for the first time. While children with earlier enrollment in childcare also experience separation anxiety, their anxiety may be less severe because they are already familiar with the surroundings and center staff. Separation anxiety may return after a vacation or school break. For some children, it might even return after a weekend.

Feelings of separation anxiety are difficult for young children to handle. Children need acceptance and emotional support during this time. As a teacher or caregiver, you can accept and describe the child's feelings for them. Reassure the child that their parent or guardian will return for them. Offer alternate activities, but be prepared for the child to refuse at first. In their own time, the child will join in. You might say, "You're sad because Daddy is leaving. He went to work, but will come back for you this afternoon. Would you like to play blocks with me?"

It can take several weeks or months for separation anxiety to diminish. Throughout this time, continue to show support and understanding. You may find yourself feeling frustrated by the child's crying or other behaviors at these times. Remind yourself that the anxiety will diminish in time and that your support is vital. Your support will help the children learn to depend on you and feel secure in the childcare environment.

When children experience separation anxiety, it is difficult for their family members, too. Parents or guardians do not enjoy seeing their children in distress. They may feel upset, sad, or guilty for having to leave their crying children. When their children cling to them, this can tug at their emotions. Remind family members that separation anxiety is normal and will diminish in time.

Share with parents or guardians any signs of progress you see. For example, if the child cries for less time or joins in with others more quickly, let the parents or guardians know. When the child settles down, take a photograph of the child. Due to confidentiality, make sure not to capture other children in the photograph. Then send the digital photograph of the child to the parent(s) or guardian(s); otherwise, you could call to help ease their minds. This gesture also tells family members that you care about their child.

29.1-7 Toys for Infants and Toddlers

When caring for infants and toddlers, teachers and caregivers should provide appropriate equipment and toys to support differing developmental needs. Toys serve as sensory stimuli for young children and are critical to brain development. For instance, by positioning an infant's toys, you can create an incentive for the child to use their memory or **locomotive** (movement) abilities (**Figure 29.14**). Even during the first few weeks of life, an infant can touch, see, and hear. Exercising these abilities fosters physical, language, and cognitive development. Gradually, young children learn concepts of cause-and-effect and learn to make things

Isbjorn/E+ via Getty Images

Figure 29.14   Crawling babies need a safe, appealing play area. *How can an infant's play area promote locomotion?*

happen. For instance, infants can learn that when they shake a rattle, it makes an interesting sound.

Filling, dumping, spilling, banging, fitting, and climbing are all exploration and discovery opportunities that toddlers enjoy. Toddlers are curious and a study in movement, so they need a range of equipment from soft blocks to climbing equipment. To promote language skills, include picture books, storybooks, audiobooks, dramatic-play props, and puppets. Media devices can promote music, movement, and sleep. Sensory materials, including nontoxic crayons, markers, and play dough, should also be available.

When planning toys for toddlers, take care to balance novel with familiar toys and materials. Be sure to provide a sufficient quantity and variety of open-ended toys, such as blocks and manipulatives, to encourage exploration and persistence. Guard the children against overstimulation, however, since many choices can overwhelm toddlers.

Display the materials so they are inviting and accessible. Cubes and blocks should be light and easy to grasp and stored in subtly colored containers so they are not a distraction. Place them on the bottom shelving unit. Avoid providing too many toys at the same time. This could be overwhelming for the children.

Many infant-toddler centers maintain a toy inventory that lists all the equipment available in the center. They subdivide the inventory into developmental sequences (**Figure 29.15**). This

Infant-Toddler Center Toy Inventory

Developmental Sequence	Types of Toys		
Looking	• dog mobile • farm animal mobile	• shape mobile • plastic mirror	• cloth and cardboard books
Squeezing/ Manipulation	• fish squeaker • pretzel squeaker • mouse squeaker • bunny squeaker	• busy box • plastic rings • plastic rattles (various colors)	• snap beads • chain of plastic disks • activity mats
Gross-Motor	• rubber balls • push toys • pull toys • small, light wagon • jumbo cardboard blocks	• wheeled train • wheeled lamb • climbing tunnel • crawling tunnel	• small gym • toy trucks big enough to ride • activity saucer
Reaching and Grasping	• ring activity gym • musical activity gym	• colored activity gym	• colored rattles
Pull/Push	• wooden train (makes a noise) • trucks • cars	• wooden dog • lawn mower	• wooden car • wooden wagon
Fine-Motor	• geometric form board • snap beads • small cards • nesting cups and boxes • shape sorting box	• strings of large beads • sand sets • water play kits • stacking rings • puzzles with large pieces • sorting box	• plastic or foam blocks • large crayons • activity center • geometric sorting box • pounding peg board
Cuddling Toys	• washable dolls • black bear • baby lamb (with chime)	• pink pig • brown pony	• black puppy • dolls
Sound	• music box • drum • jingle bells	• CD or personal media player and music • xylophone	• squeaky animals • tambourines
Kicking and Hitting	• large rubber beach balls • washable sensory balls	• colored foam balls	• bouncing clowns

Figure 29.15 An inventory of center toys and equipment is helpful when planning activities for children. *How would you make use of an equipment inventory?*

list can be helpful when planning activities for children. Since it is important to frequently rotate toys, a list will help you keep a record of the toys already used and toys that are available. Keeping a toy inventory can also be helpful when ordering new toys.

When choosing toys for the infant or toddler, safety is the first consideration. First, make sure that toys are washable. Then, check each toy carefully for sharp edges or points. Avoid small toys or toys with small parts. Children could swallow objects smaller than 1½ inches across and 1 inch in diameter, which could also cause choking.

To check whether an object is a choking risk, purchase a plastic safety tube for measuring small toys from an early childhood vendor. Try to fit each toy inside this tube. If the toy fits, it is too small to be safe for an infant or toddler. Any toy small enough to fit in the child's mouth is a choking hazard.

Each year, many infants and toddlers accidentally swallow small toys or parts. This can cause suffocation from choking on the object. Also, a child may develop intestinal or respiratory problems because of swallowing a small toy. Unfortunately, most plastic toys do not show up on X-rays. Many toy companies add *nontoxic radiopaque plastic* to toys so that toy parts will show up clearly on an X-ray. When you choose toys, check the label or package to see if the toy includes this material.

Appropriate Toys for Infants

When choosing toys, be sure to choose toys that are appropriate for the intended age level. Mobiles make excellent first toys for infants. They provide visual appeal and require a minimum of physical interaction. Select mobiles carefully and avoid mobiles that are not sturdy. If your center has such mobiles, hang them out of reach. For young infants, place toys 7 to 24 inches from the eyes.

Between six weeks and three and a half months of age, infants will discover their hands, which then become a toy for the child. Infants will study their hands as they move them back and forth. Infants between three and six months of age will continue to watch their hands. Even when infants move objects to their mouths, they will continue watching.

Smiles begin to appear at about two months of age. Infants at this age also want to touch what they see. To provide stimulation for the child, place a mirror over the changing table. It is fun to watch the child smile at his or her reflection in the mirror.

Soon, infants begin to touch objects within their reach. This behavior usually occurs between three and six months of age. As infants do this, they are taking in and organizing information about the world. During this process, they develop intelligence. Provide a variety of toys with different textures for the children to touch. These may include soft rattles and washable, stuffed, furry animals.

To provide grasping exercises, infants need a variety of toys within reach, whether in the crib or on the floor. Young children experience *object hunger*, which means they are likely to place these toys in the mouth. By placing objects in the mouth and exploring, infants gain physical knowledge about objects. Studies show that between six and ten months of age, nerve endings in an infant's mouth are very sensitive.

Rattles also promote infant development. When a rattle is handed to an infant, they follow a specific process. First, the child will use their eyes to locate the toy. After this, the child will move their hand toward the rattle. Just before contact, the infant's hand will open. In this process, the child will persist and try repeatedly to pick up a small toy. Observations have shown that infants follow a progression of hand-movement skills. First, infants learn raking motions, which appear to be random. Next, they make scissor motions. The child uses their entire hand to pick up an object. Finally, the child develops the pincer grasp. Using this method, an infant can pick up objects using only the forefinger and thumb. A child using this method shapes the hand into the grasp before reaching for the intended object.

Toys encourage the development of all these hand-movement skills. A variety of toys, such as cradle gyms, can encourage raking motions. Encourage scissor motions by providing small balls or figures that will fit into the hand. Finger foods, such as dry, ready-to-eat cereal, can also help children practice the pincer grasp.

As the child develops, they begin to experiment with cause-and-effect. Very young children are more interested in watching their hands than the objects they touch. By five to eight months, however, children are more intent on watching the effects of their actions. Around this age, children also enjoy dropping objects. They will drop objects, including utensils and toys, from a high chair or feeding table. As they do this, they will watch for the consequences of these actions. As an object hits the floor, children may wince at the sound it makes. Around this time, children also become interested in simple gadgets in the environment. They may show interest in electrical outlets (which you need to cap for safety purposes). Other appealing objects include light switches, cupboard knobs, doorknobs, fringe on rugs, and locks. The manipulation of these objects gives children a sense of magic.

Safety First

Safety Covers for Electrical Outlets

The National Fire Protection Association requires that all early centers built or renovated after 2017 have *tamper-resistant receptacles*. These receptacles have internal spring-loaded shutters that block children from inserting foreign objects into one side of the receptacle. The shutters open only when a two-bladed or ground plug is inserted into one side of the receptacle. Tamper-resistant receptacles prevent children from placing objects into the electrical outlets, preventing injury from electrical shock.

Appropriate Toys for Toddlers

Once children crawl or walk, they will continually explore the environment. To encourage this curiosity, it is important that toddler environments are safe with large, open areas where children can pull or push toys, straddle large trucks, or roll large balls.

Toddlers love to try new skills. To meet their large-muscle needs, provide them with small slides, jungle gyms, a balance beam, and sets of stairs. Make sure that you closely watch toddlers when they use the large-muscle equipment. Some children may try to walk up a slide. When this happens, take the child's hand and

direct them back to the stairs. Once children learn how to use equipment, they may use the equipment repeatedly. As they explore, children grow physically and cognitively. Small wagons, wheelbarrows, doll buggies, toddler trikes, and strollers also appeal to toddlers. If you lack indoor space, limit the use of these toys to an outdoor area.

Toddlers love to play with water. Encourage this play by providing floating toys, spoons, sponges, ladles, funnels, spray bottles, plastic pitchers, basting tubes, and unbreakable cups in a water-play area. Demonstrate how to pour water, sail a floating toy, and squeeze a sponge. For interest, add color to the water.

Books also spark the interest of toddlers (**Figure 29.16**). The books should mirror infants and toddlers like themselves. Consider images that reflect different cultures, races, and disabilities. Wordless books tell a story only through their illustrations. When toddlers begin talking, wordless books encourage them to become storytellers. When selecting books for toddlers, they enjoy stories about families, people, animals, and objects. Objects in books should be recognizable and the messages should be positive. Toddlers love the surprise of flipping the pages in a book. Since toddlers enjoy turning pages, select books with large pictures, thick pages that are easy to turn, and few words. Book bindings should be strong and sturdy.

FatCamera/iStock via Getty Images Plus

Figure 29.16 Since toddlers enjoy looking at books, provide a variety of age-appropriate and appealing books for them. ***What are three books you might use with infants and toddlers?***

Puppets also appeal to young children. Children enjoy puppets that are soft and recognizable. Puppets made of fabric, instead of plastic or rubber, are the easiest for the children to manipulate. Before buying puppets, check to see that they are machine washable.

The most time-consuming activity for toddlers is staring. Toddlers spend approximately one-fifth of their time either sitting or standing and staring. Toddlers may stare at a picture, another child, a toy, or even at you. Keep rooms visually stimulating to encourage this exploration.

Some children will lack interest in a particular toy. This is a sign of **overfamiliarity,** which results when children receive the same toy day after day and become bored. Once children are comfortable with a particular toy, they repeat the same actions repeatedly. When this happens, new skills do not develop, and it is time to provide a different toy that offers new challenges.

Young children like to have a variety of toys and need opportunities to make choices. Take care, however, not to include too many choices. Toddlers need to feel a sense of control. As the teacher or care provider, change a few toys every other day.

Lesson 29.1 Review

1. Infants and toddlers need _____, a practice where at least one teacher follows a group of children for several years. (29.1.1)
   A. object hunger
   B. overfamiliarity
   C. continuity of care
   D. community
2. **True or False.** The developmental game of serve and return is not important for an infant's brain development. (29.1.2)
3. The infant environment should include areas for all of the following *except* _____. (29.1.3)
   A. diapering
   B. sleeping
   C. feeding
   D. bicycling
4. How much of the toddlers' play area should be open space? (29.1.4)
   A. One-third to one-half
   B. One-fourth to one-third
   C. One-eighth to one-fourth
   D. All of it

5. **True or False.** Feeding practices for toddlers can differ from feeding practices for infants. (29.1.5)
6. _____ is a feeling of fear of the unknown and distress at separation from a parent or other significant person. (29.1.6)
   A. Object permanence
   B. Separation anxiety
   C. Post-partum depression
   D. Cognitive development
7. Young children experience _____, which means they are likely to place these toys in the mouth. (29.1.7)
   A. object permanence
   B. object hunger
   C. overfamiliarity
   D. cognitive development

Curriculum and Family Involvement

Essential Question

What do you need to know about planning curriculum for infants and toddlers and communicating with parents or guardians?

Learning Outcomes

After studying this lesson, you will be able to

29.2-1 **plan** the curriculum for infants and toddlers.

29.2-2 **summarize** key elements for communicating with family members.

29.2-3 **maintain** the environment to prevent illness.

Key Terms

tummy time   infant sign language

Infants and toddlers are at a special stage in their lives. The quality of care they receive is crucial to the development of their brain and health. To develop trust, infants and toddlers need consistent, predictable, positive, and caring relationships with their caregivers or teachers. And they need predictable routines. Their environment needs to balance safety and health concerns with developmental needs. Their curriculum needs to focus on supporting each child's development, culture, and home language. Age-appropriate, stimulating equipment and toys must be available. For the curriculum to be effective, daily communication with families is essential.

29.2-1 Curriculum

The early years are a critical period in learning and development. These years provide a foundation for the development of more advanced skills. To plan a developmentally appropriate antibias curriculum, you need to know the child, the family, their culture, and language. You need to honor diversity. An appropriate curriculum for infants and toddlers is based on the needs of the children attending the center. It is also based on principles of child growth and development. Curriculum is the totality of experience. Curriculum for infants and toddlers, including planned and unplanned experiences, differs from curriculum for older preschool children.

The curriculum needs to bring the children's culture, language and identities into the classroom. Consider the diversity of the classroom, too. Begin by:

- asking parents to suggest classroom equipment and play materials;
- introducing ethnic foods into the snack and lunch menus;
- selecting music, books, and songs from the children's home cultures;
- purchasing musical instruments, gender-neutral dolls, dramatic play materials; and
- adding posters showing the children's culture.

Curriculum for Infants

Rather than teachers setting learning goals, infants often set their own developmental goals. As the teacher, your role is to observe, support, and assess this growth. A curriculum for infants consists of simple, basic activities. It includes physical activities, such as feeding, cuddling, holding, rocking, and going on walks. It involves social play and positive interactions between children and their teachers. Create and implement activities for the development of social skills, including verbal and nonverbal communication, singing, chanting, talking, and listening. (**Figure 29.17**).

Curriculum for infants should include materials, activities, and time for exploring and building motor skills. Younger infants enjoy engaging in lap games that end with an expected surprise. For generations, one popular lap game has been peekaboo. During lap games, the infant exercises working memory by trying to remember who is hiding. Infants also enjoy hiding games. Hide a toy under a blanket and encourage the child to find it. Increase the challenge by changing the location and encouraging the child to find it. This game activates the child's working memory.

Tummy Time

The American Academy of Pediatrics (AAP) recommends that babies always sleep on their backs to prevent sudden infant death syndrome

Songs and Fingerplays for Infants and Toddlers

Twinkle, Twinkle, Little Star

Twinkle, twinkle, little star,
How I wonder what you are.
Up above the world so high,
Like a diamond in the sky.
Twinkle, twinkle, little star,
How I wonder what you are!

The Itsy-Bitsy Spider

The itsy-bitsy spider
Climbed up the waterspout.
Down came the rain
And washed the spider out.
Out came the sun
And dried up all the rain.
So the itsy-bitsy spider
Climbed up the spout again!

Figure 29.17 Singing with children helps promote verbal and nonverbal communication.

(SIDS). This makes tummy time an essential part of an infant's curriculum, since it encourages healthy visual, motor, and sensory development. Tummy time can be introduced in the curriculum when infants are newborns, and may continue throughout the first year of life. **Tummy time** encourages infants to lift their heads, which will help build strong head, neck, and shoulder muscles. The development of these core muscles is necessary for infants to slide on their bellies and crawl. Tummy time can also prevent the back of an infant's head from developing flat spots.

Begin introducing tummy time by spreading a clean blanket on the floor. Then place the infant, stomach down, on the blanket. Schedule only brief periods, three to five minutes, several times a day and build up to longer segments. Remain with the infant as these times require supervision. Talk, sing, and chant.

Older infants, four to seven months, need more time on their tummies to build strength, so extend their time. Try to schedule a total of one hour per day. During this time, infants will practice lifting their heads by strengthening their arms. These movements will continue to strengthen their necks, heads, and backs. As they move and their weight shifts, they gain a sense of body awareness. Move to the infant's side, encouraging them to turn their heads. Then repeat this strategy by moving to the other side. You can also lay eye level on the floor and smile at the infant. Place toys in front of the child to encourage reaching and exploration.

By six months of age, most infants are directing their own tummy time. While on their stomach, they can turn in a circle. At the same time, they are reaching for and grabbing toys within their reach. Once infants begin crawling, daily tummy time is no longer essential.

Infant Sign Language

Infant sign language is a gestural language that supports expressive language. Many infant and toddler programs use sign language to boost communication. Since language and motor skills begin before speech, it allows babies to communicate months before speaking. As a result, it helps them self-regulate by easing their frustrations in communicating their feelings and needs, particularly between eight months and two years of age. Children who learn sign language begin to regulate their own behavior and emotions. It speeds up speech development and reduces frustrations and tantrums.

American Sign Language (ASL) is now a world language like French, Italian, Portuguese, Spanish, or any other foreign language. Children who use sign language are bilingual; they can speak two languages.

When and how should you introduce sign language? Infants at six months of age can begin to learn simple sign language (**Figure 29.18**). Now they can begin to sign and imitate the adult's gestures. Often by 24 months, these children can sign compound words. To introduce infant sign language, begin by deciding with the staff what signs you should introduce first. Then communicate with the parents or guardians and include the name and description of the sign. Encourage family members to use the signs at home. Post the signs on a bulletin board in the center. This will show the center cook, visitors, volunteers, and substitutes the gestures that you are introducing.

Intentionally introduce simple signs that describe requests, objects, or activities. Use them consistently in daily routines such as eating, diapering, singing, and reading. Always state the word or phrase every time you make the sign. Be patient. Until eight or nine months, most infants lack the hand control to sign back. Once the child can sign back, share your enthusiasm with attention and praise. Use the child's interests to grow their signing vocabulary.

An easy sign is for the word "drink." Place your thumb to your mouth, tilting your head up. Every time you use the word, model the sign. Check bookstores and online. Baby sign-language books, wall charts, videos, flash cards, and dictionaries are all available.

Bilingualism

Infants have the potential for becoming bilingual. A question that family members sometimes ask the center director or teacher is, "Will hearing two languages affect my baby's language development?" The answer is *no*. Studies show infants begin their language journey in the womb. After birth, they can become bilingual by learning two languages.

Babies raised in homes that are bilingual will process the sounds of both languages. They will produce their first sounds at about the same age as most infants who only have exposure to one language. However, they are hearing fewer sounds in each language.

Teachers need to work with the families of the children enrolled in their programs to find out about their home language. It is important since it is the child's connection to the love and nurturing from his family. Chances are you will have some questions such as, "Does everyone speak the same language in the household?" Ask parents or guardians for assistance in learning words for providing basic care routines. Words such as milk, blanket, more, nap are some examples. Using phonetic spelling, print each of these words on a note card. While the children are napping, practice pronouncing the words. Once you have mastered the basic words, ask the families for help to expand your bilingual vocabulary.

Infant Sign Language

• eat	• change	• ball
• drink	• help	• please
• milk	• play	• happy
• more	• sleep	• angry
• all done	• cry	• sad
• hungry	• open	• hurt
• done	• close	
• water	• book	

Figure 29.18 Children who learn infant sign language begin to self-regulate their own behavior and emotions. *What are some other benefits of infant sign language?*

Curriculum for Toddlers

Curriculum for toddlers requires more planning. Much of toddlers' days will consist of activities that promote physical, emotional, cognitive, and social development. Nearly all these activities can take place in various activity areas within the center. It is important to encourage the toddler's sense of agency. They need to be able to make and act upon choices of what activities they want to engage in. Make the curriculum developmentally appropriate by:

- observing to identify the children's strengths and provide experiences that support those strengths;
- offering choices;
- providing culturally relevant materials;
- providing hands-on, sensory-rich materials;
- providing information to build their knowledge; and
- narrating the children's actions and emotions.

Art Activities

Art activities can be pleasurable for toddlers. In addition, art activities provide excellent opportunities for promoting small-muscle development and visual-perceptual skills. In planning art activities, consider the guidelines in **Figure 29.19**.

Tips for Art Activities

- Provide only nontoxic materials. Young children tend to put materials in their mouths.
- Allow plenty of space to prevent children from putting paint, chalk, or markers on one another.
- Use large pieces of paper.
- Cover the table and/or floor with a plastic cloth or newspapers to catch spills.
- Provide art smocks or large plastic bibs.
- Keep cloth or paper towels handy to clean children's hands as soon as they finish activities.
- Wipe spills as they occur. This prevents children from slipping or getting soiled.

Figure 29.19 Including art activities in the curriculum for toddlers helps build fine-motor skills. *What are some examples of art activities for toddlers? What art activities might you recommend for family members to use at home?*

Many young toddlers enjoy finger-painting experiences. Children can use tempera paint and colored liquid soap for finger painting. As children use these materials, they enjoy squeezing them through their fingers. During the process, they learn to sense different textures.

Older toddlers also enjoy painting. Provide a variety of brushes for this type of experience. Consider using regular art brushes, toothbrushes, small household brushes, and sponge staining brushes. Larger handles are easier for toddlers to grasp. To help prevent dripping, mix the paint with a thickener. A powdered laundry detergent will usually thicken paint well.

Toddlers also enjoy scribbling. At this age, they make simple, random marks. Provide a variety of marking tools, such as large crayons, chalk, and nontoxic markers. To help children feel some control over their movements, give younger children larger tools. As their control improves, introduce smaller tools.

According to developmental principles, large-muscle development precedes small-muscle development. To accommodate large-muscle movements, provide large sheets of paper for children to scribble or paint on. If paper is too small, drawings or paintings will run off the paper and onto the table or floor. This will require additional cleanup for you.

Sensory Activities

Sensory activities should stimulate many of the children's senses, including seeing, hearing, and touching. Many teachers also stimulate the sense of smell. They add flavorings and extracts with unique scents to some sensory-table activities.

Figure 29.20 lists sensory materials that you can use with toddlers. Avoid small objects that children can inhale or swallow. Likewise, discourage toddlers from chewing or eating any of the sensory materials.

Fine-Motor Activities

Most fine-motor activities will revolve around toys. Stacking toys, building blocks, sorting boxes, puzzles, stringing beads, and play dough are all safe toys that promote fine-motor

Sensory Materials

- Colored and/or scented water
- Soap bubbles
- Small plastic boats
- Dry or wet sand
- Shovels, strainers, and/or small-wheeled trucks
- Snow
- Ice cubes
- Musical instruments, such as drums, tambourines, bells on wristbands, and cymbals
- Common foods with strong smells, such as oranges or lemons, served at snack time

Figure 29.20 Sensory materials stimulate the toddler's senses. *What materials might you use with toddlers to promote sensory development?*

development in toddlers. Most of these toys will also provide toddlers with problem-solving opportunities. Finally, the toys may provide hand-eye coordination and visual-discrimination opportunities.

Gross-Motor Activities

Gross-motor activities can take many forms. These may involve indoor equipment, outdoor equipment, or simple movements. As children crawl, walk, and run, they develop their gross-motor skills.

Gross-motor equipment requires much space, both indoors and outdoors. Plenty of free space should surround equipment, and spaces should be large enough for several children to use at the same time. Balls, slides, tumbling mats, pull toys, small wagons, and large blocks can all promote gross-motor development. Running, crawling, or even chasing bubbles outdoors can also promote the development of children's large muscles.

Music Activities

Young children love music. Background music from a media player can soothe or comfort many toddlers. Some toddlers will even move to the music. If they do not, you may want to dance with

them. Toddlers may also enjoy hitting drums with their hands, shaking bells, tambourines, or clapping their hands.

Language and Literacy Activities

Although planned activities are not a requirement, you should always encourage language growth. During play, speak to children. Provide specific information to build their knowledge. Promote concept development by labeling things such as colors, sizes, shapes, and feelings. Encourage them to respond by asking questions such as, "What is happening?" Avoid using baby talk with toddlers. Young children will mimic your speech patterns; if they hear baby talk, chances are they will imitate it. Use complete sentences and, if possible, introduce new words. Use adverbs and adjectives to create colorful descriptions.

Puppets, unbreakable mirrors, books, pictures, posters, and dolls can all promote language development (**Figure 29.21**). Place these materials so the children can safely remove them from the shelves.

Infants and toddlers enjoy exploring and looking at books. They will manipulate books by chewing and turning pages. When sharing books, they will often point to pictures of familiar objects.

Planning Infant-Toddler Curriculums

Many teachers plan curriculum by maintaining a file that lists successful activities. This helps teachers remember the best activities. Ask other infant-toddler caregivers to share their favorite activities. Observe other caregivers in your center. Make notes of useful interactions and activities.

When planning an infant-toddler curriculum, you will also want to start your own picture collection. The best sources for obtaining pictures are calendars, children's books, magazines, the internet, and travel posters. Infants and toddlers enjoy large, simple pictures. People, animals, vehicles, and toys have the most appeal. Young children also enjoy seeing pictures of themselves.

Books for Infants and Toddlers

- *Bedtime 1 2 3* by Eric Walters and José Bisaillon
- ****Brown Bear, Brown Bear, What Do You See/Oso pardo, oso, pardo, que`ves ahi?* by Bill Martin Jr.
- ****Good Morning/Buenos Dias* by Xavier Salomo`
- *Brown Bear, Brown Bear, What Do You See?* by Bill Martin Jr.
- *Good Night Moon* by Margaret Wise
- *Ten Tiny Toes* by Caroline Jayne Church
- *Where's Spot?* by Eric Hill
- *My Very First Book of Shapes* by Eric Carle
- *Splish, Splash, Ducky!* by Lucy Cousins
- *Ten, Nine, Eight* by Molly Bang
- **I Am a Baby* by Kathryn Madeline Allen and Rebecca Gizici
- ***THINGS THAT GO* by Scarlett Wing
- *Are You My Mommy?* by Mary Murphy
- *Machines That Work* by Byron Barton
- ***Where Is Baby's Belly Button?* by Karen Katz
- ***Global Baby Bedtimes* by Maya Ajmera
- ****My Bus* by Byron Barton
- ****Las familias/Families*
- ****Baby Bear* by Kadir Nelson
- *My Feet* by Aliki
- *Peek-a-Bruce* by Ryan Higgins

*Board book
**Lift-flap book;
***Multicultural board book
****Picture book
****Bilingual books

Goodheart-Willcox Publisher

Figure 29.21 Reading books with infants and toddlers is essential for language and literacy growth. *What types of books are best to use with infants and toddlers?*

Before displaying a picture, mount it on a piece of colorful poster board. To frame each picture, leave at least a 1/2-inch border around the entire picture. Since young children enjoy touching pictures, protect the pictures by covering with clear contact paper or laminate. These pictures will provide opportunities for activities and learnings.

29.2-2 Family Involvement

Communication with the families of infants and toddlers is very important. Keep parents or guardians informed about the child's day. Also, encourage family members to update you about significant happenings in their home. When children are first enrolled, always inquire about their routines at home, food preferences, and favorite toys. You can use a form at enrollment time to record the information (**Figure 29.22**). This information will help coordinate center and home activities.

To help you provide a quality experience for children, parents or guardians need to share their goals and concerns. Changes in the home, such as illness or death in the extended family, can cause stress for children. Other changes, such as a new family pet or a grandparent visiting, may cause pleasure. Parents should also let teachers know about home routines, such as toilet learning.

When involving family members, pay close attention to record keeping. Records should track children's eating, sleeping, and eliminating routines. Also, keep track of new behaviors and skills as they occur and change. Good records provide valuable information. Unusual patterns may signal illness or a need to change the child's diet.

By maintaining a record of a child's skills and behaviors, you will note the child's progress and the start of any problems. Early detection is important for the child's development.

When reporting the child's daily routines to parents or guardians, be objective and factual. Do not be negative or judgmental. Try to state comments positively. For instance, avoid remarks such as "Mark was very crabby and difficult to be with today." Rather, say "Mark's new tooth seemed to be causing him some pain today." Always provide the parent with comments in writing whenever possible.

From time to time, you may wish to share reading materials with family members.

Infant-Toddler Center Parent Information Sheet

Child's Name _____ Birth Date _____

Home Phone _____ Home Address _____

_____

Parent's Name _____ Parent's Name _____

Address (if different from the child) _____ Address (if different from the child) _____

_____

Place of Employment_____ Place of Employment_____

Please indicate if phone numbers are home-H, cell-C, or work-W.

Primary Phone _____ H C W Primary Phone _____ H C W

Secondary Phone _____ H C W Secondary Phone _____ H C W

E-mail address _____ E-mail address _____

If there are any special family circumstances such as divorce, separation, remarriage, parental death, or adoption, please indicate them. _____

_____

In case of emergency, who should be notified and what is the best way to reach them?

Name _____ Phone _____

Name _____ Phone _____

Doctor or Clinic_____ Phone _____

Environment and Experience

Names of other people living in the home (Indicate relationship next to name – i.e., brother) and pets living in the home:

_____

_____

_____

_____

_____

_____

How does your child react when you leave him with someone other than a parent? _____

_____

List the name(s) of any previous early childhood program that your child attended. _____

_____

What was your child's response? _____

_____

(Continued)

Figure 29.22 Stress to families the importance of filling out enrollment forms. ***Why is the information on enrollment forms essential for the center staff?***

What is the primary language spoken in the home?

Physical Development

Are there any special health characteristics or problems the center should know about to best help your child and your family? Include any vision, hearing, physical difficulties, and unusual abilities or disabilities of which you are aware.

Toilet Learning

Has your child started or completed toilet learning yet?

Eating Habits

In general, describe your child's attitude toward eating.

Is your child on any special diet? i.e. vegetarian, ovo-lacto, vegan, other

What are his/her special food likes?

What are his/her special food dislikes?

Does your child have any food allergies, sensitivities, or foods that are excluded from the diet?

Sleeping Habits

What are your child's sleeping habits?

Favorite Toys

Describe your child's favorite toys.

Favorite Activities

Describe your child's favorite activities.

Information on topics such as toilet learning, separation anxiety, language development, and toy selection can be quite useful for parents or guardians. Family members also enjoy receiving information on developmental stages. Knowing and watching for stages of normal development is reassuring.

29.2-3 Maintaining the Environment to Prevent Illness

As a staff member in an early learning center, you will need to take steps to prevent illness. Disease-causing microorganisms grow in damp, dirty environments. Play equipment, cribs, changing tables, strollers, floors, tables, high chairs, and feeding tables—as well as the children's hands—all require sanitizing.

Since infants and toddlers explore with their mouths, routinely clean all toys. Saliva may form a film on the surfaces of toys where microorganisms can grow. As a result, toys such as rattles and teething rings that go into the infant's mouth require daily cleaning or after a child uses it. If your center has a dishwasher, use it. Most small toys are dishwasher safe.

Clean by hand any toys that are not dishwasher-safe. First, wash the toys in a hot, sudsy detergent and rinse well. Then mix a disinfecting solution of one gallon of water with one tablespoon of chlorine bleach. Wipe or spray each piece of equipment with the solution. Let the toys air-dry.

Depending on the frequency of use, cribs and strollers may require daily or twice weekly cleaning. Likewise, floors, tables, high chairs, and feeding tables also need cleaning each day. Food left on any of these can grow microorganisms. This process should be similar to cleaning toys. Begin by washing each piece with warm, sudsy water. Rinse well. Wipe or spray with a solution of disinfectant. Air- or sun-dry.

Contaminated hands are a common cause of the spread of illness in childcare centers. To prevent illnesses, follow proper handwashing procedures to keep your hands and the children's hands clean. Some centers also spray disinfectant on doorknobs several times a day to kill viruses and bacteria.

Sick children cannot be cared for in a center without endangering the health of other children. An environment for infants and toddlers needs to be healthful. As the teacher, it is your responsibility to maintain the best health conditions and establish a center illness policy. This policy will help staff and family members decide whether a child is too sick to be at the center.

Prior to enrollment, provide every parent a copy of the center's illness policy. At this time, stress that a primary objective of the program is to protect the children's health. **Figure 29.23** shows an example of a center illness policy. You should emphasize that center illness policies require adherence.

Infant-Toddler Center Illness Policy

To protect all the children's health, you must keep your child home when he/she has

- **Fever** — an oral temperature of 101°F or above or a rectal temperature of 102°F or above (checked with a digital thermometer)

- **Diarrhea** — stools that are more frequent or less formed than usual and cannot be contained in a diaper

- **Vomiting** that extends beyond the usual spitting up two or more times in last 24 hours

- **Bronchitis symptoms**, including hoarseness and/or cough

- **Cold** that is accompanied by a fever and nose drainage

- **Abdominal pain** that continues for two or more hours

- **Cough**, **runny nose**, or **sore throat**

- **Rash with fever** that has not been diagnosed by a doctor

- Skin sores that are weeping on an exposed body surface

- Contagious diseases including impetigo, chicken pox, mumps, measles, scarlet fever, or whooping cough

Figure 29.23   The center illness policy helps both the staff and family members decide when to keep sick children at home.

Lesson 29.2 Review

1. _____ encourages infants to lift their heads, which will help build strong head, neck, and shoulder muscles. (29.2.1)
   A. Object hunger
   B. Tummy time
   C. Continuity of care
   D. Community

2. **True or False.** Rather than teachers setting learning goals, infants often set their own developmental goals. (29.2.1)

3. Teachers should keep records that track all of children's routines *except* _____. (29.2.2)
   A. drooling
   B. sleeping
   C. eating
   D. eliminating

4. **True or False.** As a staff member in an early learning center, it will *not* be your responsibility to disinfect surfaces or take steps to prevent illness. (29.2.3)

Chapter 29 Review and Assessment

Summary

Lesson 29.1

29.1-1 Infants and toddlers need consistent loving relationships to thrive.

29.1-1 To be an effective infant-toddler caregiver, you must have a high energy level, be healthy, loving, and enjoy children.

29.1-2 An infant-toddler caregiver should take care to meet infants' and toddlers' needs in ways they understand.

29.1-3 An environment for infants should be attractive and comfortable for infants as well as for their caregivers. These environments should address daily routines by including areas for feeding, diapering, cuddling with a caregiver, sleeping, and playing.

29.1-4 Toddlers need more open areas than infants. Toddlers' environments should include receiving, playing, napping, diapering, and eating areas. Infants and toddlers may share napping, diapering, and eating areas.

29.1-5 Much of infant and toddler care will revolve around routines such as feeding, diapering, toileting, and preparing for nap time.

29.1-6 Studies support the theory that an infant's crying should always receive prompt attention. When a caregiver promptly answers these cries, the crying frequency decreases.

29.1-7 When caring for infants and toddlers, teachers and caregivers should provide appropriate equipment and toys to support differing developmental needs.

Lesson 29.2

29.2-1 To plan a developmentally appropriate antibias curriculum, you need to know the child, the family, their culture, and language.

29.2-1 The curriculum for infants comprises simple, basic activities with a responsive, caring teacher.

29.2-1 The curriculum for toddlers requires more planning. Activity areas are intentionally designed to encourage active exploration.

29.2-2 Communication with the families of infants and toddlers is very important. Encourage family members to update you about significant happenings in their home and about their goals and concerns.

29.2-3 Staff members at early learning centers need to take steps to prevent illness. Clean all toys and furniture regularly. Send sick children home to recover.

Vocabulary Activity

On a separate sheet of paper, list words that relate to each of the chapter terms. Then, work with a partner to explain how these words are related.

Critical Thinking

1. **Determine.** Imagine that your center for infants is expanding to include toddlers. Determine what types of spaces would need to be added to an infant center to accommodate these older children. What additional safety features would you need to install?

2. **Analyze.** Ask three early learning centers for examples of daily care records. Analyze what events and routines are covered and how detailed the care records are. How effective would these records be in coordinating home and center efforts? Are the levels of detail reasonable for busy childcare workers? Discuss in small groups.

3. **Evaluate.** Visit the library or search online to locate parenting and family advice magazines that address topics such as diapering and feeding. Select a sample issue of two publications and read several articles. Afterward, evaluate the accuracy of the samples based on the information covered in this chapter. Write two brief reviews recommending or not recommending the publications.

4. **Assess.** Create activities for infants that will promote development of their physical and motor, language, social, and sensory skills. If possible, use the activities in a program and ask for feedback on their effectiveness.
5. **Make Inferences.** Using reliable online or print resources, research activities for infants and toddlers that stimulate brain development. Make inferences about how some of your favorite preschool activities might be adapted for infants or toddlers.
6. **Compare and Contrast.** Collect illness policies from three early learning centers. Then, in teams, lead a discussion comparing the policies you chose. What are the advantages and disadvantages of each policy? How easy or difficult would it be to enforce each policy?

Core Skills

1. **Listening.** Interview several parents of infants and ask them about the type of characteristics they would desire in an infant or toddler caregiver. What traits were most important to the parents? Write a brief report summarizing the interview and brainstorming how caregivers could be trained to exhibit these qualities. Share your findings with the class.
2. **Technology.** Using a digital device with audio and video capabilities, have someone record you playing the developmental game of *serve and return* with an infant. After the recording, review the video with a classmate. How could you have improved your interactions?
3. **Technology.** Using graphics-editing software, design a comprehensive infant care space, including areas for feeding, diapering, and napping. Place equipment and decorations in the design and showcase your finished product to the class.
4. **Writing.** Write lesson plans incorporating activities that will promote development of toddlers' physical, vocabulary, language, math, and science skills. If possible, use the lesson plans in an early childhood setting. Make notes of any adjustments you would make to the lesson plans in the future.

5. **Research and Speaking.** Search online or at a local library for information about stranger anxiety. How should new caregivers be introduced to a child who is experiencing stranger anxiety? Based on your findings, deliver a short informational speech to the class.
6. **Financial Literacy.** Locate catalogs or internet sources for suppliers of toys for infant and toddler childcare centers. Select five toys available through different suppliers and compare them in quality, materials, and cost. Discuss your findings in class.
7. **CTE Career Readiness Practice.** Presume that you are a graphic artist and have been hired to design artwork for toddler activity areas at a local infant-toddler program. The center director has asked you to design five visually stimulating posters to be displayed in areas for sensory, art, fine-motor, gross-motor, and music learning. To prepare for your first meeting, draw thumbnail sketches of these posters. As you work on your project, keep in mind that young children enjoy patterns, color contrasts, primary colors, simple shapes, and familiar objects. Write a few sentences about your rationale for each poster and then make copies of handouts containing your miniatures and justifications. Deliver a sample of your presentation to the class.

Portfolio Project

Observe a toddler at play and write an observation describing the fine- and gross-motor skills the child uses. How does the child use his or her hands to pick up, move, or otherwise manipulate items? What fine-motor tasks does the toddler consistently perform with skill? What gross-motor skills does the child use? What equipment or materials does he or she enjoy while using movements? Be sure to indicate the exact age in months of the child. File the observation in your portfolio.

Chapter 30

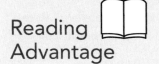
Programs for School-Age Children

Lesson 30.1: School-Age Programs, Staff, and Environments

Lesson 30.2: Implementing Curriculum and Scheduling Activities

Case Study

Priorities in Planning School-Age Programs

William Mayo has just accepted a position as the director of a before and after school program with a new YMCA center. His responsibility is to plan the indoor and outdoor environments and purchase the materials, furniture, and equipment. He will also be responsible for opening, coordinating, and teaching the school-age before and after school program. The new YMCA has indoor and outdoor spaces designed for this purpose.

After being provided with a budget, William began preparing a "to-do list." The first item on his list was to contact the National AfterSchool Association (NAA). William then went online and requested school supply catalogs for toys, shelving units, lockers, and outdoor equipment. Instead of ordering the equipment immediately since the program was scheduled to open in two months, he continued working on his "to-do list." He developed the handbook, website, parent goals, and program schedule.

William's supervisor asked for a meeting toward the end of the summer. She was concerned since the program was to open in two weeks, and there was no evidence of progress on the outdoor playground. William told her that he was waiting for the equipment to arrive. His supervisor looked concerned and continued asking him questions. She wanted to know if he could share a sketch of the indoor and indoor environments, a copy of the orders, a copy of the handbook, a link to the website, and a daily activity schedule.

Give It Some Thought

1. Would you have contacted the National AfterSchool Association (NAA) if you were William? Could the organization help him? If so, how?
2. Since William already had the money for the equipment, did he exercise good judgment in delaying ordering it? Why or why not?
3. What equipment, furnishings, and supplies should William order for the indoor and outdoor environments?
4. Describe the goals parents have for their children while attending a school-age program.
5. What are the three curriculum models used in school-age programs? Which model do you think William should choose? Why?
6. How should William schedule program activities? Why?

Opening image credit: Ridofranz/iStock via Getty Images Plus

School-Age Programs, Staff, and Environments

Essential Question

What should your priorities be in planning a before and after school program for school-age children?

Learning Outcomes

After studying this lesson, you will be able to

30.1-1 identify the characteristics of quality school-age programs for children.

30.1-2 describe the three basic program models used in school-age care.

30.1-3 identify the characteristics of an effective teacher in a school-age program.

30.1-4 discuss how to arrange indoor and outdoor space in a school-age care environment.

Key Terms

latchkey children

curriculum model

child-centered program model

adult-centered program model

unit-based program model

facilitators

school-age programs

self-care

observational learning

conscientious

microaggression

There is a critical need for **school-age programs** serving children from kindergarten through age 12. These programs are designed to meet the needs of children and their parents or guardians. They may be scheduled before and after school, during vacations, holidays, and summer. There has been significant growth in the number of working parents or guardians with children between the ages of five and 12, as in the number of single-parent families. When children do not have supervision, some parents have experienced problems. Other parents and guardians have concerns about their children's safety because of the increase in gangs, violence, and drugs in their city's neighborhoods. Often enrolling their child in a school-age program gives them peace of mind.

One in every five school-aged children is home alone after school. Children face risks being at home after school without adult supervision. Due to cost or lack of quality programs, many school-age children must care for themselves. Finn, an eight-year-old, is one example. He returns home from school at about 3:40 p.m. in the afternoon. When he arrives home, Finn unlocks the door with a key he carries. Then he enters and locks the door behind him. Finn eats processed snack foods, plays video games, and watches television until 6:00 p.m., when his mother returns home from work. Finn benefits little from this time spent alone.

Finn's mother, like many others, cannot find affordable or convenient after-school care. Children like Finn are sometimes called **latchkey children.** This term refers to school-aged children of working parents who spend part of their day without supervision. Some parents leave children in self-care for several hours each day and when school is not in session.

Yolanda is another eight-year-old child. Unlike Finn, who goes home to an empty apartment, Yolanda is fortunate. She attends a school-age program that meets in the elementary school she attends. Augustin, her cousin who lives in the same community, also attends the program.

Parents need to decide on an individual basis how old and mature their children should be before leaving them in **self-care** (Figure 30.1). State laws regarding self-care are an important consideration. The National SAFE KIDS campaign recommends that parents or guardians not leave a child under the age of 12 home alone. Children at this age may be unprepared for emergency situations. In some states, it is illegal for a child under a set age to stay home alone, especially after-school hours or during the summer. Many states consider this neglect. If no such law exists in their state, parents or guardians can use age 12 as an acceptable general guideline. However, parents or guardians may not feel comfortable leaving some immature 13- or 14-year-olds or children with diverse needs in self-care.

The focus of school-age programs has changed. Years ago, school-age care was a safe place for children before and after school. Many children were cared for in family child care homes. Today there is wide support for investing in school-age programs, which may be operated as school-based, government-based, non-profit and for-profit. United Way, local foundations, YMCAs, and other organizations may also support them. In some large cities, the mayor's office even provides support.

Program attendance and quality, and well as the quantity of centers has increased. The definition also has become broader as programs may include school vacations, holidays, and summer. Programs may also accommodate children due to early dismissals, snow days, and teacher work days. To promote quality, over half of large cities have increased funding over the past five years. Some cities have shown leadership by developing and mandating quality standards for their programs.

MBI/Shutterstock.com

Figure 30.1 In deciding whether their children are ready for self-care, parents and guardians should assess children's maturity and responsibility. *What is the general guideline for when children can be home alone to care for themselves?*

School-age programs now go beyond simple care and reflect the climate of the neighborhood, as opposed to being an extension of school. Now they are a place for school-age children to build skills, interests, and friendships, integrating their home values and culture. Exploring their passions inspires them to learn. These children are also learning about becoming part of a larger community by working as a team and sharing responsibilities.

Family members have goals for their children who attend school-age programs. They want their children to:

- feel safe;
- receive help with homework and tutoring in academic subjects;
- complete their homework and develop study skills;
- develop self-confidence, which can lead to higher self-esteem;
- improve social skills;
- develop caring, positive relationships with other children and the staff;
- gain new skills, hobbies, and interests;
- explore and study art and music;
- take part in clubs such as STEM, book, computer, gardening, drama, board games, chess, arts, and crafts; and
- perform community service.

Studies show positive outcomes for children attending high-quality school-age care programs. The time they spend in these programs is usually productive for school-age children. The children tend to earn better grades, show higher academic achievement, and strengthen their identity. They submit higher-quality homework assignments and spend more time in the learning process. They have an increased interest and ability in reading. These children also have better school attendance records, lower dropout rates, and a reduction in drug use and problem behavior. Regular participation in a high-quality program also promotes social-emotional learning. With enrollment in these programs, children develop new interests and social interaction skills.

Early Childhood Insight

Children Lacking Adult Supervision

Studies show that children who lack adult supervision tend to have a variety of problems. They are more likely to experience loneliness and unhealthy fears. They are also more likely to lack physical activity, exhibit poor school performance, show antisocial behavior, and have poor nutritional habits. Attending a quality school-age program can help children avoid these problems.

30.1-1 Quality School-Age Programs

School-age children are developing a sense of who they are and what they can do. These children need challenges. They need to be independent and accept others with an anti-bias lens. They also need opportunities to become socially, emotionally, cognitively, and academically competent. A quality school-age program will meet these needs by turning the hours after school into productive learning time and create a sense of belonging. School-age programs provide companionship, a safe and supportive environment, and activities to promote children's development. A quality school-age program has:

- low adult-child ratios;
- caring, highly trained staff members who set high expectations with age-appropriate activities;
- well-organized space with room for active play, quiet play, and interest centers;
- planned experiences to promote critical thinking skills;
- an environment that promotes curiosity and a love of learning;
- a curriculum guided by the children's strengths, needs, ideas, and interests;
- positive relationships with parents, based on mutual trust, to achieve shared goals; and
- flexible scheduling to meet the children's individual needs and interests.

Studies show that high-quality programs set goals and have strong leadership. They hire skilled staff with knowledge of child development and provide them with ongoing training. Quality programs also reach out to families.

Adult-Child Ratios

Having enough staff to meet the individual needs of children enhances program quality. Studies show that appropriate adult-child ratios and small group size improve program quality.

Children in school-age care programs must be able to get adult help when they need it. Children may need help with homework (**Figure 30.2**). They will also need adults to serve as role models and provide emotional support and encouragement.

Having more adults available benefits staff and children. Here, adults can provide the constant supervision needed to create a safe environment. While supervising, adults can use observation to gain information about each child's strengths, interests, needs, abilities, cultural background and experiences.

Most states have laws addressing adult-child ratios for children's programs, unless a public school operates and staffs the program. These ratios vary from state to state. However, the recommendation for children through six years of age is a minimum 1:10 adult-child ratio. The usual recommendation for children seven years of age and older is a minimum 1:12 adult-child ratio.

MBI/Shutterstock.com

Figure 30.2 School-age children may need or want staff to help them with homework and other tasks.

Accreditation and Standards

Accreditation and standards can measure the quality of a school-age program. The *National AfterSchool Association* (NAA) is the voice for diverse school-aged programs and has state affiliates across the nation. The organization establishes and monitors standards that reflect the best practices for children for ages five to 14. The National Afterschool Association also provides help to professionals who work with children in schools and community-based settings.

NAA's standards describe best practices that promote stimulating, supportive, and safe programs for children ages five to 14 in out-of-school care. Their standards focus on:

- human relationships;
- indoor environment;
- outdoor environment;
- activities;
- safety, health, and nutrition; and
- administration.

You can learn more about these standards on the NAA's website. Recently, the NAA also made available evidence-based standards for providing children with healthy food, beverages, and physical activity in out-of-school programs. Check to see if your own state has model standards for school-age programs.

30.1-2 Types of School-Age Programs

Parents or guardians have a variety of options when choosing after-school care (**Figure 30.3**). A nanny, an au pair, or a housekeeper can provide care in a child's home. Family childcare homes and early childhood centers provide care outside the child's home.

Many for-profit childcare centers provide school-age care and transportation. These centers offer programs during the school year. Many have special summer and out-of-school programs, too. Parents who can afford the tuition often select this type of program. Often, children taking part

tomeqs/Shutterstock.com

Andresr/Shutterstock.com

wavebreakmedia/Shutterstock.com

Antonio_Diaz/iStock via Getty Images Plus

Figure 30.3   Many childcare options are available for school-age children, including home care, care in a center, or care at a nonprofit organization. *How can families decide which type of care is best?*

in these programs have attended preschool in the same facility.

Nonprofit organizations such as United Way, YMCA, Salvation Army, and even some universities offer school-age care programs in larger communities. Faith-based organizations may also provide school-age care for their members.

There are three **curriculum models** used as a structure for decision making in school-age programs. These are the *child-centered, adult-centered,* and *unit-based models.* An excellent program uses all three models to complement children's school and home experiences. An excellent program also includes activities to promote awareness and respect for cultural diversity.

Several factors may influence the program model chosen. These include the ages, interests, abilities, culture, and experiences of the children. Staff preferences and the time children spend in the program can have an influence, too.

Workplace Connections

Summer Programs and Reading Groups

Contact the local public library to discover what summer reading groups or special summer programs are available for school-age children.

1. How long are special sessions, how often are they held, and what types of topics are typically scheduled?
2. Are the topics tied into literature or other materials on the subject that are available at the library?

Child-Centered Program Model

The **child-centered program model** is a curriculum format that allows children an opportunity to choose self-selected activities. Staff members encourage children's involvement by serving as facilitators and resource people. Together, the staff and children plan the daily activities. Resources and the children's interests help determine the activities.

Adult-Centered Program Model

The **adult-centered program model** is a more structured curriculum format that includes a high level of adult direction. The curriculum includes recreation with an emphasis on fitness and tutoring programs. Children may also have opportunities to take music, dance, art and drama lessons.

Unit-Based Program Model

The **unit-based program model** is a curriculum format that revolves around curriculum themes that reflect the children's interests. Frequently, these themes focus on special events and holidays. Staff members offer a variety of cooking, science, music, and art activities that relate to the theme. They choose children's literature and plan field trips, creative dramatics, and games to support the theme. Children can then choose many of the specific theme-related activities in which they will take part.

Regardless of the model used, school-age programs should focus on developing competence, and self-confidence (**Figure 30.4**). Self-confidence contributes to an "I-can-do-it" attitude. It will help children master reading and writing skills. Self-confidence will also help children develop positive social relationships with their peers.

30.1-3 Characteristics of School-Age Program Staff

Well-trained staff are the heart of high-quality school-age programs. These individuals

Rido/Shutterstock.com

Figure 30.4 School-age programs should encourage children to develop competence and self-confidence.

understand child growth and development. They like school-age children and enjoy conversations with them. Personnel should have age-appropriate expectations of the children's interests, behavior, and abilities. They are continuously seeking new ideas and learning new teaching techniques. These teachers also respect the cultural diversity of the children they teach.

Staff members in school-age programs need to be understanding, honest, patient, fair, trustworthy, and warm. They need to model the standards for expected behavior. Staff members need to respond positively to each child's uniqueness and changing needs. Children require encouragement to be independent and competent. School-age program staff should act as facilitators, use positive guidance, involve children, promote respect for cultural diversity, and enjoy physical activity.

Acting as Facilitators

Staff members in school-age programs act as **facilitators** (people who help or provide guidance in bringing about an intended outcome). They need excellent communication skills and should be able to listen to be able to convey messages. Teachers of school-age children need to create a sense of belonging. They need to encourage the children to share thoughts, listen to the views of others, and meet new friends.

School-age children are striving for autonomy. They want opportunities to be independent and solve their own problems. Staff members assist the children in developing skills and abilities and guide children in social-problem solving. They help by offering suggestions, providing encouragement, and recommending activities. They use demonstrations, explanations, and coaching to help children learn. Staff also ask thought-provoking questions that require children to use critical-thinking skills.

Workplace Connections

Role of Volunteers

Research the role of volunteers in local school-age programs.

1. Do the programs allow volunteers to work in their programs? If so, what are the requirements to take part as a volunteer?
2. Are there state mandated legal requirements for volunteers? How are volunteers recruited to take part in the program?
3. What role do volunteers assume in the classroom?
4. How do the school-age children in the programs respond to the volunteers?

Using Positive Guidance

School-age children enjoy being active and engaged. Unlike preschool children, there are fewer behavioral problem. Children at this stage are learning social expectations. They are learning to recognize the impact of their behavior on others and need to learn to make their own decisions. Often, they test their place in a group. By experiencing consequences, children learn to understand what is acceptable as opposed to unacceptable behavior.

Skilled staff members use positive guidance to help children achieve self-control. They encourage *pro-social behaviors* (behaviors that focus on helping others), such as taking turns, helping, cooperating, collaborating, negotiating, and talking through interpersonal problems (**Figure 30.5**). Staff work with children to develop clear and firm limits. When needed, staff members remind children of the limits. After this, they redirect the children to more acceptable behavior.

Working with school-age children can be challenging. Some children will constantly test you. They are trying to see how far they can go before you intervene. Often, these children do not understand the balance between individual rights and group rights. Take Sergio as an example.

New Africa/Shutterstock.com

Figure 30.5   Using positive guidance, staff members can teach school-age children cooperative and prosocial behaviors, such as taking turns and working together. *Give an example of positive guidance you have observed.*

While a group of children are listening to a story, Sergio keeps pounding on a drum. Several times his teacher reminds him to play the drum softly. She tells him that the other children are listening to a story and he is distracting them. Finally, Sergio has to experience the consequences. His teacher takes the drum away from him and suggests alternative activities.

Teachers also need to know how to cultivate children's friendships with one another. Although some children make friends easily, others find it challenging. Developing friendships involves the capacity to recognize that others have separate identities. Children also have feelings of their own, which include a characteristic way of reacting.

School-age children are also developing a sense of how their peers perceive them. They need to see the importance of their behavior. For example, Ian wanted the basketball Reyes was using. Ian hit Reyes hard on the back and then quickly grabbed the ball out of his hands. The teacher near him on the playground observed this happening and used the incident as a teachable moment. Miss Morrison knew Ian would need to control certain behaviors in order to cultivate friendships. She approached him and asked, "How do you think it feels to be hit and have your ball taken away?" Then she talked with Ian about the qualities that make a good friend, including alternative ways of behaving.

Involving Children

School-age children are learning to be independent. Often, they want to solve problems without help. Staff of school-age programs need to involve children in daily problem-solving activities. While developing limits, staff should involve the children in a discussion of expectations. This will help children make decisions related to their actions. Staff should also involve children by inviting them to help plan curriculum and make choices about activities (**Figure 30.6**).

Promoting Respect for Cultural Diversity

As school-age children become more aware of the world around them, they begin to make

fizkes/Shutterstock.com

Figure 30.6 Allowing children to help plan their own activities promotes self-esteem and enjoyment of the program. ***What other benefits might there be for including school-age children in program planning?***

social comparisons. Through this process, children not only define themselves, but they also identify qualities in others. As a teacher in a school-age program, you need to be culturally responsive and promote respect by embracing an antibias classroom. To be effective, you must be committed to analyzing your own cultural beliefs, biases, and antibias messages. During this process ask yourself, "How do my beliefs affect my interactions with young children and their families?" You may consider exploring your practices with another teacher. Observe each other, take notes, and then discuss your observations.

Diversity requires acceptance and celebration in every classroom. Classroom teachers need to be role models since the children are engaged in **observation learning**. This is the type of learning that occurs when children watch others and then imitate what they see and hear. Acceptance of others, regardless of their gender, disability, race, ethnicity, or socioeconomic status is important. Your role is to create an environment that promotes peaceful living. It needs to be warm, inviting and caring so the children feel welcomed, respected, valued, and protected. Likewise, children in the classroom need to treat others with respect and value.

Conscientious (effectively careful) teachers help children learn about and appreciate cultures other than their own. They help children appreciate cultural diversity by promoting unbiased perceptions regarding differences in people. Children need to learn how others express beauty through art, literature, and music (**Figure 30.7**). Teachers use toys, games, foods, and special celebrations to teach children about different cultures. They use storybooks, videos, posters, and puzzles to show people from all cultures in a variety of positive roles.

Explore diversity with the children. Children need exposure to as many people and differences as possible. One of the most effective ways is through children's literature, which is a rich source of information. Carefully chosen literature can be effective for promoting unbiased perceptions among differences in people (**Figure 30.8**). These books offer counternarratives to hurtful stereotypes. Seeing visual images of people who look like them helps children develop a sense of pride in their culture. Seeing images of people from other cultures helps children respect and value people's differences and similarities.

Microaggressions

Microaggressions are the disrespectful day-to-day comments or actions that can be unintentional or intentional, verbal or nonverbal. At their core, they are hurtful messages of disapproval of small, almost invisible acts in the classroom. Unfortunately, while developing their sense of identity, children internalize these messages. Depending on their length, severity and intensity, microaggressions can affect a child's self-esteem. These acts can make children feel unsafe, anxious, mistrust in their peers, and feel a of lack of belonging. In addition, these actions can affect their academic accomplishments. Repeated microaggressions can lead to lifelong mental-health symptoms such as lack of behavioral control and depression.

Exclusion is one form of microaggression. Teachers need to be constantly observant in the classroom and on the playground to identify these aggressions. School-age children are learning the power of words, and sometimes they use hurtful words that are intentional. Whether or not intentional, you must combat the microaggression immediately by calling it out. Inaction is not an option.

FatCamera/E+ via Getty Images

Figure 30.7   Teachers can plan activities to help children appreciate cultural diversity.

Multicultural Children's Literature

- *Yo Soy Muslim* by Mark Gonzalas (author) and Mehrdokht Amini (illustrator)
- *Where Are You From?* by Yamile Saied Méndez (author) and Jaime Kim (illustrator)*
- *El Deafo* by Cece Bell
- *Eyes that Kiss in the Corners* by Joanna Ho (author) and Dung Ho (illustrator)
- *I Love Saturdays y domingos* by Alma Flo Ada (author) and Elivia Savadier (illustrator)*
- *Amazing Grace* by Mary Hoffman (author) and Caroline Binch (illustrator)*
- *Keep Climbing Girls* by Beah E. Richards (author) and Gregory Christie (illustrator)
- *The Name Jar* by Yangsook Choi
- *Measuring Up* by Lily LaMotte (author) and Ann Xu (illustrator)
- *The Proudest Blue: A Story of Hjab and Family* by Ibtihaj Muhammad (author) and Hatem Aly (illustrator)
- *Annie's Plaid Shirt* by Stacy B. Davids (author), Rachael Balsaitis and Sam Pines (illustrators)
- *A Different Pond* by Bao Phi (author) and Thi Bui (illustrator)
- *Teach Your Dragon About Diversity* by Steve Herman

*Available in Spanish

Figure 30.8 One of the most effective ways for children to explore diversity in a multicultural world is through children's literature.

Teachers need to manage microaggressions in a way that is not an embarrassment to any child, staff member, or volunteer. Whether verbal or nonverbal, begin by exploring the incident in an attempt to understand the behavior. Direct conversation is the most effective strategy for dealing with microaggressions. Ask questions that come from curiosity, not judgement, to clarify the individual's intentions. Respond to children's microaggressions by:

- using a warm, engaging tone;
- physically getting down to the child's level if needed;
- gaining the child's full attention by looking in their eyes;
- speaking for yourself by using the word "I," as opposed to "you";
- identifying and describing the behavior you just saw or heard; and
- targeting the behavior, not the person.

Additionally, teachers use their active-listening skills to seek clarification and have children reflect on their actions by asking or saying:

- "I think I heard you saying ____."
- "I noticed you ____."
- "Why do you think that?"
- "When you say ____, (child name or names) feels hurt."
- "How would you feel if ____?"
- "Why did you ____?"
- "It's not okay to ____."
- "When you say _____, (name) feels hurt."
- "How would you feel if _____?"

Children need to learn how to recognize and speak up against microaggressions through effective teaching. Unkindness needs to be addressed and cannot be tolerated. To help children initiate conversations, role-play responses to microaggressions. During the role-playing, children will use comments to express, "This is not okay." Their comments may include, "That is not nice; we should never make fun of someone. It hurts me when you ____." By standing up for themselves, children develop a sense of independence and self-confidence by being able to solve their own problems.

Enjoying Physical Activity

Like children of all ages, school-age children thrive on physical activity. During a typical school day, they spend much time sitting in classrooms. When they arrive at after-school programs, they have pent-up energy to release. They want to move around, play games, run, and jump.

Teachers who are well suited for school-age programs enjoy physical activity. They do not have to be athletic; however, they need the energy and desire to join children in active play.

30.1-4 School-Age Children's Environments

Throughout middle childhood, children need room to practice their emerging skills. A quality school-age care environment should provide appropriate space, well-chosen materials, and equipment. The environment needs to be developmentally appropriate, reflecting the children's strengths, interests, ages, abilities, needs, and experiences. This environment will allow children to have fun, learn, and thrive as they move at their own pace.

An ideal environment is designed specifically for school-age programs. However, any facility with a large activity room and an outdoor play area can serve as a school-age program environment. Many programs are located in libraries, cafeterias, gyms, and the basements of faith-based organizations.

When a facility's design serves other purposes, restrictions may apply. Providing an appropriate environment may be difficult. Teachers in these spaces often have only a limited time to prepare the environment. They must develop creative strategies for getting the room ready each day. They may use movable carts to store games, art supplies, books, and other program materials (**Figure 30.9**). They may involve the children's help by including setup and cleanup in the children's daily schedule. School-age children's programs should have developmentally appropriate indoor and outdoor spaces.

Indoor Environment

The indoor space for a school-age program should meet the needs for the number of children enrolled. Space needs to be available for individual, small group, and large group activities. At least 35 square feet of space should be available for each child. Children become more aggressive when ample floor space is not available.

UW-Stout Child and Family Study Center

Figure 30.9   In a shared environment, staff can use wagons to store and transport art supplies. ***In what other ways might teacher transport supplies?***

Children need a secure and safe environment. For them, a school-age program is a home away from home. A quality school-age environment is informal and provides a homelike atmosphere. Some soft and comfortable furniture should be available for the children to relax. In this setting, the children can explore interests and develop one-on-one relationships.

Indoor space should be well designed and pleasing to the eye. Provide storage units for children's belongings that are separate from those used to hold classroom materials, projects, and supplies. Children are likely to bring some clothing and backpacks. Use pillows, pictures, posters, beanbag chairs, carpeting, couches, and curtains to help create a warm and inviting environment.

Children enrolled in school-age programs will represent diverse languages, cultures, and abilities. It is important to support this diversity. The environment should show evidences of the home languages. Books, music, bulletin boards, and wall posters should all represent the children's home languages.

As a teacher in a school-age program, you will need to plan how to effectively use the space in your room. As in programs for preschool children, the room needs to include interest centers. You will also need to provide space for quiet activities. Create some open areas for group activities, too. This will provide a space where the entire group can be together as needed.

Interest Centers

Interest centers are a focus of quality school-age programs. Set up centers for hobbies, blocks, cooking, science, math and manipulatives, games, music, dramatic play, and arts and crafts. Try to provide bulletin boards or display areas near each center to showcase the children's work, and feature news items and photography by the teachers and children.

Arrange interest centers to encourage independent use by the children. Place labeled open shelving units in the centers. These units will help children know where to acquire and return materials and equipment.

Quiet Areas

Your room needs to include quiet areas and privacy for individuals. Children should be able to do homework, use computers, read, and relax in these areas (**Figure 30.10**). They should feel protected from the intrusion of others. Children often enjoy flexible quiet spaces they can rearrange with movable furniture and privacy screens. Many children need their own space for a quiet study area.

Open Areas

Your room needs to include large, open areas. Children can use these areas for group planning times and special projects. They can enjoy movement activities, creative dramatics, and indoor games in open areas, too.

Outdoor Environments

Outdoor environments are just as important as indoor. The foundation for the design should be on the children's development and suitable for

TimeImage Production/Shutterstock.com

Figure 30.10 In a quiet area of the classroom, children can focus on their reading.

a wide variety of activities and ages. Space for active and quiet play must be included. Children need space to be independent, creative, and for active and quiet play. At the end of the day, they need to make noise, play, and enjoy their friends (**Figure 30.11**).

School-age children enjoy trying challenging equipment to develop new skills. Permanent equipment should be appropriate for the sizes and abilities of the children. By engaging in physical activities, children gain health benefits such as bone mass and well-being. Physical mastery of skills also promotes positive self-esteem. Playground activities encourage cooperation, communication, and friendships.

These activities require at least 75 square feet of outdoor space per child. Make sure this space offers protection from unwanted visitors and traffic. Create separate areas for running, climbing, swinging, and organized sports. Grassy areas will support running, tagging, and rolling. School-age children want to be competent at physical skills. Also, provide quiet outdoor play space where children can be with their friends, either in a group or one-to-one.

FatCamera/iStock via Getty Images Plus

Figure 30.11   School-age children enjoy physical activities and opportunities to release their energy. *What outdoor activities do you think are most beneficial for school-age children?*

Lesson 30.1 Review

1. School-aged children who spend part of their day at home during non-school times are sometimes called _____. (30.1.1)
   A. self-care children
   B. independent children
   C. latchkey children
   D. working-parent children

2. A quality school-age program has all the following qualities *except* _____. (30.1.1)
   A. high adult-child ratios
   B. well-organized spaces
   C. developmentally appropriate curriculum
   D. flexible scheduling

3. Which of the following is *not* a school-age curriculum model? (30.1.2)
   A. Unit-based
   B. Adult-centered
   C. Child-centered
   D. Development-based

4. _____ are people who help or provide guidance in bringing about an intended outcome. (30.1.3)
   A. Educators
   B. Facilitators
   C. Resource people
   D. Administrators

5. Skilled program teachers use positive guidance to encourage _____, or behaviors that focus on helping others. (30.1.3)
   A. anti-social behaviors
   B. community service
   C. pro-social behaviors
   D. random acts of kindness

6. **True or False.** Libraries, cafeterias, gyms, and the basements of faith-based organizations are all locations used for school-age programs. (30.1.4)

Essential Question

? *What do you need to know about assessing children's interests to plan and coordinate the daily schedule for a school-age program?*

Learning Outcomes

After studying this lesson, you will be able to

30.2-1 summarize ways to assess children's interests for curriculum planning.

30.2-2 plan activities and the schedule to use in a school-age program.

Key Terms

technological literacy   digital divide
digital literacy

School-age children have a different set of characteristics and interests than preschoolers. So implementing a curriculum and scheduling activities differ. Planning an engaging school-age curriculum should include involvement from the children, staff, and families. Data obtained from an assessment of the children's interests, get-acquainted and group discussions, surveys, and self-reports can all be useful. Developmentally appropriate activities must be available to help children reach their full potential. The program needs to foster positive identity and the development of problem-solving and social skills. Materials and equipment should be appropriate to the needs and interests of the age group. The daily schedule should be flexible and planned to meet the children's need for predictability and security. Rest time, activity times, snacks, and clean-up all need to be included.

30.2-1 Curriculum

A quality school-aged program has a well-planned, engaging curriculum. When you provide an inviting curriculum, everybody wins. You win because the children will enjoy participating and there will be fewer behavioral problems. The children win because they have choices and opportunities to develop new skills, interests, and friendships.

The question is, "Who should plan?" The answer is everyone—children, families, and staff should provide input. Find out what is important to each of these groups. It is important to take time to involve families in continuous two-way communication. They are assets since they are the experts on their children and their cultural and religious backgrounds. Children prosper when everyone works together in a partnership.

Parents and staff are likely to have general goals for your program. They want you to provide a safe environment for school-age children during non-school hours. They expect you to offer a variety of developmentally appropriate activities that allow children to develop new skills and higher-level thinking skills (**Figure 30.12**).

These goals will help guide your overall planning; however, the interests of the children will guide your specific day-by-day activity plans. In developing a curriculum, assess the children's interest and then plan the curriculum in a group setting.

Assess the Children's Interests

No two school-age children are exactly alike because they develop at different rates. As a teacher in a school-age program, you must consider children's individual strengths, abilities,

Memedozasian/iStock via Getty Images Plus

Figure 30.12 Activities should interest children while encouraging their development. *What activities do you think school-age children enjoy most indoors?*

interests, and needs. You must know family backgrounds and special situations. This will help you plan a meaningful curriculum built on what the children already know.

To plan a developmentally appropriate school-age program, you need to begin by assessing the children's interests, energy levels, strengths, and temperaments. Children's interests are always changing and they are interested in becoming competent. Therefore, you need to conduct assessment exercises on a continuing basis to improve teaching and learning. Informally, you can assess children by observing their play and interacting with them individually and in small groups. You can also assess interests through get-acquainted interviews, group discussions, self-reports, and surveys.

Get-Acquainted Interviews

Get-acquainted interviews can help you assess interests at the beginning of the year or when new children enroll. This assessment technique involves having a child ask one of their peer questions about their interests. Questions can focus on favorite hobbies, sports, foods, holidays, computer apps, music, books, television programs, and vacation activities.

Because school-age children enjoy using technology, you may want to video- or audio-record the interviews. Be sure to acquire family permission to create the videos. You can share the recordings during group time to help all the children learn more about their classmates.

Group Discussions

School-age children enjoy being involved in planning and implementing learning activities.

Safety First

Height Limitations for Outdoor Equipment

Outdoor play equipment has height restrictions for 5- to 12-year-olds to ensure children's safety. Balance beams should not exceed 16 inches from the ground. Upper body equipment should not exceed 84 inches in height. Check with your local and state licensing agencies to see if there are further requirements.

Group discussions can also reveal the individual interests of school-age children. Using this method regularly can also help you keep up with changes in children's interests (**Figure 30.13**).

Group discussions are particularly effective with nonreaders. Begin the process by asking the following questions:

- What are your hobbies?
- What new hobbies would you like to learn?
- What are your favorite sports?
- What new sports would you like to learn?
- What are your favorite activities at school?
- What do you like most about the program?
- What would you like to change in the program?
- What clubs would you like to join?
- What else would you like to have included in the program?

Self-Reports

Another way to learn about children is through self-reports. These reports can take the form of either stories or pictures. Ask children to focus on a theme as they write or draw. Possible themes include "All About Me," "My Family," and "When I Grow Up." Invite children to share their stories and pictures with the class. Celebrate the children's diversity. Then display stories and pictures on a bulletin board or wall.

Comeback Images/iStock via Getty Images Plus

Figure 30.13 Group discussions provide a space for children to talk about their interests. *How can discussion groups help with activity planning?*

Surveys

You can design a survey to assess children's interests. Children who are readers can complete the survey on their own. A staff member can ask questions and record the responses of nonreaders. When designing the survey, keep it brief.

Plan the Curriculum

After you have gathered information about children's interests, you are ready to make specific plans. Provide opportunities for group input. Group planning sessions are especially effective for planning themes, celebrations, special events, and field trips. Begin by asking the children to brainstorm a list of ideas. Be sure to acknowledge each suggestion. Record the ideas on the board so everyone can see them.

After children have presented all their suggestions, discuss each one. Explain your reasons for eliminating any ideas due to expense, location, safety, or lack of staff. When you have reviewed all the ideas, encourage the children to prioritize them as a group.

30.2-2 Scheduling School-Age Program Activities

Most school-age programs are open before and after school hours. Children may take part in these programs for up to five hours a day while attending kindergarten or elementary school. Some programs are available all day during vacation periods, holidays, and summer months.

As a teacher of school-age children, you must carefully plan a daily schedule that meets children's needs for predictability and security. It helps the children construct their understanding of time. Ideally, the schedule should be flexible enough to allow for children's individual differences and independence.

Organize your daily program schedule between arrival and departure times. Your schedule should include times for children to eat, relax, periods for children to take part in a variety of activities, and outdoor play. Because of the increase of time devoted to academics, many schools are reducing time for outdoor play. As a result, the NAA recommends children spend at least 30 minutes outdoors, weather permitting, for every three hours of program participation. Scheduling should also include time for children to clean up. **Figure 30.14** shows a typical schedule for a school-age program. Post your daily schedule so children and families know the routine.

Arrival and Departure Times

Arrival and departure times represent more than just the beginning and ending of the daily schedule in a school-age program. These are valuable times to share information with children and families. They serve as a bridge between home and the program. Use these moments to update families about their children and to solicit their support for program activities. Also, use these interaction times to gain insight into family values, roles, and events that may affect children.

When the children enter and leave your room, be available and intentional. Identify all children by name. Give them warm greetings. Listen to their parting comments. Be sincere. Remember that the tone of your voice and your facial expression carry a message, which tells children how you feel about seeing them.

Workplace Connections

Observing a School-Age Program

Arrange a visit to observe a local school-age program. Then, write a brief report answering the following questions.

1. Does the school-age teacher use arrival or departure times to share information with the parents? Are both indoor and outdoor activities provided? If so, how much time do the children spend indoors as opposed to outdoors?
2. Are there times for children to choose their own activities? Are snacks and a rest time provided?

School-Age Child Care Program Daily Schedule

Time Schedule	Activities
6:00–8:30 a.m.	• Arrival of children (Children will arrive at different times depending on their parent or guardian work schedules.) • Breakfast bar • Self-selected indoor activities, such as games, blocks, sewing, crafts, pegboards, art materials, books, stories, discussions, hobbies, conversation, computers, card games, puzzles, and homework • Leave for school
3:30–5:30 p.m.	• Arrive from school • Snack • Outdoor play: Field trips; organized sports; team games; water, and sand play; gardening; jumping, skipping, hopping, climbing and other physical activities involving balls and jump ropes; music and dance lessons • Tutoring: Math, language, science, social studies • Clubs • Homework and computer time
5:30–6:00 p.m.	• Group time: Discussion, program planning
6:00–6:30 p.m.	• Indoor individual and small group activities • Outside and indoor cleanup in preparation for going home

Figure 30.14 Scheduling for school-age care should include time for snacks, rest, and activities.

Snack Times

As you plan your program schedule, think of your childhood. How did you feel when you arrived home from school? Chances are you were hungry. Like you, the children in your program will probably want something to eat when they arrive.

Snack times should be a learning experience and should provide children with a sense of responsibility and community. Children can learn how to measure and prepare foods. They can assist with planning the menus, setting and decorating the tables, serving, and cleaning up. They can use the time when they gather around the table to share the events of their day, too (**Figure 30.15**).

You can use snack time as an opportunity to introduce multicultural foods. Invite children to share favorite family recipes. Ask them to help plan special foods for holidays or other celebrations. For special events, the children could invite a guest, such as a parent, guardian, grandparent, older sibling, or a special adult friend.

Rest Times

School-age programs sometimes include a daily rest time or time to relax. The amount of time you schedule for rest will depend on the children in your program. Age, health, and activity level will affect a child's need for rest.

Some children, especially those who are younger, and need time to rest. If exhausted, they may fall asleep. Other, older children may simply enjoy low-key activities. You might encourage these children to finish their homework, play quiet games, work on the computer, work in the art area, or read books. The activities they choose should not disturb children who are resting.

Soft music may help some children relax during rest time. Other children may find pleasure in having a teacher read to them.

MBI/Shutterstock.com

Figure 30.15 Snack time gives children and the early childhood staff a relaxing time to share daily events. *What snacks are a good choice for school-age children?*

Activity Times

You are likely to devote the largest part of your daily school-age program schedule to activity time. You will notice fewer conflicts among children when they are all engaged in a variety of interesting, meaningful activities. Providing a variety of familiar and unfamiliar activities will ensure that all children can find something interesting to do (**Figure 30.16**). The specific types of activities you offer will depend on the length and time of your program.

Before-school programs should focus on quiet activities. Some children may need to spend the time before school finishing or reviewing their homework. Other children may enjoy looking at books, constructing puzzles, or playing quiet games. They may also enjoy talking with friends.

After-school programs are usually longer than before-school programs, and they offer a wider variety of activities. After sitting in a classroom all day, many children enjoy physical activities that help release energy. They enjoy outdoor play, group sports, preparing snacks, and working on projects. They may want to take part in clubs, such as chess, computing, or music. They may want to join book clubs and special interest clubs.

Other children need to find space to be by themselves after school to recharge their energy. For them, being with a group of people, following directions, and completing tasks all day may

SDI Productions/E+ via Getty Images

Figure 30.16 During activity times, provide children with both familiar and unfamiliar activities to try. ***What are the benefits of having children try unfamiliar activities?***

be stressful. They may simply want to listen to music, page through a book, enjoy quiet games, do homework, or rest. When planning activity times, take care to plan group activities, plan technology (STEM) activities, include outdoor games, and carefully balance quiet and active experiences.

Planning Group Activities

Some school-age program activities will involve all the children. However, children in the middle childhood years also need opportunities to take part in small, self-selected peer group activities. Listening to a story, taking a field trip, and planning a project or celebration can all be group activities. Such activities help children communicate, develop friendships, and learn social skills.

Use different ways of dividing children into groups. You may group children according to age, interests, and needs. You may also group children according to such factors as favorite sports, recording artists, foods, pets, and hobbies.

Mixed groups representing different developmental stages benefit children at all levels. Such groups reduce competition. These groups give older children an opportunity to develop leadership skills. Older children can help younger children with such activities as board games, computer apps, and crafts. Younger children learn by observing and interacting with the older children.

Groups may undertake special activities. For example, publishing a newsletter is a special activity for a group of children. The children can write, edit, and print it using a computer. They can decide who will be the editors, reporters, photographers, illustrators and production staff. When it is published, the children can share the newsletter with their families. Other groups might want to start a science or math club. Some after-school programs feature a chef's club.

Planning Digital Learning Activities

Digital learning activities offer special learning opportunities for school-age children to develop twenty-first century skills. Many school-age students live in homes without computers or internet services. Only while attending school, do they have digital access. The **digital divide** is the term used to describe this, which is the gulf between people who have computer and internet access and those that do not. Since the internet has an increasingly important role in education, it is important for school-age children to have access. To succeed, they must develop **technological literacy,** the ability to understand and use technology.

Knowledge of **digital literacy,** the ability to use digital media for listening, speaking, reading, and writing, is important. Technology is necessary for school-age children to explore, analyze, and learn. They can use computers and other digital devices for a variety of tasks (**Figure 30.17**). They can compose letters, practice keyboarding skills, complete homework, play games, or search for information online. The design of some computer games, apps, and puzzles help to exercise children's attention and working-memory skills. Through these experiences, children improve their thinking skills by seeking information, making decisions, and solving problems.

Children need age-appropriate freedom to use the computers on their own. This helps them develop self-confidence. Supervision and protection from inappropriate content when using any digital device is necessary for children. Teachers must employ safeguards to prevent abuse of media with children. They should also investigate the use of filtering software and other technologies that keep children from accessing certain information.

Health Highlights

Ergonomics and Computer Use

Digital play has replaced physical play in the lives of many school-age children. Recent studies show an increase in *repetitive-stress injuries* in children under 12 who engage in excessive of computers, game systems, and other digital devices. These conditions are caused by placing too much stress on a joint. These injuries can occur because of poor posture when using devices or furniture that doesn't fit. For example, neck injuries may result when children must strain or hunch forward to see the computer screen. Wrists, hands, fingers, and thumb injuries may occur when children overextend their reach. Mouse pads can easily be out of reach for young children.

Computer furniture that is ergonomically designed for children age six to 12 years of age can help prevent injuries. Make sure that children sit up straight with their feet flat on the floor and backs straight against the chair backs. Crouching can place undue stress on the neck, back or spine. Arms and hands should be at a 90-degree angle and parallel with the keyboard and mouse pad.

Children may need reminders to use a light touch on the keyboard. Pounding on a keyboard is not necessary. It can hurt them and the keyboard.

FatCamera/E+ via Getty Images

Figure 30.17 Learning to use digital devices independently is a valuable skill for school-age children. *How can teachers and caregivers keep children safe while using digital devices?*

Planning Outdoor Games

Games are important for school-age children. Through age-appropriate games, they exercise self-regulation and executive-function skills. Outdoor games are especially important for allowing children time for physical activity. Physical activity is necessary to achieve optimal health benefits and physical fitness. Children improve their endurance, balance, speed, agility, and strength. They also learn about their own abilities, such as how strong or fast they are. Finally, children who get plenty of activity are more likely to grow up liking exercise.

School-age children particularly like to play group outdoor games. At this stage of development, they understand and practice rules. To be part of a group, they need to understand and abide by the rules. Sports help children monitor their own actions and those of others. They learn to make quick decisions, practice self-control, and follow rules. Outdoor games include basketball, volleyball, gymnastics, soccer, and jumping rope. Other games children enjoy outdoors include hide-and-seek, hopscotch, kickball, marbles, obstacle courses, ping-pong, and tug-of-war. Jump rope games are also popular for school-age children. To develop skills, they need focused practice. This also requires working memory to coordinate the motions with the recall of words. Such activities improve executive-function skills.

Balancing School-Age Children's Activities

An excellent school-age program does not duplicate activities that take place during the school day. Instead, it complements the child's home and school experiences. The emphasis should be on recreational activities as opposed to academic ones (**Figure 30.18**). The activities should be developmentally appropriate and provide opportunities for skill development.

The schedule for a school-age program needs to include a balance of activities. Schedule separate times for child-directed and teacher-directed activities. Allow time for small group, large group, and individual activities. Plan for gross-motor activities, such as team sports and outdoor play. Also plan for fine-motor activities, such as writing and drawing. **Figure 30.19** shows a list of indoor activities for school-age children.

Card and board games help promote the continuing development of self-regulation skills, or executive function (**Figure 30.20**). These games require strategic planning. They also promote mental flexibility, working memory, and self-control in response to peers' movements that will promote lifelong benefits. The children learn to:

- focus and sustain their attention;
- remember and follow directions;
- set goals;
- delay gratification;
- recall prior knowledge;
- think critically and solve problems;
- become flexible thinkers;
- control their impulses; and
- focus on something positive, which de-escalates frustration and anger.

Cleanup Times

Your school-age program needs to include scheduled time for cleanup. All children need to take part in cleanup activities. Everyone has a responsibility for maintaining the environment.

Outdoor Activities

	Frisbee Golf	Ring Toss
	Ghosts in the Graveyard	Sardines
	Hopscotch	Sidewalk Chalk Drawing
	Jump Rope	Simon Says
	Keep Away	Spud
	Kickball	Tag
	Obstacle Course	Color Tag
Basketball	Capture the Flag	Parachute Games	Freeze Tag
Bowling	Four Square	Red Light-Green Light	

Sunflower Light Pro/Shutterstock.com

Figure 30.18   Outdoor recreational activities provide an excellent balance after a full day of schoolwork.

Indoor Activities

	Collages	Taco vs Burrito
	Collections: Stamps, Shells, Rocks, Baseball Cards	Uno
	Cooking	Painting
	Gardening	Papier-mâché
	Map Construction	Photography
	Needlework	Puppet Constructions and Plays
	Card Games	Model Building
	War	Musical Instruments
	Go Fish	Sewing
Board Games · Chutes and Ladders	Crazy Eights	Solitaire
Sequence · Checkers	Memory	Tie-dying
Scrabble · Chess	Rummy	Tic-tac-toe
Candyland · Clay Modeling	Snap	

MBI/Shutterstock.com

Figure 30.19 Games and activities that require strategic thinking help promote the development of executive function in school-age children.

Let children know your expectations for cleanup time. Tell them they should return games and equipment to the proper storage units. Instruct them to place their belongings, projects, and artwork in their lockers or backpacks. Completing these tasks will help children develop a sense of pride.

Lesson 30.2 Review

1. Teachers should assess children's interests as part of curriculum planning because _____. (30.2.1)
   A. children know more about developmentally appropriate programs
   B. the individual interests, strengths, abilities, and needs of school-age children vary greatly
   C. parents and staff do not provide goals for school-age care
   D. teachers do not understand the needs of school-age children
2. **True or False.** Get-acquainted interviews involves the teacher asking children questions about their interests. (30.2.1)
3. Which of the following is **not** a key element in the school-age program daily schedule? (30.2.1)
   A. Outdoor play
   B. Rest time
   C. Field trip time
   D. Arrival and departure times
4. _____ is the ability to use digital media for listening, speaking, reading, and writing. (30.2.2)
   A. Digital literacy
   B. Digital divide
   C. Technological literacy
   D. Tech savvy

Summary

Lesson 30.1

30.1-1 A quality school-age program establishes non-school times as opportunities for productive learning, companionship, and activities. Most school-age programs are open before and after school hours, while others may also be available for school holidays, and during the summer. The environment should provide appropriate supervision, developmentally appropriate space, materials, and equipment, and reflect the children's interests, culture, ages, abilities, needs, and experiences. A program may demonstrate its quality by adhering to standards and seeking accreditation.

30.1-2 Parents have a variety of options when choosing before- and after-school childcare. School-age programs typically follow one of three curriculum models: child-centered, adult-centered, and unit-based. A center may choose its model based on staff preference and the ages, interests, abilities, culture, and experiences of the children.

30.1-3 Well-trained personnel who understand children's growth and development staff high-quality programs. School-age program staff should act as facilitators, use positive guidance, involve children, promote respect for cultural diversity, and enjoy physical activity.

30.1-3 Microaggressions are subtle, everyday insults that may be verbal or nonverbal which may be intentional or unintentional. They communicate negative, hurtful messages and take place in everyday conversations. Classroom teachers must address microaggressions immediately since they can disrupt the children's ability to engage in the learning process and impact children's health.

30.1-4 A quality school-age care environment should provide developmentally appropriate space, materials, and equipment that reflect the children's strengths, interests, ages, abilities, needs, and experiences. Indoor environments should be homelike and comfortable with areas for multiple interests and activity levels.

Outdoor environments should be spacious with areas for active and quiet play and developmentally appropriate for the children's age and physical skill levels.

Lesson 30.2

30.2-1 A quality school-aged program has a well-planned, engaging curriculum that has been developed with input from children, families, and staff. Parents and staff are likely to have general goals for the school-age program, including help with homework and a variety of developmentally appropriate engaging activities that allow children to develop new interests and skills.

30.2-1 When planning day-to-day activities within the curriculum, teachers should assess school-age children's interests through get-acquainted interviews, group discussions, self-reports, and surveys. Group-planning discussions are helpful in choosing themes and special events with the children.

30.2-2 A school-age program's daily schedule should be flexible and incorporate a variety of activities. Teachers must plan for arrivals, departures, mealtimes, outdoor play, relaxation periods, and interest- and group-based activities.

Vocabulary Activity

For each of the Key Terms in this chapter, identify a word or group of words describing a quality of the term—an *attribute*. Pair up with a classmate and discuss your list of attributes. Then, discuss your list of attributes with the entire class to increase understanding.

Critical Thinking

1. **Compare and Contrast.** Visit two programs for infants, toddlers, preschoolers, and school-age children. After visiting and taking detailed notes about the programs, compare them. Write a report explaining how the programs are alike and different.

2. **Evaluate.** Research the after-school programs available in your area. Are the programs part of established school-age programs or are they stand-alone businesses? Are private tutors available through your school district or through classified advertising? Choose two programs; research their

content, length, and number of sessions per week, cost, staff requirements and qualifications, location, and guarantees of success. Evaluate how effective they are. Are there areas they could improve?

3. **Critique.** Read and critique the book, *A Wrinkled Heart* by Tracy Hoexter. How does the book help teach children about empathy and friendship? How do the words children choose in relating to others impact empathy? After writing your critique of the book, create an activity you can use to teach children about empathy.

4. **Identify.** Interview a school-age care provider about the characteristics that make him or her effective at the job. Identify key characteristics of the person and then identify your key characteristics. How suited do you think you would be to school-age childcare? Share your findings in a brief oral report.

5. **Analyze.** In small groups, discuss the following question: Why is it important to promote awareness of and respect for cultural diversity in school-age programs? Make a list of your group's answers to these questions and then compare answers with other small groups. Brainstorm activities that would encourage respect for cultural diversity and then analyze how to adapt these activities for school-age children.

6. **Determine.** In small groups, determine ways of including school-age children in curriculum planning. How could a planning session be conducted? How should a teacher treat student suggestions, and in particular, unhelpful student suggestions? How much say should the teacher and the children get in planning the curriculum?

Core Skills

1. **Speaking.** In small groups, choose one school-age program model to support. Research the model and make a list of its advantages. Also consider what would realistically work in your community regarding cost and space. Prepare responses for any negatives other groups may cite about your chosen model. Finally, debate the three program models in your class. After the debate, discuss what you learned from the other teams.

2. **Math.** Measure the indoor and outdoor square footage at a school-age care facility. Calculate how much space is available for each child enrolled in the program. Is the amount of space sufficient, based on the recommendations given in this chapter? Why or why not? How much, if any, more space would need to be added for the facility to meet recommended amounts?

3. **Math.** Measure your classroom and determine how many square feet of space are available. If they used a room for an after-school program

with a minimum requirement of 35 square feet per child, how many children could participate? Also, measure the outdoor space available in your classroom. Does the play area allow for 75 square feet of space for each child that would use the indoor facility at a time?

4. **Reading and Writing.** The US Consumer Product Safety Commission publishes a handbook on playground safety. Find this handbook online and read the guidelines for playground safety. Imagine that they asked you to report to your team members about the handbook and write an easily understandable summary of what teachers need to keep in mind when planning outdoor playground spaces.

5. **Science.** Research state and USA standards for healthy eating and physical activity in out-of-school time for school-age children. How much physical activity should children get? What should they be eating? Presuming that you are a teacher at a school-age program, plan a week-long menu for after-school snacks for children. Include appropriate amounts of all nutrients.

6. **Technology.** School-age children enjoy many websites and types of media and technology. Visit a website developed for school-age children. What are its contents? For what ages is it appropriate? Which parts of the site do you think school-age children would find most interesting? If you were to set up a computer station where school-age children could access this website, what precautions would be necessary to ensure the children's safety? How would you employ safeguards to prevent abuse of media with children?

7. **CTE Career Readiness Practice.** Imagine that you are a teacher at a school-age program of twenty-five children between the ages of seven and twelve. Most of the children arrive after school at 2:00 p.m. and leave around 5:00 p.m. According to the guidelines in this chapter, draft a schedule for these children. Include arrival and departure times, mealtimes, rest times, and activity times. Remember to balance the types of activities you include.

Portfolio Project

Select a school-age program director, curriculum specialist, teacher, or aide and interview the individual about their job. What is most enjoyable about working with school-age children in the program? What presents more challenges? How important is parent communication in this position? Does the person favor a child-centered, an adult-centered, a unit-based, or a blended program? What resources do they regularly use? Write a brief review of the job and file it in your portfolio.

Chapter 31

Reading Advantage

On separate sticky notes, write five reasons how the information in this chapter will help you at school, work, or home. As you read the chapter, place the sticky notes on the pages that relate to each reason.

Guiding Children with Diverse Needs

Lesson 31.1: Education Plans and the Teacher's Role

Lesson 31.2: Hearing, Communication, Visual, and Physical Needs

Lesson 31.3: Health, Learning, and Behavior Needs

Case Study

Supporting Parents of Children with Disabilities

Tashia King walked with her two-and-a-half-year-old son, Charlie, into the center on his first day. The teacher, Tommy Rolland, immediately smiled at Charlie and cheerfully said, "Good morning, Charlie." Noticing how uncomfortable Charlie appeared, his mother asked whether she could stay. Tommy agreed and then gathered the children for story time. Before reading the story, he introduced Charlie and observed that he did not respond to his name. During the story, Charlie did not make eye contact or respond to the teacher; instead, he sat flapping his hands and had difficulties with attention. Later, Tommy also observed that Charlie's play skills seemed inappropriate for his age. He preferred solitary play, unlike the majority of the children who engaged in parallel play. Charlie only played with one toy, a rubber cow, and seemed to cause injury by biting himself during the entire morning.

Charlie's mother noticed the difference in the development of the other children in the classroom and Charlie. She had known that Charlie, an only child, had poorly developed social skills and had not started to speak. She confided to the teacher that she feared something was wrong and wondered if he could test Charlie. Tommy said he was not qualified for this task and advised her to talk to her pediatrician. He felt a diagnosis could improve the quality of Charlie's life. Within a month, a diagnosis was made, followed by an Individualized Education Plan (IEP), and an Individualized Family Service Plan (IFSP).

Give It Some Thought

1. What diverse ability does Charlie have? What are some other symptoms of this diverse ability? Why is it essential for children like Charlie to have consistency in routines and a classroom environment?
2. What is the Individuals with Disabilities Education Act (IDEA)? What services does it include?
3. What should Charlie's Individual Education Plan (IEP) contain? What is the value of an IEP to parents or guardians, teachers, and children?
4. Describe the contents of an Individualized Family Service Plan (IFSP). How can it be used to monitor progress?
5. What is the teacher's role in guiding children with diverse abilities?
6. What other types of diverse abilities might children have who are enrolled in an early childhood program?

Opening image credit: sarra22/E+ via Getty Images

Education Plans and the Teacher's Role

Essential Question

? *What do you need to know about the Individuals with Disabilities Act (IDEA), developing Individualized Education Plan (IEP), and the role of the teacher to best meet the needs of children with diverse abilities?*

Learning Outcomes

After studying this lesson, you will be able to

31.1-1 summarize the role of the Individuals with Disabilities Act (IDEA) in meeting the needs of children with disabilities.

31.1-2 explain the role of the teacher and parents or guardians in developing Individualized Education Plans and working with children who have disabilities.

Key Terms

developmental disability	Individualized Family Service Plan (IFSP)
disability	render
Individuals with Disabilities Education Act (IDEA)	Individualized Education Plan (IEP)
	referral

Miguel, a lively four-year-old, has moderate hearing loss. He can speak and understand only a few simple words. Rosie, an active five-year-old, has color deficiency. She cannot identify the primary colors. Stephen has cerebral palsy. He requires special help to develop fine-motor skills. Beyonce has been identified as a twice exceptional child. She has an orthopedic disability, but taught herself to read at age four. These are all children who have diverse needs.

Developmental disabilities affect all racial, cultural, and socioeconomic groups. According to the Center for Disease Control and Prevention (CDC), recent estimates show that about one out of every six, or 17 percent of children, have one or more developmental disabilities. Usually diagnosed in infancy or childhood, **developmental disabilities** can impact language, learning, physical abilities, socialization, and behavior. These conditions may include autism spectrum disorder, cerebral palsy, intellectual disability, blindness, or fragile X syndrome, and usually last a lifetime and affect day-to-day functioning.

There are many children with a **disability**, a mental, physical, or developmental condition that interferes with or limits how the body develops or works. Usually, these conditions have been identified with a specific class of disability such as hard of hearing or blind. Other children have communication needs. Communication needs usually fall into three categories: hearing, speech, and language problems. Visual, physical, and learning disabilities and chronic health problems are other types of diverse needs. (**Figure 31.1**).

According to the Centers for Disease Control and Prevention (CDC) most developmental disabilities begin before a baby is born and are thought to be caused by a complex mix of factors. Genetics, parental health, complications during pregnancy, and head trauma can be risk factors. Parental health and behaviors, such as drinking and smoking, are other risk factors. Children identified with disabilities, by law, need an educational plan outlining goals, services, and educational accommodations to maximize the child's education.

Addressing the needs of children with diverse needs is an evolving field. While the 1990s

Olesia Bilkei/Shutterstock.com

Figure 31.1   Many children will come to a center with known disabilities. These children may already have an IEP in place. ***What roles do teachers have in guiding children with special needs?***

recognized the rights and needs of families, the twenty-first century has recognized the value of including children with disabilities in a program with the same age peers without disabilities. Only when a routine placement would be inappropriate should these children be placed in separate schools or classrooms. Studies on early participation in high-quality programs found long-term positive effects on children's lives. Children who took part showed gains in one or more developmental areas—cognitive, emotional, behavior, and health. All early childhood teachers need to be prepared to work with children who have diverse needs and their families.

31.1-1 Educational Plans for Children with Disabilities

The **Individuals with Disabilities Education Act (IDEA)**, passed by Congress, is a law that requires a free, appropriate public education be provided to eligible children with disabilities. The IDEA ensures special education and related services are tailored to fit the needs of these children. For example, when an infant or a toddler (a child who is younger than three years of age) is diagnosed with a developmental delay, an **Individualized Family Service Plan (IFSP)** is mandated by law and is designed to help infants and toddlers. This plan is written by a group of

people, including the parents, members of the evaluation team, and teacher(s). It describes the child's current status, prescribes support services, and guidelines for the process. The IFSP is an effective tool for monitoring progress and making sure the child is getting the necessary services.

An IFSP is both a process and document, which requires a regular review. It focuses on the family's and the child's current status, strengths, resources, and prescribes support services. It includes

- the name of the person coordinating and implementing the IFSP;
- a statement about the family's needs, resources, concerns and priorities for promoting the child's development;
- a description of the child's current level of functioning and needs in the areas of physical, cognitive, social, and adaptive development;
- a description of the services to be provided to the child and/or family, including details such as who will **render** (provide) the service, where it will be provided, who will pay for it, and how often; and
- a statement of the family's concerns, resources, and priorities for promoting their child's development.

Federal law requires that children with disabilities be provided with free and appropriate public education. These services need to be provided in the least restrictive environment. The Individuals with Disabilities Education Act (IDEA) also requires that all states provide education for children who have developmental disabilities. Under this law, all three- to five-year-old children with disabilities who require special educational services must be provided with *Individualized Education Plans (IEPs)*. These same programs are also available for children from birth to three years of age who are high risk or have significant developmental problems. Infants, toddlers, and preschoolers who might have a physical, sensory, cognitive, or emotional disability are guaranteed the right to professional assessment and early intervention services under Part C of the IDEA. Services include

- audiological services to determine the child's hearing ability;
- family training, counseling, and home visits;
- medical and nursing services;
- nutritional services;
- occupational and physical therapy;
- psychological and social work services;
- respite care and other family support services;
- special education services;
- speech and language therapy;
- transportation to enable a child and family to receive early intervention services;
- vision services to assess whether the child has usable vision and what sort of low vision; and
- devices or adaptive equipment required.

The purpose of an **Individualized Education Plan (IEP)** is to ensure that each child receives an appropriate education. These plans must be written as goals that are tied to state standards. By law, parents or guardians are allowed to take part in designing their children's programs. Plans are a team effort. The teacher, the parents or guardians, and experts on the particular disability jointly develop them. After development, the parents or guardians receive a copy of the plan. Children with previously identified disabilities will usually come to an early learning center already possessing an IEP (**Figure 31.1**).

Typically, IEPs are written to cover a 12-month period extending from October 1 to September 30. Children with correctable disabilities or disabilities that require no special accommodations will not need IEPs.

Each IEP should contain the following seven components:

- a description including an assessment of the child's current level of performance and skill development;
- annual measurable goals that describe what the child will learn or do;
- short-term attainable educational objectives;
- a statement outlining the involvement of the child in the regular educational program;
- specific services that will be provided with a timeline noting the dates services will begin and end;
- supports such as accommodations and assistive technology; and
- evaluation criteria that will decide if educational objectives are met.

Workplace Connections

Investigating Early Childhood Health Policies

Investigate health policies for licensed early childhood facilities in your state.

1. Are facilities required to have a health form signed by a physician for each child in their care?
2. After admittance, are any other follow-up physicals required for children?

31.1-2 Role of the Teacher

Since federal law first mandated including children with disabilities and special needs in classrooms, teachers' roles have expanded. Now, teachers' roles in guiding children with disabilities and special needs include

- taking part in identification by monitoring developmental expectations in how children move, behave and speak;
- working with speech clinicians, school psychologists, health professionals, and other resource people to tailor individual programs;
- teaching children who have diverse abilities and children without disabilities in the same, high-quality classrooms;
- sharing information with parents and making suggestions for referrals;
- basing program decisions on input from several resources, including parents, other professionals, and personal observations; and

- encouraging parents to take part in their children's education, which may include finding out what parents or guardians are feeling as well as thinking. Teachers need to be equal partners with parents or guardians and keep them informed.

To fulfill these roles as a teacher, you will need to learn how to identify children with diverse abilities and special needs to make referrals.

Identification

Early identification of children with diverse abilities is the key to promoting their success (**Figure 31.2**). Children whose disabilities are not identified early may experience years of failure and a poor self-concept that can compound their disability.

Many young children's disabilities are identified after they enter an early childhood program. Often, an adult who is not part of the family identifies the disability. As a teacher, you may be the first to detect a speech, visual, or hearing problem. You may also be the first to note a cognitive, emotional, physical disability or giftedness.

Identifying children with disabilities and special needs requires a strong child development background. Identification involves recognizing when a child is lagging or exceeding in reaching a milestone. Observing the child and making careful notes is an important first step in collecting data. Informal observations made on note cards, paper, or a digital tablet can help in assessing a child's needs. When recording observations, mention signs of behaviors that suggest a disability or special need. These may include unusual social, cognitive, emotional, or physical development. After recording observations, ask yourself, "Could this child have _____?" Finally, consider a child's behavior compared to their usual behavior, and in comparison, to their peers.

You can collect observations and data in several ways. You might study a child's work (**Figure 31.3**). Photographs and videos can help record behaviors. Scales or checklists that name skills children of certain ages should be able to perform may help you organize your thoughts.

After you making and confirming your findings, alert the center director. The director may wish to check your observations, and may administer other tests to measure the child's abilities. If there are any concerns, the center director will schedule a conference with the child's family. These conferences may be delicate situations that you will need to handle with care and respect.

Peakstock/Shutterstock.com

Figure 31.2 Annual hearing tests are a vital tool for identifying hearing problems early. ***How does it benefit children to identify hearing loss early?***

Oksana Kuzmina/Shutterstock.com

Figure 31.3 Closely observing children's skills allows teachers to note behaviors that might indicate a special need. ***What tools do teachers use to collect data?***

During a conference, begin by introducing the suspected problem. Share your observations and provide family members with examples. Ask family members if they have noticed any of these behaviors at home. If their observations confirm yours, suggest a formal diagnosis.

For some parents, coming to terms with a child's developmental delay or disability takes time. At first, parents may not share your concern. If this is the case, keep making observations, recording data, and scheduling more conferences. It sometimes helps to ask the family to take part in structured observations in the home and school. Remember, any delay in diagnosis can hinder the child's development; however, that it is the family's choice to have their child evaluated or not. Respect their decision. You can also inform parents or guardians that many services are available for children with various disabilities. **Figure 31.4** shows disabilities that qualify a child for services.

Referrals

Once parents or guardians come to terms with a disability and agree that a problem may exist, direct them to the appropriate service. Your role as a teacher is to help them understand their children's need for treatment. Once this you accomplish this, you can direct parents or guardians to get a diagnosis. Public schools are responsible for planning and paying the costs associated with disability diagnoses unless parents or guardians choose to have their own assessments conducted. In that case, school staff must consider the results. You may suggest a professional that parents or guardians can take their child to see. This is called a **referral**. Vision or physical problems may first be referred to a county or school health nurse. Hearing, language, or speech problems may be referred to a speech clinician. Learning and behavioral problems are

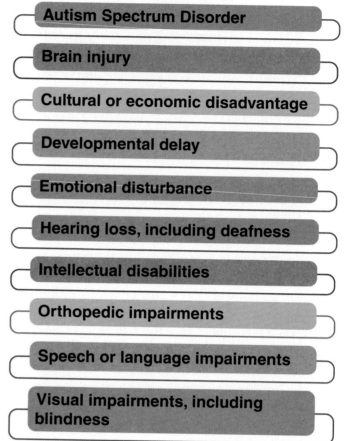

Disabilities That Qualify a Child for Services

- Autism Spectrum Disorder
- Brain injury
- Cultural or economic disadvantage
- Developmental delay
- Emotional disturbance
- Hearing loss, including deafness
- Intellectual disabilities
- Orthopedic impairments
- Speech or language impairments
- Visual impairments, including blindness

Figure 31.4   Part of the teacher's role is informing parents and guardians what services are available for various disabilities.

most often referred to a school psychologist or local agency. Depending on the state, a referral may be made to the Department of Social Services.

In both the identification and referral process and in the processes that will follow, you will need to develop a basic understanding of the learning needs of children with hearing, visual, speech, physical, learning, behavioral, and health disabilities. Understanding these needs will help you guide such children.

Focus on Careers

Special Education Teacher, Preschool

Preschool special education teachers focus on teaching academic, social, and life skills to preschool children who have learning, emotional, behavioral, or physical disabilities. This also includes teachers who specialize in teaching students who have hearing loss or are deaf, children with vision loss or who are blind, children with developmental or intellectual disabilities.

Preschool special education teachers use educational strategies and techniques to help children develop sensory- and perceptual-motor skills, language, memory and cognition. They also teach socially acceptable behavior, and encourage children with positive reinforcement. As with other children, preschool special education teachers will teach basic skills including, color, shape, number and letter recognition, social skills, and hygiene skills to children with special needs. They also help develop individual education plans (IEPs) that outline goals for children's physical, social, and educational development.

Career cluster: Education and training.

Education: Preschool special education teachers need a bachelor's degree at a minimum. Some employers require a master's degree.

Job outlook. Employment for preschool special education teachers is expected to grow 10 to 15 percent through 2030, which is faster than average for all occupations.

To learn more about a career as a special education teacher for preschool, visit US Department of Labor websites for the *Occupational Outlook Handbook (OOH)* and *O*NET OnLine.* You will be able to compare the job responsibilities, educational requirements, job outlook, and average pay for special education preschool teachers with similar occupations.

Lesson 31.1 Review

1. _____ is a law passed by Congress that requires a free, appropriate public education be provided to eligible children with disabilities. (31.1.1)
   A. Individualized Family Service Plan (IFSP)
   B. Individuals with Disabilities Education Act (IDEA)
   C. Civil Rights Act of 1964
   D. Elementary and Secondary Education Act (ESEA)

2. An Individualized Education Plan (IEP) should contain all the following *except* _____. (31.1.1)
   A. short-term attainable goals
   B. supports, such as accommodations and assistive technology
   C. the child's medical records
   D. an assessment of the child's current level of performance

3. **True or False.** Children whose disabilities are not identified early may experience years of failure and poor self-concept. (31.1.2)

4. When a teacher suggests a professional for families to visit with their child regarding a possible disability, this is called a _____. (31.1.2)
   A. referral
   B. recommendation
   C. professional courtesy
   D. school order

Essential Question

? *What do you need to know about identifying children who have hearing, communication, visual, or physical disabilities and developing strategies to meet their educational needs?*

Learning Outcomes

After studying this lesson, you will be able to

31.2-1 **identify** methods and strategies for working with children who have hearing loss or who are deaf.

31.2-2 **summarize** types of communication disorders, how to identify them, and strategies for working with children who have communication disorders.

31.2-3 **explain** types of visual impairments, how to identify them, and strategies for working with children who have visual impairments.

31.2-4 **describe** types of physical disabilities and strategies for teaching children with physical disabilities.

Key Terms

congenital disability	inarticulate
intervention	speech pathologist
hard of hearing	audiologist
deaf	articulation problem
cochlear implant	visual impairment
eclectic	ambulatory

Children come to early childhood education programs with various challenges and needs. Some children enter the program with hearing losses and communication challenges affecting all development areas. Others may have visual or communication challenges. Every child is unique and will thrive in quality programs supporting their needs, interests, and individual strengths. You will need to learn about each child's specific disabilities and classroom strategies for helping them.

Early childhood teachers must monitor children's developmental milestones to identify children with disabilities and children who are gifted. Early identification is important since young children grow and learn more in the first few years of life. Once identified, teachers must be prepared to integrate these children into their classrooms. The law entitles all children with disabilities to be provided the best and least restrictive learning environment, with typically developing peers whenever possible, and to the services needed to be successful.

31.2-1 Hearing Loss

At least 25 percent of hearing loss among babies is due to maternal infections during pregnancy, complications after birth, and head trauma, according to the Centers for Disease Control and Prevention. Children with hearing loss experience problems in one or more parts of the ear. Hearing loss prevents children from hearing adequately and is one of the most common **congenital disabilities** (disabilities present since birth, but not necessarily hereditary). These disabilities are linked with lifelong deficits in speech and language acquisition, emotional difficulties, and poor academic performance. Early detection and **intervention**, providing services to children who have disabilities or are at risk, is important for developing communication skills.

Most states mandate newborn hearing screening, which is critical. Severe hearing losses can be identified early in young children, often as newborns. Hospitals use newborn screening protocols to identify hearing loss. Congenital hearing loss is more than twice as prevalent as other conditions screened at birth. Medical staff identify one to three infants per 1,000 births with a congenital hearing defect. Children with mild hearing loss may go undetected.

A lack of vocabulary and overall delays in speech and grammar can often identify a child who has hearing loss. A child with a hearing loss may also lack interest in storytelling or other activities that require listening. This child may only speak a few simple words. Before you alter your program, learn the extent of a child's hearing loss. This information can only be learned through families and highly trained professionals. Typically, infants with a hearing loss can babble and make noises for about five months after birth (**Figure 31.5**).

Types of Hearing Loss

A child's hearing loss may range from mild to profound. With a mild to moderate hearing loss, the child is considered **hard of hearing**. Their vocabulary will not be as large as that of their peers who have normal hearing. This child might also have difficulty during large-group activities, stories, and field trips. The child may appear

Rob Marmion/Shutterstock.com

Figure 31.5 Infants with a hearing loss may still babble and make noises. *What clues can teachers observe that may indicate hearing loss?*

inattentive and distracted and may miss as much as half of what is being communicated.

Children with a mild hearing loss may go undetected. A child with a moderate hearing loss will have trouble responding to a teacher in large-group situations. A child with a severe hearing loss will have problems following directions, and frequently says, "Huh." Often, the child cannot turn their head or eyes toward the sound. They likely have a limited vocabulary. To understand the child's speech, you need to stand face to face. This will allow you to read the child's lips.

Children with severe or *profound*, hearing loss may be **deaf** (total or partial hearing loss). They often have little understandable speech. These children rely on vision, body language, and contextual clues to communicate.

When determining the extent of a child's hearing loss, professionals will often administer a hearing threshold test. The test will reveal the softest sound a child hears at different frequencies.

Assistive listening devices make up for or ease hearing loss. Infants as young as four weeks of age can be fitted with a hearing aid. *Hearing aids* are small electronic devices worn either in or behind the ear. Other children have **cochlear implants** that are surgically implanted and use both internal and external components. This device provides someone with moderate to profound hearing loss with sound perception. Their speech understanding is improved in a quiet environment.

According to the American Speech-Language-Hearing Association (ASHA), behind-the-ear (BTE) hearing aids are most commonly used with young babies and children with mild to severe hearing loss. The device has two main parts, a plastic case that holds the hearing aid and the battery. Behind-the-ear hearing devices usually last longer than other devices. The electrical components are located outside of the ear so there is less moisture and ear wax damage.

Reasons choosing BTE hearing aids include
- the BTE can use different earmold styles;
- removable earmolds can easily be replaced as the child grows;
- BTE holds larger batteries, which enables a longer battery life and stronger volume;

- controls are easy to see, and parents or guardians can easily check and adjust them; and
- parents or guardians and teachers or caregivers can easily do a listening check.

Once a child receives treatment for hearing loss, understand the type of hearing aid the child uses. Ask parents or guardians to tell you about it and about how to work the controls. Also, them what to do if the hearing aid makes a noise, falls out or is pulled out of the child's ear during program hours, or when batteries require replacement. Some children have assistive listening devices to hear what is being said more clearly.

Teaching Suggestions

If you have children with hearing loss in your classroom, you will need to modify your curriculum and interactions with the children. When approaching a child with a hearing loss, get down to the child's eye level (**Figure 31.6**). Then get the child's attention before speaking. Sometimes you can lightly touch the child's hand or arm. With practice, you will learn how close you must stand in order to be understood. Some hard-of-hearing children manage their hearing loss by reading lips, so remember to keep your

SDI Productions/E+ via Getty Images

Figure 31.6   The key to working with children who have a hearing loss is to change your teaching methods to meet the needs of the child. ***What strategies might teachers use in working with children with hearing loss?***

Early Childhood Insight

Hearing Aids

Hearing aids are tiny battery-operated digital devices that amplify and magnify sounds through a three-part process. First, the microphone receives the sound and converts it into a digital signal. Then the hearing aid's amplifier increases the strength of the digital signal. The device's speaker then produces the amplified sound into the ear. A hearing aid will not perfect a child's hearing but will amplify close sounds.

classroom well lit. In addition, follow these suggestions:

- Speak at a normal volume and speed.
- Use the child's name to gain their attention.
- Speak clearly and distinctly while looking into the child's eyes.
- Use the same vocabulary and sentence structure as you would for other children.
- Give one direction at a time.
- Pause and wait for a response after you speak.
- If the child does not understand you, repeat, rephrase, or demonstrate.
- Encourage other children to imitate you when they communicate with the child. For example, when they need to get the child's attention, teach other children to look into the child's eyes and speak at a normal volume and speed.
- Whenever needed, use gestures, facial expressions, and touch to reinforce the spoken word.
- In a group situation, have preferential seating and let the child sit in front of you. This will encourage the child to watch your body language and lips as you speak.

Beside using these teaching strategies, be aware of the background-noise level. Whether hard-of-hearing children are using an assistive device or not, they tend to be sensitive to background (environmental) sounds. When children use manual signs, learn them. Adapt the curriculum for the child with hearing loss. Before you make these changes, it might be helpful to consult a speech pathologist for teaching suggestions.

Visual skills are important for children who are deaf or have hearing loss since finely tuned visual skills help compensate for lack of hearing. Children who are have hearing loss do not automatically gain acute visual skills, though. To promote children's visual skills, stress visual activities. Use the following guidelines when incorporating visual activities into the curriculum:

- Use concrete materials as aids to demonstrate abstract concepts. For example, if you are talking about pumpkins, use a real pumpkin or a picture of a pumpkin. (Avoid drawing on the board as you are talking. Children with hearing loss need to see your face as you communicate with them.)
- Provide a variety of classification games and puzzles for the children to practice visual perception skills.
- Label classroom furniture and materials.
- Select books with simple, large, and uncluttered illustrations. Children with hearing loss rely more on vision than hearing during story time.
- Teach safety by using traffic signals with the wheeled toys in the playground.
- Teach daily routines and transitions using a light switch. Flash the light to get children's attention.
- Give one direction at a time.
- Use a picture poster or photograph to point to an upcoming activity.

Some children with hearing loss communicate manually through fingerspelling and sign language. Other children learn an oral approach, emphasizing lip-reading and speaking. Some parents feel strongly about using one approach over the other, even though most professionals today recommend a combined or **eclectic** (varied) approach to children who have hearing loss.

31.2-2 Communication Disorders

Communication needs are the most common type of disability. Communication affects all areas of child development. Communication disorders are conditions that inhibit children's abilities to communicate with adults and with each other. A child with a communication disorder may refuse to talk or may speak but be **inarticulate** (not understandable by teachers or peers) or may not recall sentences correctly. Communication disorders are varied, and early identification is key to helping children who have them.

Identification

When you have children with communication disorders in your classroom, you must identify the problem causing the disorder before you can alter a program. Informal observations are the most common method used to identify communication problems (**Figure 31.7**). You

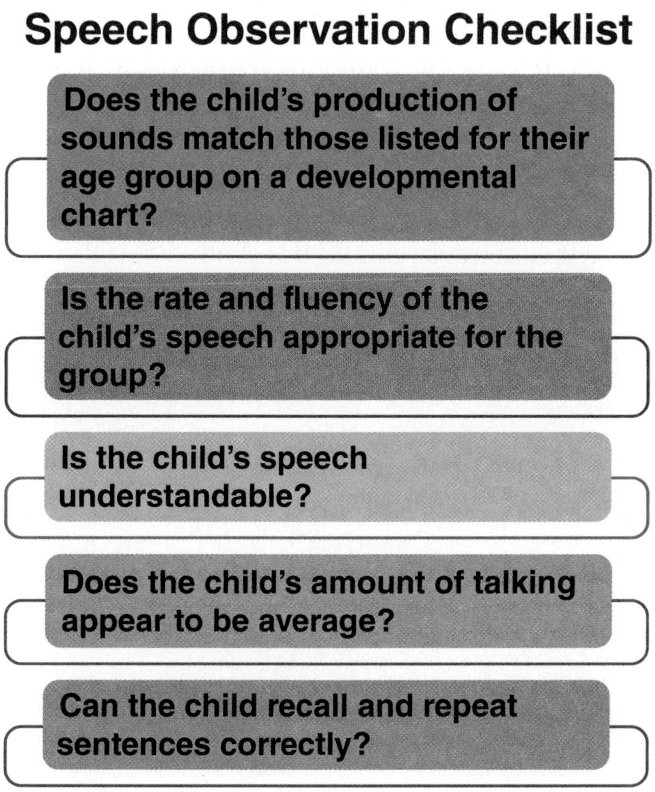

Speech Observation Checklist

Does the child's production of sounds match those listed for their age group on a developmental chart?

Is the rate and fluency of the child's speech appropriate for the group?

Is the child's speech understandable?

Does the child's amount of talking appear to be average?

Can the child recall and repeat sentences correctly?

Figure 31.7 Informal observations are the most common method used to identify communication problems.

will need to listen carefully as a child speaks, listening to both sounds and content.

At one to two years of age, children typically can make *p, b, m, n, t*, and *d* sounds. By three to four years-of-age, the child has added the k, g, f, s, y, and *d* sounds. The child's speech may be unclear to unclear to people who do not know them well. By five years of age, the child can say the following sounds *"sh", "ch", j, z, l*. Now the child's speech is usually easy to understand.

When a child is having trouble articulating words, record those sounds causing difficulty. Young children find the consonants *p, b, m, w*, and vowels the easiest to articulate. *Cr, bl, sh, ch, th, j, r, l*, and z are hard sounds to articulate and take longer to learn.

Observe and listen to children in a variety of settings: on the playground, in the dramatic play area, during lunchtime, and as they converse with others. As you identify a problem, record those sounds causing difficulty and continue observing to collect information.

A child's communication is usually impaired when it is so different from other children's that it calls attention to itself. Communication problems can also interfere with conversation and cause children to be self-conscious (**Figure 31.8**). If, after repeated observations, you conclude that a child likely has a communication problem, share your observations with your director. The center director will determine whether a parent conference should be scheduled. If the

director schedules a meeting with the parents or guardians, a follow-up appointment may be scheduled with an audiologist or speech pathologist. A **speech pathologist** assesses people with speech and language disorders; an **audiologist** identifies, assesses, and manages hearing disorders.

Types of Communication Disorders

Communication disorders can fall into many categories. Many disorders are *speech impairments*, which means they are interferences with specific sounds or sound blends. These impairments result in sounds that are missing, inappropriate, or irregular. Types of communication disorders and speech impairments include articulation problems, voice (phonation) disorders, and stuttering.

Articulation Problems

Articulation problems, often referred to as *lazy tongue* and *baby talk*, are most often omission errors, distortion problems, or substitutions of vowels or consonants or both. Articulation problems include slow, labored speech, and rapid and slurred speech. An articulation problem can result from hearing loss or lack of tongue and mouth control.

In an *omission error*, certain speech sounds are left out, distorted, or added. As a result, only a part of a word is said. For example, a child may say "oat" instead of "boat." The child may say "had" instead of the name "Thad."

A child with a *distortion problem* sometimes has trouble identifying and producing the intended sound. For example, instead of pronouncing an "s", a child may suck air in between their teeth.

Substitutions involve speech patterns such as substituting "thome" for "some" or "tate" for "cake." The most common sound substitutions include *f* for *th, t* for *k, b* for *v, th* for *s, k* for *t*, and *w* for *l* or *r*. One common substitution problem is referred to as a *lisp*. It involves substituting the *th* sound for the letter *s*.

Dragon Images/Shutterstock.com

Figure 31.8 Children who have communication problems may feel self-conscious and avoid talking.

After a child has been diagnosed as having an articulation problem, a speech clinician should be consulted. This professional will provide direct therapy and advise you. You should ask the speech clinician for advice on how to help the child.

As a teacher, your reaction to a child with articulation problems has a considerable effect. To help a child feel secure, always react positively. Ensure that other children do, too. If a child does not respond verbally, do not demand a response. Instead, provide the correct answer for him or her.

Model good listening skills and speaking skills. Use slow, deliberate speech and give the child your total attention. Look directly into the child's face as they speak (**Figure 31.9**). Verbally respond with interest to what the child is saying. If you do not understand, ask the child to repeat what they said.

Children with articulation problems need encouragement to talk. Set an example by incorporating language into activities. For example, you may say to a child, "You are placing a large red block in the square hole" as they play with a sorting box.

Use language that is proper for the child's developmental level. For example, the child may point to a large red car and say "far." You should then reframe what the child said by saying, "That is a large red car." This technique is called *expansion*. It involves taking the child's mispronounced words and correctly expanding them into sentences. Some children are more comfortable talking about objects or activities that are special to them. For example, you could have the child bring something special from home. Then have the child tell everyone about the item.

Always provide a variety of activities in your classroom. The wider the variety, the more children will have to talk about. Try to relate classroom activities to children's home experiences and cultural backgrounds.

Demand communication from all children, including those with articulation problems. Do this by asking open-ended questions. Instead of asking "Did you like the book?" ask "What did you like about the book?" During group time, however, exercise caution. Questioning can place stress on a child with a disability.

Voice (Phonation) Disorders

A person's voice involves pitch, loudness, flexibility, and quality. The lowness or highness of a voice is the *pitch*. It is not uncommon for some children to use a pitch that is too low or too high. These disorders occur less frequently than most speech problems.

Loudness is related to the amount of energy or volume used when speaking. A voice may be powerful or weak. A powerful voice will be loud and can be disturbing. A weak voice may be hard to hear and can also hinder communication.

A good speaking voice during routine conversation uses a variety of pitches and loudness levels. This is referred to as *voice flexibility*. Changes in pitch and loudness often reflect the emotions of the speaker.

Voice quality refers to the clarity of a voice. Harshness, hoarseness, breathiness, and nasality are all voice-quality disorders. A harsh voice is often louder than normal. Hoarseness may indicate a problem in the throat. A breathy voice sounds like a whisper, weak and not clearly phonated. Nasality is a condition in which sound passes through the nasal cavities instead of the throat.

FatCamera/E+ via Getty Images

Figure 31.9 Modeling good listening and speaking skills can help children who have articulation problems. ***What are two actions teachers can take to model good listening and speaking skills?***

With speech therapy and medical assistance, most voice disorders are treatable. To help prevent or correct voice disorders, promote voice control in the classroom. You can do this by:

- Encouraging children to use the correct voice volume during indoor play. You may need to say, "Teddy, you need to use your indoor voice in the building."
- Discouraging children from screaming or yelling too much during outdoor play.
- Modeling good voice characteristics. Your own voice should be the proper pitch, loudness, quality, and flexibility.

Stuttering

Stuttering in young children is often characterized by repetition, hesitation, and prolongation. While between the ages of two and five, most children may stutter slightly. Few young children stutter all the time. Most children only stutter under certain conditions, such as when they feel pressured (**Figure 31.10**).

Children who stutter function best in a warm, noncritical classroom. This type of environment helps all children speak with confidence. If you have a stuttering child in your classroom, focus on creating positive speaking conditions by:

- planning activities so all children will experience success and praising the children;

fizkes/Shutterstock.com

Figure 31.10   Children who feel pressured are more likely to stutter than children who are relaxed. ***What type of environment helps children who stutter speak with confidence?***

- providing children with enough time to say what they have to say;
- giving the child your undivided attention and using body language to show you have time to listen;
- listening closely to what the children are saying as opposed to focusing on the stuttering; and
- avoiding rushing children through a task. Do not complete a word or sentence for a child.

Unfortunately, many well-meaning adults try to provide directions to a child who stutters. "Stop and think," "Start over," and "Speak slower" are common examples. These suggestions often make the child feel even more fearful. A child's difficulty could continue because of this fear. An environment free of pressure is important. Speech therapy may be necessary when stuttering is severe.

31.2-3 Visual Impairments

The term **visual impairment** refers to any eye or nerve problem that prevents people from seeing normally. Vision problems, including amblyopia, nearsightedness, farsightedness, crossed eyes, and lazy eye, are seen in almost 20 percent of children. A color deficiency is also identified in some children. Physically, children with visual impairments are like children with normal vision; however, this disability can limit motor abilities as they take part in some physical activities.

To understand visual impairments, understand how a healthy visual system works. A person's eye does not actually *see*. Rather, the purpose of the eye is to take in light. After taking in light, the eye transmits impulses to the brain through the optic nerve. The brain then decodes visual stimuli, and "seeing" takes place. Most defects of the eye itself are correctable. If the brain or the optic nerve is damaged, however, a visual impairment may not be correctable.

Identification

Early identification of a visual impairment is important. Many early learning centers recruit a volunteer from the National Society for the Prevention of Blindness, a county or city health nurse, or some other professional to conduct a visual screening on children each year (**Figure 31.11**). Children who appear to have limited vision are referred to an eye specialist for an exam. Classroom staff should study children closely to identify vision problems. Certain symptoms may suggest problems, such as:

- excessive rubbing of the eyes;
- head tilting to look at things in front;
- short attention span;
- clumsiness and trouble moving around the classroom;
- poor hand-eye coordination;
- adjusting the head in an awkward position to view materials;
- moving materials so they are close to or far away from the eyes;
- squinting;
- frequent headaches;
- crust on the eyes;
- iris on one or both eyes appearing cloudy;
- crossed eyes or an eye that turns inward;
- red, encrusted, or swollen eyelids;
- excessive blinking; and
- inability to recognize a person or object at a distance.

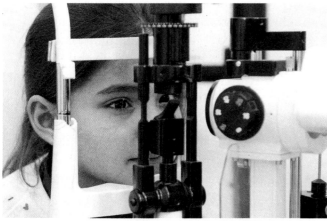

Peakstock/Shutterstock.com

Figure 31.11 Annual eye exams can mean early detection of visual impairments. *What types of vision impairments may affect children?*

Types of Visual Impairments

Many types of visual impairments exist in children. Knowing the types of impairments can help you identify and understand children's vision problems. Visual impairments in children include amblyopia, glaucoma, nearsightedness, farsightedness, color deficiency, and other uncorrectable conditions.

Amblyopia

Amblyopia, often called *lazy eye*, occurs in children younger than nine years of age. It is characterized by decreased vision in one eye. A disorder results from muscle imbalance caused by the disuse of an eye. Amblyopia occurs when the pathways between the eye and brain are not properly stimulated. Symptoms may include a wandering eye or the eyes may not appear to work together. It is one of several visual conditions that can be corrected if treated before the child is six years old. To force the use of the weaker eye, professionals place a patch over the stronger eye. The child will then wear corrective lenses when the strength is even in both eyes.

Glaucoma

Glaucoma is a condition caused by the failure of eye fluid to circulate properly. This results in increased pressure on the eye. Over time, this will destroy the optic nerve. Glaucoma that occurs before three years of age is called childhood glaucoma. If diagnosed early, this condition can be treated with medicated eye drops. Treatment can prevent loss of vision.

Nearsightedness

Some children can see things close up but have problems seeing things at a distance. Objects will appear blurred. These children are *nearsighted*. The medical term for this visual disorder is *myopia*. Myopia happens when the eye focuses in front of the retina instead of directly on it. If myopia is severe, a child must wear glasses with corrective lenses.

Farsightedness

Children who are farsighted see objects at a distance more easily, but they have difficulty seeing objects close to them. The medical term for this visual disorder is *hyperopia*. Hyperopia happens when visual images are focused behind the retina. Until age seven, most children have a small degree of farsightedness. If this problem is severe, a child will need to wear corrective lenses. **Figure 31.12** demonstrates how nearsightedness and farsightedness are caused by visual images focused on the retina.

Color Deficiency

Children with color blindness see colors differently than most people. *Color deficiency*, or *color blindness* as it is sometimes called, is the decreased ability to see or discriminate three qualities of color—brightness, saturation, and hue. Color deficiency is hereditary, meaning it is passed down through parents. The deficiency mostly affects white males, about one in 12, and is caused by a recessive gene. You should be able to quickly identify children with color deficiencies. They cannot recognize one or more primary colors. Children with color deficiency have the most difficulty distinguishing red and green, so reading traffic lights can be difficult for them. They also have trouble selecting a banana since a green and yellow one appears the same. They may also reject eating some food as the color looks like feces.

Uncorrectable Conditions

There are several visual disorders that glasses, surgery, or other means of treatment cannot correct. Any damage to the optic nerve by disease or trauma is an example. After damage, signals do not get to the brain to provide the child with sight.

Teaching Suggestions

You may need to make changes in your classroom depending on the visual needs of the children. When teaching children with vision loss, consider the following strategies:

- Always create a need to see. For instance, if children who are farsighted refuse to wear glasses, provide them with materials that have fine detail and print. The children will then realize the importance of wearing their glasses (**Figure 31.13**).

- When ordering dry-erase boards, purchase those with a dull finish. Glare can be very tiring for children who are partially sighted.

- Use colored markers on whiteboards.

- Hang children's work at their eye level so they can see what is displayed.

- Safety is important, so blocks, cars, and other items should always be picked up right after play.

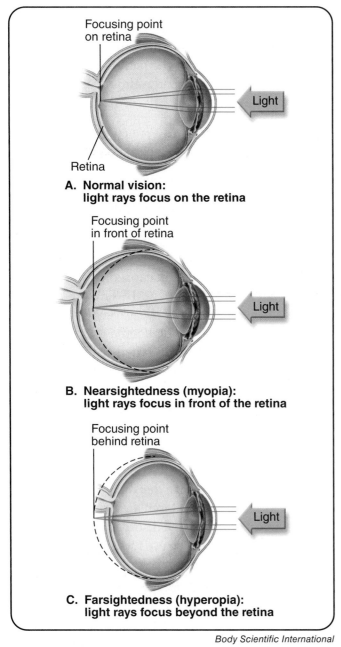

Focusing point on retina

Light

Retina

A. Normal vision:
light rays focus on the retina

Focusing point in front of retina

Light

B. Nearsightedness (myopia):
light rays focus in front of the retina

Focusing point behind retina

Light

C. Farsightedness (hyperopia):
light rays focus beyond the retina

Body Scientific International

Figure 31.12   Visual images focusing incorrectly on the retina cause nearsightedness and farsightedness.

Nikhil Patil/iStock via Getty Images Plus

Figure 31.13 Make sure children who need glasses understand the importance of wearing them at all times. ***How can teachers encourage children to wear their glasses?***

- Auditory clues are important for children with vision loss. Provide a comfortable environment by keeping the noise level low.

- Regulate light levels by adding additional lighting to areas where the children work.

- Choose large-print books with high-contrast, clear pictures.

- Provide Braille books for blind children to follow along while the teacher reads to the class.

- Provide many *tactile* (touch), *olfactory* (smell), and *auditory* (sound) clues to structure the environment for children. For instance, use a piece of shag carpeting in the story area and a bubbling aquarium or fragrant flowers in the science area.

- Use auditory reminders for transitions. These may include singing a song, beating a drum, playing a piano, or hitting tone bells.

- During activities, always encourage children to describe what they remember using their senses.

Remember that children with vision loss may need to learn some skills children with normal vision already have. For instance, children with normal vision gain eating, toileting, and dressing skills by watching others. A child who has vision loss, however, may not possess these skills when they come to the center. You will need to teach

these skills. You will also need to teach the child about classroom areas. Do this by repeatedly guiding the child from one area to another.

Once a child has been prescribed glasses, your challenge will be to keep them on their face. During the adjustment period to the new correction, the child's brain will need to recalibrate it. Gradually the brain will build up acceptance. For this reason, a doctor prescribing the first lenses may not correct to full strength. This build-up will occur over time.

31.2-4 Physical Disabilities

Most preschool children can crawl, walk, run, climb, and move their bodies in different ways. A child with a physical impairment, however, may have a limited range of motion. Because of this limitation, his or her experiences may vary from those of his or her peers. Physical disabilities are more straightforward to identify since they are often observable or result in observable changes in behavior. The surest way to identify a physical disability is to know about the physical disabilities common among young children.

Types of Physical Disabilities

Physical disabilities are orthopedic impairments of the muscles, joints, and bones that may cause spina bifida, cerebral palsy, arthritis, and spinal cord damage. Children with physical disabilities are grouped based on their abilities to function. Physical disabilities are classified as severe, moderate, or mild. Children with severe disability cannot usually move independently. Typically, they have to be carried, pushed, or moved about using a wheelchair (**Figure 31.14**). Children with moderate disability can do more for themselves, but they still require much help from staff members. Because of their need for accessible facilities and adaptations, children with severe or moderate physical disability are rarely enrolled in nonadaptive early childhood centers.

Children with mild physical disabilities can often do what most other children do. These children may need to use walking aids or other devices to help them move about. Usually, they will need more time to move or complete tasks.

SDI Productions/E+ Getty Images

Figure 31.14 Children with severe physical disabilities may use a wheelchair or other adaptive equipment.

Most children you will meet in the typical early childhood center will be **ambulatory**, meaning they can move from place to place. You may elect, however, to work in a center that caters to children with disabilities. In these centers, you will observe a higher staff-child ratio. This is necessary to meet the disability needs of these children. Many types of physical disabilities affect young children. Some that you may encounter include cerebral palsy, spina bifida, muscular dystrophy, and amputation.

Cerebral Palsy

Cerebral palsy is a neurological disorder that affects movement, posture, and balance, which results from damage to certain parts of the brain. Cerebral palsy usually causes paralysis and uncontrollable muscle movement in particular body parts. An infection or improper nutrition during pregnancy, physical injury to the brain during birth, or lack of oxygen during birth can cause this damage. It can also be acquired during the developmental years because of a tumor, head injury, or brain infection.

Children with cerebral palsy often have speech or expressive communication problems. Their inabilities to control the muscles used to make speech sounds cause these problems. If a child in your center has a speech disorder, consult with the child's family and a speech clinician. A child with severe cerebral palsy may benefit from use of an *augmentative communication device* such

as a board containing pictures of common objects. For example, the child can point to a picture of a glass of milk when thirsty.

Children with cerebral palsy also often lack fine-motor skills. Many of their self-help skills are impaired. Eating utensils and other equipment may be difficult for them to use. An occupational therapist and the child's parents or guardians can best advise what type of eating utensils, crayons, and other items are most useful. Modifications may be necessary on equipment. For example, glue large wooden knobs on puzzles so the child with cerebral palsy can remove and insert the pieces. A wide range of adaptive toys and personal care devices are available (**Figure 31.15**). Consult your nearest rehabilitation technology center for suggested adaptive aids.

Spina Bifida

Spina bifida is a defect that occurs at birth in which the bones of the spine fail to grow together, thus exposing the nerves. Nerve exposure results in paralysis. Spina bifida is a congenital problem, and its cause is unknown. Children with this problem often lack bowel and bladder control. They cannot tell when they have eliminated because of lower-body paralysis. Most children with spina bifida can walk for short distances

jarenwicklund/iStock via Getty Images Plus

Figure 31.15 Many personal care devices, such as adaptive writing utensils, are available for children with cerebral palsy. *Investigate adaptive devices online. As a teacher, what other devices might you find useful for the classroom?*

using crutches, canes, or braces. For longer distances, a wheelchair may be required.

For a child with spina bifida to focus on learning activities, they need to feel comfortable. These children need encouragement. Ask them questions such as, "Are you comfortable?" or "Do you want to sit another way?" To provide the best environment for this child, discuss positions with the parents or guardians and physical therapists. They may suggest positions that will provide the child with a sense of balance. Specific questions you may want to ask them include "Should learning activities be on the floor or table?" and "Should the classroom tables be modified?"

Muscular Dystrophy

Muscular dystrophy is a genetic condition characterized by weakness in the muscles. This results in a progressive loss of muscle tissue, especially in the legs, chest, and arms. Some children with muscular dystrophy can control their finger and hand muscles. Their fine-motor muscles skills are more easily retained and exercised than gross-motor muscles.

When working with a child with this disability, it is important to interact closely with the professionals who work with the family. There are certain therapeutic techniques that can be taught to families and caregivers. Active exercises for stretching the child's weakened muscles might help delay some of the progression.

Amputation

At some point, you may have a child in your classroom who is missing a hand, arm, or leg. Perhaps the severed limb resulted from an accident or cancer. Sometimes the limb is missing from birth. Doctors often fit a child with an artificial limb called a *prosthesis*. Research shows that young children can easily adjust to an artificial limb.

A prosthesis must fit and be cared for properly. To avoid frustrating the child, you, as a teacher, will need to know how the artificial limb works. Parents or guardians usually welcome a teacher's questions related to the device. In fact, these questions assure them of your interest in

providing the best care for their child. Other children will model their teacher's matter-of-fact acceptance of a prosthesis.

Teaching Suggestions

Although it is difficult for some, movement is important for all children. Children with physical disabilities have uncertain motor skills. They may have to crawl or move with special adaptive mobility equipment, such as wheelchairs, braces, or walkers (**Figure 31.16**). As a result, they need more time and energy for fine- and gross-motor tasks. These children will take longer to use the bathroom or finish a project. To allow for this, the classroom schedule may need to be altered. You

ktaylorg/E+ via Getty Images

Figure 31.16 Children with physical disabilities may move with the help of braces, walkers, crutches, or wheelchairs. Center staff should take care to be accessible to these children. *What accommodations and modifications might a teacher need to make in the classroom?*

may also have to make other adjustments, such as the following, in your facility:

- modify chairs to accommodate the child;
- provide space for a child's wheelchair, crutches, cane, walker, or cart;
- provide ramps so the child has access to the classroom;
- raise tables so wheelchairs fit under them;
- glue knobs on puzzle pieces so the pieces are easy to remove and replace;
- secure all carpeting or area rugs to the floor so the child does not slip or trip on them;
- provide two-handled mugs and deep-sided bowls rather than plates; and
- serve finger foods as often as possible at snack time.

Lesson 31.2 Review

1. A child with mild to moderate hearing loss is considered _____. (31.2.1)
   A. deaf
   B. heard of hearing
   C. a hearing threshold test
   D. untreatable
2. Some hard-of-hearing children may be sensitive to _____. (31.2.1)
   A. bright lights
   B. strong smells
   C. background sounds
   D. acidic foods
3. A child with a(n) _____ sometimes has trouble identifying and producing the intended sound. (31.2.2)
   A. omission error
   B. stutter
   C. phonation disorder
   D. distortion problem
4. _____ is the ability to use a variety of pitches and loudness levels when speaking. (31.2.2)
   A. Voice flexibility
   B. Pitch
   C. Voice quality
   D. Vocal range
5. Amblyopia is often called _____ and results from muscle imbalance caused by the disuse of an eye. (31.2.3)
   A. nearsightedness
   B. color blindness
   C. lazy eye
   D. farsightedness
6. **True or False.** Physical disabilities are more difficult to identify in young children since they do not result in observable changes in behavior. (31.2.4)

Health, Learning, and Behavior Needs

Essential Question

What should you know about health conditions, learning needs, and behavioral needs of children to implement strategies to meeting their needs?

Learning Outcomes

After studying this lesson, you will be able to

31.3-1 **summarize** health conditions that may impact children and strategies for meeting their health needs.

31.3.2 **describe** intellectual disabilities and their impact on children.

31.3-3 **summarize** learning disabilities, their impact on children, and strategies for working with children.

31.3-4 **explain** behavior disorders and their impact on children, including attention deficit disorder and attention deficit hyperactivity disorder.

31.3-5 **summarize** autism spectrum disorder, how it impacts children, and strategies for working with children who have this disorder.

31.3-6 **describe** giftedness, how to identify giftedness, and strategies teachers can use to support learning for children who are gifted.

31.3-7 **describe** strategies for integrating children with disabilities into a typical program.

Key Terms

chronic health needs
hemophilia
learning disability
behavioral disorder
autism spectrum disorder (ASD)
giftedness
acceleration
enrichment
asynchronous development
inclusion

Teachers need to be prepared to integrate children with health, learning, and behavior needs into their programs. Health needs are the most common type of disability in an early childhood program, and allergies are the most common health problem. Other health needs are childhood asthma, cystic fibrosis, diabetes, epilepsy, hemophilia, and pediatric leukemia. With health needs, teachers need to be prepared to handle seizures and other medical emergencies. Autism spectrum disorder and behavioral disorders are other forms of disabilities. Children who are gifted also have special needs. As a teacher, you will need to develop effective classroom strategies for working with children with these disabilities.

31.3-1 Health Conditions

Not all physical problems that affect children are physical disabilities. Some children have chronic health needs. A **chronic health need** is an illness that persists over a period of time. For some children, a problem may last a lifetime, while for others, it may last a few months.

Children with health impairments often have cycles of good and poor health. Since health needs are the most common type of diverse abilities, you should be aware of a variety of these disorders.

Allergies

The most common health problem in young children is allergies. An allergy may begin at any age, including adulthood. Researchers have estimated that as many as 40 percent of children may have nasal allergies. Over the last two decades, allergic conditions have increased significantly.

An *allergy* is a defensive reaction of the body's immune system to a harmless substance in the environment. The offending substance is called an *allergen*. Exposure to an allergen may cause rashes, swelling, sneezing, or other reactions (**Figure 31.17**). There are four categories of allergenic substances: inhalants, ingestants, contactants, and injectables. *Inhalants* are airborne substances that are inhaled. *Ingestants* are foods, drugs, or anything taken through the mouth. *Contactants* are substances that make contact with the body through touch. *Injectables* are chemicals or drugs injected into the body.

Animal dandruff, dust, feathers, fungi spores, molds, and plant pollens are types of airborne allergenic substances. If a child in your classroom has a severe allergy to animal dandruff or urine, you may have to remove any hamsters, mice, gerbils, guinea pigs, or rabbits. Typical foods to which the body reacts include beans, berries, chocolate, cinnamon, citrus fruits, corn products, cola drinks, eggs, fish, shellfish, tree nuts, milk, tomatoes, nuts, and wheat. Fabric dyes and fragrances or colorings added to soaps and shampoos are contactants that may also cause reactions. Aspirin, penicillin, and sulfa drugs are common drugs that are offenders. It is important that you ask parents at the time of enrollment whether their children have any known allergies.

If a child has food allergies, you will need to plan accordingly. Try to plan menus that avoid foods to which the child is allergic. You may have to offer food substitutes to the child with allergies. For instance, if a child has an allergy to milk, supply a substitute beverage. Many times, parents will provide the substitute to ensure their child has no temptation to have cow's milk.

Cosmetics, some detergents, wool, and starch are all substances that may cause an allergic reaction when they come in contact with the skin. Common reactions include a red rash and itching. These symptoms are a warning for the child to avoid contact with whatever substance caused the problem.

Some substances cause a reaction when they enter the body through the skin. Examples include the drug penicillin and the venom from bee or wasp stings. You need to be keenly aware of insect bites. For some children, these bites can be fatal. Bee or wasp stings usually result in redness and swelling around the wound. Usually this indicates only a mild allergy. With a severe allergy, the child may swell all over the body and have trouble breathing. If this should occur, promptly seek medical attention. Death can result if they do not immediately receive treatment.

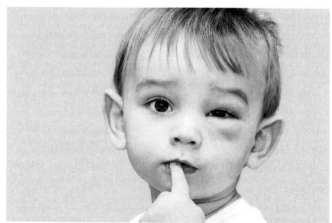

benedamiroslav/iStock via Getty Images Plus

Figure 31.17 An allergic reaction to insect bites on this child's face has caused swelling and skin irritation.

Some symptoms of allergies may be related to the season. For example, a child who is allergic to tree pollens may sneeze often in the spring. There are three major pollen seasons: early spring with tree pollens, late spring or early summer with grass pollens, and late summer and fall with weed pollens.

You may be the first to suspect allergies in a young child. **Figure 31.18** lists allergy symptoms. If you suspect a child has an allergy, discuss it with their parents or guardians.

You may be responsible for some aspects of treatment for children with allergies. There are three basic treatment methods for people with allergies. The sensitive person may avoid the allergy triggers. For instance, if a child is allergic to chocolate, avoid foods with chocolate. If the person cannot avoid the irritant, they may be *desensitized*. In this process, a doctor injects small amounts of the purified allergen into the body over a period of a few years. This builds immunities so the person can eventually withstand the irritant. Finally, depending on the symptoms, medication may be necessary to use. For example, the doctor might prescribe an over-the-counter medication for a person who has nasal congestion or a cough, such as a nasal spray, liquid, pills, or eye drops.

Children with severe allergic reactions or anaphylaxis need to carry an emergency epinephrine shot at all times. Often it is kept in a fanny pack, which makes it readily available. The shot can reduce or stop the reaction until emergency services arrive. All staff should have training to correctly administer the epinephrine shot. Be sure to check state licensing requirements.

Childhood Arthritis

Childhood arthritis is a condition brought on by chronic inflammation that produces painful swelling of the joints and surrounding tissues. The most common form of childhood arthritis is *rheumatoid arthritis*, which occurs when the body's immune system attacks its own cells and tissues. General fatigue, loss of appetite, fever, aching joints, and a stiffness of joints as they become tender from swelling are the first signs of the disease. Sometimes symptoms flare up and then disappear.

Allergy Symptoms

Body Part	Symptoms
Eyes	• pink and puffy • red from being constantly rubbed • dark circles underneath • burning feeling and watery with much tearing • lids may appear glued together by dry mucus
Skin	• frequent rashes • lesions • redness and swelling • itching and hives • blistery, swollen, or peeling
Mouth	• constant, dry hacking cough from postnasal drip • mouth breathing more common than nose breathing • wheezing • tingling • canker sores
Throat	• tickling or soreness • enlargement of lymph nodes
Nose	• inability to smell • inflammation • stuffy with nasal congestion and discharge • frequent sneezing • itchiness
Body	• chills, fever, or sweating • fatigue • light headiness • dizziness • abdominal cramps • vomiting • headache

Figure 31.18 Children can be allergic to a variety of substances or have seasonal allergies. Contact the parents or guardians if you notice these symptoms.

In children with arthritis, symptoms may come and go. They may complain of joint pain or have a limp. It is hard for the child to stay in one position for long periods of time. In the mornings or after naptime, they may lack dexterity or nimbleness. As a result, they require more space and time to move freely from one place to another. Adaptive toys, utensils, and clothing may be necessary. Activities requiring fine-motor dexterity, such as cutting paper or stringing beads, can be troublesome. Rheumatoid arthritis is typically most acute in the morning and subsides somewhat during the day. Physical activity can improve the lives of children with arthritis as it can help manage diabetes and excessive weight gain. When the disease is in its active stage, the child will need more rest.

Childhood Asthma

Asthma is a chronic inflammatory disorder of the airways that has no cure. This condition causes airways to narrow, swell, and produce extra mucus, triggering symptoms that range from mild to severe. Symptoms include coughing, wheezing, rapid or labored breathing, shortness of breath, and chest tightness. When symptoms occur, this is called an *asthma attack*, which may last minutes, hours, or weeks. Some children have a decrease in symptoms as they get older, but others do not.

Exposure to allergens, such as mold, pollen, animal dander and dust mites can trigger an asthma attack. Exposure to extreme cold or hot weather, overexertion, or excessive exercise can also cause asthma attaches. Asthma attacks are a leading cause of missed school days, emergency visits, and hospitalizations. Medications can be used to treat asthma, which are usually given in a fast-acting inhaler or a nebulizer machine (**Figure 31.19**). If the inhaled medicine does not provide relief or the child stops breathing, this is a medical emergency. You must call 911!

Depending on the severity of the disease, some children take daily medications to reduce inflammation of the airways. These medications might be a pill or an inhaler. Their purpose is to prevent attacks. Once an attack has begun, these medications provide little or no relief.

As the teacher, you should ask the parents to provide you with an asthma plan, which will help you monitor the systems. Your role might be to administer medications and to monitor the child's breathing. Try to teach the child to let you know

Nataly Belobritskaya/iStock via Getty Images Plus

Figure 31.19   A nebulizer is a machine that turns liquid medicine into a fine mist. A person with asthma can inhale the mist through the tube and mask. ***What is the role of the teacher in working with children who have asthma?***

when symptoms occur. If the child does not seem to be breathing well, take action immediately. Keep calm during the attack and help the child stay calm, too.

Ask the parents what triggers their child's asthma and try to prevent these conditions. For example, if exposure to dust is a serious trigger, be sure to keep your classroom as dust-free as possible.

Cystic Fibrosis

Cystic fibrosis is genetic disorder that causes problems with breathing and digestion that can occur almost from birth. Other people may not experience symptoms until adolescence or adulthood. This chronic condition involves persistent and serious lung infections; failure to gain weight; and loose, foul-smelling stools. A thick, sticky mucus produced in the sweat glands makes it difficult to breathe and cause some of these symptoms. This mucus interferes with the digestive and respiratory systems The mucus is also a breeding ground for fungi and bacteria.

Some parents do not enroll their child with cystic fibrosis in an early childhood program. This is because they fear the risks of developing lung infections, such as pneumonia. These children must receive treatment under the close supervision of a doctor. If children with cystic fibrosis are enrolled, they need frequent rest and a lot of fluids. They may also need to urinate frequently. The teacher should consult with the child's doctor and parents for specific care plans.

Diabetes

Juvenile diabetes is a hereditary disease, and the exact causes of the disease are unknown. It is also known as Type 1 diabetes and affects children and adults. It is a condition in which the body no longer produces insulin, which is an important hormone needed to survive. Common symptoms of diabetes include frequent urination, loss of weight, constant hunger, itching (especially around the groin), and slow-healing cuts and bruises. It is possible, however, that some children with the condition will not show any obvious symptoms.

In juvenile diabetes, the pancreas does not produce enough insulin to burn or store foods as energy. This causes the body's sugar content to increase, which increases the sugar level of the blood. When blood passes through the kidneys, the sugar is excreted in urine. Over time, this loss of carbohydrates is damaging to the body. If diabetes is uncontrolled, it can be fatal.

A careful diet is extremely important for treating diabetes. A balance of proteins, fats, carbohydrates, vitamins, and minerals is necessary. In most cases of juvenile diabetes, children need insulin injections. These are prescribed by a doctor and are usually given by the parents. Blood sugar levels may need to be checked with special medical equipment. This keeps the parents informed so they can better control the child's health.

To maintain blood sugar levels, it is necessary to balance physical activity, insulin, and diet. The child's parents and doctor must devise a plan for this. Follow this plan as closely as possible. Imbalances that occur are called *insulin reactions*. A reaction may include trembling, dizziness, headache, confusion, sweating, fatigue, and weakness.

In an insulin reaction, the body needs sugar right away to keep it from slipping into shock or a coma. For this reason, keep fast sources of sugar—such as orange juice or candy, or fast-acting glucose gel or tablets—with you at all times in case an insulin reaction occurs. If the child passes out as the result of an insulin reaction, call 911 or rush the child to the emergency room. This is a medical emergency. Several teaching suggestions are important when children with diabetes are enrolled in the program. See **Figure 31.20.**

Epilepsy

Epilepsy is a central nervous system, neurological disorder, which affects about one percent of the population of all races and ethnic backgrounds. Epilepsy disturbs the electrical rhythms of the central nervous system, causing seizures or periods of unusual behavior and sometimes loss of awareness. Epilepsy is not a disease.

Suggestions for Teaching Children with Diabetes

Ask the parents how to handle emergencies. Have them put these recommendations in writing. Place this information in the child's file.

Schedule snacks and lunch at the same time each day.

Ensure children with diabetes follow eating, medication, and activity plans daily.

Keep fast-acting carbs, such as juice boxes or candy, on hand that will raise blood sugar levels quickly if an insulin reaction occurs.

Provide information for substitute teachers in a file.

Notify parents in advance of parties, special events, or changes in the schedule.

Take the child immediately to a hospital emergency room if they become unconscious.

Figure 31.20 The child's parents or guardians will work with their doctor to devise a plan to help balance physical activity, diet, and insulin. ***What is the teacher's role in following this plan?***

Epilepsy can cause varying degrees of reactions or seizures. *Petit mal seizures* involve the convulsion of a part of the body. This type of seizure results in reactions that many times go unnoticed. Often, the only visible signs are the fluttering of the eyelids, frozen postures, a staring spell, and a temporary stop in activity. This type of seizure may only last five to ten seconds. As a teacher, you may not always notice a petit mal seizure. You may notice that the child's behavior is unusual or that he or she may not be paying attention. During the seizure, the child may have only a brief lapse of consciousness. Most of these seizures do not require medical attention.

Grand mal seizures are much more pronounced. This type of seizure involves the complete body

in a convulsion. During a grand mal seizure, a child will lose consciousness or awareness. They may also jerk, thrash, or become stiff. The child may be injured by falling and hitting objects or biting their tongue. When the child regains consciousness, they may be confused. In fact, they may not remember the seizure. Instead, the child may get up and continue with classroom activities.

Treatment for epilepsy is primarily with drugs, although sometimes surgery can control seizures. Drugs will either prevent or reduce the frequency of the seizures. Unfortunately, many drugs for epilepsy cause serious side effects, such as restlessness and lethargic behavior. Work with the child's parents and have them make a seizure action plan for you.

There may be times when you, as a teacher, have to handle a seizure. If a child falls, you should:

1. Call 911 immediately if it is a first-time seizure.
2. Let the child remain on the floor, clearing the area to provide ample room to thrash.
3. Remain calm and matter of fact.
4. Cradle the child's head in your lap. Avoid restraining movement.
5. After the seizure, turn the child's face to the side to maintain an open airway, allowing saliva to drain from the mouth. This should prevent the child from choking on secretions.
6. Never place your finger or other object in the child's mouth. This can cause injury.
7. Use your watch and time the episode. If the convulsion does not stop within two minutes, call for emergency medical help.
8. After the child regains consciousness, allow the child to remain lying down. Usually, the child is tired and wants to rest. Place a blanket over the child and allow them to sleep.
9. Call the child's doctor and family to inform them of the seizure and ask for advice regarding further actions.

Hemophilia

Hemophilia is a genetic blood disease almost always occurring in males. Most forms are hereditary. Hemophilia is a lifelong condition in which blood clots too slowly or not at all because it does not have enough blood-clotting proteins. Children with hemophilia may experience extreme internal bleeding and large deep bruising from simply bumping against something. This causes pain and swelling in the joints that may require a stay in the hospital. The real threat, however, is death caused by internal bleeding of vital organs or by blood flowing into air passages.

With the help of the parent(s), decide what equipment is safe for the child to use. You should:

- tag outdoor and indoor equipment the child can use;

- ask the parent or guardians what to do if the child is injured; and

- carefully monitor the child's play to prevent accidents.

FatCamera/E+ via Getty Images

Figure 31.21   Leukemia is the most common childhood cancer.

Workplace Connections

Child Life Specialist

The number of child life specialist positions is increasing as every children's hospital in North America has them on staff. Contact an area hospital that employs a child life specialist and arrange for an interview. Ask them:

1. What chronic health disorders affect most of the specialist's patients?
2. What services do they provide?
3. What educational preparation is necessary to become a child life specialist?

Pediatric Leukemia

Luis has the most common form of childhood cancer (**Figure 31.21**), which at one time was incurable. Today most children experience a lifelong cure. Pediatric leukemia is a cancer of the blood-forming tissues, which starts in the bone marrow. The number of abnormal white blood cells rapidly builds and crowds out normal blood cells. When this occurs, the number of healthy white blood cells decreases. Other signs and symptoms include bleeding, bruising, fever, infection, and weight loss.

There are two types of leukemia. *Acute* is fast-growing and *chronic* is slower growing. Most childhood cancer is acute, which means the abnormal cells grow quickly and need immediate treatment. Children with leukemia are treated with surgery, radiation therapy or chemotherapy, or target therapy drugs. When able, these children are encouraged to take part in the classroom.

31.3-2 Intellectual Disabilities

The term *intellectual disability* or *cognitive disability* describes a condition that causes intellectual functioning to fall significantly below developmental milestones. Intellectual disabilities may not have a specific cause, or genetic or chromosomal disorders may cause them. Other causes may include prenatal or postnatal injuries or environmental conditions. Intellectual disabilities have varying degrees of severity, as well as many potential causes.

Down syndrome is the most common cause of learning disorders in young children. It is a genetic chromosome disorder caused by a mistake in cell division. This disability is usually diagnosed before or after birth. People with

Down syndrome usually have very distinct physical features, including a small round head with a flattened midface, slightly pugged nose, and protruding tongue (**Figure 31.22**). In addition, individuals with Down syndrome typically have almond shaped eyes, small ears, and short fingers and neck. People with this condition may have low muscle tone so may have trouble holding their heads up. They may also have other physical health problems, such as heart defects, immune disorders, obesity, and sleep apnea. Cardiac problems will claim the lives of many of these children during infancy.

Children with intellectual disabilities may have problems with behavior. Often, it is hard for them to manage their feelings, so they get frustrated. They also may not pay attention and need more direct teaching techniques. Modeling and demonstrating tasks for these children is important. Likewise, these children need more repetitions to learn.

31.3-3 Learning Disabilities

Children who have learning disabilities are present in almost every classroom, even though their disabilities can be hard to define. A **learning disability** refers to a problem with one or more basic skills of learning. Children with learning disabilities, however, usually have average to above-average intellectual functioning.

SDI Productions/E+ via Getty Images

Figure 31.22   Most children with Down syndrome have distinct physical features and happy, loving personalities.

Children with learning disabilities model some common traits, such as delays in meeting developmental milestones. These children may have trouble following directions or have poor memory skills. They tend to like being in constant motion and have short attention spans. After listening to a story, some children with learning disabilities may not remember it. They may have problems storing, processing, and producing information. Other children have problems identifying or reproducing numbers and letters. Poor hand-eye coordination skills in children with learning disabilities may make them reluctant to scribble or draw.

Learning disability traits may occur in varying patterns. As a teacher, you will need to carefully observe all children for signs of possible learning disabilities. Remember, there are distinctive differences in young children. Likewise, there are distinctive differences within a normal range of development. You may find that children who have disabilities in one area of development are developing normally in other areas.

31.3-4 Behavioral Disorders

A **behavioral disorder** is a condition that affects an individual's social, emotional, and cognitive functions. These challenges include attention deficit disorder and attention deficit hyperactivity disorder.

Five to ten percent of school-age children have trouble focusing and staying on task. If children are especially easily distracted, they may have an *attention deficit disorder (ADD)*. Many children with this disorder are also overactive, inattentive, have problems taking turns, talk too much, restless, and impulsive. This condition is called *attention deficit hyperactivity disorder (ADHD)* that begins in childhood. The causes are still unknown, but current research shows that genetics may play an important role. Children with this disorder have hard time resisting temptation and make careless mistakes. Often, such children become hostile and do not follow classroom limits. They also may have difficulty getting along with other children.

Unlike some other disabilities, there is no single test to diagnose attention deficit hyperactivity disorder. It affects more males than females. The parents of preschool children identified as having ADHD are provided training in behavior therapy. Their children are usually treated with a combination of behavior therapy and medication.

31.3-5 Autism Spectrum Disorder (ASD)

Autism spectrum disorder (ASD) describes a set of developmental delays and disorders caused by differences in the brain, also called a *neurodevelopment disorder*. It is a complex disorder that may cause significant social, emotional, behavioral, and communication challenges. There is no cure, it is a lifelong condition, and it is one of the faster-growing disabilities. ASD affects one in 54 children in America, with its symptoms appearing a little different from child to child. People with ASD often have atypical language development, which affects social interaction and communication skills. They may or may not have an intellectual disability, which may be mild to severe. Children with ASD often display ritualistic and compulsive behaviors, although behaviors vary from child to child. Typically, this disorder first becomes noticeable between two and three years of age. Usually, there are more males than females who have ASD.

Because of differences is in the brain, people with the disorder may have a wide range of symptoms ranging from mild to severe. Each child with ASD is unique. One of the early signs of ASD is resistance to hugging or cuddling. When held, these children typically will not mold to the caregiver's body. Likewise, they may not make eye contact or use nonverbal communication. Self-stimulating behaviors such as rocking, head banging, hand flapping, and spinning in circles are characteristic. These children may be nonresponsive to others. Simple changes in routines, such as providing a different type of spoon, can easily upset some children with ASD. See **Figure 31.23** for a list of behaviors children with ASD might display.

Working with children who have ASD can be challenging. Some children with ASD

Possible Behavioral Symptoms of Children with Autism Spectrum Disorder

- Resists hugging and cuddling
- Avoids or does not maintain eye contact
- Lacks social gestures such as waving and smiling
- Fails to respond to name
- Exhibits unreadable facial expressions
- Becomes upset by minor changes in routines
- Plays with toys in a similar way
- Rocks body, spins self in circles, or flaps hands
- Focuses on parts of an object
- May not engage in turn-taking conversations
- Throws temper tantrums without apparent reason
- Preoccupied with repetitive behaviors
- Unaware of dangers
- Difficulty making friends and shows little interest in classmates

Figure 31.23   Children with autism spectrum disorder may experience symptoms ranging from mild to severe.

have exceptional abilities in music, visual, and academic skills. Others may experience significant disability. When working with children who have ASD, ensure consistency in both classroom routines and environment. When interacting with children with ASD, use simple and direct speech. The classroom focus should be on promoting language, appropriate behaviors, and interactions with others. Forming a partnership with the child's family and other professionals is important.

The Center for Disease Control program titled, "Learn the Signs. Act Early" includes a series of free materials that caregivers and parents or guardians can use to monitor a child's development. These materials will help to determine when there might be a problem and additional developmental screening is necessary.

31.3-6 Giftedness

No one had prepared Vivian Herr, an early childhood teacher, for all the children she would meet in her first kindergarten teaching position. Vicente, a five-year-old in her class, had taught himself to read at age three. Now he was already reading chapter books. Vicente was *gifted*, and he needed to be challenged with an individualized curriculum. To maximize his learning and achieve his potential, Vicente needed support and services. His classmate Marena is talented and excels in music. At age six, Marena is an accomplished piano player.

Giftedness can be defined in many ways. Children are considered gifted when they exhibit outstanding levels of competence in one or more areas of development. Gifted children reach milestones ahead of their peers. They may have advanced language development and may speak in sentences earlier than other children of the same age. These children need to be identified so they can receive the special education they require. The US Department of Education's office estimates that six percent of students in public schools are gifted.

Identification

Giftedness is depicted through all cultural, racial, and income levels. Identifying children who are gifted is difficult. No single test, checklist, or observation will cite all the types of giftedness. During the preschool years, usually, parents and teachers make the most observations.

A child's parents are often most familiar with their development, interests, and abilities. Because of this, they may be in a better position to identify their children as gifted. Teachers are more aware of how the child's behavior compares with that of their peers; however, teacher identification of children who are gifted is not always the best method. Studies found that teachers who identified giftedness chose

about one-third of the children incorrectly. In addition, over half the children who were gifted were not identified by their teachers. Often, gifted children's development is even. While they may excel in some areas of development, they may be at the same developmental level in others.

Figure 31.24 includes characteristics of gifted children. Many children who are gifted have a constant curiosity about many subjects. Their social and emotional behavior equals or exceeds children of the same age. They are also more independent and motivated.

Teaching Suggestions

Often, gifted children's unique educational needs are neglected in traditional education. They need constant mental stimulation, but they often spend time repeating tasks they already know. Only a small number receive instruction at the appropriate level for their needs or abilities. These children need programs and services different from those provided in the regular classroom.

The needs of a preschool child who is gifted can be met by including acceleration and enrichment in the program. Acceleration is a process in which a gifted child is assigned to a class with older children. The objective is to move the child through activities at a faster pace than children with average ability. After spending a year with older children, the child who is gifted may be ready for even older children. In enrichment, the range and depth of experiences are broadened to provide the child with a special curriculum. This process will help the child identify areas of interests.

Children who are gifted often receive enrichment through individual or small-group instruction. You or a volunteer may use audiovisual materials, games, and field trips to promote learning. The key to a useful program is to build educational experiences around children's interests. Provide open-ended learning activities for creative children. They prefer loosely structured activities that give them the chance to express ideas and inquire and discover on their own.

Children who are gifted in a certain area, such as reading, should have instruction designed

Characteristics of Gifted Children

Advanced vocabulary for age	Strong understanding of responsibility for age
Early speech and comprehension of advanced language	Self-critical
Passes intellectual milestones early	Tendency to strive toward perfection
Uses longer, more complex sentences than other children the same age	Focuses for long periods on tasks of interest
Unusual memory, hobbies, and interests	Awareness of others' feelings
Keen observation skills (sees more on field trips, in videos, or pictures than other children)	Curious, strong imagination
Unusually long attention span and memory for age	Develops reciprocal friendships earlier, usually with more mature children
Can start and carry on involved conversations with adults	Detailed memory, learns information rapidly
Creative in making up stories	Enjoys problem-solving
Solves problems in novel ways	Prefers the company of adults and older children
Inquisitive nature, constantly asking questions beyond "why" and "what if"	Plays games with more complex rules than same-age peers
Original wit and keen sense of humor	Seeks out complicated puzzles
Rapid mastery of new learning	A mature sense of humor
Flexibility, adapts quickly to new situations	Interested in cause-and-effect relationships
Persistence and intensity	Acute sensitivity to the needs and feelings of others
	Wants to have things done their way

Figure 31.24 Because parents or guardians are most familiar with their child's development, they are often better able to identify their child's giftedness. **Name four characteristics of children who display giftedness.**

to match their skills. They should be provided with a variety of books related to their special interests. It also helps to have an adult who will take the time to listen to the child read and tell the child about the story. Many small group activities can build leadership skills. These activities provide children with opportunities to learn to plan, organize, and make decisions.

Gifted children often have **asynchronous development**—or a mismatch in the areas of development. For example, they may be cognitively advanced, but they may react emotionally to situations like children of their own age.

As a teacher of children who are gifted, you need to be flexible and willing to try new things. Understand the problems these children face. Children who are gifted tend to be too hard on themselves. To help them, provide guidance so they learn to accept failure. Sometimes, because of a critical nature, a child who is gifted will not involve themselves with other children. You should help the child be considerate of others. This will help improve their social skills.

31.3-7 Integrating Children with Diverse Needs

Most times, children with diverse needs can learn through inclusion. **Inclusion** takes many forms, so a single definition of it does not exist. Inclusion, previously referred to as **mainstreaming**, involves integrating preschool, kindergarten, and Head Start children with disabilities in natural settings. This process allows children to learn in a minimally restrictive environment. All children gain skills by interacting with one another, and in this type of environment, children with disabilities can learn from those without disabilities and vice versa. Inclusionary classrooms are frequently team-taught by regular and special education teachers.

The number of children with disabilities who can be accommodated in a classroom varies. Several factors must be considered, including the teachers' training and experience, the ratio of adults to children, and the specific needs of the children. Regardless of a child's needs, they should be grouped with others based on developmental level, not age. This requires careful observation of the child before grouping.

Children with disabilities should be placed in centers that they enjoy (**Figure 31.25**). Some of these children have not had a full range of home and neighborhood experiences. Others receive painful medical treatment. For these children, the center will provide a chance for companionship and education.

To meet the individual needs of the children properly, you must ask for help from a specialist. For example, if a child has a speech problem, a speech therapist can help you plan activities for the child. In inclusionary classrooms, assistants and volunteers can also be useful. All staff members should understand the nature of a child's condition and how they are to help. Encourage adults to meet the diverse needs of children in group settings, if possible. To do this, staff may have to change or adapt classroom materials, change expectations, or give extra help when necessary.

If the parent or guardian does not remain with a child on a first visit, provide them with feedback on a child's progress at a different time. Family members should be interested in their child's adjustment to the school setting. Some teachers make a habit of either verbally sharing some positive experiences or writing a brief note each day during the child's first week or two.

The children in your classroom should be prepared for a child with disabilities. Explain any changes that will be making to the classroom. As you talk to the children, be positive and focus on benefits. This will help your group of children focus on positive expectations. Before the child arrives, inform the other children about this child. Some children are afraid of children with disabilities. They fear the disorder or illness is contagious. Create an open climate in which children are free to ask questions and discuss differences (**Figure 31.26**). Older preschoolers should be encouraged to educate classmates about their disabilities. Sometimes children's parents influence their attitudes toward a classmate who has a disability. Respond to parents' concerns or fears while maintaining the right to privacy of the child with disabilities.

Children without disabilities may assist in inclusion by helping children with disabilities adjust to the environment. Children without disabilities might introduce children with disabilities to the classroom setting. They may also help children with disabilities organize

Denis Kuvaev/Shutterstock.com

Figure 31.25 Encouraging a child with disabilities to try new experiences may help the child enjoy being at the school or center.

materials or practice a new skill. Children without disabilities also benefit from inclusionary classrooms. Children with disabilities frequently model unique adaptive skills and problem-solving abilities.

When including a child with disabilities, develop a few simple rules for classroom behavior. Stress to the children that a child with a disability needs encouragement to be independent. Young children may want to be overly helpful. This type of behavior can cause dependence and prevent a child from developing to their fullest potential. As children become more independent, they feel better about themselves.

As a teacher, your attitude toward the child with disabilities will set the classroom tone. To make yourself feel comfortable, study the disorder or illness before the child begins at the center (**Figure 31.27**). If the child is already

enrolled and the condition has just become known, learn as much as you can about it. This will help lessen any fears that you may have.

After you have learned about the disorder, arrange to have the child visit the classroom for a short period of time. This visit will reduce the fears of the child, the other children in the classroom, and perhaps the parents or guardians.

Parents or guardians of a child with disabilities may wish to remain with the child for the first, brief visit. This practice usually reduces separation anxiety the child and family members may feel. Remember that parents or guardians are the primary teachers of their children. Therefore, it is vital that they take part in planning useful, proper learning experiences. Parents or guardians should always be involved in planning for the child's individual needs, as well as planning for complementary opportunities in the home.

kali9/E+ via Getty Images

Figure 31.26   In teaching children about disabilities, teachers can provide dramatic-play materials and puppets. Through play, children can learn to grasp the concept of disability. *What other ways might the classroom teacher help prepare their students to meet a new classmate who has a disability?*

StockRocket/iStock via Getty Images Plus

Figure 31.27 You will feel more comfortable working with a child with disabilities if you study the need in advance.

Health Highlights

Health Records for Children with Disabilities

As part of the enrollment process for all children, early childhood facilities are required to maintain records regarding children's immunizations. In addition, with written parental consent, facilities must have contact information for children's health providers. For children who have disabilities, this information may include special clinics the children must attend, special therapists the children may need (such as occupational and physical therapists), and other health providers. This written consent allows an exchange of information between health providers and early childhood providers to best meet the developmental needs of children.

Lesson 31.3 Review

1. Which of the following is **not** a chronic health condition among young children? (31.3.1)
   A. Cystic fibrosis
   B. Diabetes
   C. Muscular dystrophy
   D. Asthma

2. _____ is a genetic chromosome disorder caused by a mistake in cell division. (31.3.2)
   A. Autism spectrum disorder (ASD)
   B. Hemophilia
   C. Epilepsy
   D. Down syndrome

3. **True or False.** Children with learning disabilities may demonstrate delays in meeting developmental milestones. (31.3.3)

4. Attention deficit disorder (ADD) is an example of a _____. (31.3.4)
   A. learning disorder
   B. neurodevelopment disorder
   C. behavioral disorder
   D. auditory disorder

5. Which of the following is not true of autism spectrum disorder (ASD)? (31.3.5)
   A. It is a behavioral disorder.
   B. It affects one in 54 children in America.
   C. An early sign is resistance to hugging and cuddling.
   D. Some children with ASD have exceptional abilities.

6. A teacher may offer _____ to broaden the range and depth of learning experiences in the curriculum to a child who is gifted. (31.3.6)
   A. acceleration
   B. enrichment
   C. challenges
   D. assignments

7. **True or False.** A teacher's attitude toward the child with diverse abilities will set the classroom tone. (31.3.7)

Summary

Lesson 31.1

31.1-1 The Individuals with Disabilities Education Act (IDEA) is a law that requires a free, appropriate public education be provided to eligible children with disabilities. The law entitles all children with disabilities to be provided the best and least restrictive learning environment, with typically developing peers whenever possible, and to the services needed to be successful.

31.1-1 When an infant or a toddler is diagnosed with a developmental delay, an Individualized Family Service Plan (IFSP) is mandated and used as an effective tool for monitoring progress and making sure the child is getting the necessary services.

31.1-1 Under the IDEA, all three- to five-year-old children with disabilities who require special educational services must be provided with Individualized Education Plans (IEPs).

31.1-2 Early childhood teachers must monitor children's developmental milestones to identify children with disabilities and special needs in their classrooms.

31.1-2 Teachers of children with diverse abilities work with professionals and resource people who provide individualized service to these students; create an inclusive classroom and curriculum for all children; and establish a relationship with families to include them in their children's education and provide referral suggestions when appropriate.

Lesson 31.2

31.2-1 Hearing loss prevents children from hearing adequately and is one of the most common congenital disabilities. Severe hearing losses can be identified early in young children by a lack of vocabulary and overall delays in speech and grammar.

31.2-1 Assistive devices, such as hearing aids and cochlear implants, can ease hearing loss. Understanding the child's hearing loss, sensitivities, and communication style can help the teacher better connect with and include the child in all the school-age program activities.

31.2-2 Communication disorders are conditions that inhibit children's abilities to communicate with adults and each other. A teacher recognizing a possible communication difficulty may recommend that the child be assessed by a speech pathologist or an audiologist. Types of communication disorders include articulation problems, voice (phonation) disorders, and stuttering.

31.2-3 Vision impairments, including amblyopia, nearsightedness, farsightedness, glaucoma, and color deficiency, are seen in almost 20 percent of children and can limit motor abilities during physical activities. Children who appear to have limited vision are referred to an eye specialist for an exam.

31.2-4 Physical disabilities are orthopedic impairments of the muscles, joints, and bones that may cause spina bifida, cerebral palsy, muscular dystrophy, arthritis, and spinal cord damage. Physical disabilities are classified as severe, moderate, or mild.

Lesson 31.3

31.3-1 Many children have chronic health needs, or illnesses that persist over time, and experience cycles of good and poor health. These disorders and diseases include allergies, arthritis, asthma, cystic fibrosis, diabetes, epilepsy, hemophilia, and pediatric leukemia.

31.3-2 Intellectual disabilities are conditions that cause intellectual functioning to fall significantly below developmental milestones and have degrees of severity and many potential causes.

31.3-3 Children with learning disabilities may have average to above-average intellectual functioning and model some common traits, such as delays in meeting developmental milestones, trouble following directions, poor memory skills, and difficulty storing, processing, and producing information or identifying or reproducing numbers and letters.

31.3-4 Behavioral disorders affect a child's social, emotional, and cognitive functions and include attention deficit disorder (ADD) and attention deficit hyperactivity disorder (ADHD). Children with ADHD are usually treated with a combination of behavior therapy and medication.

31.3-5 Autism spectrum disorder (ASD) is a set of delays and disorders caused by differences in the brain and may cause significant social, emotional, behavioral, and communication challenges. Symptoms may range from mild to severe. When working with children who have ASD, teachers should ensure consistency in both classroom routines and environment and use simple and direct speech.

31.3-6 Children are considered gifted when they exhibit outstanding levels of competence in one or more areas of development. Teachers may develop an individualized learning program incorporating enrichment and acceleration to meet the learning needs of gifted children.

31.3-7 Teaching children with diverse needs in an inclusive classroom can take many forms. A child may need specialists, assistants, and volunteers to provide guidance, services, and individualized attention at the center. When including a child with disabilities, the teacher should develop simple rules for classroom behavior. The teacher should involve parents or guardians in planning for the child's individual needs, as well as planning for complementary opportunities in the home.

31.3-7 Teachers need a strong child development background to identify children with diverse abilities and gifts. The teacher must provide the most effective environment and teaching strategies possible for each child in their classroom.

Vocabulary Activity

Working in small teams, locate a small image online that visually describes or explains each of the Key Terms in this chapter. To create flash cards, write each term on a note card and paste the image that describes or explains the term on the opposite side.

Critical Thinking

1. **Analyze.** Look over some of the lesson plans you have written this year for young children. Then, analyze whether the lessons are suitable for working with children who are gifted or children who have disabilities. What additional information, activities, or enrichment would you add to make the lessons appropriate for a child with a special need? Could you do this without making lessons that would be too difficult or easy for other children?

2. **Draw Conclusions.** Imagine that a child in a wheelchair recently joined a center that had never had a child with a physical disability before. Research changes the early learning center would probably have to make to become wheelchair accessible. Note such factors as carpeting or rugs; doorways, ramps, and doorknobs; space between furniture; height of furniture; and nonslip flooring, grab bars, and height of bathroom fixtures. Draw conclusions about what changes would need to be made.

3. **Compare and Contrast.** Research the qualifications required of a special education teacher. What programs or courses are available for learning to teach children with disabilities? What are the requirements for special education teachers of children in childcare centers and preschools? Compare and contrast the qualifications and requirements for becoming a special education teacher with those for becoming an early learning teacher.

Core Skills

1. **Social Studies.** Research the history of special education from its beginnings in the 1700s through today. What major events in special education history are notable? What legislative action mandated special education services? How have laws kept up with the needs of children and adults with disabilities today? How have schools responded to special education mandates? Report your findings to the class.

2. **Reading and Writing.** Many famous individuals have experienced and still experience disorders, impairments, and disabilities. Read one famous person's account of life with their disability and pay special attention to what kind of education this person received. After reading this account, write a brief reflection about what you learned.

3. **Science.** Research the ear and its hearing mechanisms. Locate a diagram of the ear structure and then write a short essay explaining how hearing works and what factors cause hearing loss or deafness.

4. **Research.** Research information on the role of the tongue in speech. Explain how parts of the tongue and tongue mobility relate to the ability to make sounds. What problems with the tongue can hinder speech? Discuss your findings in small groups and compile a group bibliography.

5. **Science and Speaking.** Research the body's response during allergic reactions. Then, adapt this information into a lesson and presentation for preschoolers. Create visuals to go with your report, such as models, posters, or slides in presentation software. Present your lesson orally to the class.

6. **Speaking.** Using reliable online or print resources, research giftedness and techniques for teaching gifted children. Based on the information you find, deliver a brief speech summarizing your research. Create a bibliography of your sources for the class to review during your speech.

7. **Technology.** Visit an early learning center that has preschool children with disabilities enrolled. Talk to the teacher and ask what assistive technology is available as well as what technology the center uses and why. Also ask the teacher to describe how the children use each of the devices. After your visit, choose one device and deliver a presentation explaining its structure, use, and benefits. Make a recommendation about whether this device should be included in the classroom.

8. **CTE Career Readiness Practice.** As center director of an early learning program in a small town, you have not had many children with disabilities in your class. This year, however, a child with moderate hearing loss, a child with Down syndrome, and a child with ASD are joining your preschool class. To prepare for the new year, you want to meet with your staff about integrating these children into the program and curriculum. Create a list of tasks that must be completed before the children arrive. Also, create a meeting agenda for your staff meeting.

Portfolio Project

In teams, research forms for Individualized Education Plans (IEPs), which vary from state to state. How specific are they? Then, choose one type of disability covered in this chapter. Consult with a specialist on this type of disability and then create an Individualized Education Plan based on that person's expertise and on the information covered in this chapter. Role-play a conference discussing the plan with parents and file a copy of the plan in your portfolio.

Engaging Families

Lesson 32.1: Communicating with Families

Lesson 32.2: Providing Family Resources and Activities

Case Study

Strategies for Engaging Families

An enthusiastic and dedicated second-year teacher, Olivia decided to commit her professional goals to paper. After evaluating her first year of teaching and consulting with the center director, she decided her family engagement skills were weak and needed improvement. As a result, she made a written improvement plan focusing on family involvement and posted it on a bulletin board above her desk in the teacher's workroom.

The first item she listed was family engagement. She needed to communicate with families more frequently since studies show children benefit from having them engaged. But this was not easy since she struggled not being able to speak or write in Spanish, and many of the families struggled with speaking and reading English. To help meet her goals, Olivia enrolled in an online Spanish class. By the end of the year, her goal is not to need an interpreter during family conferences. She also found a computer program to convert English to Spanish. Using the program would allow her to send communications to families in their home language. Olivia's goal is to send a weekly newsletter and daily news flashes.

Give It Some Thought

1. What other strategies could Olivia use to get families engaged? What are the benefits families gain from being engaged?
2. Would a home visit be an effective method of engaging families? What would be some advantages or possible disadvantages?
3. How could Olivia recruit and provide an orientation to family volunteers?
4. What are the benefits of using technology in building relationships with families?
5. What information could Olivia include in a newsletter that would interest families?
6. How should Olivia plan for a parent conference?
7. Can you think of other strategies that Olivia could use to involve families?

Opening image credit: SDI Productions/E+ via Getty Images

Lesson 32.1

Communicating with Families

Essential Question

What do you need to know and what actions do you need to take to build positive teacher-parent relationships?

Learning Outcomes

After studying this lesson, you will be able to

32.1-1 explain objectives for family engagement.

32.1-2 cite strategies for engaging families in the center through written communication.

32.1-3 plan, conduct, and **follow up** on a parent-teacher conference.

32.1-4 summarize why home visits are essential to the teacher, child, and family.

32.1-5 outline the benefits of sunshine calls in building positive relationships with families.

32.1-6 explain the advantages and disadvantages of discussion groups.

Key Terms

parent and family engagement	quibbling
newsletters	egotistical
biweekly	home visit
letters	sunshine call
daily news flash	alienated
active listening	

Frequent, two-way communication between teachers and family members creates an environment that welcomes families. When working with young children, the teacher-parent/guardian relationship is vital. Families need teachers for reassurance and emotional support.

Teachers need family members to help them create an environment that reflects children's home experiences and to help them understand families' parenting beliefs, cultural backgrounds, and linguistic abilities. This exchange can only occur when teachers and families build partnerships. Often, these unique partnerships become a valuable source for problem-solving.

The value of parent and family engagement is critical now more than ever. **Parent and family engagement** refers to parental participation in educational programs by family members, including parents or guardians, stepparents, grandparents, and siblings. There is no one model of ideal parent and family involvement. These connections will affect positive parent-child relationships, which involve a child's early learning and healthy development. Family engagement activities may include assisting in the classroom, helping with fundraising activities, home teaching, supplying classroom resources, and attending family education classes. Family involvement can be a critical factor in the success of an early childhood program (**Figure 32.1**).

Unfortunately, little information is usually available about the family-teacher relationship. At times, staff and family members fail to view each other positively. Historically, teachers have neglected to use a strength-based perspective. They sometimes failed to contact parents to praise their children's efforts and accomplishments. Likewise, family members have neglected to express their appreciation of teachers' roles.

The relationship between families and teachers should be a partnership of mutual respect and support. Often, teachers are surprised to learn that parents want unhurried time to relate with them. Parents want to learn more about their children's strengths, experiences,

814

Rawpixel/iStock via Getty Images Plus

Figure 32.1 When families are engaged in their children's school programs, both the family members and the children reap many benefits. ***What can early childhood professionals do to encourage family engagement?***

interests, peer relationships, and development. They may also want advice about working with their children at home. Teachers and families should become close partners in supporting young children's development.

To facilitate mindful parenting, you need to be an advocate for children and their families. Begin by building trusting and respectful partnerships. To do this takes time. Create opportunities to talk with family members, particularly at the beginning or ending of the day. During these casual conversations, be judgment-free and respectful of their culture, linguistic, and social aspects of the family. Share your observations and knowledge about early development behaviors. Parents also enjoy learning about their children's preferences and ways of responding to people and objects. Be sure to communicate children's strengths to family members. Families will then be more accepting when you have to share a child's needs.

Always welcome family members to the center. Include them in program functions. Family members may be observers, resource people, volunteers, or guests at special celebrations. They can share a hobby, an interest, or cultural traditions. Studies show that teachers who are confident in their skills and abilities are more inclined to include family members in program functions. Likewise, studies show that good relationships with families affect teachers' feelings of self-esteem and competence.

Children need their families and teachers to work together. A parents' or guardians' well-being is the best predictor of a child's well-being. Partnering with families can have a lasting impact on a child's development. Studies show that family involvement affects a child's later school success. Children have better attendance and homework habits. Their attitudes toward school are more positive, and they show gains in reading skills.

FatCamera/E+ via Getty Images

Figure 32.2   Being engaged in their children's programs can help adults gain increased confidence in their parenting roles. *What other benefits can family members and children reap from family engagement?*

32.1-1 Objectives for Parent and Family Engagement

Communicate frequently with parents. Young children benefit from having informed and engaged parents and family members. The purpose of family engagement is to promote family collaboration by exchanging ideas and information. This exchange should include teachers and parents, whether they are mothers or fathers. Fathers today are more active than past generations in nurturing their children. Many fathers want to be involved and are equally as important as mothers. Do not overlook them when building a family partnership. Through their involvement, family members reap many benefits, such as feeling more knowledgeable and connected. Other benefits they gain:

- a greater understanding of child growth and development;
- increased confidence and enjoyment in their parenting roles (**Figure 32.2**);
- an understanding of their child's strengths and areas of need;
- knowledge about their children's experiences at the center;
- a better understanding of their children by observing other children;
- new skills for positively interacting with their children;

- more information about community resources;
- positive interaction skills to support their children's well-being;
- learning that transfers from the center into the home;
- an understanding of how a partnership between the center and home can promote the children's development; and
- an understanding that they are their child's first and most important teacher.

Open, ongoing communication is the key to engaging families in their child's growth and development. It would help if you encouraged family engagement. One way is through daily interactions at arrival and pickup. Other methods are written communication, class videos, parent-teacher conferences, advisory committees, and discussion groups. Newsletters, emails, and text messages can also extend learning from the center to the home. When families see how their involvement can benefit their children, they are more likely to participate. This will help promote positive parent-child communication.

Benefits of Technology

Technology is an efficient tool for connecting and building a relationship with families.

Teachers use the internet to communicate and exchange information with families. Newsletters, calendars, photographs, letters, daily news flashes, and text messages are used as vehicles for communication. Some teachers have developed a website to share general classroom information. Others post videos to let families virtually experience classroom activities.

Teachers even develop e-portfolios for individual children containing assessment data, such photos, artwork, writing samples, checklists, observations, anecdotal records, rating scales, work samples, and screening tests.

Families that have technology barriers need options. Smartphones are an efficient choice. The vast majority, 96 percent of 18- to 29-year-olds, own a smartphone. Often, teachers use text since most parents or guardians have a smartphone. Email, like a text message, is fast and efficient to distribute. Adaptations also may be necessary if you have any parents or guardians with literacy problems. In this case, you may use audiotapes for newsletters; otherwise, add a QR code feature to the newsletter. A (QR) code is a two-dimensional code scannable image that can be scanned and read with a smartphone camera. It automatically will pull up text and photos.

Supporting Military Families

Military families need to cope with separation during deployment. Military deployment can affect a child's development and behavior. It also impacts a family's needs. Often these families transition from base to base. It is not unusual for their children to experience many school changes from birth through school age. For deployed military parents, videos can be made for birthdays and other celebrations and events. For family members who cannot meet in person for a conference or a child's celebration, many centers use video-conferencing.

32.1-2 Written Communications

One way that teachers can engage families is through written communication, including the use of newsletters, letters, and daily news flashes. Teachers can distribute written communication digitally by posting it on their class website, or sending emails or texts (**Figure 32.3**). When a new family enrolls, the teachers need to ask what technology tools the family prefers to use to optimize communication. To determine preferences, include a quick survey in enrollment materials. Otherwise, ask parents directly. Using this information, the teacher can determine how best to engage families. Some people will want to receive printed copies of communications and others will want emails or texts.

recep-bg/E+ via Getty Images

Figure 32.3 Depending on what mode of communication works best for the families in a center, newsletters can be mailed, emailed, or texted. ***How does using technology for communication benefit families and teachers?***

Written communications are popular for one important reason: they require less time and energy for the teacher than meetings or multiple telephone calls. However, teachers must communicate this information in the family's home language. If communication regarding an upcoming event is sent via email, sent home with children, or mailed, the teacher only needs compose one letter. Still, chances are that not every family has a digital device, so communications may still require delivery using several methods.

Families like written communication for the same reason teachers do. They can read a newsletter over a weekend, during lunch hour, or while commuting. This saves family members time and energy.

Use the active, not passive, voice when you write. The *active voice* states that the subject did something. The *passive voice* states that the subject was acted upon. For example, the active voice would say, "Reza read books and painted pictures." The passive voice would say, "Reading books and painting pictures were Reza's major activities."

Before you begin writing, think of the content headings you want to include and new emotions that you want to arouse in the families. An example of an emotion might be curiosity, pleasure, or encouragement. Content headings might include weekly or monthly themes, upcoming special days and celebrations, an interview with a teacher, a new blog post, or classroom highlights and happenings.

When writing, keep your communications short, clear, and simple for all families. Busy parents appreciate brief messages, and clear writing prevents misinterpretation of the message. After you finish writing, proofread and proofread again. You may even ask another teacher to review the communication for spelling errors or missing content.

Most schools have families from diverse cultures, so staff should prepare communications in all languages spoken by the parents (**Figure 32.4**). Computer programs are available for translating languages. Often, teachers use volunteers or support staff to translate communications into different languages.

Dragon Images/Shutterstock.com

Figure 32.4 Families in a preschool center are likely to be diverse and come from a variety of countries and cultural backgrounds. Teachers should translate letters and communicate in ways the families can understand.

Newsletters

Newsletters most often include information concerning a variety of subjects, which teachers share regularly. For example, a center might send newsletters on the first Monday of each month. Other centers, depending on budgets and resources, might send newsletters on a **biweekly** (two-week) basis. If most parents have email accounts, programs can send newsletters by email to lower their costs by saving paper and ink. A newsletter serves as a link between the home and early childhood center.

A typical newsletter may include information about:
- upcoming special events at the center;
- review of special activities;
- developmentally appropriate practices;
- importance of play;
- special classroom-related activities for children to do in the home;
- guidance tips;
- brief articles of interest;

- summaries of books or articles related to parenting;
- nutrition;
- child development information;
- a section asking for family volunteers;
- upcoming community events of interest to young children and their families;
- a "meet the staff" section;
- recognition for family contributions;
- a parent exchange section;
- reminders about center policies;
- welcomes to new families and teachers;
- classroom celebrations and birthdays;
- classroom needs; and
- links to local community services.

The design of a newsletter should include content headings in large type, which will allow families to navigate it easier. Examples of headings include the curriculum theme, classroom highlights, new teachers, children, or pets, special events and celebrations. Allow for a blank section, where a teacher can write a brief, positive, personal note. For instance, a teacher may write, "I'm so pleased with Amelia; she has learned how to tie her shoes" or "Denzel has learned to write his name and is delighted." Encourage teachers to include different children weekly and every child at some time throughout the year.

Provide another blank section for families to write their comments and thoughts. In this space, parents could respond to the newsletter or submit ideas or information for future issues. This way, a newsletter can become a two-way communication tool. Before you write your first newsletter, create a blank template to save on your computer. You can use this template each month, which gives you a head start. All you need to do is type in your content.

Letters

Teachers can also use letters to communicate with families. **Letters** most often address only one subject and are sent out as necessary. Letters are useful for reaching out to one parent or an

Workplace Connections

Unexpected Events

Unexpected events at the center may cause confusion and distress for children. Discuss situations that might require a special letter to be sent home.

1. What situations might require a special letter? How should you present these situations?
2. What suggestions could you offer for parents to help their children cope with a situation?

entire group of parents. Parent or family letters can serve as a supplement to newsletters. See **Figure 32.5** for an example of a parent or family letter.

The first letter sent to families should introduce the teachers and staff. This letter can also address classroom goals, rules, and expectations. The first letter should welcome family members to observe and take part in center activities. When writing a letter, consider the family's language and educational level. Make sure the letter is understandable to all.

After the first letter, subsequent letters should address the class's current theme. Note special center activities, along with the goals. Write out new songs and fingerplays and add the accompanying music or actions that go with them. Include field trip sites, dates, and times. Letters should also thank families for any favors and share home-learning activities for the families to do with their child. Letters can explain the rationale behind these activities to make family members feel involved in their children's education.

You may choose to send home a special letter during the week. This letter should outline something special the children did on a special day and include photographs of children engaged in the activity. It may be an event, such as a field trip, or an activity within the classroom. This letter can promote a learning experience between parents and children (**Figure 32.6**). Make sure to include all children in photographs; otherwise, individually send each child's photo.

Dear Families:

We are beginning our new curriculum theme. "Eating Well: Foods for Good Health." This will be a continuation of our Self-Awareness unit. We have previously explored how our bodies work and the importance of exercise.

The children will be involved in a wide variety of experiences. We will play "fruit basket upset," make collages of foods that are good for us, play "grocery store," take part in having a "pickle party," prepare snacks using nutritious foods and enjoy tasting a variety of fruits. Thursday will be a very special day—our trip to Connell's Orchard! The children will watch apples being washed, dried, sorted, bagged, and boxed. We will taste "Connell Reds" and drink some delicious apple cider. After the trip, we will write a language experience chart.

Center Activities

Our learning experiences will focus on "Foods for Good Health." Activities will include:
- preparing and eating mini-pizzas (with smiley faces of pepperoni and green peppers)
- having a play restaurant in our dramatic play area
- acting out a "Good Breakfast" version of *The Three Bears* (which the children heard last week)
- making applesauce
- mixing colors with eyedroppers
- reading "Ten Apples Up on Top"

Home and Community Activities

Activities you can do at home to reinforce the concepts learned at the center include:
- visiting a grocery store, identifying foods in MyPlate: grains, vegetables, fruits, dairy, and protein
- looking through old magazines, cutting out pictures, and making a collage of "good foods" for the whole family
- reading labels with your child, especially focusing on fat and sugar (in their many forms) content within certain foods
- encouraging your child to try new foods (you can, too)
- encouraging your child to help in the kitchen
- involving your child in planning the family menu

Here's to healthful eating!

Sincerely,
Miss Perez

Figure 32.5   Letters are useful for touching base with one parent or family member or a group of family members. *For what types of communication can teachers use letters?*

Parent and family letters should be inclusive and include diverse family structures. Word all family communications to include nontraditional families. Address the parent and family letter to "Families," as opposed to "Mom and Dad." When sending a letter that requires parental or guardian permission, such as a field trip, include space for more than two family member's signatures.

Daily News Flash

A **daily news flash** contains bits of news that families can discuss with their children. Family

We went to the apple orchard today.

We rode in a big yellow bus.

We saw many trees with apples on them.

We observed the beauty of apples on the trees.

The guide showed us four parts of an apple—stem, skin, meat, and core.

We tasted green, yellow, and red apples.

Tomorrow we will make applesauce.

To: Families
From: Miss Lopez
Activity: Field Trip to the Apple Orchard

Figure 32.6   Letters like this one can promote discussion between families and children.

members and teachers may be too busy for daily, in-depth, face-to-face communication, so a daily news flash may be the most effective tool for communicating with families. A flash contains news about what is going on in the program each day, including regular routines and special occasions or interesting events. News flashes cover small bits of information, such as:

- This morning we made blueberry muffins and ate them at snack time.
- Ting lost her tooth today during lunch.
- Mr. Huth is the new center cook.
- Today is Ahmad's birthday.
- Finn has a new baby brother named Ivan.
- We learned a new song today about apples.

Download digital pictures to include in the daily news flash. You can post the daily news flash at the center's main entrance, on a classroom door, or on a bulletin board. You can also email or text it to families who prefer this form of communication.

32.1-3 Teacher-Family Conferences

Teacher-family conferences are meetings to share the child's progress and involve the parents or guardians or families in the educational process. These meetings are a key way to engage them in promoting their child's development

by sharing ideas or contributing to developing a plan. Conferences help families and teachers develop a shared understanding of a child. Families will share information on what children are like at home. Teachers will share what children are like at the center. When these two viewpoints are shared, staff and families can see themselves as a team sharing developmental information (**Figure 32.7**). Together, they can then make plans to better meet the needs of the

Early Childhood Insight

Conferences and Culture

Parent-teacher or family-teacher conferences can be a way to bridge possible cultural gaps between home and center. Parents or guardians from other cultures may have different views about the approach to child-rearing. Expectations of their children or ways to help them succeed can vary from your center's practice. To strengthen family-teacher communication, teachers can explain the program goals, schedule, and competencies the children will gain. Likewise, family members need to talk about their funds of knowledge. They can talk about their values, traditions, and the role of early childhood education and expectations in their culture. Teachers can use this information to better understand the family and make learning experiences more culturally relevant for the children

Weekend Images Inc./E+ via Getty Images

Figure 32.7   Through family-teacher conferences, families can gain insights into how best to work with their child at home. *What types of information do teachers share at conferences?*

children. During the process, teachers need to understand that their role is to inform, and it is the parents' or guardians' job to decide.

There are three phases to a well-planned teacher-family conference. Planning is the first phase. The second phase is the individual conference, and the last phase is the follow-up.

Planning the Conference

Planning includes setting basic rules that will help you work successfully with the parents or guardians. Before the conference, spend time planning. An excellent conference requires careful planning if you are to win the respect of the parents or guardians and family members. As the teacher, you are responsible for the success of the conference.

Preparing for the Conference

Conferences provide an opportunity to review each child's progress and plan future goals. This time should provide an objective review of the child's total development. Begin the planning phase by selecting, preparing, and organizing assessment materials. By sharing samples of the child's work, families will learn what skills the child has achieved. Gather records on the child's emotional, social, cognitive, and physical

development. Much of this is information taken from developmental checklists and anecdotal records. Select samples of the children's artwork and writing, and photos of them in the dramatic play and block-building areas. Finally, arrange for a translator if the family speaks a language other than the teacher's language.

Some teachers use planning sheets to prepare for conferences. A planning sheet might include a record of the child's

- daily routines,
- types of play,
- activity preferences,
- fine-motor skills,
- gross-motor skills,
- social-emotional development,
- relationships with peers and adults,
- cognitive development,
- language development, and
- eating and sleeping habits.

Teachers might divide planning sheets into sections, assessing a child's ability in several areas, such as dressing, cleanup, rest patterns, eating, and toileting (**Figure 32.8**).

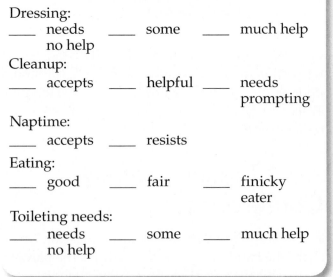

Routines

Dressing:
___ needs no help   ___ some   ___ much help

Cleanup:
___ accepts   ___ helpful   ___ needs prompting

Naptime:
___ accepts   ___ resists

Eating:
___ good   ___ fair   ___ finicky eater

Toileting needs:
___ needs no help   ___ some   ___ much help

Figure 32.8   In a planning sheet like the one shown, you can divide notes into sections. *How do planning sheets benefit teachers?*

Health Highlights

Teacher-Family Conferences

According to federal standards, early childhood providers should regularly schedule conferences with the children's families. The recommendations state that centers schedule conferences for children six years and under at least every six months.

While planning the conference, prioritize the content with the most information first. During the conference, communicate at the family members' level. Topics of primary discussion during conferences might include:

- a review of a child's strengths and abilities, focusing on the positive;
- short- and long-term goals for the child;
- a review of the child's development progression;
- a discussion about effective guidance practices;
- a review of the child's health, including special health conditions, nutrition, or sleeping problems;
- a review of the progress since the last conference; and
- any concerns or questions from the family.

The conference provides an opportunity to update the child's health record. After the conference, send a follow-up communication thanking families for attending and sharing.

Besides records and samples, teachers can share children's portfolios with their families. To start a portfolio, begin by collecting notes and data from developmental assessments and observations. Then continue by collecting some of the children's artwork to share with the parents. Make sure that the child's name and date are on each piece. Photographs, videos, audio recordings, and notes can also be useful. If developmentally appropriate, ask each child to tell you a story about a picture. Record the story as the child speaks and place the recording in the portfolio.

Teachers often show video recordings of children in teacher-family conferences. A week or two before a conference, video record each child engaging in classroom activities. Allow three to five minutes per child. Review the recording before the conference.

Checking Family Availability

In planning for a teacher-family conference, send a brief letter or e-mail to the parents explaining the purpose of the family-teacher conference. Explain to families that conferences are a routine part of communication and are a time to share progress, thoughts, and ideas. Communicate that the conferences are a time to ask questions and provide information that may be helpful to teachers. Include in the letter the dates and times the center will hold conferences.

Be flexible in scheduling conference dates. Try to accommodate parents' or guardians' schedules whenever possible. Before you schedule families for specific time slots and dates, ask about their availability. Try to schedule conferences for times most convenient for families. Your teaching schedule may also make it difficult to find times for conferences. You might try scheduling conferences:

- during nap time (teachers can alternate conferences and supervise nap time);
- before or after program hours;
- by hiring a substitute teacher for one day each month;
- by hiring a substitute teacher for lunchtime if working family members can come at this time; or
- by dismissing center activities for a day every two to three months (this may not be a desirable option for working family members who will not be able to find alternate care).

If family members do not respond to the letter, follow up with a phone call. Some parents or guardians may need extra time to adjust their schedules (**Figure 32.9**).

Each conference should last approximately half an hour. Allot 10 minutes between conferences to give you a chance to record any necessary information. This margin will also provide time if a conference runs longer than planned. If families have two or more children

fizkes/iStock via Getty Images Plus

Figure 32.9 Many parents sign up eagerly for family-teacher conferences. For others, a phone call might be necessary to set up an appointment.

at the center, try to schedule consecutive conferences. Provide care for the children when scheduling evening conferences.

You might also schedule parent-teacher conferences in each family's home. Dual-worker or single-parent families may find this appointment most convenient. Teachers can learn more about the child's home environment from this visit. This scheduling is most costly because it involves time and expense for the teacher to travel to the homes. As a result, few centers offer this alternative.

Early Childhood Insight

Supporting Absent Family Members

Some children may have family members who are absent because of military deployment, hospitalization, work, or even incarceration. Teachers should attempt to accommodate and communicate with distant family members, provided that they have custody. Tools to stay connected include copies of center emails and newsletters, videos of parent conferences or classroom celebrations, texting, and photo sharing.

Establishing a Positive Setting

A conference setting can influence its success. Establish a welcoming environment for conferences. Find an area in the center that is private with adult-sized chairs and a table. No interruptions should occur during the conference. To ensure this, place a sign on the door that states a family-teacher conference is in session and there are to be no interruptions. If you schedule the conference in an office, take the telephone off the hook or arrange for messages someone to take messages. Be sure to turn off your cell phone too.

When using an office, set chairs in a grouping that will help create a feeling of a partnership. Likewise, avoid sitting behind a desk. Sitting at a desk places you in a position of authority and will decrease the feeling of a partnership. If possible, provide light snacks, coffee, tea, and ice water.

Running the Conference

A successful conference depends on many factors, including communication skills and the information you are communicating. When running a conference, pay close attention to first impressions and questions the parents ask. Maintain a professional attitude, and always end the conference on a positive note.

Making a Good First Impression

Words and actions contribute to making a good first impression. Body language, such as facial expressions, posture, and gestures all contribute to communication. At the beginning of the conference, provide a warm welcome and greet each family member by name. The first impression you make with the children's families is important. Be prepared and individualize the conference by considering families' language and culture. Have your notes outlined, including what you would like to discuss. If needed, use your notes during the conference (**Figure 32.10**).

As you think through the conference, keep in mind you will set the tone for it. If you are nervous and anxious, family members will probably feel the same way. If you are calm, family members will likely be calm, too. Your

SDI Productions/E+ via Getty Images

Figure 32.10 During a conference, make a positive impression by bringing your notes and referencing them during the conversation. *How should teachers begin and end a conference?*

goal is to set the proper tone for a successful meeting.

Always begin and end the conference with a positive comment. Family members always enjoy hearing positive comments about their children. As you share the comment, try to be relaxed. If you are tense, the parents will know.

Listening to Families

During a teacher-family conference, provide the families with an opportunity to talk. By exchanging information, you are showing them you want to learn more about their child and family. Assume the role of an active listener. **Active listening** provides verbal and nonverbal attentiveness. It involves giving your undivided attention, using your eyes to communicate interest, listening with your ears, and caring with your heart. While listening, use positive nonverbal body language. Show interest by making eye contact appropriately and using pleasant facial expressions. Some teachers will even nod slightly to show the family members they are listening or agreeing.

When listening, never interrupt and jump ahead of the speaker. Give family members time to finish their stories or thoughts. While a family member is talking, show interest and alertness. Avoid preparing an answer while listening. The parent's or guardian's last sentence

may be a source of new information, which may put an entirely different slant on what was previously shared. Avoid **quibbling** (arguing) over words. Instead, focus intently on what the family members is trying to say. Focus on areas of agreement to encourage more friendly, open communication from the family member (**Figure 32.11**).

During the meeting, listen and watch for signs of emotion. These signs may include gestures, changes in tone of voice, or expression. If the parent or guardian appears uncomfortable, provide reassurance that you will keep all the information confidential.

Talking with Families

When talking with families, focus on the positive by sharing what the child does well. Avoid making general statements. "Ryland is doing fine" or "Jodi is doing well in school" does not give family members much information. Rather, be specific. For instance, you might say, "Leonardo has really improved in following classroom routines. He no longer needs help with his clothing when preparing to go outside. At transition time, he takes care of his personal needs in the bathroom. He no longer needs encouragement to help during cleanup. In fact, I am so pleased, because he is even encouraging other children to assist."

fizkes/iStock via Getty Images Plus

Figure 32.11 Listen attentively to parents and family members and focus on areas of agreement during conferences. You may learn vital information to help you work more effectively with their children.

Make it clear to families that you want to learn from them. Ask questions during the conference to help them think. Examples might include, "What is a strength you see in (child) at home?" or "In what area has (child) shown the most progress?" As a teacher, you must respect the family's goal(s) for their child. So, ask, "What is it you want us to do for your child?" You could also invite them to share how their children act at home and their interests. As a beginning teacher, you may feel more comfortable planning your questions before the meeting.

Ask open-ended questions if you want more than a yes or no answer. Questions that start with *why, what, when, how,* and *where* are many times the most successful. Also, provide family members opportunities to share and ask questions.

Families are also likely to ask questions during a conference, and each question can have several answers. When planning for the conference, be prepared to answer questions. Families may phrase questions differently, but most tend to ask:

- Is my child happy in the program?
- How can I help at home?
- Does my child make friends and get along with others?
- Does my child respect others' property rights?
- How long does my child nap?
- Does my child eat a nutritious diet?
- Is my child making progress in all developmental areas?
- With whom does my child play?
- Does my child have any special abilities or needs?

Watch how you word your comments and answers. As you speak, put yourself in the family's place. Try to imagine the effects of your remarks. You must evaluate the child's progress by emphasizing their strengths. While you do this, always try to use a positive expression (**Figure 32.12**).

If you have concerns about the child's development, be prepared. Make a list of resources available in the community; include

Language Expressions

Negative Expressions	More Positive Expressions
troublemaker	disturbs others at story time
below age	performs at his own level
lazy	is capable of doing more
stubborn	insistent in having his own way
mean	finds it difficult to get along with others
clumsy	lacks physical coordination
selfish	needs to learn to share with others
show-off	tries to get others' attention
messy	works too quickly

Figure 32.12   Use care when speaking with family members during conferences, evaluating the child's progress without being critical.

contact information. Also, share a list of websites with developmental resources.

Working with Challenging Families

Some families are more difficult to work with than others. It may take patience and commitment to work with them. For example, a timid family member may be speechless at the start of a meeting. Reassure them by being friendly. As you speak, provide the family member with several sincere compliments. Second meetings are often much easier.

The worried family member always needs reassurance. Hand-twirling, toe-tapping, or finger-drumming often identifies this person. If a family member expresses a concern regarding the child's developmental progress, provide reassurance. Often, family members are unaware of unevenness in a child's development. Spurts can occur in a short time.

A family member who is **egotistical** (very proud) often enters feeling self-confident and smiling. They may want to talk about what a wonderful child they have and how wonderful a parent or guardian they are. With this person, it is very important to remember that the ego is a precious possession and to comment positively on their skills.

The critical family member can be hard to work with if not handled properly. This person has expert opinions on teaching children. Be accepting. For example, do not show disapproval or surprise. Never argue with this family member or any other. Arguing only arouses resistance and creates bad feelings. Arguments will not benefit the child. Successful conferences depend on your positive relationship with family members.

When working with families, always model professional behavior (**Figure 32.13**). Never bring up or respond to negative comments about other children or parents. So, if someone makes a negative comment about another teacher or child, ignore it. Always be positive about your colleagues and the children.

Ending a Conference

Just as a conference should begin on a positive note, it should also end on one. Summarize major areas that have been discussed. Begin by repeating positive comments made at the beginning of the conference. Note areas that may need attention, including the agreed-on goals and action. Then restate your goals at the center and let family members know how they can support their child's development at home. End the conference by again making a constructive, pleasant comment. Let the family members know how appreciative you are of sharing their children's progress with them.

Invite the families to visit the center. Thank them for sharing. Stress the importance of shared information and common goals. Then walk them to the door. Leave them with a statement of encouragement or reassurance and a smile. You may say "Thank you for coming today. We all have shared information and have a better understanding of Marena. I value your perspective. Since our last conversation, she has shown growth in all developmental areas. We can work together to encourage her to become more independent."

Following Up After the Conference

Stay in touch! A follow-up involves reaching out again to the families to make sure actions agreed on in the conference are being followed.

SDI Productions/E+ via Getty Images

Figure 32.13 Always model professional behavior during a family-teacher conference. *What does modeling professional behavior involve?*

Your follow-up should also include a report of the progress made since the conference. A teacher-family conference should allow for sharing of information. Just as families will learn, so will you. Specifically, you may learn answers to:

- the child's reaction to the center, including likes and dislikes;
- how the child spends time outside the center;
- what home responsibilities the child has;
- special interests the child has shown at home;
- the status of the child's health; and
- whom the child prefers to play with at home and in school

Record conference notes and place them in the child's folder. Make a point of calling or sending a note to parents, sharing any progress the child has made (**Figure 32.14**). Some teachers schedule time each week to contact parents by phone or with a brief note.

32.1-4 Home Visits

When time and resources permit, some teachers schedule the first teacher-family conference in the child's home. Visiting a child's home is another method for learning how to support families. **Home visits** allow the teacher to enter the child's world by spending time together in the family's home. A scheduled home visit can be valuable for the teacher in obtaining helpful information. Seeing the child's home environment can provide a better understanding of the child. The teacher can observe family-child interactions and the home environment, which can promote or interfere with a child's learning. The face-to-face contact provides the teacher with firsthand insights that help them understand the "whole child" **Figure 32.15**).

Entering a child's world provides helpful information. Teachers become more sensitive to the child's linguistic, cultural, and socioeconomic diversity. They learn about the family's unique characteristics, including their daily life. The teacher observes the child's physical environment and meets other family members and household pets. The teacher also learns how the family interacts with the child in the home. Usually, families communicate more comfortably in their own homes than they do in classroom settings. By becoming more acquainted, they also feel reassured by the teacher's interest and concern. After a home visit, a child usually feels special. Seeing the teacher in their own home builds feelings of trust and intimacy. It is important for children to know their families and they are valued.

Pheelings Media/iStock via Getty Images Plus

Figure 32.14 Take the time to write a quick note or make a quick phone call to parents after a conference. They will appreciate the contact.

Heather Preston

Figure 32.15 Home visits enable teachers to see the "whole child," including who the child is outside the center. *How might the teacher use information learned during a home visit in the classroom?*

Head Start, Early Start, and other programs use home visits as a routine part of the teacher-family partnership. If you are unable to make a visit, you could use video-conferencing.

32.1-5 Sunshine Calls

Teachers can use sunshine calls to create positive family/teacher relationships and foster two-way communication. A **sunshine call** is a telephone call made by a teacher to a parent to communicate praise and support for the child. The purpose of this call is to share with families something outstanding or interesting the child has done recently. It also informs family members of the teacher's interest in and knowledge of their child. For instance, Mrs. Chavez may call Mr. Ross to let him know his child has just learned to ride a tricycle, jump rope, or tie shoelaces.

Some parents or guardians have had poor school experiences. When these family members were in school, a call from the teacher usually meant they had done something wrong. Such calls often focused on a social or learning problem. As a result, these family members may feel **alienated** (feel like they do not belong). Done well, sunshine calls can help dispel some of these negative attitudes and help build good feelings toward the teacher and center. The goal of sunshine calls should be to build feelings of cooperation.

Sunshine calls are valuable for the family, teacher, and child. For the teacher and family, sunshine calls provide two-way communication. For the child, a call is a pleasant event. The teacher has taken a personal interest in him or her. A sunshine call, however, should not replace regularly scheduled teacher-family conferences.

Before making a sunshine call, plan the call using several guidelines:
- plan the conversation by carefully choosing what to say;
- keep the call to about five minutes;
- begin the conversation by asking a family member if it is a convenient time to talk, and if it is not, arrange a time to call back;
- put the family member at ease immediately by telling the reason for the call;
- share positive statements about the child; and
- praise the family member.

Some adults are at ease with a telephone conversation. Thus, the conversation may be relaxed. Also, many teachers and family members may be more at ease on the phone than when they talk face-to-face.

32.1-6 Discussion Groups

Another method for engaging families in their children's education is group discussion. Through discussion groups, family members become familiar with child growth and development. They also learn to notice crisis points in the family cycle and learn to understand their own roles better (**Figure 32.16**).

When conducting discussions, remember that adults:
- need to integrate new information with what they already know,
- may take errors personally,
- prefer self-designed learning experiences,
- like straightforward "how-to" approaches,
- must be physically comfortable,

AYA images/Shutterstock.com

Figure 32.16 Discussion groups can help family members learn more about their parenting roles. *In what other ways can parents benefit from discussion groups?*

- learn a great deal from interacting with others, and
- enjoy learning that engages any senses.

Group discussions are useful for studying new ideas. Discussions allow several people to take part, and through discussion, may challenge individual thinking. As the group exchanges expectations during discussion, individuals have the chance to study and review their own experiences and think through their positions.

Several problems may arise in a discussion group. Some family members may not feel comfortable taking part. When this happens, ask a question that requires a response (**Figure 32.17**). For example, you may ask, "John, how do you feel?" Also, you can build on a previous comment by saying, "John, earlier you said you were opposed to physical punishment. Why do you think you feel this way?"

Another problem that occurs often is small groups debating among themselves. If this happens, redirect the group's attention by asking them to share their comments with the entire group.

Discussion groups are helpful for family members, but they have their disadvantages. First, discussion groups most often take a long time. Other methods, such as a video or lecture, can be

Techniques to Help Parents Relax

Place items of interest on the walls for parents to look at.

Provide refreshments for parents to eat and drink.

Play soft background music.

Provide name tags on which parents can write their name as well as their child's name.

Arrange the chairs in a circle.

Greet parents individually as they enter.

Introduce parents to one another.

Provide paper and pens so parents can take notes, if interested.

Figure 32.17 Techniques for helping parents and family members feel comfortable during discussion groups and promote conversation.

Focus on Careers

Parent Educator, Marriage and Family Therapist

Parent educators facilitate group instruction and discussion on parenting and family topics in a variety of setting, including early childhood centers and adult education programs through community education programs.

Parent educators who are licensed marriage and family counselors or clinical social workers may help parents and families cope with challenges in their lives. They help parents and families develop strategies for coping and may refer them to other resources and services. They may work with community organizations and policymakers to develop programs and services for families.
Career cluster: Human services.
Education: Parent educators typically need a

bachelor's degree in family counseling, social work, clinical social work, marriage and family therapy, family and consumer sciences, or other related fields. A master's degree is required for many positions.
Job outlook. Employment for parent educators and marriage and family therapists is expected to grow 10 to 15 percent through 2030, which is much faster than average for all occupations.

To learn more about a career as a parent educator or marriage and family therapist, visit US Department of Labor websites for the *Occupational Outlook Handbook (OOH)* and *O*NET OnLine*. You will be able to compare the job responsibilities, educational requirements, job outlook, and average pay for parent educators with similar occupations.

faster. Without proper handling, the discussion may wander. When deciding whether to hold discussion groups, centers should weigh the advantages and disadvantages (**Figure 32.18**).

Advantages and Disadvantages of Discussion

Advantages	
• Ideas can be carefully studied.	• Disagreement is clarified or agreement is reached.
• Many people can take part.	• Diversity of views shared.
• Parent educators can note if parents understand the discussion.	• Encourages participation.
• People are forced to think through their problems.	• Allows for more ideas to be shared.

Disadvantages	
• It is time-consuming.	• Tension and emotions may be aroused.
• Parents may pool misinformation.	• Some parents may dominate.
• Parents expecting to be told what to do may dislike this method.	• It is easy to get side-tracked.
• Parents can come to the wrong conclusion.	

Figure 32.18 To ensure discussions benefit all attending, teachers need to guide the conversations in constructive ways.

Lesson 32.1 Review

1. The purpose of _____ is to promote family collaboration by exchanging ideas and information. (32.1.1)
   A. family engagement
   B. technology
   C. newsletters
   D. supporting military families
2. **True or False.** You should use passive voice when writing a newsletter for families. (32.1.2)
3. During a teacher-family conference, whose job is it to make the decisions regarding the child? (32.1.3)
   A. Teacher
   B. Family
   C. Child
   D. Principal
4. _____ allow the teacher to enter the child's world by spending time together in the family's home (32.1.4)
   A. Newsletters
   B. Emails
   C. Teacher-family conferences
   D. Home visits
5. The purpose of a _____ is to share with families something outstanding or interesting the child has done recently. (31.1.5)
   A. Daily News Flash
   B. newsletter
   C. sunshine call
   D. teacher-family conference
6. **True or False.** Discussion groups have no disadvantages. They are the ideal method of communicating with families. (31.1.6)

Providing Family Resources and Activities

Essential Question

? *What do you need to know about providing resources to families and engaging families in classroom activities to building trusting, respectful relationships and an effective program for children?*

Learning Outcomes

After studying this lesson, you will be able to

32.2-1 **describe** how to promote family capacity-building practices.

32.2-2 **evaluate** the importance of providing take-home activities in building family engagement.

32.2-3 **describe** the process of recruiting and giving orientation to family volunteers.

32.2-4 **analyze** the importance of building trusting, respectful relationships with children and their families.

Key Terms

family-capacity building

problem-solving file

traveling backpack

theme bags

Early childhood teachers need to build trusting relationships with families and provide them with resources and activities. Knowing families and tailoring practices to meet their needs is important. All families are unique as they are diverse culturally, linguistically, and socio-economically. Your goal is to provide family capacity-building practices so they can support their children's development. Early childhood educators and staff can support family capacity-building through a resource center and problem-solving files. A bulletin board can also be an effective tool for communicating. Educators can also promote family engagement through take-home activities. Traveling backpacks, class videos, and theme bags can all be effective tools.

32.2-1 Family Capacity-Building Practices

Family capacity-building practices provide opportunities to strengthen the family's knowledge and skills. While not as detailed as meetings or discussion groups, there are many methods teachers can use to share resources and information with family members of the children in their center. Sharing these resources can help parents or guardians feel like teachers want to support them. They can also provide valuable information about child development. Teachers can share resources with families through a family resource center, a problem-solving file, and bulletin boards.

Family Resource Center

Early childhood centers play an important role in strengthening the family's knowledge and skills. They provide referrals and resources and give families access to information on child development, child guidance, and community services. Family members may want to view books, brochures, professional articles, and other media; however, many families are not aware of where to find all this information. To meet this need, some centers provide a room or space designed as a *family resource center*. Other centers provide information boards, shelves, or files. Some communities even have free magazines related to families. Government pamphlets on nutrition, health, and safety are available to everyone.

Centers work with families to identify and access information about community services. If they are not informed, families may not realize they are eligible for some of these services. Often, centers provide applications and flyers on some programs. Included may be information on:

- home-visiting programs that provide parent education and support;
- Women, Infants, and Children (WIC) program, a federal supplemental nutrition program for pregnant women, new mothers, and infants;
- Supplemental Nutrition Assistance Program (SNAP)—food purchasing help for families with lower incomes;
- nutrition, meal planning, and infant feeding;
- service programs such as Big Brothers and Big Sisters;
- Medicaid, a health care benefit for low-income families;
- dependent care tax credit for some costs related to childcare;
- hospital programs that support new parents;
- free health clinics, dental and health screenings;
- agencies that work with families in crisis, such as domestic violence and drug addiction;
- counseling and emergency housing;
- childcare resources and referral agencies;
- federal housing assistance for families with low socioeconomic status;
- federal energy assistance to help pay heating costs for low-income families; and
- family service programs from the Department of Health, Department of Human Services, licensing agency, or public library.

A family resource center may also take the form of a lending library, where family members can check out articles, magazines, and books. A lending library can help share parenting information (**Figure 32.19**). If space is not available for a lending library, consider using a few shelves in the director's office. Include current

UW-Stout Child and Family Study Center

Figure 32.19 A lending library for parents should be well organized and inviting. ***What types of resources can centers make available to parents and family members?***

books and magazines that relate to parenting in the library. Mention reading materials during daily parent contacts, at conferences, in newsletters, or on the family bulletin board. Make sure all the reading materials are available for parents in their home languages.

Problem-Solving File

Some child care directors maintain a **problem-solving file** to help families. Each file contains information on problems parents may face. Reading materials such as journal articles, magazine articles, and newspaper clippings that relate to each problem are in file folders. **Figure 32.20** lists topics you may wish to include in a problem-solving file. Teachers can publicize the file through newsletters and at family meetings.

Bulletin Board

Making a family bulletin board is a convenient way to communicate with family members. Post meeting dates, newspaper clippings, community activities, and other center information. Inform parents of local events, library resources, and educational television programs. Offer tips for choosing toys, books,

Topics for a Problem-Solving File

Aggression	Guidance
Allowance	Handedness
Anger	Language development
Baby sign language	Lying
Bedwetting	Nightmares
Behavior problems	Nutrition
Biting	Play
Bullying	Safety
Child abuse	School readiness
Childhood diseases	Selecting toys
Cognitive development	Self-esteem
Crying	Separation anxiety
Death	Shyness
Delayed speech	Sibling relationships
Disabilities	Single-parent families
Discipline	Speech problems
Diversity	Stepfamilies
Divorce	Stress
Eating difficulties	Tantrums
Emotional development	Teething
Fears	Technology
Fine-motor skills	Television
Friendships	Thumbsucking
Giftedness	Toileting issues
Gross-motor skills	

Figure 32.20   A problem-solving file contains information on problems family members face. *What topics might you include in a problem-solving file?*

UW-Stout Child and Family Study Center

Figure 32.21   A family bulletin board should be visually appealing and announce topics of interest and messages to parents or guardians. *What other types of information can a family bulletin board include?*

32.2-2 Take-Home Activities

Promote family engagement by sending children home with take-home activities and projects. These activities invite parents to take part in the learning experience of their children. Types of take-home activities include traveling backpacks, class videos, and theme bags.

Traveling Backpacks

Families are the primary teachers of their children. Teachers can involve them in their children's education using a **traveling backpack**. On a rotating basis, children can choose their favorite books, media, puzzles, or games and put these items in a backpack. Some teachers even encourage children to include paper and writing tools. When children take their backpacks home, they can share these items with their families and do activities with them. Contents of these traveling backpacks develop a connection between the early childhood program and home.

Class Videos

Class videos can show family members what activities are occurring at the center and can provide a model for them to follow in

and nutritious snacks. Attach a pocket for handouts on parenting issues such as biting, bed-wetting, and thumb-sucking. You may also include information on childhood diseases, immunizations, safety, and child development issues. Also, consider including websites for developmental resources designed for families.

Hang the bulletin board in the most visible and well-traveled area of the center. Cover it with paper or attractive fabric. Change the background color often. This alerts family members to updated information on the board (**Figure 32.21**).

encouraging children's learning. Prepare videos of children involved in activities. You may want to record special days, favorite fingerplays and songs, stories, and theme-related activities. Record children in the dramatic play area, acting out stories, building with blocks, preparing foods, or experimenting with creative media. Then, share these videos with family members to show them what their children are learning and promote that learning.

Theme Bags

Some teachers use **theme bags** to engage families in children's education. These bags contain materials and directions for activities related to a classroom theme. Include a letter introducing the purpose of the bag along with a list of its contents. The letter should describe the specific value of theme-related activities. It should also include specific suggestions for successfully involving children in the activities at home.

The theme bag can include games, puppets, storybooks, songs, and charts. You may even send home an audio recorder to have family members record children's favorite stories. Be creative. Study your theme and brainstorm a list of related activities. Then determine which would be the most successful for families to introduce. Your goal is to help family members connect what is happening at the center and reinforce it at home.

32.2-3 Family Volunteers

Many families want to be engaged in their children's education and feel a need to develop a sense of connection with their child's classroom. Because of this, teachers and directors should involve family members. One way to do this is through volunteer programs (**Figure 32.22**).

Oksana Kuzmina/Shutterstock.com

Figure 32.22 Family volunteers often feel the need to be engaged in the children's programs and care. *What actions can you take to encourage family volunteers?*

Some teachers hesitate to include family members in their program plans. Their objections include:

- family members may not have the time needed to devote to volunteer efforts,
- family members may criticize the program,
- family members may not have effective child-guidance skills,
- parents or guardians may want to take over classroom responsibilities,
- children may act up when their family members are present, and
- parents or guardians may discuss confidential information outside of school.

These concerns are all worthwhile; however, most can be addressed by carefully recruiting and then training volunteers. Each volunteer will gain:

- personal satisfaction,
- a better understanding of child development and child guidance,
- an understanding of how children learn,
- an understanding of what activities are appropriate for young children,
- an understanding of his or her own child by observing him or her playing with other children, and
- an experience of being part of a teaching team.

Recruiting Volunteers

The best volunteers are those who have an interest in working with young children. Perhaps they would have enjoyed teaching as a profession. Still, others are interested in presenting the best experiences to their children. These people are interested in supporting the center and learning more about young children. Many parents or guardians and family members have talents or interests that could be useful to your program. Parents, grandparents, and older siblings can all become helpful volunteers. When asking for parent volunteers, send out an email or letter, such as the one shown in **Figure 32.23**. Family volunteers are usually interested in what the job entails and what they need to know. Finally, they are interested in the days or dates, time, and length of time they are needed.

Ethical Responsibilities ⚖

Building Positive Relationships with Families; Maintaining Boundaries

Building positive relationships with the families of children in your care is not only a good idea, but it is also your ethical responsibility. The NAEYC Code of Ethical Conduct includes ethical concepts relating to informing families about policies, communicating with families in a language they understand, child assessments, policies on protecting confidentiality and the right to privacy, and more that impact relationship building with parents and families. As you build positive relationships with families, it is your ethical responsibility to protect them—their privacy.

Dig Deeper

Along with meeting ethical standards of conduct you will also need to establish your professional boundaries. Use online resources to investigate the meaning of *professional boundaries*. How do these boundaries impact building positive, respectful relationships children's families? Why are they important to you and the families you serve? After reading through resources on professional boundaries, write a summary of your findings. In your own words, also write your definition of professional boundaries. Discuss how you might implement professional boundaries in working with children and families.

Work schedules may prevent some families from volunteering regularly; however, think of other creative ways of involving them. Using telecommunication platforms, you can even involve deployed military parents to read or tell stories online.

Family volunteers must be dependable, fond of children, and healthy. Be sure to check with state licensing regulations regarding requirements for volunteer participation. Always meet volunteers at their comfort level. In order to take part in a program, families need and appreciate some type of orientation.

To: Parents

From: Cindy Mirro, Director

To help us provide a quality early childhood program, parents, grandparents, aunts, uncles, guardians, and older siblings are often needed as classroom resources or volunteers from time to time. If you are interested, please check those tasks with which you would like to assist.

- ☐ Sharing a hobby or job
- ☐ Repairing books
- ☐ Repairing toys and equipment
- ☐ Coordinating and assisting with field trips
- ☐ Assisting with celebrations
- ☐ Plan a Special Friends Day
- ☐ Helping with school garden
- ☐ Caring for classroom pets during holidays
- ☐ Assisting with public relations activities
- ☐ Supervising art experiences
- ☐ Cooking with the children
- ☐ Editing the newsletter
- ☐ Supervising the art area
- ☐ Sewing dramatic play costumes
- ☐ Making classroom videos
- ☐ Audio or video recording stories
- ☐ Preparing a classroom webpage
- ☐ Planning a family night

- ☐ Playing an instrument
- ☐ Singing with the children
- ☐ Reading or telling stories to children
- ☐ Sharing a musical hobby or vocation
- ☐ Participating in your child's birthday celebration
- ☐ Organizing the fall family picnic
- ☐ Organizing the spring family picnic
- ☐ Recording favorite songs
- ☐ Making puppets, doll clothes, and/or dramatic play costumes
- ☐ Serving on a parent advisory board
- ☐ Serving as a librarian
- ☐ Serving as a secretarial aide
- ☐ Monitoring playground activities
- ☐ Helping with school garden
- ☐ Other (specify):

Please return this note to the basket in my office. If you have any questions, please contact me.

Parental Signature _____   Date _____

Figure 32.23   When seeking family volunteers, sending a letter listing tasks is helpful.

Planning Orientation for Volunteers

To best prepare volunteers, plan a training session. During this session, share staff expectations, including classroom limits and state licensing rules. As you discuss these duties, make parents, guardians, and family members feel welcome. In addition, prepare a list of guidelines for volunteers (**Figure 32.24**).

If you have not met parents, guardians, or family members before an orientation session,

be prepared to make a good impression. Studies show that first impressions are lasting impressions. The tone for an entire relationship is often set in the first four minutes.

First, begin by making the parents or family members feel comfortable. Welcome them. Offer them chairs. Begin the orientation by explaining how important volunteers are in a center. People feel good when you remember their names. As you meet each volunteer, pay attention to their name. If you do not hear it, say, "Please say your name again, I want to remember it." (**Figure 32.25**).

Suggestions for Family Volunteers

Activity Categories	Suggestions for Volunteers
General participation	• Remember that the children always come first. Share your interest in the children in the following ways:
	• Provide praise with such statements as "Your painting has such wonderful colors," "Thanks for hanging your coat on the hanger," or "You are good at helping with cleanup."
	• State your suggestions positively by telling what the child should do. For example, instead of saying "Don't put the puzzle on the floor," tell the child where to place the puzzle. Say "Place the puzzle on the table."
	• When talking with the children, get down at their level by squatting or sitting. As the child speaks, give him or her your full attention.
	• Speak with other adults only when necessary.
	• Avoid doing for a child what he or she can do for himself or herself. In other words, always stress independence. If capable, let the children put on their own coats, boots, etc. Assist only when absolutely needed so the children gain independence.
	• Avoid discussing the children outside the center.
At story time	• Sit in the circle with the children.
	• Allow interested children to crawl on your lap.
	• Show your interest in the story by listening attentively.
	• If you are asked to read, hold the book so all the children can see the photographs or illustrations.
At the easel	• Children need to wear a smock while painting.
	• Only one child should use each side of the easel at a time.
	• Encourage the children to return the brushes to their proper container. (There is one brush for each container of paint.)
	• Show an interest in the children's work, but do not interpret it for them. Avoid asking the children what they have made.
	• After children finish painting, print their names in the upper left-hand corners of their work. Capitalize only the first letter of each name.
	• Hang finished paintings on the drying rack.
	• At the end of the day, encourage the children to take their artwork home.
At music time	• Participate with the children singing, dancing, and moving.
	• Observe and reinforce the teacher's actions.
	• Share your enjoyment of the music.
	• Use bells or rhythm sticks to accompany songs.

Figure 32.24 Establishing guidelines for family volunteers to follow is essential. *Why is it important to discuss classroom limits and state licensing rules and regulations with family volunteers?*

Dragana Gordic/Shutterstock.com

Figure 32.25 Family members and teachers both benefit from wearing name tags. These help everyone learn names more quickly.

Repeat the name to yourself. Memory experts claim that by repeating the name to yourself, you will improve recall by 30 percent. Use the parent's or family member's name in conversation. Through repetition, you will engrave the volunteer's name in your memory. Studies show people recall faces better than names. Another way to recall someone's name is to observe their face. Concentrate on one trait, such as the nose, eyes, or cheekbones. Then associate the names to their faces. By remembering the family member's names, you will make them feel important.

Scheduling Volunteers

When involving volunteers, pay attention to availability and scheduling. Family volunteers will only return to the classroom if they feel needed. Post a schedule such as the one shown in **Figure 32.26**. This will help detail your expectations. Also, ask volunteers if there are questions you can answer.

Thanking Volunteers

Send each volunteer a thank-you note, e-mail, or text message after volunteering. Share at least one positive comment related to their participation. This gesture will show your appreciation. It will also encourage family members to volunteer again.

32.2-4 Respecting Parent and Family Differences

As an early childhood educator, remember that you will work with families from diverse backgrounds. Building trusting relationships with them is important. You must understand their backgrounds. When communicating, consider the families' educational levels and home cultures. Families communicate in many languages, represent various cultures, and come from different economic situations. To engage all families in your program, be mindful and respectful of these differences. Parents or guardians and family members need to feel safe, competent, and appreciated by teachers.

Understanding culture and family structure and developing sensitivity to families are ongoing processes. It takes time to build partnerships with families and teachers must learn the circumstances and experiences that shape each family's unique qualities. Some families may transition from another country or culture and may need teachers to be considerate of their change. Other families need teachers to recognize and respect the family structures (for example, nuclear family, single-parent family, stepfamily, or extended family) they adhere to. With other families, building a partnership may mean being considerate of economic problems due to job loss or job change.

Building a relationship includes building *trust*—the basis of open, comfortable communication. Through communication and understanding, you can identify each family's strengths, expectations, and values. This information will assist you in establishing continuity for the child's educational experience. It will also empower families and enhance family members' self-esteem.

Building trusting relationships with families who have immigrated from other countries is important. Teachers must meet these families where they are and develop an understanding of their needs. Incorporating the families' culture and language is important. Classroom items such as chairs, tables, the clocks, and interest centers can be labeled. The labels should reflect all the home languages of children enrolled. Items reflecting culture can also be in the classroom, such as maps, flags, musical instruments, dolls of different races, bulletin boards, and music at nap time.

Experiences for children also vary depending on their families' incomes and resources. All families must budget their expenses carefully. Unexpected requests for money for supplies, a field trip, or birthday treats can seriously impact a family's finances. Remember to be respectful of all families' situations. Keep families' economic situations in mind when planning activities.

Parent Volunteer Schedule

Time	Teacher— Juana Flores	Teacher— Lisa Sung	Helper— Mo Chu Wang	Helper— Georgia Suski
Before class	Set up equipment for special free play activities. Welcome volunteers.	Set up equipment for activities other than dirt-and-water play; special, and paint activities.	Place paper on easels. Put out paint.	Fill water table.
9:00	Welcome children. Supervise free choice of activities.	Welcome children. Supervise free choice of play activities.	Supervise painting.	Supervise water table.
10:00	Serve snack.	Supervise handwashing.	Put away easels and join snack table.	Put away dirt-and-water play equipment and help with handwashing. Assist with snack.
10:30	Help with equipment or story as needed.	Read story.	Assist Judy in putting away equipment.	Assist with story and quiet time.
10:45	Help with special activity, or on alternate days, introduce it.	Introduce special activity, or on alternate days, help with it.	Assist with special activity.	Help with special activity.
11:00	Supervise movement activity.	Put away equipment from special activity.	Assist with movement activity.	Assist with movement activity.
11:15–11:45	Wash dishes and pick up the classroom.	Supervise playground.	Supervise playground.	Supervise playground.

Figure 32.26   When establishing the volunteer schedule, it is important to consider the availability of family members and their family schedules, too. *Why is it important for family members to feel needed when volunteering in your classroom?*

Lesson 32.2 Review

1. Which of the following is not a topic a director may want to include in a problem-solving file? (32.2.1)
   A. divorce
   B. aggression
   C. self-esteem
   D. employment opportunities

2. **True or False.** Theme bags contain materials and directions for activities related to a classroom theme. (32.2.2)

3. **True or False.** During a training session for classroom volunteers, share staff expectations, including classroom limits and state licensing rules. (32.2.3)

4. When communicating with families, consider each of the following except that families may _____. (32.2.4)
   A. communicate in a foreign language
   B. have varying education levels
   C. not have found a good parking space
   D. come from different economic situations

Chapter 32 Review and Assessment

Summary

Lesson 32.1

32.1-1 As a teacher, you need to honor the value of families. Families are precious resources because they have expertise about their children.

32.1-1 Families play a key role in promoting the physical, emotional, cognitive, and social development of their children. They are also their children's primary teachers, as well as partners with the center staff. Engaging them in the early childhood program strengthens their parenting competence.

32.1-2 Written communications require less time and energy for the teacher than meetings or multiple telephone calls. However, teachers must communicate this information in the family's home language.

32.1-3 Teacher-family conferences are meetings to share the child's progress and involve the parents or guardians or families in the educational process.

32.1-4 Home visits allow the teacher to enter the child's world by spending time together in the family's home. A scheduled home visit can be valuable for the teacher in obtaining helpful information.

32.1-5 The purpose of a sunshine call is to share with families something outstanding or interesting the child has done recently.

32.1-6 When deciding whether to hold discussion groups with families, centers should weigh the advantages and disadvantages.

Lesson 32.2

32.2-1 Family resource centers, problem-solving files, and bulletin boards are all useful methods for family capacity-building practices.

32.2-2 Provide take-home activities in traveling backpacks, or theme bags for them to take part in their children's learning experiences and provide a strong home-school connection.

32.2-3 Family members can assume many roles in the classroom as volunteers. With their help, extra activities that are impossible without adult help can be introduced. Like their children, families will learn.

32.2-4 Building trusting relationships with families is important. When communicating, consider the families' educational levels and home cultures. Families communicate in many languages, represent various cultures, and come from different economic situations. To engage all families in your program, be mindful and respectful of these differences.

Vocabulary Activity

Work with a partner to write the definitions of the Key Terms based on your current understanding. Then pair up with other students to discuss your definitions and any discrepancies. Finally, discuss the definitions with the class and ask your instructor for necessary correction or clarification.

Critical Thinking

1. **Evaluate.** Collect examples of preschool parent newsletters and other communications sent home to families. Review the examples for evidence of simple, clear writing; accurate spelling and grammar; and concise and useful information. As you read, correct any mistakes and change any areas that could use improvement. Write a short evaluation of each newsletter and discuss your changes in class.

2. **Draw Conclusions.** Review the list of questions that parents or guardians most often ask teachers during family-teacher conferences. Draw conclusions about how you should answer each of these questions and then role-play a family-teacher conference with a partner.

3. **Identify.** In small teams, plan a discussion group for parents and family members in a community with a large low socioeconomic status population. As you discuss, identify discussion topics for the group. What topics might be of most interest to families in this community? What resources, articles, or advice would you bring to supplement the families' discussion?

4. **Analyze.** Collect several letters for recruiting family member volunteers at a preschool center. Analyze each letter's design and content and note any especially effective or ineffective phrases. Rewrite the letter to reflect on what you think should be included in a recruiting letter.

Core Skills

1. **Writing.** In small teams, prepare a sample family newsletter. Use a desktop publishing program as an easy-to-use format for the newsletter. Write articles to fill four pages of the newsletter and illustrate the articles with images to create interest. Edit and proofread the newsletter and prepare it as an email blast to show your effective communication skills.

2. **Writing.** Choose one type of field trip and write a series of seven daily news flashes that you think would keep parents, guardians, or family members informed and excited about this learning opportunity. Highlight themes or topics that are being taught and be sure to include several at-home activity suggestions for families and children to do together. After writing your news flashes, write a follow-up article for a family newsletter summarizing the field trip and emphasizing its educational value.

3. **Speaking.** In small teams, research articles and interview two early childhood teachers about what makes an effective family-teacher conference. After gathering information, discuss in your group and identify the most helpful pieces of advice you received. Finally, deliver an oral presentation to the class by sharing the advice.

4. **Technology.** Working in teams, imagine that one of you, as a teacher, is making a home visit and observes the following situations:
   A. A mother speaks negatively about her child.
   B. The mother appears embarrassed for you to see the home.
   C. The father speaks limited English, and the mother is very uncomfortable.

5. In response to these situations, role-play how a teacher should react. How should the teacher follow up with the parents? Film role-plays for each of these scenarios and then present your films to the class.

6. **Research.** Select a topic from *Topics for a Problem-Solving File*. Then, search for informative articles about the subject you selected. Your sources, whether print or online, should be reliable and should pertain to your topic. Cite all of your sources and compile the articles into a problem-solving file. Write a brief introduction to the problem-solving file that describes the problem and summarizes the articles in the file.

7. **CTE Career Readiness Practice.** Your director has asked you and a coworker to demonstrate family-teacher conference skills for the new hires at your early childhood center. Find a partner in your class to be your coworker and prepare a role-play to illustrate family-teacher conference skills. Include at least two challenging situations in your role-play and perform your role-play for the class. Afterwards, take questions from your classmates.

Portfolio Project

Contact area early learning centers to arrange to observe a class when a volunteer will be participating. Document the classroom activities, noting the help provided by the volunteer. Interview the teacher to determine the extent volunteers are used with the programs at the center. Write a brief essay to be filed in your portfolio about the value of volunteers and your understanding of the role of volunteers in early childhood classrooms.

Chapter 33

Reading Advantage

Describe how this chapter relates to what you have learned in another class. Make a list of the similarities and differences.

Your Career in Early Childhood Education

Lesson 33.1: Preparing for Your Career Search

Lesson 33.2: Preparing for Career Success

Case Study

Seeking a Head Teacher Position in Early Childhood

Quon was excited about completing his degree at the end of the semester. After carefully examining his interests, values, and skills, he decided to pursue a career as an early childhood teacher. Although Quon lived in Colorado, he wanted to relocate to Austin, Texas, since his fiancé lived there. Quon's advisor told him that the first step in a job search was to prepare a résumé and cover letter. Knowing that his job search could be hampered if his materials are not well-written, Quon spent hours writing and rewriting them. Since he had limited work experience, he found this challenging.

Quon went online and found the addresses of 20 early childhood centers in Austin. Through online interviews, he was offered two different assistant teaching positions. But, after getting his degree, he felt that he wanted a headteacher position as the pay and benefits were better. So, he went back to his advisor to provide an update on his activities and seek advice. His advisor asked him if he was aware of the "hidden job market," and Quon responded by saying he had never heard of it.

Give It Some Thought

1. What suggestions would you give Quon for writing a résumé?
2. Quon needs to protect his personal information on a digital résumé from cybercriminals. What information needs to be protected?
3. What will prospective employers do with Quon's résumé?
4. Describe the purpose of a cover letter? What suggestions would you have for Quon since he lacks teaching experience other than student teaching?
5. Describe the *hidden job market*?
6. How should Quon prepare for the interview?
7. What is a *working interview*? Would your preference be a working interview? Why or why not?

Opening image credit: Lordn/iStock via Getty Images Plus

Essential Question

? *What do you need to know about selecting a career, seeking employment, and writing an effective résumé and cover letter to acquire meaningful employment?*

Learning Outcomes

After studying this lesson, you will be able to

33.1-1 **explain** how interests, skills, and values affect career choices.

33.1-2 **compile** your résumé.

33.1-3 **create** a cover letter.

33.1-4 **summarize** various methods for seeking employment.

Key Terms

self-assessment

values

professional priorities

résumé

cover letter

placement service

hidden job market

networking

networking letter

Preparing for your future is rewarding and exciting, and choosing a career is an important, challenging task. To be successful, approach choosing a career thoughtfully. Successful candidates often treat job hunting like a full-time job. They commit to the process 100 percent and approach the search with a plan.

Many early childhood teachers find success using several job-searching techniques. Some teachers apply directly to an employer or center director. This contact may be an e-mail request for an application, a visit to the center, or a telephone call. Usually, people make these contacts just

before completing courses to meet state licensing guidelines or early childhood certification.

Answering online or newspaper ads is another way to seek a position working with children. Check online job boards and newspaper ads daily. If you notice an appealing position, contact the center director immediately. Online postings may require you to email or digitally submit a response. If a telephone number is listed, make a call. Many times, teaching positions need to be filled immediately. Therefore, do not waste any time in making contact.

33.1-1 Choosing a Career

Choosing a career is a challenging responsibility. As you begin seeking a job, you may be thinking, "What do I want to do with my life?" Only a few people seem to know from an early age what career they will pursue; therefore, most people find this a difficult question to answer. Choosing a career takes considerable care and thought (**Figure 33.1**). People often begin choosing a job by doing a self-assessment.

A personal **self-assessment** is a focused reflection on your interests, abilities, values, skills, family and cultural influences, and personality. Your career decisions are important, affecting your health, lifestyle, sense of happiness, and self-satisfaction. As you reflect on these factors, you will gain important self-knowledge for choosing a career. You will ask yourself many questions, and your answers will help you determine whether a career working with young children is for you.

Examining Your Interests

Interests play a significant role in career choices. Primarily people seek to prepare

wavebreakmedia/Shutterstock.com

Figure 33.1 Many teens spend a great deal of time reflecting on the future and what careers they will pursue. *What careers interest you most? Is a career in early childhood education in your future? Why or why not?*

themselves for a meaningful career they will enjoy. The Chinese philosopher Confucius offered important advice concerning career decisions: He said that if you choose a job you love, you will never need to work a day in your life. You will feel fulfilled and believe you are doing something worthwhile.

Determining what work you will enjoy can be challenging. Begin this process by analyzing your interests. Start by asking yourself the following discovery questions:

- What excites you and makes you happiest in life? What brings you joy?
- How do you spend your time? What are your hobbies?
- What do you love helping people with?

- Do you enjoy learning? What has been your favorite class?
- Do you prefer working independently or working with others?
- Do you like working with people, information, or objects?
- Which career fields do you find most interesting?

Gaining experience in a career field can help you make or confirm a career decision. For example, volunteering, working part-time, or doing an internship can help you explore early childhood education as a career option. Because of this experience, you might decide it does not suit you to be an early childhood education teacher. Otherwise, you may feel more strongly that working with young children is the best career option for you.

You can also assess your interests by learning more about other careers. Research a few careers you are considering. What are the responsibilities of each job? Are these tasks you would enjoy? Interview a professional employed in the field to learn more. You might be able to arrange a job-shadowing experience where you can spend an entire day with an employee at their job. This experience can give you an overview of the job duties and rewards.

Analyzing Your Skills

The second part of self-assessment is analyzing your skills. Skills directly influence job performance—you are more likely to succeed in a job you can do well. Having interests and skills in similar areas is not uncommon. You are more likely to be interested in tasks you excel at, and you may work harder to develop skills in areas that interest you. You may have some skills that differ from your interests.

When choosing a career, analyze all your skills. These may be areas in which you have always excelled. Natural talents are called *aptitudes*. You might discover other skills by taking ability tests through a guidance or career counselor or online. Common names for these tests are *aptitude tests* and *skills assessments*. These tests can help you identify careers that might suit you and assess whether you have personal aptitudes and skills necessary for the early childhood profession.

You can also ask close friends and trusted adults for their insight. They may comment, "You're so good with children," "You relate to people so easily," or "You solve problems well." These comments can help you identify areas of strength.

Developing a solid foundation of basic skills will help you in any career. These basic skills include human relations, teamwork, leadership, communication (writing, speaking, and listening), computers, mathematics, problem-solving, decision-making, time management, stress management, and planning. With these basic skills, chances are you will become a successful employee in whatever career you choose (**Figure 33.2**).

Besides basic skills, you will need some career-specific abilities, which relate more closely to the demands of a particular job. Effective early childhood teachers need abilities to help them carry out their responsibilities, as described in earlier chapters of this book. Some of these abilities include:

- planning developmentally appropriate curriculum, lessons, activity areas, schedules, and routines;
- leading group activities and assisting children in activity areas as needed;

SDI Productions/E+ via Getty Images

Figure 33.2   Developing basic skills will make you a more valuable employee in almost any career. *What skills do you need to work on most?*

- matching guidance and communication techniques to children's developmental ages;
- setting and enforcing limits required for children's health, safety, and healthy development;
- providing comfort, nurturance, affection, and effective praise;
- offering constant supervision to all children throughout all daily activities; and
- demonstrating appropriate physical care techniques (such as diapering, feeding, dressing, toileting, and hand washing) to keep children safe and healthy.

Skills professionals need in other child-related careers may differ somewhat from those teachers' needs. For example, an early childhood director requires budgeting, record keeping, planning, organizing, leading, and supervising abilities. Learning more about particular careers will help you determine what career-specific skills are necessary.

Once you know your skills, compare them to those required of a chosen career. You may have many of the needed abilities already, but there may be others you still need to develop. If a job profoundly interests you, it may be worthwhile to identify ways to build the skills required. Taking additional classes to learn more about the subject can help. Ask a teacher, guidance counselor, supervisor, or other trusted adult to help you identify different ways to develop the needed skills.

Reflecting On Your Values

After you understand your interests and skills, look at your **values**. These are your beliefs, feelings, and ideas about what is essential. Values influence your decisions and actions. Each person is an individual with unique thoughts, feelings, experiences, and beliefs. These differences are often a reflection of their values. For example, some people desire popularity, wealth, and material possessions. Others find education, career, family life, or friendships more meaningful. Each person can value any combination of priorities in any order of importance. That makes values genuinely personal.

As you examine your values, you will better understand the importance of various people, objects, and ideas in your life. Choosing a career that aligns with your values dramatically increases your personal happiness and career success. Such a career will enhance your life by allowing you to focus on what matters most to you.

Closely related to values are **professional priorities**. These are global aspects of work that are important to a person's satisfaction. Professional priorities might include:

- opportunities to teach children;
- feeling a sense of accomplishment;
- working as a team member;
- helping others solve problems;
- having a leadership role;
- gaining recognition;
- earning a respectable salary;
- working independently; and
- contributing to your community and society.

In identifying professional priorities, ask yourself what comes to mind when you think of a fulfilling career. List these priorities and compare your list with those commonly found among workers in your chosen career field. **Figure 33.3** shows professional priorities widely shared by successful early childhood teachers.

Professionals in early childhood careers other than teaching may have different professional priorities. For example, successful directors' roles are complicated. In addition to recruiting families, one of their most critical responsibilities is hiring highly motivated, well-trained staff. **Figure 33.4** lists a director's responsibilities.

Examining your values and professional priorities will help you determine whether working with young children will be a rewarding career choice for you. This part of self-assessment can also help you propose specific short-term and long-term career goals. Then you can seek the needed education, training, and experiences to qualify you to work in the career of your choice.

Professional Priorities of Early Childhood Teachers

Successful early childhood teachers commonly share the following professional priorities:

- Independence: working on their own
- Creativity: trying out their ideas
- Responsibility: making their own decisions and solving problems
- Achievement: gaining a feeling of accomplishment
- Relationships: providing service to children and families.
- Working with coworkers in a friendly, noncompetitive environment
- Sharing knowledge: teaching and guiding young children to learn new concepts and skills

Figure 33.3   Professional priorities are global aspects of work that are important to a satisfying career. *What comes to mind for you when you think of a meaningful, fulfilling career?*

33.1-2 Preparing a Résumé

To prepare for your job search, first prepare a résumé. A **résumé** summarizes your qualifications, skills, and experience. You should tailor it to the job for which you are applying. A résumé aims to inform a potential employer of your qualifications and experience and secure an interview. If your résumé is effective, you will receive invitations to interview.

Résumés also serve many other purposes. A résumé may serve as your self-inventory. Having a factual list of your background and skills can be quite helpful when looking for a job. It can also serve as a starting point for an interview. A well-written résumé will give the employer information on which to base the discussion. After the consultation, your résumé will help the employer recall your experiences and the interview.

Director Responsibilities

Successful directors of early learning programs must fulfill the following responsibilities:

- Ensure that the early childhood center and staff adhere to all licensing rules and regulations
- Develop budget, financial policies, and procedures
- Adhere to early childhood standards
- Implement program curriculum approach
- Recruit children and families to achieve and maintain full enrollment
- Identify and report any suspected child abuse
- Hire highly motivated, well-trained staff and assign mentors
- Create strong home-family partnerships
- Provide ongoing staff training and development
- Attend professional conferences at the state and national level to remain up-to-date
- Handle conflict and confrontation among teachers, families, and staff
- Conduct regularly scheduled staff meetings
- Handle complaints
- Manage the facility with emphasis on health and safety

Figure 33.4   Directors of early learning programs have many responsibilities.

Writing a Résumé

A well-prepared résumé plays a vital role in your job search. First, it instantly creates a favorable impression of you. Second, it creates a desire in the employer to meet you. Most times, it is your ticket to a job interview.

All résumés should always contain essential information about the applicant: name, current address, email address, and a telephone number or cell phone number, including the area code.

Remember, your résumé represents you. Be accurate and neat. Use simple words and write in a clear, concise manner. Include your educational

background, employment objective, paid and volunteer work experience, professional activities, interests, and references. Always be descriptive. For instance, if you want to share that you are a hard worker, create a statement that will deliver that message: "Worked 20 hours per week during the past two semesters." **Figure 33.5** shows an example of a résumé.

Use your résumé to present yourself as an active, well-rounded person. The résumé should have an easy-to-read format. Also, correct all misspellings, grammatical errors, and typing errors. Poor computer or writing skills and grammatical errors will always reflect poorly on the applicant. Basic mistakes may cripple your job search. Some highly qualified applicants have failed to get interviews because of poor writing skills. It is always wise to ask several people who have excellent writing skills to proofread your résumé before sending it to an employer. Make sure:

- the résumé is limited to one page with a font size of 10 to 12 points;
- you use a modern font—*Arial, Calibri, Cambria, Georgia,* or *Tahoma*;
- your name is in a larger font size than any other text on the page;
- there are no grammatical or spelling errors;
- statements begin with active verbs, such as prepared, taught, planned, conducted;
- to avoid personal pronouns such as me, my, I, and our;
- to spell out your degree (Bachelor of Education);
- each institution has name, dates attended, or anticipated graduation date; and
- each experience includes the name, position title, location, and relevant date.

Recent graduates have a unique challenge in writing résumés because of their limited work experience. Those who face this challenge should not overlook any previous unpaid work experience. Any practice teaching, lab work, or volunteer work in your field of study can be included in your résumé. Involvement in

Sharon Kaminski

Phone: (715) 555-1111

Email: SKaminski@uwstout.edu

LinkedIn www.linkedin.com/in/sharon-kaminiski/

Objective

Creative and motivated graduate seeking an early childhood teaching position.

Education

University of Wisconsin-Stout

- Graduating June 20XX with a Bachelor of Science in Early Childhood Education.
- 3.83 (out of 4.0) cumulative grade point average.
- Dean's List: 20XX–present.

Valders High School

- Graduated June 20XX.
- Activities: a member of National Honor Society and school band; captain of women's volleyball team.
- Languages
- Bilingual—English and Spanish

Experiences

Internship, Wee Care Child Care Center, Atlanta, Georgia, June 20XX–September, 20XX

- Assisted headteacher with all program activities during the summer session.
- Created new teaching aids for art, science, music, and social studies activities.
- Supervised adult volunteers.

Course Assistant, Early Childhood Department at University of Wisconsin-Stout, September, 20XX–June, 20XX

- Coordinated teacher education resource room: designed room layout, ordered materials, maintained files, and developed a check-out system.

Valders Public Schools, September 20XX–June, 20XX

- Assisted four-year-old kindergarten teacher with special activities: coordinated and supervised holiday parties, prepared teaching aids, and maintained classroom centers.

Activities

International Relations Council, University of Wisconsin-Stout

- Delegate to State Model United Nations.

Dean's Student Advisory Council, University of Wisconsin-Stout

- Advised Dean on students' activities. Coordinated special school events, including Parents' Weekend.

Student Ambassador, University of Wisconsin-Stout

- Visited community high schools to recruit students for the University of Wisconsin-Stout.

Interests

Alpine and cross-country skiing, reading, gourmet cooking.

References available upon request.

Figure 33.5   Résumés should be neatly organized and evenly spaced. *Why is a well-prepared résumé important to your job search?*

professional organizations related to your field of study, such as an affiliate of the National Association for the Education of Young Children (NAEYC), should also be included in a résumé. You may wish to explain any leadership roles you assumed or any skills you developed that will help you on the job.

Safety First

Online Résumé Safety

When applying for jobs online or via email, protect your personal information. To keep your data out of the hands of cybercriminals, remember the following tips:

- Avoid using your home address and telephone number. Instead, use your email address and a prepaid cell phone for initial contact with employers.
- Never put your social security number on your résumé. Once an employer wants to hire you, you may need to provide this information.
- Consider using a separate email address only for your job search.

Read privacy policies for online job boards carefully. Some reserve the right to sell your identifiable information.

What Employers Do with Résumés

Directors will quickly look at a résumé to determine if you have the educational background and experience needed to apply. If your expertise appears to meet the job description, they will read the résumé more closely. Most employers will look for gaps in your employment, the amount of space you give to previous jobs, and the emphasis on education.

Employment gaps may make directors wary of problems in your job history. Gaps may signal that you were unemployed between jobs. You may have chosen to leave out a job on your résumé because it did not relate to the position you seek. Perhaps you were unemployed for a

legitimate reason, such as returning to school. Be sure to explain such gaps in your cover letter (**Figure 33.6**).

When you give the time of your employment, be sure to specify the month and year of each job's starting and ending date. Listing only years can confuse directors. Such a listing can also give the impression that you are concealing gaps in employment. Be accurate and honest with your résumé. Experienced center directors and employers are skilled at examining résumés, so avoid omitting facts.

A good résumé should reflect progress in a career over the years. Directors are interested in an applicant's most recent accomplishments; therefore, note the most recent job experience first. Some résumé writers devote more space to an earlier teaching position. Center directors will interpret this as either poor judgment or a hasty résumé update. Overall, these errors convey a lack of ambition and poor planning by the applicant. These errors may not always rule out an applicant from an interview; however, they may signal that the applicant requires a close review during this process.

Directors will also review a résumé to see if there is too much emphasis on education and nonjob factors. When an applicant has been out of school for several years, the résumé should stress

sturti/E+ via Getty Images

Figure 33.6   If you are not sure how to explain gaps in your employment or need help writing an effective résumé, you can visit individuals who specialize in helping job seekers. Some of these individuals might be college and career counselors or writing experts.

work experience. Applicants who emphasize post-secondary honors may focus too much on the past. If the résumé highlights emphasize non-job factors, this may show where their real interests lie.

Digital Résumés

Many employers now request that you email digital résumés in response to job ads. Employers then search the digital résumés they receive for keywords they use to identify ideal candidates. This helps employers filter through applicants more quickly, eliminating résumés that do not include the keywords. Therefore, you should be sure to word your résumé carefully and tailor it to a job description.

To create a digital résumé, save your résumé as "text-only" with no formatting. Then review the text-only résumé to make sure lines and headers break correctly. Be sure to keep this in a separate file from your formatted résumé. Digital résumés will also come in handy if you make online job applications.

33.1-3 Cover Letters

A **cover letter** is a letter of introduction usually included when sending a résumé. The primary purpose of a cover letter is to set you apart from the competition. It provides you an opportunity to showcase your thought processes and writing ability. It should capture an employer's attention and inspire them to request an interview. This letter is essential and should be carefully crafted. **Figure 33.7** shows an example of a cover letter.

When writing a cover letter, follow a business letter format. As with the résumé, use proper grammar and punctuation. Write each cover letter separately. Avoid writing one generic cover letter that you use to apply for any job. This gives the impression that you are not interested enough to write a tailored letter. It also will not stand out to the reader.

Keep in mind that no one in the early childhood community is called *Sir, Madam,* or *To Whom It May Concern.* Call, if necessary, or go

online to get the name of the center director or the person responsible for hiring. Address the cover letter to this person.

Your cover letter should be short, simple, easy to read and showcase your professional interests. Writing quality is more important than quantity. Your cover letter is an opportunity to "market yourself" to the employer. Your objective is to stand out from the other people applying for the position and earn the employer's attention. A cover letter should not be a summary of your résumé. It should convince the person hiring why you are a great match for the position.

Keep the length of your cover letter to a few paragraphs. Describe how you learned about the job opening or are familiar with the center. Explain why you want to be considered for the position and describe your interests, aptitudes, and abilities related to the job. End the letter by telling the employer what action—for instance, a phone call or interview—you would like them to take. Be polite in your request and thank the person for reviewing your cover letter and résumé. There is no best way to sign off on the cover letter to get a job interview. You could sign the letter *Sincerely,* which is a classic option, and your name. To some people, this may sound dated. Using your name may be the perfect way to sign off on the letter when in doubt.

Reread your letter several times for content, word processing, and grammatical errors. Have several other people proofread the letter for you, too. In one study, seventy-six percent of recruiters said they would not consider an applicant whose résumé or cover letter contained errors. By making an error, you could make a poor impression.

33.1-4 Avenues for Seeking Employment

Early childhood job seekers may use several methods to find employment. These methods include mailing cover letters with résumés, placing or answering ads on the internet. Career fairs and networking provide other opportunities

Cover Letter

615 Market St.
Menomonie, WI 54362
August 1, 20XX

Alex Briones, Director
Spring Hill Child Development Center
1318 Hillcrest Road
Springfield, MA 56789

Dear Mr. Briones:

While searching for job positions on the NAEYC's job board, I read your advertisement for an early childhood teacher. I am interested in obtaining a position in early childhood education and relocating to Springfield, Massachusetts.

I hold a bachelor's degree in early childhood education. My interest in early childhood education as a profession started while I was in middle school. Since then, I have cared for children, assisted with a local preschool program, and worked in an after-school program in a local center. These experiences convinced me of my interests, skills, enthusiasm, and passion for working with young children.

My résumé is enclosed for your consideration. You will see that my experience and education match the qualifications outlined in your advertisement.

Thank you for considering me for a position in your center. This is precisely the type of opportunity I am seeking, and I am sure I can make a positive contribution to your center. Please do not hesitate to call me for more information. If you would like to schedule an interview, or if you have any questions, please contact me at 789-555-5748 or email me at Kcha@uwstout.edu. Thank you for your time and consideration of this matter.

Sincerely,

Kim Cha

Kim Cha

Figure 33.7   Include a cover letter with your résumé when responding to ads. *How can a well-crafted cover letter benefit you in getting a job interview?*

to search for positions. Successful applicants also do not overlook the hidden job market.

Online Ads

Answering online ads can be helpful when looking for work. As a job seeker, make a habit of reading ads every day (**Figure 33.8**). Study a wide range of ads. Examples of titles related to child care include *childcare teacher, infant teacher, toddler teacher, preschool teacher, early childhood teacher, assistant teacher, school-age childcare teacher, program coordinator, curriculum specialist,* and *activities director.* If you are looking for an administrative position, look closely for the director, administrator, or coordinator descriptions.

rmnoa357/Shutterstock.com

Figure 33.8 Many new early childhood teachers find their first jobs through online job boards or newspaper ads. *Is there a benefit to searching job ads daily? Why or why not?*

When searching online for postings, visit many sites and job boards. Make sure to check NAEYC's Early Childhood Career Center and your state's affiliates, which are free to its membership. The site is designed to provide you access to many of the best jobs and employers. Advanced searching options are available. Once you establish an online account, your cover letter and résumé will be stored. Automatic email notifications will be sent to you when a new posting matches your criteria. Additionally, you will be shown the number of times your résumé has been reviewed.

The National Head Start's Association Career Center website posts jobs every day. The United States Department of Defense is the largest employer-sponsored system of child development centers. The Army, Marines, and Navy all post online job opportunities. LinkedIn is another source that allows employers to list jobs and search for potential candidates.

Some sites will show the distance you need to travel, or allow you to upload your résumé so employers can find you. They may also include

salary estimates. Joining a discussion group in your field is another way to find meaningful employment. Some professional associations sponsor list servers or message boards and use newsgroups.

If an ad appeals to you, respond exactly according to the instructions in the ad. If the employer requests that you fill in an online form on their company site, do so. If they want you to send your resume directly to an email address, make sure you send it to the correct address. If a cover letter is required, be sure to include one.

If an advertisement does not ask for your salary requirements, do not mention them in your letter. By including a salary figure, they could screen you out, and you would not have a chance to interview. Some ads state the exact salary or range they will pay. For instance, an ad might note the precise dollar figure per hour or a range of several thousand dollars (**Figure 33.9**). Other ads may state that salary is open "based on experience" or "based on educational background."

College or School Placement Offices

Most early childhood certificate and degree programs provide a **placement service**. This service is to find professional positions for their graduates. Placement offices are usually on campus. They encourage employers to call in, send, or email job information for the office to post (**Figure 33.10**). When employers contact the placement services on campus, they receive help finding qualified graduates.

> **» Apply Now**
> _____
>
> Head Teacher at the Sheboygan Early Childhood Center. Applicant must hold a two-year certificate from an accredited institution of higher learning. Salary range from $2,400–$3,600 per month.
>
> Call 1-414-555-4598
>
> Apply online or e-mail: eccenter@sheboygan.edu

Figure 33.9 Online job postings and ads briefly summarize the open position.

Position:

Head Teacher, Early Childhood Program

Full-Time Position

Yearly contract renewal for a maximum of three years

Date Available:

August, 20XX

Job Responsibilities:

Head Teacher in early childhood center. Plan and implement a developmentally appropriate curriculum for three- and four-year-old children. Supervise a teacher's aide and volunteers from a local community college. Assist Director in applying for accreditation. Plan and implement parent meetings, conferences, and related activities.

Qualifications:

- A Bachelor of Science degree in Early Childhood Education is required; graduate work is preferred.
- Must be certified to teach preschool in Texas.
- Experience in assessment, curriculum development, and program evaluation.
- Demonstrated excellence in teaching young children for a minimum of three years.
- Demonstrated ability to interact positively with people and work cooperatively with other staff members, families, students, volunteers, and children.
- Must be able to organize and coordinate activities with volunteers.
- Must be able to motivate children in a creative environment.
- Must be able to demonstrate initiative and continuous professional development.

Figure 33.10   Notices posted in school placement offices often give a comprehensive summary of the open position. *How can preparing a portfolio benefit you when working with a school placement office?*

As a student, you will be required to prepare a career portfolio. This portfolio will include materials on paper or as an electronic file. Regardless of the format used, this file will usually have a standard form prepared by the college or school placement service. The document

- lists your current address; schools attended, degrees earned, and past work experiences;
- contains your résumé, transcript of grades, and letters of recommendation from faculty and previous employers; and
- lists references you have contacted and confirmed.

The Hidden Job Market

Many job candidates are most successful when focusing their efforts on the **hidden job market**.

Career advisors suggest that people spend more time forging connections in their fields and less time searching job sites. Jobs frequently are advertised informally through personal contacts. Sometimes, positions are not listed in help-wanted ads, early childhood journals, or placement offices. Instead, word of mouth is used to fill positions. To find out about such openings, contact center directors or principals personally. You can do this through a letter, a telephone call, or email. Some candidates have succeeded by arranging a visit to the center and asking about job openings. Even if no position is open, some applicants receive a call later when jobs become available.

Entry-level positions are often obtained through the side door, not the front door. Get to know early childhood staff workers in the community. One way to do this is to join the local or state chapter of the NAEYC. Some counties and cities also have their own independent early childhood organizations. When you attend meetings, try to meet as many people as possible. Always let them know of your job search and when you will be available. In addition, become active in the organization(s)—volunteer for committees to show the membership your professional commitment.

Networking

Networking is the job seeker's most powerful tool. Most teachers find positions through some type of networking with others. **Networking** builds relationships with people who can help you. It involves interaction with others to share information and develop professional contacts. It is an important skill to develop.

One way to have your résumé considered is to have recommendations from respected people in the field. To find these people, you need to go where they are. Attend early childhood organizations, workshops, conferences, seminars, open houses, job fairs, and center tours. Since networking is a process, it usually takes several contacts to build relationships. These contacts may be person-to-person meetings, phone conversations, email contacts, voice mail, letters, and notes.

You might also consider writing a networking letter. Like a cover letter, carefully write **networking letters.** Send them to an assortment of people, particularly alumni in early childhood education whom you know personally. The purpose of the networking letter is to inform others that you are available for employment. After receiving the letter, these individuals could pass your name to potential employers. They could also provide you with valuable insight into potential employment opportunities.

Maintaining a Filing System

Keep a file of all the centers, schools, or job centers you have contacted (**Figure 33.11**). Make a photocopy of each cover letter you send or

maintain copies on a computer. You may also prepare index cards or a file on your computer for each contact. If you get a call from a director, you should quickly be able to retrieve the information and refresh your memory on the open position. To assist in this process, always record the school's name, address, telephone number, contact person, and date the contact letter was mailed.

If you have answered an ad, attach a copy of the advertisement to your cover letter or index card. When you receive a response (whether negative or positive), record this on your cover letter, make notes of interviews, thank-you notes, and other contacts on each letter or card.

Eva-Katalin/E+ via Getty Image

Figure 33.11 Keeping your job search information organized and up-to-date is important. *What method do you feel is best for organizing your job search information?*

Ethical Responsibilities ⚖️

Representing Yourself Accurately

Truthfully and accurately representing who you are and your credentials—including your background, education, qualifications, and experience—is essential in seeking meaningful employment. Job candidates who misrepresent themselves when applying for and accepting a job position can negatively impact the employer, coworkers, and the people they serve.

Dig Deeper

What are the consequences for job candidates who misrepresent themselves when seeking and gaining employment? Use online resources to investigate how employers handle job candidates or employees who misrepresent themselves. What actions do employers generally take? What are the long-term consequences for the person seeking employment? Write a summary of your findings and discuss the implications for job candidates with your classmates.

Lesson 33.1 Review

1. Which of the following is *not* a focused reflection of your personal self-assessment? (33.1.1)
   A. interests
   B. abilities
   C. skills
   D. favorite color
2. **True or False.** It is not important to use proper grammar in your résumé. (33.1.2)
3. **True or False.** The primary purpose of a cover letter is to set you apart from the competition. (33.1.3)

4. If an employer asks you to fill out a form on their website when you apply, you should _____. (33.1.4)
   A. fill out the form completely and correctly
   B. just email them your résumé to save time
   C. just email them your cover letter to save time
   D. skip that employer's ad

Essential Question

How can effective personal preparation lead to gaining meaningful employment in your future?

Learning Outcomes

After studying this lesson, you will be able to

33.2-1 **summarize** the basic interviewing process.

33.2-2 **explain** the rights and responsibilities of employees and employers.

33.2-3 **identify** right and wrong ways to leave a job.

33.2-4 **summarize** the importance of finding a balance among family, work, and community roles.

Key Terms

bolster	attitude
preinterview	confidentiality
traditional interview	The Family Educational Rights and Privacy Act (FERPA)
working interview	
teaching portfolio	role
candidacy	role strain
punctual	

Career success begins with preparing for the job interview, which is an essential part of the selection and hiring process. This interviewing process is critical and used worldwide for teachers obtaining employment. The interview will reveal much about your ability to work within the center or school system. Each center or school's recruitment and interview process may be different. In the teaching field,

sharing your teaching portfolio is an important step since it shows your growth and success. Be aware of potential legal problems during the interview. After, send a thank-you letter to establish goodwill. Once you gain employment, you must be aware of your responsibilities such as attendance, punctuality, and maintaining a professional appearance. Much of a teacher's success is a reflection of their commitment and attitude.

33.2-1 The Interview

Job interviews are the most critical aspect of a job search. They are opportunities to convey key information about yourself.

Preparing for an Interview

When preparing for an interview, think positively. Picture yourself walking into the interview confident and relaxed. Get in the habit of being enthusiastic. Remember, enthusiasm is catching. It shows appreciation and interest. Often, if you are excited, the interviewer will also show this feeling.

Employers want to hire self-directed people with a wide range of skills. They want people who are dependable, enthusiastic, and committed to the early childhood education profession. They want people who work hard and learn fast. They also want people who manage their time well and look for extra work. To provide high-quality programs, directors need to hire resourceful people.

Figure 33.12 outlines traits employers seek when hiring people to work in early childhood centers. To prepare for an interview, read the statements and check those that match qualities

Positive Traits of Early Childhood Teachers

Flexible	Dependable
Energetic	Effective planner
Self-confident	Committed to teaching
Enthusiastic	Open to new ideas
Mature	Self-disciplined
Willing to do extra work	Dedicated to hard work
Patient	Motivated
Cooperative	Self-reliant
Easy to get along with	Thorough
Fast learner	Self-directed
Excellent time manager	Friendly
Creative	Organized
Cheerful	Nurturing
Positive	Responsible
Resourceful	Persistent
Caring	Possessing a good sense of humor
Kind	Possessing strong interpersonal skills

Figure 33.12   Knowing the traits employers seek when hiring early childhood candidates helps you match your qualities to positions available.

you could bring to a position. Completing this task will **bolster** (strengthen) your self-image. The exercise will help you get a clear picture of your skills. It will also prepare you to make a persuasive presentation during an interview.

In nearly all interviews, applicants are provided an opportunity to ask questions. Bright applicants always prepare questions for an interview. As you prepare questions, learn

everything you can about the center. Check to see if there is a website. You might form questions by talking to teachers who have taught at the center or asking parents who have children attending the center. You can get general information about the center from the local chamber of commerce. Some questions you may wish to ask during an interview are:

- What is the educational philosophy of your center?
- To what extent may I implement my ideas?
- Is the staff encouraged to attend conferences? If so, how often may a staff member attend, and who pays the fees?
- What digital and audiovisual equipment will the school provide?
- How often are parent conferences scheduled?
- Does the center send home a weekly family letter or monthly newsletter? If so, who writes and edits the correspondence?

Asking questions tells the interviewer you are serious about a job. Practice your questions, eye contact, and posture (**Figure 33.13**).

Prospective employers usually decide what information they need to share with you about a job before the interview. Often included are job expectations, duties, and benefits. They may ask and record your response to specific questions. To prepare for an interview, think about your answers to some of the common questions asked during an interview. You may even want to write your answers. **Figure 33.14** lists common questions employers ask during interviews.

Interviews

There are three types of interviews. A **preinterview** is a conversation occurring

Figure 33.14 To prepare for an interview, practice maintaining good eye contact and posture.

before an interview, including an email, text, or telephone message. In a **traditional interview**, the person is asked a series of questions. The **working interview** is designed so the employer can see the candidates' skills. As opposed to trying to explain your qualifications, it allows you to demonstrate your teaching skills working with a group of young children to the employer.

Job interviews may take place in virtual space via video conferencing. When attending a job interview, make a positive and lasting impression. Arrive on time. Remember to take your driver's license or state ID card, résumé, portfolio, and list of questions for the interviewer. Give particular thought to your appearance. You want to make a good impression. Make sure your hair is well-groomed and attractively styled. Choose conservative jewelry, accessories, and shoes. Avoid displaying tattoos or multiple piercings, and apply makeup lightly. Be sure your clothes are clean and neat, and appropriate for the position. Choose clothes that are one step above those you would typically wear. Avoid overdressing, but do not wear a faded T-shirt, shorts, or torn jeans. Let your appearance tell the interviewer you are professional and can fit into the workplace.

At the interview, it is important to be likeable. Use body language to show enthusiasm. Make eye contact, smile, and greet the employer with a firm handshake (during in-person interviews). Many interviewers begin a discussion by introducing themselves and welcoming you to the center. Small talk might include the weather or a center activity. After this, you will probably be told information about the job. The interviewer may then ask you structured questions concerning your education or experience. Be enthusiastic; smile, nod, and give nonverbal feedback to the interviewer. Provide complete, focused answers and use the interviewer's name from time to time as you speak. Avoid answering a question with only *yes* or *no*. After you have responded to all the questions, the interviewer will ask if you have questions. You can ask those questions you prepared beforehand. Avoid asking questions about vacation time, benefits, and breaks. The interviewer may think your primary concern is with nonwork functions.

Common Questions Asked During an Interview

- Please share your educational background.
- What type of coursework did you complete?
- Do you have previous job experience? If so, describe your positions.
- Why do you want this job?
- What are the most important characteristics of a teacher of young children?
- Use three words to describe your personality.
- What are some of your negative qualities? What is the biggest mistake you ever made?
- How do people describe you?
- How would you describe your teaching style?
- Where do you see yourself professionally five years from today? Describe that job.
- Why are you interested in this job?
- What is the value of children's play?
- How would you handle a child who is always hitting others?
- How would you plan a developmentally appropriate curriculum?
- If I walked into your classroom, tell me what I would see.

- How do you think your references described you when they were contacted?
- What do you know about us?
- Why should we hire you?
- How would you handle transitions?
- How would you plan to communicate with families?
- On what basis do you plan a curriculum for young children?
- What would you do if a child kicked you and said, "I don't like you"?
- What disappointments did you face in your last teaching position?
- In what areas did your supervisor criticize you?
- In what areas did your supervisor compliment you?
- For what things did you need guidance or help from your supervisor?
- Why did you select teaching young children as a career?
- Why did you apply for this job?
- What makes you the best candidate for this position?
- What are you looking for in this position that you have not had in previous jobs?

Figure 33.13   When preparing for an interview, think about your responses to common interview questions? *Why might it be a beneficial to write down your responses prior to an interview?*

Follow the lead of the interviewer. Throughout the interview, listen with an intelligent, intent look on your face. When necessary, ask intelligent questions that will help you better understand the job. **Figure 33.15** lists other tips for successful interviewing.

Be careful not to volunteer negative information about your former employer or yourself. Employers are seeking positive people to work for them. If you were not happy in a previous job, you might not be satisfied with this job either. Therefore, it is vital not to mention anything negative. Focus on the position.

Throughout the interviewing process, you will need to sell your positive qualities. When asked what you did during your practicum, student teaching, or last job, do not recite the

daily schedule or curriculum. Instead, state specific things you did to improve the center or classroom. For example, you might talk about how you made protective education part of the curriculum. Perhaps you revised the format for family letters and reorganized the children's library.

An interviewer may ask, "What are your weaknesses?" during the interview. If this happens, sit quietly for a moment. Avoid answering the question too quickly. It is always a mistake to quickly answer a question off the top of your head. Instead, give each question some thought, then form a response in your mind. Then respond carefully and positively. Do not put yourself down while answering this question. Instead, share your growth by

Tips for a Successful Interview

- Be on time.
- Present your best appearance.
- Extend your hand to greet the interviewer with a firm handshake.
- Use the interviewer's name and smile as you speak.
- Bring your résumé and teaching portfolio with you.
- Remain relaxed and friendly.
- Listen carefully.
- Convey a positive attitude; use good posture.
- Show your enthusiasm.
- Stress your strengths.
- Use active verbs while speaking.
- Personalize your questions.
- Respond to questions carefully.
- Be truthful; if you do not know an answer, say so.
- Provide more than a "yes" or "no" response to questions, but be concise.
- Thank the interviewer for their consideration at the end of the interview.
- Send a thank-you note.

Figure 33.15 Listening intently to the interviewer throughout your interview is just one tip for successful interviewing. *Review the list of tips. Which were most unfamiliar to you? How can you take action on these tips for interview success?*

saying something like, "I have developed skills in classroom control" or "My parent interaction skills grew during the last few weeks of my student teaching." You might also express your weaknesses positively: "I care too much about the children," "I take my work too seriously," or "I try too many new ideas."

Often, the interviewer may end the interview with a final question. They might ask, "Was there anything that you were afraid that I would ask?" If this occurs, remain calm. Sometimes interviewers will share a question that they feared.

Workplace Connections

Investigating Difficult-to-Answer Interview Questions

Conduct a survey among students and teachers to discover the most difficult-to-answer questions from their job-interview experiences.

1. What were the most difficult-to-answer questions?
2. How would you answer these questions in an interview? Sometimes questions have no relation to the job because the interviewer is just trying to determine how the applicant will react under pressure.

Sharing Your Teaching Portfolio

Teaching portfolios can be created in a hard-copy format, digital, or both. Bring along your teaching portfolio to show your growth and success. Your **teaching portfolio** tells a story. It should be a professional snapshot of your efforts, progress, and achievements. Your portfolio should contain evidence of your competence. **Figure 33.16** outlines the typical contents of a teaching portfolio.

Offer to share your teaching portfolio. You may say, "I brought along my teaching portfolio. I would like to share the contents with you." While sharing the contents, use descriptions to support your materials. Explain why you chose each piece to include in the portfolio.

Teaching Portfolio

- Table of contents
- Cover page including name and a few photographs of you working with children
- Résumé
- Official transcripts
- Copies of certifications, licenses, or CDA
- Credential certificate
- Statement of educational philosophy and teaching goals
- Extracurricular activities
- Letters of recommendation
- Curriculum units and themes you have developed
- Sample lesson plans, block plans, and parent letters
- Videos of a good teaching lesson
- Teacher-made materials
- Photographs of activities with descriptions
- Photographs of bulletin boards and room arrangements you designed
- Anecdotal records
- Critical incident journals
- Teachers' evaluations

Figure 33.16 Your teaching portfolio serves as a professional snapshot of your efforts, progress, and achievements. ***What materials do you think will best showcase your abilities as a teacher?***

Workplace Connections

Developing an Effective Portfolio

Review the items listed for a teaching portfolio in Figure 33.15 and answer the following questions:

1. What items do you already have in your portfolio? What items will you still need to include?
2. What items are not on the list but should be included in your portfolio because they help showcase your skills, abilities, attitudes, and philosophies?

Exercise care, so your portfolio does not take the form of a scrapbook. This type of portfolio should include your philosophy of teaching. One way to organize a portfolio is to have a table of contents with two subheadings. Label the first subheading *Background Information*. Include your résumé and background information about your teaching experience. Also, include information about your teaching goals, letters of recommendation, and instructors' evaluations of your work.

Label the second subheading *Teaching Artifacts*. This section of the portfolio should focus on the actual process and outcomes of teaching. Include lesson plans, unit and theme plans, videos, anecdotal records, photographs, parent-family letters, and examples of teacher-made materials.

Legal Problems in Interviewing

At both the state and federal levels, there are laws to protect against discrimination. Discrimination is illegal based on age, sex, national origin, race, or religion. Most employers do not intend to use information from an interview to discriminate. However, such information could affect the hiring decision. Therefore, it is illegal for an employer to ask questions about an applicant's race, national origin, or religion.

Questions interviewers can ask are limited by law. For example, they cannot ask parents of small children how their children will be cared for while they are working. Likewise, they cannot ask about a spouse's employment or salary.

Females cannot be asked if they are planning to have a family or are currently pregnant. Interviewers are also forbidden to ask applicants for their marital status or the number of children.

Figure 33.17 lists questions that may and may not be requested. Employers should ask all applicants for a position the same questions during an interview to prevent discrimination.

Although some questions are illegal, you may still answer them. Some prospective employers may purposely ask such questions to discriminate. Others, however, may simply invite them to get to know you better or make you feel at ease. These interviewers may not even know that the questions they ask are illegal.

If you are ever asked an illegal question, it is up to you to decide what the intent of the question is. Based on your judgment, use discretion and tact to handle the situation. You may simply answer the question. If the intention was to discriminate, and then if you are offered the job, you may ask why the question was asked. If the person's answer concerns you, you may decide to decline the job offer.

You may also choose not to answer the question. Do not accuse the person of discrimination. Instead, you may say simply and calmly, "I am sorry, but I am not required to answer that question."

Early Childhood Insight

Finalizing Your Portfolio

If you haven't already filed your teaching evaluations from the early childhood lab in your portfolio, select those evaluations that best represent your skills and abilities. If you have mastered a skill or improved a weakness from an earlier lesson, you may consider filing evaluations that demonstrate this. If you have participated in an early childhood internship or work program, include assessments from those experiences. Remember to be selective in your portfolio's content, demonstrate your strengths, and minimize weaknesses.

Ending the Interview

Words or actions can end an interview. Verbally, the interviewer may thank you for coming to the interview as a signal to end the interview. Nonverbally, the interviewer may sit up straight or stand up. This gesture means the interview is over, and the interviewer has received all the needed information from you.

Legal Interview Questions

Subject	Legal Inquiries
Age	Only a question to determine if you meet state licensing requirements related to age
	Date of birth
Arrest record	No questions
Marital status	No questions
Convictions	Only convictions that would affect the job position
Education	Only questions related to training and experience related to the position
Family	Only questions related to meeting work schedule
Disabilities	Only questions related to the ability to perform the job
National origin	Only questions about ability to read, speak, and write the language the job requires
Organizations	Only questions about participation in professional organizations related to your ability to perform the job
Pregnancy	Only questions about anticipated absences from work
Religion	Only questions about anticipated absences from work

Figure 33.17 Federal and state laws help protect job-seekers from discrimination. *What questions are illegal for employers to ask?*

Respond by thanking the interviewer for their time (**Figure 33.18**). You will likely interview for several jobs before you are hired. Many people are disappointed when they learn they were unsuccessful in getting a position. If you feel this way, do not think something is wrong. It is not unusual to feel depressed or feel a slip in your self-esteem. These feelings will pass.

Thank-You Letters

Always write a brief letter thanking the people who interviewed you. Sending a thank-you letter establishes goodwill and strengthens your **candidacy** (eligibility). As few as ten percent of people who interview observe this simple courtesy. Your letter will serve as a reminder to those you met. Even if you were not hired for that position, the interviewer may remember you for future openings. Your name may be passed on to someone else searching for an early childhood employee.

More people now send thank-you letters to interviewers using email. This is quite acceptable to most employers. Whether you use email or regular mail, the key is to be prompt. Always send a thank-you letter within two days of the interview. Better yet, send it the same day to show your interest.

You should send these letters to everyone who participated in the interview process. Besides thanking them, you can restate your interest in the position and re-emphasize your qualifications. Point out the match between the job requirements and your experience. Also, provide any important information you did not share in the cover letter, résumé, or interview.

33.2-2 Employee Rights and Responsibilities

As an employee, you have certain rights that are protected by law. You also have other rights that your employer grants through personnel policies. Rights come with responsibilities, however. The law defines some of early childhood teachers' responsibilities. NAEYC has set others in the Code of Ethical Conduct. (See Appendix A for more information about the Code of Ethical Conduct.)

Knowing your employee rights will help you ensure that those rights are respected. Employees desire a work environment in where their rights are honored. Similarly, awareness of your responsibilities enables you to be the best employee possible. When you understand what employers expect of you, you can comply with all program policies and state childcare licensing requirements. Following these guidelines will ensure that your work contributes to the program's quality and builds the program's reputation.

Your employee rights parallel responsibilities your employer has to you. For example, your employer's responsibility is to ensure your right to a safe workplace under federal and state laws. Likewise, your employer has the right to receive a full day's work in exchange for a full day's pay. It is your responsibility as an employee to provide this work in a manner that meets the employer's expectations.

Employee Rights

Employers have an ethical responsibility to create a quality workplace. The employer should strive to offer a supportive early childhood environment where children and adults can reach their potential. This environment will encourage you to focus on your work and find satisfaction in it (**Figure 33.19**).

william casey/Shutterstock.com

Figure 33.18   Be sure to leave the interviewer with a positive impression of you. *What can you specifically do to leave a positive impression following an interview?*

State Licensing Requirements

Investigate how early childhood workers are licensed in your state. During your investigation, answer the following questions:
1. Does your state require early childhood staff working in licensed facilities to obtain continuing education credit each year? If so, how many hours are needed?
2. Are licensed centers required to offer classes or workshops for their employees? Are they required to pay for the employees to attend continuing education?

Your employer's policies may grant you other rights. When you begin a new position, ask for a copy of the employee handbook or other personnel papers. This information should outline your employee rights and responsibilities as defined by the employer. These are in addition to any rights and obligations protected by law.

All employees should have equal treatment according to the terms set forth by the employer. Make it a point to familiarize yourself with the handbook. This will help you obtain all the benefits to which you are entitled and adhere to the employer's rules and expectations.

FatCamera/iStock via Getty Images Plus

Figure 33.19 Early childhood teachers are happiest and most effective in a quality work environment where they can reach their potential.

Early childhood programs have an ethical responsibility to provide a job orientation program for new hires. *Job orientation programs* are activities designed to acquaint you with the workplace. You should receive an overview of the program, its policies and procedures, and your employer's expectations of you. Any other training needed for your position should be part of the orientation period.

Another ethical practice is supportive supervision for employees. Your supervisor should assist you by answering questions, solving problems, and recommending areas for improvement. Early childhood programs should provide ongoing training to meet licensing requirements and improve the program's quality. They may offer workshops or classes that include curriculum, technology, child-guidance strategies, family engagement, health, safety, microaggressions, antibias curriculum, science, technology, engineering, mathematics, assessment, and communication skills. Supervision and ongoing training promote professional growth and job satisfaction.

Besides employer-granted rights, federal and state laws protect many employees' rights (**Figure 33.20**).

Employers must understand and adhere to these laws. Your employer has a legal responsibility to observe all federal and state labor laws. Employers must follow all applicable federal and state payroll, wage, and income tax laws. You have legal rights regarding some aspects of employee benefits and insurance. Federal regulations give you the freedom to work in an environment free from discrimination and sexual harassment. You have the right to a safe work environment.

Your employer must allow you to take up to 12 weeks of unpaid leave per year and hold your job (or equivalent) until your leave ends in specified medical and family situations. These are only a few examples—you have many other employee rights protected by law.

Employee Responsibilities

You agree to fulfill specific responsibilities when accepting an early childhood teaching

Employee Rights Protected by Law

- Labor, pay, tax, and benefit administration procedures
- Equal pay for equal work regardless of gender
- Freedom from workplace discrimination
- Freedom from sexual harassment
- Safe work environment
- Reasonable workplace accommodations for workers with disabilities
- Right to take specified unpaid leave to attend to covered family and medical conditions

Figure 33.20 Federal and state laws protect many employee rights. Employers have a responsibility to follow them.

position. You agree to do the job for which your employer is paying you. You must comply with all center policies and state childcare licensing requirements. You must also adhere to the profession's ethical standards, as outlined in NAEYC's Code of Ethical Conduct.

An early childhood teacher's role is to provide the children with developmentally appropriate, responsive care. Your employer has a responsibility to create a quality work environment. You have a responsibility to maintain and contribute to the program's quality. To do this, you must have good attendance and be punctual. You should also have a professional appearance, model a positive attitude, and maintain confidentiality. When necessary, you are also responsible for seeking help from your supervisor.

Workplace Connections

Investigating Rights and Responsibilities

If possible, get a copy of an employee handbook from an early childhood center. Examine it for rights and responsibilities of both employee and employer. If a handbook cannot be obtained, list the rights you would expect as an employee of an early childhood center.
1. What do you believe are the rights and responsibilities of employers?
2. How can knowing these provide the basis for a respectful and productive employee-employer relationship?

Attendance and Punctuality

Your employer has the right to expect a full day's work from you in exchange for the pay you earn. You are responsible for maintaining good work attendance and being **punctual** (on time). The director, staff members, and parents count on you to work every day. You should arrive a few minutes early each day or be on time.

Being even a few minutes late causes extra work and stress for your coworkers and director. State licensing rules and regulations always require specific adult-child ratios. The director must make other arrangements to cover your classroom if you are absent or late. If no one can cover your absence, you and your program are at risk for noncompliance. The center can receive a licensing violation for being understaffed. If a child is seriously injured and required adult-child ratios are not met, the center legally can be at risk. Repeated violations can cause a center to lose its license. Besides legal responsibilities, you have an ethical obligation to the families and children you serve and your coworkers and director.

For these reasons, repeated absenteeism or tardiness is a severe performance problem. Many programs have attendance and tardiness policies. If you fail to follow these policies, you will likely be fired. Even if no written attendance policies are in place, you can lose your job because of repeated attendance problems.

Professional Appearance

You have an ethical obligation to your employer to maintain a professional appearance and represent your program professionally. Parents or guardians, family members, children, visitors, and coworkers may base their initial impressions of you on your appearance. For example, parents or guardians may feel that a teacher wearing a casual two-piece outfit is more intelligent and nurturing than a teacher wearing jeans. People may equate your grooming and dress with how seriously you take your work. These assessments may not be accurate, but they occur.

Looking professional requires good grooming and avoiding extremes in hairstyles and clothing. Being well-groomed involves both cleanliness and neatness (**Figure 33.21**). Follow good hygiene practices, such as showering or bathing daily. Keep your hair clean, groomed, and simply styled. If you have long hair, try to keep it out of your face. Tying your hair back while working with young children will prevent children from pulling it. This also prevents loose hair from falling into the children's faces.

When working with young children, you need comfortable, washable clothing that allows easy movement. Avoid tight or restrictive clothing in which it is difficult to move. Your clothes should be clean and neat. Avoid wrinkled, frayed, stained, or ripped clothing.

Teachers often prefer washable slacks because they are comfortable yet convey a professional appearance. Most early childhood programs consider sweatpants, shorts, and spandex leggings unacceptable. Skirts or dresses can be worn, but they are less comfortable playing with children outside or on the floor.

Casual sweaters or shirts should be washable. Most employers often consider T-shirts inappropriate, especially those with crude sayings or graphics. Tube, halter, sleeveless, cropped, and low-cut tops are always inappropriate for the early childhood workplace. Avoid wearing jewelry young children can easily grab, pull, or get scratched from.

Figure 33.21 Facility directors should present a neat, clean appearance with their professional attire and grooming. ***What would you consider to be professional attire and grooming for early childhood teachers?***

For directors, more dressy business attire may be appropriate, depending on the program. Directors interact more with parents and family members, visitors, and teachers than directly with children.

Positive Attitude

Much of your success as a child care professional will depend on your attitude. Your **attitude** is your outlook on life—how you think about or act toward others. Finding great pleasure in teaching requires a positive attitude, enabling you to see the potential in any child, parent, staff member, situation, or idea. Instead of seeing limitations, a person with a positive attitude seeks opportunities (**Figure 33.22**).

People with a positive attitude want to do well. They take responsibility for their decisions. Teachers who have a positive attitude view working with young children as an opportunity for continuous learning. They seek knowledge about child development, guidance, and curriculum. These teachers are easy to recognize on the job. They welcome suggestions on improving their skills for working with young children. Employers enjoy workers who show a positive attitude.

kali9/iStock via Getty Images Plus

Figure 33.22 Maintaining a positive attitude will make you an asset to your center and promote your relationships with coworkers. *What are some characteristics of people with positive attitudes?*

Confidentiality

As a teacher of young children, you will have access to a wide range of privileged information. You may see personal records and learn private information about others. For example, you may know which children's families receive childcare tuition assistance. Daniel's parents may share personal information about their divorce to help you work with Daniel in the most understanding way. You may know that Juana's mother has cancer, and Kevin may tell you about his father leaving the family.

In most cases, you must keep sensitive personal information private. They call this keeping **confidentiality**. It means avoiding sharing this information with others beyond what your work requires. Maintaining confidentiality protects and shows respect for children, families, coworkers, and the program itself.

Confidentiality has some limits. For example, you can share information about children and families with certain coworkers for reasons relevant to the job. You should inform other staff members who work with a child about the child's special medical, physical, or learning needs. This information helps the staff provide appropriate care and learning experiences. Likewise, you may need to inform your director about the unethical practices after trying unsuccessfully to resolve the

matter with that person. This information helps the director keep the children healthy and safe.

Child abuse and neglect present another exception to confidentiality. Early childhood professionals must report abuse and neglect cases to the appropriate state agency by law. If you suspect neglect or abuse, follow your program's policy for making this report. Your legal responsibility as a mandated reporter outweighs your responsibility to keep private information. Here, the law requires you to break confidentiality.

In most other cases, it is unacceptable to break confidentiality. For example, you should never talk about the children and their family members with your coworkers, friends, or family members. Avoid discussing the personal matters of coworkers or talking to parents about other families. These practices are unethical. If families learn you have broken confidentiality, they may feel betrayed. Their resulting suspicion could cause long-term damage to the reputations of you and your program. Broken trust can also strain coworker relationships and undermine teamwork.

Health Highlights

Employee Health Appraisals

As part of protecting the health and safety of young children, all early childhood staff members who work 40 hours or more per month should have regular health appraisals. The first screening takes place before working with children. Additional screenings take place every two years. These health appraisals include

- a complete health history;
- physical, dental, vision, and hearing exams;
- tuberculosis test;
- a review of immunization status with immunization boosters given as needed; and
- a review of occupational health concerns as related to functioning on the job, such as back problems that might interfere in caring for children.

Besides regular health appraisals, early childhood teachers are strongly recommended to get annual influenza vaccinations.

Some centers ask their employees to sign confidentiality agreements. These agreements protect the confidentiality of a program's families, children, and fellow employees. A confidentiality agreement should outline with whom you can or cannot share various types of information. If an employee violates this agreement, the employee's employment is terminated.

Knowing which information to keep private can be challenging. It is always best to err on the side of caution. When considering whether to share personal, confidential, private details about other people, ask yourself the questions in **Figure 33.23**. Base your decision on your answers to these questions.

The **Family Educational Rights and Privacy Act (FERPA)** protects the privacy of student educational records. The law applies to all schools that receive funding under an application to the US Department of Education. When turning eighteen years of age, these rights transfer to students.

Ethical Responsibilities ⚖

Confidentiality Breach

Imagine the following situation: While in the supermarket checkout lane, you overhear two of your coworkers discussing the family situation of a little girl in their class. The girl's father is in jail, and the family is now on public assistance.

Dig Deeper

What is your responsibility concerning this situation? Why should you be concerned with what your coworkers do on their own time? Write a reflective paragraph summarizing your response to this ethical dilemma.

33.2-3 Terminating Employment

You will have many jobs during your lifetime. Job changes are common today, and employee turnover is high for all age groups.

Deciding When to Share Private Information

What is my purpose for sharing the information? Does my disclosure help the child or family in any critical way?

To whom am I sharing the information? Does this person have a need or right to know?

Whose privacy is involved? How might this person feel about me sharing this information with others? If I am unsure, have I asked them?

How would my supervisor feel about me sharing this information? If I am unsure, have I asked them?

How might sharing this information negatively affect my current position and my career? Is the disclosure legally or ethically necessary enough to take these risks?

Figure 33.23 There are times when knowing which information to keep private can be challenging. *Why is it always best to err on the side of caution?*

There are many reasons why people leave their jobs. Some of these reasons include

- the desire for a better job;
- a desire for better pay, hours, or fringe benefits;
- the desire for better working conditions or hours;
- seeking opportunities for advancement;
- looking for new challenges and responsibilities;
- making better use of personal skills and abilities;
- a conflict with supervisors or coworkers; and
- transportation problems.

A change in personal lifestyle can lead to a job change. For example, a person may need to change jobs if their spouse is transferred to another city. A family move can lead to a job change. Marriage, divorce, death, or children's birth can create new job requirements. Others leave their jobs to further their education. Sometimes health problems can dictate a job or environmental change.

It is important to think through your options before making a job change. Carefully weigh the pros and cons of leaving your current job for another job. If you decide a job change is necessary, resist the urge to leave your old job immediately. Instead, start looking for a new job before leaving your current job. Be sure you have enough money to carry you over to your next paycheck. If you do not have enough money in savings, you may want to keep your current job until you find a better one.

There is a right way to leave your job. You want to leave under the best possible circumstances. Inform your employer before you tell your coworkers. Do so at least two weeks before leaving. This allows your employer time to find your replacement.

Give notice to your employer in person and provide a written letter of resignation. This letter should state your last day of work and why you are leaving. It can be brief, but it should be positive. Thank your employer for the opportunity to work there. Describe how you have benefited from your job. You might offer to train your replacement, if appropriate.

Before you leave, continue to do your job as you always have. If you work directly with children, prepare them for your departure. Be pleasant to your coworkers as you may work with them again in a different job. Do not complain about your current job, nor brag about your new one. Thank coworkers for their help and friendship.

33.2-4 Balancing Multiple Roles

One of the most challenging tasks for workers is to balance their many roles. A **role** is a set of responsibilities that accompanies a position you hold. Each person has several roles. For example, some of these roles include wage earner, spouse, parent, son, or daughter (and other family

Ethical Responsibilities

Background Checks

Federal law requires that all states implement criminal background checks on all childcare providers. The intent of these checks is to make sure that early childhood providers do not have any convictions that could endanger children's health and safety. It is a provider's legal and ethical responsibility to meet the requirements of the law.

Dig Deeper

Use online resources to investigate the requirements of criminal background checks. What is involved in this check? Do background checks apply only to new employees, or to existing employees, too? When and how often are background checks required? Do parents and guardians have the right to conduct a background check if their child's provider has not done so? Discuss the benefits of background checks for family members, children, and providers.

relationships), friend, citizen, and volunteer. Every role has demands and responsibilities. Achieving harmony among various roles is challenging but important.

Many adults feel **role strain** when they are unable to successfully balance multiple roles. Anyone can feel role strain, but it is most common in single-parent and dual-career families. In these families, parents arrive home from work and must assume home-care and parenting tasks in the evenings (**Figure 33.24**). They must also squeeze errands into evening and weekend hours. Working parents often feel they are juggling too many responsibilities with too little time to devote to them. Too many times, their personal and relationship needs go unmet. Having unmet needs adds to the level of stress they feel.

Even now, you have several roles. You are a son or daughter, sibling, student, friend, community member, and perhaps an employee or volunteer. As a family member, expectations of you may be to help with family tasks, attend family events, and spend quality time with the family. As a student, you have homework, tests, and projects to complete, and extracurricular activities, such as clubs or sports, bring additional roles. Friends will want you to spend time with them. Volunteer or part-time work creates even more demands on your time.

Making time for all these roles can be an enormous challenge. Learning to manage your time is a valuable tool. Planning can help you meet your most important duties. Although you might like to, you cannot say yes to everything. Setting priorities will help you decide which activities to let go of. Learning to say no in a positive, unapologetic way will be helpful, too.

Staying healthy will help you meet your many obligations. Getting adequate rest, nutrition, and physical activity will allow you to feel your best. It would help if you also had personal time to relax, think, and plan. Strengthening relationships with family and friends will promote your social and emotional development.

Geber86/E+ via Getty Images

Figure 33.24   When working parents come home, they often find their children are eager to spend time with them. *How can setting priorities help you balance multiple roles?*

To succeed in an early childhood career, you must balance many roles. How you do this will probably be as unique as you are. However, finding this balance matters more than exactly how you achieve it.

Lesson 33.2 Review

1. Which of the following is *not* a good question to ask at the end of an interview? (33.2.1)
   A. Can I have a higher salary than the salary posted in the job ad?
   B. What is the educational philosophy of your center?
   C. To what extent may I implement my ideas?
   D. Is the staff encouraged to attend conferences?

2. **True or False.** Knowing your employee rights will help you ensure that those rights are respected. (33.2.2)

3. **True or False.** There is no right or wrong way to leave a job. (33.2.3)

4. Many adults feel _____ when they are unable to successfully balance multiple roles. (33.2.4)
   A. hopeful
   B. confidentiality
   C. role strain
   D. employable

Chapter 33 Review and Assessment

Summary
. . . .

Lesson 33.1

33.1-1 Choosing a career involves a challenging self-assessment process. Your answers to many important questions can help you decide if you are well suited to a career in teaching. Examining your interests, analyzing your abilities, and determining your values are all involved.

33.1-2 Searching for an early childhood career is a rewarding but sometimes frustrating experience. Start by preparing a résumé. Use your résumé when you meet with or talk to prospective employers.

33.1-3 Write a cover letter; it is usually included when sending a résumé. A cover letter is the primary way to set yourself apart from the competition.

33.1-4 Use internet sites, college or school placement offices, and the hidden job market to find employment.

Lesson 33.2

33.2-1 When you get an interview, be well prepared. Recognize what strengths you would bring to the position and present your teaching portfolio. Conduct yourself professionally and show enthusiasm for working with young children. Ask intelligent questions and recognize that it is illegal to discriminate on the basis of age, sex, national origin, race, or religion.

33.2-2 Knowing your rights as an employee helps you receive the full benefits to which you are entitled. Understanding your responsibilities will help your meet your employer's expectations.

33.2-3 Think carefully before making a job change. Always announce your departure in a professional manner and leave your employer on good terms.

33.2-4 Achieving a healthy role balance will promote your success as an early education professional.

Vocabulary Activity

With a partner, use online resources to locate photos or graphics that depict the Key Terms in this chapter. Print the pictures or use presentation software to show your drawings to the class, describing how they represent the meanings of the terms.

Critical Thinking

1. **Analyze.** Why is professionalism important in early childhood education? How are professional ethics related to professionalism? Write a reflective statement summarizing your answers.

2. **Draw Conclusions.** Prepare a résumé according to the instructions provided in this chapter. When you finish, form small teams and discuss your classmates' résumés. Conclude and describe how you might improve each résumé.

3. **Identify.** In small teams, research online job boards for early childhood education. Identify at least seven job databases and make a list of titles for early childhood education positions. What are the specific keywords used? What are typical job descriptions?

4. **Determine.** Write a brief description of your teaching style from your experiences. Look at evaluations from teachers and supervisors and include remarks that show what others think about your teaching style. Determine what comments and examples you would have in a portfolio to show your style and approach to education.

5. **Analyze.** Prepare a teaching portfolio and practice describing the contents to a classmate. Afterward, discuss with a classmate to analyze how each component of your portfolio reflects your skills, interests, or abilities. Based on your classmate's analysis, are there any components you would add or replace? Why or why not?

6. **Evaluate.** Review your school or work attendance records for the last several years, paying particular attention to absences and tardiness. Write a paragraph about your understanding of the relationship between excellent attendance and successful job performance.

Core Skills

1. **Writing.** Choose one job description and write a cover letter tailored to that job. Be sure to include keywords from the description and explain why you are the best candidate.

2. **Math.** Using online resources, research salaries for early childhood teachers in at least three regions and then compile your data into a graph representing the statistics. Present your chart to the class and discuss factors contributing to teacher salaries in various regions.

3. **Speaking.** Choose a partner and then role-play a job interview for an early childhood education job you have seen posted. Prepare questions as both an interviewer and interviewee. Finally, interview each other. Give each other feedback on how to improve interviewing skills.

4. **Social Studies and Writing.** Using online or print resources, research the federal Equal Employment Opportunity (EEO) laws that protect workers' rights. What areas of discrimination fall under the Equal Employment Opportunity Commission (EEOC) jurisdiction? What current initiatives of the EEOC are helping to promote and provide employment for youth, people with disabilities, and displaced workers? After compiling your information, write a short essay summarizing your findings and citing your sources.

5. **Research.** Go online and research early childhood positions on the Head Start Job Center and the US Military One Source sites. Make a list of jobs that appeal to you. What requirements are necessary for these positions?

6. **Reading and Writing.** Locate and then read an article about confidentiality in the early childhood center. Write a brief review of the article and compare the information in the article to the information covered in this text.

7. **Writing.** Make lists of your short-term and long-term career goals. Write a summary explaining how your short-term goals will help you attain your long-term goals. Include how these career decisions will affect your caregiving qualities.

8. **Listening.** Attend a meeting of a local chapter of NAEYC. Talk with a variety of members to learn about their work.

9. **CTE Career Readiness Practice.** Locate and then attend a local job fair where early childhood organizations will be present. Before the job fair, research the organizations present and prepare a list of questions you want to ask. Talk with representatives to learn about their work and ask your questions. Ask representatives for advice on choosing and searching for a career in early childhood education.

Portfolio Project

Review all the courses you are enrolled in. Evaluate each course related to a future career in early childhood education or other work associated with children. Write next to each class how it contributes to a job working with children. Look over the portfolio you have assembled for this course and note all the projects and samples related to English, math, social studies, science, art, music, health, and physical education.

National Association for the Education of Young Children

Core Values

Standards of ethical behavior in early childhood care and education are based on commitment to the following core values that are deeply rooted in the history of the field of early childhood care and education. We have made a commitment to:

- Appreciate childhood as a unique and valuable stage of the human life cycle.

- Base our work on knowledge of how children develop and learn.

- Appreciate and support the bond between the child and family.

- Recognize that children are best understood and supported in the context of family, culture,* community, and society.

- Respect the dignity, worth, and uniqueness of each individual (child, family member, and colleague).

- Respect diversity in children, families, and colleagues.

- Recognize that children and adults achieve their full potential in the context of relationships that are based on trust and respect.

The term culture includes ethnicity, racial identity, economic level, family structure, language, and religious and political beliefs, which profoundly influence each child's development and relationship to the world.

Principles from NAEYC'S Code of Ethical Conduct and Statement of Commitment

Section I: Ethical Responsibilities to Children

Principles

P-1.1   Above all, we shall not harm children. We shall not participate in practices that are emotionally damaging, physically harmful, disrespectful, degrading, dangerous, exploitative, or intimidating to children. This principle has precedence over all others in this Code.

P-1.2   We shall care for and educate children in positive emotional and social environments that are cognitively stimulating and that support each child's culture, language, ethnicity, and family structure.

P-1.3   We shall not participate in practices that discriminate against children by denying benefits, giving special advantages, or excluding them from programs or activities on the basis of their sex, race, national origin, immigration status, preferred home language, religious beliefs, medical condition, disability, or the marital status/family structure, sexual orientation, or religious beliefs or other affiliations of their families. (Aspects of this principle do not apply in programs that have lawful mandate to provide services to a particular population of children.)

P-1.4 We shall use two-way communications to involve all of those with relevant knowledge (including families and staff) in decisions concerning a child, as appropriate, ensuring confidentiality of sensitive information. (See also P-2.4.)

P-1.5 We shall use appropriate assessment systems, which include multiple sources of information, to provide information on children's learning and development.

P-1.6 We shall strive to ensure that decisions such as those related to enrollment, retention, or assignment to special education services, will be based on multiple sources of information and will never be based on a single assessment, such as a test score or a single observation.

P-1.7 We shall strive to build individual relationships with each child; make individualized adaptations in teaching strategies, learning environments, and curricula; and consult with the family so that each child benefits from the program. If after such efforts have been exhausted the current placement does not meet a child's needs, or the child is seriously jeopardizing the ability of other children to benefit from the program, we shall collaborate with the child's family and appropriate specialists to determine the additional services needed and/or the placement option(s) most likely to ensure the child's success. (Aspects of this principle may not apply in programs that have a lawful mandate to provide services to a particular population of children.)

P-1.8 We shall be familiar with the risk factors for and symptoms of child abuse and neglect, including physical, sexual, verbal, and emotional abuse and physical, emotional, educational, and medical neglect. We shall know and follow state laws and community procedures that protect children against abuse and neglect.

P-1.9 When we have reasonable cause to suspect child abuse or neglect, we shall report it to the appropriate community agency and follow up to ensure that appropriate action has been taken. When appropriate, parents or guardians will be informed that the referral will be or has been made.

P-1.10 When another person tells us of his or her suspicion that a child is being abused or neglected, we shall assist that person in taking appropriate action to protect the child.

P-1.11 When we become aware of a practice or situation that endangers the health, safety, or well-being of children, we have an ethical responsibility to protect children or inform parents and/or others who can.

Section II: Ethical Responsibilities to Families

Principles

P-2.1 We shall not deny family members access to their child's classroom or program setting unless access is denied by court order or other legal restriction.

P-2.2 We shall inform families of program philosophy, policies, curriculum, assessment system, cultural practices, and personnel qualifications, and explain why we teach as we do—which should be in accordance with our ethical responsibilities to children (see Section I).

P-2.3 We shall inform families of and, when appropriate, involve them in policy decisions. (See also 1-2.3.)

P-2.4 We shall ensure that the family is involved in significant decisions affecting their child. (See also P-1.4.)

P-2.5 We shall make every effort to communicate effectively with all families in a language that they understand. We shall use community resources for translation and interpretation when we do not have sufficient resources in our own programs.

P-2.6 As families share information with us about their children and families, we shall ensure that families' input is an important contribution to the planning and implementation of the program.

P-2.7 We shall inform families about the nature and purpose of the program's child assessments and how data about their child will be used.

P-2.8 We shall treat child assessment information confidentially and share this information only when there is a legitimate need for it.

P-2.9 We shall inform the family of injuries and incidents involving their child, of risks such as exposures to communicable diseases that might result in infection, and of occurrences that might result in emotional stress.

P-2.10 Families shall be fully informed of any proposed research projects involving their children and shall have the opportunity to give or withhold consent without penalty. We shall not permit or participate in research that could in any way hinder the education, development, or well-being of children.

P-2.11 We shall not engage in or support exploitation of families. We shall not use our relationship with a family for private advantage or personal gain, or enter into relationships with family members that might impair our effectiveness in working with their children.

P-2.12 We shall develop written policies for the protection of confidentiality and the disclosure of children's records. These policy documents shall be made available to all program personnel and families. Disclosure of children's records beyond family members, program personnel, and consultants having an obligation of confidentiality shall require familial consent (except in cases of abuse or neglect).

P-2.13 We shall maintain confidentiality and shall respect the family's right to privacy, refraining from disclosure of confidential information and intrusion into family life. However, when we have reason to believe that a child's welfare is at risk, it is permissible to share confidential information with agencies, as well as with individuals who have legal responsibility for intervening in the child's interest.

P-2.14 In cases where family members are in conflict with one another, we shall work openly, sharing our observations of the child, to help all parties involved make informed decisions. We shall refrain from becoming an advocate for one party.

P-2.15 We shall be familiar with and appropriately refer families to community resources and professional support services. After a referral has been made, we shall follow up to ensure that services have been appropriately provided.

Section III: Ethical Responsibilities to Colleagues

Principles

A. Responsibilities to co-workers

P-3A.1 We shall recognize the contributions of colleagues to our program and not participate in practices that diminish their reputations or impair their effectiveness in working with children and families.

P-3A.2 When we have concerns about the professional behavior of a co-worker, we shall first let that person know of our concern in a way that shows respect for personal dignity and for the diversity to be found among staff members, and then attempt to resolve the matter collegially and in a confidential manner.

P-3A.3 We shall exercise care in expressing views regarding the personal attributes or professional conduct of co-workers. Statements should be based on firsthand knowledge, not hearsay, and relevant to the interests of children and programs.

P-3A.4 We shall not participate in practices that discriminate against a co-worker because of sex, race, national origin, religious beliefs or other affiliations, age, marital status/family structure, disability, or sexual orientation.

B. Responsibilities to employers

P-3B.1 We shall follow all program policies. When we do not agree with program policies, we shall attempt to effect change through constructive action within the organization.

P-3B.2 We shall speak or act on behalf of an organization only when authorized. We shall take care to acknowledge when we are speaking for the organization and when we are expressing a personal judgment.

P-3B.3 We shall not violate laws or regulations designed to protect children and shall take appropriate action consistent with this Code when aware of such violations.

P-3B.4 If we have concerns about a colleague's behavior, and children's well-being is not at risk, we may address the concern with that individual. If children are at risk or the situation does not improve after it has been brought to the colleague's attention, we shall report the colleague's unethical or incompetent behavior to an appropriate authority.

P-3B.5 When we have a concern about circumstances or conditions that impact the quality of care and education within the program, we shall inform the program's administration or, when necessary, other appropriate authorities.

Section IV: Ethical Responsibilities to Community and Society

Principles

P-4.1 We shall communicate openly and truthfully about the nature and extent of services that we provide.

P-4.2 We shall apply for, accept, and work in positions for which we are personally well-suited and professionally qualified. We shall not offer services that we do not have the competence, qualifications, or resources to provide.

P-4.3 We shall carefully check references and shall not hire or recommend for employment any person whose competence, qualifications, or character makes him or her unsuited for the position.

P-4.4 We shall be objective and accurate in reporting the knowledge upon which we base our program practices.

P-4.5 We shall be knowledgeable about the appropriate use of assessment strategies and instruments and interpret results accurately to families.

P-4.6 We shall be familiar with laws and regulations that serve to protect the children in our programs and be vigilant in ensuring that these laws and regulations are followed.

P-4.7 When we become aware of a practice of situation that endangers the health, safety, or well-being of children, we have an ethical responsibility to protect children or inform parents and/or others who can.

P-4.8 We shall not participate in practices that are in violation of laws and regulations that protect the children in our programs.

P-4.9 When we have evidence that an early childhood program is violating laws or regulations protecting children, we shall report the violation to appropriate authorities who can be expected to remedy the situation.

P-4.10 When a program violates or requires its employees to violate this Code, it is permissible, after fair assessment of the evidence, to disclose the identity of that program.

P-4.11 When policies are enacted for purposes that do not benefit children, we have a collective responsibility to work to change these practices.

P-4.12 When we have evidence that an agency that provides services intended to ensure children's well-being is failing to meet its obligations, we acknowledge a collective ethical responsibility to report the problem to appropriate authorities or to the public. We shall be vigilant in our follow-up until the situation is resolved.

P-4.13 When a child protection agency fails to provide adequate protection for abused or neglected children, we acknowledge a collective ethical responsibility to work toward the improvement of these services.

Appendix B

Developmental Continuum of Children from Birth to Age 12*

Birth to Two Years

Motor Skills Approximate Age	Widely Held Expectations
1 Month	Moves reflexively.
	Does not control body movements.
	Needs support for the head. Without support, head will flop backward and forward. Lifts head briefly from the surface to turn head from side to side when lying on tummy.
	Twitches whole body when crying.
	Keeps hands fisted or slightly open.
	May hold object if placed in the hand, but drops it quickly.
2 Months	Can keep head in mid-position of body when lying on tummy. Can hold head up for a few seconds.
	Can turn head when lying on the back. Cycles arms and legs smoothly. Movements are mainly reflexive. Grasps objects in reflex movements.
	May hold object longer, but still drops object after a few seconds.
	Uses improved vision to look at objects more closely and for a longer time.
3 Months	Shows active body movements. Can move arms and legs together. Turns head vigorously.
	Can lift head when lying on tummy. Grasps and shakes hand toys.
	Takes swipes at dangling objects with hands.
	On tummy, can lift head and chest from a surface using arms for support
4 Months	On tummy, may roll from side to side and front to back.
	Can maintain a sitting position for several minutes if given proper support. Begins to use mitten grasp for grabbing objects near the hands.
	Able to place objects in mouth.
	Looks from object to hands to object. Swipes at objects, gradually improving aim.
5 Months	On tummy, can lift head and shoulders off surface. Can roll from tummy to back.
	When supported under arms, stands and moves body up and down, stamping feet alternately.
	Helps when being pulled to a sitting position.
	Can sit supported for 15 to 30 minutes with a firm back.
	Reaches for objects such as an activity gym with good coordination and aim. Begins to grasp objects with thumb and fingers.
	Grabs objects with either hand.
	Transfers objects from one hand to the other, dropping objects often.

Motor Skills Approximate Age	Widely Held Expectations
6 Months	Rolls from back to tummy.
	On tummy, moves by pushing with legs and reaching with arms. Gets up on hands and knees, but then may fall forward.
	Is able to stand while supported.
	May be able to sit unsupported for short periods of time.
	Reaches with one arm and grasps object with hand, then transfers the object to other hand, then reaches for another object.
	Learns to drop an object at will. Able to pick up dropped objects. Holds an object in both hands.
	Sits in a tripod position using arms for support.
7 Months	Creeps awkwardly, combining movements on tummy and knees. Likes to bounce when in standing position.
	May be able to pull self to a standing position. Can lean over and reach while in sitting position.
	Has mastered grasping by using thumb in opposition to fingers. Holds an object in each hand.
	Brings objects together with banging noises. Keeps objects in hands most of the time.
	Fingers, manipulates, and rattles objects repeatedly.
8 Months	Sits alone steadily for longer periods of time.
	Creeps and may start to crawl.
	Achieves sitting position by pushing up with arms.
	Learns pincer grasp, using just the thumb and forefinger. Is able to pick up small objects and string.
9 Months	Sits alone.
	Crawls; may try to crawl up stairs.
	May be able to move along furniture, touching it for support. Uses index finger to point, lead, and poke.
10 Months	Likes to walk holding caregiver's hands. Climbs on chairs and other furniture. Stands with little support.
	Can release grasped object instead of dropping it.
11 Months	Stands alone.
	Is able to stand and pick up objects. Likes to grasp feeding utensils and cup.
	May carry spoon to mouth in feeding attempt. Takes off shoes and socks.
12 Months	Climbs up and down stairs.
	May show preference for one hand. May be able to pull off clothing. Pulls self up to stand.
	Walks holding on to furniture. Uses pincer grasp.
13 to 15 Months	Walks with one hand held.
	Builds a tower consisting of 2 one-inch cubes. Turns pages in a book 2 or 3 at a time.
	While walking, cannot maneuver around corners or stop suddenly.

Motor Skills Approximate Age	Widely Held Expectations
16 to 18 Months	Walks without assistance.
	Walks up steps while holding on with one hand without alternating feet. Walks well while carrying or pulling a toy.
	Hurls a ball.
	Can build a tower of 2 to 4 blocks. Scribbles vigorously.
19 to 22 Months	Can place pegs in pegboard.
	Walks up stairs independently, one at a time. Completes a 3-piece formboard.
	Places 4 rings on post in random order. Rolls, pounds, squeezes, and pulls clay. Kicks backward and forward.
	Jumps in place.
22 to 24 Months	Attempts to stand on balance beam.
	Carries a large toy or several toys while walking. Builds tower of 6 cubes.
	Walks alone. Begins to run. Kicks a large ball.

Cognitive Skills Approximate Age	Widely Held Expectations
1 Month	Prefers to look at human faces and patterned objects. Listens attentively to sounds and voices.
	Cries deliberately for assistance; also communicates with grunts and facial expressions.
	Is comforted by the human voice and music.
2 Months	Coordinates eye movements.
	Shows obvious preference for faces to objects.
	Makes some sounds, but most vocalizing is still crying.
	Shows some interest in sounds and will stop sucking to listen.
3 Months	Is able to suck and look at the same time, thus doing two controlled actions at once.
	Discovers hands and feet as an extension of self. Searches with eyes for sounds.
	Begins cooing one syllable, vowel-like sounds—*ooh*, *ah*, *aw*. Laughs out loud.
4 Months	Likes to repeat enjoyable acts like shaking a rattle. Enjoys watching hands and feet.
	Looks at an object, reaches for it, and makes contact with it. Makes first consonant sounds—*p*, *b*, *m*, *l*.
	Smiles and coos when caregiver talks to them. Explores toys by grasping, sucking, shaking, and banging.
5 Months	Recognizes and responds to own name. Smiles at self in mirror.
	Can recognize people by their voices. Babbles to initiate contact.
6 Months	Grabs at any and all objects in reach.
	Studies objects intently, turning them to see all sides. Varies volume, pitch, and rate while babbling. Acquires sounds of native language in babbles.

Cognitive Skills Approximate Age	Widely Held Expectations
7 Months	Anticipates events. Enjoys looking through books with familiar pictures. May begin to imitate an act. May say *mama* or *dada* but does not connect words with parents. Produces gestures to communicate. Points to desired object. May be able to play the peek-a-boo game.
8 Months	Likes to empty and fill containers. Begins putting together a long series of syllables. May label object in imitation of its sounds, such as *choo-choo* for train. Searches for a hidden object.
9 Months	Responds appropriately to a few specific words. Finds objects that are totally hidden.
10 to 12 Months	Speaks first recognizable word. Links specific acts or events to other events. Likes to look at pictures in a book. Puts nesting toys together correctly.
	Begins to find familiar objects that are not in view but have permanent locations (looks for cookies after being told he or she can have one). Likes to open containers and look at their contents. Waves good-bye.
13 to 15 Months	Identifies family members in photographs. Gives mechanical toy to caregiver to activate toy. Has an expressive vocabulary of 4 to 6 words; most refer to animals, food, and toys. Points to body parts, toys, or persons upon request.
16 to 18 Months	Demonstrates knowledge of absence of familiar person (points to door, says *gone*). Enjoys cause-effect relationships (banging drum, splashing water, turning on TV). Says 6 to 10 words.
19 to 24 Months	Has expressive vocabulary of 10 to 20 words. Sorts shapes and colors. Mimics adult behaviors. Points to and names objects in a book. Refers to self by name. Recognizes self in photo or mirror.

Social-Emotional Skills Approximate Age	Widely Held Expectations
1 Month	Reacts to discomfort and pain by crying for assistance. Recognizes a parent's voice.
	Is comforted by the human face.
2 Months	Is able to show distress, excitement, contentment, anger, and delight. Can quiet self by sucking.
	Looks at a person alertly and directly. Prefers to look at people over objects. Quiets in response to being held.
	Shows affection by looking at a person while kicking, waving arms, and smiling.
3 Months	Shows feelings of security when held or talked to. Whimpers when hungry, chortles when content. Communicates with different sounds and facial expressions. Responds with total body to a familiar face.
	Tries to attract attention of caregiver. Watches adults' facial expressions closely.
4 Months	May form an attachment to one special object. Responds to continued warmth and affection. Shows increased pleasure in social interactions. Enjoys social aspects of feeding time.
	Becomes unresponsive if left alone most of waking hours. Laughs when tickled.
5 Months	May begin to show fearful behavior as separateness is felt. Distinguishes between familiar and unfamiliar adults.
	Builds trust when cries are answered; becomes anxious and demanding when cries are unanswered.
6 Months	Enjoys playing with children.
	Responds to affection and may imitate signs of affection. Likes attention and may cry to get it.
	May begin clinging to a primary caregiver. Desires constant attention from caregiver.
	Laughs when socializing.
	Smiles at familiar faces and stares solemnly at strangers.
7 Months	May show more dependence on caregiver for security.
	Has increased drive for independence but senses frightening situations. Shows desire for social contacts.
	Thoroughly enjoys company of siblings. Begins to have a sense of humor. Expresses anger more dramatically.
8 Months	Exhibits fear of strangers.
	May anticipate being left and become disturbed.
	Values quick display of love and support from caregiver.
	Likes to explore new places, but wants to be able to return to caregiver. Enjoys playing with own image in a mirror.
	Definitely prefers caregiver to strangers.
	Is more aware of social approval or disapproval.
9 Months	May show fear of heights; may be afraid to crawl down from a chair. May show a fear of new sounds.
	Shows interest in play activities of others. Likes to play games like pat-a-cake. Recognizes the social nature of mealtimes.

Social-Emotional Skills Approximate Age	Widely Held Expectations
10 Months	Performs for others, repeats act if applauded. Cries less often. Expresses delight, happiness, sadness, discomfort, and anger. May be able to show symbolic thought by giving love to a stuffed toy or mimic behaviors of others. Is more aware of and sensitive to other children. Enjoys music and may mimic movements others make to music. Fears strange places.
11 Months	May not always want to be cooperative. Recognizes the difference between being good and being naughty. Seeks approval and tries to avoid disapproval. Imitates movements of other adults and children. Likes to say no and shake head to get response from a caregiver. Tests caregivers to determine limits. Objects to having his or her enjoyable play stopped.
12 Months	May reveal an inner determination to walk. Begins to develop self-identity and independence. Shows increased negativism. May have tantrums. Enjoys playing with siblings. Likes to practice communication with adults. Continues to test caregiver's limits. May resist napping.
13 to 15 Months	Shows pride in personal accomplishments. Likes to exhibit affection to humans and objects. Prefers to keep caregiver in sight while exploring environment. Demands personal attention. May show fear of strangers. Shows negativism. Becomes frustrated easily. Enjoys solitary play. Shows preference for family members over others. Demands personal attention.
16 to 18 Months	Is emotionally unpredictable and may respond differently at different times. Is unable to tolerate frustration. May reveal negativism and stubbornness. May exhibit fear of thunder, lightning, large animals, and strange situations. Is very socially responsive to parents and caregivers. Responds to simple requests. May punch and poke peers as if they were objects. Is unable to share.
19 to 21 Months	Likes to claim things as *mine*. Gives up items that belong to others upon request. Begins to show empathy for another child or adult. Continues to desire personal attention. Indicates awareness of a person's absence by saying *bye-bye*. May enjoy removing clothing and is not embarrassed about being naked. Plays contentedly alone if near adults. Likes to play next to other children, but does not interact with them. Is able to play some simple interacting games for short periods of time.

Social-Emotional Skills Approximate Age	Widely Held Expectations
22 to 24 Months	Displays signs of love for parents and other favorite people. Is easily hurt by criticism.
	Begins to show defiant behavior.
	Shows the emotions of pride and embarrassment.
	May show some aggressive tendencies, such as slapping, biting, hitting. May assume an increasingly self-sufficient attitude.
	Wants own way in everything.
	May dawdle but desires to please adults.
	Is more responsive to and demanding of adults.
	Still prefers to play alone, but likes to be near others. Engages in imaginative play related to parents' actions. Uses own name in reference to self when talking to others. Is continually testing limits set by parents and caregivers. Likes to control others and give them orders.

Two- and Three-Year-Olds

Gross-Motor Skills Approximate Age	Widely Held Expectations
24 to 29 Months	Runs without falling.
	Begins to use pedals on tricycle. Kicks a large ball.
	Jumps in place.
	Plays on swings, ladders, and other playground equipment with fair amount of ease.
	Throws ball without falling.
	Bends at waist to pick up object from floor.
	Walks up and down stairs, both feet on step, while holding onto railings. Stands with both feet on balance beam.
30 to 36 Months	Walks on tiptoes.
	Performs a standing broad jump 8½ inches. Attempts to balance on one foot.
	Walks to and picks up a large ball. Can balance briefly on one foot.
	Catches a large ball with outstretched arms.
	May walk up stairs with alternating feet without holding handrail. Pedals a tricycle.
	Performs 1 to 3 hops with both feet together.
37 to 48 Months	Walks toe-to-heel for 4 steps.
	Hops and stands on one foot for 8 seconds. Catches a beanbag while standing.
	Hops on one foot without losing balance. Catches a bounced ball with hands. Throws a ball overhand.
	Climbs well.
	Kicks a ball forward.
	Catches a ball most of the time.

Fine-Motor Skills Approximate Age	Widely Held Expectations
24 to 29 Months	Inserts key into lock. Holds a pencil in writing position. Copies a vertical line. Copies a horizontal line. Builds a tower consisting of 6 cubes or more. Uses 2 or more cubes to make a train.
30 to 36 Months	Turns pages in a book one at a time. Strings large beads. Builds a tower consisting of 8 cubes. Copies a circle. Imitates building a 3-block bridge. Uses one hand consistently for most activities. Holds scissors correctly. Opens and closes scissors. Snips paper with scissors.
37 to 48 Months	Pours liquid from a small pitcher. Begins to copy capital letters. Builds a tower of 9 to 10 cubes. Completes simple puzzles. Folds paper twice (in imitation). Draws circles and squares. Draws a person with 2 to 4 body parts. Uses scissors. Cuts a 5-inch piece of paper in two. Cuts along a line.

Self-Help Skills Approximate Age	Widely Held Expectations
24 to 29 Months	Cooperates in dressing. Removes shoes, socks, and pants. Pulls on simple garments. Unsnaps snap. May verbalize toilet needs. Usually remains dry during the day.
30 to 36 Months	Seldom has bowel accidents. Closes snaps. Sits on toilet without assistance. Puts on shoes. Pours well from a small pitcher. Uses a child-sized knife for spreading.
37 to 48 Months	Washes and dries face and hands. Unbuckles belt. Unzips zipper. Unbuttons large buttons. Usually remains dry at night. Turns faucet on and off.

Expressive Language Skills Approximate Age	Widely Held Expectations
24 to 29 Months	Combines 2 or more words (*boy hit*).
	Yes/no questions marked only by intonation (*Mommy go? You see me?*). No and not used to negate entire sentence (*No eat; Mommy no; No sit down*). Preposition in use (*Go in house; Ball in box*).
30 to 36 Months	Uses pronouns and plurals (*More cookies; cats*).
	Uses negative elements no, can't, and don't after subject (*I can't eat; Mommy, don't go*).
	Use of different modifiers: qualifiers (*some, a lot, all*); possessives (*mine, his, hers*); adjectives (*pretty, new, blue*). Uses 4- to 5-word sentences.
	Overgeneralization of regular past with an ed (*He eated it; I woked up*).
37 to 48 Months	Preposition on used (*book on table; sit on chair*). Possessives used (*mommy's coat; daddy's car*). When questions appear.
	Negatives cannot and do not appear.
	Uses double negatives with a negative pronoun (*nobody, nothing*) or adverb (*never, nowhere*). Examples include *I can't do nothing* or *I don't never get to go*.

Language Comprehension Skills Approximate Age	Widely Held Expectations
24 to 29 Months	Child answers routine questions (*What is that? What is your name? What is he doing?*).
	Points to 6 body parts on doll or self.
	Provides appropriate answers to yes/no questions that deal with the child's environment (*Is mommy sleeping? Is daddy cooking?*).
	Comprehends pronouns: *I, my, mine, me*.
30 to 36 Months	Follows two-step directions.
	Provides appropriate answers for where (place) questions that deal with familiar information (*Where does daddy work? Where do you sleep?*).
	Comprehends pronouns: *she, he, his, him*, and *her*.
37 to 48 Months	Provides appropriate answers for whose questions (*Whose doll is this?*). Provides appropriate answers for why (cause or reason) questions (*Why is the girl crying?*).
	Provides appropriate answers for who (person or animal) questions (*Who lives at the North Pole?*).
	Understands the pronouns you and they.
	Provides appropriate answers for how questions (*How will mother bake the pie?*).

Math Readiness Approximate Age	Widely Held Expectations
30 to 36 Months	Gives "just one" upon request.
	Comprehends concepts light and heavy in object manipulation tasks. Comprehends size concepts big and tall in object manipulation tasks. Comprehends spatial concepts on, under, out of, together, and away from in object manipulation tasks.
37 to 48 Months	Gives "just two" upon request. Distinguishes between one and many.
	Understands the quantity concept empty in object manipulation tasks. Understands smaller; points to smaller objects. Understands largest. Counts while correctly pointing to 3 objects.
	Understands quantity concepts full, more, and less in object manipulation tasks. Comprehends spatial concepts up, top, apart, and toward in object manipulation tasks.
	Comprehends spatial concepts around, in front of, in back of, high, and next to in object manipulation tasks.

Social Skills Approximate Age	Widely Held Expectations
24 to 29 Months	Likes to play near other children, but is unable to play cooperatively. Becomes a grabber, and may grab desired toys away from other children. Does not like to share toys.
	Has not learned to say please but often desires the toys of other children. Likes to give affection to parents.
	Defends a desired possession.
30 to 36 Months	Continues to have a strong sense of ownership but may give up a toy if offered a substitute.
	May learn to say please if prompted.
	Has increased desire to play near and with other children. May begin cooperative play.
	Distinguishes between boys and girls. Likes to be accepted by others.
	Enjoys hiding from others.
	Likes to play with adults on a one-to-one basis.
	Enjoys tumble play with other children and caregivers.
37 to 48 Months	Is learning to share and take turns.
	Follows directions and takes pride in doing things for others. May act in a certain way to please caregivers.
	Makes friends easily.
	Seeks status among peers.
	May attempt to comfort and remove cause of distress of playmates. Seeks friends on own initiative.
	Begins to be choosy about companions, preferring one over another. Uses language to make friends and alienate others.

Emotional Development Approximate Age	Widely Held Expectations
24 to 29 Months	Continues to be self-centered.
	May exhibit increasing independence one minute and then run back to security of parents the next.
	Likes immediate gratification of desires and finds it difficult to wait. May exhibit negativism.
	Continues to seek caregiver approval for behaviors and accomplishments. Displays jealousy.
	May develop fear of dark; needs reassurance.
30 to 36 Months	May display negative feelings and occasional bad temper. May exhibit aggressiveness.
	May dawdle but insists on doing things for self.
	Likes to dress self and needs praise and encouragement when correct. Feels bad when reprimanded for mistakes.
	Desires caregiver approval.
	Wants independence but shows fear of new experiences. May reveal need for clinging to security object.
	Needs an understanding, orderly environment.
	May have trouble sleeping if the day's events have been emotional.
37 to 48 Months	Is usually cooperative, happy, and agreeable.
	Feels less frustrated because motor skills have improved. May still seek comfort from caregivers when tired or hungry. Learns more socially acceptable ways of displaying feelings. May substitute language for primitive displays of feelings. May show fear of dark, animals, stories, and monsters.

Four- and Five-Year-Olds

Gross-Motor Skills Approximate Age	Widely Held Expectations
4 Years	Catches beanbag with hands. Hops on one foot.
	Walks down stairs with alternating feet. Throws ball overhand.
	Carries a cup of liquid without spilling. Rides bicycle with training wheels. Balances on one foot for 5 seconds.
	Walks backward toe-to-heel for 4 consecutive steps. Builds elaborate structures with blocks.
5 Years	Marches to music.
	Jumps from table height. Climbs fences.
	Skips with alternating feet.
	Skips, hops, and jumps with good balance. Attempts to jump rope.
	Attempts to skate.
	Walks forward, backward, and sideways on balance beam. Catches ball with hands.

Fine-Motor Skills Approximate Age	Widely Held Expectations
4 Years	Builds a 3-block bridge from a model. Completes a 6- to 8-piece puzzle. Folds paper diagonally (3 folds). Copies a square.
	Paints and draws freely.
5 Years	Copies a triangle. Prints first name. Prints simple words.
	Dials telephone numbers correctly. Models objects with clay.
	Colors within lines.
	Draws recognizable people, houses, and vehicles.

Self-Help Skills Approximate Age	Widely Held Expectations
4 Years	Laces shoes. Buckles belt.
	Dresses and undresses with supervision. Distinguishes front and back of clothing. Zips separating zipper.
5 Years	Dresses and undresses without assistance. Uses washcloth for wiping hands and face. Puts shoes on correct feet.
	Unbuttons back buttons.
	Cuts and spreads with knife.

Language Skills Approximate Age	Widely Held Expectations
4 Years	Joins sentences with two clauses (Then it broke and we didn't have it anymore). Understands has/doesn't have and is/is not.
	Follows three commands in proper order (clear the table, wash the table, and get ready to go outdoors).
	Understands the pronoun we.
	Uses irregular verb forms (ate, ran, went). Uses regular tense (ed) verbs.
	Uses third person present tense verbs (runs, shops). Speaks fluently with a 1,500-word vocabulary.
	Forms sentences of 4 to 8 words. Recalls parts of a story.
	Asks many when, why, and how questions. Tells simple jokes.
5 Years	Uses third person irregular verbs. (He has a ball.)
	Uses compound sentences. (I went to the grocery store and I went to my grandmother's.)
	Uses descriptions in telling a story. Uses some pronouns correctly.
	Uses words to describe sizes, distances, weather, time, and location. Asks the meaning of words.
	Recalls the main details of a story. Recognizes some verbal absurdities. Tells original stories.
	Has a 2,000-word vocabulary. Can understand and follow rules.

Math Readiness Skills Approximate Age	Widely Held Expectations
4 Years	Identifies penny, nickel, and dime.
	Understands the concepts beside, bottom, backward, and forward in object manipulation tasks.
	Understands size concepts short, fat, and thin in object manipulation tasks. Counts 1 to 4 chips and correctly answers questions such as "How many altogether?" with cardinal number.
	Says correct number when shown 2 to 6 objects and asked "How many?" Can rote count 1 through 9.
	Understands the concepts tallest and same size.
5 Years	Understands the concepts of triangle and circle. Understands square and rectangle.
	Understands the concept of same shape.
	Understands the position concepts first and last in object manipulation tasks. Understands position concept middle.
	Rote counts 1 through 20.
	Recognizes the numerals 1 through 10. Writes the numerals 1 through 5.
	May count 10 or more objects correctly.

Social-Emotional Development Approximate Age	Widely Held Expectations
4 Years	May seem less pleasant and cooperative than at age 3. May be more moody, tries to express emotions verbally. Strives for independence; resents being treated like a baby. May be stubborn and quarrelsome at times.
	Learns to ask for things instead of snatching things from others. Is increasingly aware of attitudes and asks for approval.
	Needs and seeks parental approval often. Has strong sense of family and home.
	May quote parents and boast about parents to friends. Becomes more interested in friends than in adults.
	Shares possessions and toys, especially with special friends.
	Suggests taking turns but may be unable to wait for his or her own turn.

Social-Emotional Development Approximate Age	Widely Held Expectations
5 Years	Shows increased willingness to cooperate.
	Is more patient, generous, and conscientious. Expresses anger verbally rather than physically. Is more reasonable when in a quarrel.
	Develops a sense of fairness.
	Likes supervision, accepts instructions, and asks permission. Has a strong desire to please parents and other adults.
	Still depends on parents for emotional support and approval. Is proud of mother and father.
	Delights in helping parents.
	May act protective of younger siblings.
	Shapes ideas of gender roles by watching parents' behavior. Is increasingly social and talkative.
	Is eager to make friends and develop strong friendships. May pick a best friend.
	Prefers cooperative play in small groups. Prefers friends of same age and gender.
	Stays with play groups as long as interests hold. Learns to respect the property of friends.

6 to 12 Years of Age

Physical Development Approximate Age	Widely Held Expectations
6 Years	Body becomes more slender with longer arms and legs; babyhood physique continues to disappear.
	Loses baby teeth, which are replaced by the first permanent teeth. Is constantly active.
	Prefers running over walking.
	May have frequent minor tumbles and scrapes.
7 to 8 Years	May look lanky due to thin body and long arms and legs.
	Becomes better coordinated; movements become more fluid and graceful. Develops improved sense of balance and timing.
	Enjoys sports, especially boisterous games. Enjoys skating, skipping, and jumping rope. Able to handle simple tools.
	Girls are developing faster than boys.
9 to 10 Years	Continues to improve coordination. Improves sense of balance and timing. May develop particular physical skills. Enjoys organized games.
	Can run, kick, throw, catch, and hit. Further refines fine-motor skills.
	Is able to use hands skillfully in building models, learning handcrafts, or using tools.
	Enjoys drawing.
	Spends a lot of time and energy playing physical games. Girls may start adolescent growth spurt.

Physical Development Approximate Age	Widely Held Expectations
11 to 12 Years	Likes to test strength and daring.
	Becomes very conscious of overall appearance. Boys may grow little in height.
	Girls may experience growth spurt. Girls may begin menstruation.

Cognitive Development Approximate Age	Widely Held Expectations
6 Years	Asks more complex questions and wants detailed answers. Concentrates on doing one activity for longer period of time. Has improved memory.
	Has better understanding of the concept of time. Is inquisitive and eager to learn in school.
	May begin to understand concepts of seriation, conservation, reversibility, and multiple classification.
	Can usually distinguish between fantasy and reality. Begins reading, writing, and math at school.
7 to 8 Years	Accepts idea of rules and knows harm might result if rules are not followed. Understands concept of time.
	Has longer attention span.
	Understands value of money and may be ready for an allowance. Favors reality; is less interested in fairy tales.
	Begins to show interest in collecting certain objects. Enjoys reading animal stories and science fiction stories.
	May show interest in stories about children of other countries.
	Refines concepts of seriation, conservation, reversibility, and multiple classification.
	Begins to understand cause and effect.
9 to 10 Years	Is able to consider more than one conclusion to problems or choices. Understands more about truth and honesty.
	Likes to act in a more adult manner. Is still enthusiastic about learning.
	Likes games that involve mental competition.
	Enjoys quizzing parents and impressing them with new facts. Enjoys mysteries and secrets.
	May continue to show interest in collecting certain objects. Has vocabulary of about 5,400 words.
	Has better use of language and is able to converse well with adults. Uses more abstract words.

Cognitive Development Approximate Age	Widely Held Expectations
11 to 12 Years	Is able to detect problems in daily situations and work out solutions. Grasps math concepts and applies them to daily activities.
	May like group projects and classes based on cooperative effort. Likes active learning, reading aloud, reciting, and science projects. May allow peer relationships to affect schoolwork.
	Has vocabulary of about 7,200 words.
	May enjoy lengthy conversations with teachers.
	May enjoy long periods of solitude to think or to work on projects like building models.
	May show interest in reading; mysteries, adventure stories, and biographies are favorites.
	Understands concepts of seriation, conservation, reversibility, and multiple classification.
	Applies logic to problem solving. Uses language to discuss feelings.

Emotional and Social Development Approximate Age	Widely Held Expectations
6 Years	Becomes more socially independent; chooses own friends.
	May feel less jealous of siblings as outside interests become more important. Is still egocentric, but is becoming interested in group activities.
	May still have a hard time waiting and taking turns. Wants desperately to be right and to win.
	Tattles often to check sense of right and wrong. Wants all of everything, making choices is difficult. May have nightmares.
	Often expresses sense of humor in practical jokes and riddles. Begins to see others' points of view.
	Learns to share and take turns.
7 Years	May seem withdrawn and moody.
	Likes to spend time alone or in the background. May feel that everyone is against him or her. Wants and needs approval of adults and peers. Is very conscientious; strives hard to please.
	Is sensitive and hurt by criticism. Likes to help teachers.
8 Years	Shows more spirit; is willing to try just about anything.
	May turn to tears and self-criticism upon failure, but recovers quickly. Is able to get along well with others.
	Chooses companions of same gender and age. Is very sensitive to what others think.
	Shows intense interest in groups. Wants to look and act like peers.
	Enjoys group activities in organizations and in own secret clubs. Chooses a best friend, but may change best friends often.
	Is sensitive to criticism.

Emotional and Social Development Approximate Age	Widely Held Expectations
9 Years	Is relatively quiet.
	Worries about everything.
	Forms groups with others of same gender. Complains a lot.
	Has definite likes and dislikes.
	Begins a new drive for independence; resents being "bossed" by parents. Knows right from wrong; will accept blame when necessary, but offers excuses. Shows increased interest in friends and decreased interest in family.
	Is interested in group activities and concerns. Often competes with others.
	Shows increasing capacity for self-evaluation.
10 Years	Is happy with life in general.
	Likes people and is liked by others. Is dependable and cooperative. Obeys adults easily and naturally.
	Likes to accept responsibility and tries to do things well. Likes praise and encouragement.
	Still has strong group spirit, but it may be diminishing.
	May begin to show more loyalty to a best friend than to the group, especially girls. May enjoy being part of a team.
11 to 12 Years	Is less self-centered.
	May express great enthusiasm.
	Likes to plan and carry out activities with a group. Is willing to reach out to others for friendship.
	Has improved social skills.
	May show more tact, especially with friends. Is patient and friendly with younger children.
	If puberty has begun, may become moody and show signs of emotional turmoil. Has strong desire to conform to peers in dress and behavior.
	Likes team games.
	Is becoming interested in opposite gender; girls more interested than boys.

*The items listed are based on average ages when various traits emerge. Many children may develop certain traits at an earlier or later age.

Adapted from *Parents and Their Children* by Verdene Ryder and Celia Anita Decker, Goodheart-Willcox Company, Inc.

Glossary

A

abrasion. A scrape that damages a portion of the skin. (12)

acceleration. A process in which a gifted child is assigned to a class with older children. (31)

accessibility. Ability to access and use the playground and equipment. (8)

accommodation. Adjusting what is already known to fit the new information. (3)

accreditation. Recognition that an early childhood program has met a set of professional standards. (2)

acoustic material. Material used to deaden or absorb sounds. Carpets, drapes, bulletin boards, pillows, stuffed toys, and sand are examples. (8)

acquired immunodeficiency syndrome (AIDS). A disease caused by the human immunodeficiency virus. The virus breaks down the body's immune system, leaving the body vulnerable to disease. (12)

active listening. Verbal and nonverbal feedback showing attentiveness to the speaker. Listening to what is said, then repeating it. (32)

adjoining. Next to. (29)

adult-centered program model. A structured curriculum format for school-age child care that has a high level of adult direction. (30)

adverse childhood experiences (ACEs). Toxic stress, such as extreme poverty, severe neglect, maternal depression, and exposure to violence that can undermine the developing brain with lasting effects on development. (3)

advocate. A person who defends, supports, or promotes the interests of others. (1)

aesthetic. Beautiful or pleasing in appearance. (8)

agency. The child's capacity to make choices and affect events. (21)

Air Quality Index. The AQX is the index for reporting air quality. When the AQI is within 0-50, air quality conditions are good. (12)

alienated. Feeling of not belonging. (32)

allergen. The offending substance that causes an allergic reaction. (11)

allergy. The body's negative reaction to a particular substance, possibly including rashes, swelling, or sneezing. (11)

alphabet letters. A writing system containing basic symbols called sounds. Each letter has a related sound. (22)

ambulatory. Able to move from place to place. (31)

anaphylaxis. Extreme allergic reaction that causes shock symptoms and possibly death. (11)

anecdotal record. The simplest form of direct observation; a brief narrative account of a specific incident. (17)

animal stories. Books giving animals some human qualities. Usually, the animal has some unusual success or ability. (20)

antibias curriculum. A curriculum with a many-culture approach, honoring diversity by teaching children about respect. An antibias curriculum embraces differences and acts on unfairness and bias. (25)

apprehensive. Anxious. (28)

apps. Pieces of software that can be run on the internet from a phone, computer, electronic tablet, or another type of handheld device. Also known as *applications*. (24)

articulation. The ability to speak in pronounced sounds. (6)

articulation problems. Omission errors, distortion problems, or substitutions of vowels or consonants or both. Often referred to as *lazy tongue* and *baby talk*. (31)

artifact. Tangible items collected through children's play or work that shows evidence of learning. (17)

assessment. The process of observing, recording, and documenting children's growth and behavior. (17)

assimilation. Piaget's term for adding new

Note: The number in parentheses following each definition indicates the lesson in which the term can be found.

information into an existing cognitive (mental) structure. (3)

associative play. The first type of social play where children interact with one another while engaging in a similar activity. (21)

asthma. A chronic inflammatory disease of the airways that causes airways to narrow, swell, and produce extra mucus, triggering symptoms such as labored breathing, gasping, coughing, and wheezing. (12)

asynchronous development. A mismatch in the areas of development, such as cognitive or emotional. (31)

attachment. The strong emotional connection that develops between people. Term that is often used interchangeably with bonding. (4)

attitude. A person's outlook on life; the way a person thinks about or acts toward others. (33)

attribute. A quality, characteristic, or feature that describes something such as shape, size, or number. (23)

audiologist. A non-medical expert who identifies, assesses, and manages hearing disorders. (31)

auditory discrimination skills. The ability to detect different sounds by listening. (27)

auditory learner. Those who learn best through hearing. (18)

auditory signals. Indicators that inform the children of a change through the use of sound. (16)

au pair. A person from a foreign country who lives with a family and provides child care in exchange for room, board, and transportation. (1)

authentic assessment. An informal assessment that embraces observations that occur during daily play-based activities and routines. (17)

autism spectrum disorder (ASD). A complex disorder that may cause social, emotional, behavioral, and communication impairments. (31)

autoharp. A simple chording instrument that can be used to accompany singing. (27)

autonomy. Independence. (3)

axons. Long, thin projections of the neuron or nerve cell that send information to other neurons. (3)

B

behavioral disorder. A condition that affects an individual's social, emotional, and cognitive functions, such as attention deficit disorder, hyperactivity, or conduct disorder. (31)

behavioral expectations. Limits that children are expected to follow. (28)

bicultural. The ability to hold on to the rules of one's home culture while learning the rules of the home culture. (13)

bid. The price at which vendors will sell items. (9)

bilingual. Frequently uses two languages. (20)

biweekly. Twice a week. (32)

block plan. A written, overall view of the curriculum that outlines the time period and scheduled activities. (18)

body percussion. Movements that involve using the body to make rhythm. (27)

boisterous. Loud or active. (27)

bolster. Strengthen. (33)

bonding. The closeness people develop over time. Everyday expression of affection and love between mothers and infants. (4)

bridging. A process of placing two blocks vertically a space apart and then adding the third block. (19)

bullying. Aggression that is directed at another child. (7)

burn. An injury caused by heat, radiation, electrical current, or chemical agents. (12)

C

candidacy. Eligibility. (33)

capillaries. Small veins. (12)

cardinality. The concept that the last number of the counting sequence tells how many objects exist in a set. (23)

cautious. Slower to make decisions. (18)

cephalocaudal principle. Principle of development states that development tends to proceed from the head downward. According to this principle, the child first gains control of the head, then the arms, then the legs. (3)

chalk painting. Art activity in which chalk is dipped into water and used to draw on construction paper. (19)

chant. A group of words spoken with a lively beat. (27)

chaperones. People who accompany others to ensure correct behavior. (28)

chartering. Hiring. (28)

check-in services. Services that hire workers who call the home to check whether the child has arrived safely. (2)

checklist. Designed to record the presence or absence of specific traits or behaviors. (17)

Child and Adult Care Food Program (CACFP). A program that reimburses centers and family child care homes for the nutritious meals and snacks they serve to children. (11)

child observation. Observing a child's development, behavior, interests, preferences, strengths, and/or learning. (13)

childcare centers. Full-day child care facilities that focus on basic nutritional, social, emotional, intellectual, and physical needs of children from birth to five years of age. May be operated by for-profit owners or corporation non-profit agencies. (2)

childcare license. A state-provided certificate granting permission to operate an early childhood center or a family child care home. (2)

child-centered program model. A curriculum format that allows children an opportunity to do self-selected activities. (30)

chronic health need. An illness that persists over a period of time. (31)

chronological. Describing the order in which events happened. (17)

chronological age. An age determined by birth date. Also known as *physical age*. (9)

classification. The ability to group objects by common attributes, such as size, color, shape, pattern, or function. (7, 23)

closure. The way an activity ends. (18)

coaching. Teaching skill that provides children with ideas for difficult situations. (21)

cochlear implant. A surgically implanted device that provides someone with moderate to profound hearing loss with sound perception. Speech understanding is improved in quiet and noisy areas. (31)

cognitive development. Growth in the mental processes used to gain knowledge, such as thought, reasoning, and imagination. Also called *intellectual development*. (3)

collage. A selection of interesting materials mounted on a flat surface creating two-dimensional art. (19)

collection. A group of items, including those for counting, observing, creating, sorting, discussing, construction, and comparing. (23)

communicable diseases. Illnesses that can be passed on to other people. (12)

compassion. Being aware of others' distress and wanting to help them. (7)

concept. A generalized idea or notion. (18)

concept of print. The awareness of how print works. (22)

concept picture book. Book consisting wholly or chiefly of pictures and used with pre-readers. (20)

concrete operations. The use of logic based on what has been experienced or seen; takes place during the ages of 7 to 11 years. Children develop the capacity to think systematically, but only when they can refer to actual objects and use hands-on activities. (3)

confidentiality. The keeping private of sensitive personal information involving other people. (33)

conflict. Two or more forces that oppose each other. (21)

congenital disabilities. Disabilities present at birth, but not necessarily heredity. (31)

conscientious. Effectively careful. (30)

consequence. A result that follows an action or behavior. (13)

conservation. The concept that change in position or shape of substances does not change the quantity. (7)

consistency. Quality of being the same every time. (15)

consumable supplies. Supplies that, in most cases, are used up and cannot be used again. (9)

content- and process-centered approach. A teaching philosophy in which learning is seen as a constant process of exploring and questioning the environment with hands-on curriculum stressed. (18)

context. A term used to state how something occurs. The child's context is the interconnectedness and influence of his cultural background, family, and learning environment. (14)

continuity of care. A teacher who follows a group of children for several years. (29)

controlled scribbling. The second stage of the writing process when children use symbols or drawings to represent words and ideas, such as "sticks" and "circles." (22)

conventions of print. Standardized spelling, word spacing, and upper- and lowercase letters in writing. (22)

convergent thinking. Thinking where there is only one best way or approach. (19)

cool colors. Colors, such as blue and green, that make a room appear larger and create a feeling of openness. (8)

co-op (cooperative). A group of people or organizations that join together for the mutual benefit of more buying power. (9)

cooperative play. Type of play in which two or more children interact with one another. At this stage, socio-dramatic play begins. (21)

coordination error. Occurs when the child is counting a series of objects. The same object may be labeled with more than one number word or it may not have been counted. (23)

cortisol. A steroid hormone that is produced when the body is under stress. (3)

cover letter. A letter of introduction that is usually included when sending a résumé. (33)

cubbies. Top sections of lockers used to store finished artwork, library books, parent letters, and other valuable items. (8)

cultural competence. Understanding your own cultural identity and attitudes about human differences while acquiring knowledge and appreciation of others. (4, 13)

cultural diversity. The presence of multiple different cultures or ethnicities. (1)

cultural identity. A person's sense of belonging to a certain group or culture. (25)

culture. The values, beliefs, rules, and practices of a particular group. Culture shapes the actions and are passed from generation to generation. (4)

curriculum models. A structure used for making curriculum decisions. (30)

D

daily news flash. A written communication tool used by centers to inform parents about program or center news. Contains bits of news that families can discuss with their children. (32)

dawdling. Eating slowly or having a lack of interest in food sometimes used as an attempt to gain attention. (16)

deaf. Total or partial hearing loss. (31)

deferred imitation. Watching another person's behavior and then acting out that behavior later. (4)

demand feeding. Feeding an infant in response to his or her signals. (29)

dendrites. Hair-like fibers around the cell body that receive signals. (3)

development. Change or growth that occurs in children. (3)

developmental age. A child's skill and growth level compared to what is thought of as typical for that age group. (9)

developmental disability. Disabilities that can impact language, learning, physical abilities, socialization, and behavior. (31)

developmental milestones. Characteristics and behaviors considered normal for children in specific age groups; also referred to as *emerging competencies*. (17)

developmentally appropriate practice (DAP). A framework or approach to working with young children that is based on knowledge of how children learn and develop at different ages and stages. (1)

diabetes. A condition in which the body cannot properly control the level of sugar in the blood. (11)

dietary pattern. Represents the combinations of foods and beverages representing an individual's dietary intake over time. (11)

digital divide. The gulf between those who have ready access to computers and the internet opposed to those who do not. (30)

digital literacy. The ability to use digital media for listening, speaking, reading, and writing. (30)

direct guidance. Physical and verbal actions, such as facial and body gestures, that influence behavior. (13)

direct learning experience. Learning experience planned with a specific goal in mind. (18)

disability. A mental or physical condition that impacts how the body works or develops. (31)

discipline. A term that includes both guidance and punishment. The guidance consists of direct actions to help children develop internal controls and appropriate behavior patterns. Punishment focuses on the use of unreasonable, often harsh, actions to force children into behaving the way adults want. (13)

disinfecting. The process of eliminating germs from surfaces. (12)

divergent thinking. Thinking creatively and using one's imagination to discover new possibilities and evaluate results. (19)

documentation. The process of collecting artifacts. (17)

dramatic play. A form of play in which a single child imitates another person or acts out a situation. (21)

draw and tell. A storytelling method in which drawings are made on a chalkboard, dry erase board, poster board, or an 18×24-inch newsprint pad as the story is told. Also called *chalk talk*. (20)

dual-language learners. Children who are learning to speak two or more languages at the same time. (20)

E

early childhood. The period of life from birth to nine years of age. (1)

early childhood educator. An individual who has mastered the specialized knowledge, competencies, and skills for teaching children from birth through age eight. (1)

Early Head Start. A program that includes year-round services for infants and toddlers and focuses on child development, family development, staff development, and community development. (2)

early learning standards. Used to improve professional practice by promoting high-quality learning environments for young children. (18)

early scribbling. The first stage of writing when children are more interested in the physical experience of drawing on paper than markings. (22)

e-book. An electronic book that is read on an e-reader. (20)

eclectic. Varied. (31)

ecology. The study of the chain of life. (25)

egocentric. A characteristic of people that means that they believe everyone else sees, thinks, and feels like they do. (5)

egotistical. Very proud. (32)

emergent curriculum. A child-centered curriculum that "emerges" from the children's interests and experiences. (18)

emergent writing. A term used to explain a child's knowledge before learning to write words. (19, 22)

emotional abuse. Abuse of a child's self-concept through words or actions. (10)

emotional intelligence. The ability to understand one's own emotions and recognize their causes. (25)

emotional language. Vocabulary describing emotions. (6)

empathy. The ability to understand another's feelings. (4, 5, 6)

empty set. A set with no members. (23)

engaging activities. Connect the children's interests, experience, and developmental levels. (18)

enrichment. A process to broaden the range of experiences with a special curriculum. (31)

entrepreneur. A person who creates and runs their own business. (1)

environment. All the interactions, experiences, and events that influence a child's development. (3)

environmental print. The print that surrounds kindergartners and preschoolers. (22)

epilepsy. A condition in which a person has periodic seizures. (12)

epinephrine auto-injector. A medical device that includes a spring-loaded needle and prefilled syringe of epinephrine—a drug used to treat potentially life-threatening allergic reactions. (12)

ePortfolio. An electronic portfolio containing a collection of evidence data. (17)

ethical. Conforming to accepted standards of conduct. (1)

ethics. A guiding set of moral principles, either those held personally or those determined by a professional organization for its members. (1)

evaluation. The process of reviewing the information and finding value in it. (17)

executive function. The ability to regulate self-behavior in socially and culturally appropriate ways; a critical task that develops rapidly during the early years. (3)

expressive language. The ability to produce language forms and express thoughts to others verbally or in writing. (5, 6)

F

fable. Simple story in which an animal is the main character and often points out a moral lesson. (20)

facilitator. Person who provides assistance or guidance in bringing about an intended outcome. (30)

fairy tales. Books having a theme of achievement. The characters or heroes of these stories must perform difficult tasks in order to succeed. (20)

family capacity-building practices. Providing opportunities to strengthen families' knowledge and skills. (32)

family childcare home. Child care that is provided in the caregiver's own home. Depending upon the state, the home may be licensed or exempt from licensing. (1)

family life stories. Books containing the theme of social understanding. (20)

farsighted. Able to see objects in the distance more clearly than those that are close. (7)

fast mapping. The ability of three-year-olds to absorb the meaning of a new word after hearing it just once or twice in a conversation. (5)

feely box. A box with a circle cut in it large enough for children to put their hands into and identify different objects and materials placed inside by touch. (24)

fictional books. Illustrations and text work together to tell a story. (20)

field-independent learners. Children who are more independent, prefer to work on their own, and like to try new activities. (18)

field-sensitive learners. Children who like to work with others. (18)

fine-motor development. The ability to coordinate the small muscles in the arms, fingers, and wrists to complete tasks such as grasping, holding, cutting, drawing, and writing. (3)

first aid. Immediate treatment given for injuries and illnesses, including those that are life-threatening. (12)

first-degree burn. Burn to the top layer of skin. It is the least severe of all burns. Signs include redness or mild discoloration, pain, and mild swelling. (12)

flannel board. A board covered with felt or flannel that is used as a background for placing felt characters and props to tell a story. (20)

flexible limits. Limits that can be adapted to the needs of an individual or situation. (15)

folktales. Stories typically passed by word of mouth to stimulate the children's imagination and share cultural traditions. (20)

food and nutrition experiences. Involve many activities: preparing foods, setting the table, eating snacks and meals, and cleaning up. (26)

foodborne illness. An illness caused by eating food that contains harmful bacteria, toxins, parasites, or viruses. (12)

food insecurity. Absent or inconsistent access to nutritious food. (26)

formal operations. The fourth stage of Piaget's theory. During this stage, young people develop the capacity to think in purely abstract ways. (3)

formative assessment. An ongoing process of gathering information through daily play activities. (17)

for-profit centers. Privately owned businesses in local communities that rely on parent fees to operate. (2)

frustration. The feeling that one is not in control; feeling defeated or discouraged. (14)

functional stage of play. Second stage of material use. During this stage, a child will use a prop as it was intended while playing with other children. (21)

funds of knowledge. The background experiences and knowledge that children come to school with. (20)

G

gender-neutral. Roles are not determined according to people's gender. (25)

gender roles. Behaviors that are expected of girls or boys. (5)

gender stereotypes. Based on a culture's system of female and male characteristics. (6)

germinate. Sprout. (24)

gerontology. The study of older adults. (25)

giftedness. Having exceptional skills in one or more of six areas: creative or productive thinking, general intellectual ability, leadership ability, psychomotor ability, specific academic aptitude, and/or visual or performing arts. (31)

gluten. A protein found in wheat and other grains, such as rye, barley, and graham that can cause health problems. (11)

gross-motor development. Improvement of the skills involving arms, legs, and whole-body movements. Examples include running, jumping, throwing, and climbing. (3)

guardrail. A rail enclosing an elevated platform designed to prevent falls from the device. (8)

guidance. Direct and indirect actions used by an adult to help children develop socially acceptable behavior. (13)

H

hand-eye coordination. Muscle control that allows the hand to do a task in the way the eye sees it done. (22)

hard of hearing. Mild to moderate hearing loss. (31)

head lice. Small six-legged white insects that live on people's hair and feed on blood from the scalp. (12)

Head Start. A comprehensive child development program developed by the federal government to strengthen academic skills. Provides a variety of medical and social services to promote healthy development for children in low-income families and designed mainly for four- and five-year-olds. (2)

head teacher. Responsible for all/ aspects of class functioning. These include planning a curriculum, maintaining a safe and stimulating environment, and teaching children. (1)

hemophilia. A genetic blood disease that causes blood to clot too slowly or not at all. (31)

heredity. The characteristics a child inherits genetically from parents. (3)

hidden job market. Jobs advertised informally through word of mouth. (33)

holophrase. A single word and gesture combined to express a complete thought. (4)

home language. The first language a child learns to speak. (18)

home visits. Experiences that allow the teacher to enter the child's world by spending time together in the family's home. (32)

human immunodeficiency virus (HIV). A virus that breaks down the body's immune system, eventually causing the disease AIDS. (12)

hyperactivity. Excess energy. (16)

I

imaginative stage of play. The third and final stage of material use. Children in this stage do not need real props; they are able to think of substitutes. (21)

I-message. A verbal statement that explains the effect of a child's behavior in a respectful manner. (13)

implicit bias. A bias or prejudice that is present but not consciously held or recognized. (13)

impulsive. Quick to make decisions. (18)

inarticulate. Not understandable by teachers or peers. (31)

incest. Sexual abuse by a relative. (10)

incidental learnings. Learning experiences that happen during the course of an average day. (25)

incisors. The lower and upper front teeth. (7)

inclusion. A term used to refer to an education setting in which children with and without special needs are integrated. (31)

indirect guidance. Outside factors influencing a child's behavior, such as the layout of the center. (13)

indirect learning experience. Learning experience that occurs on the spur of the moment. (18)

Individualized Education Plan (IEP). A written strategy for learning designed to ensure that each child with special needs is educated in the most appropriate manner. (31)

Individualized Family Service Plan (IFSP). Plan developed when a preschool-age child is diagnosed with a disability. It includes the family's needs in regard to enhancing the child's development, goals for the child, services to be provided to the child and/or family, and a plan for transitioning the child to other services and regular education. (31)

Individuals with Disabilities Education Act (IDEA). Federal law requiring all states to provide education and support for children who are developmentally delayed. (31)

induce. To produce on purpose. (16)

infant. Term used to refer to a child from birth through the first year of life. (3)

infant sign language. A gestural language that allows infants to communicate months before speaking. Modified gestures of American Sign Language. (4, 29)

informational books. Informs children about the natural and social environment and does not include characters. (20)

infusion. The process of integrating multiculturalism into all curricular areas. (18)

insulated. Protected from extreme temperatures. (28)

insulin. The hormone that regulates blood sugar levels. (11)

intentional. A purposeful act. (1)

interactive whiteboard. A touch-sensitive board connected to a computer and projector. (8)

internalize. Incorporate within oneself. (7)

interpretation. An attempt to explain the observed behavior and to give it meaning. (17)

intervention. Providing services to children who have disabilities or are at risk. (31)

intonation. The rise and fall of the voice. (20)

intrinsic motivation. Motivation that is driven by internal rewards that a person finds satisfying. (1)

isolation area. A special room or space in a center for children who become ill or show signs of a communicable disease. (8)

J

joint attention. Occurs when the infant attends to the same event or object as the caregiver. (4)

L

laboratory schools. Schools located on a postsecondary or college campus with the primary purpose of training future teachers and serving as a study group for research. (2)

language comprehension. A person's understanding of language. Sometimes referred to as *receptive* or *inner language*. (5)

latchkey children. Term used to describe children left in self-care or in the care of a sibling under age 15. (30)

learning disability. A problem with one or more basic skills of learning. (31)

learning expectation. The expected outcome of an activity. (18)

learning standards. Tools that are agreed upon by state boards of education with the assistance of educators in the field. (2)

learning story. A form of observation and documentation recorded in story format. (17)

lesson plan. A written plan outlining specific actions and activities that will be used to meet goals. (18)

letters. Written communications that most often address only one subject and are sent out as needed. (32)

letter string. A combination of "sticks," "circles," and "wavy lines" in a child's scribbling. (22)

licensing rules and regulations. Standards set to ensure that uniform and safe practices are followed. (2)

licensing specialist. A person employed by a state to protect and promote the health, safety, and welfare of children attending centers; sometimes referred to as *regulators*. (1)

limits. Guides to actions and behaviors that reflect the goals of a program. Sometimes called *rules*. (10, 15)

loam. A type of soil with ideal amounts of clay, silt, and sand. (24)

locomotive. Movement. (29)

logical consequences. Experiences that are deliberately set up by an adult to show what will happen if a limit is not followed. (13)

loose-fill impact-absorbing material. Materials used for protective surfacing in the use zone. Sand, shredded rubber, gravel, and engineered wood fibers are examples. (8)

M

malnutrition. A lack of proper nutrients in the diet happens when a nutrient is absent or lacking from the diet; caused by an unbalanced diet, poor food choices, or the body's inability to use certain nutrients properly. (11)

mandated reporter. People are required by law to report any known or suspected cases of child abuse or neglect. (10)

manipulative stage of play. First stage of material use; stage at which children will begin to handle props. (21)

manuscript writing. A simple form of calligraphy not requiring the sustained muscle control that cursive writing does. This writing involves unconnected letters made of simple, separate strokes. (22)

matching. A form of classification that involves putting like objects together. (23)

mathematics. The study of numbers, arithmetic, measurement, and geometry. (23)

maturation. The sequence of biological changes in children giving the child new abilities, which is based on their genetics. (3)

mentor. A more experienced person who encourages, guides, coaches, and influences the growth of a less experienced person. (1)

mesh. Fit well. (26)

microaggressions. The disrespectful comments or actions that communicate a prejudice to a historically marginalized group. Such groups include racial minorities, people with disabilities or those of a different religion, gender, nationality, socioeconomic class, or citizenship. (7, 30)

middle childhood. The span of years between ages 6 and 12. (3)

milestones. Widely held expectations of what most children are able to do at a certain age. (3)

mini-trip. A short trip that only involves a few children. (28).

mirror language. Mimicking the language of another; speaking to another using their own words. (14)

mirror neurons. These are nerve cells that allow us to mimic the feelings and body movements of other people that surround us. (29)

mitigate. Lessen. (26)

mock writing. The beginning of writing when children make vertical, circular, and wavy lines. (5, 22)

modeling. Verbal and nonverbal actions by one person, setting an example for others. (13)

molestation. Sexual contact made by someone outside the family with a child. (10)

monolingual. Speaking one language. (20)

mono-print painting. Art activity in which a piece of paper is placed over a finger painting. The two papers are patted together, then pulled apart. (19)

Montessori approach. Based on self-education in multiage groups. Schools provide children freedom within limits by a rather structured approach, and a fixed method in which materials are presented. (3)

moral development. The process of acquiring the standards of behavior considered acceptable by society. (7)

morality. Understanding and using accepted rules of conduct when interacting with others. (7)

morning meetings. Class meetings that promote a caring community at toddler, preschool, kindergarten, and school-age levels by creating and modeling a democratic environment. Sometimes referred to as *class meetings* or *gathering times*. (25)

motivation. In a lesson plan, method of gaining the children's attention. (18)

motor sequence. Order in which a child can perform new movements. The motor sequence depends on the development of the brain and nerves. (4)

multicultural. Representing a variety of cultural and ethnic groups. (9)

multiple intelligences. Theory developed by Howard Gardner that emphasizes different kinds of intelligences used by the human brain. Each intelligence functions separately, but all are closely linked. According to Gardner, a potential intelligence will not develop unless it is nurtured. (3)

music. A way of expressing ideas and feelings through sound. (27)

myelin. A white, fatty substance that coats and protects the nerve fibers, and increases the speed at which impulses are transmitted from cell to cell. (3)

MyPlate. The USDA-developed food guidance system with a set of online tools to help people plan nutritious diets to fit their individual needs. (11)

N

nanny. A child care worker who usually provides care in the child's home and may receive food and housing in addition to wages. (1)

natural consequences. Experiences that follow naturally as a result of a behavior. (13)

nearsighted. Able to see close objects more clearly than those at a distance. (7)

negativism. Negative behavior, such as apposing every request a caregiver makes. (14)

neglect. Form of child abuse when children are not given the basic needs of life, such as proper diet, medical care, shelter, and/or clothing. (10)

neophobia. The fear of something new. (11)

networking letter. A letter a person sends to an assortment of people who they know personally or who are referred to them to inform them that they are available for employment. After receiving the letter, these individuals could pass the person's name on to the appropriate people or provide them with valuable insight into possible employment opportunities. (33)

networking. A process of building relationships with people who can be helpful. (33)

neurons. Specialized nerve cells that receive and transmit neural impulses and are the building blocks of the brain. (3)

newsletters. Written communications shared on a regular basis that most often include information concerning a variety of subjects. (32)

nocturnal. Animals that usually sleep during the day and are awake at night. (24)

nonaccidental physical injury. Physical abuse inflicted on purpose. (10)

nonprofit centers. Operated for charitable purposes, often sponsored by an agency. (2)

nonverbal behavior. Communication through actions and facial expressions rather than words. (13)

novelty transition. A transition that involves the use of unusual, new actions or devices to move the children from one activity to another. (16)

number. A system for indicating quantity or amount. Each item in a group should be assigned only one number. It is used to make a judgment and solve problems. (23)

number sense. The understanding of how numbers work. (23)

numerals. The symbols that represent numbers. (23)

nursery rhymes. Short rhymes for young children that often tell a story. (20)

nutrient-dense. A diet including foods and beverages that provide health-promoting components. (11)

nutrients. The chemical substances in food that help build and maintain the body. (11)

nutrition. The science of food and how the body uses the foods taken in. (11)

nutrition concepts. Basic concepts that will help children develop good lifetime healthful eating habits. (26)

O

object permanence. The understanding that objects continue to exist even if the infant cannot see them. This skill typically emerges between 8 and 12 months of age. (3)

observational learning. A type of learning that occurs when children watch others and then imitate what they see. (30)

omission. Bias found in some teaching materials implying some groups have less value than other groups in society. (25)

one-to-one correspondence principle. The understanding that one group has the same number as another. (23)

onlookers. Those who watch others, but do not get involved. (14)

open-ended questions. Questions that promote discussion and require more than one-word answers. (13)

operation. The manipulation of ideas based on logic rather than perception. (7)

overeating. The intake of more food than is needed by the body to function properly, often causing health and emotional problems. (11)

overfamiliarity. Lack of interest in a particular toy shown by children who are given the same toy day after day. (29)

overstimulated. Overexcited. (14)

overstimulation. A flood of sounds and sights. (3)

P

palpable. Recognizable. (24)

pantomiming. Telling a story with body movements rather than words. (27)

parallel play. A type of play in which children play by themselves but stay close by other children. All the children may be involved in similar activities, but play between and among the children does not exist. (21)

parent and family engagement. Patterns of participation in educational programs by family members, including mothers, fathers, grandparents, and siblings. (32)

parent cooperatives. Preschools, usually serving children from three to five years old, that are typically formed and run by parents. (2)

parquetry blocks. Geometric pieces that vary in color and shape that are used to teach shape concepts. (23)

participation chart. Can be developed to gain information on specific aspects of children's behavior. (17)

passive voice. Sentence structure in which the object of the sentence is placed before the subject. (6)

perceptions. Ideas formed about a relationship or object as a result of what a child learns through the senses. (25)

personification. Giving human traits to nonliving objects, such as dolls or puppets. (21)

phrase method. Method of teaching songs using short sections of a long song, having children repeat these sections. These sections are increased until the children know the entire song. (27)

phrase/whole combination method. Method of teaching a song stressing key phrases with rhythmic movement or visual props. (27)

physical age. An age is determined by birth date. Also known as *chronological age*. (9)

physical aggression. An act of physically harming another person. (7)

physical development. Physical body changes in a growing individual, such as include changes in bone thickness, size, weight, vision, and coordination. (3)

pica. A craving for non-food items. (16)

picture books. Books that have single words or simple sentences and simple plots. (20)

picture story books. Words and pictures are combined to tell a story. (20)

pincer grip. Picking up objects using the forefinger and thumb. (4)

placement service. A service that finds positions for graduates. (33)

Plasticene®. A puttylike modeling material used extensively for children's play. (19)

plasticity. The ability of an infant's brain to change according to stimulation. (3)

playful learning. Describes a learning context. Children playing together in self-directed or free play can learn content. (23)

policy. A course of action that controls future decisions. (12)

portable kitchen. A kitchen is created in the classroom by placing the ingredients, tools, and other equipment on a low table so all children can watch. Also, portable appliances such as an electric skillet or a hot plate are used rather than a stove. (26)

portfolio. A purposeful collection of materials that documents a child's abilities, accomplishments, and progress over time. Portfolios are a valuable tool for communicating with families and validating the quality of instruction. (17)

positive reinforcement. Molding children's behavior by rewarding positive behavior. (13)

preinterview. A conversation occurring before an interview. (33)

prekindergarten (pre-K). The full range of early childhood programs, including school-based programs for three- to five-year-olds, is sometimes referred to as *preschool* or *junior kindergarten*. The goal is to enable every child with the skills needed to succeed in school. (1)

prelinguistic communication. Infant's comminution involving the use of facial expressions, sounds, gestures, and communication. (4)

preoperational stage. The period between ages two and seven during which children learn to classify groups and use symbols and internal images. (3)

pre-reading skills. Skills include letter knowledge, concepts of print, phonological awareness, and language. (15)

preschooler. A term referring to children ages three to six years. (3)

preverbal gestures. Intentional signals a baby uses to influence other people in their environment. (4)

primary colors. Red, blue, and yellow. (24)

principle of cardinality. The last number in a counting sequence that designates the quality of items in the set. (6)

print awareness. The understanding that print carries a message. (22)

print referencing. A strategy for calling the children's attention to the print while reading. (20)

private speech. Discussion children have with themselves when they "think out loud" as a means of guidance and direction; also referred to as *self-talk.* (3)

problem-solving file. File containing helpful information on problems families or parents may face. (32)

process-centered art. Focuses on the child's interests and development. (19)

process quality. The quality of relationships among the teachers and children, teaching strategies, curriculum, and learning environment. (2)

product-centered art. Focuses on a model and step-by-step instructions by the teacher. (19)

professional development. An ongoing process through which people update their knowledge and skills related to their professional life. (1)

professional priorities. Global aspects of work that are important to a person's satisfaction. (33)

program goals. Broad statements of purpose that state the desired end results. (18)

projection. A type of play allowing children to place feelings and emotions they feel onto another person or an object, such as a puppet. Through this play, a child may share their inner world. (21)

prompting. Making a verbal or nonverbal suggestion that requires a response; used to either stop an unacceptable action or start an acceptable one; requires a response from the child. (13)

prop box. Box containing materials and equipment that encourage children to explore various roles. (21)

props. Any items that relate to the story and would attract children's attention. (20)

prosocial behaviors. Acts of kindness that benefit others; behaviors that demonstrate cooperation, sharing, and helpfulness. (4, 13)

proximodistal principle. Principle noting that development of the body occurs in an outward direction. The spinal cord develops before the outer parts of the body; arms develop before hands; hands develop before fingers. (3)

publicly sponsored programs. Child care programs are funded by the government, school district, and/or division of social services. (2)

punctual. On time. (33)

puppetry. The use of puppets in play. (21)

Q

quality rating and improvement systems (QRIS). Established standards to assess and acknowledge program quality. (1)

quality rating specialist. A specialist that evaluates and rates the achievement of benchmarks that exceed the minimal state licensing requirements. (1)

quench. Satisfy. (26)

quibbling. Arguing. (32)

R

rabies. A disease caused by a viral infection of the nervous system and brain, transmitted through the saliva of an infected animal. (12)

rating scale. Tool used to record the degree to which a quality or trait is present. (17)

rational counting. Attaching a number to a series of grouped objects. (23)

receptive language. Grows as the children are exposed to new words or known words used in new ways. (6)

recognizing. The ability to relate past and present experiences and classify items; is made possible by using the senses to learn from repeated experiences. (23)

redirecting. A technique used to divert, or turn, a child's attention in a different direction. (13)

referral. Directing a parent to obtain a diagnosis from a professional when a problem exists with a child. (31)

reflex. An automatic body response to a stimulus controlled by the lower-brain centers that govern involuntary processes such as heart rate and breathing. (4)

regression. Showing behaviors that were typical at earlier stages of development. (14)

rehearsal. The repetition of information after it is used. (7)

relational aggression. Trying to harm the social relationships of another person by gossiping, spreading rumors, giving someone the silent treatment, or excluding them from social activities. (7)

render. Provide. (31)

resilient. Able to bounce back quickly from stress. (14)

resource people. Visitors to a classroom, field trip hosts, or people one talks to at a field trip site. (28)

résumé. A brief summary of a person's qualifications, skills, and experience. Its purpose is to secure an interview and/or inform a potential employer of a person's qualifications and experience. (33)

reviews. Lists and descriptions of books that will help you find titles, authors, and publishers of books, which can be found in public libraries. (20)

role. A set of responsibilities that accompany a position one holds in life. (33)

role strain. A type of stress created by being unable to successfully balance multiple roles. (33)

role-playing. A type of play in which children mimic the actions of others, especially adult roles. (21)

rote counting. Reciting numbers in their proper order. (6, 23)

routines. Everyday experiences such as dressing, undressing, eating, napping, toileting, and changing activities that are included in the daily schedule. (16)

S

salt painting. Art activity using salt mixed with colored tempera in shakers. (19)

sanitizing. Process of removing dirt or soil and a small amount of bacteria. (12)

scaffolding. A process in which an adult or another child provides assistance to support a child's learning. The support moves the child from his current developmental level to a higher one. (3)

schedule. The big picture includes the main events and activities that happen across the day. (16)

schemata. A term Piaget used to refer to the cognitive structures in which mental representations or concepts are organized. (3)

school-age child care programs. Program often sponsored by schools, houses of worship, or child care centers that provide care for children before and after school. They are designed for children of working families. (2)

school-age programs. Program designed to meet the needs of children and parents. They may be scheduled before or after school, during vacations, holidays, and summer. (30)

science table. A table is used to display science-related items and create a learning environment rich in materials. (24)

science. The study of natural processes and their products. (24)

secondary colors. Purple, green, and orange. (24)

second-degree burn. Burn causing damage to underlying layers of skin, requiring medical treatment. This burn is marked by pain, blistering, swelling, and discoloration. (12)

self-assessment. The process of examining interests, abilities, values, and professional priorities. (33)

self-care. Children who care for themselves at home. (30)

self-concept. Qualities a child believes they possess; are a result of beliefs, feelings, and perceptions a child has of themselves as part of the world. (5)

self-esteem. A person's belief that they are worthwhile as a person. (7)

self-help skills. Skills and abilities that help preschoolers move toward independence. (6)

self-identity. Whom a child believes themselves to be. (25)

self-regulation. The ability to regulate one's emotions, thinking, and behavior in a socially and culturally appropriate way. It lays the foundation for positive social relationships and academic success. (25)

sensitive period. In infancy, when particular experiences can best contribute to development. (4)

sensorimotor stage. Period between birth and two years of age during which infants use all their senses to explore and learn. (3)

sensory table. A table in the sensory area that gives children the opportunity to experience the sensations related to water and sand. It also allows them practice in social situations. Also known as a *water table* or *sand table*. (8, 15)

sensory training. Learning from impressions received from the five senses. (2)

separation anxiety. A child's difficulty in separating from parents, often occurring between 6 and 15 months of age. (4, 29)

sequencing error. When counting, the child may use the same number more than once, say it out of order, or skip it. (23)

sequencing. The process of ordering real-life objects from shortest to tallest or tallest to shortest. (23)

seriation. The ability to arrange items in an increasing or decreasing order based on weight, volume, or size. (7)

serve and return. Back-and-forth interactions between children and caregivers that involve an infant reaching out for interaction and the caregiver responding appropriately. (29)

set. Two or more objects that are alike in some way and, therefore, belong together. (23)

sexual abuse. Forcing a child to observe or engage in sexual activities with an adult. Rape, incest, pornography, fondling, and indecent exposure are all forms. (10)

skipped generation families. Children being raised by grandparents apart from their parents. (1)

social comparison. A process in which people define themselves in terms of the qualities, skills, and attributes they see in others. (7)

social development. The ability to make friends with others, cooperate, and resolve conflict. (25)

social-emotional development. Growth in the two related areas of social and emotional skills. Social development involves learning to relate to others. Emotional development involves refining feelings and expressions of feelings. (3)

social studies. Subjects that help children learn about themselves as well as other people. (25)

socio-dramatic play. Social play is when several children play together as they imitate others. (21)

socioeconomic status (SES). The combination of social and financial factors that affect people's ability to meet basic needs. (2)

solitary play. A type of play in which children play by themselves. Also called *independent play*. (6, 21)

sorting. The process of physically separating objects based on unique features. (23)

spatial relationships. The position of people and objects in space relative to each other. (23)

specific task assessment. Giving children set activities to determine skills and/or needs. (23)

spectator toys. Toys requiring little action on the child's part. (9)

speech pathologist. A professional who assesses and diagnoses people with speech and language disorders. (31)

speech skills. The ability to speak clearly. (27)

spice painting. Art activity in which children spread glue on a piece of paper, and then shake spices onto the paper. (19)

spiral curriculum. A curriculum based on the concept that as children grow, their circle of interests becomes larger. (18)

sportscasting. A way of communicating with an infant by reflecting on your observations. (29)

stable order. Numbers in the same sequence, as each number has a fixed meaning. (23)

staff room. Room in a child care center provided for staff to spend work-related time away from the classroom. (8)

standardized test. A test whose scores can be compared against state or national norms. (17)

standard precautions. Federal laws passed to protect staff and others from accidental exposure to bloodborne pathogens, such as HIV or hepatitis B. (12)

stationary equipment. Playground equipment permanently installed for stability, such as jungle gyms, slides, and treehouses. (8)

statute. A formal document drawn up by elected officials. (10)

STEM. An acronym that stands for the disciplines of science, technology, engineering, and math; a curriculum focusing on integrating the four disciplines that help prepare children to live and work in the twenty-first century. (24)

storybooks. Books that contain pictures but have more complex plots than picture books. (20)

storytelling. An important task for early childhood teachers involves reciting a story or reading from a book. (20)

stranger anxiety. Fear of strangers, which infants begin to experience between seven and nine months of age. (4, 29)

stress. The body's reaction to physical or emotional factors. Often takes the form of tension. (14)

string painting. A painting activity in which pieces of heavy yarn or string are dipped in paint and slid across the paper. (19)

structural quality. Teacher qualifications, teacher-child ratios, and group size. (2)

stunted. Hindered or delayed. (29)

stuttering. A speech disorder often characterized by repetition, hesitation, and prolongation. (6)

subitize. To make an immediate and accurate number of items in a group without needing to count them. (23)

subterranean. Underground. (24)

sudden infant death syndrome (SIDS). The death of a healthy infant due to unexplained causes. It is the leading cause of death for infants between one and twelve months. (29)

summative assessment. It is a process of assessing children against a standard or benchmark at the end of an experience to evaluate effectiveness. (17)

sun protection factor (SPF). A number assigned to a sunscreen that is the factor by which the time required for unprotected skin to become sunburned is increased when the sunscreen is used. (10)

sunshine calls. Telephone calls made by teachers to families or parents to communicate praise and support for children. (32)

synapses. Connections between nerve cells that pass messages in the brain. (3)

T

tactile. Related to sight and touch. (19)

teachable moment. An unexpected event the teacher can use as a learning opportunity. (18)

teacher-child ratio. The number of children per teacher or caregiver. (2)

teaching portfolio. A collection of materials that tell a story about your efforts, progress, and achievements. (33)

technological literacy. The ability to understand and use technology. (30)

technology. Focuses on using tools to make things happen, identify problems, and make things work. (24)

telegraphic speech. The term used to describe the two-word phrases toddlers begin to form when they first learn to combine words. (4)

temperament. Quality and intensity of children's emotional reactions to their environment, such as passivity, irritability, and activity patterns. (4)

tempo. The rate of speed in music in which the range can range from slow to rapid. (27)

texture painting. Art activity using liquid tempera paints mixed with sand, sawdust, or coffee grounds. (19)

The Family Educational Rights and Privacy Act (FERPA). Protects the privacy of student educational records. (33)

theme. One main topic or idea around which the classroom experiences and projects are planned. (18)

theme bags. A child's backpack filled with games, puppets, storybooks, songs, chants, and a letter of introduction for the parents. (32)

theme walks. Simple field trips taken in or near the center based on a theme. (28)

theory. A principle or idea proposed, researched, and generally accepted as an explanation. (3)

third-degree burn. Burn destroys the skin layer and nerve endings, requiring prompt medical attention. (12)

toddler. Term used to refer to a child from the first year until the third birthday. The term is used because of the awkward walking style of children in this age group. (3)

toxic stress. Abuse, neglect, violence, extreme poverty, food scarcity, and family dysfunction are examples of toxic stress. (3)

tracking error. Occurs when the child recounts an item that was counted earlier. (23)

traffic pattern. The way furniture is arranged to create movement in the classroom. (8)

transitions. Changes from one activity to another or moves from one place to another. (16)

traveling backpack. A backpack in which children take home their favorite books, media, puzzles, or games to share with their parents. (32)

trip bag. A bag that includes a teacher's essential supplies to take on a field trip. (28)

true counting. In which an object is counted for each number named. (6)

tummy time. Encourages infants to lift their heads, which will help build strong head, neck, and shoulder muscles. (29)

U

undernutrition. Not eating enough food to keep a healthy body weight and activity level. (11)

unitary surfacing material. Rubber mats or tile systems, or a blend of rubberlike materials for playground surfacing. (8)

unit-based program model. A curriculum format for school-age child care that revolves around curriculum themes that reflect the children's interests. (30)

universal prekindergarten (UPK). State-sponsored early childhood education programs that are designed for three- and four-year-old children and provide a high-quality, literary-rich environment. The goal is to enable every child with skills needed to succeed in school. (2)

unoccupied play. Play that begins at birth. There is no purpose to this type of play, but infants make random movements. (21)

V

values. Beliefs, feelings, and ideas about what is important. (33)

vendors. People and companies that sell products and supplies. (9)

verbal aggression. Involves name-calling, yelling, screaming, and swearing. (7)

verbal environment. All the communication that occurs within a setting, including verbal and nonverbal communication. (13)

verbal fluency. The ability to speak easily and well. (20)

virtual field trips. Technology-based experiences allow children an educational excursion without leaving the classroom. (28)

visual documentation. Collecting, photographing, or video recording samples of a child's work that portrays learning and development. (17)

visual impairment. Any eye or nerve problem that prevents people from seeing normally. (31)

visual learner. A child who depends a great deal on the sense of sight. (18)

visual literacy. Ability to interpret information presented through images such as photographs, symbols, and videos. (20)

visual perception. The coordination of the eye and hand. (7)

visual signals. Transition method that involves informing children of a change through signals they can see. (16)

vitality. Liveliness. (27)

voluntarily. Out of one's own will. (25)

W

wariness. Cautious fear. (29)

warm colors. Colors that make a room appear smaller including red, yellow, and orange. (8)

water-soluble. Able to dissolve in water. (19)

web. A planning tool or map that outlines major concepts and ideas related to a theme. (18)

whole song method. The method used to teach short, simple songs by having the children listen and then sing along. (27)

windows of opportunity. A specific span of time for the normal development of certain types of skills. (3)

working interview. An interview is designed so the employers can see the candidates' skills instead of explaining their qualifications. A teacher candidate would work with a group of children. (33)

wound. Damage to the surface of the skin or body tissue. (12)

writing center. An area of the classroom containing writing materials and tools that encourage children to engage in writing. (22)

Z

zone of proximal development (ZPD). Vygotsky's term that defines what children can do alone or with guidance and encouragement. (3)

Index

routines. *See also* daily routines; schedule
    arrival, 391, 766
    breaks in, 352
    culturally based, 107–108
    defined, 390

S

sadness, 145–146
safety, as human need, 72
Safety First
    age-appropriate stories, 506
    balloon ban, 608
    carbon monoxide poisoning, 237
    choking hazards, 655
    daily routines, 458
    electrical outlets, 735
    emergency lighting, 237
    facility layout, 232
    food safety, 275
    hand sanitizers, 295
    helmets, 200
    human need for safety, 72
    instruments, 677
    intergenerational care, 635
    math equipment, 575
    nonhazardous art supplies, 474
    open-door policy, 816
    play equipment height limitations, 764
    policy on aggressive behavior, 356
    policy for departure, 407
    puppet materials, 539
    safe writing tools, 553
    sensory tables, 379
    Shaken Baby Syndrome, 104
    SIDS, 89
    sports injuries, 164
    sun and hydration for infants, 240
    video recording and photographing, 428
    water table, 493
    written guidance policies, 321
safety objectives, 230–232
    adult-child ratios, 232
    building security, 235
    constant supervision, 231
    fire extinguishers, 236–237
    fire safety, 236–239
    practicing safety, 236–240
    safe environment, 233–235
    safety limits, 232
    sun safety, 239–240, 305
    transportation, 234–235
    weather or disaster emergencies, 240

salt painting, 481
sand play, 492, 494
sandbox, 199, 383
sandpaper blocks, 676–677
sandpaper sticks, 677
sanitizing, 296
schedule. *See also* daily schedule; routines
    daily, 390–393
    defined, 390
    kindergarten, 37
schemata, 74
School-Age Care Environment Rating Scale (SACERS), 48
school-age programs, 37–38
    accreditation and standards, 753
    activity times, 768–770
    adult-centered, 754, 755
    adult-child ratios, 753
    appropriate environments, 760–761
    arrival and departure times, 766
    assessing children's interests, 763–765
    balancing activities, 770
    child-centered, 754, 755
    cleanup times, 770–771
    curriculum, 763–765
    daily schedule, 766
    defined, 750
    digital learning, 768–769
    get-acquainted interviews, 764
    group activities, 768
    group discussions, 764–765
    indoor activities, 771
    indoor environment, 760–761
    outdoor activities, 770
    outdoor environments, 761
    outdoor games, 769–770
    quality, 752–753
    rest times, 767
    scheduling activities, 765–771
    self-reports, 765
    snack times, 767
    staff characteristics, 755–760
    types, 753–755
    unit-based models, 754, 755
Schurz, Margarethe, 36, 70
science
    air, 608–609
    defined, 592
    environment and weather, 609
    equipment and materials, 595–596
    field trips and guided walks, 611–612
    growth, 610–611